70-350: Implementing Microsoft Internet Security and Acceleration (ISA) Server 2004

Objective	Pages
1. Planning and Installing ISA Server 2004	
1.1. Plan an ISA Server 2004 deployment	5-3 to 5-10
1.1.1. Analyze forward proxy and reverse proxy requirements.	2-3 to 2-19
1.1.2. Analyze requirements for branch office deployment.	2-3 to 2-19
1.1.3. Analyze baseline network traffic usage.	5-3 to 5-10
1.1.4. Analyze firewall protocol requirements.	10-4 to 10-15
1.1.5. Plan a VPN deployment.	4-3 to 4-11
1.1.6. Plan for client computer connectivity.	2-3 to 2-19 and 12-20 to 12-42
1.1.7. Analyze requirements for high availability and fault tolerance.	2-3 to 2-19
1.1.8. Pilot and test an ISA Server 2004 deployment.	
1.2. Assess and configure the operating system, hardware, and network services.	
1.2.1. Analyze operating system and platform requirements.	2-20 to 2-35
1.2.2. Prepare network interfaces.	2-20 to 2-35 and 3-3 to 3-27
1.2.3. Enable required network and server services.	3-3 to 3-27
1.2.4. Analyze hardware and network requirements.	2-20 to 2-35
1.2.5. Configure operating system settings for installing ISA Server 2004.	2-20 to 2-35 and 3-3 to 3-27
1.3. Deploy ISA Server 2004.	
1.3.1. Migrate from ISA Server 2000 to ISA Server 2004.	2-36 to 2-39 and 12-20 to 12-42
1.3.2. Install ISA Server 2004 Standard Edition.	2-20 to 2-35
1.3.3. Install ISA Server 2004 Enterprise Edition.	12-43 to 12-72
1.3.4. Define the network routing requirements.	2-3 to 2-35
1.3.5. Verify the installation of ISA Server 2004.	2-20 to 2-35
1.3.6. Establish a post-installation baseline.	11-3 to 11-14
1.3.7. Plan for disaster recovery.	3-3 to 3-27
2. Installing and Configuring Client Computers	
2.1. Install Firewall Client software.	4-28 to 4-45
2.2. Configure client computers for ISA Server 2004. Types of client computers include Web Proxy, Firewall Client, and SecureNAT	4-12 to 4-45
2.2.1. Modify Firewall Client configuration files.	4-28 to 4-45
2.3. Configure a local domain table (LDT).	4-12 to 4-27
2.4. Configure ISA Server 2004 for automatic client configuration by using Web Proxy Automatic Discovery (WPAD).	
2.4.1. Configure and publish client configuration settings on ISA Server 2004.	4-12 to 4-45
2.4.2. Configure DNS and DHCP for automatic discovery.	4-12 to 4-27
2.4.3. Configure client computers for automatic discovery. Methods of configuration include Firewall Client and Web browser.	4-12 to 4-45
2.5. Diagnose and resolve client computer connectivity issues.	
2.5.1. Diagnose and resolve name resolution issues.	4-12 to 4-27
2.5.2. Diagnose and resolve protocol support issues.	4-12 to 4-45
2.5.3. Diagnose and resolve routing issues.	4-12 to 4-27
2.5.4. Diagnose and resolve authentication issues.	4-12 to 4-45
3. Configuring and Managing ISA Server 2004	
3.1. Configure the system policy.	
3.1.1. Enable infrastructure communications.	3-3 to 3-27
3.1.2. Lock down the system policy.	3-3 to 3-27
3.1.3. Modify rules.	3-3 to 3-27
3.1.4. Limit network access to the firewall.	3-3 to 3-27
3.2. Back up and restore ISA Server 2004.	
3.2.1. Backup and restore an ISA Server 2004 configuration.	3-28 to 3-37
3.2.2. Perform disaster recovery.	3-28 to 3-37
3.2.3. Transfer ISA Server 2004 configuration settings between ISA Server computers.	3-28 to 3-37
3.3. Define administrative roles.	
3.3.1. Assign and delegate administrative roles.	3-28 to 3-37 and 12-20 to 12-42
3.3.2. Remove delegation rights.	3-28 to 3-37
3.3.3. Limit access to logs and reports.	3-28 to 3-37
3.3.4. Manage access to firewall configuration.	2-20 to 2-35
3.4. Configure firewall settings.	
3.4.1. Configure intrusion detection.	7-37 to 7-45
3.4.2. Configure IP options filtering.	7-37 to 7-45
3.4.3. Configure dial-up settings.	5-11 to 5-28
3.4.4. Configure firewall chaining.	5-11 to 5-28
3.4.5. Configure IP fragmentation settings.	7-37 to 7-45
3.5. Configure ISA Server 2004 for Network Load Balancing.	12-3 to 12-19 and 12-43 to 12-72
3.6. Configure ISA Server 2004 to support a network topology.	
3.6.1. Select appropriate templates.	7-12 to 7-36
3.6.2. Define networks.	7-12 to 7-23
3.6.3. Configure route relationships between networks.	7-12 to 7-23

Objective	Pages

4. Configuring Web Caching

4.1. **Optimize performance of the ISA Server 2004 cache.**
    4.1.1. Configure cache size and location. — 6-13 to 6-30
    4.1.2. Configure cache rules. — 6-13 to 6-30
    4.1.3. Configure content download jobs. — 6-31 to 6-39
    4.1.4. Configure Cache Array Routing Protocol (CARP). — 12-3 to 12-72

4.2. **Configure forward and reverse caching.**
    4.2.1. Configure active caching. — 6-13 to 6-30
    4.2.2. Configure cache settings. — 6-13 to 6-30

4.3. **Diagnose and resolve caching issues.** — 6-13 to 6-39

5. Configuring Firewall Policy

5.1. **Plan a firewall policy.**
    5.1.1. Plan a policy to optimize performance. — 12-20 to 12-42
    5.1.2. Plan policy rules for an enterprise firewall. — 12-3 to 12-42
    5.1.3. Plan for interaction between enterprise and array-level rule deployments. — 12-3 to 12-19
    5.1.4. Validate and troubleshoot enterprise rule deployment. — 12-43 to 12-72

5.2. **Create policy elements, access rules, and connection limits. Policy elements include schedule, protocols, user groups, and network objects.** — 5-29 to 5-60 and 8-13 to 8-62

5.3. **Create policy rules for Web publishing.**
    5.3.1. Install certificates for Web publishing. — 8-33 to 8-46
    5.3.2. Configure authentication for Web access. — 8-63 to 8-75
    5.3.3. Configure HTTP filtering for Web publishing. — 7-46 to 7-64
    5.3.4. Configure bridging. — 8-33 to 8-46
    5.3.5. Configure link translator. — 8-13 to 8-32

5.4. **Create policy rules for mail server publishing.**
    5.4.1. Publish a Microsoft Outlook Web Access server. — 9-26 to 9-37
    5.4.2. Configure SMTP filtering and SMTP message screener. — 9-3 to 9-25

5.5. **Create policy rules for server publishing.**
    5.5.1. Publish a Web server by using server publishing rules. — 8-4 to 8-12
    5.5.2. Publish an RPC server. — 8-4 to 8-12
    5.5.3. Publish an FTP server. — 8-4 to 8-12
    5.5.4. Publish a Terminal Services server. — 8-4 to 8-12
    5.5.5. Publish a VPN server or device. — 8-4 to 8-12

6. Configuring and Managing Remote Network Connectivity

6.1. **Configure ISA Server 2004 for site-to-site VPN.**
    6.1.1. Add remote site networks. — 10-33 to 10-49
    6.1.2. Create a VPN router user account. — 10-33 to 10-49
    6.1.3. Configure VPN client address assignments. — 10-33 to 10-49
    6.1.4. Create site-to-site VPN access policy. — 10-33 to 10-49

6.2. **Configure ISA Server 2004 as a remote access VPN server.**
    6.2.1. Configure VPN address assignments. — 10-4 to 10-15
    6.2.2. Configure access policy for VPN client computers. — 10-4 to 10-15
    6.2.3. Configure authentication for remote client computers. Types of authentication include certificates, Windows accounts, RADIUS, and SecurID. — 10-4 to 10-15
    6.2.4. Enable network access quarantine. — 10-50 to 10-70
    6.2.5. Diagnose and resolve client computer connectivity issues. — 10-4 to 10-15

6.3. **Diagnose and resolve VPN connectivity issues.**
    6.3.1. Diagnose and resolve name resolution issues. — 10-4 to 10-15
    6.3.2. Diagnose and resolve routing issues between networks. — 10-33 to 10-49
    6.3.3. Diagnose and resolve Maximum Transmission Unit (MTU) issues. — 10-16 to 10-32
    6.3.4. Diagnose and resolve IP fragmentation issues. — 10-16 to 10-32
    6.3.5. Diagnose and resolve dial-in permission issues. — 10-16 to 10-32
    6.3.6. Diagnose and resolve issues with certificates. — 10-16 to 10-49

7. Monitoring and Reporting ISA Server 2004 Activity

7.1. **Monitor ISA Server 2004 activity.**
    7.1.1. Monitor client computer connections. — 11-29 to 11-39
    7.1.2. Monitor ISA Server 2004 performance. — 11-3 to 11-14
    7.1.3. Monitor network performance. — 11-3 to 11-14
    7.1.4. Monitor network intrusion attempts. — 7-37 to 7-45 and 11-40 to 11-57
    7.1.5. Monitor connectivity to network and services. — 11-3 to 11-14 and 11-29 to 11-39
    7.1.6. Diagnose and resolve connectivity issues. — 11-29 to 11-39

7.2. **Configure and run reports.** — 11-40 to 11-57

7.3. **Configure logging and alerts.**
    7.3.1. Create and modify alert definitions. — 11-40 to 11-57
    7.3.2. Search and filter logs by using log viewer. — 11-40 to 11-57
    7.3.3. Save log filters and session filters. — 11-40 to 11-57

Note Exam objectives are subject to change at anytime without prior notice and at Microsoft's sole discretion. Please visit Microsoft's Training & Certification Web site (*www.microsoft.com/traincert*) for the most current listing of exam objectives.

MCSA/MCSE Self-Paced Training Kit (Exam 70-350): Implementing Microsoft® Internet Security and Acceleration Server 2004

Stan Reimer

Orin Thomas

PUBLISHED BY
Microsoft Press
A Division of Microsoft Corporation
One Microsoft Way
Redmond, Washington 98052-6399

Library of Congress Control Number 2004118212

Printed and bound in the United States of America.

1 2 3 4 5 6 7 8 9   QWT   9 8 7 6 5

Distributed in Canada by H.B. Fenn and Company Ltd.

A CIP catalogue record for this book is available from the British Library.

Microsoft Press books are available through booksellers and distributors worldwide. For further information about international editions, contact your local Microsoft Corporation office or contact Microsoft Press International directly at fax (425) 936-7329. Visit our Web site at www.microsoft.com/learning/. Send comments to *tkinput@microsoft.com*.

Microsoft, Active Directory, ActiveSync, FrontPage, Microsoft Press, MSDN, MSN, Outlook, PowerPoint, SharePoint, Visual Basic, Visual Studio, Win32, Windows, Windows Mobile, Windows NT, and Windows Server are either registered trademarks or trademarks of Microsoft Corporation in the United States and/or other countries.

The example companies, organizations, products, domain names, e-mail addresses, logos, people, places, and events depicted herein are fictitious. No association with any real company, organization, product, domain name, e-mail address, logo, person, place, or event is intended or should be inferred.

Product Planner: Martin DelRe
Content Development Manager: Lori Kane
Project Manager: Julie Pickering
Project Editor: Susan McClung
Technical Editor: Kurt Dillard
Technologist: Colin Lyth
Copy Editor: Peter Tietjen
Proofreaders: Jan Cocker, Cindy Gearhart, and Kiren Valjee
Indexer: Jack Lewis

Body Part No. X11-10416

*As always, I dedicate this book to the three wonderful women in my life:
my wife, Rhonda, and my daughters, Angela and Amanda.*

Stan Reimer

*To my beautiful and lovely wife, Oksana, and my fantastic son, Rooslan.
You make this all possible.*

Orin Thomas

About the Authors

Stan Reimer, Microsoft Certified System Engineer (MCSE), and Microsoft Certified Trainer (MCT), is the president of SR Technical Services based in Winnipeg, Manitoba. Stan works as a consultant and trainer specializing in Microsoft ISA Server, Microsoft Exchange Server, and Active Directory design and implementation. Stan has worked as a consultant with some of the largest corporations in Canada, as well as some of the smallest. He is the co-author of *Active Directory for Microsoft Windows Server 2003 Technical Reference*, published by Microsoft Press, and also authors courseware and security clinics for Microsoft Learning. In the summer, Stan finds hitting the road on his motorcycle or hitting golf balls on a golf course to be excellent therapy. In the winter, he just works, because it is too cold in Winnipeg to do anything else.

Orin Thomas is a writer, editor, trainer, and systems administrator who works for the certification advice Web site Certtutor.net. His work in IT has been varied: he has done everything from providing first-level networking support to a university department to managing mission-critical servers for one of Australia's largest companies. He has co-authored several MCSA/MCSE self-paced training kits for Microsoft Learning. He holds a variety of certifications, a bachelor's degree in science with honors from the University of Melbourne, and is currently working toward the completion of a Ph.D in Philosophy of Science.

Contents at a Glance

Part 1   Learn at Your Own Pace

  1   Introduction to ISA Server 2004 1-3

  2   Installing ISA Server 2004 2-1

  3   Securing and Maintaining ISA Server 2004 3-1

  4   Installing and Managing ISA Server Clients 4-1

  5   Enabling Secure Internet Access with ISA Server 2004 5-1

  6   Implementing ISA Server Caching 6-1

  7   Configuring ISA Server as a Firewall 7-1

  8   Implementing ISA Server Publishing 8-1

  9   Integrating ISA Server 2004 and Exchange Server 9-1

 10   Configuring Virtual Private Networks for Remote
       Clients and Networks 10-1

 11   Implementing Monitoring and Reporting 11-1

 12   Implementing ISA Server 2004, Enterprise Edition 12-1

Part 2   Prepare for the Exam

 13   Planning and Installing ISA Server 2004 (1.0) 13-3

 14   Installing and Configuring Client Computers (2.0) 14-1

 15   Configuring and Managing ISA Server 2004 (3.0) 15-1

 16   Configuring Web Caching (4.0) 16-1

 17   Configuring Firewall Policy (5.0) 17-1

 18   Configuring and Managing Remote Network Connectivity (6.0) 18-1

 19   Monitoring and Reporting ISA Server 2004
       Activity (7.0) 19-1

Practices

Installing ISA Server 2004 2-29
Securing the Computer Running ISA Server 3-14
Securing ISA Server 3-24
Maintaining ISA Server 2004 3-34
Configuring SecureNAT and Web Proxy Clients 4-25
Installing and Configuring Firewall Clients 4-43
Configuring ISA Server as a Proxy Server 5-26
Configuring Access Rule Elements 5-38
Configuring ISA Server Authentication 5-45
Configuring Access Rules for Internet Access 5-56
Configuring Caching and Cache Rules 6-26
Configuring Content Download Jobs 6-36
Configuring Multiple Networking on ISA Server 7-20
Implementing Network Templates 7-33
Configuring Intrusion Detection and IP Preferences 7-43
Configuring an HTTP Web Filter 7-61
Configuring DNS for Web and Server Publishing 8-9
Configuring Web Publishing Rules 8-29
Configuring Secure Web Publishing Rules 8-42
Configuring Server Publishing Rules 8-59
Configuring ISA Server Authentication 8-71
Configuring ISA Server to Secure SMTP Traffic 9-19
Configuring ISA Server to Secure OWA Client Connections 9-34
Configuring ISA Server to Secure Outlook Client Connections 9-47
Configuring Virtual Private Networking for Remote Clients 10-29
Configuring Virtual Private Networking for Remote Sites 10-44
Configuring VPN Quarantine Control 10-61
Configuring and Managing Alerts 11-24
Configuring Session and Connectivity Monitoring 11-36
Configuring ISA Server Reporting 11-54
Installing a Configuration Storage Server 12-48
Configuring Enterprise and Array Policies 12-57
Installing ISA Server 2004, Enterprise Edition 12-62

Tables

Table 1-1: New Features in ISA Server 2004 1-19
Table 1-2: ISA Server Monitoring Components 1-36
Table 2-1: ISA Server 2004 Hardware Scalability 2-15
Table 2-2: Msisaund.ini Parameters 2-26
Table 2-3: ISA Server Unattended Setup Parameters 2-28
Table 3-1: Services Required for ISA Server 2004 3-8
Table 3-2: Optional Services 3-9
Table 3-3: ISA Server Default Configuration 3-15
Table 3-4: System Policy Settings 3-18
Table 3-5: ISA Server Roles and Tasks 3-22
Table 4-1: Comparing the ISA Server Clients 4-9
Table 4-2: Guidelines for Choosing ISA Server Clients 4-9
Table 4-3: Configuring Network Settings for SecureNAT Clients 4-13
Table 4-4: ISA Server Firewall Configuration Settings 4-34
Table 4-5: Application.ini File Settings 4-41
Table 5-1: ISA Server Internet Access Restrictions 5-8
Table 5-2: Configuring Dial-Up Preferences 5-25
Table 5-3: Access Rule Element Types 5-29
Table 5-4: Protocol Element Configuration Options 5-31
Table 5-5: Network Object Access Rule Elements 5-36
Table 5-6: Authentication Configuration Options 5-45
Table 5-7: Access Rule Format 5-49
Table 6-1: ISA Server Caching Restrictions 6-8
Table 6-2: Advanced Caching Configuration Options 6-16
Table 6-3: Cache Rule Options and the Default Cache Rule 6-18
Table 6-4: Configuring Content Retrieval Settings 6-20
Table 6-5: Configuring Content Caching 6-21
Table 6-7: Configuring HTTP Caching 6-23
Table 6-8: Configuring FTP Caching 6-23
Table 6-9: Configuring Download Frequency 6-32
Table 6-10: Configuring Content Download Job Details 6-34
Table 6-11: Configure Content Download Job Caching 6-35
Table 7-1: ISA Server Default Networks 7-15

Table 7-2: ISA Server Default Network Rules 7-18

Table 7-3: Firewall Policies Applied by the Internet-Edge Template 7-29

Table 7-4: ISA Server Intrusion-Detection Options 7-37

Table 7-5: Configuring HTTP Policy General Properties 7-51

Table 7-6: HTTP 1.1 Methods 7-52

Table 7-7: How ISA Server Evaluates Extensions 7-54

Table 7-8: Application Signatures for Common Applications .7-60

Table 8-1: Web Publishing Rule Configuration Options 8-13

Table 8-2: Web Site Configuration Options 8-24

Table 8-3: Server Publishing Rule Configuration Options 8-48

Table 8-4: Port Override Configuration Options 8-51

Table 9-1: Supported SMTP Commands 9-8

Table 9-2: Configuring the SMTP Message Screener 9-13

Table 9-3: RPC over HTTP Requirements 9-44

Table 10-1: Comparing PPTP and L2TP/IPSEC 10-8

Table 10-2: Site-to-Site VPN Configuration Components 10-33

Table 10-3: Comparing Site-to-Site Tunneling Protocols 10-35

Table 10-4: Remote-Site VPN Gateway Configuration Components 10-43

Table 11-1: ISA Server Monitoring Components 11-4

Table 11-2: ISA Server Management Console Dashboard Nodes 11-6

Table 11-3: ISA Server Performance Objects 11-10

Table 11-4: Alert Event Configuration Options 11-19

Table 11-5: Configuring an Alert Action 11-21

Table 11-6: Session Filtering Options 11-32

Table 11-7: Connectivity Monitoring Configuration Options 11-35

Table 11-8: ISA Server Log Options 11-42

Table 11-9: Configuring the ISA Server Log Summaries 11-49

Table 12-1: ISA Server Enterprise Edition Unattended Installation Files 12-62

Troubleshooting Labs

Troubleshooting Lab 3-39

Troubleshooting Lab 5-62

Troubleshooting Lab 5-71

Troubleshooting Lab 7-66

Troubleshooting Lab 8-76

Troubleshooting Lab 9-50

Case Scenario Exercises

Case Scenario Exercise. 1-37

Case Scenario Exercise. 1-45

Case Scenario Exercises. 2-37

Case Scenario Exercises. 3-38

Case Scenario Exercises. 3-46

Case Scenario Exercise. 4-46

Case Scenario Exercise. 4-51

Case Scenario Exercises. 5-61

Case Scenario Exercises. 5-70

Case Scenario Exercises. 6-39

Case Scenario Exercises. 6-45

Case Scenario Exercise. 7-65

Case Scenario Exercise 7-73

Case Scenario Exercises. 8-75

Case Scenario Exercises. 8-86

Case Scenario Exercises. 9-49

Case Scenario Exercises. 9-59

Case Scenario Exercises. 10-69

Case Scenario Exercises. 10-77

Case Scenario Exercise. 11-58

Case Scenario Exercise. 11-66

Case Scenario Exercise. 12-72

Case Scenario Exercise. 12-81

Contents

About This Book xxix

    Intended Audience xxix

    Prerequisites xxix

    About the CD-ROM. xxx

    Features of This Book xxxi

        Notes. xxxii

        Conventions xxxiii

    Getting Started xxxiii

        Hardware Requirements. xxxiv

        Software Requirements xxxiv

        Setup Instructions. xxxv

    The Microsoft Certified Professional Program xxxvii

    Technical Support xxxix

Part 1   **Learn at Your Own Pace**

1   **Introduction to ISA Server 2004**   **1-3**

    Before You Begin 1-3

    Lesson 1: Overview of ISA Server Functionality 1-4

        How ISA Server Works—An Overview 1-4

        How ISA Server Works as a Firewall 1-7

        How ISA Server Enables Secure Internet Access 1-9

        How ISA Server Enables Internal Resource Publishing 1-11

        How ISA Server Works as a VPN Server 1-14

        Lesson Summary 1-16

    Lesson 2: Overview of ISA Server 2004 Editions and Versions 1-17

        Differences Between ISA Server Standard Edition and Enterprise Edition . .1-17

        Differences Between ISA Server 2004 and ISA Server 2000 1-19

        Lesson Review 1-21

        Lesson Summary 1-21

    Lesson 3: Explaining ISA Server Deployment Scenarios 1-22

        How ISA Server Works as an Internet-Edge Firewall 1-22

        How ISA Server Works as a Back-End Firewall 1-24

        How ISA Server Works as a Branch Office Firewall 1-25

        How ISA Server Works as an Integrated Firewall, Proxy, and Caching Server 1-26

        How ISA Server Works as a Proxy- and Caching-Only Server 1-27

Lesson Review 1-29

Lesson Summary 1-30

Lesson 4: Overview of ISA Server 2004 Administration 1-31

The ISA Server Administration Process 1-31

ISA Server Management Console Features 1-34

ISA Server Monitoring Overview 1-35

Lesson Review 1-36

Lesson Summary 1-37

Scenario 1-38

Exam Highlights 1-40

Key Points 1-40

Key Terms 1-41

2   Installing ISA Server 2004   2-1

Before You Begin. 2-2

Lesson 1: Planning an ISA Server Deployment 2-3

The ISA Server Deployment Planning Process 2-3

Network Infrastructure Requirements 2-7

Server Requirements 2-13

Guidelines for Capacity Planning 2-14

Lesson Review 2-17

Lesson Summary 2-18

Lesson 2: Installing ISA Server 2004 2-19

ISA Server 2004 Installation Preparation Checklist 2-19

Guidelines for Installing ISA Server, Standard Edition 2-20

How to Verify a Successful ISA Server Installation 2-25

How to Perform an Unattended Installation of ISA Server 2004 2-26

Guidelines for Troubleshooting an ISA Server Installation 2-28

Practice: Installing ISA Server 2004 2-29

Lesson Review 2-31

Lesson Summary 2-32

Lesson 3: Overview of the ISA Server 2000 Migration Process 2-33

How the ISA Server 2000 In-Place Upgrade Process Works 2-33

How an ISA Server 2000 Configuration Migration Works 2-34

Ways to Migrate Routing and Remote Access VPN to ISA Server 2004 2-35

Lesson Review 2-35

Lesson Summary 2-36

Scenario 1 2-37

Scenario 2 2-37

Exam Highlights 2-38
    Key Points 2-39
    Key Terms 2-39
    Case Scenario Exercises 2-42

3   **Securing and Maintaining ISA Server 2004**   **3-1**
Before You Begin 3-2
Lesson 1: Securing ISA Server 2004 .3-3
    How to Harden the Server 3-5
    Practice: Securing the Computer Running ISA Server 3-14
    How to Secure the ISA Server Configuration 3-15
    Practice: Securing ISA Server 3-24
    Lesson Review 3-26
    Lesson Summary 3-27
Lesson 2: Maintaining ISA Server 2004 3-28
    How to Export and Import the ISA Server Configuration 3-28
    How to Back Up and Restore the ISA Server Configuration 3-31
    How to Implement Remote Administration 3-32
    Practice: Maintaining ISA Server 2004 3-34
    Lesson Review 3-36
    Lesson Summary 3-37
    Scenario 1 3-38
    Scenario 2 3-38
    Exercise 1: Preparing the Workstation for Remote Administration 3-39
    Exercise 2: Troubleshooting Remote Administration 3-40
Exam Highlights 3-41
    Key Points 3-41
    Key Terms 3-42

4   **Installing and Managing ISA Server Clients**   **4-1**
Before You Begin. 4-2
Lesson 1: Choosing an ISA Server Client 4-2
    ISA Server Client Options 4-3
    Lesson Review 4-10
    Lesson Summary 4-11
Lesson 2: Configuring the SecureNAT and Web Proxy Clients 4-12
    How to Configure SecureNAT Clients 4-12
    How to Configure Web Proxy Clients 4-15
    How to Troubleshoot SecureNAT and Web Proxy Clients 4-23

Practice: Configuring SecureNAT and Web Proxy Clients 4-25

Lesson Review 4-26

Lesson Summary 4-27

Lesson 3: Installing and Configuring the Firewall Client 4-28

How to Install Firewall Client 4-28

How to Automate Firewall Client Installation 4-30

How to Configure ISA Server for Firewall Clients .4-33

Advanced Firewall Client Configuration 4-38

Practice: Installing and Configuring Firewall Clients 4-43

Lesson Review 4-44

Lesson Summary 4-45

Scenario 1 4-46

Chapter Summary 4-46

Exam Highlights 4-47

Key Points 4-47

Key Terms 4-47

5   **Enabling Secure Internet Access with ISA Server 2004**   **5-1**

Before You Begin 5-2

Lesson 1: Enabling Secure Access to Internet Resources 5-3

What Is Secure Access to Internet Resources? 5-3

Guidelines for Designing an Internet Usage Policy .5-5

How ISA Server Enables Secure Access to Internet Resources 5-8

Lesson Review 5-9

Lesson Summary 5-9

Lesson 2: Configuring ISA Server as a Proxy Server 5-11

What Is a Proxy Server? 5-11

How to Configure ISA Server as a Proxy Server .5-15

How to Configure Web and Firewall Chaining 5-17

How to Configure Dial-Up Connections 5-24

Practice: Configuring ISA Server as a Proxy Server 5-26

Lesson Review 5-27

Lesson Summary 5-28

Lesson 3: Configuring Access Rule Elements 5-29

What Are Access Rule Elements? 5-29

How to Configure Access Rule Elements 5-30

Practice: Configuring Access Rule Elements 5-38

Lesson Review 5-39

Lesson Summary 5-40

Lesson 4: Configuring ISA Server Authentication 5-41
 ISA Server Authentication Options 5-41
 How to Configure Authentication 5-44
 Practice: Configuring ISA Server Authentication 5-45
 Lesson Review 5-46
 Lesson Summary 5-47
Lesson 5: Configuring Access Rules for Internet Access 5-48
 What Are Access Rules? 5-48
 How to Configure Access Rules 5-49
 Troubleshooting Internet Access 5-55
 Practice: Configuring Access Rules for Internet Access 5-56
 Lesson Review 5-59
 Lesson Summary 5-60
 Scenario 1 5-61
 Scenario 2 5-61
Exam Highlights 5-64
 Key Points 5-64
 Key Terms 5-65

6 Implementing ISA Server Caching   6-1
Before You Begin 6-2
Lesson 1: Caching Overview 6-3
What Is Caching? 6-3
 How Caching Works 6-4
 Caching Scenarios 6-5
 What Are Content Download Jobs? 6-5
 How Caching Is Implemented in ISA Server 2004 6-7
 How ISA Server Restricts Content 6-8
 What Is Web Chaining and Caching? 6-9
 Lesson Review 6-11
 Lesson Summary 6-12
Lesson 2: Configuring Caching 6-13
 How to Enable Caching and Configure Cache Drives 6-13
 How to Configure Cache Settings 6-14
 What Are Cache Rules? 6-17
 How to Create and Manage Cache Rules 6-18
 Guidelines for Troubleshooting Caching 6-25
 Practice: Configuring Caching and Cache Rules 6-26
 Lesson Review 6-29
 Lesson Summary 6-30

Lesson 3: Configuring Content Download Jobs 6-31
   How to Configure Content Download Jobs 6-31
   How to Manage Content Download Jobs 6-35
   Practice: Configuring Content Download Jobs 6-36
   Lesson Review 6-37
   Lesson Summary 6-38
   Scenario 1 6-39
   Scenario 2 6-40
Chapter Summary 6-40
Exam Highlights 6-40
   Key Points 6-41
   Key Terms 6-41

7   Configuring ISA Server as a Firewall   **7-1**
Before You Begin 7-2
Lesson 1: Introduction to ISA Server as a Firewall 7-3
   What Is Packet Filtering? 7-3
   What Is Stateful Filtering? 7-5
   What Is Application-Layer Filtering? 7-7
   What Is Intrusion Detection? 7-8
   Lesson Review 7-9
   Lesson Summary 7-10
Lesson 2: Configuring Multiple Networking on ISA Server 7-12
   ISA Server Support for Multiple Networks 7-12
   Default Networks Enabled in ISA Server 7-15
   How to Create and Modify Network Objects 7-16
   How to Configure Network Rules 7-17
   Practice: Configuring Multiple Networking on ISA Server 7-20
   Lesson Review 7-22
   Lesson Summary 7-23
Lesson 3: Implementing Perimeter Networks and
Network Templates 7-24
   What Are Perimeter Networks? 7-24
   What Are Network Templates? 7-28
   How to Implement Network Templates 7-29
   Practice: Implementing Network Templates 7-33
   Lesson Review 7-35
   Lesson Summary 7-36

Lesson 4: Configuring Intrusion Detection and IP Preferences 7-37

Intrusion-Detection Configuration Options 7-37

How to Configure Intrusion Detection 7-39

IP Preferences Configuration Options 7-40

How to Configure IP Preferences 7-41

Practice: Configuring Intrusion Detection and IP Preferences 7-43

Lesson Review 7-44

Lesson Summary 7-45

Lesson 5: Implementing Application and Web Filtering 7-46

What Are Application Filters? 7-46

What Are Web Filters? 7-48

How the HTTP Web Filter Works 7-49

How to Configure a HTTP Web Filter 7-50

Practice: Configuring an HTTP Web Filter 7-61

Lesson Review 7-63

Lesson Summary 7-64

Scenario 1 7-65

Exam Highlights 7-67

Key Points 7-67

Key Terms 7-68

8   Implementing ISA Server Publishing   8-1

Before You Begin 8-2

Lesson 1: Introduction to Publishing 8-4

What Are Web Publishing Rules? 8-4

What Are Server Publishing Rules? 8-5

Considerations for Configuring DNS for Web and Server Publishing 8-6

Practice: Configuring DNS for Web and Server Publishing 8-9

Lesson Review 8-11

Lesson Summary 8-11

Lesson 2: Configuring Web Publishing Rules 8-13

Components of a Web Publishing Rule Configuration 8-13

How to Configure Web Listeners 8-14

How to Configure Path Mapping 8-19

How to Configure Link Translation 8-21

How to Configure Web Publishing Rules 8-23

Practice: Configuring Web Publishing Rules .8-29

Lesson Review 8-31

Lesson Summary 8-32

Lesson 3: Configuring Secure Web Publishing Rules 8-33
   Components of a Secure Web Publishing Rule Configuration 8-33
   How to Install Digital Certificates on ISA Server .8-36
   How to Configure SSL Bridging 8-37
   How to Configure SSL Tunneling 8-39
   How to Configure a New Secure Web Publishing Rule 8-39
   Practice: Configuring Secure Web Publishing Rules 8-42
   Lesson Review 8-45
   Lesson Summary 8-46
Lesson 4: Configuring Server Publishing Rules 8-47
   Components of a Server Publishing Rule Configuration 8-47
   How to Configure a Server Publishing Rule 8-49
   Server Publishing Scenarios 8-52
   Guidelines for Troubleshooting Web and Server Publishing 8-58
   Practice: Configuring Server Publishing Rules 8-59
   Lesson Review 8-61
   Lesson Summary 8-62
Lesson 5: Configuring ISA Server Authentication 8-63
   How Authentication and Web Publishing Rules Work Together 8-63
   ISA Server Web Publishing Authentication Scenarios 8-64
   How to Implement RADIUS Server for Authentication 8-67
   How to Implement SecurID for Authentication 8-70
   Practice: Configuring ISA Server Authentication 8-71
   Lesson Review 8-73
   Lesson Summary 8-74
   Scenario 1 8-75
   Scenario 2 8-76
Chapter Summary 8-78
Exam Highlights 8-78
   Key Points 8-79
   Key Terms 8-79

9   Integrating ISA Server 2004 and Exchange Server   9-1
   Before You Begin 9-2
   Lesson 1: Configuring ISA Server to Secure SMTP Traffic 9-3
   Known SMTP Security Issues 9-3
   How to Configure ISA Server to Secure SMTP Traffic 9-5
   How to Configure the SMTP Application Filter 9-8
   How to Implement SMTP Message Screener 9-11
   Guidelines for Implementing SMTP Message Screener 9-16

Practice: Configuring ISA Server to Secure SMTP Traffic 9-19

Lesson Review 9-23

Lesson Summary 9-25

Lesson 2: Configuring ISA Server to Secure Web
Client Connections 9-26

Known Web Client Security Issues 9-26

How to Configure ISA Server to Enable Outlook Web
Access Connections 9-28

How to Configure Forms-Based Authentication 9-30

How to Configure ISA Server to Enable Access for Other Web Clients 9-33

Practice: Configuring ISA Server to Secure OWA Client Connections 9-34

Lesson Review 9-36

Lesson Summary 9-37

Lesson 3: Configuring ISA Server to Secure Outlook
Client Connections 9-38

Known Outlook Client Security Issues 9-39

How to Configure ISA Server to Secure Outlook RPC Connections 9-40

What Is RPC over HTTP? 9-43

How to Configure RPC-over-HTTP Connectivity .9-44

How to Configure E-Mail Access for POP3 and IMAP4 Clients 9-46

Practice: Configuring ISA Server to Secure Outlook Client Connections 9-47

Lesson Review 9-48

Lesson Summary 9-49

Scenario 1 9-49

Scenario 2 9-50

Key Points 9-54

Key Terms 9-55

**10   Configuring Virtual Private Networks for Remote
Clients and Networks   10-1**

Before You Begin 10-2

Lesson 1: Planning a Virtual Private Networking Infrastructure 10-4

What Is Virtual Private Networking? 10-4

VPN Protocol Options 10-7

VPN Authentication Options 10-8

How VPN Quarantine Control Is Used to Enforce Remote-Access
Security Policies 10-10

How Virtual Private Networking Is Implemented Using ISA Server 2004 . .10-11

Guidelines for Planning a VPN Infrastructure 10-12

Lesson Review 10-14

Lesson Summary 10-14

Lesson 2: Configuring Virtual Private Networking for Remote Clients 10-16
How to Configure VPN Client Access 10-16
How to Configure VPN Address Assignment 10-20
How to Configure VPN Authentication 10-23
How to Configure VPN Connections from Client Computers 10-27
Guidelines for Troubleshooting VPN Client Connections 10-28
Practice: Configuring Virtual Private Networking for Remote Clients 10-29
Lesson Review 10-30
Lesson Summary 10-32
Lesson 3: Configuring Virtual Private Networking for Remote Sites 10-33
Configuring a Site-to-Site VPN 10-33
What Are Site-to-Site VPNs? 10-34
Guidelines for Choosing a VPN Tunneling Protocol 10-34
How to Configure a Remote-Site Network 10-36
How to Configure Site-to-Site VPNs Using IPSec Tunnel Mode 10-39
How to Configure Network and Access Rules for Site-to-Site VPNs 10-40
How to Configure the Remote-Site VPN Gateway Server 10-42
Guidelines for Troubleshooting Site-to-Site VPNs 10-43
Practice: Configuring Virtual Private Networking for Remote Sites 10-44
Lesson Review 10-47
Lesson Summary 10-48
Lesson 4: Configuring VPN Quarantine Control 10-50
What Is Network Quarantine Control? 10-50
How Network Quarantine Control Is Implemented Using ISA Server 10-51
How to Prepare the Client-Side Script 10-53
How to Configure VPN Clients Using Connection Manager 10-55
How to Prepare the Listener Component 10-56
How to Enable Quarantine Control 10-57
How to Configure Internet Authentication Server for
Network Quarantine 10-59
How to Configure Quarantined VPN Client-Access Rules 10-60
Practice: Configuring VPN Quarantine Control 10-61
Lesson Review 10-67
Lesson Summary 10-68
Scenario 1 10-69
Scenario 2 10-69
Chapter Summary 10-70

Exam Highlights 10-71

    Key Points 10-71

    Key Terms 10-72

11   Implementing Monitoring and Reporting   11-1

Before You Begin 11-2

Lesson 1: Planning a Monitoring and Reporting Strategy 11-3

    Why You Should Implement Monitoring 11-3

    ISA Server Monitoring Components 11-4

    Guidelines for Planning a Monitoring and Reporting Strategy 11-6

    ISA Server Performance and Service Monitoring 11-9

    Lesson Review 11-12

    Lesson Summary 11-13

Lesson 2: Configuring and Managing Alerts .11-15

    What Are Alerts? 11-15

    How to Configure Alerts 11-17

    Guidelines for Managing Alerts 11-23

    Practice: Configuring and Managing Alerts 11-24

    Lesson Review 11-27

    Lesson Summary 11-28

Lesson 3: Configuring Session and Connectivity Monitoring 11-29

    What Is Session Monitoring? 11-29

    How to Monitor Sessions 11-30

    What Is Connectivity Monitoring? 11-34

    How to Configure Connectivity Monitoring .11-34

    Practice: Configuring Session and Connectivity Monitoring 11-36

    Lesson Review 11-38

    Lesson Summary 11-39

Lesson 4: Configuring Logging and Reporting 11-40

    What Is ISA Server Logging? 11-40

    How to Configure Logging 11-41

    How to View ISA Server Logs 11-44

    What Are ISA Server Reports? 11-47

    How to Configure ISA Server Reports 11-48

    Practice: Configuring ISA Server Reporting 11-54

    Lesson Review 11-55

    Lesson Summary 11-57

Exam Highlights 11-59

    Key Points 11-59

    Key Terms 11-61

12 Implementing ISA Server 2004, Enterprise Edition 12-1

Before You Begin 12-2

Lesson 1: ISA Server 2004 Enterprise Edition Overview 12-3

Why Deploy ISA Server, Enterprise Edition? 12-3

How Does ISA Server, Enterprise Edition, Store Configuration Information? .12-5

ISA Server Enterprise Edition Configuration Components 12-8

How Enterprise Policies and Array Policies Work 12-11

How Enterprise Edition Integrates with Network Load Balancing 12-13

How Enterprise Edition Enables Virtual Private Networking 12-15

How Enterprise Edition Enables Distributed Caching Using CARP 12-15

Lesson Review 12-17

Lesson Summary 12-18

Lesson 2: Planning an ISA Server 2004 Enterprise Edition Deployment 12-20

ISA Server Enterprise Edition Deployment Scenarios 12-20

Guidelines for Planning the Configuration Storage Server Deployment . . .12-22

Guidelines for Planning Enterprise and Array Policy Configuration 12-24

Guidelines for Planning for Centralized Monitoring and Management 12-26

Guidelines for Planning a Back-to-Back Firewall Deployment 12-27

Guidelines for Planning a Branch-Office Deployment 12-35

How Migrating from ISA Server 2000, Enterprise Edition, Works 12-38

Lesson Review 12-39

Lesson Summary 12-41

Lesson 3: Implementing ISA Server 2004, Enterprise Edition 12-43

Requirements for Installing Enterprise Edition 12-43

How to Install Configuration Storage Server 12-45

Practice: Installing a Configuration Storage Server 12-48

How to Configure Enterprise Policies and Networks 12-50

How to Configure Arrays and Array Policies 12-53

Practice: Configuring Enterprise and Array Policies 12-57

How to Install ISA Server 2004, Enterprise Edition 12-60

Practice: Installing ISA Server 2004, Enterprise Edition 12-62

How to Configure NLB and CARP 12-65

Lesson Review 12-70

Lesson Summary 12-71

Chapter Summary 12-73

Exam Highlights 12-74

Key Points 12-74

Key Terms 12-75

Part 2   Prepare for the Exam

13   Planning and Installing ISA Server 2004 (1.0)   13-3
   Testing Skills and Suggested Practices 13-3
   Further Reading 13-4
   Plan an ISA Server 2004 Deployment 13-6
      Objective 1.1 Questions 13-7
      Objective 1.1 Answers. 13-15
   Assess and Configure the Operating System, Hardware, and Network Services . .13-21
      Objective 1.2 Questions 13-22
      Objective 1.2 Answers. 13-26
   Deploy ISA Server 2004 13-30
      Objective 1.3 Questions 13-31
      Objective 1.3 Answers. 13-35

14   Installing and Configuring Client Computers (2.0)   14-1
   Testing Skills and Suggested Practices 14-1
   Further Reading 14-2
   Install Firewall Client Software 14-3
      Objective 2.1 Questions 14-4
      Objective 2.1 Answers. 14-6
   Configure Client Computers for ISA Server 2004 14-8
      Objective 2.2 Questions 14-9
      Objective 2.2 Answers. 14-11
   Configure a Local Domain Table (LDT). 14-13
      Objective 2.3 Questions 14-14
      Objective 2.3 Answers. 14-17
   Configure ISA Server 2004 for Automatic Client Configuration by
   Using Web Proxy Automatic Discovery (WPAD) 14-19
      Objective 2.4 Questions 14-20
      Objective 2.4 Answers. 14-22
   Diagnose and Resolve Client Computer Connectivity Issues 14-24
      Objective 2.5 Questions 14-25
      Objective 2.5 Answers. 14-29

15   Configuring and Managing ISA Server 2004 (3.0)   15-1
   Testing Skills and Suggested Practices 15-2
   Further Reading 15-3
   Configure the System Policy. 15-5
      Objective 3.1 Questions 15-6
      Objective 3.1 Answers. 15-10

Back Up and Restore ISA Server 2004 15-14

    Objective 3.2 Questions 15-15

    Objective 3.2 Answers. 15-18

Define Administrative Roles 15-21

    Objective 3.3 Questions 15-22

    Objective 3.3 Answers. 15-26

Configure Firewall Settings. 15-29

    Objective 3.4 Questions 15-30

    Objective 3.4 Answers. 15-33

Configure ISA Server 2004 for Network Load Balancing 15-36

    Objective 3.5 Questions 15-37

    Objective 3.5 Answers. 15-39

Configure ISA Server 2004 to Support a Network Topology. 15-41

    Objective 3.6 Questions 15-42

    Objective 3.6 Answers. 15-44

16   Configuring Web Caching (4.0)   16-1

Tested Skills and Suggested Practices 16-1

Further Reading 16-2

Configure Forward Caching and Reverse Caching 16-4

    Objective 4.1 Questions 16-5

    Objective 4.1 Answers. 16-7

Optimize Performance on the ISA Server 2004 Cache 16-13

    Objective 4.2 Questions 16-14

    Objective 4.2 Answers. 16-17

Diagnose and Resolve Caching Issues 16-21

    Objective 4.3 Questions 16-22

    Objective 4.3 Answers. 16-24

17   Configuring Firewall Policy (5.0)   17-1

Tested Skills and Suggested Practices 17-1

Further Reading 17-3

Plan a Firewall Policy 17-5

    Objective 5.1 Questions 17-6

    Objective 5.1 Answers. 17-10

Create Policy Elements, Access Rules, and Connection Limits 17-13

    Objective 5.2 Questions 17-14

    Objective 5.2 Answers. 17-17

Create Policy Rules for Web Publishing 17-19

    Objective 5.3 Questions 17-20

Objective 5.3 Answers 17-25

Create Policy Rules for Mail Server Publishing 17-32

Objective 5.4 Questions 17-33

Objective 5.4 Answers 17-36

Create Policy Rules for Server Publishing 17-38

Objective 5.5 Questions 17-39

Objective 5.5 Answers 17-42

18   Configuring and Managing Remote Network Connectivity (6.0)   18-1

Tested Skills and Suggested Practices 18-1

Further Reading 18-2

Configure ISA Server 2004 for Site-to-Site VPNs 18-4

Objective 6.1 Questions 18-5

Objective 6.1 Answers 18-8

Configure ISA Server 2004 as a Remote-Access VPN Server 18-12

Objective 6.2 Questions 18-13

Objective 6.2 Answers 18-16

Diagnose and Resolve VPN Connectivity Issues 18-20

Objective 6.3 Questions 18-21

Objective 6.3 Answers 18-27

19   Monitoring and Reporting ISA Server 2004 Activity (7.0)   19-1

Tested Skills and Suggested Practices 19-1

Further Reading 19-2

Monitor ISA Server 2004 Activity 19-4

Objective 7.1 Questions 19-5

Objective 7.1 Answers 19-10

Configure and Run Reports 19-15

Objective 7.2 Questions 19-16

Objective 7.2 Answers 19-18

Configure Logging and Alerts 19-20

Objective 7.3 Questions 19-21

Objective 7.3 Answers 19-24

Glossary G-1

Index I-1

Acknowledgements

Writing a book is always enjoyable because it gives me a chance to learn everything I can about an interesting product and then communicate what I have learned to you, the reader. Writing this book has been particularly enjoyable because everything that happened around the writing part went so smoothly. For that I have to thank the team that worked with me on the book.

Special thanks to my daughter, Amanda, who helped out a great deal with the technical writing of this book. And thanks to Gary Dunlop, who wrote most of the review questions and scenarios in the first part of the book.

As usual, the team at Microsoft Learning was great. Julie Pickering got me involved in the project and managed the project with her usual sense of humor. Lori Kane and Colin Lyth provided book design and technical guidance. Most of the actual editing for the book was handled by another team headquartered at nSight in Burlington, Mass. Sue McClung, the project manager, kept us all on schedule. The expertise in network security provided by Kurt Dillard, the technical editor, made this a better book. In addition, the editing team included the following: Peter Tietjen, copy editor; Peter Amirault, desktop production specialist; Jan Cocker, Cindy Gierhart, Tempe Goodhue, and Kiren Valjee, proofreaders; and Jack Lewis, indexer. Thanks to all of you.

Stan Reimer

I would love to thank my wife Oksana and son Rooslan for their love, support, and patience.

I would also like to deeply thank the following people at Microsoft Learning and nSight who have been instrumental in bringing about a successful conclusion to the writing process: Julie Pickering, Susan McClung, Stan Reimer, Kurt Dillard, Lori Kane, Randall Galloway, Peter Tietjen, Peter Amirault, Colin Lyth, and Paul Blount.

Finally, I'd like to thank Mick, Lards, Kasia, Shan, Linton, Corey, Lee, Gillian, Joan, Neil, Elena, Alex, Serge, Chris, Mike, Sergio, Michael, and Aunt Galina for all the ways in which they have made my family's life brighter.

Orin Thomas

About This Book

Welcome to *MCSA/MCSE Self-Paced Training Kit (Exam 70–350): Implementing Microsoft Internet Security and Acceleration (ISA) Server 2004*. This training kit is designed to provide the knowledge you need to pass the 70-350 certification exam. More importantly, this training kit also provides you with the knowledge and skills required to implement, manage and administer ISA Server 2004 in a real-world environment. This goal is much more important than just passing the exam; after all, passing an exam is of little value if you cannot actually use the knowledge you have gained to implement ISA Server 2004. To help you gain the required knowledge and skill, this book uses conceptual information, hands-on exercises and troubleshooting labs, real-world scenarios based on the author's consulting experiences, and questions designed to reinforce what you have learned.

Note   For more information about becoming a Microsoft Certified Professional, see the section titled "The Microsoft Certified Professional Program" later in this introduction.

Intended Audience

This book was developed for information technology (IT) professionals who plan to take the related Microsoft Certified Professional exam 70-350: *Implementing Microsoft Internet Security and Acceleration Server 2004*, as well as IT professionals who design, develop, and implement Microsoft ISA Server 2004 for Microsoft Windows-based environments.

Note   Exam skills are subject to change without prior notice and at the sole discretion of Microsoft.

Prerequisites

This training kit requires that students meet the following prerequisites:

Candidates for this exam operate in medium-sized to very large networked computing environments that use Microsoft Windows 2000 Server and Microsoft Windows Server 2003 operating systems. Candidates have a basic understanding of Active Directory directory service, DNS, DHCP, WINS, Certificate Services, RADIUS, Routing and Remote

Access Service, FTP, HTTP, HTTPS, TCP/IP, IMAP, POP3, RDP, SMTP, and SSL. They have a minimum of one year's experience implementing and administering networks and operating systems in environments that have the following characteristics:

- Between 50 and 10,000-plus supported users

- Multiple physical locations

- Outbound access for typical client services and applications, such as Web access, e-mail, Telnet, FTP, VPN, desktop management, Instant Messaging, and access control policies

- Hosting of network services, such as internal and external Web hosting, messaging, Instant Messaging, RDP, and firewall

- Connectivity requirements that include connecting individual offices and users at remote locations to the corporate network and connecting networks to the Internet

- Using ISA Server firewall or caching services, or both, in a production environment

About the CD-ROM

For your use, this book includes a Supplemental CD-ROM, which contains a variety of informational aids to complement the book content:

- The Microsoft Press Readiness Review Suite Powered by MeasureUp. This suite of practice tests and objective reviews contains questions of varying degrees of complexity and offers multiple testing modes. You can assess your understanding of the concepts presented in this book and use the results to develop a learning plan that meets your needs.

- An electronic version of this book (eBook). For information about using the eBook, see the section entitled "The eBook" later in this introduction.

A second CD-ROM contains a 180-day evaluation edition of ISA Server 2004, Standard Edition.

Features of This Book

This book has two parts. Use Part 1 to learn at your own pace and practice what you've learned with practical exercises. Part 2 contains questions and answers you can use to test yourself on what you've learned.

Part 1: Learn at Your Own Pace

Each chapter identifies the exam objectives that are covered within the chapter, provides an overview of why the topics matter by identifying how the information is applied in the real world, and lists any prerequisites that must be met to complete the lessons presented in the chapter.

The chapters are divided into lessons. Lessons contain practices that include one or more hands-on exercises. These exercises give you an opportunity to use the skills being presented or explore the part of the application being described.

After the lessons, you are given an opportunity to apply what you've learned in a case scenario exercise. In this exercise, you work through a multi-step solution for a realistic case scenario. In many chapters, you are also given an opportunity to work through a troubleshooting lab that explores difficulties you might encounter when applying what you've learned on the job.

Each chapter ends with a short summary of key concepts and a short section listing key topics and terms you need to know before taking the exam. This section summarizes the key topics you've learned, with a focus on demonstrating that knowledge on the exam.

> **Real World**   **Helpful Information**
>
> You will find sidebars like this one that contain related information you might find helpful. "Real World" sidebars contain specific information gained through the experience of IT professionals just like you.

Part 2: Prepare for the Exam

Part 2 helps to familiarize you with the types of questions you will encounter on the MCP exam. By reviewing the objectives and sample questions, you can focus on the specific skills you need to improve before taking the exam.

> **See Also**   For a complete list of MCP exams, go to *http://www.microsoft.com/learning/mcp/mcp/requirements.asp*.

Part 2 is organized by the exam's objectives. Each chapter covers one of the primary groups of objectives, referred to as Objective Domains. Each chapter lists the tested skills you need to master to answer the exam questions, and it includes a list of further readings to help you improve your ability to perform the tasks or skills specified by the objectives.

Within each Objective Domain, you will find the related objectives that are covered on the exam. Each objective provides you with several practice exam questions. The answers are accompanied by explanations of each correct and incorrect answer.

> **Note**   These questions are also available on the companion CD as a practice test.

Informational Notes

Several types of reader aids appear throughout the training kit.

- **Tip** contains methods of performing a task more quickly or in a not-so-obvious way.

- **Important** contains information that is essential to completing a task.

- **Note** contains supplemental information.

- **Caution** contains valuable information about possible loss of data; be sure to read this information carefully.

- **Warning** contains critical information about possible physical injury; be sure to read this information carefully.

- **See Also** contains references to other sources of information.

- **Planning** contains hints and useful information that should help you to plan the implementation.

- **On the CD** points you to supplementary information or files you need that are on the companion CD.

- **Security Alert** highlights information you need to know to maximize security in your work environment.

- **Exam Tip** flags information you should know before taking the certification exam.

- **Off the Record** contains practical advice about the real-world implications of information presented in the lesson.

Notational Conventions

The following conventions are used throughout this book:

■ Characters or commands that you type appear in **bold** type.

■ *Italic* in syntax statements indicates placeholders for variable information. *Italic* is also used for book titles.

■ Names of files and folders appear in Title Caps, except when you are to type them directly. Unless otherwise indicated, you can use all lowercase letters when you type a file name in a dialog box or at a command prompt.

■ File name extensions appear in all uppercase.

■ Acronyms appear in all uppercase.

■ Monospace type represents code samples, examples of screen text, or entries that you might type at a command prompt or in initialization files.

■ Square brackets [ ] are used in syntax statements to enclose optional items. For example, [filename] in command syntax indicates that you can choose to type a file name with the command. Type only the information within the brackets, not the brackets themselves.

■ Braces { } are used in syntax statements to enclose required items. Type only the information within the braces, not the braces themselves.

Keyboard Conventions

■ A plus sign (+) between two key names means that you must press those keys at the same time. For example, "Press ALT+TAB" means that you hold down ALT while you press TAB.

■ A comma (,) between two or more key names means that you must press each of the keys consecutively, not together. For example, "Press ALT, F, X" means that you press and release each key in sequence. "Press ALT+W, L" means that you first press ALT and W at the same time, and then release them and press L.

Getting Started

This training kit contains hands-on exercises to help you learn about ISA Server 2004 by performing the actual steps required to implement, configure, and troubleshoot ISA Server 2004. These exercises provide hands-on skills training that you will need to pass the exam, and to deploy ISA Server successfully in your network environment. Use this section to prepare your self-paced training environment.

To complete some of these procedures, you must have up to four networked computers or be connected to a larger network. All computers must be capable of running Microsoft Windows Server 2003 or Microsoft Windows XP. One of the computers must also be capable of running Microsoft Exchange Server 2003.

> **Caution**   Several exercises might require you to make changes to your servers. This might have undesirable results if you are connected to a larger network. Check with your Network Administrator before attempting these exercises.

Hardware Requirements

Each computer must have the following minimum configuration. All hardware should be on the Windows Server 2003 or Windows XP Hardware Compatibility List.

- A personal computer with a 550 megahertz (MHz) or higher Pentium III–compatible CPU.
- 256 megabytes (MB) of memory.
- For the computers that will be configured as ISA Server computers, you need one network adapter for communication with the internal network and an additional network adapter for each network directly connected to the ISA Server 2004 computer. You need two network adapters for most exercises, with a third network adapter required for one exercise.
- One local hard disk partition that is formatted with the NTFS file system and that has at least 150 megabytes (MB) of available hard-disk space. If you enable caching and logging, you will need additional hard-disk space.
- CD-ROM drive.
- Microsoft Mouse or compatible pointing device.

Software Requirements

The following software is required to complete the procedures in this training kit. (A 180-day evaluation edition of ISA Server 2003, Enterprise Edition, is included on the CD-ROM.)

- Microsoft Windows Server 2003, Enterprise Edition
- Microsoft Internet Security and Acceleration Server 2004, Standard Edition
- Microsoft Internet Security and Acceleration Server 2004, Enterprise Edition (required only for Chapter 12, "Implementing ISA Server, Enterprise Edition")

- Microsoft Exchange Server 2003, either Standard or Enterprise Edition (required only for Chapter 9, "Integrating ISA Server 2004 and Exchange Server," and Chapter 11, "Implementing Monitoring and Reporting")

- Microsoft Windows XP, Professional Edition

- Microsoft Outlook 2003

Caution The 180-day Evaluation Edition that is provided with this training kit is not the full retail product and is provided only for the purposes of training and evaluation. Microsoft Technical Support does not support these evaluation editions. For additional support information regarding this book and the CD-ROMs (including answers to commonly asked questions about installation and use), visit the Microsoft Press Technical Support Web site at http://www.microsoft.com/learning/support/default.asp. You can also e-mail tkinput@microsoft.com or send a letter to Microsoft Press, Attn: Microsoft Press Technical Support, One Microsoft Way, Redmond, WA 98502-6399.

Setup Instructions

Set up your computer according to the manufacturer's instructions.

For the exercises that require networked computers, you need to make sure the computers can communicate with each other. The first computer will be configured as a domain controller in the *cohovineyard.com* domain and installed as DC1. This computer should have an IP address of 10.10.0.10. If you use a different IP address, you will need to modify the practices and labs that use this IP address.

A second computer will act as an ISA Server 2004 computer for most of the procedures in this course. This computer will have Windows Server 2003 installed, use a computer name of ISA1, and will be configured as a domain member in the *cohovineyard.com* domain. This server should have two network interfaces installed. The network interface assigned to the internal network should have an IP address of 10.10.0.1. The network interface assigned to the external network can use any IP address that is compatible with the IP addresses used for your test network.

To complete some of the exercises in this training kit, you will also require a Windows XP computer installed as CLIENT1. This computer should have Outlook 2003 installed. This computer should be a member of the *cohovineyard.com* domain. This computer must have an IP address on the same network as DC1.

A third Windows Server 2003 computer named SERVER1 is required for some exercises. This computer should not be a member of the *cohovineyard.com* domain. This computer should have an IP address that is on the same network as the external interface of the ISA Server computer.

To complete the exercises in Chapter 9, you will also require a Windows Server 2003 server installed as MAIL1. This server needs to be a member of the *cohovineyard.com* domain and have a default installation of Exchange Server 2003 on it. The Exchange Server computer requires at least two mailboxes configured on it. This computer should use an IP address of 10.10.0.12.

In addition, to complete the exercises in Chapter 12, you also require two additional ISA Server computers running Windows Server 2003, using computer names of ISA2 and ISA3, and configured as a domain members in the *cohovineyard.com* domain. These servers should have two network interfaces installed. The internal network interface for ISA2 should use an IP address of 10.10.0.2, and the internal network interface for ISA3 should use an IP address of 10.10.0.3. The network interface assigned to the external network on both computers can use any IP address that is compatible with the IP addresses used for your test network.

Caution   If your computers are part of a larger network, you must verify with your network administrator that the computer names, domain name, and other information used in setting up Windows Server 2003, Windows XP, and ISA Server 2004 do not conflict with network operations. If they do conflict, ask your network administrator to provide alternative values and use those values throughout all the exercises in this book.

The Readiness Review Suite

The CD-ROM includes a practice test made up of 300 sample exam questions and an objective-by-objective review with an additional 125 questions. Use these tools to reinforce your learning and to identify any areas in which you need to gain more experience before taking the exam.

▶ **To install the practice test and objective review**

1. Insert the Supplemental CD-ROM into your CD-ROM drive.

Note   If AutoRun is disabled on your machine, refer to the Readme.txt file on the CD-ROM.

2. Click Readiness Review Suite on the user interface menu.

The eBook

The CD-ROM includes an electronic version of the Training Kit. The eBook is in portable document format (PDF). To view the document, you must have either Adobe Acrobat or Adobe Acrobat Reader, which are both available at the Adobe Web site (*http://www.adobe.com*).

▶ **To use the eBook**

1. Insert the Supplemental CD-ROM into your CD-ROM drive.

> **Note**   If AutoRun is disabled on your machine, refer to the Readme.txt file on the CD-ROM.

2. Click Training Kit eBook on the user interface menu. You can also review any of the other eBooks that are provided for your use.

The Microsoft Certified Professional Program

The Microsoft Certified Professional (MCP) program provides the best method to prove your command of current Microsoft products and technologies. The exams and corresponding certifications are developed to validate your mastery of critical competencies as you design and develop, or implement and support, solutions with Microsoft products and technologies. Computer professionals who become Microsoft-certified are recognized as experts and are sought after industry-wide. Certification brings a variety of benefits to the individual and to employers and organizations.

> **See Also**   For detailed information about the MCP program, go to *http://www.microsoft.com/learning/itpro/default.asp*.

Certifications

The Microsoft Certified Professional program offers multiple certifications, based on specific areas of technical expertise:

■ Microsoft Certified Professional (MCP). Demonstrated in-depth knowledge of at least one Microsoft Windows operating system or architecturally significant platform. An MCP is qualified to implement a Microsoft product or technology as part of a business solution for an organization.

■ Microsoft Certified Solution Developer (MCSD). Professional developers qualified to analyze, design, and develop enterprise business solutions with Microsoft development tools and technologies including the Microsoft .NET Framework.

■ Microsoft Certified Application Developer (MCAD). Professional developers qualified to develop, test, deploy, and maintain powerful applications using Microsoft tools and technologies including Microsoft Visual Studio .NET and XML Web services.

- Microsoft Certified Systems Engineer (MCSE). Qualified to effectively analyze the business requirements, and design and implement the infrastructure for business solutions based on the Microsoft Windows and Microsoft Server 2003 operating system.

- Microsoft Certified Systems Administrator (MCSA). Individuals with the skills to manage and troubleshoot existing network and system environments based on the Windows and Windows Server 2003 operating systems.

- Microsoft Certified Desktop Support Technician (MCDST). Individuals who support end users and troubleshoot desktop environments running on the Windows operating system.

- Microsoft Certified Database Administrator (MCDBA). Individuals who design, implement, and administer Microsoft SQL Server databases.

- Microsoft Certified Trainer (MCT). Instructionally and technically qualified to deliver Microsoft Official Curriculum through a Microsoft Certified Technical Education Center (CTEC).

Requirements for Becoming a Microsoft Certified Professional

The certification requirements differ for each certification and are specific to the products and job functions addressed by the certification.

To become a Microsoft Certified Professional, you must pass rigorous certification exams that provide a valid and reliable measure of technical proficiency and expertise. These exams are designed to test your expertise and ability to perform a role or task with a product, and are developed with the input of professionals in the industry. Questions in the exams reflect how Microsoft products are used in actual organizations, giving them "real-world" relevance.

- Microsoft Certified Professional (MCP) candidates are required to pass one current Microsoft certification exam. Candidates can pass additional Microsoft certification exams to further qualify their skills with other Microsoft products, development tools, or desktop applications.

- Microsoft Certified Solution Developers (MCSDs) are required to pass three core exams and one elective exam. (MCSD for Microsoft .NET candidates are required to pass four core exams and one elective.)

- Microsoft Certified Application Developers (MCADs) are required to pass two core exams and one elective exam in an area of specialization.

- Microsoft Certified Systems Engineers (MCSEs) are required to pass five core exams and two elective exams.

- Microsoft Certified Systems Administrators (MCSAs) are required to pass three core exams and one elective exam that provide a valid and reliable measure of technical proficiency and expertise.

- Microsoft Certified Desktop Support Technician (MCDSTs) are required to pass two core exams.

- Microsoft Certified Database Administrators (MCDBAs) are required to pass three core exams and one elective exam that provide a valid and reliable measure of technical proficiency and expertise.

- Microsoft Certified Trainers (MCTs) are required to meet instructional and technical requirements specific to each Microsoft Official Curriculum course they are certified to deliver. The MCT program requires on-going training to meet the requirements for the annual renewal of certification. For more information about becoming a Microsoft Certified Trainer, visit *http://www.microsoft.com/traincert/ mcp/mct/* or contact a regional service center near you.

Technical Support

Every effort has been made to ensure the accuracy of this book and the contents of the companion disc. If you have comments, questions, or ideas regarding this book or the companion disc, please send them to Microsoft Press using either of the following methods:

E-mail:	tkinput@microsoft.com
Postal Mail:	Microsoft Press
	Attn: MCSA/MSCE Self-Paced Training Kit (Exam 70-350): Implementing
	Microsoft Internet Security and Acceleration Server 2004, Editor
	One Microsoft Way
	Redmond, WA 98052-6399

For additional support information regarding this book and the CD-ROM (including answers to commonly asked questions about installation and use), visit the Microsoft Press Technical Support Web site at http://www.microsoft.com/learning/support/ default.asp. To connect directly to the Microsoft Press Knowledge Base and enter a query, visit *http://www.microsoft.com/mspress/support/search.asp*. For support information regarding Microsoft software, please connect to *http://support.microsoft.com/*.

Evaluation Edition Software Support

The 180-day Evaluation Edition provided with this training is not the full retail product and is provided only for the purposes of training and evaluation. Microsoft and Microsoft Technical Support do not support this evaluation edition.

Caution   The Evaluation Edition of ISA Server 2004, Standard Edition, that is included with this book should not be used on a primary work computer. The evaluation edition is unsupported. For online support information relating to the full version of ISA Server 2004, Standard Edition, which might also apply to the Evaluation Edition, you can connect to *http://support.microsoft.com/*.

Information about any issues relating to the use of this evaluation edition with this training kit is posted to the Support section of the Microsoft Press Web site at *http://www.microsoft.com/learning/support/default.asp*. For information about ordering the full version of any Microsoft software, please call Microsoft Sales at (800) 426-9400 or visit *http://www.microsoft.com*.

Part 1
Learn at Your Own Pace

1 Introduction to ISA Server 2004

Exam Objectives in this Chapter:

- Plan an ISA Server 2004 deployment

Why This Chapter Matters

This chapter is designed to give you the big picture of what Microsoft Internet Security and Acceleration (ISA) Server 2004 can do for your organization. In most cases when learning a new technology, it is beneficial to get a high-level overall picture of how the technology works before delving into the details of implementing and managing the technology. This chapter provides you with that overall picture–how ISA Server 2004 works, and when and how you should use it.

ISA Server is primarily a firewall designed to ensure that all unwanted traffic from the Internet is kept out of an organization's network. At the same time, ISA Server can also be used to provide internal users with selective access to Internet resources and Internet users with selective access to internal resources, such as Web or e-mail servers. ISA Server is usually deployed at the perimeter of an organization's network, which is where its internal network connects to an external network like the Internet.

Lessons in this Chapter:

- Lesson 1: Overview of ISA Server Functionality 1-4
- Lesson 2: Overview of ISA Server 2004 Editions and Versions 1-17
- Lesson 3: Explaining ISA Server Deployment Scenarios. 1-22
- Lesson 4: Overview of ISA Server 2004 Administration 1-31

Before You Begin

This chapter provides a high-level overview of ISA Server 2004 and how it can be used to secure your organization's network. There are no activities in this chapter that require you to use ISA Server, so no lab preparation is required. Later chapters will provide the details about how to implement the concepts discussed here.

Lesson 1: Overview of ISA Server Functionality

ISA Server 2004 is a valuable component in an overall plan to secure an organization's network. Because ISA Server is deployed at the connecting point between an internal network and the Internet, ISA Server's role is critical. Almost all organizations provide some level of access to the Internet for its users. ISA Server can be used to enforce security policies dealing with the types of access users should have to the Internet. At the same time, many organizations also allow remote users some type of access to internal servers. For example, almost all organizations allow e-mail servers on the Internet to connect to internal e-mail servers to send Internet e-mail. Many companies also host internal Web sites, or want employees to be able to access internal resources from the Internet. ISA Server 2004 can be used to ensure that access to these internal resources is secure.

After this lesson, you will be able to

- List the functionality provided by ISA Server 2004
- Describe how ISA Server 2004 operates as a firewall
- Describe how ISA Server 2004 can be used to enable secure access to Internet resources
- Describe how ISA Server 2004 can be used to enable secure access to internal network resources for Internet users
- Describe how ISA Server 2004 can be used to enable secure access to Microsoft Exchange Server
- Describe how ISA Server 2004 can be used to enable virtual private network (VPN) access for remote access clients and networks

Estimated lesson time: 30 minutes

How ISA Server Works—An Overview

ISA Server is designed to secure the perimeter of an organization's network. In most cases, this perimeter is between the organization's internal local area network (LAN) and a public network such as the Internet. Figure 1-1 shows an example of where ISA Server may be deployed.

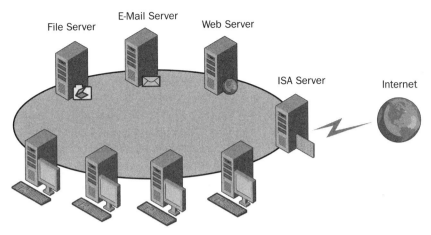

Figure 1-1 ISA Server is used to protect the perimeter of an organization's network.

Figure 1-1 shows a simple example of an ISA Server deployment. The internal network, or protected network, is usually located on an organization's premises and is under the control of the organization's IT staff. The internal network is considered to be relatively secure; that is, normally only authorized users have physical access to the internal network. Also, the IT staff have a great deal of control over the types of traffic that are allowed on the internal network.

> **Security Alert** Even though the internal network is more secure than the Internet, don't make the mistake of thinking that you just need to secure the network perimeter. To protect your network fully, you must employ a defense-in-depth strategy, which includes steps to ensure that the internal network is secure even in the event of a perimeter breach. Many recent network attacks like viruses and worms have devastated networks that have secure perimeters. ISA Server is critical in securing the network perimeter, but don't think that your job is done after you finish deploying ISA Server.

An organization has no control over who is accessing the Internet or over the security of network traffic on the Internet. Anyone in the world with an Internet connection can locate and access any other Internet connection using almost any application or protocol. Also, network packets sent via the Internet are not secure because they can be captured and inspected by anyone running a packet sniffer on an Internet network segment. A *packet sniffer* is an application that can be used to capture and view all the network traffic on a network. In order to capture network traffic, the packet sniffer must be connected to a network segment located between two routers.

Security Alert   The Internet is a fascinating and incredible invention. You can find information on literally anything online. You can locate other people who share your interests and communicate with those people regardless of national boundaries or physical distance. At the same time, the Internet is also a hazardous place, simply because anyone can access it. The very nature of the Internet makes securing it almost impossible. For example, the Internet is not designed to distinguish between the legitimate user and the hacker—both users can gain access to the Internet. This means that as soon as your organization creates a connection to the Internet, that connection is exposed to anyone on it. This may be a legitimate user looking for information on your organization's Web site, or it may be a hacker trying to deface your Web site or steal customer data from you. A good first step in securing your Internet connection is to assume the worst—begin by assuming that every user connecting to you is a hacker until proven otherwise.

Figure 1-1 showed a simple example of a network configuration where the boundary between an organization's internal network and the Internet is easy to define. In reality, defining the boundary between an organization's internal network and the rest of the world is not so simple. Figure 1-2 shows a more complicated, but more realistic, scenario.

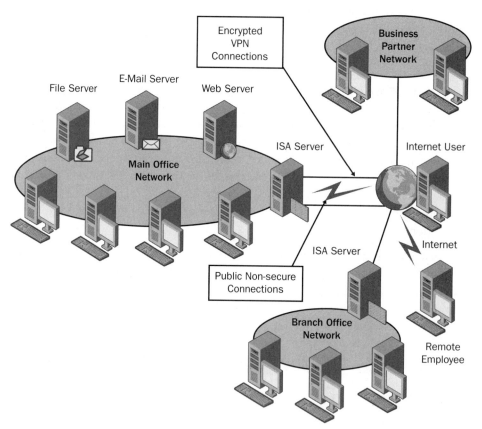

Figure 1-2   An organization's network may include multiple access points.

The network perimeter is much more difficult to define in a scenario such as the one shown in Figure 1-2. For example, company requirements may mean that the boundary between the internal network and the Internet can be crossed in several different ways:

- Any user on the Internet should be able to access the public Web site.

- Only users from a partner organization should be able to access a private Web site, and these users should be limited in what they can see on the site. These users are accessing the private Web site from the Internet.

- Users from a branch office should be able to gain full access to network resources on the internal network. The only connection between the branch office and the main office networks passes through the Internet.

- Employees that are out of the office and have an Internet connection should have access to internal network resources, including e-mail and file servers.

- Users on an internal network should be able to access the Internet, but should be limited to using only specific applications and allowed access to only specific Internet resources.

This scenario makes securing the Internet connection much more difficult. Regardless of the company scenario, ISA Server is designed to provide the required security at the network perimeter. For example, in the scenario shown in Figure 1-2, ISA Server can provide perimeter security by doing the following:

- Enabling anonymous access to the public Web site while filtering out malicious code aimed at compromising the Web site

- Authenticating users from the partner organization before granting access to the private Web site

- Enabling VPN access between the organization's locations so that users in the branch office can get access to internal network resources

- Enabling access to the internal e-mail servers for remote employees, and enabling client VPN access to internal file servers

- Enforcing the organization's Internet access policies by limiting the protocols available to users, and by filtering each user request to ensure they are accessing only the permitted Internet resources

The following sections go into more detail about how ISA Server provides this functionality.

How ISA Server Works as a Firewall

A firewall is a device that is located between one segment of a network and another, and allows only authorized traffic to pass between the segments. The firewall is configured with traffic filtering rules that define the types of network traffic that will be allowed to pass through. A firewall may be positioned and configured to protect an organization from the Internet, or it may be positioned internally to protect specific sections of an organization's corporate network.

In most cases, firewalls are deployed at the network perimeter. The primary purpose of a firewall in this configuration is to ensure that no traffic from a publicly accessible network like the Internet can enter an organization's internal network unless it has been explicitly permitted. For example, the organization may have an internal Web server that needs to be accessible to Internet users. The firewall can be configured to allow Internet traffic to access only that Web server.

ISA Server 2004 provides firewall functionality. By default, when you deploy ISA Server, it will block all traffic between networks that are attached to the server, including internal networks, perimeter networks (also known as demilitarized zones, or DMZs), and the Internet. ISA Server 2004 uses three types of filtering rules to block or allow network traffic: packet filtering, stateful filtering, and application-layer filtering.

Packet Filtering

Packet filtering works by examining the header information for each network packet that arrives at the firewall. When the packet arrives at the ISA Server network interface, ISA Server opens the packet header and checks information such as the source and destination addresses and the source and destination ports. ISA Server compares this information against its firewall rules that define which packets are allowed. If the source and destination addresses are allowed, and if the source and destination ports are allowed, the packet passes through the firewall to the destination network. If the addresses and the ports are not explicitly allowed, the packet is dropped and not forwarded through the firewall.

Stateful Filtering

Stateful filtering uses a more thorough examination of the network packet to make decisions on whether to forward it or not. When ISA Server uses a stateful inspection, it examines the Internet Protocol (IP) and the Transmission Control Protocol (TCP) headers to determine the state of a packet within the context of previous packets that have passed through ISA Server, or within the context of a TCP session. For example, a user on the internal network may send a request to a Web server on the Internet. The Web server sends a reply to that request. When the reply packet arrives at the firewall, the firewall inspects the TCP session information that is part of the packet. The firewall determines that the packet is part of a currently active session that was initiated by the internal user, so the packet is forwarded to the user's computer. If a user from outside the network attempts to connect to a computer inside the organization's network, the firewall determines that the packet is not part of a currently active session and the packet is dropped.

Application-Layer Filtering

ISA Server also uses application-layer filtering to determine whether a packet is allowed or not. Application-layer filtering examines the actual content of a packet to determine if the packet can be forwarded through the firewall. An application filter opens the entire packet and examines the actual data in it before making a forwarding decision. For example, a user on the Internet may request a page from the internal Web server using the Hypertext Transfer Protocol (HTTP) GET command. When the packet arrives at the firewall, the application filter inspects the packet and detects the GET command. The application filter checks its policy to determine if the GET command is allowed. In most cases, the GET command is allowed and the packet is forwarded to the internal Web server.

If the user sends a similar packet to the Web server, but uses the HTTP POST command, ISA Server again examines the packet. Because the POST command is used to write information to the Web server, the command is likely to be blocked. ISA Server notices the POST command, determines that the command is not allowed by the firewall policy, and drops the packet. The HTTP application filter provided with ISA Server 2004 can check for any information in the data, including virus signatures, Uniform Resource Locator (URL) length, page header content, and file extensions. ISA Server includes other application filters for securing other protocols and applications in addition to the HTTP filter.

> **Real World   Application-Layer Filtering**
>
> Virtually all firewalls available today perform packet and stateful filtering. However, many of these firewalls do not have the ability to perform application-layer filtering. And yet application-layer filtering has become one of the most critical components in securing a network perimeter. For example, virtually all organizations allow HTTP traffic (port 80) from the internal network to the Internet. As a result, many applications can now be tunneled through HTTP. For example, MSN Messenger and some peer-to-peer file sharing applications, such as Kazaa, use HTTP as a protocol. HTTP traffic can also include viruses or other malicious code.
>
> The only way to block unwanted network traffic, while still allowing legitimate HTTP usage, is to implement a firewall that is capable of application-layer filtering. The application-layer firewall can examine the contents of packets and block traffic based on HTTP methods (to block applications) or signatures (to block viruses, malicious code, or applications). ISA Server 2004 is exactly the type of sophisticated application-layer firewall that has become critical in protecting networks.

How ISA Server Enables Secure Internet Access

Almost all organizations provide Internet access for their users. The use of the World Wide Web as a source of information and as a communication tool means that most organizations cannot afford to be without access to it. At the same time, ensuring that the Internet connection is secure is critical.

Providing secure Internet access for users in an organization means the following:

- Users can access required resources. In many organizations, users must be able to access the Internet using a Web browser or other application.

- Users can access only permitted resources. Most organizations have an Internet usage policy that defines the types of applications that can be used to the Internet, and the types of Internet resources that can be accessed.

- The connection to the Internet is secure. Ideally, the connection to the Internet should not reveal any information about the internal system that can be used to launch an attack against the client computer. Information about the individual computer (for example, the computer name, user logon name, or shared folders), as well as details about the network configuration (for example, the client IP address), should be hidden.

- Data that users transfer to and from the Internet is secure. In some cases, users might send confidential personal data, such as credit card information, or confidential organizational information, such as client data, over the Internet. This data must be secure when it leaves the organization.

ISA Server 2004 can be used to secure connections for clients accessing resources on the Internet. To enable this, you must configure all client connections to the Internet so that they pass through ISA Server. When you configure this option, ISA Server operates as a proxy server between the internal client and the Internet resource.

When you configure internal clients to send all Internet requests through ISA Server, the client requests are sent to the proxy server component in ISA Server. ISA Server then sends the request to the Web server on the Internet. The Web server responds to the request and sends the reply back to the proxy server. The proxy server then forwards the reply back to the client that requested the information.

Using a proxy server means that there is no direct connection between the internal client and the Web server. The client's internal network information is not sent across the Internet. In addition to providing a secure connection, ISA Server 2004 can also filter Internet requests based on information such as user name, client IP address, protocol, and request content. This means that you can restrict which users can access information on the Internet, which applications they can use to access that information, and what types of information the users can access.

ISA Server can also operate as a caching server. The ISA Server cache is a store of frequently retrieved objects and URLs located on the cache drive of an ISA Server computer. Caching improves network performance because ISA Server can return information to a client from the cache rather than from the Internet. For example, when a user requests a page from a Web server that is not in the ISA Server cache, the ISA

Server computer retrieves the object from the Web and then retains a copy in its cache before delivering the object to the user. The benefit of caching is that when a second user requests the same Web page, ISA Server returns the object from its cache, saving time and eliminating additional Internet traffic.

How ISA Server Enables Internal Resource Publishing

Most organizations want Internet users to be able to access some resources located on their internal or protected networks. At a minimum, most organizations need to provide access to a public Web site. Organizations that are using the Internet to complete business transactions may need to make confidential information available or collect confidential information via a secure Web site. In addition, organizations may need to enable access to non-Web-based resources, such as DNS servers, media servers, or database servers.

Making internal resources accessible via the Internet increases security risks for an organization. To reduce these risks, the firewall at the perimeter of a network must be able to block all malicious traffic from entering the organization's network, and ensure that Internet users can access only the required servers. The firewall may also need to redirect traffic to more than one internal server, and provide access to multiple Web sites or internal servers while shielding the internal network configuration from the Internet.

You can use ISA Server 2004 to provide secure access to internal resources for Internet users by using ISA Server to publish the internal resources. To configure ISA Server publishing, you configure a publishing rule that specifies how ISA Server will respond to requests from the Internet. ISA Server provides three different types of publishing rules: Web publishing rules, secure Web publishing rules, and server publishing rules.

Web Publishing Rules

ISA Server 2004 uses Web publishing to enable secure access to internal Web servers for Internet clients. When you create a Web publishing rule, you are configuring ISA Server to listen for HTTP requests from the Internet. When the request for a Web page arrives, ISA Server evaluates the request. If the request matches the properties of a Web publishing rule, ISA Server forwards the request to an internal Web server. The internal Web server sends the requested Web page to ISA Server, which then forwards the Web page to the Internet client. If caching is enabled on ISA Server, subsequent requests for the Web page can be provided from the ISA Server cache.

ISA Server provides several options for securing access to the internal Web server. When you configure a Web publishing rule, you specify which Web server is being published by the Web publishing rule. Only published servers are accessible from the Internet. In addition, you can limit the URLs that ISA Server will respond to. For example, you can configure ISA Server to respond only to a URL like *www.cohovine*

yard.com. If an Internet user uses any other URL to try to connect to a Web server, the ISA Server computer will drop the request. You can also limit IP addresses and address ranges that are allowed to connect to the Web site.

ISA Server Web publishing rules can also be used to hide the complexity of the internal network from Internet users. Frequently, an organization may need to publish multiple Web sites, but may have only a single IP address that is routable on the Internet. Or a Web server may contain multiple virtual directories, but the organization may want to hide the actual names of those directories from Internet users. In some cases, a Web site may contain links to other internal servers that are not accessible from the Internet. ISA Server can be used in all of the situations to provide a single entry point to the internal Web sites, while hiding the complexity of the internal configuration from Internet users.

Secure Web Publishing Rules

Some organizations need additional security for their Web sites. The sites may contain confidential organizational data that can be accessed only by specified users, or they may collect confidential data from Internet users, including personal and credit card information. The data may need to be encrypted while it is crossing the Internet. You can help to protect such Web servers from Internet attacks by using ISA Server as a fire-wall, and by using Web publishing rules to enable access to the site. To encrypt traffic between the internal network and the Internet client, you need to configure a secure Web publishing rule.

A secure Web publishing rule is a regular Web publishing rule that uses Secure Sockets Layer (SSL) on port 443 to encrypt all traffic passed from the internal network to the Internet client. ISA Server provides multiple options for using SSL. For example, you can configure ISA Server to encrypt all traffic between ISA Server and the Internet client, but not to encrypt the traffic on the internal network. Alternatively, you can encrypt only traffic on the internal network. You can also configure ISA Server to encrypt traffic on both the internal network and to and from the Internet. You can configure ISA Server to apply application filtering on the encrypted packets as well. With this configuration, the ISA Server computer will decrypt the packet, filter it, and then encrypt the packet again.

Another important part of enabling secure access to a Web site is to ensure that only authorized personnel have access to the site. Both Web publishing rules and secure Web publishing rules can be configured to do this. ISA Server supports multiple methods for authenticating users, including certificates, Active Directory directory service, Remote Authentication Dial-In User Service (RADIUS), and RSA SecureID. You can also configure authentication at different locations. For example, you can configure ISA Server to authenticate all users before granting access to a Web site. Or you can configure ISA Server to pass the user credentials to the Web server, and then configure the

Web server to authenticate the users. In some cases, you may want to authenticate users at both ISA Server and Web server levels.

Server Publishing Rules

Web publishing and secure Web publishing can grant access only to Web servers using HTTP or Hypertext Transfer Protocol Secure (HTTPS). To grant access to internal resources using any other protocol, you must configure server publishing rules. When you create a server publishing rule, you are configuring ISA Server to listen for client requests using a particular port number. When ISA Server receives a request on the external interface for that port, it checks the server publishing rule to determine which internal server is providing the service. ISA Server then passes the request to the internal server configured in that server publishing rule. The internal server responds to the client request, forwarding the response through ISA Server.

Server publishing rules can be used to publish any server as long as ISA Server has a definition for the protocol that the server is using. ISA Server includes more than 20 protocol definitions. For some protocols, ISA Server includes both secure and non-secure definitions. For example, you can configure a server publishing rule using the Internet Mail Access Protocol version 4 (IMAP4), or you can use the Internet Mail Access Protocol Secure (IMAPS) protocol so that all the traffic will be encrypted using SSL. ISA Server also includes specific application filters for many of the supported protocols. If ISA Server does not have an existing definition for a desired protocol, you can create it.

How ISA Server Enables E-Mail Server Publishing

In addition to granting access to Web sites, almost all organizations also provide access to e-mail servers from the Internet. In order to receive e-mail from Internet users, organizations must configure their e-mail server to accept Simple Mail Transfer Protocol (SMTP) port 25 connections. In most cases, an organization's e-mail server is located on an internal network, which means that the organization must allow SMTP connections through the firewall. Many organizations use Exchange Server as their e-mail server. Exchange Server operates as an SMTP server, but also provides several options for users to access their e-mail from the Internet. This means that securing access to Exchange Server computers usually includes securing both SMTP server connections as well as client connections.

ISA Server 2004 provides the following features to help secure access to Exchange Server computers:

- SMTP server publishing rules and SMTP application and content filters. ISA Server 2004 includes a SMTP server publishing rule that can be used to publish the internal SMTP server. It also includes a SMTP application filter that can block specific SMTP commands or malformed commands. For example, attackers may attempt a buffer overflow attack on an Exchange Server computer by sending SMTP commands with larger-than-normal payloads. The SMTP application filter can block this type of attack.

■ SMTP Message Screener. Message Screener can filter out the unwanted e-mail that enters an organization. All organizations are bombarded with unwanted e-mail, either in the form of unsolicited commercial e-mail (or spam), or e-mails with virus-bearing attachments. Message Screener can block e-mail messages based on who sent the message and whether the message contains specific attachments or keywords.

■ Pre-configured Web publishing rules that can provide access to the Exchange Server computer for Microsoft Outlook Web Access (OWA) and Outlook Mobile Access (OMA) clients. OWA provides access to mailboxes on the Exchange Server computer for users using Web browsers, while OMA provides e-mail access to wireless Web clients. The specialized Web publishing rules are preconfigured so that when you create a new mail publishing rule, many of the configuration options are enabled by default. You can also use the ISA Server HTTP filter to apply application-layer filtering to Web client connections, to block potentially dangerous attachments or message contents.

■ Web or server publishing rules that make Exchange Server computers accessible to Internet clients. Exchange Server computers support many different e-mail clients. One of the most popular clients is Microsoft Outlook, which uses remote procedure call (RPC) connections to the Exchange Server computer. RPC connections are very difficult to secure because the ports used for RPC are dynamically assigned when a client connects to the server. ISA Server can provide secure access for Outlook clients with an included RPC filter that can manage dynamic RPC ports. ISA Server can also be used to publish Exchange Server computers using other e-mail protocols, such as IMAP and Post Office Protocol (POP).

How ISA Server Works as a VPN Server

In addition to granting Internet users access to specific internal servers, many organizations also need to provide remote users with access to all internal network resources. For example, an employee may be traveling and need access to resources located on the internal servers. Or an organization may have multiple locations, with employees from one office requiring access to network resources in another. To enable this level of access to the internal network, many organizations implement VPNs.

A VPN is a secure network connection created through a public network such as the Internet. The VPN is secured by using authentication and encryption, so that even if network packets are captured on the public network the packets cannot be read or replayed. VPNs can be created between a remote access user and the internal network, or between two company locations.

A remote access VPN provides an alternative to dial-up connections by providing secure access from any Internet location. This means that a user can connect to the Internet by using a local dial-up account or a high-speed Internet connection such as a DSL, and then connect to the VPN gateway. All packets sent across the Internet using the VPN are secured.

A site-to-site VPN provides an alternative to using a dedicated wide area network (WAN) to connect company locations. A site-to-site VPN is created when a VPN gateway server in one company location creates a secure VPN tunnel through the Internet to a second VPN gateway server located at another location. In most cases, using a VPN is much more cost-effective than using a WAN to connect company locations.

ISA Server provides a VPN remote access solution that is integrated within the firewall. When remote clients connect to a computer running ISA Server using a VPN, the clients are assigned to the VPN Clients network. This network is treated just like any other network on ISA Server, which means you can configure firewall rules to filter all traffic from VPN clients. ISA Server also provides VPN quarantine control functionality. VPN quarantine control delays normal remote access to a private network until the configuration of the remote access client has been examined and validated by a client-side script. If you enable VPN quarantine control, all VPN clients are assigned to the Quarantined VPN Clients network until they have passed specific security checks. You can configure firewall rules that filter all traffic from the clients in the Quarantined VPN Clients network to any other network on a computer running ISA Server.

ISA Server also enables site-to-site VPNs. In this scenario, you configure an ISA Server in each company location. When the ISA Server computer in one location receives network traffic destined for the other location, the ISA Server computer initiates a site-to-site VPN connection and routes the traffic through it to the other location. To configure site-to-site VPN connections, you create a remote-site network on ISA Server, and then define the access rules that determine the types of traffic to be allowed to flow between the networks.

Lesson Review

Use the following questions to help determine whether you have learned enough to move on to the next lesson. If you have difficulty answering these questions, review the material in this lesson before beginning the next lesson. You can find answers to the questions in the "Questions and Answers" section at the end of this chapter.

1. You have deployed ISA Server 2004 at the perimeter of your network. You need to ensure that all users are able to access the Internet through the ISA Server computer. However, you also need to ensure that users can access only approved Web sites. What should you do?

   _____

   _____

   _____

2. You have deployed ISA Server 2004 at the perimeter of your network. You now need to configure the ISA Server computer so that the organization's Web site is available to all users on the Internet. You also need to ensure that only remote

employees can access a Web site that contains confidential customer information. The data on the confidential Web site must not be readable when it is sent across the Internet. What should you do?

_____

_____

_____

3. You have deployed ISA Server 2004 as a VPN remote access server. What ISA Server feature can be used to ensure that all client computers are in compliance with the organization's security policies before granting the user access to the network?

    a. PPTP

    b. RADIUS authentication

    c. Quarantine control

    d. Application-layer filtering

Lesson Summary

- ISA Server 2004 is normally installed at a network perimeter and is used to block all unauthorized access to an internal network, as well as allow limited access from the internal network to the Internet.

- ISA Server 2004 provides firewall functionality. As a firewall, ISA Server provides packet filtering, stateful filtering, and application-layer filtering.

- ISA Server 2004 enables secure access to the Internet by ensuring that clients can access only the required resources on the Internet, and by ensuring that the connection and data transfer both to and from the Internet is secure.

- ISA Server 2004 allows secure access from the Internet to internal network resources through the use of Web publishing rules, secure Web publishing rules, and server publishing rules. These publishing rules limit who can access the internal network and what can be viewed once the internal network is accessed.

- ISA Server 2004 can enable secure access to e-mail servers by blocking attacks against those servers and filtering incoming mail for unwanted spam and attachments. ISA Server can also enable secure client connections to Exchange Server for clients using a variety of client protocols.

- ISA Server 2004 can enable secure connections to internal network resources by enabled VPN connections for remote clients and sites.

Lesson 2: Overview of ISA Server 2004 Editions and Versions

ISA Server 2004 comes in two versions, Standard Edition and Enterprise Edition. The types of functionality provided by the two editions are very similar; however, Enterprise Edition includes several enhancements that make is easy to deploy multiple ISA Server computers with the same configuration and configured for load balancing. Both editions of ISA Server 2004 are upgrades of ISA Server 2000 and include several new features.

After this lesson, you will be able to

- Describe the differences between ISA Server, Standard Edition, and ISA Server, Enterprise Edition
- Describe the differences between ISA Server 2004 and ISA Server 2000

Estimated lesson time: 15 minutes

Differences Between ISA Server Standard Edition and Enterprise Edition

ISA Server 2004 is available in two versions, Standard Edition and Enterprise Edition. In simple terms, Standard Edition is the version for you if you are deploying a single ISA Server, or if you are deploying a single ISA Server in a specific role. For example, if you are deploying a single ISA Server as a proxy server and firewall, or if you are deploying one ISA Server in one or more branch offices as well as an ISA Server in a central office, you should choose Standard Edition. However, if you are deploying multiple servers in each role, you should look at Enterprise Edition. For example, if you are working for a large organization that requires multiple servers deployed as proxy and caching servers in a central office, you should consider deploying Enterprise Edition.

ISA Server, Standard Edition, and ISA Server, Enterprise Edition, provide similar functionality. The most significant difference between the two versions is that Enterprise Edition provides enhanced scalability because it supports the following:

- Centralized storage of configuration data
- Support for the Cache Array Routing Protocol (CARP)
- Integration of network load balancing (NLB)

Centralized Storage of Configuration Data

One of the primary differences between Standard Edition and Enterprise Edition is how the two versions store their configuration information. Standard Edition stores its configuration information in the local computer registry. This means that if you want to deploy two computers running Standard Edition with the same ISA Server configuration, you install and configure one server and then export the configuration and import it in to the second server. If you need to change the configuration, you must make the changes on both servers.

ISA Server Enterprise Edition stores its configuration information in a separate directory rather than in the local registry. When you install Enterprise Edition, you must configure one or more Configuration Storage servers. The Configuration Storage server uses Active Directory Application Mode (ADAM) to store the configuration for all ISA Server computers in the organization. Because ADAM can be installed on multiple servers and the data replicated between the servers, you can have multiple Configuration Storage servers. You can also install ADAM on a server that is running ISA Server. By using ADAM, you can configure an enterprise policy that defines configuration settings for all of the ISA Server computers in the organization. You can also configure arrays and array policies. Arrays are groups of ISA Servers that share the same array policy, which is a set of configuration settings that apply to an array. After installing the Configuration Storage server and creating the enterprise and array policies, you can install ISA Server and assign them to a specific array. The enterprise and array policies will be assigned automatically to each ISA Server computer in the array.

To change the ISA Server Enterprise Edition configuration, you simply change the information in the Configuration Storage server. The Enterprise Edition computers periodically access the Configuration Storage server to check if there are any configuration changes. If there are changes, the servers will update their local (registry-based) storage to reflect the recent changes.

Support for the Cache Array Routing Protocol

ISA Server 2004 Enterprise Edition provides enhanced scalability by enabling shared Web caching across an array made up of multiple servers. With Enterprise Edition, multiple ISA Server computers can be configured as a single logical cache so that the caching capacity for all the ISA Server computers is combined.

To enable this feature, ISA Server uses the Cache Array Routing Protocol (CARP). When a user requests a page from the Internet, CARP determines which ISA Server in the array will retrieve and cache the requested item. When another user requests the same page, CARP again determines which ISA Server computer in the array has cached the page; the client request is sent to that computer. ISA Server uses CARP to optimize Web caching, which means that the ISA Server caching can be scaled to almost any size.

Integration of Network Load Balancing

The third additional feature available with Enterprise Edition is the integration of network load balancing (NLB) with ISA Server. NLB is a Windows network component available with Windows 2000 Server and Windows Server 2003 that enables load-balancing of IP traffic across a number of hosts, helping to enhance the scalability and availability of IP-based services. NLB also provides high availability by detecting host failures and automatically redistributing traffic to surviving hosts. With NLB, several computers can be clustered so that the entire group of servers shares a single IP address. A *cluster* is a group of independent computers that work together to provide a common set of services and present a single-system image to clients. When client computers connect to the NLB cluster, the client connections are automatically distributed across all of the servers in the cluster. If one of the servers is not available, the client connections are redirected to the available servers.

With ISA Server 2004, Standard Edition, you can configure NLB manually. With Enterprise Edition, NLB is integrated so that NLB can be managed from ISA Server. This means that NLB configuration is performed through ISA Server management. ISA Server also provides NLB health monitoring and manages the failover from one ISA Server in the cluster to another. During NLB failover, all the functionality provided by one of the computers in the cluster is transferred to another computer or computers in the cluster.

Differences Between ISA Server 2004 and ISA Server 2000

ISA Server 2004 is an upgrade of ISA Server 2000. While the two products share many of the same features and provide much of the same functionality, ISA Server 2004 provides numerous enhancements to the functionality provided by ISA Server 2000. Table 1-1 provides an overview of the new features available in Server 2004.

Table 1-1   New Features in ISA Server 2004

Feature	Description
Multiple network support	ISA Server 2004 supports multiple networks, each with distinct relationships to other networks. ISA Server 2000 supported only three networks, the internal network defined by the local address table (LAT), the external network, and the perimeter network. By default, ISA Server 2004 includes the VPN Clients Network and VPN Quarantined Clients network. You can also configure an unlimited number of networks on ISA Server 2004.
Policies assigned per network	In ISA Server 2004, all access policies can be defined relative to any of the networks, not just relative to the internal network. Because of limited network support in ISA Server 2000, all access policies defined access to or from the internal network or used static packet filters to configure access between the perimeter network and the external network. In ISA Server 2004, you can define distinct access rules for each network on the server. For example, you can create a perimeter network that is separate from an internal network and configure different access rules for it.
Routed and NAT network relationships	ISA Server 2004 supports both routed and network address translation (NAT) relationships between networks. In some cases, you may want more secure, less transparent communication between the networks; for these scenarios you can define a NAT relationship. In other scenarios, you may want to route traffic through ISA Server 2004; in this case, you can define a routed relationship.

Table 1-1   New Features in ISA Server 2004

Feature	Description
Extended protocol support	ISA Server 2004 extends ISA Server 2000 functionality by letting you control access and usage of any protocol, including IP-level protocols. This enhancement enables features such as publishing Point-to-Point Tunneling Protocol (PPTP) servers. In addition, IP Security (IPSec) tunnel-mode traffic can be used to create site-to-site VPN connections.
Advanced application filtering	ISA Server 2004 provides enhanced application filtering by controlling application-specific traffic with application-command and data-aware filters. Traffic can be accepted, rejected, redirected, and modified based on its contents through intelligent filtering of VPN, HTTP, File Transfer Protocol (FTP), SMTP, Post Office Protocol 3 (POP3), Domain Name System (DNS), H.323 conferencing, streaming media, and remote procedure call (RPC) traffic.
Enhanced authentication options	ISA Server 2004 supports authentication using built-in Windows, RADIUS, and RSA SecurID authentication. You can define different authentication rules for users or user groups in any namespace.
VPN and quarantine integration	ISA Server 2004 extends the Routing and Remote Access Service to provide VPN access. It also enables VPN quarantine, which can be used to provide limited network access to VPN clients until they pass a security check.
Stateful inspection for VPN	Because VPN clients are configured as a separate network in ISA Server 2004, you can create distinct policies for them. The rules engine checks requests from VPN clients, statefully inspects these requests, and dynamically opens connections based on the access policy.
Export and import	ISA Server 2004 enables the option to export and import configuration information. You can use this feature to save configuration parameters to an Extensible Markup Language (XML) file and then import the information from the file to another server, or use this file for disaster recovery.
Delegated permissions wizard for firewall administrator roles	ISA Server 2004 includes the Administration Delegation Wizard, which helps you assign administrative roles to users and groups. These predefined roles indicate the level of administrative control users are allowed over specified ISA Server 2004 services.
Enterprise Edition configuration storage	ISA Server 2000 Enterprise Edition stores its configuration information in Active Directory. This means that before you can install Enterprise Edition, you needed to modify the Active Directory schema to accommodate the ISA Server 2000 configuration. The ISA Server computers also had to be members of the Active Directory domain in order to read the configuration information. By contrast, ISA Server 2004, Enterprise Edition, stores its configuration information using ADAM rather than Active Directory. This means that the Configuration Storage server and ISA Server computers do not need to be members of an Active Directory domain.

> **Note**   Some of the features in ISA Server 2004 were first released with ISA Server 2000 Feature Pack 1. Feature Pack 1 added the SMTP filter, the RPC filter for Outlook e-mail clients, support for RSA SecureID, and more. If you have been using ISA Server 2000 without Feature Pack 1, these features will be new to you.

Lesson Review

Use the following questions to help determine whether you have learned enough to move on to the next lesson. If you have difficulty answering these questions, review the material in this lesson before beginning the next lesson. You can find answers to these questions in the "Questions and Answers" section at the end of this chapter.

1. You are considering upgrading your current ISA Server 2000 deployment to ISA Server 2004. You would like to be able to create two perimeter networks, one for all your Web servers that permit anonymous access, and another perimeter network for all servers that require authentication. What feature in ISA Server 2004 will help you to meet your requirements?

2. You are planning to deploy ISA Server 2004 and need to decide whether you want to deploy Standard Edition or Enterprise Edition. You will be deploying several ISA Servers and want to reduce the effort required to configure and manage all of them. What ISA Server version should you deploy? What ISA Server feature will address your requirement to reduce management effort?

Lesson Summary

- ISA Server 2004 comes in a Standard Edition and an Enterprise Edition. The Enterprise Edition provides enhanced scalability by using ADAM to store configuration information, supporting CARP for efficient caching and integrating NLB with ISA Server.

- ISA Server 2004 is an upgrade of ISA Server 2000. Some of the most important new features include support for an unlimited number of networks, VPN integration with the firewall, and enhanced administration tools.

Lesson 3: Explaining ISA Server Deployment Scenarios

You can use ISA Server 2004 to provide secure access to the Internet and access to internal network resources for Internet users. The exact configuration of ISA Server will be unique to each organization's security and access requirements. This lesson describes the most common deployment scenarios for ISA Server, including how ISA Server can be used as a primary security boundary or as a secondary firewall in a multiple-firewall configuration; and how ISA Server can be used for both large organizations with multiple locations and small organizations with the need for only one ISA Server computer.

After this lesson, you will be able to

- Describe how ISA Server functions as an Internet-edge firewall
- Describe how ISA Server functions as a back-end firewall
- Describe how ISA Server functions as a branch office firewall
- Describe how ISA Server functions as an integrated firewall, proxy, and caching server
- Describe how ISA Server functions as a proxy- and caching-only server

Estimated lesson time: 30 minutes

How ISA Server Works as an Internet-Edge Firewall

One of the primary deployment scenarios for ISA Server 2004 is as an Internet-edge firewall. An Internet-edge firewall is deployed at the connecting point between the Internet and the internal network. In this scenario, ISA Server provides both a secure gateway for internal users to the Internet and a firewall that prevents unauthorized access and malicious content from entering the network. Figure 1-3 shows an example of how ISA Server can be deployed as an Internet-edge firewall.

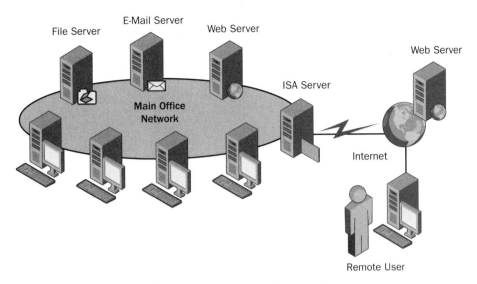

Figure 1-3   Deploying ISA Server as an Internet-edge firewall

As an Internet-edge firewall, ISA Server is the one entry point, as well as the primary security boundary, between the internal network and the Internet. ISA Server is deployed with one network interface card (NIC) connected to the Internet and a second NIC connected to the internal network. In some cases, ISA Server may also have a third NIC that is connected to a perimeter network. In this scenario, the following occurs:

- ISA Server blocks all Internet traffic from entering an organization's network unless the traffic is explicitly allowed. Because ISA Server is the primary security boundary, all components of ISA Server firewall functionality are implemented, including multilayered traffic filtering, application filtering, and intrusion detection. In addition, the operating system on the ISA Server computer must be hardened to protect against operating system–level attacks.

- ISA Server is used to make specified servers or services on the internal network accessible to Internet clients. This access is configured by publishing the server or by configuring firewall access rules. ISA Server filters all inbound requests and allows only traffic specified by the access rules.

- ISA Server may also be the VPN access point to the internal network. In this case, all VPN connections from the Internet are routed through ISA Server. All access rules and quarantine requirements for VPN clients are enforced by ISA Server.

- All client requests for resources on the Internet pass through ISA Server. ISA Server enforces an organization's policies defining which users are allowed to access the Internet, which applications and protocols can be used to do so, and which Web sites are permitted.

How ISA Server Works as a Back-End Firewall

In some cases, an organization may choose to deploy ISA Server as a second firewall in a multiple-firewall configuration. This scenario enables organizations to use their existing firewall infrastructure but also enables the use of ISA Server as an advanced application-filtering firewall. Figure 1-4 shows an example of how ISA Server can be deployed as a back-end firewall.

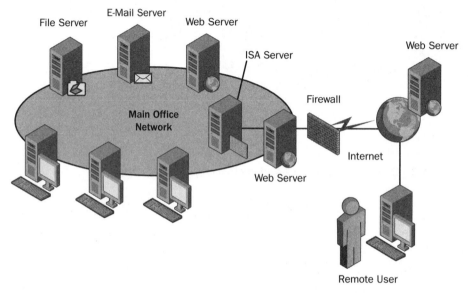

Figure 1-4   Deploying ISA Server as a back-end firewall

Many organizations implement a back-to-back firewall configuration. In this configuration, one network adapter on the front-end firewall is connected to the Internet while the second network adapter on the firewall is connected to the perimeter network. The back-end firewall has one network adapter that is connected to the perimeter network and a second network adapter connected to the internal network. All network traffic must flow through both firewalls and through the perimeter network to pass between the Internet and the internal network.

For organizations that already have a hardware-based firewall deployed as the Internet-edge firewall, ISA Server can provide valuable additional functionality as the back-end firewall. In particular, the advanced application-filtering functionality of ISA Server can ensure that specific applications are published securely. In this scenario, the following occurs:

■ ISA Server can be used to provide secure access to an organization's Exchange Server computers. Because computers running Exchange Server must be members of an Active Directory domain, some organizations prefer not to locate the Exchange Server computers in a perimeter network. ISA Server enables access to the Exchange Server computers on the internal network through secure OWA publishing, secure SMTP server publishing, and secure Exchange RPC publishing for Outlook clients.

- ISA Server may also be used to publish other secure Web sites or Web applications. If the Web servers are located on the internal network, ISA Server can be configured to publish the Web servers to the Internet. In this case, the advanced application filters on ISA Server can be used to inspect all network traffic being forwarded to the Web server.

- ISA Server may also be used as a Web proxy and caching server in the above scenario. In this case, all client requests for resources on the Internet or within the perimeter network pass through ISA Server. ISA Server enforces the organization's policies for secure Internet access.

How ISA Server Works as a Branch Office Firewall

A third deployment scenario for ISA Server is as a branch office firewall. In this scenario, ISA Server can be used to secure the branch office network from external threats as well as connect the branch office networks to the main office using site-to-site VPN connections. Figure 1-5 shows an example of how ISA Server can be deployed as a branch office firewall.

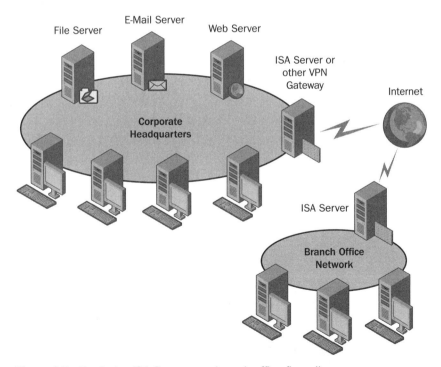

Figure 1-5   Deploying ISA Server as a branch office firewall

For organizations with multiple locations, ISA Server can function as a branch office firewall in conjunction with additional ISA Servers at other locations. If a branch office has a direct connection to the Internet, ISA Server may operate as an Internet-edge firewall for the branch, securing the branch office network and also publishing server resources to the Internet. If the branch office has only a dedicated WAN connection to the other offices, ISA Server can be used to publish servers in the branch office such as Microsoft SharePoint Portal Server or a local Exchange Server.

One of the benefits of using ISA Server as a branch office firewall is that it can operate as a VPN gateway that connects the branch office network to the main office network using a site-to-site VPN connection. Site-to-site VPN provides a cost-effective and secure method of connecting offices. In this scenario, the following occurs:

- ISA Server can be used to create a VPN from a branch office to other office locations. The VPN gateway at other sites can be either additional computers running ISA Server or third-party VPN gateways. ISA Server supports the use of three tunneling protocols for creating the VPN: IPSec tunnel mode, Point-to-Point Tunneling Protocol (PPTP), and Layer Two Tunneling Protocol (L2TP) over IPSec.

- ISA Server can perform stateful inspection and application-layer filtering of the VPN traffic between the organization's locations. This can be used to limit the remote networks that can access the local network and to ensure that only approved network traffic can access it.

How ISA Server Works as an Integrated Firewall, Proxy, and Caching Server

In a small or medium organization, a single ISA Server computer may provide all Internet access functionality. The ISA Server computer is used to create a secure boundary around the internal network, and to provide Web proxy and caching services for internal users. Figure 1-6 shows an example of how ISA Server can be deployed as an integrated firewall, proxy, and caching server.

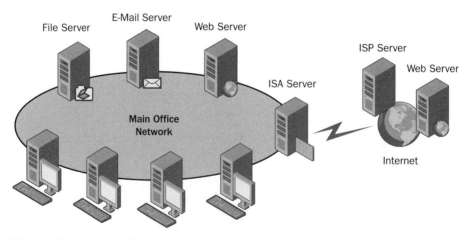

Figure 1-6 Deploying ISA Server as an integrated firewall, proxy, and caching server

Small or medium-size organizations often have significantly different Internet access requirements than larger organizations. Small organizations may have dial-up or other slow connections to the Internet. Almost all organizations provide at least some level of Internet access to employees, but these offices may need to limit access because of the slow connections. Small organizations frequently do not require any services published to the Internet because their ISP may be hosting both their organization's Web site and their e-mail servers. Other organizations may have much more complex requirements, including requirements for SMTP, FTP, and HTTP server publishing as well as VPN access. Another unique situation faced by many small or medium-size organizations is that a single network administrator performs all network administration tasks. This means that the administrator is usually not a firewall or Internet security expert.

ISA Server is flexible enough to meet almost any small or medium organization's requirements:

- Configuring caching on ISA Server computers means that Web pages are cached on the ISA Server hard disk. This can reduce the use of slow Internet connections or reduce the cost of a connection where cost is based on bandwidth usage.

- ISA Server supports the option of using dial-up connections to access the Internet or other networks. You can configure ISA Server to dial the connection automatically when a request is made for access to Internet resources.

- Installation of ISA Server is secure out of the box. By default, ISA Server 2004 will not accept any connections from the Internet after installation. This means that if the organization does not require any resources to be accessible from the Internet, the administrator does not need to configure ISA Server to block all incoming traffic. All the administrator has to do in this scenario is configure the server to enable Internet access for internal users and the configuration is complete.

- ISA Server provides network templates and server publishing wizards that can be used to configure most required settings. Configuring ISA Server to provide access to Internet resources can be as simple as applying a network template and using the wizard to configure the security settings. ISA Server provides several server publishing wizards that make it easy to securely publish internal servers to the Internet.

How ISA Server Works as a Proxy- and Caching-Only Server

A final deployment scenario for ISA Server 2004 is as a proxy server and caching server only. In this scenario, ISA Server is not used to provide a secure boundary between the Internet and the internal network, but only to provide Web proxy and caching services. Figure 1-7 shows an example of how ISA Server can be deployed as a proxy- and caching-only server.

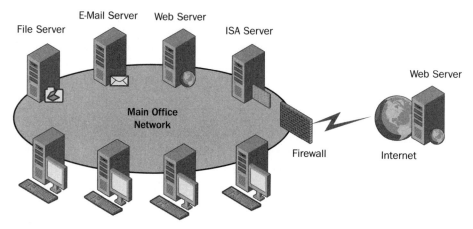

Figure 1-7   Deploying ISA Server as a proxy- and caching-only server

In most cases, computers running ISA Server are deployed with multiple network adapters to take advantage of ISA Server's ability to connect and filter traffic between multiple networks. However, if ISA Server is deployed as a Web proxy- and caching-only server, it can be deployed with a single network adapter. When ISA Server is installed on a computer with a single adapter, it recognizes only one network—the internal network.

If an organization already has a firewall solution in place, it can still take advantage of the proxy and caching functionality of ISA Server. To deploy ISA Server as a proxy and caching server, you only need to configure it to allow users to access resources on the Internet. You would then configure the Web browsers on all client computers to use the computer running ISA Server as a Web proxy server.

When you install ISA Server on a computer with a single adapter, the following ISA Server features cannot be used:

- Firewall and SecureNAT clients
- Virtual private networking
- IP packet filtering
- Multi-network firewall policy
- Server publishing
- Application-level filtering

These restrictions mean that ISA Server provides very few security benefits for the network.

Lesson Review

Use the following questions to help determine whether you have learned enough to move on to the next lesson. If you have difficulty answering these questions, review the material in this lesson before beginning the next lesson. You can find answers to these questions in the "Questions and Answers" section at the end of this chapter.

1. What features are available in ISA Server 2004 when installed on a machine with a single network adapter? (Choose all that apply.)

   a. Proxy & Caching

   b. IP Packet Filtering

   c. Server Publishing

   d. RADIUS

   e. VPN Gateway services

   f. None of the above; two network adapters are always required for ISA Server 2004

2. Your company has purchased ISA Server 2004 and has deployed it as an integrated firewall, proxy, and caching solution. You complete a default install of ISA Server 2004. What must you do next to block incoming connections from the Internet?

   a. Configure the firewall rules

   b. Configure a VPN quarantine policy

   c. Nothing

   d. Configure application-layer filtering

3. Your company wants to publish a Web site that hosts an e-commerce application. The application must have access to a SQL server on your internal network; security of the SQL database is the most important consideration. What ISA Server 2004 deployment scenario would you recommend for this environment?

   _____

   _____

   _____

Lesson Summary

- When ISA Server 2004 is deployed as an Internet-edge firewall, it blocks all Internet traffic to the internal network unless it is explicitly allowed, and allows access to only specific resources on the internal network.

- When ISA Server 2004 is deployed as a back-end firewall it can be used to provide secure access to an organization's Exchange Server computers and to publish other secure Web sites. In this scenario, ISA Server is most frequently used for application-layer filtering.

- When ISA Server 2004 is deployed as a branch office firewall for organizations with multiple locations it can be used to allow secure access to the internal network for all locations by enabling site-to-site VPNs.

- ISA Server 2004 works as an integrated firewall, proxy, and caching server by creating a secure boundary around the internal network, and by providing Web proxy and caching services for internal users. This is particularly useful in small- to medium-sized organizations where only one ISA Server is needed.

- ISA Server functions as a proxy- and caching-only server when deployed with a single network interface. In this configuration, ISA Server is not used to provide a secure boundary between the Internet and the internal network, but only to provide Web proxy and caching services.

Lesson 4: Overview of ISA Server 2004 Administration

As the ISA Server administrator in your organization, you likely are responsible for designing the ISA Server infrastructure and deploying the ISA Server computers required to meet the company requirements. After deployment, you will also be responsible for ongoing configuration and monitoring of the ISA Server computer. To do this, you will primarily use the ISA Server Management interface.

After this lesson, you will be able to

- List the phases included in deploying and managing an ISA Server environment
- Describe the features of the ISA Server Management interface
- List the monitoring features available in ISA Server 2004

Estimated lesson time: 25 minutes

The ISA Server Administration Process

In most organizations, ISA Server administrators are responsible for the initial deployment of ISA Server as well as for the ongoing management of ISA Server infrastructure. The entire ISA Server administration process consists of the following phases:

- **Designing ISA Server implementation**   Steps included in designing an ISA Server implementation are as follows:

  - In most organizations, the first step in deploying any new technology is to gather the company requirements related to the technology. With ISA Server, the organization's security requirements will be critical in designing your implementation, but you should also gather functional requirements. For example, you should determine the types of protocols users require to gain access to Internet resources, and the types of internal resources that need to be accessible from the Internet. You may also need to consider company requirements for scalability and redundancy.

  - Once you have gathered the organization's requirements, you can begin designing the ISA Server deployment. This design will include the number and placement of ISA Server computers as well as the configuration required for each server.

  - If you already have an ISA Server 2000 server in place, you need to design a migration plan for transferring the configuration to the new servers. If you are replacing another firewall or proxy server with ISA Server 2004, you also need to plan for the migration to the new servers.

  - An essential component in designing an ISA Server implementation is creating a test plan for server functionality. Before you deploy ISA Server to all users, you should know how you will test the implementation to ensure that it meets the organization's requirements.

Exam Tip As you look over this list of ISA Server administration tasks, you may be thinking that some of these tasks do not apply to you. For example, you may already have a VPN solution in place, or you may be taking over the management of an existing ISA Server infrastructure and were not involved in the design phase. However, the ISA Server 2004 exam is based on all aspects of ISA Server functionality and includes a design component as well as all the administrative tasks listed here. As you prepare for the exam, you may want to pay special attention to the ISA Server functions that you are not implementing because you may not have as much experience with these areas.

- **Installing and securing ISA Server 2004** Tasks included in installing and securing ISA Server are as follows:

  - ❑ You should secure the operating system for the computer that will be running ISA Server before installing ISA Server.

  - ❑ If you are creating a new ISA Server infrastructure using ISA Server 2004, Standard Edition, you can start deploying the servers. The default configuration for ISA Server is to block all traffic between networks, so you can begin deploying ISA Servers without compromising network security.

  - ❑ If you are creating a new ISA Server infrastructure using ISA Server 2004, Enterprise Edition, you will start the implementation by deploying the Configuration Storage server. You can then configure the enterprise and array policies and install ISA Servers into the appropriate arrays.

  - ❑ If you are upgrading an existing ISA Server 2000 implementation, then implement your migration plan. In this scenario, many of the current settings can be migrated to ISA Server 2004.

- **Installing and configuring ISA Server client computers** Tasks included in deploying ISA Server clients are as follows:

  - ❑ ISA Server supports three types of ISA Server clients: SecureNAT clients, Web proxy clients, and Firewall clients. All these clients are used to provide access to Internet resources for internal users, and each client provides different levels of functionality. As the ISA Server administrator, you will be responsible for choosing the ISA Server client and configuring the client application.

  - ❑ The Firewall Client computers require that the Firewall Client be installed on the computer. If you choose to use this client, you will need to devise a plan for deploying the client software to each client computer.

- **Configuring ISA Server 2004 to enable access to the Internet for internal users** Tasks included in configuring ISA Server to enable access to the Internet are as follows:

  - ❑ In many organizations, ISA Server is used as a proxy and caching server to provide secure access to Internet resources. Most organizations have an Internet usage policy that defines the types of access users can have to Internet resources.

❏ You can use ISA Server to enforce and monitor compliance with the organization's Internet usage policy. To enforce policy compliance, configure access rules that define the protocols that can be used to access Internet resources and the resources that will be available to users. You can also use the ISA Server logging option to monitor all access to Internet resources by internal users.

❏ To optimize Internet access, many organizations also enable Web caching on ISA Server. By default, ISA Server does not cache any client requests; you need to enable and configure caching before it is enabled.

■ **Configuring ISA Server 2004 to enable access by Internet users to internal resources**   Tasks included in enabling access to internal resources are as follows:

❏ The second primary role for ISA Server is to make internal resources accessible to Internet users. In most cases, ISA Server publishing rules provide access to internal resources.

❏ To enable access to Web sites that do not require security, create a Web publishing rule. If the Web sites require security, create a secure Web publishing rule so that all network traffic is protected by using SSL. For all internal resources that are not accessible by using HTTP or HTTPS, configure a server publishing rule.

❏ If your organization is using Exchange Server as an e-mail server, you also need to configure secure access to the Exchange Server computers for other SMTP servers on the Internet, or for clients accessing their e-mail from the Internet.

■ **Configuring ISA Server for VPN access**   Tasks included in configuring ISA Server for VPN access are as follows:

❏ Many organizations also require VPN access to the internal network. If your organization requires that users connect to your network from the Internet using a VPN, configure ISA Server to enable the client connections. For additional security, you can also enable VPN quarantine.

❏ If your organization has multiple locations, you may also need to configure a site-to-site VPN between the company locations.

■ **Monitoring ISA Server 2004**   Tasks included in monitoring ISA Server are as follows:

❏ As soon as you deploy the first ISA Server, you should begin monitoring it. ISA Server provides features such as alerts, intrusion detection, and session monitoring to detect real-time events on the ISA Server computer.

❏ You should also configure logging and reports to monitor usage of the ISA Server computer.

ISA Server Management Console Features

One of the new features in ISA Server 2004 is the management interface. The ISA Server Management Console provides a single interface for monitoring and managing ISA Server 2004. The ISA Server Management Console implements many of the components that are common to all MMCs, including the tree view for navigation with the details pane for detailed information, configuration wizards, context-sensitive help, and typical dialog boxes. Because the MMC is already a familiar interface for most administrators, the ISA Server management interface does not require any additional learning time. Figure 1-8 shows the ISA Server Management Console.

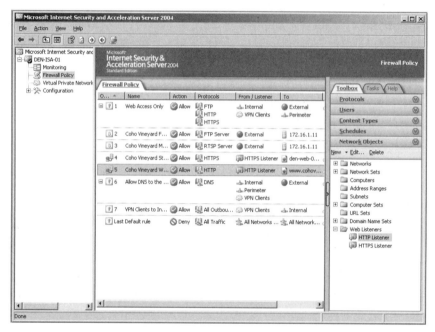

Figure 1-8   The ISA Server Management Console

The ISA Server Management Console has the following features:

■ **Getting Started page**   The ISA Server Management Console opens to a Getting Started page. This page provides an overview of the steps required to configure ISA Server with links to specific locations within the interface where configuration actions will be performed. By following the steps outlined on the Getting Started page, you can implement a secure deployment of ISA Server 2004.

■ **Monitoring dashboard**   The Management Console provides a single interface for monitoring the ISA Server performance and security-related information. The dashboard provides additional tabs that can be accessed to provide detailed monitoring information.

- **Single firewall rule base and policy editor**   All system policy and firewall rules are displayed in a single interface. From this interface you can create or modify all firewall or system policy rules, as well as manage server publishing rules.

- **Context-sensitive task lists**   Most console pages provide a context-sensitive task list that itemizes all relevant tasks. The task list includes links to wizards or dialog boxes where you can complete the tasks.

- **Context-sensitive toolbox**   Many console pages include a context-sensitive toolbox. The toolbox presents a list of relevant objects that can be modified.

- **Network templates**   Much of the management of ISA Server 2004 can be done through scenario-based wizards. One example of these wizards is the network template wizard, which enables you to pick a network scenario that matches your deployment scenario and then use the wizard to configure many of the firewall rules that are appropriate for that network template.

- **Consolidated VPN management**   ISA Server 2004 uses and extends the Routing and Remote Access Service (RRAS) on Microsoft Windows 2000 Server or Windows Server 2003 to enable VPN access. However, all VPN configurations are performed in the ISA Server management interface.

ISA Server Monitoring Overview

Monitoring is the daily task of ensuring that critical ISA Server services are running properly and ensuring that the ISA Server computer is providing the required security and functionality. The goal of daily monitoring is to identify problems before they impact your users. In addition, monitoring will also allow you to identify trends that can indicate future problems and allow you to plan for future growth.

Monitoring tasks that are performed on a daily basis allows you to determine what is normal for your ISA Server and when abnormal events occur. These tasks include the following:

- **Monitoring the Event Viewer**   Use Event Viewer to obtain information about service failures, application errors, and warnings when system resources such as virtual memory or available disk space are running low. Using Event Viewer enables you to identify problems that must be resolved and trends that will require future action.

- **Monitoring server performance**   When you install ISA Server, a pre-configured ISA Server Performance Monitor console is created. This console includes the critical ISA Server counters. Use this console to monitor server performance. Performance data can be viewed in a report or in various graph and log formats. A performance log can be useful in monitoring counters over an extended period of time. Performance alerts can be configured to create an event when counters reach certain values. These events could include creating a log entry, sending a network message, or running a program.

- **Using the ISA Server Management Console to monitor the ISA Server computer** The ISA Server Management Console provides many components that can be used to monitor the computer running ISA Server. ISA Server provides the monitoring options listed in Table 1-2.

Table 1-2 ISA Server Monitoring Components

Monitoring Components	Explanation
Alerts	Monitors ISA Server for configured events and then performs actions when the specified events occur. The alert service is configured to monitor many events by default. You may configure additional alert definitions.
Sessions	Provides information on all of the current client sessions on ISA Server. ISA Server lists sessions of the following types: Firewall client, SecureNAT, VPN client, VPN site-to-site, and Web proxy.
Logging	Provides detailed information about the Web proxy, firewall service, or SMTP Message Screener. You can use the logs to monitor the activity on ISA Server in real time, or you can review the log files at a later date.
Reports	Summarizes information about the usage patterns on ISA Server. For example, you can create reports that summarize information about the users who access the most sites through ISA Server and which sites they access, or about the protocols and applications that are being used most often. You can also use reports to monitor the security of your network. For example, you can generate reports that track malicious attempts to access internal resources.
Connectivity	Enables regular monitoring of connections from the computer running ISA Server to any other computer or URL on any network. For example, you can use connectivity options to monitor connections to domain controllers, DNS servers, published Web servers, and external Web servers. This feature provides advance warning when the connection to any required service or network fails.
Performance	Collects performance data on the computer running ISA Server. You can monitor server performance in real time, create a log file of server performance over a longer period of time for detailed analysis, or configure performance alerts to create an event when counters reach certain values.

Lesson Review

Use the following questions to help determine whether you have learned enough to move on to the next lesson. If you have difficulty answering these questions, review the material in this lesson before beginning the next lesson. You can find answers to these questions in the "Questions and Answers" section at the end of this chapter.

1. You have just finished deploying and configuring ISA Server 2004. However, now users report that one of the critical internal Web sites is no longer available from the

Internet. Which ISA Server administrative task was not completed correctly during the ISA Server deployment? What do you need to do to make the site available?

_____

_____

_____

2. You deployed ISA Server 2004 several months ago. Now your manager is asking for information on how the ISA Server computer is performing. He wants to know how much traffic is flowing through the ISA Server computer, what applications are being used to access the Internet, and which Web sites are most frequently accessed. What ISA Server monitoring feature will you use to provide this information? (Choose the best answer.)

   a. Reports

   b. Logs

   c. Alerts

   d. Sessions

Lesson Summary

- As an ISA Server administrator, you are likely to be responsible for the complete ISA Server deployment, including the initial design, ongoing configuration, and management.

- The ISA Server Management Console is used to manage and monitor almost all ISA Server activity. The console includes many features that can simplify your management tasks.

- As part of your role as an ISA Server administrator, you should constantly monitor the server. ISA Server provides several features that allow you to collect real-time information about server performance and security, as well as allow you to collect and analyze long-term usage trends.

Case Scenario Exercise

In this exercise, you will create a design for an ISA Server 2004 deployment for a fictitious organization. Read the scenario and then answer the question that follows. If you have difficulty completing this work, review the material in this chapter before beginning the next chapter. You can find answers to these questions in the "Questions and Answers" section at the end of this chapter.

Scenario

You are a systems engineer working for Contoso Pharmaceuticals, an international corporation involved in drug manufacturing and sales. Contoso Pharmaceuticals has two main offices: the European headquarters located in Berlin and the North American headquarters located in Toronto. The corporation also has offices in Johannesburg, Atlanta, and São Paolo. The Contoso Pharmaceuticals network configuration is shown in Figure 1-9.

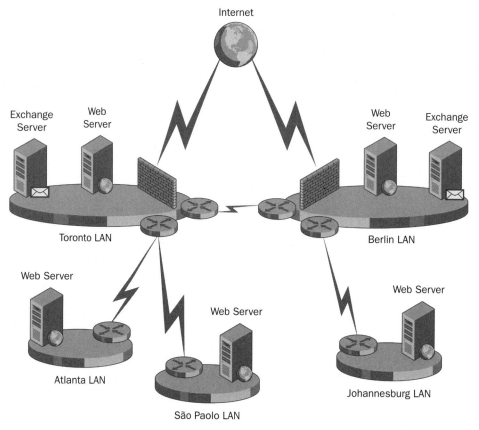

Figure 1-9   The Contoso Pharmaceutical network configuration

Contoso Pharmaceuticals is planning to deploy ISA Server 2004. Your boss hands you the following deployment requirements:

■ All current firewalls will be replaced by computers running ISA Server. Additional computers running ISA Server will be deployed if required.

■ There should be no restrictions on the flow of network traffic between any of the office locations. The existing WANs between offices will not be replaced.

- All Internet traffic flows through either Berlin or Toronto. Because the WAN links between the offices are utilized at 70 to 80 percent during business hours, this configuration needs to be changed. New Internet connections will be installed in Johannesburg, Atlanta, and São Paolo. These Internet connections must be as secure as possible.

- All company Exchange Server computers are located in Berlin and Toronto. All inbound and outbound e-mail must flow through these locations.

- Each office hosts a public Web site, as well as a secure Web site that is used by customers. These Web sites must be available through the local Internet connection.

- Contoso Pharmaceuticals is deploying a new sales application in the Toronto office. This application must be accessible to sales personnel whether they are in or out of the office. When outside the office, the sales personnel must connect to the Toronto office using a VPN before being granted access to the application. You must be able to filter all traffic that flows between this application server and other servers on the internal network. Sales personnel should not be able to access any resources on the company network except for the sales application using the VPN, unless the computer they are using passes all security requirements.

- All users need to be able to access their e-mail on the Exchange Server computers from the Internet using a Web browser.

Case Scenario Question

1. Design the ISA Server 2004 deployment to meet your company's requirements. What will you tell your boss that Contoso Pharmaceuticals should do?

_____

_____

_____

Chapter Summary

- ISA Server 2004 is normally installed at the network perimeter and is used to block all unauthorized access to the internal network, as well allow limited access from the internal network to the Internet. To secure the network perimeter:

  - ISA Server uses packet filtering, stateful filtering, and application-layer filtering to provide firewall functionality.

  - Ensures that clients can access only the required resources on the Internet and that the connection and data transfer to and from the Internet is secure.

  - Enables secure access from the Internet to internal network resources through the use of Web publishing rules, secure Web publishing rules, and server publishing rules. ISA Server 2004 also includes specialized e-mail publishing rules and application filters to secure server and client connections to Exchange Server for clients using a variety of protocols.

❑ Enables secure connections to internal network resources by enabling VPN connections for remote clients and sites.

■ ISA Server 2004 includes a Standard Edition and an Enterprise Edition. The Enterprise Edition provides enhanced scalability by using ADAM to store configuration information, supporting CARP for efficient caching, and integrating NLB. ISA Server 2004 is an upgrade of ISA Server 2000. Some of the most important new features include support for an unlimited number of networks, VPN integration with the firewall, and enhanced administration tools.

■ ISA Server 2004 can be deployed in a variety of configurations that include Internet-edge firewall; back-end firewall; branch office firewall; integrated firewall, proxy, and caching server; and proxy- and caching-only server.

■ As an ISA Server administrator, you are likely to be responsible for the complete ISA Server deployment, including its initial design and ongoing configuration and management. You can use the ISA Server Management Console to manage and monitor almost all ISA Server activity.

Exam Highlights

Because this chapter is an introduction designed to provide you with an overview of ISA Server 2004, it has not dealt with topics in detail. However, as you prepare for the exam by reading the rest of this book, pay special attention to the key points that follow.

Key Points

■ ISA Server provides advanced firewall functionality as an application filter. Understand how application filters work and how they can be used to secure your network.

■ ISA Server can be deployed in many different scenarios. As you prepare for the exam, understand the different scenarios and the different ISA Server configurations used in each scenario.

■ You will use the ISA Server Management Console to perform almost all ISA Server administrative tasks. You will become familiar with this administrative interface as you complete the hands-on exercises in this book.

Key Terms

application-layer filtering A type of filtering in which a firewall examines the actual content of a network packet to determine whether the packet will be forwarded through the firewall. The firewall opens the entire packet and examines the actual data in the packet before making a forwarding decision.

firewall A device that is located between one portion of a network and another portion, and allows only authorized network traffic to pass between the networks. The firewall is configured with traffic filtering rules that define what types of network traffic will be allowed to pass through the firewall.

proxy server A firewall component that manages Internet traffic to and from a local area network and can provide other functions, such as caching and access control.

Questions and Answers

Page
1-15

Lesson 1 Review

1. You have deployed ISA Server 2004 at the perimeter of your network. You need to ensure that all users are able to access the Internet through the ISA server. However, you also need to ensure that users can access only approved Web sites. What should you do?

   In order for all users to gain access to Internet resources using ISA Server, you must configure the client computers to use the ISA Server computer as a proxy server. To ensure that users can access only approved Web sites, configure ISA Server to block access to all sites except for the approved sites. You can use either domain names or URLs to define approved Web sites.

2. You have deployed ISA Server 2004 at the perimeter of your network. You now need to configure the ISA server so that the organization's Web site is available to all users on the Internet. You also need to ensure that only remote employees can access a Web site that contains confidential customer information. The data on the confidential Web site must not be readable when it is sent across the Internet. What should you do?

   To configure access to the organization's Web site, you should configure a Web publishing rule to publish the Web site to the Internet. This Web publishing rule should allow anonymous access to the Web site. To configure access to the confidential Web site, you should configure a secure Web publishing rule that will require the use of SSL to encrypt all network traffic to and from the Web site. To ensure that only employees have access to the confidential Web site, you should also configure ISA Server to require authentication.

3. You have deployed ISA Server 2004 as a VPN remote access server. What ISA Server feature can be used to ensure that all client computers are in compliance with the organization's security policies before granting the user access to the network?

   a. PPTP

   b. RADIUS authentication

   c. Quarantine control

   d. Application-layer filtering

   C is correct. Quarantine control limits connecting computers' access based on whether they meet security criteria defined by the administrator. A is incorrect; PPTP is a VPN tunneling protocol, but it does not test the client computer configuration before allowing the client to connect. B is incorrect; RADIUS is an authentication protocol used to confirm the user's identity. D is incorrect; application-layer filtering is used to check the contents of packets to ensure they are legitimate traffic. Application-layer filtering can block specific packets, but it cannot block a user from connecting to the network using VPN.

Page
1-21

Lesson 2 Review

1. You are considering upgrading your current ISA Server 2000 deployment to ISA Server 2004. You would like to be able to create two perimeter networks, one for all your Web servers that permit anonymous access, and another perimeter network for all servers that require authentication. What feature in ISA Server 2004 will help you to meet your requirements?

ISA Server 2004 supports an unlimited number of networks, which means that you can easily create multiple perimeter networks with different firewall rules controlling access to each network.

2. You are planning to deploy ISA Server 2004 and need to decide whether you want to deploy Standard Edition or Enterprise Edition. You will be deploying several ISA Servers and want to reduce the effort required to configure and manage all of them. What ISA Server version should you deploy? What ISA Server feature will address your requirement to reduce management effort?

You should plan on deploying ISA Server Enterprise Edition. Because Enterprise Edition stores its configuration information in ADAM on the Configuration Storage server, you can create enterprise and array policies in the directory and then deploy ISA Servers as part of an array. All the enterprise and array policies will automatically be applied to the ISA Server computers in the array.

Page
1-29

Lesson 3 Review

1. What features are available in ISA Server 2004 when installed on a machine with a single network adapter? (Choose all that apply.)

   a. Proxy & Caching

   b. IP Packet Filtering

   c. Server Publishing

   d. RADIUS

   e. VPN Gateway services

   f. None of the above; two network adapters are always required for ISA Server 2004

A is correct. All other configurations require two network adapters. Although deploying ISA Server with a single network interface is an option, remember that most of the security features included with ISA Server 2004 are not available in this configuration.

2. Your company has purchased ISA Server 2004 and has deployed it as an integrated firewall, proxy, and caching solution. You complete a default install of ISA Server 2004. What must you do next to block incoming connections from the Internet?

   a. Configure the firewall rules

   b. Configure a VPN quarantine policy

    c. Nothing

    d. Configure application-layer filtering

C is correct. By default, ISA Server 2004 will not accept connections from the Internet. A, B, and D are incorrect because these services need be configured only if you plan to accept traffic from the Internet.

3. Your company wants to publish a Web site that hosts an e-commerce application. The application must have access to a SQL server on your internal network; security of the SQL database is the most important consideration. What ISA Server 2004 deployment scenario would you recommend for this environment?

The most secure option in this case would be to deploy ISA Server as a back-end firewall with another firewall (which could be another ISA Server) as a front-end firewall. The Web server can then be placed in the perimeter network and the back-end ISA Server can be used to protect the internal network.

Page 1-36

Lesson 4 Review

1. You have just finished deploying and configuring ISA Server 2004. However, now users report that one of the critical internal Web sites is no longer available from the Internet. Which ISA Server administrative task was not completed correctly during the ISA Server deployment? What do you need to do to make the site available?

_____

_____

_____

The design phase of the deployment project was not completed correctly. During the design phase, you should identify all Web sites that need to be available on the Internet and configure the ISA Server computer to publish those sites. To make the site available, you need to determine the security requirements for the site. For example, does the site require SSL or authentication? Once you have gathered the requirements, you can create the appropriate Web publishing rule to make the Web server available from the Internet.

2. You deployed ISA Server 2004 several months ago. Now your manager is asking for information on how the ISA Server computer is performing. He wants to know how much traffic is flowing through the ISA Server computer, what applications are being used to access the Internet, and which Web sites are most frequently accessed. What ISA Server monitoring feature will you use to provide this information? (Choose the best answer.)

    a. Reports

    b. Logs

    c. Alerts

    d. Sessions

A is correct. The best ISA Server monitoring feature to use in this case is the Reports feature. A report presents information in a summary format so that you can easily show the required information to your manager. The Logs function would provide too much information because it includes details about every connection on the ISA Server computer, while the Alerts and Sessions features do not provide information on server usage, as they are used to provide real-time details on current activity.

Case Scenario Exercise

Page 1-39

1. Design the ISA Server 2004 deployment to meet your company's requirements. What will you tell your boss that Contoso Pharmaceuticals should do?

To meet the company requirements, you should deploy ISA Server computers as listed here.

In Toronto, you should do the following:

❑ Deploy an Internet-edge firewall using all the firewall functionality of ISA Server.

❑ To meet the requirement for isolating the sales application, you could either deploy a second ISA Server computer between the sales application and the internal network, or you could configure an additional network adapter and network on the Internet-edge firewall and install the sales application in the new network.

❑ To meet the VPN requirements for Toronto, deploy ISA Server as a VPN server. Configure a VPN quarantine for all clients when they connect. Allow the users access to the sales application while in the VPN quarantine, but do not allow any traffic to the internal network until the client has passed the security checks.

❑ Use the secure-server publishing functionality of ISA Server to publish the non-secure Web site and the secure customer Web site, as well as to publish the Exchange SMTP server and the Exchange Outlook Web Access server.

❑ Configure the ISA Server computer as a proxy server so that all clients in the office connect to the Internet through ISA Server.

In Berlin, you should do the following:

❑ Deploy an Internet-edge firewall using all the firewall functionality of ISA Server.

❑ Use the secure-server publishing functionality of ISA Server to publish the non-secure Web site and the secure customer Web site, as well as to publish the Exchange SMTP server and the Exchange Outlook Web Access server.

❑ Configure the ISA Server computer as a proxy server so that all clients in the office connect to the Internet through ISA Server.

In Johannesburg, Atlanta, and São Paolo, you should do the following:

❑ Deploy an Internet-edge firewall using all of the firewall functionality of ISA Server.

❑ Use the secure-server publishing functionality of ISA Server to publish the non-secure Web site and the secure customer Web site.

❑ Configure the ISA Server computer as a proxy server so that all clients in the office connect to the Internet through ISA Server.

2 Installing ISA Server 2004

Exam Objectives in this Chapter:

- Plan an ISA Server 2004 deployment
    - ❏ Analyze requirements for branch office deployment
    - ❏ Analyze baseline network traffic usage
    - ❏ Analyze requirements for high availability and fault tolerance
    - ❏ Pilot and test an ISA Server 2004 deployment
- Assess and configure the operating system and platform requirements
    - ❏ Analyze operating system and platform requirements
    - ❏ Prepare network interfaces
    - ❏ Analyze hardware and network requirements
    - ❏ Configure operating system settings for installing ISA Server 2004
- Deploy ISA Server 2004
    - ❏ Migrate from ISA Server 2000 to ISA Server 2004
    - ❏ Install ISA Server 2004, Standard Edition
    - ❏ Install ISA Server 2004, Enterprise Edition
    - ❏ Define the network routing requirements
    - ❏ Verify the installation of ISA Server 2004

Why This Chapter Matters

Before deploying Microsoft Internet Security and Acceleration (ISA) Server 2004 in your organization, you must determine what you plan to accomplish by doing so. ISA Server is a great product, but, in most organizations, merely stating this fact will not convince the top executives that it is worth the investment required to purchase, deploy, and maintain it. In most organizations, you must show that a product will address some business need. So before you think too much about what your ISA Server deployment will look like, you must gather the company's requirements. Why does your organization need ISA Server? What business goals or security requirements do you plan to satisfy with your ISA Server deployment? Once you have answered these questions, you are ready to consider where the ISA Server computers will be placed, how many ISA Server computers will be deployed, and the ISA Server configurations. Your business requirements will drive the ISA Server infrastructure design. This chapter will help you assess ISA Server in these terms—how the ISA Server design is affected by business requirements.

The second part of planning your ISA Server installation is to ensure that the deployment goes well. Your ISA Server will be integrated into an existing network, and you must determine how it will be integrated. This chapter provides guidance about how to design the network services to ensure a smooth deployment.

The third step in the planning process is ensuring that the actual hardware and server you deploy meet the company's requirements as well as the software and hardware requirements for installing ISA Server 2004. This involves dealing with the questions of scalability, redundancy, and the specific hardware and software requirements of ISA Server 2004.

Lessons in this Chapter:

- Lesson 1: Planning an ISA Server Deployment 2-3
- Lesson 2: Installing ISA Server 2004 2-20
- Lesson 3: Overview of the ISA Server 2000 Migration Process 2-36

Before You Begin

This chapter presents the skills and concepts related to planning an ISA Server installation and then deploying ISA Server computers. If you plan to complete the practices and lab in this chapter, you should prepare the following:

- A server with Microsoft Windows Server 2003 (either Standard or Enterprise Edition) installed as DC1 and configured as a domain controller in the *cohovineyard.com* domain.

- A second server with Windows Server 2003 installed as ISA1 and configured as a domain member in the *cohovineyard.com* domain. This server should have two network interfaces installed.

Lesson 1: Planning an ISA Server Deployment

Before you install ISA Server 2004, you need to plan the deployment. This lesson provides a brief summary of the planning process, and then specifically examines the planning of network infrastructure components and the server requirements. The lesson also considers capacity planning, including redundancy and availability arrangements.

After this lesson, you will be able to

- Describe the planning process for the deployment of an ISA Server infrastructure
- Describe the network infrastructure requirements for deploying ISA Server
- List the server requirements for installing ISA Server
- Perform capacity planning

Estimated lesson time: 20 minutes

The ISA Server Deployment Planning Process

Most organizations install ISA Server to address security requirements. ISA Server is a firewall that is likely to be among the critical components to ensuring that your organization's network is secure. In addition, the ISA Server computer is likely to be the primary connection point for all internal network traffic to access the Internet. This means that when you design your ISA Server deployment, you must consider a wide variety of security and functional requirements. The following is an overview of the process of planning an ISA Server deployment.

1. **Understand the current network infrastructure.**   The first step in planning an ISA Server deployment is to understand the current networking environment. When you start planning, collect network diagrams that provide details on the network infrastructure. These diagrams should include the Internet Protocol (IP) networks, router configurations, and client and server networking configuration.

   Collect information on the current configuration of network services. For example, all internal clients must be able to resolve Domain Name System (DNS) names on the Internet to connect to Internet resources. You need to understand how clients do this now. Also collect information about other network services such as Dynamic Host Configuration Protocol (DHCP) and Windows Internet Naming Service (WINS) if you have Microsoft Windows NT or Microsoft Windows 2000 clients.

   Collect information about the current domain structure. ISA Server can be integrated with Active Directory directory service to enable authentication.

2. **Review company security policies.**   Every organization should have security policies. These policies usually include general security requirements such as Internet or e-mail usage policies. The policies can also be very specific and define what protocols are not allowed through the firewall, what Web sites users can

access, and what types of information can be sent from the internal network to the Internet. For example, most organizations have policies defining what types of customer information can be sent in an e-mail.

Reviewing the company security policies is critical when planning the ISA Server deployment. ISA Server can be used to enforce at least some of the security policies. For example, you can use ISA Server to block access to a particular Web site, or to restrict which protocols can be used to access the Internet. Other policies, such as what types of information can be sent to the Internet or what sites users access when they take their mobile computers out of the company location, are more difficult to enforce using ISA Server.

> **See Also**   If your company does not have a well-defined security policy, now is a good time to develop one. There are numerous resources available on the Internet to help define the policy, including the SANS Institute Security Policy Project, located at *http://www.sans.org/resources/policies*, and the Site Security Handbook, Request for Comments (RFC) 2196, located at *http://ietf.org/rfc/rfc2196.txt* on the Internet Engineering Task Force page.

3. Plan the required network infrastructure.   For your ISA Server installation to meet the company requirements, you must plan for some specific network infrastructure components. For example, if the ISA Server computer is an Internet-edge firewall and is the only access point to the Internet, you must ensure that all client computers can connect to the ISA Server computer. If you have a single network, this solution can be as simple as configuring the default gateway on each client computer to use the internal network interface on the server running ISA Server. If you have multiple locations within your organization, or if you deploy multiple ISA Servers, this solution can be more complex.

Your ISA Server implementation may also depend on additional network infrastructure components such as DNS, DHCP, and Certificate Services. These components must be taken into account when planning an ISA Server installation.

> **Planning**   Some aspects of planning the ISA Server installation will be covered in detail in this chapter. For example, planning the network infrastructure components will be covered later in this chapter. Other aspects of planning will be covered in detail in later chapters.

4. Plan for branch office installations.   If your organization has more than one location, you must also plan for how the branch office networks will be integrated with the main office. In some cases, you may have existing wide area network (WAN) connections between the offices with routing already in place. In other cases, you may plan to replace the WAN link with a site-to-site virtual private network (VPN) or plan to deploy an ISA Server in each branch office.

See Also   Planning for branch office installations will be discussed in more detail in Chapter 5, "Enabling Secure Internet Access with ISA Server 2004," and in Chapter 10, "Configuring Virtual Private Networks for Remote Clients and Networks."

5. **Plan for availability and fault tolerance.**   Each organization will have different requirements regarding availability and fault tolerance. In some organizations (for example, organizations that are publishing e-commerce sites that are doing several million dollars of business per day), a few minutes of downtime or even slow response times can cost large amounts of money. Other organizations may be using ISA Server just to provide Internet access for internal users. In this case, downtime may not be as critical. ISA Server can be configured to enable fault tolerance, so you must understand your organization's requirements to get the right level of availability.

6. **Plan for access to the Internet.**   Most companies that deploy ISA Server use it as a proxy server for users to access the Internet. Some organizations enable full access to the Internet so that all users can use all protocols to access any Internet resource. Other organizations limit access based on protocols or applications, and users or groups, and they also limit users' access to Web sites.

   Once you have gathered your organization's requirements for granting Internet access, you can plan the ISA Server access rule configuration to meet the organization's Internet access and caching requirements.

See Also   The detailed information required to plan for access to the Internet is discussed in Chapter 5, "Enabling Secure Internet Access with ISA Server 2004," and in Chapter 6, "Implementing ISA Server Caching."

7. **Plan the ISA Server client implementation and deployment.**   An essential part of deploying an ISA Server infrastructure is to plan for ISA Server client configuration and deployment. ISA Server supports three clients: SecureNAT clients, Web Proxy clients, and Firewall clients. The use of each client has advantages and disadvantages. As part of your ISA Server deployment, you must know why you use each client and how to configure each client.

See Also   The detailed information required to plan ISA Server client implementation and deployment is discussed in Chapter 4, "Installing and Managing ISA Server Clients."

8. **Plan for server publishing.**   Most organizations also publish some internal resources to the Internet. Because this allows network traffic from the Internet to your internal network, it is essential that the connection between the internal servers is as secure as possible.

There are two components to planning server publishing. The first component is knowing what servers are going to be published and how to configure the publishing rules. The second component is a bigger question: How do you design the network connection to the Internet to ensure security? Many organizations deploy servers that are accessible from the Internet in a perimeter network. This limits access between the perimeter network and the internal network. You need to choose a perimeter network configuration as part of the planning process.

See Also   Planning for server publishing is discussed in more detail in Chapter 8, "Implementing ISA Server Publishing."

9. **Plan for VPN deployment.**   ISA Server can operate as a VPN remote access server for external clients and as a VPN gateway for site-to-site VPNs. If you plan to deploy ISA Server in either configuration, include this in your planning.

An extra level of planning is required if you choose to implement VPN network quarantine. With VPN network quarantine, you can restrict access to the internal network until the VPN clients pass a security configuration check. To perform the security configuration check, you must run a script or application on the client computer. The script can check for virtually any setting on the computer. In your planning, therefore, you must decide which security settings you will check on the client computer. This can be complicated. For example, you may decide that all clients that connect to your network must have an antivirus application installed, and that the virus detection files must be up to date. However, if you allow users to use any antivirus software, the script must check for all acceptable antivirus applications. The script that checks the security configuration on the client computer can become very complicated, so you must plan to have very competent scripting help available.

See Also   Planning for VPN deployment is discussed in more detail in Chapter 10.

10. **Plan the implementation.**   All your planning to this point has created a target state for your ISA Server implementation. The next step is to plan the actual implementation. How will you move your organization from where it is now to the target state? The following components are involved in the implementation planning:

   ❑ When you implement a new technology, you will almost always have an impact on the current environment, and you must define that impact. For example, when you deploy ISA Server, you may choose to deploy the Firewall Client to all client computers, or you may decide to implement new restrictions on what resources users can access on the Internet. Your deployment plan must identify all the ways that your implementation will affect the current environment. Whenever possible, strive to make the impact as transparent as possible; that is, your goal should be to minimize the impact on the users.

❑ Define an implementation plan. At a high level, there are two possible scenarios for implementing a new technology. One option is to deploy the new technology alongside the existing technology and complete all your testing before switching to the new technology. This is the preferred implementation plan because it carries the least risk. If you deploy ISA Server for the first time in your organization, this is probably the best approach. The second deployment scenario is to upgrade the existing technology rather than create a parallel implementation. This is a typical approach when you upgrade an existing infrastructure. For example, if you upgrade from ISA Server 2000 to ISA Server 2004, you can install ISA Server 2004 servers and migrate most of the ISA Server 2000 configuration settings to the new servers. Regardless of which approach you use, your implementation plan should clearly define how the ISA Server computers will be deployed, and how the environment will be switched over to the new technology.

❑ Another important part of your planning is a user education plan. If the end-user experience will change as a result of the implementation, you must define a process for informing users. If the impact is minimal, you may be able to inform users with a simple e-mail. For example, if the only impact on users is that they will be limited in what resources or protocols they can use to access the Internet, then an e-mail explaining the differences, with a link to an intranet site that lists the organization's security policy, may be all that is required. If the impact is significant, you may need to plan more formal training. For example, if you implement a remote access VPN for the first time, you may need to provide training about how to install and configure the remote access VPN client.

❑ Test the implementation and conduct a pilot project. Before deploying a new technology into production, it is critical that you test and pilot the implementation. A test implementation is usually performed under strict restrictions. The initial test implementation should not affect any actual users. For example, perform the tests using test accounts from test client computers. If you use ISA Server to publish internal servers, the initial testing should not include a production server, but rather a test server. In most cases, a pilot implementation uses a small group of actual users to test the configuration. For example, you may choose a small group of users and reconfigure their default gateway or Web proxy configuration to point to the ISA Server computer for Internet access. You can then use this group of users to test the access rules. If you are piloting publishing, configure a publishing rule that will publish a non-critical server before publishing all the internal servers.

Network Infrastructure Requirements

For your ISA Server implementation to succeed, you must ensure that the network infrastructure supports the ISA Server implementation. To support your ISA Server infrastructure, the following networking services must be installed and configured on your network:

- DNS
- Domain controllers
- DHCP

These supporting services are critical to the proper functioning of your ISA Server network infrastructure.

Domain Name System Requirements

To connect to resources on the Internet, client computers must be able to resolve the DNS names for servers on the Internet to IP addresses. If you publish internal servers to the Internet, users on the Internet must be able to resolve the DNS names for the published servers to an IP address. To enable both of these scenarios, a DNS infrastructure must be in place to provide name-resolution services.

> **Exam Tip**   Without DNS name resolution, users cannot connect to any resources located on a remote network. If an exam question mentions that users cannot connect to a resource, and the users are using a fully qualified domain name (FQDN) to connect to the resource, always check whether DNS name resolution could be the cause of the problem. If DNS name resolution is not the problem, then check the firewall access rule configuration.

To enable access to Internet resources, ensure that all client computers can resolve Internet DNS names. At a high level, you have two options for enabling name resolution for Internet resources: You can use an internal DNS server that can resolve both internal and Internet DNS addresses, or you can use an external DNS server to resolve IP addresses on the Internet.

To Use an Internal DNS Server   Many organizations have deployed DNS servers on their internal networks. If you have deployed Active Directory in Microsoft Windows 2000 Server or in Windows Server 2003, DNS is required for domain replication and user authentication, so all client computers running Windows 2000 or later must be able to resolve the DNS names for domain controllers. In this environment, the internal DNS server is configured with DNS zones for your Active Directory domains.

To allow internal users to access Internet resources, the internal DNS servers must also be configured to resolve Internet DNS names. One way to enable this is to configure the DNS servers to forward all requests for Internet name resolution to DNS servers on the Internet. When you configure a DNS server to use a forwarder, it sends to the forwarder requests for domains for which it is not authoritative. To configure a DNS server to use a forwarder, perform the following steps:

1. Open the DNS console from the Administrative Tools menu.

2. Right-click your server name in the left pane of the console, and then click Properties.

3. Click the Forwarders tab, as shown in Figure 2-1.

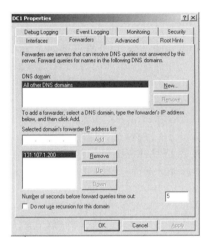

Figure 2-1   Configuring a DNS forwarder

4. Click Enable Forwarders and type the IP address of the DNS servers that you want to use as forwarders. In most cases, this will be the DNS server or servers of your Internet service provider (ISP).

Important   For the internal DNS servers to resolve Internet domain names using forwarders, ensure that the access rules on ISA Server allow the internal DNS servers to send DNS queries to the Internet.

A second option for configuring the internal DNS servers to resolve Internet names is to use root hints. The Internet root servers are authoritative for the DNS root domains, so if your DNS server is configured to use the root servers, it will use iterative queries to resolve DNS names on the Internet. By default, when you install DNS on a Windows 2000 Server or Windows Server 2003 that can connect to the Internet, the Internet root servers are automatically added to the root hints list. If you do not configure a forwarder, the DNS server will use the Internet DNS root servers to resolve Internet addresses.

> **Security Alert**   In most cases, using a DNS forwarder is considered more secure than using root hints. If you use a DNS forwarder, you can configure the firewall access rules so that DNS queries from the internal network are allowed only to the DNS servers configured as forwarders. If you use root hints, you must allow DNS queries to any DNS server on the Internet.

To Use an External DNS Server   Some organizations have not deployed internal DNS servers or have not configured the internal DNS servers to resolve Internet DNS addresses. In this situation, all Internet name resolution must be performed by DNS servers on the Internet. You have two options to enable this. If you use Web Proxy clients and Firewall clients, ISA Server can function as a DNS proxy server to resolve Internet DNS requests on the client's behalf.

When Web Proxy and Firewall clients connect to the ISA Server computer, ISA Server informs the clients which domain names are considered local. ISA Server uses the domains defined on the Domains tab on the Internal Properties dialog box to determine which resources are local and which resources are remote. To access the dialog box in ISA Server Management, expand Configuration, click Networks and the Networks tab, and double-click Internal. Figure 2-2 shows the Domains tab in the Internal Properties dialog box. When you add your internal domain to the Domains list, ISA Server instructs the Web Proxy and Firewall clients to use the internal DNS server on your network to resolve these names. When a client requests the IP address for any client that is not listed on the Domains tab, the ISA Server computer will attempt to resolve the IP address using DNS servers on the Internet. To enable this, you must configure the external network interface on the server running ISA Server with the IP addresses for DNS servers on the Internet.

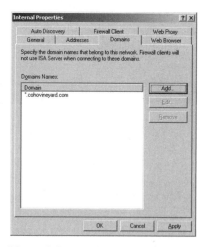

Figure 2-2   The Domains tab should list all the domains on the internal network.

SecureNAT clients cannot use ISA Server for DNS name resolution. The SecureNAT client must be configured with the IP address of a DNS server that can resolve both internal and external host names. If you have no need to resolve internal host names (for example, if you use WINS to resolve internal names), then you can configure the SecureNAT clients with the IP address of a DNS server on the Internet. In this scenario, you also need to create an access rule that allows the client computers to access the Internet using the DNS protocol. In addition, with this configuration, you cannot use DNS to resolve the IP addresses for internal network resources.

If you use ISA Server to resolve DNS names for Web Proxy and Firewall client computers, ISA Server uses its own DNS cache component that is built on top of the Windows DNS resolver. Whenever a DNS name is resolved through ISA Server by a DNS client on the internal network, ISA Server caches the lookup result. The purpose of the cache is to reduce the number of DNS queries that exit the firewall boundaries.

The DNS cache consists of three separate elements:

■ A cache of DNS name-to-address resolutions.

■ A cache of DNS address-to-name resolutions (also called the *reverse cache*).

■ A cache of failures to perform DNS address-to-name resolutions. This cache is also called the *negative cache*. Its purpose is to mitigate possible DOS attacks on the reverse cache. After a failure to locate an entry in the reverse cache, the negative cache is consulted; if the entry is found there, the firewall will not attempt a reverse DNS query against the Windows DNS resolver.

> **Exam Tip**   If you get an exam question in which the problem seems to be name resolution, but the DNS settings all appear correct, the problem may be that ISA Server has the DNS name stored in its negative cache. You can use the DNSTools.exe utility from the ISA Server Resource Kit to view and delete entries from the DNS cache.

Entries are removed from the three caches in one of the following ways:

■ When ISA Server retrieves an entry from the DNS cache, it checks the time-to-live (TTL) on the entry. If the TTL has expired, ISA Server removes the entry from the cache. ISA 2004 uses the TTL given by the DNS server. However, if the TTL is fewer than 6 minutes, it is changed to 6 minutes; if it is more than 6 hours it is changed to 6 hours.

■ When the cache size reaches the maximum threshold defined by the DnsCacheSize registry setting, 25 percent of the entries will be removed from the cache, according to the ones whose TTL is earlier. By default, the DNSCacheSize is set to 3000.

■ The firewall service also traverses the three caches once every 30 minutes and removes cache entries whose TTL has been reached.

See Also   If you are publishing internal resources to the Internet, you also need to configure DNS to resolve published resources. Details on how to configure this will be provided in
Chapter 8.

Domain Controller Requirements

If you want to restrict access to Internet resources based on user accounts, or if you want
to require authentication before users can access published servers, ISA Server must be
able to access a directory of user accounts to determine whether the user should have
access. ISA Server provides several options for authenticating the users, including
Remote Authentication Dial-In User Service (RADIUS), RSA SecureID, or the local user
account database on the computer running ISA Server. However, the easiest option to
implement for most organizations is to use a domain directory service to authenticate the
users. Most organizations already have a domain infrastructure that includes all the user
accounts; in such cases, ISA Server can use this directory service to authenticate user
accounts.

You can use Windows 2000, Windows Server 2003, or Windows NT 4 domains to perform this service. To use the domain for authentication, the server running ISA Server
must be a member of the domain. In addition, ISA Server must be able to communicate
with the domain controllers on the internal network. If you use Active Directory in
Windows Server 2003 or Windows 2000, you must configure the internal network interface on the ISA Server computer with the IP address of a DNS server that can resolve
the IP addresses for the local domain controllers.

**Real World   Should the ISA Server Computer Be a Member of the
Internal Domain?**

One of the more controversial debates when deploying ISA Server is the question
of whether the ISA Server computer should be a member of a domain or whether
it should be a stand-alone computer. Using a stand-alone computer is generally
considered more secure because of the dangers of exposing a domain member
directly to the Internet. If a computer that is a member of a domain is compromised, it is much easier for the attacker to gain access to the domain information,
including the account names for all domain user accounts. In addition, if the ISA
Server computer is a member of the internal domain, you must enable domain
authentication traffic as well as Lightweight Directory Access Protocol (LDAP) and
global catalog traffic from the ISA Server computer to the domain controllers on
the internal network.

On the other hand, configuring authentication on ISA Server is much more complicated if the ISA Server computer is not a domain member. This is particularly true if you require authentication for outgoing Internet requests. Usually, all users in the organization are granted some level of access to the Internet, and duplicating all the user accounts on the ISA Server computer or using an alternative authentication mechanism such as RADIUS is just too complicated.

It might be more reasonable to use an alternative means of authentication for granting access to published resources for Internet users. For example, if only a few users are accessing a secured Web site, then using SecurID, RADIUS, or certificate-based authentication may be feasible.

One way to meet the requirement to use domain authentication for Internet access requests for internal users, but still ensure that the ISA Server computer at the Internet-edge is not a domain member, is to use two ISA Server computers. One ISA Server computer that is not a domain member can be the Internet-edge server, and it will authenticate all user requests using a means other than domain authentication. A second ISA Server computer that is a domain member can then be used as the proxy server for all internal users, and it can use domain authentication to authenticate outgoing requests.

Dynamic Host Configuration Protocol Requirements

DHCP is not required to support an ISA Server infrastructure, but it is highly recommended to simplify network management. Even on relatively small networks of 250 or fewer computers, you will benefit from reduced administrative effort by configuring a DHCP server on your network. The advantage of using DHCP is that it can provide the IP configuration for all the client computers on your network automatically. This can make your ISA Server deployment much more efficient. For example, if you need to reconfigure the default gateway for all your client computers to point to the new ISA Server computer or to a new DNS server for Internet name resolution, you can just change the scope setting on the DHCP server and all the clients will be reconfigured automatically.

> **Tip**   The IP address configuration for all network hosts can be assigned using DHCP. However, most organizations do not configure servers as DHCP clients. In particular, domain controllers, DNS servers, and ISA Server computers must not be DHCP clients.

DHCP is also used to support VPN remote access connections to ISA Server. By default, ISA Server will use DHCP to assign IP addresses to all VPN clients. When you enable remote VPN client access on ISA Server, it will obtain a set of IP addresses from the DHCP server and assign the IP address to the VPN clients. By default, ISA Server 2004 will also assign DNS or WINS server addresses based on the DHCP scope information.

Server Requirements

To install ISA Server 2004, you must ensure that you have the correct operating system and hardware configurations.

Operating System Requirements

ISA Server 2004, Standard Edition, can be installed only on computers running Windows 2000 Server or Windows Server 2003. You can install ISA Server on the Standard Edition, Enterprise Edition, or Datacenter Edition of either Windows Server 2003 or Windows 2000 Server with Service Pack 4.

When installing ISA Server 2004 on a server running Windows 2000 Server, note the following additional requirements:

- You must install Windows 2000 Service Pack 4.

- You must install Microsoft Internet Explorer 6.

- If you installed Windows 2000 from media that included the Service Pack (SP4) files, install the hotfix specified in article KB821887, "Events for Authorization Roles Are Not Logged in the Security Log When You Configure Auditing for Windows 2000 Authorization Manager Runtime," in the Microsoft Knowledge Base at *http://support.microsoft.com/default.aspx?scid=kb;en-us;821887*.

Note   If you are installing ISA Server on a server running Windows 2000, the following options are not supported:

- Configuring the Layer 2 Tunneling Protocol (L2TP) IPSec pre-shared key is not supported.
- Quarantine mode for VPN clients is not supported when using RADIUS policy.

Hardware Requirements

The minimum hardware requirements for installing ISA Server 2004 are as follows:

- A personal computer with a 550 megahertz (MHz) or higher Pentium III–compatible CPU.

- 256 megabytes (MB) of memory.

- One network adapter for communication with the internal network.

- An additional network adapter for each network directly connected to the ISA Server 2004 computer. If you are using the ISA Server computer as a proxy and caching-only server, you do not need an additional network adapter.

■ One local hard disk partition that is formatted with the NTFS file system and that has at least 150 megabytes (MB) of available hard disk space. If you enable caching and logging, you will need additional hard disk space.

> **Tip**   As you can see from the previous list, ISA Server does not require a high-powered server in most environments. If you are deploying ISA Server in a small to medium-sized organization, you can probably reuse older hardware that has been replaced. Just ensure that you have all the appropriate Windows drivers if you are using older hardware.

ISA Server Enterprise Edition Installation Requirements

ISA Server 2004, Enterprise Edition, must be installed on a computer that is running Windows Server 2003. In addition to the hardware requirements listed above, you will need the following minimum disk space requirements for the ISA Server components:

■ ISA Server Services—106 MB

■ Configuration Storage server—58 MB

■ ISA Server Services and Configuration Storage server—156 MB

■ ISA Server management—32 MB

> **Planning**   These hard disk specifications are the minimum requirements for installing the Configuration Storage server or ISA Server. By default, ISA Server logs all connections or attempted connections. On a busy ISA Server computer, these log files can amount to several hundred megabytes (MB) per day. During a denial-of-service (DoS) attack or a virus outbreak, these logs can be several gigabytes (GB) per day, so ensure that you have sufficient hard-disk space for the log files. In addition, if you activate caching, ensure that you have enough hard-disk space to store a cache file that meets your requirements.

Guidelines for Capacity Planning

ISA Server can be scaled to support an organization of almost any size, either by increasing the hardware level on individual ISA Server computers or by deploying multiple ISA Server computers. The following factors should influence your choice in hardware configuration:

■ Bandwidth of the Internet connection

■ Firewall policy configuration

■ Logging requirements

■ Availability and redundancy requirements

See Also   For more information about scaling ISA Server, see the article "ISA Server Performance Best Practices" at *http://www.microsoft.com/technet/prodtechnol/isa/2004/plan/bestpractices.mspx*.

Internet Connection Bandwidth

ISA Server is designed to provide very fast data throughput, even if each packet is inspected at multiple layers. In most cases, the throughput of ISA Server will exceed the throughput of the Internet connection. A typical default deployment of ISA Server securing outbound Web access (Hypertext Transfer Protocol [HTTP] traffic) requires the hardware configurations for various Internet links shown in Table 2-1.

Table 2-1   ISA Server 2004 Hardware Scalability

Internet Link Bandwidth	Up to 5 T1 7.5 Mbps	Up to 25 Mbps	Up to T3 45 Mbps
Processors	1	1	2
Processor type	Pentium III 550 MHz or higher	Pentium 4 2.0–3.0 GHz	Xeon 2.0–3.0 GHz
Memory	256 MB	512 MB	1 GB
Disk space	150 MB	2.5 GB	5 GB
Network adapters	10/100 Mbps	10/100 Mbps	100/1000 Mbps
Concurrent VPN remote access connections	150	700	850

In most situations, a single computer has enough processing power to secure traffic going through standard Internet links. If you are using ISA Server primarily as a Web proxy server with minimal packet filtering, ISA Server running on a single Pentium 4, 2.4-GHz processor can provide a throughput of approximately 25 megabits per second (Mbps) at 75 percent CPU utilization. This means that, for each T1 Internet link (1.5 Mbps), the firewall service will use only 4.5 percent of CPU capacity. Dual Xeon 2.4-GHz processors can provide a throughput of approximately 45 Mbps (T3) at 75 percent of CPU, or 2.5 percent of CPU for every T1.

As you increase the level of application filtering, or if you are publishing multiple servers, the processor usage will increase. However, unless if you have an Internet connection faster than 25 Mbps, the throughput on a single computer running ISA Server will exceed the capacity of the network connection.

Firewall Policy Configuration

ISA Server uses application filters to perform application level security inspection. An application filter is a dynamic-link library (DLL) that registers to a specific protocol port. Whenever a packet is sent to this protocol port, it is passed to the application filter, which inspects it according to application logic and decides what to do according to policy.

When no application filter is assigned to a protocol, data undergoes TCP stateful filtering. At this level, ISA Server only checks the Transmission Control Protocol/Internet Protocol (TCP/IP) header information.

In general, application level filtering requires more processing than TCP stateful filtering for several reasons:

- Application filters inspect the data payload, while TCP stateful filtering looks only at the TCP/IP header information. Application filters can perform other actions with the data payload, such as looking at it and blocking it, or changing content according to application logic.

- Application filters work in user mode space. Transport level filtering works in kernel mode. This means extra processing overhead for passing the data through the full operating system networking stack.

Because application filters extend firewall processing, they can affect performance. To optimize the performance of your ISA Server computers when using application filters, do the following:

- Obtain performance information for the filters you use and tune them to be as efficient as possible. One example is the HTTP Web filter that can be configured to look at HTTP payload and search for specific signatures. You can configure the HTTP filter to examine both request and response headers as well as the body of the request and response. If you are trying to block a specific signature (for example, to stop users from using a particular application that uses HTTP), configure the HTTP filter to examine only the relevant request or response component. When you configure the HTTP filter to search request or response bodies, you can configure how many bytes will be scanned by the filter. If you know that the particular signature that you want to block always appears in the first 100 bytes of the response body, configure the HTTP filter to examine only the first 100 bytes rather than the entire response.

- Where applicable, consider using ISA Server rules instead of a filter. For example, site blocking using access rule destination sets may be more efficient than a Web filter that does the same thing.

The number and type of published servers can also affect your ISA Server performance. The more servers you publish on ISA Server, the more server resources are needed. This is especially true if you publish secure Web sites because of the extra resources required to decrypt and encrypt Secure Sockets Layer (SSL) traffic.

Logging Requirements

ISA Server provides two options for logging firewall activity:

- **MSDE logging**   This method is the default logging method for firewall and Web activity. ISA Server writes log records directly to a Microsoft SQL Server Desktop Engine (MSDE) database to enable online sophisticated queries on logged data.

■ **File logging**   With this method, ISA Server writes log records to a text file in a sequential manner.

MSDE has more features, but it uses more system resources. Specifically, you can expect an overall 10 percent to 20 percent improvement in processor utilization when switching to file logging from MSDE. MSDE logging also consumes more disk storage resources. MSDE logging performs about two disk accesses on every megabit. File logging will require the same amount of disk accesses for 10 megabits. One way to improve ISA Server performance is to switch from MSDE to file logging. This is recommended only when there is a performance problem caused by saturated processor or disk access.

Redundancy and Availability Requirements

A single high-end server running ISA Server can meet the performance requirements for most organizations. However, in addition to server performance, an organization might also have redundancy and availability requirements. Even if one server can provide more throughput than can the connection to the Internet, your organization may still want to consider installing additional ISA Server computers to ensure that an ISA Server computer is always available in the event of a single server failure.

ISA Server 2004, Enterprise Edition, is designed for these deployment scenarios. Enterprise Edition integrates network load balancing (NLB), which can be used to distribute the load on the ISA Server computers across multiple computers. If one of the ISA Server computers in the NLB cluster fails, the other servers in the cluster provide redundancy. In most cases, the server failure will be transparent to users. Enterprise Edition also uses the Configuration Storage server, so you can add and remove servers from arrays without configuring each individual server.

Lesson Review

Use the following questions to help determine whether you have learned enough to move on to the next lesson. If you have difficulty answering these questions, review the material in this lesson before beginning the next lesson. You can find answers to these questions in the "Questions and Answers" section at the end of this chapter.

1. You want to implement SecureNAT clients for Internet access for all employees and provide for Internet and internal name resolution. You want to minimize the number of DNS servers that are accessed from the internal network. What steps must you take? (Choose all that apply.)

    a. Configure the clients' TCP/IP settings to point to the internal DNS server.

    b. Configure delegation on the internal DNS server.

    c. Configure the internal DNS server to forward irresolvable queries to an external DNS server.

   d. Configure the clients' default gateway to point to the internal interface on ISA Server.

   e. Configure root hints on the internal DNS server.

   f. Configure the clients' default gateway to point to the external interface on ISA Server.

2. Your organization's IT security policy states that the internal DNS server supports only Active Directory and should never perform iterative queries to the Internet. Your clients run the Web Proxy client for Internet access. What steps must you take to ensure that your clients can access Internet resources without violating the IT security policy? (Choose all that apply.)

   a. Configure the client's Web browsers to use the ISA Server computer as a proxy server.

   b. Configure the external interface on ISA Server with the IP address of an external DNS server.

   c. Configure the client computer's default gateway to use the internal interface on ISA Server.

   d. Configure the internal interface on ISA Server to use an external DNS server.

   e. Configure the internal DNS server to forward irresolvable queries to the ISA Server computer.

Lesson Summary

- The deployment of ISA Server is one of the critical aspects of ensuring that your organization's network is secure; therefore, the planning process is crucial. There is a wide variety of security and functional requirements that must be considered when planning your ISA Server deployment.

- To ensure the success of your ISA Server installation, make sure that your network infrastructure will support ISA Server implementation. DNS, Domain controllers, and DHCP are essential.

- To install ISA Server 2004, ensure that you have the correct operating system and hardware configurations. ISA Server, Standard Edition, can be installed on Windows 2000 Server or Windows Server 2003 with a relatively low level of hardware (see the lesson for details). ISA Server, Enterprise Edition, must be installed on Windows Server 2003.

- A single server running ISA Server 2004 will provide enough throughput for most small to medium-sized organizations. However, larger organizations with fast Internet connections, complex firewall configurations that require application filtering, or high availability requirements might want to deploy ISA Server, Enterprise Edition, on multiple servers to meet their requirements.

Lesson 2: Installing ISA Server 2004

After you complete your planning, you are ready to install your first computer running ISA Server 2004. This lesson describes how to install ISA Server 2004 and how to verify and troubleshoot an ISA Server installation. It also describes how to perform both a manual and an unattended installation of ISA Server 2004. Finally, this lesson provides an overview of how to migrate from ISA Server 2000 to ISA Server 2004.

After this lesson, you will be able to

- List the steps in the ISA Server 2004 installation preparation process
- Install ISA Server, Standard Edition
- Verify a successful installation of ISA Server 2004
- Perform an unattended installation of ISA Server 2004
- Troubleshoot an ISA Server 2004 installation

Estimated lesson time: 45 minutes

ISA Server 2004 Installation Preparation Checklist

As you prepare to install ISA Server 2004, use the following checklist to ensure that you are ready to complete the installation:

- Install Windows 2000 Server or Windows Server 2003 on the server. Ensure that Microsoft Internet Information Services (IIS) is not installed during the installation unless you plan to publish a Web site on the ISA Server computer. As a best practice, install all service packs and security updates on the server before installing ISA Server.

- Ensure that you have the ISA Server installation media available.

- Log on as a local administrator. You must be a local administrator on the server in order to install ISA Server.

- Configure the network interfaces on the server.

- Understand the installation types and the implications of choosing each option. Choose one of the installation types.

- Understand the installation options and the implications of choosing each option. Choose which options you will select during installation.

- Prepare a plan for verifying the ISA Server installation.

Important   Before installing ISA Server 2004, review the Release Notes file that is located on the ISA Server 2004 installation CD-ROM. This file contains important information on installation issues that you could encounter.

Guidelines for Installing ISA Server, Standard Edition

Installing ISA Server, Standard Edition, is a fairly simple process if you have planned the installation carefully. You will begin by configuring the network interface cards on the ISA Server computer and then complete the installation. This section shows the overall process and provides some guidelines for performing the installation. You will install ISA Server, Standard Edition, as part of the practice.

To Configure the ISA Server Network Interfaces

In most cases, the server running ISA Server is situated between multiple networks. At a minimum, when ISA Server is deployed as an Internet-edge firewall, it will have two network interfaces, one connected to the Internet and the other connected to the internal network. You can also configure ISA Server to support additional networks, for example, you may have a perimeter network (also known as a demilitarized zone, or DMZ) attached to the server running ISA Server. The configuration of the network interfaces depends on which network the network interface is connected to.

> **Exam Tip**   One of the more common reasons explaining why an ISA Server computer does not perform as expected is that the network interfaces are not correctly configured. If you see an exam question that asks you to troubleshoot a problem, and you are provided with the configuration settings for the network interfaces, you can be fairly certain that the problem is with the network interface configuration.

The Internal Interface   Use the following guidelines to configure the internal interface of the ISA Server computer:

- The internal interface of the ISA Server computer must have an IP address that is on the local network. If you are using network address translation (NAT) on the ISA Server computer, you can use addresses from the private IP address range for the internal network.

> **Note**   The private IP address ranges are 10.0.0.0, 172.16.0.0—172.32.0.0 and 192.168.0.0—192.168.255.0. These addresses cannot be routed on the Internet, so you can use any of these addresses internally.

- The internal interface of the ISA Server computer should be configured with a DNS server address that can resolve internal host names. When incoming requests from external clients are forwarded to the internal network, the ISA Server computer will use the DNS server configured on the internal interface to resolve the internal host name. This is especially important if you choose to use host names when publishing internal servers using Web publishing rules.

■ Do not configure a default gateway on the internal interface of the ISA Server computer. The only interface that should have a default gateway is the external interface of the ISA Server computer.

The External Interface   Use the following guidelines to configure the external interface of the ISA Server computer:

■ The IP address assigned to the external interface must be routable on the Internet. In most cases, this IP address is provide by your ISP.

■ Only the external interface on the ISA Server computer should be configured with a default gateway. If that interface is directly attached to the Internet, then configure the network interface to use the default gateway provided by your ISP.

■ If you want ISA Server to provide DNS proxy services for internal Web Proxy and Firewall clients, then configure the external interface with the IP addresses of DNS servers on the Internet.

> **Tip**   By default, the network interfaces on Windows servers are named Local Area Connection, Local Area Connection 2, and so on. To make it easier to distinguish between the network interfaces, you should rename them with more descriptive names, such as Internal, External, and Perimeter.

Perimeter Network Interfaces   Use the following guidelines to configure the external interface of the ISA Server computer:

■ If you are using NAT between the Internet and the perimeter network, you can use private IP addresses for the perimeter network. In this case, assign one of the private IP addresses to the ISA Server interface on that network. If you are using a route relationship between the Internet and perimeter network, then you must use an address that is routable on the Internet (that is, you cannot use an address from the private IP address range).

> **See Also**   The differences between a NAT and a route network relationship, and recommendations for using each option, will be discussed in Chapter 7, "Configuring ISA Server as a Firewall."

ISA Server Installation Options

When you install ISA Server 2004, you must choose the type of installation to perform and determine the components to install. When you start the ISA Server installation, you have a choice of three installation types:

■ **Typical Installation**   This type installs Firewall Services and ISA Server Management.

■ **Full Installation**   This type installs all four ISA Server components: Firewall services, ISA Server Management, Firewall Client Installation Share, and the SMTP Message Screener.

■ **Custom Installation**   This type enables you to select which components will be installed.

If you choose to perform a custom installation, you can select which ISA Server components are installed during the installation. Figure 2-3 shows the interface where you can choose the components. The following components are available:

■ **Firewall Services**   These services control access and traffic between networks. Services must be installed on the ISA Server computer.

■ **ISA Server Management**   ISA Server Management is the management console used to manage the ISA Server configuration.

■ **Firewall Client Installation Share**   This option installs a shared folder named *ServerName**mspclnt*, from which client computers can install the Firewall Client software. The client installation files are typically installed on a computer other than the ISA Server computer, so it is not part of the Typical Installation option. You can install the Firewall Client share on computers running Windows Server 2003, Windows 2000 Server, or Microsoft Windows XP.

■ **Message Screener**   This feature performs content filtering on Simple Mail Transfer Protocol (SMTP) traffic arriving on an ISA Server computer. Configure this component to screen e-mail messages for keywords and attachments. You can install this feature on the computer running ISA Server only if the IIS SMTP service is installed on the computer.

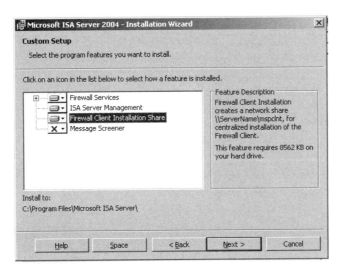

Figure 2-3   Options for installing the ISA Server components

Configuration Choices During Installation

When you install ISA Server 2004, you must make several decisions regarding the installation. One of the more important configuration options is to configure the IP addresses associated with the internal network. In addition, you can choose whether to allow earlier versions of the Firewall client.

> **Exam Tip** Getting the IP address assignment for the Internal network right is critical to ensure a functional ISA Server installation. When you get a troubleshooting exam question that includes information about the IP addresses assigned to the Internal network, check the IP address configuration carefully.

Choices for Configuring the Internal Network IP Addresses One of the options that you must configure during the ISA Server installation is the configuration of the internal network. The internal network can contain the IP addresses associated with all the network interfaces on the ISA Server computer except the network adapter connected to the Internet. You can also configure the internal network to contain a set of IP addresses associated with only one network interface, while the IP addresses assigned to other network interfaces are used to create additional networks. By default, ISA Server Setup also assigns the private IP address ranges as part of the internal network.

During the ISA Server installation, you must choose which IP addresses are associated with the internal network, as shown in Figure 2-4.

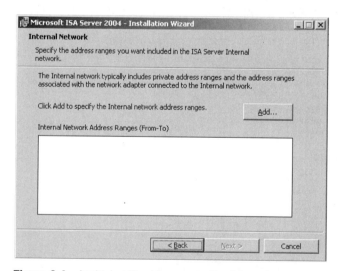

Figure 2-4 Assigning IP addresses to the internal network

To add the IP addresses associated with the internal network, click Add on the Internal Network page, producing the interface shown in Figure 2-5.

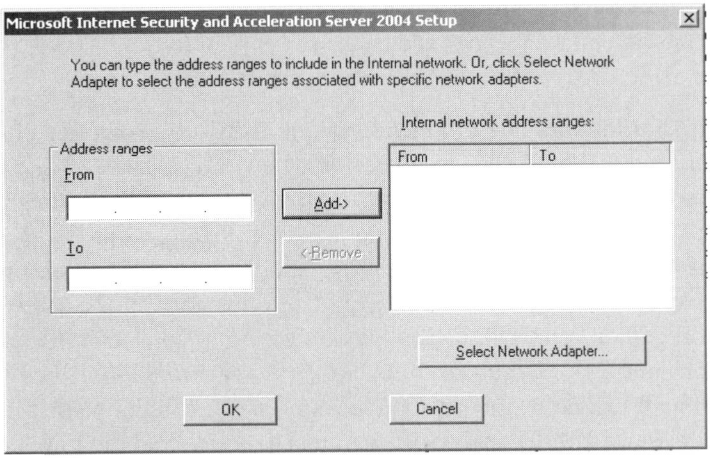

Figure 2-5   Adding IP addresses to the internal network

In this dialog box, you can either type the IP address ranges that comprise the internal network, or you can click Select Network Adapter. If you choose Select Network Adapter, the interface shown in Figure 2-6 appears.

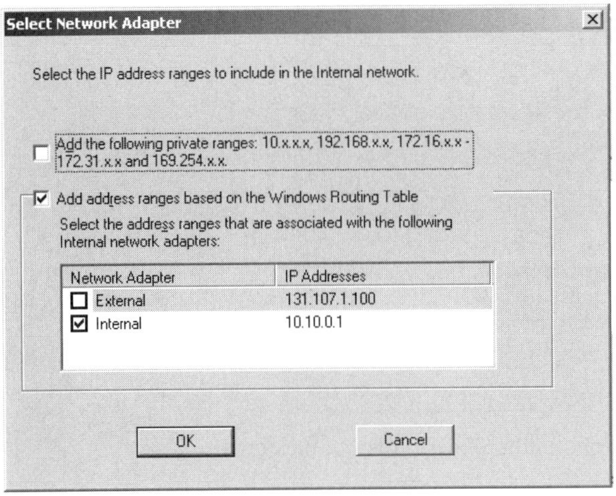

Figure 2-6   Using a network adapter to add IP addresses to the internal network

On the Select Network Adapter page, you can choose which adapter or adapters are connected to the internal network. When you choose this option, ISA Server Setup constructs the internal network based on the network adapter, and it uses the Windows routing table to determine which address ranges are internal. You can also choose to include the private IP address ranges in the internal network.

> **Caution**   If the routing table is not set correctly, the ISA Server internal network may not be built correctly. This can result in a client request for an internal IP address being routed to the Internet or being redirected through the Microsoft Firewall service. Before starting the installation of ISA Server, ensure that the routing table on the server is correct.

Choices for Allowing Earlier Versions of Firewall Client Software   Another choice that you must make during the ISA Server installation is whether to allow earlier versions of the Firewall Client software. ISA Server supports earlier versions of the software, including Firewall Client for ISA Server 2000 and the Winsock Proxy client (from Microsoft Proxy Server 2). However, these clients cannot use encryption when connecting to the ISA Server computer, so you may want to prevent these versions of the Firewall Client software installed on earlier versions of Windows operating systems from connecting to your ISA Server computer. By default, the ISA Server 2004 installation does not allow non-encrypted Firewall Client connections. The interface for making this installation decision is shown in Figure 2-7. To enable older clients to connect to the ISA Server computer during the installation, select the option Allow Firewall Clients Running Earlier Versions Of The Firewall Client Software To Connect.

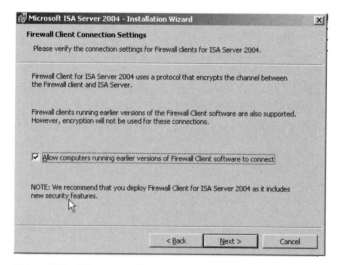

Figure 2-7   Allowing earlier versions of the Firewall Client software

> **Note**   When you use the ISA Server 2004 version of the Firewall Client software, only network traffic sent using the control channel is encrypted. When a Firewall client connects to the Firewall service on ISA Server, information such as authentication credentials, name-resolution queries, and port negotiations are sent along the control channel. Firewall clients use TCP and UDP Port 1745 to connect to the control channel. After the initial connection, data sent between the Firewall client and the ISA Server computer is not encrypted.

Additional Services Disabled or Stopped During Installation

As part of the ISA Server 2004 installation process, the following services are disabled:

- Internet Connection Firewall or Internet Connection Sharing
- IP Network Address Translation

In addition, the following services are stopped during installation. These services are restarted after the installation finishes:

- Simple Network Management Protocol (SNMP) service
- File Transfer Protocol (FTP) Publishing service
- Network News Transfer Protocol (NNTP)
- Internet Information Services (IIS) Admin service
- World Wide Web Publishing service

Important   In most cases, it is recommended that you not run IIS or any of the IP services on the ISA Server computer. This is particularly important if you are deploying ISA Server as an Internet-edge firewall.

How ISA Server Is Installed Using Remote Desktop

You can install ISA Server 2004 on a server running Windows 2000 using Terminal Services, or on a server running Windows Server 2003 using Remote Desktop. The installation process is the same as if you perform the installation from the server console, except that the System Policy on ISA Server will be configured to allow remote administration only from the computer that you used to install ISA Server.

Note   The MSDE component is not properly installed when you use Terminal Services in application server mode to install ISA Server remotely on a server running Windows 2000. Use Terminal Services in administration mode to install MSDE properly. The MSDE component is properly installed if you install ISA Server 2004 using Remote Desktop on a server running Windows Server 2003.

How to Verify a Successful ISA Server Installation

After completing the ISA Server installation, you should verify that the installation was successful and included all expected components. Verification is essential to ensure that all ISA Server Services and MSDE were installed and started, as well as to ensure that

Firewall Service has been started. There are several steps that you can perform to verify that the ISA installation completed successfully. These steps include the following:

1. Use the Services console from the Administrative Tools folder to verify that the ISA Server services are installed and started. Performing a default installation of ISA Server creates and starts the following services:

    ❑ Microsoft Firewall

    ❑ Microsoft ISA Server Control

    ❑ Microsoft ISA Server Job Scheduler

    ❑ Microsoft ISA Server Storage

2. Use the Services console from the Administrative Tools folder to verify that the MSDE services are installed and started. ISA Server installs the MSDE and adds the following services:

    ❑ *MSSQL$MSFW*—This service is started and set for automatic start.

    ❑ *MSSQLServerADHelper*—This service is not started and is set for manual start.

3. Installing the MSDE service also creates the initial log files for ISA Server. By default, these log files are located in C:\Program Files\Microsoft ISA Server\ISALogs. Use Windows Explorer to ensure that these files exist.

4. The ISA Server installation creates three setup log files. These files are located in the %Windir%/temp directory and are named ISAWRAP_###, ISAMSDE_###, and ISAFWSV_###, where ### is a three-digit number. The ISAWRAP file contains a summary of the installation, including a statement on whether the installation was successful. The other two files provide detailed information about the installation of MSDE and ISA Server. Check the ISAWRAP file to ensure that the last entry in the file indicates a successful installation.

5. Check the Application Log in the Event Viewer. If the installation was a success, the Event Log will include events indicating that the ISA Services started successfully.

6. Using the ISA Server Management Console, check for ISA Server Alerts. If the installation completed successfully, an ISA Server alert is created showing that the Firewall Service started.

Important   By default, the ISA Server computer will deny all access to Internet resources after the installation. This means that you cannot use a client to test access through the ISA Server computer until you have configured a firewall rule enabling access.

How to Perform an Unattended Installation of ISA Server 2004

In some cases, you may want to perform an unattended installation of ISA Server. There are several scenarios in which you may want to use an unattended, rather than a manual, installation of ISA Server 2004:

- **To ensure an identical and error-free installation** If you deploy multiple ISA Server computers that all require the same configuration, you can configure the installation information file once, and you can then use that file repeatedly to ensure that all servers are installed the same way.

- **To rapidly rebuild a failed server** If a server fails, you can use the installation information file that you used to build the server to rapidly install ISA Server on another server. You can configure the installation file to use an exported XML file to configure the ISA Server settings.

To perform the unattended installation, create or modify the Msisaund.ini file and then configure the ISA Server installation process to use this file when completing the setup.

To Modify the Msisaund.ini file

The Msisaund.ini file contains the configuration information that is used by ISA Server setup in unattended mode. The entries and values in the Msisaund.ini file are described in Table 2-2. If a value is not specified in this file, a default value is used.

Table 2-2   Msisaund.ini Parameters

File Entry	Description
PIDKEY	Specifies the tnbaroduct key. This is the 25-digit number located on the back of the ISA Server CD-ROM case.
INTERNALNETRANGES	Specifies the range of addresses in the internal network. Msisaund.ini must specify at least one IP address. Otherwise, setup fails. The syntax specifies the number of internal networks and the network numbers. For example, if you have two internal network ranges, you would use a line such as the following: INTERNALNETRANGES=2 192.168.1.0 – 192.168.1.255, 192.168.2.0 – 192.168.2.255.
InstallDir = {install_directory}	Specifies the installation directory for ISA Server. If not specified, it defaults to the first disk drive with enough space. The syntax is *Drive:\Folder*. The default folder is: %Program Files%\Microsoft ISA Server.
COMPANYNAME = Company_Name	Specifies the name of the company installing the product.
DONOTDELLOGS = {0 | 1}	If set to 1, log files on the computer are not deleted. The default is 0.

Table 2-2   Msisaund.ini Parameters

File Entry	Description
DONOTDELCACHE = {0 | 1}	If set to 1, cache files on the computer are not deleted. The default is 0.
ADDLOCAL = {MSFirewall_Management}, {MSFirewall_Services}, {Message_Screener}, {Publish_Share_Directory}, {MSDE}	Specifies a list of components (delimited by commas) that should be installed on the computer. To install all the components, set ADDLOCAL = ALL.
REMOVE = {MSFirewall_Management}, {MSFirewall_Services}, {Message_Screener}, {Publish_Share_Directory}, {MSDE}	Specifies a list of components (delimited by commas) that should be removed from the computer. To remove all the components, set REMOVE = ALL.
IMPORT_CONFIG_FILE = Importfile.xml	Specifies a configuration file to import. This can be used to apply an ISA Server Configuration to the server after installation.

A sample Msisaund.ini file is located on the ISA Server 2004 CD-ROM in the FPC folder. To modify the file, you can open the file using a text editor such as Notepad. In the sample file, all the configuration lines are prefaced by a semicolon (;). To enable a setting, remove the semicolon and then modify the file to meet your requirements. For example, to install ISA Server with the Firewall Services, the ISA management tools, MSDE with a single internal network range, and a company name of Coho Vineyards, you would modify the following lines.

```
ADDLOCAL=MSFirewall_Management,MSFirewall_Services,MSDE
INTERNALNETRANGES =1 192.168.1.0-192.168.1.255
COMPANYNAME=Coho Vineyards
```

To Run an Unattended Setup

After modifying the Msisaund.ini file, use the ISA server setup program with the appropriate parameters to complete the unattended installation. The command-line syntax is shown here:

```
PathToISASetup\Setup.exe [/[X|R]] /V" /Q[b|n]
FULLPATHANSWERFILE=\"PathToINIFile\MSISAUND.INI\""
```

The parameters for the unattended setup are described in Table 2-3.

Table 2-3   ISA Server Unattended Setup Parameters

Parameter	Description
PathToISASetup	The path to the ISA Server 2004 installation files. The path may be the root folder of the ISA Server CD-ROM or a shared folder on the network that contains the ISA Server files.
/Q [b|n]	Performs a quiet, unattended setup. If *b* is specified, the exit dialog box displays when setup completes. If *n* is specified, no dialog boxes are displayed.
/R	Performs an unattended reinstallation.
/X	Performs an unattended uninstallation.
/V	Provides verbose logging during the installation.
PathToINIFile	The path to the folder containing the unattended installation information.

For example, to perform an unattended installation of ISA Server 2004 with the source files on the CD-ROM and the Msisaund.ini file at the root of the C:\ drive, you can use this command:

```
D:\FPC\Setup.exe" /V /Qb FULLPATHANSWERFILE=\C:\MSISAUND.INI"
```

Guidelines for Troubleshooting an ISA Server Installation

In most cases, the ISA Server installation will complete without error. However, occasionally the installation may fail, or the services may not start after the installation is complete. Use the following guidelines to troubleshoot the ISA Server installation:

■ When you start the installation, you may receive a message that says, "The system administrator has set policies to prevent this installation." This message appears when you do not have sufficient permissions to install ISA Server. To install ISA Server, you must be a member of the local Administrators group.

■ If the installation fails, check the error message. Usually, the error message contains information explaining why the ISA Server installation failed, and it also provides information about how to correct the problem.

■ If the installation fails, check Application Log. The installation process writes events to the Application Log that may provide useful information for troubleshooting the error.

Exam Tip   When you see a troubleshooting question on the exam, always read the question carefully and look for evidence within the question that will point you to the right answer. When you are troubleshooting a problem in the real world, always collect as much information as possible to determine the cause of the problem. Use the same approach when you take the exam.

■ If the installation fails, check the installation log files. When you install ISA Server 2004, the Setup program automatically generates log files that contain detailed installation information. The information in the ISA Server 2004 Setup log file is based on Windows Installer logging. Windows Installer logs errors and other events that occur when the ISA Server 2004 Setup program runs. Review these log files for detailed information on when the ISA Server installation failed. In addition, the log files frequently contain details on why the installation failed. When you install ISA Server 2004, the following three log files are created:

❑ %Windir%\Temp\ISAWRAP_###.log (where ### is a three-digit number) — The setup wrapper log file records general information about the success or failure of the Firewall and MSDE installation.

❑ %Windir%\Temp\ISAFWSV_###.log (where ### is a three-digit number) — The Firewall service setup log file records events and errors related to the configuration of the ISA 2004 Firewall service.

❑ %Windir%\Temp\ISAMSDE_number.log — The ISA 2004 database setup log file records events and errors related to MSDE.

Practice: Installing ISA Server 2004

In this practice, you will install ISA Server 2004 on the ISA1 computer. You will then verify that ISA Server installed correctly on the server.

> **Important**   You must complete this practice to complete other practices in this book.

Exercise 1: Installing ISA Server

1. Log on to the ISA1 server using an Administrator account.

2. Insert the ISA Server CD-ROM into the server's CD-ROM drive. If Autorun is enabled, the Microsoft ISA Server 2004 Setup page will open automatically. If it does not open, open Windows Explorer, browse to the CD-ROM drive, and double-click Isaautorun.exe.

3. On the Microsoft ISA Server 2004 Setup page, click Install ISA Server 2004.

4. On the Welcome To The Installation Wizard For Microsoft ISA Server 2004 Setup page, click Next.

5. On the License Agreement page, review the terms and conditions stated in the End-User License Agreement (EULA). Then select the I Accept The Terms In The License Agreement check box, and click Next.

6. On the Customer Information page, enter the User Name, Organization, and Product Serial Number information, and then click Next.

7. On the Setup Type page, chose the type of installation you want to perform. For this practice, click Custom. Click Next.

8. On the Custom Setup page, click Firewall Client Installation Share, click the menu for Firewall Client Installation Share, and then select the This Feature Will Be Installed On Local Hard Drive option. Click Next.

9. On the Internal Network page, click Add.

10. Click Select Network Adapter.

11. Click the check box for the network card that is attached to your internal network, clear the Add The Following Private Ranges: check box, and then click OK.

12. Review the Setup Message and then click OK.

13. Review the internal network address ranges. If you are using the network addresses suggested in "About This Book," the internal network address range should include 10.10.0.0 – 10.10.0.255 and 10.255.255.255. Click OK.

14. On the Internal Network page, click Next.

15. On the Firewall Client Connections Settings page, click Next.

16. On the Services page, click Next. The Services page states that during the installation the SNMP Service and IIS Admin Service will be stopped, and that the Internet Connection Firewall (ICF)/Internet Connection Sharing (ICS) and the IP Network Address Translation services will be disabled.

17. On the Ready To Install The Program page, click Install.

18. On the Installation Wizard Completed page, click Finish.

19. Click Yes to restart the computer.

Exercise 2: Verifying the ISA Server 2004 Installation

1. After the server restarts, log on using the Administrator account.

2. In the Internet Explorer dialog box, select the In The Future, Do Not Show This Message check box and then click OK. Close Internet Explorer.

3. Open the Services management console from the Administrative Tools folder. Ensure that the following services are installed and running:

   ❑ Microsoft Firewall

   ❑ Microsoft ISA Server Control

   ❑ Microsoft ISA Server Job Scheduler

   ❑ Microsoft ISA Server Storage

   ❑ MSSQL$MSFW

4. Ensure that the MSSQLServerADHelper is installed and configured for manual startup, but not running. Close the Services management console.

5. On the desktop, ensure that the MSDE icon is displayed in the System Tray. To remove the MSDE icon from the System Tray, right-click the icon and click Exit.

6. Open Windows Explorer and browse to the C:\Program Files\Microsoft ISA Server\ISALogs folder. Ensure that several .mdf and .ldf files are in this folder.

7. Browse to the C:\Windows\Temp folder. Open the ISAWRAP_###.log file (where ### is a three-digit number). Review the log file, ensuring that the log indicates that the firewall installation ended successfully. Close all open windows.

8. Open the Event Viewer from the Administrative Tools folder. Open the Application log and review the events listed. You may see two error messages from the Firewall Service indicating network routing errors. These error messages can be safely ignored. Close the Event Viewer.

9. Open ISA Server Management from the All Programs\Microsoft ISA Server folder. Expand ISA1. Click Monitoring and then click Alerts. Review the alerts that were created during the installation. If a configuration error alert is listed that indicates the same network routing error as was displayed in the Application log, it can be safely ignored. Close all open windows.

Lesson Review

Use the following questions to help determine whether you have learned enough to move on to the next lesson. If you have difficulty answering these questions, review the material in this lesson before beginning the next lesson. You can find answers to these questions in the "Questions and Answers" section at the end of this chapter.

1. What file can provide information to an unattended install of ISA Server 2004?

    a. Winnt.sif

    b. Unattend.txt

    c. ISAMSDE###

    d. Msisaund.ini

2. You have just finished an installation of ISA Server 2004. The server's external network card is connected to the Internet and the internal network card is connected to the internal network. You install the Firewall Client software on a client computer and configure it to use the ISA Server computer. You try to connect to the Internet from the client that is running the Firewall Client software. You cannot connect to the Internet but receive an error message from the ISA Server computer. Why are you getting the error message?

    _____

    _____

    _____

Lesson Summary

- There are three ISA Server 2004 installation types:

  - A typical installation installs Firewall Services as well as ISA Server Management.

  - A full installation installs all four components of ISA Server including the Firewall Client file share and the SMTP Message Screener.

  - A custom installation allows you to select which components will be installed.

- There are several configuration choices that must be made when installing ISA Server 2004. You must configure the IP addresses associated with the internal network. Another choice that must be made during installation is whether to allow earlier versions of Firewall Client software.

- To verify that ISA Server 2004 has been installed, there are several checks that must be done. Verify that the ISA Server Services are installed and started, that MSDE services is installed and started, and that no error messages are listed in the Application log or in the ISA Server Alerts view.

- To perform an unattended installation of ISA Server 2004, create or modify the Msisaund.ini file and then configure ISA Server Installation process to use this file in the setup.

- To troubleshoot the ISA Server installation, ensure that you are logged on as a local administrator, and then use the Application Log error messages and the ISA Server setup logs to determine the cause of the installation failure.

Lesson 3: Overview of the ISA Server 2000 Migration Process

ISA Server 2004, Standard Edition, supports an upgrade path for ISA Server 2000, Standard Edition. Most ISA Server 2000 rules, network settings, monitoring configurations, and cache configurations will be upgraded to ISA Server 2004.

There are three options for upgrading from ISA Server 2000 to ISA Server 2004:

- Perform an in-place upgrade

- Migrate an ISA Server 2000 configuration to ISA Server 2004

- Migrate a Routing and Remote Access (RRAS) configuration to ISA Server 2004

See Also   Upgrading ISA Server 2000, Enterprise Edition, to ISA Server 2004, Enterprise Edition, is not supported. More details about how to migrate a ISA Server 2000, Enterprise Edition, infrastructure to ISA Server 2004 are provided in Chapter 12, "Implementing ISA Server 2004, Enterprise Edition."

After this lesson, you will be able to

- Explain the ISA Server 2000 in-place upgrade process
- Explain how ISA Server 2000 configuration migration works
- Describe the ways to migrate Routing and Remote Access to ISA Server 2004

Estimated lesson time: 15 minutes

How the ISA Server 2000 In-Place Upgrade Process Works

To perform an in-place upgrade, you install ISA Server 2004 on the computer that is already running ISA Server 2000. Before doing this, ensure that ISA Server 2000 Service Pack 1 (SP1) is installed on the computer. When you perform an in-place upgrade, ISA Server 2000 is removed and ISA Server 2004 is installed with the migrated configuration. When you perform an in-place upgrade, you do not have to run any migration tool to migrate the ISA Server configuration.

When you perform an in-place upgrade, the following ISA Server 2000 objects and configuration settings are not migrated to ISA Server 2004:

- Bandwidth rules are no longer supported in ISA Server 2004, so the rules are not migrated.

- Permission settings, such as system access control lists (SACLs), are not upgraded.

- Logging and reporting configuration and information are not migrated.

In addition, the following settings are modified when you upgrade from ISA Server 2000 to ISA Server 2004:

- IP packet filters are replaced by access rules or system policy rules that provide the same filtering functionality.

- Protocol rules are replaced by access rules that provide the same functionality.

- Site and content rules are replaced by access rules and access rule elements such as computer sets.

- Server and Web publishing rules are migrated with some modifications for where ISA Server access rule elements are different than ISA Server 2000 components.

See Also   For detailed information about how configuration options and settings are migrated from ISA Server 2000 to ISA Server 2004, see "Upgrading from Microsoft Internet Security and Acceleration (ISA) Server 2000 Standard Edition." This document is included on the ISA Server 2004 CD-ROM and can be accessed by selecting Read Migration Guide from the Autorun startup screen.

How an ISA Server 2000 Configuration Migration Works

When you perform an ISA Server configuration migration, you install ISA Server 2004 and then migrate the ISA Server 2000 configuration to the new ISA Server computer. To migrate the ISA Server 2000 configuration to ISA Server 2004, complete the following high-level steps:

1. Run the ISA Server Migration Wizard on the ISA Server 2000 computer. The wizard creates an .xml file with the configuration information.

2. If you are moving ISA Server to another server, install ISA Server 2004 on the new server. If you are installing ISA Server 2004 on the same server, completely uninstall ISA Server 2000 and then install ISA Server 2004.

3. Import the .xml file to the ISA Server 2004 computer. Before you import the .xml file, perform a full backup of the current settings on the ISA Server 2004 computer.

Tip   The actual IP address of the external network adapter on the original ISA Server 2000 computer is saved in the .xml file with the configuration information. If ISA Server 2004 is installed on a different computer, you must correct the IP address after you import the .xml file.

When you perform a configuration migration, the ISA Server 2000 configuration is migrated with the same limitations as when you perform an in-place upgrade.

Ways to Migrate Routing and Remote Access VPN to ISA Server 2004

If you have a Windows Server computer providing VPN access through RRAS, you can upgrade some of the VPN settings to ISA Server 2004. If you install ISA Server 2004 on a server running RRAS, the VPN configuration is migrated into ISA Server automatically. The server does not need to be running ISA Server 2000. You can also use the ISA Server Migration Wizard to migrate the RRAS settings to a new installation of ISA Server 2004.

When you upgrade RRAS to ISA Server 2004, the following limitations apply:

- The maximum number of remote VPN clients allowed to connect to ISA Server 2004 is set to whichever is larger on RRAS: the number of Point-to-Point Tunneling Protocol (PPTP) ports or the number of L2TP ports.

- If the number of IP addresses statically assigned is smaller than the number of VPN clients, the number of VPN clients is reduced to fit the size of the static address pool.

- Pre-shared keys configured for RRAS and for site-to-site connections are not exported.

- If an invalid IP address is configured for the DNS or WINS servers, the addresses are not exported. The DHCP settings are used instead, and a warning message is issued.

- If a site-to-site connection on RRAS is configured as PPTP first (and then L2TP), it is upgraded to a remote site network on ISA Server 2004 that uses PPTP only. If a site-to-site connection on RRAS is configured as L2TP first (and then PPTP), it is upgraded to a remote site network on ISA Server 2004 that uses L2TP only.

- Credentials configured for site-to-site connections in Routing and Remote Access are not exported. On ISA Server 2004, outgoing VPN connections are disabled until you reconfigure them.

Warning   Application filters and Web filters supplied by third-party vendors for ISA Server 2000 are not compatible with ISA Server 2004. Some third-party vendors have created new versions for ISA Server 2004. To upgrade to the new versions, uninstall the application filters and Web filters from the ISA Server 2000 computer. Then perform the upgrade to ISA Server 2004 and install the new version of the application filter or Web filter.

Lesson Review

Use the following questions to help determine whether you have learned enough to move on to the next lesson. If you have difficulty answering these questions, review the material in this lesson before beginning the next lesson. You can find answers to these questions in the "Questions and Answers" section at the end of this chapter.

1. Your organization is currently running ISA Server 2000, installed on servers running Windows 2000. You plan to install ISA Server 2004 to replace your current ISA Server. However, to minimize the disruption caused by the migration, you need to migrate the current ISA Server 2000 configuration to the new ISA Server 2004. You also decide that you want to install ISA Server 2004 on a computer running Windows Server 2003. The standard operating procedure for your organization states that server operating systems should not be upgraded unless there is no other way to perform an application migration to a new operating system. How can you complete your migration? (Choose two correct answers, both of which are required to complete the migration.)

   a. Upgrade the operating system on the computers running Windows 2000 servers to Windows Server 2003.

   b. Install ISA Server 2004 on computers running Windows Server 2003.

   c. Perform an in-place upgrade of ISA Server 2000 to ISA Server 2004.

   d. Export the configuration from ISA Server 2000. Import the configuration on ISA Server 2004.

2. You have migrated from ISA Server 2000 to ISA Server 2004 successfully. You run a streaming video application which uses a vendor-specific application filter. The application appears to have stopped functioning. What is the problem?

   _____

   _____

   _____

Lesson Summary

- There are three options for upgrading to ISA Server: an in-place upgrade, a migration of the ISA Server 2000 configuration to ISA Server 2004, and a migration of the RRAS VPN configuration to ISA Server 2004.

- When you perform an in-place upgrade, you install ISA Server 2004 on the same computer that is running ISA Server 2000. Most of the configuration settings are migrated to ISA Server 2004.

- When you migrate the ISA Server 2000 configuration to ISA Server 2004, you either install ISA Server 2004 on a different computer, or completely remove ISA Server 2000 before installing ISA Server 2004. In either case, you must use the Migration Tool to export the ISA Server 2000 configuration, and then transfer the configuration information to ISA Server 2004.

- To migrate the RRAS VPN configuration to ISA Server 2004, you can either install ISA Server on the computer running RRAS to perform an in-place upgrade or you can use the Migration Tool to copy the RRAS VPN information to ISA Server 2004.

Case Scenario Exercises

In these exercises, you will read two scenarios about installing and configuring ISA Server 2004, and then answer the questions that follow. If you have difficulty completing this work, review the material in this chapter before beginning the next chapter. You can find answers to these questions in the "Questions and Answers" section at the end of this chapter.

Scenario 1

Your organization's security department has just completed a security audit. During the audit, several violations were discovered where users were using unapproved applications to access Internet resources and were also downloading inappropriate material from the Internet. In some cases, users were downloading files that contained viruses or Trojan horse applications. In addition, the security audit found that the publicly accessible Web servers are located on the internal network.

You have been asked to incorporate the following changes using ISA Server 2004:

- Users must have restricted access to the Internet. Users must be authenticated before they get access to the Internet and must be prevented from accessing inappropriate Internet resources.

- Users must not be able to use unapproved applications to access the Internet. For example, peer-to-peer file sharing applications and MSN Messenger should be blocked from accessing the Internet.

- All publicly accessible Web servers must be removed from the internal network, but must still be protected from Internet access by a firewall. Your corporate public Web site must be accessible to all users on the Internet.

- The DNS administrator for your organization also requests that the internal DNS server should not be used to resolve Internet names.

Scenario 1 Question

1. What configuration would you recommend?

_____

_____

_____

Scenario 2

You are currently using ISA Server 2000 and have made the decision to move up to ISA Server 2004. You currently run ISA Server 2000 on a 450 MHz processor with 512 MB RAM. You support Internet access using Web Proxy clients and you publish a secure Web site. In addition, you support site-to-site VPN connections from a branch office to the head office through RRAS. You want to migrate to ISA Server 2004.

Scenario 2 Question

1. What steps should you take to perform the upgrade?

_____

_____

_____

Chapter Summary

- To ensure the success of your ISA Server installation, you must ensure that:

  - Your network infrastructure will support ISA Server implementation. DNS, domain controllers, and DHCP are essential.

  - You have the correct operating system and hardware configurations. ISA Server, Standard Edition, can be installed on Windows 2000 Server or Windows Server 2003. ISA Server, Enterprise Edition, must be installed on Windows Server 2003.

  - Your ISA Server provides sufficient performance. A single server running ISA Server 2004 will provide enough throughput for most small to medium-sized organizations.

- There are three ISA Server 2004 installation types. A typical installation installs ISA Server Services as well as ISA Server Management. The full installation installs all four components of ISA Server including the Firewall Client file share and the SMTP Message Screener. A custom installation allows you to select which components will be installed. When you install ISA Server, ensure that you configure the IP addresses for the internal network correctly.

- When you perform an in-place upgrade, you install ISA Server 2004 on the same computer that is running ISA Server 2000. When you migrate the ISA Server 2000 configuration to ISA Server 2004, you install ISA Server 2004, use the Migration Tool to export the ISA Server 2000 configuration, and then transfer the configuration information to ISA Server 2004. In either scenario, most configuration settings are migrated to ISA Server 2004.

Exam Highlights

Before taking the exam, review the key points and terms that are presented in this chapter. You need to know this information.

Key Points

- Planning your ISA Server installation is always driven by requirements. When you see an exam question that asks you to configure ISA Server, make sure that you have a clear understanding of the requirements.

- One of the key requirements that you may see when planning an ISA Server installation is for redundancy and availability. The only way to meet these requirements with ISA Server 2004 is to deploy multiple servers. Ideally, you should use ISA Server 2004, Enterprise Edition, to simplify the management of multiple servers.

- DNS name resolution is critical for both internal users accessing Internet resources and for Internet users accessing published resources. To enable Internet name resolution, you can use an internal DNS server that can resolve Internet addresses, or use the DNS proxy functionality of ISA Server.

- ISA Server 2004, Standard Edition, can be installed on Windows 2000 Server and Windows Server 2003. ISA Server 2004, Enterprise Edition, can be installed on Windows Server 2003 only. ISA Server 2004 has fairly minimal hardware requirements.

- When migrating from ISA Server 2000 to ISA Server 2004, or from a Windows 2000 RRAS VPN server implementation to ISA Server 2004, you can perform an in-place upgrade or use the ISA Server Migration Wizard to migrate the server configuration.

Key Terms

DNS forwarder   A Domain Name System (DNS) server on a network used to forward DNS queries for external DNS names to DNS servers outside of that network.

ISA Server clients   Client computers that access network resources by passing the request through an ISA Server computer. ISA Server 2004 supports three types of clients: SecureNAT, Web Proxy, and Firewall clients.

unattended installation   An automated installation method in which a setup information file provides the information required by the installation program to complete the product installation.

Questions and Answers

Page
2-18

Lesson 1 Review

1. You want to implement SecureNAT clients for Internet access for all employees and provide for Internet and internal name resolution. You want to minimize the number of DNS servers that are accessed from the internal network. What steps must you take? (Choose all that apply.)

    a. Configure the clients' TCP/IP settings to point to the internal DNS server.

    b. Configure delegation on the internal DNS server.

    c. Configure the internal DNS server to forward irresolvable queries to an external DNS server.

    d. Configure the clients' default gateway to point to the internal interface on ISA Server.

    e. Configure root hints on the internal DNS server.

    f. Configure the clients' default gateway to point to the external interface on ISA Server.

    A, C, and D are correct. B is incorrect because delegation is used to delegate authority for portions of the DNS namespace. E is incorrect because this would mean that the internal DNS servers would need to be able to send queries to any DNS server on the Internet. F is incorrect because internal clients can only point to a default gateway that is on their subnet; the external card is not.

2. Your organization's IT security policy states that the internal DNS server supports only Active Directory and should never perform iterative queries to the Internet. Your clients run the Web Proxy client for Internet access. What steps must you take to ensure that your clients can access Internet resources without violating the IT security policy? (Choose all that apply.)

    a. Configure the clients' Web browsers to use the ISA Server computer as a proxy server.

    b. Configure the external interface on ISA Server with the IP address of an external DNS server.

    c. Configure the client computers' default gateways to use the internal interface on ISA Server.

    d. Configure the internal interface on ISA Server to use an external DNS server.

    e. Configure the internal DNS server to forward irresolvable queries to the ISA Server computer.

    A and B are correct. C would be correct only for Secure NAT clients; D is incorrect because the internal card should point to an internal DNS server; and F is incorrect because you cannot forward queries to an ISA Server computer.

Lesson 2 Review

1. What file can provide information to an unattended install of ISA Server 2004?

    a. Winnt.sif

    b. Unattend.txt

    c. ISAMSDE###

    d. Msisaund.ini

    D is correct. Winnt.sif and Unattend.txt are answer files, but not for ISA Server 2004. ISAMSDE### provides information about the install of MSDE.

2. You have just finished an installation of ISA Server 2004. The server's external network card is connected to the Internet and the internal network card is connected to the internal network. You install the Firewall Client software on a client computer and configure it to use the ISA Server computer. You try to connect to the Internet from the client that is running the Firewall Client software. You cannot connect to the Internet but receive an error message from the ISA Server computer. Why are you getting the error message?

    The default installation of ISA Server does not allow any network traffic to flow through the server. The only firewall rule that is created on the server is the default rule that denies all network traffic for everyone. You would need to configure a firewall rule to enable access to the Internet.

Lesson 3 Review

1. Your organization is currently running ISA Server 2000, installed on servers running Windows 2000. You plan to install ISA Server 2004 to replace your current ISA Server. However, to minimize the disruption caused by the migration, you need to migrate the current ISA Server 2000 configuration to the new ISA Server 2004. You also decide that you want to install ISA Server 2004 on a computer running Windows Server 2003. The standard operating procedure for your organization states that server operating systems should not be upgraded unless there is no other way to perform an application migration to a new operating system. How can you complete your migration? (Choose two correct answers, both of which are required to complete the migration.)

    a. Upgrade the operating system on the computers running Windows 2000 servers to Windows Server 2003.

    b. Install ISA Server 2004 on computers running Windows Server 2003.

    c. Perform an in-place upgrade of ISA Server 2000 to ISA Server 2004.

    d. Export the configuration from ISA Server 2000. Import the configuration on ISA Server 2004.

    B and D are correct. Although A and D would upgrade the ISA Server computer, it would violate the organization's operating procedure, which says that server operating systems should be upgraded only as a last resort. Doing B and D will meet the request to have ISA Server 2004 running on Windows Server 2003 with the same configuration as the ISA Server 2000 computer had.

2. You have migrated from ISA Server 2000 to ISA Server 2004 successfully. You run a streaming video application which uses a vendor-specific application filter. The application appears to have stopped functioning. What is the problem?

Third-party application filters were not migrated to the ISA Server 2004 installation. You will have to get an updated version of the filter from the vendor.

Case Scenario Exercises

Page 2-40
Scenario 1 Question

1. What configuration would you recommend?

Use ISA Server 2004 to create a perimeter network. You can configure a back-to-back configuration with two computers running ISA Server 2004 to establish the perimeter network, or you can create a third network on the ISA Server computer as the perimeter network. Place the Web server in the perimeter network and configure Web publishing rules on the ISA Server computer for the corporate Web site.

Then configure the Web Proxy client on all client computer Web browsers. Enable the Web Proxy service on ISA Server and configure ISA Server to require all users to authenticate. Configure the external card on the ISA Server computer with the IP address of an external DNS server. Configure application layer filters on the ISA Server computer to allow only authorized HTTP traffic.

Page 2-41
Scenario 2 Question

1. What steps should you take to perform the upgrade?

You must upgrade the hardware to meet the requirements of ISA Server 2004. Because you must use new hardware, run the ISA Server Migration Wizard on the ISA Server 2000 server and import the .xml file to the new installation of ISA Server 2004. You will use the same wizard to migrate the RRAS settings. After you complete the migration, you must still configure any pre-shared keys and configure credentials for site-to-site VPN access.

3 Securing and Maintaining ISA Server 2004

Exam Objectives in this Chapter:

- Assess and configure the operating system, hardware, and network services
    - ❑ Prepare network interfaces
    - ❑ Enable required network and server services
    - ❑ Configure operating system settings for installing ISA Server 2004
- Deploy ISA Server 2004
    - ❑ Plan for disaster recovery
- Configure the system policy
    - ❑ Enable infrastructure communications
    - ❑ Lock down the system policy
    - ❑ Modify rules
    - ❑ Limit network access to the firewall
    - ❑ Limit access to logs and reports
- Back up and restore ISA Server 2004
    - ❑ Backup and restore an ISA Server 2004 configuration
    - ❑ Perform disaster recovery
    - ❑ Transfer ISA Server 2004 configuration settings between ISA Server computers
- Define administrative roles
    - ❑ Assign and delegate administrative roles
    - ❑ Remove delegation rights
    - ❑ Manage access to firewall configuration

Why This Chapter Matters

Microsoft Internet Security and Acceleration (ISA) Server 2004 is a core component in your organization's overall security strategy. When you deploy ISA Server as an Internet-edge firewall, your ISA Server computer is accessible to everyone on the Internet. Even if your ISA Server computer is not an Internet-edge firewall, it is likely to be accessible from the Internet. Because ISA Server is the gateway to the Internet, a security compromise on the ISA Server computer can have significant repercussions for your entire network.

Securing and maintaining ISA Server is therefore a critical topic for you as you deploy your ISA Server infrastructure. You need to ensure that the ISA Server computer is secure. This starts with the physical security of the computer running ISA Server and includes network layer security and operating system security. Once the computer on which ISA Server is running is secured, you must address securing the ISA Server configuration.

Lessons in this Chapter:

- Lesson 1: Securing ISA Server 2004 3-3
- Lesson 2: Maintaining ISA Server 2004. 3-28

Before You Begin

This chapter presents the skills and concepts related to securing and maintaining ISA Server. If you plan to complete the practices and lab in this chapter, prepare the following:

- A Microsoft Windows Server 2003 (either Standard Edition or Enterprise Edition) computer installed as DC1 and configured as a domain controller in the *cohovine yard.com* domain.

- Download the Windows Server 2003 Security Guide from *http://go.microsoft.com/ fwlink/?linkid=14846*. Create a folder named Security Templates at the root of the C drive on DC1. Copy the Security Guide templates to the Security Templates folder.

- A second Windows Server 2003 computer installed as ISA1 and configured as a domain member in the *cohovineyard.com* domain. This server should have two network interfaces installed. You must have completed the exercises from Chapter 2, "Installing ISA Server 2004," on this server.

- To complete the troubleshooting lab, you will also need a Microsoft Windows XP computer installed as CLIENT1. This computer should be a member of the *cohovineyard.com* domain.

Lesson 1: Securing ISA Server 2004

Securing the computer running ISA Server is vital to ensuring your organization's security. To secure the ISA Server computer, ensure the security of the computer itself, the operating system running on the computer, and the ISA Server configuration. After installation, ISA Server starts with a default configuration that blocks all traffic between networks connected to ISA Server but enables some traffic between the ISA Server computer and other networks. As an ISA Server administrator, you will need to modify the default configuration. The third step in ensuring ISA Server security is to manage the administrative permissions users have on ISA Server.

Real World   **Defense in Depth**

Deploying ISA Server 2004 is a critical component of an organization's overall security design. However, merely deploying ISA Server 2004 at the perimeter of the network does not guarantee security throughout the network. For example, you may use ISA Server at the network perimeter to block all attacks from the Internet. However, the ISA Server computer is not effective if a user brings an infected laptop computer to work and connects it to the network. To provide security throughout the network, you must implement a defense-in-depth security strategy.

A defense-in-depth security strategy means that you use multiple levels of defense to secure your network. If one level is compromised, it does not necessarily mean that your entire organization is compromised. As a general guideline, you design and build each level of your security on the assumption that every other layer of security has been breached, and that the level you're working on is the final roadblock to an attacker's gaining access to resources on your network. If you assume that, you will ensure that each layer is as secure as possible.

When you use a defense-in-depth strategy, you increase an attacker's risk of detection and reduce an attacker's chance of success. Because you monitor for illegitimate activity at many levels, you are more likely to detect an attacker's actions. In addition, because you monitor at many levels, you can correlate related events from various monitoring sources to identify the attack and determine which levels have been compromised. The defense-in-depth strategy also reduces the attacker's chance of success. The attacker may use a particular strategy to defeat one level of defense, but must then use a completely different strategy to compromise the next level. The defense-in-depth layers are illustrated on the next page.

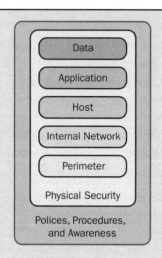

Each level in the defense-in-depth strategy forms part of the overall strategy, as follows:

- *Policies, procedures, and awareness*—Many network attacks succeed because an organization's employees deliberately or inadvertently create a breach. One of the first components in creating the security strategy is to develop organizational policies and procedures dealing with security and then to train users about them.

- *Physical security*—Ensure that only authorized personnel can gain physical access to the resources. At a minimum, all critical network resources should be located in a secured facility.

- *Perimeter*—Almost all companies provide some form of access to the Internet, so it is critical that the connecting point between the Internet and the internal network is as secure as possible. Options for providing this security include firewalls or multiple firewalls, secure virtual private network (VPN) access that uses quarantine procedures, and secure server publishing to provide required access to internal resources. ISA Server can have a primary role in providing perimeter security.

- *Internal networks*—Even if the perimeter is secure, you must still ensure that the internal networks are secure for cases in which the perimeter is compromised or when the attacker is within the organization. Options include network segmentation to isolate networks that carry highly confidential network traffic, using Internet Protocol Security (IPSec) to encrypt network traffic, and a network intrusion-detection system (NIDS) at each network access point.

- *Operating systems*—Many security attacks take advantage of security vulnerabilities that are available within operating systems. These attacks can be prevented by hardening server and client operating systems, ensuring that all security updates are efficiently deployed, requiring strong authentication methods, and using a host-based intrusion-detection system (HIDS).

- *Applications*—Security attacks also take advantage of vulnerabilities in application security. These attacks can be mitigated by ensuring that applications are designed with security in mind, hardening the applications so that the applications are secure and run with the least possible permissions, and ensuring that appropriate antivirus software is deployed on each application server. Using a firewall, such as ISA Server 2004 with application filtering functionality, can further help secure applications.

- *Data*—The final level in the defense-in-depth strategy is protecting the data that is located on network resources. This data can be protected by using access control lists (ACLs), and using a data encryption mechanism such as Encrypting File System (EFS) to ensure that only authorized users can gain access to the data.

ISA Server 2004 is a critical component in the overall defense-in-depth security strategy. When designing your ISA Server implementation, consider how ISA Server will fit into your defense-in-depth strategy. However, don't make the mistake of thinking that once you have deployed ISA Server, your network is secure.

After this lesson, you will be able to

- Harden the operating system components on the server running ISA Server
- Modify the ISA Server default configuration to enhance security
- Configure ISA Server administrative roles for delegated permissions

Estimated lesson time: 60 minutes

How to Harden the Server

ISA Server runs on computers running Microsoft Windows 2000 Server or Windows Server 2003, so the first step of securing ISA Server is to ensure that the computer and operating system are as secure as possible. Securing the computer includes the following components:

- Securing the network interfaces

- Ensuring that only required system services are enabled

- Ensuring that security updates are applied

Security Alert   One of the critical components in securing ISA Server is to ensure that the ISA Server computer is stored in a physically secure location. If an attacker can gain physical access to a server, the attacker can circumvent the operating system security fairly easily. To maintain a secure environment, restrict physical access to the ISA Server computer.

How to Secure the Network Interfaces

To secure ISA Server, begin by securing the network interfaces connected to the server. By default, network interfaces in both Windows 2000 Server and Windows Server 2003 are configured to facilitate connecting other computers on the network to the server. On an ISA Server computer, ensure that clients can connect to the network interfaces only to access specific resources. Although both the interface connected to the Internet and the interface connected to the Internal network need to be secured, it is particularly important to secure the interface that is connected to the Internet.

Securing the External Network Interface   The external interface of your ISA Server computer is likely to be directly attached to the Internet, where it may be exposed to an attack from anywhere on the Internet. To secure the external interface on the ISA Server computer, complete the following actions:

- **Disable File and Printer Sharing for Microsoft Networks and Client for Microsoft Networks.**   File and Printer Sharing for Microsoft Networks allows the machine to share Server Message Block/Common Internet File System (SMB/CIFS) resources. The Client for Microsoft Networks allows the machine to access SMB/CIFS resources. These options can enable NetBIOS and Direct Hosting ports, both of which are used for conventional file sharing and access on Microsoft networks.

- **Disable NetBIOS over TCP/IP.**   NetBIOS over TCP/IP is required if the computer needs to be configured as a Windows Internet Naming Service (WINS) client, needs to send out NetBIOS broadcasts, needs to send out browser service announcements, or needs to access NetBIOS resources. The ISA Server computer should not send or receive any NetBIOS packets to the Internet.

- **Disable the LMHOSTS Lookup option.**   The LMHOSTS file is used to enable NetBIOS name lookups. The ISA Server computer should not connect to any computers on the Internet using NetBIOS. If you disable LMHOSTS lookup, be aware that this option is disabled for all network interfaces on the ISA Server computer.

- **Disable automatic Domain Name System (DNS) name registration.**   By default, Windows 2000 and Windows Server 2003 computers attempt to register their IP addresses with a DNS server. The ISA Server computer should not register the IP address for its external interface with DNS servers on the Internet or with DNS servers inside the network.

Securing the Internal Network Interface   In addition to securing the external interface, you should secure the internal interface on the computer running ISA Server.

However, in many cases, you may require more functionality on the internal interface, so you must ensure that you disable only the components that are not required.

- Leave File and Printer Sharing for Microsoft Networks enabled on the internal interface if you want internal network clients to access the Firewall Client software. If the client installation files are stored on another computer, you can disable File and Printer Sharing.

- Client for Microsoft Networks must also be enabled if you want to access resources on the internal network or authenticate to internal resources.

- Disable NetBIOS over TCP/IP if you do not have any legacy client computers or NetBIOS-based applications on the network that need access to the ISA Server computer.

- Leave automatic DNS name resolution enabled on the internal network interface so that the ISA Server computer's IP address is registered in DNS. If you do not have automatic updates enabled on the DNS zone, disable this option and manually configure the host record in DNS.

> **Note** If you have additional interfaces on the computer running ISA Server, disable as many services as possible on these interfaces. If the network interface is connected to a perimeter network, configure it as you would the Internet interface.

Managing System Services on the ISA Server Computer

A second step in securing the computer running ISA Server is to disable all services on the computer that are not required. Several core services are required for ISA Server to run properly, and additional services can be enabled depending on the functionality required. All other services should be disabled.

> **Security Alert** This lesson is focused on reducing the attack surface of the computer running ISA Server and of ISA Server itself. Reducing the attack surface means that you eliminate as many of the avenues of attack as possible without losing the required functionality. For example, you disable a system service so that an attacker can never gain access to the server using that service. You avoid running non-essential applications on the computer running ISA Server to ensure that a security flaw in that application cannot be used to compromise the server. Reducing the attack surface can also mean that you reduce the larger risk to your organization in the event of a security breach on the ISA Server computer. For example, never install ISA Server on a domain controller because Windows domain controllers require many different ports to be accessible to client computers, resulting in a complicated configuration. In addition, if an attacker can gain access to the domain database, the attacker may be able to compromise all user accounts, or perhaps damage the database so that no one can log on. As much as possible, your ISA Server computer should be dedicated to operating only as an ISA Server computer with all other functionality disabled.

Services Required by ISA Server   Table 3-1 lists the core services that must be enabled for ISA Server and the ISA Server computer to function properly.

Table 3-1   Services Required for ISA Server 2004

Service Name	Rationale	Startup Mode
COM+ Event System	Core operating system	Manual
Cryptographic Services	Core operating system	Automatic
Event Log	Core operating system	Automatic
IPSec Services	Core operating system	Automatic
Logical Disk Manager	Core operating system	Automatic
Logical Disk Manager Administrative Service	Core operating system	Manual
Microsoft Firewall	Required for ISA Server	Automatic
Microsoft ISA Server Control	Required for ISA Server	Automatic
Microsoft ISA Server Job Scheduler	Required for ISA Server	Automatic
Microsoft ISA Server Storage	Required for ISA Server	Automatic
MSSQL$MSFW	Required when MSDE logging is used	Automatic
Network Connections	Core operating system	Manual
NTLM Security Support Provider	Core operating system	Manual
Plug and Play	Core operating system	Automatic
Protected Storage	Core operating system	Automatic
Remote Access Connection Manager	Required for ISA Server	Manual
Remote Procedure Call (RPC)	Core operating system	Automatic
Secondary Logon	Core operating system	Automatic
Security Accounts Manager	Core operating system	Automatic
Server	Required for ISA Server Firewall Client Share	Automatic
Smart Card	Core operating system	Manual
SQLAgent$MSFW	Required when MSDE logging is used	Manual
System Event Notification	Core operating system	Automatic
Telephony	Required for ISA Server	Manual
Virtual Disk Service (VDS)	Core operating system	Manual
Windows Management Instrumentation (WMI)	Core operating system	Automatic
WMI Performance Adapter	Core operating system	Manual

You may need to enable additional services on ISA Server, depending on the functionality you require from the server. The ISA Server computer may need to provide additional server functionality such as operating as a VPN remote access server, or as a terminal server for remote desktop. The ISA Server computer, in some cases, also acts as a network client. For example, the ISA Server computer may need to be a DNS client, or you may want to be able to access shared folders on the Internal network from the ISA Server computer. Table 3-2 lists additional services that may need to be enabled on the computer running ISA Server.

Table 3-2   Optional Services

Functionality Required	Services Required	Startup Mode
Routing and Remote Access Server	Routing and Remote Access	Manual
Terminal Server for Remote Desktop Administration	Server Terminal Services	Automatic (for Server); Manual (for Terminal Services)
To install applications using the Microsoft Installer Service	Windows Installer	Manual
To collect performance data on the ISA Server computer	Performance Logs and Alerts	Automatic
To enable remote management of the Windows server	Remote Registry	Automatic
To allow the ISA Server computer to register its IP address with a DNS Server automatically	DHCP Client	Automatic
To perform DNS lookups	DNS Client	Automatic
To assign the ISA Server computer to a domain	Network location awareness Net Logon	Manual Automatic
To allow the ISA Server computer to connect to other Windows clients	Workstation	Automatic
To allow the ISA Server computer to perform WINS-based name resolution	TCP/IP NetBIOS Helper	Automatic

See Also   Table 3-2 lists the most common optional services that you may need to enable. For a complete list of all the services that may be required, and a description of the specific situations when you may require the services, see the Security Hardening Guide, located at *http://www.microsoft.com/technet/prodtechnol/isa/2004/plan/securityhardeningguide.mspx.*

To manage system services on the computer running ISA Server, follow this procedure:

1. Open the Services console from the Administrative Tools folder.

2. Right-click the service that you are configuring and click Properties.

3. On the service Properties page, on the General tab, select the Startup type. You can also start, stop, pause, or resume the service.

> **Tip**   Many system services require that other services be running before the service can start. If you have configured a service to start automatically and it will not start, check for service dependencies on the Dependencies tab on the service Properties dialog box. The Dependencies tab also includes information detailing which services depend on the service with which you are working.

Using Security Templates to Manage Services   You can manage the system services manually on the computer running ISA Server 2004. However, if you have multiple computers running ISA Server, you should automate the process of managing the services. One option for managing the system services is to use security templates. Security templates are preconfigured sets of security settings that can be applied to users and computers. Security templates can be used to configure the following:

- **Audit Policy settings**   These settings specify the security events that are recorded in the Event Log. You can monitor security-related activity such as who accesses or attempts to access an object, when a user logs on or logs off a computer, or when changes are made to an Audit Policy setting.

- **User Rights Assignment**   These settings specify which users or groups have logon rights or privileges on the member servers in the domain.

- **Security Options**   These settings are used to enable or disable security settings for servers, such as digital signing of data, administrator and guest account names, driver installation behavior, and logon prompts.

- **Event Log settings**   These settings specify the size of each event log and actions to take when each event log becomes full.

- **System services**   These settings specify the startup behavior and permissions for each service on the server.

Implementing Security Templates   If your computer is a member of an Active Directory directory service domain, you can apply security templates using Group Policy at a domain or organizational unit (OU) level. If your computer is not a member of a domain, you can use the Security Configuration and Analysis Microsoft Management Console (MMC) snap-in or the Secedit command-line tool.

> **Exam Tip**   For the exam, you need not worry about how the security templates are being applied, but you must be aware of the security template settings, especially how the template relates to system services.

Microsoft has released the Windows Server 2003 Security Guide, which includes several templates that you can use to secure servers on your network. The templates are grouped into three categories:

■ Enterprise Client templates are designed for most networking environments that contain only Windows 2000 or later computers.

■ Legacy Client templates are designed for networking environments that contain older computers.

■ High Security templates are designed to be deployed only in networks that require very high security.

Caution   The High Security templates set very restrictive security policies that may interfere with network functionality. These policies should be deployed only in environments that require this level of security, and only after thorough testing.

The Security Guide also provides multiple templates based on server roles, as follows:

■ For member servers in a domain, the Security Guide recommends that you first apply the Member Server Baseline template, which provides a set of baseline security settings that can be applied to all member servers in the domain.

■ After you have applied baseline security settings, you can use additional security templates provided in the Security Guide to apply additional, incremental, security settings to member servers that perform specific roles, such as infrastructure servers, file servers, print servers, and Microsoft Internet Information Services (IIS) servers.

See Also   The Windows Server 2003 Security Guide can be found at *http://go.microsoft.com/fwlink/?LinkId=14845*. The Microsoft Windows 2000 Security Hardening Guide can be found at *http://go.microsoft.com/fwlink/?LinkID=22380*.

ISA Server and Security Templates   Security templates are the ideal means to configure the security settings on an ISA Server computer. By applying these templates, you can ensure a consistently high level of security on the ISA Server computer. To apply the security templates to the ISA Server computer, perform the following steps:

1. Using the Security Templates MMC snap-in, shown in Figure 3-1, analyze the security templates included with the Windows Server 2003 Security Guide and determine which template most closely meets your organization's requirements. Modify those parts of the template that do not match your requirements.

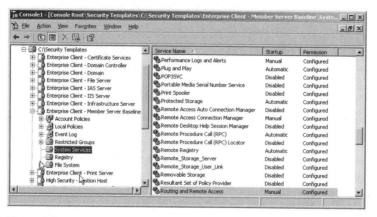

Figure 3-1 Configuring the security template services

2. Apply the security templates to your ISA Server computer or computers. If your ISA Server computers are members of an Active Directory domain, create an OU that contains only the ISA Server computers and then create a Group Policy Object (GPO) to apply the security template to the servers. If your ISA Server computer is not a member of the domain, use the Security Analysis and Configuration tool to apply the security policy to the ISA Server computer.

Applying Security Updates

Another critical component in keeping the computer running ISA Server secure is to ensure that all security updates and patches are applied. Security updates are product updates that eliminate known security vulnerabilities. To keep ISA Server secure, you must ensure that the security updates for both ISA Server and the operating system are current by installing the latest fixes. If the operating system is vulnerable, ISA Server is also vulnerable. When a security update becomes available, quickly evaluate your system to determine if the update is relevant to your current situation.

Monitor and install security patches for multiple components for the computer running ISA Server. These include the latest updates for the operating system, for ISA Server, and for other components installed by ISA Server, including Microsoft SQL Server 2000 Desktop Engine (MSDE) and Office Web Components 2002 (OWC).

Monitoring Security Updates   The first step in applying security updates is to be aware of which security updates are available and the security issues that each update is designed to fix. Resources that help you stay aware of the latest security updates include the following:

■   Microsoft and many third-party antivirus vendors provide security bulletins that enable you to stay current on security issues and fixes. To receive the Microsoft notifications, register at Microsoft Security Notification Service, which is located at *http://www.microsoft.com/technet/security/bulletin/notify.mspx*.

■ Monitor the Microsoft Security Web site, located at *http://www.microsoft.com/security*.

■ For ISA Server–specific information, monitor the Microsoft Internet Security and Acceleration Security Center, located at *http://www.microsoft.com/technet/security/ prodtech/isa/default.mspx*. You can also check the ISA Server 2004 Download Center, located at *http://go.microsoft.com/fwlink/?LinkId=28791*.

■ Search for the latest updates for MSDE and OWC, at Microsoft Security Bulletin Search, located at *http://go.microsoft.com/fwlink/?LinkId=28687*.

ISA Server and Security Updates   Because ISA Server security is critical, you must ensure that the most recent security patches for the operating system, ISA Server, and other components such as MSDE are installed on the ISA Server computer. At the same time, you need to ensure that you don't install a security patch that breaks something else on the ISA Server computer or prevents users from using the ISA Server computer. Follow these guidelines when deploying security patches on your ISA Server computer:

■ Evaluate the security update severity and risk. When a new security update is released, evaluate the severity of the security issue that it is fixing and evaluate the risk to your organization. If the security patch is fixing a security hole that is extremely difficult to exploit, or if the fix pertains to a feature that you have not implemented, you may choose to wait until the next service pack to apply the patch. In some cases, you may also be able to mitigate the vulnerability by disabling a service or feature instead of using the patch. However, if the patch fixes a critical security issue that directly affects your organization, you should implement the patch immediately.

■ Apply the security update in a test environment. Maintain a test environment that closely mirrors your production environment, and install the patch in this environment first to see if it disrupts any ISA Server functionality.

■ Monitor others' experience with the security patch. Monitor Internet newsgroups and forums to see if other people are having problems with the patch. This will reveal not only problems with the patch itself, but with the patch installation as well. If the patch causes problems, you may be able to avoid the vulnerability by implementing an alternative control, such as disabling the relevant service or feature.

■ Prepare a backup plan. Despite your best efforts, deploying the security update may interfere with ISA Server functionality. Be prepared with a backup plan that enables you to restore ISA Server functionality as rapidly as possible.

■ Deploy the security update in the production environment. Once you are confident that the patch will not interfere with the functionality in the production environment, deploy the patches to the production ISA Server computers.

Practice: Securing the Computer Running ISA Server

In this practice, you will secure the ISA Server computer's external network interface. You will then use security templates to manage the system services running ISA Server.

▶ **Exercise 1: Securing the Network Interface**

1. Log on to ISA1 as an Administrator.

2. Open Network Connections from the Control Panel, and then click External. Click Properties.

3. On the External Properties page, clear the check box for Client for Microsoft Networks and File and Printer Sharing for Microsoft Networks.

4. Click Internet Protocol (TCP/IP) and click Properties. The Internet Protocol (TCP/IP) Properties dialog box opens.

5. Click Advanced. On the DNS tab, clear the check box for Register This Connection's Address In DNS.

6. On the WINS tab, clear the check box for Enable LMHOSTS Lookup and select Disable NetBIOS Over TCP/IP. Click OK twice and close all open windows.

▶ **Exercise 2: Using Security Templates and Group Policy to Manage System Services**

1. Log on to DC1 as an Administrator.

2. Open Active Directory Users and Computers from the Administrative Tools folder on the Start menu.

3. Create a new OU in the *cohovineyard.com* domain named ISA Servers.

4. Right-click ISA Servers and click Properties.

5. On the Group Policy tab, click New.

6. Type **ISA Server Security Settings** and then click Edit.

7. Expand Computer Configuration and then click Windows Settings.

8. Right-click Security Settings and select Import policy.

9. In the Import Policy From dialog box, browse to the C:\Security Templates folder. Click Enterprise Client—Member Server Baseline and click Open.

Tip When you move the ISA Server computer account into the ISA Servers OU, the member server baseline security template settings will be applied. This template disables several services required for ISA Server, so you must modify the template to enable the ISA Services to run.

10. Expand Security Settings, and then click System Services. Double-click Remote Access Connection Manager.

11. Click Manual and then click OK.

12. Enable the Routing and Remote Access service and configure it for manual start.

13. Enable the Telephony service and configure it for manual start.

14. Enable the Secondary Logon service and configure it for automatic start.

15. Close the Group Policy Object Editor and close the ISA Servers Properties page.

16. Move the ISA1 computer object from the Computers container to the ISA Servers OU.

17. Reboot ISA1.

How to Secure the ISA Server Configuration

After securing the computer running ISA Server, the next step is to ensure that your ISA Server configuration is as secure as possible. After installation, ISA Server, Standard Edition, starts with a default configuration that provides a high level of security. As an ISA Server administrator, you must understand what the default configuration is and how you may need to modify it to provide additional security or functionality.

> **Note**   This default configuration information applies only to ISA Server, Standard Edition. When you install ISA Server 2004, Enterprise Edition, you assign the server to an array, and the enterprise and array policies are applied to the server.

The ISA Server Default Configuration

After a standard installation, ISA Server starts with a default configuration. This configuration provides a high level of security because it does not allow access to any Internet or internal resources through the ISA Server computer. However, the default configuration also includes several other settings. Table 3-3 summarizes the default configuration.

Table 3-3   ISA Server Default Configuration

ISA Server Feature	Default Configuration
Administrator permissions	Members of the Administrators group on the local computer can configure all ISA Server settings. If the ISA Server computer is a member of a domain, the Domain Admins group is a member of the local Administrators group, so the Domain Admins also has full ISA Server management rights. No other users have any Administrator permissions on ISA Server.

Table 3-3 ISA Server Default Configuration

ISA Server Feature	Default Configuration
Default networks	The following networks are configured: *Local Host.* This network represents the ISA Server computer. *External.* This network includes all computers (IP addresses) that are not explicitly associated with any other network. The external network is generally considered an untrusted network and represents all hosts on the Internet. *Internal.* This network includes all computers (IP addresses) that were specified as internal during the installation process. *VPN Clients.* This network contains addresses of currently connected VPN clients. The range of possible addresses is configured when you configure the VPN properties. *Quarantined VPN Clients.* This network contains addresses of VPN clients that have not yet cleared quarantine.
Network settings	The following network relations are created: *Local Host Access.* Defines a network rule that states that all traffic between the Local Host (the ISA Server computer) and all networks will be routed. This does not enable the routing of traffic, but it states that traffic between the ISA Server computer and any other network will be routed rather than use network address translation (NAT). *Internet Access.* Defines a NAT network relationship from the Internal network, the Quarantined VPN Clients network, and the VPN Clients network, to the External network. Again, this does not grant any access; it only states that NAT will be used for traffic between these networks. *VPN Clients to Internal Network.* Defines a routed network relationship between the VPN Clients network and the Internal network.
Firewall Access Rules	The following default rules are created: *System policy rules.* A series of rules that enable interaction between the ISA Server computer and other network resources. *Default rule.* This rule denies all traffic between all networks. Because this is the only firewall access rule that is created by default, all traffic between different networks on the ISA Server computer is blocked.
Publishing	No internal servers are accessible to external clients.

Table 3-3   ISA Server Default Configuration

ISA Server Feature	Default Configuration
Caching	The cache size is set to 0. All caching is therefore disabled.
Firewall Client Install Share	When you install the Firewall Client Share, a system policy rule named Allow Access To Firewall Client Share To Trusted Computers, which allows clients on the Internal network to access the share, is enabled. This rule must be enabled to allow the clients to install the software from the share.

The default configuration of a newly installed ISA Server means that traffic can occur between the ISA Server computer and other networks. For example, Lightweight Directory Access Protocol (LDAP) traffic is permitted from the ISA Server computer to the internal network. This enables the ISA Server computer to operate as a member of an Active Directory domain. However, by default, no traffic is permitted through the ISA Server computer from one network to another.

Because ISA Server blocks all network traffic between connected networks, you must modify the default ISA Server configuration to use ISA Server. Modify the default settings by configuring firewall access rules and publishing rules so that users can access resources on other networks through the ISA Server computer. You may also want to modify the default configuration by modifying the system policies on the server or by assigning administrative roles.

Configuring System Policies

When ISA Server 2004 is installed, a default system policy is configured on the server. This system policy includes a variety of access rules that provide an initial configuration for ISA Server 2004. Depending on your organization's requirements, you may need to modify the system policy configuration, either by disabling some of the rules or enabling and modifying the rules.

System policy rules are used to define what traffic is allowed between the ISA Server computer and the connected networks. All the system policies define access between the Local Network, which is the ISA Server computer itself, and the connected networks rather than defining access between networks.

Exam Tip   System policies are the primary means for restricting or enabling access to the ISA Server computer. When you see questions on the exam that relate to accessing the ISA Server computer (called the Local Network in the ISA Server Management interface), check the system policy settings.

The firewall access rules defined by the system policy function the same way as other access rules in that they enable or disable access. However, the implementation of the system policy rules is different. When you create an access rule, you must define all components for that rule. The system policy rules are defined in advance; all you need to do is decide whether to enable or disable the rule and then choose which networks are affected by the rule.

System Policy Settings   A default system policy is applied when you install ISA Server 2004. This policy enables the functionality needed to manage the ISA Server computer and provide network connectivity. Table 3-4 summarizes the system policy configuration options.

Table 3-4   System Policy Settings

Configuration Group	Configuration Options
Network Services	Defines which networks are accessible from the ISA Server computer for DNS, Dynamic Host Configuration Protocol (DHCP), and Network Time Protocol (NTP). You can modify the system policy so that only particular computers on the internal network can be accessed, or add networks if the services are found on a different network.
Authentication Services	To authenticate users, ISA Server must be able to communicate with the authentication servers. By default, ISA Server can communicate with Active Directory servers (for Windows authentication) and with Remote Authentication Dial-In User Service (RADIUS) servers located on the internal network. You can modify which networks are accessible for authentication as well as limit which authentication options can be used.
Remote Management	By default, ISA Server can be managed by running a remote MMC snap-in or by using Terminal Services on any computer in the built-in Remote Management Computers computer set. When ISA Server is installed, this empty computer set is created. Add all computers that will manage ISA Server remotely to this set. Until this is done, remote management is not available from any computer.
Firewall Client	If the Firewall Client Share component was installed when you installed ISA Server, the Firewall Client Installation Share configuration group is enabled by default. All computers on the Internal network can access the shared folder.

Table 3-4 System Policy Settings

Configuration Group	Configuration Options
Diagnostic Services	The system policy rules that allow access to diagnostic services are enabled, with the following permissions: ■ *Internet Control Message Protocol (ICMP) is allowed to all networks.* This service is important for determining connectivity to other computers. ■ *Windows networking.* This allows NetBIOS communication to computers on the Internal network. ■ *Microsoft error reporting.* This allows Hypertext Transfer Protocol (HTTP) access to the Microsoft Error Reporting sites Uniform Resource Locator (URL) set to allow reporting of error information. By default, this URL set includes specific Microsoft sites.
Logging and Remote Monitoring	These system policy rules allow remote logging and monitoring. The following configuration groups are disabled by default: ■ Remote Logging (NetBIOS) ■ Remote Logging (SQL) ■ Remote Performance Monitoring ■ Microsoft Operations Manager
SMTP	The Simple Mail Transfer Protocol (SMTP) configuration group is enabled, allowing SMTP communication from ISA Server to computers on the Internal network. This is required to send alert information in an e-mail message.
Scheduled Download Jobs	The scheduled download jobs feature is disabled. When a content download job is created, the administrator is prompted to enable this system policy rule.
Allowed Sites	By default, the allowed sites configuration group is enabled, allowing ISA Server to access content on specific sites that belong to the System Policy Allowed Sites URL set. This URL set includes various Microsoft Web sites by default. The URL set can be modified to include additional Web sites.

Modifying System Policy   After installing ISA Server, you should analyze the default system policy configuration and modify the policy to meet your organization's requirements. The default system policy enables more options than are required for most organizations. If your organization does not require a specific type of functionality enabled by a system policy rule, then disable the rule. For example, the default system policy enables both RADIUS and Active Directory authentication, and most organizations will use one or the other. If you are using only one type of authentication, then disable the rule pertaining to the other.

Modify the default system policy settings to match your organization's requirements. First, identify the functionality that you require on the ISA Server computer. Then review the system policy settings and disable all the system policy rules that you do not require. For example, if no users will ever access ISA Server using Remote Desktop, then disable the Terminal Server system policy that enables Remote Desktop connections.

Second, for the system policy rules that you leave enabled, you should limit which networks are included in the system policy setting. For example, by default, the DNS system policy allows ISA Server to perform DNS lookups on any connected network. If you want the ISA Server computer to be able to perform lookups only on the Internal network, then modify the system policy setting. You can limit the scope of some system policy rules even more. For example, Remote Desktop connections are permitted only from the computers listed in the Remote Management Computer set. You should add the IP addresses for the computers used by the ISA Server administrators to this group, rather than allow access based on a network.

To modify the default system policy, use the following procedure:

1. In the console tree of ISA Server Management, click Firewall Policy.

2. On the Tasks tab, click Edit System Policy. The interface is shown in Figure 3-2.

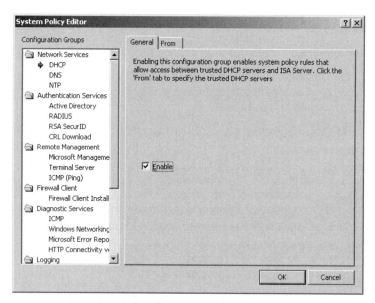

Figure 3-2   Modifying the ISA Server system policy

3. Click the configuration group that you want to configure. For example, to configure the DHCP settings, click DHCP in the Configuration Groups box.

4. On the General tab, click Enable or clear the Enable check box to enable or disable the configuration group.

5. On the From tab, configure the source of network traffic. You can use any network entity to configure the source network. You can also define exceptions to the rule.

> **Note**   The system policy settings all configure traffic to or from the Local Host network. For some configuration groups, such as DHCP, you define the source network for the traffic on the From tab. For other configuration groups, such as Active Directory authentication, you configure the destination network on the To tab.

6. When you enable a system policy setting, ISA Server configures one or more system policy rules. To display the system policy rules, click Firewall Policy in ISA Server Management and then, on the Tasks tab, click Show System Policy Rules.

> **Security Alert**   In addition to configuring system policy to reduce the attack surface, disable the ISA Server features that you do not use. For example, if you do not require caching, disable caching. If you do not require the VPN functionality of ISA Server, disable VPN client access. Both options are disabled by default.

How to Configure ISA Server Administrative Roles

Another component to securing the ISA Server computer is to configure the ISA Server administrative permissions. As a general rule, user accounts should always be configured with the minimum privileges necessary to perform a specific task. You can use role-based administration to organize your ISA Server administrators into separate, defined roles, each with its own set of privileges and corresponding tasks. The roles assigned in ISA Server are based on Windows users and groups. If the ISA Server computer is a member of a domain, these users and groups can be either local accounts or domain accounts. If the ISA Server computer is not a member of a domain, you must assign local users and groups to the roles.

ISA Server includes three administrative roles that are defined in advance:

- **ISA Server Basic Monitoring**   Users and groups assigned this role can monitor the ISA Server computer and network activity, but cannot configure specific monitoring functionality.

- **ISA Server Extended Monitoring**   Users and groups assigned this role can perform all monitoring tasks, including log configuration, alert-definition configuration, and all monitoring functions available to the ISA Server Basic Monitoring role.

- **ISA Server Full Administrator**   Users and groups assigned this role can perform any ISA Server task, including rule configuration, application of network templates, and monitoring.

Exam Tip   The only way to assign permissions in ISA Server is to use administrative roles. If an exam question mentions a user's having too many or too few permissions, check the administrative role configuration.

Each ISA Server role has a specific list of ISA Server tasks associated with it. Table 3-5 lists some ISA Server administrative tasks, as well as the roles in which they are performed.

Table 3-5   ISA Server Roles and Tasks

Activity	ISA Server Basic Monitoring	ISA Server Extended Monitoring	ISA Server Full Administrator
View Dashboard, alerts, connectivity, sessions, services	X	X	X
Acknowledge alerts	X	X	X
View log information		X	X
Create alert definitions		X	X
Create reports		X	X
Stop and start sessions and services		X	X
View firewall policy		X	X
Configure firewall policy			X
Configure cache			X
Configure VPN			X

Any Windows user can be a member of these ISA Server administrative groups. No special privileges or Windows permissions are required. The only exception is that to view the ISA Server performance counters using either Performance Monitor or the ISA Server Dashboard, the user must be a member of the Windows Server 2003 Performance Monitor Users group.

Security Alert   When configuring ISA Server administrative roles, apply the principle of least privilege, whereby a user has the minimum privileges necessary to perform a specific task. This helps ensure that if a user account is compromised, the impact is minimized by the limited privileges granted that user. In particular, remember that the users in the Administrators local group on the computer running ISA Server are assigned the role of ISA Server Full Administrator, meaning that they also have full rights to configure and monitor ISA Server. This group should contain as few users as possible.

To assign administrative roles, use the following procedure:

1. In the console tree of ISA Server Management, click the ISA Server computer name.

2. On the Tasks tab, click Define Administrative Roles.

3. On the Welcome to the ISA Server Administration Delegation Wizard page, click Next.

4. On the Delegate Control page, to add groups, click Add. Figure 3-3 shows the interface.

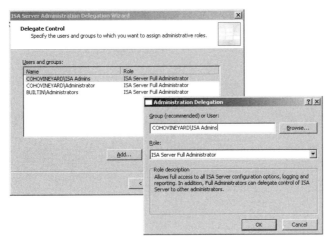

Figure 3-3   Using the Administration Delegation Wizard to assign administrative roles

5. On the Administration Delegation page, click Browse to locate the group or user account.

6. On the Select User Or Group page, click Locations and select the appropriate directory location. Click OK.

7. Type the name of the user or group that you want to add, and then click OK.

8. In the Role box, select the ISA Server role that you want to assign to this user or group. Click OK.

9. Click Next, review the changed roles, and then click Finish.

10. To remove or change the roles assigned to a user or group, run the ISA Server Administration Delegation Wizard again. Select the user or group whose role you want to change. If you are removing the user or group's administrative role, click Remove. If you are changing the administrative role, click Edit and change the role.

Practice: Securing ISA Server

In this practice, you will examine the configuration of an ISA Server computer after installation. Then you will examine and modify the default system policies. Finally, you will create a new user and group in your domain and assign an ISA Server administrative role to the user.

▶ **Exercise 1: Examining the Default ISA Server Configuration**

1. On ISA1, open ISA Server Management. Right-click ISA1 and click Administration Delegation.

2. On the Welcome To The ISA Server Administration Delegation Wizard page, click Next.

3. What roles have been assigned to the following groups?

   a. Cohovineyard\Administrator

   b. Builtin\Administrators

4. Click Cancel.

5. Expand Configuration and click Networks. In the details pane, click Network Rules.

6. Review the Network Rules. List the network relationships between the networks listed below:

   a. Local Host and All Networks

   b. Quarantined VPN Clients, VPN Clients, and Internal

   c. Quarantined VPN Clients, VPN Clients, Internal, and External

7. In the console tree, click Firewall Policy. What rule(s) are listed? Describe the rule configuration.

8. On the Tasks tab, click Show System Policy Rules. Locate the rule named Allow Access From Trusted Computers To The Firewall Client Installation Share On ISA Server. Double-click the rule. What does this rule enable? What network is included in this rule?

9. In the console tree, expand Configuration and click Cache. Under Tasks, click Define Cache Drives. What is the default size of the maximum cache size? What does this indicate about the default cache configuration? Click OK.

10. Close all open windows. If you receive a message about unsaved changes, click Discard Changes.

▶ **Exercise 2: Examining and Modifying the Default System Policy**

1. On ISA1, open ISA Server Management and click Firewall Policy.

2. On the Tasks tab, click Edit System Policy.

3. In the Configuration Groups box, ensure that DHCP is selected. On the From tab, ensure that Internal is listed in the This Rule Applies To Traffic From These Sources box.

4. On the General tab, clear the check box for Enable.

5. In the Configuration Groups box, click Microsoft Management Console. On the From tab, ensure that Remote Management Computers is listed in the This Rule Applies To Traffic From These Sources box.

6. Click Remote Management Computers, and then click Edit. Click Add, and then click Computer.

7. In the New Computer Rule Element dialog box, type **DC1** as the computer name, and **10.10.0.10** as the IP Address. Click OK twice.

8. Under Authentication Services, click RADIUS. Clear the check box for Enable. Click OK.

9. Click Apply to apply the changes and click OK when the changes have been applied.

10. Locate the rule named Allow DHCP Requests From ISA Server To All networks. Right-click the rule and then click Properties. Confirm that the rule is disabled and that you cannot modify the rule. Click OK.

▶ **Exercise 3: Configuring Administrative Roles**

1. Log on to DC1 as an Administrator.

2. Create a group in the Users container named ISA Admins. You will assign ISA Server administrative permissions to this group.

3. Create a user in the Users container. Use your first name and last initial as the user logon name. Add this user account to the ISA Admins group.

4. On ISA1, open ISA Server Management. Right-click ISA1 and click Administration Delegation.

5. On the Welcome To The ISA Server Administration Delegation Wizard page, click Next.

6. On the Delegate Control page, click Add.

7. In the Administration Delegation dialog box, click Browse. Click Locations, expand Entire Directory and then click Cohovineyard.com. Click OK.

8. In the Enter The Object Name To Select box, type ISA Admins and then click OK. Select ISA Server Full Administrator from the Role drop-down list. Click OK.

9. On the Delegate Control page, click Next.

10. On the Completing The Administration Delegation Wizard page, click Finish.

11. Click Apply to apply the changes and click OK when the changes have been applied. Close all open windows.

Lesson Review

Use the following questions to help determine whether you have learned enough to move on to the next lesson. If you have difficulty answering these questions, review the material in this lesson before beginning the next lesson. You can find answers to these questions in the "Questions and Answers" section at the end of this chapter.

1. You want your Help Desk group to be able to monitor the ISA Server Dashboard. Your organization has a security policy that requires that all users be assigned as few permissions as possible to complete their tasks. You assign the ISA Server Basic Monitoring role to the Help Desk group on the ISA Server computer. However, none of your help desk employees can view the performance information in the ISA Server Dashboard. What is the problem and how would you resolve it?

   a. The Help Desk group needs to be added to the local Administrators group on the computer running ISA Server.

   b. You need to create an access rule to allow the Help Desk group to connect to the ISA Server computer.

   c. The Help Desk group needs to be added to the local Performance Monitor Users group on the computer running ISA Server.

   d. The Help Desk group needs to be added to the Server Operators domain local group.

2. You work for a large company with several branch offices. Each of the locations has an Internet connection as well as a dedicated wide area network (WAN) connection to the corporate head office. You install and configure ISA Server 2004 in each branch office. The ISA Server computers are not members of an Active Directory domain. You need to ensure that the same operating system security settings are applied to each ISA Server. What should you do?

   a. Create a script that shuts down all the services that are not required on one of the servers running ISA Server. Run the same script on all the computers running ISA Server.

   b. Document the security settings on one of the servers. Send the document to an administrator in each office, asking them to duplicate the configuration.

   c. Create a security template with your security settings. Apply the security template using Group Policy.

   d. Create a security template with your security settings. Apply the security template using Security Configuration and Analysis.

3. Your organization has deployed ISA Server 2004. You install a third-party product on the server running ISA Server. However, when you try to access the company Web site from the ISA Server computer, you cannot connect to the site. You need to connect to the company Web site from ISA Server to download updates. How can you configure your server to support this requirement?

   a. Enable Schedule Download Jobs on the ISA Server computer.

   b. Add the company Web site to the System Policy Allowed Sites domain name set on the ISA Server computer.

   c. Configure an access rule that enables access from the internal network to the company Web site.

   d. Configure the Web browser on the ISA Server computer as a Web Proxy client.

Lesson Summary

■ The first step in securing ISA Server is to harden the network interfaces and the operating system on the computer that hosts ISA Server. To harden the network interfaces, remove all services and functionality that is not required.

■ The second step to securing ISA Server is to ensure that only required services are running on the computer. To function properly, ISA Server requires some system services; all other services should be disabled. The best way to manage system services on the ISA Server computer is to use security templates.

■ The default configuration of ISA Server 2004 is secure and does not allow access to any Internet or internal resources. It also is configured to allow traffic to flow between the ISA Server computer and other networks.

■ The system policy is a set of firewall policy rules that control how the ISA Server computer interacts with the connected networks. Following installation, the policy should be modified to meet your organization's requirements. You may need to enable some system policy settings, and you should disable all system policies that are not required.

■ Securing ISA Server also means ensuring that users do not have more administrative permissions on the ISA Server computer than they require. ISA Server provides three administrative roles that enable different levels of administrative permissions. Use the Administration Delegation Wizard to assign appropriate roles on ISA Server.

Lesson 2: Maintaining ISA Server 2004

After the ISA Server computer has been deployed and secured, you need to continuously maintain your ISA Server infrastructure. As part of this maintenance, you must ensure that you can recover your ISA Server installation as quickly as possible in the event of a configuration error or a server failure. ISA Server 2004 provides two options for saving and restoring an ISA Server configuration. This lesson explains how to export and import the ISA Server configuration as well as how to back up and restore the configuration. In addition, this lesson discusses how to implement remote administration on ISA Server 2004.

See Also   Another important part of maintaining an ISA Server implementation is monitoring ISA Server. This topic is explored in Chapter 11, "Implementing Monitoring and Reporting."

After this lesson, you will be able to

- Import and export the ISA Server configuration
- Back up and restore the ISA Server configuration
- Implement remote administration of ISA Server 2004

Estimated lesson time: 45 minutes

How to Export and Import the ISA Server Configuration

Among the new features in ISA Server 2004 is the option to export and import the ISA Server configuration. With this option, you can save and restore the ISA Server configuration information. When you use the ISA Server export feature, the configuration parameters are exported and stored in an .xml file.

The import and export features are useful in several scenarios:

- **Cloning a server**   You can export a configuration from one ISA Server computer and then import the settings on another computer, thereby easily duplicating a server configuration. For example, after configuring an ISA Server computer at one branch office, you can export the configuration to an .xml file. Then you can import the file on a computer running ISA Server at another branch office. The two ISA Server computers will have a duplicate configuration.

- **Saving a partial configuration**   You can export and import any part of the ISA Server configuration. For example, you can export a single rule, an entire policy, or an entire configuration. This is helpful when you want to copy all the firewall policy rules, but not the monitoring configuration, from one ISA Server to another. This is also useful when you want to modify a specific rule. You can export that rule and have the exported configuration available in case you need to roll back the rule modification.

- **Sending a configuration for troubleshooting**   You can export your configuration information to a file and send it to support professionals for analysis and troubleshooting.

- **Rolling back a configuration change**   As a best practice, before modifying any ISA Server settings you should export the specific component that you are modifying. If your modification is not successful, you can easily restore the previous configuration by importing the policy file.

Exporting the ISA Server Configuration

You can export the entire ISA Server configuration, or just parts of it, depending on your specific needs. You can export the following objects:

- The entire ISA Server configuration
- All the connectivity verifiers, or one selected connectivity verifier
- All the networks, or one selected network
- All the network sets, or one selected network set
- All the network rules, or one selected network rule
- All the Web chaining rules, or one selected Web chaining rule
- Cache configuration
- All the content-download jobs, or one or more selected content-download jobs
- The entire firewall policy, or one selected rule

Tip   The system policy rules are not exported when you export the firewall policy. To export the system policy configuration, you must select the Export System Policy task.

When you export an entire configuration, all general configuration information is exported. This includes access rules, publishing rules, rule elements, alert configuration, cache configuration, and ISA Server properties. In addition, you can choose to export user permission settings and confidential information such as user passwords. Confidential information included in the exported file is encrypted.

Caution   When you export an entire configuration, certificate settings are also exported. However, if you import the configuration to an ISA Server computer with different certificates, the Microsoft Firewall service will fail to start and an event message will be logged. To avoid this, use the Certificates MMC snap-in to copy the certificates from the first server to the second server, or modify the ISA Server computer settings that require certificates.

To export the ISA Server configuration, complete the following procedure:

1. Open ISA Server Management.

2. Select the object the settings of which you want to export. Remember if you select a container object (such as the Firewall Policy), all the objects in the container will be exported.

3. On the Tasks tab, click the Export task. The exact name for the task will vary depending on the type of object that you select.

4. Enter a file name for the exported .xml file and click Export.

Security Alert   Ensure that you save the exported files to a secure location on the local server or on a network share. Only administrators of the ISA Server computer should have read permissions to the location. If an attacker can access the configuration file, the intruder will have complete information about your ISA Server configuration.

Importing the ISA Server Configuration

When you import a previously exported file, all properties and settings defined in the file are imported, overwriting the current configuration on the ISA Server computer. However, if you export only a specific component, such as a specific firewall rule, the file import overwrites only that particular rule.

Note   When you import the configuration, the configuration file must be imported at the appropriate node. For example, after you export a rule, you must import the configuration file at the Firewall Policy node level or by selecting another rule.

To import the ISA Server configuration, complete the following procedure:

1. Open ISA Server Management.

2. Select the object whose settings you want to import. You must select the correct type of object for the configuration file that you are using.

3. On the Tasks tab, click the import task. The exact name for the task will vary, depending on the type of object that you selected.

4. Select the exported .xml file and click Import.

5. Click Apply to apply the changes and click OK when the changes have been applied.

How to Back Up and Restore the ISA Server Configuration

ISA Server 2004 also includes backup and restore features that enable you to save and restore the ISA Server configuration information. The backup procedure also stores the configuration information in an .xml file.

The primary use of the backup and restore option in ISA Server is for disaster recovery. You should regularly back up the configuration on the ISA Server computer so that you can restore the computer with the same settings in case of a computer failure. The backup functionality saves the appropriate information to ensure that an identical configuration can be restored.

> **Real World   Disaster Recovery with ISA Server 2004**
>
> Disaster recovery is often a complicated and painful process for an organization. In my experience, many organizations do not have a documented disaster recovery plan in place. Even if an organization has such a plan, disaster recovery is usually very difficult and results in significant downtime for the network and often a loss of data. As a result, most network administrators find the whole topic of disaster recovery very stressful.
>
> The good news is that disaster recovery with ISA Server 2004 is really quite easy. Because you can back up an entire ISA Server configuration to an .xml file, you can restore ISA Server functionality very rapidly on another server. In the simplest scenario, you configure a replacement server with the same IP address configuration as the failed server. If you use Group Policy to assign a security template to the ISA Server computers, you can move the new ISA Server into the applicable OU to apply all the Windows security settings. Then install ISA Server on the replacement server and import the ISA Server settings from the failed server.
>
> This doesn't mean that you need not plan for handling a disaster. For example, ensure that you have a recent backup of the ISA Server configuration. This backup must be stored in a network location other than the ISA Server computer in case of a hard-disk failure on the server. You must also have a replacement server available. The good news is that because you are not restoring any operating system components, the replacement server need not be running on the same hardware as the failed server.
>
> If you are using digital certificates for Secure Sockets Layer (SSL) on the ISA Server computer, you also need to have backup copies of the digital certificates available. If you do not have a backup copy of the original certificate, you will need to obtain another certificate with the same name before you can restore full ISA Server functionality. Because of this, use the Certificates MMC snap-in to export all the certificates on the ISA Server computer and store these certificates with the ISA Server backups.

Backing up an ISA Server configuration backs up all configuration options on the server. This includes firewall policy rules, rule elements, alert configuration, cache configuration, system policy and VPN configuration. One of the differences between backing up the server configuration and exporting the configuration is that you can only back up the entire ISA Server configuration, not individual components or groups of components.

The restore process reconstructs the configuration information that was backed up. By restoring a backup, you can rebuild the ISA Server configuration or restore it after a configuration error.

To back up and restore the ISA Server configuration, complete the following procedure:

1. Open ISA Server Management and click the server name. The option to back up and restore the ISA Server configuration is available only when you select the server name.

2. On the Tasks tab, click Backup This ISA Server Configuration.

3. Enter a file name for the backup file and click Backup.

4. You must provide a password for the ISA Server backup

5. To restore the backup, click the server name in ISA Server Management. Then click Restore this ISA Server Configuration and select the appropriate ISA Server backup file.

6. Click Apply to apply the changes and click OK when the changes have been applied.

How to Implement Remote Administration

In most organizations, you will not perform ISA Server administration directly from the ISA Server computer console. The ISA Server computer should be located in a physically secure server room and you should administer the server from your client computer. If your organization has multiple locations with ISA Servers installed in each location, you may need to manage all the servers from your desktop. Remote administration enables you to administer ISA Server in all these cases.

You have two options for remotely administrating ISA Server. You can use a Terminal Services or Remote Desktop connection to administer the server, or you can install the ISA Server Management Console on another computer and use it to manage the ISA Server computer.

If you have installed ISA Server on a server running Windows 2000, you can use Terminal Services to manage the ISA Server computer. If ISA Server is installed on a computer running Windows Server 2003, you can use Remote Desktop in the same way. When you use Terminal Services or Remote Desktop to administer the ISA Server computer, you can view the desktop of the ISA Server computer as if you were in front of the monitor attached to the ISA Server computer. The advantage of using Terminal Services or Remote Desktop to administer ISA Server is that you can manage virtually all the settings on the server, not just ISA Server.

> **Security Alert** Remote Desktop also has additional benefits related to security. For example, the Remote Desktop Protocol (RDP) uses TCP Port 3389 by default, but you can modify this setting. RDP traffic is also encrypted. If you want to use the ISA Server Management Console to administer ISA Server remotely, you must enable File And Printer Sharing on the ISA Server computer. In addition, the MMC traffic is not encrypted.

To enable remote administration of ISA Server on computers running Windows Server 2003, you must be a member of the Administrators group or Remote Desktop Users group on the ISA Server computer, or be granted permission to use Remote Desktop to connect to the server. To enable remote administration of ISA Server running on a Windows 2000 computer, you must install Terminal Services on the server in either Application or Remote Administration mode. Then the user properties must be configured to allow remote connections using Terminal Services.

You can also perform remote administration of ISA Servers using the ISA Server Management Console snap-in. To install the MMC snap-in on a computer not running ISA Server, perform a custom installation, installing only ISA Server Management. After installation, you can connect to any computer with ISA Server installed.

There are advantages to remote administration with ISA Server Management. Using ISA Server Management, you can connect to and display information from many ISA Server computers at once. This is useful for central administration of geographically dispersed ISA Server computers.

To run ISA Server Management, you need the following:

- A personal computer with a 300-megahertz (MHz) or higher, Pentium II–compatible CPU

- Windows Server 2003, Windows 2000 Server or Windows 2000 Professional, or Windows XP

- 256 megabytes (MB) of memory

- 19 MB of available hard-disk space

When you install ISA Server, the default system policy allows remote administration from all members of a computer set named Remote Management Computers. This computer set is used to assign remote access permissions in both the MMC system policy configuration group and the Terminal Services configuration group. By default, no computers are in this group, so no computers can connect to the ISA Server computer for remote management. To enable remote management on the ISA Server computer, you must configure remote administration by editing the appropriate MMC or Terminal Server configuration group in the System Policy editor.

> **Exam Tip**   Remember that to use the ISA Server Management Console from a remote computer, your computer must be added to the Remote Management Computers computer set. Similarly, to use Terminal Services or Remote Desktop to administer ISA Server, your computer must be added to the Remote Management Computers computer set, and you must also have permission to create a terminal session to the server. Just to complicate matters further, you must also ensure that the Terminal Services or Microsoft Management Console system policy configuration groups are enabled. And there is one more thing to be aware of: If you installed ISA Server using Terminal Services or Remote Desktop, the IP address of the computer from which you performed the install is automatically added to the Remote Management Computers computer set. Keep all this in mind when you see a question dealing with remote access permissions.

Practice: Maintaining ISA Server 2004

In this practice, you will install the ISA Server Management Console on another server and then use the MMC to back up the ISA Server configuration. You will then connect to the ISA Server computer using Remote Desktop and export and import settings on the ISA Server computer.

▶ **Exercise 1: Using the ISA Server Management Console for Remote Administration**

1. Log on to the DC1 computer as an Administrator.

2. Insert the ISA Server CD-ROM into the server CD-ROM drive. If Autorun is enabled, the Microsoft ISA Server 2004 Setup page will open automatically. If it does not open, open Windows Explorer, browse to the CD-ROM, and double-click Isaautorun.exe.

3. On the Microsoft ISA Server 2004 Setup page, click Install ISA Server 2004.

4. On the Welcome To The Installation Wizard for Microsoft ISA Server 2004 Setup page, click Next.

5. On the License Agreement page, review the terms and conditions stated in the end-user license agreement. Then click I Accept The Terms In The License Agreement and click Next.

6. On the Customer Information page, click Next.

7. On the Setup Type page, click Custom and then click Next.

8. On the Custom Setup page, modify the Firewall Services option so that it will not be installed. Ensure that ISA Server Management is configured to be installed on the local hard drive and click Next.

9. On the Ready To Install The Program page, click Install.

10. When the program is installed, click Finish. Close all open windows.

11. Open ISA Server Management. In the console tree, right-click Microsoft Internet Security And Acceleration Server 2004 and click Connect To.

12. In the Connect To dialog box, type **ISA1** and click OK.

13. Click ISA1. On the Tasks tab, click Back Up This ISA Server Configuration.

14. In the Backup Configuration dialog box, in the File name box, type **ISA1 Backup** and then click Backup.

> **Note**   The backup .xml file is stored on the local computer, not on the computer running ISA Server.

15. In the Set Password dialog box, type a password in the Password and Confirm password boxes. Click OK.

16. When the backup is complete, click OK. Close all open windows.

▶ **Exercise 2: Using Remote Desktop for Remote Administration**

1. On DC1, open Remote Desktop Connection from the Communications folder.

2. In the Remote Desktop Connection screen, in the Computer box, type **ISA1** and then click Connect. The connection will fail.

3. When the Remote Desktop Disconnected message appears, review the contents of the message and click OK.

4. On ISA1, open the System control panel.

5. On the Remote tab, select the check box for Allow Users To Connect Remotely To This Computer. Click OK to clear the Remote Sessions warning.

6. Click Select Remote Users. Notice that the Administrator account already has access. Close all open windows.

7. On DC1, in the Remote Desktop Connection box, click Connect.

8. The connection should succeed. In the Logon Warning dialog box, click OK.

9. Log on using the Administrator account.

10. Within the Remote Desktop, open ISA Server Management.

11. Expand ISA1, then expand Configuration, click Networks, select the Tasks tab, and then click Export Existing Networks.

12. In the Export Configuration dialog box, in the File Name box, type **Networks Export**. Click Export.

> **Note**   Notice that the export file this time is stored on the ISA Server computer, not on the local computer.

13. After the export completes, click OK.

14. Click Internal and then click Edit Selected Network. On the Addresses tab, remove all Address ranges. Click OK.

15. Click Apply to apply the changes and click OK when the changes have been applied. Check the Internal network properties to ensure that the addresses have been deleted.

16. Click Networks and on the Tasks tab, click Import Networks.

17. Select Networks Export.xml and click Import. Click OK to acknowledge the successful import.

18. Click Apply to apply the changes and click OK when the changes have been applied.

19. Confirm that all of the Address ranges have been restored to the Internal network. Close all open windows and log off the Remote Desktop connection.

Lesson Review

Use the following questions to help determine whether you have learned enough to move on to the next lesson. If you have difficulty answering these questions, review the material in this lesson before beginning the next lesson. You can find answers to these questions in the "Questions and Answers" section at the end of this chapter.

1. You work for a large company with several branch offices. Each location has an Internet connection as well as a dedicated WAN connection to the corporate head office. You install and configure ISA Server 2004 on a computer running Windows Server 2003 in each branch office. You need to ensure that you can administer all the ISA Server computers. You need to be able to manage all components on the servers, not just ISA Server. You should be able to administer the ISA Server computers only from your desktop computer. What should you do? (Choose two correct answers, both of which are required to complete the configuration.)

    a. Configure a system policy rule on each ISA Server that allows Remote Desktop connections from your desktop computer's IP address.

   b. Configure a system policy rule on each ISA Server that allows MMC connections from your desktop computer's IP address.

   c. Configure the computer to support Remote Desktop connections.

   d. Install ISA Server Management on your desktop computer.

2. You have exported your entire ISA Server configuration for the purpose of cloning the ISA Server computer in your branch offices. When you go to import the configuration to the branch server, the option to import the user permissions is unavailable. What has happened?

   _____

   _____

   _____

3. You recently backed up your ISA Server computer. Since then, you have changed several firewall rules. Now you would like to restore one of those rules from the backup. How would you do this?

   _____

   _____

   _____

Lesson Summary

- You can use the export and import features in ISA Server 2004 to save and restore most ISA Server configuration information. The import and export features can be useful when rolling back a configuration change, sending a configuration for troubleshooting, saving a partial configuration, and cloning a server.

- ISA Server 2004 includes backup and restore features that enable you to save and restore the ISA Server configuration information, primarily for disaster recovery. These features back up the server's firewall policy rules, rule elements, alert configuration, cache configuration, and VPN configuration.

- You can perform all ISA Server administrative tasks remotely. You can use a Terminal Services or Remote Desktop connection to administer the server, or you can install the ISA Server Management Console on another computer and use it to manage an ISA Server computer.

Case Scenario Exercises

Scenario 1

You have successfully installed ISA Server 2004 and now must configure it to meet your organization's needs. Your company's security policy states the following:

1. Users must be able to ping the ISA Server computer from the Internal network only.

2. ISA Server will use Active Directory only for authentication.

3. Administrators must be able to administer ISA Server remotely using an MMC installed on a computer on the Internal network.

4. ISA Server Firewall clients will not be deployed.

5. Microsoft Operations Manager will be used for remote monitoring.

6. Remote logging will be done to an internal SQL database.

7. You need to be able verify connectivity to a published Web site from the ISA Server computer.

Scenario 1 Question

1. You want all your ISA Server computers to have the same system policies. How must system policies be modified, disabled, or enabled to meet your requirements? How will you ensure that all ISA servers have the same policy configuration?

Scenario 2

You work for a large insurance company. Your company needs to deploy a firewall solution and has decided to use ISA Server 2004. Currently you have a head office and 10 branch offices in a multiple-domain environment.

Scenario 2 Question

1. What steps should you take to ensure that ISA Server is protected from Internet attacks? How can you ensure that only authorized users have administrative permissions on the ISA Server computers and that these users can provide remote management using Remote Desktop and MMCs? How can you most efficiently configure all ISA Server computers in the branch offices with a standard configuration?

Troubleshooting Lab

In this lab, you will install ISA Server Management Console on a workstation running Windows XP. You will then attempt to use the MMC and Remote Desktop to administer the ISA Server computer. You will then identify the reasons why you cannot administer the ISA Server computer remotely from the workstation and correct the problems so that you can do so.

Exercise 1: Preparing the Workstation for Remote Administration

1. Log on to CLIENT1 as an Administrator.

2. Add the ISA Admins group from the *cohovineyard.com* domain to the local Administrators group on CLIENT1.

3. Log off CLIENT1 and log back on using your user name.

4. Insert the ISA Server CD-ROM into the server CD-ROM drive. If Autorun is enabled, the Microsoft ISA Server 2004 Setup page will open automatically. If it does not open, open Windows Explorer, browse to the CD-ROM, and double-click Isaautorun.exe.

5. On the Microsoft ISA Server 2004 Setup page, click Install ISA Server 2004.

6. On the Welcome To The Installation Wizard for Microsoft ISA Server 2004 Setup page, click Next.

7. On the License Agreement page, review the terms and conditions stated in the end-user license agreement. Click I Accept The Terms In The License Agreement and then click Next.

8. On the Customer Information page, click Next.

9. On the Installation Requirements Summary page, review the issues and click Next.

10. On the Custom Setup page, ensure that ISA Server Management is configured to be installed on the local hard drive and click Next.

11. On the Ready To Install The Program page, click Install.

12. When the program is installed, click Finish. Close all open windows.

13. Open ISA Server Management. In the console tree, right-click Microsoft Internet Security And Acceleration Server 2004 and click Connect To.

14. In the Connect To dialog box, type **ISA1** and click OK. The connection will fail. Review the details of the error message and close all open windows.

15. Open Remote Desktop Connection from the Communications folder.

16. In the Remote Desktop Connection screen, in the Computer box, type **ISA1** and then click Connect. The connection will fail.

17. When the Remote Desktop Disconnected message appears, review the contents of the message, click OK, and close Remote Desktop Connection.

Exercise 2: Troubleshooting Remote Administration

1. Log on to ISA1 as an Administrator.

2. Open ISA Server Management.

3. If necessary, expand ISA1 and click Firewall Policy. On the Tasks tab, click Edit System Policy.

4. Under Remote Management, click Microsoft Management Console (MMC).

5. On the From tab, click Remote Management Computers and then click Edit. Notice that remote ISA Management Console connections are allowed only from DC1.

6. Click Add and then click Subnet. In the New Subnet Rule Element dialog box, in the Name box, type **Internal Computers**.

7. In the Network Address box, type **10.10.0.0**. In the Network Mask box, type **255.255.255.0**. Click OK twice.

8. Click OK to close the System Policy Editor dialog box.

9. Apply the configuration changes.

10. Open ISA Server Management Console. In the console tree, right-click Microsoft Internet Security And Acceleration Server 2004 and click Connect To.

11. In the Connect To dialog box, type **ISA1** and click OK. The connection will succeed. Close ISA Server Management.

12. Open Remote Desktop Connection from the Communications folder.

13. In the Remote Desktop Connection screen, in the Computer box, type **ISA1** and click Connect. The connection will succeed.

14. Try to log on using your user name and password. The logon will fail. Review the contents of the logon message and click OK.

15. On ISA1, add the ISA Admins group from the *cohovineyard.com* domain to the local Administrators group.

16. On Client1, in the Remote Desktop Connection screen, in the Computer box, type **ISA1** and click Connect. The connection will succeed.

17. Try to log on using your user name and password. The logon will succeed. Log off and close all open windows.

Chapter Summary

- Securing ISA Server includes the following components:

  ❑ Hardening the network interfaces and the operating system on the computer that is hosting ISA Server.

  ❑ Ensuring that only required services are running on the computer. ISA Server requires some system services in order to function, but all other services should be disabled.

  ❑ Modifying the default ISA Server configuration to allow only required network traffic.

  ❑ Modifying the system policy to meet your organization's requirements. You may need to enable some system policy settings, and you should disable all system policies that are not required.

  ❑ Ensuring that users do not have more administrative permissions on the ISA Server computer than they require. ISA Server provides three administrative roles that enable different levels of administrative permissions.

- To manage the ISA Server computer, you can use the export and import features in ISA Server 2004 to save and restore most ISA Server configuration information. ISA Server 2004 also includes backup and restore features that enable you to save and restore the ISA Server configuration information, primarily for disaster recovery. You can manage ISA Server computers remotely. You can use a Terminal Services or Remote Desktop connection to administer the server, or you can install the ISA Server Management Console on another computer and use it to manage an ISA Server computer.

Exam Highlights

Before taking the exam, review the key topics and terms that are presented in this chapter. You need to know this information.

Key Points

- To ensure ISA Server security, you need to ensure that the operating system on the host computer is secure. This includes configuring the network interfaces, disabling all system services that are not required, and installing security updates. However, you can also lock down the operating system components too much.

For example, if you disable a system service that is required by ISA Server, ISA Server will not function correctly.

- ISA Server administrative roles are the only way that you can assign ISA Server administrative permissions.

- Use the export and import features in ISA Server to save part of the ISA Server configuration. The backup and restore feature saves the entire ISA Server configuration.

- To perform remote administration on ISA Server, you must be assigned to the appropriate ISA Server administrative role. In addition, the system policy configuration groups must be configured to enable remote desktop, and your workstation must be added to the Remote Management Computers computer set. To use Terminal Services or Remote Desktop, you must also have permission to make this type of connection to the server.

Key Terms

administrative role   Used to assign permissions on ISA Server. Each administrative role has a predefined set of permissions that allow the user to perform specific tasks on the ISA Server computer.

firewall access rule   A configuration object on ISA Server that defines what types of network traffic will be allowed on the ISA Server computer. By default, all network traffic is blocked unless a firewall access rule allows the specific traffic.

Remote Management Computers   A computer set that is used to provide remote management access to ISA Server. This computer set should include all the IP addresses of the computers that are used to perform remote administration on the ISA Server computer.

system policy   A set of firewall access rules that controls how the ISA Server computer communicates with computers on the attached networks.

Questions and Answers

Page
3-24

Lesson 1 Practice

Exercise 1: Examining the Default ISA Server Configuration

1. On ISA1, open ISA Server Management. Right-click ISA1 and click Administration Delegation.

2. On the Welcome To The ISA Server Administration Delegation Wizard page, click Next.

3. What roles have been assigned to the following groups?

   a. Cohovineyard\Administrator

   ISA Server Full Administrator

   b. Builtin\Administrators

   ISA Server Full Administrator

4. Click Cancel.

5. Expand Configuration and click Networks. In the details pane, click Network Rules.

6. Review the Network Rules. List the network relationships between the networks listed below:

   a. Local Host and All Networks

   Route

   b. Quarantined VPN Clients, VPN Clients, and Internal

   Route

   c. Quarantined VPN Clients, VPN Clients, Internal, and External

   NAT

7. In the console tree, click Firewall Policy. What rule(s) are listed? Describe the rule configuration.

   Last Default rule. The rule blocks denies all traffic from All Networks to All Networks.

8. On the Tasks tab, click Show System Policy Rules. Locate the rule named Allow access from trusted computers to the Firewall Client installation share on ISA Server. Double-click the rule. What does this rule enable? What network is included in this rule?

   The rule enables access to the Firewall Client installation share on the computer running ISA Server. Only the Internal network is included in the rule.

9. In the console tree, expand Configuration and click Cache. Under Tasks, click Define Cache Drives. What is the default size of the Maximum cache size? What does this indicate about the default cache configuration? Click OK.

The cache drive size is set to 0, which means that caching is disabled.

Page 3-26 **Lesson 1 Review**

1. You want your Help Desk group to be able to monitor the ISA Server Dashboard. Your organization has a security policy that requires that all users be assigned as few permissions as possible to complete their tasks. You assign the ISA Server Basic Monitoring role to the Help Desk group on the ISA Server computer. However, none of your help desk employees can view the performance information in the ISA Server Dashboard. What is the problem and how would you resolve it?

   a. The Help Desk group needs to be added to the local Administrators group on the computer running ISA Server.

   b. You need to create an access rule to allow the Help Desk group to connect to the ISA Server computer.

   c. The Help Desk group needs to be added to the local Performance Monitor Users group on the computer running ISA Server.

   d. The help desk group needs to be added to the Server Operators domain local group.

   C is correct. The Help Desk group needs to be added to the Performance Monitor Users group on the computer running ISA Server. Users that are assigned to the ISA Server Basic Monitoring role can view all ISA Server Dashboard information except the performance counters. Adding the Help Desk group to the local Administrators group would give them the required permissions, but would also give them full administrative rights on the ISA Server computer, so this would violate the company policy.

2. You work for a large company with several branch offices. Each of the locations has an Internet connection as well as a dedicated wide area network (WAN) connection to the corporate head office. You install and configure ISA Server 2004 in each branch office. The ISA Server computers are not members of an Active Directory domain. You need to ensure that the same operating system security settings are applied to each ISA Server. What should you do?

   a. Create a script that shuts down all the services that are not required on one of the servers running ISA Server. Run the same script on all the computers running ISA Server.

   b. Document the security settings on one of the servers. Send the document to an administrator in each office, asking them to duplicate the configuration.

   c. Create a security template with your security settings. Apply the security template using Group Policy.

d. Create a security template with your security settings. Apply the security template using Security Configuration and Analysis.

D is correct. The only way to ensure a consistent application of the security settings is to create a security template. Because these servers are not members of an Active Directory domain, you cannot use Group Policy to apply the template; you must use Security Configuration and Analysis or Secedit. Answer B would not guarantee a consistent application of the security settings because of the potential for human error. Answer A is not correct because the security settings include more than just which services are running.

3. Your organization has deployed ISA Server 2004. You install a third-party product on the server running ISA Server. However, when you try to access the company Web site from the ISA Server computer, you cannot connect to the site. You need to connect to the company Web site from ISA Server to download updates. How can you configure your server to support this requirement?

a. Enable Schedule Download Jobs on the ISA Server computer.

b. Add the company Web site to the System Policy Allowed Sites domain name set on the ISA Server computer.

c. Configure an access rule that enables access from the internal network to the company Web site.

d. Configure the Web browser on the ISA Server computer as a Web Proxy client.

B is correct. The default system policy on the ISA Server computer enables access from the ISA Server computer to all Web sites listed in the System Policy Allowed Sites domain name group. By adding the Web site to this group, you will be able to access it. Enabling Schedule Download Jobs will not enable access to any additional Web sites. Configuring an access rule for the internal network does not allow access from the ISA Server computer. And configuring the Web browser as a Web Proxy client does not bypass the system policy that is blocking access.

Page
3-36

Lesson 2 Review

1. You work for a large company with several branch offices. Each location has an Internet connection as well as a dedicated WAN connection to the corporate head office. You install and configure ISA Server 2004 on a computer running Windows Server 2003 in each branch office. You need to ensure that you can administer all the ISA Server computers. You need to be able to manage all components on the servers, not just ISA Server. You should be able to administer the ISA Server computers only from your desktop computer. What should you do? (Choose two correct answers, both of which are required to complete the configuration.)

a. Configure a system policy rule on each ISA Server that allows Remote Desktop connections from your desktop computer's IP address.

b. Configure a system policy rule on each ISA Server that allows MMC connections from your desktop computer's IP address.

c. Configure the computer to support Remote Desktop connections.

d. Install ISA Server Management on your desktop computer.

A and C are correct. The only way to administer all components on a server remotely is to use Remote Desktop. To enable Remote Desktop on a server running ISA Server, you must configure a system policy rule and configure the server to allow Remote Desktop connections. You can use ISA Server Management Console only to administer the ISA Server computer.

2. You have exported your entire ISA Server configuration for the purpose of cloning the ISA Server computer in your branch offices. When you go to import the configuration to the branch server, the option to import the user permissions is unavailable. What has happened?

The Import User Permission setting is available only if the Export User Permission Settings check box was selected in the Export Configuration dialog box during the original export procedure.

3. You recently backed up your ISA Server computer. Since then, you have changed several firewall rules. Now you would like to restore one of those rules from the backup. How would you do this?

You cannot restore individual items from a backup of ISA Server. You would have had to export the elements prior to making the changes and import individual elements back into the configuration.

Case Scenario Exercises

Page 3-38 **Scenario 1 Question**

1. You want all your ISA Server computers to have the same system policies. How must system policies be modified, disabled, or enabled to meet your requirements? How will you ensure that all ISA servers have the same policy configuration?

Networking services may be left at the default settings. Authentication services must be changed to disable the RADIUS policy. Remote Management policy must be changed to disable Terminal Services connections. The Firewall Client policy must be disabled. Diagnostic services must be modified to allow ICMP traffic from the Local Network only, and HTTP Connectivity Verifiers must be enabled to allow HTTP GET requests to test connectivity. The logging policy must be modified to enable Remote SQL logging. Remote monitoring must be modified to enable Microsoft Operations Manager.

Once system policy is configured properly, it can be exported to an .xml file and imported to all ISA Server computers.

Page 3-38 **Scenario 2 Question**

1. What steps should you take to ensure that ISA Server is protected from Internet attacks? How can you ensure that only authorized users have administrative permissions on the ISA Server computers and that these users can provide remote

management using Remote Desktop and MMCs? How can you most efficiently configure all ISA Server computers in the branch offices with a standard configuration?

The first step will be to secure the external interface by disabling unneeded services like File and Printer Sharing and NetBIOS over TCP/IP. This could be accomplished manually on each machine or by configuring the settings on the initial server and exporting those registry settings to a custom security template.

Then you will need to harden the operating system by disabling all services that are not required for server functionality. This could be accomplished by configuring the services in a custom security template.

For ISA Administrators to have remote management access, you must assign the proper administrative role to them and add their computers' names and IP addresses, or the appropriate subnet, to the Remote Management Computers group in the ISA Server system policy. You must also ensure that the ISA Administrators are in the Remote Desktop Users group on each ISA Server computer.

To configure all branch office ISA Server computers to be the same, you could export the configuration of the original server to an .xml file and then import it on all other servers. You could apply the custom security policy that you created to the OU in each domain that contains the ISA Server computer accounts.

4 Installing and Managing ISA Server Clients

Exam Objectives in this Chapter:

- Plan an ISA Server 2004 deployment.

  - Plan for client computer connectivity.

- Install Firewall Client software.

- Configure client computers for ISA Server 2004. Considerations include Web Proxy client, Firewall Client, and secure network address translation (SecureNAT) client.

  - Modify Firewall Client configuration files.

- Configure a local domain table (LDT).

- Configure ISA Server 2004 for automatic client configuration by using Web Proxy Automatic Discovery (WPAD).

  - Configure and publish client configuration settings on ISA Server 2004.

  - Configure Domain Name System (DNS) and Dynamic Host Configuration Protocol (DHCP) for Automatic Discovery.

  - Configure client computers for Automatic Discovery. Methods of configuration include Firewall Client and Internet Explorer.

- Diagnose and resolve client computer connectivity issues.

  - Diagnose and resolve name-resolution issues.

  - Diagnose and resolve protocol support issues.

  - Diagnose and resolve routing issues.

  - Diagnose and resolve authentication issues.

Why This Chapter Matters

Now that you have installed and secured Microsoft Internet Security and Acceleration (ISA) Server 2004, the next step is to configure the server to perform a useful function. In most organizations, ISA Server is used to provide secure access to Internet resources. This means that, to gain access to the Internet, users must go through ISA Server. You can then use ISA Server to restrict which applications users can use to access the Internet, block access to specific types of content, or limit which users can access Internet resources.

To set up such restrictions, you must first configure the internal computers as ISA Server clients. An ISA Server client is simply any computer that accesses resources on another network through ISA Server. ISA Server supports three types of clients: Firewall clients, Web Proxy clients, and SecureNAT clients. Each of these clients has some advantages, as well as some disadvantages, so you need to know when to use each type of client. You must also know how to configure and troubleshoot each type of client.

Lessons in this Chapter:

- Lesson 1: Choosing an ISA Server Client. 4-3
- Lesson 2: Configuring the SecureNAT and Web Proxy Clients 4-12
- Lesson 3: Installing and Configuring the Firewall Client 4-28

Before You Begin

This chapter presents the skills and concepts related to deploying and configuring ISA Server clients. If you plan to complete the practices and lab in this chapter, you should prepare the following:

- A Microsoft Windows Server 2003 (Standard Edition or Enterprise Edition) computer installed as DC1 and configured as a domain controller in the *cohovineyard.com* domain.

- A second Windows Server 2003 computer installed as ISA1 and configured as a domain member in the *cohovineyard.com* domain. This server should have two network interfaces installed. You must have completed the exercises from Chapter 2, "Installing ISA Server 2004," on this server.

- A Microsoft Windows XP computer installed as CLIENT1. This computer should be a member of the *cohovineyard.com* domain.

Lesson 1: Choosing an ISA Server Client

Before you configure ISA Server to grant access to Internet resources, you must choose which ISA Server clients to use within your network. ISA Server 2004 supports three clients: SecureNAT clients, Firewall clients, and Web Proxy clients. The Firewall client provides the highest level of functionality but also requires that the Firewall Client application be installed and configured on all client computers. SecureNAT and Web Proxy clients are easier to deploy because they do not require a client application installation, but SecureNAT clients and Web Proxy clients also provide more limited functionality. One of your tasks as an ISA Server administrator is to choose the client that best suits your organization.

After this lesson, you will be able to

- Describe the three types of clients supported by ISA Server 2004.
- Choose the most appropriate ISA Server client for your organization.

Estimated lesson time: 25 minutes

ISA Server Client Options

An ISA Server client is a client computer that connects to resources on another network by going through the ISA Server computer. In most cases, ISA Server clients are used to provide access to the Internet for users on the Internal network. The type of client you use on your network depends primarily on your security requirements and on whether you want to deploy Firewall Client software to each client computer on your network.

ISA Server supports three types of clients:

- **Firewall clients**   Firewall clients are computers on which Firewall Client software has been installed and enabled. When a computer with the Firewall Client software installed requests resources on the Internet, the request is directed to the Firewall service on the ISA Server computer. The Firewall service authenticates and authorizes the user and filters the request based on Firewall rules and application filters or other add-ins. Firewall clients provide the highest level of functionality and security.

- **SecureNAT clients**   SecureNAT clients do not require any client installation or configuration. SecureNAT clients are configured to route all requests for resources on other networks to the internal Internet Protocol (IP) address of the ISA Server computer. If the network includes only a single segment, the SecureNAT client is configured to use the internal IP address on the computer running ISA Server as the default gateway. SecureNAT clients are easiest to configure because only the default gateway on the client computers must be configured.

■ **Web Proxy clients**   Web Proxy clients are any computers that run Web applications that comply with Hypertext Transfer Protocol (HTTP) 1.1, such as Web browsers. Requests from Web Proxy clients are directed to the Firewall service on the ISA Server computer. Because most client computers already run Web Proxy–compatible applications, Web Proxy clients do not require the installation of special software. However, the Web application must be configured to use the ISA Server computer.

Both Firewall client computers and SecureNAT client computers may also be Web Proxy clients. If the Web application on the computer is configured explicitly to use ISA Server for proxy services, all HTTP, File Transfer Protocol (FTP), and Hypertext Transfer Protocol Secure (HTTPS) are sent to the Web Proxy listener on ISA Server.

What Is a Firewall Client?

The Firewall client computer uses the Firewall Client application when initiating connections to the ISA Server computer. This means that the Firewall Client application must be installed on each client computer.

Many applications running on Windows computers use the Winsock application programming interface (API) to communicate with services running on other computers. Winsock applications use sockets to connect to applications running on another computer. For example, for a Web browser to connect to a Web server, the Web browser uses a Transmission Control Protocol (TCP) socket to connect to the Web server. In this case, the socket includes the IP address of the destination computer, the protocol used (TCP), and the port number on which the server is listening (Port 80). All applications use the same sockets to connect to the same services regardless of the operating system that is running on the client computer and the application server.

The Firewall Client application changes how a client computer connects to resources on the Internet using Winsock applications. After you install the Firewall Client, when the client computer initiates a Winsock application, the Firewall Client intercepts the application calls. The Firewall Client checks the destination computer name or IP address and determines whether to route the request to the ISA Server computer or to a server on the local network. If the destination computer is not local, the request is sent to the Firewall service on the ISA server computer. The Firewall service accepts the request and authenticates the user. The Firewall service also checks whether any filtering rules apply to the request. If the request is allowed, the Firewall service initiates a new socket connection with the destination server. The destination server responds to the ISA Server computer, which then replies to the client computer.

When the client makes a request for a resource that is located on the local network, the Firewall Client checks the destination address and confirms that the address is in the range of addresses included in the local network. In this case, the application request is sent directly to the application server rather than through the ISA Server computer.

The Firewall client provides the highest level of security and functionality of any of the ISA Server clients. The advantages of using Firewall clients include the following:

- Firewall clients enable user or group based access control and logging. This means that you can limit access to Internet resources based on the user or the groups to which the user belongs. You can also log, by user name, what the user can access.

- When a Firewall client connects to ISA Server, the Firewall service automatically authenticates the user.

- You can use the Firewall Client software to configure the Web Proxy browser automatically.

- Firewall clients support all Winsock applications. Web Proxy clients can only be used to connect to Internet resources using HTTP, HTTPS, and FTP. SecureNAT clients can use a wider variety of protocols than Web Proxy clients, but SecureNAT clients cannot use some applications that will fail when they must traverse a network device that uses network address translation (NAT) or that requires secondary protocol connections. Therefore, Firewall clients support the broadest range of protocols and applications

However, the Firewall client also has some disadvantages:

- You must install the Firewall Client software on the client computers. If you have a large number of client computers in your organization and have no means of automating the client installation, it will require a significant effort to deploy the client. Once the software has been distributed, you can automatically configure all client settings.

- The Firewall client can only be installed on Windows computers. If you have other clients on your network, you will need to use a different ISA Server client.

Exam Tip   Keep this last point in mind when you write the exam. If the exam question asks you to choose an ISA Server client and there are any clients on the network other than Windows computers, you must choose a client other that the Firewall client.

What Is a SecureNAT Client?

Client computers that do not have Firewall Client software are secure network address translation, or SecureNAT, clients. SecureNAT clients do not require any software installation or configuration, but the clients must be able to route requests for Internet resources through the ISA Server computer. To enable this, you must configure the default gateway on the SecureNAT clients and configure network routing, so that all traffic destined to the Internet is sent through the ISA Server computer.

When a SecureNAT client connects to the ISA Server computer, the request is directed first to the NAT driver, which substitutes the external IP address of the ISA Server computer for the internal IP address of the SecureNAT client. The client request is then directed to the Firewall service to determine whether access is allowed. Finally, the request may be filtered by application filters and other extensions. The Firewall service may also cache the requested object or deliver the object from the ISA Server cache.

Because SecureNAT clients require no software deployment and configuration, SecureNAT clients are the easiest to deploy. SecureNAT clients have other advantages:

- SecureNAT clients also provide almost as much functionality as Firewall clients. For example, because SecureNAT client requests are passed through the Firewall Service, almost all options for filtering Internet requests apply to SecureNAT clients. If you block access to a specific Web site, or enable access for a specific protocol such as DNS, these rules will also be applied to SecureNAT clients.

- Requests from SecureNAT clients can be passed to application filters, which can modify the requests to enable handling of complex protocols. For example, the FTP application filter in ISA Server manages the secondary connections for SecureNAT clients as well as for Firewall clients.

- SecureNAT can use the Web Proxy service for Web access filtering and caching. The Firewall service can pass all HTTP requests to the Web Proxy service, which handles caching and ensures that site and content rules are applied appropriately.

- Any operating system that supports Transmission Control Protocol/Internet Protocol (TCP/IP) can be configured as a SecureNAT client.

SecureNAT clients have two primary limitations:

- You cannot control access to Internet resources based on users and groups. SecureNAT clients cannot pass authentication credentials to the ISA Server computer, so users cannot be authenticated. This means that if you configure access rules that require authentication, SecureNAT clients cannot access the resources enabled by the rule.

- SecureNAT clients may not be able to use all protocols. Some protocols and applications require secondary connections. For example, when you use FTP, by default, the client initiates a primary connection to the server and the server then initiates a secondary connection to the client. ISA Server must use an application filter that edits the data stream to allow SecureNAT clients to use such protocols and applications. ISA Server includes several application filters, such as an FTP filter and an H.323 filter. If ISA Server does not include the appropriate application filter for a protocol or an application, SecureNAT clients cannot use this protocol or application.

Important   When you publish servers to the Internet, ensure that the servers are configured as SecureNAT clients. One reason for this is that the Firewall Client software can interfere with the publishing. Moreover, by configuring the published server as a SecureNAT client, no special configuration is required on the server after you create the publishing rule on ISA Server. Just ensure that published servers use the IP address assigned to the internal network interface of the ISA Server computer as the default gateway.

What Is a Web Proxy Client?

A Web Proxy client is a client computer that has an HTTP 1.1–compliant Web browser application and is configured to use the ISA Server computer as a Web Proxy server. Virtually all current Web browsers comply with this HTTP standard, so any client computer can be configured as a Web Proxy client, including computers which are SecureNAT or Firewall clients.

When a Web Proxy client tries to access resources on the Internet, the requests are directed to the Firewall service on the ISA Server computer. If the access rule is configured to require authentication, the ISA Server computer requests authentication from the Web Proxy client. The Firewall service then determines whether the user is allowed to access the Internet and checks the access rules to determine whether the request is allowed. For example, you can configure access to rules to block access to specified sites, or to block requests with certain keywords in the client request. The Firewall service may also cache the requested object or serve the object from the ISA Server cache.

One of the advantages of using Web Proxy clients is that most client computers already run compatible Web browsers, so Web Proxy clients require no special software to be installed. However, you must configure the Web browser to use the ISA Server computer as a proxy server. In most cases, this is a simple configuration. If you install Firewall Client software, you can use it to configure the Web browser to use the ISA Server computer as a proxy server. After you have completed the initial configuration of the Web Proxy client, you can also automate the configuration of the Web Proxy client using the ISA Server Management Console.

Using Web Proxy clients provides several advantages:

■ As mentioned earlier, almost all client computers already run compatible Web browsers, which means you do not need to install any software on the client computers. All you need to do is configure the software, and this can be automated.

■ Web Proxy clients support authentication, so you can restrict access to Internet resources based on users and groups.

■ Client computers can be running any operating system that supports compatible Web browsers.

■ All client requests and responses are passed through the Web Proxy filter on ISA Server. This means that you can use application layer filtering to filter all traffic from the Web Proxy clients to the Internet, and from the Internet to the Web Proxy clients.

The primary disadvantage of using Web Proxy clients is that the clients can use only HTTP, HTTPS, and FTP over HTTP to access Internet resources. No other protocols are allowed, so if you want to enable access to Internet resources using any other protocol, you must configure the client computers as SecureNAT clients or Firewall clients.

Exam Tip   If an exam question asks you to choose an ISA Server client, and the required protocols include anything other than HTTP, HTTPS, or FTP over HTTP, you must choose a client other than the Web Proxy client.

Guidelines for Choosing an ISA Server Client

ISA Server clients are used to provide access to Internet resources. This means that one of the choices that you must make as you deploy ISA Server 2004 is which ISA Server client you will deploy. Table 4-1 compares the ISA Server clients.

Table 4-1 Comparing the ISA Server Clients

Feature	SecureNAT Client	Firewall Client	Web Proxy Client
Client installation	No client installation but some client computer configuration	Client installation required	No client installation but application configuration
Operating system support	All operating systems that support TCP/IP	Only Windows clients	All operating systems that support compatible Web applications
Protocol support	Application filters required for multiple-connection protocols	All Winsock applications	HTTP, HTTPS, and FTP over HTTP
User level authentication	No, except for VPN connections	Yes	Yes

Table 4-2 lists some guidelines to use as you decide which clients to deploy.

Table 4-2 Guidelines for Choosing ISA Server Clients

If You Need To	Then Use
Avoid deploying or configuring client software	SecureNAT clients. SecureNAT clients do not require any software or specific configuration. Firewall clients require that you deploy Firewall Client software and Web Proxy clients require that you configure Web applications on client computers.
Use ISA Server only for accessing Web resources using HTTP or HTTPS	SecureNAT or Web Proxy clients. If you use SecureNAT clients in this scenario, you need not deploy any special software or configure the client computers. Web Proxy clients require some application configuration but also support Web access.
Allow access only for authenticated clients	Firewall clients or Web Proxy clients. For Firewall clients, you can configure user-based firewall policy rules. You can also configure user-based rules for Web Proxy clients, but the rule will be effective only if the Web application can pass the authentication information.
Publish servers that are located on your Internal network	SecureNAT clients. Internal servers can be published as SecureNAT clients. This eliminates the need for creating special configuration files on the publishing server.
Improve Web performance in an environment with non-Windows operating systems	Web Proxy or SecureNAT clients. Non-Windows operating systems cannot be configured as Firewall clients, but can be configured as SecureNAT and Web Proxy clients. Both of these clients improve Web performance by enabling caching.

Real World   Choosing an ISA Server Client

For most of the organizations that I work with, the decision on which ISA Server client to deploy usually depends on whether the organization wants to make the extra effort of deploying the Firewall Client application. The Firewall Client provides more security and functionality than the other clients, but for most organizations, the effort required to deploy the software is not worth the trouble. As with any other deployment decision, this decision becomes a question of functionality versus effort of deployment.

In my experience, most organizations opt for using SecureNAT clients and Web Proxy clients. This combination provides all the functionality that most organizations need. With this configuration, you can enforce security policies based on user accounts for access to Web-based resources because the Web Proxy clients can be authenticated. Web Proxy clients are also easy to configure. You can use the Automatic Discovery option, or you can use Group Policy in Active Directory directory service to configure the Web Proxy settings if you use Microsoft Internet Explorer. If the ISA Server computer is a member of the internal domain, user authentication is transparent to users.

Most companies also have very few requirements to access any resources on the Internet using any protocols other than HTTP, HTTPS, or FTP. When this functionality is required, the client computers are configured as SecureNAT clients. Again, SecureNAT clients are easy to configure. In most cases, you can complete this configuration by making a change to the DHCP server and waiting a day or two until the client computers refresh their IP addresses.

All this means that most organizations that I work with do not deploy the Firewall client. Organizations that deploy the Firewall client usually have an effective means of distributing software to client computers, or they are organizations that have a strong requirement for the extra functionality that the Firewall client provides.

Lesson Review

Use the following questions to help determine whether you have learned enough to move on to the next lesson. If you have difficulty answering these questions, review the material in this lesson before beginning the next lesson. You can find answers to the questions in the "Questions and Answers" section at the end of this chapter.

1. You have deployed ISA Server 2004 as your enterprise firewall solution. Your enterprise consists of multiple operating systems, including UNIX and Novell clients. You run TCP/IP as your network protocol. The client IP addresses and options are assigned through DHCP. All clients have HTTP 1.1–compliant Web

browsers installed. All internal employees will require the same level of access to the Internet. You need to minimize the effort required to deploy the ISA Server clients. What ISA Server client will work best to provide simple Internet access for your internal employees?

_____

_____

_____

2. You have deployed ISA Server 2004 as your enterprise firewall solution. You use Active Directory and all your client computers run Microsoft operating systems. Due to limited Internet bandwidth, you must restrict Internet access to selected departments during business hours. Your employees also need access to a Real-Player streaming media application on an external Web site. What ISA Server client works best for your situation?

_____

_____

_____

Lesson Summary

- ISA Server supports three types of clients: Firewall clients, SecureNAT clients, and Web Proxy clients. Firewall clients provide the highest level of functionality but do require the installation of the Firewall Client software. SecureNAT clients are the easiest to configure because they do not require any application installation or configuration, but SecureNAT clients do not support user authentication. Web Proxy clients are any computers that run HTTP 1.1–compatible Web browsers. The applications must be configured to use the ISA Server computer as a proxy server.

- As you prepare to deploy ISA Server, you must choose an ISA Server client that best meets your organization's requirements. Factors that you should consider when choosing the client include protocol and operating system support, support for authentication, and the effort required to deploy the clients.

Lesson 2: Configuring the SecureNAT and Web Proxy Clients

The biggest advantage of using the SecureNAT client or Web Proxy client is that you do not need to deploy special software for either. Both the SecureNAT client and the Web Proxy client, however, still require some configuration. This lesson describes how to configure SecureNAT and Web Proxy clients, how to use ISA Server to automate the configuration of the Web Proxy clients, and how to troubleshoot issues for both clients.

After this lesson, you will be able to

■ Configure SecureNAT clients

■ Configure Web Proxy clients

■ Configure Automatic Discovery

■ Troubleshoot Web Proxy and SecureNAT clients

Estimated lesson time: 45 minutes

How to Configure SecureNAT Clients

SecureNAT clients are the easiest ISA Server clients to configure because you need only configure the network settings on the client computers. If your network consists of a single subnet, configuring SecureNAT clients may be as simple as configuring the client computers to use the internal address of the ISA Server computer as their default gate-way. The primary concern, when using SecureNAT clients, is to ensure that the clients can route Internet requests to the ISA Server computer, and to ensure that the clients can resolve Internet names using DNS.

Exam Tip   If you see an exam question in which a SecureNAT client cannot access resources on the Internet, look for hints in the question that suggest that the client cannot route the requests to the ISA Server computer. If the client can route the requests, but still cannot connect, then look for hints that suggest that the client cannot resolve Internet names.

Configuring SecureNAT Clients to Route Internet Requests

For SecureNAT clients to access Internet resources, the client computers must be able to route Internet requests to the ISA Server computer. If the SecureNAT client is on the same network as the ISA Server computer, you must configure the client computer so that all traffic destined for the Internet is sent through the ISA Server computer. To do this, set the SecureNAT client's IP default gateway settings to the IP address of the ISA Server computer's internal network interface. You can configure clients manually or by using the DHCP service.

Most medium-sized or large organizations have more than one IP network separated by routers. For example, Figure 4-1 shows an example of a typical network for a larger organization.

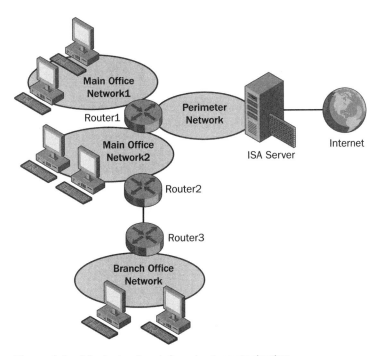

Figure 4-1   A typical network for a larger organization

In this environment, configuring the SecureNAT clients to route Internet requests to the ISA Server computer is more complicated. For example, none of the client computers are on the same network as the ISA Server computer. This means that you must configure the client computers and the routers correctly to route the SecureNAT client requests. For example, Table 4-3 shows the network configuration required to enable the clients to access Internet resources.

Table 4-3 Configuring Network Settings for SecureNAT Clients

SecureNAT Client	Required Network Configuration
Located on the Branch Office Network	The client computers must be configured with Router3 as the default gateway. Router3 must be configured with Router2 as the default gateway. Router2 must be configured to route Internet requests to Router1. Router1 must be configured to route Internet requests to the ISA Server computer.
Located on Main Office Network2 or Main Office Network1	The client computers must be configured to route all Internet requests to Router1. Router1 must be configured to route Internet requests to the ISA Server computer.

Configuring SecureNAT Clients for Internet Name Resolution

In order for SecureNAT clients to access Internet resources, the client computers must also be able to resolve the DNS names for computers on the Internet. You have two options for configuring name resolution:

- **Configure an internal DNS server to enable Internet DNS name resolution, and then configure the SecureNAT clients to use the internal DNS server for name resolution.** If your internal DNS servers can resolve Internet DNS names, then the easiest option is to configure the SecureNAT clients to use the internal DNS server. If you choose this option, the SecureNAT clients will be able to resolve both internal and Internet names.

> **Exam Tip** If the SecureNAT clients are using an internal DNS server, you need to ensure that the internal DNS server can resolve Internet names. By default, ISA Server does not allow requests from internal DNS servers to the Internet, so you need to configure an access rule that allows this access.

- **Configure the SecureNAT clients to use a DNS server on the Internet for name resolution.** If you do not have an internal DNS server that can resolve Internet names, then you need to configure the SecureNAT clients with the IP address of a DNS server on the Internet that they can use for Internet name resolution. In this case, you must also configure an access rule that allows all SecureNAT clients to send DNS queries to the Internet.

> **Important**   If you configure the SecureNAT clients to use an Internet DNS server to resolve DNS queries, the client will not be able to resolve internal DNS names. If you have deployed Active Directory, Windows 2000 and Windows XP clients must be able to use DNS to locate domain controllers. The domain controller records should never be stored on the Internet DNS servers. Obviously these two configurations are not compatible. This means that if you are deploying Active Directory, you must configure an internal DNS server, and you must con-figure the SecureNAT clients to use that DNS server. To also provide Internet access for those SecureNAT clients, you really have no option other than enabling Internet name resolution on those internal DNS servers.

How to Configure Web Proxy Clients

A Web Proxy client is a client computer that has a Web Proxy application installed and configured to use the ISA Server computer as a proxy server. The most common type of Web Proxy application is a Web browser. You do not have to install any software to configure Web Proxy clients. However, you must configure the Web applications on the client computers to use the ISA Server computer as a proxy server. You can config-ure the Web Proxy client application manually or you can automate the configuration using Automatic Discovery. However, before the Web Proxy clients can connect to the ISA Server computer, you must configure the ISA Server computer to accept Web proxy connections.

How to Configure ISA Server for Web Proxy Clients

The first step in enabling Web Proxy clients is to configure the ISA Server computer to allow connections from these clients. By default, ISA Server allows Web Proxy client connections, but you should confirm this setting. To do this, use the following procedure:

1. In the console tree of ISA Server Management, expand Configuration, and click Networks.

2. In the details pane, click the Networks tab and select the applicable network. In this case, select the Internal network.

3. On the Tasks tab, click Edit Selected Network and then click the Web Proxy tab. Figure 4-2 shows the interface.

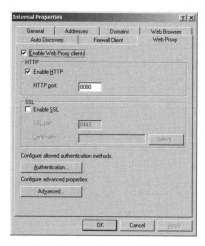

Figure 4-2   Configuring ISA Server to allow Web Proxy clients

4. On the Web Proxy tab, ensure that Enable Web Proxy clients is selected. You can also enable or disable HTTP and HTTPS connections and configure the relevant ports and the authentication options for Web Proxy clients.

> **See Also**   This chapter examines the client configuration to enable Web Proxy clients. Chapter 5, "Enabling Secure Internet Access with ISA Server 2004," provides more details about configuring the Web Proxy settings such as authentication on ISA Server 2004.

Configuring Web Proxy Clients Manually

To configure a Web Proxy client, you must configure the Web Proxy applications on the client to use the ISA Server computer as a proxy server. Each Web Proxy application will require its own unique configuration. For example, to configure the Web Proxy settings in Internet Explorer 6, use the following procedure:

1. Open Internet Explorer, click the Tools menu, and then click Internet Options.

2. On the Connections tab, click LAN Settings. Figure 4-3 shows the interface.

3. On the LAN Settings page, click Use A Proxy Server For Your LAN. In the Address box, type the name or IP address of the proxy server. In the Port box, type the port number that the client will use to connect to the proxy server. By default, ISA Server uses Port 8080 for Web Proxy client connections.

4. Select Bypass Proxy Server For Local Addresses to configure the Web Proxy to bypass the proxy server when accessing resources on the local network. When this option is selected, Internet Explorer sends requests directly to Web servers located on the same network segment as the client rather than forwarding the request to the proxy server.

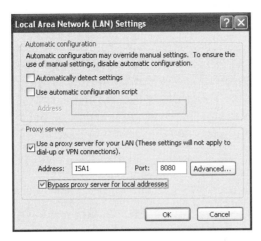

Figure 4-3   Configuring Internet Explorer 6 to use a proxy server

5. To configure additional settings, click Advanced. Figure 4-4 shows the interface. On the Proxy Settings page, you can configure different proxy servers for various types of servers, and specify addresses that the Web Proxy client should connect to directly rather than through the proxy server. When you add names to the Exceptions list, you can enter a full Uniform Resource Locator (URL), such as **www.contoso.com**, or you can use wildcards as part of the address. For example, you can enter *.**contoso.com** to configure an exception for all hosts in the *contoso.com* domain, **www.*.com** to configure an exception for all www sites in the top-level *.com* domain, or **10.10.*** to configure an exception for all sites that are part of the 10.10.x.x network (when you try to connect to the IP address rather than to the host name).

Figure 4-4   Configuring advanced proxy server settings for Internet Explorer 6

Configuring Web Proxy Clients Automatically

In addition to configuring Web Proxy clients manually, you can also automate the configuration of the Web Proxy clients. When you enable the Web Proxy client for automatic configuration, the client downloads a configuration script every time the computer starts, or every six hours. By enabling the automatic configuration on the Web Proxy client, you can modify the Web Proxy configuration on the ISA Server computer without having to reconfigure each individual Web browser.

To configure the client to download the configuration script, use the following procedure:

1. Open Internet Explorer, click the Tools menu, and then click Internet Options.

2. On the Connections tab, click LAN Settings. The interface is shown in Figure 4-3.

3. On the LAN Settings page, click the Automatically Detect Settings and Use Automatic Configuration Script options. In the Address box, type in the URL for the configuration script. The default configuration URL is *http://ISA_Server/ array.dll?Get.Routing.Script*, where *ISA_Server* is the fully qualified domain name (FQDN) or IP address of the ISA Server computer.

Automating the configuration of the Web Proxy clients can be useful in many situations. If you have a large number of Web Proxy clients and you need to change a Web Proxy configuration, you can make the configuration change to the ISA Server network properties and the change will be applied automatically to all the Web Proxy clients on that network. For example, you may want to change the ISA Server computer and port to which the Web Proxy clients on the Internal network connect. By changing the configuration on ISA Server, all clients will be updated automatically.

You cannot directly edit the automatic configuration script; instead, use the ISA Server Management Console to modify the Web Proxy settings. ISA Server then changes the configuration script, which is downloaded by the Web Proxy clients. To modify the ISA Server settings that are sent to the Web Proxy clients, use the following procedure:

1. In the console tree of ISA Server Management, expand Configuration, and click Networks.

2. In the details pane, click the Networks tab and select the applicable network. In this case, you should select the Internal network.

3. On the Tasks tab, click Edit Selected Network and click the Web Browser tab. The interface is shown in Figure 4-5.

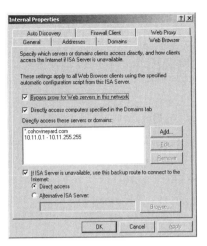

Figure 4-5   Configuring the Web Browser settings for the Internal network

On the Web Browser tab, you can configure the following settings:

- **Bypass Proxy For Web Servers In This Network**   If you select this option, the Web Proxy clients will connect directly to Web servers on the same network as the client instead of going through the proxy server.

- **Directly Access Computers Specified In The Domains Tab**   This setting applies to Firewall client computers. You can add domain names on the Domains tab so that the Firewall clients will connect directly to the computers rather than connecting through the proxy server.

- **Directly Access These Servers Or Domains**   You can add domain names or IP address ranges for servers that Web Proxy clients and Firewall clients should access directly. For example, if you add *.**cohovineyard.com** to the list, all client requests for any server in the *cohovineyard.com* domain will not be sent through the proxy server. You can also add IP addresses or IP address ranges. For example, if you have Web servers on a different subnet than the Web Proxy clients, you can add the IP addresses for that subnet to this list so that the Web Proxy clients can directly access the servers.

- **If ISA Server Is Unavailable, Use This Backup Route To Connect To The Internet**   If you have multiple ISA Servers, or if the clients can connect directly to the Internet without going through an ISA Server computer, you can configure a backup route for Web proxy clients. If the original ISA Server is not available, the clients will automatically try the backup connection to the Internet.

If you have the Firewall Client software installed on a client computer, you can also use the Firewall Client to automate the configuration of the Web browser settings. To enable this, you modify the Firewall Client settings in the ISA Server Management Console using the following procedure:

1. In the console tree of ISA Server Management, expand Configuration, and click Networks.

2. In the details pane, click the Networks tab and select the applicable network. In this case, select the Internal network.

3. On the Tasks tab, click Edit Selected Network and click the Firewall Client tab. Figure 4-6 shows the interface. From this interface, you can configure which Web proxy server the Web Proxy clients will connect to and how the Web Proxy clients will be automatically configured.

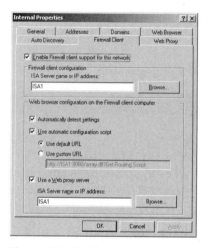

Figure 4-6   Configuring Web Proxy client settings using Firewall Client

When the Firewall Client software is installed, and the client connects to the ISA Server computer, the Web browser on the client computer is configured with those settings.

How to Configure Automatic Discovery

In addition to automating the configuration of the Web Proxy client, you can also configure your environment so that the Web Proxy clients can discover the correct location to download the configuration automatically. This also applies to Firewall clients. For a Web Proxy client or a Firewall Client to connect to an ISA Server computer, you must configure the browser or Firewall Client to forward Internet requests to a specific ISA Server computer. If the ISA Server computer becomes unavailable or if you want to use a different ISA Server computer, you must change this configuration before the client will connect to an ISA Server computer.

When you enable Automatic Discovery, Firewall clients and Web Proxy clients can automatically find an ISA Server computer on the network. Using Automatic Discovery can help you minimize the time spent troubleshooting connection problems on client computers. Web Proxy clients enable Automatic Discovery by using Web Proxy Automatic Discovery (WPAD) protocol information. Firewall clients use the Winsock Proxy AutoDetect (WSPAD) protocol. To enable Automatic Discovery, you must configure either a DHCP server or a DNS server with information specifying the ISA Server computer to which Web Proxy or Firewall clients should connect. The ISA Server client computers can then retrieve the information from DHCP or DNS, connect to the appropriate ISA Server computer, and download the automatic configuration script.

> **Planning**   Using Automatic Discovery is especially useful if your organization has multiple locations and users that travel between the locations. If a client computer is configured to use the ISA Server computer in one location, it will always try to access that ISA Server computer even if it is connected to the network in another location. If you configure Automatic Discovery, the client computer will automatically discover the ISA Server computer in its current location.

How Automatic Discovery Works   The Automatic Discovery process works as follows:

1. When Automatic Discovery is enabled, the Firewall client or the Web Proxy client requests an object from the ISA Server computer that is configured to fulfill requests. If the ISA Server computer does not respond, and if Automatic Discovery is enabled for the client, it starts the Automatic Discovery process.

2. A client connects to a DNS or DHCP server for the ISA Server computer location information.

3. The client uses a WPAD entry from the DNS or DHCP server to locate an ISA Server computer.

4. The client connects to the ISA Server computer specified in the WPAD entry to retrieve configuration information by using the WPAD protocol or the WSPAD protocol.

5. The client configures itself by using the configuration information that it retrieved.

How to Enable Automatic Discovery   To enable Automatic Discovery, complete these steps:

1. Enable the ISA Server computer to publish automatic configuration information. To do this, access the Auto Discovery tab in the Internet Network Properties dialog box, and select the Publish option to publish Automatic Discovery information, as shown in Figure 4-7.

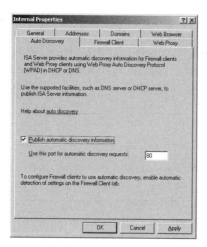

Figure 4-7   Configuring ISA Server to publish Automatic Discovery information

2. Configure the DHCP server or DNS server to provide Automatic Discovery server names for ISA Server clients. If you use a DHCP server, follow these steps:

   a. Open DHCP from the Administrative Tools folder.

   b. Expand the *Servername* in the left-hand pane of the Microsoft Management Console (MMC), and then right-click the server name. Click Set Predefined Options.

   c. In the Predefined Options and Values dialog box, click Add.

   d. In the Option Type dialog box, in the Name box, type **WPAD**. In the Data type box, click String and, in the Code box, type **252**. Click OK. In the Value area, in the String box, type the URL to which the client should connect. For example, you could use **http://ISA1.cohovineyard.com:80/wpad.dat**.

   e. Expand the DHCP scope where you want to assign the WPAD option. Right-click scope options and click configure options. Select the check box for 252 WPAD and click OK.

Figure 4-8 shows the completed configuration.

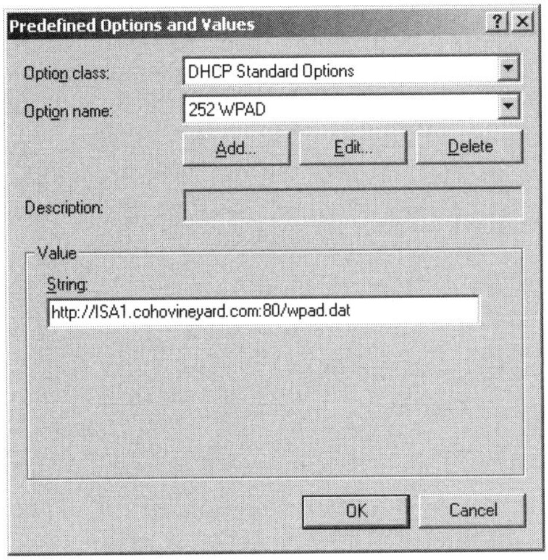

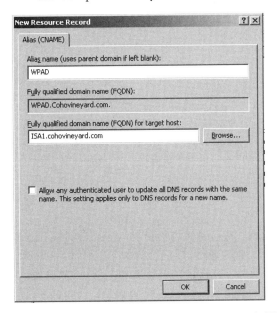

Figure 4-8   Configuring DHCP to support Automatic Discovery

3. If you use DNS, complete this procedure:

   a. Open DNS from the Administrative Tools folder.

   b. Expand Forward Lookup Zones, expand the domain in which you want to create the resource record, right-click the domain name, and click New Alias.

   c. In the New Resource Record dialog box, in the Alias name box, type **WPAD**.

   d. In the Fully Qualified Domain Name (FQDN) box for the target host, type the fully qualified domain name of the ISA Server computer. Figure 4-9 illustrates the completed entry.

Figure 4-9   Configure DNS to support Automatic Discovery

> **Important**   The Automatic Discovery values must be assigned on each DHCP scope used by ISA Server clients. With a DNS server, the DNS values are assigned to DNS zones. This means you must configure each DNS zone, including delegated zones, which the ISA Server clients use.

How to Troubleshoot SecureNAT and Web Proxy Clients

SecureNAT and Web Proxy clients are easy to deploy and configure. However, these clients can also fail to connect to Internet resources. When this happens, use the following guidelines to troubleshoot the client connections.

Test for Name Resolution

One of the more common reasons why an ISA Server client cannot access resources on the Internet is that the client cannot resolve the DNS name for the resource.

- If you are using SecureNAT clients, you must configure the client computer network settings to use a DNS server that can resolve Internet names. So the first detail to check is whether the DNS Server setting is correct and ensure that the client computer can connect to the DNS server. Use tools such as NSLookup to query the DNS server to ensure that the client can connect to the server, and to ensure that the DNS server has the correct information. If the DNS configuration appears correct, but the SecureNAT client still cannot connect, you may need to clear that local DNS client cache by using the Ipconfig /Flushdns command.

- If you use Web Proxy clients, remember that the ISA Server computer can perform Internet name resolution for the client. If you cannot connect to an Internet Web site using a Web Proxy client, try connecting to the site from a SecureNAT client. If the SecureNAT client can access the Web site, the Web Proxy client, or the ISA Server DNS cache may contain the wrong IP address. Try clearing the local DNS Client cache, and if that doesn't work, try clearing the ISA Server DNS cache.

- If no internal clients can access the Internet through the ISA Server computer and you are using internal DNS servers, then ensure that the DNS servers can resolve Internet addresses. Ensure that the forwarders or root hints on the DNS servers are configured correctly. Ensure that there is an access rule on the ISA Server computer that allows the DNS servers to send DNS queries to the Internet.

Test for Network Connectivity

A second common reason why SecureNAT clients cannot connect to the Internet is due to network routing configuration. SecureNAT clients must be able to connect to the internal network interface on the ISA Server computer. If you have a single subnet on your network, check the client default gateway configuration. If you have multiple subnets, then check the routing configuration.

Review the Access Rule Configuration

If the DNS configuration is correct, and the client computer can connect to the ISA Server computer, the next step is to check the access rule configuration on ISA Server. By default, all access to the Internet is blocked by ISA Server, so you must enable access before the client computers can connect.

> **See Also**   We will explore access rule configuration and issues such as access rule order in much more detail in Chapter 5.

Remember the ISA Server Client Limitations

When troubleshooting SecureNAT and Web Proxy connection problems, remember that these clients are limited in their functionality. Web Proxy clients can only access resources using HTTP, HTTPS, or FTP over HTTP. SecureNAT clients do not support authentication, so clients will not be able to use any access rule that requires authentication. SecureNAT clients also do not support all protocols.

> **Exam Tip**   Because SecureNAT clients do not support authentication, any access rule that requires authentication will block access to SecureNAT clients. For example, you could have an access rule that allows all protocol traffic from the Internal network to the Internet. If that rule is applied to Authenticated Users, all SecureNAT clients will be blocked. If that rule is the first rule evaluated by ISA Server, all SecureNAT client connections will be blocked.

Practice: Configuring SecureNAT and Web Proxy Clients

In this practice, you will configure logging using the ISA Server Management Console to monitor client connections to the server. You will then configure a SecureNAT client and a Web Proxy client and test the client connections. Because you do not have an access rule defined on ISA Server to enable access to Web resources on other networks, you cannot actually connect to Web resources.

Exercise 1: Configuring ISA Server 2004 to Log Client Connections

1. On ISA1, open ISA Server Management, expand ISA1, and then click Monitoring.

2. On the Logging tab, in the Details pane, click Start Query. When you click Start Query, ISA Server will show all client connections on the Logging tab.

Exercise 2: Configuring and Testing a SecureNAT Client

1. On DC1, log on to the *cohovineyard.com* domain as an administrator.

2. Open a Command Prompt and type **IPConfig /all**. Verify that the server's default gateway is configured to use the ISA Server internal IP address.

3. Open Internet Explorer. Try connecting to *http://131.107.1.200.* The connection will fail.

4. Close the open windows.

5. On ISA1, in ISA Server Management, locate the events logged that used the HTTP protocol. Confirm that the HTTP request was denied by the Default rule.

Exercise 3: Configuring and Testing a Web Proxy Client

1. On CLIENT1, log on as an Administrator.

2. Open Internet Explorer. Click Tools, and then click Internet Options.

3. In the Internet Options dialog box, click the Connections tab.

4. Click LAN Settings. On the LAN Settings page, click Use A Proxy Server For Your LAN. In the Address box, type **ISA1**. In the Port box, type **8080**.

5. Select Bypass Proxy Server For Local Addresses. Click OK twice.

6. In the Address box, type **131.107.1.200**. The connection will fail.

7. Review the Proxy Message.

8. Switch to the ISA1 virtual machine and locate the events logged that used the HTTP protocol and the Destination Port of 8080. Confirm that the request was denied by the Default rule.

9. On the Tasks tab, click Stop Query. Close all open windows.

Lesson Review

Use the following questions to help determine whether you have learned enough to move on to the next lesson. If you have difficulty answering these questions, review the material in this lesson before beginning the next lesson. You can find answers to the questions in the "Questions and Answers" section at the end of this chapter.

1. You use ISA Server 2004 to publish a public Web site on an internal Web server. What ISA Server client, if any, needs to be configured on the Web server?

    a. Firewall client.

    b. SecureNAT client.

    c. Web Proxy client.

    d. No client configuration is required.

2. Your organization wants to use the Web Proxy client to allow clients access to the Internet using Port 8888. All the client computers are located in a single Active Directory domain. How can you automate the distribution of the client configuration? What steps must you take to implement it?

_____

_____

_____

3. Your network includes multiple subnets in a routed environment. You are using DHCP to supply IP addresses and standard TCP/IP options for all internal clients. You have configured all clients to be SecureNAT clients. All users are connecting to the Internet except users from one subnet. What would you do to troubleshoot the problem?

_____

_____

_____

Lesson Summary

- SecureNAT clients can be configured manually or by using the DHCP service. These clients do not require special software, but you must configure the default gateway so that all traffic destined for the Internet is sent through the ISA Server computer.

- Web Proxy clients also do not need any special software installation. However, you must configure the Web applications on the client computers to use the ISA Server computer as the proxy server. You can configure the Web Proxy client settings manually or you can configure many of the Web Proxy client configurations automatically.

- Web Proxy and Firewall clients must be configured with the name or IP address of an ISA Server computer. You can automate the discovery of the ISA Server computer by configuring Automatic Discovery using DHCP or DNS.

- To troubleshoot SecureNAT and Web Proxy client connections, ensure that you have network connectivity and that the clients can resolve Internet server names using DNS. After that, check the client configuration and the access rule configuration.

Lesson 3: Installing and Configuring the Firewall Client

The third type of client supported by ISA Server 2004 is a Firewall client. Firewall clients provide the highest level of functionality and security, but also require a client installation on each computer. This lesson describes how to install and configure the Firewall Client software. It also describes the advanced Firewall client configuration options, and the options for automating the installation of Firewall Client.

After this lesson, you will be able to

- Install and configure the Firewall Client software
- Identify options for automating the installation of the Firewall Client
- Configure the Firewall Client settings on the ISA Server computer
- Configure the advanced Firewall Client options
- Troubleshoot Firewall Clients

Estimated lesson time: 45 minutes

How to Install Firewall Client

When you install ISA Server, you have the option of installing the Firewall Client Share on the ISA Server computer. When you choose this option, the Firewall Client installation files are copied to the server in the C:\Program Files\Microsoft ISA Server\Clients folder. The folder is then shared with a share name of Mspclnt. Moreover, the system policy rule that enables access to the shared folder is enabled. To install the Firewall Client manually, users can connect to the share and run the setup program.

Note   You can also copy the Firewall Client installation files to a shared folder on another server on the network and then instruct the users to connect to that share to install the Firewall Client.

Important   The permissions on the Mspclnt share allow the Authenticated Users group to connect to the share and read and execute the setup program. However, you must be a member of the local Administrators group on the client computer to install the Firewall Client.

To install the Firewall Client software from a shared folder, use the following procedure:

1. Connect to the shared folder that contains the Firewall Client installation files. If you use the shared folder on the ISA Server computer, the default share name is ISA_Server_name/MSPClnt.

2. Right-click MS_FPC.msi and click Install. Alternatively, you can double-click Setup.exe.

3. On the Welcome To The Install Wizard For The Microsoft Firewall Client page, click Next.

4. On the Destination Folder page, review the default installation folder location. Click Change if you want to change the installation folder. Click Next to continue.

5. On the ISA Server Computer Select screen, you can select how the Firewall Client will locate the ISA Server computer, as shown in Figure 4-10. To configure the server name or IP Address manually, select Connect To This ISA Server and type the ISA Server name or the IP address. To enable Automatic Discovery of the ISA Server computer, select Automatically Detect The Appropriate ISA Server Computer. Click Next.

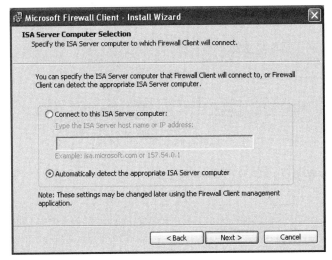

Figure 4-10   Configuring the ISA Server selection during the Firewall Client installation

6. On the Ready to Install the Program page, click Install.

7. When the installation wizard finishes, click Finish.

Note   You can install Firewall Client software on client computers that run Microsoft Windows Server 2003, Windows 2000 Server, Windows XP, Microsoft Windows 98 Second Edition, Microsoft Windows Millennium Edition, or Microsoft Windows NT 4.0. You cannot install Firewall Client software on the ISA Server computer.

After the installation is complete, the Firewall Client application is enabled. The Microsoft Firewall Client Management icon is added to the system tray. To modify the Firewall Client configuration on the client, right-click the icon and click Configure. On the General tab (shown in Figure 4-11), you can enable or disable the Firewall Client and configure it to detect the ISA Server computer automatically or configure the ISA Server computer manually. On the Web Browser tab, you can enable or disable automatic configuration of the Web browser.

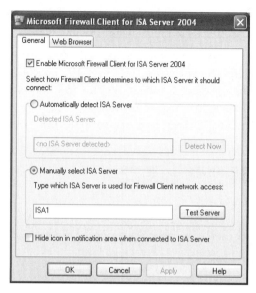

Figure 4-11   Configuring the Firewall Client after installation.

How to Automate Firewall Client Installation

If you deploy the Firewall Client to a large number of clients, you may choose to automate the Firewall Client installation. You have several options for automating the installation of the Firewall Client. You can perform an unattended installation, use Group Policy in Active Directory, or Microsoft Systems Management Server (SMS) to automate the installation.

Tip   Before deploying Firewall Client, configure the Firewall Client settings using ISA Server Management. By first configuring these settings, all the clients will get the desired Firewall Client configuration when the installation completes. The next section describes how to configure the Firewall Client settings.

Performing an Unattended Installation of the Firewall Client

One option for automating the deployment of the Firewall Client is to perform an unattended installation. To perform an unattended installation, you must ensure that the Firewall Client installation files are accessible from the client computer and then run the setup program from a command prompt with the appropriate parameters.

To complete an unattended installation of Firewall Client when running the setup program from the command prompt, use the following syntax:

```
Path\Setup.exe /v" [SERVER_NAME_OR_IP=ISA_Server_Name] [ENABLE_AUTO_DETECT={1|0}]
[REFRESH_WEB_PROXY={1|0}] /qn"
```

where

- *Path* is the path to the shared ISA Server 2004 client installation files.

- *ISA_Server_Name* is the name of the ISA Server computer to which the Firewall Client should connect. This parameter, as well as the next two, is optional.

- *ENABLE_AUTO_DETECT=1* specifies that the Firewall Client automatically detects to which computer the ISA Server computer should connect.

- *REFRESH_WEB_PROXY=1* indicates that the Firewall Client configuration should be updated with the Web Proxy configuration specified on the ISA Server computer.

- */qn* means that the application will install without showing the user interface.

For example, to complete the unattended installation from the Firewall Client share on an ISA Server computer named ISA1 and configure the Firewall Client to use the same ISA Server computer for Firewall Client and Web Proxy configuration, use the following command:

```
\\isa1\mspclnt\Setup.exe /v" SERVER_NAME_OR_IP=ISA1 ENABLE_AUTO_DETECT=0
REFRESH_WEB_PROXY=1 /qn"
```

You can use this option to install the Firewall Client in several scenarios. For example, you can provide users with a link on a Web page that will run the unattended installation from a network location. Or you can use a command such as this in a logon script to install the application. You can also copy the Firewall Client installation files to a CD-ROM and then launch the command when users insert the CD-ROM into their computers.

Note Users must be logged on as local Administrators to complete an unattended installation of the Firewall Client. If the users in your organization are not local Administrators on their computers, use one of the following options to distribute the software.

Using Active Directory Group Policy to Distribute the Firewall Client

You can also use the Software Installation option in Active Directory Group Policy to automate the installation of the Firewall Client. To distribute the Firewall Client using this option, perform the following procedure:

1. Copy the Firewall Client installation files to a network share. You can use the Firewall Installation share on the ISA Server computer or on a file server. If you are installing the Firewall Client on a large number of client computers, use a separate file server.

2. Determine whether you wish to distribute the client software to users or computers. If you distribute the software to users, you can choose whether the software will be installed the next time the user logs on or whether the user can initiate the installation from Add/Remove Programs. If you distribute the software to computers, the software will be installed the next time the computer restarts.

3. Create a new software distribution package. Configure the software distribution package to use the installation files on the shared folder. You can also configure the distribution options for the software package.

4. When users log on or the client computers reboot, the Firewall Client is installed. The Firewall Client will then automatically discover the ISA Server computer and download the configuration information.

> **See Also**   One advantage of using Active Directory Group Policy to distribute software is that the software installation process can run even if the logged-on user is not an Administrator. For detailed information about using Active Directory Group Policy to distribute software installations, see the *Group Policy Software Installation Extension Technical Reference* at *http://www.microsoft.com/resources/documentation/WindowsServ/2003/all/techref/en-us/ Default.asp?url=/Resources/Documentation/windowsserv/2003/all/techref/en-us/ W2K3TR_gp_intro.asp*.

Using Systems Management Server 2003

Organizations that have deployed SMS 2003 can use the software distribution feature of SMS to distribute the ISA Firewall Client. Software distribution in SMS 2003 provides the ability to deploy Microsoft Windows Installer (.msi) or Package Definition Format (.pdf, .sms) files to any computer that is assigned to the SMS environment. To deploy the ISA Firewall Client using SMS, perform the following procedure:

1. Create a collection that includes any computer that is to receive the ISA Firewall Client software. A collection is a logical group of resources such as computers or users that are gathered together to be managed within SMS. You can set specific

requirements such as IP address, hardware configuration, or add clients directly by name to group all resources that are to have the ISA Firewall Client installed.

2. Create an SMS package by importing the ISA Firewall Client Windows Installer file (MS_FWC.msi). The Windows Installer file automatically creates attended and unattended installation program options that can be deployed on a per-system or per-user basis. Programs are also created to uninstall the client if the need arises. The per-system programs are configured to install the client with administrative rights regardless of whether the user is logged on. The per-user programs install the client using the credentials of the logged-on user.

3. Create an SMS advertisement, which specifies the target collection and program to install. To control deployment, you can schedule a time for the program to be advertised to collection members.

Off the Record   If you are using a non-Microsoft application to distribute applications, you can certainly use that application to deploy the Firewall Client. The Firewall Client includes a Windows Installer setup information file (MS_FWC.msi) that can be distributed using any software distribution application.

How to Configure ISA Server for Firewall Clients

When you first install the Firewall Client on a client computer, it will connect to the ISA Server computer configured during the installation to complete the Firewall Client configuration. After installation, each time a computer running the Firewall Client restarts, the Firewall Client checks for any new client configuration settings on the server. This means that you can modify the Firewall Client by configuring the settings using ISA Server Management. The settings are then applied to the client when the client connects, or updated every six hours on the client computer if the client computer remains connected.

Firewall Client Configuration Options

Almost all Firewall Client settings can be modified using ISA Server Management. The Firewall Client settings that you can configure are summarized in Table 4-4.

Table 4-4   ISA Server Firewall Configuration Settings

Firewall Client Configuration	Explanation
Enable or disable Firewall Client support.	You can specify whether Firewall Client support is enabled for a specific network. If Firewall Client support is enabled, ISA Server will accept incoming requests on TCP or UDP Port 1745.
Application settings.	These settings define how the Firewall Client connects to ISA Server for specific applications.
Internal network and local domains.	These settings define the set of IP addresses and domains that the Firewall Client recognizes as local. The Firewall Client will connect to resources in these locations directly, without going through the ISA Server computer.
Automatic discovery.	By enabling Automatic Discovery, Firewall clients will automatically discover the appropriate ISA Server computer.
Web browser settings for the Firewall client.	The Firewall Client application can automatically update the Web Proxy settings on the Firewall Client computer. These settings are obtained from ISA Server when the Firewall Client settings are updated.
Support for older versions of Firewall Client.	ISA Server supports earlier versions of the Firewall Client software, including Firewall Client for ISA Server 2000 and the Winsock Proxy client (from Microsoft Proxy Server 2.0). You can enable or disable support for these clients on the ISA Server computer.

How to Configure Firewall Client Settings

The Firewall Client settings are configured in two different locations within ISA Server Management. To configure which versions of the Firewall Client are supported and to configure the application settings, use the following procedure:

1. Open ISA Server Management, expand the Configuration folder, and click General.

2. Click Define Firewall Client Settings.

3. On the Connection tab (as shown in Figure 4-12), configure whether or not earlier versions of the Firewall Client software are supported. Because older Firewall clients do not support encryption, you must enable the Allow Non-Encrypted Firewall Client Connections option.

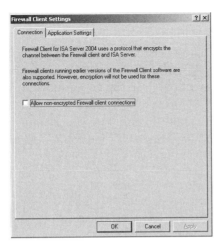

Figure 4-12   Configuring ISA Server support for earlier Firewall Client versions

Exam Tip   By default, ISA Server 2004 requires encrypted Firewall client connections. If you see an exam question in which client computers are running older Firewall Clients, remember that you must change the default configuration to allow these clients to connect.

4. On the Application Settings tab as shown in Figure 4-13, configure the settings for applications that run on Firewall Clients. To configure a specific application, click the application name and then click Edit.

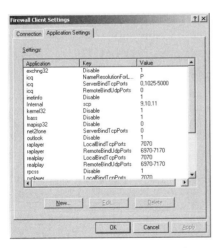

Figure 4-13   Configuring Firewall Client application settings

The application settings are used to configure how the Firewall Client will respond when specific Winsock applications are started on the client computer. Some applications require specific port number assignments. For example, the RealPlayer application from RealNetworks requires that the Firewall client use Port 7070 when connecting to RealServer streaming media servers. The streaming media server will respond on any port between 6970 and 7170. As Figure 4-13 illustrates, the application settings for the RealPlayer application (the application name in the interface is Realplay) configure the LocalBindTcpPorts key with a value of 7070 and the RemoteBindUdpPorts key with a value of 6970-7170. Other applications are disabled in the application settings. For example, the Exchng32 application, the Mapisp32 application, and the Outlook application are all disabled by default, which means that the Firewall Client cannot establish the RPC and MAPI connections required for Microsoft Outlook e-mail clients through the ISA Server computer.

> **Note**   RealPlayer can also use Port 554 to connect to RealServers. ISA Server 2004 enables this connection by enabling the Real-Time Streaming Protocol (RTSP) which uses Port 554 to establish the initial client connection and the RTSP application filter to manage secondary connections.

To configure the other Firewall Client settings using ISA Server Management Console, use the following procedure:

1. Open ISA Server Management, expand the Configuration folder, and click Networks.

2. In the details pane, click the Networks tab.

3. To edit the internal network settings, double-click Internal.

4. To configure the internal addresses, click the Addresses tab. You originally configured the IP addresses for the Internal network when you installed ISA Server, but you can use this option to change the configuration, as shown in Figure 4-14. You can configure the following settings for this network:

   a. To add a specific range of IP addresses, click Add. Then, type the first address of the network address range in Starting Address and the last address of the network address range in Ending Address.

   b. To add IP addresses associated with a specific adapter, click Add Adapter and then, in Network Interfaces, select one or more adapters.

   c. To add private address ranges, click Add Private and then select a range from the list.

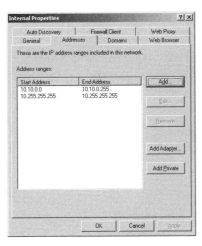

Figure 4-14   Configuring IP addresses for the Internal network

5. To configure the internal domains, click the Domains tab, as shown in Figure 4-15. Click Add to add the domain names for the internal network. When a firewall client connects to any computer with a domain name listed on the Domains tab, the Firewall client will connect to the computer directly rather than go through ISA Server.

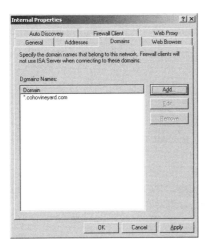

Figure 4-15   Configuring the Domains for the Internal network

6. You can use the Firewall Client to configure the Web browser settings for Web Proxy clients. To configure the Web browser settings, click the Firewall Client tab, as shown in Figure 4-16. You can use this interface to configure the following settings:

    a. To enable Firewall Client support for this network, verify that the Enable Firewall Client Support For This Network check box is selected. When you enable this option, ISA Server will accept incoming requests on TCP or UDP Port 1745.

b. Select Automatically Detect Settings if the client computer should automatically attempt to find the ISA Server computer.

c. Select Use Automatic Configuration Script if the Web browser on the Firewall Client computer should use configuration information that is contained in the specified automatic configuration script. If you select this option, specify Use Default URL or Use Custom URL.

d. To specify the name of the ISA Server computer, select Use a Web Proxy Server and type the ISA Server name or IP Address.

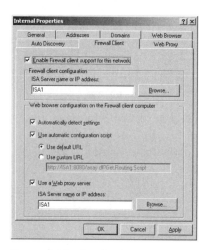

Figure 4-16   Configuring the Firewall Client settings for the Internal network

Advanced Firewall Client Configuration

In addition to the Firewall Client settings that you can configure on the ISA Server computer for distribution to all clients, there are also advanced settings that you can configure on the client computer running the Firewall Client. As much as possible, use the ISA Server settings to configure the Firewall Client settings, but in some cases, you may need a unique configuration for one or more clients.

Configuring Local Addresses

One of the advanced options that you can configure is the local address table. By default, Firewall Client considers all addresses on its local network, as well as the addresses specified in the local routing table on the Firewall client computer, as local. Each time a Winsock application on that client attempts to establish a connection to an IP address, the Firewall Client uses this information plus the Internal network information on ISA Server to determine whether the IP address is on the local network. If the server IP address is local, the Firewall Client will connect to the server directly; if the address is not local, the Firewall Client will go through the ISA Server computer to access the server.

You can modify this client behavior by creating a client computer–specific file that defines local addresses for that client. Using a text editor, you can create a custom client local address table (LAT) file named Locallat.txt and place it in the \Documents and Settings\All Users\Application Data\Microsoft\Firewall Client 2004 folder on the Firewall client computer. You can add additional IP address ranges to the file so that the client will recognize these addresses as part of the local network. If this file exists, the client uses its own routing table, the server-specific settings, and the Locallat.txt file to determine the IP addresses that are part of the local network.

When you create the Locallat.txt file, enter IP address pairs in the file. Each address pair defines either a range of IP addresses or a single IP address. The following example shows a Locallat.txt file that has two entries. The first entry is an IP address range and the second entry is a single IP address. Note that the second entry on each line is an IP address and not a subnet mask.

```
10.51.0.0      10.51.255.255

10.52.144.103  10.52.144.103
```

Advanced Firewall Client Settings

For most Winsock applications, the default Firewall Client configuration that is downloaded from the ISA Server computer works with no further modification needed. However, in some cases, you will need to add specific client configuration information. For example, if one Firewall client computer requires an application setting that is different from all other clients, you will need to configure the application settings on that particular computer. The configuration is done by making changes to Firewall Client .ini files.

The Firewall Client configuration information is stored in a set of files, which are installed on the Firewall client computer. The following files are used to configure the local Firewall client settings:

- **Common.ini** Specifies the common configuration for all applications
- **Management.ini** Specifies Firewall Client Management configuration settings
- **Application.ini** Specifies application-specific configurations settings

The Common.ini file and the Management.ini file are created for all users logged on to the computer and can also be created manually for each specific user on the computer. By default, the Application.ini file is not created, so you must create it manually. The per-user settings override the general configuration settings. These files are created in different locations, depending on the operating system. For example, on Windows XP computers, the files may be located in one of two places:

- \Documents and Settings\All Users\Application Data\Microsoft\Firewall Client 2004 folder

- \Documents and Settings\user_name\Local Settings\Application Data\Microsoft\ Firewall Client 2004 folder

The settings in these files are applied as follows:

1. The .ini files in the user's folder take precedence. Any configuration settings specified in the user's profile are used by Firewall Client to determine how the application will function.

2. The .ini files in the All Users folder are applied next. If a specified configuration setting contradicts the user-specific settings, it is ignored.

3. Finally, Firewall Client examines the server-level settings. Any configuration settings specified on ISA Server are applied. If a specified configuration setting contradicts the user-specific or computer-specific settings, it is ignored.

If a specific client computer requires unique Firewall Client settings, you can modify these .ini files on the client computer to meet the requirements. For example, the Common.ini file specifies common configuration for all applications. In most cases, the Common.ini file very simply consists of lines such as the following:

```
[Common]

ServerName=ISA1

Disable=0

Autodetection=0
```

The *ServerName* value is used to configure the ISA Server computer from which the Firewall Client should download its configuration. The Disable option specifies whether the Firewall Client is disabled, with a value of 1 indicating that it is disabled. And the Autodetection value specifies whether the Firewall Client is configured to detect ISA Servers automatically.

By default, the Management.ini file contains only a setting that specifies whether the Firewall Client is enabled to modify the Web Proxy settings on the client.

The Application.ini file specifies configuration settings for specific applications and also the file that is most often modified. For example, you may have several users on your network running a Winsock application, but only a subset of those users should be able to use that application to access Internet resources. One way to enable this is to configure the Application.ini files on the client computers used by the users that should use the application to gain access to Internet resources.

The following is an example of part of an Application.ini file showing possible configuration settings for an application:

```
[FW_Client_App]

Disable=0

NameResolution=R

LocalBindTcpPorts=7777

RemoteBindTcpPorts=30

KillOldSession=1

Persistent=1

ForceCredentials=1
```

Table 4-5 defines the settings included in this Application.ini file.

Table 4-5   Application.ini File Settings

Option	Sample Value	Explanation
Disable	0	Specifies that the Firewall Client is enabled for this application. A value of 1 means that the Firewall Client is disabled for this application.
NameResolution	R	When the value is set to R, all names are redirected to the ISA Server computer for resolution. When the value is set to L, all names are resolved on the local computer.
LocalBindTcpPorts	7777	Specifies the TCP port used by the application.
RemoteBindTcpPorts	30	Specifies the TCP port used on the remote server.
KillOldSession	1	Specifies that before a new session is started by the application, any existing session will be terminated. A setting of 0 means that old sessions are not terminated.
Persistent	1	Specifies that the server state is maintained if the server becomes unavailable. A value of 0 means that the server state is not maintained.
ForceCredentials	1	Forces the use of user credentials other than the credentials of the logged-on user.

See Also   For detailed information about all the settings that you can configure in the .ini files, see the Advanced Firewall Client Configuration Settings topic in ISA Server Online Help.

How to Troubleshoot Firewall Clients

You can use many of the same steps when troubleshooting Firewall clients as you would when troubleshooting any other clients. However, the Firewall client configuration is more complicated then configuring other ISA Server clients, so there are also some specific troubleshooting steps for Firewall clients.

Check Compatibility with Older Firewall Clients and Proxy Servers   The version of Firewall Client included with ISA Server 2004 is different from earlier Firewall and Proxy Server clients in two ways. First, the ISA Server 2004 Firewall Client is the only client that supports encrypting the Firewall Client control channel. Secondly, the ISA Server 2004 Firewall Client uses only TCP Port 1745 for the client control channel, while earlier clients also used UDP Port 1745.

The first difference can lead to compatibility problems if you have older Firewall or Proxy Server clients deployed. To fix these problems, ensure that you allow nonencrypted client connections to the ISA Server computer.

The second difference can lead to compatibility issues if you have deployed ISA Server 2004 Firewall clients, but these clients are connecting to ISA Server 2000 or Proxy Server computers. In this scenario, the ISA Server 2004 Firewall Client cannot connect to a Proxy 2.0 server or to an ISA Server 2000 computer because the Firewall client cannot use UDP. You can enable UDP control channel support by defining the following registry value:

```
HKEY_LOCAL_MACHINE\Software\Microsoft\Firewall Client 2004\EnableUdpControlChannel = 1.
```

Check the Firewall Configuration Files   The Firewall Client can be configured in several different locations. You can configure the client using files on the local computer such as the .ini files or the Locallat.txt file. You can even have multiple copies of the local files, one in the All Users profile, and one in the profile for the user who is logged on. The Firewall Client also downloads a configuration from the ISA Server computer, including settings such as the domain table, the local address information, and the application settings. Because the client configuration can come from several sources, troubleshooting client connections can be quite difficult. If you are using all the different configuration options, remember that the local files are applied after the server settings, overwriting any conflicting changes. So start by checking the local files for configuration problems and then move on to checking the ISA Server configuration. As a best practice, try to eliminate the local files as much as possible, and use only the ISA Server configuration.

See Also   Microsoft provides a very useful set of tools for troubleshooting Firewall Client connections. The tools, called Firewall Client Tools for ISA Server 2004, can be downloaded from *http://www.microsoft.com/downloads/details.aspx?familyid=f20f6267-273d-4870-b1e8-799b261b4786&displaylang=en*

Practice: Installing and Configuring Firewall Clients

In this practice, you will configure the Firewall Client settings on the ISA Server computer and then install the Firewall Client software from a shared folder on the ISA Server computer.

Exercise 1: Configuring the Firewall Client Settings on ISA Server

1. On ISA1, open ISA Server Management, expand Configuration, and click General.

2. Click Define Firewall Client Settings.

3. On the Connection tab, click Allow Non-Encrypted Firewall Client Connections. Click OK.

4. Apply the changed configuration.

5. In ISA Server Management, under Configuration, click Networks.

6. In the details pane, click the Networks tab, and then click Internal.

7. On the Tasks tab, click Edit Selected Network.

8. Click the Domains tab, and click Add to add the domain names for the internal network. Type ***.Cohovineyard.com**, and then click OK.

9. Click the Firewall Client tab and verify that the Enable Firewall Client Support For This Network check box is selected. On the Firewall Client tab, perform the following steps:

    a. Clear the Automatically Detect Settings option.

    b. Clear the Use Automatic Configuration Script option.

    c. Ensure that Use A Web Proxy Server is selected and ISA1 is listed in the ISA Server Name Or IP Address box.

10. Click OK.

11. Apply the changed configuration.

Exercise 2: Installing the Firewall Client

1. On CLIENT1, log on as a local Administrator.

2. On the Start menu, click Run. Type **\\ISA1\MSPClnt** and then click OK.

3. Right-click MS_FWC.msi and click Install.

4. On the Welcome To The Install Wizard For The Microsoft Firewall Client page, click Next.

5. On the Destination Folder page, review the default installation folder location. Click Next to continue.

6. On the ISA Server Computer Select screen, select Connect To This ISA Server and type **ISA1**. Click Next.

7. On the Ready To Install The Program page, click Install.

8. On the Install Wizard Completed page, click Finish.

9. Close all open windows.

Lesson Review

Use the following questions to help determine whether you have learned enough to move on to the next lesson. If you have difficulty answering these questions, review the material in this lesson before beginning the next lesson. You can find answers to the questions in the "Questions and Answers" section at the end of this chapter.

1. Your organization has deployed ISA Server 2004 and has installed the Firewall Client software on all Windows XP client computers. All users on the network are running a Winsock application, but some of the users need a customized configuration to run the Winsock application using a server on another network protected by the ISA Server firewall. How would you provide the configuration settings for the Winsock application?

   a. Create a file named Management.ini and place it in the All Users profile.

   b. Create a file named Application.ini and place it on the ISA Server computer.

   c. Create a file named Management.ini on the ISA Server computer and enable Automatic Discovery.

   d. Create a file named Application.ini and place it in the specific user's profile.

2. You have recently upgraded from ISA Server 2000 to ISA Server 2004. Most of your client computers still run the Firewall Client software from ISA Server 2000. What must you do to enable support for this version of the Firewall Client?

_____

_____

_____

3. Your client computer is located on the 172.16.0.0 network. The client computer is configured as a Firewall client. You need to modify the configuration of the client computer so that a single IP address, 192.168.7.1 will be considered as a local address by the firewall client. What entry needs to be in the Locallat.txt?

    a. 192.168.7.1   255.255.255.0

    b. 192.168.7.1   192.168.7.254

    c. 192.168.7.1   192.168.7.1

    d. 192.168.7.1   255.255.255.255

Lesson Summary

■ To perform a manual installation of the Firewall Client, connect to the Firewall Client Share on the ISA Server computer or to an alternate location that contains the Firewall Client installation files. You can then run setup using the Ms_fwc.msi file or the Setup.exe file. You can configure the name of the ISA Server computer during the client installation.

■ You can perform an unattended installation of Firewall Client using command-line options, Active Directory Group Policy, or SMS to automate the installation.

■ You can modify the Firewall Client by configuring the settings using ISA Server Management. The following Firewall Client Settings can be modified: application settings, internal network and local domains, Automatic Discovery, and Web browser settings.

■ You can modify advanced settings for the Firewall Client to be specific for certain clients. One of the advanced options that you can configure is the local address table which is used by the Firewall client to determine whether to connect to the server directly or through the ISA Server computer. You can also modify the configuration .ini files to configure unique settings for the Firewall client.

■ Troubleshooting Firewall Client computers is similar to troubleshooting other ISA Server clients. However, you also need to be aware of compatibility issues between the Firewall Client included with ISA Server 2004 and previous ISA Server or Proxy Server versions. As well, you may need to review the local client configuration files when troubleshooting Firewall Client issues.

Case Scenario Exercise

In this exercise, you will plan an ISA Server 2004 client deployment for a fictitious organization. Read the scenario and then answer the question that follows. If you have difficulty completing this work, review the material in this chapter before beginning the next chapter. You can find answers to these questions in the "Questions and Answers" section at the end of this chapter.

Scenario 1

Your organization has a single location with 2000 employees. You have a single Active Directory domain. You have installed and configured two computers running ISA Server 2004 to distribute the client load and provide fault tolerance. You need to ensure that only Authenticated Users have access to Internet resources. The purchasing department needs to run a Web-based application that is located at a partner organization, and is accessible only over the Internet. The application uses a custom port and protocol that need to be defined. You need to decide what type of ISA Server client you will deploy in the organization. You also need to ensure that the clients are deployed and configured with the least amount of administrative effort.

Scenario 1 Question

1. Design the ISA Server client deployment to meet your organization's requirements. What clients will you deploy, and how will you configure them?

_____

_____

_____

Chapter Summary

- ISA Server supports three types of clients: Firewall clients, SecureNAT clients, and Web Proxy clients. As you prepare to deploy ISA Server, you need to choose an ISA Server client that best meets your organization's requirements. Factors that you should consider when choosing the client include protocol and operating system support, support for authentication and the effort required to deploy the clients.

- SecureNAT clients do not require special software, but you must configure the default gateway and network routing so that all traffic destined for the Internet is sent through the ISA Server computer. Web Proxy clients also do not need any special software installation. However, you must configure the Web applications on the client computers to use the ISA Server computer as the proxy server. You can manually configure the Web Proxy client settings or you can automatically configure many of the Web Proxy client configurations. To troubleshoot SecureNAT and Web Proxy client connections, ensure that you have network connectivity and that the clients can resolve Internet server names using DNS.

■ Firewall clients require the installation of the Firewall Client application. You can perform a manual installation of the Firewall Client or you can automate the Firewall Client installation of Firewall Client using command-line options, Active Directory Group Policy, or Systems Management Server (SMS). You can modify the Firewall Client by configuring the settings using ISA Server Management. You can also modify the Firewall Client settings to be specific for certain clients by modifying the local configuration files on the client computer.

Exam Highlights

Before taking the exam, review the key points and terms that are presented in this chapter. You need to know this information.

Key Points

■ The ISA Server client that you choose for your organization will be based on your security requirements and on whether you want to deploy the Firewall Client application. Remember that for maximum security and functionality if you are using just Windows clients, you should deploy the Firewall Client.

■ SecureNAT clients are the easiest to deploy. The two most important components to deploying SecureNAT clients are Internet name resolution and network routing. Understand how to configure these two options and you will be able to deploy SecureNAT clients.

■ Web Proxy clients can be manually configured, but you also need to understand how the client configuration can be automated. Understand how to configure the settings on ISA Server, and then how to configure the Web Proxy clients to download this configuration from ISA Server.

■ Automatic discovery simplifies the configuration of Web Proxy and Firewall clients. Understand how to enable Automatic Discovery using DHCP and DNS, and how the clients use Automatic Discovery.

■ Firewall clients are the most work to deploy, but you can also automate the client installation using unattended setups, Group Policy, or a software distribution tool such as SMS.

■ Firewall Clients get their configuration from the ISA Server computer when they connect to the server. To configure Firewall Clients, configure the settings on the ISA Server computer and all the clients will be updated within six hours.

Key Terms

Automatic Discovery   Automatic Discovery is a feature in ISA Server that enables Firewall and Web Proxy clients to discover an ISA Server computer automatically.

Firewall clients   Firewall clients are computers that have Firewall Client software installed and enabled. Firewall clients provide the highest level of functionality and security of the various types of clients.

SecureNAT clients   SecureNAT clients do not require any client installation or configuration. SecureNAT clients are configured to route all requests for resources on other networks to the internal IP address of the computer running ISA Server.

Web Proxy clients   Web Proxy clients are any computers that run HTTP 1.1 compatible Web applications such as Web browsers. The Web applications must be configured to use the ISA Server as a proxy server.

Winsock applications   Winsock applications use sockets to communicate with services running on other computers. The Firewall Client intercepts Winsock application requests and redirects them to the ISA Server computer.

Questions and Answers

Page
4-10
Lesson 1 Review

1. You have deployed ISA Server 2004 as your enterprise firewall solution. Your enterprise consists of multiple operating systems, including UNIX and Novell clients. You run TCP/IP as your network protocol. The client IP addresses and options are assigned through DHCP. All clients have HTTP 1.1–compliant Web browsers installed. All internal employees will require the same level of access to the Internet. You need to minimize the effort required to deploy the ISA Server clients. What ISA Server client will work best to provide simple Internet access for your internal employees?

   Although either the Web Proxy client or the SecureNAT client will work, the SecureNAT client is the better solution because of the ease of deployment and because there is no requirement for authentication. You only need to configure the default gateway and you can easily use DHCP to provide the gateway address. The Firewall Client software can only be deployed to Microsoft clients and would require software installation and configuration.

2. You have deployed ISA Server 2004 as your enterprise firewall solution. You use Active Directory and all your client computers run Microsoft operating systems. Due to limited Internet bandwidth, you must restrict Internet access to selected departments during business hours. Your employees also need access to a RealPlayer streaming media application on an external Web site. What ISA Server client works best for your situation?

   To restrict access to only certain employees, you must use a client that supports authentication. In this case, you must use the Firewall Client software because it provides support for authentication and support for multiple protocols such as the RealPlayer streaming media application. The SecureNAT client does not support authentication, and the Web Proxy client only supports HTTP, HTTPS, and FTP over HTTP.

Page
4-26
Lesson 2 Review

1. You use ISA Server 2004 to publish a public Web site on an internal Web server. What ISA Server client, if any, needs to be configured on the Web server?

   a. Firewall client.

   b. SecureNAT client.

   c. Web Proxy client.

   d. No client configuration is required.

   B is correct. The SecureNAT client should be configured on the Web server to point to the internal network interface of your ISA Server computer.

2. Your organization wants to use the Web Proxy client to allow clients access to the Internet using Port 8888. All the client computers are located in a single Active Directory domain. How can you automate the distribution of the client configuration? What steps must you take to implement it?

You must enable the Web Proxy client on ISA Server 2004 and configure the HTTP port on the Internal network Web Proxy property pages. Then the client Web browser application must be configured to detect settings and use the configuration script automatically. You can do this manually, or by using the Firewall Client.

3. Your network includes multiple subnets in a routed environment. You are using DHCP to supply IP addresses and standard TCP/IP options for all internal clients. You have configured all clients to be SecureNAT clients. All users are connecting to the Internet except users from one subnet. What would you do to troubleshoot the problem?

Use standard TCP/IP troubleshooting techniques. Run Ipconfig and check the client settings. Ensure that the default gateway address is correct. Check that the router options on the DHCP server are configured properly. Test network connectivity by using a client on the affected network to ping the default gateway. If the client connections work on the local subnet, then check the routing table on the router.

Page
4-44

Lesson 3 Review

1. Your organization has deployed ISA Server 2004 and has installed the Firewall Client software on all Windows XP client computers. All users on the network are running a Winsock application, but some of the users need a customized configuration to run the Winsock application using a server on another network protected by the ISA Server firewall. How would you provide the configuration settings for the Winsock application?

   a. Create a file named Management.ini and place it in the All Users profile.

   b. Create a file named Application.ini and place it on the ISA Server computer.

   c. Create a file named Management.ini on the ISA Server computer and enable Automatic Discovery.

   d. Create a file named Application.ini and place it in the specific user's profile.

   D is correct. A and C are incorrect because Management.ini only specifies whether the Firewall Client can modify Web Proxy settings. B is incorrect because creating Application.ini on the ISA Server computer will not configure the clients. The Application.ini file should be placed in the specific users profile so that only that user will receive the settings. It will override any settings coming from ISA Server.

2. You have recently upgraded from ISA Server 2000 to ISA Server 2004. Most of your client computers still run the Firewall Client software from ISA Server 2000. What must you do to enable support for this version of the Firewall Client?

You must enable support for the previous version of the Firewall Client software in the ISA Server Management Console. To do this, click the Define Firewall Client Settings link in the General container, and check the Allow Non-Encrypted Firewall Client Connections box.

3. Your client computer is located on the 172.16.0.0 network. The client computer is configured as a Firewall client. You need to modify the configuration of the client computer so that a single IP address, 192.168.7.1 will be considered as a local address by the firewall client. What entry needs to be in the Locallat.txt?

   a. 192.168.7.1   255.255.255.0

   b. 192.168.7.1   192.168.7.254

   c. 192.168.7.1   192.168.7.1

   d. 192.168.7.1   255.255.255.255

C is correct. Entries in the Locallat.txt use the first IP address and the last IP address in the range of addresses to be considered local. To specify a single entry, the first and last number in the range should be identical. A and D are incorrect because Locallat.txt does not use subnet mask entries. B is incorrect because is identifies the whole subnet as being local.

Case Scenario Exercise

Page
4-46
Scenario 1 Question

1. Design the ISA Server client deployment to meet your organization's requirements. What clients will you deploy, and how will you configure them?

You cannot use SecureNAT clients in this scenario because SecureNAT clients cannot be authenticated and the company policy states that only Authenticated Users are allowed to access the Internet.

Employees that need only basic Web access can be configured as Web Proxy clients. You could automate the configuration of these clients by using a WPAD entry in DHCP to configure the browser settings.

The purchasing department needs to run the Firewall Client software because it is using an application that is not using a protocol supported by the Web Proxy client. You can distribute the Firewall Client application to the users by using Group Policy.

On both ISA Server computers, you must configure the properties of the Internal network to enable Automatic Discovery. The special port and protocol settings for the Winsock application can be configured on the ISA Server computers.

5 Enabling Secure Internet Access with ISA Server 2004

Exam Objectives in this Chapter:

- Plan an ISA Server 2004 deployment.

    - Analyze forward proxy and reverse proxy requirements.

    - Analyze firewall protocol requirements.

    - Configure dial-up settings.

    - Configure firewall chaining.

- Create policy elements, access rules, and connection limits. Policy elements include schedule, protocols, user groups, and network objects.

Why This Chapter Matters

Well, you are finally ready to do something with Microsoft Internet and Security Acceleration (ISA) Server 2004. Users in your organization have been clamoring for Internet access and now you are ready to give it to them. Granting access to the Internet using ISA Server is relatively easy, especially if you want to give all users access to all resources on the Internet. All you have to do is to create an access rule that says all users on the Internal network have permission to use all protocols to connect to any resource on the Internet.

However, you may want to be more restrictive in the level of access users have to the Internet. Or more likely, your organization has a security policy that says you need to be more restrictive. For example, you may need to prevent employees from using certain protocols or applications to access the Internet. You may need to restrict which Web sites users can access, or what time of day they can access the Internet. You may even need to apply one set of restrictions to one group of users and another set of restrictions to another group.

Configuring all these restrictions is possible with ISA Server 2004. To do this, however, you must understand how ISA Server access rules work — that is, what types of objects you must configure to enable these restrictions, and how you can put the objects together to ensure that users get the right level of access.

Lessons in this Chapter:

- Lesson 1: Enabling Secure Access to Internet Resources 5-3

- Lesson 2: Configuring ISA Server as a Proxy Server. 5-11

- Lesson 3: Configuring Access Rule Elements. 5-29

- Lesson 4: Configuring ISA Server Authentication. .5-41

- Lesson 5: Configuring Access Rules for Internet Access. 5-48

Before You Begin

This chapter presents the skills and concepts related to configuring ISA Server to enable secure access to the Internet. If you plan to complete the practices and lab in this chapter, you should prepare the following:

- A server with Microsoft Windows Server 2003 (either Standard Edition or Enterprise Edition) installed as DC1 and configured as a domain controller in the *cohovineyard.com* domain. DC1 must be able to resolve the Domain Name System (DNS) names for resources located on the ISA Server external network.

- Use Active Directory Users and Computers to create and configure the following users and groups.

  ❑ Managers global group

  ❑ Manager1 user account. Add the account to the Managers group.

  ❑ Sales global group

  ❑ Sales1 user account. Add the account to the Sales group.

- A second server with Windows Server 2003 installed as ISA1 and configured as a domain member in the *cohovineyard.com* domain. ISA Server Standard Edition should be installed on this server, which should also have two network interfaces installed. The external interface should be connected to a network that contains one or more Web servers. If possible, the network interface should be attached to the Internet.

- A Microsoft Windows XP computer installed as CLIENT1. This computer should be a member of the *cohovineyard.com* domain.

Lesson 1: Enabling Secure Access to Internet Resources

Before you can configure ISA Server to enable secure access to the Internet, you must understand what secure access means. Every organization defines this concept slightly differently because an important part of configuring secure access is defining limits to what resources users can access on the Internet. To define secure access, the organization needs to develop an Internet usage policy that prescribes how users can use the Internet. Then you can use this policy to design your ISA Server configuration to ensure that users have only the required access to the Internet. This chapter provides an overview of what is meant by secure access to the Internet, some high-level guidelines for developing an Internet usage policy and an overview of how you can use ISA Server to enforce the policy. The other lessons in the chapter provide the details of how to configure ISA Server to implement the policy.

After this lesson, you will be able to

- Describe secure access to Internet resources
- List guidelines for creating an Internet usage policy
- Describe how ISA Server can provide secure access to Internet resources

Estimated lesson time: 15 minutes

What Is Secure Access to Internet Resources?

Almost all organizations provide some level of Internet access for their users. The use of the Internet as a source of information and e-mail as a communication tool means that most organizations cannot afford to be without access to the Internet. At the same time, ensuring that the connection to the Internet is secure is critical.

So what is secure access to the Internet? At a minimum, providing secure Internet access for users in an organization means the following:

- Users can access the resources that they need. To do their jobs, users in many organizations must be able to use a Web browser or other application to access Internet resources.

- The connection to the Internet is secure. Users must be reasonably sure that they will not be attacked through the Internet connection. Ideally, the connection to the Internet should not reveal any information about the internal system that can be used to launch an attack against the client computer. Information about the computer, such as the computer name, user logon name, and shared folders, as well as details about the network configuration for the client computer, such as the client Internet Protocol (IP) address, should be hidden.

■ The data that users transfer to and from the Internet is secure. In some cases, users might send confidential personal information such as credit card information to the Internet or they might send private or confidential organizational information such as client data to the Internet. This data must be secured when it leaves the organization. If the data cannot be protected, you must prevent users from sending the information to the Internet.

■ Users cannot download malicious programs from the Internet. One of the ways attackers gain access to your network is by getting users to download malicious content. You must prevent users from inadvertently or deliberately causing damage to the network by downloading viruses or Trojan horse applications to their client computers.

Secure access to the Internet also means that the user's actions comply with the organization's security or Internet usage policy. This means the following:

■ Only users who have permission to access the Internet can access the Internet.

■ These users can use only approved protocols and applications to access Internet resources.

■ These users can gain access only to approved Internet resources, or these users cannot gain access to denied Internet resources.

■ These users can gain access to the Internet only in accordance with any other restrictions the organization may establish, such as when and from which computers access is permitted.

Real World   Security Trade-Offs

Implementing secure access to the Internet is rarely simple because you must always find a balance between competing interests within the organization. The people responsible for security want to have the most secure network possible. Often, it seems that the only way to satisfy them would be to disconnect your network from the Internet and not allow anyone to leave or enter the building carrying a mobile computer. On the other hand, you have the employees who are interested only in getting their jobs done (and maybe having a bit of fun on the Internet). And these users don't want any restrictions in place to prevent them from doing so. These users seem remarkably adept at presenting a situation in which almost any restriction you put in place will prevent them from doing their work.

Obviously, this overstates the case, but I have worked with organizations in which this was close to reality. You can never please both groups completely, but in most cases, you can find a compromise. To do this, you must develop a plan that balances the following key trade-offs:

- *The benefit versus the security risk of different types of Internet access*—Applications and protocols, such as Web browsers using Hypertext Transfer Protocol (HTTP) or Hypertext Transfer Protocol Secure (HTTPS), can provide a great deal of benefit to an organization. Therefore, most organizations accept the risk of enabling this type of access to the Internet. However, many organizations do not see the benefits of enabling chat-room clients or peer-to-peer file-sharing applications, or of providing Internet access for users using the ICQ protocol. For these companies, the risk of enabling these types of access exceeds the benefit, so access to the Internet using these methods is denied.

- *Ease of use versus the security of the system*—Systems that are the easiest to use are often also the least secure; the most secure systems, on the other hand, may be almost impossible to use or to administer. Balance the requirement for security with the need for usability. If getting Internet access is too difficult, many users won't even try, and the organization will lose the potential benefit, while other users will spend a lot of time trying to figure out how to get around your security restrictions.

- *The cost of providing security versus risk of loss without security*—Implementing a completely secure solution can be very expensive, both in terms of money spent on purchasing and managing the security solution, and in terms of performance—a highly secure system might provide much slower performance. If an organization is working with highly confidential or private information, this cost is required. For other organizations, the cost of providing an excessively high level of security may be higher than the actual loss if the security is breached.

Exam Tip   You may see exam questions that ask you to balance security requirements and requested functionality. For example, you may get an exam question in which users require a certain level of access, but the security requirements set limits to the level of access. In this situation, configure the access rules so that users get the least level of access to meet their requirements, and you will have the most secure configuration possible. If users require access to the Internet using a particular protocol, then enable only that protocol.

Guidelines for Designing an Internet Usage Policy

One of the first steps that an organization must take, as it prepares to grant access to Internet resources, is to define an Internet usage policy. An Internet usage policy defines what actions users are allowed to perform while they are connected to the Internet. The Internet usage policy becomes the basis for configuring the ISA Server settings to provide secure access to the Internet.

Internet usage policies should do the following:

- **Describe the need for an Internet usage policy.**   At first, users may resist the policy because they may interpret the policy as arbitrarily and without any business reason limiting what they can do. The policy should define exactly why the policy is being created. For many organizations, there are clear legal requirements for creating a policy that limits what users can do, especially for organizations that work with confidential and private client information. Frequently, understanding the rationale for a policy greatly decreases the resistance to the policy.

- **Describe what the policy covers.**   The policy must include specific descriptions of what is acceptable and unacceptable Internet usage. This policy may define which applications can be used to access Internet resources, or what Internet resources can be accessed, as well as what applications and resources are denied by the policy.

- **Identify the people within the organization who are responsible for creating and enforcing the policy.**   If users have questions about the policy, or if policy restrictions prevent users from accessing resources that they need to do their jobs, users must have the means of resolving these issues. The easiest way to ensure this resolution is to provide users with the contacts they can use to get their answers quickly.

- **Define how violations are handled.**   The policy must define exactly what will happen to users who violate the security policy. Many security policies include levels of disciplinary action depending on the severity or recurrence of policy violations.

Each organization is unique, so each Internet usage policy will be slightly different. However, there are general guidelines that you can use to create a usage policy.

1. Identify vulnerabilities to the network that users introduce when connecting to the Internet. What damage can users do to your network or to your organization if allowed to connect to the Internet? This list should include damage to the network itself; for example, what damage could users cause by downloading a virus or malicious programs? The list should also include damage to the organization, which may include damage related to the company's reputation or productivity, as well as legal or privacy issues. Your Internet usage policy will define countermeasures for mitigating these risks.

2. Determine how much access to resources you want to grant users. Users must be able to do their jobs, and the policy should not prevent users from doing so. However, in most cases, users do not need access to all Internet resources to do their jobs. The policy should define the access that users need to perform their jobs, but also define the access that users do not need.

3. Create clear and concise Internet usage policies. Based on the information gained from completing the first two steps, create policies that are plainly written and easily followed.

4. Determine how to enforce the Internet usage policy. In some cases, the policy can be enforced using technology solutions. For example, you may use ISA Server to enforce policies that identify the users who can access the Internet and the protocols that they can use. Using technology to enforce security policies helps prevent employees from unwittingly violating security policies. However, technology is not the only method of enforcement and may not be an option in some cases. You may be able to use ISA Server to enforce an Internet usage policy while the user is at the office, but will need to use another method to enforce the policy when the user is working on a company laptop to connect to the Internet from a hotel or from home.

5. Define the incentives for policy adherence and the consequences for policy violation. Create incentives for following or exceeding security policies. For example, consider making a portion of an employee's bonus contingent on following security polices. At the same time, ensure that the consequences of violating the policy are consistent with the severity of the violation and with your organization's culture. Ensure that managers are empowered to enforce the consequences of violating security policy.

6. Gather feedback from users, managers, and human resources and legal departments about proposed policies. To ensure that the policies are appropriate, enforceable, and do not violate employee rights, have management, human resources, and legal departments review and approve acceptable use policies. Involving the senior management in the development of the policy is essential for the implementation and enforcement of security policies. To ensure that the policies do not disrupt business processes, and to obtain backing from employees, gather feedback from users about proposed policies.

7. Revise policies based on feedback and create detailed procedures before implementing the policies. After incorporating the feedback from all stakeholders, work with human resources personnel to create and implement the policies. Whenever possible, write simple procedures that demonstrate how to comply with the policies.

8. Implement the policies. Distribute your security policies so that employees can refer to them easily. For example, give employees printed copies of policies or post the policies to convenient internal Web sites, and update the policies regularly.

See Also   There are many resources available to guide you in your policy development, including the SANS Institute Security Policy Project located at *http://www.sans.org/resources/policies*, and the Site Security Handbook located at *http://ietf.org/rfc/rfc2196.txt? number=2196*.

How ISA Server Enables Secure Access to Internet Resources

Now that you have developed the Internet usage policy, you are ready to implement that policy. Many of the restrictions that you have defined in the policy can be implemented using ISA Server to block access to specified resources.

ISA Server provides the following functionality to enable secure access:

- **Implementing ISA Server as a firewall**   ISA Server provides a complete firewall solution that enables multilayer filtering. As a firewall, ISA Server secures access to the Internet by ensuring that no unauthorized traffic can enter the internal network.

- **Implementing ISA Server as a proxy server**   When Firewall clients and Web Proxy clients connect to the ISA Server to gain access to Internet resources, ISA Server acts as a proxy server. ISA Server accepts the client request for Internet content, and then creates a new request that it sends to the Internet server. ISA Server hides the details of the internal network from the Internet. Only the ISA Server's external IP address is transmitted on the Internet.

- **Using ISA Server to implement the organization's Internet usage policy**   ISA Server can be used to implement many Internet-use restrictions. Table 5-1 lists some of the restrictions you can implement using ISA Server.

Table 5-1   ISA Server Internet Access Restrictions

Options for Restricting Access	Explanation
Restrictions based on users and groups	ISA Server can limit access to the Internet based on users and groups. These user or group accounts can be defined in Active Directory directory service or on the ISA Server computer.
Restrictions based on computers	ISA Server can limit access to specific computers, a group of computers, or all computers on a particular network. For example, you can set restrictions for Internet access from servers on the network, or for computers located in a public location.
Restrictions based on protocols	ISA Server can enable or disable access to the Internet based on the protocols used to access the Internet. For example, you can enable access only for HTTP or HTTPS and disable all other protocols. Or you can enable all protocols, and define the protocols that will not be allowed.

Table 5-1   ISA Server Internet Access Restrictions

Options for Restricting Access	Explanation
Restrictions based on Internet destinations	ISA Server can limit access based on Internet destinations. You can block or enable destinations based on domain names or Uniform Resource Locators (URLs).
Restrictions based on content being downloaded from the Internet	ISA Server can also scan all network packets coming from the Internet to ensure that users are not downloading inappropriate or dangerous content.

Lesson Review

Use the following questions to help determine whether you have learned enough to move on to the next lesson. If you have difficulty answering these questions, review the material in this lesson before beginning the next lesson. You can find answers to these questions in the "Questions and Answers" section at the end of this chapter.

1. What is the purpose of an Internet usage policy?

2. You are the network administrator for your organization. The organization is using a packet-filtering firewall with limited functionality to provide access to the Internet. The organization is planning an ISA Server 2004 implementation and wants to exploit some of its advanced filtering options to limit the access users have to the Internet. What should be the first step for implementing ISA Server 2004?

   a. Install ISA Server 2004.

   b. Design the access rules that will enable access to the Internet.

   c. Create an Internet usage policy that defines the organization's security requirements.

   d. Design a server publishing strategy.

3. How can an Internet usage policy be enforced by ISA Server 2004?

Lesson Summary

- Providing secure Internet access for users in an organization means that users can gain access to the resources they need, the connection to the Internet is secure, the data that users transfer to and from the Internet is secure, and users cannot download malicious programs from the Internet.

- Internet usage policies should explain the need for an Internet usage policy and describe what the policy addresses. It should also identify the people within the organization who are in charge of creating and maintaining the policy. Finally, an Internet usage policy should clearly define how violations of the policy will be handled.

- ISA Server can be used to provide secure Internet access for internal clients. ISA Server provides several options for enabling this secure access. These options include using ISA Server as a firewall, using ISA Server as a proxy server, and using ISA Server to implement the organization's Internet usage policy.

Lesson 2: Configuring ISA Server as a Proxy Server

One of the primary deployment scenarios for ISA Server 2004 is as a proxy server that enables secure access to Internet resources. ISA Server operates as a proxy server for both Web proxy and Firewall clients. This lesson provides an overview of how a proxy server works and how to configure ISA Server 2004 to operate as a proxy server. The lesson also considers two specialized configurations that you might use in an Internet access scenario: configuring multiple ISA Servers in a Web chain, and configuring ISA Server to use a dial-up connection for Internet access.

After this lesson, you will be able to

- Describe how a proxy server works
- Configure ISA Server 2004 as a proxy server
- Configure Web chaining
- Configure dial-up connections

Estimated lesson time: 30 minutes

What Is a Proxy Server?

A proxy server is a server that is situated between a client application, such as a Web browser or a Winsock application, and a server to which the client connects. All client requests are sent to the proxy server. The proxy server creates a new request and sends the request to the specified server. The server response is sent back to the proxy server, which then replies to the client application. A proxy server can provide enhanced security and performance for Internet connections.

The most important reason for using a proxy server is to make the user's connection to the Internet more secure. Proxy servers make the Internet connection more secure in the following ways:

- **User authentication**   When a user requests a connection to an Internet resource, the proxy server can require that the user authenticate, either by forcing the user to enter a user name and password or by using the cached credentials stored on the client computer. The proxy server can then grant or deny access to the Internet resource, based on the authenticated user.

- **Filtering client requests**   The proxy server can use multiple criteria to filter client requests. In addition to filtering the request based on the user making the request, the proxy server can filter requests based on the IP address, the protocol or application that is being used to access the Internet, the time of day, and the Web site the user requests.

- **Content inspection** Proxy servers can inspect all traffic to and from the Internet connection and determine if there is any traffic that should be denied. This may include examining the traffic content for inappropriate words, scanning for viruses, or scanning for file extensions.

- **Logging user access** Because all traffic flows through the proxy server, the server can log whatever the user does. For HTTP requests, this can include logging every URL visited by each user. The proxy server can be configured to provide detailed reports of user activity that can be used to ensure compliance with the organization's Internet usage policies.

- **Hiding the internal network details** Because all requests for Internet resources come from the proxy server rather than from the internal client computer, the details of the internal network are hidden from the Internet. In almost all cases, no client computer information, such as computer name or IP address, is sent to the Internet resource. In some cases, such as when creating a Remote Desktop Protocol connection to a server on the Internet, the client computer name is transmitted on the Internet.

Another benefit of using a proxy server is to improve Internet access performance. The Web proxy server improves performance by caching requested Internet pages on the Web proxy server's hard disk. When another user requests the same information, the proxy server provides the page from the cache rather than retrieving it from the Internet.

> **Note** For more information about configuring proxy server caching on ISA Server, see Chapter 6, "Implementing ISA Server Caching."

How Proxy Servers Work

Proxy servers can be used to secure both inbound and outbound Internet access. When a proxy server is used to secure outbound Internet access, it is configured as a forwarding proxy server. When a proxy server is used to secure inbound Internet access, it is configured as a reverse proxy server.

How Does a Forward Proxy Server Work?

Forward proxy servers are usually located between a Web or Winsock application running on a client computer on the internal network and an application server located on the Internet. The proxy server may be running at the connection point between the Internet and the internal network. In this case, the client computers may have no physical connection to the Internet other than through the proxy server. In other cases, a firewall may be deployed between the Internet and the proxy server, but all client computers will still be configured to use the proxy server.

Note   As described in Chapter 4, "Installing and Managing ISA Server Clients," when you install Firewall Client software on a client computer, the Firewall Client intercepts all Winsock application calls and forwards them to the ISA Server computer if the destination server is on a remote network. When connecting to a proxy server, the Firewall Client acts just like any other Winsock application. The only difference is that the Firewall Client can handle all connections from all Winsock applications, so you do not need to modify the application to use the proxy server.

Figure 5-1 illustrates how a forward proxy server works.

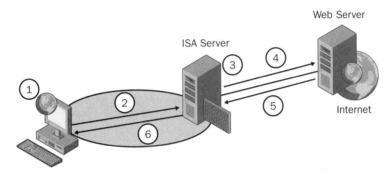

Figure 5-1   How a forward proxy server works

The following steps outline how a forward Web Proxy server works for a Web application:

1. A client application, such as a Web browser, makes a request for an object located on a Web server. The client application checks its Web proxy configuration to determine whether the request destination is on the local network or on an external network.

2. If the requested Web server is not on the local network, the request is sent to the proxy server.

3. The proxy server checks the request to confirm that there is no policy in place that blocks access to the requested content.

4. If caching is enabled, the proxy server also checks if the requested object exists in its local cache. If the object is stored in the local cache and it is current, the proxy server sends the object to the client from the cache. If the page is not in the cache or if the page is out of date, the proxy server sends the request to the appropriate server on the Internet.

5. The Web server response is sent back to the proxy server. The proxy server filters the response based on the filtering rules configured on the server.

6. If the content is not blocked and it is cacheable, ISA Server saves a copy of the content in its cache and the object is then returned to the client application that made the original request.

> **Important** When the proxy server accepts a request from the client application, it does not just forward the client request to the destination server. Instead, it creates a completely new request. When the destination server responds to the proxy server, the proxy server responds to the original client request. Because the request to the destination server comes from the proxy server, and not the original client, client configuration information is not sent to the Internet.

How Does a Reverse Web Proxy Server Work?

A reverse Web proxy server operates in much the same way as a forward Web proxy server. However, instead of making Internet resources accessible to internal clients, reverse proxy makes internal resources accessible to external clients.

Figure 5-2 illustrates how a reverse proxy server works.

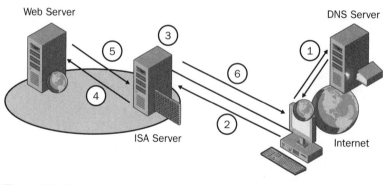

Figure 5-2 How a reverse proxy server works

The following steps outline how a reverse Web proxy server works:

1. A user on the Internet makes a request for an object located on a Web server that is on an internal network protected by a reverse proxy server. The client computer performs a DNS lookup using the fully qualified domain name (FQDN) of the hosting server. The DNS name will resolve to the IP address of the external network interface on the proxy server.

2. The client application sends the request for the object to the external address of the proxy server.

3. The proxy server checks the request to confirm that the URL is valid and to ensure that there is a policy in place that allows access to the requested content.

4. The proxy server also checks whether the requested object already exists in its local cache. If the object is stored in the local cache and it is current, the proxy server sends the object to the client from the cache. If the object is not in the cache, the proxy server sends the request to the appropriate server on the internal network.

5. The Web server response is sent back to the proxy server.

6. The object is returned to the client application that made the original request.

> **Note**   Before ISA Server 2004 will operate as a reverse proxy server, you must configure Web publishing rules. Web publishing is discussed in detail in Chapter 8, "Implementing ISA Server Publishing."

How to Configure ISA Server as a Proxy Server

You can deploy ISA Server 2004 as a Web proxy and a Winsock proxy server. In fact, as soon as you enable access to Internet resources for internal clients, ISA Server begins to operate as a Web proxy server. However, there are also several Web proxy server settings that you can modify on ISA Server.

You can configure several Web proxy settings on ISA Server. To do so, perform the following procedure:

1. In the Microsoft ISA Server Management Console tree, expand the Configuration node and select Networks.

2. Click the network whose Web access properties you want to configure. If you are configuring access to the Internet for internal clients, select the Internal network. Click Edit Selected Network.

3. Click the Web Proxy tab to configure the Web Proxy settings for ISA Server. The interface is shown in Figure 5-3. First, ensure that Enable Web Proxy Clients is selected. This is selected by default.

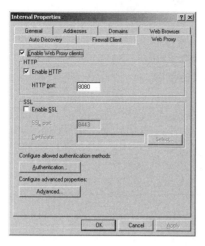

Figure 5-3   Configuring ISA Server as a proxy server

On the Web Proxy tab, you can choose to enable or disable HTTP connections on the specified port number. You can also enable or disable Secure Sockets Layer (SSL) connections. If you select this option, ISA Server will listen for HTTPS connections on the port specified. If you enable SSL, you must also configure a certificate that will be used for SSL authentication and encryption. Web browsers cannot use this setting for Internet access, but it can be used for Web chaining scenarios.

4. To configure the Advanced Settings, click Advanced. The interface is shown in Figure 5-4. On this tab, you can configure the number of connections, which will limit the number of users that can connect to the ISA Server at one time. You can also specify a connection timeout value, which sets a timeout limit for idle connections.

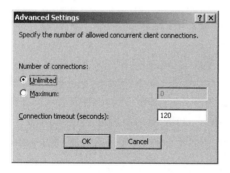

Figure 5-4   Configuring advanced proxy server settings

Exam Tip   Notice that one of the advanced configuration options limits the number of connections that the ISA Server computer will accept. If you get an exam question that includes information about the number of users, and some of those users cannot connect, check to see if you are given any information about this setting. However, by default, ISA Server is configured to accept an unlimited number of connections, so if you are not given any information about the number of connections allowed, assume that this setting is not the problem.

5. To configure ISA Server as a Winsock proxy server, you must configure the Internal network properties so that Firewall clients are supported. To configure this, click the Firewall Client tab on the Internal network properties and ensure that Enable Firewall Client Support For This Network is selected. The configuration options for Firewall Clients were discussed in Chapter 4.

Note   Configuring authentication for Internet access requests will be discussed later in this chapter in Lesson 4, "Configuring ISA Server Authentication."

How to Configure Web and Firewall Chaining

ISA Server 2004 Standard Edition supports the chaining of multiple servers running ISA Server together to provide flexible Web proxy services. These servers can be chained in a hierarchical manner so that one ISA Server computer routes Internet requests to another ISA Server computer, rather than routing the request directly to the Internet. ISA Server also supports Firewall chaining to allow requests from SecureNAT and Firewall clients to be forwarded to another ISA Server computer.

Tip   With ISA Server Standard Edition, you can use Web chaining to define how Web requests will be routed to the Internet from one ISA Server computer to another. However, each individual ISA Server still has to be configured, and the ISA Servers have no way of sharing the Web cache across multiple computers. The advantage of deploying ISA Server Enterprise Edition is that you can configure arrays so that groups of ISA Servers can be managed by one set of policies, and so that the ISA Servers can distribute the Web cache across multiple computers.

Why Use Web Chaining?

Web chaining is useful if your organization has multiple branch office locations, but all Internet requests are routed through one location at the head office. In this scenario, you can install ISA Server in each office and then configure ISA Server at the branch offices to route all Internet requests to the server running ISA Server at the head office. Figure 5-5 shows an example of this configuration.

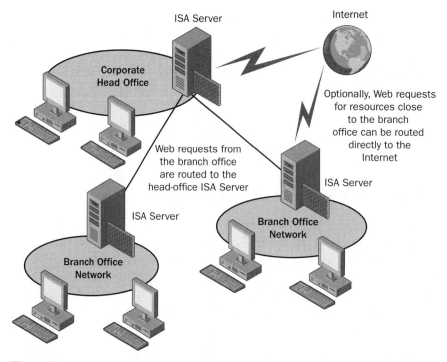

Figure 5-5   Configuring Web Proxy chaining in a branch office

> **Note**   In this configuration, the ISA Server computers at the branch offices are identified as downstream servers, while the ISA Server computer at the head office is the upstream server. Think of it as having to swim upstream to access the Internet.

You can also configure Web chaining so that not all Web requests are sent to the upstream server. For example, you can configure rules for conditionally routing Internet requests, depending on the destination Web server. This is useful if the head office and the branch offices are in different countries. If one of the branch offices has a direct Internet connection and many of the Web sites used by users in that branch office are in the same country as the branch office, you may choose to have the branch office ISA Server computer route all requests for specific domain names directly to the Internet. You can still have the branch office server route all other requests to the head-office ISA server.

One of the benefits of using Web chaining is the accumulated caching on ISA Server. If all the servers running ISA Server in the branch offices are configured to forward their requests to the head-office ISA Server, the head-office ISA Server will develop a large cache that contains many requested items. The combination of caching at the local branch office and at head office increases the chances that the Internet content can be delivered to the client with the least use of network bandwidth.

Tip   Another scenario in which Web chaining is useful is for configuring a test lab. Many organizations run a test lab that needs to be isolated from the production environment but may also need access to the Internet. By configuring ISA Server at the edge of the test lab network, and configuring it to forward all Internet requests to the production ISA Server, you can accomplish both goals.

Configuring Web Chaining Rules

To configure Web chaining rules, use the following procedure:

1. In the Microsoft ISA Server Management Console tree, expand the Configuration node, select Networks, and then click the Web Chaining tab.

Note   Notice the Web chaining rule named Last Default that was created when ISA Server was installed. This rule specifies that the ISA Server will route all requests directly to all networks. In other words, it will not use Web chaining unless you create a new rule.

2. To create a new Web chaining rule, on the Tasks tab, click Create New Web Chaining Rule.

3. On the Welcome To The New Web Chaining Rule Wizard page, in the Web Chaining Rule Name box, type a name for the Web chaining rule. Click Next.

4. On the Web Chaining Rule Destination page, as shown in Figure 5-6, click Add to specify the destinations that will be affected by this rule.

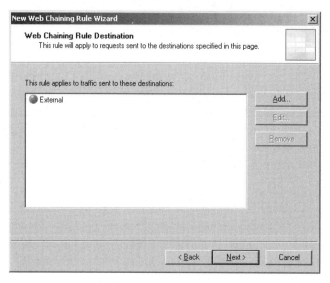

Figure 5-6   Configuring the Web chaining destination rules

5. In the Add Network Entities dialog box, select the destinations that this rule will apply to. For example, if the rule should apply to all Internet requests, expand Networks, then click External. Click Close.

6. On the Web Chaining Rule Destination page, click Next.

7. On the Request Action page, shown in Figure 5-7, select how the request should be processed. You have three options:

   ❑ *Retrieve Requests Directly From The Specified Destination*—In this case, the Web request is routed directly to the Internet.

   ❑ *Redirect Requests To A Specified Upstream Server*—In this case, the Web request is routed to the server that you specify.

   ❑ *Redirect Requests To*—In this case, the request is routed to the specified Web site.

Note   When configuring Web chaining, you can also configure chained authentication by selecting Allow Delegation Of Basic Authentication Credentials. By default, if both the downstream and upstream proxy servers require authentication, users with Web Proxy clients will be prompted for credentials by both ISA Server computers. If you use basic authentication for user authentication, you can configure the downstream server to pass the credentials to the upstream server by enabling basic authentication delegation.

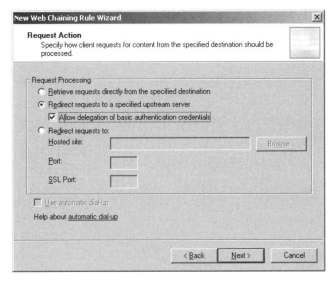

Figure 5-7   Configuring the Web chaining action

To configure Web chaining, select Redirect Requests To A Specified Upstream Server and then click Next.

8. On the Primary Routing page, shown in Figure 5-8, in the Server box, type the name of the server to which this server will send the requests. You can also specify the port numbers for HTTP and SSL and configure an account that will be used to authenticate at the upstream ISA Server. Click Next.

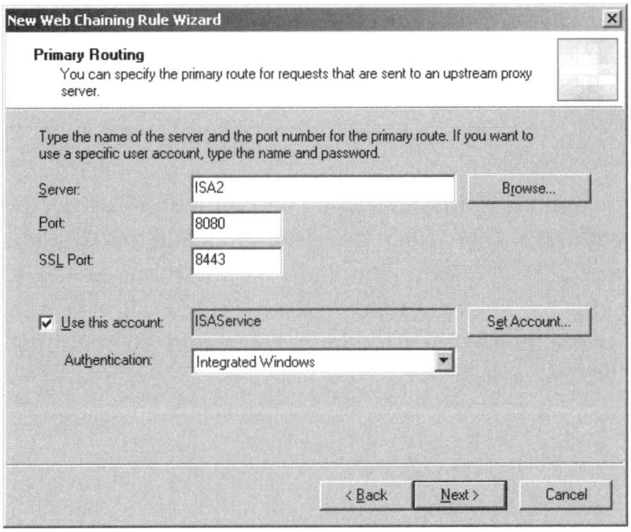

Figure 5-8   Configuring the primary Web chaining route

9. On the Backup Action page shown in Figure 5-9, configure what ISA Server should do if the upstream ISA Server is unavailable. You have three choices:

❑ *Ignore Requests*—In this case, ISA Server will not respond to client requests.

❑ *Retrieve Requests Directly From The Specified Destination*—In this case, ISA Server will route the request to the Internet.

❑ *Route Requests To An Upstream Server*—In this case, you can specify an alternative upstream server.

Select the option you require and then click Next.

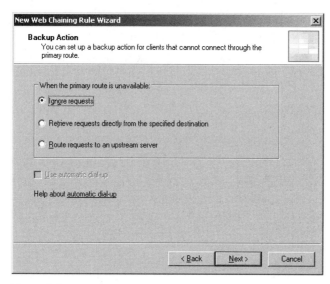

Figure 5-9   Configuring the backup action for Web chaining

10. On the Completing The New Web Chaining Rule Wizard page, review the configuration and then click Finish.

11. After creating the Web Chaining rule, you can configure how the ISA Server computer will bridge HTTP and HTTPS requests when using the Web chaining rule. To configure bridging, click the Web chaining rule and then, on the Tasks tab, click Define SSL Bridging For Selected Rule. The interface is shown in Figure 5-10. On this page, you can configure how to redirect HTTP and SSL requests when sending the requests to the upstream server.

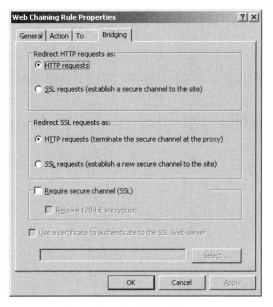

Figure 5-10   Configuring SSL bridging for a Web chaining rule

How to Configure Firewall Chaining

ISA Server 2004 also supports firewall chaining for SecureNAT and Firewall clients. To enable firewall chaining, use the following procedure:

1. In the Microsoft ISA Server Management Console tree, expand the Configuration node, and then click Configure Firewall Chaining.

2. On the Firewall Chaining dialog box shown in Figure 5-11, you can configure the firewall chaining. If you select Use The Primary Connection, ISA Server will try to route client requests directly to the Internet. If you select Chain To This Computer, you can specify the upstream server to which the firewall requests will be sent. If the upstream ISA Server server requires authentication, you must configure a user account that the downstream server will use to authenticate to the upstream server.

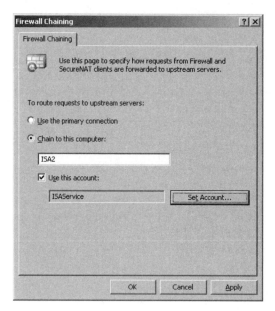

Figure 5-11   Configuring firewall chaining

How to Configure Dial-Up Connections

ISA Server 2004 also supports the use of a dial-up connection to another network. For example, if you do not have a dedicated Internet connection that is always available, you can configure a dial-up connection so that when a user makes a request for a resource on the Internet, the ISA Server computer can dial an Internet connection automatically. You can also configure the dial-up connection as a backup route, so that the dial-up connection is used only if the primary Internet connection is not available. In a Web chaining scenario, either the primary or backup route can be a dial-up connection.

How to Configure Dial-Up Connections

To configure an automatic dial-up connection, use the following procedure:

1. In the Microsoft ISA Server Management Console tree, expand the Configuration node and select General.

2. In the details pane, select Specify Dial-Up Preferences. The Dialing Configuration dialog box is shown in Figure 5-12.

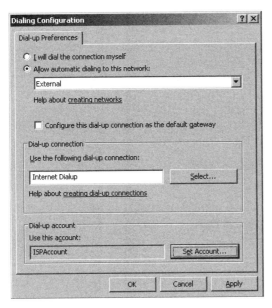

Figure 5-12   Configuring dial-up preferences

Note   Before you can configure ISA Server to use a dial-up connection, you need to config-ure the dial-up connection using the Network Connections Control Panel. You can then config-ure ISA Server to dial the connection automatically as required.

Table 5-2 describes dial-up configuration settings.

Table 5-2   Configuring Dial-Up Preferences

Choose This Setting	To Do This
Allow Automatic Dialing To This Network	Configure ISA Server to use the dial-up connection automatically for connecting to the specified network.
Configure This Dial-Up Connection To Be The Default Gateway	Configure this connection as the primary way to connect to the Internet. If you choose this option, all ISA Server traffic intended for the external network is sent on the connection.
Use The Following Dial-Up Connection	Specify the name of the dial-up connection.
Use This Account	Specify the name and password used to authenticate the dial-up connection. Normally, this is a dial-up account assigned by an Internet service provider (ISP).

After you configure the dial-up connection, you can specify this connection when configuring Web chaining rules.

Practice: Configuring ISA Server as a Proxy Server

In this practice, you will modify the default Web proxy server settings on ISA Server. You will also configure a new Web chaining rule.

Exercise 1: Configuring ISA Server Proxy Server Settings

1. In the Microsoft ISA Server Management Console tree, expand ISA1, then expand the Configuration node and select Networks.

2. On the Networks tab, click the Internal network. On the Tasks pane, click Edit Selected Network.

3. On the Web Proxy tab, ensure that Enable Web Proxy Clients and Enable HTTP are selected. Ensure that the HTTP port is 8080.

4. To configure the advanced options, click Advanced.

5. In the Advanced Settings dialog box, under Number Of Connections, click Maximum. In the Maximum text box, type **10**.

6. Click OK to close the Advanced Settings dialog box. Click OK to close the Internal Properties dialog box.

7. Click Apply to apply the changes.

Exercise 2: Configuring Web Chaining

1. In the ISA Server Management Console tree, expand the Configuration node, select Networks, and then click the Web Chaining tab.

> **Note** In this exercise, you will complete the configuration of a new Web chaining rule, and then discard the changes you make to the ISA Server configuration. One of the new features in ISA Server 2004 is that no changes are applied to the configuration until you commit the changes.

2. To create a new Web chaining rule, on the Tasks tab, click Create New Web Chaining Rule.

3. On the Welcome To The New Web Chaining Rule Wizard page, in the Web Chaining Rule Name box, type a name for the Web chaining rule. Click Next.

4. On the Web Chaining Rule Destination page, click Add to specify the destinations that will be affected by this rule.

5. In the Add Network Entities dialog box, expand Networks, click External, and then click Add. Click Close.

6. On the Web Chaining Rule Destination page, click Next.

7. On the Request Action page, select Redirect Requests To A Specified Upstream Server and click Next.

8. On the Primary Routing page, in the Server box, type **ISA2** as the name of the server to which this server will send the requests. Accept the default port numbers for HTTP and SSL. Click Next.

9. On the Backup Action page, click Retrieve Requests Directly From The Specified Destination.

10. On the Completing The New Web Chaining Rule Wizard page, review the configuration and click Finish.

11. Click Discard to discard the changes you made. Click Yes in the Microsoft ISA Server dialog box.

Lesson Review

Use the following questions to help determine whether you have learned enough to move on to the next lesson. If you have difficulty answering these questions, review the material in this lesson before beginning the next lesson. You can find answers to these questions in the "Questions and Answers" section at the end of this chapter.

1. Your organization has a high-speed Internet connection as your main method of access to the Internet. You also have a dial-up account with your ISP to provide a backup route. How should you configure ISA Server to use the dial-up connection in case the primary route fails?

    a. Configure the Dial-Up Preferences to specify the dial-up connection as the backup route.

    b. Create a network for the dial-up connection and designate it as the backup route.

    c. Configure a Web Chaining rule to specify the dial-up connection as the backup route.

    d. Modify the Web Browser properties of the Internal network to designate the dial-up connection as the alternate route.

2. All the Web browser applications in your organization are configured to be Web Proxy clients. You are the network administrator and you have received reports that some employees are viewing and downloading information from inappropriate Web sites. How could you identify the employees responsible and prevent further infractions?

3. Your company has seven branch offices that have no direct Internet connection. All Internet requests are routed to the ISA Server at the head office over a 128-kilo-byte-per-second (Kbps) Integrated Services Digital Network (ISDN) link. The ISDN link is heavily used during business hours. What can you do to minimize the bandwidth usage for Internet requests?

_____

_____

_____

Lesson Summary

- A proxy server is a server that is situated between a client application, such as a Web browser, and a server that the client is connecting to. Forward proxy servers accept requests for resources from clients on the internal network and forward the requests to servers located on the Internet. A reverse Web proxy server makes internal resources accessible to external clients.

- By default, ISA Server is configured to operate as a proxy server for Web proxy and Firewall client computers. You can modify the proxy server settings to enable or disable HTTP, enable or disable SSL, define the authentication method you wish to use and define the connection settings.

- ISA Server 2004 supports chaining multiple ISA Server computers together so that Internet requests are passed from one computer to another computer. You can use Web chaining when your organization has multiple branch office locations, but all Internet requests are routed through one location at the head office. One of the benefits of using Web chaining is the accumulated caching on ISA Server.

- ISA Server 2004 also supports the use of a dial-up connection to another network. If you do not have an Internet connection that is always available, ISA Server can automatically dial up when a user makes a request for a resource from the Internet.

Lesson 3: Configuring Access Rule Elements

By default, ISA Server 2004 denies all network traffic between networks connected to the ISA Server computer. Configuring an access rule is the only way to configure ISA Server so that it will allow traffic to flow between networks. An access rule defines the conditions for when traffic will be allowed or denied between networks.   ISA Server enables a great deal of flexibility when creating access rules. You can define the protocols allowed, which users can use those protocols, what resources users can access, and what time of day users can do all this. Each option is defined by creating access rule elements, and then combining the elements into access rules. This lesson describes the access rule elements that you can create in ISA Server 2004.

After this lesson, you will be able to

- Describe the access rule elements available in ISA Server 2004
- Configure access rule elements

Estimated lesson time: 30 minutes

What Are Access Rule Elements?

Access rule elements are configuration objects in ISA Server that you use to create access rules. For example, you may want to create an access rule that allows only HTTP traffic. To do this, ISA Server provides an HTTP protocol access rule element that you can use when creating the access rule. Or you may want to limit access to the Internet to certain users or computers. To enable this, you can create a subnet or user set access rule element, and then use this element in an access rule to limit access to the Internet to only computers on the specified subnet, or to only the specified users.

Access Rule Element Types

Table 5-3 describes the five types of access rule elements:

Table 5-3   Access Rule Element Types

Access Rule Element	Description
Protocols	This rule element defines protocols that you can use in an access rule. You can allow or deny access on one or more protocols.

Table 5-3 Access Rule Element Types

Access Rule Element	Description
User Sets	This rule element defines a group of one or more users to which a rule will be explicitly applied, or which can be excluded from a rule. For example, you may want to create a rule that enables Internet access to all users within an organization with the exception of all temporary staff. By using an Active Directory domain or Remote Authentication Dial-In User Service (RADIUS) server for authentication, you can configure an access rule that grants the Domain Users group access to the Internet, but denies access to the TempEmployees group.
Content Types	This rule element provides common content types to which you may want to apply a rule. For example, you can use a content type rule element to block all content downloads that include .exe or .vbs file extensions.
Schedules	This rule element allows you to designate hours of the week during which the rule applies. If you need to define an access rule that allows access to the Internet only during specified hours, you can create a schedule rule element that defines those hours, and then use this schedule rule element when creating the access rule.
Network Objects	This rule element allows you to create sets of computers to which a rule will apply, or which will be excluded from a rule. You can also configure URL sets and domain name sets that you can use to allow or deny access to specific URLs or domains.

How to Configure Access Rule Elements

ISA Server includes several default access rule elements. For example, ISA Server includes a large number of protocol elements that you can use when creating an access rule. However, in some cases, you must create new access rule elements or modify existing elements.

How to Configure Protocol Elements

In some cases, you may want to create an access rule that allows or denies access to the Internet, depending on which protocol the client uses. To do this, you can use one of the protocol elements provided with ISA Server or create your own protocol definition.

In almost all cases, the preconfigured protocols defined by the ISA Server configuration provide all the flexibility you need when configuring access rules. The protocols included with ISA Server cannot be deleted. You can modify which application filters are applied to the preconfigured protocols, but you cannot modify any other settings.

You can also create new protocols by using the ISA Server Management Console. For example, you may be using a custom application that requires a specific port. You can create a protocol element that uses this port number and then use the protocol in an access rule. User-defined protocols can be edited or deleted.

To create a protocol object, use the following procedure.

1. In the Microsoft ISA Server Management Console tree, click Firewall Policy.

2. On the Toolbox tab, click Protocols.

3. Click New, and then click Protocol or RPC Protocol. The New Protocol Definition Wizard starts. When you create a protocol, you specify settings listed in Table 5-4.

Table 5-4   Protocol Element Configuration Options

Options	Explanation
Protocol Type	This includes protocol types for Transmission Control Protocol (TCP), User Datagram Protocol (UDP), Internet Control Message Protocol (ICMP), or IP levels.
Direction	For UDP, this includes Send, Receive, Send Receive, or Receive Send. For TCP, this includes Inbound and Outbound. For ICMP and IP, this includes Send and Receive.
Port Range	For TCP and UDP protocols, this is a range of ports between 1 and 65535 that is used for the initial connection.
Protocol Number	For IP-level protocols, this is the protocol number.
ICMP Properties	For ICMP, this is the ICMP code and type.
Secondary Connections	This setting is optional; it is the range of ports, protocol types, and direction used for additional connections or packets that follow the initial connection. You can configure one or more secondary connections.

To modify an existing protocol definition, click the protocol in the Protocols box, and then click Edit.

How to Configure User Set Elements

The second criterion that you may want to apply to an access rule specifies which users will be allowed or denied access by the access rule. To limit access to Internet resources based on users or groups, you must create a user set element. When you limit an access rule to specific users, users must authenticate before they are granted access. For each group of users, you can define the type of authentication required. You can mix different types of authentication within a user set. For example, a user set might include a Windows user or group based on domain membership, a user from a RADIUS namespace, and another user from the SecurID namespace.

ISA Server is preconfigured with the following user sets:

- **All Authenticated Users** This set includes all users who have authenticated using any type of authentication. SecureNAT clients are not authenticated unless they connect through a virtual private network (VPN). This means that this group does not include non-VPN SecureNAT clients.

- **All Users** This set includes all users, both authenticated and unauthenticated. If you want to allow access for SecureNAT clients, you should use this user set.

- **System and Network Service** This user set includes the Local System service and the Network service on the computer running ISA Server. This user set is used in some system policy rules.

To create a new user set, use the following procedure:

1. In the Microsoft ISA Server Management Console tree, click Firewall Policy.

2. On the Toolbox tab, click Users.

3. Click New. On the Welcome To The New User Sets Wizard, in the User Set Name box, type the user set name. Click Next.

4. On the Users page, click Add, and then click the type of user that you are adding to the set. The interface is shown in Figure 5-13. There are three options:

   ❑ *Windows Users And Groups*—Use this option to add users and groups from a Windows domain or from the local accounts on the computer running ISA Server.

   ❑ *RADIUS*—Use this option to add specific users or all users from a specific RADIUS namespace.

   ❑ *SecurID*—Use this option to add specific users or all users from a specific SecurID namespace.

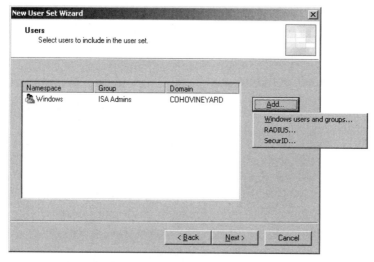

Figure 5-13   Configuring a user set

To modify an existing user set, click the user set in the Users box, and click Edit.

How to Configure Content Type Elements

You may also want to limit the types of content that users can access on the Internet. To do this, create a new content type element, or use one of the existing content type elements when you create an access rule. Content type elements define Multipurpose Internet Mail Extensions (MIME) types and file name extensions. When a client such as Microsoft Internet Explorer downloads information from the Internet using HTTP or File Transfer Protocol (FTP), the content is downloaded in either MIME format or as a file with a specified file name extension.

Content type elements apply only to HTTP and FTP traffic that is tunneled in an HTTP header. When a client requests HTTP content, ISA Server sends the request to the Web server. When the Web server returns the object, ISA Server checks the object's MIME type or its file name extension, depending on the header information returned by the Web server. ISA Server determines if a rule applies to a content type that includes the requested filename extension, and processes the rule accordingly. FTP traffic is tunneled in an HTTP header when a client is configured as a Web Proxy client. When a client requests FTP content, ISA Server checks the filename extension of the requested object. ISA Server determines if a content type that includes the file extension is linked to the access rule. If a content type applies, ISA Server applies the rule.

ISA Server is preconfigured with the following content types: Application, Application data files, Audio, Compressed files, Documents, Hypertext Markup Language (HTML) documents, Images, Macro documents, Text, Video, and Virtual Reality Modeling Language (VRML). In most cases, you need not configure additional content types, and can merely apply the existing types.

To create a new content type object, use the following procedure:

1. In the Microsoft ISA Server Management Console tree, click Firewall Policy.

2. On the Toolbox tab, click Content Types.

3. Click New.

4. In the New Content Type Set dialog box, shown in Figure 5-14, fill in the following information:

   ❏ *Name*—Type the content type set name.

   ❏ *Available Types*—Select the appropriate content types from the drop-down list. You can choose either MIME types or application extensions. Click Add.

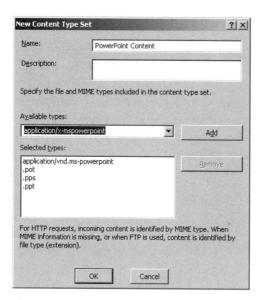

Figure 5-14   Configuring a content type set

> **Note**   When you configure a content type and specify the MIME type, you can use an aster-
> isk (*) as a wildcard character. For example, to include all application types, enter **applica-
> tion/***. The asterisk wildcard character can be used only with MIME types and not with file
> extensions. The asterisk can be specified only once, at the end of the MIME type after the
> slash mark (/).

To modify an existing content type set, click the content type set in the Content Types
box, and then click Edit.

How to Configure Schedule Elements

In some cases, you may also want to configure access to the Internet based on the time
of day. To do this, configure a schedule element and apply it or one of the existing
schedules to an access rule. Schedule elements define a schedule that you can use to
grant or deny Internet access as part of an access rule.

ISA Server 2004 is preconfigured with the following two schedules:

- **Weekends**   Defines a schedule that includes all times on Saturday and Sunday

- **Work Hours**   Defines a schedule that includes the hours between 09:00 (9:00 A.M.)
  and 17:00 (5:00 P.M.) on Monday through Friday

To create a new schedule element, use the following procedure.

1. In the Microsoft ISA Server Management Console tree, click Firewall Policy.

2. On the Toolbox tab, click Schedules.

3. Click New. In the New Schedule dialog box, as shown in Figure 5-15, fill in the following information:

   ❑ Type the content type set name in the Name box.

   ❑ Configure the schedule by selecting the times when the rule will be active or inactive and then clicking Active or Inactive.

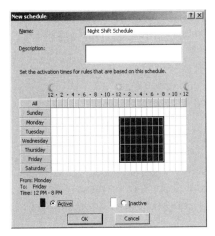

Figure 5-15   Configuring a new schedule

To modify an existing schedule element, click the schedule element in the Content Types box, and then click Edit.

How to Configure Network Objects

You may also want to define which Web sites or servers users can or cannot access. You can configure this by creating either a domain name set or a URL set and then applying these sets to an access rule. Moreover, you can create groups of computers that you can use when creating access rules. For example, you may want to allow access to specific Internet resources only to certain computers. You can create computer objects, computer sets, address ranges, or subnets to define groups of one or more computers, and then use these objects to allow or deny access to Internet resources. These computer objects can be used both as the source object and the destination object when defining access rules.

Table 5-5 describes the types of network objects available in ISA Server 2004 when creating access rules.

Table 5-5 Network Object Access Rule Elements

Network Object	Description	Examples
Networks	A network rule element represents a network, which is all the computers connected (directly or through one or more routers) to a single ISA Server computer network adapter.	Internal, External, Branch Office.
Network Sets	A network-set rule element represents a grouping of one or more networks. You can use this rule element to apply rules to more than one network.	All Protected Networks.
Computer	A computer rule element represents a single computer, identified by its IP address.	DC1 (IP Address: 192.168.1.10).
Address Ranges	An address range is a set of computers represented by a continuous range of IP addresses.	All DCs (IP Address Range: 192.168.1.10 – 192.168.1.20).
Subnets	A subnet represents a network subnet, specified by a network address and a mask.	Branch Office Network (IP Addresses 192.168.2.0/24).
Computer Sets	A computer set includes a collection of computers identified by their IP addresses, a subnet object, or an address-range object.	All DCs and Exchange Servers.
URL Sets	URL sets specify one or more URLs grouped together to form a set.	Microsoft Web Site (*http:// www.microsoft.com/**)
Domain Name Sets	Domain name sets define one or more domain names as a single set, so that you can apply access rules to the specified domains.	Microsoft Domain (*.microsoft.com) Microsoft Error Reporting Sites - A predefined domain name set used to allow error reporting. System Policy Allowed Sites - A predefined domain name set used to allow access to trusted sites for maintenance and management.

Note For more information about configuring networks and network sets, see Chapter 7, "Configuring ISA Server as a Firewall."

You can use any of these access rule elements when defining access rules. Note the following configuration restrictions:

- When specifying the domain name, you can use an asterisk (*) to specify a set of computers. For example, to specify all computers in the *cohovineyard.com* domain, type the domain name as ***.cohovineyard.com**. The asterisk can appear only at the start of the domain name, and can be specified only once in the name. You must use the FQDN when specifying a domain name.

- When you create a URL set, you can specify one or more URLs in URL format. For example, you specify a URL such as *http://www.cohovineyard.com*. You can also specify a path and use wildcard characters in the path, but only at the end. For example, *www.cohovineyard.com/** is acceptable. However, *www.cohovineyard.com/*/sales* is not.

Tip   ISA Server processes rules that apply to URL sets only for client requests for HTTP or FTP over HTTP. When a client uses any other protocol, ISA Server does not process rules that apply only to a URL set.

To create a new Network Object, use the following procedure:

1. In the Microsoft ISA Server Management Console tree, click Firewall Policy.

2. On the Toolbox tab, click Network Objects.

3. Click New, and then click the type of object that you want to create. All the network objects have a similar configuration interface. The configuration interface for creating a domain set is shown in Figure 5-16.

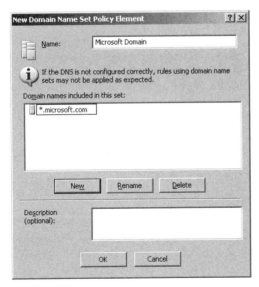

Figure 5-16   Configuring a domain set

To modify an existing network object, click the object in the Network Objects box, and then click Edit.

Practice: Configuring Access Rule Elements

In this practice, you will configure several access rule elements. You will be using these access rule elements in a later practice to create access rules to grant and deny access to Internet resources.

Exercise 1: Configuring a New User Set

1. In the Microsoft ISA Server Management Console tree, click Firewall Policy.

2. On the Toolbox tab, click Users.

3. Click New. On the Welcome To The New User Sets Wizard, in the User Set Name box, type **Managers**. Click Next.

4. On the Users page, click Add, and then click Windows Users And Groups.

5. In the Select Users And Groups dialog box, click Locations. In the Locations dialog box, expand Entire Directory, then click Cohovineyard.com and then click OK.

6. In the Select Users And Groups dialog box, in the Enter The Object Names To Select box, type **Managers**.

7. Click OK, and then click Next.

8. On the Completing The New User Set Wizard, review the configuration and click Finish.

Exercise 2: Configuring a New Content Type Element

1. On the Toolbox tab, click Content Types.

2. Click New.

3. In the New Content Type Set dialog box, in the Name box, type **Powerpoint Content Type**. In the Available Types drop-down list, click .ppt. Click Add. Repeat for the following available types: application/vnd.ms-powerpoint, application/x-mspowerpoint, .pot, .pps.

4. Click OK.

Exercise 3: Configuring a New Schedule Element

1. On the Toolbox tab, click Schedules.

2. Click New.

3. In the New Schedule dialog box, in the Name box, type **Night Shift Schedule**. Configure the Active time on the schedule to be from midnight to 8 A.M. every weekday.

4. Click OK.

> **Note**   In the following two exercises, you will create a URL set and a domain name set. To test the access rules that you will create later in this chapter, the Web sites listed in the URL set and domain name set must be accessible on the external network of the ISA Server computer. The following exercises assume that the Internet is accessible from the ISA Server computer. If you are using a test environment where the Internet is not accessible, configure the URL set and the domain set to use a Web address that is accessible from the ISA Server computer.

Exercise 4: Configuring a New URL Set

1. On the Toolbox tab, click Network Objects.

2. To create a new URL set, click New, and then click URL Set.

3. In the New URL Set Rule Element dialog box, in the Name box, type **Microsoft URL**. Click New and then, in the URLs Included In This URL Set box, type **http://www.microsoft.com/***.

4. Click OK.

Exercise 5: Configuring a New Domain Name Set

1. On the Toolbox tab, click Network Objects.

2. To create a new domain name set, click New, and then click Domain Name Set.

3. In the New Domain Set Policy Element dialog box, in the Name box, type **Microsoft Domain**. Click New and then, in the Domain Names Included In This Set box, type ***.microsoft.com**.

4. Click OK.

Exercise 6: Configuring a New Computer Set

1. On the Toolbox tab, click Network Objects.

2. Click New, and then click Computer.

3. In the New Computer Rule Element dialog box, in the Name box, type **DC1**. In the Computer IP Address box, type **10.10.1.10**.

4. Click OK.

5. Click Apply to apply all the changes made in this practice.

Lesson Review

Use the following questions to help determine whether you have learned enough to move on to the next lesson. If you have difficulty answering these questions, review the material in this lesson before beginning the next lesson. You can find answers to these questions in the "Questions and Answers" section at the end of this chapter.

1. Your organization has an Internet usage policy specifying that only managers and executives have unrestricted Internet access. All other employees are allowed Internet access during the lunch hour and after business hours with restrictions on the type of content that should be accessible. How can you enforce this policy?

   _____

   _____

   _____

2. Your organization has limited bandwidth available for Internet connections. The users who require Internet access to do their jobs are complaining about the speed of the connection. After reviewing the logs you discover that many employees are downloading large image libraries for their desktop wallpaper on a daily basis from a specific Web site. What can you do to prevent this?

   _____

   _____

   _____

3. Your organization has a single domain running Active Directory. Your organization has four branch offices, all of which use ISA Server 2004 as their Internet edge firewall and proxy server. All branch offices require the same access rules. Managers at the branch offices must be able to connect to a custom Web application at your head office using a specific TCP port. No other users should be able to access the application. How would you configure all the ISA Server 2004 servers in the most efficient manner?

   _____

   _____

   _____

Lesson Summary

- An access rule defines the conditions for when traffic will be allowed or denied between networks. An access rule element is one of the configuration options in an access rule. You use access rule elements to configure the access rule

- ISA Server 2004 supports the following access rule elements for enabling Internet access: protocol, user set, content type, schedule, and network objects. ISA Server provides several default access rule elements, but you can also create and configure new elements.

Lesson 4: Configuring ISA Server Authentication

Many organizations need to limit access to Internet resources based on users or groups. To configure access rules based on users, you must configure ISA Server to require authentication. You have several options when configuring authentication on ISA Server 2004.

> **After this lesson, you will be able to**
> - Describe the ISA Server authentication options
> - Choose the correct type of authentication based on the Internet client you are using
> - Configure authentication for Internet access
>
> **Estimated lesson time: 20 minutes**

ISA Server Authentication Options

You can configure which authentication method ISA Server will use to authenticate users that connect using Web Proxy clients. ISA Server supports the following authentication methods:

- **Basic authentication**   Basic authentication sends and receives user information as plaintext and does not use encryption. Basic authentication is the least secure authentication method that ISA Server supports. However, because basic authentication is part of the HTTP specification, most browsers support it.

- **Digest authentication**   Digest authentication passes authentication credentials through a process called hashing. Hashing creates a string of characters based on the password but does not send the actual password across the network, ensuring that no one can capture a network packet containing the password and impersonate the user. Digest authentication currently works only in a domain in which all the domain controllers are running Microsoft Windows 2000 or Windows Server 2003 and client computers are running Internet Explorer 5 or later. Digest authentication also works only if the domain controller has a reversibly encrypted copy of the requesting user's password stored in Active Directory. This is not the default configuration, and so you must enable this. Storing a password in reversible encryption is significantly less secure than the Active Directory default, in which the password is stored in a one-way hash.

Note   ISA Server 2004 also supports a new version of Digest authentication named WDigest authentication. WDigest does not require that passwords be stored in reversible encryption. WDigest is supported only for ISA Server computers running on Windows Server 2003. When both ISA Server and the domain controllers are running Windows Server 2003, the default authentication is WDigest. This means that when you select Digest authentication in a Windows Server 2003 environment, you are actually selecting WDigest.

- **Integrated Windows authentication** Uses either the Kerberos version 5 authentication protocol or NTLM protocol, both of which do not send the user name and password across the network. Integrated Windows authentication works with Internet Explorer 2.0 or later. Use Integrated Windows authentication when all the client computers use Internet Explorer. Integrated Windows authentication is the default authentication method used by members of the Windows 2000 Server and Windows Server 2003 families.

- **Digital certificates authentication** Requests a client certificate from the client before allowing the request to be processed. Users obtain client certificates from a certification authority that can be internal to your organization or a trusted external organization. Client certificates usually contain identifying information about the user and the organization that issued the client certificate. Client certificates are more commonly used to authenticate Internet users rather than internal users trying to access the Internet. Web Proxy clients do not support client certificate authentication.

- **Remote Authentication Dial-In User Service** RADIUS is an industry-standard authentication protocol. A RADIUS client (typically a dial-up server, VPN server, or wireless access point) sends user credentials and connection parameter information in the form of a RADIUS message to a RADIUS server. The RADIUS server authenticates the RADIUS client request, and sends back a RADIUS message response. RADIUS authentication is more frequently used to provide authentication for accessing resources on the internal network from the Internet.

ISA Server Clients and Authentication

The ISA Server authentication that you choose depends on the type of ISA Server client you have deployed in your organization.

SecureNAT Clients For SecureNAT clients, there is no user-based authentication. You can restrict access to the Internet based only on network rules and other access rules. If an access rule requires authentication, SecureNAT clients will be blocked from accessing the resources defined by the rule.

> **Exam Tip** Keep this SecureNAT client restriction in mind when you write the exam. Any access rule that requires authentication, or any requirement that states that you must limit access based on users or groups, cannot be applied to SecureNAT clients.

Firewall Clients When ISA Server authenticates a Firewall client, it uses the credentials of the user making the request on the computer running the Firewall client. Because ISA Server requests credentials when a session is established, no client configuration is required to enable authentication of users who gain access to ISA Server by using a Firewall client. When the Firewall client requests an object, ISA Server does not ask the client to authenticate, because the session already has an identity.

Web Proxy Clients   Web Proxy clients do not automatically send authentication information to the ISA Server computer. By default, ISA Server requests credentials from a Web Proxy client only when processing a rule that restricts access based on a user set element. You can configure which method the client and ISA Server use for authentication.

You can also configure ISA Server to require authentication for all Web requests. When a Web Proxy client requests HTTP content and all users are required to authenticate, ISA Server will always ask for user credentials before checking the firewall policy. Otherwise, ISA Server will try to determine if the first rule (of the ordered firewall policy) matches the client request. If the rule seems to match, but ISA Server requires client authentication to validate the match, ISA Server will request that the client authenticate.

Otherwise, if the rule applies to the All Users user set, or the rule applies to the IP address of the specific client, ISA Server will not request user credentials and will try to apply the firewall policy.

Real World   What Type of Authentication Should You Use?

By default, ISA Server 2004 enables only Integrated authentication for Internet access authentication. Most organizations never need to change that setting. Integrated authentication is the most secure and the most flexible authentication option available, with two very important restrictions.

The first restriction is that all your clients must be using Internet Explorer. All versions of Internet Explorer currently in use support Integrated authentication but no other Web browsers support it.

The second important restriction is that the ISA Server computer must be a member of the internal domain to use Integrated authentication. As discussed in the last chapter, this is often a controversial decision, but the easiest way to enable authentication for Internet access is to use an ISA Server computer that is a member of the same domain, or in a trusting domain. If the ISA Server computer is a member of the internal domain, you can use the domain users and groups to define user sets to limit access.

So if you are using Internet Explorer as your Web browser, and your ISA Server computer is a member of your internal domain, then just leave the default configuration. If you are not using Internet Explorer as your Web browser, then your most feasible options are to use Basic authentication or Digest authentication. Basic authentication is supported by virtually all Web browsers, so implementing Basic authentication is a matter of enabling the option on ISA Server. However, Basic authentication is not secure, because all user logon traffic is passed in clear text. Digest authentication is supported by most recent Web browsers and it does not pass the user name in clear text, but storing user passwords in reversible encryption is not secure either.

> If your organization is using a Web browser other than Internet Explorer, you might want to consider deploying the Firewall Client to all client computers. When a Firewall client connects to the ISA Server computer, the user is authenticated using the encrypted control channel. Then you can use any browser to access Internet resources without requiring additional authentication.

Exam Tip   It is always a good idea to keep the default setting for any configuration item in mind when writing the exam. For example, the fact that the default authentication method for Internet access is Integrated authentication means that, by default, only Internet Explorer Web browsers can be used if authentication is required.

How to Configure Authentication

When access rules that apply to Web Proxy clients are configured to apply to users (and not to IP addresses), at least one authentication mechanism must be specified so that the users making the requests can be authenticated. If no authentication mechanism is specified, then all requests will be denied.

To configure authentication for Internet requests, complete the following steps:

1. In the Microsoft ISA Server Management Console tree, expand the Configuration node and select Networks.

2. On the Networks tab, click Internal. Click Edit Selected Network.

3. Click the Web Proxy tab, and then click Authentication to access the Authentication dialog box, shown in Figure 5-17. The configuration options are described in Table 5-6.

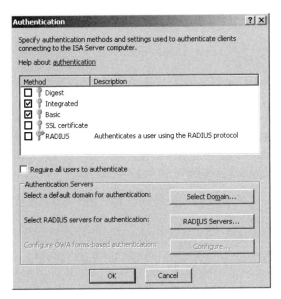

Figure 5-17   Configuring authentication for Internet requests

Table 5-6   Authentication Configuration Options

Configuration Option	Explanation
Authentication Method	Configure the method or methods of authentication supported by the ISA Server computer.
Require All Users To Authenticate	Configure ISA Server to allow only authenticated users to access other networks. If you choose this option, SecureNAT clients will not be able to access the Internet using this ISA Server.
Authentication Domain	Configure the default domain that will be used for authentication when using Basic, Digest, or RADIUS authentication.
RADIUS Servers	Configure the RADIUS server that will be used for authentication.

Practice: Configuring ISA Server Authentication

1. In the Microsoft ISA Server Management Console tree, expand the Configuration node and select Networks.

2. On the Networks tab, click Internal. Click Edit Selected Network.

3. Click the Web Proxy tab, and then click Authentication.

4. Select the check box beside Require All Users To Authenticate.

5. Click Basic. Click OK to accept the warning message.

6. Click Select Domain. In the Select Domain dialog box, in the Domain Name text box, type **cohovineyard.com**. Click OK.

7. Click OK to close the Authentication dialog box, and then click OK to close the Internal Properties dialog box.

8. Click Apply to apply the changes.

Lesson Review

Use the following questions to help determine whether you have learned enough to move on to the next lesson. If you have difficulty answering these questions, review the material in this lesson before beginning the next lesson. You can find answers to these questions in the "Questions and Answers" section at the end of this chapter.

1. Your organization has a mixture of Windows 2000 and Windows 2003 domain controllers. You have deployed ISA Server 2004 as your firewall solution. Your Internet usage policy states that all users accessing the Internet will be authenticated using Digest authentication. You have configured the properties of the Internal network to require Digest authentication. Now none of your users can access the Internet. How can you correct this problem?

   _____

   _____

   _____

2. All the clients in your organization are configured as SecureNAT clients. You have created content type elements to prevent users from downloading executables, MP3 and video file types. You use those elements in an access rule and assign it to the All Authenticated Users group. After applying the access rule, you discover that all your clients still have unrestricted access to download the content types. Why can users still download the content types that you are trying to block? What should you do to prevent this?

   _____

   _____

   _____

3. Your organization has a multiple-domain forest running Active Directory. You support various browser applications including Internet Explorer and Netscape Navigator. All browsing software is configured to use an ISA Server computer as a proxy server. You have configured access rules to allow HTTP and HTTPS traffic for all internal clients, but have not changed any other settings on the ISA Server. Some of your users have Internet access while others are always denied connections. How can you resolve this problem?

_____

_____

_____

Lesson Summary

■   ISA Server supports five authentication methods for restricting Internet access: Basic authentication, Digest authentication, Integrated Windows authentication, Digital Certificates authentication, and RADIUS authentication.

■   SecureNAT clients do not support user-based authentication. You can only restrict access to the Internet based on network rules and other access rules. Firewall client authentication is performed when the client connects to the ISA Server computer. Web Proxy clients do not automatically send authentication information to ISA Server. ISA Server requests credentials from a Web Proxy client to identify a user only when processing a rule that restricts access based on a user element.

■   If you want to restrict access to the Internet based on users and groups, you must configure ISA Server authentication to meet your organization's needs.

Lesson 5: Configuring Access Rules for Internet Access

Now that you understand how to configure the access rule elements and how to configure authentication, you are ready to put the elements together to create access rules to enable Internet access. Access rules are used to configure all network traffic on ISA Server. Access rules define whether clients on the source network will be able to access resources on the destination network. This lesson describes how to implement access rules.

After this lesson, you will be able to

- Describe what access rules are
- Configure access rules that enable Internet access

Estimated lesson time: 30 minutes

What Are Access Rules?

Access rules are used to configure all traffic flowing through ISA Server, including all traffic from the internal network to the Internet, and from the Internet to the internal network. An access rule is graphically represented in Figure 5-18.

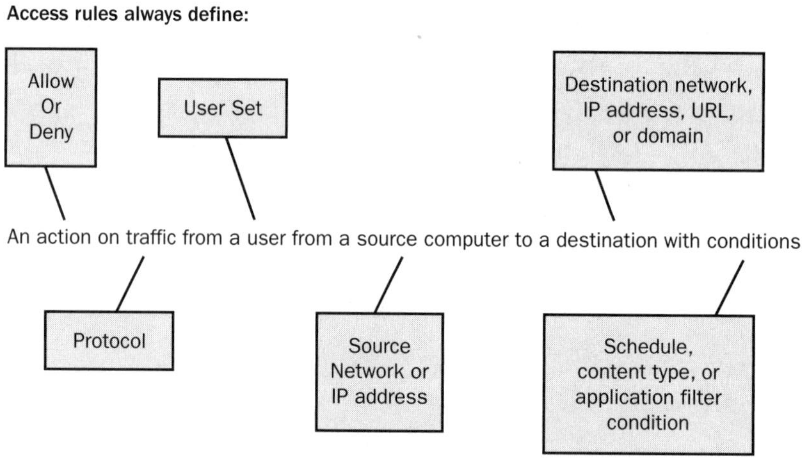

Access rules always define:

Figure 5-18 All access rules have the same structure.

All access rules have the same overall structure, as described in Table 5-7.

Table 5-7   Access Rule Format

Access Rules Define	Explanation
An action	Access rules are always configured to either allow or deny access.
To be performed on specified traffic	Access rules can be applied to all protocols, to specified protocols, or to all protocols except specified protocols.
From a particular user	Access rules can be applied to specific users or all users, whether they have authenticated or not.
Coming from a particular computer	Access rules can be applied to computers based on their network locations or IP addresses.
Going to a particular destination	Access rules can be applied to specific destinations, including networks, destination IP addresses, and domain names or URLs.
Based on particular conditions	Access rules can set additional conditions, including schedules, content-type filtering, or application layer filtering

How to Configure Access Rules

To enable access for internal clients to access the Internet, you must configure an access rule that grants this type of access. You can configure the access rule using the access rule elements.

Configuring a New Access Rule

To configure a new access rule that grants access to the Internet, use the following procedure:

1. In the ISA Server Management Console tree, select Firewall Policy.
2. In the task pane, on the Tasks tab, select Create New Access Rule.
3. On the Welcome To The New Access Rule page, in Access Rule Name, enter the name for the access rule; then click Next.
4. On the Rule Action page, shown in Figure 5-19, click Allow, and then click Next.

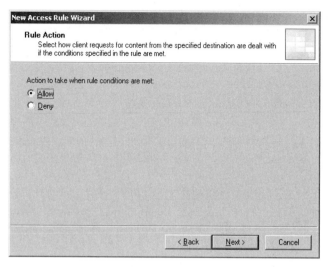

Figure 5-19   Configuring the access rule action

5. On the Protocols page, shown in Figure 5-20, configure the protocols to which this access rule applies. You have three options that you can allow:

   ❑ *All Outbound Protocols*—If you choose this option, the access rule applies to all protocols coming from the source network to the destination network.

   ❑ *Selected Protocols*—Click Add to add the specific protocol elements from the Add Protocols dialog box. With this option, you can specify which protocols will be allowed by this access rule.

   ❑ *All Outbound Protocols Except Selected*—Click Add to add the specific protocol elements from the Add Protocols dialog box. With this option, all protocols will allowed except for the protocols that you specify.

   When you have made these selections, click Next.

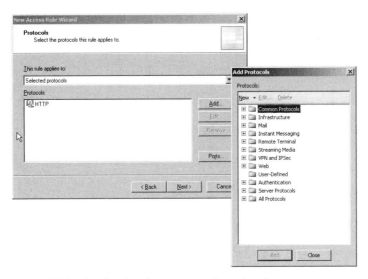

Figure 5-20   Configuring the access rule protocols

6. On the Access Rule Sources page, shown in Figure 5-21, click Add to open the Add Network Entities dialog box. You can choose from any of the network objects defined on ISA Server. Select the network object or objects that you want, click Add, and then click Close. On the Access Rule Sources page, click Next.

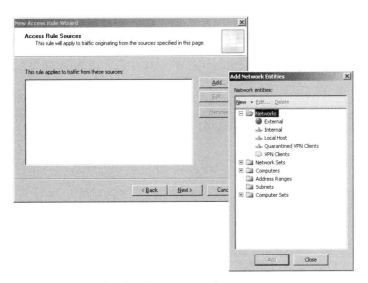

Figure 5-21   Configuring the access rule source

7. On the Access Rule Destinations page, shown in Figure 5-22, click Add to open the Add Network Entities dialog box, click Networks, select the External network (representing the Internet), click Add, and then click Close. On the Access Rule Destinations page, click Next.

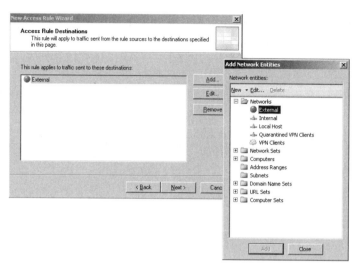

Figure 5-22   Configuring the access rule destination

8. On the User Sets page, shown in Figure 5-23, you configure which users will be able to use the access rule. If you want to grant access to the Internet for all users, you can leave the user set All Users in place and proceed to the next page of the wizard. If the rule applies to specific users, select All Users, and then click Remove. Then, click Add to open the Add Users dialog box, from which you can add the user set to which the rule applies. When you have completed the user set selection, click Next.

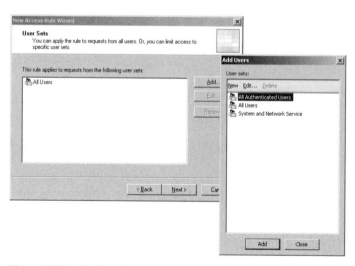

Figure 5-23   Configuring the access rule users

9. On the Completing The New Access Rule Wizard page, review the information in the wizard summary, and then click Finish.

10. To configure the content types for the access rule, double-click the access rule. On the Content Types tab, shown in Figure 5-24, either accept the default setting that applies the rule to all content types or select the content types that the rule applies to.

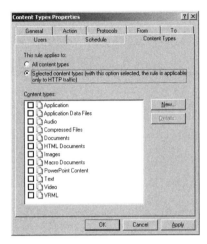

Figure 5-24   Configuring the access rule content types

11. To configure the schedule, on the Schedule tab, select the appropriate schedule from the Schedule list or click New to configure a new schedule element. Click OK.

12. To change the order of your access rules, select the access rule on the Firewall Policy tab and click Move Selected Rules Up or Move Selected Rules Down.

13. In the Firewall Policy details pane, click Apply to apply the new access rule.

See Also   For detailed walk-throughs of a variety of Internet access scenarios, see the article "Controlling Secure Internet Access Using ISA Server 2004," located at *http://www.microsoft. com/technet/prodtechnol/isa/2004/plan/controllingsecureinternetaccess.mspx*.

How to Assign Access Rule Priorities

Because access rules are evaluated in order based on the priority assigned in the ISA Server Management Console interface, it is important that you assign these priorities correctly.

Exam Tip   One of the more common reasons why access rules do not operate as expected is because of the access rule priorities. ISA Server evaluates the access rules listed in the ISA Server Management Firewall Policy from the top down. As soon as ISA Server encounters a rule that corresponds with the client request, ISA Server evaluates that rule and grants or denies access. When you get an exam question in which users cannot access resources on another network, examine the access rule properties and examine the access rule order. If an access rule that denies access is evaluated before an access rule that enables access, the client connection will be denied.

In general, you should apply deny rules first, followed by the more specific rules, followed by general rules. For example, you may have the following requirements when configuring Internet access:

- All computers should be able to access the Internet except for selected file servers.

- All users should be able to access the Internet except temporary employees.

- Users who access the Internet from a public kiosk computer located in the organization's reception area should be able to use only HTTP and HTTPS to access the Internet.

- Users should be able to access the Internet using all protocols.

Tip   If you have worked as a Windows server administrator for a while and configured permissions using NTFS permissions, you are used to the idea that Windows always applies the deny permissions first, and then evaluates the allow permissions. This is not the case with ISA Server 2004. ISA Server evaluates all the access rules in order, regardless of whether the access rule allows or denies access.

To configure the access rules in this scenario, you could configure the rules with the following priorities:

1. Create an access rule that blocks Internet access to a computer set that includes all the file servers.

2. Create an access rule that blocks Internet access to the domain group that contains all temporary employees.

3. Create an access rule that allows only HTTP or HTTPS traffic from the public kiosk computer to access the Internet.

4. Create an access rule that allows all users to access the Internet using any protocol.

> **Important**   ISA Server includes one default access rule that denies access to all protocols going to any network. This rule cannot be modified, and it is always the last rule to be applied.

Troubleshooting Internet Access

ISA Server uses access rules to grant internal users access to Internet resources. In some cases, you may need to troubleshoot these access rules to ensure that a user can access the required resources. Use the following guidelines to troubleshoot Internet access issues:

- **Check DNS name resolution**   If the client cannot resolve the DNS name of the Internet resource, the client will not be able to connect to the resource. To check if the client can resolve the DNS name, ping the FQDN of the Internet resource. Even if you can not ping the server, you can use the ping to determine if the client resolved the FQDN to the correct IP address. If the client did not resolve the DNS name correctly, then check the client DNS configuration and the DNS server used by the client. Also check the access rules on ISA Server to ensure that DNS queries from the internal network can be forwarded to the Internet DNS servers.

- **Determine the extent of the problem**   An important troubleshooting step is to attempt to identify the cause of the problem by isolating who is affected by the problem. For example, if only one user or group of users is affected then the issue is likely a configuration error on an ISA Server access rule. If only one Web site is inaccessible, then the problem may be with an access rule configuration, or the Web site may be unavailable. If all computers are affected, then you must check the ISA Server configuration and network connectivity. If only one computer is affected, then check the network connectivity and client configuration on that one computer.

- **Review access rule objects and access rule configuration**   After determining the extent of the problem, review the access rule configurations that specifically relate to the affected users. For example, if a group of users is affected, then look for access rules or access rule elements that apply specifically to that group.

- **Review access rule order**   ISA Server evaluates access rules in the order listed in ISA Server Management. The first rule that matches the client request is applied to the request. For example, if an access rule that allows access to all Web sites using HTTP is listed first, other access rules that set restrictions on which Web sites can be accessed will not be evaluated.

- **Check access rule authentication**   If an access rule requires authentication, then ensure that the ISA Server clients support the authentication protocol configured for the access rule. Also ensure that all users are using Web Proxy or Firewall clients because SecureNAT clients do not support authentication. The access rule order is also important when using access rules that require authentication. For example, if an access rule that allows Internet access using all protocols but only for members of a particular group is evaluated first, all users that are not members of that group will not be able to access the Internet.

Planning Configuring access rules can be quite difficult if you have complicated require-ments. The only way to ensure that the access rules will work as expected is to thoroughly test the access rule configuration. As you work on your ISA Server deployment project plan, make sure to include lots of time for testing.

One of the useful tools provided with ISA Server for troubleshooting access to resources on other networks is the logging feature. By default, ISA Server logs all Web Proxy and Firewall client connections to the Internet. You can use these logs to deter-mine which access rules are allowing or blocking access.

To view the information logged by ISA Server, complete the following steps:

1. In ISA Server Management, click Monitoring.

2. Click the Logging tab.

3. To view the information being logged at the current time, click Start Query. To use this option, start the query and then attempt to access the Internet resource from the client computer. You can view the client connection attempts in the log viewer.

4. To view archived information or to limit the number of entries in the log viewer, configure a filter to view specific information contained within the log files. For example, you could configure a filter that allowed you to view all the client con-nection attempts from a specific client computer over a specified period.

Note For more details about configuring and using ISA Server monitoring tools including logging, see Chapter 11, "Implementing Monitoring and Reporting."

Practice: Configuring Access Rules for Internet Access

In this practice, you will configure access rules that allow internal users at Coho Vine-yard to access Internet resources.

Exercise 1: Creating a DNS Lookup Rule

All clients on the Coho Vineyard network are configured to use DC1 as a DNS server. For these clients to be able to access resources on the Internet, DC1 must be able to resolve DNS requests for Internet resources. To enable this, you must enable an access rule that enables DNS lookups to the Internet from DC1.

1. In the Microsoft ISA Server Management Console tree, click Firewall Policy.

2. In the Firewall Policy list, click Last Default rule. In the task pane, on the Tasks tab, click Create New Access Rule.

> **Tip**   When you create an access rule, ISA Server always places the new rule just above the rule that is selected when you create the new rule.

3. On the Welcome To The New Access Rule Wizard, type **DNS Lookup Policy** as the Access rule name, and then click Next.

4. On the Rule Action page, click Allow, and then click Next.

5. On the Protocols page, in the This Rule Applies To drop-down box, click Selected Protocols, and then click Add.

6. In the Add Protocols dialog box, expand Common Protocols, click DNS, and then click Add. Click Close.

7. On the Protocols page, click Next.

8. On the Access Rule Sources page, click Add.

9. In the Add Network Entities dialog box, expand Computers, click DC1, and then click Add. Click Close. Click Next.

10. On the Access Rule Destinations page, click Add.

11. In the Add Network Entities dialog box, expand Networks, click External, and then click Add. Click Close. Click Next twice.

12. On the Completing The New User Sets Wizard page, review the settings and click Finish.

Exercise 2: Creating a Managers Access Rule

The Internet usage policy at Coho Vineyard states that managers must have access to all Internet resources using any protocols.

1. In the task pane, on the Tasks tab, click Create New Access Rule.

2. On the Welcome To The New Access Rule Wizard, type **Managers Access Policy** as the Access rule name, and then click Next.

3. On the Rule Action page, click Allow, and then click Next.

4. On the Protocols page, ensure that the rule applies to All outbound traffic. Click Next.

5. On the Access Rule Sources page, click Add.

6. In the Add Network Entities dialog box, expand Networks, click Internal, and then click Add. Click Close. Click Next.

7. On the Access Rule Destinations page, click Add.

8. In the Add Network Entities dialog box, expand Networks, click External, and then click Add. Click Close. Click Next.

9. On the User Sets page, click All Users, and then click Remove.

10. Click Add and click Managers, and then click Add. Click Close. Click Next.

11. On the Completing The New Access Rule Wizard page, review the settings and click Finish.

12. Ensure that the Mangers Access Policy is listed after than the DNS Lookup Policy. If it is not, right-click the Managers Access Policy, and then click Move Down.

13. Click Apply to apply the changes.

Exercise 3: Configure an All Employees Access Rule

All employees other than Managers should be able to use only HTTP and HTTPS to access the Internet. All users should be required to authenticate to access the Internet.

1. In the task pane, on the Tasks tab, click Create New Access Rule.

2. On the Welcome To The New Access Rule Wizard, type **All Employees Access Policy** as the Access rule name, and then click Next.

3. On the Rule Action page, click Allow, and then click Next.

4. On the Protocols page, in the This Rule Applies To drop-down box, click Selected Protocols, and then click Add.

5. In the Add Protocols dialog box, expand Common Protocols, click HTTP, and then click Add. Click HTTPS, and then click Add. Click Close.

6. On the Protocols page, click Next.

7. On the Access Rule Sources page, click Add.

8. In the Add Network Entities dialog box, expand Networks, click Internal, and then click Add. Click Close. Click Next.

9. On the Access Rule Destinations page, click Add.

10. In the Add Network Entities dialog box, expand Networks, click External, and then click Add. Click Close. Click Next.

11. On the User Sets page, click All Users, and then click Remove.

12. Click Add and click All Authenticated Users, and then click Add. Click Close. Click Next.

13. On the Completing The New Access Rule Wizard page, review the settings and click Finish.

14. Click Apply to apply the changes.

Exercise 4: Testing Internet Access

Manager1 is a member of the Managers group. Use this account to test the Managers access rules that you have configured. Sales1 is a member of the Sales group. Use this account to test Internet access for other employees.

1. On the CLIENT1 computer, log on to the *cohovineyard.com* domain as Manager1.

2. Open Internet Explorer and attempt to connect to *www.microsoft.com*. The connection should be successful.

3. Attempt to connect to *ftp://ftp.microsoft.com*. To view the contents of the ftp site, click Internet Options on the Tools menu. On the Advanced tab, clear the check box for Enable folder view for FTP sites. The connection should be successful.

4. Log off and log on to the CLIENT1 computer as Sales1.

5. Open Internet Explorer and attempt to connect to *www.microsoft.com*. The connection should be successful.

6. Attempt to connect to *ftp://ftp.microsoft.com*. The connection should not be successful. Why can Manager1 connect to the FTP site, while Sales1 cannot?

Manager1 is a member of the Managers user set, which is allowed to use all protocols to connect to Internet resources. Sales1 is not a member of any specific user set, so the All Employees Access Policy applies to this user. This access policy allows only HTTP and HTTPS access.

Lesson Review

Use the following questions to help determine whether you have learned enough to move on to the next lesson. If you have difficulty answering these questions, review the material in this lesson before beginning the next lesson. You can find answers to these questions in the "Questions and Answers" section at the end of this chapter.

1. Your Internet usage policy specifies that all users will be allowed full Internet access except that users are not allowed to download any executable files or Visual Basic script files. The IT Administration group is exempted from this restriction. You configure an access rule to prevent the All Users user set from downloading .exe and .vbs file types. Then you create a access rule that allows the IT Administration group to download these files. Then you configure an access rule

that allows Internet access for All Users. You soon discover that any user is able to download executable files from the Internet. Why is this happening and how can you change the configuration to meet the company requirements?

_____

_____

_____

2. Your Internet usage policy states that all employees should have full Internet access except that users should not be able to use the ICQ protocol to connect to the Internet. How will you accomplish this?

_____

_____

_____

3. Your organization has bought a new building and set up new offices in that building. The network in the new building is directly connected to the current network, but all the computers in the new building are on a different subnet, and all the offices in the new building are assigned to one company department that has Internet access requirements different from any other department. You install a new network card on the ISA Server computer and connect it to the network from the new office. You configure a new network on ISA Server for the new network. However, when you test Internet access from the new office, you cannot get access. What do you need to do?

_____

_____

_____

Lesson Summary

- Access rules determine how clients on a source network can access resources on a destination network. Access rules are used to configure all traffic flowing through ISA Server, including all traffic from the internal network to the Internet, and from the Internet to the internal network.

- In order to allow internal clients to access the Internet, you must configure an access rule that allows Internet access. To configure restrictions to Internet access, use access rule elements to create the required rules.

- To troubleshoot access rules for Internet access, check for DNS name resolution, and then check the access rule and access rule elements configuration. Another common problem with access rules is access rule order. ISA Server always evaluates the access rules based the access rules priorities.

Case Scenario Exercises

In this exercise, you will read two scenarios about installing ISA Server 2004, and then answer the questions that follow. If you have difficulty completing this work, review the material in this chapter before beginning the next chapter. You can find answers to these questions in the "Questions and Answers" section at the end of this chapter.

Scenario 1

Your organization's network includes a single Active Directory domain. Clients in your organization use Web browser applications from multiple vendors. You have implemented ISA Server 2004 as your proxy and firewall solution. Your organization's Internet usage policy states the following:

- All users will have Internet access from 12:00 noon to 1:00 P.M. and after regular business hours. Users should be able to use all protocols to access the Internet during these times.

- Managers and Executives and Domain Admins will have Internet access at all times.

- Two computers in the cafeteria area and two in the front lobby are set up for public access. These computers will only be able to use HTTP and HTTPS to access the Internet.

- MP3 file types will be blocked for all users at all times.

- Executable files will be blocked for all users except for the Domain Admins group.

Scenario 1 Question

1. How must you configure ISA Server 2004 to meet these requirements?

   _____

   _____

   _____

Scenario 2

Your organization has three branch offices, all of which are connected to the head office with dedicated high-speed links. Moreover, all ISA Server computers have a 128-Kbps ISDN connection available that is used as a backup connection to the head office. The head office has a high-speed Internet connection. All access to the Internet from all offices must use this head-office Internet connection. You have implemented ISA Server 2004 as your proxy and firewall solution in all offices. All users in the organization require Internet access, but they should be required to authenticate before getting access to the Internet. All users use a recent version of Internet Explorer as their Web browser. You want the branch offices to be able to take full advantage of ISA Server's caching ability. The ISDN connection will be implemented as a backup route.

Scenario 2 Question

1. How will you configure the ISA Server computers at all locations?

_____

_____

_____

Troubleshooting Lab

In this lab, you will troubleshoot an Internet access issue. This issue is related to Internet access requirements for users at Coho Vineyards. Domain administrators have reported that they cannot access any Internet resources when they are logged on to DC1. They need to be able to access resources on the Internet. However, the Internet usage policy states that the administrators should only be able to access resources on the Microsoft Web site. The DC1 computer cannot be configured as a Web Proxy client.

Exercise 1: Testing the Configuration

1. Log in to DC1 as an Administrator.

2. Open Internet Explorer and try to access *www.microsoft.com*. The connection will fail. Why? How would you fix this problem?

Exercise 2: Enabling Internet Access on DC1

1. On ISA1, open ISA Server Management. Click Firewall Policy, and then click Managers Access Policy.

2. On the Tasks tab, click Create New Access Rule.

3. In the task pane, on the Tasks tab, click Create New Access Rule.

4. On the Welcome To The New Access Rule Wizard, type **DC Access Policy** as the Access rule name, and then click Next.

5. On the Rule Action page, click Allow, and then click Next.

6. On the Protocols page, ensure that the rule applies to All outbound traffic. Click Next.

7. On the Access Rule Sources page, click Add.

8. In the Add Network Entities dialog box, expand Networks, expand Computers, click DC1, and then click Add. Click Close. Click Next.

9. On the Access Rule Destinations page, click Add.

10. In the Add Network Entities dialog box, expand Networks, expand Domain Name Sets, click Microsoft Domain, and then click Add. Click Close. Click Next.

11. On the User Sets page, click All Users, and then click Next.

12. On the Completing The New Access Rule Wizard page, review the settings and click Finish.

13. Click Apply to apply the changes.

14. On DC1, open Internet Explorer and try to access *www.microsoft.com*. The connection should fail. Why can you not connect to the Web site?

15. On ISA1, in ISA Server Management, move the DC Access Policy so that it is listed before the All Employees Access Policy.

16. Click Apply to apply the changes.

17. On DC1, open Internet Explorer and try to access *www.microsoft.com*. The connection should fail. Why can you not connect to the Web site?

18. On ISA1, in ISA Server Management, expand Configuration, then click Networks. On the Networks tab, double click Internal.

19. On the Web Proxy tab, click Authentication. Clear the check box for Require All Users To Authenticate. Click OK twice.

20. Click Apply to apply the changes.

21. On DC1, open Internet Explorer and try to access *www.microsoft.com*. The connection should succeed. Try to access *msdn.microsoft.com*. Again the connection should succeed. Try to access *www.msn.com*. In this case, the connection should fail because the Microsoft Domain domain name set only enables access to the *microsoft.com* domain.

Chapter Summary

■ Providing secure Internet access for users in an organization means that users can gain access to the resources they need, the connection to the Internet is secure, the data that users transfer to and from the Internet is secure, and users cannot download malicious programs from the Internet. ISA Server can be used to provide secure Internet access for internal clients and to implement the organization's Internet usage policy.

- A proxy server is a server that is situated between a client application, such as a Web browser, and a server that the client is connecting to. By default, ISA Server is configured to operate as a proxy server for Web Proxy and Firewall client computers. ISA Server 2004 supports chaining multiple ISA Server computers together so that Internet requests are passed from one computer to another computer. ISA Server 2004 also supports the use of a dial-up connection to another network.

- Access rule elements are used to configure access rules. ISA Server 2004 supports the following access rule elements for enabling Internet access: protocol, user set, content type, schedule, and network objects. ISA Server provides several default access rule elements, but you can also create and configure new elements.

- ISA Server supports five authentication methods for restricting Internet access. They are: Basic authentication, Digest authentication, Integrated Windows authentication, digital certificates authentication, and RADIUS authentication. If you want to restrict access to the Internet based on users and groups, you must configure ISA Server authentication to meet your organization's needs and the types of ISA Server clients used by your organization.

- Access rules determine how clients on a source network can access resources on a destination network. In order to allow internal clients to access the Internet, you must configure an access rule that allows Internet access. To configure restrictions to Internet access, use access rule elements to create the required rules.

Exam Highlights

Before taking the exam, review the key points and terms that are presented in this chapter. You need to know this information.

Key Points

- An organization's Internet usage policy is based on the organization's security requirements and the level of access required for employees to do their work. ISA Server 2004 can be used to implement many of the usage policy requirements.

- By default, ISA Server is configured as a proxy server for Web Proxy and Firewall clients.

- By default, ISA Server enables only integrated authentication. This means that if you want to use any Web browser clients other than Internet Explorer without deploying the Firewall client, you must enable additional authentication options.

- Access rules are built using access rule elements. Creating access rules is like building a puzzle. First you have to create puzzle pieces (the access rule elements), then you put the pieces together to create an access rule.

■ Configuring access rules can be difficult if you have complicated requirements. You have to consider not only the rule elements but also rule order. The access rule order is most critical when troubleshooting access rule problems.

Key Terms

access rule   Defines the conditions for when traffic will be allowed or denied between networks.

access rule element   An ISA Server configuration object that you can use when creating an access rule. Access rule elements include protocols, user sets, network objects, and schedules.

Internet usage policy   A policy defined by an organization that sets restrictions on the types of activities users at the organization can perform on the Internet.

Questions and Answers

Page
5-9

Lesson 1 Review

1. What is the purpose of an Internet usage policy?

   The Internet usage policy defines what constitutes acceptable usage of Internet resources. The policy must be clear and concise, describing who can use the Internet and what applications are allowed or not allowed. It must also explain how violations of the policy will be handled and who is responsible for enforcing the policy.

2. You are the network administrator for your organization. The organization is using a packet-filtering firewall with limited functionality to provide access to the Internet. The organization is planning an ISA Server 2004 implementation and wants to exploit some of its advanced filtering options to limit the access users have to the Internet. What should be the first step for implementing ISA Server 2004?

   a. Install ISA Server 2004.

   b. Design the access rules that will enable access to the Internet.

   c. Create an Internet usage policy that defines the organization's security requirements.

   d. Design a server publishing strategy.

   C is correct. The first step in implementing ISA Server 2004 is to create an Internet usage policy that defines the organization's security requirements. This policy becomes the basis for designing the access rules and for designing the server publishing strategy. ISA Server should be deployed only after the policy has been created and the Internet access and server publishing design have been completed.

3. How can an Internet usage policy be enforced by ISA Server 2004?

   ISA Server 2004 can be used to implement restrictions based on many different criteria including users, computers, content, URLs and protocols that are allowed or disallowed.

Page
5-27

Lesson 2 Review

1. Your organization has a high-speed Internet connection as your main method of access to the Internet. You also have a dial-up account with your ISP to provide a backup route. How should you configure ISA Server to use the dial-up connection in case the primary route fails?

   a. Configure the Dial-Up Preferences to specify the dial-up connection as the backup route.

   b. Create a network for the dial-up connection and designate it as the backup route.

    c. Configure a Web Chaining rule to specify the dial-up connection as the backup route.

    d. Modify the Web Browser properties of the Internal network to designate the dial-up connection as the alternate route.

C is correct. Web chaining rules allow you to specify that a dial-up connection should be used if the primary route is not available. A is incorrect because Dial-Up Preferences only specify what dial-up connections are available to ISA Server and what credentials to use. B is incorrect because you cannot create a network for a dial-up connection. D is incorrect because the Web Browser properties can only specify an alternate ISA Server computer.

2. All the Web browser applications in your organization are configured to be Web Proxy clients. You are the network administrator and you have received reports that some employees are viewing and downloading information from inappropriate Web sites. How could you identify the employees responsible and prevent further infractions?

ISA Server can log all HTTP requests and provide information on the user and the Web sites visited. You can use the log files to determine which users accessed the inappropriate Web sites and take any further action as prescribed by your Internet usage policy. You can also configure ISA Server to block access to those Web sites and to filter content to prevent the downloading of inappropriate material.

3. Your company has seven branch offices that have no direct Internet connection. All Internet requests are routed to the ISA Server at the head office over a 128-kilo-byte-per-second (Kbps) Integrated Services Digital Network (ISDN) link. The ISDN link is heavily used during business hours. What can you do to minimize the bandwidth usage for Internet requests?

Install an ISA Server in each branch office and configure a Web chaining rule to pass Internet requests to the head office ISA Server. Over time, the cache of objects on the branch office ISA Server computer will build up and reduce the need to use the ISDN connection to access Internet resources.

Lesson 3 Review

Page
5-39
1. Your organization has an Internet usage policy specifying that only managers and executives have unrestricted Internet access. All other employees are allowed Internet access during the lunch hour and after business hours with restrictions on the type of content that should be accessible. How can you enforce this policy?

Create a user set that contains the Managers and Executives groups and create an access rule that allows them unrestricted Internet access. Create schedule and content type elements to define the time of day and the prohibited content that will apply to all other employees. Use those elements in an access rule to restrict their Internet access according to your Internet usage policy.

2. Your organization has limited bandwidth available for Internet connections. The users who require Internet access to do their jobs are complaining about the speed of the connection. After reviewing the logs, you discover that many employees are downloading large image libraries for their desktop wallpaper on a daily basis from a specific Web site. What can you do to prevent this?

Create a URL Set for the specific Web site and create an access rule to deny this URL Set to the All Users group.

3. Your organization has a single domain running Active Directory. Your organization has four branch offices, all of which use ISA Server 2004 as their Internet edge firewall and proxy server. All branch offices require the same access rules. Managers at the branch offices must be able to connect to a custom Web application at your head office using a specific TCP port. No other users should be able to access the application. How would you configure all the ISA Server 2004 servers in the most efficient manner?

On one of the branch office ISA Server computers, create a user set to represent the Managers group. Then create a protocol element that defines outbound TCP connections to the specified port. Then create an access rule to allow access to the application using the access rule elements. The most efficient way to distribute the configuration is to export the configuration on one server and import it to the other three ISA Server computers.

Page
5-46
Lesson 4 Review

1. Your organization has a mixture of Windows 2000 and Windows Server 2003 domain controllers. You have deployed ISA Server 2004 as your firewall solution. Your Internet usage policy states that all users accessing the Internet will be authenticated using Digest authentication. You have configured the properties of the Internal network to require Digest authentication. Now none of your users can access the Internet. How can you correct this problem?

Because you have domain controllers running on both Windows 2000 and Windows Server 2003 servers, your domain cannot be running in Windows Server 2003 mode. Therefore, you must configure the user properties in Active Directory to store the user's password using reversible encryption.

2. All the clients in your organization are configured as SecureNAT clients. You have created content type elements to prevent users from downloading executables, MP3 and video file types. You use those elements in an access rule and assign it to the All Authenticated Users group. After applying the access rule, you discover that all your clients still have unrestricted access to download the content types. Why can users still download the content types that you are trying to block? What should you do to prevent this?

SecureNAT clients cannot be authenticated and therefore the rule will not be applied to anyone. You must assign the rule to the All Users group. The All Users group includes everyone, whether they are authenticated or not.

3. Your organization has a multiple-domain forest running Active Directory. You support various browser applications including Internet Explorer and Netscape Navigator. All browsing software is configured to use an ISA Server computer as a proxy server. You have configured access rules to allow HTTP and HTTPS traffic for all internal clients, but have not changed any other settings on the ISA Server. Some of your users have Internet access while others are always denied connections. How can you resolve this problem?

Only Internet Explorer can support Integrated Windows authentication. To support Netscape Navigator and other browsing software, you must select a different authentication method, such as Basic or Digest.

Page
5-59

Lesson 5 Review

1. Your Internet usage policy specifies that all users will be allowed full Internet access except that users are not allowed to download any executable files or Visual Basic script files. The IT Administration group is exempted from this restriction. You configure an access rule to prevent the All Users user set from downloading .exe and .vbs file types. Then you create a access rule that allows the IT Administration group to download these files. Then you configure an access rule that allows Internet access for All Users. You soon discover that any user is able to download executable files from the Internet. Why is this happening and how can you change the configuration to meet the company requirements?

The problem is in the priority of the rules. If the allow rule for Internet access to All Users is at the top of the list then no other rules will be evaluated and users will have full access. Deny rules or specific allow rules need to be first. The most general rules should be just before the default deny rule. You need to put the allow rule for IT Administration at the top, then the deny rule for .vbs and .exe extensions next, and then the general allow rule for All Users.

2. Your Internet usage policy states that all employees should have full Internet access except that users should not be able to use the ICQ protocol to connect to the Internet. How will you accomplish this?

Create an access rule that denies access for All Users from the Internal network to the External network for the ICQ protocol. Then create an access rule that allows full access to the Internet using any protocol. Place the rule blocking the ICQ protocol at the top of the priority list.

3. Your organization has bought a new building and set up new offices in that building. The network in the new building is directly connected to the current network, but all the computers in the new building are on a different subnet, and all the offices in the new building are assigned to one company department that has Internet access requirements different from any other department. You install a new network card on the ISA Server computer and connect it to the network from

the new office. You configure a new network on ISA Server for the new network. However, when you test Internet access from the new office, you cannot get access. What do you need to do?

You must configure a new access rule that meets the new office requirements. By default, ISA Server will not allow any network traffic from the new network to the Internet until you configure an access rule.

Case Scenario Exercises

Page 5-61

Scenario 1 Question

1. How must you configure ISA Server 2004 to meet these requirements?

Configure all Web browsers to be Web Proxy clients of ISA Server. Because of the need to support multiple browser types, configure the Internal Network Web proxy settings to use Basic authentication.

Create access rule elements to define the schedule for 12:00 noon to 1:00 P.M. and after business hours. Create user sets to define the Managers and Executives and Domain Admins groups. Create an access rule element to define MP3 file extensions and one to define executable file types. Create a computer set network object that includes the IP addresses of the public computers.

Create access rules as follows:

a. Deny access to MP3 files to All Users.

b. Allow access to Domain Admins to executable files.

c. Deny access to All Users to executable files.

d. Allow access to HTTP and HTTPS only for the public computers.

e. Allow Internet access to Managers and Executives and Domain Admins at any time.

f. Allow Internet access to All Users for the scheduled times.

Page 5-61

Scenario 2 Question

1. How will you configure the ISA Server computers at all locations?

Configure all users in all domains as Web Proxy clients for Internet access. On all ISA Server computers, create a rule that allows access to the External Network to the All Authenticated Users user set. Accept the default of using Integrated Windows authentication. At the branch offices, create a Web chaining rule to direct all Internet requests to the head office ISA Server computer; and in that rule, configure the ISDN connection as the backup route.

Troubleshooting Lab

Page
5-62
Exercise 1

1. Open Internet Explorer and try to access *www.microsoft.com*. The connection will fail. Why? How would you fix this problem?

   The DNS Lookup Policy, which applies to the DC1 computer, only allows DNS lookups to the Internet. The All Employees Access Policy which allows access to the Internet using the HTTP and HTTPS protocol applies to All Authenticated Users. Because DC1 is a SecureNAT client, the user cannot be authenticated to gain access to the Internet. To fix this, you will need to create an access rule that does not require authentication that allows access from DC1 to the Microsoft.com Web sites.

Page
5-62
Exercise 2

1. On DC1, open Internet Explorer and try to access *www.microsoft.com*. The connection should fail. Why can you not connect to the Web site?

   One problem is with rule order. When ISA Server evaluates the access rules, it evaluates the All Employees Access Policy before it evaluates the DC Access Policy. The All Employees Access Policy enables access for HTTP, but requires authentication. Because DC1 does not support authentication, access is blocked.

2. On DC1, open Internet Explorer and try to access *www.microsoft.com*. The connection should fail. Why can you not connect to the Web site?

   In an earlier exercise, you configured the Internal network properties to require all users to authenticate. When you try to access an Internet resource using HTTP, access will be blocked. You need to remove this configuration before you can access the Internet using HTTP.

6 Implementing ISA Server Caching

Exam Objectives in this Chapter:

- Configure forward and reverse caching
  - ☐ Configure cache size and location
  - ☐ Configure cache rules
  - ☐ Configure content download jobs
- Optimize performance of the ISA Server 2004 cache
  - ☐ Configure active caching
  - ☐ Configure cache settings
- Diagnose and resolve caching issues

Why This Chapter Matters

So far, this book has focused primarily on the security features provided by Microsoft Internet Security and Acceleration (ISA) Server 2004. ISA Server, however, is not only a firewall but can also be configured to accelerate Internet access by providing caching functionality. One benefit of using ISA Server 2004 as a Web proxy server is that ISA Server can cache much of the Internet content that clients request. ISA Server stores frequently accessed Web objects in memory and in a cache file on the ISA Server computer's hard disk. Much of the content on the Internet is dynamic content that cannot be efficiently cached. This has reduced the importance of using caching, but there are still several scenarios in which ISA Server caching can improve Internet access performance.

Lessons in this Chapter:

- Lesson 1: Caching Overview 6-3
- Lesson 2: Configuring Caching. 6-13
- Lesson 3: Configuring Content Download Jobs 6-31

Before You Begin

This chapter presents the skills and concepts related to configuring ISA Server to cache Web content. If you plan to complete the practices and lab in this chapter, you should prepare the following:

■ A server with Microsoft Windows Server 2003 (either Standard Edition or Enterprise Edition) installed as DC1 and configured as a domain controller in the domain *cohovineyard.com*. DC1 must be able to resolve the Domain Names System (DNS) names for resources located on the ISA Server External network.

■ A second server with Windows Server 2003 installed as ISA1 and configured as a domain member in the domain *cohovineyard.com*. This server should have ISA Server, Standard Edition as well as two network interfaces installed. The external interface should be connected to a network that contains one or more Web servers. If possible, the network interface should be attached to the Internet.

■ A Microsoft Windows XP computer installed as CLIENT1. This computer should be a member of the *cohovineyard.com* domain.

Lesson 1: Caching Overview

ISA Server supports caching as a way to improve the speed of retrieving information from the Internet. From the internal user's point of view, caching improves Internet access performance. From the network administrator's point of view, caching provides the added benefit of reducing the use of network bandwidth. ISA Server extends the benefits of caching by enabling scheduled content download jobs in which ISA Server downloads Internet content to the cache before any user requests the object. You can also combine Web caching with Web proxy chaining to optimize performance further if your organization has multiple locations. This lesson provides an overview of how caching works and how ISA Server 2004 implements caching.

After this lesson, you will be able to

- Describe what caching is
- Describe how content download jobs work
- Describe how caching is implemented with ISA Server 2004
- Describe how Web chaining and caching work together

Estimated lesson time: 20 minutes

What Is Caching?

One of the primary deployment scenarios for ISA Server 2004 is as a Web proxy server in which ISA Server retrieves information from the Internet for internal clients. ISA Server supports Web caching as a way to improve the speed with which this information is returned to Web clients.

Caching stores Web content on the ISA Server computer in memory or on the server's hard disk. When a user requests Web information that is in the cache, ISA Server provides the information from the cache, enabling a quicker response to the client. ISA Server 2004 can be configured to enable the caching of Hypertext Transfer Protocol (HTTP) and File Transfer Protocol (FTP) objects.

ISA Server 2004 caching provides the following benefits:

- **Improved performance** Web caching speeds client response for Internet access by bringing the Web content closer to the user. When a user behind the ISA Server 2004 firewall requests Web content, ISA Server checks to see whether the content is contained in its cache. If it is, the cached content is returned to the user. Accessing Web content from a cache on the corporate network is faster than requiring a connection to a remote Web server located on the Internet. Recently accessed information is stored in the cache and remains in the cache as long as that content continues to be accessed by users.

■ **Reduced bandwidth usage**   Web caching can help reduce the overall bandwidth usage on the organization's Internet connection. When users request Web content already contained in cache, that content is returned to the user immediately from the cache without requesting the content again from the Internet.

How Caching Works

When a user requests an HTTP or FTP object, the Web proxy client sends the request to the Web proxy filter on ISA Server, as illustrated in Figure 6-1.

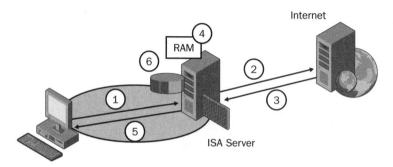

Figure 6-1   Forward caching caches Internet content for internal clients

In a forward caching scenario, the following actions occur to complete the client request:

1. The Web proxy client sends a request for content located on an Internet Web server. The Web request is intercepted by ISA Server 2004 and forwarded to the Web proxy filter.

> **Note**   By default, the Microsoft Firewall service forwards HTTP requests from Firewall clients and secure network address translation (SecureNAT) clients to the Web proxy service. This means that, when caching is enabled, Web content from all ISA Server clients can be cached.

2. ISA Server checks whether the requested content is contained in its cache. If the content is not in the cache, or if the content has expired (that is, the header information in the content indicates that it should no longer be served from a cache), ISA Server 2004 forwards the request to the Web server on the Internet.

3. The Web server on the Internet returns the information requested.

4. The ISA Server Web proxy filter places the Web content in its in-memory cache. ISA Server 2004 uses an in-memory cache to store the most frequently requested content.

5. After placing the Web content in the in-memory cache, ISA Server 2004 Web caching server returns the content to the requesting user.

6. After a time, the ISA Server 2004 Web proxy filter will copy the contents of the in-memory cache to the disk-based cache. If the content is not frequently accessed, the in-memory cache will flush the content and the only copy of the content on ISA server will reside in the disk-based cache.

> **Note**   The time for an object to remain in the cache is called Time-to-Live (TTL). When ISA Server places an object into its cache, it sets a TTL for the object. ISA Server returns the HTTP object that is stored in its cache to clients until the TTL has expired. ISA Server can set the TTL based on the creation date and the modification date of the object or by using the settings that you configure when you enable Web caching or configure caching rules. Many Web pages use metatags to set expiration dates for content. When a Web page has an expiration date, ISA Server sets the TTL of the object to match the Web page's expiration date.

Caching Scenarios

ISA Server supports both forward and reverse caching.

- Forward caching occurs when a user on the corporate network makes a request for Web content located on an Internet Web server. The user initiates an HTTP, Hypertext Transfer Protocol Secure (HTTPS), or FTP request to an Internet Web server and the request is intercepted by ISA Server. ISA Server retrieves the content from the Internet Web server, stores that content in its cache, and returns the content to the user.

- Reverse caching occurs when users on the Internet request Web content located on a server on the corporate network that is accessible through a Web publishing rule. When an Internet user requests content from the internal server, ISA Server forwards the request to the Web server. The Web server sends the requested content to ISA Server, which then returns the content to the Internet user who made the request. In this scenario, ISA Server will cache a copy of the requested information so that the next request for the same information can be provided from the ISA Server cache rather than again accessing the internal Web server.

> **Note**   When caching is enabled, both forward and reverse caching are enabled. There is no way to disable either forward or reverse caching specifically. If you want to disable the caching of content from a particular Web site, then you must create a caching rule that prohibits it.

What Are Content Download Jobs?

ISA Server extends caching performance by enabling content download jobs. By monitoring and analyzing Internet access, you can determine which Web content is most likely to be requested by internal clients. You can then create a content download job to download the Web content to the ISA Server cache before any client requests the object. Content download jobs allow you to schedule content for download at a specific time or at recurring times.

Benefits of Using Content Download Jobs

The main reasons for using content download jobs are to improve Internet access performance and decrease the use of bandwidth to the Internet. There are several possible scenarios in which content download jobs can provide this functionality. For example, you can create a content download job at a branch office ISA Server so that the entire main-office intranet site is downloaded from the main office Web server. The content download job can be configured to take place during non-working hours so that the branch-office link to the main office is not used for the download during working hours. When branch-office users arrive at the office, the main-office Web site's content is stored in the branch-office cache. Branch office users can quickly download even large files from cache, while freeing the branch-office link to the main office during work hours for other business-related network activity.

You can also use content download jobs to update information from Internet Web sites. For example, users may frequently request a price list from the Web site of a business partner. You can configure a scheduled content download so that ISA Server retrieves the price list each night. By using a scheduled content download, the most recent version of the price list will be in the cache each morning.

You can also use scheduled content downloads to ensure that Web content is always available to users, even when they cannot connect to the Internet. For example, users may need constant access to a particular Web site, and any disruption in that access may disrupt business processes. In this case, you can configure ISA Server to download the content and provide that content for users even when the Internet connection is not available.

Scheduled download jobs can also be useful in reverse proxy scenarios. For example, if you are publishing an internal Web site that is modified every night, you can schedule a content download job every morning so that the new Web content is stored in the ISA Server cache. The ISA Server computer then does not need to access the internal Web site to provide the content to clients.

How Content Download Jobs Work

When you enable content download jobs, the actions listed in Figure 6-2 occur:

1. You create a content download job that specifies Web content to be retrieved from the Internet and when content retrieval occurs.

2. At the scheduled time, ISA Server uses a background process to retrieve the content from the Web server. The content is stored in the ISA Server cache based on the settings specified by the content download job.

3. A user on the internal network sends a request for the Web content to the ISA Server computer. The Firewall service passes the request to the Web proxy filter.

4. The ISA Server Web proxy filter determines that the content is in the Web cache, so ISA Server retrieves the content from the cache.

5. Content retrieved from cache is returned to the requesting user.

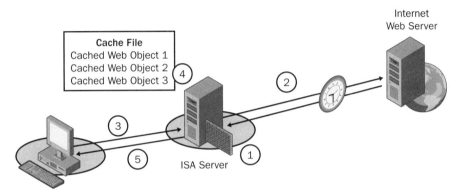

Figure 6-2   Content download job

How Caching Is Implemented in ISA Server 2004

When you enable Web caching, you configure ISA Server to store Web objects in its cache. ISA Server includes the following features that optimize cache performance:

- **RAM and disk caching**   ISA Server allocates RAM for caching popular objects and caches other objects on disk. When caching an object, ISA Server first places an object into the RAM cache and then writes objects to disk. RAM and disk caching help to improve users' access speed to popular Web sites. By default, ISA Server 2004 uses 10 percent of the RAM on the server to cache Web content.

- **Maintaining the RAM cache in physical memory**   ISA Server never writes the cached information stored in RAM to the operating system paging file. This optimizes access to the cache stored in RAM.

- **Directory of cached object**   ISA Server maintains a directory of cached objects in RAM to optimize the process of determining whether the server has an object in its cache.

- **Single cache file**   ISA Server maintains a single cache file per disk partition to retain cached objects so that gaining access to objects does not use additional system resources that are needed for opening and closing multiple files. The cache file size can be configured for each disk partition. The maximum size of a single cache file is 64 gigabytes (GB). If you require a larger cache store, you can distribute it over different drives.

- **Quick recovery**   ISA Server quickly rebuilds the directory of cached objects at startup, even after an abnormal termination.

- **Efficient cache updates**   ISA Server automatically determines which objects to retain in the RAM cache. This decision is based on the likelihood of a user's again requesting the same object, which is determined by how recently and how frequently an object is accessed.

- **Automatic cleanup**   ISA Server removes objects that have not been accessed recently or frequently when the disk space that is allocated to the cache approaches capacity.

See Also   ISA Server Enterprise Edition uses Cache Array Routing Protocol (CARP) to distribute the cache efficiently across multiple ISA Server computers. ISA Server Enterprise Edition is discussed in detail in Chapter 12, "Implementing ISA Server 2004, Enterprise Edition."

How ISA Server Restricts Content

ISA Server does not cache all content that is requested by Web clients. Table 6-1 describes how ISA Server restricts the content that it caches.

Exam Tip   As you write the exam, remember that ISA Server does not cache all content. If you see an exam question in which some content is not being cached, one possible reason is that the content is not cacheable. You can modify which types of content are cached.

Table 6-1   ISA Server Caching Restrictions

Restriction	Description
ISA Server does not cache responses to requests that contain the following HTTP response headers.	Cache-control: no-cache Cache-control: private Pragma: no-cache www-authenticate Set-cookie
ISA Server does not cache responses to requests that contain the following HTTP request headers.	Authorization, unless the origin server explicitly allows this by including the "cache-control: public" header in the response Cache-control: no-store.

> **Note**   For more information about Web pages and caching, see the article "HOW TO: Prevent Caching in Internet Explorer," in the Microsoft Knowledge Base at *http://support.microsoft.com/ support/kb/articles/Q234/0/67.asp*.

What Is Web Chaining and Caching?

Some organizations include multiple locations with computers running ISA Server deployed in each location. In this scenario, you can combine caching with Web proxy chaining to optimize caching performance. Web proxy chaining is useful when your organization has multiple branch-office locations, but all Internet requests are routed through one location at the head office. In this scenario, you can install ISA Server in each office and then configure ISA Server at the branch offices to route all Internet requests to the ISA Server computer at the head office.

One of the benefits of using Web chaining is the accumulated caching on ISA Server. If all the servers running ISA Server in the branch offices are configured to forward their requests to the head-office ISA Server, the head-office ISA Server will develop a large cache that contains many requested items. Moreover, the local ISA Server will build up a cache of the most requested items from the branch office. The combination of caching at the local branch office and at the head office increases the chances that the Internet content can be delivered to the client without downloading it again from the Internet.

The following steps and Figure 6-3 describe how Web proxy chaining works in this branch-office/main-office scenario:

1. The client sends a request for Web content to the Web caching server at the branch office. If the Web caching server at the branch office contains a valid version of the Web content in its cache, it will return the content to the requesting user.

2. If the content requested by the branch-office user is not contained in the branch-office server's cache, the request is forwarded to an upstream Web caching server in the Web proxy chain.

3. If the upstream Web caching server has a valid copy of the requested content in cache, the content is returned to the branch-office Web caching server. The branch-office Web caching server places the content in its own Web cache and then returns the content to the branch-office user who requested the content.

4. If the upstream Web caching server at the main office does not contain the requested content in its cache, it will forward the request to the Web server on the Internet. The Internet Web server returns the requested content to the main-office Web caching server. The Web caching server at the main office places the content in cache.

5. The main office returns the content to the branch-office Web caching server. The branch-office Web caching server places the content in its cache.

6. The branch-office Web caching server returns the content from its cache to the requesting user.

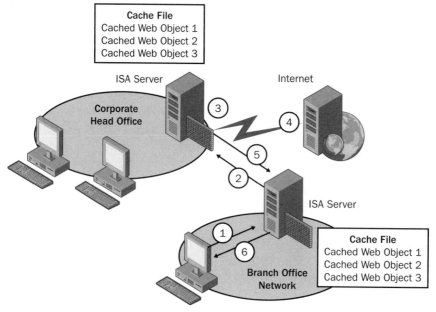

Figure 6-3   Web chaining and caching for branch offices

Planning   One of the common deployment scenarios for ISA Server in organizations with multiple locations is the Web chaining and caching scenario. Often the branch offices are connected to central offices using fairly slow wide area network (WAN) connections. By deploying an ISA Server in each branch office and enabling caching on the server, these organizations can reduce the use of the WAN bandwidth. You have several options when deploying this configuration. One option is to deploy the ISA Server computer with a single network interface. If you already have a router at the branch office, and you don't require ISA Server to filter network traffic, you can configure the ISA Server computer with a single network interface and then configure all the clients in the branch offices to use the ISA Server computer as a proxy server. You can also take advantage of content download jobs in this scenario. If you have an Intranet Web site to which all users need access, you can download the content to the local ISA Server overnight. If you are deploying ISA Server Enterprise Edition, you can also configure an array of multiple ISA Server computers at the head office and use CARP to ensure that as much content as possible is cached.

Lesson Review

Use the following questions to help determine whether you have learned enough to move on to the next lesson. If you have difficulty answering these questions, review the material in this lesson before beginning the next lesson. You can find answers to these questions in the "Questions and Answers" section at the end of this chapter.

1. You have deployed ISA Server 20004 in a large office with a relatively slow Internet connection. The ISA Server computer is to be used only for caching content. What can you do to maximize cache response time?

   _____

   _____

   _____

2. You have deployed ISA Server 2004 and configured the server as a Web proxy server. All internal client computers are configured as Web proxy clients. You have limited bandwidth to the Internet, so you enable caching on ISA Server, using the default caching configuration. Many users in your organization, you notice, access a partner organization's Web site several times a day. The Web site contains many large files that are changed every few days; when users download the files, much of the available bandwidth to the Internet is used. You need to make sure that users have access to the partner Web site, yet you must limit the amount of bandwidth used to access the Web site as much as possible during working hours. What should you do?

   a. Install the Firewall client on each client computer.

   b. Configure caching to cache only small files from the partner Web site.

   c. Configure a content download job to download the partner Web site every night.

   d. Configure the ISA Server to cache content with a TTL of one day.

3. Users in your organization must download files from an FTP site on the Internet twice a day. Your users report that they frequently download outdated versions of the file. What is happening and how will you fix it?

   _____

   _____

   _____

Lesson Summary

■ ISA Server 2004 uses caching to retrieve and store cacheable Web content so that the next time a client requests the same content it can be retrieved from the cache file to provide faster response and reduce bandwidth consumption. Forward caching stores Web content from the Internet for internal clients. Reverse caching stores Web content from an internal published Web site for Internet clients.

■ Content download jobs allow you to retrieve in advance Web content based on your analysis of usage. Jobs can be scheduled to run at off-peak hours to populate the ISA Server cache content prior to a user's requesting the data.

■ When caching is enabled on ISA Server, it stores the cache both in the server memory and on the server hard disk. ISA Server optimizes the use of the cache.

■ Web proxy chaining can allow branch offices to take advantage of a larger cache maintained at head office and use it to build up cached content at the branch office.

Lesson 2: Configuring Caching

By default, caching is disabled on ISA Server 2004. To enable caching, you must configure a cache drive. You can also optimize caching by creating and modifying cache rules. This lesson explains how to enable and optimize caching and provides guidelines for how to troubleshoot caching.

After this lesson, you will be able to

- Enable caching and configure cache drives
- Configure cache rule settings
- Create and manage cache rules
- Troubleshoot caching

Estimated lesson time: 20 minutes

How to Enable Caching and Configure Cache Drives

By default, a new installation of ISA Server is configured with a maximum cache size of 0 megabytes (MB), which means that ISA Server will not cache any content. To enable caching, you must define a cache drive. To define a cache drive, complete the following procedure:

1. Open ISA Server Management, expand Configuration, and then click Cache.

2. In the details pane, click the Cache Rules tab.

3. On the Tasks tab, click Define Cache Drives, as shown in Figure 6-4.

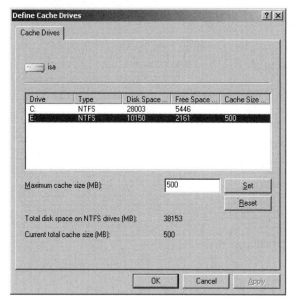

Figure 6-4   Configuring a cache drive

4. In the Define Cache Drives dialog box, select one of the drives listed in the list box.

5. In Maximum cache size, type the amount of space on the selected drive to allocate for caching.

6. Click Set to configure the cache drive.

> **Note**   The drive you use for caching must be a local drive that is formatted using NTFS. To optimize performance, use a drive different from the one on which the main ISA Server system, the operating system, and the page file are installed.

When you configure a drive to be used for caching, ISA Server creates a file with a .cdat extension in the \Urlcache folder on that drive. The .cdat file is as large as the amount of space you dedicated for caching on that drive. As ISA Server caches the objects, it places the objects into the .cdat file. If the .cdat file is too full to hold a new object, ISA Server removes older objects from the cache by using a formula that evaluates age, popularity, and size. The .cdat file can be accessed only by the Web proxy service.

How to Configure Cache Settings

After you define the cache drives, ISA Server will begin caching Web content based on the default caching configuration. This default configuration can be modified to meet your organization's requirements. You can modify how ISA Server caches specific types of HTTP objects. By limiting certain types of content, you can improve the efficiency of the caching process. For example, you can configure ISA Server to limit the size of cached objects to reserve cache space for additional smaller objects.

> **Important**   The ISA Server Management Console interface provides the option to configure active caching, but the functionality has been disabled in ISA Server 2004. Active caching, which was available in ISA Server 2000, is used by ISA Server to download popular content from the Internet before the TTL expired. This feature is not available in ISA Server 2004, even though the feature still appears in the interface.

To configure content settings for caching:

1. In ISA Server Management Console, in the console tree, click Cache, and then, in the details pane, click Configure Cache Settings.

2. In the Cache Settings dialog box, on the Advanced tab, shown in Figure 6-5, configure the settings listed in Table 6-2.

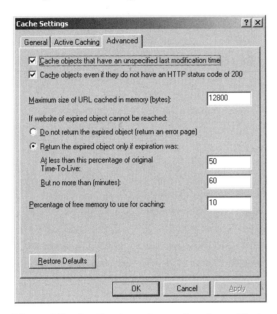

Figure 6-5   Configuring advanced cache settings

Table 6-2   Advanced Caching Configuration Options

Configuration Option	Use This Option To
Cache Objects That Have An Unspecified Last Modification Time	Configure ISA Server to cache objects that do not have a TTL defined in the page header. If you select this option, ISA Server will cache these objects and clean them up based on the parameters defined by the cache rule that applies to content retrieved from the specific Web site.
Cache Objects Even If They Do Not Have An HTTP Status Code Of 200	Configure responses by ISA Server to requests that failed to return an object. This type of caching is referred to as negative caching. When you configure negative caching, ISA Server returns error messages to clients and caches the negative results, even if the Web site is only temporarily unavailable. Until the TTL for the negative response expires, clients may receive an error message from ISA Server even if the object is actually available again. When you configure negative caching, HTTP objects with the following status codes are cached: 203 Partial information 300 Redirection 301 Object has moved permanently 410 Object is gone
Maximum Size Of URL Cached In Memory (Bytes)	Configure the Uniform Resource Locators (URLs) that ISA Server will store in memory. When you increase the amount of memory that a single object may occupy, ISA Server will store fewer Web objects. ISA Server will cache objects larger than this limit on disk.
If Web Site Of Expired Object Cannot Be Reached: Do Not Return The Expired Object (Return An Error Page)	Configure ISA Server to never return an expired item to a user. For example, ISA Server may have a cached copy of a Web page that has expired. If the Web server is available when a user requests the same page, ISA Server would retrieve a fresh page from the Internet Web server. However, if the Internet Web server is not available and this option is selected, ISA Server will return an error message to the user. If this option is not selected, then ISA Server will return the expired content to the user.
At Less Than This Percentage Of Original Time-To-Live	Configure the time period for when ISA Server will return an expired object based on the original TTL. For example, if a Web page has a TTL of 100 minutes and this option is set at 50 percent, ISA Server will return the page for 50 minutes after it expires.

Table 6-2   Advanced Caching Configuration Options

Configuration Option	Use This Option To
But No More Than (Minutes)	Configure the maximum time period for when ISA Server will return an expired object. For example, if a page has a TTL of 24 hours, and the percentage value is set at 50 percent, but this value is set at 60 minutes, ISA Server will respond with an error message to all requests for objects that have been expired for more than 60 minutes.
Percentage Of Free Memory To Use For Caching	Configure the amount of RAM the computer running ISA Server will use for caching. If this server is used primarily as a caching server, you should increase this number. If you are using ISA Server for reverse caching, you should configure the RAM cache to be equal to your internal Web site size so that all client requests can be provided from the RAM cache.

Exam Tip   If you get an exam question in which users cannot access a Web site, even though the Web site is available from a client that is not using the ISA Server computer as a Web proxy server, the reason may be negative caching. If negative caching is enabled, ISA Server caches the fact that the Web site is not available until the TTL expires. To avoid this, you must disable negative caching.

What Are Cache Rules?

In some cases, you may have different caching requirements for specific Web content. You can use cache rules to define the types of Web content that is stored in the cache and how Web content is stored and returned to users from the cache.

Why Use Cache Rules?

The default caching configuration, including the cache settings and the default cache rule, is sufficient for many organizations. If these settings are not modified, the default settings apply to all Web content cached in the ISA Server cache for both forward and reverse caching scenarios.

However, in some cases, you may need to configure a more specific caching configuration. For example, users in your organization may frequently access a Web site, so you may want to configure the cache so that all content from that Web site is cached on the computer running ISA Server. If the Web site contains critical information that changes frequently, you may need to implement the opposite solution, that is, configure the Web site to never be cached.

Cache Rule Settings

When you enable caching on ISA Server, a default cache rule is enabled. You can also configure a wide variety of settings that enable you to fine-tune caching performance on ISA Server. Table 6-3 describes how you can change options to fine-tune caching performance and how the default cache rule is configured.

Table 6-3   Cache Rule Options and the Default Cache Rule

Cache Rule Options	The Default Cache Rule
Apply to content retrieved from all Internet locations, or limit the rule to apply to specific destination sets. You can also configure the rule to apply to all Internet content except specific destination sets.	Applies to content requested from all network locations
Define how Web content is returned to the user. For example, you can define a cache rule that will always return the content from the cache, whether the information has expired or not.	Will return unexpired content to a Web user who requests the content. If the content has expired, ISA Server will route the request to the Web server.
Define whether Web content is stored in the cache. You can configure the cache rule so that the Web content is never cached, or so that specific parameters are applied defining what type of content is cached.	Will cache the default cacheable objects.
Define whether HTTP content, FTP content, or both types of content are cached and configure the caching configuration for each protocol.	Enables both HTTP and FTP caching with a default TTL setting. You can enable or disable HTTP or FTP caching on the default rule, or modify the default TTL settings. These settings are the only settings that you can modify on the default cache rule.
Define the maximum size for cached objects.	Does not set limits on the maximum size of cached objects.
Define whether Secure Sockets Layer (SSL) content will be cached.	Caches SSL responses.

Exam Tip   Remember that the default cache rule applies to all cached content on the ISA Server computer. The only way that you can change this default behavior for a specific Web site is by configuring a cache rule for that site. So if you see an exam question that defines different caching requirements for a particular Web site, you must create a caching rule. If you want to enable caching, yet need to ensure that users always get the most recent data from a particular Web site, configure a cache rule that prevents caching for that Web site.

How to Create and Manage Cache Rules

To create a caching rule, complete the following procedure:

1. In ISA Server Management Console, click Cache, and then choose the option to Create a Cache Rule.

2. The New Cache Rule Wizard starts. All the cache rule settings can be configured using the wizard.

3. The first option is to define the Cache Rule Destination, as shown in Figure 6-6. The cache rule destination uses destination sets defining to which Web content this rule applies. You can use any destination set that is available on ISA Server, or create a new destination set. For example, if you want to apply this rule to a specific Web site, you can use or create a URL set or a domain name set and apply the rule only to that destination set.

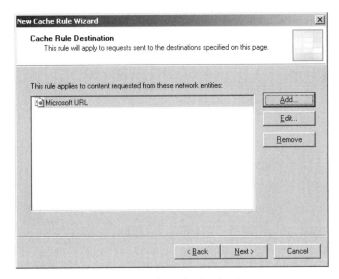

Figure 6-6   Configuring cache rule destinations

4. The second option you must define is the content retrieval settings, as shown in Figure 6-7. The settings are described in Table 6-4.

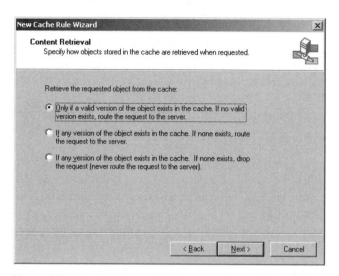

Figure 6-7 Configuring cache rule content retrieval settings

Table 6-4 Configuring Content Retrieval Settings

Content Retrieval Options	Choose This Option To
Only If A Valid Version Of The Object Exists In The Cache. If No Valid Version Exists, Route The Request To The Server	Configure ISA Server to retrieve the requested object from the cache if it has not expired. If the object has expired, ISA Server will retrieve the content from the Internet.
If Any Version Of The Object Exists In The Cache. If None Exists, Route The Request To The Server	Configure ISA Server to retrieve the requested object from its cache if any version exists, even if the version is expired. If no version exists, ISA Server will retrieve the content from the Internet.
If Any Version Of The Object Exists In The Cache. If None Exists, Drop The Request (Never Route The Request To The Server)	Configure ISA Server to retrieve the requested object from its cache if any version exists, even if the version is expired. If no version exists, ISA Server will return an error to the client.

5. You can also configure what content will be stored in the cache on the Cache Content page, as shown in Figure 6-8. The options are listed in Table 6-5.

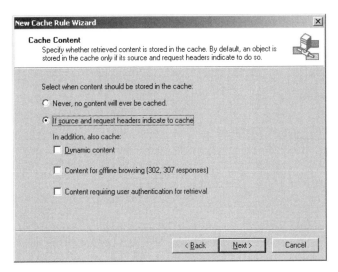

Figure 6-8   Configuring cache rule content caching settings

Table 6-5   Configuring Content Caching

Cache Content Options	Choose This Option To
Never, No Content Will Ever Be Cached	Configure ISA Server to not cache any of the requested content but to always retrieve it from the Internet.
If Source And Request Headers Indicate To Cache	Configure ISA Server to cache all content that is marked as cacheable.
In Addition, Also Cache: Dynamic Content	Configure ISA Server to also cache dynamic content that would normally not be cached.
In Addition, Also Cache: Content For Offline Browsing (302, 307 Responses)	Configure ISA Server to cache content with 302 and 307 response codes. These response codes indicate that the content has been temporarily relocated or the client has been temporarily redirected.
In Addition, Also Cache: Content Requiring User Authentication For Retrieval	Configure ISA Server to cache content that may require authentication to be accessed.

6. On the Cache Advanced Configuration page shown in Figure 6-9, you can configure the settings listed in Table 6-6.

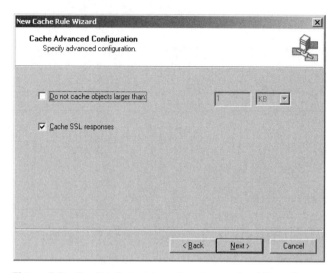

Figure 6-9   Configuring cache rule advanced configuration

Table 6-6   Configuring the Advanced Caching Settings

Advanced Caching Options	Choose This Option To
Do Not Cache Objects Larger Than:	Limit the size of objects that ISA Server will cache.
Cache SSL Responses	Configure ISA Server to cache SSL content. ISA Server can only cache SSL content in an SSL bridging configuration.

7. On the HTTP Caching page, as shown in Figure 6-10, you can configure the settings listed in Table 6-7.

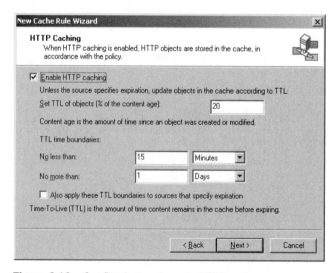

Figure 6-10   Configuring cache rule HTTP caching

Table 6-7   Configuring HTTP Caching

HTTP Caching Options	Choose This Option To
Enable HTTP Caching	Enable or disable the caching of HTTP content.
Set TTL Of Objects (Percent Of The Content Age)	Configure the TTL for HTTP content. The time is expressed as a percentage of the TTL provided by the content.
TTL Time Boundaries	Configure the minimum and maximum amount of time that the content should be cached.
Also Apply These TTL Boundaries To Sources That Specify Expiration	Configure the ISA Server TTL settings to override the expiration data included with the content.

8. On the FTP Caching page, as shown in Figure 6-11, you can configure the settings listed in Table 6-8.

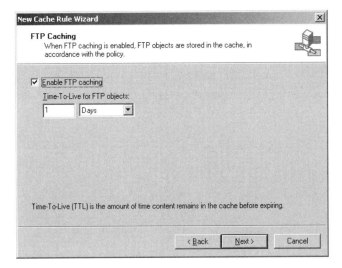

Figure 6-11   Configuring cache rule FTP caching

Table 6-8   Configuring FTP Caching

FTP Caching Options	Choose This Option To
Enable FTP Caching	Enable or disable the caching of FTP content.
TTL For FTP Objects	Configure how long the TTL is for FTP content.

Managing Cache Rules

After you configure caching rules, you may need to modify the cache rule settings or manage the cache rules. There are several actions that you may need to perform to manage cache rules. These include the following:

■ **Modifying settings**   You may need to modify a cache rule after creating it. To modify the cache rule settings, open ISA Server Management, expand the Cache container, and click the cache rule on the Cache Rules tab. Then click Edit Selected Rule, as shown in Figure 6-12. The configuration options when modifying the rule are the same as the options when creating the rule, with one additional option. When you modify the cache rule properties, you can use destination sets to configure exceptions to the network entities that the rule applies to. For example, if you need to configure a rule that applies to all Web sites except one, you can configure a destination set for the Web site's URL and add it to the Exceptions list.

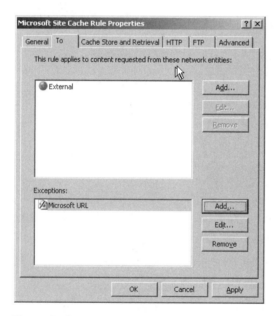

Figure 6-12   Adding exceptions to a cache rule

■ **Managing rule order**   Just like firewall access rules, you may need to modify the cache rule order to achieve a desired result. When ISA Server receives a Web request, it evaluates the cache rules in order. The first cache rule that matches the client request is applied. For example, you may have a cache rule that specifies the caching criteria for all Internet Web sites and another rule that specifies different caching requirements for a specific Web site. If the caching rule controlling caching for all Web sites is listed before the more specific rule, the more specific rule will never be applied. In general, you should configure the more specific rules so that they are evaluated first. The default caching rule will always be the last rule to be applied. To modify the rule order, click the rule you want to reorder and click either Move Selected Rules Up or Move Selected Rules Down.

- **Disabling or deleting cache rules**   If a cache rule is no longer required, you can disable or delete the rule. To do this, click the rule you want to modify and then click Disable Selected Rules or Delete Selected Rules.

- **Export and import cache rules**   Just as with any other ISA Server configuration setting, you can export the cache rule configuration to an .xml file and import cache rule settings. Use this option to create a backup copy of your cache rules before modifying the configuration.

Guidelines for Troubleshooting Caching

Caching is an important feature of ISA Server 2004 and, if configured correctly, caching can provide benefits in speed of response and in reduction of bandwidth usage. At the same time, ISA Server caching there are also situations in which you may need to troubleshoot caching on ISA Server. Use the following guidelines when troubleshooting ISA Server caching:

- If users are accessing the Internet to retrieve objects rather than retrieving the objects from the ISA Server cache, check to see if caching is enabled. To do this, check the cache configuration to ensure that a cache drive has been created. And confirm that the client computers are configured to use the ISA Server computer as a Web proxy server.

- If only some objects are cached and the cache contents are deleted frequently, ensure that the cache drive is large enough. Cached content may be being discarded due to lack of space. You can use Performance Monitor to check the Total URLs Cached and Total Memory URLs Retrieved. A low number could indicate a cache drive that is too small.

- If some Web sites are not being cached at all and you have caching rules configured, ensure that the caching rule order is correct. Check to see that one rule is not blocking another rule from being evaluated. Rules are evaluated in the order that they are listed in the ISA Server Management interface.

- If users cannot retrieve content from specific Web sites, check to see if negative caching is enabled. Intermittent network problems may have caused one negative response to be cached, thereby affecting all subsequent users.

- If users are receiving outdated content from a particular Web site that is included in a cache rule, decrease the TTL for the caching rule.

■ If objects are being cached but not returned to clients from the cache, check to see if the cache has become corrupted. Use Performance Monitor to check caching statistics. If Performance Monitor indicates that Web content is being cached, but no content is being retrieved from the cache, you may need to clear the ISA Server cache. You can clear the cache by disabling caching and enabling it again.

See Also   You can also download a script from Microsoft TechNet that you can use to clear the contents of the cache file. The file is available as part of the Deleting Cache Contents article located at *http://www.microsoft.com/technet/prodtechnol/isa/2004/plan/ deletecachecontents.mspx.*

Practice: Configuring Caching and Cache Rules

In this practice, you will configure ISA Serve caching and then configure a cache rule. You will use Microsoft Internet Explorer, ISA Server logging, and the Performance Microsoft Management Console (MMC) to monitor caching.

Exercise 1: Enabling and Configuring Caching

1. Log on to ISA1 as an ISA Server Administrator. Open ISA Server Management. Expand ISA1, expand Configuration, and then click Cache.

2. In the details pane, click Cache Rules tab.

3. On the Tasks tab, click Define Cache Drives.

4. In the Define Cache Drives dialog box, ensure that the C drive is selected.

5. In Maximum cache size, type **50**. Click Set to configure the cache drive.

6. Click OK, and then click Apply. In the ISA Server Warning dialog box, click Save The Changes And Restart The Services, and then click OK.

7. After the changes are applied, click OK.

8. Click Configure Cache Settings.

9. In the Cache Settings dialog box, on the Advanced tab, clear the check box for Cache Objects even if they do not have an HTTP status code of 200. Click OK.

10. Click Apply to apply the changes.

Exercise 2: Configuring Cache Rules on ISA Server

1. In the ISA Server Management Console, click the Cache Rules tab.

2. On the Tasks tab, click Create a Cache Rule.

3. On the Welcome To The New Cache Rule Wizard page, type **Microsoft Site Cache Rule** as the name for the rule, and then click Next.

4. On the Cache Rule Destination page, click Add to open the Add Network Entities dialog box. Expand URL Sets, and then click Microsoft URL. Click Add, and then click Close.

5. On the Cache Rule Destination page, click Next.

6. On the Content Retrieval page, click Next.

7. On the Cache Content page, click Next.

8. On the Cache Advanced Configuration page, click Next.

9. On the HTTP Caching page, ensure that HTTP caching is enabled, and then click Next.

10. On the FTP Caching page, disable FTP caching, and then click Next.

11. On the Completing The New Cache Rule Wizard page, review the settings, and then click Finish.

12. Click Apply to apply the changes.

Exercise 3: Monitoring ISA Server Caching

1. On CLIENT1, log on as a domain user.

2. Click Start and then right-click Internet. Click Internet Properties.

3. On the Advanced tab, under Security, select the check box for Empty Temporary Internet Files When Browser Is Closed. Click OK.

4. On ISA1, in ISA Server Management, click Monitoring.

5. Click the Logging tab. On the Tasks tab, click Configure Web Proxy Logging.

6. In the Web Proxy Logging Properties dialog box, on the Fields tab, select the check box for Cache Information. Click OK.

7. Click Apply to apply the changes.

8. On the Logging tab, click Start Query.

9. Right-click Log Time and click Add/Remove Columns.

10. In the Add/Remove Columns dialog box, click Cache Information, and then click Add to add the column to the Displayed Columns list.

11. Click Cache Information in the Displayed Columns list and move it up so that it is second in the list.

12. Click URL in the Displayed Columns list and move it up so that it is third in the list.

13. Click OK.

14. On ISA1, open the Performance Console from the Administrative Tools folder.

15. Ensure that the Pages/Sec counter is selected and press DELETE. Press DELETE two more times, deleting all the performance counters.

16. Click Add (+) on the Performance Console toolbar.

17. In the Add Counters dialog box, in the Performance Object list, click ISA Server Cache.

18. Click All counters, and then click Add.

19. Click Close to close the Add Counters dialog box.

20. Press CTRL-R to switch the performance view to a report view.

21. On CLIENT1, open Internet Explorer and access *http://www.microsoft.com.*

22. Close Internet Explorer.

23. On ISA1, in ISA Server Management, click Stop Query.

24. Review information in the Cache Information and Destination IP columns. A cache information value of 800000 means that the content was retrieved from the Internet, but that the content is cacheable and that the response included the Last-Modified header. A destination Internet Protocol (IP) that is the actual IP address of the server on the Internet also indicates that the page was retrieved from the Internet. A value of 40840000 indicates that this content should not be cached because it contains the Cache-Control: No-Cache header or the Pragma: No-Cache header. A value of a00000 indicates that this content should be cached but it has a time limit defined.

25. Switch to the Performance Console. Notice that ISA Server has cached several URLs.

26. In ISA Server Management, click Start Query.

27. On CLIENT1, open Internet Explorer and access *http://www.microsoft.com.*

28. Close Internet Explorer.

29. On ISA1, click Stop Query.

30. Review information in the Cache Information and Destination IP columns for each of the Tailspin Toys URLs. A cache information value of 0 means that the content was retrieved from the ISA Server cache. A destination IP of 0.0.0.0 also indicates that the page was retrieved from the ISA Server cache.

31. Switch to the Performance Console. Notice that the Total URLs Retrieved from Memory Cache and the Total Bytes Retrieved from Memory Cache (KB) counters show that ISA Server retrieved the cached content from the memory cache.

32. Close the Performance Console.

Lesson Review

Use the following questions to help determine whether you have learned enough to move on to the next lesson. If you have difficulty answering these questions, review the material in this lesson before beginning the next lesson. You can find answers to these questions in the "Questions and Answers" section at the end of this chapter.

1. You have deployed ISA Server 2004 and configured the server as a Web proxy server. All internal client computers are configured as Firewall clients. You enable caching on ISA Server, using the default caching configuration. After you enable caching, users report that they are getting more error messages when they try to access some Web sites. You investigate and determine that the error messages appear when a Web site is temporarily unavailable. Users continue to get the error messages for some time after the Web site is available. You need to ensure that the users can access the Web sites as soon as they are available on the Internet. How can you do this?

   _____

   _____

   _____

2. You have deployed ISA Server and configured the server as a Web proxy server. After you enable caching, some users report that they get out-of-date information from a partner Web site. The Web site contains information that changes frequently, sometimes several times a day. The users say that the information from the Web site that they see is sometimes more than a day old. You must ensure that users always get the most recent information from the partner Web site, but you do not want to affect the caching configuration for other Web sites. What should you do?

   a. Modify the cache settings so that data that has expired for more than 30 minutes will not be returned to the client.

   b. Create a cache rule for this Web site. Configure the cache rule to never cache content from the Web site.

   c. Create a cache rule for this Web site. Configure the cache rule to cache dynamic content.

   d. Create a cache rule that will apply to all Web sites except this Web site. Configure the cache rule to not cache dynamic content.

3. You have configured ISA Server to cache content from a Web site that is updated regularly. You want to ensure that your users never receive an outdated page from cache if the Web site is unavailable. You also want them to be informed if the Web site is unavailable. What settings should you configure?

_____

_____

_____

Lesson Summary

- Caching is not enabled by default on ISA Server 2004. To enable caching, you must configure a cache drive. You can then configure additional cache settings for Web content.

- The default caching rule is in effect as soon as caching is enabled. If you need different caching configurations for specific Web sites, you can configure cache rules to define the types of Web content that will be cached and how it is stored and returned to users.

- Cache rules can be modified, disabled, or deleted as requirements and conditions change.

- When troubleshooting ISA Server caching, determine the extent of the problem and then check the caching and cache rule configurations.

Lesson 3: Configuring Content Download Jobs

In addition to managing caching and configuring cache rules, you may also need to configure and manage content download jobs. As described earlier, content download jobs are used to populate the ISA Server cache with content before any user requests the information. This lesson describes how to configure and manage content download jobs.

After this lesson, you will be able to

- Configure content download jobs
- Manage content download jobs

Estimated lesson time: 15 minutes

How to Configure Content Download Jobs

By default, no content download jobs are configured on ISA Server when you enable caching. You can configure a content download job to download all content or some of the content from a specific Web site. To configure a content download job, complete the following procedure:

1. In ISA Server Management, expand Configuration, click Cache and then select the Content Download Jobs tab.

2. Click Schedule A Content Download Job. If this is the first time you are enabling a content download job, you will receive a message stating the requirements for enabling schedule download jobs. The following two requirements must be met to enable content download jobs:

   ❑ The Local Host network must be configured to listen for Web proxy client requests. This option is enabled by default.

   ❑ The Scheduled Download Job configuration group must be enabled. This option is not enabled by default but can be enabled from the warning screen or by editing system policy.

3. After applying the change, click Schedule A Content Download Job again. The New Scheduled Content Download Job Wizard starts.

4. The first configuration option is to configure the download frequency, as shown in Figure 6-13. The options are described in Table 6-9.

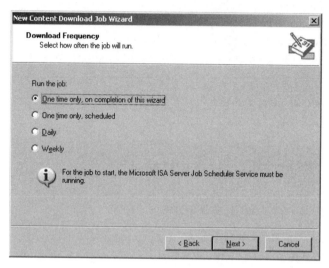

Figure 6-13   Configuring download frequency for a content download job

Table 6-9   Configuring Download Frequency

Download Frequency Options	Choose This Option To
One Time Only, On The Completion Of This Wizard	Configure ISA Server to download the content once, immediately after you apply the changes made by the wizard.
One Time Only, Scheduled	Configure ISA Server to download the content once, based on a schedule that you configure.
Daily	Configure ISA Server to download the content every day at a configured time.
Weekly	Configure ISA Server to download the content on a weekly schedule. You can configure the schedule to download on specific days during the week and at particular times.

5. The next page in the wizard depends on the choice you made in the previous step. If you chose any option other than the first option, you will be asked to configure the download schedule, as shown in Figure 6-14.

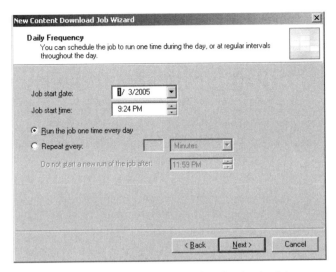

Figure 6-14   Configuring a content download schedule

6. Next, on the Content Download page, as shown in Figure 6-15, you configure the content download job details. You can configure the options listed in Table 6-10.

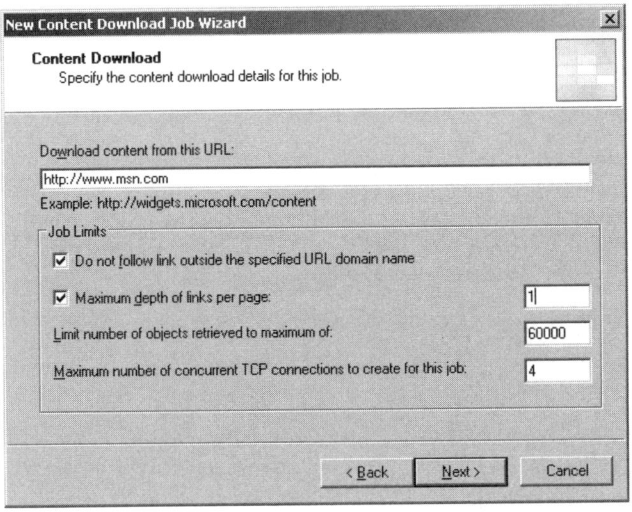

Figure 6-15   Configuring Content Download Job details

Table 6-10   Configuring Content Download Job Details

Content Download Options	Choose This Option To
Download Content From This URL	Specify the URL that will be downloaded to the ISA Server cache.
Do Not Follow Link Outside The Specified URL Domain Name	Specify that only content from the domain name in the URL will be downloaded. If this option is not selected, ISA Server will download content from all links up to the maximum depth-of-links setting.
Maximum Depth Of Links Per Page	Specify the number of links ISA Server will follow to download content.
Limit Number Of Objects Retrieved To Maximum Of	Specify the maximum number of Web objects that will be downloaded by this job.
Maximum Number Of Concurrent TCP Connections To Create For This Job	Specify the maximum number of connections that will be used to download content at the same time.

7. On the Content Caching page, you can choose how the content is cached on ISA Server, as shown in Figure 6-16. You can configure the options listed in Table 6-11.

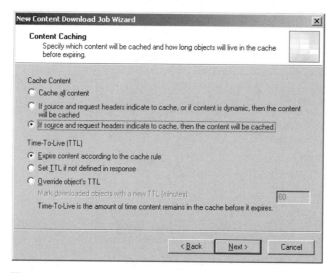

Figure 6-16   Configuring Content Download Job caching

Table 6-11   Configure Content Download Job Caching

Content Caching Options	Choose This Option To
Cache All Content	Specify that all content will be cached even if the source and request headers indicate that the content is not cacheable.
If Source And Request Headers Indicate To Cache, Or If Content Is Dynamic, Then The Content Will Be Cached	Specify that all content will be cached if the source and request headers indicate that the content is cacheable, or if the content is dynamic.
If Source And Request Headers Indicate To Cache, Then The Content Will Be Cached	Specify that all content will be cached if the source and request headers indicate that the content is cacheable.
Expire Content According To The Cache Rule	Specify that the content will expire based on the cache rule that applies to this content.
Set TTL If Not Defined In Response	Specify that the content will expire based on the TTL defined in the response header and the associated cache rule. If there is no TTL defined in the response header, configure the TTL based on the value configured in the Mark downloaded objects with a new TTL (minutes) text box.
Override Object's TTL	Specify that the content will expire based on the TTL value configured in the Mark downloaded objects with a new TTL (minutes) text box.

Exam Tip   If an exam question deals with a content download job that does not work as expected, look for details that will help you to locate the problem. If none of the expected content is cached, then check the job schedule or the URL specified in the job configuration. If some of, but not all, the content is cached, then check the job configuration to ensure that it is downloading the expected content.

How to Manage Content Download Jobs

After you configure content download jobs, you may need to modify the job setting or configure other content download job settings. There are several actions that you may need to perform to manage content download jobs. These include the following:

- **Modifying settings**   You may need to modify a content download job after creating it. To modify the cache rule settings, open ISA Server Management, expand the Cache container, and click the content download job on the Content Download Jobs tab. Then click Edit The Selected Job. The configuration options when modifying the job are the same as the options when creating the job.

- **Starting and stopping content download jobs** Regardless of the schedule configured for the content download job, you can force the job to start immediately or stop a job that's running. To start a content download job, click the job you want to start and click Start the Selected Job. To stop a currently running job, click the job you want to stop and click Stop the Selected Job.

- **Disabling or deleting content download jobs** If a content download job is no longer required, you can disable or delete the job. To do this, click the job you want to modify, and then click Disable the Selected Jobs or Delete the Selected Jobs.

Practice: Configuring Content Download Jobs

In this practice, you will configure a content download job and then you will use Internet Explorer and ISA Server logging to confirm that the content download job was successful.

Exercise 1: Creating a Content Download Job

1. On ISA1, In the ISA Server Management Console, click Cache, and then click the Content Download Jobs tab.

2. On the Tasks tab, click Schedule A Content Download Job.

3. On the Enable Schedule Content Download Jobs dialog box, click Yes.

4. Click Apply to apply the changes.

5. On the Content Download Jobs tab, click the Tasks tab, and then click Schedule A Content Download Job.

6. On the Welcome To The New Scheduled Content Download Job Wizard page, type **Download MSN.com** as the name of the rule, and then click Next.

7. On the Download Frequency page, click One Time Only, Scheduled, and then click Next.

8. On the Daily Frequency page, configure a Job Start Date with today's date, and a Job Start Time of five minutes from now. Click Next.

9. On the Content Download page, in the Download content from this URL text box, type **http://www.msn.com**. Click Do Not Follow Link Outside The Specified URL Domain Name, and click Maximum Depth Of Links Per Page. Type **1** as the maximum depth of links per page. Click Next.

10. On the Content Caching page, click Next.

11. On the Completing The New Scheduled Content Download Job Wizard page, review the configuration and click Finish.

Exercise 2: Testing the Content Download Job

1. On ISA1, in the ISA Server Management Console, click Cache Monitoring and, on the Logging tab, click Start Query.

2. On CLIENT1, open Internet Explorer and access *www.msn.com*.

3. Click several links listed on the page.

4. Close Internet Explorer.

5. On ISA1, click Stop Query.

6. Review information in the Cache Information and Destination IP columns for each of the MSN.com URLs. Notice that most of the pages for *www.msn.com* were retrieved from the ISA Server cache while pages from URLs outside of *www.msn.com* were retrieved from the Internet.

Lesson Review

Use the following questions to help determine whether you have learned enough to move on to the next lesson. If you have difficulty answering these questions, review the material in this lesson before beginning the next lesson. You can find answers to these questions in the "Questions and Answers" section at the end of this chapter.

1. Users need to access a price list that is published at a public Web site. Bandwidth usage from your office is tightly restricted during business hours. The page is dynamic content and not normally cacheable material. The site is updated once every 24 hours. How can you force ISA Server to download and cache dynamic content and minimize the use of network bandwidth during business hours?

   _____

   _____

   _____

2. You have many branch offices with slow connections to the Internet and no direct connection to head office. You have implemented ISA Server 2004 as a firewall solution at all branch offices. You also want to take advantage of the caching ability of ISA Server to allow branch office ISA Server computers to update content from the corporate Web site twice a day during business hours. Due to hardware restrictions, you want the branches to cache only content from your corporate Web site. How would you configure that?

   _____

   _____

   _____

3. Many users in your organization need access to a partner organization's Web site, so you create a content download job for that Web site. Because the content on the Web site changes daily, you configure the content download job to run every night. After the first time the content download job runs, you notice that the job included much more content than you expected. You notice that many Web sites that are not part of the partner Web site were included in the content download job. You need to ensure that only content from the partner Web site is included in the content download job. How can you do this?

   a. Configure the content download job to use a maximum depth of links per page of 1.

   b. Configure the content download job to limit the number of objects retrieved to a low number.

   c. Configure the content download job to not follow links outside the partner organization's Web site URL.

   d. Configure the content download job to cache only the content that is configured as cacheable.

Lesson Summary

- Content download jobs are used to populate the ISA Server cache with content before any user requests the information. Content download jobs are configured on a site-by-site basis and include several configuration options such as scheduling the download, and configuring what types of data are cached and how long the data is kept stored in the cache.

- After you configure content download jobs, you can modify the job setting or configure other content download job settings.

Real World   What Is the Future of Caching?

Caching is a valuable function of ISA Server 2004. However, as the Internet becomes more dynamic and interactive, the amount of cacheable content will decrease and with it, the value of caching Web content. The use of Active Server Pages, .NET programming technologies, and more user-friendly programming languages means that there is less static content on public Web sites. Software packages such as Microsoft FrontPage 2003 have made sophisticated Web site development available to almost everyone. No longer do you need to be a programming wizard to include dynamic content on your site. Often, the only cacheable content on a public Web site is a home page that merely provides links to dynamic content.

Perhaps the most useful feature of caching today, and the long-term future of caching, may be between business partners or for internal use. The branch-office scenarios, in which branch offices with slow links make use of content download jobs to download head-office Web content to their local ISA Server computer, will always have value. Reports and other types of information can be generated at the head office and published to an internal site to be downloaded to branch offices on a regular schedule to give employees access to up to date information without many individuals using bandwidth during the day to access the same content. Similar situations can exist between clients and vendors in which updated price lists or other information can be downloaded to clients on a regular basis.

Case Scenario Exercises

In this exercise, you will read two scenarios about configuring caching on ISA Server 2004, and then answer the questions that follow. If you have difficulty completing this work, review the material in this chapter before beginning the next chapter. You can find answers to these questions in the "Questions and Answers" section at the end of this chapter.

Scenario 1

You work for an organization with branch offices located across the country. Some of those offices are in remote areas and are connected to the Internet by a dial-up connection with expensive daytime rates. Users in all branch offices need to access a number of public and partner Web sites to do their jobs. These users report that they must wait for extended periods to access those sites. Some of those sites contain dynamic content.

Scenario 1 Question

1. You want to increase response times for users at the branch offices and reduce the costs for the Internet connections. What steps should you take?

Scenario 2

You publish a Web site in your perimeter network using a Web publishing rule. The content on the Web site is updated frequently throughout the day as you perform random updates of your page as new data becomes available. The content is accessed and used by your business partners.

Scenario 2 Question

1. Because you perform unscheduled updates of the data, you must ensure that the content cannot be cached by your business partners so that they always get the most up-to-date information. What steps must you take?

_____

_____

_____

Chapter Summary

- Caching is the ability of the ISA Server 2004 to retrieve and store cacheable Web content so that, the next time a client requests the same content, it can be retrieved from the cache file to provide faster response and reduce bandwidth consumption. Content download jobs allow you to prepopulate the ISA Server cache content. ISA Server also enables Web proxy chaining that can allow branch offices to take advantage of a larger cache maintained at head office and use it to build up cached content at the branch office.

- Caching is not enabled by default on ISA Server 2004. To enable caching, you need to configure a cache drive. You can also configure cache rules to specify custom rules for how content is downloaded from a specific Web site.

- Content download jobs are configured on a site-by-site basis. When you configure content download jobs, you can specify what Web sites are downloaded as well as configure settings for how the content is cached.

Exam Highlights

Before taking the exam, review the key points and terms that are presented in this chapter. You need to know this information.

Key Points

- By default, caching is disabled on ISA Server 2004.

- The only way to configure caching for one Web site so that it is different from other Web sites is to create a cache rule for the Web site. The default cache rule is applied to all Web sites that are not specified in another cache rule.

- ISA Server does not cache all content. For example, dynamic content, SSL encrypted content or content that requires authentication may not be cached. You can modify how ISA Server caches all of these types of content.

- You can use ISA Server logging or the Performance MMC to monitor ISA Server caching. Use these tools to optimize and troubleshoot caching.

- Content download jobs are used to retrieve Web content in advance. If content download jobs do not work as expected, check when the job is scheduled to run, and check the job configuration to ensure that it is downloading and caching the expected content.

Key Terms

cache rule   Define the types of Web content that is stored in the cache and how Web content is stored and returned to users from the cache. Rules can be configured to allow or deny caching from particular sites.

content download jobs   Are used to retrieve Web content from selected Web sites in advance to provide faster response for internal clients. Jobs can be configured to download any content on a flexible schedule.

forward caching   Forward caching occurs when a user on the corporate network makes a request for Web content located on an Internet Web server and the request is intercepted by ISA Server. ISA Server retrieves the content from the Internet Web server, stores it in its cache, and returns the content to the user.

reverse caching   Reverse caching occurs when users on the Internet request Web content located on the corporate network. When an Internet user requests content from the internal server, ISA Server forwards the request to the Web server. ISA Server will cache a copy of the requested information so that the next request for the same information can be provided from the ISA Server cache rather than accessing the internal Web server again.

Questions and Answers

Page
6-11
Lesson 1 Review

1. You have deployed ISA Server 2004 in a large office with a relatively slow Internet connection. The ISA Server computer is to be used only for caching content. What can you do to maximize cache response time?

    You can allocate as much disk space as possible on the ISA Server computer for caching. You can also assign a higher percentage of RAM on the server to cache Web contents.

2. You have deployed ISA Server 2004 and configured the server as a Web proxy server. All internal client computers are configured as Web proxy clients. You have limited bandwidth to the Internet, so you enable caching on ISA Server, using the default caching configuration. Many users in your organization, you notice, access a partner organization's Web site several times a day. The Web site contains many large files that are changed every few days; when users download the files, much of the available bandwidth to the Internet is used. You need to make sure that users have access to the partner Web site, yet you must limit the amount of bandwidth used to access the Web site as much as possible during working hours. What should you do?

    a. Install the Firewall client on each client computer.

    b. Configure caching to cache only small files from the partner Web site.

    c. Configure a content download job to download the partner Web site every night.

    d. Configure the ISA Server to cache content with a TTL of one day.

    C is correct. To minimize the effect of accessing the partner Web site during working hours, you must configure a content download job that will download the Web site at night. A is incorrect because Web proxy client requests are also cached, so installing the Firewall client will not improve performance. B is incorrect; in fact, this option would decrease Internet performance because none of the large files would be cached. D is incorrect. It will not improve performance because the clients still need to access the Web site to download the files every time the files change.

3. Users in your organization must download files from an FTP site on the Internet twice a day. Your users report that they frequently download outdated versions of the file. What is happening and how will you fix it?

    By default, when you enable caching on ISA Server, it will cache FTP content for one day. This means that the users are retrieving the content from the ISA Server cache. You can solve the problem by reducing the TTL for FTP objects so that content is updated more often or by disabling FTP caching.

Lesson 2 Review

1. You have deployed ISA Server 2004 and configured the server as a Web proxy server. All internal client computers are configured as Firewall clients. You enable caching on ISA Server, using the default caching configuration. After you enable caching, users report that they are getting more error messages when they try to access some Web sites. You investigate and determine that the error messages appear when a Web site is temporarily unavailable. Users continue to get the error messages for some time after the Web site is available. You need to ensure that the users can access the Web sites as soon as they are available on the Internet. How can you do this?

   By default, ISA Server enables negative caching, which means that it will cache error messages from the Internet and return these responses to clients even after the Web site is available. To disable this, you must configure ISA Server to not cache objects that do not have a status code of 200.

2. You have deployed ISA Server and configured the server as a Web proxy server. After you enable caching, some users report that they get out-of-date information from a partner Web site. The Web site contains information that changes frequently, sometimes several times a day. The users say that the information from the Web site that they see is sometimes more than a day old. You must ensure that users always get the most recent information from the partner Web site, but you do not want to affect the caching configuration for other Web sites. What should you do?

   a. Modify the cache settings so that data that has expired for more than 30 minutes will not be returned to the client.

   b. Create a cache rule for this Web site. Configure the cache rule to never cache content from the Web site.

   c. Create a cache rule for this Web site. Configure the cache rule to cache dynamic content.

   d. Create a cache rule that will apply to all Web sites except this Web site. Configure the cache rule to not cache dynamic content.

   B is correct. In this case, there is likely a problem with the partner Web site, in that it contains information that changes frequently yet the data is still being cached. This can happen if the Web pages do not contain TTL information. To ensure that this data is not cached, configure a cache rule for this Web site. A is incorrect; this option only configures ISA Server's response to expired content when the Internet Web server is not available. C and D will not change the caching behavior in this scenario.

3. You have configured ISA Server to cache content from a Web site that is updated regularly. You want to ensure that your users never receive an outdated page from cache if the Web site is unavailable. You also want them to be informed if the Web site is unavailable. What settings should you configure?

On the Cache Settings, Advanced tab under the heading If Website of Expired Object Cannot be Reached select Do Not Return the Expired Object (Return an Error Page).

Page
6-37

Lesson 3 Review

1. Users need to access a price list that is published at a public Web site. Bandwidth usage from your office is tightly restricted during business hours. The page is dynamic content and not normally cacheable material. The site is updated once every 24 hours. How can you force ISA Server to download and cache dynamic content and minimize the use of network bandwidth during business hours?

   Schedule a Content Download job to retrieve the material from the partner's site in advance during non-business hours after it has been updated. It will be available for your users by configuring the download job to Cache if Content is Dynamic in the properties of the job.

2. You have many branch offices with slow connections to the Internet and no direct connection to head office. You have implemented ISA Server 2004 as a firewall solution at all branch offices. You also want to take advantage of the caching ability of ISA Server to allow branch office ISA Server computers to update content from the corporate Web site twice a day during business hours. Due to hardware restrictions, you want the branches to cache only content from your corporate Web site. How would you configure that?

   Create a Content Download Job for your corporate Web site. Then create a Cache Rule to cache content from your corporate Web site. Create another cache rule to block content caching for all other Web sites. Ensure that the corporate cache rule is listed first.

3. Many users in your organization need access to a partner organization's Web site, so you create a content download job for that Web site. Because the content on the Web site changes daily, you configure the content download job to run every night. After the first time the content download job runs, you notice that the job included much more content than you expected. You notice that many Web sites that are not part of the partner Web site were included in the content download job. You need to ensure that only content from the partner Web site is included in the content download job. How can you do this?

   a. Configure the content download job to use a maximum depth of links per page of 1.

   b. Configure the content download job to limit the number of objects retrieved to a low number.

   c. Configure the content download job to not follow links outside the partner organization's Web site URL.

   d. Configure the content download job to cache only the content that is configured as cacheable.

   C is correct. To ensure that only pages from the partner Web site are downloaded, you must configure the job to not download any links outside the Web site URL. A is incorrect because this option would limit the amount of content downloaded from the partner site, and if a link on the first page pointed to an outside Web site, that link would still be downloaded. B is incorrect because this option would limit the amount of content downloaded from the partner site, and would not prevent pages from an outside Web site from being downloaded. D is incorrect because most content is configured as downloadable.

Case Scenario Exercises

Page
6-39

Scenario 1 Question

1. You want to increase response times for users at the branch offices and reduce the costs for the Internet connections. What steps should you take?

Install ISA Server 2004 at each branch office and enable caching. Create caching rules as required to cache dynamic content from particular sites. Analyze the ISA Server usage reports to determine which sites are most frequently used and then create Content Download jobs for those sites to download content overnight to take advantage of lower telephone rates.

Page
6-40

Scenario 2 Question

1. Because you perform unscheduled updates of the data, you must ensure that the content cannot be cached by your business partners so that they always get the most up-to-date information. What steps must you take?

Create a cache rule to ensure that nothing is cached for requests for the published Web site from outside your enterprise.

7 Configuring ISA Server as a Firewall

Exam Objectives in this Chapter:

- Configure firewall settings
    - Configure intrusion detection
    - Configure IP options filtering
    - Configure IP fragmentation settings
- Configure ISA Server 2004 to support a network topology
    - Select appropriate templates
    - Define networks
    - Configure route relationships between networks
- Create policy rules for Web publishing
    - Configure HTTP filtering for Web publishing

Why This Chapter Matters

For much of its development cycle, Microsoft Internet Security and Acceleration (ISA) Server 2004 was called Microsoft Firewall Server 2004. This name reflects one of the primary deployment scenarios for ISA Server 2004. Many organizations are taking a look at ISA Server as an Internet-edge firewall. Another common scenario is to use another firewall as the Internet-edge firewall and use ISA Server as a second firewall, chiefly for application filtering.

ISA Server 2004 is a full-featured firewall. ISA Server provides advanced filtering functionality and intrusion detection. ISA Server supports an unlimited number of networks, and a user-friendly interface for configuring the access rules that define what types of network traffic will be allowed between networks. ISA Server also provides network templates as a means for simplifying the deployment of networks and firewall access rules. But the most powerful feature of using ISA Server as a firewall is its application-layer filtering. Many of the recent security breaches and attacks occur at the application layer, so an application-layer firewall is crucial to protecting your network.

Lessons in this Chapter:

- Lesson 1: Introduction to ISA Server as a Firewall. 7-3
- Lesson 2: Configuring Multiple Networking on ISA Server. 7-12
- Lesson 3: Implementing Perimeter Networks and Network Templates 7-24
- Lesson 4: Configuring Intrusion Detection and IP Preferences. 7-37
- Lesson 5: Implementing Application and Web Filtering. 7-46

Before You Begin

This chapter presents the skills and concepts related to deploying ISA Server 2004 as a firewall. If you plan to complete the practices and lab in this chapter, prepare the following:

- A Microsoft Windows Server 2003 (Standard Edition or Enterprise Edition) computer installed as DC1 and configured as a domain controller in the *cohovineyard.com* domain.

- A second Windows Server 2003 computer installed as ISA1 and configured as a domain member in the *cohovineyard.com* domain. Three network interfaces should be installed on this server. The external interface should be connected to a network that contains one or more Web servers. If possible, the network interface should be attached to the Internet.

- A Microsoft Windows XP computer installed as CLIENT1. This computer must be a member of the *cohovineyard.com* domain. The Windows Server 2003 Resource Kit tools must be installed on the client computer.

- To complete the troubleshooting lab at the end of the chapter, MSN Messenger or Windows Messenger must be installed on CLIENT1 and a user account configured to use MSN Messenger. The external interface on ISA1 must have access to the Internet.

Lesson 1: Introduction to ISA Server as a Firewall

Firewalls are deployed to limit network traffic from one network to another. To distinguish between network traffic that should be allowed and network traffic that should be blocked, firewalls use packet filters, stateful filters, application filters, and intrusion detection. This lesson describes this core functionality provided by firewalls and how this functionality is implemented in ISA Server 2004.

After this lesson, you will be able to

■ Describe packet filtering and the benefits of using packet filtering

■ Describe stateful filtering the benefits of using stateful filtering

■ Describe application filtering and the benefits of using application filtering

■ Describe intrusion detection and the benefits of using intrusion detection

Estimated lesson time: 30 minutes

What Is Packet Filtering?

A firewall's primary role is to prevent network traffic from entering an internal network unless the traffic is explicitly permitted. One way that a firewall ensures this is through packet filtering. Packet filters control access to the network at the network layer by inspecting and allowing or denying the Internet Protocol (IP) packets. When the firewall inspects an IP packet, it examines only information in the network and transport layer headers.

A packet-filtering firewall can evaluate IP packets using the following criteria:

■ **Destination address**   The destination address may be the actual IP address of the destination computer in the case of a routed relationship between the two networks being connected by ISA Server. The destination may also be the external interface of ISA Server in the case of a network address translation (NAT) network relationship.

■ **Source address**   This is the IP address of the computer that originally transmitted the packet.

■ **IP protocol and protocol number**   You can configure packet filters for Transmission Control Protocol (TCP), User Datagram Protocol (UDP), Internet Control Message Protocol (ICMP), and any other protocol. Each protocol is assigned a number. For example, TCP is protocol 6, and the Generic Routing Encapsulation (GRE) protocol for Point-to-Point Tunneling Protocol (PPTP) connections is protocol 47.

- **Direction**   This is the direction of the packet through the firewall. In most cases, the direction can be defined by inbound, outbound, or both. For some protocols, such as File Transfer Protocol (FTP) or UDP, the directional choices may be Receive Only, Send Only, or Both.

- **Port numbers**   A TCP or UDP packet filter defines a local and remote port. The local and remote ports can be defined by a fixed port number or a dynamic port number.

Advantages and Disadvantages of Packet Filtering

Packet filtering has advantages and disadvantages. Among its advantages are the following:

- Packet filtering must inspect only the network and transport layer headers, so packet filtering is very fast.

- Packet filtering can be used to block a particular IP address or to allow a particular IP address. If you detect an application-level attack from an IP address, you can block that IP address at the packet-filter level. Or, if you need to enable access to your network and you know that all access attempts will be coming from a particular address, you can enable access only for that source address.

- Packet filtering can be used for ingress and egress filtering. Ingress filtering blocks all access on the external interface of the firewall to packets that have a source IP address that is logically on the internal network. For example, if your internal network includes the 192.168.20.0 network, an ingress filter will block a packet arriving at the external interface that claims to be coming from 192.168.20.1. An egress filter prevents packets from leaving your network that have a source IP address that is not on the internal network.

Disadvantages of packet filtering are the following:

- Packet filters cannot prevent IP address spoofing or source-routing attacks. An attacker can substitute the IP address of a trusted host as the source IP address and the packet filter will not block the packet. Or the attacker can include routing information in the packet that includes incorrect routing information for return packets so that the packets are not returned to the actual host, but to the attacker's computer.

- Packet filters cannot prevent IP-fragment attacks. An IP-fragment attack splits a single IP packet into multiple fragments. Most packet-filtering firewalls check only the first fragment and assume that the other fragments of the same packet are acceptable. The additional fragments may contain malicious content.

- Packet filters are not application-aware. You may be blocking the default Telnet port (Port 23) on your firewall, but allowing access to the Hypertext Transfer Protocol (HTTP) port (Port 80). If an attacker can configure a Telnet server to run on Port 80 on your network, the packets would be passed to the server.

ISA Server 2004 and Packet Filtering

ISA Server 2004 does not have an option for directly configuring packet filtering. However, ISA Server does operate as a packet filter firewall, inspecting traffic at the network and transport layers. For example, if you define a firewall access rule that enables all protocol traffic from an IP address on one network to an IP address on another network, ISA Server uses a packet filter to allow that traffic. Or, if you configure a firewall access rule that denies the use of the default Telnet port (TCP Port 23), ISA Server will use a packet filter to block that port. ISA Server also enables ingress and egress filtering by default. ISA Server 2000 supports direct configuration of packet filters. If you upgrade to ISA Server 2004 from ISA Server 2000, the packet filter definitions are replaced by access rules.

> **Exam Tip**   You may get an exam question that states a company requirement to block all connection attempts from a specific host, or to allow a specific protocol from a particular host. Remember that, with ISA Server 2004, you can only configure this type of access using an access rule.

What Is Stateful Filtering?

When a firewall uses stateful filtering, the firewall examines not only the packet header information, but the status of the packet as well. For example, the firewall can inspect a packet at its external interface and determine whether the packet is a response to a request from the internal network. This check can be performed at both the transport and the application layers.

Stateful filtering uses information about the TCP session to determine whether a packet should be blocked or allowed through the firewall. TCP sessions are established using the TCP three-way handshake, the purpose of which is to synchronize the sequence number and acknowledgment numbers and to exchange other information defining how the two hosts will exchange packets. The following steps outline the process:

1. The initiator of the TCP session, typically a client, sends a TCP segment to the server. The client sends its sequence number and requested that the server provide its sequence numbers (by setting the SYN bit to 1).

2. The responder of the TCP session, typically a server, sends back a TCP segment containing its initial sequence number and an acknowledgment (ACK) of the client's sequence number. The server sets both the SYN bit and ACK bit to 1. The ACK bit indicates that the server has received the client's sequence number.

3. The initiator sends the server a TCP segment containing an acknowledgment of the server's sequence number. Once the client and server have agreed on the sequence numbers, they will use the sequence numbers to track all packets. TCP uses the information to recover from errors, such as packets arriving out of order or packets not arriving.

TCP uses a similar handshake process to end a connection. This guarantees that both hosts have finished transmitting and that all data was received.

A firewall uses this TCP information to perform stateful filtering. When a client on the internal network sends the first packet in the three-way handshake, the server forwards the packet and records that the packet has been sent. When the response comes back from the server, the firewall accepts the packet because it is in response to an internal request. If a packet arrives with only the SYN bit set, or with the SYN and ACK bits set, and the firewall does not have a record of a client request, the firewall blocks the packet.

The firewall can also use other characteristics of TCP session to control traffic. For example, when the client initiates the session, the firewall can set a timer and keep the session open only as long as specified by the timer. The firewall can also analyze application-level data to perform stateful filtering. For example, when a client sends a GET command for a specific Uniform Resource Locator (URL) on a Web server, the firewall can track the request and allow a response. An HTTP packet that arrives without a corresponding client request is dropped.

Advantages and Disadvantages of Stateful Filtering

Using stateful filtering has several advantages. For example, stateful filtering ensures that all network traffic forwarded by the firewall is part of an existing session, or matches the rules for creating a new session. In addition, stateful filtering implements dynamic packet filtering, which ensures that specific ports are available only when a valid session exists. For example, if the Web Proxy filter requests that a Web server respond on Port 1159, ISA Server will listen on Port 1159 for only as long as the connection exists.

However, stateful filtering still does not provide enough protection against the threats to network security. Many of the newest attacks occur at the application level. For example, a client computer may download malicious code in an HTTP packet that is part of a legitimate session. Only application-layer stateful inspection can block these types of attacks.

ISA Server Connection Rules

ISA Server uses connection rules to keep track of sessions. Whenever a packet arrives at the server, ISA Server attempts to associate the packet with a connection rule, based on the protocol, source, and destination. A connection rule has the following attributes:

- Protocol number

- Source (IP address and port/endpoint)

- Destination (IP address and port/endpoint)

- Source address translation (used for NAT connections)

- Destination address translation (used for NAT connections)

- Statistics (number of bytes transferred, last access time)

- Misc. (checksum delta, used when doing address translation)

If the packet matches a connection rule, the packet is forwarded. If the packet does not match a connection rule, ISA Server checks the firewall access rules to determine if a new connection rule can be created. If no firewall access rule blocks the creation of the connection rule, ISA Server creates the connection and forwards the packet. If a firewall rule blocks the creation of the connection rule, the packet is dropped.

See Also   You can use the Firewall Kernel Mode Tool to monitor the current connections on the ISA Server computer, and to view the connection creation objects that define what new connections can be created. You can download the Firewall Kernel Mode Tool from *http://www.microsoft.com/isaserver/downloads/2004.asp.*

What Is Application-Layer Filtering?

Application-layer filtering enables the firewall to inspect the application data in a TCP/IP packet for unacceptable commands and data. For example, a Simple Mail Transport Protocol (SMTP) filter intercepts network traffic on Port 25 and inspects it to make sure the SMTP commands are authorized before passing the communication to the destination server. An HTTP filter performs the same function on all HTTP packets. Firewalls that are capable of application-layer filtering can stop dangerous code at the edge of the network before it can do any damage.

Note   Application filters are described in more detail in the last section of this chapter.

Advantages and Disadvantages of Application-Layer Filtering

Application-layer filtering can be used to stop attacks from sources such as viruses and worms. To the packet-filtering firewall, most worms look like legitimate network traffic. The headers of the packets are identical in format to those of legitimate traffic. It is the payload that is malicious; only when all the packets are put together can the worm be identified as malicious code, so these exploits often travel straight through to the private network because the firewall allowed what appeared to be legitimate application data.

> ### Real World   Why Use an Application Filtering Firewall?
>
> An application-layer firewall has become critical in securing a network from attack. For years, companies deployed firewalls that provide packet filtering and stateful filtering. Many excellent firewalls that provide this level of filtering are available. The problem is that these firewalls are so good that attackers no longer bother to attack the firewall at the network layer, but at the application layer, where many of the most serious security breaches have occurred.
>
> Attacks at the application layer use legitimate application-level protocols and ports. To a firewall that performs only packet and stateful filtering, the network packets appear to be normal application data. For example, an SMTP message that contains a virus is just an SMTP message with an attachment. Or the Web page that downloads a worm to your computer is just a series of HTTP packets. The problem is not evident until the application client or server removes the network layer information and starts processing the application data.
>
> Most organizations that I work with realize the need for an application-layer filter for e-mail and have deployed advanced SMTP filtering servers that can examine the contents of every e-mail message and block messages based on message contents or attachments. These organizations have become increasingly aware of the need for the same level of filtering for HTTP packets. HTTP has become the protocol of choice for many applications. HTTP traffic is allowed through virtually every firewall and every user's computer already has the HTTP client software installed. This makes using HTTP very attractive to an attacker. An important step in securing your network from these types of attacks is to ensure that the Web browsers installed on your client computers are fully patched and configured for optimal security. The second way to secure your network against this type of attack is to implement a firewall that can examine each HTTP packet and block the packet based on the application data. ISA Server 2004 is one of the best application-layer firewalls available today.

But the advantages of application-layer filtering transcend the prevention of attacks. It can also be used to protect your network and systems from the harmful actions often taken by unaware employees. For example, you can configure filters that prevent potentially harmful programs from being downloaded through the Internet, or ensure that critical customer data does not leave the network in an e-mail.

Application-layer filtering can also be used to more broadly limit employee actions on the network. You can use an application filter to restrict common types of inappropriate communication on your network. For example, you can block peer-to-peer file-exchange services. These types of services can consume substantial network resources and raise legal liability concerns for your organization.

The most significant disadvantage of application-filtering firewalls is performance. Because an application-layer filtering firewall examines the actual payload of each packet, application-layer filtering is usually slower than packet or stateful filtering.

What Is Intrusion Detection?

Intrusion detection is a means of detecting when an attack against a network is attempted or in progress. If you detect an intrusion attempt early enough, you may be able to prevent a successful intrusion. If an intrusion does occur, you must be alerted as soon as possible to reduce the potential impact of the intrusion and to eliminate the vulnerability in your network security.

An intrusion-detection system (IDS) that is located at the edge of a network inspects all traffic in and out of the network and identifies patterns that may indicate a network or system attack. An IDS is usually configured with information about a wide variety of known attacks, then monitors the network traffic for signatures indicating that a known attack is occurring. An IDS can also be configured with information about normal network traffic and then be configured to detect variations from the normal traffic.

A complete IDS includes several layers. One device may be located at the network perimeter and monitor all traffic entering and leaving the network. Additional devices may be deployed on the internal networks, or on routers connecting networks. A final layer of protection is provided by host-based systems in which an IDS is configured on individual computers. The most sophisticated IDS can collect information from all the layers and correlate data to make the most accurate intrusion-detection decisions.

Intrusion-detection systems also provide options for configuring alerts or responses to intrusion attempts. At the very least, an IDS should alert an administrator when an attack is detected. More sophisticated IDSs provide additional responses to attacks, including shutting down or limiting the functionality of the systems under attack.

Although both an IDS and a firewall relate to network security, an IDS differs from a firewall in that a firewall looks for intrusions to stop them from happening. The firewall limits the access between networks to prevent intrusion and does not signal an attack from inside the network. An IDS evaluates a suspected intrusion as it occurs and signals an alarm.

ISA Server and Intrusion Detection

ISA Server includes intrusion-detection functionality that monitors for several well-known vulnerabilities. ISA Server detects intrusions at two different network layers. First, ISA Server detects intrusions at the network layer. This enables ISA Server to detect vulnerabilities that are inherent to the IP layer. Second, ISA Server uses application filters to detect intrusions at the application layer. You can use third-party application filters to add more intrusion detection or create your own application filters using the filter application programming interfaces (APIs) defined in the ISA Server software development kit (SDK).

Lesson Review

Use the following questions to help determine whether you have learned enough to move on to the next lesson. If you have difficulty answering these questions, review the material in this lesson before beginning the next lesson. You can find answers to these questions in the "Questions and Answers" section at the end of this chapter.

1. You are the ISA Server administrator of your organization. You have deployed ISA Server 2004 as the firewall and configured it so that the users have unrestricted access to the Internet. You suspect that some of your users have installed a peer to peer file sharing application which is not an approved application. The application uses a custom protocol and port number to communicate with other computers. You need to ensure that traffic from that application is not allowed into your network from the Internet. What is the easiest way for you to accomplish this?

    a. Create a packet filter to block the port used by the application.

    b. Do nothing. The traffic is blocked by default.

    c. Configure an application filter to block the traffic.

    d. Create an access rule to block the port used by the application.

2. How does application filtering protect the internal network?

    a. By blocking IP fragments

    b. By inspecting the data in a packet for unacceptable commands and data

    c. By blocking connections to particular ports

    d. By allowing or disallowing traffic based on connection rules

3. What feature of ISA Server prevents IP addresses that logically appear on the Internal network from entering your network through the external interface?

    a. Egress filtering

    b. Ingress filtering

    c. Application-layer filtering

    d. Stateful filtering

Lesson Summary

- Firewalls are used to limit network traffic from one network to another. Firewalls use packet filters, stateful filters, application filters, and intrusion detection to distinguish network traffic that should be allowed from network traffic that should be blocked.

- Packet filters control access to the network by inspecting the packet network and transport layer information and allowing or denying the IP packets based on that inspection.

- Stateful filtering not only examines the packet header information, but examines the status of the packet as well. This check can be performed at both the transport and application layers.

- Application filtering enables the firewall to inspect the application data in a TCP/IP packet for unacceptable commands and data. Application-layer filtering can be used to stop attacks from sources such as viruses and worms.

- An intrusion-detection system is located at the edge of a network or at different points in the network and inspects all traffic in and out of the network by identifying patterns that may indicate a network or system attack.

Lesson 2: Configuring Multiple Networking on ISA Server

The role of a firewall is to block all traffic from flowing from one network to another unless that traffic is explicitly permitted. To understand how ISA Server works as a firewall, you first need to know how ISA Server implements networks.

After this lesson, you will be able to

- Describe multinetworking
- Describe the default networks configured in ISA Server 2004
- Create and modify network objects
- Configure network rules

Estimated lesson time: 25 minutes

ISA Server Support for Multiple Networks

ISA Server 2004 uses networks to define blocks of IP addresses that may be directly attached to the ISA Server computer or IP addresses that may be remote networks. ISA Server uses these networks as components when you create access rules. ISA Server supports an unlimited number of networks.

> **Note**   ISA Server 2000 supports only three networks: the Internal network, the External network, and a perimeter network (also known as a demilitarized zone, or DMZ, or a screened subnet). One of the significant enhancements in ISA Server 2004 is that it supports an unlimited number of networks.

What Is Multinetworking?

Multinetworking means that you can configure multiple networks on ISA Server, and then configure network and access rules that inspect and filter all network traffic between all networks. Multinetworking enables flexible options for network configuration. One common network configuration is a three-legged firewall, as shown in Figure 7-1.

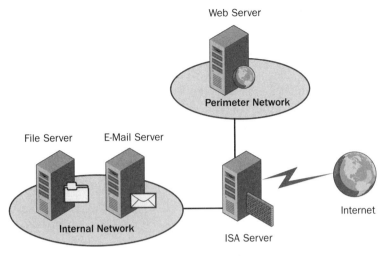

Figure 7-1   A three-legged firewall configuration

In this configuration, you create three networks:

- The servers that are accessible from the Internet are usually isolated on their own network, such as a perimeter network.

- The internal client computers and servers that are not accessible from the Internet are located on an internal network.

- The third network is the Internet.

ISA Server multinetworking functionality supports this configuration. You can configure how clients on the corporate network access the perimeter network, and how external clients access the perimeter network. You can also define access rules for all network traffic flowing from the Internal network to the Internet. You can also configure the relationships between the various networks, defining different network rules between each network.

Note   The client's membership in a network is automatically assigned. In the case of local area network (LAN)–connected clients, a computer becomes a network member based on the computer's IP address; in the case of virtual private network (VPN) clients, a computer becomes a network member based on its connection method.

You might also need to configure a more complicated network environment such as the one shown in Figure 7-2. In this scenario, you could have the following:

- **Two perimeter networks**   Perhaps you are deploying some servers that are domain members and other servers that are stand-alone servers. The domain members need to be able to communicate with domain controllers that are located on your internal network. In this scenario, you could configure a second perimeter network for the servers that need to be members of the domain.

- **Two internal networks**   You might have a group of client computers that needs to access the Internet using a different application or with security rules different from the other client computers. You can create an additional internal network and configure specific Internet access rules for each network.

- **VPN client and VPN remote-site networks**   ISA Server defines a network for VPN clients, and you can define a network for each remote site connected with a site-to-site VPN connection.

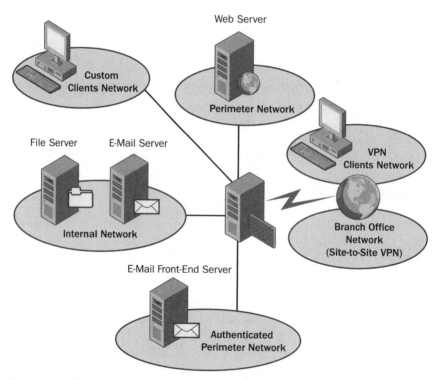

Figure 7-2   ISA Server 2004 supports an unlimited number of networks.

Because ISA Server supports per-network policies, you can configure unique access rules for each of these networks.

Planning   ISA Server does not support separate networks and access rules for networks that are not directly attached to the ISA Server computer. For example, organizations often have multiple IP networks associated with the internal corporate network. For example, you may have an internal network such as 10.10.0.0/16 and another network such as 192.168.1.0/24. If both networks are accessible through the same network interface on the ISA Server computer (for example, the IP address for the internal interface may be 192.168.1.1), both networks must be defined on the Internal network properties.

Default Networks Enabled in ISA Server

When you install ISA Server 2004 on a server with at least two network cards, it is configured in advance with a default set of networks. Table 7-1 lists the default networks.

Table 7-1   ISA Server Default Networks

Network	Description
Local Host	This network represents the ISA Server computer. Use this network to control all traffic to and from ISA Server rather than traffic that flows through ISA Server. The Local Host network cannot be modified. In most cases, you will use the system policy to define what network traffic will flow to and from the ISA Server computer, but you can also create access rules that use the Local Host network.
External	This network includes all computers (IP addresses) that are not explicitly associated with any other network. The External network is generally considered an untrusted network and represents all hosts on the Internet. The default External network cannot be modified.
Internal	This network includes all computers (IP addresses) that were specified as internal during the installation process.
VPN Clients	This network contains addresses of currently connected VPN clients. The range of possible addresses is configured when you configure the VPN properties.
Quarantined VPN Clients	This network contains addresses of VPN clients that have not cleared quarantine.

Note   A network set rule element represents a grouping of one or more networks. You can use this rule element to apply rules to more than one network. By default, ISA Server includes two network sets: All Networks, which includes all the networks attached to ISA Server, and All Protected Networks, which includes all networks except the External network. You can also create network sets that include any combination of networks on the server.

How to Create and Modify Network Objects

For a small organization with a fairly simple network, the default network objects may provide all the configuration options required. However, in a larger organization with a more complex network environment and more complicated requirements, you may need to create and modify the network objects.

To create a new network object, use the following procedure:

1. In the Microsoft ISA Server Management Console tree, expand the Configuration node and click Networks.

2. In the Details pane, click the Network tab.

3. On the Tasks tab, click Create a New Network.

4. On the Welcome to the New Network Wizard page, in the Network Name: box, type the name for the network. Click Next.

5. On the Network Type page, as shown in Figure 7-3, select the type of network you are creating. Select one of the following options:

   ❑ External Network

   ❑ Internal Network

   ❑ Perimeter Network

   ❑ VPN Site-To-Site Network

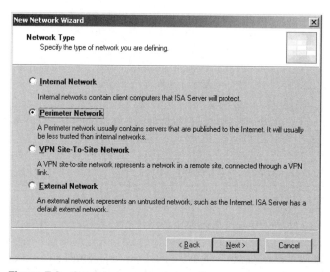

Figure 7-3   Choosing a network type for a new network

See Also   Configuring VPN site-to-site networks will be discussed in detail in Chapter 10, "Configuring Virtual Private Networks for Remote Clients and Networks."

6. After selecting the network type, click Next.

7. If you selected an internal, perimeter, or external network type, on the Network Addresses page, click Add.

8. In the IP Address Range Properties page, type the starting and ending addresses, and then click OK.

9. On the Completing The New Network Wizard page, review the settings and then click Finish.

To modify a network, click the network in ISA Server Management Console and then click Edit Selected Network.

How to Configure Network Rules

When you enable networks or network objects on ISA Server, you can configure network rules that define how network packets will be passed between networks or between computers. Network rules determine whether there is a relationship between two network entities and what type of relationship is defined. Network relationships can be configured as follows:

- **Route**   When you specify this type of connection, client requests from the source network are directly routed to the destination network. The source client address is included in the request. A route relationship is bidirectional. That is, if a routed relationship is defined from network A to network B, a routed relationship also exists from network B to network A.

- **Network Address Translation (NAT)**   When you specify this type of connection, ISA Server replaces the IP address of the client on the source network with its own IP address. A NAT relationship is directional. It indicates that the addresses from the source network are always translated when passing through ISA Server. For example, by default a NAT network relationship is defined between the Internet and the internal network. When a client makes a request on the Internet, the IP addresses of the internal client computer are replaced by the address on the ISA Server computer before the request is passed to the server on the Internet. On the other hand, when a packet from the Internet is returned to the client computer, the address of the server is not translated. Client computers on the internal network can access the actual addresses of computers on the Internet, but computers on the Internet cannot access the internal IP addresses.

Planning   If you are using the private IP addresses on any network that is protected by ISA Server, you must define a NAT relationship between that network and the Internet. This is because the private IP addresses are not routable on the Internet. In this configuration, only the IP address assigned to the external network adapter on the ISA Server computer is accessible from the Internet so all other addresses must be translated.

When no relationship is configured between networks, ISA Server drops all traffic between the two networks.

Default Network Rules

When you install ISA Server 2004, the default network rules listed in Table 7-2 are created.

Table 7-2   ISA Server Default Network Rules

Network Rule	Network Relationship
Local Host Access	This rule defines a route relationship between the Local Host network and all other networks.
VPN Clients to Internal Network	This rule defines a route relationship among the Internal network and the Quarantined VPN Clients and the VPN Clients networks.
Internet Access	This rule defines a NAT relationship among the internal network, the Quarantined VPN Clients, and the VPN Clients networks and the External network.

How Network Rules and Access Rules Are Applied

ISA Server uses both network rules and access rules to determine whether a client request is passed from one network to another. Together, the network rules and access rules comprise the firewall policy. The firewall policy is applied in the following way:

1. A user using a client computer sends a request for a resource located on another network. For example, a client on the Internal network sends a request to a server located on the Internet.

2. ISA Server checks the network rules to verify that the two networks are connected. If no network relationship is defined between the two networks, the request is refused.

3. If a network rule defines a connection between the source and destination networks, ISA Server next processes the access rules. The rules are applied in order of priority as listed in the ISA Server Management Console interface. If an allow rule allows the request, then the request is forwarded without checking any additional access rules. If no access rule allows the request, the final default access rule is applied, which denies all access.

4. If the request is allowed by an access rule, ISA Server checks the network rules again to determine how the networks are connected. ISA Server checks the Web chaining rules (if a Web Proxy client requested the object) or the firewall chaining configuration (if a SecureNAT client or a Firewall client requested the object) to determine how the request will be serviced.

5. The request is forwarded to the Internet Web server.

> **Exam Tip**   Remember that both access rules and network rules can block access to a net-
> work resource. If an exam question presents you with a scenario in which a user cannot
> access a resource on another network, look for information on both the access rule configura-
> tion and the network rule configuration.

Creating a New Network Rule

To create a new network rule, use the following procedure:

1. In the Microsoft ISA Server Management Console tree, expand the Configuration node and click Networks.

2. In the Details pane, click the Network Rules tab.

3. On the Tasks tab, click Create a New Network Rule.

4. On the Welcome to the New Network Rule Wizard page, in the Network Rule Name: box, type the name for the network rule. Click Next.

5. On the Network Traffic Sources page, click Add, as shown in Figure 7-4.

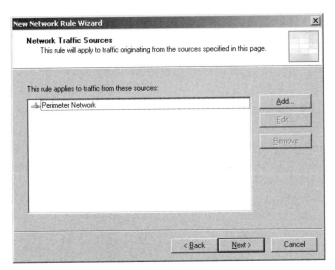

Figure 7-4   Configuring the network traffic source for a network rule

6. On the Add Network Entities page, select the Network Entity to which this rule will apply. Click Add, and then click Close.

7. On the Network Traffic Sources page, click Next.

8. On the Network Traffic Destinations page, click Add.

9. On the Add Network Entities page, select the Network Entity to which this rule will apply. Click Add, and then click Close.

10. On the Network Traffic Destinations page, click Next.

11. On the Network Relationship page, as shown in Figure 7-5, click Network Address Translation or Route. Click Next.

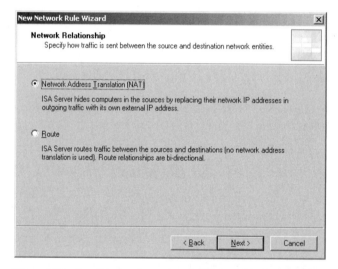

Figure 7-5   Configuring the network relationship for a network rule

12. On the Completing The New Network Rule Wizard page, review the settings and then click Finish.

Planning   To determine the address relationship between two computers on different networks, ISA Server processes network rules according to the order that the rules are listed in the ISA Server Management Console interface, looking for a rule that matches the computer addresses. The first rule that matches the computer addresses defines the network relationship. This means that you may have a routing relationship configured between two networks, but a NAT relationship configured between a specific computer on the network and the other network. In this case, the network rule defining the NAT relationship should be listed first to ensure that this specific rule is applied

Practice: Configuring Multiple Networking on ISA Server

In this practice, you will configure a new network on the ISA Server computer. You will then configure a new network rule that defines a NAT relationship between the Internet and the perimeter network and another network rule that defines a route relationship between the Internal network and the perimeter network.

> **Note** To complete this practice, you need three network adapters installed on the computer running ISA Server. This practice assumes that the third network adapter is assigned the IP address 172.6.1.1. All other practices only require two network adapters. Later practices do not depend on this practice.

Exercise 1: Configuring a New Network on ISA Server

1. Log on to ISA1 as an Administrator. Open ISA Server Management Console.

2. In the Microsoft ISA Server Management Console tree, expand the Configuration node and click Networks.

3. In the details pane, click the Networks tab.

4. On the Tasks tab, click Create a New Network.

5. On the Welcome To The New Network Wizard page, in the Network Name: box, type **Perimeter Network**. Click Next.

6. On the Network Type page, click Perimeter Network, and then click Next.

7. On the Network Addresses page, click Add.

8. In the IP Address Range Properties page, type **172.16.1.0** as the Starting Address and **172.16.1.255** as the Ending Address. Click OK.

9. On the Network Addresses page, click Next.

10. On the Completing The New Network Wizard page, review the settings and then click Finish.

11. Click Apply to apply the changes.

Exercise 2: Configuring New Network Rules on ISA Server

1. In the Details pane, click the Network Rules tab.

2. On the Tasks tab, click Create a New Network Rule.

3. On the Welcome To The New Network Rule Wizard page, in the Network Rule Name: box, type **Perimeter to External Network Rule**. Click Next.

4. On the Network Traffic Sources page, click Add.

5. On the Add Network Entities page, expand Networks, click Perimeter Network, and click Add. Click Close.

6. On the Network Traffic Sources page, click Next.

7. On the Network Traffic Destinations page, click Add.

8. On the Add Network Entities page, expand Networks, click External and then click Add. Click Close.

9. On the Network Traffic Destinations page, click Next.

10. On the Network Relationship page, click Network Address Translation. Click Next.

11. On the Completing The New Network Rule Wizard page, review the settings and click Finish.

12. Configure another network rule named Internal To Perimeter Network, which defines a route relationship between the Internal network and the Perimeter Network that you created in the previous practice.

13. Click Apply to apply the changes.

Lesson Review

Use the following questions to help determine whether you have learned enough to move on to the next lesson. If you have difficulty answering these questions, review the material in this lesson before beginning the next lesson. You can find answers to these questions in the "Questions and Answers" section at the end of this chapter.

1. The research department in your organization has unique network access requirements. All the computers used by the department users are on a separate subnet that must be isolated from the production environment. The users need unrestricted Internet access. What should you do to facilitate that?

_____

_____

_____

2. You have configured four different internal networks on your ISA Server. Each network represents a different department in your organization. The different departments have some unique Internet access rule requirements, but you also want some of the access rules to be the same for all departments. What is the easiest way to accomplish this?

_____

_____

_____

3. All users in your organization require access to the Internet from their desktop computers. From their desktop computers, the users should be able to use any protocol to access the Internet. However, when the users are using one of the publicly accessible computers located in the office lobby, they should be able to use only HTTP to access the Internet. What are two possible ways to configure this?

    a. Configure a network that includes the internal network and the publicly accessible computers. Enable only HTTP access to the Internet from that network.

    b. Configure a computer set that includes the publicly accessible computers. Enable only HTTP access to the Internet from that computer set.

    c. Configure a domain name set that includes the publicly accessible computers. Enable only HTTP access to the Internet from that computer set.

    d. Configure a new network that includes the publicly accessible computers. Enable only HTTP access to the Internet from that network.

Lesson Summary

- ISA Server 2004 supports multinetworking, which means that you can configure multiple networks on ISA Server, and then configure network and access rules that inspect and filter all network traffic between all networks.

- ISA Server is configured in advance with the following networks: Local Host, External, Internal, VPN Clients, and Quarantined VPN Clients.

- Network rules determine whether there is a relationship between two network entities and whether the relationship is a route and NAT relationship.

Lesson 3: Implementing Perimeter Networks and Network Templates

Many organizations use perimeter networks to isolate servers and resources from both the Internet and the internal network. In this configuration, servers that need to be accessible from the Internet are placed in a separate network behind a firewall. These servers might also be separated from the internal network by another firewall or by connecting the perimeter network and the internal networks to different interfaces on the firewall. ISA Server enables the configuration of almost any perimeter network configuration. To simplify the task of implementing ISA Server as a firewall, ISA Server 2004 provides several network templates. This lesson describes how to implement a perimeter network with ISA Server 2004.

After this lesson, you will be able to

- Describe what a perimeter network is
- Describe the network templates included with ISA Server 2004
- Implement network templates

Estimated lesson time: 30 minutes

What Are Perimeter Networks?

A perimeter network is a network that is separated from an internal network and the Internet. Perimeter networks allow external users to gain access to specific servers that are located on the perimeter network while preventing direct access to the internal network. Perimeter networks have the following characteristics:

- **Protected by one or more firewalls** Perimeter networks are separated from the Internet by one or more firewalls or routers. The perimeter network is usually also separated from the internal network by a firewall. The firewall protects the servers in the perimeter network from the Internet and filters traffic between the perimeter network and the internal network.

- **Contain publicly accessible servers and services** The servers in the perimeter network are usually accessible to users from the Internet. The types of servers or services that are often located in the perimeter network include VPN servers and clients, remote access servers (RASs) and clients, Web servers, application front-end servers, SMTP gateway servers, and proxy servers.

- **Must be accessible from the Internet** Because the servers on the perimeter network must be accessible from the Internet, the firewall protecting the perimeter network must allow network traffic from the Internet. This traffic must be filtered to ensure that only legitimate traffic enters the perimeter network. Because almost all network traffic will flow from the Internet to the perimeter network, most firewall rules can be configured to allow only inbound traffic.

- **Require network connectivity to the internal network**   Frequently, the computers on the perimeter network must be able to connect to resources on the internal network. For example, VPN or RAS Clients connect to the VPN or RAS server, but then must gain access from that server to the internal network. An SMTP gateway server must be able to forward messages to internal e-mail servers. An application front-end server may need to connect to a database server on the internal network. Often, users on the internal network must also be able to connect to servers in the perimeter network. This means that you must configure firewall access rules on the firewall between the perimeter network and the internal network to enable the required network traffic.

- **Require some level of network protection**   The servers on the perimeter network must be partially isolated both from the Internet and the internal network. The firewalls on both sides of a perimeter network should not forward all traffic, but should filter traffic flowing in both directions. Only required network traffic should be allowed to pass between networks.

Benefits of Using a Perimeter Network

The main reason for using a perimeter network is to provide an additional layer of security. A perimeter network is commonly used for deploying publicly accessible servers while servers that should never be accessed from the Internet are located on the internal network. In this way, even if an attacker penetrates the perimeter network security, only the perimeter network servers are compromised.

The servers in the perimeter network usually do not contain confidential or private organization data. This data and critical applications are located on the internal network. By implementing a perimeter network, you ensure that there is an additional layer of security between the Internet and the internal servers.

The perimeter network can also be used to secure other connections to the internal network. For example, many organizations are using mobile clients such as wireless devices or cell phones to access information such as e-mail on the internal network. These devices greatly increase the security risks; one way to reduce that risk is to install the wireless access servers for these devices in the perimeter network and then use the internal firewall to filter traffic from these servers to the internal network. VPN servers and clients can be secured using the same method.

Important   Although a well-designed perimeter network can greatly enhance your network's security, you must ensure that it is not your only level of defense. Because of the importance of the Internet both for providing services to customers and for providing access to business partners, many organizations deploy multiple servers in the perimeter network. Often the configuration of the access rules on both the external and internal networks can be quite complicated. This can lead to configuration errors or reduced security due to the number of ports that must be open. To reduce the risk, you must implement all other defense-in-depth components

Network Perimeter Configuration Options

Perimeter networks provide an additional layer of network security by protecting publicly accessible servers from unauthorized access while also partially isolating these servers from the internal network. The design of a secure network perimeter includes protection for the internal network as well as for servers that must be accessible from the Internet. There are three broad types of network perimeter configurations:

- **Bastion host**   In this configuration, there is only a single firewall between the Internet and the internal network, as shown in Figure 7-6. The bastion host acts as the main connection for computers on the internal network that are accessing the Internet. As a firewall, the bastion host is designed to defend against attacks that are aimed at the internal network. A bastion host uses two network adapters, one connected to the internal network and one connected to the Internet. This configuration physically isolates the internal network from potential intruders on the Internet. However, the bastion host is only a single line of defense between an internal network and the Internet.

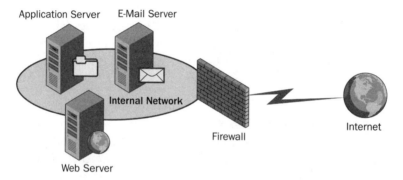

Figure 7-6   A bastion host perimeter configuration uses a single firewall with two network interfaces

- **Three-legged configuration**   A three-legged configuration creates a perimeter network that gives users on the Internet limited access to network resources on the perimeter network while preventing unwanted traffic to computers that are located on the internal network (Figure 7-1 shows ISA Server deployed in a three-legged perimeter configuration). A three-legged configuration uses a firewall with three network adapters—one connected to the internal network, one connected to a perimeter network, and one connected to the Internet. Frequently, each server in the perimeter network has IP addresses that are routable on the Internet, so the firewall routes traffic to the perimeter network. The firewall screens and routes packets to the perimeter as defined by the firewall configuration. However, the firewall computer does not allow direct access to resources that are located on the internal network. One advantage of a three-legged firewall is that it gives you a single point of administration to configure access to both your perimeter network and your internal network. A disadvantage of a three-legged firewall is that it presents a single point of access to all parts of your network. If the firewall is compromised, both the perimeter network and the internal network might be compromised.

■ **Back-to-back configuration** This perimeter network configuration places the perimeter network between two firewalls, as shown in Figure 7-7. The two firewalls are connected to the perimeter network with one firewall connected to the Internet and the other firewall connected to the internal network. In this configuration, there is no single point of access from the Internet to the internal network. To reach the internal network, an attacker would need to get past both firewalls. It is common to use two different firewall vendors in this configuration for maximum security. This dual-vendor configuration prevents an exploit on one firewall from being easily exploited on both firewalls. A back-to-back configuration allows the creation of very granular rules for internal and external access to the network. For example, you can create rules that allow only HTTP and SMTP traffic access to the screened subnet from the Internet and rules that allow only Internet Protocol security (IPSec)–encrypted traffic access to the back-end servers on the internal network from the screened subnet.

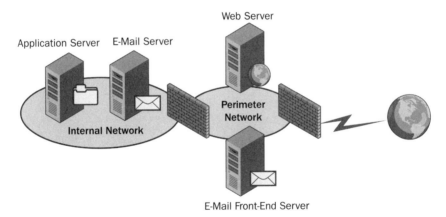

Figure 7-7 A back-to-back perimeter configuration uses multiple firewalls

Caution One of the more common reasons for firewall security breaches is incorrect configuration of the firewall. Regardless of how good your firewall is, it is only as secure as your configuration. One of the problems with deploying a back-to-back perimeter network is that the firewall configurations can be quite complex. The problem can be compounded if you deploy two firewalls and you are not thoroughly familiar with both firewalls. If you do not have the training or experience to configure two firewalls, then consider becoming an expert in only one firewall and using just that firewall. A single firewall with a secure configuration is more secure than two incorrectly configured firewalls.

What Are Network Templates?

ISA Server 2004 can be deployed in any of the perimeter network configurations. To simplify the deployment, ISA Server 2004 includes several network templates that you can use to configure ISA Server based on one of the perimeter network scenarios. A network template is stored in an Extensible Markup Language (XML) file that includes the following:

- Networks and network sets
- Network rules that describe the relationships between networks and network sets
- Access rule elements
- Access rules

To apply a network template, run the Network Template Wizard. When you run the wizard, you can choose the level of access that will be enabled between networks. For example, you may want internal users to be able to access resources on the Internet using all protocols, but only use HTTP or HTTPS to access the perimeter network. The access rules created by the wizard are based on the level of access you grant.

> **Important**   When you apply a network template, the Network Template Wizard overwrites your current ISA Server configuration with the settings provided in the template. If you have configured access rules that you want to retain, export the access rules before applying the network template, and then import the access rules after applying the template.

ISA Server Template Types

ISA Server 2004 provides the following templates:

- **Edge Firewall**   This template assumes a network topology with ISA Server configured as a bastion host. One network interface is connected to the internal network, the other is connected to an external network (Internet). When you select this template, you can allow all outgoing traffic, or limit outgoing traffic to allow only Web access.

- **3-Leg Perimeter**   This template assumes a network topology with ISA Server configured as the firewall for a three-leg perimeter configuration. In this configuration, ISA Server has three network interfaces, one connected to the internal network, one connected to the external network, and one connected to a perimeter network.

- **Front End**   This template assumes a network topology with ISA Server at the edge of a network, with another firewall configured at the back end, protecting the internal network.

■ **Back End**   This template assumes a network topology with ISA Server deployed between a perimeter network and the internal network, with another firewall located between the perimeter network and the Internet.

■ **Single Network Adapter**   This template assumes a single network adapter configuration within a perimeter or corporate network. In this configuration, ISA Server is used as a Web proxy and caching server.

> **Exam Tip**   Be familiar with each of these network templates and the default settings applied by the templates. When you see an exam question that mentions a network template, you should have a clear idea what the template does so that you can troubleshoot any problems with the template.

How to Implement Network Templates

To implement a network template, run the Network Template Wizard. When you apply the template, you can select a firewall access policy that best matches your corporate security guidelines. For example, Table 7-3 lists the firewall policies available when you select the Edge Firewall network template and also details the rules that are created when you select the policy.

Table 7-3   Firewall Policies Applied by the Internet-Edge Template

Policy Name	Description	Rules Created
Block all	This policy blocks all network access through ISA Server. This option does not create any access rules other than the default rule that blocks all access. Use this option when you want to define firewall policy on your own.	None
Block Internet access, allow access to Internet service provider (ISP) network services	This policy blocks all network access through ISA Server except for access to external network services such as DNS. This option is useful when services are provided by your ISP. Use this option when you want to define firewall policy on your own.	Allow DNS from Internal network and VPN Clients network to External network (Internet).
Allow limited Web access	This policy allows limited Web access using HTTP, Hypertext Transfer Protocol Secure (HTTPS), and FTP only. All other network access is blocked	Allow HTTP, HTTPS, and FTP from Internal network to External network.

Table 7-3   Firewall Policies Applied by the Internet-Edge Template

Policy Name	Description	Rules Created
Allow limited Web access and access to ISP network services	This policy allows limited Web access using HTTP, HTTPS, and FTP, and allows access to ISP network services. All other network access is blocked.	Allow HTTP, HTTPS, and FTP from Internal network and VPN Clients network to External network. Allow DNS from Internal network and VPN Clients network to External network (Internet). Allow all protocols from VPN Clients network to Internal network.
Allow unrestricted access	This policy allows unrestricted access to the Internet through ISA Server. ISA Server will prevent access from the Internet to protected networks.	Allow all protocols from Internal network and VPN Clients network to External network (Internet). Allow all protocols from VPN Clients network to Internal network.

To apply the Edge Firewall template, use the following procedure:

1. In the ISA Server Management Console tree, select Networks.

2. In the Task pane, on the Templates tab, shown in Figure 7-8, click Edge Firewall.

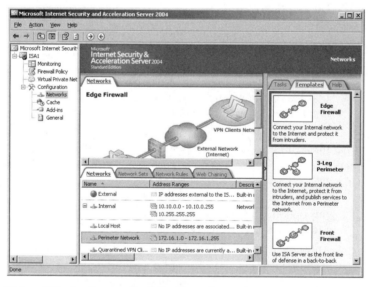

Figure 7-8   Configuring the Edge Firewall template

3. On the Welcome To The Network Template Wizard page, click Next.

4. On the Export The ISA Server Configuration page, click Export to export the network configuration before modifying it.

> **Tip**   Before implementing a significant change to the ISA Server configuration, you should export the firewall settings. The export performed during the Network Template Wizard exports the entire ISA Server configuration, including networks and network rules.

5. In the Export Configuration dialog box, choose a location and name for the .xml file and click Export. When the export finishes, click OK.

6. On the Export The ISA Server Configuration page, click Next.

7. On the Internal Network IP Address page, shown in Figure 7-9, confirm that all internal network addresses are listed. Modify the address ranges if required. Click Next.

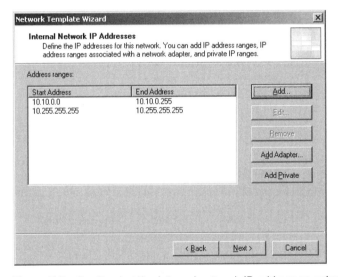

Figure 7-9   Configuring the Internal network IP addresses using a network template

8. On the Select A Firewall Policy page, select the appropriate firewall policy (see Figure 7-10). Click Next.

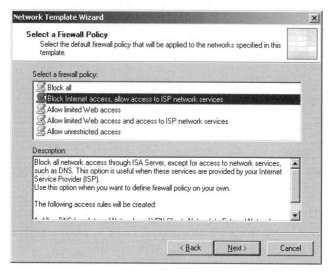

Figure 7-10   Configuring the firewall policy using a network template

9. On the Completing The Network Template Wizard page, review the configuration and click Finish.

10. In the Details pane, click Apply to apply the new access rule.

Modifying Access Rules Applied by Network Templates

Network templates simplify the configuration of ISA Server 2004 network and access rules. However, in most cases, the access rules applied by the template may not meet your requirements exactly. In these cases, you must modify the access rules implemented by the template. There are many scenarios in which you may need to define Internet access more precisely by modifying the access rules, such as the following:

- **Modifying Internet access based on user or computer sets**   The default network template defines the same access rules for all users and all computers on the internal network. If all client computers are Firewall clients or Web Proxy clients and you want to ensure that all users authenticate before gaining access to the Internet, you may want to change the rule created by the wizard to apply to All Authenticated Users. If you want to apply more or less restrictive policies based on user or computer groups, you can create a user set or computer set, and then create an access rule that applies the settings you need.

- **Modifying Internet access for different protocols**   The network template either allows all protocols, or a selected group of the most common Internet protocols. If you want to allow all users to use a different set of protocols, you can modify the default rule created by the network template. If you want a selected user group to be able to use other protocols, create the user set, then create a new access rule granting the required access.

- **Modifying network rules to change network relationships**   In some cases, you may also need to change the default network rules that are created by the network templates. For example, the 3-Leg Perimeter network template creates a route relationship between the perimeter network and the external network and a NAT relationship between the perimeter network and the internal network. If you use private IP addresses in the perimeter network, you must change the perimeter network to external network rule to a NAT relationship.

- **Configuring publishing rules or access rules for inbound access**   The network template only enables Internet and perimeter network access from the internal networks. To enable access to internal resources from the Internet, you must configure publishing rules.

To simplify the configuration of the additional access rules, choose the network template that most closely meets your requirements when you run the wizard. For example, if you are implementing a three-legged perimeter network configuration in which almost all users must be able to access the Internet using all protocols, then choose the 3-Leg Perimeter network template and enable unrestricted access when you run the wizard. Then create additional access rules that apply the exceptions. For example, you may need to create a more restrictive policy for some users.

Practice: Implementing Network Templates

In this practice, you will apply the Edge Firewall template. Then you will review the access and network rules created by the template. Finally, you will test the template settings to ensure that you have Internet access.

Exercise 1: Applying the Edge Firewall Template

1. In the ISA Server Management Console tree, expand ISA1, then expand Configuration, and then click Networks.

2. In the Task pane, on the Templates tab, click Edge Firewall.

3. In the Welcome to the Network Template Wizard, click Next.

4. On the Export the ISA Server Configuration page, click Export to export the network configuration before modifying it.

5. In the Export Configuration dialog box, type **Network Configuration Pre-Template** in the File Name box. Click the check boxes for Export user permission settings and Export confidential information (encryption will be used) and then click Export.

6. Type a password in the Password and Confirm Password boxes. Click OK. When the export finishes, click OK.

7. On the Export the ISA Server Configuration page, click Next.

8. On the Internal Network IP Address page, confirm that the start address is 10.10.0.0 and the end address is 10.10.0.255. Also ensure that the network broadcast address (10.255.255.255) is listed. Click Next.

9. On the Select a Firewall Policy page, click Allow limited Web access and access to ISP network services. Click Next.

10. On the Completing the Network Template Wizard page, review the configuration and click Finish.

11. Click Apply to apply the changes.

Exercise 2: Reviewing the Access and Network Rules Created by the Edge Firewall Template

1. In the ISA Server Management Console tree, click Firewall Policy.

> **Note**   Notice that all the access rules you previously configured were overwritten by the template. Moreover, the perimeter network and network rule that you created in the previous practice were overwritten by the template.

2. In the Task pane, double-click Web Access Only and examine the properties of the access rule. Click OK.

   The Web Access Only access rule allows HTTP, HTTPS, and FTP traffic from the Internal and VPN Clients network to the External network.

3. In the Task pane, double-click Allow DNS To The Internet and examine the properties of the access rule. Click OK.

   The Allow DNS To The Internet access rule allows DNS traffic from the Internal and VPN Clients network to the External network.

4. In the Task pane, double-click VPN Clients To Internal Network and examine the properties of the access rule. Click OK.

   The VPN Clients To Internal Network access rule allows all protocols from the VPN Clients network to the Internal network.

5. Click Networks. In the details pane, click Network Rules.

6. Double-click the Internet Access Network Rule and examine the properties of the access rule. Click OK.

   The Internet Access Network Rule defines a NAT relationship between the Internal, Quarantined VPN Clients and VPN Clients networks, and the External network.

Exercise 3: Testing Internet Access

1. Switch to the CLIENT1 virtual machine and log on to the *cohovineyard.com* domain.

2. Open Microsoft Internet Explorer and attempt to connect to *www.microsoft.com*.

3. Attempt to connect to *www.msn.com*.

4. Attempt to connect to *ftp://ftp.microsoft.com*. You may need to clear the Enable Folder View for FTP Sites on the Advanced tab in Internet Options to view the FTP directory listing. All connections should be successful.

Lesson Review

Use the following questions to help determine whether you have learned enough to move on to the next lesson. If you have difficulty answering these questions, review the material in this lesson before beginning the next lesson. You can find answers to these questions in the "Questions and Answers" section at the end of this chapter.

1. You are the network administrator of a small company. Your company does not publish any servers to the Internet and your ISP handles all Internet services for your organization. You need to enable Internet access for your internal users using only HTTP and HTTPS. What network template and policy would work best for you?

   _____

   _____

   _____

2. You use a third-party firewall solution as your Internet-edge firewall. You have installed ISA Server 2004 and you are using it just to take advantage of the caching capabilities. What network template will you choose?

   a. Front Firewall

   b. Bastion Host

   c. Edge Firewall

   d. Single Network Adapter

3. Your organization is designing a new perimeter network configuration. The organization is planning on deploying several Web servers and other application servers that need to be accessible from the Internet. At the same time, the organization requires that these servers be isolated from the internal network so that only selected traffic can pass from the publicly accessible servers to the internal network. The company must implement the most secure solution possible. What perimeter network configuration should the organization implement?

   a. Configure a bastion host firewall.

   b. Configure a three-leg perimeter network.

   c. Configure a back-to-back perimeter network with two firewalls from the same vendor.

   d. Configure a back-to-back perimeter network with two firewalls from different vendors.

Lesson Summary

■ A perimeter network is a network that you set up separately from an internal network and the Internet. Perimeter networks are used to isolate servers and resources from both the Internet and the internal network.

■ There are three general types of network perimeter configurations; bastion host, three-legged configuration, and back-to-back configuration.

■ The network templates included with ISA Server 2004 include preconfigured networks and network sets, network rules, access rules, and access rule elements. The templates are designed to simplify the process of configuring ISA Server. After applying the network template, you may need to modify the access rules or add additional access rules to meet your company requirements.

Lesson 4: Configuring Intrusion Detection and IP Preferences

ISA Server 2004 provides two additional options for increasing security; these options are intrusion detection and IP preferences. These options are used to configure how ISA Server will respond to various attacks or malformed IP packets. This lesson describes how to configure these options.

After this lesson, you will be able to

- Describe the intrusion-detection configuration options
- Configure intrusion detection
- Describe the IP preferences configuration options
- Configure IP preferences

Estimated lesson time: 20 minutes

Intrusion-Detection Configuration Options

To protect your network, you will also need to know how to configure your ISA Server for intrusion detection. Intrusion detection identifies when an attack is attempted against your network and performs a set of configured actions, or alerts, in case of an attack. To detect potential attacks, ISA Server compares network traffic and log entries to well-known attacks. When ISA Server detects suspicious activities, it triggers an alert. You can configure the actions that ISA Server will perform in the event of an alert. These actions include connection termination, service termination, e-mail alerts, logging, and others.

Intrusion Detection at the IP Level

ISA Server provides intrusion detection for well-known IP attacks listed in Table 7-4.

Table 7-4   ISA Server Intrusion-Detection Options

IP Attack	Description
Windows out-of-band attack	This alert notifies you that there was an out-of-band, denial-of-service (DoS) attack attempted against a computer protected by ISA Server. An out-of-band attack occurs when a Windows system receives a packet with the "URGENT" flag set. The system expects data will follow that flag. The exploit consists of setting the URGENT flag, but not following it with data. The port most susceptible is TCP Port 139, the NetBIOS Session Service port. If mounted successfully, this attack causes the computer to fail or causes a loss of network connectivity on vulnerable computers.

Table 7-4   ISA Server Intrusion-Detection Options

IP Attack	Description
Land attack	This alert notifies you that a TCP SYN packet was sent with a spoofed source IP address and port number that match those of the destination IP address and port. If the attack is successfully mounted, it can cause some TCP implementations to go into a loop that causes the computer to fail.
Ping-of-death attack	This alert notifies you that an IP fragment was received with more data than the maximum IP packet size. If the attack is successfully mounted, a kernel buffer overflows, which causes the computer to fail.
Port scan	This alert notifies you that an attempt was made to access more than the preconfigured number of ports. You can specify a threshold, indicating the number of ports that can be accessed.
IP half scan	This alert notifies you that repeated attempts to send TCP packets with invalid flags were made. During an IP half-scan attack, the attacking computer does not send the final ACK packet during the TCP three-way handshake. Instead, it sends other types of packets that can elicit useful responses from the target host without causing a connection to be logged. This is also known as a stealth scan, because it does not generate a log entry on the scanned host. If this alert occurs, log the address from which the scan occurs. If appropriate, configure the ISA Server rules to block traffic from the source of the scans.
UDP bomb	This alert notifies you that there is an attempt to send an illegal UDP packet. These UDP packets will cause some older operating systems to fail when the packet is received. If the target machine does fail, it is often difficult to determine the cause.

Intrusion Detection at the Application Layer

ISA Server also provides built-in application filters that detect DNS networking protocol and Post Office Protocol (POP) intrusions. The DNS intrusion-detection filter detects the following known DNS exploits:

■ **DNS host name overflow**   A DNS host name overflow occurs when a DNS response for a host name exceeds a certain fixed length (255 bytes). Applications that do not check the length of the host names may overflow internal buffers on the server when copying this host name, allowing a remote attacker to execute arbitrary commands on a targeted computer. This filter inspects the response that an internal client receives from an external DNS server.

■ **DNS length overflow**   DNS responses for IP addresses contain a length field, which should be 4 bytes. By formatting a DNS response with a larger value, some applications executing DNS lookups will overflow internal buffers, potentially allowing a remote attacker to execute arbitrary commands on a targeted computer. This filter inspects the response that an internal client receives from an external DNS server.

■ **DNS zone transfer**   A malicious user executes a zone transfer to gather a list of all the host names in a domain. This filter detects when an Internet user attempts to execute a zone transfer from an internal DNS server through ISA Server.

The POP filter intercepts and analyzes POP traffic destined for the published servers. The application filter checks for POP buffer overflow attacks. A POP buffer overflow attack occurs when a remote attacker attempts to gain root access to a POP server by overflowing an internal buffer on the server.

How to Configure Intrusion Detection

By default, ISA Server is configured with most of the intrusion-detection options already enabled. To review and configure intrusion detection of common attacks, use the following procedure:

1. In the ISA Server Management Console tree, click General.

2. In the Details pane, click Enable Intrusion Detection and DNS Attack Detection.

3. On the Common Attacks tab, shown in Figure 7-11, ensure that Enable Intrusion Detection is selected.

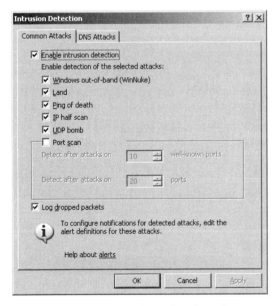

Figure 7-11   Configuring intrusion detection

4. Select one or more of the attack options. The only option that is not configured by default is the Port Scan. If you select this option, you can also specify when the alert will be raised. You can choose to raise the alert after a specified number of attacks on well-known ports or after a specified number of attacks on all ports.

5. To enable intrusion detection of DNS attacks, click the DNS Attacks tab, and then click Enable Detection And Filtering Of DNS Attacks.

6. Select one or more of the attack options. The only option that is not enabled by default is DNS Zone Transfer.

7. When you finish configuring intrusion detection, click OK.

> **Note**   After configuring intrusion detection, you can also configure the alert settings. For more information about configuring alerts and responses to alerts, see Chapter 11, "Implementing Monitoring and Reporting."

IP Preferences Configuration Options

Another option on ISA Server 2004 that you can use to improve security is to configure the IP preferences. IP preferences are used to configure how ISA Server will handle specific types of IP packets. Configuring IP preferences is more complicated than configuring intrusion detection because, in most cases, IP preferences can be used to block normal packets that may or may not be used by attackers. You can configure the following IP preferences on ISA Server:

- **IP option**   You can configure ISA Server to refuse all packets that have the IP options flag set in the header, or you can configure ISA Server to drop packets with only specific IP options enabled. The IP options flags that are most commonly used by attackers are the source routing options. The source route option in the IP header allows the sender to override routing decisions that are normally made by the routers between the source and destination machines. An attacker can use source routing to reach addresses on the internal network that normally are not reachable from other networks, by routing the traffic through another computer that is reachable from both the other network and the internal network. Because source routing can be used in this way, you should disable source routing on your ISA Server computer.

- **IP fragments**   You can also configure ISA Server to drop all IP fragments. A single IP datagram can be separated into multiple datagrams of smaller sizes known as IP fragments. If you enable this option, then all fragmented packets are dropped when ISA Server filters packet fragments. A common attack that uses IP fragments is the teardrop. In the teardrop attack, multiple IP fragments are sent to a server. However, the IP fragments are modified so that the offset fields within the packet overlap. When the destination computer tries to reassemble these packets, it is unable to do so. It may fail, stop responding, or restart. Enabling IP fragment filtering can interfere with streaming audio and video. In addition, Layer Two Tunneling Protocol (L2TP) over IPSec connections may not be established successfully because packet fragmentation may take place during certificate exchange.

Exam Tip   Blocking IP fragments is an example of a configuration option that may provide some additional security but at the cost of some functionality. If you get an exam question in which users cannot use streaming media, yet need this functionality, one of the possible explanations is that IP fragments are being blocked. By default, IP fragment blocking is not enabled on ISA Server.

- **IP routing**   When IP routing is enabled, ISA Server sends the original network packet from one network to another. ISA Server can filter the network packet. When IP routing is disabled, ISA Server sends only the data (and not the original network packet) to the destination. Also, when IP routing is disabled, ISA Server sends each packet through the firewall in user mode. Disabling IP routing is more secure, but can also decrease router performance.

How to Configure IP Preferences

By default, ISA Server is configured with the most important IP preferences set. You can modify the default settings. To configure IP preferences, use the following procedure:

1. In the ISA Server Management Console tree, click General.

2. In the Details pane, click Define IP Preferences.

3. On the IP Options tab, ensure that Enable IP Options Filtering is selected, as shown in Figure 7-12. You can then configure the level of IP options filtering by denying all packets with the IP option flag configured or by denying packets with specific IP options set. By default, packets with IP options Record Route, Time Stamp, Loose Source Route, and Strict Source Route are denied.

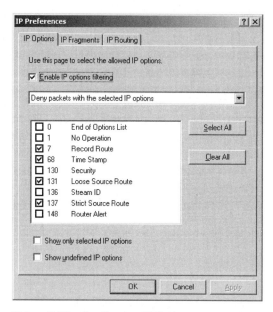

Figure 7-12   Configuring IP Options

4. On the IP Fragments tab, shown in Figure 7-13, click Block IP Fragments to block all IP fragments. By default, this option is not enabled.

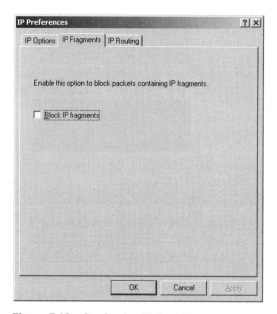

Figure 7-13   Configuring IP Fragments

5. On the IP Routing tab, as shown in Figure 7-14, clear the check box for Enable IP Routing to disable IP routing. By default, IP routing is enabled.

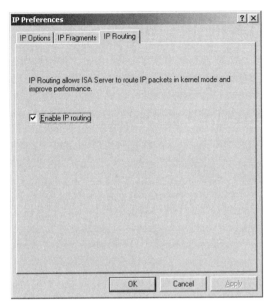

Figure 7-14   Configuring IP Routing

Practice: Configuring Intrusion Detection and IP Preferences

In this practice, you will modify the intrusion-detection configuration on ISA Server 2004. You will then test the intrusion-detection configuration.

Exercise 1: Modifying the Default Intrusion Detection

1. In the ISA Server Management Console tree, expand ISA1, then expand Configuration, and then click General.

2. In the Details pane, click Enable Intrusion Detection And DNS Attack Detection.

3. On the Common Attacks tab, ensure that Enable Intrusion Detection is selected.

4. Select Port Scan and configure ISA Server to detect after five attacks on well-known ports.

5. On the DNS Attacks tab, select DNS Zone Transfer. Click OK.

6. Click Apply to apply the changes.

Exercise 2: Testing Intrusion Detection

In this exercise, you will use the Portqry.exe utility that is included with the Windows Server 2003 Resource Kit to perform a port scan on the internal network interface of the ISA Server computer.

1. On CLIENT1, open a command prompt and configure user context to be the C:\Program Files\Windows Resource Kits\Tools folder (or in the folder where the resource kit is installed).

2. Type **portqry.exe –n 192.168.1.1 –r 1:20**.

3. On the ISA1 virtual machine, in the Microsoft ISA Server Management Console tree, click Monitoring.

4. On the Alerts tab, locate the Intrusion Detected alert. You may need to wait a few minutes for the alert to appear. Expand the alert and read the Alert Information at the bottom of the Details pane.

Lesson Review

Use the following questions to help determine whether you have learned enough to move on to the next lesson. If you have difficulty answering these questions, review the material in this lesson before beginning the next lesson. You can find answers to these questions in the "Questions and Answers" section at the end of this chapter.

1. Your organization has just deployed an ISA Server computer as a firewall. The security policy for your organization requires that all settings on the ISA Server computer be configured as securely as possible. After you implement a secure configuration, users report that they can no longer access a streaming media site. Access to this site is critical for the company, so you must enable access to the site. What security setting should you change to enable access to the site?

    a. Enable IP routing

    b. Disable all filtering based on IP options

    c. Disable filtering of IP fragments

    d. Disable filtering based on the source-routing IP options

2. You have configured intrusion detection to detect when the ISA Server interfaces are being exposed to a port scan. You configure the alert to send an e-mail to your account when the alert is triggered. You are now receiving a high number of e-mails from the ISA Server computer. You want to reduce the number of e-mails sent to your account, but still want to know when there are frequent port scans of your ISA Server. What should you do?

_____

_____

_____

3. You have configured ISA Server 2004 as a bastion host. You are concerned about the security of your DNS database. One of the internal DNS servers must be accessible from the Internet but you want to ensure that zone transfers will never be allowed to clients that are not on your internal network. How will you accomplish this?

_____

_____

_____

Lesson Summary

- The purpose of intrusion detection is to detect network attacks as early as possible to ensure that appropriate corrective actions can be taken. ISA Server provides intrusion detection for well-known IP attacks and also provides built-in application filters that detect DNS networking protocol and POP intrusions.

- By default, the most important intrusion detection options are enabled in ISA Server 2004. You can configure additional options.

- IP preferences are used to configure how ISA Server will handle specific IP packets. You can configure the following IP preferences on ISA Server: IP Option, IP Fragments, and IP Routing.

- Configuring IP preferences can be difficult because for some of the options you will block some functionality when you enable the IP preference. You need to balance the need for security versus functionality when configuring IP preferences.

Lesson 5: Implementing Application and Web Filtering

An important advantage of ISA Server over traditional firewalls is its ability to filter the application data in the network packets as they enter or leave the network. This feature is especially important because of the near-universal use of HTTP. Almost all organizations allow users on the internal network to use HTTP to access Web resources. Most organizations also allow HTTP traffic into the network as Internet users access internal Web resources. The fact that HTTP is so widely used means HTTP-based attacks have become increasingly popular and sophisticated. Moreover, many applications which have traditionally used another protocol are now using HTTP to carry the application data. Because of this, it is critical to examine all HTTP traffic entering or leaving the organization's network. This lesson provides an overview of how application and Web filters work in ISA Server 2004 and then focuses on how to implement and manage HTTP filtering in ISA Server 2004.

After this lesson, you will be able to

- Define an application filter
- Define a Web filter
- Describe how the HTTP Web filter works
- Configure an HTTP Web filter

Estimated lesson time: 30 minutes

What Are Application Filters?

Application filters work with the firewall service in ISA Server to intercept and process network packets as they pass through ISA Server. Application filters examine the application-level data within those packets and then filter the packets based on firewall rules. ISA Server application filters are implemented as Component Object Model (COM)–server dynamic link libraries (DLLs) that run in the same process space as the firewall service. When the firewall service starts, all application filters that are registered with the firewall service are also loaded.

Application filters are add-ons to the firewall service. When a packet arrives, the firewall service uses firewall rules defined in the rules engine to check the packet. One check is to see if an application filter is associated with the protocol used by the packet. If there is, the firewall service passes the packet to the application filter for further inspection. An application filter can perform protocol- or system-specific tasks such as authentication and checking for viruses.

See Also   To view all the application filters included with ISA Server 2004, open the ISA Server Management Console, expand Configuration, and then click Add-ins. The application filters are listed on the Application Filters tab. You can enable or disable the Web filters from this interface, but most applications filters cannot be modified.

Application filters can be used in several different ways on ISA Server, including:

- **Enabling firewall traversal for complex protocols**   Application filters can extend the ability of ISA Server to handle complicated protocols that require more than a single TCP connection. Some applications, such as FTP or media streaming applications, initiate a connection with a server using a specified port number. However, once the initial connection has been established, the server and client negotiate one or more dynamic ports that will be used for further communications. An application filter can enable the firewall traversal of these protocols. ISA Server uses the application filter to track the negotiation between the client and server as they determine the secondary connections, and then ISA Server can dynamically configure the ports required for the secondary connections. An example of such a filter is the built-in FTP application filter that handles all aspects of configuring a firewall to automatically allow a secondary FTP data channel. The FTP filter can also be modified to control whether users can download and upload files using FTP. By default, the FTP filter only allows users to download files.

- **Enabling protocol-level intrusion detection**   Application filters can examine the contents of application packets to check for protocol-level intrusion detection. A common example of this type of filtering is based on filtering commands to protect against buffer overflow attempts. ISA Server provides POP3, SMTP, and DNS application filters that provide this type of functionality.

- **Enabling protocol-level content filtering**   Application filters can parse high-level application protocols, look for actual data (the payload), and apply rules and processing based on the content. For example, you can use the feature to provide protocol-level syntax validation, antivirus scanning on file transfers, or scans of the content based on defined strings. The SMTP filter provided with ISA Server is an example of these types of application filters.

- **Generating alerts and log events**   Application filters can also be used to create alerts and log events based on the activity discovered by the application filter. For example, if a DNS application filter detects repeated attack attempts, the filter can create an alert or log the information.

> **Note**   Many third-party vendors use application filters to implement features such as content filtering, access control, specialized authentication methods, and intrusion detection. For a listing of many of the third-party products that are compatible with ISA Server, see *http://www.isaserver.org* and the Partners Web site at *http://www.microsoft.com/isaserver/partners*.

What Are Web Filters?

Web filters also extend the functionality of the firewall service in ISA Server by providing advanced filtering capability for HTTP packets as they pass through ISA Server. Web filters are DLLs that are based on the Microsoft Internet Information Services (IIS) Internet Server Application Programming Interface (ISAPI) model. The Web filters are loaded by the Web proxy filter, which is an application filter. When a Web filter is loaded, it passes information to the Web proxy filter that specifies the types of events that the filter is configured to monitor. Each time one of those events occurs, the Web filter is notified.

Web filters can be used to perform a number of different tasks, including the following:

- **Request scanning and modification**   A Web filter can scan HTTP client requests and modify or add a header to a request. For example, you could use a Web filter to add a cookie header to the request, or remove a header sent by the client.

- **Response scanning and modification**   Web filters can scan and modify the server responses. For example, during link translation, ISA Server substitutes the externally accessible server names for the internal names. The link translation filter included with ISA Server is a Web filter.

- **Block specific responses**   Web filters can be used to block access to particular sites based on the content of the server response. These features can also be used to scan HTTP packets for viruses.

- **Traffic logging and analysis**   Web filters can be used to log specific information about HTTP traffic and to create reports based on the logged information.

- **Data encryption or compression**   Web filters can be used to apply custom data encryption or compression schemes to HTTP packets.

- **Custom authentication schemes**   Outlook Web Access (OWA) forms-based authentication, RSA SecurID authentication, and Remote Authentication Dial-In User Service (RADIUS) authentication are all implemented as Web filters in ISA Server. Third-party vendors can use Web filters to implement additional authentication schemes.

See Also   To view all the Web filters included with ISA Server 2004, open the ISA Server Management Console, expand Configuration, and then click Add-ins. The Web filters are listed on the Web Filters tab. You can enable or disable the Web filters from this interface but most Web filters cannot be modified.

How the HTTP Web Filter Works

One of the more important Web filters included with ISA Server 2004 is the HTTP filter. Many Internet applications now use HTTP to tunnel the application traffic. For example, Microsoft MSN Messenger uses HTTP as the application-layer protocol. The only way to block these types of applications without blocking all HTTP traffic is to use HTTP filtering.

HTTP filtering can be applied in two general scenarios:

- Clients on an internal network accessing HTTP objects on another network through ISA Server. This access is controlled by ISA Server access rules, to which an HTTP policy can be applied using the HTTP filter.

- Clients on the Internet accessing HTTP objects on a Web server that is published through ISA Server. This access is controlled by ISA Server Web publishing rules, to which an HTTP policy can be applied using the HTTP filter.

HTTP filtering is rule-specific, so that you can apply different levels and types of filtering depending on the specific requirements of your firewall policy. For example, you can use HTTP filtering to block the use of a particular peer-to-peer file-sharing service for one set of users, but allow it for another set, or you can allow Internet users to use specific HTTP methods such as POST for one Web publishing rule, but deny the method on another Web publishing rule. (Table 7-6, later in this chapter, lists HTTP 1.1 methods.)

Note   HTTP filters can also filter HTTPS traffic in a Web publishing Secure Sockets Layer (SSL) bridging scenario. In this case, ISA Server decrypts the packet and inspects it before re-encrypting the packet. HTTP filters cannot filter HTTPS traffic in an SSL tunneling scenario. For more details about configuring SSL bridging and tunneling, see Chapter 8, "Implementing ISA Server Publishing."

HTTP Filter Options

The HTTP filter can block HTTP requests based on the following options:

- **Length of request headers and payload**   Limits the maximum HTTP header size and request body size for a client request.

- **Length of Uniform Resource Locator (URL)**   Limits the maximum URL size for client requests.

- **HTTP request method**   Specifies the HTTP method, such as POST, GET, or HEAD, that will be blocked.

- **HTTP request file-name extension**   Prevents the downloading of any content using HTTP based on file extensions such as .exe, .asp, or .dll.

- **HTTP request or response header**   Specifies how server headers will be returned or forwarded when the server responds to the client. For example, the request or response header may be Location, Server, or Via.

- **Signature or pattern in the requester response headers or body**   Specifies HTTP access based on specific strings in the response header or body.

The HTTP filter is initially configured with defaults that help ensure secure HTTP access. However, depending on the specific deployment scenario, these options should be customized.

> **See Also**   To fully understand how the HTTP filter works, you must understand how HTTP works. For more information about HTTP, see Request for Comments (RFC) 2616: Hypertext Transfer Protocol HTTP/1.1, located at *http://www.ietf.org/rfc/rfc2616.txt.*

How to Configure a HTTP Web Filter

HTTP filters are applied on a per-rule basis. To configure the HTTP filters on a particular access rule or Web publishing rule, modify the HTTP policy for that rule.

> **Important**   The one exception to the per-rule application of the HTTP filter is the Maximum headers length setting on the General tab of the Configure HTTP Policy For Rule dialog box. This setting is applied to all rules globally, which means that if you change it in one rule, it is changed in all rules.

Configuring HTTP Policy General Properties

To access the HTTP policy associated with a specific rule, right-click the rule in ISA Server Management Console and select Configure HTTP, as shown in Figure 7-15.

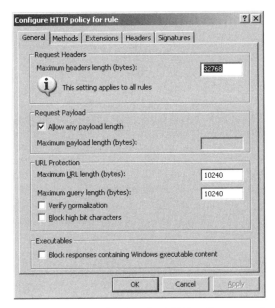

Figure 7-15   Configuring the HTTP policy general properties

Table 7-5 describes the configuration options available on the General tab of an HTTP policy.

Table 7-5   Configuring HTTP Policy General Properties

Setting	Configuration Options	Explanation
Request Headers, Maximum headers length (bytes)	Specify the maximum number of bytes that a request can have in its headers (URL and headers) before it is blocked.	Reducing the allowed header size mitigates the risk of attacks that require complex and long headers, such as buffer overflow attacks and some denial-of-service attacks. If you set the maximum header length too low, it could break some legitimate applications that use long headers.
Request Payload, Allow any payload length	To block requests exceeding a specified maximum payload length, clear the Allow Any Payload Length (Bytes) check box. Then, in Maximum Payload Length (Bytes), specify the maximum number of bytes.	By limiting the request payload you can restrict the amount of data a user can POST to your Web site in a Web publishing scenario. To determine what limit to set, estimate the maximum size of a file that would constitute a legitimate POST based on your site usage and use that as the allowed payload length.

Table 7-5   Configuring HTTP Policy General Properties

Setting	Configuration Options	Explanation
URL Protection, Maximum URL length (bytes)	Specify the maximum URL length allowed.	Use this option to limit the length of URLs used in a request. You may want to limit the URL length if you learn of an attack based on a long URL string. By default the maximum query length is set to 10240.
URL Protection, Maximum query length (bytes)	Specify the maximum query length allowed in a request.	The query is the part of a URL that follows "?". You may want to limit the query length if you learn of an attack based on a long query string. By default the maximum query length is set to 10240.
URL Protection, Verify normalization	Use this to block requests with URLs containing escaped characters after normalization.	Web servers receive requests that are URL encoded. This means that certain characters may be replaced with a percent symbol (%) followed by a particular number. For example, %20 corresponds to a space. Normalization is the process of decoding URL-encoded requests. Because the percent symbol (%) itself can be URL-encoded, an attacker can submit a URL request to a server that is double-encoded. When you select Verify Normalization, the HTTP filter normalizes the URL twice. If the URL after the first normalization is different from the URL after the second normalization, the filter rejects the request.
URL Protection, Block high bit Characters	Specify that URLs with high-bit characters will be blocked.	When you select Block high-bit characters, URLs that contain double-byte character sets (DBCS) or Latin 1 characters will be blocked. These are typically characters from languages that require more than 8 bits to represent the characters of the language, and therefore use 16 bits.
Executables, Block responses containing Windows executable content	Specify that responses containing Windows executable content are to be blocked.	This option blocks all Windows executable content (responses that begin with MZ). In most cases, it is recommended to use file extensions to block specific types of files.

How to Configure HTTP Web Filter Methods

HTTP methods (also known as *HTTP verbs*) are instructions sent in a request message that notify an HTTP server of the action to perform on the specified resource. For example, "GET" specifies that a resource is being retrieved from the server. Table 7-6 lists the HTTP 1.1 methods defined in RFC 2616.

Table 7-6   HTTP 1.1 Methods

Method	Description
GET	Retrieves the specified Uniform Resource Identifier (URI).
HEAD	Retrieves only the header of the specified URI.
POST	Asks the server to accept the enclosed information, such as a bulletin board message of form data.
PUT	Asks the server to accept the enclosed information as the specified URI.
DELETE	Asks the server to delete the specified URI.
TRACE	Asks the server to return the request message (used for diagnostics).
CONNECT	Reserved for requesting a proxy tunnel.

To configure HTTP methods, follow this procedure.

1. To access the HTTP policy associated with a specific rule, right-click the rule in ISA Server Management Console and select Configure HTTP.

2. To modify the HTTP methods settings on the HTTP policy, click the Methods tab, as shown in Figure 7-16.

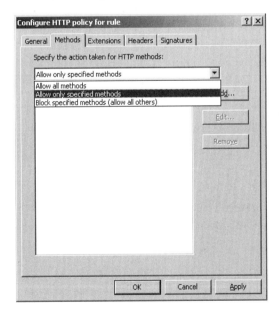

Figure 7-16   Configuring the HTTP methods

3. In Specify The Action Taken For HTTP Methods, select one of the following options:

   ❑ *Allow All Methods*—No blocking according to method will be applied.

❑ *Allow Selected Methods*—All requests will be blocked except those with the specified methods.

❑ *Block Specified Methods (Allow All Others)*—All requests will be allowed except those with methods specified in the list.

4. If you have selected either of the last two options, click Add to add a method to the list.

5. When you click Add, the Method dialog box opens, as shown in Figure 7-17. Provide the method (case-sensitive) and a description, and then click OK.

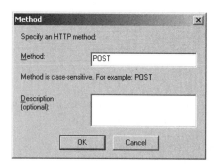

Figure 7-17   Configuring a specific HTTP method

An example of blocking by method would be to block POST so that internal clients cannot post data to an external Web page. This is useful in a secure network scenario where you want to prevent sensitive information from being posted on a Web site. This can also be useful in Web publishing, to prevent attackers from posting malicious material to your Web site.

How to Configure HTTP Web Filter Extensions

You can configure ISA Server to allow or deny HTTP downloads based on file extensions. When the HTTP filter is configured in this way, it analyzes each HTTP request to see if the request includes a configured extension. ISA Server considers an extension to be any character or characters that fall after the last period (.) of a URL and that end with a slash (/) or question mark (?) or the end of the URL if there is no slash or question mark.

In addition, if ISA Server identifies characters following a period that seem to be an extension (for example, .exe, .dll, or .com), the HTTP filter uses those as the extension. If there are multiple entries that appear to be extensions, ISA Server evaluates only the first extension.

Table 7-7 lists some examples of client requests and how ISA Server evaluates the extensions.

Table 7-7 How ISA Server Evaluates Extensions

Client Request	Extension
http://server/path/file.ext	.ext
http://server/path/file.htm/additional/path/info.asp	.asp
http://server/Path.exe/file.ext	.exe

In the last example listed in the table, if the HTTP filter allows .exe extensions, the request will be allowed (even if the filter does not allow .ext extensions). To work around this issue, configure a signature setting that denies the .ext signature in the URL.

To specify file extensions, follow this procedure:

1. To access the HTTP policy associated with a specific rule, right-click the rule in ISA Server Management Console and select Configure HTTP.

2. To modify the HTTP extensions settings on the HTTP policy, click the Extensions tab, as shown in Figure 7-18.

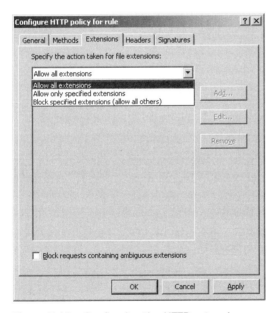

Figure 7-18 Configuring the HTTP extensions

3. In Specify The Action Taken For File Extensions, select one of the following options:

- ❏ *Allow All Extensions*—No blocking according to requested file extensions will be applied.

- ❏ *Allow Selected Extensions*—All requests will be blocked except those with specified requested file extensions.

- ❏ *Block Specified Extensions (Allow All Others)*—All requests will be allowed except those with requested file extensions specified in the list.

4. Click Add to add an extension to the list.

5. When you click Add, the Extension dialog box opens, as shown in Figure 7-19. Provide the extension (which is case-sensitive) and a description, and then click OK.

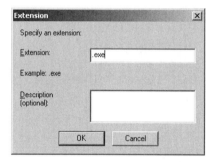

Figure 7-19   Configuring a specific HTTP extension

6. Select Block Requests Containing Ambiguous Extensions if you want to block content when ISA Server cannot determine the extension.

A typical use of extension blocking is to block executable files such as .exe, .bat, or .cmd files. Another example is to use extension blocking to prevent worm attacks. For example, the Code Red Worm uses a header that included "GET http://<ipaddress>/ default.ida?" so you could stop the worm from entering the network by blocking .ida extensions. You can also use file extensions to enforce organizational policies that restrict the types of data that can be downloaded.

How to Configure HTTP Web Filter Headers

When a client sends a request to a Web server, or when the server responds, the first part of that response is always the HTTP request or response.

- ■ The HTTP request from the client includes the client's HTTP method (such as GET) as well as the URI that the client is requesting and the protocol version.

- ■ The server HTTP response contains the protocol version followed by a numeric status code and its associated textual phrase. For example, if the server responds with a 2xx code, the server is indicating that the request was successfully received, understood, and accepted. A 4xx code is a client error that indicates that the request contains bad syntax or cannot be fulfilled.

After the HTTP request or response, the client and server send an HTTP header. The request-header fields allow the client to pass additional information about the request, and about the client itself, to the server. Headers contain information about the client, including browser and operating system data, authorization information, and the format types that client supports for the server response. The client header can also use the User-Agent to indicate the specific application that is making the request. You can use this header information to block HTTP packets.

To configure how the HTTP filter will manage headers, follow this procedure:

1. To access the HTTP policy associated with a specific rule, right-click the rule in ISA Server Management Console and select Configure HTTP.

2. To modify the HTTP headers settings on the HTTP policy, click the Headers tab, as shown in Figure 7-20.

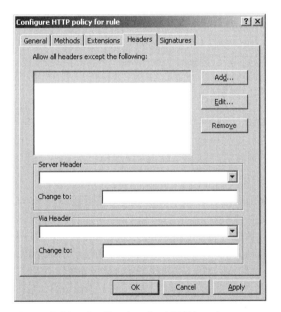

Figure 7-20   Configuring the HTTP headers

3. In Headers, list the headers that will be blocked. Click Add to add a header to the list. When you click Add, the Header dialog box opens. Specify whether the response or request header will be checked, provide the header, and then click OK.

4. In Server Header, specify how the server header will be returned in the response. The server header is a response header that contains information such as the name

of the server application and software version information, for example, HTTP: Server = Microsoft-IIS/6.0. The possible settings are the following:

❑ *Send Original Header*—The original header will be returned in the response.

❑ *Strip Header From Response*—No header will be returned in the response.

❑ *Modify*—A modified header will be returned in the response. If you select this option, in Change To, type the value that will appear in the response.

5. In Via Header, specify how the Via header will be forwarded in the request or returned in the response. Via headers provide a way for proxy servers in the path of a request to ensure that they are also included in the path of the response. Each server along the request's path can add its own Via header. Each sender along the response path removes its own Via header and forwards the response to the server specified in the next Via header on the stack. For example, you can use this feature to avoid disclosing the name of your computer running ISA Server in a response. The possible settings are:

❑ *Send Default*—The default header will be used.

❑ *Modify Header In Request And Response*—The Via header will be replaced with a modified header. If you select this option, in the Change too box, type the header that will appear instead of the Via header.

How to Configure HTTP Web Filter Signatures

An HTTP signature can be any string of characters in the HTTP header or body. To block an application based on signatures, you must identify the specific patterns the application uses in request headers, response headers, and body, and then modify the HTTP policy to block packets based on that string.

One of the difficulties in configuring the HTTP policy to block packets based on the signature is ensuring that the signature contains the specific information you need to block the chosen HTTP packet while not blocking other packets. For example, if you create an HTTP policy to block the word "Mozilla," you would block most Web browsers as well as other applications. This is because most Web browsers are Mozilla-compatible and include this term in HTTP headers. In most cases, you should use a more application-specific string. For example, to block MSN Messenger, configure the rule to block User-Agent: MSN Messenger in the request header.

To configure how the HTTP filter will manage signatures, follow this procedure:

1. To access the HTTP policy associated with a specific rule, right-click the rule in ISA Server Management Console and select Configure HTTP.

2. To modify the HTTP signatures settings on the HTTP policy, click the Signatures tab as shown in Figure 7-21. The Signatures tab shows the signatures that will be blocked.

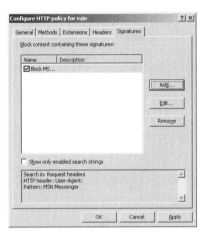

Figure 7-21   Configuring the HTTP policy signatures

3. Click Add to add a signature to the list as shown in Figure 7-22. In the Signature dialog box, in the Name text box, type a name for the signature search.

Figure 7-22   Configuring a specific HTTP signature

4. Under Signature search criteria, in the Search In drop-down list, select the part of the client request or server response you want the Web filter to search. Then, in the Signature text box, type the string that you want to filter.

5. When you have added signatures to the list on the Signatures tab, you can enable or disable specific signatures using the check boxes next to the signature names.

> **Note**   When you configure the HTTP policy to search the HTTP request body or response body, you can also specify how much of the body will be scanned for the signature and what format to use when scanning. By default, the filter will scan only the first 100 bytes of the request or response body. Increasing this number can negatively affect the server performance. You can also specify whether to search using text or binary format.

You can use HTTP signatures to block access to specific applications or to specific content. For example, if you configure the policy to block User-Agent: MSN Messenger in the request header, users will not be able to use MSN Messenger through the firewall. You can also block access to sites that might contain malicious code if you are aware of common malicious code. For example, a Web page containing <iframe src="?"/> will cause Internet Explorer to use up central processing unit (CPU) resources in an infinitely nested iframe element. To prevent access to Web pages containing this code, use a signature that searches in the response body for the text <iframe src="?"/>.

HTTP signature filtering assumes that all HTTP requests and responses are Uniform Transformation Format-8 (UTF-8, a transformation of Unicode character encoding) encoded. If a different encoding scheme is used, signature blocking cannot be performed.

Table 7-8 shows some of the signatures used by common HTTP-based applications.

> **Tip**   If you do not know the application signature for an application that you want to block, you can use a network sniffer, such as Network Monitor, to capture the traffic between the application client and a server. Then you can analyze the traffic to determine which signature you should block.

Table 7-8   Application Signatures for Common Applications

Application	Search In	HTTP Header	Signature
MSN Messenger	Request headers	User-Agent:	MSN Messenger
Windows Messenger	Request headers	User-Agent:	MSMSGS
Netscape 7	Request headers	User-Agent:	Netscape/7
Netscape 6	Request headers	User-Agent:	Netscape/6
AOL Messenger (and all Gecko browsers)	Request headers	User-Agent:	Gecko/
Yahoo Messenger	Request headers	Host:	msg.yahoo.com
Kazaa	Request headers	P2P-Agent:	Kazaa Kazaaclient:
Kazaa	Request headers	User-Agent:	KazaaClient

Table 7-8   Application Signatures for Common Applications

Application	Search In	HTTP Header	Signature
Kazaa	Request headers	X-Kazaa-Network:	KaZaA
Gnutella	Request headers	User-Agent:	Gnutella Gnucleus
Edonkey	Request headers	User-Agent:	e2dk
Internet Explorer 6.0	Request headers	User-Agent:	MSIE 6.0
Morpheus	Response header	Server:	Morpheus
Bearshare	Response header	Server:	Bearshare
BitTorrent	Request headers	User-Agent:	BitTorrent
Simple Object Access Protocol (SOAP) over HTTP	Request headers Response headers	User-Agent:	SOAPAction

See Also   For more information about configuring HTTP filtering in ISA Server 2004, see the HTTP Filtering in ISA Server 2004 article at *http://www.microsoft.com/technet/prodtechnol/ isa/2004/plan/httpfiltering.mspx*. This article includes excellent information on best practices for configuring HTTP filtering and includes an XML file that can be imported into ISA Server to configure the HTTP filter based on the best practices.

Practice: Configuring an HTTP Web Filter

In this practice, you will test the default HTTP filtering policy on the computer running ISA Server. Then you will modify the HTTP filter configuration in several ways and then test the results.

Note   In this practice, you are working with the HTTP Web Filter for an outbound Internet access rule. You can apply the same HTTP policies to inbound Web access after you configure a Web publishing rule.

Exercise 1: Testing HTTP Connections with the Default HTTP Filter

1. On CLIENT1, open Internet Explorer and, in the Address box, type **http:// www.microsoft.com/abc** and then press ENTER. The Microsoft Web server response indicates that there is no Microsoft.com Web page matching your

request. HTTP Filtering allowed the request, and the error message was returned from the Microsoft Web server because the requested object does not exist.

2. In Internet Explorer, in the Address box, type **http://www.microsoft.com/%252e** and then press ENTER. The HTTP request that you typed contains a double-encoded hexadecimal representation, which is often used in Unicode canonicalization attacks. Again, the HTTP filter did not block the request.

> **Tip** The HTTP policy that is assigned by default to a Web publishing rule blocks this type of request, but it is not blocked on Internet access rules.

3. In Internet Explorer, in the Address box, type **http://www.microsoft.com/scripts/root.exe?/dir+c** and then press ENTER. The Microsoft Web server response indicates that there is not Microsoft.com Web page matching your request.

Exercise 2: Configuring the HTTP Filter Settings

1. On ISA1, open ISA Server Management Console. Click Firewall Policy

2. Right-click Web Access Only and click Configure HTTP.

3. On the General tab, click Verify Normalization. This option will block the double-decoded request (*http://www.microsoft.com/%252e*).

4. On the Extensions tab, click Block Specified Extensions (Allow All Others) in the Specify The Action Taken For File Extension drop-down list.

5. Click Add. In the Extension dialog box, in the Extension text box, type **.exe**. Click OK.

6. On the Signatures tab, click Add. In the Signature dialog box, fill in the following information and then click OK.

   ❑ Name: **Block ABC**

   ❑ Search In: **Request URL**

   ❑ Signature: **abc**

7. Click OK and then click Apply to apply the changes.

Exercise 3: Testing HTTP Connections with the Modified HTTP Filter

1. On CLIENT1, open Internet Explorer and, in the Address box, type **http://www.microsoft.com/abc** and then press ENTER. Internet Explorer displays an error message from ISA Server. HTTP filtering blocked the request and returned an error that indicates that the attempt was blocked by the HTTP filter.

2. In Internet Explorer, in the Address box, type **http://www.microsoft.com/%252e** and then press ENTER. The HTTP filter blocked the request and returned an internal server error that indicates that the attempt was blocked by the HTTP Security filter.

3. In Internet Explorer, in the Address box, type **http://www.microsoft.com/ scripts/root.exe?/dir+c** and then press ENTER. Again, the HTTP filter blocked the request because of the .exe file extension in the request header.

Lesson Review

Use the following questions to help determine whether you have learned enough to move on to the next lesson. If you have difficulty answering these questions, review the material in this lesson before beginning the next lesson. You can find answers to these questions in the "Questions and Answers" section at the end of this chapter.

1. You are the ISA Server 2004 administrator for your organization. You create a Web publishing rule to allow access to your Web site. You want to ensure that no one from the external network can post any content or create any unauthorized links to other pages. You want to configure this on the ISA Server that you used to publish the Web site. What must you do?

   _____

   _____

   _____

2. You have deployed ISA Server and are using it as a proxy server for all client connections to the Internet. All users are allowed to use HTTP, HTTPS, and FTP to access the Internet. You review the firewall logs on the computer running ISA Server and notice that some users are accessing Web sites that contain information that is not acceptable under the organization's security policy. You need to block the user access to these Web sites based on the URL that the users type into Internet Explorer. How can you do this?

   a. Configure the HTTP policy to block access based on signatures.

   b. Configure the HTTP policy to block access based on methods.

   c. Configure the HTTP policy to block access based on headers.

   d. Configure the HTTP policy to block access based on extensions.

3. You use the Edge Firewall network template to configure Internet Access for your internal users. You used the template to enable HTTP, HTTPS, and FTP access to the Internet. Your users need to place files on an FTP server at a partner FTP site.

Now your users report that they are unable to put files on the FTP server. What must you do to correct the problem?

_____

_____

_____

Lesson Summary

- Application filters work with the firewall service in ISA Server to intercept and process network packets as they pass through ISA Server. ISA Server application filters can be used to implement various types of functionality on ISA Server.

- Web filters extend the functionality of the firewall service in ISA Server by providing advanced filtering capability for HTTP packets as they pass through ISA Server.

- One of the most important Web filters included with ISA Server 2004 is the HTTP filter. Many Internet applications now use HTTP to tunnel the application traffic. The only way to block these types of applications without blocking all HTTP traffic is to use HTTP filtering.

- HTTP filters are applied on a per-rule basis. To configure the HTTP filters on a particular access rule or Web publishing rule, you must modify the HTTP policy for that rule.

Case Scenario Exercise

In this exercise, you will plan an ISA Server configuration for a fictitious organization. Read the scenario and then answer the question that follows. If you have difficulty completing this work, review the material in this chapter before beginning the next chapter. You can find answers to these questions in the "Questions and Answers" section at the end of this chapter.

Scenario 1

You are the ISA Server administrator for your organization. You need to set up ISA Server 2004 to protect your network from unwanted traffic and you want to deal with any attacks from the Internet in a proactive manner. You also need to publish a public Web site. You have only one IP address that you can use that is routable on the Internet. Your ISP hosts the Internet DNS records for your domain. Your internal clients use your corporate DNS server on the internal network to resolve all queries. Your organization's security policy states the following:

- Authenticated Users are allowed access to the Internet using HTTP and HTTPS and FTP only.

- No peer-to-peer file-sharing applications are allowed to run on your network.

- Only members of the Administrators group should be able to download executable files from the Internet.

- The Web server that is accessible from the Internet must be isolated from the internal network.

- No one must be able to post objects to your Web server from the Internet.

Scenario 1 Question

1. How will you configure ISA Server 2004 to meet the security requirements?

_____

_____

_____

Troubleshooting Lab

In this lab, you will troubleshoot an HTTP Web filter problem. The new security policy in your organization prohibits the use of MSN Messenger and Windows Messenger from your internal network to the Internet. You need to block the use of these applications on your firewall.

Exercise 1: Testing Internet Access Using MSN Messenger

1. On CLIENT1, start MSN Messenger or Windows Messenger from the Start menu.

2. Log on using your account. Ensure that you can access the Internet using MSN Messenger or Windows Messenger.

Exercise 2: Configuring the HTTP Web Filter to Block an Application

1. On ISA1, start ISA Server Management Console. Click Firewall Policy.

2. Right-click the Web Access Only access rule and click Configure HTTP.

3. In the Configure HTTP Policy For Rule dialog box, click the Signature tab. Click Add.

4. In the Name text box, type **Block MSN Messenger**.

5. From the Search In list, click Request Headers.

6. In the HTTP header box, type **User-Agent**.

7. In the Signature box, type **MSN Messenger**.

8. Click Add again.

9. In the Name text box, type **Block Windows Messenger**.

10. From the Search In list, click Request Headers.

11. In the HTTP header box, type **User-Agent**.

12. In the Signature box, type **MSMSGS**.

13. Click OK to close the Signature box and then click OK to close the Configure HTTP Policy For Rule dialog box.

14. Click Apply to apply the changes.

Exercise 3: Testing the HTTP Web Filter Signature Block

1. On CLIENT1, try to access the Internet using MSN Messenger or Windows Messenger.

2. Confirm that you cannot access the Internet using these applications.

Chapter Summary

- Firewalls are used to limit network traffic from one network to another. Firewalls use packet filters, stateful filters, application filters, and intrusion detection to distinguish between network traffic that should be allowed and network traffic that should be blocked.

- ISA Server 2004 supports multi-networking, which means that you can configure multiple networks on ISA Server, and then configure network and access rules that inspect and filter all network traffic between all networks. ISA Server comes pre-configured with the following networks: Local Host, External, Internal, VPN Clients, and Quarantined VPN Clients. Network rules determine whether there is a relationship between two network entities and whether the relationship is a route and network address translation (NAT) relationship.

- A perimeter network is a network that you set up separately from an internal network and the Internet. There are three general types of network perimeter configurations; bastion host, three-legged configuration, and back-to-back configuration. The network templates included with ISA Server 2004 include preconfigured networks and network sets, network rules, access rule elements, and access rules. The templates are designed to simplify the process of configuring ISA Server.

- The purpose of intrusion detection is to detect network attacks as early as possible to ensure that appropriate corrective actions can be taken. ISA Server provides intrusion detection for well-known IP attacks and also provides built-in application filters that detect DNS protocol and Post Office Protocol (POP) intrusions. IP preferences are used to configure how ISA Server will handle specific IP packets. You can configure the following IP preferences on ISA Server: IP Option, IP fragments, and IP Routing.

- Application filters work with the firewall service in ISA Server to intercept and process network packets as they pass through ISA Server. ISA Server application filters can be used to implement various types of functionality on ISA Server. Web filters extend the functionality of the firewall service in ISA Server by providing advanced filtering capability for HTTP packets as they pass through ISA Server. One of the most important Web filters included with ISA Server 2004 is the HTTP filter. HTTP filters are applied on a per-rule basis. To configure the HTTP filters on a particular access rule or Web publishing rule, you must modify the HTTP policy for that rule.

Exam Highlights

Before taking the exam, review the key points and terms that are presented in this chapter. You need to know this information.

Key Points

- ISA Server does not support the direct configuration of a packet filter. To block all connection attempts from a specific host, or to allow a specific protocol from a particular host you must configure an access rule.

- Both access rules and network rules are processed by ISA Server before network traffic is passed through the firewall. Check the configuration of both types of rules when troubleshooting network access.

- ISA Server network templates simplify the configuration of the ISA Server settings. However, the templates also enable only outbound access and have a limited set of configuration options. You should have a clear idea what each template does so that you can troubleshoot any problems with the template.

- Blocking IP fragments is an example of a configuration option that may provide some additional security but at the cost of some functionality. If users cannot use a streaming media application one of the possible explanations is that IP fragments are being blocked. By default, IP fragment blocking is not enabled on ISA Server.

- HTTP Web filter rules are applied on a per rule basis. Just because you have configured filtering on one rule, does not mean that filtering is applied to all rules. If you have multiple rules that grant access to the Internet, you need to configure the filter for all the rules.

Key Terms

intrusion detection   A means to detect when an attack is attempted or in progress against a network. If you detect an intrusion attempt early enough, you may be able to prevent a successful intrusion.

network rule   Defines how network packets will be passed between networks. Network rules determine whether there is a relationship between two network entities and what type of relationship is defined.

network template   A set of ISA Server configuration options that define networks and network sets, network rules, access rule elements, and access rules.

packet filtering   Filters network packets by inspecting and allowing or denying the IP packets based on information in the IP packet network layer header.

perimeter network   A network that is separated from an internal network and the Internet. Perimeter networks allow external users to gain access to specific servers that are located on the perimeter network while preventing direct access to the internal network.

stateful filtering   Filters network packets by using information about the TCP session to determine if a packet should be blocked or allowed through the firewall.

Web filters   Extend the functionality of the firewall service in ISA Server by providing advanced filtering capability for HTTP packets as they pass through ISA Server.

Questions and Answers

Page
7-10

Lesson 1 Review

1. You are the ISA Server administrator of your organization. You have deployed ISA Server 2004 as the firewall and configured it so that the users have unrestricted access to the Internet. You suspect that some of your users have installed a peer-to-peer file sharing application which is not an approved application. The application uses a custom protocol and port number to communicate with other computers. You need to ensure that traffic from that application is not allowed into your network from the Internet. What is the easiest way for you to accomplish this?

   a. Create a packet filter to block the port used by the application.

   b. Do nothing. The traffic is blocked by default.

   c. Configure an application filter to block the traffic.

   d. Create an access rule to block the port used by the application.

   D is correct. You can block the application by creating an access rule to block the port used by the application. A is incorrect because you cannot specifically create packet filters in ISA Server 2004. B is incorrect because, if the application is already installed, the request is coming from an internal user and stateful filtering will allow the connection. C may be possible if you have an application filter that blocks the protocol used by the application, but just blocking the port is easier in this scenario.

2. How does application filtering protect the internal network?

   a. By blocking IP fragments

   b. By inspecting the data in a packet for unacceptable commands and data

   c. By blocking connections to particular ports

   d. By allowing or disallowing traffic based on connection rules

   B is correct. The advantage of using an application filter is that it can inspect the data in an IP packet. A and C are incorrect because application filters do not block IP fragments or ports. D is incorrect because connection rules track session status.

3. What feature of ISA Server prevents IP addresses that logically appear on the Internal network from entering your network through the external interface?

   a. Egress filtering

b. Ingress filtering

c. Application-layer filtering

d. Stateful filtering

B is correct. Ingress filtering blocks all packets on the external interface that have a source address that is logically on the Internal network. Egress filtering is the opposite of ingress filtering—it blocks packets on the Internal interface that have a source address which is logically on the external network. Application-layer filtering filters traffic based on application data, while stateful filtering filters traffic based on its state in the context of previous network packets.

Page
7-22
Lesson 2 Review

1. The research department in your organization has unique network access requirements. All the computers used by the department users are on a separate subnet that must be isolated from the production environment. The users need unrestricted Internet access. What should you do to facilitate that?

   Create a new internal network that is defined by the range of IP addresses for the research department subnet. Then define a network rule between the research department network and the Internet and define an access rule that allows full access to the Internet from the research department network.

2. You have configured four different internal networks on your ISA Server. Each network represents a different department in your organization. The different departments have some unique Internet access rule requirements, but you also want some of the access rules to be the same for all departments. What is the easiest way to accomplish this?

   Create a network set that includes the four network objects. Then configure the common access rules and assign them to the network set. Configure the unique access rules for each department and assign them to the department network. Ensure that the access rules for the department networks are listed before the access rules that apply to the network set.

3. All users in your organization require access to the Internet from their desktop computers. From their desktop computers, the users should be able to use any protocol to access the Internet. However, when the users are using one of the publicly accessible computers located in the office lobby, they should be able to use only HTTP to access the Internet. What are two possible ways to configure this?

   a. Configure a network that includes the internal network and the publicly accessible computers. Enable only HTTP access to the Internet from that network.

   b. Configure a computer set that includes the publicly accessible computers. Enable only HTTP access to the Internet from that computer set.

    c. Configure a domain name set that includes the publicly accessible computers. Enable only HTTP access to the Internet from that computer set.

    d. Configure a new network that includes the publicly accessible computers. Enable only HTTP access to the Internet from that network.

B and D are correct. You can group all the publicly accessible computers by creating a computer set or network that includes all the computers. After you have grouped the computers, you can apply an access rule to those computers. A network object that includes both internal and the publicly accessible computers would apply the rule to both groups of computers. A domain name set can only be used to define what Web sites can be accessed.

Page
7-35

Lesson 3 Review

1. You are the network administrator of a small company. Your company does not publish any servers to the Internet and your ISP handles all Internet services for your organization. You need to enable Internet access for your internal users using only HTTP and HTTPS. What network template and policy would work best for you?

Because your company does not publish servers, there is no need for a perimeter network. The Edge Firewall template, with the Block Internet Access, Allow Access To Internet Service Provider Network Services policy, would be the best choice because it allows DNS traffic through to your ISP. Then create an access rule to allow HTTP and HTTPS traffic from the Internal network. Any other policies also allow FTP access or unrestricted access.

2. You use a third-party firewall solution as your Internet-edge firewall. You have installed ISA Server 2004 and you are using it just to take advantage of the caching capabilities. What network template will you choose?

    a. Front Firewall

    b. Bastion Host

    c. Edge Firewall

    d. Single Network Adapter

D is correct. If you only want caching functionality then the Single Network Adapter template will apply the Allow Web Proxy and Caching policy. Then you must configure your clients to be Web Proxy clients. All the other deployment scenarios listed as possible answers are used to provide firewall functionality, not just caching.

3. Your organization is designing a new perimeter network configuration. The organization is planning on deploying several Web servers and other application servers that need to be accessible from the Internet. At the same time, the organization requires that these servers be isolated from the internal network so that only selected traffic can pass from the publicly accessible servers to the internal network. The company must implement the most secure solution possible. What perimeter network configuration should the organization implement?

   a. Configure a bastion host firewall.

   b. Configure a three-leg perimeter network.

   c. Configure a back-to-back perimeter network with two firewalls from the same vendor.

   d. Configure a back-to-back perimeter network with two firewalls from different vendors.

D is correct. A back-to-back firewall configuration with firewalls from two different vendors is the most secure configuration. Even if attackers get past one firewall, they will need to use a different attack to bypass the second firewall. Both the bastion host and a three-leg perimeter use a single firewall, which is less secure than multiple firewalls. In addition, the bastion host configuration does not provide any isolation between the publicly accessible servers and the internal network.

Page
7-44

Lesson 4 Review

   1. Your organization has just deployed an ISA Server computer as a firewall. The security policy for your organization requires that all settings on the ISA Server computer be configured as securely as possible. After you implement a secure configuration, users report that they can no longer access a streaming media site. Access to this site is critical for the company, so you must enable access to the site. What security setting should you change to enable access to the site?

   a. Enable IP routing

   b. Disable all filtering based on IP options

   c. Disable filtering of IP fragments

   d. Disable filtering based on the source-routing IP options

C is correct. Streaming media frequently requires the use of IP fragments, so filtering all IP fragments may block access to streaming media content. Enabling or disabling IP routing will not affect access to streaming media. Streaming media also does not require any IP options, including the source-routing options.

   2. You have configured intrusion detection to detect when the ISA Server interfaces are being exposed to a port scan. You configure the alert to send an e-mail to your account when the alert is triggered. You are now receiving a high number of e-mails from the ISA Server computer. You want to reduce the number of e-mails sent to your account, but still want to know when there are frequent port scans of your ISA Server. What should you do?

On the Intrusion Detection–Common Attacks Property page, you can increase the number of attacks before an alert is triggered. In this way, you will not receive as many e-mails, but will still receive an e-mail after multiple attacks have been detected.

3. You have configured ISA Server 2004 as a bastion host. You are concerned about the security of your DNS database. One of the internal DNS servers must be accessible from the Internet but you want to ensure that zone transfers will never be allowed to clients that are not on your internal network. How will you accomplish this?

On the General Configuration settings on the Intrusion Detection–DNS Attacks properties page, Select Enable Detection And Filtering of DNS Attacks and ensure that DNS Zone Transfers is enabled.

Page
7-63

Lesson 5 Review

1. You are the ISA Server 2004 administrator for your organization. You create a Web publishing rule to allow access to your Web site. You want to ensure that no one from the external network can post any content or create any unauthorized links to other pages. You want to configure this on the ISA Server that you used to publish the Web site. What must you do?

Configure your Web publishing rule's HTTP Policy to block the POST and LINK Methods.

2. You have deployed ISA Server and are using it as a proxy server for all client connections to the Internet. All users are allowed to use HTTP, HTTPS, and FTP to access the Internet. You review the firewall logs on the computer running ISA Server and notice that some users are accessing Web sites that contain information that is not acceptable under the organization's security policy. You need to block the user access to these Web sites based on the URL that the users type into Internet Explorer. How can you do this?

    a. Configure the HTTP policy to block access based on signatures.

    b. Configure the HTTP policy to block access based on methods.

    c. Configure the HTTP policy to block access based on headers.

    d. Configure the HTTP policy to block access based on extensions.

A is correct. To block access to Web sites based on the URL typed by the user, configure the HTTP policy to block access based on the signatures that you want to block.

3. You use the Edge Firewall network template to configure Internet Access for your internal users. You used the template to enable HTTP, HTTPS, and FTP access to the Internet. Your users need to place files on an FTP server at a partner FTP site. Now your users report that they are unable to put files on the FTP server. What must you do to correct the problem?

You must modify the configuration of the FTP Web filter to enable the users to upload FTP content. By default, the FTP policy only allows downloads. To modify the FTP policy, right-click the access rule and click Configure FTP. You must clear the Read Only option.

Case Scenario Exercise

Page
7-65

Scenario 1 Question

1. How will you configure ISA Server 2004 to meet the security requirements?

You should start by applying the 3-Leg Perimeter network template on the ISA Server computer. Since you have only one IP address that you can use on the Internet, you must use a private IP subnet in the perimeter network. You must modify the network rule created by the network template to define a NAT relationship between the perimeter network and the Internet. When you apply the wizard, chose the Allow Limited Web Access option. Modify the Web Access Only rule created by the wizard to apply to Authenticated Users instead of All Users and configure HTTP Filtering for the rule to block the signatures for all peer-to-peer file-sharing applications and to block all executable content. Create an access rule to allow DNS traffic from your internal DNS server to the Internet and then configure your internal DNS server to forward all queries to your ISP's DNS server. Finally, configure a Web publishing rule for the public Web site and set the HTTP Policy to block the POST method on the rule.

8 Implementing ISA Server Publishing

Exam Objectives in this Chapter:

- Create policy elements, access rules, and connection limits. Policy elements include schedule, protocols, user groups, and network objects.

- Create policy rules for Web publishing.
    - ❏ Install certificates for Web publishing.
    - ❏ Configure authentication for Web access.
    - ❏ Configure bridging.
    - ❏ Configure link translator.

- Create policy rules for server publishing.
    - ❏ Publish a Web server by using server publishing rules.
    - ❏ Publish an RPC server.
    - ❏ Publish an FTP server.
    - ❏ Publish a Terminal Services server.
    - ❏ Publish a VPN server or device.

Why This Chapter Matters

Now that you have configured Microsoft Internet Security and Acceleration (ISA) Server 2004 to allow internal clients to access the Internet, and understand how to configure ISA Server as a firewall, you are ready for the next step in your ISA Server deployment. That step is configuring ISA Server to publish internal servers to the Internet, so that users on the Internet can access those internal resources. Many organizations now host corporate Web sites or make messaging servers accessible from the Internet. Other organizations have much more complex requirements. Perhaps they are hosting multiple Web sites, or they may need to enable access to a wide variety of servers on the internal or perimeter network.

Making internal resources accessible to the Internet increases the security risks for the organization. By default, firewalls such as ISA Server block all traffic from the Internet to the protected networks. When you make external resources available, you deliberately allow network traffic from the Internet onto your internal or perimeter network. To reduce this risk, the firewall at the perimeter of the network must be able to block all malicious network traffic from entering the organization's network from the Internet and ensure that users from the Internet can access only the required servers.

ISA Server 2004 uses Web and server publishing rules to publish internal network resources to the Internet. Web publishing rules determine how ISA Server deals with Hypertext Transfer Protocol (HTTP) and Hypertext Transfer Protocol Secure (HTTPS) requests from the Internet intended for internal Web servers. Server publishing rules define how ISA Server responds to requests from the Internet for other network resources on the internal network. You must know how to use these rules to securely publish internal network resources to the Internet.

Lessons in this Chapter:

- Lesson 1: Introduction to Publishing 8-4
- Lesson 2: Configuring Web Publishing Rules. 8-13
- Lesson 3: Configuring Secure Web Publishing Rules 8-33
- Lesson 4: Configuring Server Publishing Rules 8-47
- Lesson 5: Configuring ISA Server Authentication. 8-63

Before You Begin

This chapter presents the skills and concepts related to publishing internal Web sites and other internal services to the Internet. If you plan to complete the practices and lab in this chapter, you should prepare the following:

- A Microsoft Windows Server 2003 (Standard Edition or Enterprise Edition) computer installed as DC1 and configured as a domain controller in the *cohovineyard.com* domain. This server must have the following configuration:

  ❑ Microsoft Internet Information Services (IIS) installed, with a default Web and file transfer protocol (FTP) site configured.

  ❑ Remote Desktop connections must be enabled.

  ❑ Routing And Remote Access must be enabled and configured for virtual private network (VPN) connectivity.

- A second Windows Server 2003 computer installed as ISA1 and configured as a domain member in the *cohovineyard.com* domain. This server should have two network interfaces installed.

- A Microsoft Windows XP computer installed as CLIENT1. This computer must be a member of the *cohovineyard.com* domain.

- A Microsoft Windows Server 2003 (Standard Edition or Enterprise Edition) computer installed as SERVER1. This computer should not be a member of the *cohovineyard.com* domain. This server should be located on the same network as the external interface of the ISA Server computer. This server should run the Domain Name System (DNS) Service and the DNS client setting should be configured to use the server's Internet Protocol (IP) address as the DNS server.

Lesson 1: Introduction to Publishing

Most organizations want users from the Internet to be able to access some resources that are located on the organization's internal or perimeter network. You can use ISA Server 2004 to provide secure access to internal resources for Internet users. ISA Server 2004 uses publishing to provide this secure access. This lesson introduces the concepts of Web publishing and server publishing. It also provides an overview of how to configure DNS to enable Web and server publishing.

After this lesson, you will be able to

- Describe a Web publishing rule
- Describe a server publishing rule
- Describe how to integrate DNS with the Web publishing scenarios

Estimated lesson time: 25 minutes

What Are Web Publishing Rules?

ISA Server uses Web publishing rules to make Web sites on protected networks available to users on other networks, such as the Internet. A Web publishing rule is a firewall rule that specifies how ISA Server will route incoming requests to internal Web servers.

Web publishing rules provide the following functionality:

- **Access to Web servers running HTTP protocol** When you configure a Web publishing rule, you configure ISA Server to listen for HTTP or HTTPS requests from the Internet and to forward or proxy that request to a Web server on a protected network. To publish servers using any other protocols, you need to use a server publishing rule.

- **HTTP application-layer filtering** HTTP application-layer filtering enables ISA Server to inspect the application data in each packet passing through ISA Server. This includes filtering of Secure Sockets Layer (SSL) packets if you enable SSL bridging. This provides an additional layer of security not provided by most server publishing rules.

- **Path mapping** Path mapping enables you to hide the details of your internal Web site configuration by redirecting external requests for parts of the Web site to alternate locations within the internal Web site. This means that you can limit access to only specific areas within a Web site.

- **User authentication**   You can configure ISA Server to require that all external users authenticate before their requests are forwarded to the Web server hosting the published content. This protects the internal Web server from authentication attacks. Web publishing rules support several methods of authentication, including Remote Authentication Dial-In User Service (RADIUS), integrated, basic, digest, digital certificates, and RSA SecurID.

- **Content caching**   The content from the internal Web server can be cached on ISA Server, which improves the response time to the Internet client while decreasing the load on the internal Web server.

- **Support for publishing multiple Web sites using a single IP address**   Many organizations use a single external IP address that is routable on the Internet. You can configure multiple Web publishing rules that can make multiple internal Web sites available to Internet clients using that single IP address.

- **Link translation**   With link translation, you can provide access to complex Web pages that include references to other internal Web servers that are not directly accessible from the Internet. Without link translation, any link to a server that is not accessible from the Internet would appear as a broken link. Link translation can be used to publish complex Web sites providing content from many servers while hiding the complexity from the Internet users.

> **Note**   ISA Server 2004 also provides secure Web publishing rules. These rules are Web publishing rules that use SSL to encrypt network traffic. ISA Server provides multiple options for using SSL. For example, you can configure ISA Server to encrypt all the traffic from ISA Server to the Internet client but not to encrypt the traffic on the internal network. Or you can encrypt just the traffic on the internal network. You can also configure ISA Server to encrypt the traffic on both the internal network and the Internet. You can also configure ISA Server to apply application filtering on the encrypted packets. With this configuration, the ISA Server computer will decrypt the packet, filter it, and then encrypt the packet again.

What Are Server Publishing Rules?

Web publishing and secure Web publishing rules can grant access only to Web servers using HTTP or HTTPS. To grant access to internal resources using any other protocol, you must configure server publishing rules. When you create a server publishing rule, you are configuring ISA Server to listen for client requests using a particular port number. When ISA Server receives a request on the external interface for that port, it checks the server publishing rule to determine which internal server is providing the service. ISA Server then passes the request to the internal server. The internal server responds to the client request, forwarding the response to ISA Server, which forwards the response to the client.

Server publishing rules to provide the following functionality:

- **Access to multiple protocols** Server publishing rules provide access to protocols that Web publishing rules cannot. Web publishing rules can only publish servers using HTTP or HTTPS; for all other protocols, you must use a server publishing rule. ISA Server is configured in advance with a variety of protocol definitions for commonly used protocols that can be incorporated within server publishing rules. You can also create custom protocol definitions. Any protocol definition in which the primary connection is defined as inbound can be used for a server publishing rule.

- **Application-layer filtering for specified protocols** Application-layer filtering enables ISA Server to inspect the application data in each packet passing through ISA Server. ISA Server can apply application-layer inspection for server publishing when an application filter is registered for a specific protocol. For all other network traffic, ISA Server can apply packet and stateful filtering. ISA Server cannot inspect incoming SSL packets for servers published by server publishing rules.

- **Support for encryption** Some of the protocol definitions provided with ISA Server are secure protocols. For example, ISA Server includes definitions for secure Internet Message Access Protocol (IMAPS) and secure Post Office Protocol (POPS). When a server publishing rule is configured to use these protocols, ISA Server can forward encrypted data between the client computer and the internal published server.

- **IP address logging for the client computer** By default, when you publish a server using server publishing rule, the source IP address that is received by the internal server is the IP address of the client computer on the Internet.

Considerations for Configuring DNS for Web and Server Publishing

One of the complicating considerations when publishing internal Web servers as well as other servers to the Internet is DNS name resolution. Often, clients from the internal network, as well as clients from the Internet, must connect to the same internal server using the same DNS name. However, the internal clients usually need to connect to a different IP address than the external clients.

> **Exam Tip** One of the more common reasons for Web publishing rule failures is DNS resolution errors. If you see an exam question in which users on one network can access a resource using the fully qualified domain name (FQDN) but users on another network cannot, check the DNS resolution configuration. Because some users can access the server, you know that the server is functional; therefore, the problem may be name resolution. If name resolution seems to be set up correctly, check the publishing rule configuration.

For example, you may have a corporate Web server located on a perimeter network that needs to be accessible to both internal users and Internet users. A possible configuration is shown in Figure 8-1. In this configuration, a route configuration is configured between the internal network and the perimeter network, so when the internal clients try to access *www.cohovineyard.com*, they must connect to the IP address of 172.16.10.1. However, users from the Internet must access *www.cohovineyard.com* by connecting to the external network interface on the ISA Server computer (131.107.1.1). ISA Server then uses a Web publishing rule to provide access to the corporate Web server. The solution to providing access to the same server using two different IP addresses is to deploy a split DNS.

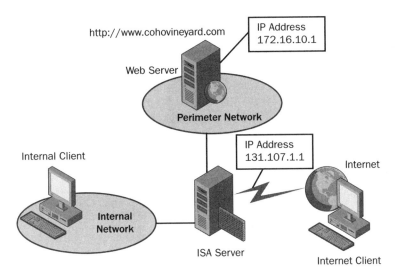

Figure 8-1   Enabling access to a Web site for internal and Internet clients

A split DNS uses two different DNS servers with the same DNS domain name to provide name resolution for internally and externally accessible resources. Both DNS servers are authoritative for the same domain name. For example, in the Web publishing scenario shown in Figure 8-1, one DNS server, used by all the internal clients, has a host record for the Web server that points to the actual IP address of the Web server. The second DNS server, accessible to Internet clients, has a host record for the Web server that points to the IP address of the external interface of the server running ISA Server.

Security Alert   To implement a split DNS, you need two DNS servers, both of which are authoritative for the same domain. However, these two servers should not have the same resource records. For example, your internal DNS server will have the IP addresses for all the internal servers (including the domain controllers if you have deployed Active Directory directory service). This information should never be made available on the Internet DNS server. The Internet DNS server should only have resource records for the hosts that must be accessible from the Internet. If you are exposing a single Web site and a single messaging server to the Internet, then the Internet DNS server should have only the resource records required to resolve the IP addresses for those two servers.

With a split DNS, users from both the Internet and the internal network can access the corporate Web site, as illustrated in Figure 8-2.

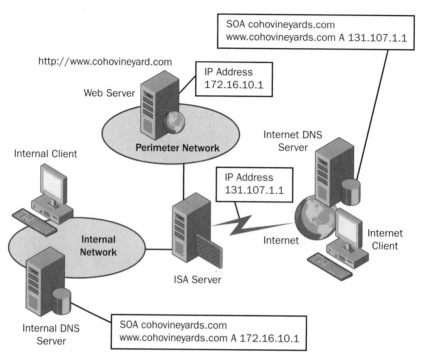

Figure 8-2 Implementing a split DNS

When the Internet client wants to access the Web server, it must resolve the name *www.cohovineyard.com*. The client sends a query to the DNS server on the Internet. Because the DNS server has a Start of Authority (SOA) record for the *cohovineyard.com* domain, the DNS server checks its zone files for the requested information. The server responds with the IP address of the external interface of the server running ISA Server. The client will then send the Web request to the IP address provided by the DNS server, and ISA Server will forward the request to the Web server.

Note The scenario described here assumes a Network Address Translation (NAT) relationship between the external network and the perimeter network and a route relationship between the internal network and the perimeter network. If the network relationships were reversed, then the host record on the external DNS would point to the actual IP address for the Web server, while the host record on the internal DNS would point to the IP address of the internal network interface on ISA Server.

When the internal client wants to access the Web server, it will query the internal DNS server for the IP address of *www.cohovineyard.com*. The internal DNS server will check its zone files, and provide the client with the actual IP address of the Web server. The internal client will then directly connect to the internal Web server. If the Web server is located on a perimeter network, the request will be passed through ISA Server.

> **Important**   Firewall clients and Web proxy clients do not require a split DNS configuration to access the internal Web sites as they can use the Internet IP address to access the internal server. In this configuration, the Web requests are passed through ISA Server. However, Secure Network Address Translation (SecureNAT) clients cannot connect to the internal Web servers using an Internet IP address as SecureNAT client requests cannot be routed back through the ISA Server computer. Even if you do not need to implement a split DNS, it is still a best practice to implement a split DNS, especially if you publish Web servers on the internal network. In this way, Web Proxy and Firewall clients can access the internal Web servers directly rather than through the ISA Server computer.

Practice: Configuring DNS for Web and Server Publishing

In this practice, you will configure the DNS servers on the internal and external network (representing the Internet in your practice configuration) to correctly resolve the addresses for the Web site and FTP site located on DC1. SERVER1 is configured as the external DNS server in this scenario. You will use these DNS records in later exercises when testing the publishing rules.

Exercise 1: Creating the Internet DNS Records for Cohovineyard.com

1. Log on to SERVER1 using an administrator account.

2. Open the DNS Management Console from the Administrative Tools folder.

3. Right-click Forward Lookup Zones, and then click New Zone.

4. On the Welcome To The New Zone Wizard page, click Next.

5. On the Zone Type page, accept the default of Primary Zone and click Next.

6. On the Zone Name page, type **cohovineyard.com** as the zone name. Click Next.

7. On the Zone File page, accept the default zone file name and click Next.

8. On the Dynamic Update page, accept the default and click Next.

9. On the Completing The New Zone Wizard page, review the configuration and then click Finish.

10. Expand cohovineyard.com, then right-click cohovineyard.com and click New Host (A).

11. In the New Host dialog box, type **www** in the Name box. Type the IP address assigned to the external interface of the ISA Server computer in the IP address box. Click Add Host.

12. In the New Host dialog box, type **ftp** in the Name box. Type the IP address assigned to the external interface of the ISA Server computer in the IP address box. Click Add Host.

13. In the New Host dialog box, type **secure** in the Name box. Type the IP address assigned to the external interface of the ISA Server computer in the IP address box. Click Add Host.

14. In the DNS dialog box, click OK.

15. Click Done. Close the DNS Management Console.

Exercise 2: Creating the Internal DNS Records for Cohovineyard.com

1. Log on to DC1 using an administrator account.

2. Open the DNS Management Console from the Administrative Tools folder.

3. Expand Forward Lookup Zones and then expand cohovineyard.com.

4. Right-click cohovineyard.com and click New Host (A).

5. In the New Host dialog box, type **www** in the Name box. Type **10.10.0.10** in the IP address box. Click Add Host.

6. In the New Host dialog box, type **ftp** in the Name box. Type **10.10.0.10** in the IP address box. Click Add Host.

7. In the New Host dialog box, type **secure** in the Name box. Type **10.10.0.10** in the IP address box. Click Add Host.

8. In the DNS dialog box, click OK.

9. Click Done, then close the DNS Management Console.

Exercise 3: Testing Internal Access to Cohovineyard.com Web Sites

1. Log on to CLIENT1 using a domain user account.

2. Open Internet Explorer and type **www.cohovineyard.com** into the Address box. The connection should be successful.

3. Connect to *secure.cohovineyard.com* and *ftp://ftp.cohovineyard.com*. All connections should be successful.

Note   You cannot access the internal Web sites from the Internet (SERVER1) at this point because you have not configured any publishing rules that allow this access.

Lesson Review

Use the following questions to help determine whether you have learned enough to move on to the next lesson. If you have difficulty answering these questions, review the material in this lesson before beginning the next lesson. You can find answers to the questions in the "Questions and Answers" section at the end of this chapter.

1. You have deployed ISA Server 2004 as a Bastion Host. You need to provide a secure method of publishing your Web site. You also need to be able to configure ISA Server to inspect the contents of the packets to and from the Web server using application filters. What feature of ISA Server 2004 makes this possible?

   a. SSL Tunneling

   b. Link Translation

   c. SSL Bridging

   d. Path Mapping

2. You implement a split DNS configuration to support a Web site in your perimeter network. ISA Server 2004 is your external firewall. There is a NAT relationship between the external network and the perimeter network. What IP address should the Internet DNS record return for external clients to access the Web site?

   a. The internal IP address of the ISA Server computer

   b. The actual IP address of the Web server

   c. The IP address of your internal DNS server for name resolution

   d. The external IP address of the ISA Server computer

3. You have a Web server in a perimeter network that hosts multiple Web sites that have links to each other. How can you enable access to these sites to users on the Internet using ISA Server 2004?

   _____

   _____

   _____

Lesson Summary

- A Web publishing rule is a firewall rule that specifies how ISA Server routes incoming requests to internal Web servers. Web publishing is used to provide access to Web servers running HTTP and HTTPS. Web publishing rules also enable application-layer filtering, path mapping, user authentication, content caching, support for publishing multiple Web sites using a single IP address, and link translation.

- Server publishing rules are firewall rules that specify how ISA Server routes incoming requests to internal servers using any available protocol. Server publishing rules are used to provide access for multiple protocols, application-layer filtering for specified protocols, support for encryption, and IP address logging for the client computer.

- A split DNS configuration uses two different DNS servers to provide name resolution for internally and externally accessible resources. Implementing a split DNS requires two DNS servers that both host the zone files for the same DNS domain name but have host records with different IP addresses for the required servers.

Lesson 2: Configuring Web Publishing Rules

ISA Server uses Web publishing rules to provide a secure and flexible way to publish the content on internal Web servers to the Internet. When you enable Web publishing rules, you can configure a variety of options, including Web listeners, path mapping, and link translation. This lesson describes how to configure Web publishing.

After this lesson, you will be able to

- Identify Web publishing rules configuration components
- Configure Web listeners
- Configure path mapping
- Configure link translation
- Configure Web publishing rules

Estimated lesson time: 30 minutes

Components of a Web Publishing Rule Configuration

Web publishing rules map incoming HTTP or HTTPS requests to the appropriate Web servers located on a network protected by ISA Server. Web publishing rules determine what incoming requests for HTTP objects will be accepted by ISA Server and how ISA Server will respond to those requests. If the HTTP request matches a Web publishing rule, the request is forwarded to the Web server located on the internal or perimeter network.

Web Publishing Configuration Options

When you configure Web publishing rules, you must configure the components listed in Table 8-1.

Table 8-1   Web Publishing Rule Configuration Options

Configuration Option	Explanation
Action	Defines whether the Web publishing rule will allow or deny access.
Name (or IP address)	Defines the name or IP address of the Web server that is published by this rule.
Users	Defines which users can access the Web site.
Traffic source	Defines the network objects that can access the published Web server. The network objects that you specify must also be included in the Web listener specified for this Web publishing rule.

Table 8-1 Web Publishing Rule Configuration Options

Configuration Option	Explanation
Public name	Defines the Uniform Resource Locator (URL) or IP address that is made accessible by this rule. You can configure ISA Server to allow access based on a specific URL or allow access to all URLs. If you specify a URL, ISA Server will respond only to requests using that URL. If you allow access to all URLs, ISA Server will respond to all requests using the appropriate protocol.
Web listener	Defines the IP address on the computer running ISA Server that listens for requests from clients.
Path mappings	Defines how ISA Server will modify the external path specified in the request and map it to a corresponding internal path.
Bridging	Defines how HTTP requests are forwarded to the published server. You can configure the requests so that they are redirected using HTTP, SSL, or FTP.
Link translation	Defines how ISA Server updates Web pages that include references to internal server names.

Note The following sections describe these configuration options. In the last section of this lesson, you will see how to put all the options together to create a Web publishing rule.

How to Configure Web Listeners

Web listeners are used by Web and secure Web publishing rules. A Web listener is an ISA Server configuration object that defines how the ISA Server computer listens for HTTP requests and SSL requests. The Web listener defines the network, IP address, and the port number on which ISA Server listens for client connections.

Web listeners are required for Web publishing rules to function. If the ISA Server computer receives a HTTP or HTTPS on a network adapter and no Web listener is configured for the IP address associated with the network adapter, ISA Server will discard all the requests before applying Web server publishing rules. If the computer running ISA Server has multiple network adapters or IP addresses, you can configure the same listener configuration for all IP addresses, or you can configure separate listener configurations for different IP addresses.

A Web listener can be used in multiple Web publishing rules so long as the publishing rules share a common configuration. For example, if you have two Web publishing rules that both use HTTP and require basic authentication, then both Web publishing rules can use the same Web listener. However, if one publishing rule requires all users to authenticate, and the other rule requires anonymous access, then you must configure two different Web listeners.

To configure a Web listener, you must configure the following options:

- **Network**   This option specifies the network on which ISA Server will listen for incoming Web requests. The network that you select depends on the origin of the Web requests. For example, if the published Web site allows client requests from the external network (Internet), then the external network should be selected for the Web listener. After selecting a network, you can also specify whether the Web listener will listen for requests on all IP addresses on ISA Server that are part of that network, or on specified IP addresses.

- **Port numbers**   This option specifies the port number on which the Web listener will listen for incoming Web requests. By default, ISA Server listens on Port 80 for HTTP requests, but this setting can be modified. You can also enable the Web listener to listen for SSL requests (the default is Port 443). If you choose SSL, an appropriate certificate must be installed on the computer running ISA Server so that the computer running ISA Server can authenticate itself to the client.

- **Client authentication methods**   This option specifies the supported authentication methods if you are going to require authentication on the Web listener. If you select the option to require authentication, all users must authenticate using one of the authentication methods specified for the incoming Web requests. The authentication that you configure for the computer running ISA Server is in addition to any authentication that the published Web server requires. ISA Server authentication determines whether a request is passed to the Web server. The authentication method that you configure for the Web server determines whether a user is allowed to gain access to content on the Web server.

- **Client Connection Settings**   This option specifies the number of concurrent client connections and connection timeout values for the Web listener.

How to Configure a Web Listener

> **Note**   You can create a Web listener before creating a Web publishing rule, or you can create the Web listener while you create the Web publishing rule. The following procedure describes how to configure the Web listener first.

To create a Web listener, complete the following procedure:

1. In the ISA Server Management Console tree, click Firewall Policy.

2. On the Toolbox tab, expand Network Objects and then right-click Web Listeners and click New Web Listener.

3. On the Welcome To The New Web Listener Wizard page, in the Web Listener Name text box, type the name for the Web Listener.

4. On the IP Addresses page, shown in Figure 8-3, select the network on which the listener will listen for requests. If you are publishing a Web site for Internet access, select External.

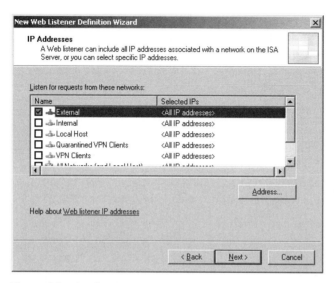

Figure 8-3   Configuring the network on which the Web listener will listen

5. If you have multiple network adapters or multiple IP addresses associated with the network you selected, you can configure the specific IP address on which this Web listener will listen by clicking the Address tab to display the External Network Listener IP Selection dialog box, shown in Figure 8-4. In this dialog box, you can configure the ISA Server computer to listen on all IP addresses or only some IP addresses associated with the selected network.

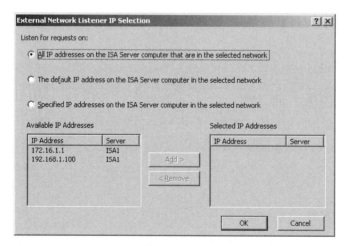

Figure 8-4   Configuring the network on which the Web listener will listen

> **Exam Tip**   If an exam scenario describes the ISA Server computer as having multiple net-work adapters or multiple IP addresses associated with a specific network, remember this configuration option. If a client tries to access a Web site using a particular IP address, but the Web listener is listening on a different IP address on the same network, the client will not be able to connect to the Web site.

6. On the Port Specification page, select the protocol and port number used by the Web listener, shown in Figure 8-5. By default, the Web listener will listen on for HTTP requests on Port 80. If this listener is used for a secure Web publishing rule, you must also enable SSL and configure a certificate.

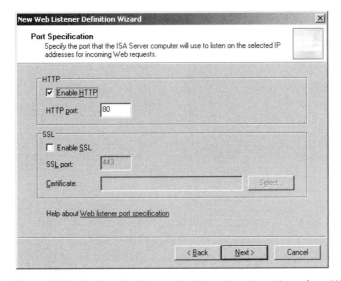

Figure 8-5   Configuring the protocols and port numbers for a Web listener

> **Caution**   Be careful about changing the default port numbers for the protocols. All Web browsers use the standard port numbers, and if you change the port numbers, you must instruct each user to use the new port number. For example, if you change the port number to 8888 and you are using the Web publishing rule to publish the *www.cohovineyard.com* site, you would have to instruct the users to use *http://www.cohovineyard.com:8888* to connect to the site.

7. On the Completing The New Web Listener Wizard page, review the configuration and then click Finish.

After you create the Web listener, you can modify the Web listener settings by double-clicking the Web Listener object in the Toolbox. In addition to the settings that you can configure during the Web listener creation, you can also configure the authentication methods supported on the Web listener and the connection settings. The settings are accessible on the Preferences tab, as shown in Figure 8-6.

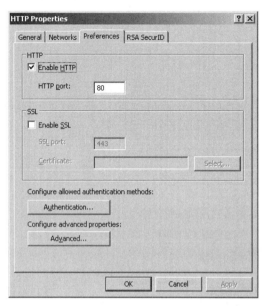

Figure 8-6 Configuring the Web listener preferences

 Note Figure 8-6 should look familiar to you because it is almost identical to the Web Proxy tab on the Internal Network Properties dialog box. Although you may not have known it at the time, when you configured the Web proxy settings, you were actually configuring a Web listener for the Internal network.

To configure the client connection options, click Advanced on the Preferences tab to get to the Advanced Settings dialog box, as shown in Figure 8-7. In this dialog box, you can configure the maximum number of concurrent client connections that will be accepted by the Web listener and the connection time-out for idle connections.

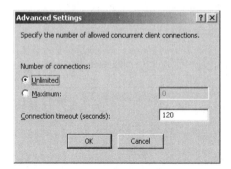

Figure 8-7 Configuring the Web listener advanced settings

> **See Also**   The authentication options will be discussed in Lesson 5, "Configuring ISA Server Authentication," later in this chapter.

How to Configure Path Mapping

Path mapping is an ISA Server feature that enables ISA Server to redirect user requests to an alternate path on internal Web servers. When a user connects to a Web site published on ISA Server, the user types a specific URL. Before forwarding a request to the published Web server, ISA Server checks the URL specified in the request. If a path mapping is configured for that URL, ISA Server will replace the path specified in the request with an internal path name and forward it to the appropriate Web server.

> **Note**   Path mapping is used for both Web publishing and secure Web publishing rules but not for server publishing rules.

How Path Mapping Works

Path mapping can be used in several different scenarios. For example, an organization may have a Web site that is accessible on the Internet using the URL *http://www.cohovineyard.com*. If the entire Web site is located on a single Web server, you can use path mapping to redirect client requests to different virtual directories on that server. The URL *http://www.cohovineyard.com/catalog* can be redirected to a virtual directory named CurrentCatalog on the Web server while the URL *http://www.cohovineyard.com/sales* is redirected to the SalesData virtual directory. If you rename the virtual directory on the Web server, you can just reconfigure the path mapping on ISA Server without interfering with client connectivity.

You can also use path mapping to redirect client requests to multiple internal Web servers. For example, when users request the URL *http://www.cohovineyard.com/sales*, they can be directed to the Sales virtual directory on one Web server. When users request the URL *http://www.cohovineyard.com/catalog*, they are redirected to a Catalog virtual directory on another Web server.

> **Important**   To redirect client requests to multiple back-end servers, you must configure multiple Web publishing rules. Each Web publishing rule can only redirect client requests to a single Web server. To redirect the client requests described above, you would configure a Web publishing rule that publishes the Sales virtual directory on one Web server, and another Web publishing rule that publishes the Catalog virtual directory on another server.

ISA Server 2004 performs this redirection transparently. Internet users see only that they are connecting to the Web sites and paths they entered into the browsers or accessed by clicking links to those URLs. ISA Server tracks these requests and forwards them to the appropriate Web server.

How to Configure Path Mapping

> **Note**   The procedure described here assumes that you have already created a Web publishing rule and are modifying its configuration. You can also configure path mappings while creating the Web publishing rule.

To configure path mapping, complete the following procedure:

1. In the ISA Server Management Console tree, click Firewall Policy.

2. In the details pane, click the applicable Web publishing rule.

3. On the Tasks tab, click Edit Selected Rule.

4. Path mapping is configured on the Paths tab, shown in Figure 8-8. By default, the /* internal path is published, which means that the entire Web site is available. To modify path mapping, click the listed path mapping and click Remove. Then click Add.

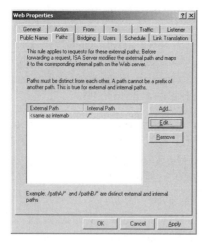

Figure 8-8   Configuring path mapping on a Web publishing rule

5. In the Path Mapping dialog box, shown in Figure 8-9, type the path on the Web server. This path is the actual internal path to which the ISA Server computer will send the request.

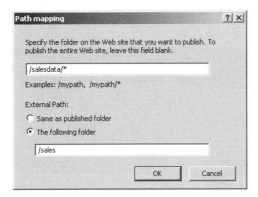

Figure 8-9   Configuring an additional path mapping

6. Under External Path, select one of the following:

❑ Same As Published Folder. If the path specified in the user request is identical to the path on the published Web server.

❑ The Following Folder. If the path specified in the user request needs to be mapped to a virtual directory with a different name on a Web server. Type the path to which requests on the published Web server will be mapped. When specifying the internal path to which the request will be mapped, use this format: /path/*.

Important   The paths used for path mapping on a Web publishing rule cannot overlap. For example, you cannot use an internal path of /* and an internal path of /salesdata/* on the same Web publishing rule because the salesdata path overlaps with the root directory. You can use an internal path of /salesdata/* and an internal path of /catalog/* on the same Web publishing rule. The same rules apply to the external path.

7. Click OK to close the Web Publishing Rule Properties dialog box.

How to Configure Link Translation

Path mapping allows you to redirect client requests from the ISA Server computer to different locations on one or more Web servers. By using path mapping you can mask a complex internal Web server configuration and present a simple Web site view to the Internet. Link translation can provide the same end result, but is used in different situations. Link translation is used when the Web pages published on ISA Server contain links to other Web servers on the protected network, and those Web servers are not accessible from the Internet.

Link translation is an ISA Server configuration object that enables ISA Server to replace internal server names on Web pages with server names that are accessible from the

Internet. Some published Web sites may include references to internal names of computers other than the server listed in the Web publishing rule. If these internal computer names are not accessible to clients outside the network, these references will appear as broken links. ISA Server includes a link translation feature to ensure that the information on these servers is accessible to Internet clients without requiring that the internal server names be revealed or accessible.

Link Translation Levels

ISA Server provides several levels of link translation functionality so that you can provide the appropriate level of link connectivity:

- **Header link translation**   Header link translation ensures that any URL returned in a header to the client is translated to an externally recognizable URL. When the user accesses the link, it is recognized by the Web publishing rule and forwarded to the correct internal server. This link translation is always enabled by default in any Web publishing rule.

- **Translation of links in the body of a returned Web page**   This functions in the same manner as the header link translation, but includes links returned in the body of Web pages, not just in the header. For example, a Web page on a server named Web1 that is accessed through the URL *www.cohovineyard.com* may include a reference to an image using *http://Web1.cohovineyard.com/images/image1.jpg*. This link needs to be translated to *http://www.cohovineyard.com/images/image1.jpg* in order to be accessible from the Internet. To enable this link translation, you need to enable the replacement of absolute links in Web pages on a Web publishing rule.

- **Translation of links to other internal Web pages**   Link translation works only for links to the Web server specified in the Web publishing rule. If you want links to other internal Web servers to also be translated, you have to provide information about how to translate each link. This information is stored by ISA Server in a link dictionary.

  For example, Coho Vineyard may have two internal Web servers named WEB1 and WEB2. The Web site on WEB1 may include cross-references to pages on the other server. For example, WEB1 may have a reference to *http://Web2/images/image1.jpg*. This link will not work on the Internet. You can create a link translation dictionary entry for the www.cohovineyard.com Web publishing rule substituting any reference to WEB2 with *www.cohovineyard.com*.

How to Configure Link Translation

To configure link translation on an existing Web publishing rule, complete the following procedure:

1. In the ISA Server Management Console tree, click Firewall Policy.

2. In the details pane, click the applicable Web publishing rule.

3. On the Link Translation tab, shown in Figure 8-10, click Replace Links In Web Pages To Enable Link Translation. Clicking this option enables link translation for Web page bodies.

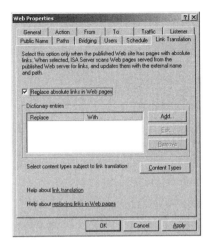

Figure 8-10   Configuring link translation on a Web publishing rule

4. To enable link translation to other internal Web pages, click Add to open the Add/Edit Dictionary Item dialog box, shown in Figure 8-11.

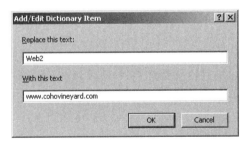

Figure 8-11   Configuring link dictionary entries on a Web publishing rule

5. In Replace This Text, provide the internal name of the server to be translated, such as WEB2. In With this text, provide the replacement value, such as www.cohowinery.com. Click OK.

Note   You can configure link translation only after you have created the Web publishing rule.

How to Configure Web Publishing Rules

Now that you understand most of the complicated pieces that comprise a Web publishing rule, you are ready to create the rule. To create a Web publishing rule, complete the following procedure:

1. In the ISA Server Management Console, click Firewall Policy. On the Tasks tab, click Publish A Web Server.

2. On the Welcome To The New Web Publishing Rule Wizard page, type the name for the Web publishing rule, and then click Next.

3. On the Select A Rule Action page, click Allow and click Next.

4. On the Define Web Site To Publish page, as shown in Figure 8-12, configure the options listed in Table 8-2.

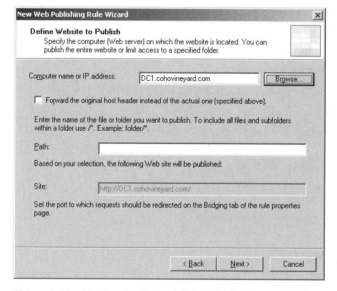

Figure 8-12   Configuring the published Web site on a Web publishing rule

Table 8-2   Web Site Configuration Options

Configuration Option	Explanation
Computer Name Or IP Address	Specifies the Web server computer name or IP address for the server that hosts the Web site that you want to publish.

Table 8-2   Web Site Configuration Options

Configuration Option	Explanation
Forward The Original Host Header Instead Of The Actual One	Specifies that ISA Server forward the host header that it received from the client. By default, ISA Server substitutes a host header that it uses to refer to the internal Web server, rather than sending the original host header that ISA Server received. This means that a client request that includes the host header of Host: www.cohovineyard.com is replaced with Host: DC1.cohovineyard.com as specified in the Web publishing rule. All requests are then routed to the same Web site on the published server.
	To publish more than one Web site on a Web server, configure the Web publishing rule to forward the original host header to the published server. For example, if client requests for *www.cohovineyard.com* and *www.cohowinery.com* need to be forwarded to two different Web sites on the same internal server, configure the Web publishing rule to forward the original host header.
Path	Specifies the Web site folder that you want to publish, such as Sales. If you leave this field blank, you will be publishing the entire site.

> **Exam Tip**   If you use a server name as the published server when you configure a Web publishing rule, the ISA Server computer must be able to resolve the DNS name for the internal Web server. If ISA Server is configured to use an internal DNS server, ensure that the name you use on the Web publishing rule is available in DNS. If you do not want to configure ISA Server to use an internal DNS server, you can use a hosts file on the DNS server to provide name resolution. If you get an exam question where users cannot access the Web site that is being published, check for information that would indicate that the ISA Server computer cannot resolve the server name.

  5. On the Public Name Details page, shown in Figure 8-13, configure a public name, which defines what requests will be received by the ISA Server computer and forwarded to the Web server. You have two options:

   ❑ *Any Domain Name*—This option means that any request that is resolved to the IP address of the external Web listener of the ISA Server computer will be forwarded to your Web site.

   ❑ *This Domain Name (Type Below)*—This option means that the ISA Server computer will forward only requests for a specific URL. To configure this, type the specific domain name in Public Name. You can also specify a specific folder in Folder that would also be required in the request. For example, if you configure the *www.cohovineyard.com* as the public name and Sales as the folder, then only requests for *www.cohovineyard.com/sales* will be forwarded by this rule.

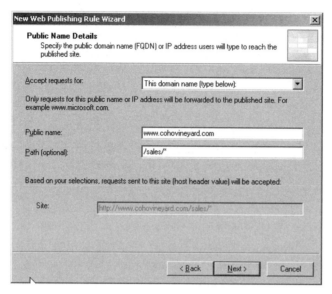

Figure 8-13   Configuring the public name for a Web publishing rule

Security Alert   In almost every case, you should use a specific public name rather than use any domain name when publishing a Web site. Choosing a specific public name means that ISA Server will only accept requests that use that name in the request header, and that all other requests will be dropped.

6. On the Select Web Listener page, select a preconfigured Web listener or click New to create a Web listener.

7. On the User Sets page, configure the user sets that will be allowed to access the published Web site. By default, the All Users user set, which includes anonymous users is granted access.

8. On the Completing the New Web Publishing Rule Wizard page, review the configuration and then click Finish.

You can also modify the configuration for the Web publishing rule after you configure the rule. To modify the configuration of the Web publishing rule, select Firewall Policy in the ISA Server Management Console and double-click the rule. Most of the configuration options are identical to the options available when you created the rule, with some additional options. For example, you can configure a schedule for when the publishing rule will be available. Moreover, you can configure how ISA Server will forward requests to the published Web server. To configure this option, open the Web publishing rule properties and select the To tab, as shown in Figure 8-14.

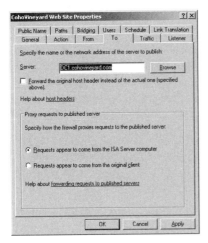

Figure 8-14   Configuring ISA Server proxy requests to a Web server

Note   For an explanation of when to use the option to forward the original host header, see Table 8-2.

ISA Server provides two options for proxying requests to the published server:

- **Requests Appear To Come From The ISA Server Computer**   This is the default option. When this is configured, the ISA Server computer substitutes its own IP address for the original client IP address when forwarding the request to the Web server. This means that if you enable logging on the Web server, all client connections will appear to come from the ISA Server computer.

- **Requests Appear To Come From The Original Client**   When you select this option, ISA Server sends the original client IP address to the published Web server. Some applications require that the actual client IP address be sent to the Web server. In addition if you want to log the client IP addresses for all connections to the Web server, you need to enable this option.

Exam Tip   Remember that, by default, client IP addresses are not sent to the published Web server. If you see an exam question that requires the logging of the client IP address in a Web publishing scenario, you must change the default configuration.

Real World   Implementing Complex Web Publishing Scenarios

ISA Server 2004 provides a great deal of flexibility when configuring Web publishing rules. In fact, you can enable almost any Web publishing scenario with single ISA Server computer. This includes some of the complicated scenarios that I have encountered when working with large corporations. Some requirements that can complicate Web publishing include the following:

- The need to publish multiple Web sites that have different domain names. These Web sites may be hosted on a single Web server, or on multiple Web servers.

- The need to use a single IP address to publish multiple Web sites.

- The need to publish a Web site with a single domain name that is distributed across multiple internal Web servers.

For most of these scenarios, there is more than one way to solve them. You can use path mapping and link translation to deal with some complex situations. Here are some other suggestions:

- If you need to publish multiple Web sites that have different domain names or different host names, you have to configure multiple Web publishing rules. For example, if you are publishing *www.cohovineyard.com* and *www.cohowinery.com* on the ISA Server computer, you will need two different Web publishing rules, each with a different public name. The same is true if you are publishing the *www.cohovineyard.com* site and the *store.cohovineyard.com* site. The configuration is easy when the Web sites are on different Web servers; you just create two Web publishing rules pointing to the two Web servers, and correctly configure the public name for each publishing rule. If the Web server has multiple IP addresses assigned to it, you can configure the Web server to listen for HTTP requests on a different IP address for each Web site, and then configure ISA Server to forward the Web requests to the appropriate IP address.

- If the two Web sites are on the same server and the Web server only has one IP address, the configuration is a bit more complex. You will still need two Web publishing rules, each configured with the appropriate public name. However, when you configure the Web publishing rule, you need to configure it to forward the original host header to the published server. Then on the Web server, ensure that the Web sites are distinguished by the host headers.

■ Another alternative when publishing multiple Web sites on the same Web server is to change the ports on which ISA Server will forward HTTP requests to the Web server. By default, all HTTP requests are forwarded using Port 80. However, you can configure the Web server to listen on an alternate port for one of the Web sites and then configure ISA Server to forward requests to that alternate port for the appropriate Web publishing rule.

■ In some cases, you may also need to publish a Web site with multiple virtual directories with the virtual directories distributed across multiple Web servers. For example, *www.cohovineyard.com/sales* may be configured on one Web server, while *www.cohovineyard.com/updates* is configured on another server. Just *www.cohovineyard.com* may be hosted on a third Web server. To configure this, you need to configure three Web publishing rules and then use path mapping on each rule to distribute client requests to the appropriate Web server. So you need to create one Web publishing rule that will respond to requests sent to the sales virtual directory and configure the rule to forward the request to the correct Web server. You need to configure another Web publishing rule for the updates virtual directory and another for the *www.cohovineyard.com* site. In this case, you must ensure that the publishing rule for the *www.cohovineyard.com* domain is listed after the first two rules to ensure that this rule is processed last.

All these scenarios have assumed that you have a single IP address on the ISA Server computer that is connected to the Internet. If you have multiple IP addresses available on the ISA Server computer, you can configure multiple Web listeners and use each of these Web listeners to configure multiple rules. As I mentioned, just about any Web site configuration can be published using ISA Server.

Exam Tip   Any of these complicated scenarios could show up on the exam. If you see an exam question that requires access to multiple URLs remember that you need to create multiple Web publishing rules for each URL with the correct public name information. Then just ensure that the requests from the ISA Server computer are forwarded to the appropriate Web server, or to the appropriate Web site on the Web server.

Practice: Configuring Web Publishing Rules

In this practice, you will configure a new Web listener and then configure and test a Web publishing rule.

Exercise 1: Configuring a New Web Listener

1. On ISA1, in the ISA Server Management Console, click Firewall Policy.

2. On the Toolbox tab, expand Network Objects, click New, and then click Web Listener.

3. On the Welcome To The New Web Listener Wizard page, in the Web listener name field, type **HTTP Listener** and then click Next.

4. On the IP Addresses page, select External and then click Next.

5. On the Port Specification page, ensure that Enable HTTP is selected and that HTTP port is 80. Click Next.

6. On the Completing The New Web Listener Wizard page, review the configuration and click Finish.

7. Click Apply to apply the changes.

Exercise 2: Configuring a New Web Publishing Rule

1. On the Tasks tab, click Publish a Web Server.

2. On the Welcome To The New Web Publishing Rule Wizard page, in the Web Publishing Rule Name field, type **Coho Vineyard Web Site** and click Next.

3. On the Select Rule Action page, ensure that the default Allow is selected. Click Next.

4. On the Select Web Site To Publish page, in the Computer Name Or IP Address box, type **DC1.cohovineyard.com**. Accept the default settings for the other options and click Next.

5. On the Public Name Details page, in the Accept Requests For drop-down list, click This Domain Name (Type Below). In the Public Name box, type **www.cohovineyard.com** and then click Next.

6. On the Select Web Listener page, click HTTP Listener from the Web listener list. Click Next.

7. On the User Sets page, accept the default. Click Next.

8. On the Completing The New Web Publishing Rule Wizard page, review the configuration settings and click Finish.

9. Click Apply to apply the changes.

Exercise 3: Testing Internet Access to the Cohovineyard.com Web Site

1. On SERVER1, open Microsoft Internet Explorer and type **www.cohovineyard.com** into the Address box.

2. The connection should be successful. Close Internet Explorer.

Lesson Review

Use the following questions to help determine whether you have learned enough to move on to the next lesson. If you have difficulty answering these questions, review the material in this lesson before beginning the next lesson. You can find answers to the questions in the "Questions and Answers" section at the end of this chapter.

1. You are the network administrator for your organization and you use Active Directory in a single-domain environment. Your organization includes five branch offices that need access to the Web site that is hosted on a server in the perimeter network at your head office. These branch offices connect to the head office through the Internet. You need to ensure that only Authenticated Users can access the site. How will you configure ISA Server?

   _____

   _____

   _____

2. You have published your company's Web site under the public name of *www.cohovineyard.com*. The internal name of the Web server hosting the site is WebSrv01. The site does not contain any references to other servers. What must you configure in your Web Publishing rule to allow Internet clients to access the site properly?

   a. Configure a link translation dictionary entry to replace *www.cohovineyard.com* with WebSrv01 in the HTTP request header.

   b. Create a path mapping entry to map *www.cohovineyard.com* to WebSrv01.

   c. Configure a link translation dictionary entry to replace WebSrv01 with *www.cohovineyard.com* in the response header.

   d. Do nothing; the required level of link translation is enabled by default.

3. You have just published two separate Web sites on one Web server by implementing Host Headers. The server is located on your perimeter network. You use ISA Server 2004 as your external firewall. Internet clients report that they always get the default Web site on the server, regardless of which two URLs they enter into their Web browser. What is the problem and how will you fix it?

   _____

   _____

   _____

Lesson Summary

- Web publishing rules map incoming requests to the appropriate Web servers located on the internal or perimeter network. Web publishing rules determine how ISA Server will intercept incoming requests for HTTP objects on a Web server, and how ISA Server will respond on behalf of the Web server.

- A Web listener is an ISA Server configuration object that defines how the ISA Server computer listens for HTTP requests and SSL requests. The Web listener defines the IP address and the port number on which ISA Server listens for client connections.

- Path mapping is an ISA Server feature that enables ISA Server to redirect user requests to multiple internal Web servers or to multiple locations on the same Web server.

- Link translation is an ISA Server configuration object that enables ISA Server to replace internal server names on Web pages with server names that are accessible from this Internet. ISA Server provides several levels of link translation functionality so that you can provide the appropriate level of link connectivity.

- To configure a new Web publishing rule, use the New Web Publishing Rule Wizard.

Lesson 3: Configuring Secure Web Publishing Rules

Secure Web publishing provides an additional layer of security when publishing an internal Web site by enabling the option to use SSL to encrypt all network traffic to and from the Web site. Secure Web publishing is critical when securing Web sites that contain confidential information, or when the Web site asks clients to submit confidential information such as credit-card numbers. This lesson describes how to configure secure Web publishing.

After this lesson, you will be able to

- List the components to configuring secure Web publishing rules
- Install digital certificates on ISA Server
- Describe SSL bridging
- Describe SSL tunneling
- Configure secure Web publishing rules

Estimated lesson time: 45 minutes

Components of a Secure Web Publishing Rule Configuration

Secure Web publishing rules are a special type of Web publishing rule. Because of this, many of the same configuration options apply to both types of rules. The most important additional configuration you must address is how to configure SSL for the secure Web publishing rule.

What Is Secure Sockets Layer?

Secure Sockets Layer (SSL) is used to validate the identities of two computers involved in a connection across a public network, and to ensure that the data sent between the two computers is encrypted. To do this, SSL uses digital certificates and public and private keys. SSL enables the following features:

- **Server authentication**   Server authentication allows a client to confirm a server's identity. SSL-enabled client software can use standard techniques of public-key cryptography to check that a server's certificate and public ID are valid and have been issued by a certificate authority (CA) that the client is configured to trust.

- **Client authentication**   Client authentication allows a server to confirm a user's identity. Using the same techniques as those used for server authentication, SSL-enabled server software can check that a client's certificate and public ID are valid and have been issued by a CA listed in the server's list of trusted CAs. Client authentication is optional for most secure Web sites.

■ **Encrypted SSL connections**   All network traffic, including the confidential parts of the authentication process, is sent using an encrypted SSL connection that is created between the client and server. In addition, the client and server will automatically detect if the data sent over an encrypted SSL connection has been altered in transit.

> **See Also**   SSL requires the use of digital certificates and public and private keys that are issued by a CA. To understand how these components work together, you need to understand Public Key Infrastructure (PKI) concepts. For detailed information about PKI, see the technical reference named PKI Technologies located at *http://www.microsoft.com/resources/documentation/WindowsServ/2003/all/techref/en-us/W2K3TR_sec_pki_over.asp.*

SSL Configuration Options

As you prepare to implement secure Web publishing rules, you need to decide how you want to configure SSL on ISA Server. ISA Server supports two SSL configurations:

■ **SSL tunneling**   With SSL tunneling, the SSL connection is set up directly between the client computer and the Web server. In this scenario, the ISA Server computer does not encrypt or decrypt the network packets but merely forwards encrypted packets between the client and the Web server. ISA Server cannot inspect the content of the packets because the contents are encrypted as they pass through the ISA Server computer.

■ **SSL bridging**   With SSL bridging, the ISA Server computer acts as the end point for one or more SSL connections. The network packets can still be encrypted from the Web client to the Web server, however, in an SSL bridging scenario, the ISA Server computer will decrypt network traffic from the client computer and then re-encrypt it before sending it to the Web server. The ISA Server computer will accept the encrypted reply packets from the Web server, decrypt them, and then encrypt the packets again before sending them back to the client. ISA Server can be configured to require SSL connections from clients, or SSL connections when connecting to Web server, or both. In an SSL bridging scenario, ISA Server can inspect the HTTP packets while they are not encrypted.

Enabling SSL on ISA Server

Before you can enable SSL in a secure Web publishing scenario, you must obtain one or more digital server certificates issued by a CA. The number and placement of the digital certificates depends on what SSL configuration option you choose. Follow these guidelines:

- If you plan to use SSL in an SSL tunneling configuration, you must install a digital certificate only on the Web server. The Web server and the client will use this certificate and the associated keys to create the SSL connection.

- If you plan to use SSL in a SSL bridging configuration, you must install a digital certificate on the ISA Server computer, and possibly, on the Web server. To create an SSL connection with the client, the ISA Server computer must have a certificate installed. If you are also configuring an SSL connection between the ISA Server computer and the published Web server, then the Web server must have a certificate installed.

- If you require client certificates, you also need install digital certificates on each client computer. In this configuration, the ISA Server computer or the Web server will use the client certificate to authenticate the client.

Planning   If you plan to implement client certificates, ensure that you have an efficient process in place for issuing and managing client certificates. Each client certificate must be stored on the client computer or on a device like a smart card. In large organizations with thousands of client computers, distributing and managing the client certificates can be a great deal of work. However, client certificates do provide an extra level of security if you have a Web site that requires a very high level of security.

The most important decision that you need to make when obtaining the server certificates is deciding from where you will get the certificates. You have essentially two choices: you can obtain server certificates from a commercial CA, or you can deploy a CA inside your organization and use it to issue the server certificates. Both Microsoft Windows 2000 Server and Microsoft Windows Server 2003 include a Certificate Services component that you can use to create a CA.

Creating your own CA and using it to issue the server certificates has a couple of advantages. First, if you use the Certificate Services included with Windows Server, you do not have to pay for the Certificate Server software or any of the certificates. Second, if you install your own CA, you have complete control of issuing and managing the certificates.

Security Alert   If you do decide to deploy your own CA infrastructure, you need to ensure that your CA infrastructure is very secure. If an attacker can ever compromise your root CA, or obtain a subordinate CA certificate from the root CA, every certificate issued by the CA becomes suspect. If this happens, you will need to rebuild your entire CA infrastructure and reissue all client certificates.

Despite these advantages, however, you probably should not use your own CA to issue certificates for your ISA Server or public Web server. This is especially true if users from outside your organization will be accessing the Web site. The reason for this is that the client software will not be configured to trust your internal CA and the users will get an error message every time they access your Web site. PKI is built on the concept of trust; when a client computer connects to a Web server, the client checks to see if it trusts the CA that issued the server certificate. If the client is configured to trust the CA, then the SSL negotiation begins. If the client is not configured to trust the CA, the user will receive an error message, or the connection will fail. Most Web browsers are preconfigured with certificates for the most popular commercial CAs.

> **Planning** Using an Enterprise CA installed on Windows Server 2003 or Windows 2000 Server can greatly simplify the process of managing certificates. The Enterprise CA requires, and is tightly integrated with Active Directory. You can configure policies in Active Directory that automate the process of issuing and renewing certificates. Moreover, certificates issued to domain users are stored in Active Directory so the public keys can easily be retrieved by other clients. If you are running Active Directory, and only internal clients will connect to your ISA Server or Web servers, an Enterprise CA can greatly simplify your certificate management processes.

How to Install Digital Certificates on ISA Server

Once you have decided where you will get the certificate from, the next step is obtaining and installing the server certificate on ISA Server. Depending on the required configuration, you may also need to install a certificate on the internal Web server.

The procedure for installing a server certificate on the computer running ISA Server varies depending on the CA you are using and on the ISA Server computer configuration, as follows:

- If you use an internal CA that provides a Web site for clients to obtain certificates, you can connect to the Web site from the ISA Server computer and apply for and install the certificate. You will complete this procedure in the practice that follows this lesson.

- If you use an external CA, you need to create a certificate request and forward it to the external CA. You can create the certificate request on the server running ISA Server. However, this requires that IIS be installed on the computer running ISA Server. This is not recommended, so you should prepare the request on the Web server computer, install the certificate on the Web server computer, and then export it and import it to the ISA Server computer.

See Also   For more information about how to request and install a certificate from a commercial CA, see the Knowledge Base article, Generating a Certificate Request File Using the Certificate Wizard in IIS 5.0, located at *http://support.microsoft.com/kb/228821/EN-US* and the Knowledge Base article named Installing a New Certificate with Certificate Wizard for Use in SSL/TLS, located at *http://support.microsoft.com/kb/228836/EN-US*.

When you request the certificate, the name on the certificate must be the FQDN that users use to access the Web site. For example, if you are deploying the certificate on an ISA Server computer named *ISA1.cohovineyard.com*, but users will be using an FQDN of *secure.cohovineyard.com* to connect to the server, the certificate name must be *secure.cohovineyard.com*. If the common name on the certificate does not match the FQDN used by client computers to access the Web site, clients will receive an error message when they send HTTPS requests.

If you plan to use SSL tunneling or if you plan to configure a secure connection between the ISA Server computer and the Web server, you will need to request and install a server certificate on the Web servers. The name on the certificate must be the FQDN that ISA Server uses to access the Web site. For example, if the Web publishing rule specifies *Web1.cohovineyard.com* as the internal server name, then this must be the FQDN on the certificate. This must also be the FQDN used by clients to connect to the server in an SSL tunneling scenario. You must install this certificate before the Web servers can accept SSL tunneling connections and before the Web servers can accept secure connections from ISA Server.

How to Configure SSL Bridging

One of the options that ISA Server provides for securing network traffic is SSL bridging. SSL bridging means that the ISA Server computer operates as the end point for an SSL connection. The SSL connection could be between ISA Server and the client or between ISA Server and the internal Web server. The primary benefit of using SSL bridging is that it enables application filtering of SSL traffic.

How SSL Bridging Works

SSL bridging is used when ISA Server ends or initiates an SSL connection. This connection can be with the client computer, with the internal Web server, or both.

A common scenario in which SSL bridging is used is in a Web publishing scenario. The scenario works as follows:

1. An external client uses HTTPS to request an object from a Web server located on the internal network. By default, the client connects to ISA Server on the standard SSL port, Port 443. ISA Server responds with a server-side SSL certificate to the client and the client authenticates the server. After authentication, the client and server create a secure encryption channel.

2. ISA Server accepts the client's request and decrypts it, terminating the SSL connection. ISA Server inspects the client request to ensure that the request is not blocked by a firewall access rule. If the request is not blocked, ISA Server continues processing the request. If ISA Server is configured to enable caching, and the object is in the cache, ISA Server returns the object to the client.

3. If the object is not in the cache, ISA Server forwards the request to the internal Web server specified in the Web publishing rule. The Web publishing rule also defines how ISA Server communicates the request to the published Web server (FTP, HTTP, or SSL). If the secure Web publishing rule is configured to forward the request using HTTPS, ISA Server initiates a new SSL connection with the Web server, sending a request to Port 443. Because the ISA Server computer is now an SSL client, the Web server responds with a server-side certificate.

4. After the SSL connection has been created, the Web server responds by sending the requested object back to ISA Server.

5. ISA Server receives the object and decrypts it. At this point, ISA Server inspects the information based on the firewall access rules and the HTTP policy. If the reply is acceptable, ISA Server then encrypts the object again and passes it to the requesting client.

One of the important benefits of using SSL bridging is that it allows stateful inspection of SSL connections and application-layer filtering of the contents of HTTPS packets. Because ISA Server decrypts each packet, it can inspect the application-layer data before re-encrypting the packet. This prevents attackers from hiding malicious code inside SSL packets. The most significant disadvantage with using SSL bridging is that encrypting and decrypting network traffic is CPU-intensive, so the ISA Server computer performance may be affected.

SSL Bridging Options

You can configure the SSL bridging options when you configure a secure Web publishing rule or you can change the Web publishing rule after the initial configuration. ISA Server supports three SSL bridging options:

- **SSL bridging from ISA Server to the client**   A client requests an SSL object. ISA Server decrypts the request and forwards it to the Web server. The Web server returns the HTTP object to ISA Server. ISA Server encrypts the object and sends it to the client. In this scenario, SSL is used to secure only the connection between ISA Server and the client.

- **SSL bridging from ISA Server to the Web server**   A client requests an HTTP object from an internal Web server. ISA Server accepts the request, encrypts it, and forwards it to the Web server. The Web server returns an encrypted object to ISA Server. Then, ISA Server decrypts the object and sends it to the client. In this scenario, SSL is used to secure only the connection between ISA Server and the Web server.

■ **SSL bridging from client to Web Server**   The client requests an SSL object. ISA Server decrypts the request, and then encrypts it again and forwards it to the Web server. The Web server returns the encrypted object to ISA Server. ISA Server decrypts the object and then encrypts it again and sends it to the client. In this scenario, SSL is used to encrypt all connections.

How to Configure SSL Tunneling

In an SSL tunneling scenario, ISA Server does not encrypt or decrypt packets, but simply forwards SSL packets from the client to the Web server. SSL tunneling means that ISA Server does not need to decrypt SSL packets, but it also means that the encrypted packets cannot be inspected by ISA Server.

How SSL Tunneling Works

In SSL tunneling mode, a client can establish a tunnel through the computer running ISA Server directly to the internal Web server. In tunneling mode, the connection between the client and the Web server is encrypted. Because ISA Server does not decrypt the packet, it cannot inspect the application-layer contents of the packet. SSL tunneling can also be used in a Web publishing scenario as follows:

1. An external client uses HTTPS to request an object from a Web server located on the internal network. The request is sent to an external IP address on the ISA Server computer.

2. ISA Server checks the Web publishing rule for the request. If the rule specifies SSL tunneling mode, ISA Server forwards the request to the internal Web server without decrypting the packet.

3. The Web server responds with a server-side SSL certificate to the client and the client authenticates the server. After authentication, the client and server create a secure encryption channel.

4. The Web server then encrypts the requested object and sends it to ISA Server, which forwards it to the client.

> **Note**   You can configure SSL tunneling only when you initially create the secure Web publishing rule. When you configure an SSL tunneling for a secure Web publishing rule using the ISA Server Wizard, you are actually configuring a server publishing rule that uses HTTPS. For more details on this, see the section "How to Publish a Web Server," later in this chapter.

How to Configure a New Secure Web Publishing Rule

To configure a new secure Web publishing rule, complete the following procedure:

1. To configure a secure Web publishing rule that will require the ISA Server to terminate the client SSL connection, you must first install a server certificate on the ISA Server computer.

2. After installing the server certificate, create or configure a Web listener that will listen for SSL connections. When you configure the Web listener to listen for SSL connections, you need to configure the server certificate that ISA Server will use when responding to client SSL requests.

3. In the ISA Server Management Console, click Firewall Policy. On the Tasks tab, click Publish A Secure Web Server.

4. On the Welcome To The SSL Web Publishing Rule Wizard page, in the SSL Web Publishing Rule name field, type **rule name** and click Next.

5. On the Publishing Mode page, shown in Figure 8-15, configure the publishing mode to use either SSL bridging or SSL tunneling.

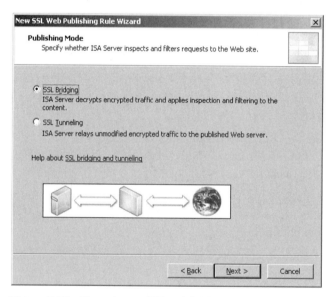

Figure 8-15 Choosing an SSL publishing mode

6. On the Select Rule Action page, ensure that the default Allow is selected. Click Next.

7. On the Bridging Mode page, shown in Figure 8-16, choose one of the following options:

❑ *Secure Connection To Clients*—When you select this mode, ISA Server establishes a secure HTTPS connection with the client, but forwards the request as standard HTTP to the published Web server.

❑ *Secure Connection To Web Server*—When you select this mode, ISA Server establishes a standard HTTP connection with the client, but forwards the request as secure HTTPS to the published Web server.

❑ *Secure Connection To Client And Web Server*—When you select this mode, ISA Server establishes a secure HTTPS connection with the client, and also forwards the request as secure HTTPS to the published Web server.

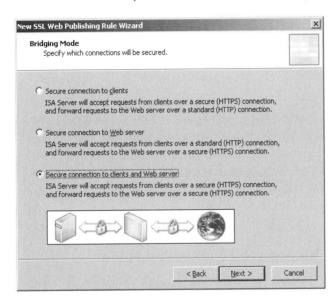

Figure 8-16   Choosing an SSL bridging mode

8. The remaining steps in the wizard are almost identical to the steps for configuring a Web publishing rule. The only difference is that you need to choose or create a Web listener that listens for SSL requests.

You can modify the SSL bridging configuration for the secure Web publishing rule after you create the Web publishing rule. If you decide that you no longer need SSL connections between the ISA Server computer and the client computers, change the Web listener to support HTTP rather than HTTPS connections. If you decide to change the SSL configuration for the ISA Server to Web server connection, access the Bridging tab on the Web Publishing Rule Properties dialog box, shown in Figure 8-17. On this tab, if you choose the option Redirect Requests To SSL Port, the connection between the ISA Server computer and the Web server will be secured. If the Web server is configured to require client certificates, you must also select Use a Certificate to Authenticate to the SSL Web Server, and select a certificate that ISA Server will use to authenticate to the Web server.

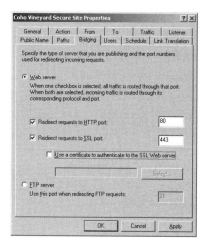

Figure 8-17 The Bridging tab of the Web Publishing Rule Properties dialog box

Tip Notice that the SSL settings are configured on each publishing rule. This means that you have a great deal of flexibility about how you will deploy SSL. You can have one Web publishing rule that requires SSL connections to both client and server, and have another rule that requires only SSL connections between the ISA Server and the client computers. If you have multiple Web listeners (which requires multiple IP addresses on the relevant network), you can even use different certificates to authenticate the ISA Server computer.

Practice: Configuring Secure Web Publishing Rules

In this practice, you will configure a secure Web Publishing rule. This publishing rule will require SSL connections from the client computer to the ISA Server, but not SSL connections from the ISA Server to the Web server (*DC1.cohovineyard.com*). To begin, install an Enterprise CA on *DC1.cohovineyard.com*. Then use the Certification Authority to issue a certificate for the ISA Server computer. Once the certificate is in place, you will configure and test the secure Web publishing rule.

Exercise 1: Installing an Enterprise CA

1. On DC1, log on as an Administrator.

2. Open Control Panel and open Add Or Remove Programs.

3. Click Add/Remove Windows Components. On the Components list, click Certificate Services.

4. In the Microsoft Certificate Services warning box, click Yes and then click Next.

5. On the CA Type page, click Enterprise Root CA and then click Next.

6. On the CA Identifying Information Page, type **Coho Vineyards CA** as the common name for the CA and click Next.

7. On the Certificate Database Settings page, click Next.

8. Click OK to clear the warning message, and then wait for the installation to finish. You may need to provide the Windows Server 2004 installation CD to complete the installation.

9. When the installation completes, click Finish.

Exercise 2: Enabling Access to the Certification Authority Web Site

By default, the system policy on ISA Server prevents you from accessing the certificate services Web site on DC1. Therefore, you have to change the system policy before you can access the Web server to obtain the certificate.

1. On ISA1, open the ISA Server Management Console if necessary, and click Firewall Policy.

2. On the Tasks tab, click Edit System Policy.

3. In the System Policy Editor dialog box, in Configuration Groups, click Allowed Sites.

4. On the To tab, click System Policy Allowed Sites and then click Edit.

5. Click New, and type ***.cohovineyard.com**.

6. Click OK and then click OK again to close the System Policy Editor.

7. Click Apply to apply the changes.

Exercise 3: Installing a Certificate on ISA Server

1. On ISA1, open Internet Explorer.

2. In the Address bar, type **http://DC1.cohovineyard.com/certsrv**.

3. Log on as cohovineyard\administrator with the appropriate password.

4. On the Welcome page, under Select A Task, click Request A Certificate.

5. On the Request A Certificate page, click Advanced Certificate Request.

6. On the Advanced Certificate Request page, click Create And Submit A Request To This CA.

7. On the Advanced Certificate Request page, in the Certificate Template drop-down list, click Web Server. Complete the form using the following information:

   ❑ Name: **Secure.cohovineyard.com**

   ❑ E-Mail: **Administrator@cohovineyard.com**

❑ Company: **Coho Vineyard**

❑ Country/Region: **US**

8. Under Key Options, select Store Certificate In The Local Computer Certificate Store.

9. Submit the request by clicking Submit. Review the two warning dialog boxes that appear, and click Yes for both.

10. Click Install This Certificate. Review the warning dialog box that appears, and then click Yes. When you receive the message that the certificate is successfully installed, close Internet Explorer.

Exercise 4: Configuring a New Secure Web Publishing Rule

1. In the ISA Server Management Console, ensure that Firewall Policy is selected under the ISA1 node.

2. On the Tasks tab, click Publish A Secure Web Server.

3. On the Welcome To The SSL Web Publishing Rule Wizard page, in the SSL Web Publishing Rule name field, type **Coho Vineyard Secure Site** and click Next.

4. On the Publishing Mode page, accept the default configuration of SSL Bridging and click Next.

5. On the Select Rule Action page, ensure that the default Allow is selected. Click Next.

6. On the Bridging Mode page, click Secure Connection To Clients. Click Next.

7. On the Select Web Site To Publish page, in the Computer Name or IP Address box, type **DC1.cohovineyard.com**. Accept the default settings for the other options and click Next.

8. On the Public Name Details page, ensure This Domain Name (Type Below) is selected in the Accept Requests From box. Then, in the Public Name box, type **Secure.cohovineyard.com**. Click Next.

9. On the Select Web Listener page, click New to create a Web listener.

10. On the Welcome To The New Web Listener Wizard page, in the Web Listener Name field, type **HTTPS Listener** and click Next.

11. On the IP Addresses page, click External and then click Next.

12. On the Port Specification page, clear the check box for Enable HTTP and select the check box for Enable SSL. Ensure that the SSL port is 443. Click Select.

13. In the Select Certificate dialog box, select the certificate issued by the Coho Vineyards CA and then click OK.

14. Click Next.

15. On the Completing The New Web Listener Wizard page, review the configuration and click Finish.

16. On the Select Web Listener page, click Next.

17. On the User Sets page, accept the default, All Users. Click Next.

18. On the Completing The New SSL Web Publishing Rule Wizard page, review the configuration settings, and click Finish.

19. Click Apply to apply the changes.

Exercise 5: Testing the Secure Web Publishing Rule

1. On SERVER1, open Internet Explorer and type **https://secure.cohovineyard.com** into the Address box.

> **Exam Tip**   You should get a Security Alert message stating that the certificate used by the Web server was issued by a Certification Authority that you have not chosen to trust. This is the warning message other clients would receive if they connect to your Web site and you have used an internal CA. Click Yes to continue. Remember this warning message for the exam.

2. The connection should be successful.

Lesson Review

Use the following questions to help determine whether you have learned enough to move on to the next lesson. If you have difficulty answering these questions, review the material in this lesson before beginning the next lesson. You can find answers to the questions in the "Questions and Answers" section at the end of this chapter.

1. True or False? ISA Server 2004 always requires a digital server certificate to be installed in order for Internet clients to connect to a Web site using SSL.

_____

_____

_____

2. You publish two Web sites in your perimeter network. You need to configure secure access to both of them. There are many domain laptop users in your organization who work from the office and from home. You must ensure that only users who can authenticate to your domain from the Internet can get to one site, but allow public access to the other. You have installed Microsoft Certificate Server as an Enterprise Root Authority. What else must you do?

_____

_____

_____

3. You are publishing a secure Web site that hosts a Web application that requires the actual IP address of the requesting client. You have installed a commercial CA certificate on the ISA Server computers. Users report that although they are able to establish a session to the Web site, they cannot use the application. How will you address this problem?

_____

_____

_____

Lesson Summary

- Secure Web publishing rules are a special type of Web publishing rules that use SSL to encrypt traffic between the server and client. When you configure a Secure Web publishing rule, you need to decide how you are going to configure SSL. Before you can use SSL, you must install a server certificate on ISA Server. Depending on the required configuration, you may also need to install a certificate on the internal Web server.

- SSL bridging means that the ISA Server computer operates as the end point for an SSL connection. The SSL connection could be between ISA Server and the client or between ISA Server and the internal Web server. ISA Server supports three SSL bridging options: SSL bridging from ISA Server to the client, SSL bridging from ISA Server to the Web server, and SSL bridging from client to Web Server.

- In SSL tunneling mode, a client establishes a tunnel through the computer running ISA Server directly to the internal Web server. ISA Server does not decrypt the packet, it cannot inspect the application-layer contents of the packet.

- Configuring a secure Web publishing rule is similar to configure a Web publishing rule. The primary differences are that you need to use a Web listener that is enabled for SSL, and you need to choose an SSL tunneling or bridging mode.

Lesson 4: Configuring Server Publishing Rules

Web publishing rules are used on ISA Server to enable access to HTTP and HTTPS content on internal Web servers. Server publishing rules are used to enable access to internal applications that use other protocols. Server publishing is a secure and flexible way to publish the content or services provided by internal servers to the Internet. This lesson describes how to configure server publishing.

After this lesson, you will be able to

- List the server publishing rule configuration options
- Configure a new server publishing rule
- Implement server publishing rules to publish various services
- Troubleshoot Web and server publishing

Estimated lesson time: 45 minutes

Components of a Server Publishing Rule Configuration

Server publishing rules are used on ISA Server to map a port number on an external interface of the ISA Server computer to the IP address of an internal server providing a specific service. When ISA Server receives a request on the external IP address for a specific port, it passes the request to the internal server defined on the server publishing rule.

ISA Server performs the following steps when a client accesses a server that is published using a server publishing rule:

1. A client computer on the Internet needs to access an application server on a network protected by the ISA Server computer. In most cases, the client computer will perform a DNS lookup to locate the IP address for the server that is providing the service. The IP address provided to the clients is the IP address of the external network interface of the ISA Server computer. The client request is sent to the IP address.

2. ISA Server checks the destination port number and then uses the server publishing rule to map the request to an IP address of an internal server. The request is forwarded to the internal server.

3. The internal server returns the object to the ISA Server computer, which passes it on to the requesting client.

When you configure server publishing rules, you need to configure the components listed in Table 8-3.

Table 8-3   Server Publishing Rule Configuration Options

Configuration Option	Explanation
Action	Enables a server publishing rule to be configured to allow or deny network traffic that matches the publishing rule.
Traffic	Defines the protocol that is allowed by this server publishing rule. Each server publishing rule can enable only one protocol.
Traffic source	Defines the network objects that can access the published server. You can limit access to the published server based on networks, network sets, computers, computer sets, address ranges, or subnets.
Traffic destination	Defines the IP address of the published server. You can also configure whether the client requests will appear to come from the client computer or from ISA Server. On a server publishing rule, the default is that the client requests appear to come from the original client.
Networks	Defines the network on which ISA Server will listen for connections on the protocol port. You can also configure ISA Server to listen on all IP addresses on the specified network, or only on specific IP addresses.
Schedule	Defines when the server publishing rule will be active.

Port Override Options

When you create a server publishing rule, ISA Server listens for client requests on the default port for that protocol. However, you can modify the ports used by ISA Server. For example, you can configure the server publishing rule for FTP services to listen for client connections on Port 2121 rather than on Port 21. You can also specify that ISA Server redirect the client request to an alternate port number on the internal server. You could configure ISA Server to send all FTP requests to Port 2111 on the internal server (assuming that the internal FTP server has been modified to provide FTP services on that port). In either case, ISA Server receives client requests for the published service on the firewall port specified, and then forwards requests to the designated port on the published server.

> **Tip**   The port override option can be useful when multiple services are using the same default port number on one ISA Server. For example, you can publish one FTP server on the default port for one set of users, and publish another FTP server on another, nonstandard port for a different set of users.

SSL for Server Publishing

Server publishing rules use SSL in the same way that Web publishing rules use SSL tunneling. When a client connects to ISA Server using SSL with a protocol other than HTTP, ISA Server simply redirects the SSL connection to the internal server. The client computer will establish the SSL connection directly with the internal server, not with ISA Server.

> **Note**   ISA Server does not support SSL bridging when configuring a server publishing rule. SSL bridging is available only when publishing Web servers using a secure Web publishing rule.

There is little configuration required on ISA Server to enable SSL for server publishing. To enable secure server publishing, you need only configure the server publishing rule to use a secure protocol. For example, to enable SSL access to an IMAP server, you just configure the server publishing rule to allow the secure IMAP (IMAPS) Server protocol rather than the IMAP4 Server protocol. This means that ISA Server will listen for client connections on Port 993 rather than on Port 143. You do not need to configure a server certificate on ISA Server, but you do need to configure a server certificate on the internal server providing this service.

How to Configure a Server Publishing Rule

To configure a new server publishing rule, complete the following procedure:

1. Ensure that the internal server that you are publishing is correctly configured. The server must be configured as a SecureNAT client and have the required service installed and configured.

> **Exam Tip**   If a server publishing rule looks like it is configured properly, but users still cannot access the server, check the server IP address configuration. The published server must be a SecureNAT client.

2. Open the ISA Server Management Console, and click Firewall Policy.

3. On the Tasks tab, click Create New Server Publishing Rule to start the New Server Publishing Rule Wizard.

4. On the Welcome To The New Server Publishing Rule Wizard page, in the Server Publishing Rule Name box, type a name for the publishing rule and click Next.

5. On the Select Server page, in the Server IP Address box, type the IP address of the internal server. Click Next.

6. On the Select Protocol page, shown in Figure 8-18, in the Selected Protocol list, select the appropriate protocol and click Next.

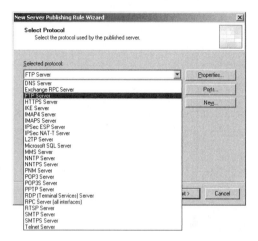

Figure 8-18   Selecting a protocol for a server publishing rule

7. After you select a protocol, you can also override the port mappings for the protocol. To do this, click Ports. In the Ports dialog box that opens (shown in Figure 8-19), you can modify the settings listed in Table 8-4.

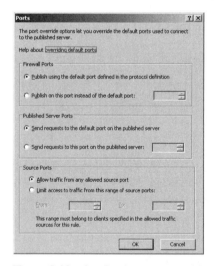

Figure 8-19   Configuring port override on a server publishing rule

Table 8-4   Port Override Configuration Options

Category	Configuration Option	Use This Option To
Firewall Ports	Publish Using The Default Port Defined In The Protocol Definition	Configure ISA Server to listen for connections on the default protocol port.
	Publish On This Port Instead Of On The Default Port	Configure ISA Server to listen for connections on an alternative port.
Published Server Ports	Send Requests To The Default Port On The Published Server	Configure ISA Server to forward requests to the default protocol port on the published server.
	Send Requests To This Port On The Published Server	Configure ISA Server to forward requests to an alternative port on the published server.
Source Ports	Allow Traffic From Any Allowed Source Port	Configure ISA Server to accept connection attempts on any port.
	Limit Access To Traffic From This Range Of Source Ports	Configure ISA Server to accept connection attempts on a limited range of ports.

8. On the IP Addresses page, select the network on which the ISA Server computer will listen for client requests. Click Next.

> **Note**   If you have multiple IP addresses connected to the appropriate network on the ISA Server computer, you can also configure the server publishing rule to listen on all IP addresses for the network, or only a specific address.

9. On the Completing The New Server Publishing Rule Wizard page, review the settings and click Finish.

You can also modify the configuration for the server publishing rule after you configure the rule. To modify the configuration of the server publishing rule, select Firewall Policy in the ISA Server Management Console and double-click the rule. Most of the configuration options are identical to the options you used when creating the rule. However, like a Web publishing rule, you can also configure a schedule for the server publishing rule, and configure how the server will forward client requests. Server publishing rules are different than Web publishing rules in that, by default, the original client IP address is sent to the published server rather than the ISA Server computer IP address.

> **Important** Server publishing rules do not provide the option of authenticating users. This is because server publishing is implemented using NAT, and the internal servers must be configured as SecureNAT clients. If you need to limit which users can access the published server, you must configure authentication on the published application or server. The only option you have for restricting access to the application on the server publishing rule is to limit which IP addresses are allowed to connect to the application.

Server Publishing Scenarios

Server publishing rules are fairly straightforward to configure in most scenarios. The configuration options for all server publishing rules are very much the same — you need to configure a port number, enter the published server IP address, and select on which network or networks the ISA Server computer will listen for the protocol connections.

> **Exam Tip** The following server publishing rules are explicitly mentioned in the objectives for the ISA Server exam. Make sure you understand when to use each type of rule and how to configure the rule.

How to Publish a Web Server

You cannot use a server publishing rule to publish an HTTP server. However, you can use either the SSL Web Publishing Rule Wizard or the Server Publishing Rule Wizard to publish a Web server using HTTPS. In fact, if you choose to use SSL tunneling when you use the SSL Web Publishing Wizard, you are actually configuring a server publishing rule.

To use the Server Publishing Rule Wizard to publish an HTTPS server, you must ensure that the appropriate certificate is configured on the Web server. Then start the wizard and enter the IP address of the Web server as the published server, and HTTPS server as the protocol. Because the rule will use SSL tunneling, you cannot configure the HTTP Web filter to filter any of the network traffic.

How to Publish a Remote Procedure Call Server

One of the more complicated server publishing scenarios is publishing a Remote Procedure Call (RPC) server. Many client applications use RPCs to connect to a server-based application. The most common of these applications is an Outlook client communicating with Microsoft Exchange Server.

Publishing an RPC server is difficult because RPCs use multiple ports to create the connection between the client and server. A single server may be hosting multiple

RPC-based applications so the client and server must have some means of determining which application the client wants to connect to. To do this, the RPC client initiates communication with the server using Port 135, which is the endpoint mapping service port. The RPC client then sends the server a universally unique identifier (UUID) that identifies the specific application or service that the client wants to gain access to, and requests that the endpoint mapper send it a port number that the server will use for that application. The endpoint mapper returns an available port number to the RPC client. This port is randomly chosen and could be any port over 1024. The client then uses that port number to connect to the server application.

To provide secure access to an RPC server, ISA Server must be able to manage the UUIDs and the dynamic assignment of ports. To do this, ISA Server provides an RPC filter. The RPC application filter works as follows:

1. The RPC client issues a request over TCP Port 135 through ISA Server to the RPC server. As part of the request the client sends the UUID for the service with which it wants to communicate.

2. The application server sends a response back with a port number on which the client can communicate with the specified application.

3. ISA Server uses the RPC application filter to capture this information, and maintains it in a table. ISA Server allocates a new port on external interface of the ISA Server computer, and changes the response that it sends to the RPC client to reflect this change. This information is also maintained in the table.

4. The RPC client establishes a connection to the port that ISA Server instructed it to use. ISA Server screens the RPC commands to ensure that no exploits are contained within the channel. The RPC filter matches the client response and port number to the information it maintains in its table.

5. The RPC client response is forwarded by ISA Server to the application server.

6. The application server responds to the RPC client. ISA Server intercepts the response and changes the source port number to match the information contained in its table.

7. ISA Server forwards the responses to the RPC client.

To publish an RPC server, you need to configure an RPC protocol and then configure a server publishing rule that uses the RPC protocol. You need to define the RPC protocol to define which UUIDs the ISA Server will accept. To configure an RPC protocol, complete the following procedure:

1. In the ISA Server Management Console, click Firewall Policy, and then select the Toolbox tab.

2. Click Protocols, click New, then click RPC Protocol.

3. On the Welcome To The New RPC Protocol Definition Wizard page, type a name for the new protocol, and then click Next.

4. On the Select Server page, shown in Figure 8-20, you can configure the UUID interfaces that will be included with this protocol definition. To get a list of supported UUID server names from a server on the network, type the server name in the Server Name text box and click Next.

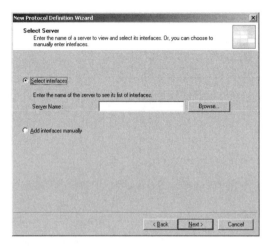

Figure 8-20 Configuring the server for an RPC protocol

5. On the Server interfaces page, shown in Figure 8-21, select some of or all the interfaces available on the server. If you are publishing a specific application, choose only the UUID interface associated with that application, and then click Next.

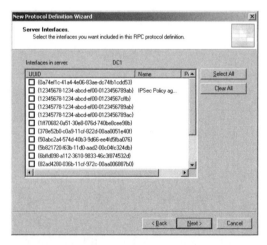

Figure 8-21 Configuring the UUID interfaces for an RPC protocol

6. On the Completing The New RPC Protocol Definition Wizard page, review the configuration and then click Finish.

After configuring the RPC protocol, use the protocol in a server publishing rule to publish the application server.

> **See Also**   The most common scenario for publishing an RPC server is to publish Exchange Server for Outlook e-mail clients. To simplify the configuration of the Exchange Server publishing rules, ISA Server 2003 is preconfigured with a protocol object named Exchange RPC protocol, which already includes all the UUIDs used by Exchange Server clients. ISA Server also includes a mail publishing wizard that can be used to publish the Exchange Server computer for Outlook clients. For more information, see Chapter 9, "Integrating ISA Server 2004 and Exchange Server."

How to Publish an FTP Server

You can also use a server publishing rule to publish an FTP server. Configuring an FTP publishing rule is the same as configuring any other server publishing rule. However, when you configure a server rule to publish the FTP protocol, the FTP application filter is automatically applied to the filter. Enabling FTP at the firewall can be complex because FTP uses multiple ports and connections to transfer data. The FTP filter is specially designed to handle this complexity and securely manage all needed connections.

The following steps describe how an FTP connection is set up:

1. The FTP client creates a connection to an FTP server using Port 21. As part of the request, the FTP client also indicates on which port it will listen for a response. This port will be a random port over 1023.

2. The server responds on the port indicated by the client, and the client and server complete the three-way handshake.

3. Once the three-way handshake is complete, the server initiates a connection with the client on Port 20. This port will be used as the data channel to actually transmit the data. The server also indicates a port greater than 1023 to which the client should respond.

4. The client and server complete a three-way handshake on the new ports and then begin to transmit data.

The first two steps in the process are similar to most protocol connections. However, when the FTP server initiates a connection back to the client on Port 20, the connection is not part of any existing TCP session. The FTP filter enables the FTP connections by monitoring the initial FTP connection between the FTP client and server and then enables the server connection attempt to set up the data channel.

There are several different configuration options available with the FTP filter:

- You can disable the FTP filter on any access rule or server publishing rule. By default, the FTP filter is enabled on all rules that enable FTP. If you want to disable the FTP filter on a particular rule, access the protocol properties on the rule and disable the FTP filter.

- You can disable the FTP filter for all rules. To disable the FTP filter, access the Add-ins container in ISA Server Management. Right-click FTP Access Filter and select Disable.

- You can configure the FTP filter to allow read-only access or read-write access for each rule using FTP. By default, the FTP filter allows only read access to FTP servers. If you want to enable write access, locate the access rule in the Firewall Policy container. Right-click the rule and click Configure FTP and then clear the Read Only check box.

How to Publish a Terminal Services Server

Another possible server publishing scenario is to publish a Terminal Services server to the Internet. Terminal Services is a Windows 2000 Server and Windows Server 2003 feature that allows multiple users to run applications on a Windows Server computer. The application runs on the Windows Server computer with only keystrokes and pointer actions sent from the client to the server, and screen display information sent to the client from the server. Remote Desktop, which is included with Windows Server 2003 and Windows XP, is a limited version of Terminal Services.

Microsoft Terminal Services uses the Remote Desktop Protocol (RDP), which uses Port 3389 to communicate between the client and server. To publish a Terminal Services computer, you need to create a server publishing rule that allows access using the RDP protocol to the Terminal Services server IP address.

> **Security Alert**   By default, a Windows Server 2003 Terminal Server will try to negotiate encryption of all network traffic between the server and but will accept nonencrypted connections. If you are accessing the Terminal Server across the Internet, you should configure the Terminal Server to require encryption.

One interesting Terminal Services scenario is one where you want to use Terminal Services to manage ISA Server from the Internet. You can enable this configuration by enabling a server publishing rule that enables RDP access to the ISA Server computer. If you want to publish both the ISA Server computer and an internal computer using RDP, you need to configure two IP addresses on the ISA Server computer that are accessible from the Internet. Then configure two different server publishing rules, one to allow RDP access to the ISA Server computer, and one to allow RDP access to the internal Terminal Services computer. If you do not have multiple IP addresses available on the external interface, then you can publish each terminal server on a different port.

How to Publish a VPN Server

You can also use ISA Server 2004 to publish VPN servers on the internal network to the Internet. ISA Server can operate as a VPN remote-access server, but you can also use it to publish other VPN servers. When you choose to publish a VPN server, you need to choose which tunneling protocol you will use. You have two options: Point-to-Point Tunneling Protocol (PPTP) or Layer-Two Tunneling Protocol over IP Security (L2TP over IPSec).

> **See Also**   For more information about these tunneling protocols, see Chapter 10, "Configuring Virtual Private Networks for Remote Clients and Networks." Chapter 10 provides details about how to configure the ISA Server computer as a VPN server.

To publish a VPN server, you need to configure the following:

■ Configure a computer to serve as the VPN endpoint. If you are using a Windows Server computer, enable and configure Routing and Remote Access to allow VPN connections. On the VPN server, set the default gateway to the internal interface of the ISA Server computer.

■ To publish a VPN server running PPTP, you just need to configure a server publishing rule that allows PPTP connections from the Internet to the VPN server.

■ Deploying an L2TP over IPSec VPN server is more complicated. First of all, L2TP requires either a pre-shared key or digital certificate for authentication. Because the pre-shared key has to be identical for all clients, the use of digital certificates is strongly recommended. This means that a digital certificate must be installed on the VPN server and on each VPN client. Secondly, L2TP over IPSec does not support NAT connections without the NAT traversal (NAT-T) update. This means that all L2TP over IPSec clients must have the NAT-T update installed and you need to configure ISA Server to enable NAT-T connections.

> **See Also**   For more information about the NAT-T update, see the article, "L2TP/IPSec NAT-T Update for Windows XP and Windows 2000," located at *http://go.microsoft.com/fwlink/?LinkId=28084*.

L2TP over IPSec requires two publishing rules. One rule is used to publish Internet Key Exchange (IKE) negotiation and a second rule to publish NAT-T. The first rule uses the IKE Server protocol, while the second rule uses the IPSec NAT-T Server protocol.

Guidelines for Troubleshooting Web and Server Publishing

By using the ISA Server publishing wizards, you can easily publish internal resources to the Internet. However, there are also many situations in which you may need to troubleshoot connectivity to those published resources. Use the following guidelines to troubleshoot ISA Server Web and server publishing issues:

■ **Check the resource availability**   Can you access the published resource directly? For example, if you are publishing a Web site, try connecting to the Web site from a computer that is located on the same network as the Web server. If the Web site is not available from the same network, then the primary issue is related to the Web server and not to the ISA Server configuration.

■ **Check the DNS records**   Does the resource named on the Internet resolve to an IP address on the external network adapter of the computer running ISA Server? If not, then check the zone information on the Internet DNS server that is authoritative for your domain name.

■ **Check the error message**   When you fail to connect to the published resource, check the error message that you receive. This is particularly useful when troubleshooting Web publishing rules because HTTP defines a standard set of error messages. For example, if you fail to connect to the Web site and receive an Error 403 page, you know that the connection to the external IP of the computer running ISA Server has succeeded. The issue will therefore be an ISA Server Web publishing issue or an IIS issue. If you receive a 500 Internal Server Error page, there is likely a problem with the SSL certificate on the Web server.

■ **Check on which ports the ISA Server is listening for connections**   You can check this by using the Netstat utility. To use Netstat, type **netstat -an** at a command prompt on the ISA Server computer. If ISA Server is not listening on a Port 80 or a Port 443, check the Web listener configuration. For other ports, check the server publishing rules configurations.

■ **Check the publishing rule configuration**   When configuring a Web publishing rule, ensure that the public name matches the name that an external user specifies to access the Web site. Also confirm that the internal destination server name or IP address is correct. If you are using a server name for the internal Web server, ensure that ISA Server can resolve the IP address for the server name. You can accomplish this by configuring ISA Server to use an internal DNS server that can provide name resolution, or configuring the server name in the HOSTS file on the computer running ISA Server.

■ **Check SSL configuration and certificates**   If a connection to a secure resource is failing, check the SSL configuration and the installed server certificates. In a secure Web publishing scenario, check the SSL bridging configuration and ensure that ISA Server and the Web server both have certificates if required. Also, check that the name on the certificate matches the FQDN that is used to connect to the certificate. In a server publishing scenario, check the certificate on the published server, and check the server publishing rule to ensure that it is configured to use a secure protocol rather than the nonsecure protocol. Any one of the following problems will result in the Web client receiving a 500 Internal Server Error page:

❑ The certificate on the internal Web server is not valid on the date of the request.

❑ The Certification Authority that issued the Web site certificate for the internal Web server is not trusted by the ISA Server 2004 firewall.

❑ The server name provided on the Web publishing rule To tab does not match the name on the certificate installed on the published Web site.

Exam Tip   In most cases, when you see a 500 Internal Server error in a secure Web publishing scenario, the problem is with the certificate configuration.

Practice: Configuring Server Publishing Rules

In the following practice, you will configure several server publishing rules and then test the rules to ensure that they are correctly configured. You will publish an FTP server, a VPN server that is using PPTP, and a Remote Desktop server.

Note   This practice assumes that DC1 is configured as an FTP server and as a VPN server using Routing And Remote Access. Remote Desktop also should be enabled on DC1.

Exercise 1: Configuring a New Server Publishing Rule

1. If necessary, open ISA Server Management Console, expand the ISA Server computer node, and click Firewall Policy.

2. On the Tasks tab, click Create New Server Publishing Rule to start the New Server Publishing Rule Wizard.

3. On the Welcome To The New Server Publishing Rule Wizard page, in the Server Publishing Rule Name box, type **Coho Vineyard FTP Site** and click Next.

4. On the Select Server page, in the Server IP Address box, type **10.10.0.10**. Click Next.

5. On the Select Protocol page, in the Selected Protocol list, click FTP Server and click Next.

6. On the IP Addresses page, select the check box for External. Click Next.

7. On the Completing The New Server Publishing Rule Wizard page, review the settings and click Finish.

8. Configure another server publishing rule named Coho Vineyard VPN Server that uses the PPTP Server protocol to enable connections to 10.10.0.10.

9. Configure another server publishing rule named Coho Vineyard Remote Desktop Server that uses the RDP (Terminal Services) Server to enable connections to 10.10.0.10.

10. Click Apply to apply the changes.

Exercise 2: Testing the Server Publishing Rules

1. Switch to the SERVER1 virtual machine.

2. Open Internet Explorer. On the Tools menu, click Internet Options. On the Advanced tab, ensure Enable Folder View For FTP Sites is not selected and click OK.

3. In the Address box, type **ftp://ftp.cohovineyard.com** into the Address box. The connection should be successful. Close Internet Explorer.

4. Click Start, point to Control Panel, then point to Network Connections and click New Connection Wizard.

5. On the Welcome To The New Connection Wizard page, click Next.

6. On the Network Connection Type page, click Connect To The Network At My Workplace, and then click Next.

7. On the Network Connection page, click Virtual Private Network Connection and click Next.

8. On the Connection Name page, type **Coho Vineyard VPN** and click Next.

9. On the VPN Server Selection page, type the IP address for the external interface of the ISA Server computer and click Next.

10. On the Connection Availability page, click Next.

11. On the Completing The New Connection Wizard page, click Finish.

12. On the Connect Coho Vineyard VPN dialog box, type the password for the administrator account and then click Connect. The connection should be successful.

13. Right-click the connection icon and click Disconnect.

14. Click Start, point to Accessories, point to Communications and click Remote Desktop Connection.

15. In the Remote Desktop Connection dialog box, type the IP address for the external interface of the ISA Server computer and click Connect. The connection should be successful.

16. In the Remote Desktop desktop, click Cancel.

Lesson Review

Use the following questions to help determine whether you have learned enough to move on to the next lesson. If you have difficulty answering these questions, review the material in this lesson before beginning the next lesson. You can find answers to the questions in the "Questions and Answers" section at the end of this chapter.

1. You have installed ISA Server 2004 as a front-end firewall protecting a perimeter network. You need to publish two separate FTP servers in the perimeter network. One of the FTP servers is for public users to download evaluation versions of your product. The other needs to be restricted to the Web Developers group in your domain so they can post code revisions from the Internet. You have only one IP address that you can use on the Internet. How will you configure ISA Server to meet these requirements?

   _____

   _____

   _____

2. You have just published a secure Web site on your perimeter network using a server publishing rule. Internal users are able to access the site without receiving any error messages, but Internet users receive a warning whenever they access the site. You confirm that the ISA Server certificate is valid and that it was issued by a well-known commercial CA. What is the most likely cause for the warning message?

   _____

   _____

   _____

3. You need to enable SSL access to an IMAP Server computer. What steps must you take to do this? (Choose two answers.)

   a. Install a server certificate on the ISA Server computer.

   b. Create a server publishing rule for IMAPS Server protocol.

   c. Install a server certificate on the IMAP Server computer.

   d. Create a server publishing rule for IMAP Server protocol.

   e. Install a server certificate on both the IMAP Server computer and the ISA Server computer.

Lesson Summary

- Server publishing rules are used on ISA Server to map a port number on an external interface of the ISA Server computer to the IP address of an internal server providing a specific service.

- Server publishing rules are fairly easy to configure. For most rules, all you need to do is choose the protocol that you want to publish and enter the IP address for the server that you are publishing.

- There are many possible scenarios where you can use a server publishing rule. Some examples include publishing a secure Web site, an FTP server, an RPC server, a VPN server, and a Terminal Services server.

- There are many situations in which you may need to troubleshoot Web and server publishing. To troubleshoot ISA Server Web and server publishing issues check whether the resource is available on the local network, check name resolution, and then check the publishing rule configuration.

Lesson 5: Configuring ISA Server Authentication

In many cases, the network resources that are published by Web or server publishing rules are confidential and should be available only to authorized users. To enforce this, you can configure ISA Server 2004 to require authentication for all users accessing a published resource. This lesson describes the types of authentication supported by ISA Server 2004 and how to configure authentication.

After this lesson, you will be able to

- Describe how access rules and authentication work together to provide secure Internet access
- Identify the Web publishing authentication options on ISA Server 2004
- Describe how RADIUS authentication works and how to implement it
- Implement SecurID for ISA authentication

Estimated lesson time: 30 minutes

How Authentication and Web Publishing Rules Work Together

Authentication is an integral part of any firewall policy. You can limit access to internal resources by limiting access based on the IP address of a computer. However, in most cases, it is much more effective to provide access only to specific users who have authenticated themselves.

Important   Authentication applies only to Web publishing rules. You cannot configure authentication on server publishing rules.

Authentication and Web publishing rules work together in the following ways:

- Users can gain access to an internal resource protected by ISA Server only if an access rule or publishing rule grants access to that resource. When you create a publishing rule, you can limit which users can gain access to the resource using the rule. Whenever a rule is configured to grant access to a specific set of users other than the All Users user set, authentication becomes an important part of how the rule is evaluated.

- For Web publishing and secure Web publishing rules, you must configure a Web listener as part of the rule definition. The Web listener defines which authentication methods are enabled. You can configure a Web listener to use more than one authentication mechanism. These authentication mechanisms can be used simultaneously on a Web listener: Basic, Digest, Integrated, and Client Certificate Authentication. RADIUS, SecurID, or forms-based authentication methods must be the only authentication mechanism configured on a Web listener. Once you have configured the Web listener for a Web publishing or secure Web publishing rule, you can then specify which users can gain access to resources based on the rule.

■   When ISA Server receives a request for an internal resource, it processes the firewall policy rules in order. When a firewall rule matches the client request, but ISA Server requires client authentication to validate the match, ISA Server will request that the client authenticate. In other words, if the firewall rule limits access to users other than the All Users user set, then the user must provide credentials to prove his or her identity.

> **Important**   By default, Web publishing rules and secure Web publishing rules grant access to the All Users user set, which includes anonymous, or unauthenticated, users. To limit access to a Web publishing rule, remove the All Users user set and add the All Authenticated Users or a specific user set.

ISA Server Web Publishing Authentication Scenarios

When designing an authentication strategy for ISA Server Web publishing rules, you have several options. You can configure ISA Server to perform the authentication, or you can configure the published server to perform the authentication. In some cases, you may want to require authentication on both ISA Server and the published server.

Configure Authentication on ISA Server

In some cases, you may want users to authenticate before they reach the internal network. To enable this, you can configure the Web listener associated with the publishing rule to require authentication. Once the users authenticate with ISA Server, they can then access the Web server on the internal network. This is a secure configuration because if users cannot successfully authenticate with ISA Server, they cannot access anything on the internal network.

Use ISA Server authentication if you have fairly simple authentication requirements. For example, if you want to ensure that only authenticated users can access all your published Web servers, then configure the Web listener to allow access to the All Authenticated Users user set. This option also has the added benefit of offloading authentication activity to the ISA Server computer.

See Also   For information about how to configure authentication, see Chapter 5, "Enabling Secure Internet Access with ISA Server 2004." Although Chapter 5 deals specifically with how to configure authentication for outbound Internet access, the options and procedures for configuring authentication are the same when configuring authentication for inbound access. The only differences are that you need to configure the authentication protocols on the Web listener rather than on the Internal network properties, and you can configure OWA Forms-Based authentication and SecurID authentication on the Web listener. OWA Forms-Based authentication will be discussed in detail in Chapter 9.

Configure Authentication on the Internal Web Server

Another option for configuring authentication is to configure the internal Web server to require authentication. In this scenario, ISA Server allows anonymous access to the published server, but the server requests authentication. In this configuration, ISA Server uses pass-through authentication to complete the authentication. Pass-through authentication refers to the ability of ISA Server to pass a client's authentication information to the destination server. The following steps describe how pass-through authentication works in a Web publishing scenario:

1. The client sends a request for an object on a Web server protected by ISA Server. Because the publishing rule allows anonymous access, ISA Server does not prompt for authentication but passes the request to the Web server.

2. The Web server receives the request and responds that authentication is required.

3. ISA Server passes the authentication-required response to the client.

4. The client returns authentication information to ISA Server.

5. ISA Server passes the client authentication information to the Web server.

6. After successful authentication, the client communicates with the Web server.

This option transfers all authentication activity to the internal server. This is a recommended solution when you have complex authentication requirements. For example, you may be publishing multiple Web sites with some allowing anonymous access, while others require authentication. In this scenario, it is easier to configure authentication on the internal Web server.

Important   If you are publishing resources using a server publishing rule, you can only configure authentication on the server hosting the internal resource. You cannot configure authentication on a server publishing rule.

Configure Authentication on ISA Server and on the Internal Web Server

You can also design an authentication strategy that requires that users authenticate on ISA Server as well as on the internal Web server. You may choose to implement this solution if you have a Web site with varying types of confidential information. For example, you may want to limit access to a private Web site in your organization to only users who have valid domain user accounts. However, the Web site may also contain a confidential area that should be accessible only to executives. In this case, you could enable ISA Server authentication to limit access to the Web site to the Domain Users group, and then use authentication on the Web server to limit access to confidential information.

When you configure authentication using an authentication option other than basic authentication on both servers, the users have to provide their credentials more than once. If you are using basic authentication on both ISA Server and the internal Web server, you can use basic authentication delegation to enable single sign-on for the users. When you enable basic authentication delegation, ISA Server authenticates the users, and then forwards the user credentials to the Web server, allowing the Web server to authenticate users without requesting credentials a second time.

To enable basic authentication delegation, select the check box for Forward Basic Authentication Credentials (Basic Delegation) on the Users tab of the Web publishing or secure Web publishing rule, as shown in Figure 8-22.

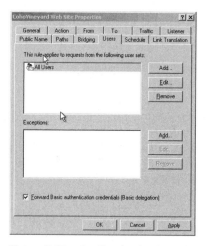

Figure 8-22 Configuring basic authentication delegation

How to Implement RADIUS Server for Authentication

ISA Server enables the use of RADIUS to authenticate users. RADIUS is an industry-standard protocol used to provide authentication in heterogeneous environments. To implement RADIUS authentication, you need to implement the following components:

- **RADIUS server**   A RADIUS server has access to all the user accounts within a defined namespace. The RADIUS server passes authentication requests to an authentication server (such as an Active Directory domain controller) and can also be used to apply policies to user connections. Microsoft includes Internet Authentication Server (IAS), which is a RADIUS server with Windows 2000 Server and Windows Server 2003.

- **RADIUS client**   A RADIUS client is typically a dial-up server, VPN server, or wireless access point. The RADIUS client is the server that users connect to when they want to access a network. The RADIUS client collects the user credentials and sends them in the form of a RADIUS message to a RADIUS server. The RADIUS server authenticates the RADIUS client request, and sends back a RADIUS message response. If the RADIUS message response indicates that the user has been successfully authenticated, the user is granted access.

ISA Server can be configured as a RADIUS client. This means that when users connect to ISA Server, ISA Server will send the user logon information to a RADIUS server rather than to an Active Directory domain controller.

The most important benefit of using RADIUS for ISA Server authentication is that you can authenticate users based on their Active Directory user names without requiring that ISA Server be a member of the Active Directory domain. In organizations that have deployed Active Directory, most user accounts are stored in Active Directory. One of the benefits of using ISA Server as a firewall is that you can use those Active Directory accounts to authenticate user access, for both inbound and outbound access. However, for ISA Server to authenticate Active Directory users, the computer running ISA Server must be a member of the Active Directory domain. Security best practices specify that the firewall should not be located on a server that is a member of a Windows domain. The problem with using a firewall that is a member of a domain is that if an attacker were able to compromise the firewall, the attacker could potentially leverage the firewall's domain member status to launch a successful attack against other internal network servers.

You can use RADIUS to gain the benefit of using the Active Directory domains for authentication without joining the server running ISA Server to the domain. When ISA Server is configured to use RADIUS authentication for incoming Web requests, the firewall forwards the request to a RADIUS server located on a protected network. The RADIUS server can forward the authentication requests to an Active Directory domain controller, another RADIUS server, or a directory server created by a third party that accepts RADIUS authentication messages.

How to Implement RADIUS Authentication

Configuring ISA Server to use RADIUS for authentication requires several steps. The high-level steps are described here (you will complete the detailed steps in the following practice):

1. Install IAS on a computer running Windows Server 2003 or Windows 2000 Server. IAS is one of the Networking Services installed by using Add Or Remove Programs from Control Panel.

2. Configure IAS to accept ISA Server as a RADIUS client. To configure this option, open the Internet Authentication Service console from the Administrative Tools menu. Right-click RADIUS clients and click New RADIUS client. To complete the configuration, you need to provide the ISA Server name and IP address and configure a shared secret that will be used to authenticate the connection between the ISA Server and the RADIUS server.

3. Configure IAS to use Active Directory for its user account database. To do this, you must register the IAS server in the Active Directory domain.

4. Configure the Active Directory user accounts and remote access policies. When the user attempts to authenticate on a RADIUS server, the RADIUS server checks the user account properties and the remote access policies to determine if the user can authenticate. The user account must be configured to allow dial-in access or configured so that dial-in access is controlled by a remote access policy. Then a remote access policy must be created that will allow the user dial-in access.

5. Configure ISA Server to use a RADIUS server for authentication. To do this, expand the Configuration container in ISA Server management, click General and then click Define RADIUS Servers. To add a RADIUS server, click Add and then specify the RADIUS server name, shared secret, and port number, as shown in Figure 8-23.

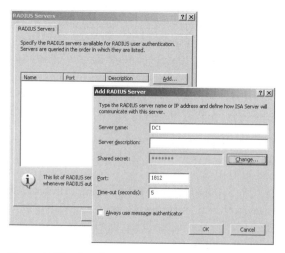

Figure 8-23   Configuring ISA Server to use a RADIUS server for authentication

6. Configure a Web listener to use RADIUS authentication. To do this, perform the following steps:

   a. Access the Web Listener properties on the Firewall Policy Toolbox tab.

   b. On the Web Listener Properties dialog box, select the Preferences tab and click Authentication, as shown in Figure 8-24.

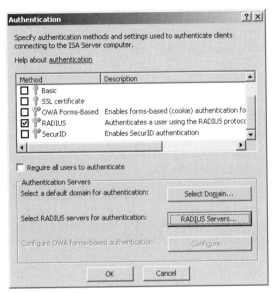

Figure 8-24   Configuring a Web listener to use a RADIUS server for authentication

   c. Select RADIUS authentication and then click RADIUS Servers to select the RADIUS server that will be used by the Web listener.

Off the Record   Although RADIUS authentication does enable you to configure authentication based on domain groups without joining the ISA Server computer to the Active Directory domain, the current implementation of RADIUS authentication on ISA Server is too limited to be feasible in a complex environment. When you configure the RADIUS remote access policy, you can choose to which group the policy will apply. You can also configure whether the group has permission to connect or not. However, you can apply only one remote access policy for ISA Server authentication. For example, if you create a remote access policy that allows members of the Managers group to access the server, and then configure the Web Listener to use RADIUS, only members of the Members of the Managers group will be able to access the Web site. That may be what you want but once you configure this rule, you cannot enable RADIUS authentication for another Web publishing rule and provide access to another group of users. You can configure a user set on the ISA Server computer, but there is no way for ISA Server to pass the user set information to the RADIUS server. Because of this limitation, RADIUS cannot be used to configure complex authentication requirements on ISA Server. About the best you can do is configure RADIUS to grant access to the Domain Users group, and then use more granular permissions on the Web site.

How to Implement SecurID for Authentication

The RSA SecurID authentication system is a two-factor user authentication system. Two-factor authentication means that users need to identify themselves with two unique factors: something they know (a password or PIN) and something they have (in this case, an RSA SecurID token that generates a unique six-digit passcode every minute). ISA Server 2004 enables the option to authenticate users based on authentication credentials from the RSA SecurID product from RSA Security, Inc.

To implement RSA SecurID authentication, you need the following components:

- **RSA ACE/Server** This computer retains information about users, groups, hosts, and tokens. For each user, the RSA ACE/Server maintains a list of hosts to which the user can log on, and a logon name, which can differ from one host to the other.

- **RSA ACE/Agent** This computer provides Web content, and requires the user to provide credentials for RSA SecurID. When using SecurID authentication with ISA Server, ISA Server is the RSA ACE/Client.

- **Client** Usually, this is a Web browser that receives Web content.

When a user attempts to access Web pages that are protected by RSA SecurID, the ISA Server computer requests a Web browser cookie. This cookie will only be present if the user has authenticated recently. If the user's cookie is missing, the user is prompted for a username and passcode for SecurID. The passcode consists of a combination of the user's PIN and tokencode. The tokencode is displayed on the user's token and changes once every minute. The RSA ACE/Agent on the ISA Server computer passes these credentials to the RSA ACE/Server computer for validation. If the credentials are successfully validated, a cookie is delivered to the user's browser for subsequent activity during the session, and the user is granted access to the content.

Configuring ISA Server to use RSA SecurID is similar to configuring ISA Server to use a RADIUS server for authentication. The high-level steps are described here (to complete the detailed steps, you need access to an RSA ACE/Server):

1. On the RSA ACE/Server, set up ISA Server as an RSA ACE/Agent. To do this, you need to add the ISA Server computer name and IP address as an Agent Host. Then copy the Sdconf.rec file, located in the ACE\Data folder on the RSA ACE/Server computer, to the %Windir%\System32 folder on the ISA Server computer. ISA Server uses this file when connecting to the RSA ACE/Server.

2. Add users to the ISA Server Host record on the ACE Server computer. Users with valid authentication credentials must be specified on the ACE Server computer.

3. Configure a Web listener to use SecurID for authentication.

Practice: Configuring ISA Server Authentication

In this practice, you will install and configure Internet Authentication Service on DC1. Then you will configure ISA Server to use RADIUS for authentication and to use the IAS server as the RADIUS server. Then you will configure a Web publishing rule to use RADIUS authentication. Finally, you will test RADIUS authentication.

Exercise 1: Installing and Configuring IAS Server

1. On DC1, log on as an administrator.

2. Open Control Panel and open Add Or Remove Programs.

3. Click Add/Remove Windows Components. On the Components list, click Networking Services and then click Details.

4. Click the check box for Internet Authentication Service and then click OK.

5. Click Next, and then wait for the installation to finish. You may need to provide the Windows Server 2004 installation CD to complete the installation.

6. When the installation finishes, click Finish.

7. Open Internet Authentication Services from the Administrative Tools folder.

8. Right-click Internet Authentication Service (Local) and click Register Server in Active Directory.

9. Read the notice explaining that IAS will be able to read users' dial-in settings, and click OK.

10. When you receive the Server registered message, click OK.

11. Right-click RADIUS Clients and click New RADIUS Client.

12. In the New RADIUS Client dialog box, in the Friendly Name text box, type **ISA1**. In the Client Address (IP or DNS) text box, type **10.10.0.1**. Click Next.

13. In the Additional Information dialog box, in the Client-Vendor list, ensure that RADIUS Standard is selected. Type a password for the Shared Secret and the Confirm Shared Secret. Click Finish.

14. Close Internet Authentication Service.

Exercise 2: Configure ISA Server to Use the RADIUS Server for Authentication

1. On ISA1, in the ISA Server Management Console, expand Configuration and then click General.

2. Under Additional Security Policy, click Define RADIUS Servers.

3. In the RADIUS Servers dialog box, click Add.

4. In the Add RADIUS Server dialog box, in the Server Name box, type **DC1.cohovineyard.com**.

5. Click Change to change the Shared Secret.

6. In the Shared Secret dialog box, type the same password you used earlier as the New Secret and Confirm New Secret and then click OK.

7. In the Add RADIUS Servers dialog box, click OK.

8. In the RADIUS Servers dialog box, click OK.

9. Click Firewall Policy, double-click the Coho Vineyard Secure Site to open the Web publishing rule's properties.

10. On the Listener tab, click Properties to access HTTPS Web listener properties.

11. On the Preferences tab, click Authentication.

12. Configure the Authentication settings to allow only RADIUS authentication and to require all users to authenticate.

13. Click Select Domain and type **Cohovineyard.com**. Click OK.

14. Click RADIUS Servers and ensure that *DC1.cohovineyard.com* is configured as the RADIUS server. Click OK until the HTTPS dialog box is closed.

15. In the Coho Vineyard Store Site Properties dialog box, on the Users tab, remove All Users. Add the All Authenticated Users user set. Click OK.

16. Click Apply to apply the changes.

Exercise 3: Configure the Remote Access Policy on IAS

1. On DC1, open Internet Authentication Services from the Administrative Tools folder.

2. Right-click Remote Access Policies and click New Remote Access Policy.

3. On the Welcome To The New Remote Access Policy Wizard page, click Next.

4. On the Policy Configuration Method page, click Set Up a Custom Policy, and type **Secure Site Access Policy** in the Policy Name: text box and click Next.

5. On the Policy Conditions page, click Add.

6. In the Select Attributes dialog box, click Windows-Groups and click Add.

7. In the Groups dialog box, click Add.

8. In the Enter the Object Names To Select text box, type **Domain Users**. Click OK.

9. In the Group dialog box, click OK.

10. On the Policy Conditions page, click Next.

11. On the Permissions page, click Grant Remote Access Permission, and then click Next.

12. On the Profile page, click Edit Profile.

13. In the Edit Dial-in Profile Dialog box, click the Authentication tab.

14. Select Unencrypted Authentication (PAP,SPAP). Click OK.

15. In the Dial-in Settings box, click No and then click Next.

Security Alert   The option you just selected shows another limitation with the RADIUS server implementation. You must enable nonsecure authentication in order to pass credentials from the ISA Server to the RADIUS server.

16. On the Completing The New Remote Access Policy Wizard page, click Finish.

17. Ensure that the Secure Site Remote Access Policy is listed first in the Remote Access Policy list. If it is not, right-click the policy and click Move Up.

Exercise 4: Test the RADIUS Authentication

1. On SERVER1, open Internet Explorer.

2. Connect to *https://secure.cohovineyard.com*. When prompted to log on, enter the user name and password of a domain user that has access.

3. After you connect to the Web site, change the HTTPS Web listener to use Basic and Integrated authentication.

Tip   If you cannot access the Web site, ensure that the user account you are using has Allow Dial-in permissions set on the user account in Active Directory.

Lesson Review

Use the following questions to help determine whether you have learned enough to move on to the next lesson. If you have difficulty answering these questions, review the material in this lesson before beginning the next lesson. You can find answers to the questions in the "Questions and Answers" section at the end of this chapter.

1. You have deployed Active Directory in a single-domain environment. You want to use RADIUS authentication for your internal Web site. What steps do you take to configure this? (Choose two answers.)

   a. Configure the ISA Server 2004 computer as a RADIUS Server computer.

   b. Register the RADIUS Server computer in Active Directory.

   c. Register the ISA Server 2004 computer in Active Directory.

   d. Configure the ISA Server 2004 computer as a RADIUS Client computer.

2. You are configuring a Web site that contains some confidential information. Most of the information on the Web site should be available to all users with user accounts in your domain, while some folders should be accessible only to managers. You are configuring a Web listener and a Web publishing rule to enable this access. How can you configure authentication on ISA Server and the Web server?

    a. Configure ISA Server to require authentication for all users. Allow the managers access to the Web site. Use Internet Information Server (IIS) authentication to allow access to all authenticated users.

    b. Configure ISA Server to allow all users access to the Web site. Use IIS authentication to restrict access to the manager's folders.

    c. Configure ISA Server to require authentication for all users. Allow all authenticated users access to the Web site. Use IIS authentication to restrict access to the managers' folders.

    d. Configure ISA Server to allow all users access to the Web site. Use IIS authentication to restrict access to authenticated users.

3. You have deployed ISA Server 2004 in a 3-Leg perimeter firewall configuration. The ISA Server computer is not a member of your Active Directory domain. You need to provide access to a Web site in your perimeter network. Only Domain Users should be able to access the site. What authentication method should you implement?

    a. RADIUS

    b. Digest

    c. Basic

    d. Integrated

Lesson Summary

- Authentication and Web publishing rules work together to ensure that users can gain access to an internal resource protected by ISA Server only if an access rule or publishing rule grants access to that resource. If the access rule requires authentication, then the user must provide authentication credentials before they will be granted access.

- In some cases, you may want users to authenticate before they reach the internal network. To enable this, you can configure the Web listener associated with the publishing rule to require authentication. Another option for authentication is to configure the internal Web server to require authentication. In this scenario, ISA Server allows anonymous access to the published server, but the server requests authentication. The third option is an authentication strategy that requires that users authenticate on ISA Server as well as on the internal Web server.

- ISA Server enables the use of RADIUS to authenticate users connecting to Web servers. To implement RADIUS authentication, you need to implement a RADIUS Server, configure ISA Server as a RADIUS client and then configure a Web listener to use RADIUS authentication.

- ISA Server 2004 enables the option to authenticate users based on authentication credentials from the RSA SecurID product from RSA Security, Inc. The RSA SecurID authentication system is a two-factor user authentication system. To implement RSA SecurID authentication, you need to configure an RSA ACE/Server, configure ISA Server as an RSA ACE/Client, and then configure a Web listener to use SecurID authentication.

Case Scenario Exercises

In these exercises, you will plan an ISA Server 2004 publishing configuration for a fictitious organization. Read the scenario and then answer the question that follows. If you have difficulty completing this work, review the material in this chapter before beginning the next chapter. You can find answers to these questions in the "Questions and Answers" section at the end of this chapter.

Scenario 1

You are the network administrator for your organization. You publish a public Web site and a secure Web site on two separate servers in your perimeter network. Your organization has a head office and two branch offices. You have deployed a single Active Directory domain. Users at the branch offices use the Internet to access your Web sites. You need to ensure that only Domain Users have access to the secure site and only members of the Managers group have access to the Sales folder of the secure site. You need to ensure that all network traffic is encrypted from the client to the Web server that is hosting the secure Web site. However, you also need to ensure that ISA Server can inspect all traffic coming to the secure site from the Internet. You have deployed ISA Server 2004 as an Internet-edge firewall at the branch offices and as a front-end firewall at the head office. You want to provide access to the secure site in the most cost-effective manner.

Scenario 1 Question

1. How will you configure the head office ISA Server computer and how will you configure DNS to enable the required access?

_____

_____

_____

Scenario 2

You are the network administrator for your organization. Your organization has just opened a branch office. You have deployed ISA Server 2004 in a 3-Leg perimeter configuration at the head office and now deploy ISA Server as a Bastion Host at the branch office. Users at the branch office need secure access to the IMAP and SMTP servers at the head office. No other users or servers require secure access to the IMAP and SMTP server from the Internet. You also host a Streaming Media server. You also need to publish a Web site for public access. The Web site includes links that reference content on the Streaming Media server by its Universal Naming Convention (UNC) path.

Scenario 2 Question

1. How will you configure the head office ISA Server computer to publish these Web services?

_____

_____

_____

Troubleshooting Lab

In this lab, you will troubleshoot an ISA Server Web publishing issue. You have configured the Coho Vineyard Secure Site Web publishing rule to require SSL connections from the Internet clients to the ISA Server computer. You have also configured the Web publishing rule to require authentication. However, because the Web site contains confidential information, you also need to configure SSL connections from the ISA Server computer to the back-end Web server.

Exercise 1: Configuring SSL Connections

1. On ISA1, in the ISA Server Management Console, click Firewall Policy.

2. Double-click Coho Vineyard Secure Site.

3. On the Bridging tab, clear the check box for Redirect Requests To HTTP Port. Select the check box for Redirect Requests To SSL Port. Click OK.

4. Click Apply to apply the changes.

Exercise 2: Testing the Configuration

1. On SERVER1, open Internet Explorer.

2. Connect to *https://secure.cohovineyard.com*. When prompted to log on, enter the user name and password of a domain user.

3. You will not be able to access the Web site.

Exercise 3: Enabling the SSL Connection

The reason why the SSL connection to the Web server failed is because there is no certificate installed on DC1 so when the ISA Server tried to bridge the SSL connection and establish a new SSL connection with DC1, the connection failed.

1. On DC1, open Internet Information Services (IIS) Manager.

2. Expand DC1 and then expand Web Sites.

3. Right-click Default Web Site and click Properties.

4. On the Directory Security tab, click Server Certificate.

5. On the Welcome To The Web Server Certificate Wizard page, click Next.

6. On the Server Certificate page, click Create A New Certificate and then click Next.

7. On the Delayed or Immediate Request page, click Send The Request Immediately To An Online Certification Authority. Click Next.

8. On the Name And Security Settings page, accept the default and click Next.

9. On the Organization Information page, type **Coho Vineyards** as the Organization Name and **Security** as the Organizational Unit Name. Click Next.

10. On the Your Site's Common Name page, type **DC1.Cohovineyard.com**. This name must match the name that ISA Server is using to connect to the Web server.

11. On the Geographical Information page, enter your country and region information. Click Next.

12. On the SSL Port page, click Next.

13. On the Choose A Certification Authority page, click Next.

14. On the Certificate Request Submission page, click Next.

15. On the Completing The Web Server Certificate Wizard page, click Finish.

16. Under Secure Communications, click Edit. Click Require Secure Channel and then click OK twice.

17. Close all open windows.

Exercise 4: Testing the Configuration

1. On SERVER1, open Internet Explorer.

2. Connect to *https://secure.cohovineyard.com*. When prompted to log on, enter the user name and password of a domain user. The connection should be successful.

Chapter Summary

- A Web publishing rule is a firewall rule that specifies how ISA Server will route incoming requests to internal Web servers. Server publishing rules are firewall rules that specify how ISA Server will route incoming requests to internal servers using any available protocol. To provide name resolution for internally and externally accessible resources, you may need to implement a split DNS configuration.

- Web publishing rules map incoming requests to the appropriate Web servers located on the internal or perimeter network. A Web listener is an ISA Server configuration object that defines how the ISA Server computer listens for HTTP requests and SSL requests. Path mapping is an ISA Server feature that enables ISA Server to redirect user requests to multiple internal Web servers or to multiple locations on the same Web server. Link translation is an ISA Server configuration object that enables ISA Server to replace internal server names on Web pages with server names that are accessible from the Internet.

- Secure Web publishing rules are a special type of Web publishing rules that use SSL to encrypt traffic between the server and client. SSL bridging means that the ISA Server operates as the end point for an SSL connection. The SSL connection could be between ISA Server and the client or between ISA Server and the internal Web server. In SSL tunneling mode, a client establishes a tunnel through the computer running ISA Server directly to the internal Web server.

- Server publishing rules are used on ISA Server to map a port number on an external interface of the ISA Server computer to the IP address of an internal server providing a specific service. Server publishing rules are fairly easy to configure. For most rules, all you need to do is choose the protocol that you want to publish and enter the IP address for the server that you are publishing. To troubleshoot ISA Server Web and server publishing issues check whether the resource is available on the local network, check name resolution and then check the publishing rule configuration.

- Authentication and Web publishing rules work together to ensure that users can gain access to an internal resource protected by ISA Server only if an access rule or publishing rule grants access to that resource. If the access rule requires authentication, then the user must provide authentication credentials before they will be granted access. You can configure authentication on ISA Server, on the internal Web server, or on both. ISA Server enables the use of RADIUS as well as the use of the RSA SecurID product from RSA Security, Inc. to authenticate users connecting to Web servers.

Exam Highlights

Before taking the exam, review the key points and terms that are presented in this chapter. You need to know this information.

Key Points

- One of the most common reasons why Web and server publishing rules fail is because of DNS resolution errors. If you see an exam question where users on one network can access a resource using the FQDN but users on another network cannot, then check the DNS resolution configuration.

- Firewall clients and Web proxy clients do not require a split DNS configuration to access the internal Web sites as they can use the Internet IP address to access the internal server. However, SecureNAT clients cannot connect to the internal Web servers using an Internet IP address so you must deploy a split DNS configuration for SecureNAT clients to access internal Web sites.

- If the ISA Server computer has multiple network adapters or multiple IP addresses associated with a specific network, remember that you can configure Web listeners or server publishing rules to listen on one or all of the IP addresses on that network.

- If you use a server name as the published server when you configure a Web publishing rule, the ISA Server computer must be able to resolve the DNS name for the internal Web server.

- SSL settings are configured on each publishing rule. This means that you can have one Web publishing rule that requires SSL connections to both client and server, and have another rule that requires only SSL connections between the ISA Server and the client computers. If you have multiple Web listeners (which requires multiple IP addresses on the relevant network), you can even use different certificates to authenticate the ISA Server computer.

- In order to redirect client requests to multiple back-end servers, you must configure multiple Web publishing rules. Each Web publishing rule can only redirect client requests to a single Web server.

- By default, Web publishing rules and secure Web publishing rules grant access to the All Users user set, which includes anonymous, or unauthenticated, users. To limit access to a Web publishing rule, remove the All Users user set and add the All Authenticated Users or a specific user set.

- If you are publishing resources using a server publishing rule, you can only configure authentication on the server hosting the internal resource. You cannot configure authentication on a server publishing rule.

Key Terms

link translation An ISA Server configuration object that enables ISA Server to replace internal server names on Web pages with server names that are accessible from this Internet.

pass-through authentication Refers to the ability of ISA Server to pass a client's authentication information to the destination server.

path mapping An ISA Server feature that enables ISA Server to redirect user requests to multiple internal Web servers or to multiple locations on the same Web server.

Remote Authentication Dial-In User Service (RADIUS) An industry-standard protocol used to provide authentication in heterogeneous environments.

server publishing rules Firewall rules that specify how ISA Server will route incoming requests to internal servers using any available protocol.

split DNS Uses two different DNS servers with the same DNS domain name to provide name resolution for internally and externally accessible resources. Both DNS servers are authoritative for the same domain name.

SSL bridging Occurs when the ISA Server computer operates as the endpoint for an SSL connection. The SSL connection could be between ISA Server and the client or between ISA Server and the internal Web server.

SSL tunneling Occurs when a client establishes an SSL tunnel through the ISA Server computer directly to the Web server using HTTPS.

Web listener An ISA Server configuration object that defines how the ISA Server computer listens for HTTP requests and SSL requests. The Web listener defines the network, IP address, and the port number on which ISA Server listens for client connections.

Web publishing rule A firewall rule that specifies how ISA Server will route incoming requests to internal Web servers.

Lesson 1 Review

1. You have deployed ISA Server 2004 as a Bastion Host. You need to provide a secure method of publishing your Web site. You also need to be able to configure ISA Server to inspect the contents of the packets to and from the Web server using application filters. What feature of ISA Server 2004 makes this possible?

   a. SSL Tunneling

   b. Link Translation

   c. SSL Bridging

   d. Path Mapping

   C is correct. SSL bridging allows ISA Server to accept SSL requests from clients and decrypt them to be inspected. A is incorrect because SSL tunneling simply passes SSL packets without looking at them. B is incorrect because link translation provides references to other internal Web servers and D is incorrect because path mapping redirects requests to alternate locations within your site.

2. You implement a split DNS configuration to support a Web site in your perimeter network. ISA Server 2004 is your external firewall. There is a NAT relationship between the External network and the perimeter network. What IP address should the Internet DNS record return for external clients to access the Web site?

   a. The internal IP address of the ISA Server computer

   b. The actual IP address of the Web server

   c. The IP address of your internal DNS server for name resolution

   d. The external IP address of the ISA Server computer

   D is correct. In a NAT relationship, the address of the external interface of the ISA Server computer should be returned to the client. A is incorrect because Internet clients cannot access the internal interface, and C is incorrect because the internal DNS would return the wrong address. B is incorrect because the client cannot directly access the address of the Web site.

3. You have a Web server in a perimeter network that hosts multiple Web sites that have links to each other. How can you enable access to these sites to users on the Internet using ISA Server 2004?

   Configure a Web publishing rule for each Web site that needs to be accessible from the Internet and use link translation to translate the links to the pages on the different sites.

Page
8-31

Lesson 2 Review

1. You are the network administrator for your organization and you use Active Directory in a single-domain environment. Your organization includes five branch offices that need access to the Web site that is hosted on a server in the perimeter network at your head office. These branch offices connect to the head office through the Internet. You need to ensure that only Authenticated Users can access the site. How will you configure ISA Server?

   Create a Web Listener for the External network and configure it to Require All Users to Authenticate. Then configure a Web publishing rule that allows traffic to the site and change the rule to apply to All Authenticated Users.

2. You have published your company's Web site under the public name of *www.cohovineyard.com*. The internal name of the Web server hosting the site is WebSrv01. The site does not contain any references to other servers. What must you configure in your Web Publishing rule to allow Internet clients to access the site properly?

   a. Configure a link translation dictionary entry to replace *www.cohovineyard.com* with WebSrv01 in the HTTP request header.

   b. Create a path mapping entry to map *www.cohovineyard.com* to WebSrv01.

   c. Configure a link translation dictionary entry to replace WebSrv01 with *www.cohovineyard.com* in the response header.

   d. Do nothing; the required level of link translation is enabled by default.

   D is correct. In this scenario the Link Translation Web Filter will automatically create a dictionary to replace references to WebSrv01 in the HTTP responses headers with the public name. A and C are incorrect because there are no absolute links that must be replaced. B is incorrect because path mapping redirects clients to other virtual directories.

3. You have just published two separate Web sites on one Web server by implementing Host Headers. The server is located on your perimeter network. You use ISA Server 2004 as your external firewall. Internet clients report that they always get the default Web site on the server, regardless of which two URLs they enter into their Web browser. What is the problem and how will you fix it?

   You must configure the Web Publishing Rule properties to Forward The Original Host Header Instead Of The Actual One. If not, all requests are routed to the Default Web site.

Page
8-45

Lesson 3 Review

1. True or False? ISA Server 2004 always requires a digital server certificate to be installed in order for Internet clients to connect to a Web site using SSL.

   False. When configured to use SSL tunneling, the ISA Server 2004 computer does not open or inspect the packets and therefore does not require a certificate to be installed. In all other Web publishing SSL scenarios where the client is establishing an SSL connection, a certificate must be installed on the ISA Server computer.

2. You publish two Web sites in your perimeter network. You need to configure secure access to both of them. There are many domain laptop users in your organization who work from the office and from home. You must ensure that only users who can authenticate to your domain from the Internet can get to one site, but allow public access to the other. You have installed Microsoft Certificate Server as an Enterprise Root Authority. What else must you do?

For the restricted site, issue a server certificate from your internal Certification Authority to your Web server and then export it and install in on the ISA Server computer. Then install client certificates from your internal CA on your users' laptops. For the public site, you should request a server certificate from a commercial CA to install on the ISA Server. Then configure two secure Web publishing rules, one for each Web site. Configure a Web Listener for the Public site to apply to All Users and another Web Listener for the Authenticated site that applies to All Authenticated Users. Configure the Web listener to Require Users to Authenticate and to use certificate authentication.

3. You are publishing a secure Web site that hosts a Web application that requires the actual IP address of the requesting client. You have installed a commercial CA certificate on the ISA Server computers. Users report that although they are able to establish a session to the Web site, they cannot use the application. How will you address this problem?

Configure the secure Web publishing rule to have Requests Appear to Come From the Original Client. Because ISA Server substitutes its own IP address in the header of the packet destined for the Web server, the application cannot determine the identity of the client.

Page
8-61

Lesson 4 Review

1. You have installed ISA Server 2004 as a front-end firewall protecting a perimeter network. You need to publish two separate FTP servers in the perimeter network. One of the FTP servers is for public users to download evaluation versions of your product. The other needs to be restricted to the Web Developers group in your domain so they can post code revisions from the Internet. You have only one IP address that you can use on the Internet. How will you configure ISA Server to meet these requirements?

You must create two server publishing rules for FTP. One of the publishing rules will allow anonymous access using the default ports to the public FTP site. The other rule will use an alternate port to publish the Web Developers site. The FTP filter for the second rule will have to be modified to allow read and write access to the site. You cannot restrict access to the Web Developers group using a server publishing rule, so you will need to configure the NTFS folder permissions on the FTP server. Note that this solution means that the passwords for the users in the Web Developers group are sent across the Internet in clear text when they authenticate to the FTP server. Ensure that this is an acceptable risk. As an alternative, you could require that the Web Developers use a VPN to connect to the FTP server and not publish the second FTP server to the Internet.

2. You have just published a secure Web site on your perimeter network using a server publishing rule. Internal users are able to access the site without receiving any error messages, but Internet users receive a warning whenever they access the site. You confirm that the ISA Server certificate is valid and that it was issued by a well-known commercial CA. What is the most likely cause for the warning message?

The probable reason for the warning message is that the certificate installed on the Web server is not trusted by the Internet clients. The server publishing rule can only be used in a SSL tunneling configuration, so the ISA Server certificate is not used by the rule. To fix the problem, you must replace the publishing rule with one that uses SSL bridging, or you must install a certificate from a commercial CA on the Web server.

3. You need to enable SSL access to an IMAP Server computer. What steps must you take to do this? (Choose two answers.)

   a. Install a server certificate on the ISA Server computer.

   b. Create a server publishing rule for IMAPS Server protocol.

   c. Install a server certificate on the IMAP Server computer.

   d. Create a Server publishing rule for IMAP Server protocol.

   e. Install a server certificate on both the IMAP Server computer and the ISA Server computer.

B and C are correct. You need to create a Server publishing rule for the IMAPS Server protocol and install a Server certificate on the IMAP Server computer so that it can accept SSL connections. A is incorrect because ISA Server just forwards the secure traffic to the messaging server and does not operate as an SSL endpoint. D is incorrect because the IMAP publishing rule will not use to the right port. E is incorrect because the SSL connection cannot be terminated on the ISA Server computer in a server publishing rule scenario.

Page 8-73
Lesson 5 Review

1. You have deployed Active Directory in a single-domain environment. You want to use RADIUS authentication for your internal Web site. What steps do you take to configure this? (Choose two answers.)

   a. Configure the ISA Server 2004 computer as a RADIUS Server computer.

   b. Register the RADIUS Server computer in Active Directory.

   c. Register the ISA Server 2004 computer in Active Directory.

   d. Configure the ISA Server 2004 computer as a RADIUS Client computer.

B and D are correct. You must install Internet Authentication Service and register the server in Active Directory, then configure the ISA Server computer to be a RADIUS Client computer. A is incorrect because the ISA Server computer never acts as the RADIUS Server computer. C is incorrect because the ISA Server computer does not need to be registered in Active Directory.

2. You are configuring a Web site that contains some confidential information. Most of the information on the Web site should be available to all users with user accounts in your domain, while some folders should be accessible only to managers. You are configuring a Web listener and a Web publishing rule to enable this access. How can you configure authentication on ISA Server and the Web server?

   a. Configure ISA Server to require authentication for all users. Allow the managers access to the Web site. Use IIS authentication to allow access to all authenticated users.

   b. Configure ISA Server to allow all users access to the Web site. Use IIS authentication to restrict access to the manager's folders.

   c. Configure ISA Server to require authentication for all users. Allow all authenticated users access to the Web site. Use IIS authentication to restrict access to the managers' folders.

   d. Configure ISA Server to allow all users access to the Web site. Use IIS authentication to restrict access to authenticated users.

   C is correct. Because only authenticated users should have access to the Web site, you can use ISA Server to enforce this requirement. Then use IIS authentication to limit access to the managers' folders. A would result in just managers being able to access the Web site. B would allow all anonymous access to the Web site except for the managers' folders. D would not restrict access to the managers' folders.

3. You have deployed ISA Server 2004 in a 3-Leg perimeter firewall configuration. The ISA Server computer is not a member of your Active Directory domain. You need to provide access to a Web site in your perimeter network. Only Domain Users should be able to access the site. What authentication method should you implement?

   a. RADIUS

   b. Digest

   c. Basic

   d. Integrated

   A is correct. RADIUS authentication would be the best solution because it allows ISA Server to pass domain credentials through a RADIUS server without being a domain member. All the other answers are incorrect because they require the ISA Server computer to be a domain member.

Case Scenario Exercises

Page
8-75
Scenario 1 Question

1. How will you configure the head office ISA Server computer and how will you configure DNS to enable the required access?

Implement a split DNS configuration. Configure the internal DNS server at the head office to return the internal addresses of the Web sites. Configure the Internet DNS server to return the IP address of the ISA Server external interface. Install Certification Services as an Enterprise CA on a Windows server and use it to issue a certificate to the ISA Server computer and to the Web server. Configure a secure Web publishing rule and configure a Web listener that accepts only SSL connections. Configure the Web listener to require all users to authenticate, and configure the Web publishing rule to use the All Authenticated Users user set. On the Web server, ensure that only members of the Managers group have access to the Sales folder by configuring the NTFS permissions on the folder. Finally, configure another Web publishing rule and Web listener for the public site that accepts HTTP connections and anonymous access.

Page
8-76
Scenario 2 Question

1. How will you configure the head office ISA Server computer to publish these Web services?

You need to configure four publishing rules. For secure IMAP access, create a server publishing rule that accepts IMAPS connections from the branch office network to the IMAP server. Then create a publishing rule for SMTPS from the branch office network to the SMTP server. Then create a Web publishing rule and Web listener for the public site. Configure the Web publishing rule to translate any UNC links to the Streaming Media server with its Web address. Finally, create a server publishing rule to publish the streaming media server.

9 Integrating ISA Server 2004 and Exchange Server

Exam Objectives in this Chapter:

- Create policy rules for mail server publishing
  - Publish a Microsoft Outlook Web Access server
  - Configure SMTP filtering and SMTP Message Screener

Why This Chapter Matters

If you ask most users in a corporate environment what the most important application they have running on their computers is, they will probably tell you it is their e-mail application. In many organizations, e-mail has become a business-critical application; if the e-mail server is not available, work seems to stop and everyone picks up the phone to call the help desk. A great deal of business communication is done by e-mail, both internally and with external clients or customers. At the same time, many users also spend time outside the office and would like to have the same access to e-mail when they are out of the office as they have in the office.

Just to make life interesting for messaging administrators, e-mail has also become one of the primary means of disrupting corporate networks. E-mail is the most common means for spreading viruses and other malicious software. And e-mail seems to be the advertising medium of choice, as our mailboxes are filled with unsolicited commercial e-mail or spam.

Microsoft provides a great messaging server—Microsoft Exchange Server 2003. Exchange Server is a powerful e-mail and collaboration server that can be accessed using a wide array of messaging clients. Any of these clients can be used on the internal network, as well as from the Internet. And this is where Microsoft Internet Security and Acceleration (ISA) Server 2004 comes in—ISA Server does an admirable job of securing connections from the Internet to the Exchange Server computers. Moreover, ISA Server can be used to secure connections from other Simple Mail Transport Protocol (SMTP) servers on the Internet to the Exchange Server computer. In this role, ISA Server can also be used to block unwanted e-mail.

Lessons in this Chapter:

- Lesson 1: Configuring ISA Server to Secure SMTP Traffic. 9-3
- Lesson 2: Configuring ISA Server to Secure Web Client Connections 9-26
- Lesson 3: Configuring ISA Server to Secure Outlook Client Connections 9-38

Before You Begin

This chapter presents the skills and concepts related to publishing Exchange Server to the Internet. If you plan to complete the practices and lab in this chapter, you should prepare the following:

- A Microsoft Windows Server 2003 (Standard Edition or Enterprise Edition) computer installed as DC1 and configured as a domain controller in the *cohovineyard.com* domain.

- A second Windows Server 2003 computer installed as ISA1 and configured as a domain member in the *cohovineyard.com* domain. This server should have two network interfaces installed.

- A Windows Server 2003 server installed as MAIL1. This server needs to be a member of the *cohovineyard.com* domain and have a default installation of Exchange Server 2003 installed on it. The Exchange Server computer requires at least two mailboxes configured on it.

- A Microsoft Windows Server 2003 (Standard Edition or Enterprise Edition) computer installed as SERVER1. This computer should not be a member of the *cohovineyard.com* domain. This server should be located on the same network as the external interface of the ISA Server computer. This server should be running the Domain Name System (DNS) Server and the DNS client setting should be configured to use the server's Internet Protocol (IP) address as the DNS server.

- To complete the Outlook publishing practices, you also need to have a computer running Microsoft Outlook 2003 available on the same network as the external interface of the ISA Server computer. You can run Outlook 2003 on SERVER1 or, if you have Outlook 2003 installed on CLIENT1, you can configure the IP address for CLIENT1 so that it is on the external network.

Lesson 1: Configuring ISA Server to Secure SMTP Traffic

One way that ISA Server can secure Exchange Server is by providing enhanced options for filtering all SMTP messages sent from the Internet to the computers running Exchange Server. This lesson explains how to publish SMTP servers and how to configure SMTP filtering.

After this lesson, you will be able to

- Describe known SMTP messaging security issues
- Implement ISA Server to secure SMTP traffic
- Configure SMTP application filter
- Implement SMTP Message Screener
- Plan an SMTP Message Screener implementation

Estimated lesson time: 40 minutes

Known SMTP Security Issues

Virtually all e-mail sent on the Internet is sent using SMTP. To receive e-mail from the Internet, your organization must have an SMTP server that is accessible to other SMTP servers. However, SMTP has some security weaknesses, both at a protocol level and in terms of the content sent using SMTP messages.

SMTP Protocol-Level Exploits

SMTP servers are vulnerable to several protocol level exploits including buffer-overflow attacks and SMTP command attacks.

Buffer-overflow attacks   A buffer-overflow attack is triggered when a program or process tries to store more data in a memory buffer than the buffer's designed capacity. The extra information can spill into adjacent buffers, corrupting or overwriting the valid data that they hold. In buffer-overflow attacks, the extra data may contain code designed to trigger specific actions, in effect sending new instructions to the attacked computer. Buffer-overflow attacks can be mounted against an organization's SMTP server by sending large SMTP commands. The best deterrent to a buffer-overflow attack against the SMTP server is to stop the attacker at the network perimeter, before the exploit ever finds its way into the corporate network.

Attackers use buffer-overflow exploits to disable specific server services with the intent of mounting a denial-of-service (DoS) attack, either by disabling a specific service on the target computer or by taking the entire machine offline. More elaborate buffer-overflow exploits can be used to disable key security features and allow the attacker to run commands of his choice on the targeted machine.

> **Important**   These SMTP vulnerabilities are well known, and most SMTP servers are either not vulnerable to the exploits or can be patched so that they are not vulnerable. However, ISA Server can block the attack at the network perimeter so that the attack does not reach the SMTP server.

SMTP command attacks   SMTP servers must support a standard set of commands that are used to send and receive SMTP messages. Attackers can use the commands to mount buffer-overflow attacks or to send malformed commands that the system programmers did not anticipate. Command-manipulation attacks can lead to system compromise by giving an attacker access to key files, the ability to overwrite files, or to inject Trojan horse programs onto a mail server.

Some SMTP commands are optional. Some commands, such as EXPN and VRFY, if configured incorrectly, can be used to find a list of recipients on the server. If these commands are not required, they can be disabled at the firewall so that the SMTP server does not receive them.

Unwanted or Malicious E-Mail Attacks

The most prominent security challenge related to e-mail is the number of unwanted and malicious e-mails that are sent across the Internet. These e-mails can be grouped in two categories: unwanted junk e-mail that consumes computer resources and user time but does not harm the computer, and malicious e-mails that contain viruses, worms, or Trojan horse programs.

Unwanted E-Mail   It has been estimated that unwanted e-mail messages consume more than 50 percent of total bandwidth usage on the Internet today. Unwanted e-mail leads to the following problems:

- Wasted bandwidth on both internal and Internet networks, which may lead to increased Internet bandwidth cost, and increased nonproductive traffic on the corporate network

- Increased resource usage, including disk space, processor, and memory use on e-mail servers

- Decreased employee productivity due to reading and deleting unwanted e-mail

- Increased administrative costs as network administrators attempt to reduce the negative effects of unwanted e-mail

- Increased exposure to legal liability to users who may view offensive unwanted e-mail messages

Most organizations attempt to filter unwanted e-mail before it gets to the e-mail servers. The challenge is to determine which e-mail messages are unwanted, yet allow valid e-mail messages into your mail systems. To filter junk e-mail, you must use an application-layer filter. These filters can inspect the SMTP messages transporting unwanted e-mail messages and filter out messages based on factors such as source e-mail address, keywords in the subject line or message body, and attachment name or extension.

Malicious E-Mail   Viruses and worms sent by e-mail can cause a tremendous amount of damage to corporate networks. Viruses and worm attacks are responsible for the following:

- Destruction of data on servers and workstations

- DoS attacks on servers and workstations

- Lost employee productivity because a workstation or network server is unavailable

- Distribution of corporate secrets by means of mass-mailing worms

- Increased administrative costs due to repairing damaged workstations and servers

- Increased bandwidth use on the corporate network and Internet connection secondary to mass-mailing worms and DoS attacks

Viruses and worms most commonly access an organization's network through e-mail. Virus writers realize that e-mail is a critical service in most organizations and they exploit this fact by crafting viruses and worms that spread by e-mail. When a user opens an e-mail attachment that contains dangerous code, the code is released to the user's computer and then spreads to the rest of the network. A single infected host can damage virtually every networked device in a short period.

Effective prevention of viruses and worms requires organizations to deal with the viruses at multiple levels. Antivirus programs should be installed on the e-mail servers as well as on the client computers. Another level in the defense is to block all e-mail attachments at the perimeter. An SMTP application filter on the network perimeter can then examine all e-mail attachments and scan the attachment for viruses, worms, and other dangerous code. Based on the results of the scan and its rule configuration, the application filter can delete the message, quarantine the message for further inspection, or forward the message to the e-mail server.

How to Configure ISA Server to Secure SMTP Traffic

ISA Server provides three components for securing SMTP traffic. The first is the Mail Server Wizard, which can be used to publish the SMTP server to the Internet. The second component is the SMTP Message Screener, which can help reduce the amount of unwanted e-mail entering the organization. The third component is the SMTP application filter, which can be used to block buffer-overflow attacks or SMTP command-based attacks on Exchange Server.

Mail Server Wizard

You can use the Mail Server Wizard to make Exchange Server computers available to Internet clients. The Mail Server Wizard includes several options, one of which is publishing an SMTP server. When publishing an Exchange Server computer as an SMTP server, you create a server publishing rule that accepts SMTP traffic on the ISA Server computer's external interface and forwards the packets to the Exchange Server computer.

> **Tip** The Mail Server Wizard can be used to configure all types of access to your organization's Exchange Server computers. When you run the wizard, you choose the access required based on server or client type and the Mail Server Wizard configures a Web or server publishing rule with the required protocols and settings.

To configure ISA Server to publish an Exchange Server computer as an SMTP Server computer, complete the following procedure:

1. In the ISA Server Management Console, click Firewall Policy. On the Tasks tab, select Publish a Mail Server.

2. On the Welcome To The New Mail Server Publishing Wizard page, type a name for the publishing rule, and then click Next.

3. On the Select Access Type page, shown in Figure 9-1, click Server-To-Server Communication: SMTP, NNTP, and then click Next.

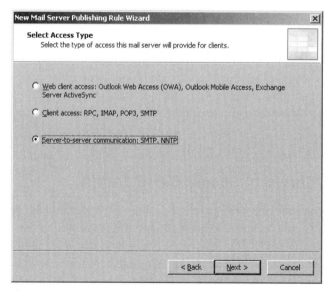

Figure 9-1 Configuring a mail server publishing rule

4. On the Select Services page, select SMTP, as shown in Figure 9-2. Click Next.

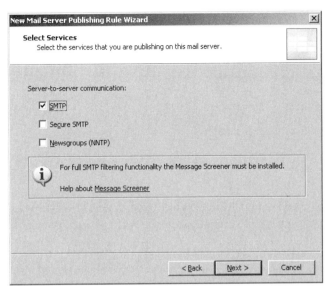

Figure 9-2   Configuring a mail server publishing rule to publish an SMTP server

5. On the Select Server page, type the IP address of the computer running Exchange Server, and then click Next.

6. On the IP Addresses page, select External, and then click Next.

7. On the Completing The New Mail Server Publishing Rule Wizard page, review the configuration, and then click Finish.

Note   This procedure describes how to configure a publishing rule for inbound SMTP traffic. To send SMTP messages to other servers on the Internet, you must also configure an access rule that allows SMTP traffic from the SMTP servers on your internal network to the External network.

SMTP Application Filter

ISA Server 2004 provides application-layer filtering to help prevent Internet attackers from using buffer-overflow commands to disable or take control of your computer running Exchange Server. The SMTP application-layer filter inspects the commands included in all incoming SMTP communications. You can configure the SMTP filter to limit the size of the SMTP command sequences as well to block specific commands.

SMTP Message Screener

The ISA Server 2004 SMTP Message Screener can be used to control incoming SMTP mail by performing application-layer inspection of all SMTP messages. The Message

Screener can scan the messages and examine the attachments and then block or hold messages for later inspection.

You can configure the SMTP Message Screener to block or hold incoming or outgoing e-mail using the following parameters:

- Source or destination e-mail domain
- Source or destination e-mail address
- Attachment size, file extension, or file name
- Keywords in the mail subject or body

The SMTP Message Screener can block or hold messages sent from the internal network in the same way that it does for messages entering the network.

> **Note** All the options for securing SMTP e-mail are available regardless of which SMTP server you use in your organization. You can use Microsoft Exchange Server in this situation, or you can use any other SMTP server.

How to Configure the SMTP Application Filter

To make an Exchange Server computer accessible to other SMTP servers on the Internet, you must configure a publishing rule that publishes the Exchange Server computer using the SMTP port. When you configure a rule that uses SMTP, the SMTP application filter is enabled for that rule automatically. The SMTP application filter accepts the traffic, inspects it, and forwards it to internal SMTP servers only if the SMTP filter allows it.

What Is SMTP Command Filtering?

SMTP servers use a set of commands (also called *verbs*) to initiate an SMTP connection between servers and then to transmit SMTP messages. The SMTP application filter filters SMTP traffic by examining these SMTP commands. The SMTP commands supported by most SMTP servers are listed in Table 9-1.

Table 9-1   Supported SMTP Commands

SMTP Command	Command Function
HELO	Sent by an SMTP client or server to identify itself, usually with a domain name.
EHLO	Used by an SMTP server to identify its support for Extended Simple Mail Transfer Protocol (ESMTP) commands.
MAIL FROM	Identifies the sender of the message; used in the form MAIL FROM:.
RCPT TO	Identifies the message recipients; used in the form RCPT TO:.

Table 9-1   Supported SMTP Commands

SMTP Command	Command Function
TURN, ATRN, ETRN	These commands are used to download messages from an SMTP server that has queued messages sent to a domain name. TURN does not require any security, ATRN requires authentication, and ETRN can confirm the requesting server's identity based on IP address.
SIZE	Provides a mechanism by which the SMTP server can indicate the maximum-size message supported.
PIPELINING	Provides the ability to send a stream of commands without waiting for a response after each command.
CHUNKING	An ESMTP command that replaces the DATA command. This command sends a BDAT command with an argument that contains the total number of bytes in a message. The receiving server counts the bytes in the message and, when the message size equals the value sent by the BDAT command, the server assumes it has received all of the message data.
DATA	Sent by a client to initiate the transfer of message content
DSN	An ESMTP command that enables delivery status notifications
RSET	Nullifies the entire message transaction and resets the buffer
VRFY	Verifies that a mailbox is available for message delivery on the destination server
HELP	Returns a list of commands that are supported by the SMTP service
QUIT	Terminates the session

See Also   Exchange Server supports several additional commands. For a complete list of commands supported by Exchange Server, see Appendix A of the *Exchange Server 2003 Transport and Routing Guide* located at *http://www.microsoft.com/technet/prodtechnol/ exchange/2003/library/extransrout.mspx*.

The SMTP filter can be configured to disable specific SMTP commands. When an SMTP server or client uses a command that is defined but disabled, the filter stops the command and closes that connection. For example, if you disable the VRFY command, ISA Server will block all SMTP connections that use this command. When a client uses a command that is not recognized by the SMTP filter, the connection is also denied. For example, the SMTP filter does not define the TURN command, so TURN commands will be blocked by the SMTP filter.

Exam Tip   If you disable or delete an SMTP command, that command will be blocked by ISA Server. If you get an exam question in which SMTP messages are not flowing through the ISA Server computer, and you are given some information about how the SMTP filter is configured, make sure that configuration is not blocking the message flow. By default, the SMTP filter allows all required SMTP commands.

Each SMTP command also has a maximum length that specifies the number of bytes allowed for each command. If an attacker sends a command that exceeds the number of bytes allowed for the command, ISA Server drops the connection and prevents the attacker from communicating with the SMTP server. For example, the default maximum length for the RCPT TO command is 266 bytes. If an SMTP connection uses a longer RCPT TO command than this limit, the connection is dropped.

Note   The SMTP Request for Comment (RFC) considers the AUTH command to be part of the MAIL FROM command. For this reason, the SMTP filter blocks MAIL FROM commands only when they exceed the length of the MAIL FROM and AUTH commands issued (when AUTH is enabled). For example, if you specify the maximum length of MAIL FROM as 266 bytes and AUTH as 1024 bytes, the message will be blocked only if the MAIL FROM command exceeds 1290 bytes.

If an SMTP command is blocked because it violates one of the SMTP filter's conditions, the blocked message will only be logged when the SMTP Filter event alert is enabled. This alert is disabled by default.

How to Configure the SMTP Application Filter

The SMTP filter is installed and enabled by default. When you publish an SMTP mail server, or enable an SMTP access rule, all SMTP messages are filtered using the default policy. To modify the default configuration of the SMTP filter, complete the following procedure:

1. In the ISA Server Management Console, click Add-ins.

2. In the Details pane, on the Applications Filters tab, double-click SMTP Filter.

3. On the SMTP Commands tab, as shown in Figure 9-3, click the applicable command, and then click Edit.

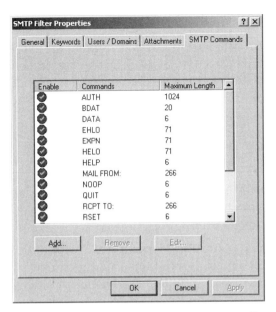

Figure 9-3   Configuring the SMTP application filter

4. In the SMTP Command Rule dialog box, shown in Figure 9-4, you can disable the command by clearing the Enable SMTP command check box.

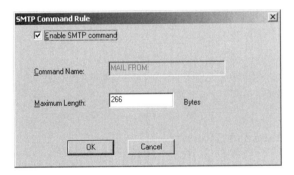

Figure 9-4   Configuring the SMTP command rule

5. To modify the maximum length for the SMTP command, type the maximum length of the command line (in bytes) for the command in the Maximum Length field.

6. To add an SMTP command to the filter, on the SMTP Commands tab, click Add and enter the command name and maximum length of the command line.

How to Implement SMTP Message Screener

The SMTP Message Screener works with the SMTP filter to intercept and filter SMTP traffic. The Message Screener provides additional functionality by inspecting the SMTP message contents and enabling the filtering of unwanted and malicious e-mail.

How Message Screener Filters Messages

The Message Screener must be installed on a server running the Microsoft Internet Information Services (IIS) 5.0 or IIS 6.0 SMTP service. The Message Screener component can be installed on the computer running ISA Server, on a computer running Exchange Server, or on any other IIS 5.0 or IIS 6.0 SMTP server in the internal network or in a perimeter network (also known as a demilitarized zone, or DMZ).

SMTP Message Screener can be configured to filter incoming mail based on the following:

- **The information in the MAIL FROM SMTP command**   The MAIL FROM command specifies the source SMTP address for the e-mail message. This is used for sender and domain name filtering.

- **The information in the Content-Disposition header field for each attachment**   This field commonly contains the attachment file name and extension. SMTP Message Screener can filter attachments by extension, by name, or by size.

- **Keywords in the message subject or body**   This is used for filtering the message subject and the body, either text/plain or text/html content type.

SMTP Message Screener can be configured to delete e-mail messages, hold e-mail messages for later inspection, or forward e-mail messages to a specific e-mail account for further examination and analysis.

> **Important**   If SMTP Message Screener is installed but not enabled and configured, Message Screener will drop all messages.

How to Implement SMTP Message Screener

SMTP Message Screener is an optional component that is included with ISA Server. This component is unique in that it need not be installed on a server running ISA Server but can be installed on any server running the SMTP service included with IIS 5.0 or IIS 6.0. The following steps provide a high-level overview of how to implement SMTP Message Screener:

1. Install the SMTP service on the IIS server on which you will install the SMTP Message Screener. Only the SMTP service and the default components included with this service are required.

2. Install the SMTP Message Screener on the IIS server. To install the Message Screener, run Setup from the ISA Server CD-ROM and choose a custom installation. Install only the Message Screener component.

3. Configure a user account on the Message Screener computer with access to the ISA Server computer. Do this by running the SMTPCred.exe program from the FPC\Program Files\Microsoft ISA Server directory on the ISA Server 2004 CD. When you run SMTPCred.exe, enter the username, domain, and password of a user who has administrative permissions on ISA Server.

> **Note**   This user account is required in order for the SMTP service to interact with the ISA Firewall service. If you install Message Screener on the ISA Server computer, this step is not required.

4. Configure an SMTP mail server publishing rule that publishes the SMTP server running Message Screener. If Message Screener is installed on an IIS Server on your internal network, then configure the SMTP publishing rule to forward all SMTP messages to that server.

> **Exam Tip**   If you install Message Screener on the ISA Server computer, you must configure the SMTP server to listen only on the IP address assigned to the Internal network, and then configure the server publishing rule to forward all SMTP messages to that IP address. You must also configure the SMTP server to forward all messages for the internal domain to the internal Exchange Server computers. The practice at the end of this lesson provides the detailed steps used to complete this configuration.

5. Configure the Message Screener properties on the SMTP filter. To configure the Message Screener properties in the ISA Server Management Console, expand Configuration, and then click Add-ins.

6. On the Application Filters tab, double-click SMTP Filter. You can configure the settings listed in Table 9-2.

Table 9-2   Configuring the SMTP Message Screener

Tab	Use This Setting To
Keywords (see Figure 9-5)	Provide a string that the Message Screener will look for in e-mails. You can select whether the action is applied if the keyword is found in the message header, the body, or both. You can also specify an action for when a message meets the keyword criteria. You can configure the Message Screener to delete the message, hold the message, or forward the message to a specified mailbox.
Users/Domains (see Figure 9-6)	Add the names of senders or of entire domains for which e-mail will be blocked. When the SMTP sender address matches the blocked senders or domains list, the message will be deleted.

Table 9-2   Configuring the SMTP Message Screener

Tab	Use This Setting To
Attachments (see Figure 9-7)	Configure how Message Screener will filter attachments. You can configure Message Screener to filter attachments based on attachment name, attachment extension, or attachment size limit. You can also specify an action for when a message meets the attachment criteria. You can configure the Message Screener to delete the message, hold the message, or forward the message to a specified mailbox.

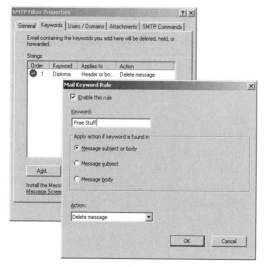

Figure 9-5   Configuring the keyword option on the SMTP Message Screener

Exam Tip   Notice that you can configure the SMTP Message Screener to delete a message, hold a message, or forward a message to a specified mailbox if it meets the Message Screener criteria. Check this setting if Message Screener is blocking messages from getting to a user mailbox as expected, but other expected actions are not happening.

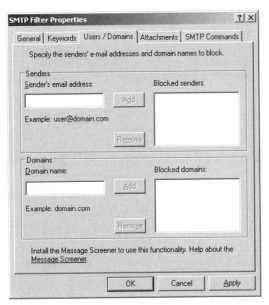

Figure 9-6   Configuring the user/groups option on the SMTP Message Screener

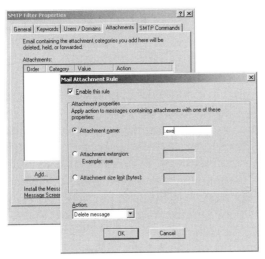

Figure 9-7   Configuring the attachments option on the SMTP Message Screener

See Also   For more information about configuring the SMTP application filter and Message Screener, see the Technet article, Using the ISA Server 2004 SMTP Filter and Message Screener, located at *http://www.microsoft.com/technet/prodtechnol/isa/2004/plan/smtpfilter.mspx.*

Guidelines for Implementing SMTP Message Screener

The SMTP filter must be installed on the ISA Server that is used to publish SMTP servers and used to configure access rules for sending SMTP messages to the Internet. However, because Message Screener need not be installed on a computer running ISA Server, you have several options for deploying Message Screener. One of the questions that you must address when deploying SMTP Message Screener is where to install the Message Screener component. You have two options:

■ **Install Message Screener on ISA Server**   You can install Message Screener on the server running ISA Server and configure it to filter inbound messages. In this configuration, ISA Server Firewall services forwards all messages to the SMTP service which scans the messages. This configuration is less secure than installing Message Screener on another server because Message Screener requires that the SMTP service be installed on the ISA Server computer. Moreover, this configuration is not scalable for larger organizations. For these reasons, installing Message Screener on ISA Server is recommended only for situations in which no additional servers are available and in which ISA Server is not operating as an Internet-edge firewall.

■ **Install Message Screener on another IIS server**   This is the more secure configuration because the IIS Server running the SMTP service is not directly accessible from the Internet. The configuration is shown in Figure 9-8. The ISA Server can filter the SMTP commands, and only allowed packets will reach the SMTP Message Screener server. This option is also scalable because the Firewall service and SMTP Message Screener are separated. For maximum security, the IIS Server running Message Screener should be located in a perimeter network and the server should not be a member server in the internal domain. However, if the SMTP server is not a member of the internal domain and is also configured as the SMTP relay server for Post Office Protocol 3 (POP3) or Internet Message Access Protocol 4 (IMAP4) clients, users will not be able to authenticate to this server to relay messages. Installing the Message Screener component on a server in the perimeter network requires additional ISA Server configuration because you must configure server publishing rules or access rules between the perimeter network and the internal network, but this option is more secure.

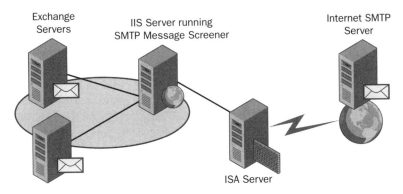

Figure 9-8   Deploying the SMTP Message Screener on a protected IIS Server computer

 Important   Exchange Server 2003 enables the option to block an SMTP connection based on the IP address of the connecting SMTP server. If you configure the SMTP Message Screener, you will not be able to use this feature on Exchange Server 2003, because all messages will come from the computer that is running Message Screener.

The second design question is whether to scan inbound messages only or both inbound and outbound messages. Here again, you have two options:

■ **Use Message Screener for inbound messages only**   In this configuration, you configure ISA Server to publish the server running Message Screener, and configure Message Screener to forward all allowed messages to the computers running Exchange Server on the internal network. You also configure the access rule on ISA Server to allow the internal computers running Exchange Server to send SMTP messages to the Internet. Use this configuration if your organization has no requirement to scan outbound message contents.

■ **Use Message Screener for inbound and outbound messages**   In this configuration, you configure ISA Server to publish the server running Message Screener, and configure Message Screener to forward all approved messages to the computers running Exchange Server on the internal network. You also configure the internal computers running Exchange Server to send all SMTP messages to the server running Message Screener. Message Screener scans outbound messages and then forwards the messages through ISA Server to the Internet. In this scenario, the server running Message Screener must be able to use DNS to locate the mail servers for both the internal and external DNS domains. Use this configuration to ensure the security of outbound e-mail. For example, you can use Message Screener to scan outbound messages for specific content or to block messages with specified attachments.

Real World   Keeping Unwanted E-Mail Out of Your Organization

If you are using Internet e-mail, it is virtually inevitable that you will be exposed to unwanted e-mail. If you are responsible for managing a messaging infrastructure for your organization, one of your biggest headaches will be keeping such unwanted e-mail out of your organization. Although you can use ISA Server to provide some protection against spam and viruses, the ISA Server Message Screener just doesn't provide enough functionality for most organizations.

There are much better options available for keeping unwanted e-mail out of your organization. One option is to make use of the spam-filtering features included with Exchange Server 2003. One of the options available in Exchange Server 2003 is the use of a real-time block list (RBL). To configure RBL support, configure the Exchange Server computer to send a query to an RBL provider. The RBL provider maintains a list of all the IP addresses for known sources of spam. When you enable RBL filtering, the Exchange Server computer will send a query to the RBL provider to check if the IP address of the SMTP server that is attempting to make a connection is on the RBL. If the address is on the list, the connection is dropped. Exchange Server 2003 also supports Intelligent Message Filter, which allows you to configure what levels of spam will be blocked at the Exchange Server computers and what messages will be sent to the Junk E-Mail folder in Outlook 2003.

There are also excellent third-party products available for message screening using SMTP gateway servers. These products provide RBL support, advanced message scanning functionality and advanced management options so that administrators and users can configure white lists (e-mail senders whose messages should never be blocked) and black lists (e-mail senders whose messages should always be blocked). Many of these products integrate smoothly with ISA Server. (For a list of these products, see *http://www.microsoft.com/isaserver/partners*.)

A critical component in your efforts to keep unwanted e-mail out of your network is to implement multiple-level antivirus scanning. You should configure an antivirus scanner to scan all SMTP messages on the ISA Server or SMTP server through which the e-mail enters your organization. You should also enable an Exchange-specific antivirus product on your Exchange Server computers. Finally, make sure that the antivirus software on every user's desktop is functioning and up-to-date.

Practice: Configuring ISA Server to Secure SMTP Traffic

In this practice, you will configure the SMTP application filter and Message Screener to block SMTP messages. To do this, you will configure a client on the external network in your test environment to send messages to the Exchange server on your internal network. Then you will configure an SMTP publishing rule and an SMTP access rule to enable the flow of SMTP traffic through ISA Server. Finally, you will configure the Message Screener and test its functionality.

> **Note**   This practice demonstrates how to configure ISA Server to secure SMTP traffic in the test environment and does not include all of the steps required to enable SMTP messaging in a production environment. For example, in order to receive e-mail from the Internet, you must configure Mail Exchanger (MX) records on the DNS servers that host your DNS zone on the Internet.

Exercise 1: Configuring an SMTP Mail Server Publishing Rule

1. Log on to ISA1 as an Administrator.

2. Open the ISA Server Management Console, expand ISA1 if necessary, and click Firewall Policy.

3. On the Firewall Policy task pane Tasks tab, select Publish A Mail Server.

4. On the Welcome To The New Mail Server Publishing Wizard page, type **Coho Vineyard Mail** as the rule name, and then click Next.

5. On the Select Access Type page, click Server-To-Server Communication: SMTP, NNTP, and then click Next.

6. On the Select Services page, select SMTP. Click Next.

7. On the Select Server page, type **10.10.0.12** as the Server IP address of the computer running Exchange Server, and then click Next.

8. On the IP Addresses page, select External, and then click Next.

9. On the Completing The New Mail Server Publishing Rule Wizard page, review the configuration, and then click Finish.

> **Note**   Because you do not have an SMTP server configured on the external network of the ISA Server computer, you will use Microsoft Outlook Express to test SMTP message flow. Outlook Express uses SMTP to send messages, but uses POP3 or IMAP4 to receive messages. To enable POP3 access, you must configure a server rule that publishes the internal Exchange Server computer as a POP3 server.

10. On the Tasks tab of the Firewall Policy task pane, select Publish A Mail Server.

11. On the Welcome To The New Mail Server Publishing Wizard page, type **POP3 Access** as the rule name, and then click Next.

12. On the Select Access Type page, click Client Access: RPC, IMAP, POP3, SMTP, and then click Next.

13. On the Select Services page, select POP3 under Standard Ports. Click Next.

14. On the Select Server page, type **10.10.0.12** as the Server IP address of the computer running Exchange Server, and then click Next.

15. On the IP Addresses page, select External, and then click Next.

16. On the Completing The New Mail Server Publishing Rule Wizard page, review the configuration, and then click Finish.

> **Note**   By default, the Microsoft Exchange POP3 Service is disabled on Exchange Server 2003. You must enable this service before testing e-mail flow.

Exercise 2: Configuring Outbound SMTP Traffic

1. On the Tasks tab, click Create New Access Rule.

2. On the Welcome To The New Access Rule Wizard, type **SMTP Outbound** as the name for the access rule, and then click Next.

3. On the Rule Action page, select Allow, and then click Next.

4. On the Protocols page, in the This Rule Applies To list, click Selected Protocols, and then click Add.

5. In the Add Protocols dialog box, expand Mail, and then select SMTP. Click Add, and then click Close to close the Add Protocols dialog box. On the Protocols page, click Next.

6. On the Access Rule Sources page, click Add to open the Add Network Entities dialog box, expand Networks, select Internal, click Add, and then click Close. On the Access Rule Sources page, click Next.

7. On the Access Rule Destinations page, click Add to open the Add Network Entities dialog box, click Networks, select the External network (representing the Internet), click Add, and then click Close. On the Access Rule Destinations page, click Next.

8. On the User Sets page, accept the default user set of All Users and click Next.

9. On the Completing The New Access Rule Wizard page, review the configuration, and then click Finish.

10. Click Apply to apply the changes.

Exercise 3: Testing SMTP Traffic Flow

1. On SERVER1, open the DNS Administration Console.

2. In the *Cohovineyard.com* zone, create a new resource record for *Mail .cohovineyard.com*. Configure the resource record with the IP address of the external interface of the ISA Server computer.

3. On the Start menu, point to All Programs, and then click Outlook Express.

4. The Internet Connection Wizard starts. On the Your Name page, in the Display Name field, type the name of a user with a mailbox on MAIL1. Click Next.

5. On the Internet E-mail Address page, in the E-mail Address field, type the e-mail address for the user account you are using, and then click Next.

6. On the E-mail Server Names page, enter **Mail.cohovineyard.com** as both the Incoming mail (POP3, IMAP, or HTTP) server and the Outgoing mail (SMTP) server. Click Next.

7. On the Internet Mail Logon page, type the user name and password. Click Next.

8. On the Congratulations page, click Finish.

9. Send an e-mail to the user account that you are using (use the format *user@cohovineyard.com*).

10. Click Send/Recv. The message you sent should be returned to your Inbox.

Exercise 4: Installing the SMTP Service on the ISA Server Computer

1. On ISA1, open Add Or Remove Programs from the Control Panel.

2. Click Add/Remove Windows Components.

3. In the Windows Components dialog box, click Application Server, and then click Details. Do not select the check box for Application Server.

4. In the Application Server dialog box, click Internet Information Services (IIS), and then click Details. Do not select the check box for Internet Information Services (IIS).

5. In the Internet Information Services (IIS) dialog box, click the SMTP Service check box, and then click OK.

6. Click OK in the Internet Information Services (IIS) dialog box, and then click OK to close the Application Server dialog box. In the Windows Components dialog box, click Next.

7. If you see an Insert Disk dialog box, provide the Windows Server 2003 installation CD-ROM.

8. When the installation completes, click Finish.

> **Note** Because the SMTP Message Screener component is installed on the same server as ISA Server, you must configure the SMTP server to listen only on the internal IP address of the computer running ISA Server. Then you will configure ISA Server to publish that IP address as the SMTP server. You must also configure the SMTP server to relay messages for the internal domain, *cohovineyard.com*.

9. Open Internet Information Services (IIS) from the Administrative Tools folder.

10. Expand ISA1 (local computer), then right-click Default SMTP Virtual Server and click Properties.

11. On the General tab, in the IP address list, click 10.10.0.1.

12. Click OK to close the Default SMTP Virtual Server Properties.

13. Expand Default SMTP Virtual Server, then right-click Domains and point to New, and then click Domain.

14. On the Welcome To The New SMTP Domain Wizard page, accept the default of Remote, and then click Next.

15. On the Domain Name page, type **cohovineyard.com** and click Finish.

16. Expand Domains, right-click *cohovineyard.com*, and click Properties.

17. On the General tab, click Allow incoming mail to be relayed to this domain. Under Route domain, click Forward All Mail To Smart Host and type **[10.10.0.12]**. Click OK.

18. Right-click Default SMTP Virtual Server and click Stop. Right-click Default SMTP Virtual Server again and click Start.

19. Close Internet Information Services (IIS) Manager.

Exercise 5: Installing the SMTP Message Screener

1. On ISA1, in the Add Or Remove Programs dialog box, click Microsoft ISA Server 2004. Click Change/Remove.

2. On the Welcome To The Installation Wizard For Microsoft ISA Server 2004 page, click Next.

3. On the Program Maintenance page, click Modify, and then click Next.

4. On the Custom Setup page, click the icon next to Message Screener and select This Feature Will Be Installed On Local Hard Drive. Click Next.

5. On the Services page, click Next.

6. On the Ready To Modify The Program page, click Install.

7. On the Installation Wizard Completed page, click Finish.

Exercise 6: Configure the SMTP Publishing Rule and the Message Screener

1. Open the ISA Server Management Console. In the console tree, click Firewall Policy.

2. Right-click Coho Vineyard Mail SMTP Server, and click Properties. On the To tab, type **10.10.0.1** as the server IP address. Click OK.

3. Expand Configuration, and then click Add-ins. On the Application Filters tab, right-click SMTP Filter and click Properties.

4. On the Keywords tab, click Add to open the Mail Keyword Rule dialog box. In Keyword, type **test**. In the Action drop-down list, select Hold Message. Click OK.

5. Click OK to close the SMTP Filter Properties dialog box.

6. Click Apply to apply the changes.

Exercise 7: Test the SMTP Message Screener Configuration

1. On SERVER1, open Outlook Express.

2. Create an e-mail and send it to *user@cohovineyard.com*. Use a subject of Test.

3. Click Send/Recv. Confirm that the message is not delivered to the user Inbox. This is because the message was blocked by the SMTP Message Screener.

4. On ISA1, open Windows Explorer and browse to the C:\Inetpub\Mailroot\Badmail directory. Locate the file with the .bad extension and open the file using Notepad. This file is the archived copy of the message you just sent that was filtered by the SMTP Message Screener.

Lesson Review

Use the following questions to help determine whether you have learned enough to move on to the next lesson. If you have difficulty answering these questions, review the material in this lesson before beginning the next lesson. You can find answers to these questions in the "Questions and Answers" section at the end of this chapter.

1. What criteria can the Message Screener use to filter e-mail messages? (Choose all that apply.)

    a. IP address of the sending SMTP server

    b. Keywords in the message body

    c. Source SMTP address

    d. IP address of the destination SMTP server

2. You have deployed ISA Server 2004 and configured access rules on your ISA Server 2004 to limit Internet access. You need to allow your internal SMTP server to send mail to the Internet. What steps must you take? (Choose two.)

    a. Install the Message Screener on the ISA Server.

    b. Configure the SMTP server as a SecureNAT client.

    c. Create an access rule to allow SMTP traffic outbound.

    d. Install the Firewall Client software on the SMTP server.

    e. Enable the SMTP filter on ISA Server.

    f. Create an SMTP server publishing rule.

3. You have deployed ISA Server, and you are using it to publish the internal computers running Exchange Server as SMTP servers. You have configured both the SMTP application filter and Message Screener. You have just received a notification that a new virus has been detected on the Internet. The virus is spread by e-mail as an attachment named Clickhere.vbs. Programmers within the company frequently e-mail messages to each other with attachments with .vbs extensions, and you should not stop this. You need to protect your network from this virus. What should you do?

    a. Configure the SMTP application filter to block all SMTP commands.

    b. Configure the SMTP application filter to block all MAIL FROM: commands.

    c. Configure Message Screener to block messages based on keywords.

    d. Configure Message Screener to block messages based on attachment extensions.

4. You have created the appropriate rules and DNS records to allow your SMTP Server to send e-mail to and receive e-mail from the Internet. You have installed the message screener on a server running the IIS SMTP service, and you have configured it to inspect incoming e-mail and block certain domains known for relaying spam e-mail. You configure the publishing rule to send all SMTP messages to the message screener computer. You discover that the message screener is not functioning. What else must you do to configure the message screener?

_____

_____

_____

Lesson Summary

■ SMTP servers are vulnerable to several protocol level exploits including buffer-overflow attacks and SMTP command attacks. Attackers can use the standard SMTP commands to perform buffer overflow attacks or to send malformed commands that the system programmers did not anticipate.

■ ISA Server provides three components for securing SMTP traffic. The first is the Mail Server Wizard, which can be used to publish the SMTP server to the Internet. The second component is the SMTP Message Screener, which can help reduce the amount of unwanted e-mail entering the organization. The third component is the SMTP application filter, which can be used to block buffer overflow attacks or SMTP command-based attacks on Exchange Server.

■ When you configure a publishing rule that uses SMTP, the SMTP application filter is automatically enabled for that rule. The SMTP application filter scans SMTP connection attempts for the use of appropriate SMTP commands and command length.

■ The Message Screener inspects the SMTP message contents and enables the filtering of unwanted and malicious e-mail. SMTP Message Screener can be configured to filter incoming mail based on the message sender, attachments, or keywords in the message subject or body.

■ Because Message Screener need not be installed on a computer running ISA Server, you have several options for deploying Message Screener. You can install Message Screener on the ISA Server computer, or install Message Screener on another IIS server. You can also configure your environment so that only inbound messages are scanned or both inbound and outbound messages.

Lesson 2: Configuring ISA Server to Secure Web Client Connections

Providing user access to e-mail from anywhere has become an important service for many organizations. Many of these organizations have chosen to use Web-based clients to give remote users access to their Exchange Server mailboxes. One of the most popular ways to provide access to e-mail on Exchange Server computers for users outside the internal network is to deploy an Outlook Web Access (OWA) server that is accessible from the Internet. With OWA, users can access their mailboxes on an Exchange server from any computer with an Internet connection and a Web browser. In addition, Exchange Server 2003 also enables access to mailboxes for wireless mobile clients, including Outlook Mobile Access (OMA) and Microsoft ActiveSync clients. This lesson describes how to use ISA Server to secure Web client connections.

After this lesson, you will be able to

- Discuss known Web client security issues
- Configure ISA Server to publish an Outlook Web Access server
- Configure forms-based authentication for OWA
- Configure ISA Server to enable access for other Web clients

Estimated lesson time: 40 minutes

Known Web Client Security Issues

The most popular options for providing Web-based client access to Exchange Server mailboxes are using Outlook Web Access (OWA) and Outlook Mobile Access (OMA) and Microsoft Exchange ActiveSync.

Outlook Web Access Features and Security Issues

OWA provides access to the mailboxes on an Exchange Server computer through a Web browser. Although OWA does not provide all the functionality provided by a full Outlook client, the fact that it is easy to deploy and requires no special client makes OWA an attractive option for providing remote access.

By default, all servers running Exchange 2000 Server and Exchange Server 2003 are OWA servers. To install Exchange Server, Microsoft Internet Information Services (IIS) must be installed on the computer. When the user connects to a computer running Exchange Server from the Web browser, the request is passed from IIS to the Exchange Server services on the computer. The requested content is returned to the IIS service, where it is forwarded to the Web browser.

OWA is frequently deployed using front-end and back-end servers. To do this, the front-end server must be running Exchange 2000 Server, Enterprise Edition, or Exchange Server 2003, Enterprise Edition. In this configuration, clients connect to the front-end server. This server authenticates the user, and then queries Active Directory directory service to determine which back-end computer running Exchange Server hosts the user mailbox. The front-end server then forwards the request to the back-end server. The back-end server replies to the front-end server, which replies to the client.

The use of OWA raises several issues with e-mail security, including the following:

- **Securing the user logon**   By default, OWA is configured to use Hypertext Transfer Protocol (HTTP). This means that all user logon information is passed in clear text to the computer running Exchange Server. This issue can be easily addressed using Secure Sockets Layer (SSL) to encrypt all user sessions. However, some clients may cache the user logon credentials so that if the user does not close all Web browser sessions, another user may be able to access the user's e-mail without logging on.

- **Securing e-mail contents**   Because all messages are sent in clear text using HTTP, the e-mail contents may not be secure while crossing the Internet. You can use Hypertext Transfer Protocol Secure (HTTPS) to secure the e-mail. However, some Web browsers may cache the e-mail contents on the local computer. For example, when you open an attachment using OWA, it is stored in the temporary Internet files on the computer. Another user may be able to gain access to the files.

Exchange Server 2003 Wireless Device Support

Exchange Server 2003 allows users of wireless and small devices, such as mobile phones, personal digital assistants (PDAs), or smart phones (hybrid devices that combine the functionality of mobile phones and PDAs), access to Exchange data. Exchange ActiveSync and Outlook Mobile Access (OMA) are two of the mobile service components that are built into Exchange Server 2003.

Exchange ActiveSync is a service provided in Exchange Server 2003 that allows users to synchronize their Exchange information (inbox, subfolders, calendar, contacts, and tasks) with their ActiveSync-enabled mobile device (such as Pocket PC 2002, Smartphone 2002, and Windows Mobile 2003 devices).

OMA is a service provided in Exchange Server 2003 that allows users to access their Exchange mailbox by using a browser-enabled mobile device. Devices such as mobile phones and PDAs that use extensible Hypertext Markup Language (XHTML), compact HTML (cHTML), or standard HTML browsers allow your users to connect to their inbox, calendar, contacts, and tasks, and perform global address list (GAL) searches. In addition to mobile phones, Windows Mobile devices using Microsoft Pocket Internet Explorer and desktop personal computers using Microsoft Internet Explorer 6.0 or later also support OMA.

Like OWA, OMA and ActiveSync require that the computer running Exchange Server 2003 be accessible from the Internet using HTTP. When accessing a mailbox using OMA, the wireless device connects to a wireless access point that provides access to the Internet. Then the Web browser on the wireless device is used to access the computer running Exchange Server.

The use of wireless clients raises similar security issues to OWA including the following:

- **Securing the user logon**   By default, OMA is configured to use HTTP. This means that all user logon information is passed in clear text to the computer running Exchange Server. In addition, authentication to the SMTP server is passed in clear text. This issue can be easily addressed using SSL to encrypt all user sessions.

- **Securing e-mail contents**   Because all messages are sent in clear text using HTTP or SMTP, the e-mail contents may not be secure while crossing the Internet. SSL can secure the e-mail in this case.

How to Configure ISA Server to Enable Outlook Web Access Connections

For the most part, publishing OWA is similar to publishing any other Web server. The easiest way to publish an OWA server is to use the Mail Server Publishing Wizard on ISA Server 2004 to make an internal OWA server accessible to Internet clients.

To publish an OWA server using ISA Server, complete the following procedure:

1. Install a certificate on the OWA server and on the computer running ISA Server. These certificates will be used to configure SSL that's bridged between the OWA clients and the ISA Server, and between the ISA Server and the OWA server. On the OWA server, configure IIS to require SSL connections for the /Exchange, /Exchweb, and the /Public virtual directories under the default Web site. These are the virtual directories used by Exchange to provide OWA access.

2. Start the Mail Server Publishing Rule Wizard from the ISA Server Management Console. On the Welcome To The Mail Server Publishing Rule Wizard Page, type a name for the rule and click next.

3. On the Select Access Type page, as shown previously in Figure 9-1, select Web Client Access: Outlook Web Access (OWA), Outlook Mobile Access, Exchange Server ActiveSync, and then click Next.

4. On the Select Services page, shown in Figure 9-9, ensure that Outlook Web Access is selected. Click Next.

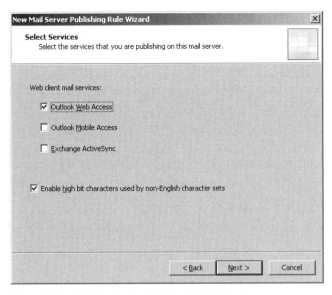

Figure 9-9   Configuring an OWA publishing rule

5. On the Bridging Mode page, shown in Figure 9-10, choose one of the following three options:

   ❑ *Secure Connection To Clients*—Specifies that ISA Server establish a secure connection with the client computers and a standard connection to the mail server

   ❑ *Secure Connection To Mail Server And Clients*—Specifies that ISA Server establish a secure connection with both the mail server and the clients

   ❑ *Standard Connections Only*—Specifies that ISA Server establish a standard connection with both the mail server and the clients

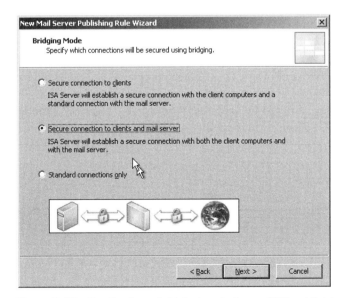

Figure 9-10   Configuring a bridging mode for an OWA publishing rule

The most secure option is to require a secure connection from ISA Server to the clients and from ISA Server to the OWA server. This option allows HTTP application filtering on the computer running ISA Server and secures the network traffic both on the Internet and on the protected network.

6. On the Specify the Web Mail Server page, type the name or IP address of the OWA server. Click Next.

7. On the Public Name Details page, ensure that This Domain Name (Type Below) is configured in the Accept Request For drop-down list. In the Public Name box, type the URL the users will use when connecting to the ISA Server computer and click Next.

8. On the Select Web Listener page, select or create a Web listener. If you are requiring secure connections with clients, the Web listener must be enabled for SSL. Click Edit.

9. On the User Sets page, choose which users can access the OWA server. Because only domain users can have mailboxes on an Exchange Server computer, you should choose the All Authenticated Users user set. Click Next.

10. On the Completing the New Mail Server Publishing Rule Wizard page, click Finish.

How to Configure Forms-Based Authentication

When users try to access OWA, they will be forced to authenticate by the Exchange Server computer. You can also enable authentication on the ISA Server computer and use any of the available authentication methods. The most secure option for enabling authentication for an OWA publishing rule is to configure the Web listener to use OWA forms-based authentication. Forms-based authentication ensures that the user credentials are not cached on the client computer after the user logs off, or after a time-out period expires. In addition, OWA forms-based authentication can be used to restrict whether users can view or download e-mail attachments.

> **Planning**   If you choose not to use OWA forms-based authentication but still want to enable authentication on the ISA Server computer, the best option is to use basic authentication with SSL. When you configure the Web listener used by the OWA Web publishing rule to use basic authentication, you can also configure the Web publishing rule to forward the basic authentication credentials to the Exchange Server computer. By doing this, users will be asked to authenticate once rather than authenticating for both ISA Server and Exchange Server. However, if you use Basic authentication, then you must use SSL to encrypt network traffic; if you don't, all network traffic will be sent in clear text.

When a user logs on using OWA forms-based authentication, the user password is never sent across the network in clear text. Rather, a session cookie is created and stored on the OWA client computer. This cookie stores the OWA user credentials in an encrypted format. When the user logs off from OWA, the cookie is cleared and it is no longer valid for authentication. This means that if a user logs off OWA, no one else can access the mailbox without being asked to authenticate.

> **Important**   Exchange Server 2003 also enables the option of using forms-based authentication when connecting to OWA. You cannot enable forms-based authentication on both the Exchange Server 2003 and ISA Server. On the other hand, Exchange 2000 Server and Exchange Server 5.5 do not support forms-based authentication, but you can configure forms-based authentication on ISA Server when publishing these Exchange Servers.

You can also limit how long the credentials are stored if the user does not log off. The automatic time-out is valuable for keeping a user mailbox secure from unauthorized access. For example, if you do not use forms-based authentication, or use an alternate authentication method, the user credentials on the client computer will be valid as long as the Web browser session is open. This means that if the Web browser is not closed, another user could reconnect to the user's mailbox without being asked for authentication credentials. Although this time-out does not completely eliminate the risk of an unauthorized user accessing an account if an Outlook Web Access session is left running on a public computer, the time-out greatly reduces this risk.

Another option that is enabled with forms-based authentication is the option to prevent users from opening or saving attachments. You can configure attachment blocking for public computers, private computers, or both. Blocking attachments, particularly on public computers, is recommended.

> **Security Alert**   If users are allowed to receive e-mail attachments, and a user opens an attachment on the client computer, the attachment is stored in the Temporary Internet Files on the client computer. This file is not removed when the attachment is closed or when the Web browser session is closed so another user can access the attachment. ISA Server and Exchange Server do not provide the means of stopping this, other than blocking all attachments. At a minimum, you should block all attachments on public machines.

When you configure OWA forms-based authentication, the user logon experience will change when they connect the OWA site, as shown in Figure 9-11. The logon page enabled by forms-based authentication allows the user to select the security option that best fits the client they are connecting from. The two options available are as follows:

- **Public Or Shared Computer**   Public or shared computer is the default setting. It provides a short default timeout option of 22 minutes of user inactivity before the cookie times out. The user is allowed to download attachments.

■ **Private Computer**   The private computer option allows for a longer period of inactivity before automatically ending the session, with a default value of 36 hours. The user is allowed to download attachments. This option should be used if the user is the only operator of the computer, and the computer adheres to the security policies of the user's company.

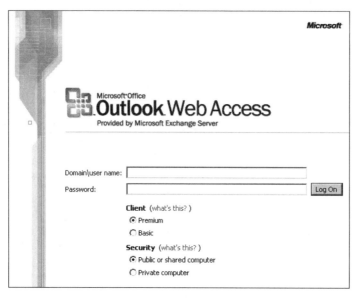

Figure 9-11   Logging on to OWA using forms-based authentication

Note   The Client option on the OWA logon form is used to select the client display format. If you are running Internet Explorer 5.0 or later, you can select Premium to enable the advanced OWA client display options. If you are running an older Internet Explorer client, or a non-Microsoft client, choose Basic.

Off the Record   There is obviously a problem with allowing the user to select what type of computer they are connecting from. For example, if you allow users to access attachments if they select Private Computer but block attachments if they choose Public Or Shared Computer, nothing stops users from selecting the private computer option even though they are on a public kiosk computer. You can try to prevent this from happening with security policies, but be aware that you really cannot enforce this with ISA Server.

Configuring Forms-Based Authentication

To configure ISA Server to require forms-based authentication for OWA connections, complete the following steps:

1. In the ISA Server Management Console, click Firewall Policy.

2. In the task pane, on the Toolbox tab, in the Network Objects pane, expand Web Listeners, right-click the Web Listener that is used for OWA connections, and then click Properties.

3. In the Web Listener Properties dialog box, on the Preferences tab, click Authentication.

4. In the Authentication dialog box, in the Method list, enable OWA Forms-Based Authentication, and then click Configure, as shown in Figure 9-12.

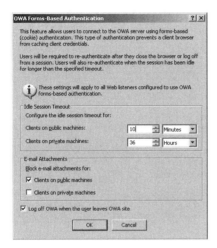

Figure 9-12   Configuring the OWA forms-based authentication settings

5. In the OWA Forms-Based Authentication dialog box, you can configure the Idle Session Timeout setting for public and private computers as well as configure whether users will be allowed to open e-mail attachments box on private and public computers. If you select Log Off OWA When The User Leaves The OWA Site, the user will be logged off when the user connects to a Web site other than the OWA site.

How to Configure ISA Server to Enable Access for Other Web Clients

ISA Server can also be configured to publish OMA and Exchange ActiveSync services on Exchange Server 2003 computers to the Internet. Configuring access to OMA and Active-Sync on ISA Server is almost identical to enabling access to OWA. When you run the Mail Server Publishing Wizard, you can choose to enable the OMA and Exchange ActiveSync Web client mail services. When you choose these options, the /Microsoft-Server-Active-Sync virtual directory and the /OMA virtual directories are mapped to the OWA server. If you have forms-based authentication configured for the Web listener that's used for OWA, you must use a different Web listener for OMA and ActiveSync access, because OMA and ActiveSync do not support forms-based authentication.

Practice: Configuring ISA Server to Secure OWA Client Connections

In this practice, you will configure ISA Server to secure OWA client connections to the Exchange Server computer. To use SSL bridging from the ISA Server computer to the Exchange Server computer, you must first install a certificate on MAIL1. Then you will configure and test the OWA connection.

Exercise 1: Install a Certificate on the Exchange Server

1. Log on to MAIL1 as an Administrator.

2. Open Internet Information Services (IIS) Manager. Expand MAIL1, and then expand Web Sites.

3. Right-click Default Web Site and click Properties.

4. On the Directory Security tab, click Server Certificate.

5. On the Welcome To The Web Server Certificate Wizard page, click Next.

6. On the Server Certificate page, click Create A New Certificate. Click Next.

7. On the Delayed Or Immediate Request page, click Send The Request Immediately To An Online Certification Authority and click Next.

8. On the Name And Security Settings page, accept the defaults and click Next.

9. On the Organization Information page, type **Coho Vineyard** as the Organization name and **Messaging** as the Organizational unit name. Click Next.

10. On the Your Site's Common Name page, type **MAIL1.cohovineyard.com** as the Common name. Click Next.

11. On the Geographic Information page, enter your location information. Click Next.

12. On the SSL Port page, accept the default and click Next.

13. On the Choose A Certification Authority page, accept the default and click Next.

14. On the Certification Request Submission page, review the settings, and then click Next.

15. On the Completing To The Web Server Certificate Wizard page, click Finish. Click OK.

Exercise 2: Configuring IIS to Require SSL on the Virtual Directories Used by OWA

1. In the IIS Manager console, expand Default Web Site, right-click Exchange, and then click Properties.

2. In the Exchange Properties dialog box, on the Directory Security tab, in the Secure communications box, click Edit.

3. In the Secure Communications box, enable Require Secure Channel (SSL), and then click OK.

4. Click OK to close the Exchange Properties dialog box.

5. Configure the ExchWeb virtual directory to require SSL.

6. Configure the Public virtual directory to require SSL.

7. Close the IIS Manager console.

Exercise 3: Configuring an Outlook Web Access Publishing Rule

1. On ISA1, open the ISA Server Management Console and click Firewall Policy.

2. On the Firewall Policy tasks pane, on the Tasks tab, click Publish A Mail Server.

3. On the Welcome To The New Mail Server Publishing Rule Wizard page, type **OWA Access Rule**, and then click Next.

4. On the Select Access Type page, select Web client access: Outlook Web Access (OWA), Outlook Mobile Access, Exchange Server ActiveSync, and then click Next.

5. On the Select Services page, ensure that Outlook Web Access is selected. Click Next.

6. On the Bridging Mode page, accept the default to create a secure connection to clients and mail server, and then click Next.

7. On the Specify The Web Mail Server page, in the Web Mail Server text box, type **MAIL1.cohovineyard.com**. Click Next.

8. On the Public Name Details page, ensure that This Domain Name (Type Below) is configured in the Accept Request For drop-down list. In the Public Name box, type **secure.cohovineyard.com** and click Next.

9. On the Select Web Listener page, in the Web Listener drop-down list, click HTTPS Listener. Click Edit.

10. On the HTTPS Listener Properties page, on the Preferences tab, click Authentication. Configure the Web listener to use only OWA Forms-Based authentication and to Require All Users To Authenticate. Click OK twice.

11. On the Select Web Listener page, click Next.

12. On the User Sets page, accept the default and click Next.

13. On the Completing the New Mail Server Publishing Rule Wizard page, click Finish.

14. Double-click OWA Access Rule. On the Users tab, click Forward Basic Authentication Credentials (Basic Delegation). Click OK.

15. Ensure that the OWA Access Rule is listed before the Coho Vineyard Secure Site rule. If it is not, click OWA Access Rule and click Move Selected Rule Up.

16. Click Apply to apply the changes.

Exercise 4: Testing the Outlook Web Access Publishing Rule

1. Switch to SERVER1.

2. Open Internet Explorer and type **https://secure.cohovineyard.com/exchange** in the Address bar. Press ENTER.

3. Log on using the user account with a mailbox on MAIL1. You should be able to access the mailbox on MAIL1.

Lesson Review

Use the following questions to help determine whether you have learned enough to move on to the next lesson. If you have difficulty answering these questions, review the material in this lesson before beginning the next lesson. You can find answers to these questions in the "Questions and Answers" section at the end of this chapter.

1. What authentication method allows you to control a user's ability to view or save attachments?

    a. Digest authentication

    b. OWA forms-based authentication

    c. RADIUS authentication

    d. SSL certificates

2. You are configuring ISA Server 2004 to publish an OWA server. You have enabled SSL Bridging Mode as a secure connection to mail server and clients. You have requested and installed SSL certificates on the ISA Server computer and the OWA server. However, your users report that they cannot connect to Exchange Server and are receiving a 500 Internal Server Error page. What is the most likely cause of the error?

    a. The external DNS record is incorrect.

    b. There is a problem with the OWA server certificate.

    c. You are using an unsupported authentication method.

    d. The OWA server has not been published correctly.

3. You need to allow access to the corporate Exchange Server computer for your users with PDA's to retrieve e-mail. How can you ensure the client's logon information will be secure while traversing the Internet?

    a. Use OWA forms-based authentication.

    b. Use SSL to encrypt user sessions.

    c. Configure Internet Protocol Security (IPSec) to encrypt logon traffic.

    d. Use RADIUS authentication.

Lesson Summary

- Exchange Server 2003 provides access to the mailboxes on an Exchange Server to clients using a Web browser or using a wireless or mobile device. The use of these clients raises several issues with e-mail security, including securing the user logon, and securing e-mail contents.

- To publish an Outlook Web Access server, use the Mail Server Publishing Wizard on ISA Server 2004 and select the options to publish an OWA server. For maximum security, configure SSL connections from ISA Server to the OWA client and from ISA Server to the Exchange Server computer.

- The most secure option for enabling authentication for an OWA publishing rule is to configure the Web listener to use OWA forms-based authentication. Forms-based authentication ensures that the user credentials are not cached on the client computer after the user logs off, or after a timeout period expires. Moreover, forms-based authentication can be used to block access to e-mail attachments.

- ISA Server can also be configured to publish Outlook Mobile Access and Exchange ActiveSync services to the Internet. When you run the Mail Server Publishing Wizard, you can choose to enable the Outlook Mobile Access and Exchange ActiveSync Web client mail services. OMA and ActiveSync do not support forms-based authentication.

Lesson 3: Configuring ISA Server to Secure Outlook Client Connections

The Outlook messaging client provides the highest level of functionality of any messaging client that can be used with Exchange Server. However, because the Outlook client requires remote procedure call (RPC) connectivity to the computer running Exchange Server, it is difficult to provide secure access to Exchange Server from the Internet for Outlook clients. ISA Server can be used to secure the Outlook RPC connections as well as enable RPC over HTTP connections.

After this lesson, you will be able to

- Discuss known Outlook client security issues
- Configure ISA Server to secure Outlook RPC connections
- Describe how RPC over HTTP works
- Configure ISA server to enable RPC over HTTP
- Configure e-mail access for POP3 and IMAP4 clients

Estimated lesson time: 40 minutes

Real World   ISA Server and Outlook Clients

As you may have noticed, the exam objectives include no mention of configuring ISA Server to secure Outlook client connections. However, I decided to provide at least an overview of this topic because it is becoming an increasingly relevant topic for ISA Server administrators. After years of avoiding this topic, many organizations are getting ready to take another look at exposing their Exchange Server computers to the Internet for Outlook clients.

Firewall administrators have steadfastly resisted enabling Outlook client connections from the Internet. And they have very good reason for doing so. Outlook clients are Messaging Application Programming Interface (MAPI) clients, and MAPI uses RPCs to connect to the Exchange Server computer. As discussed in Chapter 8, "Implementing ISA Server Publishing," to enable RPC connections, you must open too many ports for secondary connections. And though you can specify which ports the Exchange Server computer and Outlook clients will use by modifying the Exchange Server computer and domain controller registries, most firewall administrators were just not interested. ISA Server can be used to securely publish the Exchange Server computers for Outlook RPC clients, but even then, the traffic between the Outlook client and the ISA Server computer is not secure because of the low level of encryption available to secure RPC traffic.

> The reason that organizations are ready to look again at this question is because of the RPC-over-HTTP feature that is available if you are running Exchange Server 2003 and Outlook 2003. With this feature, the RPC traffic is tunneled through HTTP or HTTPS, so all you have to do is configure an RPC proxy server, and then configure a secure Web publishing rule to publish the server. This provides a very high level of security, and it allows users to use the full Outlook client from anywhere. All they need is an Internet connection.

Known Outlook Client Security Issues

The Outlook client is the only Exchange Server client that can take full advantage of all the features available with Exchange Server 2003. The Outlook client enables access to all mailbox and collaboration features such as calendaring, public folder access, and task and contact management. Another significant benefit to using Outlook compared to OWA is that Outlook provides offline access. With Outlook, you can perform most e-mail tasks while you are not connected to the network, and then automatically synchronize with Exchange Server when connected to the network.

Because the Outlook client has the highest level of functionality, most users prefer to use it not only at work, but while traveling and from home as well. However, to take full advantage of all the available client functionality, Outlook must be configured as a MAPI client, and MAPI requests are sent as an RPC to the computer running Exchange Server. Using RPC across the Internet raises some significant security concerns.

MAPI clients, like other RPC clients, connect to servers over Port 135, which is the endpoint mapper service port. The MAPI client and the Exchange Server computer then use universally unique identifiers (UUIDs) to determine a port number for subsequent connections to the required services. The client sends the UUID to the endpoint mapper service and requests the port number for the application that it needs. The endpoint mapper returns an available port number to the MAPI client and the client then uses that port number to connect to the server application that it needs.

On an internal network, there are usually no restrictions on the ports that a MAPI client can use. However, when a firewall exists between the MAPI client and the server, it would defeat the purpose of the firewall to open every possible port that a MAPI client might need. To maintain the integrity of your firewall, you need to limit the ports that the MAPI client can use. You can do this by modifying the registry to assign static port numbers on the Exchange Server computers and Active Directory domain controllers that are used by the Outlook clients. Then you can enable only those ports and the endpoint mapper port on your firewall. This reduces the number of ports that you will need to open in the firewall but still means that those ports are always open to the Internet.

Another potential security risk for MAPI Outlook clients is that the encoding used for RPC is not secure. If an attacker captures the packets sent using RPC, they will be able to decode the packets and read the messages. Additional security can be enabled by configuring the Outlook client to use encrypted RPC connections.

How to Configure ISA Server to Secure Outlook RPC Connections

To provide additional security for the Outlook client connections to the Exchange Server computers, you can configure an Outlook RPC publishing rule on ISA Server. When you configure this publishing rule, ISA Server uses the RPC filter to manage the port number assignments for the RPC ports.

How the RPC Application Filter Works

When an Outlook MAPI client from the Internet connects to a computer running Exchange Server through ISA Server, the RPC application filter works as follows:

1. The Outlook client issues a request over TCP Port 135 through ISA Server to the computer running Exchange Server to find the service port number associated with the Exchange RPC UUID.

2. The computer running Exchange Server sends a response back with a port number on which the client can communicate. The response includes all the UUIDs and associated port numbers that the client will use to connect to the required Exchange services.

3. ISA Server uses the RPC application filter to capture this information, and maintains it in a table. ISA Server allocates a new port on the ISA Server computer, and changes the response that it sends to the Outlook client to reflect this change. This information is also maintained in the table.

4. The Outlook MAPI client establishes a connection to the MAPI ports that ISA Server instructed it to use. ISA Server screens the RPC commands to ensure that no exploits are contained within the channel.

5. Information sent by the Outlook MAPI client is forwarded by ISA Server to the computer running Exchange Server.

6. The computer running Exchange Server responds to the Outlook MAPI client and ISA Server intercepts the responses. The RPC filter screens these responses and changes the source port number.

7. ISA Server forwards the responses to the Outlook MAPI client.

Configuring an Outlook RPC Publishing Rule

To configure an Outlook RPC publishing rule on ISA Server, complete the following procedure:

1. In the ISA Server Management Console, click Firewall Policy.

2. On the Firewall Policy task pane, on the Tasks tab, select Publish A Mail Server to start the New Mail Server Rule Wizard.

3. On the Welcome To The New Mail Server Publishing Rule Wizard page, type a name for the rule, and then click Next.

4. On the Select Access Type page (shown previously in Figure 9-1), click Client Access: RPC, IMAP, POP3, SMTP, and then click Next.

5. On the Select Services page, shown in Figure 9-13, select Outlook (RPC), and then click Next.

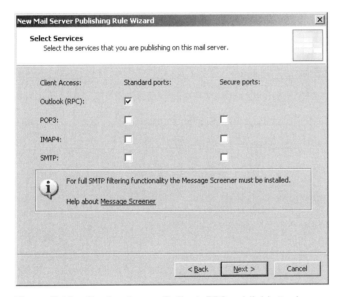

Figure 9-13   Configuring an Outlook RPC publishing rule

6. On the Select Server page, type the IP address for the published Exchange Server computer, and then click Next.

7. On the IP Addresses page, click External, and then click Next.

8. On the Completing The New Mail Server Publishing Rule Wizard page, review the configuration, and then click Finish.

9. After you configure the Outlook RPC publishing rule, you can also configure the rule to accept connections only from Outlook clients that are configured to use encryption. To do this, right-click the Outlook RPC publishing rule and click Configure Exchange RPC. Select Enforce Encryption.

When you use the Mail Publishing Wizard to create an Outlook RPC publishing rule, the publishing rule enables access to the Exchange Server computers using the Exchange RPC Server protocol. To examine the protocol configuration, open the Properties for the publishing rule. On the Traffic tab, notice that the Exchange RPC Server protocol is listed and then click Properties. On the Parameters tab, shown in Figure 9-14, notice that the protocol is configured to allow inbound connections on Port 135, and that the RPC Filter is applied to the protocol.

Figure 9-14 Configuring the Exchange RPC Server protocol

On the Interfaces tab, shown in Figure 9-15, you can see all the UUID interfaces enabled by the Exchange RPC Server protocol.

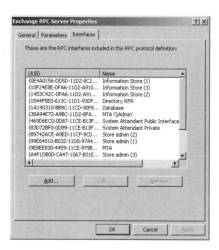

Figure 9-15 Viewing the RPC interfaces enabled by the Exchange RPC Server protocol

What Is RPC over HTTP?

With the newest versions of Exchange Server and Outlook, you can enable access to Exchange Server for Outlook clients using RPC over HTTP, which provides all the benefits of using an Outlook client without needing multiple ports open on the firewall. Users running Outlook 2003 can connect directly to a computer running Exchange Server 2003 over the Internet by using HTTP or HTTPS, even if both the computer running Exchange Server and Outlook are behind firewalls and located on different networks. Only the HTTP and HTTPS ports need to be opened on the firewall.

Security Alert   Although the official name for this feature is RPC over HTTP, you should never consider implementing it over HTTP. Always use HTTPS to secure the network traffic sent from the Outlook client to the ISA Server computer.

RPC over HTTP is usually deployed using front-end and back-end servers. The front-end server is an RPC proxy server that converts the RPC over HTTP packets into normal RPC packets, which are forwarded to the back-end computer running Exchange Server. The back-end server replies to the front-end server, which converts the response back into HTTP packets and replies to the client. In this case, the RPC proxy server need not be running Exchange Server. RPC over HTTP can also be deployed in a single server configuration where the Exchange Server is also configured as the RPC proxy server.

Important   You should not configure the ISA Server computer as the RPC proxy server because to do so you would need to install IIS on the server. Moreover, the access rule configuration would be quite complex.

When you enable RPC over HTTP, only Port 80 or Port 443 need be accessible from the Internet. You can configure ISA Server to publish the RPC proxy server, so that all RPC over HTTP requests are forwarded to the RPC proxy sever. To enable this, you configure a Web publishing rule, or a secure Web publishing rule, on ISA Server that publishes the RPC virtual directory on the RPC proxy server.

Requirements for RPC over HTTP

The requirements for RPC over HTTP and the computers and servers to which those requirements apply are shown in Table 9-3.

Table 9-3   RPC over HTTP Requirements

These Computers	Must Meet These Requirements
Clients	Outlook 2003 Windows XP with Service Pack 1 with Windows XP update Q331320 Windows XP with Service Pack 2
Servers	Exchange 2003 on Windows Server 2003 for front-end servers (if front-end servers are deployed) Exchange 2003 on Windows Server 2003 for back-end servers Exchange 2003 on Windows Server 2003 for public folders Exchange 2003 on Windows Server 2003 for system folders Windows Server 2003 for all Active Directory global catalog servers accessible to the RPC over HTTP clients

How to Configure RPC-over-HTTP Connectivity

Before configuring ISA Server to publish the RPC over HTTP proxy server, you must configure the computers running Exchange Server and the Outlook clients to support RPC over HTTP. Then you can create secure Web publishing rule to publish the \Rpc virtual directory on the RPC proxy server through ISA Server.

Configuring Exchange Server 2003 for RPC over HTTP

When you deploy RPC over HTTP, you must configure a computer running Windows Server 2003 as an RPC proxy server. The RPC proxy server accepts the RPC over HTTP or HTTPS connections and translates them into regular RPCs. In a scenario in which you have deployed Exchange Server front-end and back-end servers, the Exchange Server front-end servers should be configured as RPC proxy servers.

The high-level steps to configure Exchange Server 2003 for RPC over HTTP are as follows:

1. Configure the Exchange front-end server as an RPC proxy server by adding the RPC over HTTP subcomponent to the Windows Networking Services component. If you have Exchange Server 2003 Service Pack 1 installed, then use Exchange System Manager to configure the server as an RPC front-end server.

2. Configure the Authentication Method in the RPC virtual directory in IIS to use Basic authentication. Also configure the virtual directory to require SSL connections.

3. Modify the registry on the RPC proxy server and global catalog server to use specified port numbers. To communicate with the domain controllers and computers running Exchange Server, the RPC proxy server specifies which ports to use for communicating with the domain controllers, global catalog servers, and all the computers running Exchange Server with which the RPC client must communicate.

If you have Exchange Server 2003 Service Pack 1 installed, you can avoid editing the registry by using the Exchange System Manager to configure the back-end servers as RPC back-end servers.

> **See Also**   For detailed steps about how to configure the Exchange Server computer, see the article "How to Configure RPC over HTTP on a Single Server in Exchange Server 2003," located at *http://support.microsoft.com/default.aspx?scid=kb;en-us;833401*. For detailed steps about how to configure the Outlook client to support RPC over HTTP, see the Office 2003 Resource Kit chapter, "Configuring Outlook 2003 for RPC over HTTP," located at *http://www.microsoft.com/office/ork/2003/three/ch8/OutC07.htm*.

After you have completed these steps, your Exchange Server environment is configured to accept and respond to requests from clients that are using RPC over HTTP.

Configuring Outlook 2003 for RPC over HTTP

If you want your users to be able to use RPC over HTTP to connect to their mailboxes, your users must create an Outlook profile on their computers that contains the necessary settings for RPC over HTTP. These settings enable SSL communication with Basic authentication, which is necessary when using RPC over HTTP.

The steps to configure Outlook 2003 for RPC over HTTP are as follows:

1. Create an Outlook profile that will use RPC over HTTP.
2. Configure the Outlook profile to connect to a computer running Exchange Server and to use cached mode.
3. Configure the Outlook profile to connect to the mailbox by using HTTP.
4. Configure the profile's Exchange proxy settings with the fully qualified domain name (FQDN) of the RPC proxy server, and then configure the SSL options.

Configuring ISA Server for RPC over HTTP

You can configure ISA Server to enable RPC over HTTP by using a Web publishing rule to publish the \Rpc virtual directory on the RPC proxy server. To make the connection more secure, use a Web listener configured for SSL and configure SSL bridging to encrypt the client connection to ISA Server and the connection from ISA Server to the RPC proxy server.

> **See Also**   For detailed steps about how to configure ISA Server to enable RPC over HTTP connectivity, see the article "Using ISA Server 2004 with Exchange Server 2003," located at *http://www.microsoft.com/technet/prodtechnol/isa/2004/plan/exchage2003.mspx*.

To publish the \Rpc virtual directory, create a secure Web publishing rule by performing the following steps:

1. Open the ISA Server Management Console and click Firewall Policy.

2. In the task pane, on the Tasks tab, click Publish A Web Server to start the New Web Publishing Rule Wizard.

3. On the Welcome To The New Secure Web Publishing Rule Wizard page, in the Name field, type a name for the rule, and then click Next.

4. On the Select Rule Action page, ensure that Allow is selected. Click Next.

5. On the Select Web Site To Publish page, in Web server, specify the RPC proxy server that you want to publish. This can be the computer name or the IP address of the computer. Select Send The Original Host Header. Click Next.

6. On the Select Public Domain Name page, type the public name with which users will connect to the ISA Server computer, and configure the rule to publish the \Rpc folder.

7. On the Select Web Listener page, select a Web listener that is configured to listen for HTTPS connections, and then click Next.

8. On the User Sets page, either accept the default of All Users or use the Remove button to remove All Users, and add the appropriate users. Click Next.

9. On the Completing The New Web Publishing Rule Wizard page, review the configuration, and then click Finish.

How to Configure E-Mail Access for POP3 and IMAP4 Clients

In addition to publishing Exchange Server computers so they can be accessed using Outlook as a MAPI client, ISA Server can also be used to publish Exchange Server for clients such as Outlook Express. These clients use POP3 or IMAP4 to read messages in the Exchange Server mailboxes and use SMTP to send messages to the computers running Exchange Server. Alternatively, these clients can be configured to use the secure versions of these protocols: POP3S, IMAP4S, and SMTPS.

You can use the New Mail Server Publishing Rule Wizard to create a new server publishing rule for Internet protocol clients. When running the wizard, choose to create a client access rule, and then choose IMAP4 or POP3 as the client access protocols. If no publishing rule is configured allowing access to an SMTP server, then you also need to configure the publishing rule to support SMTP.

When you configure the publishing rule, you can choose to enable the POP3, IMAP4, and SMTP secure ports. If you choose to use secure ports, all user logon and message transfer traffic is encrypted using SSL. This means that you must have a server certificate configured on the computer running Exchange Server.

If you configure access for multiple protocols using the New Mail Server Publishing Rule Wizard, the wizard automatically creates a server publishing rule for each protocol that you published.

Practice: Configuring ISA Server to Secure Outlook Client Connections

In this practice, you will configure ISA Server to publish the Exchange Server for Outlook RPC clients. You will then test the publishing rule.

Exercise 1: Configuring an Outlook RPC Publishing Rule

1. On ISA1, in the ISA Server Management Console, click Firewall Policy.

2. On the Firewall Policy task pane, on the Tasks tab, select Publish A Mail Server to start the New Mail Server Publishing Rule Wizard.

3. On the Welcome To The New Mail Server Publishing Rule Wizard page, type **Outlook Client Access** as the name for the rule, and then click Next.

4. On the Select Access Type page, click Client Access: RPC, IMAP, POP3, SMTP, and then click Next.

5. On the Select Services page, select Outlook (RPC), and then click Next.

6. On the Select Server page, type **10.10.0.12**, and then click Next.

7. On the IP Addresses page, click External, and then click Next.

8. On the Completing The New Mail Server Publishing Rule Wizard page, review the configuration, and then click Finish.

9. Click Apply to apply the changes.

Exercise 2: Testing the Outlook RPC Publishing Rule

> **Note**   To test the Outlook RPC publishing rule, you need a computer running the Outlook client that is located on the same network as the external network interface of the ISA Server computer. The client computer should be configured to use SERVER1 for DNS name resolution.

1. On the External client, log on as an Administrator.

2. Open Outlook from the Start menu.

3. On the Outlook 2003 Startup page, click Next.

4. On the E-mail Accounts page, click Next.

5. On the Server Type page, click Microsoft Exchange Server, and then click Next.

6. On the Exchange Server Settings page, in the Microsoft Exchange Server field, type **Mail1.cohovineyard.com**. In the User Name field, type the user name of a user with a mailbox on MAIL1, and then click Next.

7. On the Congratulations page, click Finish.

8. In the Connect To MAIL1.cohovineyard.com dialog box, log on as the mailbox user.

9. On the User Name dialog box, click OK. You should be able to access the Exchange Server computer using Outlook.

Lesson Review

Use the following questions to help determine whether you have learned enough to move on to the next lesson. If you have difficulty answering these questions, review the material in this lesson before beginning the next lesson. You can find answers to these questions in the "Questions and Answers" section at the end of this chapter.

1. Your company uses Exchange Server 2003 and Outlook 2003 as a MAPI client. You must securely publish RPC over HTTP. What ports must be accessible on the ISA Server computer?

   a. Port 80

   b. Port 443

   c. Port 135

   d. Ports 80 and 443

2. You need to configure ISA Server to publish internal Exchange servers for Outlook clients that are located on the Internet. You have both Exchange Server 2000 and Exchange Server 2003 in your organization. Users in your company all use Outlook 2003 and need to be able to access all the mailbox and public folder contents when out of the office. The security officer for your organization is concerned about making the internal computers running Exchange Server accessible for Outlook clients because of the number of ports that need to be opened on the firewall. What can you tell the security officer?

   a. Tell him that you will configure ISA Server to use RPC over HTTP so that only one port needs to be opened on the firewall.

   b. Tell him that you will configure ISA Server to publish the computers running Exchange Server as IMAP4 servers, so only one port needs to be opened on the firewall.

   c. Tell him that you will configure ISA Server to publish the computers running Exchange Server using an Outlook RPC publishing rule, so only one port needs to be opened on the firewall.

   d. Tell him that you will configure ISA Server to publish the computers running Exchange Server as Outlook Web Access servers, so only one port needs to be open on the firewall.

Lesson Summary

- The Outlook client provides the highest functionality of any messaging client that can be used with Exchange Server, but also introduces some security risks when used to provide access from the Internet. The most significant security issue with using MAPI Outlook clients to provide remote access has to do with the nature of RPC communications. Another potential security risk for MAPI Outlook clients is that the encoding used for RPC is not secure.

- The ISA Server RPC filter enables secure Outlook MAPI connections from the Internet by dynamically managing the assignment of the ports required. The RPC filter uses the Exchange RPC protocol which includes the UUID interfaces for all the Exchange Server services.

- Outlook 2003 with Exchange Server 2003 running on Windows Server 2003 supports RPC over HTTP, which provides MAPI client access to the computer running Exchange Server without using the RPC ports. Users running Outlook 2003 can connect directly to a computer running Exchange Server over the Internet by using HTTP or HTTPS.

- To enable RPC over HTTP, you must configure an RPC over HTTP proxy server, and then configure an Outlook client profile. Then you must configure ISA Server to support this feature by using a Web publishing rule to publish the \Rpc virtual directory on the RPC proxy server.

- ISA Server can also be used to publish Exchange Server for clients such as Outlook Express. These clients use POP3 or IMAP4 to read messages in the Exchange server mailboxes and use SMTP to send messages to the computers running Exchange Server. These clients can also be configured to use POP3S, IMAP4S, and SMTPS.

Case Scenario Exercises

In these exercises, you will read two scenarios about using ISA Server 2004 to publish Exchange Server computers, and then answer the questions that follow. If you have difficulty completing this work, review the material in this chapter before beginning the next chapter. You can find answers to these questions in the "Questions and Answers" section at the end of this chapter.

Scenario 1

You are the network administrator of your company. You use Exchange Server 2003 to provide messaging functionality for your users. You have deployed ISA Server 2004 as a bastion host. You must configure ISA Server so that your Exchange Server computer can send and receive e-mail from the Internet. You also need to configure ISA Server to enforce the corporate security policy that states the no e-mail attachments that are executables or Microsoft Visual Basic Scripting Edition scripts should be allowed from the Internet. Several users in your organization must be able to read and send e-mail from remote locations using both private and public machines. You need to ensure that confidential files attached to e-mails will not be cached on public machines.

Scenario 1 Question

1. How will you configure ISA Server to meet these requirements?

_____

_____

_____

Scenario 2

You have deployed Exchange Server 2003 as a front-end server in your perimeter network. You are using ISA Server 2004 as your front-end firewall. Several users in your organization with laptops require remote access to update their Outlook calendar and send and receive e-mail. All users use Outlook 2003. You need to ensure that the client connection to the Exchange Server computer is as secure as possible.

Scenario 2 Question

1. How will you configure your environment to meet the company requirements?

_____

_____

_____

Troubleshooting Lab

In this lab, you will troubleshoot a Web site access issue. Since you configured the OWA access rule, users on the Internet report that they can no longer access the Coho Vineyard secure Web site. When they try to access the Web site, the users are presented with a logon screen. Because most of the users do not have user accounts in your domain, they cannot authenticate and cannot access the secure site. You need to ensure that both the secure Web site and the OWA Web site are accessible to Internet clients, and that access to both Web sites is as secure as possible.

Exercise 1: Testing Access to the Secure Web Site

1. On SERVER1, open Internet Explorer and type **https://secure.cohovineyard.com** into the Address box. Notice that you receive the OWA forms-based authentication screen.

2. On ISA1, open the ISA Server Management Console, and click Firewall Policy.

3. Click the Coho Vineyard Secure Site publishing rule and click Move Selected Rule up. Repeat until the secure site publishing rule is listed above the OWA Access Rule.

4. Click Apply to apply the changes.

5. On SERVER1, open Internet Explorer and type **https://secure.cohovineyard.com** into the Address box. Notice that you still receive the OWA forms-based authentication screen.

Exercise 2: Enabling Access to the Secure Web Site and the OWA Site

In this scenario, the problem is that the HTTPS listener used by the OWA publishing rule is configured to require OWA forms-based authentication. To use OWA forms-based authentication for the OWA site while using no authentication for the Coho Vineyard secure Web site, you will need to configure an additional Web listener that will require SSL, but not require authentication.

To enable this configuration, you must add an additional IP address to the network interface on the ISA Server computer that is connected to the external network.

1. On ISA1, access the properties for the network interface connected to the external network.

2. Click Internet Protocol (TCP/IP), and then click Properties. Click Advanced.

3. In the Advanced TCP/IP Settings dialog box, add an additional IP address to the network interface. Click OK and close the open dialog boxes.

   Because you will need to use two DNS names on the Internet to distinguish between the OWA Web site and the Secure Web site, you need to add a certificate on ISA1. In this case, you will obtain and install a new certificate for ISA1 that is issued to Mail.cohovineyard.com.

4. On ISA1, open Internet Explorer.

5. In the Address bar, type **http://DC1.cohovineyard.com/certsrv**.

6. Log on as cohovineyard\administrator with the appropriate password.

7. On the Welcome page, under Select a task, click Request a certificate.

8. On the Request A Certificate page, click Advanced Certificate Request.

9. On the Advanced Certificate Request page, click Create and submit a request to this CA.

10. On the Advanced Certificate Request page, in the Certificate Template drop-down list, click Web Server. Complete the form using the following information:

    ❑ Name: **Mail.cohovineyard.com**

    ❑ E-Mail: **Administrator@cohovineyard.com**

    ❑ Company: **Coho Vineyard**

    ❑ Country/Region: **US**

11. Under Key Options, select Store Certificate in the local computer certificate store.

12. Submit the request by clicking Submit. Review the two warning dialog boxes that appear, and click Yes for both.

13. Click Install This Certificate. Review the Warning dialog box that appears, and then click Yes. When you receive the message that the certificate is successfully installed, close Internet Explorer.

Now you will configure the Web listener used by the OWA access rule to use the newly installed certificate, and to listen on the new IP address that you configured on ISA1. To do this, perform the following steps:

1. On ISA1, open ISA Server Management and click Firewall Policy.

2. Right-click OWA Access Rule and click Properties.

3. On the Public Name tab, click secure.cohovineyard.com and click Edit.

4. Type **mail.cohovineyard.com** and click OK.

5. On the Listener tab, click Properties.

6. On the Networks tab, click External, and then click Address.

7. In the External Network Listener IP Selection dialog box, click Specified IP addresses on the ISA Server computer in the selected network.

8. Click the new IP address that you assigned to the external interface and click Add. Click OK.

9. On the Preferences tab, click Select.

10. Select the certificate issued to mail.cohovineyard.com and click OK.

11. Click OK twice and then click Apply to apply the changes.

The final step is to create a new Web listener that will be used by the Secure Web site. This Web listener will use the certificate issued to *secure.cohovineyard.com* and listen for Web connections on the original IP address. To do this, perform the following steps:

1. Right-click Coho Vineyard Secure Site, and click Properties.

2. On the Listener tab, click New to create a new Web listener.

3. On the Welcome To The New Web Listener Wizard page, in the Web listener name field, type **HTTPS Listener** and click Next.

4. On the IP Addresses page, click External and then click Address.

5. On the Networks tab, click External, and then click Address.

6. In the External Network Listener IP Selection dialog box, click specified IP addresses on the ISA server computer in the selected network.

7. Click the original IP address assigned to the external interface and click Add. Click OK.

8. On the IP Address page, click OK.

9. On the Port Specification page, clear the check box for Enable HTTP and select the check box for Enable SSL. Ensure that the SSL port is 443. Click Select.

10. In the Select Certificate dialog box, select the certificate issued to *secure .cohovineyard.com* and then click OK.

11. Click Next.

12. On the Completing To The New Web Listener Wizard page, review the configuration and click Finish.

13. On the Web Listener tab, select HTTPS Listener. Click OK and then click Apply to apply the change.

Exercise 3: Testing Access to the Secure Web Site and the OWA Site

Before testing access to the two secure Web sites, you must change the information in DNS on SERVER1 to reflect the changes you made on ISA1. To do this, perform the following steps:

1. On SERVER1, open DNS and create a new host record in the cohovineyard.com zone for the host mail.cohovineyard.com. Assign the new IP address on ISA1 to the host record.

2. Open Internet Explorer and type **https://secure.cohovineyard.com** into the Address box. The connection should be successful.

3. Type **https://mail.cohovineyard.com/exchange** into the Address box. You should see the OWA logon form.

Chapter Summary

- SMTP servers are vulnerable to several protocol level exploits including buffer-overflow attacks and SMTP command attacks. ISA Server provides three components for securing SMTP traffic. The first is the Mail Server Wizard, which can be used to publish the SMTP server to the Internet. The second component is the SMTP Message Screener, which can help reduce the amount of unwanted e-mail entering the organization. The third component is the SMTP application filter, which can be used to block buffer overflow attacks or SMTP command-based attacks on Exchange Server.

- Exchange Server 2003 provides access to the mailboxes on an Exchange Server to clients using a Web browser by enabling Outlook Web Access. Use the Mail Server Publishing Wizard to publish an OWA server. For maximum security, configure SSL connections from ISA Server to the OWA client and from ISA Server to the Exchange Server computer. To increase the authentication security, configure the Web listener to use OWA forms-based authentication. Forms-based authentication ensures that the user credentials are not cached on the client computer after the user logs off, or after a timeout period expires. ISA Server can also be configured to publish Outlook Mobile Access and Exchange ActiveSync services to the Internet.

- The Outlook client provides the most functionality, but also introduces some security risks when used to provide access from the Internet. The most significant security issue with using MAPI Outlook clients to provide remote access has to do with the nature of RPC communications. The ISA Server RPC filter enables secure Outlook MAPI connections from the Internet by dynamically managing the assignment of the ports required. Outlook 2003 with Exchange 2003 running on Windows Server 2003 also supports RPC over HTTP, which provides MAPI client access to the Exchange Servers using HTTP or HTTPS.

Exam Highlights

Before taking the exam, review the key points and terms that are presented in this chapter. You need to know this information.

Key Points

- If you disable or delete an SMTP command, that command will be blocked by ISA Server. If a required command is disabled, SMTP messages will not flow through the ISA Server to the SMTP servers. By default, the SMTP filter allows all required SMTP command.

- If you install Message Screener on the ISA Server computer, you have to configure the SMTP server to listen only on the IP address assigned to the Internal network, and then configure the server publishing rule to forward all SMTP messages to that IP address. You must also configure the SMTP server to forward all messages for the internal domain to the internal Exchange Server computers.

■ You can configure the SMTP Message Screener to delete a message, hold a message, or forward a message to a specified mailbox if it meets the Message Screener criteria.

■ Exchange Server 2003 also enables the option of using forms-based authentication when connecting to OWA. You cannot enable forms-based authentication on both the Exchange Server 2003 computer and ISA Server.

Key Terms

Outlook Web Access (OWA)   An Exchange Server feature that provides access to the mailboxes on an Exchange Server through a Web browser.

OWA forms-based authentication   A cookie-based authentication method that ensures that user credentials are not cached on the client computer after the user logs off, or after a timeout period expires. In addition, OWA forms-based authentication can be used to restrict whether users can view or download e-mail attachments.

SMTP application filter   Provides application-layer filtering that can be used to block buffer overflow attacks and to disable SMTP commands that are not required.

SMTP Message Screener   Provides application layer filtering that can be used to filter SMTP mail. The Message Screener can scan the messages and examine the attachments and then block or hold messages for later inspection.

Questions and Answers

Page
9-23
Lesson 1 Review

1. What criteria can the Message Screener use to filter e-mail messages? (Choose all that apply.)

   a. IP address of the sending SMTP server

   b. Keywords in the message body

   c. Source SMTP address

   d. IP address of the destination SMTP server

   B and C are correct. A and D are not correct because the Message Screener does not block messages based on IP addresses.

2. You have deployed ISA Server 2004 and configured access rules on your ISA Server 2004 to limit Internet access. You need to allow your internal SMTP server to send mail to the Internet. What steps must you take? (Choose two.)

   a. Install the Message Screener on the ISA Server.

   b. Configure the SMTP server as a SecureNAT client.

   c. Create an access rule to allow SMTP traffic outbound.

   d. Install the Firewall Client software on the SMTP server.

   e. Enable the SMTP filter on ISA Server.

   f. Create an SMTP server publishing rule.

   B and C are correct. You need to configure the SMTP server as a SecureNAT client and create an access rule to allow SMTP traffic outbound. A is incorrect because the Message Screener is used to block unwanted traffic. D is incorrect because the Firewall Client software is not required and should not be installed. E is incorrect because the SMTP filter allows you to filter SMTP commands, and F is incorrect because an SMTP publishing rule allows SMTP server to receive mail.

3. You have deployed ISA Server, and you are using it to publish the internal computers running Exchange Server as SMTP servers. You have configured both the SMTP application filter and Message Screener. You have just received a notification that a new virus has been detected on the Internet. The virus is spread by e-mail as an attachment named Clickhere.vbs. Programmers within the company frequently e-mail messages to each other with attachments with .vbs extensions, and you should not stop this. You need to protect your network from this virus. What should you do?

   a. Configure the SMTP application filter to block all SMTP commands.

   b. Configure the SMTP application filter to block all MAIL FROM: commands.

c. Configure Message Screener to block messages based on keywords.

d. Configure Message Screener to block messages based on attachment extensions.

D is correct. To block the virus, configure Message Screener to delete all messages that include an attachment with a .vbs extension. The Message Screener only filters messages entering or leaving the organization, so this configuration will not prevent the programmers from sending their files. A and B would block all incoming e-mail from the Internet. C would not block the virus because it does not use a particular keyword in the body or header.

4. You have created the appropriate rules and DNS records to allow your SMTP Server to send e-mail to and to receive e-mail from the Internet. You have installed the message screener on a server running the IIS SMTP service, and you have configured it to inspect incoming e-mail and block certain domains known for relaying spam e-mail. You configure the publishing rule to send all SMTP messages to the message screener computer. You discover that the message screener is not functioning. What else must you do to configure the message screener?

You must run the SMTPCred.exe on the server where the Message Screener is installed and configure it with a user account that has administrative permissions on the ISA Server. The SMTPCred.exe is located on the ISA Server CD.

Page
9-36
Lesson 2 Review

1. What authentication method allows you to control a user's ability to view or save attachments?

   a. Digest authentication

   b. OWA forms-based authentication

   c. RADIUS authentication

   d. SSL certificates

   B is correct. Only OWA forms-based authentication allows you to control how attachments will be handled.

2. You are configuring ISA Server 2004 to publish an OWA server. You have enabled SSL Bridging Mode as a secure connection to mail server and clients. You have requested and installed SSL certificates on the ISA Server computer and the OWA server. However, your users report that they cannot connect to Exchange Server and are receiving a 500 Internal Server Error page. What is the most likely cause of the error?

   a. The external DNS record is incorrect.

   b. There is a problem with the OWA server certificate.

   c. You are using an unsupported authentication method.

   d. The OWA server has not been published correctly.

B is correct. The most likely problem is that the name that the ISA Server computer is using to connect to the OWA server is not the same as the name of the published site on the certificate. All the other answers are incorrect because they would generate different error codes.

3. You need to allow access to the corporate Exchange Server computer for your users with PDA's to retrieve e-mail. How can you ensure the client's logon information will be secure while traversing the Internet?

   a. Use OWA forms-based authentication.

   b. Use SSL to encrypt user sessions.

   c. Configure Internet Protocol Security (IPSec) to encrypt logon traffic.

   d. Use RADIUS authentication.

   B is correct. SSL encryption will secure traffic as traffic crosses the Internet. A and D are incorrect because these authentication methods do not encrypt traffic. C is incorrect because IPSec requires policies set up on both client and server.

Page
9-48
Lesson 3 Review

1. Your company uses Exchange Server 2003 and Outlook 2003 as a MAPI client. You must securely publish RPC over HTTP. What ports must be accessible on the ISA Server computer?

   a. Port 80

   b. Port 443

   c. Port 135

   d. Ports 80 and 443

   B is correct. Only Port 443 should be opened if you want secure access.

2. You need to configure ISA Server to publish internal Exchange servers for Outlook clients that are located on the Internet. You have both Exchange Server 2000 and Exchange Server 2003 in your organization. Users in your company all use Outlook 2003 and need to be able to access all the mailbox and public folder contents when out of the office. The security officer for your organization is concerned about making the internal computers running Exchange Server accessible for Outlook clients because of the number of ports that need to be opened on the firewall. What can you tell the security officer?

   a. Tell him that you will configure ISA Server to use RPC over HTTP so that only one port needs to be opened on the firewall.

   b. Tell him that you will configure ISA Server to publish the computers running Exchange Server as IMAP4 servers, so only one port needs to be opened on the firewall.

    c. Tell him that you will configure ISA Server to publish the computers running Exchange Server using an Outlook RPC publishing rule, so only one port needs to be opened on the firewall.

    d. Tell him that you will configure ISA Server to publish the computers running Exchange Server as Outlook Web Access servers, so only one port needs to be open on the firewall.

C is correct. Although all these options would mean that only one port needs to be opened on the firewall, only C would allow the users to use Outlook to access all their mailbox contents. A would work only for those users with mailboxes on computers running Exchange 2003 Server. B would not allow full access to all mailbox contents because this is not supported by IMAP4. D would not allow the remote users to use Outlook.

Case Scenario Exercises

Page
9-50
Scenario 1 Question

    1. How will you configure ISA Server to meet these requirements?

    To meet these requirements, you should perform the following steps:

        a. Create an SMTP publishing rule to publish the Exchange Server to the Internet.

        b. Create a Firewall Access rule to allow outbound SMTP traffic from the Exchange Server computer.

        c. Install the message screener on an internal server running IIS and use SMTPCred.exe to configure a user to authenticate to ISA Server. Enable the message screener and configure it to delete e-mails with executable or VB script attachments.

        d. Create a Web listener to use OWA forms-based authentication and configure it to block attachments to public machines. Create a new Mail Server publishing rule that publishes the OWA site.

Scenario 2 Question

    1. How will you configure your environment to meet the company requirements?

    To provide full messaging client functionality, you must enable the use of the Outlook MAPI client. Because your users are running Outlook 2003 and you have deployed Exchange Server 2003, you can enable Outlook access using RPC over HTTPS. Configure your Outlook 2003 clients to use RPC over HTTP by creating a custom profile. Configure the front-end Exchange Server computer as an RPC proxy server and configure the RPC virtual directory to require Basic authentication. Install an SSL certificate on the OWA server. Export the certificate and install it on the ISA Server or configure another SSL certificate on the ISA Server. Create a Secure Web publishing rule for the RPC directory on the Exchange Server computer. Finally, create a rule on the internal firewall to allow RPC traffic from the front-end Exchange Server computer to the back-end Exchange Server computers.

10 Configuring Virtual Private Networks for Remote Clients and Networks

Exam Objectives in this Chapter:

- Plan an ISA Server 2004 deployment.
    - ❑ Plan a VPN deployment.
- Configure ISA Server 2004 for site-to-site VPN.
    - ❑ Add remote site networks.
    - ❑ Create a virtual private network (VPN) router user account.
    - ❑ Configure VPN client address assignments.
    - ❑ Create site-to-site VPN access policy.
- Configure ISA Server 2004 as a remote-access VPN server.
    - ❑ Configure VPN address assignments.
    - ❑ Configure access policy for VPN client computers.
    - ❑ Configure authentication for remote client computers. Types of authentication include certificates, Windows accounts, RADIUS, and SecurID.
    - ❑ Enable network access quarantine.
    - ❑ Diagnose and resolve client computer connectivity issues.
- Diagnose and resolve VPN connectivity issues.
    - ❑ Diagnose and resolve name-resolution issues.
    - ❑ Diagnose and resolve routing issues between networks.
    - ❑ Diagnose and resolve Maximum Transmission Unit (MTU) issues.
    - ❑ Diagnose and resolve IP fragmentation issues.
    - ❑ Diagnose and resolve dial-in permission issues.
    - ❑ Diagnose and resolve issues with certificates.

Why This Chapter Matters

You can use Microsoft Internet Security and Acceleration (ISA) Server 2004 to enable Internet user access to internal network resources such as Web servers or Microsoft Exchange servers. To do this, you need only configure the appropriate publishing rule. However, in many cases, organizations must enable a higher level of access to the internal network. In some cases, the remote user may need access to virtually all resources on the internal network, including domain controllers and file servers. These types of resources should never be published using a publishing rule; rather you should enable a virtual private network (VPN) between the client and the internal network so that clients can operate as if they are directly attached to the internal network.

In addition to having individual users connecting the internal network, many organizations also need a secure means of connecting to multiple locations. Although many large companies use dedicated wide area network (WAN) connections to link the organization's locations, a much less expensive option in some cases is to create a site-to-site VPN connection between the company locations.

You can use ISA Server 2004 to enable both remote client VPN and site-to-site access to the internal network. By integrating the VPN solution with the secure filtering of a firewall, you can provide another option for remote users to connect to your internal network.

Lessons in this Chapter:

- Lesson 1: Planning a Virtual Private Networking Infrastructure 10-4
- Lesson 2: Configuring Virtual Private Networking for Remote Clients. 10-16
- Lesson 3: Configuring Virtual Private Networking for Remote Sites 10-33
- Lesson 4: Configuring VPN Quarantine Control 10-50

Before You Begin

This chapter presents the skills and concepts related to publishing internal Web sites and other internal services to the Internet. If you plan to complete the practices and lab in this chapter, you should prepare the following:

- A Microsoft Windows Server 2003 (Standard Edition or Enterprise Edition) computer installed as DC1 and configured as a domain controller in the *cohovineyard.com* domain.

- A second Windows Server 2003 computer installed as ISA1 and configured as a domain member in the *cohovineyard.com* domain. This server should have two network interfaces installed. To complete the network quarantine control practice, you also need to complete the following steps:

    a. Create a folder named C:\VPNQuarantine.

    b. Download the Configurerqsforisa.vbs script from *http://www.microsoft.com/ downloads/details.aspx?FamilyId=3396C852–717F–4B2E–AB4D– 1C44356CE37A&displaylang=en* and add it to the C:\VPNQuarantine folder.

    c. Ensure that you have the Windows Server 2003 Resource Kit tools installed. The tools are available at *http://www.microsoft.com/downloads/ details.aspx?FamilyID=9d467a69–57ff–4ae7–96ee–b18c4790cffd&display lang=en*.

    d. Download and install the updated Remote Access Quarantine Agent from *http://www.microsoft.com/downloads/details.aspx?FamilyID=d4ec94b2–1c9d– 4e98–ba02–b18ab07fed4e&DisplayLang=en*.

- A Microsoft Windows Server 2003 (Standard Edition or Enterprise Edition) computer installed as SERVER1. This computer should not be a member of the *cohovineyard.com* domain. This server should be located on the same network as the external interface of the ISA Server computer. This server should be running the DNS Service and the DNS client setting should be configured to use the server's Internet Protocol (IP) address as the DNS server.

Lesson 1: Planning a Virtual Private Networking Infrastructure

Before you deploy a virtual private network solution using ISA Server 2004, you must plan the deployment so that you can take full advantage of the ISA Server VPN features. This lesson discusses the protocols and authentication methods available when using ISA Server 2004 to implement virtual private networking. Moreover, the chapter describes how VPN quarantine control works. The chapter then describes how you can use ISA Server 2004 to implement a VPN solution and provides guidelines for planning the deployment.

After this lesson, you will be able to

- Describe a VPN and when to use it
- List the VPN protocol options
- List the VPN authentication options
- Describe how VPN quarantine control works
- Describe how to use ISA Server 2004 to implement VPNs
- List guidelines for deploying a VPN solution using ISA Server 2004

Estimated lesson time: 30 minutes

What Is Virtual Private Networking?

Virtual private networking allows secure remote access to resources on an organization's internal network for users outside the network. These resources would otherwise be available only if the user were directly connected to the corporate network. A VPN is a virtual network that enables communication between a remote access client and computers on the internal network or between two remote sites separated by a public network such as the Internet.

How VPNs Work

When you configure a VPN, you create a secured, point-to-point connection across a public network such as the Internet. A VPN client uses special tunneling protocols, which are based on Transmission Control Protocol/Internet Protocol (TCP/IP), to connect to a virtual connection port on a VPN server. The tunneling protocols use encryption protocols to provide data security as the data is sent across the public network. The two VPN protocols supported by ISA Server are Microsoft Point-to-Point Tunneling Protocol (PPTP) or the Layer Two Tunneling Protocol with Internet Protocol Security (L2TP/IPSec).

PPTP and L2TP create "virtual" direct connections between a VPN client and VPN remote-access server, or between two VPN gateways. This connection allows a computer connected over the virtual network to send and receive TCP/IP messages in the same way as it does on other directly connected networks, such as computers located on the same Ethernet local area network (LAN). The actual network connection is transparent to the applications running on the client computer.

PPTP and L2TP use encryption protocols to ensure that the connection is private or secure by encrypting all traffic sent across a public network. PPTP uses the Microsoft Point-to-Point Encryption (MPPE) protocol to protect data moving through the PPTP virtual networking connection. The L2TP/IPSec VPN protocol uses Internet Protocol Security (IPSec) to encrypt data moving through the L2TP virtual network.

VPN scenarios

VPNS are used in two primary scenarios, as shown in Figure 10-1:

- **Network access for remote clients**   In this scenario, a remote user establishes a connection to the Internet and then creates a tunneling protocol connection to the VPN remote-access server. The remote user can use any available technology to connect to the Internet, including dial-up connection to an Internet service provider (ISP) or a direct connection such as a cable or digital subscriber line (DSL) connection. Once connected to the Internet, the VPN client makes a virtual private network connection to the VPN remote-access server that is also connected to the Internet. The remote-access server authenticates the user and possibly the remote computer, establishes a secure connection and transfers encrypted data between the virtual private networking client and the organization's network.

- **Site-to-site VPNs**   A site-to-site VPN connection connects two or more networks in different locations using a VPN connection over the Internet. In this scenario, each site requires a VPN gateway and an Internet connection. When the gateways establish a VPN connection with one another, the site-to-site VPN link is established. Users can then communicate with other networks over the VPN site-to-site link. The VPN gateways act as VPN routers that route the packets to the appropriate network. In most cases, a site-to-site VPN connection is made between branch-office and main-office networks.

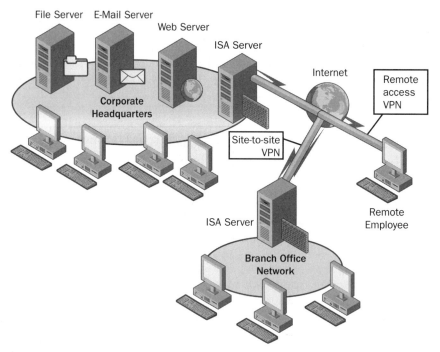

Figure 10-1   Virtual private network scenarios

Benefits of Using VPNs

The primary benefits of using VPNs are as follows:

- **Reduced costs**   Using the Internet as a connection medium saves long-distance phone expenses and requires less hardware than a dial-up networking solution. In the case of a site-to-site VPN, using the Internet as a WAN is also less expensive than using a dedicated WAN connection.

- **Security**   Authentication prevents unauthorized users from connecting to the VPN servers. Strong encryption methods make it extremely difficult for an attacker to interpret the data sent across a VPN connection.

- **Flexibility**   By using VPNs, the organization does not need to manage Internet connections or dial-up servers for remote users. The users need only be able to connect to the Internet using whatever technology is available.

- **Transparency to applications**   One of the significant advantages of using a VPN connection, rather than an alternative solution such as a client/server Web application, is that VPN users at remote locations can potentially access all protocols and servers on the corporate network. The remote-access VPN user does not need special software to connect to each of these services, and the network and firewall administrator does not need to create special proxy applications to connect to these resources.

VPN Protocol Options

VPN security is based on the tunneling and authentication protocols that you use and the level of encryption that you apply to VPN connections. ISA Server 2004 supports two VPN tunneling protocols for remote-access connections: PPTP and L2TP/IPSec.

> **Note**   ISA Server 2004 also supports IPSec tunnel mode for site-to-site VPNs. For more details about IPSec tunnel mode, see the section "Site-To-Site VPN Protocol Options," later in this chapter.

PPTP

PPTP uses Point-to-Point Protocol (PPP) user authentication methods and Microsoft Point-to-Point Encryption (MPPE) to encrypt IP traffic. PPTP supports the use of Microsoft Challenge Handshake Authentication Protocol Version 2 (MS-CHAP v2) for password-based authentication. For stronger authentication for PPTP connections, you can use smart cards or certificates to implement Extensible Authentication Protocol/ Transport Level Security (EAP/TLS) authentication.

PPTP is widely supported and easily deployed, and it works with most network address translators (NATs). Although it is not considered as secure as IPSec, a PPTP-based VPN solution can reduce costs associated with implementing a certificate infrastructure and is less complex to administer than IPSec because it does not require digital certificates.

L2TP/IPSec

L2TP/IPSec is the more secure of the two VPN protocols, using PPP user authentication methods and IPSec encryption to encrypt IP traffic. You can also use certificate-based computer authentication to create IPSec security associations in addition to PPP-based user authentication. L2TP/IPSec provides data integrity, data origin authentication, data confidentiality, and replay protection for each packet.

> **Note**   Support for L2TP/IPSec is provided with Windows Server 2003, Microsoft Windows 2000 and Windows XP. To use L2TP/IPSec with Microsoft Windows 98, Windows Millennium Edition (Windows Me), or Microsoft Windows NT Workstation 4.0, download and install Microsoft L2TP/IPSec VPN Client (Ms12tp.exe). For information about Mls12tp.exe, see the Microsoft L2TP/IPSec VPN Client link on the Web Resources page at *http:// www.microsoft.com/windows2000/server/evaluation/news/bulletins/l2tpclient.asp*.

L2TP/IPSec and PPTP Considerations

When implementing a VPN solution, you must choose which tunneling protocol to use. Table 10-1 lists factors that you should consider as you plan and implement a VPN solution. It also describes the advantages and disadvantages of using PPTP or L2TP/IPSec.

Table 10-1   Comparing PPTP and L2TP/IPSEC

Factor	PPTP	L2TP/IPSec
Client operating systems supported	Windows 2000, Windows XP, Windows Server 2003, Windows NT Workstation 4.0, Windows Me, or Windows 98.	Windows 2000, Windows XP, or Windows Server 2003.
Certificate support	Requires a certificate infrastructure only for EAP/TLS authentication.	Requires a certificate infrastructure or a pre-shared key.
Security	Provides data encryption. Does not provide data integrity.	Provides data encryption, data confidentiality, data origin authentication, and replay protection.
NAT support	To locate PPTP-based VPN clients behind a NAT, the NAT should include an editor that can translate PPTP.	To locate L2TP/IPSec–based clients or servers behind a NAT, both client and server must support IPSec NAT-T.

Exam Tip   L2TP/IPSec requires a certificate or pre-shared key to authenticate the client computer. If a user can connect from one computer, but not from another, the problem may be that the client computer is not configured with the correct certificate or pre-shared key.

VPN Authentication Options

In addition to selecting a VPN tunneling protocol, you must also choose an authentication protocol and choose whether to use a RADIUS or RSA SecurID for authentication. Choosing the appropriate authentication mechanism is essential when designing a VPN implementation because not all VPN clients support the most secure authentication options. The authentication mechanism should be as secure as possible while still enabling VPN client access.

VPN Authentication Method Options

The authentication protocol is used to verify the identity of the remote-access client. ISA Server 2004 supports the following VPN authentication protocols:

- **PAP**   Password Authentication Protocol (PAP) uses plaintext passwords and is the least secure authentication protocol. PAP is typically used if the remote-access client and remote-access server cannot negotiate a more secure form of authentication.

- **SPAP**   The Shiva Password Authentication Protocol (SPAP) is a reversible encryption mechanism employed by Shiva. When a computer running Windows XP Professional connects to a Shiva LAN Rover, it uses SPAP, as does a Shiva client that connects to a server running Routing and Remote Access. This form of authentication is more secure than plaintext but less secure than CHAP or MS-CHAP.

- **CHAP**   The Challenge Handshake Authentication Protocol (CHAP) is a challenge-response authentication protocol that uses the Message Digest 5 (MD5) algorithm to hash the response to a challenge that the remote-access server issues. CHAP is used by various vendors of dial-in servers and client computers, including Macintosh and UNIX. Data cannot be encrypted when you use the CHAP protocol. Therefore, CHAP is not considered a secure option.

- **MS-CHAP**   Microsoft CHAP (MS-CHAP) is similar to CHAP, except that MS-CHAP can be used with MPPE to encrypt data. MS-CHAP is more secure than CHAP, but use MS-CHAP only if you run earlier Microsoft operating systems that require it. Both CHAP and MS-CHAP are only as secure as the strength of the user's password.

- **MS-CHAP version 2**   MS-CHAP version 2 (MS-CHAP v2) was designed to fix many of the security issues with MS-CHAP, including the lack of mutual authentication. MS-CHAP v2 uses mutual authentication, so both the client and the server are authenticated. In addition, data is encrypted by using separate session keys for transmitted and received data, which makes it more difficult for an attacker to sniff the traffic and use a brute-force attack on the key. The session-key generation is not entirely based on the user's password, so a weak password will not necessarily leave the session vulnerable. MS-CHAP v2 is supported by VPN clients running Windows XP, Windows Server 2003, Windows 2000, Windows NT Workstation 4.0 with Service Pack 4 (SP4) and later, Windows Me or Windows 98.

- **EAP**   Extensible Authentication Protocol (EAP) is the most secure remote authentication protocol. It uses certificates on both the client and the server to provide mutual authentication, data integrity, and data confidentiality. It negotiates encryption algorithms and secures the exchange of session keys. Use EAP if you are implementing multifactor authentication technologies such as smart cards or universal serial bus (USB) token devices.

Exam Tip   By default, ISA Server 2004 enables only MS-CHAP v2 authentication for VPN access. If a client computer does not support this level of authentication, then the user cannot connect. For a client to connect, the server and client must both be enabled for at least one common authentication protocol.

Choosing an Authentication Server

In addition to choosing the authentication method and protocol, you also need to decide whether you will use RADIUS or RSA SecurID for authentication. Just like ISA Server can be configured to use these services to enable authentication for Web publishing rules, it can also use them to authenticate VPN users. ISA Server can use IAS servers or any other RADIUS-compliant server.

Windows 2000 Server and Windows Server 2003 both include Internet Authentication Service, which is a RADIUS-compliant server. When ISA Server is configured to use the IAS server for authentication, the VPN server component forwards the credentials presented to it by the VPN client to the IAS server on the internal network. The IAS server forwards these credentials to a domain controller that authenticates the user.

The most important advantage for using RADIUS to authenticate VPN clients is so that you can use domain credentials for authentication when the server running ISA Server is not a member of the network domain. This adds a layer of security to the ISA Server firewall/VPN server solution because, if the firewall is compromised in any way, the machine's domain membership cannot be leveraged to attack the internal network.

A second advantage for using RADIUS for authentication is that this configuration allows you to centralize Remote Access Policy administration. For example, you could have five servers running ISA Server configured as VPN remote-access servers configured in a network load-balancing (NLB) array. You could configure the settings manually on each server, or you could configure each of the servers to use an IAS server for authentication and then configure the Remote Access Policies once on the IAS server. By doing this, the same remote-access policies are automatically applied to each computer running ISA Server.

You can also configure ISA Server to use RSA SecurID for authenticating VPN remote-access clients. To enable ISA Server to use RSA SecurID, you must install and configure an RSA ACE/Server. Then, configure the ISA Server computer as an RSA ACE/Agent and then configure the EAP authentication method to use RSA SecurID.

Using RSA SecurID provides similar advantages to using RADIUS for authentication. In addition, because SecurID uses a remote-access token to generate new pass codes for each connection, it provides an additional layer of security that is not available with the other authentication methods, which use the same password for each connection from the same client.

How VPN Quarantine Control Is Used to Enforce Remote-Access Security Policies

In most cases, a VPN remote-access server can only validate the credentials of remote-access users and computers. If the remote-access users successfully authenticate, they can access all resources on the internal network. However, the remote-access client computer may not comply with corporate security policies. In this situation, you can use VPN quarantine control to prevent remote access to a private network until a client-side script validates the remote-access client configuration.

VPN quarantine control allows you to scan the VPN client computer configuration before allowing them access to the organization's network. To enable VPN quarantine, you create a Connection Manager Administration Kit (CMAK) package that includes a VPN client profile and a VPN-quarantine client-side script. This script runs on the remote-access client when the client connects to the VPN server. The script checks the security configuration of the client and reports the results to the VPN server. If the client passes the security configuration check, the client is granted access to the organization's network.

If you use ISA Server as the VPN server, and the script reports that the client meets the software requirements for connecting to the network, the VPN client is moved from the Quarantined VPN Clients network to the VPN Clients network. You can set different access policies for hosts on the Quarantined VPN Clients network compared to the VPN Clients network. In this way, you can limit network access until the clients have cleared quarantine, and then provide full access.

Although quarantine control does not protect against attackers, computer configurations for authorized users can be verified and, if necessary, corrected before they can access the network. A timer setting is also available, which you can use to specify an interval at which the connection is dropped if the client fails to meet configuration requirements.

The following clients can use VPN quarantine:

- Windows Server 2003
- Windows XP Home Edition and Windows XP Professional
- Windows 2000
- Windows Me
- Windows 98 Second Edition

How Virtual Private Networking Is Implemented Using ISA Server 2004

When you configure ISA Server 2004 as a VPN server, it relies on and enhances the basic VPN functionality provided by Routing and Remote Access, available with Microsoft Windows Server 2003 and Windows 2000. ISA Server supports two types of VPN connections:

- **Remote-client access VPN connection**   A remote-access client makes a remote-access VPN connection that connects to a private network. ISA Server provides access to the internal network to which the VPN server is attached. To configure remote-client VPN access on ISA Server, configure the computer running ISA Server to accept VPN connections and define the parameters for what types of connections will be accepted.

- **Site-to-site VPN connection**   A VPN gateway server makes a site-to-site VPN connection that connects two private networks. To configure site-to-site VPN connections, you configure a remote-site network on the computer running ISA Server and then define how the VPN connection to the remote network will be created. You also define access rules that determine what types of traffic will be allowed to flow from the remote network to the other networks protected by ISA Server.

ISA Server assigns computers to networks and then uses network rules, network access rules, and publishing rules to restrict the movement of network traffic between networks. These concepts are also used by ISA Server to manage VPN connections. ISA Server uses the following networks for VPN connections:

- **VPN Clients network**   This network contains the IP addresses of all the VPN clients that have connected using VPN client access.

- **Quarantined VPN Clients network**   This network contains the IP addresses of all the VPN clients that have connected using VPN client access but have not yet cleared quarantine.

- **Remote-site networks**   These networks contain the IP addresses of all the computers in remote sites when a site-to-site VPN connection is configured. Additional remote-site networks are created for each remote-site connection.

ISA Server uses these networks just as it uses any other directly connected networks. That means that you can use network rules and access rules to define the conditions under which network packets will be passed from one network to another.

ISA Server uses Routing and Remote Access Service (RRAS) to provide some of the VPN functionality, so RRAS must be running on ISA Server to enable VPN access. Although most VPN configuration is done by using ISA Server Management, you can also configure some advanced settings using Routing and Remote Access; however, you must be careful not to override specific settings that should be configured only in ISA Server. In particular, note the following:

- If you use RRAS to enable NAT, some ISA Server features may not function properly.

- Do not use RRAS to enable or disable IP routing. ISA Server always synchronizes RRAS settings, but RRAS does not check how ISA Server configures this functionality.

- RRAS packet filters are not applied when ISA Server is running. It is recommended that you copy the functionality defined by the packet filters used for quarantine in RRAS to ISA Server.

Guidelines for Planning a VPN Infrastructure

Implementing a VPN infrastructure must be planned carefully because you are deliberately exposing your internal network to the Internet. In many cases, VPN clients have complete access to the internal network, just as if the client computer were connected to the internal network behind the ISA Server computer. This means that your VPN implementation must be as secure as possible.

Use the following guidelines when planning your ISA Server VPN implementation:

- For the highest level of security, implement a VPN solution that uses L2TP/IPSec, MS-CHAP v2, or EAP/TLS for user authentication and certificate-based authentication for computer authentication. With this configuration, you must deploy certificates to all remote-access clients. However, the certificate authentication means that only computers that have the appropriate certificate will be able to connect.

- You can also deploy PPTP using certificate-based authentication. In this scenario, you can use two-factor authentication, with devices such as smart cards, to ensure the identity of the remote client. Although this option provides a more secure means to authenticate the remote-access user, it does not provide an option for authenticating the remote-access client computer.

- If you do not have the option of deploying client certificates to all VPN clients or using smart cards, the most secure option is to use PPTP with password authentication. When you use PPTP, the data is encrypted; however, the authentication mechanism is not as secure. If you use password-based authentication, ensure that you enforce strong passwords by using Group Policy.

 Security Alert   To ensure network security, you should always require complex passwords for user accounts. This becomes especially important when you enable remote access to your internal network using VPNs. If users do not use secure passwords, an attacker may be able to guess the passwords and gain access to the internal network.

- Always use the most secure protocols that both your VPN access servers and clients can support and configure the remote-access server and the authenticating server to accept only secure authentication protocols. If you have older VPN clients that do not support secure authentication protocols, consider not enabling VPN access for these clients. Only enable VPN access for these clients if there is a strong business need to do so, and if you do not have the option of upgrading the clients.

■ ISA Server 2004 allows you to use pre-shared keys in place of certificates when creating remote-access and gateway-to-gateway VPN connections. Pre-shared key-support for IPSec-based VPN connections should be used only for testing purposes. A single remote-access server can use only one pre-shared key for all L2TP/IPSec connections requiring a pre-shared key for authentication. This means that you must issue the same pre-shared key to all L2TP/IPSec VPN clients. Unless you distribute the pre-shared key within a Connection Manager profile, each user must manually enter the pre-shared key into the VPN client software settings. This reduces the security of the L2TP/IPSec VPN deployment.

■ Using RADIUS for authentication does not increase the level of security for VPN connections. The only advantage of using RADIUS is that you can centralize policy management for multiple ISA Server computers acting as VPN remote-access servers.

■ Using SecurID can significantly increase the level of security for the VPN connections because SecurID requires access to the token that provides a one use password. However, deploying SecurID significantly increases the complexity of the VPN server deployment.

Lesson Review

Use the following questions to help determine whether you have learned enough to move on to the next lesson. If you have difficulty answering these questions, review the material in this lesson before beginning the next lesson. You can find answers to these questions in the "Questions and Answers" section at the end of this chapter.

1. Your company needs to support VPN clients that use Microsoft Windows 98, Windows 2000, and Windows XP to connect to ISA Server 2004. The computers are all configured with smart-card readers, and each user has been issued a smart card. What is the most secure authentication protocol that is available for these clients?

   a. CHAP

   b. MS-CHAP

   c. MS-CHAP v2

   d. EAP

2. You need to ensure that your VPN clients attempting to connect have the Windows Firewall installed and enabled. How would you accomplish this?

   _____

   _____

   _____

3. You want to use L2TP/IPSec as your tunneling protocol. Some of your VPN clients are running Windows NT 4.0 Workstation. What must you do to enable L2TP/IPSec support with the least amount of effort?

   a. Do nothing. L2TP/IPSec support is built into NT 4.0 Workstation.

   b. Download and install the Ms12tp.exe on the clients.

   c. You must upgrade the clients to Windows 2000 Professional or Windows XP.

   d. Install a Connection Manager package to deliver the L2TP/IPSec client.

Lesson Summary

■ Virtual private networking allows secure remote access to resources on an organization's internal network for users outside the network. The VPN is a virtual network that enables communication between a remote-access client and computers on the internal network or between two remote sites even though the computers might be in different locations and separated by a public network such as the Internet.

■ ISA Server 2004 supports two VPN tunneling protocols: Point-to-Point Tunneling Protocol (PPTP) and Layer Two Tunneling Protocol with Internet Protocol security (L2TP/IPSec). PPTP uses Point-to-Point Protocol (PPP) user authentication methods and Microsoft Point-to-Point Encryption (MPPE) to encrypt IP traffic. L2TP/IPSec uses PPP user authentication methods and IPSec encryption to encrypt IP traffic.

■ ISA Server 2004 supports a variety of VPN authentication protocols. Whenever possible, you should use MS-CHAP version 2 or Extensible Authentication Protocol (EAP).

■ VPN quarantine control allows you to scan the VPN client computer configuration before allowing it access to the organization's network. You can use VPN quarantine control to prevent remote access to a private network until a client-side script validates the remote-access client configuration.

■ ISA Server supports two types of VPN connections: remote-client access VPN connection, and site-to-site VPN connections. When you enable VPN access on ISA Server, it uses the VPN Clients network, the Quarantined VPN Clients network and remote site networks to filter network traffic.

■ Implementing a VPN infrastructure must be planned carefully because you are deliberately exposing your internal network to the Internet. For the highest level of security, implement the most secure authentication and tunneling protocols possible.

Lesson 2: Configuring Virtual Private Networking for Remote Clients

One of the most common deployment scenarios for VPNs is to provide a remote-access solution for remote or mobile clients. In this scenario, a VPN is a cost-effective and secure alternative to using dial-up networking. This lesson describes how to enable VPNs for remote clients using ISA Server 2004.

After this lesson, you will be able to

- Configure VPN client access
- Configure VPN address assignment
- Configure VPN authentication
- Configure VPN connections from client computers
- Troubleshoot VPN client connections

Estimated lesson time: 45 minutes

How to Configure VPN Client Access

Before any users can access ISA Server using a VPN, you must enable VPN client access. When you enable this option, ISA Server enables VPN access using a default configuration that you can modify to meet your organization's requirements.

> **Important**   If your ISA Server computer is a member of an Active Directory domain, you must add the computer account to the RAS and IAS Servers group in Active Directory. If the computer is not a member of this group, ISA Server cannot read the user attributes to determine if users have permission to dial in to the network.

The VPN client access configuration is managed using the Configure VPN Client Access dialog box in ISA Server Management. To access this dialog box, open ISA Server Management and click Virtual Private Networks (VPN), as shown in Figure 10-2.

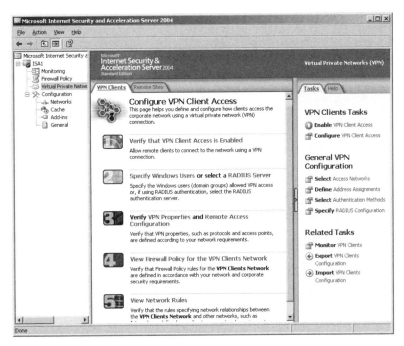

Figure 10-2   Configuring VPN client access

To enable and configure VPN client access, complete the following procedure:

1. In ISA Server Management, click Virtual Private Networks (VPN).

2. To enable VPN client access, click Enable VPN Client Access in the Tasks pane, and then click Apply to apply the changes to the ISA Server configuration.

3. After you enable VPN client access, you can also modify the default configuration. To do this, click Configure VPN Client Access in the Tasks pane.

4. On the General tab, you can enable or disable VPN client access as well as change the value for the Maximum number of VPN clients allowed.

5. On the Groups tab, as shown in Figure 10-3, you can add or remove users and groups who have permission to connect to the ISA Server computer using VPN. By default, no groups are allowed to access ISA Server using a VPN. To assign this permission to a group, click Add. If the computer running ISA Server is a member of an Active Directory domain, then add the Active Directory groups. Click OK.

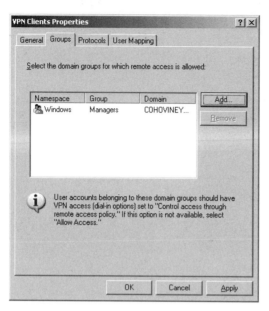

Figure 10-3   Configuring VPN remote-access permissions

 Exam Tip   In order for the users to be able to authenticate for a VPN connection, they must be a member of a group that has been granted access. However, the user account must also have dial-in permissions configured in Active Directory, or on the local computer. Access must be enabled in both places for the user to connect.

6. On the Protocols tab, select the protocols that you want to enable for VPN access. You can choose to enable PPTP, L2TP/IPSec, or both. Click OK.

7. On the User Mapping tab, as shown in Figure 10-4, click the Enable User Mapping check box if you want to enable user mapping. If you want to use a domain to authenticate users who do not enter a domain name when they authenticate, click the When Username Does Not Contain A Domain, Use This Domain check box and then enter the domain name in the Domain Name text box. Click OK.

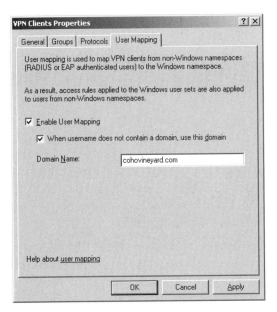

Figure 10-4   Configuring VPN user mapping

User mapping is used to map VPN clients connecting to the ISA Server using an non-Windows authentication method such as RADIUS or EAP authentication to the Windows namespace. When user mapping is enabled and configured, firewall policy access rules specifying user sets for Windows users and groups are also applied to authenticated users that do not use Windows authentication. If you do not define user mapping for users from namespaces that are not based on Windows, default firewall policy access rules will not be applied to them.

When user mapping is enabled and a user tries to create a VPN connection, the user is prompted for his or her credentials. The credentials are passed to the RADIUS server and the user name and domain supplied by the user are mapped to the same user name and domain in Active Directory and the user is authenticated as if Windows credentials had been presented.

Default VPN Client Access Configuration

When you enable VPN client access, the following default settings are applied:

- **System policy rules**   When VPN client access is enabled, a system policy rule named Allow VPN Client Traffic To ISA Server is enabled. Depending on which protocols are configured for remote-client access, the system policy rule allows the use of PPTP, L2TP, or both, from the external network to the computer running ISA Server (Local Host network).

- **VPN access network**   By default, ISA Server will listen for VPN client connections only on the external network. This property can be modified. When this property is modified, the system policy rule is changed automatically to apply to the additional or changed networks.

- **VPN protocol**   By default, only PPTP is enabled for VPN client access. This can be modified to include L2TP/IPSec only or both protocols. When this setting is modified, the system policy rule is updated to allow the appropriate protocol.

- **Network rules**   Enabling VPN client access does not modify the network rules configured on ISA Server. When you install ISA Server, two network rules are created that include the VPN Clients network, one specifying a route relationship between the VPN Clients network and the internal network, and one specifying a NAT relationship between the VPN Clients network and the external network. The second rule is part of the Internet access rule that also defines the relationship between the internal network and external network.

- **Firewall-access rules**   By default, clients on the VPN Clients network cannot access any resources on any other network. You can manually configure a firewall-access rule that enables this access, or you can use a network template to configure the rule. If you use a network template, a firewall-access rule named VPN Clients to Internal Network is created. This rule allows access from the VPN Clients network to the internal network using all protocols. The VPN Clients network is also included in any rule that you create using a network template to grant Internet access. For example, if you use a network template to enable Internet access using all protocols, clients on the VPN Clients network will be able to access the Internet using that rule.

- **Remote-access policy**   When you enable ISA Server for VPN client access, a remote-access policy named ISA Server Default Policy is created in Routing and Remote Access. This default policy denies access to all VPN connections except those explicitly allowed by the remote-access profile. The remote-access profile for the default policy enables MS-CHAP v2 authentication and requires authentication for all VPN connections.

How to Configure VPN Address Assignment

When VPN clients connect to the VPN server, they must be assigned an IP address configuration that enables them to access the resources on the internal network or other networks. ISA Server can be configured to assign the IP address configuration directly, or to use a Dynamic Host Configuration Protocol (DHCP) server to assign the addresses.

When you use DHCP, VPN clients are assigned IP addresses that are part of the internal network subnet. The advantage of this addressing scheme is that you do not need to create special routing table entries to support the VPN clients and all VPN clients will automatically be able to access the internal network and the Internet (using the protocols specified in the access rules). In this configuration, ISA Server acts as an Address

Resolution Protocol (ARP) proxy for VPN clients. For example, when addresses assigned to the VPN Clients network are part of the internal network segment, computers from the internal network will send ARP queries to VPN clients. ISA Server will intercept the queries and reply on behalf of the connected VPN client. The network traffic will then be transparently routed to the VPN client.

Assigning IP Addresses to VPN Clients

When VPN clients connect to ISA Server, the client must be assigned an IP address. There are two ways that ISA Server can assign the addresses:

- **Dynamic address assignment**   To enable dynamic address assignment, a DHCP server must be accessible from the computer running ISA Server. Any computer running Windows Server 2003 or Windows 2000 Server on the internal network can serve as the DHCP server. If you use a DHCP server for address assignment, ISA Server retrieves a group of available IP addresses from the DHCP server. When a VPN client connects, ISA Server assigns one of these addresses to the VPN client. As part of the IP address assignment, ISA Server also assigns other TCP/IP properties such as the Domain Name System (DNS) servers and Windows Internet Naming Service (WINS) servers. The IP address assigned to the client is automatically moved from the internal network to the VPN Clients network (or Quarantined VPN Clients network if quarantine is enabled and the client is quarantined).

- **Static address assignment**   You can also configure ISA Server with a static pool of addresses to assign to VPN clients. In this configuration, you do not need a DHCP server; rather, you configure the IP addresses on the computer running ISA Server. When a client connects, ISA Server assigns one of the IP addresses to the VPN client. If you use a static address pool for address assignment, the addresses that you want to assign to the pool must first be removed from other defined networks, because overlapping of IP addresses between networks is not allowed. You must also provide one more IP address in the static address pool than the expected number of remote VPN connections because the VPN interface on ISA Server requires an IP address.

Tip   If you try to configure static IP addresses for VPN clients that are part of the Internal network, you will receive an error message indicating that the address ranges are overlapping. You can address this error by removing the required addresses from the Internal network, or by using a different address range. For example, if your Internal network includes all addresses 10.10.0.0 to 10.10.255.255, you can remove the IP addresses from 10.10.255.0 to 10.10.255.255 from the Internal network and then assign those to VPN clients. Or you can configure a static IP address range for VPN clients on the 10.11.0.0 network.

Configuring IP Address Assignment

To configure ISA Server to assign IP addresses, complete the following procedure:

1. In the ISA Server Management Console, click Virtual Private Networking.

2. On the Tasks tab, click Define Address Assignment.

3. On the Address Assignment tab, as shown in Figure 10-5, select one of the following options:

   ❑ *Static Address Pool*—To assign static addresses to the remote VPN gateway or the remote VPN clients. If you select Static Address Pool, click Add to specify the IP address range. In the IP Address Range Properties dialog box, in Starting Address, type the first address in the range of addresses to assign to the VPN clients. In Ending Address, type the last address in the range of addresses to assign to the VPN clients.

   ❑ *Dynamic Host Configuration Protocol*—To assign addresses dynamically to the remote VPN gateway or the remote VPN clients.

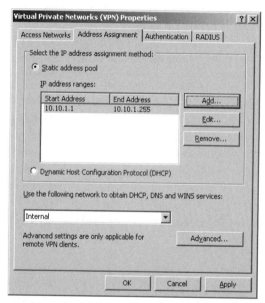

Figure 10-5   Configuring VPN IP addresses for VPN clients

4. In the Use The Following Network To Obtain DHCP, DNS, And WINS Services drop-down list, select the network on which the name-resolution servers are located. In most cases, this will be the Internal network.

5. To configure the DNS and WINS server IP addresses that will be assigned to VPN clients, click Advanced, as shown in Figure 10-6. By default, the DNS and WINS servers assigned by DHCP are also assigned to VPN clients, but you can modify this so that ISA Server assigns alternate DNS and WINS server addresses for VPN client connections only.

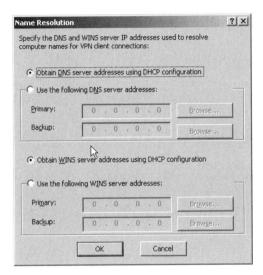

Figure 10-6   Configuring name resolution for VPN clients

 Exam Tip   VPN clients must be able to resolve the IP addresses for all servers to which they need to connect. This could include internal servers and Internet servers if the clients are accessing the Internet through the VPN. If you see an exam question in which users cannot access resources using fully qualified domain names, ensure that the VPN configuration is using the correct DNS servers.

How to Configure VPN Authentication

ISA Server supports multiple authentication protocols for VPN clients. You can enable one of or all the authentication protocols. As a best practice, you should enable only the most secure protocols that are supported by your remote-access clients.

Configuring VPN Authentication

To configure ISA Server authentication, use the following procedure:

1. In the ISA Server Management Console, click Virtual Private Networking.

2. On the Tasks tab, click Select Authentication Methods.

3. On the Authentication tab, shown in Figure 10-7, select the authentication methods you want to enable.

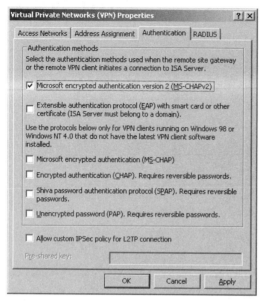

Figure 10-7 Configuring the VPN authentication method

4. To enable a pre-shared key for L2TP/IPSec connections with ISA Server 2004, click Allow Custom IPSec Policy For L2TP Connection. Then type the pre-shared key into the Pre-Shared Key text box.

> **Note** If you configure ISA Server to use a pre-shared key for L2TP connections, all L2TP clients must use that pre-shared key. These clients will not be able to use certificates for authentication.

Configuring RADIUS Server Authentication

In addition to configuring a VPN authentication method, you may also need to configure ISA Server to use a RADIUS server for authentication. To configure ISA Server authentication, complete the following procedure:

1. In the ISA Server Management Console, click Virtual Private Networking.

2. On the Tasks tab, click Specify RADIUS Configuration.

3. On the RADIUS tab, shown in Figure 10-8, click Use RADIUS For Authentication to configure ISA Server to forward authentication requests to the RADIUS server. Click Use RADIUS For Accounting (Logging) to configure RADIUS logging to log VPN connections on the RADIUS server.

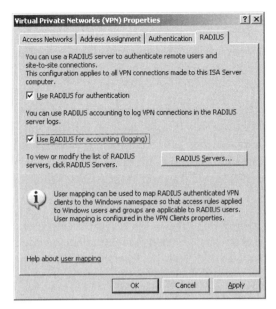

Figure 10-8   Configuring ISA Server to use RADIUS for authentication and logging

4. Click RADIUS Servers. In the RADIUS Servers dialog box, you can add one or more RADIUS servers as well as configure the port number and secret used to communication with the server.

Note   In addition to configuring ISA Server to use a RADIUS server for authentication, you must also configure the RADIUS server to accept ISA Server as a RADIUS client. For more information about configuring the RADIUS server, see Chapter 8, "Implementing ISA Server Publishing."

Configuring RSA SecurID Authentication

You can also configure ISA Server 2004 to use RSA SecurID to authenticate remote-access VPN clients. To enable SecurID authentication, complete these high-level steps:

1. Enable and configure VPN client access in ISA Server.

2. Install RSA ACE/Server. The RSA ACE/Server is an authentication server that manages the authentication process for users.

3. Configure ISA Server as an RSA ACE/Agent. You install the agent on each resource you want to protect with RSA ACE/Server authentication.

4. Enable the system policy rule to allow access from the ISA Server computer to the RSA ACE/Server computer. By default, the RSA SecurID system policy rule allows access from the Local Host network (ISA Server computer) to the Internal network. The rule is disabled by default. You need to enable the rule, and should indicate a specific RSA ACE/Server computer instead of the entire Internal network.

5. Configure EAP (RSA SecurID) authentication. In ISA Server Management, you can configure various VPN authentication methods, including Extensible Authentication Protocol (EAP) with a smart card or other certificate. You cannot enable EAP authentication with RSA SecurID using this interface. Instead, you need to enable EAP authentication on the ISA Server Default Policy in the Routing and Remote Access console.

See Also For more information about how to enable RSA SecurID authentication for VPN clients, see the article, "Authenticating VPN Clients with RSA SecurID Authentication," located at *http://www.microsoft.com/technet/prodtechnol/isa/2004/plan/vpnrsa.mspx*.

Configuring Dial-In Permissions in Active Directory

In addition to configuring ISA Server to enable VPN connections, you must also configure Active Directory user accounts to enable dial-in permissions for those accounts. Until this is configured, users will be unable to connect to ISA Server using a VPN.

The default user account configuration in Active Directory varies depending on the domain being used to authenticate users.

- In Windows 2000 mixed-mode domains, or in Windows Server 2003 domains at the Windows 2000 mixed-functional level, all user accounts have dial-in access disabled by default. You must enable dial-in access on a per-account basis for these Active Directory domains.

- In Windows 2000 native-mode domains, or in Windows Server 2003 domains at the Windows 2000 native or Windows Server 2003 functional levels, all user accounts, by default, have dial-in access controlled by Remote Access Policy. You can control dial-in access by just modifying the remote-access policy.

- Windows NT 4.0 domains always have dial-in access controlled on a per-user account basis.

Tip When a domain is switched to a higher functional level, the dial-in permission for existing user accounts is not modified. The default settings mentioned above are only applied to new user accounts created after raising the domain functional level.

Perform the following steps to modify the user account properties for dial-in access:

1. Open Active Directory Users And Computers from the Administrative Tools folder.

2. Locate the user account you want to modify, and access the user account properties.

3. On the Dial-in tab, choose one of the following options:

   ❏ *Deny Access*—If you choose this option, the user will not be able to connect using VPN regardless of the remote-access policy configuration.

   ❏ *Allow Access*—This option will override permissions set on the remote-access policy, so users will have permission to connect to the VPN server even when they are not granted permission in a remote-access policy. Other settings in the remote-access policy profile may still prevent users from connecting.

   ❏ *Control Access Through Remote Access Policy*—Use this option to configure remote-access permissions using remote-access policies. This option is available only when the domain is at the Windows 2000 native or Windows Server 2003 functional level.

How to Configure VPN Connections from Client Computers

After configuring ISA Server to enable VPN client access, you need to configure VPN connections on the remote-access clients. The exact steps to enable VPN connections will vary, depending on the client operating system.

To configure a client computer running Windows XP as a VPN client, perform the following steps to connect to the VPN remote-access server:

1. On the Start menu, click Control Panel, right-click Network Connections, and then click Open. The Network Connections window opens.

2. In the Network Connections window, click Create A New Connection.

3. In the Welcome To The New Connection Wizard dialog box, click Next.

4. On the Network Connection Type page, click Connect To The Network At My Workplace, and then click Next.

5. On the Network Connection page, click Virtual Private Network Connection, and then click Next.

6. On the Connection Name page, in the Company Name text box, type a name for the connection, and then click Next.

7. On the VPN Server Selection page, in the Host Name or IP Address text box, type the server name or IP address for the VPN access server, and then click Next.

8. On the Connection Availability page, click Next.

9. On the Completing The New Connection Wizard page, click Finish.

10. The wizard creates a connection in the Network Connections window.

> **Note**   To configure a PPTP connection, you need only supply a user name and a password to connect. To configure an L2TP/IPSec connection, you also need to install a client certificate on the client computer or configure a pre-shared secret.

Guidelines for Troubleshooting VPN Client Connections

Enabling VPN connectivity requires a complex interplay between several server components such as the ISA Server configuration and the RRAS configuration. In addition, you have several configuration options such as authentication methods and tunneling protocols. All these components and options must be configured correctly to allow users to connect to the ISA Server computer using a VPN.

Use the following guidelines when troubleshooting VPN client connections:

- The most common problems with VPN connections are user authentication problems. Start by checking the user configuration. Does the user have permission to dial in? Is the user part of a group that has permission to use VPN on the ISA Server computer? Is the user account locked out? Is the user using the correct password?

- If the user account is not the problem, then check the authentication method configuration. If the user is connecting to a PPTP connection, ensure that the client and server share an authentication method. By default, ISA Server only enables MS-CHAP v2 authentication, so if users are using an older Windows client such as Windows 98 or Windows NT, they may not be able to support the authentication method. The best solution in this case is to install the appropriate security patches on the clients so they support MS-CHAP v2 authentication.

- If the users are connecting to an L2TP/IPSec connection, ensure that the client has the correct certificate installed or is configured to use the appropriate pre-shared key.

- L2TP/IPSec clients may also not be able to authenticate if ISA Server is configured to block IP fragments. In this scenario, users will get an error message that indicates that the security negotiation timed out. IPSec uses the Internet Key Exchange (IKE) protocol for mutual computer authentication and for the exchange of session keys in an L2TP VPN connection. The IKE negotiation information cannot fit inside an MTU. Because of this, the IKE negotiation packet is fragmented into smaller packets. When you filter fragmented packets in ISA Server, the IKE negotiation packets are dropped by ISA Server. Therefore, the VPN connection cannot be completed successfully. To enable client connections, you must configure ISA Server not to block IP fragments.

- If the users can connect to the VPN remote-access server and authenticate, but cannot get access to any network resources, check the name resolution for the

VPN clients. The VPN clients must be configured with a DNS server (and possibly a WINS server) address to resolve server names on the internal network.

- If the DNS configuration is accurate, check the configuration of the access rules defined on the ISA Server computer. Remember that the VPN Clients network is used by ISA Server like any other network, so you must configure access rules in order to enable network traffic to flow between networks.

Practice: Configuring Virtual Private Networking for Remote Clients

In this practice, you will enable and configure VPN client remote access on ISA Server. You will then configure a remote VPN client and test the VPN connection.

Exercise 1: Configuring VPN Client Access on ISA Server

1. On DC1, log on as Administrator. Open Active Directory Users And Computers from the Administrative Tools folder.

2. Click Users, and double-click RAS And IAS Servers. On the Members tab, click Add.

3. In the Select Users, Contacts, Computers Or Groups dialog box, click Object Types.

4. On the Object Types dialog box, click Computers, and then click OK.

5. In the Enter The Object Names To Select text box, type **ISA1**. Click OK.

6. Click OK to close the RAS And IAS Servers Properties dialog box.

7. On ISA1, log on as an ISA Server Administrator.

8. Open ISA Server Management, expand ISA1, and then select Virtual Private Networks (VPN).

9. In the task pane, on the Tasks tab, click Enable VPN Client Access.

10. On the Tasks tab, click Configure VPN Client Access.

11. In the VPN Client Properties dialog box, on the Groups tab, click Add. In the Select Groups dialog box, click Locations.

12. In the Locations dialog box, click cohovineyard.com and then click OK.

13. In the Enter The Object Names To Select field, type **Managers**. Click OK.

14. On the Protocols tab, ensure that only Enable PPTP is selected.

15. Click OK to close the VPN Clients Properties dialog box.

16. In the left pane, right-click Virtual Private Networks (VPN), and then click Properties.

17. In the Virtual Private Networks (VPN) Properties dialog box, on the Access Networks tab, notice that ISA Server is configured to accept only incoming VPN connections from the External network.

18. On the Address Assignment tab, click Static Address Pool, then click Add.

19. In the IP Address Range Properties dialog box, type **10.10.1.10** as the Starting Address, and **10.10.1.20** as the Ending Address. Click OK.

20. On the Authentication tab, notice that ISA Server is configured to allow only MS-CHAP v2 authentication for incoming VPN connections.

21. Click OK to close the Virtual Private Networks (VPN) Properties dialog box.

22. Click Apply to apply the changes.

23. Restart ISA1.

Exercise 2: Configuring and Testing a VPN Client Connection

1. While ISA1 reboots, on DC1, locate the Manager1 user account in Active Directory Users And Computers. Double-click the account.

2. On the Dial-In tab, click Allow Access.

3. Log on to SERVER1 using a local administrator account.

4. On the Start menu, point to Control Panel, and then point to Network and click New Connection Wizard.

5. Click Create A Connection To The Network At Your Workplace. Click Next.

6. On the Network Connection page, click Virtual Private Network Connection and then click Next.

7. On the Connection Name page, in the Company Name text box, type **Coho Vineyard VPN**, and then click Next.

8. On the VPN Server Selection page, in the Host Name Or IP Address text box, type the IP address for the external network interface on ISA1, and then click Next.

9. On the Connection Availability page, click Next.

10. On the Completing The New Connection Wizard page, click Finish.

11. Wait until ISA1 finishes rebooting. Once the server is back online, click My Network Places in the left pane, and then click View Network Connections.

12. Double-click Coho Vineyard VPN.

13. In the Connect Cohovineyard VPN dialog box, log on as Manager1, and then click Connect.

14. After creating the VPN connection to the computer running ISA Server, an icon that represents the established connection appears in the System tray. Right-click the icon and click Disconnect.

Lesson Review

Use the following questions to help determine whether you have learned enough to move on to the next lesson. If you have difficulty answering these questions, review the material in this lesson before beginning the next lesson. You can find answers to these questions in the "Questions and Answers" section at the end of this chapter.

1. You have deployed three different ISA Server computers and configured them to accept VPN connections. You want to log information about all connection attempts in a single log file. What is the best way to accomplish this?

_____

_____

_____

2. You are the network administrator for your organization. You have deployed ISA Server to accept VPN connections. You have remote-access policies in place so that only specified Windows security groups can connect to the VPN server. Users in those groups are reporting that they are unable to get a connection. The error message they receive tells them they do not have dial-in permission. The remote-access policies are configured correctly. What is the most likely cause of the error message? How will you resolve the problem?

_____

_____

_____

3. You have deployed ISA Server 2004. Several users within the organization travel frequently and must be able to access resources on the internal network. These resources include accessing their mailboxes through Microsoft Exchange Server by using client computers running Microsoft Office Outlook, accessing internal Web sites that contain confidential information, and accessing file shares on internal file servers. You need to enable access to these internal resources while minimizing the complexity of the client configuration as much as possible. Users should require only a user name and password to connect to internal resources. All the users should also be granted immediate access to the network after authentication. What should you do?

   a. Configure ISA Server to support VPN client access to the internal network. Configure the VPN connection to require L2TP over IPSec. Provide the users with instructions on how to configure each of these connections.

   b. Configure ISA Server to support VPN client access to the internal network. Configure the VPN connection to require L2TP over IPSec. Use the Connection Manager Administration Kit to create a profile for all the remote users.

    c. Configure ISA Server to support quarantined VPN access to the internal network. Configure the VPN connection to require PPTP. Provide the users with instructions about how to configure each of these connections.

    d. Configure ISA Server to support VPN client access to the internal network. Configure the VPN connection to require PPTP. Use the Connection Manager Administration Kit to create a profile for all the remote users.

Lesson Summary

- ISA Server enables VPN access using a default configuration that you can modify to meet your organization's requirements. Most of the VPN client access configuration is managed using the Configure VPN Client Access dialog box in ISA Server Management.

- When VPN clients connect to the VPN server, they must be assigned an IP address configuration that allows them to access the resources on the internal network or other networks. This IP address configuration can be assigned by ISA Server directly, or you can use a Dynamic Host Configuration Protocol (DHCP) server to assign the addresses.

- ISA Server supports multiple authentication protocols for VPN clients. You can enable one of or all the authentication protocols. To obtain the most secure network, you should enable only the most secure protocols that are supported by your remote-access clients.

- After ISA Server is configured to enable client access, VPN connections need to be configured on the remote-access clients. The exact steps to enable VPN connections will vary, depending on the client operating system.

- Troubleshooting VPN access to ISA Server 2004 requires a thorough understanding of the ISA Server configuration and the authentication methods and tunneling protocols. All these components and options must be configured correctly to allow users to connect to the ISA Server using a VPN.

Lesson 3: Configuring Virtual Private Networking for Remote Sites

Another common deployment scenario for VPNs is to provide a secure connection between company locations through a public network such as the Internet. A VPN is often a cost-effective and secure alternative to using a dedicated WAN connection between company locations. This lesson describes how to enable VPNs between remote sites using ISA Server 2004.

After this lesson, you will be able to

- Describe remote-site VPN access configuration options
- Describe a site-to-site VPN
- Choose a VPN tunneling protocol
- Configure a remote-site network on ISA Server
- Configure a site-to-site VPN using IPSec tunnel mode
- Configure network and access rules for site-to-site VPNs
- Configure the remote-site VPN gateway server
- Troubleshoot site-to-site VPNs

Estimated lesson time: 45 minutes

Configuring a Site-to-Site VPN

Configuring a site-to-site VPN is more complex than configuring VPN client access because ISA Server does not include a default remote-site network such as the VPN Clients network. This means that you must configure all the remote site network properties and configure access rules for traffic flow between the networks. In addition, you must configure both sides of a site-to-site VPN connection. When you configure site-to-site VPNs, you need to configure the components listed in Table 10-2.

Table 10-2   Site-to-Site VPN Configuration Components

Configuration Components	Explanation
Determine the tunneling protocol to use	ISA Server supports several tunneling protocols. You need to choose the appropriate protocol based on your organization's security requirements and the VPN gateway servers that you will deploy in each site.
Configure a remote-site network	To enable site-to-site VPNs, you need to create a remote-site network on ISA Server. All the client computers in the remote site are located in this network. You can use this network when applying rules to limit access to other networks.

Table 10-2   Site-to-Site VPN Configuration Components

Configuration Components	Explanation
Configure VPN client access	When a remote VPN gateway server connects to ISA Server, the remote server is treated like any other VPN client. This means that you must enable VPN client access to enable site-to-site access.
Configure network rules and firewall access rules	Because ISA Server uses the remote-site network just like it uses any other network, you need to configure access settings on ISA Server to enable clients at one site access to resources in another site. You can use access rules or publishing rules to make internal resources accessible to remote office users.
Configure the remote site VPN gateway	Once you have configured ISA Server in one of the sites, you also need to configure the VPN gateway server in the other site. This gateway server could be another computer running ISA Server, a computer running RRAS on Windows Server, or a third-party VPN gateway server. The exact configuration of this server will depend on the type of server used in the remote site.

What Are Site-to-Site VPNs?

A site-to-site VPN is a point-to-point tunnel created between a VPN gateway server in one location to a VPN gateway server in another location. In most cases, the VPN tunnel is created across a public network such as the Internet. All data sent across the VPN tunnel is encrypted. When computers from one network send traffic to computers in the other network, the traffic is sent to the VPN gateway server, which encrypts the network traffic and then forwards it to the remote gateway server. The remote gateway server decrypts the network traffic, and forwards it to the appropriate network host.

When you configure a site-to-site VPN on ISA Server 2004, a demand-dial interface is created in Routing and Remote Access. In addition, a static routing entry is added to the routing table on the ISA Server computer that defines how to route network traffic to the remote network. The demand-dial interface is only initiated when required. For example, if the VPN tunnel is not active when a client makes a request that needs to be routed to the remote site, the VPN gateway server in the client site will initiate the VPN connection. After the two servers establish the VPN tunnel, the network traffic can be sent across the VPN tunnel.

Guidelines for Choosing a VPN Tunneling Protocol

ISA Server supports three tunneling protocols. You need to choose the appropriate protocol based on your organization's security requirements and the VPN gateway servers that you deploy at each site.

A tunneling protocol is a protocol that encapsulates a network packet inside a new packet. This new packet might have new addressing and routing information, which enables it to travel through a network. Often, tunneling is combined with encryption to provide data confidentiality—in this case, the original packet data (as well as the original source and destination) is encrypted so that the packets cannot be captured and read. After the encapsulated packets reach their destination, the encapsulation is removed, and the original packet header is used to route the packet to its final destination.

Site-to-Site VPN Protocol Options

ISA Server supports the following three protocols for site-to-site VPN connections:

- **Point-to-Point Tunneling Protocol (PPTP)**   Point-to-Point Tunneling Protocol (PPTP) is a network protocol that enables the secure transfer of data between remote sites. PPTP-based VPNs can be encrypted by using Microsoft Point-to-Point Encryption (MPPE). The primary advantage of using PPTP to create a site-to-site VPN connection is that PPTP connections require only user-level authentication through a PPP-based authentication protocol. This means that the VPN gateway servers do not need any certificates or other authentication mechanism.

- **Layer Two Tunneling Protocol (L2TP) over Internet Protocol security (IPSec)**   Layer Two Tunneling Protocol (L2TP) is an industry-standard Internet tunneling protocol that provides encapsulation for sending Point-to-Point Protocol (PPP) traffic across IP networks. The Microsoft implementation of the L2TP protocol uses Internet Protocol security (IPSec) encryption to protect the data stream between the VPN gateway servers. L2TP/IPSec connections require user-level authentication and computer-level authentication using computer certificates or a pre-shared key.

- **IPSec tunnel mode**   When Internet Protocol security (IPSec) is used in tunnel mode, IPSec itself provides encapsulation for IP traffic only. The primary reason for using IPSec tunnel mode is interoperability with other routers, gateways, or end systems that do not support L2TP over IPSec or PPTP VPN tunneling.

Table 10-3 compares the three tunneling protocols supported by ISA Server.

Table 10-3   Comparing Site-to-Site Tunneling Protocols

Protocol	When To Use	Comments
IPSec tunnel mode	Connecting to third-party VPN server	Provides high security if certificates are used for authentication, moderate if pre-shared keys are used. This is the only option you can use if you are connecting to a server running a non-Microsoft VPN. Requires certificates or pre-shared keys.
L2TP over IPSec	Connecting to a computer running ISA Server 2000 or ISA Server 2004, or a server running Windows RRAS	Provides high security if certificates are used for authentication, moderate if pre-shared keys are used. Requires that the remote VPN server be a computer running ISA Server or a server running a Windows RRAS. Requires user name and password and certificates or pre-shared keys for authentication.

Table 10-3   Comparing Site-to-Site Tunneling Protocols

Protocol	When To Use	Comments
PPTP	Connecting to a computer running ISA Server 2000 or ISA Server 2004, or a server running Windows RRAS	Provides moderate security. Requires that the remote VPN server be a computer running ISA Server or a server running a Windows RRAS. Requires only a user name and password for authentication.

How to Configure a Remote-Site Network

To configure ISA Server to support site-to-site VPNs, you must configure one or more remote-site networks. A remote-site network will contain the IP addresses for all computers connecting from the remote office. In addition, the remote site network also includes tunnel attributes such as the tunneling protocol and the address for the remote site VPN gateway server.

To configure a site-to-site VPN in ISA Server, you need to create a new remote-site network. To create a remote site, complete the following procedure:

1. Open the ISA Server Management Console and click Virtual Private Networks (VPN).

2. In the details pane, click the Remote Sites tab.

3. On the Tasks tab, click Add Remote Site Network to start the New Network Wizard. On the Welcome page, type a name for the remote site network and click Next.

4. On the VPN Protocol page, shown in Figure 10-9, choose the VPN protocol that will be used to create a tunnel to the remote network. Click Next.

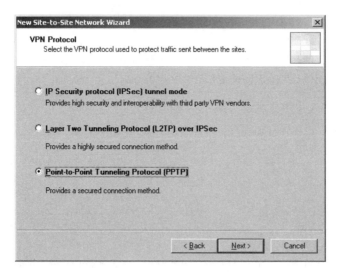

Figure 10-9   Choosing a VPN tunneling protocol

5. On the Remote Site Gateway page, type the name or IP address of the VPN gateway server on the remote network. Click Next.

6. On the Remote Authentication page, shown in Figure 10-10, configure whether the local site can initiate connections to the remote site and then configure user account to be used for the connection. When you configure a site-to site VPN, you can configure which VPN gateway can initiate the VPN connection. You can configure the VPN so that one or both servers can initiate the connection. If you want the server that you are configuring to initiate the connection, you must enter the authentication credentials on the Remote Authentication page. These credentials will be used to initiate the connection on the destination VPN gateway server, so this account must be created on the destination server or in the domain in which the destination server is a member. This user account name must also exactly match the name of the VPN network you create on the destination VPN gateway.

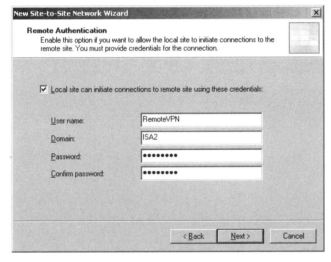

Figure 10-10   Configuring remote authentication for a site-to-site VPN

Exam Tip   One of the common reasons that site-to-site VPNS do not work is authentication errors. Remember that the user name used to authenticate on the remote computer must be the same as the network name defined on the remote computer. For example, on the branch-office VPN gateway server, if you configure an account named HeadOfficeVPN, then the name of the remote site network configured on the branch office VPN server must also be HeadOfficeVPN.

7. On the Local Authentication page, review the information provided on the user account that must be created on the local VPN server or in the local domain and then click Next.

8. If you are configuring an L2TP/IPSec tunnel, you will see the L2TP/IPSec authentication page. If you choose to use L2TP/IPSec as the tunneling protocol, you have the option of configuring a pre-shared key that will be used to authenticate the computers when creating the tunnel. If you are using a pre-shared key, enable this option and then type in the pre-shared key that will be used by all remote VPN gateway servers.

Important   By default, L2TP/IPSec tunnels will use digital certificates to authenticate the servers. Pre-shared keys are simple to deploy because they do not require any certificates and are easy to configure on a VPN server. However, pre-shared keys are not as secure as certificates. If you want a long-term, strong authentication method, consider using certificates.

9. On the Network Addresses page, shown in Figure 10-11, click Add to configure the address ranges assigned to the remote network.

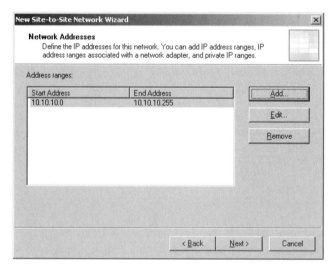

Figure 10-11   Configuring the remote site IP address range

10. On the Completing The New Network Wizard page, review the configuration and click Finish.

Note   If you have not enabled VPN client access on ISA Server, you must enable this before the remote office VPN gateway servers can connect to the ISA Server VPN service. ISA Server considers the remote VPN gateway server connection to be the same as any other VPN client connection.

After you create the remote site network, it is listed on the Remote Sites tab in ISA Server Management. You can modify the remote site network configuration, including changing the authentication methods, the tunneling protocol, the remote site network IP addresses, and the remote gateway server name or IP address. All these options are the same as when you created the rule, with one exception. On the network properties page, you can configure the VPN tunnel to be terminated after a set period of inactivity.

How to Configure Site-to-Site VPNs Using IPSec Tunnel Mode

There are only two differences between configuring a site-to-site VPN using IPSec tunnel mode and configuring a PPTP or L2TP/IPSec–based VPN.

- When you configure the remote VPN gateway IP address, you must also configure a local VPN gateway IP address used by the computer running ISA Server to listen for VPN connections.

- You can configure the VPN gateways to use a certificate for authentication or a pre-shared key for authentication.

Advanced IPSec Protocol Configuration

After you configure the remote-site network, you can also configure advanced IPSec settings. The settings specify the settings IPSec will use when creating the VPN tunnel and can be used to maximize VPN security. To access the advanced IPSec configuration, open the Properties dialog box for the remote-site network that is using IPSec tunneling mode. On the Connection tab, click IPSec Configuration.

In the IPSec Configuration dialog box, as shown in Figure 10-12, you can configure the Phase I or Phase II tabs. On the Phase I tab, you can configure the main mode settings of the Internet Key Exchange protocol. This protocol is used to create an initial secure channel between the VPN gateway servers to secure authentication traffic and the traffic that is used to negotiate the encryption settings for the other traffic that will be sent between the gateways.

On the Phase II tab, you can configure the quick mode settings of the Internet Key Exchange protocol. This protocol defines the configuration settings for the encryption of network traffic using Encapsulating Security Payload (ESP).

Figure 10-12   Configuring advanced IPSec settings

Note   For more information about the configuration of advanced IPSec configuration options, see "Configure IPSec Networks" in the ISA Server documentation. For more information about IPSec, see the IPSec Technical Reference, which is one of the technical reference documents located at *http://www.microsoft.com/resources/documentation/WindowsServ/2003/all/techref/en-us/Default.asp?*

How to Configure Network and Access Rules for Site-to-Site VPNs

When you configure a site-to-site VPN in ISA Server, a new network is established. This network is created for the remote site, but it is treated by ISA Server in the same way as any directly attached network is treated. This means that you can configure access rules to limit the flow of network traffic from the remote site to any other network.

System Policies for Site-to-Site Networks

When a remote network is created, the VPN site-to-site connection is enabled. When this happens, ISA Server enables two system policy rules. One of the rules, named Allow VPN Site-To-Site Traffic To ISA Server, allows access from all external networks to the computer running ISA Server (Local Host network), using the VPN tunneling protocols. You can modify the networks from which the ISA Server computer accepts VPN client connections. When this is modified, the system policy rule is changed automatically to apply to the additional or changed networks.

The second system policy rule that is created is Allow VPN Site-To-Site Traffic From ISA Server. This policy rule allows all VPN tunneling protocols from the Local Host network to the external network and to a computer set named IPSec Remote Gateways. IPSec Remote Gateways is a computer set, defined in advance, that cannot be modified. When an IPSec site-to-site network is added, the IP address configured as the remote tunnel endpoint is added to the IPSec Remote Gateways computer set.

Configuring Network Rules for Remote-Site Networks

After you have created the remote-site network, ISA Server views it as it does any other network connected to the computer running ISA Server. This means that you need to create a network rule establishing whether the network has a NAT or route relationship with the other networks connected to the computer running ISA Server. You should establish a route relationship between the remote-site network and the internal network if two-way communication is required. If the computers that must communicate across the various networks have public IP addresses, a route relationship can be created without concern about address duplication, because public IP addresses are unique. When the computers have private IP addresses, there is a risk that there will be duplicate addresses across the VPN networks. You must ensure that there is no duplication of IP network numbers between the computers that have to connect across the two VPN networks, so that a route relationship can be established.

Configuring Access Rules for Remote-Site Networks

After you create the remote-site networks, you also need to configure access rules to regulate traffic between the remote site and the other networks connected to your computer running ISA Server. You can use any access rule or publishing rule to configure access. There are two high-level options: you can allow all network traffic between the sites, or you can allow only selected network traffic between the sites.

Open Communication Between Networks   One option is to configure the branch office to have full access to the internal network. To enable full access, create an access rule allowing all traffic from the remote-site network to the internal network. You also need to create an access rule that enables all network traffic to flow in the other direction.

Controlled Communication Between Networks   In some situations, you may not want the branch office users to have complete access to the internal network but want to limit access based on users, computers, or traffic destination. For example, you may want to create a firewall policy that allows the following types of communication:

- Some users will have full access to the internal network of the main office, while others have limited access.

- Specific users will have access to an application server on the internal network of the main office.

- All users will have access to the computer running Microsoft Exchange Server on the internal network of the main office.

- The domain controller in the branch office will communicate with the domain controller in the main office, so that users from the branch office can be authenticated for access to the computer running Exchange Server in the main office.

Follow these general steps to create this firewall-access policy:

- Create computer sets representing the client computers who will have differing access rights. Where there is only one computer, such as a single domain controller, you can create a computer object rather than a computer set.

- Create computer objects representing the computers that users will have access to on the internal network of the main office. In this example, you will need computer objects for the application server, one for the computer running Exchange Server, and one for the internal domain controller. Where there is more than one server providing the same network services, such as two computers running Microsoft SQL Server, create a computer set rather than a computer object.

- Create an access rule allowing all traffic for the users who need full access to the internal network of the main office.

- Create an access rule allowing application-specific network traffic from the application user computer set to the application server on the internal network of the main office.

- Publish Exchange Server on the internal network of the main office, using the Exchange Server remote procedure call (RPC) protocol.

- Create an access rule allowing Lightweight Directory Access Protocol (LDAP), LDAP (UDP), LDAPS, LDAP GC, LDAPS GC, DNS, Kerberos (TCP), and Kerberos (UDP) traffic from the remote-site domain controller to the internal domain controller of the main office.

How to Configure the Remote-Site VPN Gateway Server

After configuring one of the VPN gateways, you must also configure the other VPN gateway. The specific steps in configuring the VPN gateway for the remote site will depend on the type of VPN gateway used in the remote office.

ISA Server can support a variety of VPN gateway servers in the remote site, including the following:

- ISA Server 2004 or ISA Server 2000 configured as a VPN gateway server

- Windows Server 2003 or Windows 2000 Server with RRAS configured as a VPN gateway server

- Non-Microsoft VPN gateways that support IPSec tunnel-mode VPN connections

> **See Also**   Microsoft provides detailed instructions for how to configure several non-Microsoft VPN gateway servers to interoperate with ISA Server 2004. For more information, see the VPN page located at *http://www.microsoft.com/isaserver/techinfo/guidance/2004/vpn.asp*.

Regardless of what type of VPN gateway you use in the remote site, you need to configure the components listed in Table 10-4.

Table 10-4   Remote-Site VPN Gateway Configuration Components

Configuration Components	Explanation
Configure the VPN gateway to use the same tunneling protocol	The remote-site gateway must use the same protocol as the main-office gateway. If you use L2TP/IPSec or IPSec tunneling protocols, ensure that the two gateways are configured with the same pre-shared key or have digital certificates that are trusted by the other VPN gateway.
Configure the connection to the main site VPN gateway	If you use ISA Server as the remote office VPN gateway, then configure a remote site network for the main office. If you use RRAS or a non-Microsoft VPN gateway, then configure the connection to the main office VPN gateway. As part of this configuration, create a user account that will be used by the computer running ISA Server at the main office to initiate connections to the remote office, and configure the remote office VPN gateway to initiate connections to the main office.
Configure network routing	If you use ISA Server as the remote office VPN gateway, then you need to configure network rules and access rules or publishing rules to make network resources accessible to main office users. If you use RRAS or a non-Microsoft VPN gateway, then configure the routing rules that you want to apply for traffic from the main office network.

> **Note**   In some cases, the remote office may use a dial-up connection to the Internet rather than a dedicated connection. You can configure both ISA Server and RRAS on a Windows Server to initiate the dial-up connection when the VPN gateway detects traffic intended for the main office. If you use ISA Server, access the dial-up settings on the General tab in the ISA Server Management Console.

Guidelines for Troubleshooting Site-to-Site VPNs

Many of the guidelines for troubleshooting remote-access VPN connections also apply to troubleshooting site-to-site VPNS. However, troubleshooting site-to-site VPN connections may require some additional steps:

■ If the site-to-site VPN connection cannot be established, or if it can be established in only one direction, then check the authentication credentials used to create the connection. As mentioned earlier, the logon user accounts must match the remote-site network names. If you use IPSec tunnel mode, or L2TP/IPSec, check the certificates or pre-shared keys.

■ You can use RRAS to troubleshoot authentication and connection issues. To use RRAS, locate the demand-dial connection and force a connection. If the connection fails, check the error message in RRAS and in the Application log in the Event Viewer.

■ If you use a non-Microsoft VPN gateway, you may also need to modify the MTU on the ISA Server computer to enable the site-to-site connection. Microsoft Windows Server 2003, Microsoft Windows 2000, and Microsoft Windows XP use a fixed MTU size of 1500 bytes for all PPP connections and use a fixed MTU size of 1400 bytes for all VPN connections. If the remote-site gateway requires a different MTU, you can use the registry editor to change the default setting on the ISA Server computer.

 See Also For more information on how to configure the MTU settings for VPN connections, see the article "HOW TO: Change the Default Maximum Transmission Unit (MTU) Size Settings for PPP Connections or for VPN Connections," located at *http://support.microsoft.com/ default.aspx?scid=kb;en-us;826159*.

Practice: Configuring Virtual Private Networking for Remote Sites

In this practice, you will configure the head-office computer running ISA Server to enable site-to-site VPN connections. You will configure the remote site network on the computer and then configure the access rules to enable full access from the remote site to the head-office internal network.

Exercise 1: Creating a User Account for the Remote-Site Connection

1. On DC1, open Active Directory Users And Computers.

2. In the Users container, create a user account named BranchOfficeVPN. Assign a password to the account. Clear the check box for User Must Change Password At Next Logon and do not create a mailbox for the user.

> **Important**   The BranchOfficeVPN user account will be used by the remote computer to authenticate when connecting to ISA1.

3. Open the BranchOfficeVPN User properties. On the Dial-In tab, configure Remote-Access Permissions as Allow Access. Click OK and close Active Directory Users And Computers.

Exercise 2: Configuring the Remote-Site Network

1. On ISA1, open the ISA Server Management Console.

2. Expand ISA1, and then click Virtual Private Networks (VPN).

3. Click the Remote Sites tab.

4. In the tasks pane, on the Tasks tab, click Add Remote Site Network to start the New Network Wizard.

5. On the Welcome To The New Network Wizard page, type **BranchOfficeVPN**, and then click Next.

6. On the VPN Protocol page, click Point-to-Point Tunneling Protocol (PPTP), and then click Next.

7. On the Remote Site Gateway page, type an IP address as the IP address for the remote VPN server, and then click Next. The IP address can be any IP address that is reachable from the external IP address of the ISA Server computer.

8. On the Remote Authentication page, click Local Site Can Initiate Connections To Remote Site Using These Credentials. Fill in the following information and click Next:

   ❏ User Name: HeadOfficeVPN

   ❏ Domain: enter the remote domain name or server name

   ❏ Password and Confirm Password: enter a password and then re-enter it to confirm it

> **Important**   The HeadOfficeVPN account will be used to authenticate to the remote-site VPN gateway server. The remote network that you configure on the remote VPN server must be named HeadOfficeVPN. The user name used to authenticate on the remote computer must be the same as the network name defined on the remote computer.

9. The Local Authentication page provides a reminder that a user with dial-in properties must be configured on the local network for the remote network to be able to initiate a connection to the local network. Click Next.

10. On the Network Addresses page, click Add.

11. In the IP Address Range Properties dialog box, type **10.10.2.0** as the Starting Address and **10.10.2.255** as the Ending Address. Click OK and then click Next.

12. On the Completing The New Network Wizard page, review the configuration, and then click Finish.

13. Read the ISA Server 2004 warning message and click OK.

14. Click Apply to apply the changes.

Exercise 3: Configuring Access Rules for the Remote-Site Network

After you have created the remote-site network, ISA Server views that network as it does any other network connected to the computer running ISA Server. You now need to create network rules and access rules enabling access from the remote-office network to the internal network.

1. On ISA1, in the ISA Server Management Console, expand Configuration, and then click Networks.

2. Click the Network Rules tab in the details pane. On the Tasks tab, click Create A New Network Rule.

3. On the Welcome To The New Network Rule Wizard page, type **Branch-OfficeVPN** in the Network Rule Name text box. Click Next.

4. On the Network Traffic Sources page, click Add.

5. In the Add Network Entities dialog box, click the Networks folder. Double-click the Internal network. Click Close.

6. Click Next on the Network Traffic Sources page.

7. On the Network Traffic Destinations page, click Add.

8. In the Add Network Entities dialog box, click Networks, then double-click the BranchOfficeVPN network. Click Close.

9. Click Next on the Network Traffic Destinations page.

10. On the Network Relationship page, click Route, and then click Next.

11. Click Finish on the Completing The New Network Rule Wizard page.

12. Click Apply to apply the changes.

 Note In this scenario, you will configure access rules so that users on both the main-office and branch-office networks have full access to all resources on each network. Therefore, you must create access rules to allow traffic from the main office to the branch office and from the branch office to the main office.

13. Click Firewall Policy. On the Tasks tab, click Create New Access Rule.

14. On the Welcome To The New Access Rule Wizard page, type **Head Office To Branch Office** in the Access Rule name text box. Click Next.

15. On the Rule Action page, click Allow, and click Next.

16. On the Protocols page, select All Outbound Traffic in the This Rule Applies To list. Click Next.

17. On the Access Rule Sources page, click Add.

18. In the Add Network Entities dialog box, click the Networks folder, and double-click the Internal network. Click Close.

19. On the Access Rule Sources page, click Next.

20. On the Access Rule Destinations page, click Add.

21. In the Add Network Entities dialog box, click the Networks folder, and then double-click the BranchOfficeVPN network. Click Close.

22. On the Access Rule Destinations page, click Next.

23. On the User Sets page, accept the default entry All Users, and then click Next.

24. On the Completing The New Access Rule Wizard page, click Finish.

25. Repeat steps 13 through 25, creating another remote-access rule. The access rule name should be configured with a name of Branch Office to Head Office and the access rule should allow all traffic from the BranchOfficeVPN network to the Internal network.

26. Click Apply to apply the changes.

27. To enable the remote-site network, you must restart ISA1.

Lesson Review

Use the following questions to help determine whether you have learned enough to move on to the next lesson. If you have difficulty answering these questions, review the material in this lesson before beginning the next lesson. You can find answers to these questions in the "Questions and Answers" section at the end of this chapter.

1. Your organization has a head office and one branch office. You have deployed ISA Server 2004 in both locations and configured a site-to-site VPN between the two locations. Currently all users at the branch office can access the Exchange Server computer located at the head office. You need to modify the configuration so that

only managers at the branch office can access a file server at the head office. The managers should be able to access only the file server and the Exchange Server computer at the head office. What steps must you take to accomplish this?

_____

_____

_____

2. You are connecting your branch office to a third-party VPN gateway at the head office. Which tunneling protocol should you use?

_____

_____

_____

3. You have deployed ISA Server and have created a site-to-site VPN between the organization's head office and one of the branch offices. The users in the remote office need to access resources on the head-office network. These resources include accessing their mailboxes through Exchange Server by using client computers running Outlook, accessing internal Web sites that contain confidential information, and accessing file shares on internal file servers. The organization's security requirements state that users in remote offices should have the same access to the head-office network as users in the head office. In addition, the domain controllers in the head office must be able to replicate with the domain controllers in the remote offices. What should you do? (Choose two correct answers.)

   a. Configure an access rule that enables Port 80 and Port 443 traffic from the remote-site network to the internal network at the head office. Configure an Exchange Server publishing rule for Outlook RPC publishing and configure an access rule that enables traffic on Port 139.

   b. Configure an access rule that enables all protocols from the remote-site network to the head-office internal network.

   c. Configure a network rule that enables a NAT relationship between the remote-site network and the head-office internal network.

   d. Configure a network rule that enables a route relationship between the remote-site network and the head-office internal network.

Lesson Summary

- When you configure a site-to-site VPN, you must configure all the remote-site network properties and configure access rules for traffic flow between the networks. In addition, you must configure both sides of a site-to-site VPN connection.

- A site-to-site VPN is a point-to-point secure tunnel created through the Internet between a VPN gateway server in one location and a VPN gateway server in another location.

- A tunneling protocol is a protocol that encapsulates a network packet inside a new packet. ISA Server supports the following three protocols for site-to-site VPN connections: Point-to-Point Tunneling Protocol (PPTP), Layer Two Tunneling Protocol (L2TP), and Internet Protocol security (IPSec) tunnel mode.

- A remote-site network will contain the IP addresses for all computers connecting from the remote office. To configure ISA Server to support site-to-site VPNs, you must configure one or more remote-site networks.

- There are only two differences between configuring a site-to-site VPN using IPSec tunnel mode and configuring a PPTP or L2TP/IPSec–based VPN. When you configure the remote VPN gateway IP address, you must also configure a local VPN gateway IP address used by ISA Server computer to listen for VPN connections and you can configure the VPN gateways to use a certificate or pre-shared key for authentication or a pre-shared key for authentication.

- When you configure a site-to-site VPN in ISA Server, a new network is established. You can configure network rules and access rules to limit the flow of network traffic from the remote site to any other network.

- After configuring one of the VPN gateways in a site-to-site VPN, you also need to configure the other VPN gateway. The specific steps in configuring the VPN gateway for the remote site will depend on the type of VPN gateway used in the remote office but most of the steps are similar for both VPN gateways.

- Troubleshooting site-to-site VPN connections is similar to troubleshooting remote-access VPN connections. In addition, you must ensure that the user name and network names are identical, and you can use RRAS to troubleshoot some connectivity issues.

Lesson 4: Configuring VPN Quarantine Control

Windows Server 2003 provides a quarantine service that is used to confirm the security configuration of a remote client before granting the client full access to the internal network. This functionality has been extended by ISA Server 2004, which integrates the VPN quarantine control feature with the firewall. This lesson describes what the quarantine service is, how it works, and how to implement VPN quarantine control using ISA Server 2004.

After this lesson, you will be able to

- Describe a network quarantine
- List the components required for network quarantine using ISA Server
- Configure the client-side script
- Configure VPN clients using Connection Manager
- Configure the listener component on ISA Server
- Enable quarantine control on ISA Server
- Configure Internet authentication server for network quarantine
- Configure quarantined VPN client-access rules

Estimated lesson time: 60 minutes

What Is Network Quarantine Control?

The VPN network quarantine control feature allows you to screen VPN client machines before allowing them access to the organization's network. VPN quarantine control can delay normal remote access to a private network until the remote-access client configuration has been validated by a client-side script.

Figure 10-13 illustrates and the following steps describe how ISA Server quarantine control works when the remote listener and remote-client component provided with Windows Server 2003 Resource Kit and ISA Server policies are used to implement quarantine control:

1. The user on the quarantine-compatible remote-access client uses the installed quarantine Connection Manager (CM) profile to connect with the computer running ISA Server with quarantine control enabled.

2. The remote-access client passes its authentication credentials to the computer running ISA Server. The computer running ISA Server validates the authentication credentials of the remote-access client and, assuming that the credentials are valid, checks its remote-access policies.

3. If the connection attempt matches the quarantine policy, the connection is accepted with quarantine restrictions, and the client is assigned an IP address and placed in the Quarantined VPN Clients network. At this point, the remote-access client can only connect to resources that are enabled by the firewall policy for the Quarantined VPN Clients network. The client has up to the number of seconds specified in the ISA Server quarantine properties to notify the computer running ISA Server that the script has run successfully.

4. After connecting, the CM profile on the VPN client runs the quarantine script. The quarantine script verifies that the remote-access client computer's configuration complies with network policy requirements.

5. If all the tests for network policy compliance pass, the script runs Rqc.exe with its command-line parameters, one of which is a text string for the version of the quarantine script included within the CM profile. Rqc.exe sends a notification to the computer running ISA Server, indicating that the script was successfully run.

6. The notification is received by the listener component (Rqs.exe) on ISA Server. The listener component verifies the script version string in the notification message with those configured in the registry and sends back either a message indicating that the script version was valid or a message indicating that the script version was invalid. If the script version was valid, the listener component informs ISA Server that the client has been accepted, which causes ISA Server to move the client from the Quarantined VPN Clients network to the VPN Clients network. The client can now access all resources that are accessible from the VPN Clients network.

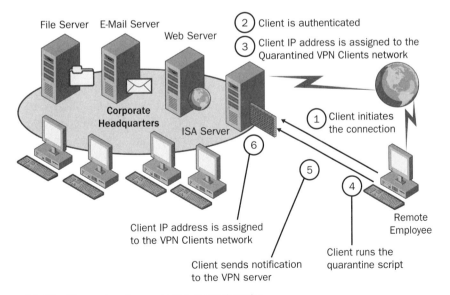

Figure 10-13   How network quarantine control works

How Network Quarantine Control Is Implemented Using ISA Server

Configuring quarantine control on ISA Server requires several configuration steps. Before you enable quarantine mode, you must complete the following steps:

1. Create a client-side script that will be used to validate the client configuration information.

2. Use CMAK to create a Connection Manager profile that includes a notification component and the client-side script. The notification component provides verification to the computer running ISA Server that the script has successfully run. If you do not want to create your own notification component, you can use Rqc.exe from the Windows Server 2003 Resource Kit. Distribute the CM profile to all users who need to access your network through the VPN connection.

3. Create and install a listener component on the ISA Server computer. The listener component is installed on the computer running ISA Server, and receives notification from the client that the script has successfully performed all configuration checks. After the listener component receives notification, it removes the client from quarantine mode, and the ISA Server computer moves the client IP address from the Quarantined VPN Clients network to the VPN Clients network. If you do not want to create your own listener component, you can use the Rqs.exe sample from the Windows Server 2003 Resource Kit.

4. Enable quarantine control on ISA Server. After completing all the previous steps, you can then enable quarantine control on ISA Server. When you enable quarantine for ISA Server, you can configure a time-out setting that specifies the amount of time a client attempting to create a VPN connection is allowed to remain in quarantine mode and an exception list of users to whom quarantine is not applied. Users in this list are automatically joined to the VPN Clients network.

5. Configure network rules and access rules for the Quarantined VPN Clients network. Before a client computer clears quarantine, the client's IP address is added to the Quarantined VPN Clients network. For the client to have access to any network resources, you need to configure network and access rules so that clients on this network can gain access to the internal network. At a minimum, you should configure the firewall policy so that the client can perform name resolution using DNS, obtain the latest version of the CM profile, or access instructions and components needed to make the remote-access client compliant with network policies.

6. Configure network rules and access rules for the VPN Clients network. After the client computer clears quarantine, the client IP address is moved to the VPN Clients network. To enable access to the internal network, you need to define access rules that enable the appropriate level of access.

Exam Tip   By default, a route relationship is configured between the Internal network and both the VPN Clients and the Quarantined VPN Clients network when you install ISA Server. However, no access rule is created for network traffic between the VPN Clients network, the Quarantined VPN Clients network and the Internal network. If you use a network template to configure the ISA Server computer, an access rule is created that enables all protocol access from the VPN Clients network to the Internal network. Remember these default configurations if you see an exam question dealing with the network traffic restrictions between a VPN client and the Internal network.

How to Prepare the Client-Side Script

The quarantine script or program that you create to validate client configuration during remote access can be an executable file (*.exe), a script file (*.vbs) or a simple command file (*.cmd or *.bat). When you create the script, you need to configure it to perform a set of tests to ensure that the remote-access client complies with network security policy. For example, you could configure the script to ensure that a personal firewall is installed on the client computer, that the antivirus software on the computer is running and all files are current, or to check for any other option on the ISA Server computer.

Real World   **Preparing the Client-Side Script**

The most complicated component of enabling quarantine control is planning and creating the client-side script. Part of the reason for this complexity is that the script can query almost any information on the client computer. For example, you can query the network configuration on the computer to determine if Internet Connection Sharing is enabled and whether a client firewall is installed and enabled. You can query computer attributes such as screen saver configuration or the password policies on the computer. One of the critical components that you should query is the antivirus software; is it installed and are all the detection files up-to-date?

To query these components, you can use scripting tools such as VBScript to query registry values, and to look for specific files on the client computers. If you use Windows 2000 and Windows XP clients, you can use Windows Management Instrumentation (WMI) interfaces to query virtually any operating system and many hardware values.

However, the fact that these scripts can be so relatively powerful can also make writing them very complicated. For example, if your company supports more than one antivirus application, your script would have to check for all supported antivirus applications and ensure that at least one of them is installed and current. If you support more than one client firewall, you must scan for all supported versions. If users are allowed to install their own applications, they may have selected nonstandard installation locations so your script may have to be very flexible.

Because writing these scripts can be so complicated, you need considerable scripting expertise to plan and create the script. Ensure that your team includes an experienced script writer. In addition, start with a simple script and gradually implement more complexity. For example, you may want to start by checking for the presence of the antivirus software, and modify the script to check for the detection file versions only after you are sure that the script is working. You should also strictly limit the types of software that you will support. To simplify the script, you may choose to require all VPN clients to use the same antivirus software. Or you may choose to allow VPN access to only Windows XP clients with Service Pack 2 installed and Windows Firewall enabled.

In addition, there are other concerns that you need to plan for in your VPN network quarantine deployment. For example, there are some configuration settings that you may want to check on the client computer that require Administrator privileges for the user. If you give your users Administrator privileges, you significantly increase the risk that the computers will be infected by malware and also make it harder to control what users do on their machines. If you want the users to be able to correct any configuration problems, they might need Administrator privileges. Another concern with network quarantine is that Rqs.exe and Rqc.exe may not be as secure as you would like; a malicious user may be able to spoof the approval message to the VPN server bypassing the quarantine without actually passing the checks.

If you are using the Windows Server Resource Kit notification component, the script must run Rqc.exe if all the tests specified in the script are successful. Rqc.exe uses the following parameters:

```
rqc ConnName TunnelConnName TCPPort Domain UserName ScriptVersion
```

The command-line parameters of Rqc.exe are as follows:

- **ConnName** The name of the remote-access connection on this host. The value of this parameter can be inherited from the Connection Manager profile *%DialRasEntry%* variable.

- **TunnelConnName** The name of the tunnel connection on this host. The value of this parameter can be inherited from the Connection Manager profile *%Tunnel RasEntry%* variable.

- **TCPPort** The TCP port used to send the notification message. The default TCP port used by Rqs.exe is 7250. If you configure Rqs.exe to use a TCP port other than 7250, you must specify that TCP port number here.

- **Domain**   The domain of the connecting user. The value of this parameter can be inherited from the Connection Manager profile *%Domain%* variable.

- **UserName**   The user name of the connecting user. The value of this parameter can be inherited from the Connection Manager profile *%UserName%* variable.

- **ScriptVersion**   A text string that contains the script version. You can specify a text string using keyboard characters, except the */0* character sequence. This script version is used to ensure that the client is using the latest version of the script. If rqc.exe does not return the correct script version, the client will not be released from quarantine.

> **Note**   For more information about creating quarantine control scripts and a sample script, see Network Access Quarantine Control in Windows Server 2003 located at *http://www.microsoft.com/windowsserver2003/techinfo/overview/quarantine.mspx*
>
> For additional script examples, see the article "VPN Quarantine Sample Scripts for Verifying Client Health Configurations," located at *http://www.microsoft.com/downloads/details.aspx?FamilyID=a290f2ee-0b55-491e-bc4c-8161671b2462&displaylang=en*

How to Configure VPN Clients Using Connection Manager

The Connection Manager family of programs is a set of optional components included with Windows Server 2003 and Windows 2000 Server than can be used to create a managed remote-access solution. You can use Connection Manager to create a client installation file that will pre-configure remote-access clients. The Connection Manager family of products includes the Connection Manager client, CMAK, and Connection Point Services (CPS).

To enable clients to use quarantine mode, you must configure a Connection Manager profile using CMAK. The profile contains the following components:

- **A post-connect action that runs a network policy requirements script**   This functionality is configured when the CM profile is created with CMAK.

- **A network policy requirements script**   This script performs validation checks on the remote-access client computer to verify that it conforms to network policies. It can be a custom executable file or a simple command file (also known as a *batch file*). When the script has run successfully and the connecting computer has satisfied all the network policy requirements (as verified by the script), the script runs a notification component (an executable) with the appropriate parameters.

> **Tip**   If the script does not run successfully, you should consider using the script to display information to the remote-access user that directs them to a quarantine resource, such as an internal or external Web page, that describes how to install the components that are required for network policy compliance.

- **A notification component**   The notification component sends a message that indicates a successful execution of the script to the quarantine-compatible remote-access server. You can use your own notification component or you can use Rqc.exe, which is provided with the Windows Server 2003 Resource Kit.

To configure the quarantine CM profile, run the Connection Manager Administration Kit Wizard. Only two parts of the configuration process are specific to creating a quarantine CM profile:

- **Define a custom action**   You can use the Connection Manager Administration Kit Wizard to define a custom action. This action can occur before the client connects, or at any stage during or after the connection. To create a profile that will enable quarantine control, you must configure a custom action that will run the quarantine requirements script after the client connects.

- **Add the notification component as an additional file**   As part of the CM profile, you can install additional files on the client computer. To enable a quarantine profile, you need to add the Rqc.exe or a custom notification component to the profile.

> **Note**   You will configure a CM profile in the practice that follows this lesson.

Distributing the CM Profile

After you create the quarantine Connection Manager profile, it must be distributed and installed on all your remote-access client computers. The profile itself is an executable file that must be run on the remote-access client to install the profile and configure the quarantine network connection.

There are many methods to distribute and run the profile on remote-access client computers, including the following:

- Send the profile executable file, or a link to the profile, to your remote-access users with instructions to run the executable that installs the quarantine connection.

- Place the profile executable file on a secure Web page and instruct your users to run the profile that installs the quarantine connection.

- Have the profile run as part of a startup script or as part of the domain logon script.

- Put the executable file on a CD or a floppy disk and provide the installation media to the remote-access users.

- Use a software distribution application such as SMS to distribute the profile.

In addition to distributing the profile to your remote-access users, place the profile on a file share or Web site that is accessible from the Quarantined VPN Clients network. If the profile is placed on a share or a Web site, you can instruct remote-access clients who do not have the current profile installed and are in quarantine mode to install the latest profile and then reconnect.

How to Prepare the Listener Component

The Network Quarantine Service (Rqs.exe) provides the listener service for computers running ISA Server to support VPN Quarantine. This component must be installed on all computers running ISA Server that will provide quarantine services. In addition, the computer running ISA Server must be configured to enable network traffic intended for the listener service.

The easiest way to install the Network Quarantine Service and configure ISA Server to support listener network traffic is to use the ConfigureRQSForISA.vbs script provided for ISA Server 2004.

> **Note**   You can download the Configurerqsforisa.vbs script from *http://www.microsoft.com/ downloads/details.aspx?FamilyId=3396C852-717F-4B2E-AB4D-1C44356CE37A&displaylang=en*

The syntax to use this script is:

```
Cscript ConfigureRQSForISA.vbs /install SharedKey1\0SharedKey2 pathto RQS.exe
```

- The /install command-line switch installs the listener service. To uninstall the listener service, use /remove.

- The SharedKey value is the key that the notification component will send to the listener component. The notification message sent by Rqc.exe contains a text string that indicates the version of the quarantine script being run. This string is configured for Rqc.exe as part of its command-line parameters, as run from the quarantine script. Rqs.exe compares this text string to a set of text strings stored in the registry of the computer running ISA Server. If there is a match, the quarantine conditions are removed from the connection. If the client provides a shared key that is not in the allowed set, it will be disconnected. There can be more than one shared key, separated by "\0".

- The pathto value defines where the listener executable is located.

The ConfigureRQSForISA.vbs script performs the following actions:

- Installs RQS as a service and sets it to run in the security context of the local system account. The service name is Network Quarantine Service.

- Creates an ISA Server access rule that allows communication on the RQS port (7250) from the VPN Clients and Quarantined VPN Clients networks to the Local Host network. This is necessary so that the computer running ISA Server can receive notice that the client has met the connection requirements.

- Modifies registry keys on the computer running ISA Server so that RQS will work with ISA Server.

- Starts the RQS service.

How to Enable Quarantine Control

After configuring all the other components, you are finally ready to enable quarantine service on ISA Server. To enable quarantine service, complete the following steps.

1. In the tree of the ISA Server Management Console, click Networks.

2. In the details pane, click the Networks tab, and then select the Quarantined VPN Clients network.

3. On the Tasks tab, click Edit Selected Network.

4. On the Quarantine tab, shown in Figure 10-14, click Enable Quarantine Control, and then select one of the following options:

   ❏ *Quarantine According To RADIUS Server Policies*—When a VPN client attempts to connect, Routing and Remote Access policy determines whether the connection request is passed to ISA Server. After Routing and Remote Access policy has been verified, the client unconditionally joins the VPN Clients network. To use this option, you must configure ISA Server to use RADIUS for authentication and configure the quarantine policies on the RADIUS server.

   ❏ *Quarantine According To ISA Server Policies*—When a VPN client attempts to connect to the computer running ISA Server, Routing and Remote Access unconditionally passes the request to ISA Server. ISA Server places the connecting client in the Quarantined VPN Clients network, subjecting the client to the firewall policy defined for that network. When the client clears quarantine, it moves into the VPN Clients network.

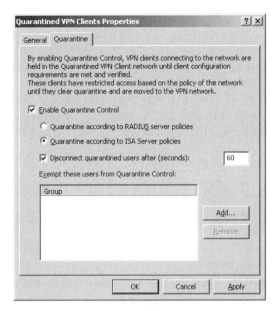

Figure 10-14   Enabling VPN quarantine control

5. If quarantined clients should be disconnected after a specified time, select Disconnect Quarantine Users After (Seconds) and type the number of seconds that will pass before a client will be removed from the Quarantined VPN Clients network and disconnected from ISA Server.

6. If specific users should be exempted from quarantine control, click Add under Exempt These Users From Quarantine Control. Add the user sets that represent the users who are not required to go through quarantine control.

> **Important**   Note that when quarantine mode is disabled, all remote VPN clients with appropriate authentication permissions are placed in the VPN Clients network and will have the access you have allowed the VPN Clients network in your firewall policy. However, once you enable quarantine mode, all client connections will be forced to use the quarantine mode. If a client does not support quarantine mode, the client will not be able to connect. If the Network Quarantine Service is not running, users will not be able to connect. The only exception to this is if you configure a user set in the Exempt These Users From Quarantine Control panel.

How to Configure Internet Authentication Server for Network Quarantine

If you are running ISA Server on Windows Server 2003, you can enable quarantine by using RADIUS policy or by using ISA Server policy. When you run ISA Server on Windows 2000 Server, you can only enable quarantine using ISA Server policy. If you enable quarantine using RADIUS policy, you can use Internet Authentication Service on Windows Server 2003 or Windows 2000 Server to act as the RADIUS server.

IAS is a RADIUS-compliant service that is available with Windows Server 2003 or Windows Server and can be used to control remote access by authenticating users and enforcing policies. When you use IAS to restrict remote access, you need to define a remote-access policy. Remote-access policies are ordered sets of rules that define how remote-access connections are either authorized or rejected. You can use remote-access policies to specify the groups or individuals that are allowed remote access and to set different types of connection constraints. A remote-access policy consists of the following three components:

- **Conditions** The conditions of remote-access policies are a list of parameters, such as the time of day, user groups, caller IDs, or IP addresses, that are matched to the parameters of the client that is connecting to the server. The first set of policy conditions that match the parameters of the incoming connection request are processed for access permission and configuration. If none of the condition sets are matched, the access attempt will fail.

- **Remote-access permission** Remote-access connections are permitted based on a combination of the dial-in properties of a user account and remote-access policies. The permission setting on the remote-access policy works with the user's dial-in permissions in Active Directory directory service.

- **Profile** Each policy includes a profile of settings, such as authentication and encryption protocols, that are applied to the connection. The settings in the profile are applied to the connection immediately and may cause the connection to be denied. For example, if the profile settings for a connection specify that the user can only connect for 30 minutes at a time, the user will be disconnected from the remote-access server after 30 minutes. Where applicable, connection restrictions for a user account override the connection restrictions for the remote-access policy profile.

Using IAS for Quarantine Control

If your organization has several branch offices, each running ISA Server 2004, you may want to enable quarantine using RADIUS policy to centralize the quarantine control in a single RADIUS server that serves all branch offices.

If you use RADIUS to manage the quarantine settings, you must install the listener component on the RADIUS server and then configure a remote-access policy that configures the quarantine settings. RADIUS uses two settings in a remote-access policy to enforce the quarantine:

- **MS-Quarantine-IPFilter setting** This setting is used to configure the packet filters that quarantine the remote-access client until the notifying component on the remote-access client indicates that the computer is in compliance with quarantine policies. You can use the MS-Quarantine-IPFilter attribute to configure input and output packet filters to allow the client computer to connect using TCP Port 7250 (for the notification component to connect to the RADIUS server) and other traffic needed to access the quarantine resources. This includes filters that allow the remote-access client to access name resolution servers (such as DNS servers), file shares, or Web sites.

■ **MS-Quarantine-Session-Timeout**   You can use the MS-Quarantine-Session-Timeout attribute to specify how long the remote-access server must wait to receive the notification that the script has run successfully before terminating the connection.

After you configure IAS and ISA Server to use RADIUS, VPN client requests are passed by ISA Server to the IAS server. The remote-access policy on IAS determines whether the connection request is accepted on ISA Server. After the remote-access policy has been verified, the client unconditionally joins the VPN Clients network.

> **Tip**   In most cases, you should use ISA Server policies when enabling VPN quarantine control. With RADIUS policies, you are limited to using packet filters to restrict access to the internal network while enabling access to the resources that the client requires in order to clear quarantine. If you use ISA Server policies, you can configure any access or publishing rule with the Quarantined VPN Clients network as the source address.

How to Configure Quarantined VPN Client-Access Rules

The final step in configuring quarantine control for VPN clients is to configure the access rules for the Quarantined VPN Clients network to access required resources on other networks.

To allow access to a resource, create an access rule with the Quarantined VPN Clients network as the source and the server to which access is required as the destination. To configure this rule, create a computer rule element for each server, so that it can be used in access rules. Alternatively, you can create a computer set containing all the computers to which the quarantined clients require access, and create an access rule with the Quarantined VPN Clients network as the source and the computer set as the destination.

The following are examples of the types of access you may want to allow the Quarantined VPN Clients network:

■ For Rqc.exe-notification traffic, use destination TCP Port 7250. (This is the default TCP port used by Rqs.exe.)

- Allow queries to LDAP servers on the internal network.

- Allow traffic to domain controllers or RADIUS servers.

- Allow quarantined VPN clients to issue DNS queries to DNS servers.

- Allow quarantined VPN clients to access WINS servers.

- Allow quarantined VPN clients to use Hypertext Transfer Protocol (HTTP) to access internal Web servers. Use this option if you have a Web page that explains how the user can configure his or her computer so that it meets the quarantine security requirements, or if the Web page contains any other resource that can be used to configure the quarantined VPN client.

- Allow quarantined VPN clients to use NetBIOS over TCP/IP using destination TCP Port 139 to enable access to file shares on the internal network. Use this option to enable client access to a share that contains resources that can be used to configure the quarantined VPN client.

Another option is to design your network so that all the servers to which access is required are on a subnet, and define a Subnet rule element for use in the access rule. In this configuration, you may enable access using all protocols to the specific subnet, or limit access to only the required protocols.

Practice: Configuring VPN Quarantine Control

In this practice, you will configure ISA Server to enable VPN quarantine control. For testing purposes, you will use a simple script that will check for the existence of a specific file on the client computer and grant access to the network if the file exists. You will then use Configurerqsforisa.vbs to configure ISA Server to support quarantine control and then you will enable quarantine control. You will then create a Connection Manager profile and distribute it to the VPN remote-access clients. Finally, you will configure access rules to enable access for the Quarantined VPN Clients network.

Exercise 1: Creating the Quarantine Client-Side Script

1. Copy the file Rqsscript.cmd located in the \Labs folder on the companion CD-ROM of this book to ISA1.

2. Save the file as Rqsscript.cmd in the C:\VPNQuarantine folder.

 Note   This script is a simple script that just checks for the presence of a file called Access.txt on the root of C: drive. In the real world, you will need to use a different script.

Exercise 2: Installing and Configuring the Network Quarantine Service Using ConfigureRQSForISA.vbs

1. Open a command prompt and switch to the C:\VPNQuarantine directory.

2. At the command prompt, type **Cscript configurerqsforisa.vbs /install Version7a "c:\program files\windows resource kits\tools"** and press ENTER.

3. Wait until the script finishes running and then close the command prompt.

Exercise 3: Confirming the ISA Server Configuration

1. On the Start menu, click Run.

2. In the Run dialog box, type **regedit.exe**, and then press ENTER.

3. In the Registry Editor window, select the HKEY_LOCAL_MACHINE\SYSTEM\ CurrentControlSet\Services\rqs key.

4. Confirm that the AllowedSet key was created and configured with a value of Version7a. Version7a is the identifier of the script (Rqscript.vbs) that this practice uses to check the security configuration of the client computer.

5. Confirm that the Authenticator key was created and configured with a value of C:\Program Files\Microsoft ISA Server\vpnplgin.dll.

6. Close the Registry Editor window.

7. On the Start menu, click Administrative Tools, and then click Services.

8. In the Services console, in the right pane, right-click Network Quarantine Service, and then click Properties.

9. Ensure that Network Quarantine Service is set to start automatically and that it is started. Click OK.

10. Close the Services console.

> **Note**   When the security configuration of the VPN client computer meets the security policy, the Rqc.exe application on the client computer notifies the Rqs.exe service on ISA Server that the quarantine restrictions can be removed. This requires an access rule to allow communication (using TCP Port 7250) from the Quarantined VPN Clients network to the Local Host network (ISA Server).

11. In ISA Server Management, click Firewall Policy.

12. In the task pane, on the Toolbox tab, click Protocols and expand User-Defined.

13. Double-click RQS and on the Parameters tab, confirm that the configuration matches the following settings and then click OK:

   ❑ Protocol type: TCP

   ❑ Direction: Outbound

   ❑ Port Range From: 7250

   ❑ Port Range To: 7250

> **Note**   A new firewall-access rule is required that allows RQS communication from a VPN client computer on the Quarantined VPN Clients network to ISA Server.

14. In the task pane, on the Firewall Policy tab, double-click Network Quarantine (RQS).

15. On the Action tab, confirm that Allow is selected.

16. On the Protocols tab, confirm that the access rule applies to the RQS protocol only.

17. On the From tab, confirm that the rule accepts traffic from the Quarantined VPN Clients, VPN Clients networks.

18. On the To tab, confirm that the rule applies to traffic sent to the Local Host network.

19. Click OK.

Exercise 4: Enabling Quarantine Control

1. In the ISA Server Management Console, in the left pane, expand Configuration and select Networks.

2. In the right pane, on the Networks tab, right-click the Quarantined VPN Clients network, and then click Properties.

3. In the Quarantined VPN Clients Properties dialog box, on the Quarantine tab, select Enable Quarantine Control.

4. In the message box, click OK to confirm that enabling quarantine requires configuration on both the computer running ISA Server and VPN client computers.

5. Ensure that Quarantine According To ISA Server Policies is selected.

6. Click Disconnect Quarantine Users After (seconds) and type **60** in the text box. Click OK.

7. Click Firewall Policy, and then click the Coho Vineyard VPN Server publishing rule. On the Tasks tab, click Disable Selected Rule.

8. Click Apply to apply the changes.

Exercise 5: Installing Connection Manager Administration Kit

1. On ISA1 on the Start menu, point to Control Panel, and then click Add Or Remove Programs.

2. In the Add Or Remove Programs window, click Add/Remove Windows Components.

3. On the Windows Components page, select the Management And Monitoring Tools component, and then click Details.

4. In the Management And Monitoring Tools dialog box, select the Connection Manager Administration Kit check box, and then click OK.

5. On the Windows Components page, click Next.

6. If the Insert Disk dialog box appears, insert the Windows Server 2003 installation CD-ROM and click OK.

7. On the Completing The Windows Components Wizard page, click Finish.

8. Close the Add Or Remove Programs window.

Exercise 6: Configuring a Connection Manager Profile

1. On the Start menu, click Administrative Tools, and then click Connection Manager Administration Kit.

2. On the Welcome To The Connection Manager Administration Kit Wizard page, click Next.

3. On the Service Profile Selection page, accept the default of New Profile, and then click Next.

4. On the Service And File Names page, type the following information:

    ❑ Service Name: **VPN to Cohovineyard**

    ❑ File Name: **VPN_RQ**

    Click Next.

5. On the Realm Name page, click Next.

6. On the Merging Profile Information page, click Next.

7. On the VPN Support page, click the check box for Phone Book From This Profile. Under Always Use The Same VPN Server, type the external IP address for the ISA Server computer and then click Next.

8. On the VPN Entries page, click Next.

9. On the Phone Book page, clear the Automatically Download Phone Book Updates check box, and then click Next.

10. On the Dial-Up Networking Entries page, click Next.

11. On the Routing Table Update page, click Next.

12. On the Automatic Proxy Configuration page, click Next.

13. On the Custom Actions page, click New.

14. In the New Custom Action dialog box, enter the following information:

    ❑ Description: **Quarantine policy checking**

    ❑ Program To Run: **C:\VPNQuarantine\rqsscript.cmd**

    ❑ Parameters: *%ServiceDir% %DialRasEntry% %TunnelRasEntry% %Domain% %UserName%*

    ❑ Action Type: Post-Connect

    ❑ Run This Custom Action For: All Connections (Accept Default)

    ❑ Include The Custom Action Program With This Service Profile: Enable

    ❑ Program Interacts With The User: enable (Accept Default)

    Click OK.

15. On the Custom Actions page, click Next.

16. On the Logon Bitmap page, click Next.

17. On the Phone Book Bitmap page, select Default Graphic, and then click Next.

18. On the Icons page, select Default icons, and then click Next.

19. On the Notification Area Shortcut Menu page, click Next.

20. On the Help File page, select Default Help File, and then click Next.

21. On the Support Information page, click Next.

22. On the Connection Manager Software page, select Install Connection Manager 1.3, and then click Next.

23. On the License Agreement page, click Next.

24. On the Additional Files page, click Add.

25. Browse to the C:\Program Files\Windows Resource Kits\Tools folder, select the Rqc.exe file and then click Open.

26. On the Additional Files page, click Next.

27. On the Ready To Build The Service Profile page, click Next. A command prompt window opens and closes as the new Connection Manager profile (VPN_RQ.exe) is created in the C:\Program Files\Cmak\Profiles\VPN_RQ folder.

28. On the Completing The Connection Manager Administration Kit Wizard page, click Finish.

29. Open Windows Explorer and browse to C:\Program Files\Cmak\Profiles and copy the VPN_RQ folder to a floppy disk or other removable media.

Exercise 7: Installing a Connection Manager Profile

1. Copy the VPN_RQ folder to the SERVER1 computer desktop.

2. Open the VPN_RQ folder, right-click VPN_RQ (the Win32 Cabinet Self-Extractor file), and then click Open.

3. In the VPN To Coho Vineyard message box, click Yes to confirm that you want to install the Connection Manager profile.

4. In the next VPN To Coho Vineyard dialog box, accept the default of My Use Only, and then click OK.

5. The Connection Manager profile is installed on SERVER1. After the installation is completed, the Network Connections window opens, and the VPN To Coho Vineyard connection dialog box is shown.

Exercise 8: Testing a VPN Quarantine Connection

1. In the VPN To Coho Vineyard connection dialog box, type the following information:

    ❑ User Name: **Manager1**

    ❑ Password: Manager1's password

    ❑ Logon Domain: **cohovineyard**

    ❑ Save Password: Enable

    ❑ Connect Automatically: Disable (Accept Default)

    Click Connect.

2. The quarantine script displays a message box to indicate that the security configuration of the client computer does not meet the security policy (the C:\Access.txt file does not exist).

3. Click OK to close the Remote Access Quarantine message box.

4. The connection stays in quarantine mode and is dropped after 60 seconds. Wait for the connection to be dropped. In the Reconnect dialog box, click No.

5. Open Windows Explorer and create a file named Access.txt on the C drive.

6. In the Network Connections window, under Connection Manager, right-click VPN To Cohovineyard, and then click Connect.

7. In the VPN To Cohovineyard Connection dialog box, ensure that the User Name and Password information is still present, and then click Connect. This time the quarantine script displays a message box to indicate that the security configuration of the client computer meets the security policy.

8. The quarantine script successfully notifies the Rqs.exe service. ISA Server removed the quarantine restrictions by moving the VPN client computer from the Quarantined VPN Clients network to the VPN Clients network.

9. Click OK to close the Remote Access Quarantine message box.

10. At the command prompt, type **ping 10.10.0.10**, and then press ENTER. Four ping replies are returned from the DC1 (10.10.0.10) on the internal network.

11. Close the command prompt window.

12. In the Run dialog box, type **10.10.0.10** and then press ENTER. A Windows Explorer window opens for \\10.10.0.10. These results show that the VPN client computer can now connect to resources on the internal network.

13. Close all open windows.

Lesson Review

Use the following questions to help determine whether you have learned enough to move on to the next lesson. If you have difficulty answering these questions, review the material in this lesson before beginning the next lesson. You can find answers to these questions in the "Questions and Answers" section at the end of this chapter.

1. You are configuring ISA Server to support quarantined VPN client access. Your organization's security policy states that client computers should not be able to access the internal network if the antivirus software on the client computer is not up-to-date and if Windows Firewall is not enabled on all network connections. What quarantine control component can you use to enforce this configuration?

   a. Configure a remote-access policy on IAS Server that sets limits to the IP ports that can be used by quarantined VPN clients.

   b. Configure ISA Server to limit the ports that can be used from the Quarantined VPN Clients network to access the internal network.

   c. Configure a client-side script that checks for the required settings.

   d. Configure the listener component on the ISA Server computer to listen for the required response from the client notification component.

2. Your organization's security policy states that all VPN clients that connect to your network must have the corporate antivirus application installed and updated with the latest definitions. You have set up a quarantine network and issued the CM profile to your clients with all the correct scripts. You have set up a private FTP site that the users can use to download and install the corporate antivirus program. How will you allow users to do this while they are in quarantine?

_____

_____

_____

3. Your company has several branch offices. You want to centralize quarantine control to a single RADIUS server. Where must you install the listener component?

   a. On each branch-office ISA Server computer

   b. On the head-office ISA Server computer

   c. On the RADIUS server

   d. On the RRAS server

Lesson Summary

- The VPN quarantine control feature allows you to screen VPN client machines before allowing them access to the organization's network. VPN quarantine control can delay normal remote access to a private network until the remote-access client configuration has been validated by a client-side script.

- Configuring quarantine control on ISA Server requires a number of configuration steps on the ISA Server computer and on the VPN clients.

- The quarantine script or program that you create to validate client configuration during remote access can be an executable file (*.exe), a script file (*.vbs) or a simple command file (*.cmd or *.bat). When you create the script, you need to configure it to perform a set of tests to ensure that the remote-access client complies with network security policy.

- The Connection Manager family of programs is a set of optional components used to create a managed remote-access solution. Connection Manager enables a network administrator to pre-configure remote-access clients including VPN quarantine clients.

- The Network Quarantine Service (Rqs.exe) provides the listener service for computers running ISA Server to support VPN Quarantine. The easiest way to install the Network Quarantine Service and configure ISA Server to support listener network traffic is to use the Configurerqsforisa.vbs script provided with ISA Server 2004.

- If you enable quarantine using RADIUS policy, you can use Internet Authentication Service on Windows Server 2003 or Windows 2000 Server to act as the RADIUS server. Use RADIUS for VPN quarantine control if you want to centralize the configuration of quarantine policies for multiple ISA Servers.

- The final step in configuring quarantine control for VPN clients is to configure the access rules for the Quarantined VPN Clients network to access required resources on other networks. To allow access to a resource, create an access rule with the Quarantined VPN Clients network as the source and the server to which access is required as the destination.

Case Scenario Exercises

In these exercises, you will plan an ISA Server 2004 VPN solution for a fictitious organization. Read the scenario and then answer the question that follows. If you have difficulty completing this work, review the material in this chapter before beginning the next chapter. You can find answers to these questions in the "Questions and Answers" section at the end of this chapter.

Scenario 1

You are the network administrator for your organization. You need to allow VPN access to an application server on your Internal network for remote users. You do not have the option to distribute certificates to all the remote users, and do not want to configure a pre-shared key on each client computer. Your ISA Server computer is configured as an Internet-edge firewall and is not a member of your internal domain. You need to ensure that only authenticated domain users will be able to connect using the VPN connections. Due to limited bandwidth, the maximum number of concurrent VPN connections is 50.

Scenario 1 Question

1. What steps will you take to deploy this solution?

_____

_____

_____

Scenario 2

Your organization has a single branch office. You must provide VPN access from the branch office to the head office using the highest security available. Only Authenticated Users should be able to access the Exchange Server computer in the head office using Outlook Express, and only the Sales group should be able to access selected file servers in the head office. You have deployed ISA Server 2004 at both locations. The branch office administrator will configure their ISA Server computer and you must configure the head-office ISA Server computer.

Scenario 2 Question

1. How will you configure the ISA Server computer at the head office to enable the required functionality?

_____

_____

_____

Chapter Summary

- Virtual private networking allows secure remote access to resources on an organization's internal network for users outside the network. ISA Server 2004 supports two VPN tunneling protocols: Point-to-Point Tunneling Protocol (PPTP) and ISA Server 2004 supports a variety of VPN authentication protocols. Whenever possible, you should use MS-CHAP v2 or Extensible Authentication Protocol (EAP). VPN quarantine control allows you to scan the VPN client computer configuration before allowing them access to the organization's network. ISA Server supports two types of VPN connections: remote-client access VPN connections, and site-to-site VPN connections.

- ISA Server enables VPN access using a default configuration that you can modify to meet your organization's requirements. When VPN clients connect to the VPN server, they must be assigned an IP address configuration that enables them to access the resources on the internal network or other networks. This IP address configuration can be assigned by ISA Server directly, or you can use a Dynamic Host Configuration Protocol (DHCP) server to assign the addresses. After ISA Server is configured to enable client access, VPN connections need to be configured on the remote-access clients.

- When you configure a site-to-site VPN, you must configure all the remote site network properties and configure access rules for traffic flow between the networks. In addition, you must configure both sides of a site-to-site VPN connection. ISA Server supports the following three protocols for site-to-site VPN connections: Point-to-Point Tunneling Protocol (PPTP), Layer Two Tunneling Protocol (L2TP), and Internet Protocol security (IPSec) tunnel mode. A remote-site network will contain the IP addresses for all computers connecting from the remote office. When you configure a site-to-site VPN in ISA Server, a new network is established.

You can configure network rules and access rules to limit the flow of network traffic from the remote site to any other network.

■ The VPN quarantine control feature allows you to screen VPN client machines before allowing them access to the organization's network. VPN quarantine control can delay normal remote access to a private network until the remote-access client configuration has been validated by a client-side script. The quarantine script can perform a set of tests to ensure that the remote-access client complies with network security policy. To enable quarantine control, you must distribute a remote-access client, configure the listener service on ISA Server and configure access rules for the Quarantined VPN Clients network.

Exam Highlights

Before taking the exam, review the key points and terms that are presented in this chapter. You need to know this information.

Key Points

■ L2TP/IPSec requires a certificate or pre-shared key to authenticate the client computer. If a user is able to connect from one computer, but not from another, the problem may be that the client computer is not configured with the correct certificate or pre-shared key.

■ By default, ISA Server 2004 enables only MS-CHAP v2 authentication for VPN access. If a client computer does not support this level of authentication, then the user will not be able to connect. In order for a client to be able to connect, the server and client must both be enabled for at least one common authentication protocol.

■ If your ISA Server computer is a member of an Active Directory domain, you must add the computer account to the RAS and IAS Servers group in Active Directory. If the computer is not a member of this group, ISA Server cannot read the user attributes to determine if users have permission to dial in to the network.

■ In order for the users to be able to authenticate for a VPN connection, they must be a member of a group that has been granted access on the ISA Server computer. However, the user account must also have dial-in permissions configured in Active Directory, or on the local computer. Access must be enabled in both places for the user to connect.

■ If you use static IP addresses for VPN clients ensure that the addresses assigned to VPN clients do not overlap with the IP addresses assigned to the Internal network.

■ VPN clients must be able to resolve the IP addresses for all servers that they need to connect to. This could include internal servers and Internet servers if the clients are accessing the Internet through the VPN.

■ One of the common reasons explaining why site-to-site VPNS do not work is authentication errors. The user name used to authenticate on the remote computer must be the same as the network name defined on the remote computer.

■ By default, a route relationship is configured between the internal network and both the VPN Clients and the Quarantined VPN Clients network when you install ISA Server. However, no access rule is created for network traffic between the VPN Clients network, the Quarantined VPN Clients network, and the Internal network.

■ When quarantine mode is disabled, all remote VPN clients with appropriate authentication permissions are placed in the VPN Clients network and will have the access you have allowed the VPN Clients network in your firewall policy. However, once you enable quarantine mode, all client connections will be forced to use the quarantine mode. If clients do not support quarantine mode, they will not be able to connect. If the Network Quarantine Service is not running, users will not be able to connect. The only exception to this is if you configure a user set in the Exempt These Users From Quarantine Control panel.

Key Terms

Quarantine Control   A remote-access feature that can be used to restrict VPN client access. Quarantine Control allows you to screen VPN client machines using a client-side script before allowing them access to the organization's network.

Quarantined VPN Clients network   Contains the IP addresses of all the VPN clients that have connected using VPN client access but have not yet cleared quarantine.

remote-site network   Contains the IP addresses of all the computers in remote sites when a site-to-site VPN connection is configured. Additional remote-site networks are created for each remote-site connection.

site-to-site VPN   A point-to-point secure tunnel created through the Internet between a VPN gateway server in one location and a VPN gateway server in another location.

tunneling protocol   Uses encryption protocols to provide data security as the data is sent across the public network. The two VPN protocols supported by ISA Server are Microsoft Point-to-Point Tunneling Protocol (PPTP) or the Layer 2 Tunneling Protocol (L2TP).

virtual private network (VPN)   A virtual network that enables communication between a remote-access server and computers on the internal network or between two remote sites separated by a public network such as the Internet.

VPN Clients network   Contains the IP addresses of all the VPN clients that have connected using VPN client access.

Questions and Answers

Page
10-14

Lesson 1 Review

1. Your company needs to support VPN clients that use Microsoft Windows 98, Windows 2000, and Windows XP to connect to ISA Server 2004. The computers are all configured with smart-card readers, and each user has been issued a smart card. What is the most secure authentication protocol that is available for these clients?

    a. CHAP

    b. MS-CHAP

    c. MS-CHAP v2

    d. EAP

    D is correct. Although you can use any of these protocols, the most secure form of authentication for these clients is Extensible Authentication Protocol because it can use the smart cards for authentication.

2. You need to ensure that your VPN clients attempting to connect have the Windows Firewall installed and enabled. How would you accomplish this?

    Implement network quarantine control by enabling quarantine control and then using a script on each client to test if the client has the Windows Firewall installed and enabled. Only allow VPN access if the client has the firewall enabled.

3. You want to use L2TP/IPSec as your tunneling protocol. Some of your VPN clients are running Windows NT 4.0 Workstation. What must you do to enable L2TP/IPSec support with the least amount of effort?

    a. Do nothing. L2TP/IPSec support is built into NT 4.0 Workstation.

    b. Download and install the Ms12tp.exe on the clients.

    c. You must upgrade the clients to Windows 2000 Professional or Windows XP.

    d. Install a Connection Manager package to deliver the L2TP/IPSec client.

    B is correct. Download and install Ms12tp.exe. A is incorrect because L2TP/IPSec is not available in Windows NT 4.0 by default. C is incorrect because the VPN client can be installed to provide support for L2TP/IPSec so you do not have to upgrade the client to a newer operating system. D is incorrect because the Connection Manager package is used to deliver a client side script to test client configuration and cannot be used to distribute an upgraded client.

Page
10-31

Lesson 2 Review

1. You have deployed three different ISA Server computers and configured them to accept VPN connections. You want to log information about all connection attempts in a single log file. What is the best way to accomplish this?

Install Internet Authentication Service on a server in your domain. Then configure the ISA Server computers to Use RADIUS for Accounting (Logging) and configure them to use the IAS server. RADIUS servers allow you to log all connection information on the RADIUS server.

2. You are the network administrator for your organization. You have deployed ISA Server to accept VPN connections. You have remote-access policies in place so that only specified Windows security groups can connect to the VPN server. Users in those groups are reporting that they are unable to get a connection. The error message they receive tells them they do not have dial-in permission. The remote-access policies are configured correctly. What is the most likely cause of the error message? How will you resolve the problem?

The most likely cause is that the domain is running in mixed mode. While in mixed mode, all users' dial-in permissions are set to Deny and remote-access policies are ignored. You must raise the domain level or manually configure each user's dial-in permission.

3. You have deployed ISA Server 2004. Several users within the organization travel frequently and must be able to access resources on the internal network. These resources include accessing their mailboxes through Microsoft Exchange Server by using client computers running Microsoft Office Outlook, accessing internal Web sites that contain confidential information, and accessing file shares on internal file servers. You need to enable access to these internal resources while minimizing the complexity of the client configuration as much as possible. Users should require only a user name and password to connect to internal resources. All the users should also be granted immediate access to the network after authentication. What should you do?

   a. Configure ISA Server to support VPN client access to the internal network. Configure the VPN connection to require L2TP over IPSec. Provide the users with instructions on how to configure each of these connections.

   b. Configure ISA Server to support VPN client access to the internal network. Configure the VPN connection to require L2TP over IPSec. Use the Connection Manager Administration Kit to create a profile for all the remote users.

   c. Configure ISA Server to support quarantined VPN access to the internal network. Configure the VPN connection to require PPTP. Provide the users with instructions about how to configure each of these connections.

   d. Configure ISA Server to support VPN client access to the internal network. Configure the VPN connection to require PPTP. Use the Connection Manager Administration Kit to create a profile for all the remote users.

D is correct. To provide access to several internal resources while simplifying the client configuration, use a VPN. Because the users require immediate access after authentication, you cannot use a quarantine control. Point-to-Point Tunneling Protocol (PPTP) is the only protocol that requires only a user name and password because Layer Two Tunneling Protocol (L2TP) over Internet Protocol Security (IPSec) requires a certificate or pre-shared key. And to simplify the client configuration, use the Connection Manager Administration Kit (CMAK) to configure a profile for each user.

Lesson 3 Review

1. Your organization has a head office and one branch office. You have deployed ISA Server 2004 in both locations and configured a site-to-site VPN between the two locations. Currently all users at the branch office can access the Exchange Server computer located at the head office. You need to modify the configuration so that only managers at the branch office can access a file server at the head office. The managers should be able to access only the file server and the Exchange Server computer at the head office. What steps must you take to accomplish this?

   Create a Computer Object to represent the file server. Create a firewall-access rule that allows traffic from the remote site to the file server computer. Configure the rule to apply only to the Managers group.

2. You are connecting your branch office to a third-party VPN gateway at the head office. Which tunneling protocol should you use?

   IPSec tunnel mode must be used to operate with a third-party VPN gateway.

3. You have deployed ISA Server and have created a site-to-site VPN between the organization's head office and one of the branch offices. The users in the remote office need to access resources on the head-office network. These resources include accessing their mailboxes through Exchange Server by using client computers running Outlook, accessing internal Web sites that contain confidential information, and accessing file shares on internal file servers. The organization's security requirements state that users in remote offices should have the same access to the head-office network as users in the head office. In addition, the domain controllers in the head office must be able to replicate with the domain controllers in the remote offices. What should you do? (Choose two correct answers.)

   a. Configure an access rule that enables Port 80 and Port 443 traffic from the remote-site network to the internal network at the head office. Configure an Exchange Server publishing rule for Outlook RPC publishing and configure an access rule that enables traffic on Port 139.

   b. Configure an access rule that enables all protocols from the remote-site network to the head-office internal network.

   c. Configure a network rule that enables a NAT relationship between the remote-site network and the head-office internal network.

   d. Configure a network rule that enables a route relationship between the remote-site network and the head-office internal network.

   B and D are correct. To enable the same level of access for remote office users as head-office users have, you must enable all protocols to pass between the remote-office network and the head-office internal network. In addition, you must enable a route relationship between the networks for the domain controllers at the head office to replicate with the domain controllers on the remote-office network. A NAT relationship enables traffic to flow in only one direction.

Lesson 4 Review

1. You are configuring ISA Server to support quarantined VPN client access. Your organization's security policy states that client computers should not be able to access the internal network if the antivirus software on the client computer is not up-to-date and if Windows Firewall is not enabled on all network connections. What quarantine control component can you use to enforce this configuration?

   a. Configure a remote-access policy on IAS Server that sets limits to the IP ports that can be used by quarantined VPN clients.

   b. Configure ISA Server to limit the ports that can be used from the Quarantined VPN Clients network to access the internal network.

   c. Configure a client-side script that checks for the required settings.

   d. Configure the listener component on the ISA Server computer to listen for the required response from the client notification component.

   C is correct. The only way to check a client configuration in a quarantined VPN client scenario is to use a client-side script to check the client configuration. Internet Authentication Service (IAS) remote-access policies and ISA Server access rules can be used to limit client access while in quarantine, but not to check the client configuration. And the listener component can only receive the information from the client notification component; it cannot check the client configuration.

2. Your organization's security policy states that all VPN clients that connect to your network must have the corporate antivirus application installed and updated with the latest definitions. You have set up a quarantine network and issued the CM profile to your clients with all the correct scripts. You have set up a private FTP site that the users can use to download and install the corporate antivirus program. How will you allow users to do this while they are in quarantine?

   Create a firewall-access rule to allow DNS queries and FTP traffic from the quarantine network to the internal network. Provide a message in the network policy requirements script directing the users to the FTP site to download and install your corporate antivirus program.

3. Your company has several branch offices. You want to centralize quarantine control to a single RADIUS server. Where must you install the listener component?

   a. On each branch-office ISA Server computer

   b. On the head-office ISA Server computer

   c. On the RADIUS server

   d. On the RRAS server

   C is correct. The listener component must be installed on the RADIUS server. In this situation, the ISA Server computers will just forward the client request to the RADIUS server, so you do not need to install the listener component on the ISA Server computers. In this scenario, you do not need to deploy RRAS servers.

Case Scenario Exercises

Page
10-70
Scenario 1 Question

1. What steps will you take to deploy this solution?

Install the IAS service on an internal server that is a member of the internal domain. Configure the IAS Server to accept the ISA Server computer as a client and configure the ISA Server computer as a RADIUS client. On ISA Server, enable VPN Client access and configure the properties to allow a maximum of 50 connections. Configure the VPN properties to use a RADIUS for authentication and configure ISA Server to use the server running IAS on the Internal network. Create a firewall-access rule to allow Authenticated Users from the VPN Client network access to the application server. On the RADIUS server create a remote-access policy to give Authenticated Users permission to connect to the VPN connection. Ensure that all required users have dial-in permission enabled in the domain. Finally, provide instructions for all remote users on how to configure a PPTP VPN connection.

Page
10-70
Scenario 2 Question

1. How will you configure the ISA Server computer at the head office to enable the required functionality?

On the ISA Server computer at head office, create a remote-site network defining the IP addresses for the branch-office network. Configure the remote-site network to use L2TP/IPSec. Obtain and distribute certificates to both ISA Server computers to support computer authentication and encryption. Create a user account in your domain that will be used to authenticate the VPN gateway server from the remote site.

Then create computer objects to represent the Exchange server and create a computer set to represent the file servers and domain controllers. Publish the Exchange server in the head office to allow Authenticated Users access to SMTP and IMAP4 (or POP3) to the Exchange computer object. Configure an access rule to allow LDAP and Kerberos traffic to the domain controllers from the remote site. Create another firewall-access rule to allow the Sales group access to the Network set for the file servers.

11 Implementing Monitoring and Reporting

Exam Objectives in this Chapter:

- Monitor ISA Server 2004 activity
    - ❑ Monitor client computer connections
    - ❑ Monitor ISA Server 2004 performance
    - ❑ Monitor network performance
    - ❑ Monitor network intrusion attempts
    - ❑ Monitor connectivity to network and services
    - ❑ Diagnose and resolve connectivity issues
- Configure and run reports
- Configure logging and alerts
    - ❑ Create and modify alert definitions
    - ❑ Search and filter logs by using the Log Viewer
    - ❑ Save log filters and session filters

Why This Chapter Matters

Now that you have Microsoft Internet Security and Accelerator (ISA) Server 2004 up and running, and all the access rules and publishing rules are working, you may think that your work is done. Actually, that is not the case. ISA Server is now an important part of your network infrastructure. It may be the only route your users have to the Internet, or it may be the only way users on the Internet have to access resources on your internal network. Because of the role ISA Server has on your network, you must monitor it constantly to ensure that it is functioning as expected.

ISA Server may also be a critical component of your network security. Because your ISA Server computer is accessible from the Internet, it will be the target of attacks, many trivial, some serious. This means that you must apply an additional layer of monitoring on the ISA Server computer.

ISA Server monitoring includes real-time monitoring and configuring alerts that provide immediate information of the current activity on the ISA Server computer. Moreover, you can configure connectivity monitoring by which the ISA Server computer monitors its connections to services on the internal network or on the Internet. Monitoring also includes configuring logging and reports that provide complete or summary information on the ISA Server activity.

Lessons in this Chapter:

- Lesson 1: Planning a Monitoring and Reporting Strategy 11-3
- Lesson 2: Configuring and Managing Alerts 11-15
- Lesson 3: Configuring Session and Connectivity Monitoring 11-29
- Lesson 4: Configuring Logging and Reporting. 11-40

Before You Begin

This chapter presents the skills and concepts related to monitoring ISA Server 2004. If you plan to complete the practices and lab in this chapter, you should prepare the following:

- A Microsoft Windows Server 2003 (Standard Edition or Enterprise Edition) computer installed as DC1 and configured as a domain controller in the *cohovineyard.com* domain.

- A second Windows Server 2003 computer installed as ISA1 and configured as a domain member in the *cohovineyard.com* domain. Two network interfaces should be installed on this server.

- A Windows Server 2003 server installed as MAIL1. This server must be a member of the *cohovineyard.com* domain and have a default installation of Exchange Server 2003 on it. The Exchange server requires at least two mailboxes configured on it.

- A Microsoft Windows Server 2003 (Standard Edition or Enterprise Edition) computer installed as SERVER1. This computer should not be a member of the *cohovineyard.com* domain. This server should be located on the same network as the external interface of the ISA Server computer. This server should be running the DNS Service and the Domain Name System (DNS) client setting should be configured to use the server's Internet Protocol (IP) address as the DNS server.

Lesson 1: Planning a Monitoring and Reporting Strategy

ISA Server 2004 provides several monitoring options that can be accessed through the Microsoft ISA Server Management Console and through other administration tools on the server. This lesson provides an overview of what components can be monitored on ISA Server and how to design a monitoring and reporting strategy.

After this lesson, you will be able to

- Describe why monitoring ISA Server is important
- List components that can be monitored on ISA Server
- Plan a monitoring and reporting strategy
- Implement ISA Server performance monitoring

Estimated lesson time: 25 minutes

Why You Should Implement Monitoring

ISA Server is a critical component in an organization's network infrastructure. If ISA Server is deployed as an Internet-edge firewall, it operates as a firewall that secures the internal network. ISA Server may also be providing secure access to Internet resources for internal clients and access to specified internal resources for Internet clients. If ISA Server is not available, this functionality is disrupted. If ISA Server is being attacked from the Internet, the internal network may be at risk.

There are many reasons for monitoring ISA Server. Some of these include the following:

- **Monitoring traffic flow between networks**   You must monitor traffic between networks to ensure that your access rules are correctly configured and that only the expected traffic passes through ISA Server. You also need to monitor ISA Server regularly to identify normal and legitimate traffic passing through the server. After you identify a typical traffic pattern, you can detect any variation that might indicate a potential problem.

- **Troubleshooting network connectivity**   Monitoring ISA Server is a critical component of troubleshooting network connectivity. For example, if users report that they cannot access resources on the Internet, you can connect to ISA Server to help locate the problem. In this scenario, the problem might be with the client configuration, the ISA Server configuration, or the availability of the Internet resource. By monitoring ISA Server, you can begin troubleshooting by identifying the option most likely to be the source of the problem.

- **Investigating attacks**   If ISA Server is operating as a firewall, it will inevitably be exposed to attacks from the Internet. If ISA Server is configured correctly, it can detect and block most attacks. However, even if ISA Server successfully blocks the attacks, you should still be aware that the attacks are occurring and be aware of any variations in the normal attack patterns. If a new attack is launched against ISA Server, you must be alerted as quickly as possible that the attack is occurring so that you can determine how to respond to the attack. After the attack is finished, you should also have enough information logged on the ISA Server computer to investigate the attack. Even if the attack fails, investigate the attack pattern to detect possible patterns that may lead to additional attack attempts.

■ **Planning** By monitoring the computer running ISA Server, you can also gather information you can use for planning modifications to the current ISA Server infrastructure. By collecting performance data over a period of time, you can identify trends and use this information for planning future deployments of ISA Server.

ISA Server Monitoring Components

One of the significant improvements to the ISA Server Management Console is the improvement to the monitoring functionality. You can use the ISA Server Management Console to monitor several components on the ISA Server computer. The monitoring options are listed in Table 11-1.

Table 11-1   ISA Server Monitoring Components

Monitoring Components	Explanation
Alerts	Monitors ISA Server for configured events and then performs actions when the specified events occur. The alert service is configured with many events that are monitored by default. You can also configure additional alert definitions and define the events that occur when the alert is triggered.
Sessions	Provides information on all the current client sessions on ISA Server. ISA Server lists sessions of the following types: Firewall client, secure network address translation (SecureNAT) client, virtual private network (VPN) client, VPN site-to-site, and Web Proxy client.
Logging	Provides detailed information about the Web proxy, Microsoft Firewall service, or Simple Mail Transfer Protocol (SMTP) Message Screener. ISA Server logs all client connections and all blocked client connections by default. You can use the logs to monitor the activity on ISA Server in real time, or you can review saved log files.
Reporting	Summarizes information about the usage patterns on ISA Server. For example, you can create reports that summarize information about the users who access the most sites through ISA Server and what sites are accessed, as well as information about what protocols and applications are used most often. You can also use reports to monitor the security of your network. For example, you can generate reports that track malicious attempts to access internal resources.

Table 11-1   ISA Server Monitoring Components

Monitoring Components	Explanation
Connectivity	Enables regular monitoring of connections from the ISA Server computer to any other computer or Uniform Resource Locator (URL) on any network. For example, you can use connectivity options to monitor connections to domain controllers, DNS servers, published Web servers, and external Web servers. This feature provides advance warning when the connection to any required service or network fails.
Performance	Collects performance data on the computer running ISA Server. You can monitor server performance in real time, create a log file of server performance over a longer period for detailed analysis, or configure performance alerts to create an event as a result of counters reaching certain values.

ISA Server Dashboard

The Dashboard view in ISA Server Management Console displays a summary of the information that is available for real-time monitoring in ISA Server. The interface is shown in Figure 11-1. Most of the nodes in the Dashboard display a summary of the information that is available on the other views under the Monitoring node. The Dashboard nodes are described in Table 11-2.

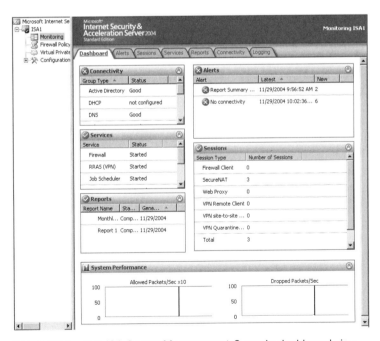

Figure 11-1   The ISA Server Management Console dashboard view

Table 11-2   ISA Server Management Console Dashboard Nodes

Node	Description
Connectivity	Displays a summary of the status of the connectivity verifiers on the ISA Server computer. To configure the connectivity verifiers, access the Connectivity view on the Monitoring pane.
Services	Displays a summary of which services are started on the ISA Server computer. To manage the services, access the Services view.
Reports	Display a list of reports that have been generated on the ISA Server computer. To open the reports, access the Reports view.
Alerts	Displays a summary of the alerts on the ISA Server computer. To view the actual alerts, access the Alerts view.
Sessions	Displays a summary of all the client sessions connected to the ISA Server computer. For more details on which clients are connected, access the Sessions view.
System Performance	Displays the Allowed packets/sec and the Blocked packets/sec performance counters on the ISA Server computer. This provides a real-time view of how much network traffic is passing through or being blocked on the ISA Server computer. For more detailed performance information, use the Performance Console.

In each node, the Dashboard provides visual information on the status of each monitoring component. An "X" in a red circle indicates a potential problem, a yellow icon indicates a warning, a blue "i" in a white circle on the Alerts box indicates there are unacknowledged alerts, and a check mark in a green circle indicates that everything is functioning as expected.

Guidelines for Planning a Monitoring and Reporting Strategy

If you configure ISA Server to collect all the possible types of monitoring information, it will be virtually impossible to analyze or understand the data collected on a busy ISA Server computer. You must develop a monitoring strategy that identifies the information is most important, and then determine how you will collect that information. You must also develop a plan of how and when you will review the collected information.

Real World   Planning a Monitoring Strategy

One of the more difficult parts of implementing any new technology is developing the strategy to monitor the system after you deploy it. Most operating systems and applications can provide a great deal of monitoring information, often far more than you can analyze. Many of the organizations that I have worked with have started with very ambitious monitoring plans when they deploy a new technology. Often they know that they did a poor job of monitoring the older technology and they see the deployment of a new technology as a chance for a fresh start. So when they deploy the new technology, they turn on every auditing and monitoring option available.

Usually, when I check with these organizations six months later I find that no one has looked at the monitoring information for months. In many cases, the reason is that there is just too much information, and it is really difficult to find the important information in the mass of data that can accumulate. To avoid this, you need to create a monitoring strategy.

The first step in creating a monitoring strategy is to decide what information is critical. This is the information that you need to see in real time or you need to know about in real time. On an ISA Server computer, the most critical information is security-related. You must also determine what information you don't want to know about immediately, but want to retain. ISA Server logs all connections and blocked connections, most of which are of no interest to you. However, by archiving the logs, you have all the information available.

Your monitoring strategy is apt to have its weaknesses on your first try, so be prepared to fine-tune your strategy. If you find that you are collecting too much information, and you cannot detect what is important, reduce the data you collect rather than abandon monitoring. If you notice that you are not collecting an important piece of information, start collecting that data. If you are getting too many alerts on your pager in the middle of the night, and most of those alerts are not significant, fine-tune the alerting procedure rather than turn off the pager.

An excellent solution to monitoring ISA Server, especially if you have multiple servers deployed, is to use an automated monitoring tool. These monitoring tools can collect information from many sources and analyze the information. Microsoft Operations Manager is one example of an automated monitoring solution that can monitor ISA Server computers for you.

Monitoring Real-Time Information

You can monitor real-time information by configuring alerts that are raised when specific events occur. You can also collect real-time information about client connections, server performance, and connectivity on ISA Server. Consider the following when you create a monitoring and reporting strategy:

- **Decide the events to which you must be alerted in real time**   ISA Server can raise alerts based on almost any event that occurs. In most cases, you do not need to be apprised in real time about every alert. For example, if ISA Server blocks a single spoofing attack, you probably do not need to receive an alert. However, if the connection between ISA Server and a business-critical published Web server fails, you might decide that you must receive an alert. If you are using SMTP Message Screener, and suddenly the volume of e-mail passing through the message screener increases tenfold, you must be notified about this immediately to reduce the impact of a potential virus outbreak.

- **Determine the threshold for the alert**   As part of deciding which events will raise alerts, you must also determine the threshold for when ISA Server will raise the alerts. If ISA Server detects hundreds of spoofing attacks within minutes, then you probably want to receive an alert. If a single VPN client fails to authenticate once, you are probably not interested. However, if the same client tries to authenticate many times, you may want to be alerted.

- **Monitor ISA Server using the ISA Server Management Console and Performance Monitor**   You can also collect real-time information from ISA Server using the ISA Server Management Console and the Performance Monitor. In many cases, you might use these tools for real-time analysis only when a problem is reported. For example, if users report that the Internet connection is slower than usual, you can use these tools to determine why. If you use the Performance Monitor, use the preconfigured ISA Server Performance Monitor to monitor the most important counters on ISA Server.

> **Tip**   You can delegate ISA Server monitoring without allowing administrative access to the ISA Server configuration. If you assign users to the ISA Server Basic Monitoring role, they can view all the ISA Server monitoring information, but cannot change any settings. If you assign users to the ISA Server Extended Monitoring role, they can monitor the ISA Server computer, and change the monitoring configuration, but cannot modify other ISA Server settings such as access or publishing rules.

Collecting Long-Term Information

In addition to the real-time information that you can collect on ISA Server, you should also develop a strategy to collect long-term information on ISA Server. Categories of information that you should collect include the following:

- **Performance-related information**   To prepare for future modifications to the ISA Server infrastructure, regularly collect information about ISA Server performance. As a best practice, collect information about the performance to establish a baseline and then regularly collect the same types of information to determine how the performance on ISA Server is changing.

- **Usage information**   Regularly collect usage reports. This is useful for future planning and to monitor the current activity on the server.

- **Security-related information**   Collect information about security-related events. This information allows you to develop a baseline of the normal security events, which makes it easier to detect an anomaly to that regular pattern. This information may also be useful to track the progress of a successful attack so that you can prevent such an attack in the future.

As part of collecting long-term information, also develop a strategy for archiving and regularly review the information. The time line for reviewing this information will depend on the types of information collected. For example, you may want to review the security-related information on a daily basis, the usage information on a weekly basis, and the performance data only once per month.

Developing a Response Strategy

As part of your monitoring strategy, create a strategy for how to respond to critical events that occur on the ISA Server computer. These events could include:

- Network security breaches
- Denial-of-service (DoS) attacks
- Unusual usage patterns

In each case, develop a strategy for how you will detect these activities and then how you will respond when the event is detected. As part of this strategy, create an immediate-response plan, such as isolating servers or networks, or shutting down services, in the event of a security breach and a longer-term plan for investigating and mitigating the attacks.

ISA Server Performance and Service Monitoring

ISA Server 2004 uses the Microsoft Windows 2000 or Microsoft Windows Server 2003 Performance Monitor to assess server performance. When you install ISA Server

Management Console on a computer, the ISA Server Performance Monitor is also installed, providing a preconfigured Performance console that includes the most important ISA Server counters. You can use this monitor to add the ISA Server counters that you want to track to the Performance Console.

Monitoring ISA Server Performance

When you install ISA Server, the installation configures several new performance objects that you can use to monitor ISA Server performance on the computer. You view the performance objects and their associated performance counters in real time in System Monitor, which is a monitoring tool that is included with Windows 2000 and Windows Server 2003. You can also log performance data and create alerts from the data by using Performance Log and Alerts.

To access the ISA Server Performance Monitor, click ISA Server Performance Monitor in the Microsoft ISA Server menu on the Start menu. The Microsoft Management Console (MMC), with the preconfigured counters, is shown in Figure 11-2.

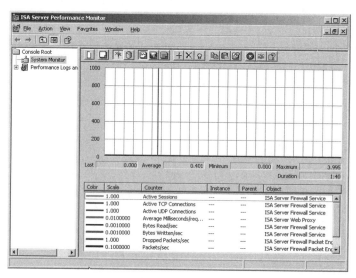

Figure 11-2   The ISA Server Performance Monitor

   See Also   If you are not familiar with using Performance Monitor in Windows 2000 Server or Windows Server 2003, refer to the Performance Monitoring chapter in the Server Operations Guide that is part of the Windows 2000 Server Resource Kit. The chapter is available at *http://www.microsoft.com/resources/documentation/windows/2000/server/reskit/en-us/ default.asp*. Although this reference deals specifically with Windows 2000 Server, the concepts and monitoring interface have not changed significantly for Windows Server 2003.

The ISA Server performance objects that are installed are listed in Table 11-3.

Table 11-3   ISA Server Performance Objects

Object	Explanation
ISA Server Firewall Engine	Includes performance counters to monitor connections and throughput for the Firewall engine. Use these counters to monitor the number of client connections, the number of allowed and dropped packets, and the number of bytes passed through the Firewall engine. For example, use the Active Connections counter to monitor the number of clients currently connected to ISA Server.
ISA Server Cache	Includes performance counters to monitor the memory, disk, and URL activity associated with the cache. Use these performance counters to monitor the effectiveness of the cache. For example, you can use the Disk URL Retrieve Rate performance counter to determine the rate at which URLs are retrieved from the disk cache.
ISA Server Firewall Service	Includes performance counters to monitor Firewall service connections and associated services such as DNS. This object monitors only Firewall client connections. For example, you can use the Active Sessions performance counter to monitor the number of Firewall client sessions that are running simultaneously.
ISA Server Web Proxy Service	Includes counters to monitor the number of users and the rate at which ISA Server transfers data to remote and upstream servers. For example, you can use the Total Users performance counter to monitor the total number of users that are connected to the Web proxy service.
ISA Server H.323 Filter	Includes counters that monitor the total and the active H.323 calls on the ISA Server computer.

In addition to monitoring the ISA Server–specific performance counters, also monitor the other performance counters such as memory usage, CPU usage, and disk usage. Use the combination of ISA Server performance information and the Windows server performance information to detect potential performance problems and bottlenecks on the computer running ISA Server.

Exam Tip   To use Performance Monitor to monitor ISA Server, you must be a local Administrator. The System Performance information on the ISA Server Dashboard is provided by Performance Monitor, so if you are not a local Administrator, you cannot view the System Performance information.

Monitoring ISA Server Services

When ISA Server 2004 is installed, the following Windows services are also installed:

- Microsoft Firewall service

- Microsoft ISA Server Control service

- Microsoft ISA Server Job Scheduler service

- Microsoft Data Engine (MSDE)

- Microsoft ISA Server Storage

You can use the Services view in ISA Server Management Console to view and control the status of some of the ISA Server services. By default, the Microsoft Firewall, Microsoft ISA Server Job Scheduler, and MSDE services are listed in the Services view. As additional services are installed or enabled on ISA Server, these services may also appear in the Services view. For example, when ISA Server is configured as a VPN server, the Remote Access Service is added to the Services view.

The services listed in the Services view can be monitored or managed in the ISA Server Management Console. Other services, such as the ISA Server Control service and the Microsoft ISA Server Storage service, must be managed using the Services console from the Administrative Tools folder, or by using a command line.

Lesson Review

Use the following questions to help determine whether you have learned enough to move on to the next lesson. If you have difficulty answering these questions, review the material in this lesson before beginning the next lesson. You can find answers to these questions in the "Questions and Answers" section at the end of this chapter.

1. You have deployed ISA Server 2004. You are the only network administrator in your organization and do not have time for constantly monitoring the computer running ISA Server. However, you do need to be notified immediately whenever there is a security problem on ISA Server and when the services on ISA Server stop. How can you implement this functionality?

   a. Configure ISA Server logging

   b. Configure ISA Server connectivity

   c. Configure ISA Server alerts

   d. Configure ISA Server reports

2. You are the network administrator for your organization. Users report that they are unable to use the Internet and are receiving a DNS error message. You investigate and discover that the DNS server used to resolve Internet names has failed. What proactive measure could you have taken to ensure that you were aware of the DNS server failure as soon as possible?

_____

_____

_____

3. You have deployed ISA Server and configured it to allow user access to the Internet. You have deployed the Firewall client to some of the client workstations in your organization. You now need to monitor the number of active Firewall client sessions on ISA Server. What performance objects should you monitor on ISA Server?

   a. ISA Server Firewall Engine

   b. ISA Server Cache

   c. ISA Server Firewall Service

   d. ISA Server Web Proxy

4. You are the ISA Server administrator for your organization. Your manager wants information about the trends in Web usage provided to him on a monthly basis. What can you do to provide this?

_____

_____

_____

Lesson Summary

■ Implementing monitoring on ISA Server is a critical component of a successful ISA Server deployment. You can monitor traffic between networks to ensure that your access rules are configured correctly and that only the expected traffic is passing through ISA Server. By monitoring the computer running ISA Server, you can also gather information to use for planning modifications to the current ISA Server infrastructure.

■ You can use the ISA Server Management Console to monitor several components on the ISA Server computer. The Dashboard view in ISA Server Management displays a summary of the information that is available for real-time monitoring on ISA Server.

- To ensure that your monitoring strategy is as effective as possible, you must develop a monitoring plan. This plan should define what information you need to monitor in real time, how you will configure the ISA Server alerts and what long-term information about client connections, server performance, and connectivity on ISA Server you must collect. The monitoring strategy should also define how you will review the collected information and how you will respond to specific events that occur on the ISA Server.

- ISA Server 2004 uses the Windows 2000 or Windows Server 2003 Performance Monitor to monitor server performance. When you install the Microsoft ISA Server Management Console on a computer, the ISA Server Performance Monitor is also installed. This console provides a preconfigured Performance console that includes the most important ISA Server counters.

Lesson 2: Configuring and Managing Alerts

One of the important components of an ISA Server monitoring strategy is configuring and managing alerts. ISA Server is configured to create an alert when specific server-related events occur. You can configure additional alerts as well as configure the alerts to perform specific actions when the alert occurs. This lesson explains how to configure and manage ISA Server 2004 alerts.

After this lesson, you will be able to

- Describe an ISA Server alert
- Configure alert definitions and alert actions
- Manage alerts

Estimated lesson time: 30 minutes

What Are Alerts?

To maintain the functionality and security of ISA Server and the networks protected by ISA Server, you must know when specific events occur on the ISA Server computer. For example, you need to know if an ISA Server service stops responding, or if a specific type of intrusion is detected. You can use the ISA Server alert service to notify you when specific events occur, as well as to configure alert definitions to trigger a series of actions when an event occurs.

An alert is a notification of an event or action that has occurred on ISA Server. When the event occurs, an alert is triggered according to the conditions and trigger thresholds specified for the event. Some examples of default events that trigger alerts include the following:

- **Service Started** This informational event provides an alert concerning the proper startup of a specific ISA Server–related service.

- **IP Spoofing** This warning event provides an alert that indicates that an IP packet source address is not valid. In most cases, the IP packet arrives on one of the ISA Server computer interfaces, but has an address that logically belongs to the network attached to another interface.

- **Intrusion Detected** This warning event provides an alert that indicates that ISA Server has detected an external user attempting an intrusion attack.

- **DNS Intrusion** This warning event provides an alert that indicates that a host-name overflow, length overflow, zone high-port, or zone-transfer attack occurred.

> **See Also** For a complete list of events available when configuring alerts in ISA Server 2004, see "Alerts" in ISA Server 2004 Help.

As a response to a specific event, you can configure an alert to send an e-mail notification, run a program, report to the Microsoft Windows event log, or start and stop a service. For example, you can configure ISA Server to send you an e-mail message when a specified number of intrusion attempts has occurred.

You can also use scripts to configure advanced responses to the alerts. For example, you can create a program that is triggered by the detection of an intrusion attack. When the alert is triggered, the program could scan the ISA Server logs for the IP address of the intruder and then create an access rule that blocks connections from the intruder's IP address.

Viewing Alerts

When a server event occurs and records an alert, the ISA Server Management Console displays the alert in the Alerts view of the Monitoring node. A summary of all the most recent alerts is also listed in the Alerts area of the Dashboard view.

When an alert is triggered, an entry appears in the Alerts view that lists the following information, as shown in Figure 11-3:

- **Alert** The Alert column indicates the type of alert that has occurred based on a predefined list of configured alerts and events. As alerts occur, all identical alerts are grouped by category for ease of use. You can expand or collapse a category to display or hide each individual alert within each category.

- **Latest** The Latest column shows the date and time that an alert occurred. If multiple alerts are grouped together, the main category heading illustrates the latest date and time of the most current alert.

- **Status** The Status column illustrates the status of the alert. Any alert that has a New status is also displayed in the Dashboard Alerts snapshot pane. You can acknowledge an alert to remove the notification entry in the Dashboard snapshot pane. When an alert is acknowledged, the entry is not removed from the Alerts view; only the status is changed to reflect the state.

- **Category** The Category column illustrates the category to which the alert belongs. Valid categories include Security, Cache, Routing, Firewall, Service, and Other.

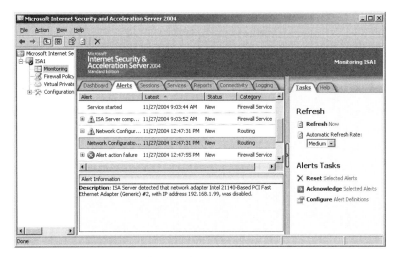

Figure 11-3   Viewing ISA Server alerts

You can view more information about each alert by accessing the Add/Remove Columns command from the View menu. You can add other columns to the Alerts view, including the following:

- **Severity**   Valid severity categories include Information, Warning, and Error.
- **Server**   The Server column lists the name of the ISA Server that has generated the alert.
- **Count**   The Count column lists the number of times a specific alert has been recorded.

When you click each registered alert, the bottom of the Alerts view provides Alert Information, which contains a detailed description of the selected alert.

How to Configure Alerts

ISA Server includes a large number of predefined alerts. You can modify the existing alert definitions by defining events that will trigger the alert, and by defining the actions when the alert is triggered. You can also create new alert definitions.

What Are Alert Definitions?

An alert definition lists the specific actions or notifications that occur when an event takes place on the ISA Server computer. During ISA Server installation, alert definitions are defined for a variety of built-in general events. Several of these events allow you to define a more specific alert by configuring conditions related to the event. For example, ISA Server includes the preconfigured Intrusion Detected event. The associated alert is configured to report on any intrusion detected. You may want to redefine this general alert to provide additional specific notifications related to all port-scan attacks, ping-of-death attacks, or other conditions.

What Are Alert Events and Conditions?

Alert events define actions that occur on the computer running ISA Server that can raise alerts. Alert conditions are additional criteria applied by ISA Server when alert events happen. For example, DNS intrusion is an alert event. Additional conditions that you can apply to the alert event include raising an alert when any DNS intrusion attempt is detected, or raising an alert only when specific DNS intrusion attempts are detected. You can also modify the event trigger-threshold limits. The trigger threshold refers to how many times the event should occur before the alert is triggered and how long to wait before issuing the alert again.

Configuring Alert Events and Conditions

To configure alert events and conditions, complete the following steps:

1. In ISA Server Management Console, click Monitoring and then click the Alerts view.

2. In the Task pane, click Configure Alert Definitions. The Alert Definitions dialog box, shown in Figure 11-4, displays all the alert definitions.

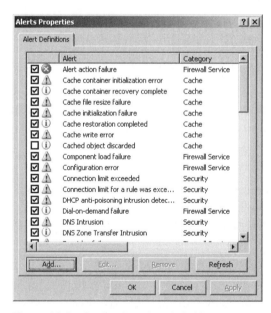

Figure 11-4   Configuring alert definitions

3. To enable or disable an Alert Definition that is already configured, click the check box next to the desired alert.

4. Select the Alert Definition you want to configure and then click Edit.

5. On the General tab, shown in Figure 11-5, you can edit the Name, Description, Category, or Severity of the alert definition. You can also enable or disable the alert by clicking the Enable check box.

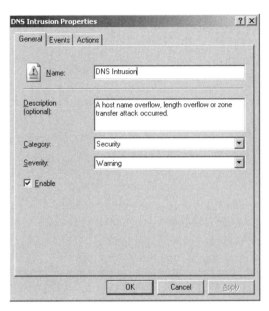

Figure 11-5   Configuring alert definition general properties

6. On the Events tab, shown in Figure 11-6, you can configure the options described in Table 11-4.

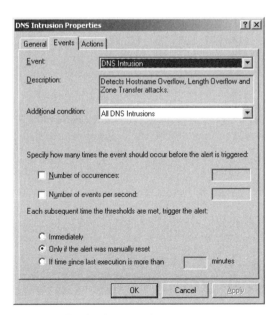

Figure 11-6   Configuring alert events

Table 11-4   Alert Event Configuration Options

Event Options	Choose This Option To
Event	Configure the event that is to be associated with the selected Alert definition. The Description text box explains what each event refers to.
Additional Condition	Configure specific conditions for events that have additional conditions available.
Alert Action Trigger Threshold/ Number Of Occurrences	Specify how many times the event should occur before the alert is triggered.
Alert Action Trigger Threshold/ Number Of Events Per Second	Specify how many times per second an event should occur before the alert is triggered.
Immediately	Specify that a subsequent alert is sent immediately when a threshold is met after the initial alert is triggered.
Only If The Alert Was Manually Reset	Specify that a subsequent alert is sent when a threshold is met and the initial alert was manually reset.
If Time Since Last Execution Is More Than	Specify that a subsequent alert is sent when a threshold is met after a specified amount of time.

What Is an Alert Action?

An alert action is an optional task that takes place when an alert condition is met. Actions that can be configured are the following:

- Send an e-mail message
- Run a program
- Log the event in the Windows event log
- Stop or start the Microsoft Firewall service or the Microsoft ISA Server Job Scheduler

Exam Tip   By default, almost all the ISA Server alerts only write events to the Windows event log. If you want to receive the alert in any other way, or if you want to shut down the ISA Server services if an alert occurs, you must modify the existing alert definition. The only alerts that are configured to stop the ISA Firewall service are alerts that would prevent the ISA Server from logging connections.

Configuring Alert Actions

To configure alert actions, complete the following steps:

1. In the ISA Server Management Console, click the Alerts view under the Monitoring node.

2. In the Task pane, click Configure Alert Definitions.

3. Select the Alert Definition you want to configure, and then click Edit.

4. Click the Actions tab, shown in Figure 11-7. The options on the Actions tab are described in Table 11-5.

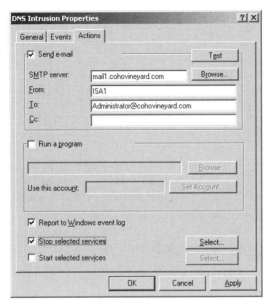

Figure 11-7   Configuring alert actions

Table 11-5   Configuring an Alert Action

Actions Tab Options	Choose This Option To
Send E-Mail	Specify that an e-mail message be sent when the alert conditions are met.
SMTP Server	Provide the IP address or name of the SMTP server.
From	Provide the e-mail address of the sender.
To	Provide the e-mail address of the recipient.
Cc	Provide the e-mail address of the person who receives a copy of the e-mail alert.
Test	Send a test e-mail message to the recipient.
Run Program	Specify that a program will be executed when the alert conditions are met.
Use This Account	Configure the name of a specific user account or local system account that will be used to run the specified program. The specified user must have Logon as batch-job permissions.

Table 11-5   Configuring an Alert Action

Actions Tab Options	Choose This Option To
Report To Windows Event Log	Specify that the event will be written to the Windows event log when the alert conditions are met.
Stop Selected Services	Specify that the selected services will be stopped when the alert conditions are met. The two services that can be stopped are the Microsoft Firewall service or the Microsoft ISA Server Job Scheduler.
Start Selected Services	Specify that the selected services will be started when the alert conditions are met. The two services that can be started are the Microsoft Firewall service or the Microsoft ISA Server Job Scheduler.

Important   If you configure an SMTP server located on the internal network, you must enable the system policy rule that allows the Local Host network to access the internal network using the SMTP protocol. In the System Policy Editor, in the Remote Monitoring configuration group, select SMTP, and then click Enable. The Allow SMTP protocol from firewall to trusted servers rule is enabled. If you configure an e-mail action to use an external SMTP server, you must create an access rule that allows the Local Host network to access the external network (or the network on which the SMTP server is located), using the SMTP protocol.

Configuring New Alert Definitions

To configure a new alert definition, complete the following procedure:

1. In the ISA Server Management Console, click Monitoring and then click the Alerts view.

2. In the Task pane, click Configure Alert Definitions.

3. To add an Alert Definition, click Add in the Alerts Properties dialog box to open the New Alert Wizard. When you configure a new alert definition, you must do the following:

   ❑ Provide an Alert name.

   ❑ Choose a specific Event and additional condition that will trigger the alert. You cannot add any event that is already configured as an alert and that does not have any additional conditions.

   ❑ Assign the Category and Severity level for the alert that you are configuring. These options provide a way to group together alert instances in the Alerts view according to category type and severity level.

❑ Specify an alert action for the event. Your choices include Send An E-mail Message, Run A Program, Report The Event To The Windows Event Log, Stop Selected ISA Server Services, and Start Selected ISA Server Services.

❑ Depending on which alert actions you have selected, you may have additional steps such as SMTP server and e-mail configuration settings, program startup parameters, or the selection of ISA Server services to stop or start.

Guidelines for Managing Alerts

After you configure alert definitions, you must manage the alerts that are created. Many of the ISA Server alerts are used to report on detected intrusion attempts. If you configure the intrusion-detection alerts to shut down the ISA Firewall Service, then ISA Server will go into lockdown mode when the service is shut down. You will need to manage the ISA Server lockdown mode. You can manage all alerts in the Alerts view of the Monitoring Node in the ISA Server Management Console. It is important to manage this list to easily recognize the most recent alerts as well as to purge alerts that are no longer relevant.

Alerts and Intrusion Detection

A primary reason for using alerts is for intrusion detection. Intrusion detection identifies when an attack is attempted against your network and then triggers an alert. You can configure the alert actions that ISA Server will perform in the event of a detected intrusion attempt.

See Also   For more information about the intrusion-detection options available with ISA Server, see Chapter 7, "Configuring ISA Server as a Firewall."

If your ISA Server is exposed to the Internet, it is almost inevitable that it will be exposed to intrusion attempts. When an attack occurs, it may seem that the first line of defense is to disconnect from the Internet, isolating the compromised network from the attack. However, this is not recommended for most attacks. By default, ISA Server raises an alert when it detects an intrusion attempt and writes an event to the event log. In most cases, you should not modify the default as ISA Server is capable of blocking the known intrusion attempts. In some cases, you may get hundreds of intrusion attempts in a day, all of which are successfully blocked.

However, there may be some cases where you want to enable additional actions when ISA Server detects an intrusion attempt. For example, if a new vulnerability is discovered in an application server, you may want to configure ISA Server to detect an attack aimed at the vulnerability and shut down the ISA Server Firewall Service if it detects the attack. This should be a temporary measure until you can fix the application server vulnerability.

When you configure an alert to stop the ISA Server Firewall Service, or when you manually stop the service, ISA Server goes into a lockdown mode. When in lockdown mode, the following restrictions apply:

- The following system policy rules are still applicable:

    - Allow ICMP from trusted servers to the local host.

    - Allow remote management of the firewall using MMC (RPC through Port 3847).

    - Allow Dynamic Host Configuration Protocol (DHCP) replies from DHCP servers to ISA Server

    - Allow remote management of the firewall using RDP.

- Outgoing traffic from the Local Host network to all networks is allowed. If an outgoing connection is established, that connection can be used to respond to incoming traffic. For example, a DNS query can receive a DNS response, on the same connection.

- No incoming traffic is allowed.

- VPN remote access clients cannot access ISA Server. Moreover, access is denied to remote site networks in site-to-site VPN scenarios.

- Any changes to the network configuration while in lockdown mode are applied only after the Firewall Service restarts and ISA Server exits lockdown mode.

- ISA Server does not trigger any alerts.

Troubleshooting ISA Server when the Firewall Service is not running is difficult because of these restrictions. However, you can access the ISA Server computer using an MMC from a remote computer, or you can log on directly to the ISA Server computer. After you have access to the ISA Server Management Console, review the alerts and logs to see what triggered the lockdown mode.

Managing Alerts

Alerts are managed by performing two types of tasks:

- **Acknowledge registered alerts**   You can indicate that you have addressed a specific alert by acknowledging the event. When you mark an event as acknowledged, the status for the event is changed in the Alerts view and the event is no longer displayed on the Dashboard. To acknowledge an event, right-click the alert and then click Acknowledge. You can also click Acknowledge Selected Alerts from the Task pane.

- **Reset registered alerts**   To reset an alert means to remove it from the Alerts view. To reset an alert, right-click the alert and then click Reset. You can also click Reset Selected Alerts from the Task pane. You can reset or acknowledge an entire group of alerts by selecting the group heading and specifying the desired task.

> **Tip**   All alerts are reset when ISA Server restarts.

> **See Also**   In some cases, the alert actions may not be as expected. For information about how to troubleshoot the alert actions, see the article "Troubleshooting Alert Action Failures," located at *http://www.microsoft.com/technet/prodtechnol/isa/2004/plan/ troubleshootingAlertActionFailures.mspx.*

Practice: Configuring and Managing Alerts

In this practice, you will create a new alert as well as modify the default configuration for an existing alert. You will then test the alert action by triggering the alert.

Exercise 1: Creating a New Alert Definition

1. On ISA1, open ISA Server Management Console. Expand ISA1, click Monitoring, and then click the Alerts view.

2. In the Task pane, click Configure Alert Definitions.

3. Click Add in the Alerts Properties dialog box to open the New Alert Wizard.

4. On the Welcome To The New Alert Configuration Wizard page, type **Network Configuration Change** as the alert name. Click Next.

5. On the Events And Conditions page, in the Event list, choose Network Configuration Changed. In the Additional Condition list, choose NIC Disabled. Click Next.

6. On the Category And Severity page, in the Category list, click Routing. In the Severity list, click Warning. Click Next.

7. On the Actions page, click Send An E-Mail Message And Report The Event To The Windows Event Log. Click Next.

8. On the Sending E-Mail Messages page, fill in the following information:

   ❑ SMTP Server: **MAIL1.cohovineyard.com**

   ❑ From: **ISAServerAlert**

   ❑ To: Type the SMTP address for a user with a mailbox on MAIL1

   Click Next.

9. On the Completing The New Alert Configuration Wizard page, review the configuration, and then click Finish.

10. On the Alert Definitions tab, enable the new alert definition by clicking the check box for Network Configuration Changed.

Exercise 2: Modifying an Existing Alert Definition

1. On the Alerts Properties page, click VPN Connection Failure and then click Edit.

2. On the Events tab, click the check box for Number Of Occurrences. In the text box, type **3**. Click Apply.

3. On the Actions tab, click Send E-Mail and fill in the following information:

   ❑ SMTP Server: **Mail1.cohovineyard.com**

   ❑ From: **ISAServerAlert**

   ❑ To: Type the SMTP address for a user with a mailbox on MAIL1

   Click OK.

4. Click OK on the VPN Connections Failure Properties page. Click OK on the Alerts Properties page.

5. Click Apply to apply the changes.

Exercise 3: Test the ISA Server Alerts

1. On ISA1, open the Control Panel and then open Network Connections.

2. Disable the network interface connected to the external network.

3. Open ISA Server Management Console, click Monitoring, and then click the Alerts tab. Click Refresh Now.

4. When the alert appears, click the alert and read the alert description.

5. Right-click the alert, and then click Acknowledge.

6. Open Event Viewer and then open the Application Log. Notice the event created by Microsoft Firewall.

7. Re-enable the network interface.

8. On one of the other computers on the internal network, open Microsoft Internet Explorer.

9. Connect to *http://Mail1.cohovineyard.com/exchange*.

10. Log on using the account that you configured as the alert recipient.

11. Confirm that the e-mail messages from ISAServerAlerts have arrived.

Lesson Review

Use the following questions to help determine whether you have learned enough to move on to the next lesson. If you have difficulty answering these questions, review the material in this lesson before beginning the next lesson. You can find answers to these questions in the "Questions and Answers" section at the end of this chapter.

1. You are the network administrator at the branch office of your company. ISA Server 2004 is installed as your Internet-edge firewall. You have configured the alerts on the ISA Server computer to send an e-mail to your e-mail account at an Internet service provider (ISP). What else must you do to receive the e-mail notifications?

   _____

   _____

   _____

2. You have deployed ISA Server 2004. You have configured ISA Server alerts to notify you through your e-mail account whenever a security-related alert is raised. However, you discover that you are receiving too many e-mail messages. For example, on one weekend, you received several dozen e-mail messages about the same type of attack that was successfully blocked by ISA Server. You need to decrease the number of e-mail messages you receive about the same types of attacks. However, you do need to receive an e-mail when a new type of attack is detected, and you need to be notified if a specific type of attack continues. What should you do?

   a. Configure ISA Server to increase the threshold limit for the events associated with network attacks.

   b. Configure ISA Server to raise additional alerts only after a specified period.

   c. Configure ISA Server to raise additional alerts immediately.

   d. Configure ISA Server to raise additional alerts only if the alert has been manually reset.

3. You have configured a script to run with a set of user credentials when an alert threshold is reached. Later you discover that the alerts are triggering, but that your script is not running. What is the most likely cause?

   _____

   _____

   _____

Lesson Summary

- An alert is a notification of an event or action that has occurred on ISA Server. When the event occurs, an alert is triggered according to the conditions and trigger thresholds specified for the event. You can view the alerts in the ISA Server Management Console in the Alerts view of the Monitoring node.

- An alert definition lists the specific actions or notifications that occur when an event takes place on the computer running ISA Server. Alert events define actions that occur on the computer running ISA Server that can raise alerts. Alert conditions are additional criteria applied by ISA Server when alert events occur. You can also define the actions that will occur after the alert is triggered.

- Many of the ISA Server alerts are used to report on detected intrusions attempts. You can configure the intrusion detection alerts to shut down the ISA Firewall Service. You can manage all alerts in the Alerts view of the Monitoring Node in ISA Server Management Console.

Lesson 3: Configuring Session and Connectivity Monitoring

ISA Server 2004 provides the ability to monitor real-time information about the current sessions open on the server. Session monitoring provides information on all clients that are connected to the ISA Server. You can also enable ISA Server to monitor connections with other servers on the internal network or on the Internet by configuring connectivity monitors. This lesson describes how to configure and manage session monitoring and connectivity monitoring on ISA Server.

After this lesson, you will be able to

- Define session monitoring
- Implement session monitoring
- Define connectivity monitoring
- Implement connectivity monitoring

Estimated lesson time: 30 minutes

What Is Session Monitoring?

You can use session monitoring to identify the users or computers that are connected to the ISA Server computer. These clients may be internal SecureNAT, Firewall, or Web Proxy clients, or they may be Internet clients connected to an internal Web resource, or through a VPN connection.

Session monitoring provides real-time information about the client sessions. This information is accessible on the Session view of the Monitoring node in the ISA Server Management Console, as shown in Figure 11-8. The type of information that is presented includes the following:

- **Activation**   This column shows the date and time that the session has been established.

- **Session Type**   This column shows the type of session that has been established. Session types include SecureNAT, Firewall Client, VPN Client, VPN Site-To-Site, and Web Proxy.

- **Client IP**   This column displays the IP address of the client initiating the session.

- **Source Network**   This column displays the network from which the session has been initiated.

- **Client Username**   This column displays the name of the client that has initiated the session. The client name is displayed only for Web Proxy and Firewall Client connections. Moreover, if the access rule or publishing rule does not require authentication, the client name for Firewall Client is followed by a question mark in parentheses.

- **Client Host Name**   This column displays the name or IP address of the client host computer. The client name is only displayed for Firewall Clients, and the IP address is displayed for SecureNAT.

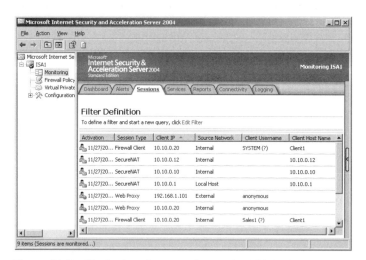

Figure 11-8   Monitoring client sessions using ISA Server Management Console

 Note   All connections from the Internet that access internal Web sites are displayed as Web Proxy connections. Other client connections from the Internet are shown as SecureNAT connections.

You can add two other column headings to provide additional information about the server and application. To add the headings, click Add/Remove Columns from the View menu of the ISA Server Management Console. You can also right-click the headings in the Sessions view and then select the columns you want to view.

These additional headings are as follows:

- **Server Name**   This column displays the name of the computer running ISA Server that is hosting the session.

- **Application Name**   This column displays the name of any application maintaining a session through ISA Server. The application name is only available for Firewall Client connections.

All session details are listed in the Sessions view of the ISA Server Management Console. A summary of total Firewall Client, SecureNAT, and Web Proxy sessions is displayed on the Dashboard.

How to Monitor Sessions

You can use session monitoring for more than just viewing the client connections. You can also disconnect unwanted connections between a client and your network, as well as pause or stop current sessions. To decrease the number of sessions visible in the Sessions view, you can also filter the client sessions.

You can also perform several tasks on the client sessions. These tasks include the following:

- **Disconnecting the session**   This task allows you to stop unwanted sessions immediately. When you stop a session, all associated connections from that client are closed. Note that this does not prevent a client from reactivating the session. If you want to prevent the client from reconnecting, you must change the firewall policy configuration so that it specifically denies access to the unwanted client.

- **Pausing monitoring sessions**   This task allows you to pause monitoring. Any sessions that are currently displayed in the Sessions view are not removed; however, new sessions are not added to the view. When you resume session monitoring, ISA Server updates the view with the relevant, new session information.

- **Stopping monitoring sessions**   This task allows you to stop session monitoring, which clears the sessions view. When session monitoring is stopped, all information about any monitored session is lost. When you restart session monitoring, ISA Server starts to collect all information about active sessions.

> **Exam Tip**   If you disconnect a client session, most clients will just reconnect the session without the user even being aware of the disconnection. To prevent users from accessing a resource, modify the access rule that grants them access, and then disconnect the session.

To manage the client session on the ISA Server, complete the following procedure:

1. In the ISA Server Management Console, click Monitoring.

2. Click the Sessions tab.

3. Identify the current sessions that are listed in the Sessions view.

4. To disconnect a specific session, click the session and then, in the Task pane, click Disconnect Session. You can also right-click the session and then click Disconnect Session.

5. To pause session monitoring, click Pause Monitoring Sessions, which can be found in the Task pane or by right-clicking a session and clicking Pause Monitoring Sessions.

6. To resume session monitoring, click Resume Monitoring Sessions, which can be found in the Task pane or by right-clicking a session and clicking Resume Monitoring Sessions.

7. To stop session monitoring, click Stop Monitoring Sessions, which can be found in the Task pane or by right-clicking a session and clicking Stop Monitoring Sessions.

8. To start session monitoring again, click Start Monitoring Sessions, which can be found in the Task pane.

> **Note**   When you pause session monitoring, the items displayed in the Sessions view are not removed. When you stop monitoring sessions, all sessions in the window are removed.

Filtering Sessions

If you have a large number of users in your organization, you can use a filter definition to determine the sessions to display in the Sessions view. You can create a filter based on a set of conditions to focus on specific issues. For example, if you want to view sessions only by a specific client, you can create a filter to view only sessions initiated by that specific client. Or if you want to view only sessions from the Internet, you can configure the filter to show only connections from the External network.

To configure session filtering, complete the following procedure:

1. In ISA Server Management Console, click Monitoring.

2. Click the Sessions tab.

3. Click Edit Filter, which can be found in the Task pane or as a link under the Filter Definition heading.

4. In the Edit Filter dialog box, as shown in Figure 11-9, select the filter criteria.

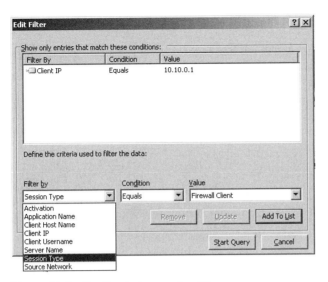

Figure 11-9 Configuring a session filter

Table 11-6 lists the options.

Table 11-6 Session Filtering Options

Criteria	Explanation
Filter By	Select a specific heading to filter, such as Session Type, Client IP, Client Username, or others. You can create a filter based on any of the columns in the Sessions view.
Condition	Select a specific condition to apply to the filtered heading. Some examples of conditions include Equals, Contains, Not Contains, and Not Equal.
Value	The Value field provides a text box for you to enter a specific value to filter. For example, if you are filtering by session type, you can select the various session types available in ISA Server 2004. If you are filtering based on IP addresses, then you can type in the specific IP address.

5. Click Add To List to add it to the filter list.

6. Continue to add additional filters as required.

7. After creating a filter definition, you can export the definition for future use. To export the filter definitions, in the Task pane, click Export Filter Definitions. When you want to use the same filter again, click Import Filter Definitions and select the appropriate exported .XML file.

What Is Connectivity Monitoring?

In addition to monitoring the client activity on the ISA Server computer, you can also use connectivity monitoring to monitor the availability of connections between the ISA Server computer and other servers on the network. Connectivity verifiers regularly monitor connections from the ISA Server computer to any computer or URL on any network.

When you configure a connectivity verifier, you can configure the method the verifier will use to determine connectivity. The following options are available:

- **Ping** When you configure a connectivity verifier to use this method, ISA Server sends an ICMP ECHO_REQUEST to the specified server and waits for an ICMP ECHO_REPLY. This test checks for simple network connectivity.

- **TCP connection** When you configure a verifier to use this method, ISA Server tries to establish a Transmission Control Protocol (TCP) connection using a specified port number on the specified server. For example, if you are testing connectivity with a domain controller, ISA Server will try to establish a connection using the Lightweight Directory Access Protocol (LDAP) port (Port 389). This test not only checks for network connectivity but also verifies that a specific service is running on the server and can be reached by ISA Server.

- **HTTP GET request** When you configure a verifier to use this method, ISA Server sends an HTTP GET request to the specified server or URL and waits for the reply. This tests for network connectivity and verifies that a Web server is running on the destination server and can be reached by ISA Server. When you configure a connectivity verifier that issues an HTTP request to check connectivity, ISA Server enables a system policy rule that allows Hypertext Transfer Protocol (HTTP) and Hypertext Transfer Protocol Secure (HTTPS) traffic from the Local Host network to All Networks.

When you configure a connectivity verifier, it is categorized into one of the following groups: Active Directory, DHCP, DNS, Published Servers, Web (Internet), and Others. The server group status for each group is displayed on the Dashboard view so you can quickly identify whether there is a problem with a particular service.

How to Configure Connectivity Monitoring

To configure connectivity monitoring, complete the following procedure:

1. In ISA Server Management Console, click Monitoring, and then click Connectivity.

2. On the Tasks tab, click Create New Connectivity Verifier.

3. On the Welcome To The New Connectivity Verifier Wizard page, type a name and then click Next.

4. On the Connectivity Verification Details page, shown in Figure 11-10, fill in the information listed in Table 11-7.

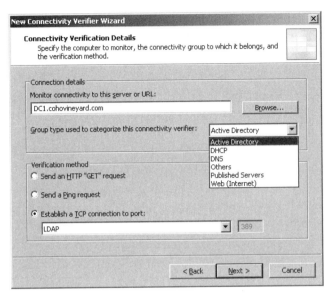

Figure 11-10   Configuring a connectivity verifier

Table 11-7   Connectivity Monitoring Configuration Options

Configuration Option	Use This Option To
Monitor Connectivity To This Server Or URL	Type the name or URL of the server.
Group Used To Categorize This Connectivity Verifier	Select the group this verifier belongs to. When you choose a particular group, a default verification method for that group is automatically selected.
Verification Method	Choose the verification method used for this verifier. You can choose to use an HTTP GET request, Ping request, or a TCP connection. If you choose the TCP connection method, you can also choose the protocol and port number used to create the TCP connection.

5. Click Next, and then click Finish to complete the wizard.

6. By default, the connectivity verifier will test connectivity with the specified server every 5000 milliseconds. You can modify this setting by right-clicking the verifier in the Connectivity view and then clicking Properties. On the Properties page, modify the value for Specify The Timeout Response (Msec). You can also configure whether the verifier will trigger an alert if the connection fails.

Practice: Configuring Session and Connectivity Monitoring

In this practice, you will configure session monitoring by viewing the sessions open on the ISA Server computer, and by configuring a session filter. You will also configure and test four connectivity verifiers.

Exercise 1: Monitoring Sessions

1. On CLIENT1, open Internet Explorer and connect to *http://www.microsoft.com*.

2. On DC1, open Internet Explorer and connect to *http://www.msn.com*.

3. On ISA1, open ISA Server Management Console, and click Monitoring.

4. Click the Sessions tab. Notice the client sessions open on ISA1.

5. Click Edit Filter. In the Filter By drop-down list, click Session Type. In the Condition drop-down list, click Equals. In the Value drop-down list, click Firewall Client. Click Add To List, and then click Start Query.

6. Notice that only the session from CLIENT1 is displayed.

7. Right-click the session from CLIENT1, and then click Disconnect Session. In the Warning dialog box, click Yes.

8. On CLIENT1, refresh the page for *http://www.microsoft.com*.

9. On ISA1, notice that the CLIENT1 session has been reestablished.

Exercise 2: Configuring Connectivity Monitoring

1. On ISA1, in ISA Server Management Console, click Monitoring, and then click Connectivity.

2. On the Tasks tab, click Create New Connectivity Verifier.

3. On the Welcome To The New Connectivity Verifier Wizard page, type **Internet Connection Test**, and then click Next.

4. On the Connectivity Verification Details page, fill in the following information:

   ❑ Monitor Connectivity To This Server Or URL: **www.microsoft.com**

   ❑ Group Used To Categorize This Connectivity Verifier: Web (Internet)

   ❑ Verification Method: Send An HTTP GET Request

   Click Next.

5. On the Completing The New Connectivity Verifier .Wizard page, review the configuration and then click Finish.

6. In the Enable HTTP Connectivity Verification dialog box, click Yes.

7. Double-click Internet Connection Test. On the Properties page, under Timeout, change the Response Threshold to 10000 milliseconds. Click OK.

8. Create another connectivity verifier with the following configuration:

   ❏ Connectivity Verifier Name: **DC Connection Test**

   ❏ Monitor Connectivity To This Server Or URL: **DC1.cohovineyard.com**

   ❏ Group Used To Categorize This Connectivity Verifier: Active Directory

   ❏ Verification Method: Establish A TCP Connection Using This Protocol: LDAP

9. Create another connectivity verifier with the following configuration:

   ❏ Connectivity Verifier Name: **DNS Connection Test**

   ❏ Monitor Connectivity To This Server Or URL: **DC1.cohovineyard.com**

   ❏ Group used to categorize this connectivity verifier: DNS

   ❏ Verification Method: Establish A TCP Connection Using This Protocol: DNS

10. Create another connectivity verifier with the following configuration:

    ❏ Connectivity Verifier Name: **Network Connection Test**

    ❏ Monitor Connectivity To This Server Or URL: **10.10.0.10**

    ❏ Group Used To Categorize This Connectivity Verifier: Others

    ❏ Verification Method: Send A Ping Request

11. Click Apply to apply the changes.

12. Open Network Connections from the Control Panel. Disable the network interface connected to the external network.

13. In ISA Server Management Console, click the Alerts tab. Wait for the No Connectivity alert to appear. Review the contents of the alert and then right-click the alert. Click Reset.

14. Enable the network interface connected to the external network.

15. On DC1, open a command prompt.

16. Type **sc stop DNS**.

17. On ISA1, wait for the No Connectivity alert to appear. Review the contents of the alert and then right-click the alert. Click Acknowledge.

18. On DC1, type **sc start DNS** in the command prompt window.

19. On DC1, disable the Local Area Connection.

20. On ISA1, wait for the No Connectivity alert to appear. Review the contents of the alert. Notice that all three alerts associated with DC1 report an error. Right-click the alerts and click Acknowledge.

21. On DC1, enable the Local Area Connection.

Lesson Review

Use the following questions to help determine whether you have learned enough to move on to the next lesson. If you have difficulty answering these questions, review the material in this lesson before beginning the next lesson. You can find answers to these questions in the "Questions and Answers" section at the end of this chapter.

1. While monitoring sessions on your ISA Server computer, you notice a Firewall Client session that has been inactive for an unusually long time. How can you find out which application is maintaining the session?

   _____

   _____

   _____

2. While monitoring the sessions on your ISA Server computer, you notice that a specific user is accessing the Internet using a chat application that is prohibited by the organization's security policy. You disconnect the session but notice that the session is reconnected almost immediately. You need to ensure that the application cannot be used to access the Internet without affecting Internet access for legitimate applications. What should you do?

   a. Disconnect the client and then configure ISA Server to stop monitoring sessions.

   b. Configure an access rule that prevents users from using the application to access the Internet. Then disconnect the client session.

   c. Disconnect the client session and then stop the Microsoft Firewall service on ISA Server.

   d. Configure an HTTP filter to prevent users from using the application to access the Internet, and then disconnect the client session.

3. How would you configure a filter to view only external users coming to your published FTP site?

   _____

   _____

   _____

4. You have deployed ISA Server and configured it to enable access to several servers in the perimeter network (also called a demilitarized zone, or DMZ). A user reports that he cannot access one of the servers in the perimeter. The server is running a custom-built application using a specific port number. You determine that the server is running but that the application has stopped responding to user requests. You restart the application. The application is a business-critical application, so you would like to configure ISA Server to raise an alert whenever the application on the server fails. What should you do?

    a. Configure an ISA Server connectivity verifier to ping the server every 30 seconds.

    b. Configure an ISA Server connectivity verifier to send an HTTP GET request to the server every 30 seconds.

    c. Configure an ISA Server connectivity verifier to send a Transmission Control Protocol (TCP) request to the server every 30 seconds.

Lesson Summary

- Session monitoring provides real-time information about client sessions being hosted through ISA Server. You can view the session information on the Sessions View in the ISA Server Management Monitoring node.

- You can perform several tasks on the session entries. These tasks include disconnecting the session, pausing monitoring sessions, and stopping monitoring sessions. Moreover, you can configure session filters to limit which sessions are displayed.

- You can use connectivity monitoring to monitor the availability of connections between the ISA Server computer and other servers on the network. Connectivity verifiers regularly monitor connections from the ISA Server computer to any computer or URL on any network.

- You can configure connectivity verifiers to use an HTTP GET request, perform a ping, or to connect to other servers using specified protocols. When a connectivity monitor cannot establish a connection, an alert is raised.

Lesson 4: Configuring Logging and Reporting

ISA Server enables the option to log all activity related to the Firewall service, Web proxy service, and the SMTP Message Screener. These logs can be used to provide usage information and also to provide information about malicious or inappropriate activity on the server. You can view this detailed log information in the Log Viewer, or you can create a summary of the information in a report. This lesson describes how to configure logging and reporting on ISA Server 2004.

After this lesson, you will be able to

- Describe ISA Server logging functionality
- Configure logging
- View ISA Server logs
- Describe ISA Server reporting functionality
- Configure ISA Server reports

Estimated lesson time: 30 minutes

What Is ISA Server Logging?

In addition to session monitoring, you can also monitor ISA Server activity by configuring logging. By default, when ISA Server 2004 is installed, logging is enabled for all available components. The main benefit of ISA Server logging is that, in addition to viewing current log information from within the ISA Server Management Console, you can also use logs to generate reports, analyze trends, or investigate security issues.

ISA Server 2004 enables the following logging options:

- **Firewall Logging**   Records all connections and connection attempts to the Firewall service.

- **Web Proxy Logging**   Records all connections and connection attempts to the Web proxy service.

- **SMTP Message Screener Logging**   Records SMTP Message Screener events and status information.

You can store ISA Server log information in one of the following locations:

- **MSDE database**   Storing a log in MSDE format provides the ability for events to be viewed in the Log Viewer. MSDE database size is limited to 2 gigabytes (GB). When a log exceeds the size limit, ISA Server automatically creates a new database. Also, at the beginning of each day a new log-file database is created. However, the Log Viewer displays the data as if it were in a single database.

Note   By default, the log information for Web proxy and Firewall Service logs are saved in MSDE format.

- **SQL database**   You can store log information in a SQL database to provide advanced storage and analysis capabilities. The use of a SQL database also provides the ability to store the logs on a remote server or storage location.

- **File**   You can save ISA Server logs to a file in either the World Wide Web Consortium (W3C) format or ISA Server format. W3C logs contain both data and directives describing the version, date, and logged fields. The tab character is used as a delimiter. Date and time are in Universal Time Coordinate (UTC) format. ISA Server format logs contain only data with no directives. All fields are always logged and the comma character is used as a delimiter. The date and time fields are in local time.

 Note   The SMTP Message Screener log information is saved by default in the W3C file format. It cannot be saved to a database format.

You can use the ISA Server Log Viewer to monitor and analyze current activity on the ISA Server computer. When you start a query in the Log Viewer, it will display all activity on the server, including all successful connections and all blocked connections. You can also filter the data displayed in the Log Viewer to only show data that meets specific criteria. In addition to real-time monitoring, you can also use the Log Viewer to view the archived logs to examine previous server activity.

 Note   The SMTP Message Screener log information is not displayed in the Log Viewer because the information is stored in a text log file. To view the SMTP Message Screener log, you can use any text editor. Only logs that are stored in MSDE format can be viewed using the Log Viewer.

How to Configure Logging

By default, ISA Server begins logging information immediately after installation. However, you can modify some of the logging configuration after installation. To configure logging for the Firewall service, Web proxy service, or the SMTP Message Screener, complete the following procedure:

1. In ISA Server Management Console, click Monitoring.

2. Click the Logging view.

3. On the Tasks tab, choose one of the following tasks, depending on which service you are configuring:

❏ Configure Firewall Logging

❏ Configure Web Proxy Logging

❏ Configure SMTP Message Screener Logging

4. Configure the Log options, as shown in Figure 11-11. The options are described in Table 11-8.

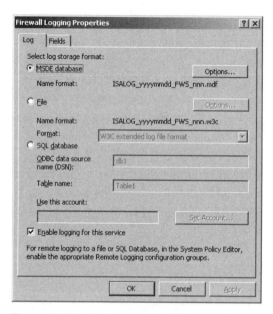

Figure 11-11   Configuring the ISA Server log type

Table 11-8   ISA Server Log Options

Log Option	Choose This Option To
MSDE Database	Configure the log to use the MSDE format. Click Options to configure additional settings such as the log file storage location and log file storage limits.
File	Configure the log to be stored in a file format. You can choose to save the file in either the W3C extended log file format or the ISA Server file format. Click Options to configure additional settings such as the storage location of the log file and log file storage limits. This is the only option available if you are configuring the SMTP Message Screener log.
SQL Database	Configure the log file to be stored in an Open Database Connectivity (ODBC)–compliant database. Additional settings include the ODBC data source name, the table name, and the account name to use when logging on to the log database.

Table 11-8   ISA Server Log Options

Log Option	Choose This Option To
Enable Logging For This Service	Specify whether logging is enabled for this service. If not selected, no events are recorded in the log.

5. On the Log tab, click Options to modify the logging options. In the Options dialog box, shown in Figure 11-12, you can perform either of the following actions:

❏ Modify the location of the log files. By default, the log files are located in the ISA Logs folder in the ISA Server installation directory. For improved performance, you should move the logs to a separate hard drive.

❏ Define log storage limits. By default, ISA Server will use up to 8 GB to store the logs. Each log file is a maximum of 2 GB in size. You can change how much space ISA Server will use to store the log files as well as define how ISA Server will maintain the log file space. By default, when the log files reach the defined maximum size, or when the space on the hard drive reaches the Maintain Free Disk Space limit, ISA Server will begin deleting older log files. You can modify the default setting to increase the total log file storage limit, or to stop logging new information when the limit is reached. You can also define when ISA Server will begin deleting log files when the disk space limitation is not reached. ISA Server checks every 10 minutes that logs do not exceed the specified limits.

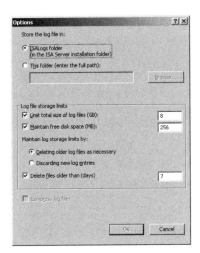

Figure 11-12   Configuring the logging options

Exam Tip   If you do not use the option to Maintain Free Disk Space, ISA Server logs can fill the entire hard drive with log files. When this happens, ISA Server will stop the Firewall Service rather than continue without logging. By default, the only events that will trigger an alert to stop the Firewall Service are events that prevent logging.

Planning   You need to ensure that you plan the log file archiving and disk usage to meet your organization's requirements. The log files are the only place where ISA Server stores detailed information about the activity on the ISA Server computer, so you need to ensure that you have access to the log files for as long as you require. For example, if your organization requires that you can track Internet access for at least seven days, you need to ensure that you configure enough hard disk space to maintain that many logs. For most busy ISA Server computers, this will require a significant increase in the maximum size for the log files. To ensure that you log all information, do not select the option to discard logging data when the logs reach the maximum size. Moreover, you should back up the log files as part of your regular backup to ensure that you have access to log files after they have been deleted from the ISA Server computer.

6. You can also modify which fields will be logged in the log files. Click the Fields tab to configure the fields to include in the log. By default, ISA Server logs almost all available fields.

How to View ISA Server Logs

The method you use to view an ISA Server log depends on the type of log and the storage format. Any log stored in the MSDE format can be viewed using the Log Viewer. Logs that are stored in the file format can be viewed with a standard text editor, such as Notepad. Logs that are stored in a SQL database can be viewed using SQL reporting software such as Microsoft SQL Server 2000 Reporting Services, located at *http://www.microsoft.com/sql/reporting/default.asp*.

Real World **Troubleshooting Client Connections Using ISA Server Logs**

As you work with ISA Server 2004, you will find yourself spending a fair amount of time working with the Log Viewer. ISA Server stores all connection related data in the log files, so when you need to troubleshoot or investigate connection-related problems, the best place to look is in the log files.

I have found that I use the Log Viewer a great deal at the beginning of an ISA Server deployment. Despite the best planning efforts, there are usually some cases with every deployment were a specific client connection does not work as expected. Sometimes this is an internal client who cannot get access to the Internet; sometimes it is a publishing rule that does not grant the right level of access. Among the best ways to troubleshoot these problems is to use the Log Viewer to view the client connection attempt. You can either view the logs in real time, or you can examine the archived logs to see why the connection attempt failed.

If you do not see a client connection attempt in the log, you know that the client connection is not even getting to the ISA Server computer. This may be due to a client configuration error or a DNS configuration error. If you notice a client connection attempt in the log, but the client connection is blocked, you can use the logged information to determine which firewall rule is blocking the client connection. In some cases, the problem may be with the firewall rule order. In other cases, the problem may be with the firewall rule configuration. In either case, you can see why the client attempt is not successful and begin troubleshooting the firewall rule configuration.

Sometimes, the problem is not with the client or the firewall rules, but with the destination server. In this case, you will see the client connection in the ISA Server log, and the client connection will be allowed through the firewall, but you don't see a corresponding response from the destination server. In this case, you know that the problem is not with your ISA Server configuration, and you need to look elsewhere to resolve the problem.

Viewing Log Files Stored in the File Format

To view a log file stored in the file format, browse to C:\Program Files\Microsoft ISA Server\ISALogs or an alternate location if you moved the log files. Use Notepad to open one of the following file types:

- **ISALOG_yyyymmdd_FWS_nnn.w3c** This file type refers to logs stored in the W3C format. In this file type, *yyyy* represents the year, *mm* represents the month, *dd* represents the day, and *nnn* represents multiple log files created on the same day.

- **ISALOG_yyyymmdd_FWS_nnn.iis** This file type refers to logs stored in the ISA Server file format. In this format, *yyyy* represents the year, *mm* represents the month, *dd* represents the day, and *nnn* represents multiple log files created on the same day.

> **Note** If you use text logs to store all the ISA Server logs, you will see three current logs. In the log file names, FWS refers to the Firewall service, WEB refers to the Web proxy service, and EML refers to the SMTP Message Screener.

Viewing Log Files Stored In the MSDE Format

To view a log file stored in the MSDE format, complete the following steps:

1. In the ISA Server Management Console, click Monitoring.

2. Click the Logging tab.

3. To view the information being logged at the current time, click Start Query. When you choose this option, you are viewing the client connections in real time, so all the current client connection attempts are displayed in the logging window.

4. To limit which client connections are displayed in the log or to look at the archived log, click Edit Filter. You can apply a filter to the logged information based on any of the log fields. For example, you can filter the log based on Client IP, Log Record Type, Object Source, HTTP Method, and so on. You can also filter the log based on the log time, as shown in Figure 11-13. Use this option to view the archived logs.

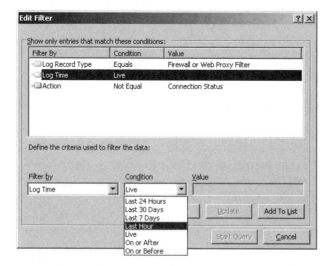

Figure 11-13 Configuring the logging filter

5. You can also copy the logged information into another application. To do this, click Copy Selected Results To Clipboard or Copy All Results To Clipboard, and then paste the results into another application.

Exam Tip   When you examine the ISA Server logs, you will notice that in some cases, the Web client connections include a URL, and in some cases, they include only an IP address. Only clients that are configured as Web Proxy clients resolve sites through the ISA Server computer. Other clients handle name resolution themselves, and so the ISA Server computer only knows about the IP address. If you need to log the URLs, ensure that the required clients are configured as Web Proxy clients.

What Are ISA Server Reports?

In addition to the logs, ISA Server also provides reports that you can use to analyze ISA Server activities. ISA Server reports provide a summary of the information collected from the ISA Server log files. ISA Server reports are accessible on the Reports view of the Monitoring node in the ISA Server Management Console. You can generate a report on demand or you can schedule reports to be generated on a recurring basis. The reports can include daily, weekly, monthly, or yearly data.

ISA Server provides the following report content options:

- **Summary reports**   Summary reports include a set of statistics about ISA Server usage. Summary reports combine data from the Web proxy service logs and Firewall service logs.

- **Web usage reports**   Web usage reports include a set of reports that display top Web users, common responses, and Web browsers. These reports show how an organization uses the Web and are based on the Web proxy service logs.

- **Application usage reports**   Application usage reports display Internet application usage, including incoming and outgoing traffic, top users, client applications, and destinations. Application usage reports can help you to plan network capacity and determine bandwidth policies. Application usage reports are based on the Firewall service logs.

- **Traffic and utilization reports**   Traffic and utilization reports display total Internet usage by application, protocol, and direction; average traffic and peak simultaneous connections; cache hit ratios; errors; and other statistics. Traffic and utilization reports can help you plan and monitor network capacity and determine bandwidth policies. Traffic and utilization reports combine data from the Web proxy service logs and the Firewall service logs.

■ **Security reports** Security reports list attempts to breach network security. Security reports can help identify attacks or security violations after they have occurred. Security reports are based on the Web proxy service logs and the Firewall service logs.

How Reporting Works

ISA Server reports are based on the Web proxy and Microsoft Firewall service logs. Once per day, ISA Server creates a summary database of these logs and stores the summary in the ISASummaries folder. When a report is created, all relevant summary databases are combined into a single report database. The report is then created based on the combined summaries.

> **See Also**   For information about what log fields are included in the reports, see "How the report mechanism works," in ISA Server Help. You can also modify the information that is stored in the summary logs by customizing the reports.

How to Configure ISA Server Reports

ISA Server creates the log summary databases every day but you need to configure the reports in order to view the information. You can modify how ISA Server creates the log summary information. Moreover, you can generate reports on demand, or schedule and publish ISA Server reports.

How to Configure the Log Summary Database

The report summary database contains the report information created daily from the ISA Server log files. Every day, an application called Dailysum.exe summarizes the Web proxy and Firewall service log information. Two log summaries are saved; one with a daily summary and one with a monthly summary. At the beginning of each month, Dailysum.exe creates another monthly summary that summarizes all the past month's daily summaries. By default, daily and monthly log summaries are generated automatically at 12:30 A.M. You can change these parameters to fit your organization's needs. To configure the log summary database settings, complete the following procedure:

1. In ISA Server Management Console, click Monitoring.

2. Click the Reports tab.

3. In the Task pane, scroll to the Related Tasks section and then click Configure Log Summary.

4. The Log Summary Properties dialog box, shown in Figure 11-14, contains the options listed in Table 11-9.

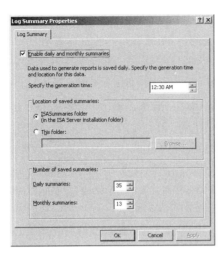

Figure 11-14   Configuring the ISA Server log summaries

Table 11-9   Configuring the ISA Server Log Summaries

Log Summary Options	Choose This Option To
Enable Daily And Monthly Summaries	Enable or disable the creation of the daily and monthly log summaries.
Specify The Generation Time	Specify the time that the log summaries are generated.
Location Of Saved Summaries	Specify a location to save the summary database information. By default, the ISASummaries folder is used.
Number Of Saved Summaries	Specify the number of saved daily and monthly summaries to save.

How to Generate a Report

You can generate a new report at any time using the ISA Server Management console. When you generate a new report, ISA Server displays the information that you select from the summary logs.

Exam Tip   Because ISA Server reports are based on the log summary information, any information that is added to the logs after the log summary is created is not included in the report. By default, these log summaries are created at 12:30 A.M. daily. This means that the reports do not contain the current day's information.

To generate a new report, complete the following procedure:

1. In ISA Server Management Console, click Monitoring.
2. Click the Reports tab.

3. In the Task pane, click Generate A New Report. The New Report Wizard starts.

4. On the Welcome To The New Report Wizard page, type a name for the report.

5. On the Report Content page, shown in Figure 11-15, select the check box next to the content you want to include in the report. The content choices are as follows:

   ❑ *Summary*—This section includes summarized information about network traffic usage, sorted by application.

   ❑ *Web Usage*—This section includes information about top Web users, common responses, and browsers.

   ❑ *Application Usage*—This section includes Internet application usage information about top users, client applications, and destinations.

   ❑ *Traffic And Utilization*—This section includes total Internet usage by application, protocol, and direction. These reports also show average traffic and peak simultaneous connections, cache hit ratio, errors, and other statistics.

   ❑ *Security*—This section lists attempts to breach network security.

Figure 11-15   Choosing a report content type

6. On the Report Period page, specify the start and end dates for the report. Click Next.

7. On the Report Publishing page, you can choose to publish reports to a directory. If you choose this option, the report will be generated and then copied to the specified directory. You can also specify the name that will be used to write the report to the directory. If you do not choose this option, the report will be listed in the ISA Server Management console, and stored on the ISA Server computer.

8. On the Send E-Mail Notification page, shown in Figure 11-16, you can configure an e-mail address and SMTP server. If you choose this option, an e-mail will be sent to the recipient notifying the recipient that the report has been generated. You can also include a link to the report if you published the report to a directory.

Figure 11-16   Configuring an e-mail notification for a report

9. Click Finish to close the wizard.

The new report is shown in Report view. The status column shows the report as Generating. When the generation is complete, the status will show as Completed.

Note   The Microsoft ISA Server Job Scheduler service must be running to create a report.

Viewing Reports

As each report is generated, the report is listed in the Reports view. You can view a report by double-clicking the report name in the Report view of ISA Server Management. You can also select the report and then click View Selected Report in the Task pane. The report is displayed in Internet Explorer.

The following columns are displayed by default:

- **Report Name**   This column displays the name of the report.
- **Period**   This column displays how frequently the report is generated.
- **Start Date**   This column displays the start date of the report. Information is shown only from this start date.
- **End Date**   This column displays the end date of the report. Information is shown only up to this end date.
- **Status**   This column displays whether the report is being generated or completed.

An additional column is available to be displayed if required:

- **Generation Date**   This column displays the date on which the report was created.

> **Exam Tip** When a report is generated but not published to a shared folder, it can be viewed only on the computer running ISA Server Management. On any other computer, the report shows either empty data or a page with empty frames and a message that "Page cannot be displayed."

Creating Recurring Report Jobs

In addition to creating on-demand reports, you can also create recurring report jobs. You can use this option if your organization needs weekly or monthly reports for auditing and trend analysis requirements. Instead of creating reports manually, you can create a recurring report job that will create the reports automatically based on a configure schedule.

To create a recurring report job, complete the following steps:

1. In ISA Server Management Console, click Monitoring. Click the Reports tab.

2. Click Create And Configure Report Jobs.

3. In the Report Jobs Properties dialog box, click Add. The New Report Job Wizard starts.

4. On the Welcome To The New Report Job Wizard page, type a name for the report job. Click Next.

5. On the Report Content page of the wizard, choose the option to customize the report content. Select the check box next to the content you want to include in the report. Click Next.

6. On the Report Job Schedule page, as shown in Figure 11-17, specify the schedule. The schedule determines how frequently the report job will run. The options include

   ❑ Daily

   ❑ Weekly, On Specified Days

   ❑ Monthly, On This Date Every Month

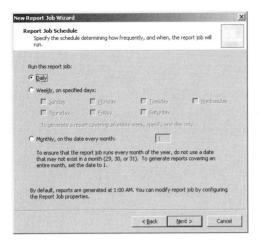

Figure 11-17   Configuring a recurring report schedule

Note   By default, reports are generated at 1:00 A.M. You can change the report job by configuring the Report Job properties.

7. On the Report Publishing page, you can choose the option to publish reports to a directory as well as the user name used to publish the report. Click Next.

8. On the Send E-Mail Notification page, choose the option to configure e-mail notification for when a report is generated. Click Next.

9. Click Finish to close the wizard.

After you create the report, the report job is listed in the Report Job page of the Report Jobs Properties dialog box. After the scheduled report job runs, a new report appears in the Reports view of ISA Server Management.

Tip   If you choose to create the report on either the 29th, 30th, or 31st day of the month, you will get a warning message when you create the report indicating that not all months include those dates. If a month does not include the date, a report will not be published for that month. As a best practice, do not select these dates when configuring a recurring report job.

How to Publish Reports

To make reports more available, you can publish them to a shared folder. Any individual who needs access to the reports needs to have Read permissions to this folder. Users do not need to have the ISA Server Management Console installed on their computers to view the reports.

To successfully publish a report, the Isarepgen.exe process must have Write permissions to the publishing folder. If you publish a report manually, the Isarepgen.exe process uses the credentials of the user publishing the report. When you publish a recurring report, you need to configure the credentials Isarepgen.exe uses to publish the reports.

You can publish a report when you configure an on-demand report or when you configure a recurring report job. You can also publish reports that you have created previously. To do this, locate the report in the Reports review and then click Publish Selected Report.

To view a published report, browse to the folder where the report was published and open the Report.htm file. This file contains links to all the other information in the report.

Practice: Configuring ISA Server Reporting

In this practice, you will configure an ISA Server report and view the report contents. You will also configure a recurring report job and configure it to publish the report to a shared folder. You will then view the report from the shared folder.

Exercise 1: Generating a Report

1. On ISA1, in ISA Server Management Console, click Monitoring.

2. Click the Reports tab.

3. In the Task pane, click Generate a New Report. The New Report Wizard starts.

4. On the Welcome To The New Report Wizard page, type **Daily Report** and click Next.

5. On the Report Content page, ensure that all the check boxes for the report content are selected. Click Next.

6. On the Report Period page, in the Start Date box, select the date on which this course started. Click Next.

7. On the Report Publishing page, click Next.

8. On the Send E-Mail Notification page, click Next.

9. Click Finish to close the wizard.

10. Wait until the Daily Report status is Completed and then double-click the report. In the Internet Explorer dialog box, view the information that is provided in the report and then close the report.

Exercise 2: Creating a Recurring Report Job

1. On DC1, create a folder on the C drive named WebReports. Share the folder and configure the Share Permissions on the folder to grant Change and Read permissions to the user account that you are using to manage ISA Server. Modify the Security settings on the folder to grant the same user account Modify permissions.

2. On ISA1, in ISA Server Management Console, click Create And Configure Report Jobs.

3. In the Report Jobs Properties dialog box, click Add. The New Report Job Wizard starts.

4. In the Welcome To The New Report Job Wizard page, type **Monthly Report** and click Next.

5. On the Report Content page, ensure that all the check boxes for the report content are selected. Click Next.

6. On the Report Job Schedule page, click Monthly, on this date every month. In the text box, enter today's date. Click Next.

7. On the Report Publishing page, click Publish Reports To A Directory. In the Published Reports Directory text box, type **DC1\webreports**.

8. Click Publish Using This Account and then click Set Account. Enter **cohovineyard***yourusername* and your password and click OK.

9. On the Report Publishing page, click Next.

10. On the Send E-Mail Notification page, click Send E-Mail Notification For Completed Reports and fill in the following information:

    ❑ SMTP Server: **Mail1.cohovineyard.com**

    ❑ From: **ISAServerReports**

    ❑ To: **administrator@cohovineyard.com**

    ❑ Message: **The monthly report has been generated.**

11. Click Include A Link To The Completed Report In The Message.

12. Click Test and click OK.

13. Click Next. On the Completing The New Report Job Wizard, review the configuration and then click Finish.

14. On the Report Jobs tab, click Monthly Report and click Edit.

15. On the Schedule tab, set the Generation Hour: Value to a time five minutes from now.

16. Click OK twice.

17. On DC1, open the C:\Webfolders folder. When the report information is written to the directory, open the report folder, and then open Report.htm to view the report.

Lesson Review

Use the following questions to help determine whether you have learned enough to move on to the next lesson. If you have difficulty answering these questions, review the material in this lesson before beginning the next lesson. You can find answers to these questions in the "Questions and Answers" section at the end of this chapter.

1. You are a new ISA administrator with your organization. The previous administrator deployed ISA Server and configured it to allow user access to the Internet. When you try to check the ISA Server log files using the ISA Server Log Viewer, you cannot see any information. You need to be able to view the ISA Server logs using the Log Viewer. What should you do?

   a. Configure the ISA Server logs to be stored in an MSDE database.

   b. Configure the ISA Server logs to be stored in a Microsoft SQL Server database.

   c. Configure the ISA Server logs to be stored in a text file in ISA Server format.

   d. Configure the ISA Server logs to be stored in a text file in World Wide Web Consortium (W3C) format.

2. Your corporate security policy requires that you keep two years' worth of Monthly Summaries of logged activity. What will you do to adhere to corporate policy?

   _____

   _____

   _____

3. Your application server is published on the Internet and hosts multiple applications. You want to view information about connections to a particular application that have occurred today. How would you accomplish this?

   a. Generate a Web Usage report for today.

   b. Start a log query and filter it for the destination port of the application.

   c. Generate an Application Usage report for today.

   d. Monitor sessions and filter for the name of the application.

4. The Information Technology (IT) manager for your organization is interested in getting information about the Internet usage for the organization. He wants to have weekly reports that include information about which employees access the Internet most frequently and the Web sites that are accessed most frequently. You need to make this information available for the IT manager, but you want to do this with the least administrative effort. The IT manager does not have any administrative rights on ISA Server, and you should not change this configuration. What should you do?

   a. Configure a recurring report job to publish a report once a week to a shared folder that the IT manager can access.

   b. Once a week, publish a report from ISA Server to a shared folder that the IT manager can access.

   c. Configure a recurring report job to create a report once a week.

   d. Once a week, generate a report on ISA Server.

Lesson Summary

- You can monitor ISA Server activity by configuring logging. By default, when ISA Server 2004 is installed, logging is enabled for all available components. With ISA Server logging you can view current log information from within the ISA Server Management console and also use logs to generate reports, analyze trends, or investigate security issues.

- By default, ISA Server begins logging information immediately after installation. However, you can modify some of the logging configuration such as the log file types and log file locations after installation.

- Any log stored in the MSDE format can be viewed using the Log Viewer. You can use the Log Viewer to view current activity on the ISA Server computer, or you can use it to view archived logs. Logs that are stored in the file format can be viewed with a standard text editor, such as Notepad.

- ISA Server reports provide a summary of the information collected from the ISA Server log files. The reports can include daily, weekly, monthly, or yearly data.

- You need to configure reports in order to view the log summary information. You can generate a report on-demand or you can schedule reports to be generated on a recurring basis. You can also publish reports to a folder on the ISA Server computer or to a shared folder on the network.

Case Scenario Exercise

In this exercise, you will troubleshoot an ISA Server 2004 installation for a fictitious organization. Read the scenario and then answer the questions that follow. If you have difficulty completing this work, review the material in this chapter before beginning the next chapter. You can find answers to these questions in the "Questions and Answers" section at the end of this chapter.

Scenario 1

Your company has deployed ISA Server 2004 in a 3-Leg perimeter configuration. You are publishing a public Web site in your perimeter network. You also have several remote users who connect to your ISA Server using a VPN. Users are reporting the following problems with your ISA Server implementation:

- Users report that sometimes your Web site is not available. On investigation, you determine that the Web service on the server occasionally stops responding to client requests and needs to be restarted. You need to automate restarting the Web service.

- Some users report that they are unable to access an external Web site that other users are able to access.

- Some remote users report that they are not able to access some resources on the internal network. You need to determine whether the VPN client connection is successful.

- The security department wants to be able to use SQL Reporting Services to process the Firewall and Web Proxy logs.

- In addition, you want to generate a monthly report that provides information on Internet usage by internal clients and another report to provide information on cache hits. You want to publish these reports to an internal Web site where they can be viewed by the Admin group.

- You need to be able to provide an analysis of current bandwidth usage to plan for future hardware requirements.

Scenario 1 Question

1. How would you use the reporting and monitoring features of ISA Server 2004 to deal with these ISA Server issues?

_____

_____

_____

Chapter Summary

- Implementing monitoring on ISA Server is a critical component of a successful ISA Server deployment. Your monitoring plan should define what information you need to monitor in real time, how you will configure the ISA Server alerts and what long-term information about client connections, server performance, and connectivity on ISA Server you need to collect. By monitoring the computer running ISA Server, you can also gather information you can use for planning modifications to the current ISA Server infrastructure.

- An alert is a notification of an event or action that has occurred on ISA Server. When the event occurs, an alert is triggered according to the conditions and trigger thresholds specified for the event. You can view and manage the alerts in the ISA Server Management Console in the Alerts view of the Monitoring node. You can also modify the existing alerts or create new alerts.

- Session monitoring provides real-time information about client sessions being hosted through ISA Server. You can view and manage the session information on the Sessions View in the ISA Server Management Monitoring node. You can use connectivity monitoring to monitor the availability of connections between the ISA Server computer and other servers on the network. Connectivity verifiers regularly monitor connections from the ISA Server computer to any computer or URL on any network.

- You can monitor ISA Server activity by configuring logging. By default, when ISA Server 2004 is installed, logging is enabled for all available components. With ISA Server logging you can view current log information from within the ISA Server Management Console as well also use logs to generate reports, analyze trends, or investigate security issues. ISA Server reports provide a summary of the information collected from the ISA Server log files. The reports can include daily, weekly, monthly, or yearly data. You can generate a report on-demand or you can schedule reports to be generated on a recurring basis. You can also publish reports to a folder on the ISA Server computer or to a shared folder on the network.

Exam Highlights

Before taking the exam, review the key points and terms that are presented in this chapter. You need to know this information.

Key Points

- You can delegate ISA Server monitoring without allowing administrative access to the ISA Server configuration. If you assign users to the ISA Server Basic Monitoring role, they can view all the ISA Server monitoring information, but cannot change any settings. If you assign users to the ISA Server Extended Monitoring role, they can monitor the ISA Server computer, and change the monitoring configuration, but cannot modify other ISA Server settings such as access or publishing rules.

■ You must be a local Administrator in order to monitor ISA Server using Performance Monitor. The System Performance information on the ISA Server Dashboard is provided by Performance Monitor, so if you are not a local Administrator, you will not be able to view the System Performance information.

■ By default, almost all the ISA Server alerts only write events to the Windows event log. If you want to receive the alert in any other way, or if you want to shut down the ISA Server services if an alert occurs, you must modify the existing alert definition.

■ If you configure ISA Server to send SMTP messages based on alerts or to report the generation of ISA Reports, you need to enable the appropriate system policy or access rule so that ISA Server can send the messages.

■ If you disconnect a client session, most clients will just reconnect the session without the user even being aware of the disconnection. To stop users from accessing a resource, modify the access rule that grants them access, and then disconnect the session.

■ If you do not use the option to Maintain Free Disk Space, ISA Server logs can fill the entire hard drive with log files. When this happens, ISA Server will stop the Firewall Service rather than continue without logging.

■ The ISA Server logs are very useful for troubleshooting ISA Server client connections. Understand how to view current logs and archived logs and how to filter the logs to locate the required information.

■ Because ISA Server reports are based on the log summary information, any information that is added to the logs after the log summary is created is not included in the report. By default, these log summaries are created at 12:30 A.M. daily. This means that the reports do not contain the current day's information.

■ When a report is generated but not published to a shared folder, it can be viewed only on the computer running ISA Server Management. On any other computer, the report shows either empty data or a page with empty frames and a message that "Page cannot be displayed."

Key Terms

alert   A notification of an event or action that has occurred on ISA Server. When the event occurs, an alert is triggered according to the conditions and trigger thresholds specified for the event.

connectivity verifier   An ISA Server object used to test connections from the ISA Server computer to any computer or URL on any network regularly. When you configure a connectivity verifier, you can configure the method the verifier will use to determine connectivity.

log   Provides detailed information about the Web proxy, Microsoft Firewall service, or Simple Mail Transfer Protocol (SMTP) Message Screener. ISA Server logs all client connections and all blocked client connections by default.

report   Provides summarized information about the usage patterns on ISA Server. The report information is extracted from the ISA Server logs.

session monitoring   Used to provide real-time information about the users or computers that are connected to the ISA Server computer. These clients may be internal SecureNAT, Firewall, or Web proxy clients, or they may be Internet clients connected to an internal Web resource, or through a VPN connection.

Questions and Answers

Page
11-12
Lesson 1 Review

1. You have deployed ISA Server 2004. You are the only network administrator in your organization and do not have time for constantly monitoring the computer running ISA Server. However, you do need to be notified immediately whenever there is a security problem on ISA Server and when the services on ISA Server stop. How can you implement this functionality?

   a. Configure ISA Server logging

   b. Configure ISA Server connectivity

   c. Configure ISA Server alerts

   d. Configure ISA Server reports

   C is correct. ISA Server alerts are designed to provide immediate information whenever specified events happen on ISA Server. ISA Server logging and reports provide information about the activity on ISA Server but do not have functionality to notify the administrator of events on the server. ISA Server connectivity monitors the connections between ISA Server and other computers and may raise alerts, but these are not security-related alerts.

2. You are the network administrator for your organization. Users report that they are unable to use the Internet and are receiving a DNS error message. You investigate and discover that the DNS server used to resolve Internet names has failed. What proactive measure could you have taken to ensure that you were aware of the DNS server failure as soon as possible?

   You could have configured ISA Server to monitor connectivity to the DNS server and then set up an alert to trigger an e-mail in the event of a server failure.

3. You have deployed ISA Server and configured it to allow user access to the Internet. You have deployed the Firewall client to some of the client workstations in your organization. You now need to monitor the number of active Firewall client sessions on ISA Server. What performance objects should you monitor on ISA Server?

   a. ISA Server Firewall Engine

   b. ISA Server Cache

   c. ISA Server Firewall Service

   d. ISA Server Web Proxy

   C is correct. The Firewall Service performance objects monitor the Firewall client connections. The Firewall Engine objects monitor all client connections, including SecureNAT and Web Proxy client connections, whereas the Web Proxy counters monitor only the Web Proxy client connections. The ISA Server Cache counters monitor the efficiency of the Web Proxy cache on the server.

4. You are the ISA Server administrator for your organization. Your manager wants information about the trends in Web usage provided to him on a monthly basis. What can you do to provide this?

The reporting features of ISA Server can provide recurring reports to summarize Web usage.

Page
11-27

Lesson 2 Review

1. You are the network administrator at the branch office of your company. ISA Server 2004 is installed as your Internet-edge firewall. You have configured the alerts on the ISA Server computer to send an e-mail to your e-mail account at an Internet service provider (ISP). What else must you do to receive the e-mail notifications?

Because your Exchange Server computer is on the External network, you must create a firewall access rule that allows the Local Host network access to the External network using SMTP.

2. You have deployed ISA Server 2004. You have configured ISA Server alerts to notify you through your e-mail account whenever a security-related alert is raised. However, you discover that you are receiving too many e-mail messages. For example, on one weekend, you received several dozen e-mail messages about the same type of attack that was successfully blocked by ISA Server. You need to decrease the number of e-mail messages you receive about the same types of attacks. However, you do need to receive an e-mail when a new type of attack is detected, and you need to be notified if a specific type of attack continues. What should you do?

   a. Configure ISA Server to increase the threshold limit for the events associated with network attacks.

   b. Configure ISA Server to raise additional alerts only after a specified period.

   c. Configure ISA Server to raise additional alerts immediately.

   d. Configure ISA Server to raise additional alerts only if the alert has been manually reset.

B is correct. To meet the requirements, you must configure ISA Server to raise additional alerts about a specific event after a specified period. This means that if the same event happens repeatedly, you will continue to receive alerts, but not as frequently. A would decrease the chances that you would receive an alert in the event of a new attack. C would increase, rather than decrease, the number of alerts you would receive. D would mean that you would not receive any alerts about attacks that continue for an extended period.

3. You have configured a script to run with a set of user credentials when an alert threshold is reached. Later you discover that the alerts are triggering, but that your script is not running. What is the most likely cause?

The most likely cause of the problem in this case is a user permissions error. Ensure that the user account you chose has the Logon as a Batch Job user right on the ISA Server computer.

Lesson 3 Review

1. While monitoring sessions on your ISA Server computer, you notice a Firewall
    Client session that has been inactive for an unusually long time. How can you find
    out which application is maintaining the session?

    You can customize the view on the Session view page to include the Application Name column.

2. While monitoring the sessions on your ISA Server computer, you notice that a
    specific user is accessing the Internet using a chat application that is prohibited by
    the organization's security policy. You disconnect the session but notice that the ses-
    sion is reconnected almost immediately. You need to ensure that the application
    cannot be used to access the Internet without affecting Internet access for legitimate
    applications. What should you do?

    a. Disconnect the client and then configure ISA Server to stop monitoring sessions.

    b. Configure an access rule that prevents users from using the application to
    access the Internet. Then disconnect the client session.

    c. Disconnect the client session and then stop the Microsoft Firewall service on
    ISA Server.

    d. Configure an HTTP filter to prevent users from using the application to access
    the Internet, and then disconnect the client session.

    B is correct. To ensure that the client does not connect again by using the application, you need
    to configure an access rule that prevents the use of the application to access the Internet. A is
    incorrect because this just configures ISA Server to stop monitoring sessions but does not pre-
    vent the application from reconnecting. C is incorrect because this would disrupt all other
    users' access to the Internet. D is incorrect because the application is not using HTTP to
    access the Internet.

3. How would you configure a filter to view only external users coming to your
    published FTP site?

    You would edit the session filter to include two conditions. One condition would specify the cli-
    ent application as FTP and the other condition would specify the source network as External.

4. You have deployed ISA Server and configured it to enable access to several servers
    in the perimeter network (also called a demilitarized zone, or DMZ). A user reports
    that he cannot access one of the servers in the perimeter. The server is running a
    custom-built application using a specific port number. You determine that the server
    is running but that the application has stopped responding to user requests. You
    restart the application. The application is a business-critical application, so you
    would like to configure ISA Server to raise an alert whenever the application on the
    server fails. What should you do?

    a. Configure an ISA Server connectivity verifier to ping the server every
    30 seconds.

  b. Configure an ISA Server connectivity verifier to send an HTTP GET request to the server every 30 seconds.

  c. Configure an ISA Server connectivity verifier to send a Transmission Control Protocol (TCP) request to the server every 30 seconds.

C is correct. To check if the custom application is running, you must configure the connectivity verifier to check for connectivity using a TCP request and using the specific port number. The ping check will test only whether the server is online or not. The HTTP GET command will work only if there is a Web server running on the server, and this will test only the Web server availability.

Page
11-56
Lesson 4 Review

 1. You are a new ISA administrator with your organization. The previous administrator deployed ISA Server and configured it to allow user access to the Internet. When you try to check the ISA Server log files using the ISA Server Log Viewer, you cannot see any information. You need to be able to view the ISA Server logs using the Log Viewer. What should you do?

  a. Configure the ISA Server logs to be stored in an MSDE database.

  b. Configure the ISA Server logs to be stored in a Microsoft SQL Server database.

  c. Configure the ISA Server logs to be stored in a text file in ISA Server format.

  d. Configure the ISA Server logs to be stored in a text file in World Wide Web Consortium (W3C) format.

A is correct. For the log files to be visible in ISA Server Log Viewer, you must store the data in the MSDE database installed by ISA Server. The other options are all acceptable formats for storing the logged information, and you can view the logs using different tools, but Log Viewer supports only the MSDE database format.

 2. Your corporate security policy requires that you keep two years' worth of Monthly Summaries of logged activity. What will you do to adhere to corporate policy?

Configure the Log Summary properties on the Reporting Tasks tab to keep 24 monthly summaries.

 3. Your application server is published on the Internet and hosts multiple applications. You want to view information about connections to a particular application that have occurred today. How would you accomplish this?

  a. Generate a Web Usage report for today.

  b. Start a log query and filter it for the destination port of the application.

  c. Generate an Application Usage report for today.

  d. Monitor sessions and filter for the name of the application.

B is correct. The log query can filter on the destination port of the application. A and C are incorrect because reports cannot be generated until the next day. D is incorrect because the Session Monitor only provides information about current sessions.

4. The Information Technology (IT) manager for your organization is interested in getting information about the Internet usage for the organization. He wants to have weekly reports that include information about which employees access the Internet most frequently and the Web sites that are accessed most frequently. You need to make this information available for the IT manager, but you want to do this with the least administrative effort. The IT manager does not have any administrative rights on ISA Server, and you should not change this configuration. What should you do?

    a. Configure a recurring report job to publish a report once a week to a shared folder that the IT manager can access.

    b. Once a week, publish a report from ISA Server to a shared folder that the IT manager can access.

    c. Configure a recurring report job to create a report once a week.

    d. Once a week, generate a report on ISA Server.

A is correct. To provide this report with minimal administrative effort, configure a recurring report job; this means that ISA Server will generate the report automatically based on the configured schedule. By publishing the report on a shared folder, the IT manager can get access to the reports without requiring any administrative permissions on ISA Server. B is incorrect because this would require you to manually generate and publish the report once a week. C and D are incorrect because both these options mean that the report can be viewed only on ISA Server, which would require administrative rights on the server.

Case Scenario Exercise

Page
11-58
Scenario 1 Question

1. How would you use the reporting and monitoring features of ISA Server 2004 to deal with these ISA Server issues?

To restart the Web service on the server hosting the Web site, set up a connectivity verifier to send an HTTP GET request at regular intervals to your Web server. If the connectivity verifier fails to get a response, have an alert generated that will run a script to restart the Web service.

To determine why some users cannot connect to an external Web site while others can, use the Web Proxy log to view connection attempts for the users to determine which firewall access rule is responsible for the connections failing.

To determine whether the VPN client connections are successful, use the Session view to check if the clients are connected. You will need to configure the session filter to view VPN client sessions.

To use SQL Reporting Services to process the Firewall and Web Proxy logs, configure the log properties to use a SQL database by specifying the ODBC data source and Table Name and a user account for authentication.

To generate a monthly report that provides information on Internet usage by internal clients and another report to provide information on cache hits, create two report jobs, one for Web Usage and one for Traffic and Utilization. Configure them both to be generated monthly and published to the virtual directory of the Web site using the proper credentials.

To provide an analysis of current bandwidth usage, use the Performance Monitor counters that come with ISA Server 2004 to log data about Internet usage trends and to measure the ability of hardware to keep up with demand.

12 Implementing ISA Server 2004, Enterprise Edition

Exam Objectives in this Chapter:

- Deploy ISA Server 2004
    - ❑ Migrate from ISA Server 2000 to ISA Server 2004
    - ❑ Install ISA Server 2004, Enterprise Edition
- Define administrative roles
    - ❑ Assign and delegate administrative roles
- Configure ISA Server 2004 for network load balancing (NLB)
- Configure forward and reverse caching
    - ❑ Configure Cache Array Routing Protocol (CARP)
- Plan a firewall policy
    - ❑ Plan policy rules for an enterprise firewall.
    - ❑ Plan for interaction between enterprise- and array-level rule deployments
    - ❑ Validate and troubleshoot enterprise-rule deployment

Why This Chapter Matters

If you are working for a small or medium-sized business, and have just completed your Microsoft Internet Security and Acceleration (ISA) Server Standard Edition deployment, you are probably done with your ISA Server deployment. However, if you are working for a large organization or for an organization that has high redundancy requirements, you are probably considering deploying ISA Server 2004, Enterprise Edition.

ISA Server, Enterprise Edition, is virtually identical to ISA Server, Standard Edition, with one very important difference. Enterprise Edition is designed for scalability and redundancy. With Standard Edition, each ISA Server computer is a stand-alone server, and each server stores its own configuration information. One ISA Server computer cannot communicate with other ISA Server computers except in scenarios such as Web chaining.

Enterprise Edition enables scalability by storing the configuration information in a central location so that configuration settings can be applied to multiple servers at one time and by enabling such options as network load balancing (NLB) and distributed caching using Caching Array Routing Protocol (CARP).

You may believe that you have spent all this time learning about ISA Server, Standard Edition, and now you will have to relearn everything for Enterprise Edition. No need to worry about this, though, because most of what you have learned so far applies to Enterprise Edition. You will still configure access rules and publishing rules in Enterprise Edition; the main difference is that now these rules will be applied at the enterprise or array level. You will notice that many of the wizards and configuration options are identical. The only change lies in where you configure the settings, and that the settings can be applied to all ISA Server computers in the enterprise or all the ISA Server computers in an array.

Lessons in this Chapter:

- Lesson 1: ISA Server 2004 Enterprise Edition Overview 12-3
- Lesson 2: Planning an ISA Server 2004 Enterprise Edition Deployment 12-20
- Lesson 3: Implementing ISA Server 2004, Enterprise Edition 12-43

Before You Begin

This chapter presents the skills and concepts related to deploying and configuring ISA Server 2004, Enterprise Edition. If you plan to complete the practices and lab in this chapter, prepare the following:

- A Microsoft Windows Server 2003 (Standard Edition or Enterprise Edition) computer installed as DC1 and configured as a domain controller in the *cohovineyard.com* domain. This server should be configured as an Enterprise Certification Authority.

- A second Windows Server 2003 computer installed as ISA2. This server should be a domain member in the *cohovineyard.com* domain. Two network interfaces should be installed on this server. The external interface should be connected to a network that contains one or more Web servers. If possible, the network interface should be attached to the Internet.

- A third Windows Server 2003 computer installed as ISA3. This server should not be a domain member in the *cohovineyard.com* domain. The network configuration for this server must be identical to ISA2.

Lesson 1: ISA Server 2004 Enterprise Edition Overview

Exam Objectives in this Chapter:

- List reasons for deploying ISA Server, Enterprise Edition
- Describe how ISA Server, Enterprise Edition, stores its configuration information
- List the ISA Server Enterprise Edition configuration components
- Describe how enterprise and array policies work
- Describe how ISA Server, Enterprise Edition, integrates with NLB
- Describe who ISA Server, Enterprise Edition, enables virtual private networking
- Describe how ISA Server, Enterprise Edition, enables distributed caching using CARP

Estimated lesson time: 30 minutes

Why Deploy ISA Server, Enterprise Edition?

Both ISA Server, Standard Edition, and ISA Server, Enterprise Edition, provide full firewall functionality to enable secure access to the Internet for internal users and secure access to published servers for Internet users. Both editions can be used as virtual private network (VPN) remote access servers, and as remote gateway servers in a site-to-site VPN configuration. The most significant difference between the two versions is that Enterprise Edition provides enhanced scalability. ISA Server, Standard Edition, provides firewall and proxy server services on a single computer while Enterprise Edition provides the same services on multiple servers. This lesson describes why you might choose to deploy Enterprise Edition rather than Standard Edition.

One of the primary differences between Standard Edition and Enterprise Edition is how the two editions store their configuration information. Standard Edition stores its configuration information in the local computer registry. ISA Server, Enterprise Edition, stores its configuration information in a separate directory located on one or more Configuration Storage servers. The Configuration Storage servers use Active Directory Application Mode (ADAM) to store the configuration information.

On the Configuration Storage server, you can configure enterprise policies, networks and network objects, and arrays and array policies. Then you can install ISA Server on multiple computers and assign each of them to a specific array. The enterprise and array policies are assigned automatically to each ISA Server computer in the array. To change the ISA Server configuration, you simply change the information on the Configuration Storage server. You can also configure array level permissions so that you can delegate the management and monitoring of ISA Server computers in each array.

ISA Server 2004, Enterprise Edition, also enhances scalability by enabling shared Web caching across an array of multiple servers. With Enterprise Edition, multiple ISA Server computers can be configured as a single logical cache, so that the caching capacity for all the ISA Server computers is combined. To enable this feature, ISA Server uses the

Cache Array Routing Protocol (CARP), which is used to manage the distribution and retrieval of Web information across multiple ISA Server computers.

The third feature available with Enterprise Edition is the integration of NLB with ISA Server. With NLB, several computers can be clustered so that the entire group of servers shares a single Internet Protocol (IP) address in addition to the unique IP addresses assigned to each computer. When client computers connect to the NLB cluster, they connect to that shared IP address. NLB delivers scalability by distributing the client connections across all the servers in the cluster and delivers high availability by redirecting incoming network traffic to working cluster members if one of the servers in the cluster fails or is offline. Any connections to the failed computer are lost, but the services remain available.

With ISA Server 2004, Standard Edition, you can configure NLB manually and manage it using Microsoft Windows management tools. With Enterprise Edition, NLB is integrated so that NLB can be managed using the ISA Server Management Console. This means that NLB configuration is performed through ISA Server management. ISA Server also provides NLB health monitoring and manages the failover from one ISA Server computer in the cluster to another.

These Enterprise Edition features mean that you can deploy ISA Server Enterprise Edition in many scenarios, including the following:

- **Deploying multiple ISA Server computers that require the same configuration**   Some organizations require multiple ISA Server computers with the same configuration. For example, a large organization may want to deploy multiple servers in a large office to provide scalable access to Internet resources, or to provide fault-tolerant publishing access to public Web sites. To deploy this configuration, you can configure an array, and enable NLB and CARP on the array. Then, install as many ISA Server computers as needed into the array; all servers will have the same configuration.

- **Deploying ISA Server computers in a distributed administration scenario**   Some organizations require the option to enable distributed administration. For example, an organization with multiple branch offices or divisions may require the ability to configure some configuration settings at an organization level, while delegating some administrative rights to other administrators. ISA Server, Enterprise Edition, enables this configuration by using enterprise policies for the organization's configuration and allowing for the delegation of administrative rights at an array level.

- **Deploying ISA Server computers without Active Directory**   ISA Server 2000, Enterprise Edition, uses Active Directory directory service to store its configuration information. This means that each ISA Server 2000 computer had to be a member of an Active Directory domain. Because ISA Server 2004 uses ADAM, you can deploy Enterprise Edition without storing any information in Active Directory. You can deploy Configuration Storage Server and ISA Server computers as domain members or as workgroup members.

Real World   Should You Deploy ISA Server, Enterprise Edition?

For many of its products, Microsoft provides multiple editions. Usually there is a standard build that is intended for small and medium-sized organizations, and an enterprise build, which is intended for larger companies with more complex requirements. The enterprise build of the product is more expensive, but also usually provides some functionality that is critical for the enterprise customer.

ISA Server is no exception. You can buy Standard Edition or Enterprise Edition. For many companies, the decision whether to deploy Standard Edition or Enterprise Edition is easy. Small companies that deploy only one ISA Server computer have no need for Enterprise Edition. Very large organizations with high performance and redundancy requirements know that they need to spend the extra money on Enterprise Edition. But there are many companies in the middle for which the choice is more complicated.

For most companies, ISA Server performance is not an important reason to implement Enterprise Edition. A single ISA Server computer can examine and forward network traffic at a much faster rate than most Internet connections for medium-sized businesses. A more important consideration for many companies is redundancy or failover functionality. If you publish a business-critical Web site through ISA Server, or if your business is directly affected by any downtime in Internet connectivity, you should consider Enterprise Edition. ISA Server, Enterprise Edition, enables NLB, which means that if one ISA Server computer fails or if you need to take one ISA Server computer offline, the other servers in the NLB cluster can automatically assume the load. If your published Web site does even a few thousand dollars' worth of business every hour, this feature alone may make Enterprise Edition worthwhile.

The second feature that is important in many companies is manageability. If you deploy more than one ISA Server computer in a particular role, the fact that you can just configure the policy in one location and have it applied to multiple ISA Server computers can save a significant amount of time. In some cases, you may have lots of time to configure your ISA Server computers. However, if you need to make a configuration change immediately to prevent an attack from succeeding, you will appreciate the benefits of Enterprise Edition. Moreover, the fact that you can monitor all the ISA Server computers in your enterprise from a single interface is important to many organizations.

How Does ISA Server, Enterprise Edition, Store Configuration Information?

ISA Server, Enterprise Edition, uses a Configuration Storage server to store the configuration for all the arrays in the enterprise. You can deploy multiple Configuration Storage servers in an organization with all Configuration Storage servers in the same enterprise storing the same configuration information. Each Configuration Storage server replicates any updates to the enterprise configuration to the other Configuration Storage servers.

What Is Active Directory Application Mode?

The Configuration Storage server uses ADAM to store and replicate configuration data for all the ISA Server computers in an ISA Server enterprise. When you install the Configuration Storage server, you also automatically install ADAM on the computer.

> **Note**   An ISA Server enterprise is a collection of all ISA Server 2004 computers that use the same Configuration Storage directory to store configuration information.

ADAM is a special mode of Active Directory that is designed for directory-enabled applications. Compatible with Lightweight Directory Access Protocol (LDAP), ADAM is a directory service that runs on Microsoft Windows Server 2003 computers. ADAM is designed to be a stand-alone directory service; it does not require the deployment of Domain Name System (DNS), domains, or domain controllers. ADAM enables the replication of data between multiple servers using a multiple-master replication model. This means that when ADAM servers are configured as replication partners, changes to the directory data can be made on any server and the data will be replicated to all other replication partners.

> **Note**   ADAM also runs on computers running Windows XP Professional, but this deployment is not supported with ISA Server. For detailed information about ADAM, see the Windows Server 2003 Active Directory Application Mode site at *http://www.microsoft.com/windowsserver2003/adam/default.mspx*.

Although ISA Server 2004, Enterprise Edition, uses ADAM to store its configuration information, you do not need to install ADAM directly. Instead, it is installed when you install a Configuration Storage server. You will rarely directly access the directory information using the ADAM tools. Instead, you will use ISA Server Management to modify the directory data.

Deploying Configuration Storage Server

You can deploy multiple configuration storage servers in an enterprise. When you deploy the first Configuration Storage server, you must choose the option to create an enterprise. For a subsequent installation, you should choose to join an existing enterprise.

When you create an array, you must specify a Configuration Storage server from which the array will receive updates. After you create an array you can change the array's Configuration Storage server. In addition to a primary Configuration Storage server, an array may be assigned a backup Configuration Storage server.

> **Note**   If your Configuration Storage Server is a member of a workgroup, rather than a domain, you can deploy only one Configuration Storage server in your enterprise.

When the ISA Server Firewall Service starts, it initiates a connection to its designated Configuration Storage server. If the Configuration Storage server is available, the latest configuration is downloaded and applied to the registry of the ISA Server computer. If a Configuration Storage Server is not available, the Firewall Service will initiate a connection to its backup Configuration Storage server, if one has been designated for use. If the backup Configuration Server is unavailable or has not been designated, the Firewall Service will use its last known configuration. No configuration updates are applied to the ISA Server computer until it can connect to a Configuration Storage server.

Whenever you change a configuration in the ISA Server Management Console, the change is replicated to available Configuration Storage servers. The configuration changes are retrieved by the ISA Server computers and applied to the local registry. By default, ISA Server computers will check for configuration changes every 15 seconds. You can modify this setting for each array.

The servers in an array use the following protocols to communicate with each other and with the Configuration Storage server:

- **MS Firewall Storage**   This protocol is an inbound LDAP-based protocol. It uses Port 2172 [for Secure Sockets Layer (SSL) protocol connections] and Port 2171 (for non-SSL connections). Array members communicate with the Configuration Storage server using the MS Firewall Storage protocol. Computers running the ISA Server Management Console also use the MS Firewall Storage protocol to read from and write to the Configuration Storage server.

- **MS Firewall Storage Replication**   This protocol is an outbound Transmission Control Protocol (TCP), which is defined on Port 2173. MS Firewall Storage Replication is used for configuration replication between Configuration Storage servers.

- **MS Firewall Control** This is another outbound TCP protocol and is defined on Port 3847. It is used for communications between the ISA Server Management Console and computers running ISA Server services.

- **Remote Procedure Call (RPC)** To monitor server performance, the ISA Server Management computer requires remote procedure call (RPC) connectivity to the ISA Server computers.

ISA Server Enterprise Edition Configuration Components

When deploying ISA Server, Enterprise Edition, you must configure additional components that are not available in Standard Edition. These additional components include the following:

- **ISA Server enterprise** An ISA Server enterprise is a collection of all ISA Server 2004 computers that use the same Configuration Storage directory to store configuration information. The enterprise defines the replication boundary between Configuration Storage servers. All Configuration Storage servers in the same enterprise share the same configuration information, but the information is not replicated outside the enterprise.

> **Planning** You can deploy more than one enterprise in an organization, but this is not recommended because the ISA Server computers in the two enterprises cannot share configuration information.

- **Enterprise policies** An enterprise policy is a policy defined at the enterprise level that can be applied to any array. An enterprise policy, like any firewall policy, contains an ordered set of policy rules such as access rules or publishing rules. These rules can be applied before or after firewall rules that are defined at the array level. In most cases, you should define one or more enterprise policies and then apply the enterprise policies to arrays.

- **Enterprise networks and network objects** The enterprise policy can also include policy elements such as networks, computer sets, Uniform Resource Locator (URL) sets, or subnets. An enterprise network is a range of IP addresses defined on the enterprise level. You can define enterprise networks and network objects, and then use these objects when configuring array networks or enterprise or array firewall rules.

- **ISA Server arrays** An array is a group of ISA Server 2004 computers that shares the same configuration. An array includes:

  ❑ One or more Configuration Storage servers that store the configuration information for the array.

  ❑ One or more array members that are computers with ISA Server services installed.

- **Array policies**   An array policy is a set of rules that is defined on the array level and is specific to the array. These rules include access rules, publishing rules, and policy elements, as well as array networks and other network objects.

> **Tip**   The array configuration displayed in ISA Server Manager is almost exactly the same as the configuration displayed in ISA Server Manager when connected to a computer running ISA Server 2004, Standard Edition. The only new item in the interface is a Servers container that lists all the servers in the array. However, many of the objects in an array have additional configuration options related to Enterprise Edition features such as NBL and CARP.

Configuring Enterprise Networks

When you create an enterprise network, the only configuration option you have is to configure the IP address range. For example, you can create an enterprise network named Internal that includes all the IP addresses that are internal to your organization, but you cannot configure options such as Web Proxy client or Firewall client settings. After you create the enterprise network, you can assign the network to an array-level network.

The IP addresses assigned to an enterprise network cannot cross any security boundary, such as a firewall or a VPN connection. However, you can create an enterprise network that contains the IP addresses in a perimeter network (also known as a demilitarized zone, or DMZ), or the IP addresses for a remote site.

When you install ISA Server, Enterprise Edition, several enterprise networks are created that act as placeholders for array-level networks of the same name. These enterprise networks cannot be explicitly used when creating array-level firewall policy rules. Instead, they are typically used in the enterprise policy. Any rule applied by the enterprise administrator to the predefined enterprise network will be applied to the array-level network of the same name. For example, an enterprise rule that allows HTTP access to the External network will be applied to the External network for each array. ISA Server includes the following predefined enterprise networks:

- External
- Local Host
- Quarantined VPN Clients
- VPN Clients

Enterprise networks can be used in several different scenarios:

- Enterprise networks can be used to create enterprise-level rules. For example, you can create an enterprise network named Internal Network that includes all the IP addresses for computers on your network. Then you can create an enterprise-level rule that controls Internet access. This rule applies to any computer on any internal network. If you add an array, the rule would automatically apply to the internal network of that array, so long as it is within the IP address range of the enterprise network.

- Enterprise networks enable communication between arrays. When an array's networks are defined as part of an enterprise network, ISA Server can recognize the communication between the networks as internal traffic. Otherwise, ISA Server will consider the request to be from an external source, and the request will be rejected by the ISA Server spoof-detection feature.

- Enterprise networks allow the enterprise administrator to manage the IP address space of the enterprise, so that if a network is added on one array, there is no need to configure every other array to recognize that new network. So long as the new network is in an enterprise network and the other arrays built their networks based on the IP ranges defined in the enterprise networks, the new network will be recognized by all the arrays in the enterprise. To enable this, the array administrator must define the array networks using the enterprise networks. For example, if there is an enterprise network called Internal Network, the array administrator can create an array network and choose the Internal Network enterprise network as the IP range for that array network.

> **Exam Tip** If you configure an enterprise network that includes IP addresses that are not included in any array-level network, any traffic coming from those IP addresses is considered spoofed and the traffic will be blocked. All IP addresses must be defined in an array network, either explicitly or by assigning an enterprise network as the address range for the array network.

Configuring Arrays

All ISA Server computers in an array must have the same server configuration including:

- The same number of network adapters connected to array-level networks.
- The same time-zone configuration, with synchronized clocks (for logging).
- The same hard-disk partitions (for logging).
- The same certificates installed on each array member (for SSL communications).
- The same network services available to each array member (for example, the servers must use the same DNS servers, the same servers for Certificate revocation list checking, and have access to the same Active Directory domain controllers).
- The same language version of ISA Server and Windows Server 2003 installed, with the same locale set for the computer and for the logged-on user.

■ The same ISA Server updates installed.

■ The same domain and site configuration (or belong to a workgroup).

You cannot move a server from one array to another after you install ISA Server services. To move the server, uninstall ISA Server services, and then reinstall ISA Server services.

You can define any access rules or publishing rules at the array level. These rules will be applied to all array members. You can also create array policy elements that can be used to create array-level rules. You can also define array networks for each array. The IP addresses of an array network can contain IP ranges as well as enterprise networks, including more than one enterprise network.

How Enterprise Policies and Array Policies Work

Deploying ISA Server, Enterprise Edition, can be more complicated that deploying Standard Edition because you can configure ISA Server policies and policy objects at both the enterprise and array levels. You can create one or more enterprise policies that contain firewall rules. Then you can apply the policy to an array, and all the firewall rules defined by the enterprise policy will also be applied to the array members.

When you create an enterprise, an enterprise policy named Default Policy is created. This policy does not contain any firewall rules other than a final access rule named Default Rule, which denies all network traffic. Because this enterprise policy does not contain any additional policy rules, if you apply this policy to an array, only the array policy rules and the Default Rule will be applied on that array. You cannot modify the Default Policy.

As an enterprise administrator, you can define additional enterprise policies. In most cases, you would define enterprise policies that can be applied across the entire enterprise. For example, you can define an enterprise policy that blocks the downloading of executables using Hypertext Transfer Protocol (HTTP), or an enterprise policy that allows HTTP and secure Hypertext Transfer Protocol (HTTPS) access to the Internet for all users. After you create the enterprise policies, you can assign the enterprise policies to the arrays in the enterprise. Only one enterprise policy can be assigned to each array.

After you create the enterprise policy, you can also configure enterprise firewall rules. The enterprise policy rules, together with the array policy rules, make up the rule base for the ISA Server computers in the array. When you define the enterprise policy, you can define the enterprise policy rules so that they are applied before or after the array policy rules (see Figure 12-1 for an example of how the rules are displayed in the ISA Server Management Console). Because ISA Server processes the rules in order, the rule order and the placement of enterprise rules, affects the final policy. The first rule to match a request received by ISA Server will be used to determine access, and subsequent rules will not be checked.

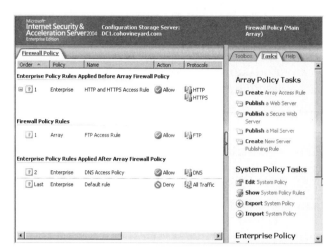

Figure 12-1   Both enterprise and array rules are applied to array members

What Is the Effective Policy?

The effective policy for an array is a combination of enterprise and array policies. When you define enterprise policy rules, you can configure the rules to be applied before the array policy rules are applied, or you can configure the enterprise rules to be applied after the array rules. Where you place the rules determines how the rules are applied.

Enterprise Edition, like Standard Edition, always evaluates the policy rules shown in the Firewall Policy list in a specified order. When the ISA Server computer receives a client request, ISA Server starts evaluating all the policy rules. The first rule that applies to the client request is applied, whether the rule explicitly allows or explicitly denies access. For example, if an access rule that allows all HTTP access to the Internet is evaluated before an access rule blocking access to a particular Web site, access to the Web site will be allowed.

When ISA Server 2004, Enterprise Edition, evaluates the policy rules, it begins by evaluating the enterprise rules that are applied before the array policy rules. Then the array firewall policy rules are evaluated, followed by the enterprise rules that applied after the array policy. Finally, if no other rules apply to the client request, the final Default Rule is applied.

To understand how the effective policy works, consider the following example of an enterprise policy and a branch-office array policy configuration:

- Enterprise Policy Rules Applied Before Array Firewall Policy

  ❑ Allow HTTP and HTTPS access from All Protected Networks to the Internet for all users

- Branch-Office Array Firewall Policy Rules

  - Allow all protocol access from the array's Internal network to the Internet for all authenticated users

  - Allow DNS protocol traffic from a computer set that includes all DNS servers at the branch office to the Internet

- Enterprise Policy Rules Applied After Array Firewall Policy

  - Enable DNS protocol traffic from a computer set that includes all DNS servers at the main office to the Internet.

  - Default Rule

With this rule configuration, the following actions would occur:

- When a user from the branch office tries to access the Internet using HTTP, the user is granted access without requiring authentication.

- When a user from the branch office tries to access the Internet using any protocol other than HTTP or HTTPS, the user will be required to authenticate.

- The DNS servers in the branch office are configured to forward DNS queries directly to the Internet. This is enabled using the array DNS rule. If the DNS servers in the branch office were configured to forward all queries to the DNS servers at the main office, the array DNS rule would not be required as the enterprise rule enables the main-office DNS servers to send queries to the Internet.

Exam Tip   Be prepared for exam questions that use a combination of enterprise and array access rules. Remember that ISA Server always evaluates the rules in order, regardless of whether the rule is defined at the enterprise level or the array level, and that the first rule that corresponds to the request is applied.

How Enterprise Edition Integrates with Network Load Balancing

NLB is a Windows network feature that is used to create a cluster of computers that can be addressed by a single cluster IP address. NLB provides load balancing and high availability for IP-based services. ISA Server, Enterprise Edition, integrates with NLB so that you can configure and manage the NLB functionality using the ISA Server Management Console tools.

NLB provides the following benefits:

- NLB delivers high availability by redirecting incoming network traffic to working cluster members if one of the servers in the cluster fails or is offline. Any connections to the failed computer are lost, but the services remain available.

- NLB delivers scalability by distributing the incoming network traffic among one or more virtual IP addresses (the cluster IP addresses) assigned to the cluster.

- NLB employs an algorithm for statistically mapping incoming clients to the cluster hosts based on their IP address. So long as the number of computers in the NLB cluster does not change, the same cluster member will always respond to the same client.

- Clients accessing the NLB cluster are unable to distinguish the cluster from a single server so that no client configuration is required.

Integrating NLB with ISA Server

ISA Server NLB is based on Windows Server 2003 NLB. When you configure NLB through ISA Server, NLB is integrated with ISA Server. This provides important functionality that is not available in Windows NLB alone, as follows:

- NLB configuration is performed through the ISA Server Management Console.

- ISA Server provides NLB health monitoring, and discontinues NLB on a particular computer if the server is not available or if the Firewall Service on the server has stopped.

- When NLB integration is enabled, each network in an array can be configured as an NLB cluster. Because NLB is enabled per network and configured at an array level, you can configure how a specific network is load-balanced.

- ISA Server enables single affinity by default. When you enable NLB on an array network, the network is configured for single affinity. This means that all connections from the same client to the same NLB cluster will always be handled by the same ISA Server computer in the array. This will continue indefinitely until a host is either added or removed from the array, at which time the connections originating from that IP address could get mapped to a different host in the cluster.

- ISA Server enables bidirectional affinity as needed. In some cases, single affinity does not provide sufficient functionality. For example, you can configure a server publishing rule that is publishing an internal server located behind an NLB cluster. In this scenario, NLB can be configured on both the external interface facing the Internet and the internal interface facing the published servers. Because the internal published servers are configured as SecureNAT clients, they must use the shared IP address for the NLB cluster as their default gateway. However, NLB has to ensure that the response from the published server is always routed to the same ISA server that handled the request from the Internet client because this is the only ISA server in the cluster that has the security context for that particular session. ISA Server enables this functionality by using bidirectional affinity.

How Enterprise Edition Enables Virtual Private Networking

Enterprise Edition, like Standard Edition, supports remote-access VPNs, including network quarantine control, and site-to-site VPNs. The added feature that is available in Enterprise Edition is the option to use NLB for VPN connections.

When you enable NLB for an array and configure the array policy to enable remote-access VPNs, the VPN client must be configured to connect to the NLB shared IP address. When a remote access client initiates a VPN connection to an array, it initiates the connection on the shared IP address. One of the array members establishes the VPN connection and allocates an IP address for that client. From then on, that array member maintains the VPN connection, and all traffic for that remote client passes through that array member. As additional remote access VPN clients connect, the connections are distributed across all available ISA Server computers in the array.

To enable NLB for site-to-site VPNs, the remote site network must be configured to connect to the shared IP address for the NLB cluster in the destination site. At the destination site, one of the ISA Server computers accepts the VPN connection and becomes the VPN gateway server for the site. If the source network is also configured for NLB, ISA Server automatically assigns one array member to handle the VPN tunnel. The VPN gateway server in each site will maintain the VPN tunnel. In this way, parallel tunnels between two sites are not created. Moreover, when a client on one network tries to access resources on another remote site network, the client request is automatically directed to the array member that is hosting the VPN connection. If the server that owns a site-to-site VPN connection fails, ISA Server automatically shifts the connection to another ISA Server array member.

You can also enable site-to-site VPNs without integrating the VPN service and NLB. In this scenario, you must select the one of the array members as the ISA Server computer that will initiate the VPN connection to the remote site, and the remote-site ISA Server must be configured to use the specified ISA Server as the tunnel destination. This scenario does not provide any fault tolerance; if the server designated as the VPN tunnel owner fails, you must configure another ISA Server to manage the connection.

How Enterprise Edition Enables Distributed Caching Using CARP

ISA Server provides distributed caching through the use of the Cache Array Routing Protocol (CARP). CARP distributes the cache used by Web Proxy clients across an array of ISA Server computers. CARP is used by Web browsers and by ISA Server to increase performance when accessing a Web site using a Web Proxy client. CARP uses hash-based routing to determine which ISA Server computer will respond to a client request and cache specific Web content.

CARP provides the following benefits:

- CARP eliminates the duplication of cache contents across multiple ISA Server computers. The result is a faster response to queries and a more efficient use of server resources.

- Because CARP determines which ISA Server will cache any specific content, no traffic is required between ISA Server computers to determine which server is caching the content.

- CARP automatically adjusts when array members are added or removed. The hash-based routing means that when a server is either taken offline or added, only minimal reassignment of URL caches is required.

- CARP ensures that the cache objects are either distributed evenly between all servers in the array or by the load factor that you configure for each server.

How CARP Works

The CARP process provides efficient routing for Web requests on the client side and on the server side. When client-side CARP is enabled, the Web browser downloads the Array.dll?Get.Routing.Script from an ISA Server computer in the array. When a user types a URL into a Web browser, the URL is submitted to the script, which calculates which ISA Server in the array will be used to cache the content. The script always returns the same server list for a given URL, ensuring that each URL is cached on one array server only.

The script generated by ISA Server implements the CARP algorithm. The script includes information about the configuration and current status of the array. By default, the script ensures that the URL space is distributed evenly across the available ISA Server computers. You can also configure a load factor for each array member that allows you to distribute the cache based on server configuration.

ISA Server also enables server-side CARP for Web clients that do not use client-side CARP. In this situation, when a client sends a Web request to an array member, the server runs the CARP script with the requested URL and determines the array member that can best serve the request. The request is forwarded to that server.

> **Note** NLB can be used to load-balance all types of network traffic going into the array. When clients connect to an NLB cluster, they use the shared IP address for the cluster. However, CARP cannot use the shared IP address because the client requests must be sent to a specific ISA Server. Because of this, CARP does not include the virtual IP address in the script sent to clients or when server-side requests are forwarded to other array members. Instead, CARP uses the specific IP address for the ISA Server computer.

Lesson Review

Use the following questions to help determine whether you have learned enough to move on to the next lesson. If you have difficulty answering these questions, review the material in this lesson before beginning the next lesson. You can find answers to these questions in the "Questions and Answers" section at the end of this chapter.

1. You have installed ISA Server 2004, Enterprise Edition, and have configured multiple arrays for different departments. Administrators have been assigned to each array to create access rules based on departmental needs. You need to ensure that no employees can use the ICQ protocol for online chatting or instant messaging. How will you accomplish this with the least administrative effort?

   a. Request that the array administrators create a firewall access rule to deny ICQ to Authenticated Users.

   b. Create an enterprise policy rule to deny ICQ to All Users and have it applied after the array rules.

   c. Request that the array administrators create a firewall-access rule to deny ICQ to All Users.

   d. Create an enterprise policy rule to deny ICQ to All Users and have it applied before the array rules.

2. You have implemented ISA Server 2004, Enterprise Edition, as your firewall solution. You want to ensure fault tolerance in case of server failure. What feature of ISA Server 2004 can provide this?

   a. Enterprise Policies

   b. NLB

   c. Arrays

   d. Configuration Storage Servers

3. You are the network administrator for your organization. You are deploying ISA Server 2004, Enterprise Edition, and have created your first enterprise policy rules and array policy rules. You have configured the following enterprise rules and branch-office array rules:

   Enterprise Policy Rules Applied Before Array Firewall Policy

   ❑ Allow HTTP and HTTPS access from All Protected Networks to the Internet for all users

   Branch-Office Array Firewall Policy Rules

   ❑ Allow all protocol access from the array's Internal network to the Internet for all authenticated users

❑ Allow FTP traffic from a computer set that includes all client computers at the branch office to the Internet

Enterprise Policy Rules Applied After Array Firewall Policy

❑ Enable all protocol access from All Protected Networks to the Internet for all users

Which of the following actions can users in the branch office perform? (Choose all that apply.)

1. Users on computers configured as secure network address translation (SecureNAT) clients will be able to access the Internet using FTP.

2. Users on computers configured as Web Proxy clients will be able to access the Internet using FTP.

3. Users on computers configured as SecureNAT clients will be able to access the Internet using HTTP.

4. Users on computers configured as Web Proxy clients will be able to access the Internet using MSN Messenger.

Lesson Summary

- ISA Server, Standard Edition, and ISA Server, Enterprise Edition, provide similar functionality. The most significant difference between the two versions is that Enterprise Edition provides enhanced scalability. ISA Server, Standard Edition, provides firewall and proxy server services on a single computer, while Enterprise Edition provides the same services on multiple servers.

- ISA Server, Enterprise Edition, uses a Configuration Storage server to store the configuration for all the arrays in the enterprise. There can be multiple Configuration Storage servers deployed in the organization. Configuration Storage server uses Active Directory Application Mode (ADAM) to store and replicate configuration data for all the ISA Server computers in an ISA Server enterprise.

- When deploying ISA Server, Enterprise Edition, you must configure additional components that are not available in Standard Edition. These additional components include enterprise policies and networks, and arrays and array policies.

- When you deploy ISA Server, Enterprise Edition, you can configure ISA Server policies and policy objects at both the enterprise level and the array level. Enterprise policy rules can be evaluated before or after the array rules. The effective policy is the combination of enterprise and array policies.

- Network load balancing (NLB) is a Windows network feature that is used to create a cluster of computers that can be addressed by a single cluster IP address. ISA

Server, Enterprise Edition, integrates with NLB so that you can configure and manage NLB functionality using the ISA Server Management Console tools.

- ISA Server, Enterprise Edition, supports remote-access virtual private networks (VPN), including network quarantine control, and site-to-site VPNs. With Enterprise Edition, you can configure the option to use NLB for VPN connections.

- ISA Server provides distributed caching through the use of the Cache Array Routing Protocol (CARP). CARP distributes the cache used by Web Proxy clients across an array of ISA Server computers.

Lesson 2: Planning an ISA Server 2004 Enterprise Edition Deployment

ISA Server 2004, Enterprise Edition, can be deployed in a variety of scenarios that require a scalable configuration. As you prepare to deploy Enterprise Edition in these scenarios, you will find that some aspects of planning the ISA Server Enterprise Edition deployment are quite different from planning a Standard Edition deployment. This lesson provides an overview of the ISA Server Enterprise Edition deployment scenarios and the planning components for deploying ISA Server in each scenario.

After this lesson, you will be able to

- Describe the primary ISA Server Enterprise Edition deployment scenarios
- Plan a Configuration Storage server deployment
- Plan an enterprise and array policy deployment
- Plan for centralized monitoring and management
- Plan a back-to-back firewall deployment
- Plan a branch-office site-to-site VPN deployment
- Describe how to migrate from ISA Server 2000, Enterprise Edition, to ISA Server 2004, Enterprise Edition

Estimated lesson time: 45 minutes

ISA Server Enterprise Edition Deployment Scenarios

You can deploy ISA Server 2004, Enterprise Edition, in the same scenarios as you can deploy ISA Server, Standard Edition. If you only need to deploy one ISA Server computer and want to use Enterprise Edition, you can deploy Configuration Storage server and the ISA Server services on the same computer and configure an array that contains only one server. However, there are some scenarios in which ISA Server, Enterprise Edition, offers maximum benefit.

Multiple ISA Server Computers in Identical Roles

One of the deployment scenarios in which Enterprise Edition offers the most benefit is where you require multiple ISA Server computers that will perform identical roles. For example, a large organization with a very fast Internet connection might require multiple ISA Server computers to provide Internet access and to publish internal resources. In this scenario, Enterprise Edition offers the following benefits:

- **Centralized management using arrays**   Because you are deploying multiple ISA Server computers in the same role, you can create an array for each role, and configure the array policies. Then you can add as many ISA Server computers as required for that array.

- **NLB**   If the ISA Server computers are being used to provide access to Internet resources or to publish internal resources to the Internet, you can take advantage of the load balancing and redundancy provided by NLB.

- **CARP**   If the ISA Server computers are being used to provide access to Internet resources and you require caching, you can take advantage of the caching scalability provided by CARP.

- **Centralized monitoring**   You can monitor multiple ISA Server Enterprise Edition computers using a single ISA Server Management Console workstation.

> **Tip**   You can use network templates to configure ISA Server, Enterprise Edition; however, you will configure the network template at the array level and the settings will be applied to all array members.

Workgroup Scenario

A workgroup is a group of computers that do not share a common directory. Although workgroups do not offer the centralized user accounts and authentication offered by domains, you may choose to deploy your ISA Server computers in a workgroup rather than a domain for additional security. In this scenario, even if an attacker gains access to the ISA Server computer, the attacker will not have access to any domain accounts. Moreover, workgroup computers do not need to connect to domain controllers, so you can reduce the number of system policy rules and access rules that need to be enabled.

ISA Server, Enterprise Edition, supports three different domain and workgroup configurations:

- The installation of an ISA Server array in a workgroup, where the Configuration Storage server is a member of a domain but the ISA Server computers are not. In this scenario, you can deploy multiple Configuration Storage servers and implement certificate authentication between the Configuration Storage servers and the ISA Server computers.

- The installation of both the Configuration Storage server and the ISA Server computers in a workgroup, creating an isolated enterprise. In this scenario, you can only deploy a single Configuration Storage server for the enterprise, and will need to implement certificate authentication between the Configuration Storage servers and the ISA Server computers.

- A mixed installation of multiple ISA Server computer arrays, where the Configuration Storage server is a member of a domain, and some of the ISA Server computers are also domain members, but some ISA Server computers are not. In this scenario, you can create one or more arrays that include ISA Server computers that are domain members and one or more arrays that contain ISA Server computers that are in a workgroup.

> **See Also** For more information about configuring ISA Server in different domain and workgroup configurations, see the section "Guidelines for Planning a Back-to-Back Firewall Deployment," later in this chapter.

Branch Office Site-to-Site VPN Scenario

ISA Server, Enterprise Edition, can also optimize the ISA Server deployment in a branch-office scenario if you require multiple ISA Server computers in each branch. In this scenario, you can take advantage of NLB for site-to-site VPNs. In addition, you can implement CARP for the branch office array, for the main office array, or both.

In this scenario, the ISA Server computers at the main office can be deployed as domain members, while the branch office ISA Server computers can be in the same domain as the main office: in a child domain, in a separate domain with trust between the domains, or in a workgroup. In a branch-office scenario, you can also deploy a Configuration Storage server in each branch office so that the ISA Server computers can always access a local copy of the ISA Server configuration.

When you deploy an ISA Server array in a branch office, you need to consider how to connect the branch office computers to the main office so as to access the Configuration Storage servers required to install the ISA Server computers. ISA Server provides secure site-to-site VPN functionality between the locations, however, that functionality cannot be provided to the branch before ISA Server is installed. ISA Server provides several options for deploying the first ISA Server computers in the branch office.

> **See Also** For more information about configuring ISA Server in a branch-office scenario, see the section, "Guidelines for Planning a Branch-Office Deployment," later in this chapter.

Guidelines for Planning the Configuration Storage Server Deployment

Because the ISA Server enterprise configuration information is stored in the Configuration Storage server directory, it is critical that you plan the Configuration Storage server implementation carefully. You have the following options when planning your Configuration Storage server deployment:

- Deploy a single Configuration Storage server to manage the entire enterprise. You must deploy at least one Configuration Storage server to create an ISA Server enterprise. If you deploy only one server, that server will be used by all ISA Server computers when requesting configuration information.

■ Deploy multiple Configuration Storage servers in the same enterprise. You can also deploy multiple Configuration Storage servers. In this configuration, each server will store the configuration information for the entire enterprise, but you can configure each array to use a different Configuration Storage server to obtain configuration updates. You can also deploy the Configuration Storage servers across multiple offices. ADAM multiple-master replication means that you can perform updates on any Configuration Storage server and the changes will be replicated to all other servers.

■ Deploy multiple Configuration Storage Servers in different ADAM sites. If your organization has multiple locations and you are deploying Configuration Storage servers in each location, you can create multiple ADAM sites for each location. When you create a site, you can configure how frequently replication occurs between the sites. You can use this option to manage the bandwidth between organization locations.

■ Install the Configuration Storage server in a domain or workgroup. You can deploy Configuration Storage server in either a domain or workgroup. If you deploy Configuration Storage server in a workgroup, you can deploy only one server in your ISA Server enterprise and will need to use certificates to authenticate between the ISA Server computers and the Configuration Storage server. If you deploy the Configuration Storage server in a domain, you can use domain authentication and deploy multiple servers.

■ Install the Configuration Storage server as a dedicated server. You can install Configuration Storage server on a dedicated server that does not have any other ISA Server components installed on the server.

■ Install the Configuration Storage server on a server also running ISA Server. You can also install Configuration Storage server on a computer that is also running the ISA Server services. In this configuration, the server can operate as a firewall as well as a Configuration Storage server.

Configuration Storage Server Design Guidelines

Use the following guidelines when planning your Configuration Storage server deployment:

■ **Deploy multiple Configuration Storage servers**   Configuration Storage servers provide redundancy for each other so that if one server fails, another server is still available. The Configuration Storage server computers also provide redundancy through replication. If you make a change on one server, that change will be replicated to the other Configuration Storage server computers so that even if the first server fails, the change is retained. You should back up all your Configuration Storage servers on a regular basis, but if you do not have multiple Configuration Storage servers, the backup is much more critical because it will be the only means of recovering the enterprise information in the event of a server failure.

- **Install the Configuration Storage server on a dedicated computer that has no other ISA Server services running on it**   This is particularly important if the ISA Server computer is being deployed at the Internet edge. You should place the Configuration Storage server on the internal network where it is protected by ISA Server computers.

- **Install the Configuration Storage server on a domain member**   To take advantage of domain authentication you must join the computer running as the Configuration Storage server to a domain. Doing so allows you to use domain accounts to configure administrative delegation and user sets. This also allows you to configure multiple Configuration Storage servers in your enterprise.

- **Consider network speed when deploying Configuration Storage servers**   You should ensure that every ISA Server computer has a fast LAN network connection to a Configuration Storage server. The ISA Server Management Console computer also should have a fast network connection to the Configuration Storage server. Usually this means that you should deploy at least one Configuration Storage server per office location.

- **Test and verify communication among all computers in the ISA Server enterprise**   The Configuration Storage servers must be able to communicate with each other using the MS Firewall Storage Replication protocol. The Configuration Storage servers and all ISA Server computers must be able to communicate using the MS Firewall Storage protocol. ISA Server Management Console computers must be able to communicate with the Configuration Storage server using the MS Firewall Control protocol, and with the ISA Server computers using the RPC protocol. If your Configuration Storage servers and ISA Server computers are separated by firewalls, ensure that the firewall configuration enables the required protocols.

Guidelines for Planning Enterprise and Array Policy Configuration

Because ISA Server, Enterprise Edition, supports both enterprise and array policies you need to plan the implementation of policies at both levels as well as plan for the interaction between the two different policies.

Planning Enterprise Policies

You can create one or more enterprise policies and then apply that enterprise policy to the arrays in your ISA Server enterprise. Each array can have only one enterprise policy applied to it.

When you create enterprise policies, start by considering what types of arrays you will deploy. If you deploy only one array, or if all the arrays that you deploy are similar, you should create a single enterprise policy. For example, if you need to define similar access and publishing rules for all your arrays, you should configure a single enterprise policy and apply it to all arrays.

However, if you deploy arrays with different requirements, you may need to implement multiple enterprise policies. For example, if you deploy several front-end firewall arrays, several back-end firewall arrays and an array for site-to-site VPN servers, you may want to configure an enterprise policy for each type of array.

> **Tip**   If you deploy just one array of each type, consider not using enterprise policies at all and configuring all the policies at the array level. There is little benefit in configuring an enterprise policy if each array requires a unique policy.

After you have determined how many enterprise policies you will need, you can define the policy rules for each policy. The enterprise policy rules will apply to all the array members, so ensure that the rules meet the requirements. In most cases, you are likely to define few enterprise policy rules.

After creating the policy rules, determine the order in which the rules will be applied. Each rule in the policy can be defined so that it applies either before or after the array policy. If a rule must always be applied to the array, configure the rule so that it is applied before the array policy. If you want to give the array administrator the option of applying the rule, or of overriding the rule by creating an array level rule, then configure the enterprise rule to be configured after the array rules.

You also need to create the arrays in the enterprise. When you create an array, you configure which enterprise policy will be applied to the array. Moreover, you can configure what types of policy rules can be created for the array. You can choose whether deny access rules, allow access rules and publishing rules can be created for the array. You could choose this option when only enterprise policies should be applied to the array.

> **Exam Tip**   If you do not allow the creation of a particular type of rule for an array, no one, not even an enterprise administrator, can create that type of rule. If you want to configure that type of rule, you must enable the option to create the rule and then create the rule.

Planning Array Policies

Planning array policies is similar to planning the configuration of a single ISA Server Standard Edition computer. The array policy defines the networks, network elements, access rules, and publishing rules that apply to all the ISA Server computers in the array, just as these components can be used to apply a policy to a single ISA Server computer. When planning these policies, you need to consider the organization's security policies, business requirements, and publishing requirements.

The only additional factor that you need consider when planning the array policy is how the policy will interact with the enterprise policy. You need to consider which access rules are applied before the array policy because you cannot override those rules at the array level. You also need to consider the rules applied after the array policy and choose to either use those rules or override them by configuring an array policy rule.

Guidelines for Planning for Centralized Monitoring and Management

One of the benefits of deploying ISA Server, Enterprise Edition, is that you can manage and monitor multiple ISA Server computers from a central location. In most organizations, the Configuration Storage server and ISA Server computers will be located in a secured server room. If your organization includes multiple locations, the servers may be located in a different office location than where you are. In either case, you will need to use remote administration to administer ISA Server. Like ISA Server, Standard Edition, you have two options that you can use for remote administration:

- **Remote administration using Remote Desktop**   Use this approach when you need to configure Windows Server settings or when you need to restart ISA Server services that may interfere with Microsoft Management Console (MMC) connectivity.

- **Remote administration using the ISA Server Management Console**   ISA Server Management can be installed on an administrator workstation. The Enterprise Edition version of the ISA Server Management Console is similar to the Standard Edition version, but also displays the enterprise-level information. When you use the monitoring tools in the Enterprise Edition, the monitoring information for all ISA Server computers in the array is displayed.

Regardless of which solution you choose, you should deploy a client computer that you will use to manage the ISA Server configuration. Install the ISA Server Management Console on this computer. If you intend to use this client computer to manage all ISA Server computers in the enterprise, add the computer to the Enterprise Remote Management Computers computer set defined in the enterprise policy. If you intend to administer only ISA Server computers in a particular array, add the client computer to the Remote Management Computers set defined for each array.

Configure Administrative Roles

ISA Server, Standard Edition, enables administrative roles that can be configured on each server. ISA Server, Enterprise Edition, also enables role-based administration, but does so at the enterprise and array levels. ISA Server provides the following roles for enterprise administration:

- **ISA Server Enterprise Administrator**   Users and groups assigned this role have full control over the enterprise and all array configurations. The Enterprise Administrator can also assign roles to other users and groups.

- **ISA Server Enterprise Auditor**   Users and groups assigned this role can view the enterprise configuration and all array configurations but cannot modify any settings.

In addition, ISA Server includes an Enterprise Policy Editor role that can be assigned to a specific enterprise policy. A user assigned to this role can create policy rules for the enterprise policy.

> **See Also**   For detailed information about the specific rights assigned to each role, see the topic "Administrative Roles," in ISA Server Enterprise Edition Online Help.

You can also organize your array-level administrators into separate, predefined roles, each with its own set of tasks. ISA Server provides the following roles for array administrators:

- **ISA Server Array Monitoring Auditor**   Users and groups assigned this role can monitor the ISA Server computer and network activity, but cannot configure specific monitoring functionality.

- **ISA Server Array Auditor**   Users and groups assigned this role can perform all monitoring tasks, including log configuration, alert definition configuration, and all monitoring functions available to the ISA Server basic monitoring role.

- **ISA Server Administrator**   Users and groups assigned this role can perform any ISA Server task, including rule configuration, applying of network templates, and monitoring.

> **Important**   If the computer running ISA Server services belongs to a workgroup, but the Configuration Storage Server belongs to a domain, then user accounts configured on the domain should be used to access the Configuration Storage server. However, you will need to create mirrored accounts on each ISA Server computer to facilitate intra-array communication and administration.

Guidelines for Planning a Back-to-Back Firewall Deployment

One of the possible scenarios for ISA Server in an enterprise environment is in a back-to-back firewall deployment. In a back-to-back firewall deployment, one firewall is connected to the Internet and a perimeter network. This firewall manages traffic flowing between the Internet and the perimeter network. The other firewall is attached to the perimeter network and the internal network. This firewall manages traffic flowing between the internal network and the perimeter network. Deploying a back-to-back firewall solution is significantly more complicated than deploying a single Internet-edge firewall. In a back-to-back scenario, you need to ensure that both the front-end and the back-end firewalls are configured correctly to ensure security and functionality.

Exam Tip The exam objectives do not specifically mention deploying ISA Server in a back-to-back firewall configuration. However, this is one of the more complicated scenarios for an ISA Server deployment, so if you understand how to configure ISA Server in this scenario, you shouldn't have any trouble with the planning questions on the exam. Notice that this is not just an Enterprise Edition deployment scenario. This section describes how to configure the front-end and back-end arrays, but you could use Standard Edition and configure one front-end firewall and one back-end firewall.

As you prepare to deploy a back-to-back firewall solution using ISA Server 2004, Enterprise Edition, there are a variety of considerations that must be addressed in your planning. These include the following:

- Should you deploy the ISA Server computers in a domain or workgroup configuration?

- How will you configure the front-end array?

- How will you configure the back-end array?

Off the Record Many organizations that deploy a back-to-back firewall configuration use two different firewalls, one for the front-end firewall and one for the back-end firewall. In most cases where companies do this, the front-end firewall is a non-Microsoft firewall while the back-end firewall might be ISA Server. In this configuration, ISA Server is often used for application filtering and as a proxy server. If you deploy this type of firewall configuration, you can still apply the principles discussed in this section. The exact configuration of the non-Microsoft firewall will vary, but many of the same principles apply.

Deploying ISA Server in a Domain or Workgroup

ISA Server, Enterprise Edition, can be deployed in a domain configuration or in a workgroup configuration. In a back-to-back firewall scenario, you have the following deployment options:

- Install the Configuration Storage server or servers and all ISA Server services on computers that are members in a domain, or in trusted domains.

- Install the Configuration Storage server or servers and all ISA Server services on computers that are in a workgroup.

- Install the Configuration Storage server or servers on computers that are members in a domain and all or some of the ISA Server services on computers that are in a workgroup. For example, you can install Configuration Storage server on a domain member, install the ISA Server services for the back-end array on domain members, and then install ISA Server services for the front-end array on computers in a workgroup.

Deploying All ISA Server Components on Domain Members   The easiest deployment option is to deploy all ISA Server components on computers that are members of the same domain or in trusted domains. In this scenario, you can use domain authentication for the ISA Server administrators and for all ISA Server clients. In addition, the ISA Server computers can use the domain computer accounts to authenticate with other array members and to authenticate with the Configuration Storage servers. All network traffic between ISA Server computers is encrypted and digitally signed using keys derived from the domain authentication, so you do not need to configure any certificates for ISA Server communication.

The most significant limitation with deploying all ISA Server components on domain members is the concern about deploying a domain member where it can be directly accessed from the Internet. This configuration increases the risk that an attacker will be able to gain access to the domain accounts if the Internet-edge firewall is compromised. Moreover, a domain member requires that additional services are running on the server. If you deploy ISA Server on a domain member in a front-end array, you must also open additional ports on the back-end array for the server to connect to the domain controllers on the internal network.

Deploying All ISA Server Components on Workgroup Members   The second option is to deploy all ISA Server components on computers that are members of a workgroup. This configuration has the advantage that no domain accounts are accessible on the ISA Server computer, so even if the server is compromised in an attack, the attacker does not have access to domain resources.

However, deploying all the ISA Server components on workgroup computers makes the deployment more complicated in the following ways:

- You can only deploy one Configuration Storage server in your enterprise. This means that you will not have Configuration Storage server redundancy and all computers running ISA Server services and ISA Server Management must be able to communicate with the single Configuration Storage server.

- Because the workgroup computers cannot access domain user accounts, workgroup clients cannot be authenticated using Windows authentication. You can use Remote Authentication Dial-In User Service (RADIUS) or RSA SecurID authentication to authenticate users. Firewall clients depend on access to domain user accounts, therefore, Firewall client will not work in a workgroup configuration.

■ To use centralized administration, you must create mirrored user accounts on all the computers in the array. Mirrored accounts are local users with identical user names and passwords. You will use the credentials of this user when you use ISA Server management to connect to the workgroup array. As a best practice, these accounts should have user names and passwords that are different from any domain user accounts.

■ To assign ISA Server roles, you need to create a local user on each workgroup array member that can be assigned to an ISA Server role. If you use the same user account for each role on each computer, you can connect to the Configuration Storage server and each ISA Server computer using the same logon credentials and have access to the same ISA Server administrator role.

■ Because the ISA Server computers in a workgroup cannot use domain authentication to create a secure channel between servers, you need to configure any array containing workgroup members to use authentication over an SSL encrypted channel. To enable this option, you must install a server certificate on the Configuration Storage server and configure the computers running ISA Server services with a root certificate of a mutually trusted certification authority (CA). You must also configure the array so that a user account is used to authenticate the connections between array members, rather than using the domain user account.

Deploying ISA Server Components in a Mixed Configuration   The third deployment option is to install Configuration Storage server on a computer that is a member of a domain, and then to install the ISA Server services on either domain members or workgroup members. This scenario takes advantage of some of the benefits of deploying ISA Server components on domain members, while enabling the more secure workgroup configuration for workgroup members.

When deploying this configuration, remember the following:

■ All members of an array must have the same workgroup or domain configuration. You can deploy an array with domain members or an array with workgroup members, but one array cannot have both types of members.

■ For the arrays where the ISA Server computers are members of a domain, you can use domain authentication for the ISA Server administrators and for ISA Server clients, as well as for intra-array authentication.

■ For the arrays in which the ISA Server computers are members of a workgroup, you need to consider all the requirements of deploying ISA Server computers in a workgroup. You need to configure the array to enable SSL authentication, install a certificate on all Configuration Storage servers, and configure the root certificate on each computer running ISA Server services.

Changing Your Configuration to Allow Workgroup Arrays   You can modify the ISA Server domain or workgroup configuration after deployment. If you installed the Configuration Storage server without a certificate, you can modify the configuration to support workgroup arrays. To do this, obtain a server authentication certificate for each Configuration Storage server. Then associate the certificate with the appropriate service on the Configuration Storage server. You can do this in one of two ways:

- Rerun ISA Server setup. When you run ISA Server setup, select Repair on the Program Maintenance page. Then, select the option to deploy ISA Server in a workgroup and configure the service to use the server.

- Use ISACertTool to install the certificate and associate it with the Configuration Storage service. The ISACertTool is available as part of the ISA Server Resource Kit.

Configuring the Front-End and Back-End Arrays

When you deploy ISA Server, Enterprise Edition, in a back-to-back firewall configuration, you must plan the network configuration for the front-end and back-end arrays, and then configure both the front-end firewall array and the back-end firewall array.

Plan the Array Network Configuration   The first step in deploying a back-to-back firewall is to plan the ISA Server networks for both arrays. On the back-end array, the Internal network should include the IP addresses for all networks connected to the internal network interface on the ISA Server computer. The External network on the back-end array includes the IP addresses in the perimeter network, as well as the IP addresses on the Internet. Figure 12-2 illustrates how networks look from the perspective of the back-end array.

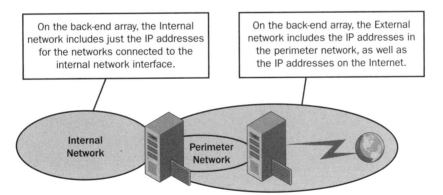

Figure 12-2   Defining the Internal and External addresses on the back-end array

On the front-end array, the Internal network always includes the IP addresses used in the perimeter network. If you use a NAT relationship between the perimeter network and the Internal network on the back-end array, the Internal network for the front-end array includes only the perimeter network IP addresses. If you define a route relationship between the perimeter network and the Internal network for the back-end array, the Internal network on the front-end array includes the perimeter network IP addresses and the back-end array Internal network IP addresses. On the front-end array, the External network includes just the Internet IP addresses. Figure 12-3 illustrates how networks look from the perspective of the front-end array.

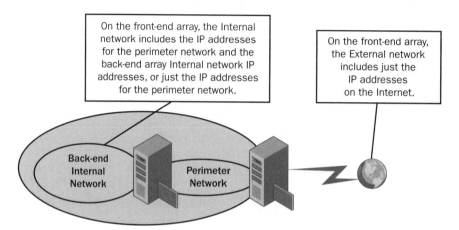

On the front-end array, the Internal network includes the IP addresses for the perimeter network and the back-end array Internal network IP addresses, or just the IP addresses for the perimeter network.

On the front-end array, the External network includes just the IP addresses on the Internet.

Back-end Internal Network

Perimeter Network

Figure 12-3   Defining the Internal and External addresses on the front-end array

Configuring the Front-End Array   When configuring the front-end firewall array, consider the following guidelines:

- **Configure network routing**   If you define a route relationship between the perimeter network and the Internal network (as defined on the back-end array), the front-end array servers may need to be able to route network traffic to the servers on the back-end Internal network using the actual IP addresses of the servers. In this case, before installing ISA Server services on the front-end array servers, you should configure network routing. In most cases, the front-end array servers need to be configured to use a router connected to the Internet as its default gateway. This means that you must configure a static route on the ISA Server computers so that they can route incoming traffic to the back-end Internal network. If you use a NAT relationship between the perimeter network and the back-end Internal network, the front-end ISA Server computers can route all requests by using the IP address for a network adapter connected to the perimeter network on the back-end ISA Server computers, so no additional routing is required.

- **Configure the network relationship**   You need to define a network relationship between the External network on the front-end array and the perimeter network. If you use private IP addresses for the perimeter network, you must configure a NAT relationship between the two networks. If you use public IP addresses for the perimeter network, you can define either a NAT or route relationship.

- **Configure access to resources on the perimeter network**   After you configure the network relationship, you can begin configuring access to servers or services on the perimeter network. If you configure a NAT relationship, you should use publishing rules to enable access. If you configure a route relationship, you can use either access rules or publishing rules for the same purpose. If you use access rules, external clients must be able to resolve the actual IP address of the servers on the perimeter network. If you use publishing rules, all client connections will use the external IP addresses for the front-end array.

- **Configure access to resources on the back-end array Internal network**   In some cases, you may need to configure access to resources on the Internal network located behind the back-end array. In this case, the front-end ISA Server computers will forward the client requests to the back-end array's external IP address. To enable this, you need configure access or publishing rules that forward the client requests to the appropriate address for the back-end array.

- **Configure SSL publishing for perimeter network servers**   You may also need to configure access to secure Web sites or other resources on the perimeter network. If you are using SSL to secure a Web site on the perimeter network, you can use the SSL Web publishing to publish the Web site and configure either SSL bridging or SSL tunneling. Just as when you publish secure Web sites in an Internet-edge firewall scenario or in a 3-Legged firewall scenario, you need to ensure that you install all the required server certificates and that the correct Web server names are used for the certificates.

- **Configure SSL publishing for network servers located on the Internal network behind the back-end array**   You may also need to configure secure access to the resources on the back-end Internal network. In this scenario, you can deploy SSL in the following ways:

  - ❏ You can terminate the SSL connection at the front-end array and enable non-SSL connections to the back-end firewall. To enable this option, you only need server certificates on the front-end array servers. This option is not recommended because this means that traffic will be sent in clear text across the perimeter network.

  - ❏ You can enable SSL bridging between the front-end array and the back-end array, so that the front-end ISA Server computers will decrypt the packet, then re-encrypt it before sending it to the back-end array. In this case, you will need certificates on both the back-end and front-end array members.

  - ❏ You can enable SSL tunneling on the front-end array and use SSL bridging on the back-end array. In this case, you will need certificates only on the back-end array members. This option is not recommended because this means that the front-end ISA Server computers cannot apply application filtering to incoming traffic.

❑ In any case, you may also need server certificates on the server that is being published to provide end-to-end SSL encryption.

> **Important** Before you configure any publishing rules that require SSL termination on the front-end array, you must install the required server certificates on all members of the array. You must install the same server certificates on all array members.

■ **Configuring authentication** If you are publishing a Web site on the perimeter network that requires authentication, you can enable authentication on the ISA Server computer or on the published resource. If the ISA Server computers in the front-end array are members of a trusted domain, you can use domain accounts to enable authentication. However, if the front-end servers are in a workgroup, you cannot use domain accounts unless you use RADIUS authentication.

Configuring the Back-End Array When configuring the back-end firewall array, consider the following guidelines:

■ **Configure routing for the back-end array members** In most cases, you can just configure the default gateway on the back-end array to use the front-end array servers.

■ **Configure the perimeter network on the internal array** This network should include only the IP addresses for the perimeter network. After configuring the perimeter network, configure a network rule that defines the relationship between the back-end array's Internal network and the perimeter network. This step is required only if you need to define firewall rules that allow access to or from the entire perimeter network.

■ **Configure network objects** Instead of configuring a network object for the perimeter network, you can configure network objects for the computers in the perimeter network. For example, if you deploy a Web server in the perimeter network and that Web server will need access to the internal network, you should configure a computer set for the Web server. Then configure the firewall rule granting access to the back-end Internal network to use the computer set rather than the entire perimeter network. You should also configure a network object for the front-end ISA Server computers that contains the IP addresses for the network adapters connected to the perimeter network (as well as the virtual IP address if NLB is configured). Then use this network object when configuring firewall rules for the front-end servers to access resources such as Configuration Storage servers on the back-end Internal network.

■ **Configure access to perimeter network resources** In some cases, you may need to provide access to servers in the perimeter network for internal users. To enable this, you can either configure a publishing rule or an access rule.

- **Configure access for ISA Server computers in the front-end array**   In order for the ISA Server computers in the front-end array to access the Configuration Storage servers on the internal network, you need to configure an access rule that allows the MS Firewall Storage protocol from the front-end array computers to the Configuration Storage server. If you use the ISA Server Management Console on the front-end computers, this rule should also allow access for the MS Firewall Control protocol. To manage the front-end-array ISA Server computers, you also need to configure an access rule that allows the MS Firewall Control and RPC (all interfaces) protocols from the Configuration Storage server and the ISA Server management workstations to the front-end array computers.

- **Configure access to resources on the back-end array Internal network**   In some cases, you may need to configure access to resources on the Internal network from the Internet or the perimeter network. To enable this, you need configure access or publishing rules that forward the client requests from the perimeter network or the front-end ISA Server computers. You can also enable SSL bridging or SSL tunneling.

- **Configure back-end array Internal network access for domain members**   In some cases, you may also need to provide access to the Internal network for domain member servers located in the perimeter network. For example, you may have a Web server in the perimeter network that is a member of the internal domain and needs to use domain user accounts to authenticate access to a Web site. Or the front-end ISA Server computers may be members of the internal domain and may require access to internal domain controllers. To enable this type of access, you must configure an access rule that allows DNS, Kerberos-Sec (TCP) and Kerberos-Sec (User Datagram Protocol, or UDP), LDAP, LDAP UDP, and LDAP GC traffic from the domain members to the internal domain controllers. To join a computer in the perimeter network to the internal domain, you must also enable RPC (all interfaces) and Microsoft Common Internet File System (CIFS) access.

Caution   Deploying domain members in a perimeter network is considered a security risk if anonymous user connections are allowed to the perimeter network.

Guidelines for Planning a Branch-Office Deployment

In many ways, implementing a site-to-site VPN using ISA Server, Enterprise Edition, is similar to deploying the VPN using ISA Server, Standard Edition. In both cases, you need to configure the VPN gateway on both networks, define a remote-site network, and define how the two VPN gateway servers connect to each other. You also need to choose a tunneling protocol and ensure that both ISA Server editions support the same options. However, there are also some differences in how you configure site-to-site VPNs in the two ISA Server editions. One simple difference is that, in ISA Server,

Enterprise Edition, you configure VPN settings at an array level rather than on individual servers. There are also more complicated considerations, including the following:

■ How will you establish a connection between the branch office and the main office so that you can install a Configuration Storage server or ISA Server computer with access to the enterprise configuration information?

■ How will you configure Configuration Storage server replication between the offices?

> **Planning**   When you configure the access rules for the remote-site network, ensure that the Configuration Storage servers have the required access to the main-office computers. The Configuration Storage servers in the branch office must be able to communicate with the main-office Configuration Storage servers. The Configuration Storage servers also require access to an Active Directory domain controller and to appropriate DNS servers so as to use domain authentication. You must configure an appropriate firewall policy that allows this access.

Establishing Remote Office Connectivity

One of the factors that makes deploying ISA Server, Enterprise Edition, in a site-to-site VPN configuration more complicated is the fact that all the ISA Server configuration information for the enterprise is stored on the Configuration Storage server, which is likely located in the main office. To install a Configuration Storage server or computer running ISA Server services in the branch office, the computer must have access to the configuration information. However, until you deploy the ISA Server computer in the branch office, you cannot use ISA Server to establish the site-to-site VPN that enables communication between the offices. You have several options for addressing this issue:

■ **Use a third-party VPN**   If you are currently using a third-party site-to-site VPN solution, you can use the existing VPN connection to access the Configuration Storage server in the main office. Just ensure that the computer on which you install the components uses the third-party VPN gateway server as its default gateway. Once you've installed the ISA Server services in the branch office, you can either leave the existing VPN connection, or remove it and create a new connection using ISA Server.

■ **Use Routing and Remote Access Service (RRAS)**   You can also use RRAS to establish the VPN tunnel to the main office. In this case, use a Windows 2000 Server or Windows Server 2003 computer that is not going to have ISA Server installed on it, because the ISA Server installation stops the Routing and Remote Access Service, thereby ending the VPN connection. Once you've created the VPN connection, set it as the default gateway for the computer on which you install the ISA Server components.

> **Note**   You can install a replicate Configuration Storage server in the branch on the computer that hosts RRAS if it is running Windows Server 2003. Installing Configuration Storage server does not stop RRAS.

- **Use server publishing**   You can publish the Configuration Storage server in the main office to the Internet, and then access the Configuration Storage server from the branch office through the Internet. If you choose this option, create a computer object for the remote-office computer and enable access to the server publishing rule only to that IP address. The server publishing rule needs to enable access for the MS Firewall Storage Server protocol. After installing the branch-office ISA Server computers, disable the server publishing rule.

- **Use a temporary enterprise**   You can also create a combined ISA Server installation in a separate enterprise in the branch office and use it to establish a VPN connection to the main office. After you've created the VPN connection, install a replicate Configuration Storage server that uses the main Configuration Storage server, then use that server as the Configuration Storage server for the branch array. Finally, you can remove the combined server.

- **Use an ISA Server backup file**   To deploy this option, use Windows Backup on the Configuration Storage server in the main office to create a backup file (.bkf). When you run Backup, choose to back up only the ADAMData folder located in the Microsoft ISA Server folder. Then, when you install the Configuration Storage server on the computer in the branch office you can choose to use the backup file as the replication source, as shown in Figure 12-4. This option is recommended in an environment where you have many ISA Server computers and the network connection between the branch office and main office is slow because, after you restore the data, only the changes to the enterprise since the backup need to be replicated, rather than the entire configuration.

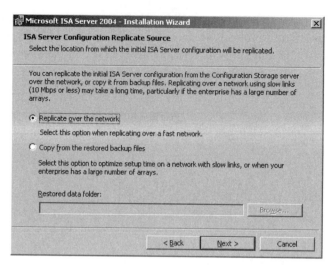

Figure 12-4   Choosing the replication sources during Configuration Storage server installation

Managing Configuration Storage Server Replication

The Configuration Storage servers use multiple-master replication to maintain consistent enterprise information on all Configuration Storage servers in the enterprise. One of the problems that you may face in this situation is that the replication may use up much of the bandwidth between the main office and the branch offices, particularly if you have a large ISA Server enterprise and the network connection is slow. In these scenarios, you can optimize the replication of the configuration information stored on the Configuration Storage servers by establishing ADAM sites. You can then configure how often the configuration information is replicated between the sites.

> **Tip**   ADAM is a specialized mode of Active Directory, so it uses the same replication mechanisms as Active Directory. When deploying Active Directory, one of the main reasons for creating sites is to control replication between domain controllers. After you can create the sites, you can also configure site links that define when replication occurs between sites. ADAM works in the same way. You can create ADAM sites, move servers in to the appropriate sites, and then configure replication between the sites.

To configure ADAM sites, you must use the Adamsites.exe tool that is included with the ISA Server 2004 Resource Kit. To move a Configuration Storage server to a different site, perform the following steps:

1. Install the Configuration Storage server on a Windows Server 2003 computer.

2. Use the Adamsites.exe tool to create a site. To do this, open a command prompt and type **AdamSites Site Create *NewSite***, where *NewSite* is the name of the new site.

3. Then, use the Adamsites.exe tool to move the server to a new site. At a command prompt, type **AdamSites MoveServer *ConfigStgServer Site1 NewSite***, where *ConfigStgServer* is the name of the Configuration Storage server, *Site1* is the name of the existing site, and *NewSite* is the name of the new site.

4. You also use the Adamsites.exe tool to configure replication between the sites. At a command prompt, type **AdamSites Sitelink create *LinkName 2 Site1 Site2 50 480***, where *Linkname* is the name of the link that you are creating, *2* defines the number of sites connected by this link, *Site1* and *Site2* are the site names, *50* defines a site link cost, and *480* defines the replication interval in minutes.

> **Note**   By default, the site link cost is 100 and the replication interval between sites is 180 minutes.

How Migrating from ISA Server 2000, Enterprise Edition, Works

ISA Server 2004 supports a upgrade path from ISA Server 2000, Enterprise Edition, to ISA Server 2004, Enterprise Edition. Most ISA Server 2000 configuration information will be upgraded to ISA Server 2004.

ISA Server 2000, Enterprise Edition, stores its configuration information in Active Directory. When ISA Server 2000, Enterprise Edition, is installed as an array member, ISA Server setup modifies the Active Directory schema to include ISA Server–specific classes and attributes. Because ISA Server 2004 stores the same information in ADAM, you cannot upgrade the ISA Server 2000 infrastructure merely by upgrading the ISA Server computers. Instead, you must migrate the ISA Server 2000 configuration to ISA Server 2004. To do this, complete these steps:

1. Run the ISA Server Migration Wizard on the ISA Server 2000 computer. The wizard creates an .xml file with the configuration information.

2. Install ISA Server 2004, Enterprise Edition, selecting the option to install the Configuration Storage server.

3. Import the .xml file to the ISA Server 2004 computer.

After you migrate the ISA Server configuration to the Configuration Storage server, you can start deploying servers running ISA Server 2004 services. You can also perform an in-place upgrade of the individual ISA Server 2000 computers to ISA Server 2004. When you perform the upgrade, you will need to choose the Configuration Storage server to use for configuration information and the ISA Server 2004 array of which the server will be a part.

Note   If ISA Server 2000 is currently installed on a Windows 2000 Server computer, verify that ISA Server 2000 Service Pack 1 (SP1) or ISA Server 2000 Service Pack 2 (SP2) is installed. If ISA Server 2000 SP1 is installed, verify that the hot fix described in the Microsoft Knowledge Base article 331962, "Running ISA Server on Windows Server 2003," is also installed. Then, upgrade the operating system to Windows Server 2003 before installing ISA Server 2004, Enterprise Edition.

See Also   For detailed information about how to upgrade an ISA Server 2000 Enterprise Edition infrastructure to ISA Server 2004, Enterprise Edition, and on how each specific item is upgraded, see the Upgrading to Microsoft Internet Security and Acceleration (ISA) Server 2004 Enterprise Edition guide that is included on the ISA Server 2004 Enterprise Edition CD-ROM. To access the guide, run Isaautorun.exe from the CD-ROM and click Read Migration Guide.

Lesson Review

Use the following questions to help determine whether you have learned enough to move on to the next lesson. If you have difficulty answering these questions, review the material in this lesson before beginning the next lesson. You can find answers to these questions in the "Questions and Answers" section at the end of this chapter.

1. Your company has two branch offices connected to the head office by a slow network connection. You have configured ISA Server 2004, Enterprise Edition, with one array for the head-office ISA Server computers, and an array for the branch-office ISA Server computers. You need to ensure that the branch-office ISA Server computers have fast, reliable access to the array configuration information. What is the best way to accomplish this?

_____

_____

_____

2. You administer an ISA Server array at the branch office of your company. Some of your users have requested access to an FTP site to download a file they require. You create a firewall access rule to allows the required access, yet users report they are still not able to access the FTP site. What is the most likely cause?

_____

_____

_____

3. You are deploying ISA Server, Enterprise Edition, in your organization. You are deploying multiple arrays and need to ensure that array level administrators can install ISA Server computers into the array. The array level administrators should not be able to modify any enterprise policies. What role and permissions will you assign to the array level administrators? (Choose all that apply.)

    a. ISA Server Administrator

    b. ISA Server Enterprise Policy Editor

    c. Local Administrator on the ISA Server computers

    d. ISA Server Enterprise Administrator

4. You need to deploy ISA Server 2004, Enterprise Edition, so that domain accounts are not exposed on the Edge Firewall ISA Server array. You also want to grant Array Administrator rights based on Windows group membership. What is the best way to accomplish this?

    a. Deploy the Configuration Storage server and ISA Server array in a workgroup and create mirrored user accounts on the ISA Server computers.

    b. Deploy the ISA Server array and Configuration Storage server in the domain.

    c. Deploy the Configuration Storage server in the domain and the ISA Server array in a workgroup and create mirrored user accounts on the ISA Server computers.

    d. Deploy the ISA Server array in the domain and the Configuration Storage server to a workgroup and create mirrored domain user accounts.

Lesson Summary

■ You can deploy ISA Server 2004, Enterprise Edition, in the same scenarios as you can deploy ISA Server, Standard Edition. However, there are some scenarios in which ISA Server, Enterprise Edition, offers maximum benefit. These scenarios include deploying multiple ISA Server computers in identical roles, deploying ISA Server computers in a workgroup, and deploying multiple ISA Server computers in a site-to-site VPN configuration.

■ Because the ISA Server enterprise configuration information is stored in the Configuration Storage server directory, it is critical that you plan the Configuration Storage server implementation carefully. You should deploy multiple Configuration Storage servers in the same enterprise, deploy Configuration Storage Servers in each remote office, install the Configuration Storage server on a domain member, and install the Configuration Storage server as a dedicated server.

■ Because ISA Server, Enterprise Edition, supports both enterprise and array policies, you must plan the implementation of policies at both levels as well as plan for the interaction between the two different policies.

■ One of the benefits of deploying ISA Server, Enterprise Edition, is that you can manage and monitor multiple ISA Server computers from a central location. Like ISA Server, Standard Edition, you can use Remote Desktop or ISA Server Management to remotely administer ISA Server computers. You can also assign enterprise-level, policy-level, and array-level administrative roles.

■ One of the possible scenarios for ISA Server in an enterprise environment is in a back-to-back firewall deployment. In a back-to-back firewall deployment, one firewall is connected to the Internet and a perimeter network and the other firewall is attached to the perimeter network and the internal network. Deploying a back-to-back firewall solution is complicated because you need to ensure that both the front-end and the back-end firewalls are configured correctly to ensure security and functionality.

■ When implementing a site-to-site VPN using ISA Server, Enterprise Edition, configure VPN settings at an array level rather than on individual servers. You also need to determine how you will establish a connection between the branch office and the main office so that you can install a Configuration Storage server or ISA Server computer with access to the enterprise configuration information. You can manage Configuration Storage server replication between the offices.

■ ISA Server 2004 supports an upgrade path from ISA Server 2000, Enterprise Edition, to ISA Server 2004, Enterprise Edition. Most ISA Server 2000 configuration information will be upgraded to ISA Server 2004. To migrate the configuration, you need to export the ISA Server 2000 configuration using the ISA Server Migration Wizard, and then import the .xml file to the ISA Server 2004 computer.

Lesson 3: Implementing ISA Server 2004, Enterprise Edition

Once you have completed the planning for your ISA Server Enterprise Edition deployment, you are ready to start deploying ISA Server. To start deployment, you need review the requirements for installing ISA Server, Enterprise Edition, and understand how to install and configure the ISA Server components. In this lesson, you will learn how to install a Configuration Storage server, create enterprise and array policies, and install and configure ISA Server 2004, Enterprise Edition.

After this lesson, you will be able to

- List the requirements for installing Enterprise Edition
- Install the Configuration Storage Server
- Configure enterprise policies and networks
- Configure array policies
- Install ISA Server 2004, Enterprise Edition
- Configure NLB and CARP

Estimated lesson time: 60 minutes

Requirements for Installing Enterprise Edition

The requirements for installing ISA Server, Enterprise Edition, are similar to the requirements for Standard Edition. ISA Server 2004, Enterprise Edition, requires the following Windows operating systems:

- The ISA Server Enterprise Edition Configuration Storage Server and ISA Server services must be installed on a computer running Windows Server 2003. Enterprise Edition is not supported on Windows 2000 Server.

- You can install the Message Screener component on computers running Windows Server 2003 or Windows 2000 Server.

- You can install the Firewall Client Share and ISA Server Management on computers running Windows Server 2003, Windows 2000 Server, or Windows XP

ISA Server 2004, Enterprise Edition, also has the following additional requirements:

- Like Standard Edition, Enterprise Edition requires at least one network adapter for each network connected to the ISA Server computer.

- If you plan to configure NLB, you should allow for an additional network adapter for intra-array communication. Load balancing should not be configured for this network.

- One local hard-disk partition that has at least 150 megabytes (MB) of available hard disk space. The disk should be formatted with the NTFS file system.

- In addition, you will need to allow additional disk space for logging or Web caching. At a minimum, you should allow an additional of 4 gigabytes (GB) disk space.

The ISA Server Enterprise Edition deployment requires more steps than a Standard Edition deployment. With Standard Edition, you can just install ISA Server on a server and complete the configuration after deployment. With ISA Server, Enterprise Edition, actually installing the ISA Server services is one of the last steps you will take.

Installation Overview

To implement ISA Server 2004, Enterprise Edition, complete these high-level steps:

1. Install a Configuration Storage server. When you install a Configuration Storage server, you can join the server to an existing enterprise or create a replica of an existing enterprise. When installing the first Configuration Storage server in your enterprise, choose to create a new enterprise.

2. On the Configuration Storage server, define the enterprise policies and policy rules and enterprise networks. Also create the required arrays and array policies. This step is optional: you can create the arrays when you install the ISA Server services but if you configure the arrays before installing array members, you can join the servers to arrays that already exist and that have the array policies already configured.

3. If required, install additional Configuration Storage servers. By default, when you choose to install a replica of an existing configuration, ADAM replication will immediately begin populating the configuration information on the new server.

4. Install ISA Server services on one or more computers. When you install a computer running ISA Server services as the first member of a new array, you need to specify addresses for the Internal network.

5. Install ISA Server Management on the workstations that you will use to administer the ISA Server Configuration Storage server and ISA Server computers.

Note You can install all ISA Server services on a single Windows Server 2003 server by installing both the Configuration Storage server and ISA Server services on the computer. You can also install the ISA Server Management Console on the same computer. You can then configure the enterprise policies and array policies after the installation.

How to Install Configuration Storage Server

The Configuration Storage server stores the configuration information for the entire enterprise so the first step in implementing ISA Server, Enterprise Edition, is to install and configure this server. To install Configuration Storage server, complete the following high-level steps on the computer that you have designated as the Configuration Storage server:

1. Access the ISA Server Enterprise Edition installation CD-ROM and start the installation by running Isaautorun.exe and clicking Install ISA Server.

2. Accept the terms and conditions stated in the user license agreement.

3. Enter your customer information.

4. On the Setup Scenarios page, you are given four installation options, as shown in Figure 12-5:

   ❑ *Install ISA Server Services*—Choose this option when you are configuring a server that will operate as a firewall or proxy server.

   ❑ *Install Configuration Storage Server*—Choose this option when you are installing a server that will operate as a Configuration Storage server only.

   ❑ *Install Both ISA Server Services And Configuration Storage Server*—Choose this option when you are installing a server that will operate as a Configuration Storage server and as a firewall or proxy server.

   ❑ *Install ISA Server Management*—Choose this option when you are installing a computer that will be used only to manage the ISA Server configuration and monitor ISA Server computers.

   Click Install Configuration Storage Server, and then click Next.

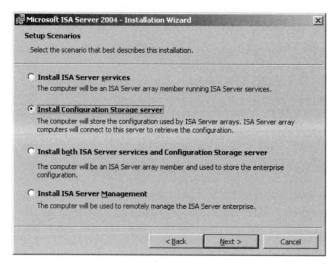

Figure 12-5 Choosing an installation scenario

5. On the Component Selection page, you are given a choice about what components to install, as shown in Figure 12-6. You have the following options:

   ❑ ISA Server

   ❑ ISA Server Management

   ❑ Firewall Client Installation Share

   ❑ Message Screener

   ❑ Configuration Storage Server

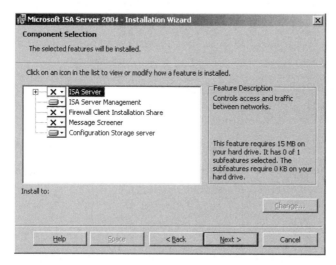

Figure 12-6 Choosing installation components

Depending on your selection in step 4, the required components will be selected. If you are installing a Configuration Storage server, Configuration Storage Server and ISA Server Management are selected. Click Next.

6. On the Enterprise Installation Options page, as shown in Figure 12-7, select Create A New ISA Server Enterprise, and then click Next.

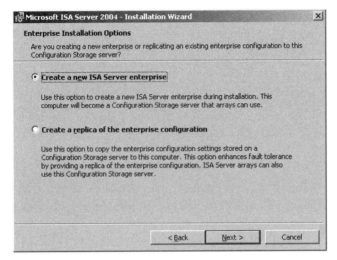

Figure 12-7   Choosing to create or join an enterprise

7. On the New Enterprise Warning page, click Next. This page warns you not to install more than one enterprise. Because you are creating a new enterprise, you can ignore the warning.

8. On the Create a New Enterprise page, enter a name and description for the enterprise. Click Next.

9. On the Enterprise Deployment Environment page, you can choose what type of enterprise you are creating, as shown in Figure 12-8. You have two options:

   ❑ *I Am Deploying In A Single Domain Or In Domains With Trust Relationships*—If you choose this option, then you will use Windows authentication between all the computers in the enterprise.

   ❑ *I Am Deploying In A Workgroup Or In Domains Without Trust Relationships*— If you choose this option, then you can use either Windows authentication or choose a certificate that will be used to authenticate computers in the enterprise.

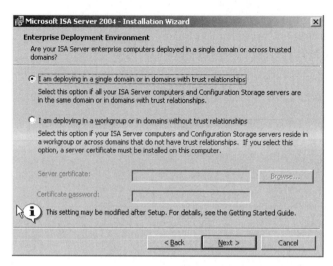

Figure 12-8   Choosing the enterprise deployment environment

10. On the Service Account Selection page, you can choose to have Configuration Storage server service run under the Network Service account or choose another service account.

> **Important** Normally, when you install Configuration Storage server on a computer that is not designated a domain controller, the service will run in the security context of the Network Service account. However, when you install Configuration Storage server on a domain controller, you must create a separate service account. One option is to use an account that is a member of the Domain Admins group, but this is not a security best practice. As an alternative, create a regular user account and then run the .bat file created during the Configuration Storage server installation to configure the account with the required permissions. The .bat file is named *Yourdnsdomainname*.bat and is located in the C:\Program Files\Microsoft ISA Server\ADAMData directory. The .bat file adds the account that you chose as a service principal name in the ADAM directory. You will complete the specific steps in the practice that follows.

11. On the Ready To Install The Program page, click Install to begin the installation.

Practice: Installing a Configuration Storage Server

In this practice, you will install a Configuration Storage server to begin the ISA Server Enterprise Edition deployment. You will also be configuring delegated administrative rights for the various arrays. To prepare the lab environment, you need to do the following:

- Configure administrative user accounts for ISA Server management
- Install Configuration Storage server on DC1

Exercise 1: Configure the Required User and Group Accounts

1. On DC1, log on to the *cohovineyard.com* domain as an administrator.

2. Open Active Directory Users and Computers from the Administrative Tools.

3. Create two users, one named EntAdmin and one named ArrAdmin.

4. Create two groups, one named ISA EntAdmins and one named ISA ArrAdmins.

5. Add the EntAdmin user account to the Domain Admins group and to the ISA EntAdmins group.

6. Add the ArrAdmin user account to the ISA ArrAdmins group.

7. Create a user account named ISAService.

8. On ISA2 and ISA3, log on to the *cohovineyard.dom* domain as a domain administrator.

9. Open Computer Management and add ISA ArrAdmins to the local Administrators group.

Exercise 2: Install the Configuration Storage Server on DC1

1. On DC1, log on as EntAdmin. Access the ISA Server Enterprise Edition CD-ROM and double-click Isaautorun.exe.

2. In Microsoft ISA Server Setup, click Install ISA Server.

3. On the Welcome page, click Next.

4. Review the terms and conditions stated in the user license agreement, click I Accept The Terms In The License Agreement, and then click Next.

5. On the Customer Information page, click Next.

6. On the Setup Scenarios page, select Install Configuration Storage Server, and then click Next.

7. On the Component Selection page, review the settings, and then click Next.

8. On the Enterprise Installation Options page, select Create A New ISA Server Enterprise, and then click Next.

9. On the New Enterprise Warning page, click Next. This page warns you not to install more than one enterprise. Because you are creating a new enterprise, you can ignore the warning.

10. On the Create A New Enterprise page, type **Coho Vineyards Enterprise** as the Enterprise name. Click Next.

11. On the Enterprise Deployment Environment page, click I Am Deploying In A Single Domain Or In Domains With Trust Relationships, then click Next.

12. On the Configuration Storage Server Service Account page, in the User Name text box, type **ISAService**. In the Password text box, type the password that you assigned to the ISAService account. Click Next.

13. On the Ready To Install The Program page, click Install to begin the installation.

14. After the installation is complete, click Finish.

15. Open a command prompt and switch to the C:\Program Files\Microsoft ISA Server\Adamdata directory.

16. Type **Cohovineyard.com.bat** and press ENTER. Close the command prompt window.

How to Configure Enterprise Policies and Networks

After you install the Configuration Storage server, the next step in the implementation is to configure the enterprise administrator roles and configure enterprise networks and enterprise policies and rules.

Delegate Enterprise Administrator Permissions

After installing the Configuration Storage server, you can delegate the enterprise administrative permissions. By default, the user account used to create the enterprise is the only account that has enterprise administrator permissions. To assign enterprise administrator permissions to a group, complete the following procedure:

1. In the ISA Server Management Console, right-click Enterprise and click Properties.

2. In the Enterprise Properties dialog box, on the Assign Roles tab, as shown in Figure 12-9, click Add.

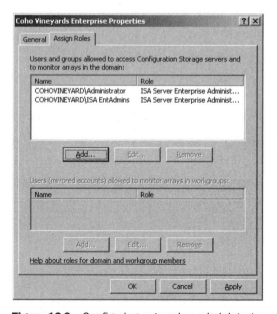

Figure 12-9   Configuring enterprise administrator roles

3. In the Administration Delegation dialog box, in the Group or User text box, type the name of the group to which you are assigning permissions.

4. Under Role, select the appropriate role, and click OK.

Configuring an Enterprise Network

An enterprise network is a range of IP addresses defined on the enterprise level. This network can then be used to create enterprise rules or added to array network objects. When you create a new enterprise network, the only configuration option you have is to configure the IP address range. To configure an enterprise network, complete these steps:

1. In ISA Server Management, expand the Enterprise node, and click Enterprise Networks.

2. In the task pane, on the Tasks tab, select Create a New Network to start the New Network Wizard.

3. Provide a name for the new network, and then click Next.

4. On the Network Addresses page, click Add Range to open the IP Address Range Properties dialog box, shown in Figure 12-10. In Start Address, type the low end of the IP address range, and in End Address, type the high end of the IP address range. Click OK. On the Network Addresses page, click Next.

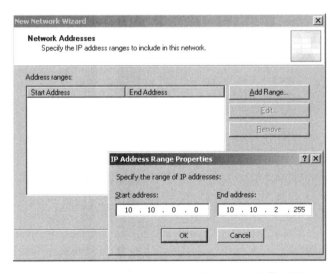

Figure 12-10   Configuring an enterprise network IP address range

5. On the summary page, review the properties of the enterprise network you are creating, and then click Finish.

In addition to creating enterprise networks, you can also create enterprise policy elements such as computer sets, URL sets, and domain name sets. To do this, click Enterprise Policy and, on the Toolbox tab, create the policy element.

Creating an Enterprise Policy and Policy Rules

The next step is to create an enterprise policy that can be applied to arrays. To configure an enterprise policy, complete these steps:

1. In the ISA Server Management Console, expand Enterprise, and click Enterprise Policies.

2. In the task pane, on the Tasks tab, click Create New Enterprise Policy to start the New Enterprise Policy Wizard.

3. On the Welcome page, provide a name for the new policy and click Next.

4. On the Completing The New Enterprise Policy Wizard page, click Finish.

The enterprise policy is essentially just a container object; to make it effective, you need to configure policy rules that comprise the policy. When you configure the policy rules, you can choose to apply the rules before or after the array policy rules are applied. To configure an enterprise policy rule, complete these steps:

1. In ISA Server Management, expand Enterprise, expand Enterprise Policies, and select an existing enterprise policy.

2. In the task pane, on the Tasks tab, select Create Enterprise Access Rule to start the New Access Rule Wizard.

3. On the Welcome page of the wizard, enter the name for the access rule, and then click Next.

4. On the Rule Action page, select Allow or Deny, and then click Next.

5. On the Protocols page, configure the protocols that apply to this rule, and click Next.

6. On the Access Rule Sources page, select the network or network object from which the access requests will come and click Next.

> **Tip**   If you are creating an access rule that will enable Internet access for all arrays in the enterprise, choose All Protected Networks as the source. The advantage of using All Protected Networks as the source, rather than listing specific networks, is that this rule will include any future networks that are added to your enterprise, without requiring you to modify the rule.

7. On the Access Rule Destinations page, select the network or network object to which the traffic will flow and click Next.

8. On the User Sets page, choose the appropriate user set and then click Next.

9. Review the information on the wizard summary page and then click Finish.

> **Note**   The steps to configure an enterprise access rule are virtually identical to creating an access rule on an ISA Server Standard Edition server. The only difference is that you can use only enterprise-level networks when you create the access rule.

Depending on which access rule you selected when you started the New Access Rule Wizard, the access rule may be created under Enterprise Policy Rules Applied Before Array Firewall Policy, or under Enterprise Policy Rules Applied Before Array Firewall Policy, as shown in Figure 12-11. You can change the location of the access rule by right-clicking the rule and selecting Move Up or Move Down.

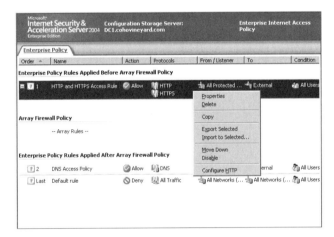

Figure 12-11   Moving enterprise access rules

> **Note**   You cannot create publishing rules at the enterprise level. You can create only access rules at this level.

How to Configure Arrays and Array Policies

After you create enterprise policy and enterprise policy rules, the next step is to create one or more arrays and then assign array policy rules.

Creating an Array

An array is a group of computers running the ISA Server services that share the same configuration. Although you can create an array when you install ISA Server services, as a best practice you should configure the array first and then install ISA Server computers into the array. To create an array, complete the following procedure:

1. In the ISA Server Management Console, expand Arrays.

2. In the task pane, on the Tasks tab, click Create New Array to start the New Array Wizard.

3. On the Welcome page, provide a name for the new array, and then click Next.

4. On the Array DNS Name page, type the DNS name that will be used by Firewall clients and Web Proxy clients to connect to the array. Click Next

5. On the Array Enterprise Policy page, shown in Figure 12-12, from the drop-down menu, select the enterprise policy that will be applied to the new array. You can choose to either apply the default policy or any other enterprise policy that you have created. Click Next.

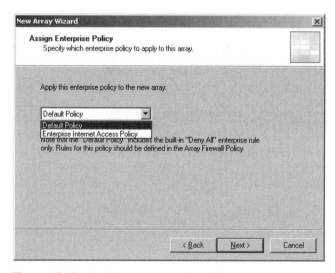

Figure 12-12   Applying an enterprise policy to an array

6. On the Array Policy Rule Types page, as shown in Figure 12-13, select the types of rules that can be configured for the array. You can choose to enable or disable allow access rules, deny access rules, and publishing rules. Click Next.

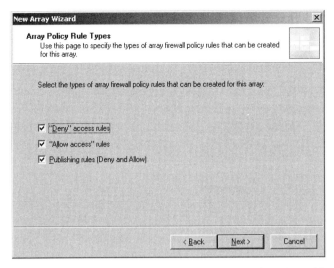

Figure 12-13   Defining the policy rules that can be created for an array

7. On the summary page, review the array configuration and then click Finish.

Configuring an Array

After you create the array, you can modify the array configuration by completing the following procedure:

1. In the ISA Server Management Console, expand Arrays.

2. Right-click the array that you are configuring and click Properties.

3. On the Policy Settings tab, shown in Figure 12-14, configure the enterprise policy that will apply to the array, and modify the types of firewall policy rules that can be configured for the array.

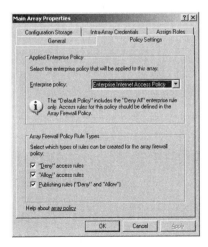

Figure 12-14   Modifying the policy settings for an array

4. On the Configuration Storage tab, as shown in Figure 12-15, configure which Configuration Storage server will be used by the ISA Server computers that are members of the array. You can also configure an Alternate Configuration Storage server and configure how frequently the ISA Server computers will check for updates. You can also modify the authentication type.

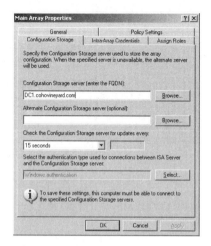

Figure 12-15   Modifying the Configuration Storage settings for an array

5. On the Intra-Array Credentials tab, as shown in Figure 12-16, configure the account that will be used to authenticate for intra-array communication. If the array contains computers that are members of a trusted domain, you can use Authenticate using the computer account of the array member. If the array contains computers that are members of a workgroup, select Authenticate Using This Account (For Workgroup Configuration Only) and then click Set Account to specify a user account. This user account must be mirrored on all array members.

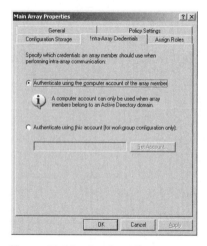

Figure 12-16   Configuring intra-array credentials

6. After configuring the array, you may choose to delegate the array administrative permissions. By default, the enterprise administrators have full administrative rights to the array. On the Assign Roles tab, as shown in Figure 12-17, click Add.

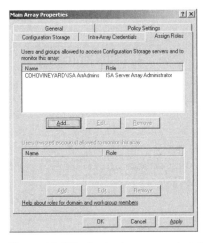

Figure 12-17 Assigning array administrative roles

7. In the Administration Delegation dialog box, in the Group or User text box, type the name of the group to which you are assigning permissions.

8. Under Role, select the appropriate role, and click OK

Creating Array Policy Rules

The next step in configuring the array is to create the policy rules for the array policy. To create the access rules, click the Firewall Policy container under the array name and on the Tasks tab, click Create Array Access Rule or click the option to create one of the publishing rules. The procedures for creating array access rules or publishing rules in an array are identical to creating these rules on an ISA Server Standard Edition computer.

Practice: Configuring Enterprise and Array Policies

In this practice, you will prepare your ISA Server environment for the deployment of ISA Server Enterprise Edition computers by configuring an enterprise network and enterprise policy. Then you will then create an array and configure an array policy.

Exercise 1: Configure an Enterprise Network and Enterprise Policy

1. On DC1, open the ISA Server Management Console.

2. Expand Enterprise and click Enterprise Networks.

3. In the task pane, on the Tasks tab, select Create A New Network to start the New Network Wizard.

4. In Network name, type **Internal** as the network name, and then click Next.

5. On the Network Addresses page, click Add Range to open the IP Address Range Properties dialog box. In Starting Address, type **10.10.0.0** and in Ending Address, type **10.10.0.255**, and then click OK.

6. On the Network Addresses page, click Next.

7. On the summary page, review the properties of the enterprise network you are creating, and then click Finish.

8. In the ISA Server Management Console, click Enterprise Policy. On the Toolbox tab, click Network Objects.

9. Click New, and then click Computer.

10. In the New Computer Rule Element dialog box, under Name, type **DC1**. In Computer IP Address, type **10.10.0.10**. Click OK.

11. Click Enterprise Policies.

12. In the task pane, on the Tasks tab, click Create New Enterprise Policy to start the New Enterprise Policy Wizard.

13. On the Welcome page, type **Enterprise Internet Access Policy** as the name of the new policy. Click Next.

14. On the Completing The New Enterprise Policy Wizard page, click Finish.

15. Expand Enterprise Policies and click Enterprise Internet Access Policy. In the task pane, on the Tasks tab, select Create Enterprise Access Rule to start the New Access Rule Wizard.

16. On the Welcome page of the wizard, type **HTTP and HTTPS Access Rule** as the name of the access rule. Click Next.

17. On the Rule Action page, select Allow, and then click Next.

18. On the Protocols page, in This Rule Applies To, select Selected Protocols. Click Add to open the Add Protocols dialog box.

19. Expand Web, click HTTP, click Add, click HTTPS, and then click Add. Click Close to close the Add Protocols dialog box. On the Protocols page, click Next.

20. On the Access Rule Sources page, click Add to open the Add Network Entities dialog box, expand Network Sets, select All Protected Networks, click Add, and then click Close. On the Access Rule Sources page, click Next.

21. On the Access Rule Destinations page, click Add to open the Add Network Entities dialog box, expand Enterprise Networks, select External, click Add, and then click Close. On the Access Rule Destinations page, click Next.

22. On the User Sets page, because your rule applies to all users, you can leave the All Users user set in place and then click Next.

23. Review the information on the wizard summary page and then click Finish.

24. The rule is created under Enterprise Policy Rules Applied After Array Firewall Policy by default. Now, you will move HTTP and HTTPS Access Rule under Enterprise Policy Rules Applied Before Array Firewall Policy. Right-click the rule and select Move Up.

25. Create another access rule with the following properties:

   ❑ Access rule name: **DNS Access Policy**

   ❑ Rule action: Allow

   ❑ Selected protocol: DNS

   ❑ Access Rule Sources: DC1

   ❑ Access Rule destination: External

   ❑ User sets: All Users

26. If necessary, move the rule so that it is listed under Enterprise Policy Rules Applied After Array Firewall Policy.

27. Click Apply to apply the changes.

Exercise 2: Creating and Configuring an Array

   1. In the ISA Server Management Console, click Arrays. In the task pane, on the Tasks tab, click Create New Array to start the New Array Wizard.

   2. On the Welcome page, type Main Array as the name for the new array and then click Next.

   3. On the Array DNS Name page, click Next.

   4. On the Array Enterprise Policy page, select Enterprise Internet Access Policy from the drop-down menu and then click Next.

   5. On the Array Policy Rule Types page, accept the default. Click Next.

   6. On the summary page, review the array configuration and then click Finish. When the array is created, click OK.

   7. Right-click Main/Back-End Array and click Properties.

   8. In the Array Properties dialog box, on the Assign Roles tab, click Add.

   9. In the Administration Delegation dialog box, in the Group Or User text box, type ISA ArrAdmins.

   10. Under Role, select ISA Server Array Administrator, and click OK.

   11. Click Firewall Policy (Main Array) and then click Create Array Access Rule.

   12. Create an array access rule with the following properties:

   ❑ Access rule name: **FTP Access Policy**

   ❑ Rule action: Allow

❑ Selected protocol: FTP

❑ Access Rule Sources: Internal

❑ Access Rule destination: External

❑ User sets: All Users

13. Click Apply to apply the changes.

How to Install ISA Server 2004, Enterprise Edition

Once you have prepared the enterprise and create the required arrays, you are ready to start installing the ISA Server services. Installing the ISA Server services enables the servers to operate as firewall servers. To install ISA Server services, complete the following steps on a Windows Server 2003 computer:

1. Access the ISA Server Enterprise Edition installation files and start the installation by running Isaautorun.exe and clicking Install ISA Server.

2. Accept the terms and conditions stated in the user license agreement.

3. Enter your customer information.

4. On the Setup Scenarios page, click Install ISA Server Services and then click Next.

5. On the Component Selection page, the ISA Server and ISA Server Management components are selected. You can choose to add additional components such as the Firewall Client Installation Share. Click Next.

6. On the Locate Configuration Storage Server page, shown in Figure 12-18, type the fully qualified domain name (FQDN) of a Configuration Storage server. Click Next.

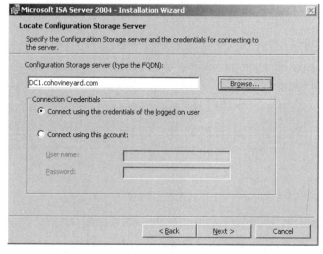

Figure 12-18   Configuring the Configuration Storage server during ISA Server installation

7. On the Array Membership page, select either Join An Existing Array or Create a New Array, and then click Next.

8. If you selected Join an Existing Array page, shown in Figure 12-19, you will see the Join An Existing Array page. Click Browse, and then click the array that the ISA Server computer will join. Click OK, and then click Next.

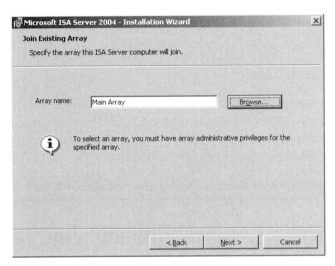

Figure 12-19   Configuring the array membership during ISA Server installation

9. On the Configuration Storage Server Authentication Options page, shown in Figure 12-20, you can choose how the ISA Server services computer will authenticate with the Configuration Storage server. Click Next.

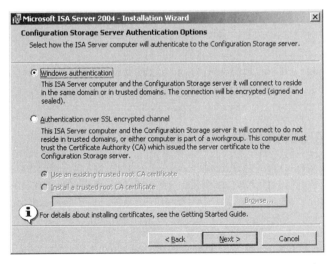

Figure 12-20   Configuring Configuration Storage server authentication during ISA Server installation

10. On the Internal Network page, click Add to open the Addresses dialog box.

11. You can configure the Internal Network by either adding an Enterprise network, adding an IP address range, or selecting an adapter address range.

12. On the Internal Network page, click Next.

13. On the Services Warning page, review the list of services that will be stopped or disabled during installation of ISA Server. To continue the installation, click Next.

14. On the Ready To Install The Program page, click Install.

Performing an Unattended Setup

You can install ISA Server 2004, Enterprise Edition, by using the UNATTENDED SERVER SETUP command. The files listed in Table 12-1 are located in the FPC folder on the ISA Server installation CD-ROM. The files contain the configuration information that can be used by server setup in unattended mode.

Table 12-1   ISA Server Enterprise Edition Unattended Installation Files

File name	Description
Installjoinedserver.ini	Install a computer running ISA Server services and join it to a specific array
InstallNewArrayAndServer.ini	Install a computer running ISA Server services and create a new array
Installnewmanagementserver.ini	Install a Configuration Storage server
Installstandaloneserver.ini	Install ISA Server services and Configuration Storage server
Uninstallserver.ini	Uninstall a server

See Also   For detailed information about how to modify the configuration files to perform an unattended installation, see ISA Server Online Help.

Practice: Installing ISA Server 2004, Enterprise Edition

In this practice, you will install ISA Server 2004 on both ISA2 and ISA3. For ISA2, you will install the ISA Server services, the ISA Server Management Console, and the ISA Server Client Installation share. On ISA3, you will install a replica Configuration Storage server, the ISA Server services, and ISA Server Management.

Exercise 1: Installing ISA Server, Enterprise Edition, on ISA2

1. On ISA2, log on to the *cohovineyard.com* domain using the ArrAdmin account.

2. Browse to the ISA Server Enterprise Edition CD-ROM and double-click ISAautorun.exe.

3. In Microsoft ISA Server Setup, click Install ISA Server 2004.

4. After the setup program prompts that it has completed determining the system configuration, on the Welcome page, click Next.

5. To accept the terms and conditions stated in the user license agreement, click I Accept The Terms In The License Agreement, and then click Next.

6. On the Customer Information page, click Next.

7. On the Setup Scenarios page, select Install ISA Server Services, and then click Next.

8. On the Component Selection page, click the icon for Firewall Client Installation Share, click This Feature Will Be Installed On The Local Hard Drive, and then click Next.

9. On the Locate Configuration Storage Server page, type **DC1.cohovineyard.com**. Click Next.

10. On the Array Membership page, select Join An Existing Array, and then click Next.

11. On the Join An Existing Array page, click Browse and then click Main Array. Click OK and then click Next.

12. On the Configuration Storage Server Authentication Options page, click Next.

13. On the Internal Network page, click Add to open the Addresses dialog box.

14. Click Add Network to open the Select Enterprise Networks dialog box.

15. Click Internal, and then click OK.

16. On the Internal Network page, click Next.

17. On the Services Warning page, review the list of services that will be stopped or disabled during installation of ISA Server. To continue the installation, click Next.

18. On the Ready To Install The Program page, click Install.

19. After the installation is complete, click Finish.

20. You will be prompted to restart the computer. Click Yes to restart the computer.

Exercise 2: Installing ISA Server, Enterprise Edition, on ISA3

1. On ISA3, log on to the *cohovineyard.dom* domain using the EntAdmin account.

> **Exam Tip**   To install Configuration Storage server on a server, you need to be logged in as an ISA Server Enterprise Administrator.

2. Browse to the ISA Server Enterprise Edition CD-ROM and double-click ISAautorun.exe.

3. In Microsoft ISA Server Setup, click Install ISA Server 2004.

4. After the setup program prompts that it has completed determining the system configuration, on the Welcome page, click Next.

5. To accept the terms and conditions stated in the user license agreement, click I Accept The Terms In The License Agreement, and then click Next.

6. On the Customer Information page, click Next.

7. On the Setup Scenarios page, select Install Both ISA Server Services And Configuration Storage Server, and then click Next.

Caution   Normally, you should not install Configuration Storage server on an ISA Server computer deployed as an Internet-edge firewall.

8. On the Component Selection page, click Next.

9. On the Enterprise Installation Options page, click Create A Replica Of The Enterprise Configuration, and click Next.

10. On the Locate Configuration Storage Server page, type **DC1.cohovineyard.com**. Click Next.

11. In the ISA Server Warning dialog box, click OK.

12. On the ISA Server Configuration Replicate Source page, ensure that the option to Replicate over the network is selected and click Next.

13. On the Enterprise Deployment Environment page, click Next.

14. On the Array Membership page, select Join An Existing Array, and then click Next.

15. On the Join An Existing Array page, click Browse, then click Main Array. Click OK, and then click Next.

16. On the Configuration Storage Server Authentication Options page, click Next.

17. On the Services Warning page, review the list of services that will be stopped or disabled during installation of ISA Server. To continue the installation, click Next.

18. On the Ready To Install The Program page, click Install.

19. After the installation is complete, click Finish.

20. You will be prompted to restart the computer. Click Yes to restart the computer.

21. After the computer restarts, log on to ISA3 as EntAdmin. Open ISA Server Management.

22. Click Enterprise Policies. On the Toolbox tab, click Network Objects, expand Computer Sets, and double-click Replicate Configuration Storage servers.

23. On the Replicate Configuration Storage Servers Properties dialog box, click Add and select Computer.

24. In the New Computer Rule Element, type **DC1** as the Name and type **10.10.0.10** as the Computer IP Address. Click OK.

25. Add another computer element with a name of **ISA3** and an IP address of **10.10.0.3**.

26. Apply the changes.

How to Configure NLB and CARP

After you install multiple computers in an ISA Server array, you can then enable support for NLB and CARP. To enable NLB, you should first configure a dedicated network for intra-array communication, and then enable and configure NLB for the networks that are attached to the array. You can also configure CARP for the networks attached to the array.

Configuring Intra-Array Addressing

Before implementing NLB for an array, you should configure the intra-array communication between the ISA Server computers in each array. The ISA Server computers that are part of an array must be able to communicate with each other to enable features such as such as CARP and NLB.

The servers in the array communicate with each other using the intra-array address. This address is automatically configured during setup and is configured as the first network interface on the internal network. You can modify the intra-array address.

> **Note** A default system policy, named Allow Intra-array Communications, allows communication using the MS Firewall Control and RPC (All Interfaces) protocols to and from all members of the Array Servers computer set. By default, the Array Servers computer set includes the intra-array address of each member server. When you modify the intra-array address, the Array Servers computer set is automatically updated.

When configuring the intra-array address for a server, follow these guidelines:

- If you do not plan to enable NLB for the array, specify the intra-array address as the primary IP address of the first network adapter on the Internal network.

- If you plan to enable NLB for the array, use a dedicated network adapter that is located on the Internal network for intra-array traffic. Use a different network adapter on the Internal network for NLB.

■ The best option is to use a dedicated network adapter in a network used only for intra-array communication. To do this, configure a network used for intra-array traffic that includes only the intra-array addresses used by all servers in the array.

To configure the intra-array address that is using a dedicated network, you need at least three network interfaces on the ISA Server computer. Then you need to create a network used for intra-array communication, and configure the ISA Server computers to use IP addresses associated with that network for intra-array communications. To configure these options, complete the following procedure:

1. In the ISA Server Management Console, expand Arrays, and then expand the array that you are configuring.

2. Expand Configuration and click Networks.

3. On the Tasks tab, click Create A New Network.

4. On the Welcome page, type a name for the intra-array communication network and then click Next.

5. On the Network Type page, ensure that Internal Network is selected and click Next.

6. On the Network Addresses page, click Add Adapter.

7. On the Network Adapters page, select the check box for the adapter that will be used for intra-array communications and click OK.

8. On the Network Addresses page, click Next.

9. On the Completing The New Network Wizard page, review the configuration and click Finish.

10. Expand Configuration and click Servers and then double-click the ISA Server name.

11. On the Communication tab, shown in Figure 12-21, under Intra-Array Communication, select the IP address connected to the intra-array network from the drop-down list. Click OK.

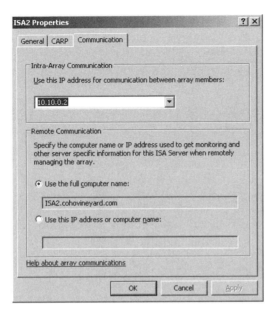

Figure 12-21   Configuring the intra-array communication IP address

12. Complete these steps on all other array members.

Configuring NLB

After you configure the intra-array addresses for an array, you can enable and configure NLB for the other networks connected to the array. When you configure NLB for a network, you must specify one virtual IP address for the network. The dedicated IP address and the virtual IP address must belong to the same subnet and have the same subnet mask.

When configuring and deploying NLB-enabled networks, follow these guidelines:

■ Do not use a layer-2 switch to connect the array members. The reason is that NLB uses a virtual physical address for the virtual IP address. None of the ISA Server network adapters registers that physical address on the switch, so incoming packets are flooded to all ports on the switch. Instead, connect the network adapters to a hub and uplink that hub to the network switch.

■ When NLB is enabled on all the networks in the array, you must add a network adapter that is dedicated for intra-array traffic. Place this network adapter on a separate network subnet. In this way, all outgoing traffic to other array members will pass only through this network adapter and not through load-balanced networks.

■ When the Configuration Storage server is installed on an array member, the IP address that the array members use to access the Configuration Storage server should be set to the intra-array address of the Configuration Storage server. Otherwise, the other array members may lose connectivity to the Configuration Storage server.

To enable NLB on the ISA Server array, complete the following procedure:

1. In the ISA Server Management Console, expand Arrays, and then expand the array that you are configuring.

2. Expand Configuration and click Networks.

3. On the Tasks tab, click Enable Network Load Balancing Integration.

4. On the Welcome page, click Next.

5. On the Select Load Balanced Networks page, shown in Figure 12-22, select the network for which you want to enable NLB.

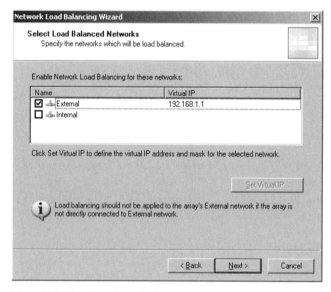

Figure 12-22   Configuring NLB

6. Click Set Virtual IP, and on the Set Virtual IP Address dialog box, type the virtual IP address and mask. Click OK.

7. Repeat steps 5 and 6 for the other networks on the array that you want to load-balance.

8. Click Next, and then click Finish.

9. Click Apply to apply the changes. When you enable NLB, the firewall services on all array members need to be restarted.

Enabling CARP Support

You can also enable CARP on the ISA Server arrays. When you enable CARP, the cache drives on all the servers in the array are treated as a single logical cache drive. In this way, cached objects can be efficiently distributed among the member servers.

ISA Server, Enterprise Edition, changes some of the options for configuring Web Proxy client and Firewall client connections. When deploying Web Proxy or Firewall clients with ISA Server, Standard Edition, you configure the clients to use the IP address or name of the ISA Server computer when connecting to remote resources. However, when deploying Web Proxy or Firewall clients with ISA Server, Enterprise Edition, the clients must connect to the array rather than the individual servers.

To enable this, configure the ISA Server clients to use the array DNS name to connect to the array. When you create an array, the array is assigned a DNS name. You can modify the array DNS name after deployment.

For the ISA Server clients to connect to the array DNS name, the clients must be able to resolve the name using DNS. This means that you must add the array DNS name to the DNS zone files used by the ISA Server clients. If the array contains more than one server, you should configure a DNS host record using the dedicated IP address for each array member.

If you have CARP enabled for the array, the Web Proxy clients connect to the array using the array DNS name to download the CARP script. The clients use the script to determine which array member to connect to when accessing Web content.

> **Note**   The default gateway for SecureNAT clients should be configured to use the shared virtual IP address for the array if NLB is enabled, and the IP address of one of the array members if NLB is not enabled.

To enable CARP, you need to enable caching on at least one member server and then enable CARP for the array network. Complete the following procedure:

1. In the ISA Server Management Console, expand Arrays, and then expand the array that you are configuring.

2. Expand Configuration, and then click Cache.

3. Select one of the computers in the array, and click Define Cache Drives (Enable Caching).

4. In the Cache Drives dialog box, configure a maximum cache size and click Set. Then click OK. Apply the changes and accept the option to restart the services.

5. Enable caching on all the servers in the array.

6. Expand Configuration, and then click Networks. Double-click the network for which you want to enable caching.

7. In the network Properties dialog box, click the CARP tab, as shown in Figure 12-23, and click Enable CARP On This Network. You can also configure CARP exceptions to specify Web sites that will not be cached using CARP. Click OK.

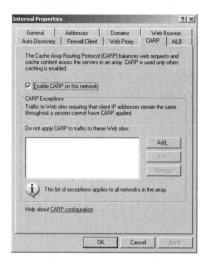

Figure 12-23 Configuring CARP

8. You can also configure the CARP load distribution by modifying the load factor for each ISA Server computer in the array. By default, the load factor on each server is set to 100. You can configure a higher load factor if you want more objects to be cached to a specific server. Alternatively, configure a lower load factor if fewer objects should be cached to the server. To modify the load factor on a computer, expand Configuration, click Servers, and then double-click the server name. On the CARP tab, configure the load factor.

Lesson Review

Use the following questions to help determine whether you have learned enough to move on to the next lesson. If you have difficulty answering these questions, review the material in this lesson. You can find answers to these questions in the "Questions and Answers" section at the end of this chapter.

1. You are preparing to deploy ISA Server, Enterprise Edition, in your organization. The design documentation for the ISA Server infrastructure that you are deploying states that the server roles required for ISA Server, Enterprise Edition, must be distributed across multiple servers. What action do you need to perform first when you deploy ISA Server, Enterprise Edition?

    a. Deploy a workstation running ISA Server Management

    b. Deploy a server running ISA Server services and Configuration Storage server

    c. Deploy a server running ISA Server services

    d. Deploy a Configuration Storage server

2. You have deployed ISA Server 2004, Enterprise Edition, and have created an array for the branch office. You have delegated a branch office administrator as an ISA Server Administrator for the array. You want to ensure that the array administrator cannot publish any servers in the branch office. The array administrator should be able to modify access rules for the array. What is the best way to achieve this?

_____

_____

_____

3. You have deployed ISA Server 2004, Enterprise Edition, and configured multiple arrays. All arrays have firewall access rules that allows HTTP traffic to all users. You receive reports that some users are accessing a peer-to-peer file sharing application that tunnels over HTTP. In response, you create a firewall access rule that denies access to HTTP application signature in the enterprise policy that is being applied to all arrays. Later you discover that users are still able to access the file-sharing application. What is the most likely reason that the rule is not having the desired effect?

_____

_____

_____

Lesson Summary

- The requirements for installing ISA Server, Enterprise Edition, are similar to the requirements for Standard Edition except that ISA Server Enterprise Edition Configuration Storage Server and ISA Server services must be installed on a computer running Windows Server 2003.

- The Configuration Storage server stores the configuration information for the entire enterprise so the first step in implementing ISA Server, Enterprise Edition, is to install and configure this server. When installing the first Configuration Storage server, choose the option to create a new enterprise.

- After you install the Configuration Storage server, the next step in the implementation is to configure the enterprise administrator roles and configure enterprise networks and enterprise policies and rules.

- After you create enterprise policy and enterprise policy rules, the next step is to create one or more arrays and then assign array policy rules.

- Once you have prepared the enterprise and created the required arrays, you are ready to start installing the ISA Server services. Installing the ISA Server services enables the servers to operate as firewall servers.

- After installing the ISA Server computers, you can also enable NLB and CARP on the ISA Server arrays. To configure NLB, enable the service and then configure a shared IP address for each network attached to the array. To configure CARP, enable the service and then configure a CARP load-balancing factor.

Case Scenario Exercise

In this exercise, you will plan an ISA Server 2004, Enterprise Edition, deployment in a back-to-back configuration for a fictitious organization. Read the scenario and then answer the questions that follow. If you have difficulty completing this work, review the material in this chapter before beginning the next chapter. You can find answers to these questions in the "Questions and Answers" section at the end of this chapter.

Scenario 1

Coho Vineyards is implementing a back-to-back firewall solution using ISA Server 2004 Enterprise Edition as both the front-end and back-end firewall. A Configuration Storage server has been deployed on the internal network at Coho Vineyards. Coho Vineyards has the following three IP addresses available to connect to the Internet: 131.107.1.101 to 131.107.1.103.

Coho Vineyards has the following security and functional requirements:

- All users in the organization use Firewall clients to access Internet resources. The organization must be able to restrict access to Internet resources based on domain user accounts.

- The connection to the Internet should not be disrupted if a single ISA Server computer fails.

- The ISA Server computers in the front-end array should not be members of the *cohovineyard.com* domain.

- Users on the internal network must be able to access resources on the Internet using HTTP, HTTPS, and FTP.

- All users on the Internet must be able to access a company Web site located on a Web server in the perimeter network.

- Users on the internal network must also be able to a access company Web site located on a Web server in the perimeter network.

- Users on the Internet must be able to access the Exchange server on the internal network using Microsoft Outlook Web Access (OWA). The connection must be secured from the client to the Exchange server using SSL.

- Users on the Internet must be able to access a secure Web site located on a Web server in perimeter network. The connection must be secured from the client to the Web server using SSL. Access to the secure Web site must be restricted to domain user accounts.

Scenario 1 Questions

1. Based on these requirements, how will you configure the back-end array and the ISA Server computers that are members of the back-end array?

2. How will you configure the front-end array and the ISA Server computers that are members of the front-end array?

3. What other configurations must you enable?

Chapter Summary

- ISA Server, Enterprise Edition, uses a Configuration Storage server to store the configuration for all the arrays in the enterprise. When you deploy ISA Server, Enterprise Edition, you can configure ISA Server policies and policy objects at both the enterprise and array level. Enterprise policy rules can be evaluated before or after the array rules. The effective policy is the combination of enterprise and array policies. ISA Server, Enterprise Edition, integrates with NLB so that you can configure and manage NLB functionality using the ISA Server Management tools. ISA Server, Enterprise Edition, supports remote access VPNs, including network quarantine control and site-to-site VPNs using NLB for VPN connections. ISA Server provides distributed caching through the use of the Cache Array Routing Protocol (CARP).

- ISA Server Enterprise Edition deployment scenarios include deploying multiple ISA Server computers in identical roles, deploying ISA Server computers in a workgroup, and deploying multiple ISA Server computers in a site-to-site VPN configuration. Because the ISA Server enterprise configuration information is stored in the Configuration Storage server directory, you should deploy multiple Configuration Storage servers in the same enterprise, deploy Configuration Storage Servers in each remote office, install the Configuration Storage server on a domain member, and install the Configuration Storage server as a dedicated server. One of the benefits of deploying ISA Server, Enterprise Edition, is that you can manage and monitor multiple ISA Server computers from a central location using Remote Desktop or ISA Server Management. ISA Server 2004 supports an upgrade path from ISA Server 2000, Enterprise Edition, to ISA Server 2004, Enterprise Edition. Most ISA Server 2000 configuration information will be upgraded to ISA Server 2004.

■ The requirements for installing ISA Server, Enterprise Edition, are similar to the requirements for Standard Edition except that ISA Server Enterprise Edition Configuration Storage Server and ISA Server services must be installed on a computer running Windows Server 2003. The Configuration Storage server stores the configuration information for the entire enterprise so the first step in implementing ISA Server, Enterprise Edition, is to install and configure this server. After you install the Configuration Storage server, the next step in the implementation is to configure the enterprise administrator roles, and configure enterprise networks and enterprise policies and rules, then to create one or more arrays, and then assign array policy rules. Once you have prepared the enterprise and created the required arrays, you are ready to start installing the ISA Server services and enabling NLB and CARP on the ISA Server arrays.

Exam Highlights

Before taking the exam, review the key points and terms that are presented in this chapter. You need to know this information.

Key Points

■ If you deploy Configuration Storage Server on a member of a workgroup rather than a domain, you can only deploy one Configuration Storage server in your enterprise.

■ All the Configuration Storage servers in an enterprise share the same configuration information. You can deploy more than one enterprise in an organization, but this is not recommended as the ISA Server computers in the two enterprises cannot share configuration information.

■ If you configure an enterprise network that includes IP addresses that are not included in any array level network, any traffic coming from those IP addresses is considered spoofed and the traffic will be blocked. All IP addresses must be defined in a array network, either explicitly or by assigning an enterprise network as the address range for the array network.

■ Remember that ISA Server always evaluates the rules in order, regardless of whether the rule is defined at the enterprise or array level, and that the first rule that corresponds to the request is applied.

■ Configuration Storage server plays a central role in an Enterprise Edition deployment. If ISA Server computers are not performing as expected, ensure that the servers can access a Configuration Storage server and that the most recent configuration is downloaded to the servers. It is also critical that you plan the Configuration Storage server implementation carefully.

■ If you do not allow the creation of a particular type of rule for an array, no one, not even an enterprise administrator, can create that type of rule. If you want to configure that type of rule, you must enable the option to create the rule and then create the rule.

■ If the computer running the ISA Server services belongs to a workgroup, but the Configuration Storage Server belongs to a domain, you need to create mirrored accounts on each ISA Server computer to facilitate intra-array communication and administration.

■ Before you configure any publishing rules that require SSL termination on the front-end or back-end array, you must install the required server certificates on all members of the array. You must install the same server certificates on all array members.

■ Normally, when you install Configuration Storage server on a computer that is not designated a domain controller, the service will run in the security context of the Network Service account. However, when you install Configuration Storage server on a domain controller, you must create a separate service account that is a member of the Domain Admins group. Or, you can run the .bat file created during the Configuration Storage server installation to configure the account with the required permissions.

■ You must be an array-level ISA Server Administrator to install ISA Server in an array. As well, you must be a local Administrator on the ISA Server computer to install ISA Server services. If you are also installing Configuration Storage server on the computer, you must be an Enterprise ISA Server Administrator.

Key Terms

Active Directory Application Mode (ADAM)   ADAM is a special mode of Active Directory that is designed for directory-enabled applications. Compatible with Lightweight Directory Access Protocol (LDAP), ADAM runs on computers on which Microsoft Windows Server 2003 is installed.

array   A group of ISA Server 2004 computers that share the same configuration. An array includes one or more Configuration Storage servers that store the configuration information for the array and one or more array members that are computers with ISA Server services installed.

Cache Array Routing Protocol (CARP)   CARP distributes the cache used by Web proxy clients across an array of ISA Server computers. CARP uses hash-based routing to determine which ISA Server computer will respond to a client request and cache specific Web content.

enterprise   A collection of all ISA Server 2004 computers that use the same Configuration Storage directory to store configuration information. An enterprise includes one or more arrays.

enterprise policy   A policy defined at the enterprise level that can be applied to any array.

MS Firewall Control Protocol   An outbound TCP protocol defined on Port 3847. It is used for communications between ISA Server Management and computers running ISA Server services.

MS Firewall Storage Protocol   An inbound LDAP-based protocol that uses Ports 2171 (for non-SSL connections) and 2172 (for SSL connections). Array members communicate with the Configuration Storage server using the MS Firewall Storage protocol. Computers running ISA Server Management also use the MS Firewall Storage protocol to read from and write to the Configuration Storage server.

MS Firewall Storage Replication Protocol   An outbound TCP protocol defined on Port 2173. MS Firewall Storage Replication is used for configuration replication between Configuration Storage servers.

network load balancing (NLB)   A Windows network feature that is used to create a cluster of computers that can be addressed by a single cluster IP address. NLB provides load balancing and high availability for IP-based services.

Questions and Answers

Page
12-17

Lesson 1 Review

1. You have installed ISA Server 2004 Enterprise Edition and have configured multiple arrays for different departments. Administrators have been assigned to each array to create access rules based on departmental needs. You need to ensure that no employees can use the ICQ protocol for online chatting or instant messaging. How will you accomplish this with the least administrative effort?

   a. Request that the array administrators create a firewall access rule to deny ICQ to Authenticated Users.

   b. Create an enterprise policy rule to deny ICQ to All Users and have it applied after the array rules.

   c. Request that the array administrators create a firewall-access rule to deny ICQ to All Users.

   d. Create an enterprise policy rule to deny ICQ to All Users and have it applied before the array rules.

   D is correct. An enterprise policy rule that denies the ICQ protocol applied before the array rules will ensure that it is the first rule applied and therefore will match all requests. B is incorrect because if the rule applies after the array rules then an array rule that might allow ICQ will be applied first. A and C are incorrect because, although array rules would work, they would not be the least administrative effort and would allow array administrators to change the rules.

2. You have implemented ISA Server 2004, Enterprise Edition, as your firewall solution. You want to ensure fault tolerance in case of server failure. What feature of ISA Server 2004 can provide this?

   a. Enterprise Policies

   b. NLB

   c. Arrays

   d. Configuration Storage Servers

   B is correct. The NLB feature provides fault tolerance in case of server failure. A is incorrect because Enterprise policies allow you to use common configuration rules for all arrays. C is incorrect because arrays have common configuration but are not fault tolerant. D is incorrect because the Configuration Storage server holds the array configuration properties but does not provide fault tolerance.

3. You are the network administrator for your organization. You are deploying ISA Server 2004 Enterprise Edition and have created your first enterprise policy rules and array policy rules. You have configured the following enterprise rules and branch-office array rules:

Enterprise Policy Rules Applied Before Array Firewall Policy

❑ Allow HTTP and HTTPS access from All Protected Networks to the Internet for all users

Branch-Office Array Firewall Policy Rules

❑ Allow all protocol access from the array's Internal network to the Internet for all authenticated users

❑ Allow FTP traffic from a computer set that includes all client computers at the branch office to the Internet

Enterprise Policy Rules Applied After Array Firewall Policy

❑ Enable all protocol access from All Protected Networks to the Internet for all users

Which of the following actions can users in the branch office perform? (Choose all that apply.)

a. Users on computers configured as secure network address translation (SecureNAT) clients will be able to access the Internet using FTP.

b. Users on computers configured as Web Proxy clients will be able to access the Internet using FTP.

c. Users on computers configured as SecureNAT clients will be able to access the Internet using HTTP.

d. Users on computers configured as Web Proxy clients will be able to access the Internet using MSN Messenger.

B, C, and D are correct. Because SecureNAT clients do not support user authentication, A is not possible, even though the final rule enables all protocol access for all users. The first rule in the array policy will be applied first, and it requires authentication. SecureNAT clients will be able to access the Internet using HTTP because of the first rule, and Web proxy clients support authentication, so users can authentication to gain access to the Internet for FTP and MSN Messenger connections.

Page
12-40

Lesson 2 Review

1. Your company has two branch offices connected to the head office by a slow network connection. You have configured ISA Server 2004, Enterprise Edition, with one array for the head-office ISA Server computers, and an array for the branch-office ISA Server computers. You need to ensure that the branch-office ISA Server computers have fast, reliable access to the array configuration information. What is the best way to accomplish this?

To enable fast and reliable access to the array configuration, deploy a Configuration Storage server in each branch office. You can install both the Configuration Storage server and ISA Server services components on the branch office computers, or you can install these components on two different computers in the branch office.

2. You administer an ISA Server array at the branch office of your company. Some of your users have requested access to an FTP site to download a file they require. You create a firewall access rule to allows the required access, yet users report they are still not able to access the FTP site. What is the most likely cause?

The most likely cause is that an enterprise policy rule that is preventing FTP access is being applied before the array policy. To enable access to the FTP site, the enterprise policy rule may need to be modified, or moved so that it is applied after the array policies.

3. You are deploying ISA Server, Enterprise Edition, in your organization. You are deploying multiple arrays, and need to ensure that array level administrators can install ISA Server computers into the array. The array level administrators should not be able to modify any enterprise policies. What role and permissions will you assign to the array level administrators? (Choose all that apply.)

   a. ISA Server Administrator

   b. ISA Server Enterprise Policy Editor

   c. Local Administrator on the ISA Server computers .

   d. ISA Server Enterprise Administrator

A and C are correct. You must be an ISA Server Administrator to add a server to an array. Moreover, you must be a local Administrator on the ISA Server computer to install ISA Server services. B is incorrect because it does not grant enough permissions, and D is incorrect because it would enable the administrators to modify enterprise-level policies.

4. You need to deploy ISA Server 2004, Enterprise Edition, so that domain accounts are not exposed on the Edge Firewall ISA Server array. You also want to grant Array Administrator rights based on Windows group membership. What is the best way to accomplish this?

   a. Deploy the Configuration Storage server and ISA Server array in a workgroup and create mirrored user accounts on the ISA Server computers.

   b. Deploy the ISA Server array and Configuration Storage server in the domain.

   c. Deploy the Configuration Storage server in the domain and the ISA Server array in a workgroup and create mirrored user accounts on the ISA Server computers.

   d. Deploy the ISA Server array in the domain and the Configuration Storage server to a workgroup and create mirrored domain user accounts.

C is correct. To use domain accounts to assign array level permissions, you must deploy the Configuration Storage server in the domain. Then configure the ISA Server array in a workgroup with mirrored accounts for authentication. These accounts should be different than the domain user accounts. A and D are incorrect because placing the Configuration Storage server in a workgroup will not let you use domain accounts. B is incorrect because if the ISA Server array is in the domain, then domain accounts may be exposed.

Lesson 3 Review

1. You are preparing to deploy ISA Server, Enterprise Edition, in your organization. The design documentation for the ISA Server infrastructure that you are deploying states that the server roles required for ISA Server, Enterprise Edition, must be distributed across multiple servers. What action do you need to perform first when you deploy ISA Server, Enterprise Edition?

    a. Deploy a workstation running ISA Server Management

    b. Deploy a server running ISA Server services and Configuration Storage server

    c. Deploy a server running ISA Server services

    d. Deploy a Configuration Storage server

    D is correct. The first server that you must deploy in the ISA Server infrastructure is a Configuration Storage server. Then you can configure a workstation with the ISA Server Management console, and use it configure the enterprise. Then install the servers running ISA Server services. If you deploy a server running both ISA Server services and Configuration Storage server you would be violating the design requirement to distribute the services across multiple servers.

2. You have deployed ISA Server 2004, Enterprise Edition, and have created an array for the branch office. You have delegated a branch office administrator as an ISA Server Administrator for the array. You want to ensure that the array administrator cannot publish any servers in the branch office. The array administrator should be able to modify access rules for the array. What is the best way to achieve this?

    Configure the array properties so that publishing rules cannot be configured for the array.

3. You have deployed ISA Server 2004, Enterprise Edition, and configured multiple arrays. All arrays have firewall access rules that allows HTTP traffic to all users. You receive reports that some users are accessing a peer-to-peer file sharing application that tunnels over HTTP. In response, you create a firewall access rule that denies access to HTTP application signature in the enterprise policy that is being applied to all arrays. Later you discover that users are still able to access the file-sharing application. What is the most likely reason that the rule is not having the desired effect?

    The most likely problem is that the access rule is created in the post-array Enterprise Policy and therefore is not being applied before the array policy that allows HTTP access to the Internet. You can move the access rule to the pre-array Enterprise Policy by right-clicking it and selecting Move Up until it is in the correct location.

Case Scenario Exercise

Page
12-73

Scenario 1 Questions

1. Based on these requirements, how will you configure the back-end array and the ISA Server computers that are members of the back-end array?

    a. At least two ISA Server computers must be deployed in the back-end array, and NLB must be configured for the array.

    b. The back-end ISA Server computers must be members of the *cohovineyard.com* domain in order to use Firewall clients and restrict user access.

    c. Create a perimeter network that includes the perimeter network IP addresses. Create a network rule between Internal network and the perimeter network. The network rule will define a route relationship between the two networks.

    d. Configure an access rules that enables the MS Firewall Storage and the MS Firewall Control protocols from the front-end ISA Server computers to the Configuration Storage server.

    e. Configure an access rule that enables the MS Firewall Control and the RPC (All Interfaces) protocols from the to the Configuration Storage server to the front-end ISA Server computers.

    f. Configure access rules allowing access from the Internal network to the External network using HTTP, HTTPS, and FTP.

    g. Configure an access rule enabling access to the Web server on the perimeter network for the internal network clients.

    h. Obtain and install a certificate on each of the back-end array ISA Server computers that will be used to secure access to the OWA site.

    i. Configure secure Web publishing rule that allows access to the OWA site.

    j. Configure access rules that enable the Web server in the perimeter network hosting the secure Web site to join the *cohovineyard.com* domain.

2. How will you configure the back-end array and the ISA Server computers that are members of the front-end array?

    a. At least two ISA Server computers must be deployed in the front-end array, and NLB must be configured for the array.

    b. Configure the front-end array to use SSL authentication and configure the ISA Server computers in the front-end array with a root certificate.

    c. Configure access rules allowing access from the Internal network to the External network using HTTP, HTTPS, and FTP.

    d. Publish the public Web site on the perimeter network. Allow anonymous access.

    e. Obtain and install a certificate used to secure access to the secure Web site on both front-end ISA Server computers.

    f. Configure a secure Web publishing rule to publish the Coho Vineyard Secure Web site for Internet users.

    g. Configure a secure Web publishing rule that publishes the OWA site.

3. What other configurations must you enable?

    a. Configure the Configuration Storage server to certificate-based authentication for the ISA Server computers in the front-end array.

    b. Configure the Web server hosting the secure Web site to be a member of the cohovine-yard.com domain.

    c. Obtain and install a certificate on the Web server hosting the secure Web site.

    d. Obtain and install a Web Server certificate on the Exchange server for the OWA Web site. Configure IIS on the Exchange server to require SSL on the virtual directories used by OWA.

Part 2
Prepare for the Exam

13 Planning and Installing ISA Server 2004 (1.0)

The old adage "measure twice, cut once" applies to the installation of any network infrastructure. When dealing with the important areas of network security that ISA Server 2004 addresses, proper care in the planning process is even more important. Implementing a well-thought-out plan will produce far better results for your organization than a more *ad hoc* installation of ISA Server 2004.

One of the first questions you need to address is, "What problems are we trying to solve by implementing ISA Server 2004?" You should have a thorough understanding of the current environment and how ISA Server 2004 will fit into that environment. The last thing you want is to discover that some heretofore unknown mission-critical application on the network suddenly broke the moment your new ISA Server 2004 installation became active. You should ensure that the hardware on which you install ISA Server 2004 is appropriate. Plan ahead and assume that the load on the ISA Server will only increase over the coming years. If you spend a little more on provisioning a server now, you're likely to save the organization more money in the long run. A well-provisioned server is less likely to need replacement in several years than one that currently meets only the minimum specifications. Finally, your choice of whether to implement ISA Server 2004, Standard Edition, or Enterprise Edition will depend very much on the feature set your organization requires. For the most part, the products are very similar, but there are several advantages to the Enterprise Edition that are worth the extra licensing cost if you know that you will be able to implement them effectively.

Testing Skills and Suggested Practices

The skills that you need to successfully master the Planning and Installing ISA Server 2004 objective domain of Exam 70-350, *Implementing Microsoft Internet Security and Acceleration (ISA) Server 2004*, include:

- Planning and Installing ISA Server 2004.
  - ❏ Practice 1: Install and configure a virtual machine using Microsoft VirtualPC. You have the option of using a separate computer to do this, but most candidates find it easier to use virtual machines for practice labs rather than having separate computers. A 45-day evaluation version of VirtualPC can be obtained from *http://www.microsoft.com/virtualpc/*. The virtual machine that you create should have three separate network adapters and should run the evaluation version of Microsoft Windows Server 2003 Enterprise Edition. If you do not have the Windows Server 2003 Enterprise Edition evaluation version, you

can obtain it from Microsoft by visiting *http://www.microsoft.com/ windowsserver2003/evaluation/trial/evalkit.mspx*. Label one network adapter EXTERNAL and give it the IP Address 10.10.10.1, subnet mask 255.255.255.0. Label the second network adapter PERIMETER and give it the IP address 172.16.10.1, subnet mask 255.255.255.0. Label the third network adapter INTERNAL and give it the IP address 192.168.10.1, subnet mask 255.255.255.0.

❑ Practice 2: On the computer you installed in Practice 1, install the SMTP component of Microsoft Internet Information Services (IIS) 6.0. Once this is completed, install the evaluation version of ISA Server 2004. Be sure when installing to correctly designate the external interface of the server as the network adapter named EXTERNAL.

❑ Practice 3: Perform a packet capture on your network using the Network Monitor utility. Make a note of the different protocols in use. While the packet capture is in process, navigate to a Web site and check your e-mail. See what impact this has on the protocols captured by Network Monitor.

■ Deploy ISA Server 2004.

❑ Practice 1: Examine the ISA Server installation logs located in the %Windir%\Temp directory of the computer you installed ISA Server 2004 on earlier. Compare each log and determine the function of each based on its contents.

❑ Practice 2: Install an enterprise management configuration server on a member server in your domain. You will be unable to install this software on either a domain controller or a stand-alone server.

❑ Practice 3: Install ISA Server 2004, Enterprise Edition. When installing, you will need to enter the address of the enterprise management configuration server installed in Practice 2.

Further Reading

This section lists supplemental readings by objective. We recommend that you study these sources thoroughly before taking this exam.

Objective 1.1   Review ISA Server 2004 Online help, "Deployment Scenarios."

A list of port numbers and their associated protocols: *http://www.iana.org/ assignments/port-numbers*

Objective 1.2   Review ISA Server 2004 Online help, "Installation and Upgrade."

Microsoft Corporation, ISA Server 2004 Quickstart Guide: *http://down load.microsoft.com/download/3/7/b/37b0cbc4-e578-4082-a779-de4fbe876f06/ ISA2004SE_quickstartguide-Rev%201%2003.doc*

Microsoft Corporation, ISA Server 2004 Configuration Guide: *http://down load.microsoft.com/download/3/7/b/37b0cbc4-e578-4082-a779-de4fbe876f06/ ISA2004SE_configguide-Rev%201%2003.doc*

Objective 1.3   Review ISA Server 2004 Online help, "Installation and Upgrade."

Microsoft Corporation, ISA Server 2004 Quickstart Guide: *http://down load.microsoft.com/download/3/7/b/37b0cbc4-e578-4082-a779-de4fbe876f06/ ISA2004SE_quickstartguide-Rev%201%2003.doc*

Microsoft Corporation, ISA Server 2004 Configuration Guide: *http://down load.microsoft.com/download/3/7/b/37b0cbc4-e578-4082-a779-de4fbe876f06/ ISA2004SE_configguide-Rev%201%2003.doc*

Plan an ISA Server 2004 Deployment

Part of the planning process for ISA Server 2004 deployment is performing an analysis of the pre-existing network environment. This analysis should cover several broad areas: existing network infrastructure and usage patterns, the caching and firewall requirements that implementing ISA Server 2004 will address, and the way that existing clients will integrate with the new security infrastructure.

The first step in gaining an accurate picture of how the current network infrastructure functions is to generate a baseline of the current network traffic. A baseline is a snapshot of the network that describes typical usage over a period of time. Generating a baseline will provide you information about which applications are running on the internal network, what protocols these applications use, and what access to external locations is required. Also important is gaining an understanding of how the organization's current virtual private network (VPN) setup works. The answers to the questions "What type of VPN connections exist to branch offices?" and "What sort of VPN access to remote clients is required?" will affect your eventual ISA Server 2004 deployment.

Next, you need to get an understanding of the expectations that exist for ISA Server 2004 in terms of its use as a proxy and as a firewall. You need to determine what requirements exist for both forward and reverse proxies on the network. You also have to determine the firewall requirements of the network. The primary factor that will influence the configuration of the firewall is which protocols and applications need access to the perimeter network (also known as a demilitarized zone, or DMZ, and a screened subnet) and external networks through the firewall.

Objective 1.1 Questions

1. Your organization has two existing hardware-based firewalls providing protection to the network. These existing firewalls are configured so that one acts as a front-end firewall and the other acts as a back-end firewall. A perimeter network exists between the two. To reduce the organization's Internet costs, in the future you will cache Web content. To this end you wish to deploy ISA Server 2004 on the perimeter network purely as a Web-caching-only server. In this situation, what is the minimum number of network interfaces required on the server that will host ISA Server 2004? (Choose the correct answer.)

   A. Three.

   B. Four.

   C. Two.

   D. One.

   E. Zero.

2. Your organization is located on a large campus several miles in diameter. Currently your organization's Internet connection enters the campus at Building A. Building A has a secured server room that hosts an ISA Server 2004 computer. The ISA Server 2004 computer is configured as an edge firewall with three network interfaces. One interface is configured as the connection to the perimeter network. Presently there are two Web servers and a mail server located on the perimeter network. Unlike the ISA Server 2004 computer, which is located in Building A, the perimeter network servers are located in Building B. Buildings A and B are connected via CDDI. In the last two hours, construction work between Buildings A and B has cut the CDDI cable. It will be two weeks before this connection can be restored. In the meantime, a 128-kilobit microwave connection has been implemented between Buildings A and B. You have investigated the possibility of moving the perimeter network servers to Building A, but it will be several days before this can be arranged. Presently the low-bandwidth microwave link is being flooded by traffic from the Internet to the two Web servers. Which of the following presents a way that you could use the ISA Server in Building A to ameliorate this problem with a minimum of administrative effort? (Choose the correct answer.)

   A. Install IIS 6.0 on the ISA Server computer and migrate the two Web sites from the servers in Building B.

   B. Install ISA Server 2004 in Building B and configure a site-to-site VPN between it and the computer running ISA Server in Building A.

   C. Install ISA Server 2004 in Building B and configure it to perform reverse caching for the two Web servers.

    D. Configure the ISA Server 2004 computer in Building A to perform reverse caching for the content hosted on the two Web servers in Building B.

3. Your organization is spread out across Australia, with a head office located in Melbourne and branch offices located in Sydney, Brisbane, Adelaide, and Perth. Currently each branch office has four dedicated modem lines. One modem line connects to the head office in Melbourne, and the other modem lines are for direct connections to the other branch offices. Modems are configured to dial automatically whenever data from one location needs to be forwarded to another. The organization is connected to the Internet only at the Melbourne head office using a digital subscriber line (DSL).

Your boss has called you in and asked you to come up with a plan to improve communication with the branch offices. It is important that you reduce the organization's reliance on long-distance modem calls. It is also important that in any new plan the computers at the branch offices are secure from the Internet. Users from the head office should be able to connect to branch offices as easily as users from branch offices connect to the head office. It is preferable that users at branch offices be able to browse the Internet at a reasonable speed, though this is not a necessity. Which of the following recommendations should you make? (Choose the correct answer.)

    A. Remove the modems. Install ISA Server at the Melbourne office. Install DSL connections at the branch offices. Configure a VPN server on a Windows Server 2003 computer at the head office. Configure all hosts at branch offices as VPN clients and configure them to connect to the VPN server at the head office.

    B. Remove the modems. Install ISA Server at the Melbourne office. Install DSL connections at the branch offices. Configure ISA Server at the Melbourne office to function as a VPN server. Configure all hosts at branch offices as VPN clients and configure them to connect to the VPN server at the head office.

    C. Remove the modems. Install DSL connections at each branch office. Install ISA Server 2004 at the head office and at the branch offices. Configure each ISA Server as a VPN server and configure site-to-site VPNs between each ISA Server at the branch offices and the ISA Server computer at the head office.

    D. Remove the modems. Install ISA Server at the head office and at branch office locations. Configure the ISA Server at the head office as a VPN server. Configure all clients at branch office locations as VPN clients that are able to connect to the VPN server at the head office.

4. You are planning the proxy and caching configuration for a series of scientific bases to be located in Antarctica. The primary base is connected to a satellite Internet link. Several smaller research stations are connected to the primary base via land line. Each of the smaller research stations employs 20 scientists. The primary base has a staff of 100 scientists. All scientists require access to hosts on the World Wide Web. Which of the following scenarios might you use to make the scientists' access to the World Wide

Web most efficient in terms of minimizing the amount of content that needs to be downloaded from the Internet or transmitted across the land lines? (Choose the correct answer.)

A. Install a single ISA Server 2004 server at the primary base. Configure all clients at the primary base and the research stations to use this server as their Web proxy.

B. Install a single ISA Server 2004 server at the primary base. Install a single ISA Server 2004 server at each research station. Configure clients at the primary base to use the ISA Server server at the primary base. Configure clients at each research station to use their local ISA Server computer. Configure each ISA Server computer to download frequently requested content from the Internet after hours.

C. Install a single ISA Server 2004 server at the primary base and a single ISA Server computer at each of the research stations. Configure the ISA Server computers at the research stations to forward all traffic requests to the ISA Server computers located at the primary base. Configure the ISA Server computer at the primary base to download frequently requested content from the Internet after hours. Configure all clients to use the ISA Server computer at the primary base as their Web proxy server.

D. Install a single ISA Server 2004 server at the primary base and a single ISA Server computer at each of the research stations. Configure the ISA Server computers at the research stations to forward all traffic requests to the ISA Server computer located at the primary base. Configure the ISA Server computer at the primary base to download frequently requested content from the Internet after hours. Configure clients to use their local ISA Server computer as their Web proxy server.

5. Contoso currently maintains a bank of 40 modems at headquarters that remote salespeople connect to using laptops while traveling around the country. Recently, a consultant has identified the costs involved in supporting the modem bank and the associated long-distance changes as an area that can be rationalized. You have the national telephone number of an Internet service provider (ISP) that has a point-of-presence in each location that Contoso salespeople travel to. How could you use ISA Server 2004 to rationalize the costs of remote access to the Contoso network? (Choose the correct answer.)

A. Install the Firewall Client software on each salesperson's laptop. Configure each laptop with the dial-up information for the national ISP. Instruct salespeople to connect to the ISP when working remotely.

B. Configure each salesperson's laptop as a SecureNAT client of the ISA Server computer. Configure each laptop with the dial-up information for the national ISP. Instruct salespeople to connect to the ISP when working remotely.

C. Configure each salesperson's laptop as a Web proxy client of the ISA Server computer. Configure each laptop with the dial-up information for the national ISP. Instruct salespeople to connect to the ISP when working remotely.

D. Configure the ISA Server computer as a VPN server and configure each of the laptops as a VPN client. Configure each laptop with the dial-up information for the national ISP. Instruct salespeople to connect to the ISP when working remotely and then to launch the VPN connection.

6. Which of the following utilities can be used on a perimeter network to audit the protocols that are currently in use? (Choose the correct answer.)

A. Ping

B. Arp

C. Netstat

D. Performance Monitor

E. Network Monitor

7. You are the network administrator for Tailspin Toys. You have recently installed an ISA Server 2004 computer as an edge firewall and have configured all the Microsoft Windows XP Professional computers on your network as Web proxy clients. Until recently, you used a Software Update Services (SUS) server on your internal network to keep a list of approved updates. Although you continue to manage the update list, none of the Windows XP Professional clients on your network has been able to download updates since you installed the ISA Server 2004 computer. Which of the following steps can you take to ensure that Windows XP Professional clients are able to receive operating system updates while retaining network security? (Choose the correct answer.)

A. Configure the SUS Server computer to download and store updates locally. Configure the Windows XP clients to download updates from the SUS Server computer.

B. Configure a download job on the ISA Server computer to download recently released updates from the Windows Update Servers.

C. Install SUS on the ISA Server computer.

D. Remove the ISA Server computer.

8. You are going to implement ISA Server 2004 as an edge firewall for a small manufacturing company named Tailspin Toys. The ISA Server computer will be configured with three network interface cards (NICs). One NIC will be connected to the public Internet, the second to a perimeter network, and the third to the Tailspin Toys internal network. Two servers are located on the perimeter network. The first server runs IIS 6.0 and hosts Tailspin Toys' public Internet site. The public Internet has a section where clients can log on and view special pages over Secure Sockets Layer (SSL). The second server runs Windows Server 2003 and hosts the Post Office Protocol 3 (POP3) service. This allows Tailspin Toys employees to send and receive e-mail via the Internet. Employees using hosts on the internal network access e-mail using Microsoft Outlook Express. E-mail is

not accessed by employees from any other network location. Given this information, which Transmission Control Protocol/Internet Protocol (TCP/IP) ports need to be opened between the external network and the perimeter network on the ISA Server computer? (Choose all that apply.)

    A. 80

    B. 110

    C. 25

    D. 443

    E. 21

9. You are planning the implementation of ISA Server 2004 for a small publishing company that has 10 full-time employees. Authors who write books for the publishing company currently log on to a server running IIS 6.0 and upload their manuscripts to the server using Web-based Distributed Authoring and Versioning (WebDAV). Authentication is controlled via Integrated Windows Authentication, and each author has a local account on the server running IIS 6.0. There will be only two network interfaces on the server running ISA Server 2004; the server running IIS 6.0 will be located on the company's internal network. When you implement ISA Server 2004, which of the following ports will need to be accessible from the Internet to the server running IIS 6.0? (Choose the correct answer.)

    A. 21

    B. 25

    C. 80

    D. 443

    E. 110

10. You are planning a site-to-site VPN for Tailspin Toys. The site-to-site VPN will connect a branch office located in Volgograd with the head office located in Melbourne. After discussing the issue with your manager, you have come up with the following goals:

First Goal: Data transmitted over the VPN between Volgograd and Melbourne must be encrypted.

Second Goal: Data transmitted over the VPN between Volgograd and Melbourne must be protected against replay attacks.

Third Goal: Solution should function using Windows 2000 Advanced Server as an operating system platform for ISA Server 2004.

You decided to implement a VPN solution using Point-to-Point Tunneling Protocol (PPTP) and Microsoft Point-to-Point Encryption (MPPE). Which of your goals have you met? (Choose the correct answer.)

A. All three goals have been met.

B. The first and third goals have been met.

C. Only the first goal has been met.

D. The first goal has not been met. The second and third goals have been met.

E. None of the goals have been met.

11. Your organization has a single TCP/IP subnet used for the internal network. You have an ISA Server 2004 computer configured as an edge firewall. The ISA Server computer is correctly configured with the following addresses for its internal network interface:

IP: 172.16.98.85

Subnet mask: 255.255.255.240

The computer hosting ISA Server 2004 is configured as a caching-only DNS server. You are attempting to configure a Windows XP Professional computer as a SecureNAT client. The TCP/IP configuration of the Windows XP Professional computer is shown here.

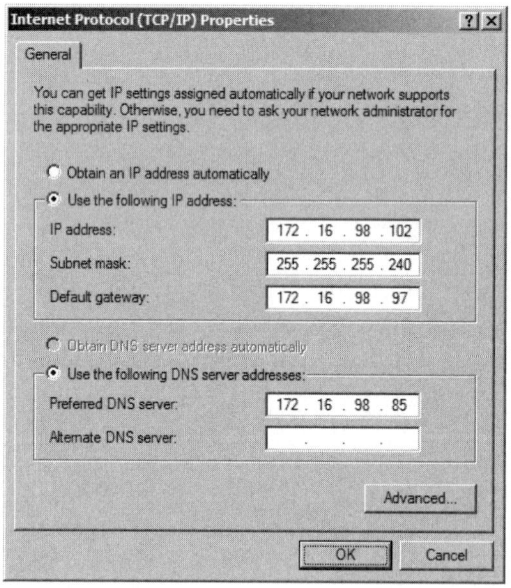

Currently the Windows XP Professional computer is without Internet connectivity. Which of the following modifications need to be made to the Windows XP Professional computer to allow it to connect to the Internet as a SecureNAT client? (Choose all that apply.)

   A. Change the IP address to 172.16.98.92.

   B. Change the IP address to 172.16.98.85.

   C. Change the default gateway to 172.16.98.81.

   D. Change the subnet mask to 255.255.255.224.

   E. Change the default gateway to 172.16.98.85.

12. You have configured an ISA Server 2004 computer on the Contoso internal network as an edge firewall. The ISA Server computer has the fully qualified domain name (FQDN) *isaserver.contoso.internal*. All clients on your network are running Windows XP Professional and Microsoft Internet Explorer 6. You want all clients on the Contoso internal network to have their Web proxy settings configured automatically. Which of the following steps do you need to take? (Choose two correct answers.)

   A. On the LAN settings page, click Automatically Detect Settings and Use Automatic Configuration Script.

   B. On the LAN settings page, click Use A Proxy Server For Your LAN.

   C. In the address box, enter the address **http://isaserver.contoso.internal/ array.dll?Get.Routing.Script**.

   D. In the address box, enter the address **http://isaserver.contoso.internal/ configuration.html**.

   E. In the address box, enter **isaserver.contoso.internal**. In the port box, enter the number **8080**.

13. You are the network administrator for Tailspin Toys. Tailspin Toys is a very large company located on a single campus. Employees need to be able to access the Internet on a continuous basis as part of their job function. You are planning to implement ISA Server 2004 as a caching and proxy server. You have the following three goals:

First Goal: Ensure that Tailspin Toys clients are able to access Internet content via ISA Server 2004 even if one of the ISA Server 2004 servers fails.

Second Goal: That clients are able to locate quickly which proxy and Web caching server is storing cached content.

Third Goal: That load will be distributed evenly between servers providing proxy and Web caching services.

You make the following decisions. You install ISA Server 2004, Standard Edition, on two Windows Server 2003 Enterprise Edition computers and configure them as Web caching servers. You manually configure network load balancing (NLB).

Which of your goals have you achieved? (Choose the correct answer.)

A. All three goals have been achieved.

B. The first and third goals have been achieved.

C. Only the first goal has been achieved.

D. The second and third goals have been achieved, but not the first.

E. None of the listed goals has been achieved.

14. You are considering implementing ISA Server 2004 for Contoso, Ltd., as an edge firewall. Currently Contoso uses a hardware-based firewall. Proxy and cache services are handled by Microsoft Proxy Server 2.0. Both the hardware-based firewall and the proxy server will eventually be replaced. Rather than switch all users at Contoso over to the new ISA Server computer at once, you wish to run a pilot program with a small percentage of the total users. You want to test the functionality of the Firewall Client software, ensure that users from each of the five departments at Contoso are able to use the new proxy and firewall solution, maintain network security, and not interrupt the functionality of other workers on the network. Which of the following steps should you consider implementing as a part of your pilot program? (Choose all that apply.)

A. Install the firewall client on every computer in the IT, Accounting, and HR departments and configure it to use the new ISA Server computer.

B. Install the Firewall Client on five computers each in the IT, Accounting, Management, HR, and Sales department. Configure the Firewall Client to use the new ISA Server computer.

C. Obtain a second public IP address from your ISP. Configure the ISA Server computer so that one interface is connected directly to the Internet and the second is connected to the internal network.

D. Install the ISA Server 2004 computer on the perimeter network as a back-end firewall.

E. Install the ISA Server 2004 computer on the internal network as a firewall in a branch office.

Objective 1.1 Answers

1.   **Correct Answers: D**

    A. Incorrect: To perform the Web-caching-only server role, ISA Server 2004 requires only a single network interface.

    B. Incorrect: To perform the Web-caching-only server role, ISA Server 2004 requires only a single network interface.

    C. Incorrect: To perform the Web-caching-only server role, ISA Server 2004 requires only a single network interface.

    D. Correct: To perform the Web-caching-only server role, ISA Server 2004 requires only a single network interface.

    E. Incorrect: To perform the Web-caching-only server role, ISA Server 2004 requires a single network interface. A server without any network interfaces is unable to communicate with the network and hence is unable to cache Web content for other hosts on the network.

2.   **Correct Answers: D**

    A. Incorrect: Although possible, this solution does not minimize administrative effort. Best practice also dictates that you not run a service like IIS 6.0 on the server running ISA Server 2004.

    B. Incorrect: This would not solve the problem of the low-bandwidth microwave link being flooded by Web server traffic.

    C. Incorrect: The same amount of Web server traffic will still travel across the low-bandwidth microwave link in this scenario, which doesn't solve the problem.

    D. Correct: By caching the content of the Web servers in Building B on the computer running ISA Server in Building A, you will reduce the amount of Internet traffic that needs to pass across the low-bandwidth microwave link.

3.   **Correct Answers: C**

    A. Incorrect: This will not protect the networks at the branch offices. This will also not allow the head office to connect to branch offices.

    B. Incorrect: This will not protect the networks at the branch offices. This will also not allow the head office to connect to branch offices.

    C. Correct: This will protect the networks at the branch offices and will allow the head office to connect to branch offices. It will remove the necessity to use modems as site connections, which will now occur over VPN. It has the added benefit of allowing users at the branch offices to connect to the Internet using their local ISA Server computer as a proxy and caching server.

D. Incorrect: Although this will protect the branch office sites, it will not allow the head office to connect to branch offices because no VPN servers exist at these locations.

4.   Correct Answers: D

A. Incorrect: Although this will minimize the amount of traffic downloaded from the Internet, it will not minimize the amount of Web traffic downloaded across the land lines.

B. Incorrect: Configuring the infrastructure in this manner could lead to the same content being downloaded from the Internet several times by ISA Server computers at different research stations. It is not the most efficient use of the land lines or of the primary research station's Internet connection.

C. Incorrect: Clients should use their local ISA Server computer, rather than the ISA Server computer located at the primary base. In this configuration, the ISA Server computers located at each research station will be ignored by their local clients.

D. Correct: This process is known as *Web proxy chaining* and allows the most efficient use of the organization's Internet and land-line links. If a client at a research station requests content, it will check the local ISA Server computer first. If the content isn't found there, the primary base server is checked. Finally, if the content isn't found, it is retrieved from the Internet. It will then be stored on the primary base server and the original research station server.

5.   Correct Answers: D

A. Incorrect: Configuring the laptops in this way will not allow remote salespeople access to the internal Contoso network.

B. Incorrect: Configuring the laptops in this way will not allow remote salespeople access to the internal Contoso network.

C. Incorrect: Configuring the laptops in this way will not allow remote salespeople access to the internal Contoso network.

D. Correct: ISA Server 2004 can function as a VPN server, which allows clients to access the internal network via the Internet. This is the perfect solution to the situation outlined in the question, as it will save on long-distance calls and will also enable Contoso to retire the modem bank.

6.   Correct Answers: E

A. Incorrect: Ping is used to determine whether or not connectivity exists between two hosts. It cannot be used to determine which protocols are currently in use on a perimeter network.

B. Incorrect: Arp is used to convert between Internet Protocol (IP) and media access control (MAC) addresses. It cannot be used to determine which protocols are currently in use on a perimeter network.

C. **Incorrect:** Netstat is used to display the current active connections made to a particular computer. Although it does provide some port information, it cannot be used to audit the protocols that are currently in use on a perimeter network.

D. **Incorrect:** Although Performance Monitor can provide information about selected protocols for which it has counters, it cannot be used to audit the protocols currently in use on a perimeter network.

E. **Correct:** Through the process of packet capture, Network Monitor can be used to provide information about protocols that are in use on a perimeter network.

7. **Correct Answers: A**

A. **Correct:** Background Intelligent Transfer Service (BITS), the protocol used by Windows Update to download updates, cannot authenticate against a proxy. The most practical solution is to store updates on the SUS server; that way, they are not being downloaded constantly over the Internet.

B. **Incorrect:** This process would not work because there is no way to tie the downloaded content to the SUS Server computer itself. It is better to download the content to the SUS server computer locally and then distribute to the Windows XP clients.

C. **Incorrect:** Although this could be done, it would not resolve the problem with clients being unable to download updates from the Windows Update Servers.

D. **Incorrect:** Although clients would be able to receive updates, this would not provide the internal network with any level of security.

8. **Correct Answers: A, C, and D**

A. **Correct:** Port 80 will need to be opened to support Web site traffic between hosts on the Internet and the Tailspin Toys public Internet site, hosted on the perimeter network.

B. **Incorrect:** Although a POP3 server is located on the perimeter network, access to POP3 is not required from the Internet. Access to POP3, which uses Port 110, is required only from hosts on the internal network.

C. **Correct:** For mail servers on the Internet to transfer mail to the Tailspin Toys mail server located on the perimeter network, Port 25 will need to be open between the Internet and the perimeter network.

D. **Correct:** The question states that some aspects of the Tailspin Toys Web site are accessible via SSL. Port 443 provides Hypertext Transfer Protocol/Secure Sockets Layer (HTTP/SSL) functionality.

E. **Incorrect:** Port 21 is used for File Transfer Protocol (FTP). Hosts on the Internet do not require FTP access to hosts on the perimeter network.

9.   Correct Answers: C

A. Incorrect: WebDAV, a technology that allows authors to upload and download files from a server running IIS 6.0, only requires that Port 80, used for HTTP, be open. Port 21 is used for FTP and is not required in this case.

B. Incorrect: WebDAV, a technology that allows authors to upload and download files from a server running IIS 6.0, only requires that Port 80, used for HTTP, be open. Port 25 is used for Simple Mail Transfer Protocol (SMTP) and hence is not required in this case.

C. Correct: WebDAV, a technology that allows authors to upload and download files from a server running IIS 6.0, only requires that Port 80, used for HTTP, be open.

D. Incorrect: WebDAV, a technology that allows authors to upload and download files from a server running IIS 6.0, only requires that Port 80, used for HTTP, be open. Port 443 is used for Hypertext Transfer Protocol Secure (HTTPS). HTTPS is not required in this case, as no mention has been made of SSL connections.

E. Incorrect: WebDAV, a technology that allows authors to upload and download files from a server running IIS 6.0, only requires that Port 80, used for HTTP, be open. Port 110 is used for POP3 and is not required in this case.

10.   Correct Answers: B

A. Incorrect: In choosing to use PPTP and MPPE, the first goal, ensuring that data transmitted over the VPN is encrypted, has been met. PPTP and MPPE can be used with ISA Server 2004 installed on Windows 2000 Advanced Server. PPTP and MPPE cannot be used to protect against replay attacks, so the second goal is not met.

B. Correct: In choosing to use PPTP and MPPE, the first goal, ensuring that data transmitted over the VPN is encrypted, has been met. PPTP and MPPE can be used with ISA Server 2004 installed on Windows 2000 Advanced Server. PPTP and MPPE cannot be used to protect against replay attacks, so the second goal is not met.

C. Incorrect: In choosing to use PPTP and MPPE, the primary goal, ensuring that data transmitted over the VPN is encrypted, has been met. PPTP and MPPE can be used with ISA Server 2004 installed on Windows 2000 Advanced Server. PPTP and MPPE cannot be used to protect against replay attacks, hence the second goal is not met.

D. Incorrect: In choosing to use PPTP and MPPE, the first goal, ensuring that data transmitted over the VPN is encrypted, has been met. PPTP and MPPE can be used with ISA Server 2004 installed on Windows 2000 Advanced Server. PPTP and MPPE cannot be used to protect against replay attacks, hence the second goal is not met.

E. Incorrect: In choosing to use PPTP and MPPE, the first goal, ensuring that data transmitted over the VPN is encrypted, has been met. PPTP and MPPE can be used with ISA Server 2004 installed on Windows 2000 Advanced Server. PPTP and MPPE cannot be used to protect against replay attacks, hence the second goal is not met.

11.   Correct Answers: A & E

A. Correct: The IP address of the Windows XP Professional computer is currently on a different subnet from that of the ISA Server 2004 computer's internal interface. As the question specifies that a single TCP/IP subnet is in use, the currently assigned IP address is incorrect.

B. Incorrect: This is the IP address of the ISA Server's internal interface; it cannot be assigned to the Windows XP Professional computer.

C. Incorrect: To configure a client as a SecureNAT client, you need to change the default gateway so that it is set to the ISA Server's internal interface.

D. Incorrect: The question states that the ISA Server's internal interface is correctly configured. This means that the internal network utilizes a subnet mask of 255.255.255.240 and that this should not be changed.

E. Correct: To configure a client as a SecureNAT client, you need to change the default gateway so that it is set to the ISA Server's internal interface.

12.   Correct Answers: A and C

A. Correct: This is the first step in allowing proxy configuration to occur automatically.

B. Incorrect: If you choose the Use A Proxy Server For Your LAN option, the proxy configuration will not be handled automatically.

C. Correct: This is the location of the configuration script that is used to automatically configure Web proxy settings.

D. Incorrect: This is the incorrect URL for the configuration script. The correct URL is *http://isaserver.contoso.internal/array.dll?Get.Routing.Script.*

E. Incorrect: You would use this option if you did not want the proxy configuration to be handled automatically.

13.   Correct Answers: B

A. Incorrect: In configuring NLB for the two servers manually, the first and third goals have been achieved. Unless ISA Server 2004, Enterprise Edition, was used, the second goal of being able to locate which server has cached particular content is unable to be achieved.

B. **Correct:** In configuring NLB for the two servers manually, the first and third goals have been achieved. Unless ISA Server 2004, Enterprise Edition, was used, the second goal of being able to locate which server has cached particular content is unable to be achieved.

C. **Incorrect:** In configuring NLB for the two servers manually, the first and third goals have been achieved. Unless ISA Server 2004, Enterprise Edition, was used, the second goal of being able to locate which server has cached particular content is unable to be achieved.

D. **Incorrect:** In configuring NLB for the two servers manually, the first and third goals have been achieved. Unless ISA Server 2004, Enterprise Edition, was used, the second goal of being able to locate which server has cached particular content is unable to be achieved.

E. **Incorrect:** In configuring NLB for the two servers manually, the first and third goals have been achieved. Unless ISA Server 2004, Enterprise Edition, was used, the second goal of being able to locate which server has cached particular content is unable to be achieved.

14. **Correct Answers: B and C**

A. **Incorrect:** This will not test the functionality of all departments at Contoso, only those of all users in three departments. Pilot programs should use a small number of users from each department, not all users in several departments.

B. **Correct:** Pilot programs should use a small number of users from each department so that the project is tested under a variety of conditions.

C. **Correct:** During the pilot program, you will need to run both the original and the new firewall and proxy solution in parallel. If you ran the ISA Server computer on the perimeter network, the firewall would not be tested under the conditions it would be used in when the project went live.

D. **Incorrect:** During the pilot program, you will need to run both the original and the new firewall and proxy solution in parallel. If you ran the ISA Server computer on the perimeter network, the firewall would not be tested under the conditions it would be used in when the project went live.

E. **Incorrect:** During the pilot program, you will need to run both the original and the new firewall and proxy solution in parallel. If you ran the ISA Server computer on the perimeter network, the firewall would not be tested under the conditions it would be used in when the project went live.

Assess and Configure the Operating System, Hardware, and Network Services

The next step after completing the planning process is to assess and prepare the hardware, network, and operating system environment for the installation of ISA Server 2004. A correctly configured operating system is the bedrock upon which you build a solid ISA Server 2004 deployment. Understanding how to configure the operating system for ISA Server 2004 correctly means understanding how to analyze the operating system requirements and check that network interfaces on the server are prepared. You will need to make sure that services and components required by ISA Server 2004, such as the SMTP service, need to be installed and running prior to installation. You should also ensure that the hardware that ISA Server 2004 will run on is adequately provisioned for the service to run. Without the proper preparation, the installation of ISA Server 2004 could fail or the performance of the server might be so lackluster that implementation provides more of a hindrance than a help to the organization.

Objective 1.2 Questions

1. Your organization is going to implement ISA Server 2004 at one central and five branch office locations. Connections between branch and central offices will be via site-to-site VPN connection. These VPN connections will utilize L2TP and IPSec, with IPSec being authenticated via pre-shared keys. Which of the following ISA Server configurations will support this type of VPN connection? (Choose all that apply.)

    A. ISA Server 2004, Enterprise Edition, installed on Windows Server 2003, Enterprise Edition.

    B. ISA Server 2004, Standard Edition, installed on Windows Server 2003, Enterprise Edition.

    C. ISA Server 2004, Standard Edition, installed on Windows 2000 Server.

    D. ISA Server 2004 Enterprise Edition, installed on Windows 2000 Advanced Server.

    E. ISA Server 2004, Standard Edition, installed on Windows 2000 Advanced Server.

2. You are planning on installing ISA Server 2004 on a computer running Windows 2000 Server. The Windows 2000 Server is patched to Service Pack 3. Prior to the installation of ISA Server 2004, what steps should you take to prepare the Windows 2000 Server computer? (Choose all that apply.)

    A. Install IIS 5.0 on the Windows 2000 Server computer.

    B. Install SUS Server on the Windows 2000 Server computer.

    C. Install Service Pack 4 or later on the Windows 2000 Server computer.

    D. Install Internet Explorer 6 or later on the Windows 2000 Server computer.

    E. Install the .NET Framework 1.1 or later on the Windows 2000 Server computer.

3. Which of the following statements about network interfaces on an ISA Server 2004 computer functioning as an edge firewall are correct? (Choose two correct answers.)

    A. The ISA Server's external interface must use statically assigned IP address information.

    B. The ISA Server's external interface can use dynamically assigned IP address information.

    C. The ISA Server's internal network interface can use dynamically assigned IP address information.

    D. The ISA Server's internal network interface must use statically assigned IP address information.

4. You are preparing your server's external interface for the installation of ISA Server 2004 and have run into some problems. Prior to the installation of ISA Server 2004, you were unable to use the external interface connection to download the latest updates to Windows Server 2003 from the Windows Update servers. The TCP/IP Properties of the external interface are shown here.

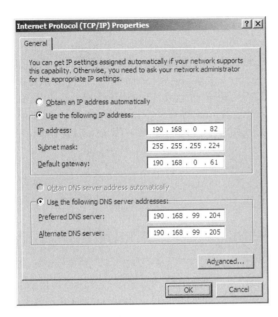

Which of the following changes could you make to the IP address configuration of the external interface to resolve the connectivity problem?

A. Change the subnet mask to 255.255.255.240.

B. Change the subnet mask to 255.255.255.192.

C. Change the IP address to 190.168.0.66.

D. Change the primary DNS server address to 190.168.0.74.

E. Change the default gateway address to 190.168.0.65.

5. You are planning the installation of ISA Server 2004 on a Windows Server 2003 computer. ISA Server 2004 will be supporting the edge firewall role. You want to install the Message Screener component so that you can filter incoming and outgoing e-mail based on keywords and attachments. Which of the following Windows Server 2003 components must be installed prior to installing the Message Screener component of ISA Server 2004? (Choose the correct answer.)

A. Certificate Services

B. E-Mail Services

    C. ASP.NET

    D. Message Queuing

    E. SMTP Service

6. As part of an ISA Server 2004 pilot program, you will be installing ISA Server 2004 on an older computer running Windows 2000 Server. The ISA Server computer will function as an edge firewall. If the pilot program is successful, you will be allocated the funds by your manager to purchase a newer, better provisioned server. Presently you have the budget to improve some of the hardware on the older test Windows 2000 Server computer. The test server has the following specifications: 300 MHz Pentium II CPU; 256 MB RAM; One 100 Mb NIC; NTFS-formatted hard disk drive with 1.5 GB free space available. Which of the following components do you need to upgrade to meet the minimum requirements for running ISA Server 2004? (Choose all that apply.)

    A. Add a second NIC.

    B. Upgrade to 512 MB RAM.

    C. Add a 10 GB hard disk drive.

    D. Upgrade the CPU to a Pentium III 600 MHz.

    E. Upgrade to Windows Server 2003.

7. You are about to begin deploying eight ISA Server Enterprise Edition computers. Prior to installing these computers, you wish to set up an enterprise configuration storage server. Which of the following computers would make a suitable host for an ISA Server 2004 enterprise configuration storage server? (Choose all that apply.)

    A. Windows Server 2003 domain controller

    B. Windows Server 2003 stand-alone server

    C. Windows Server 2003 member server

    D. Windows 2000 Server domain controller

    E. Windows 2000 Server member server

8. You are preparing to deploy 10 ISA Server computers at a state university. You want to be able to manage all these servers centrally. To do this, you must install a configuration storage server. Which of the following are properties of an ISA Server 2004 configuration storage server? (Choose all that apply.)

    A. A configuration storage server must be a member of an Active Directory directory service domain.

    B. You must install a configuration storage server before installing the second ISA Server 2004 Enterprise Edition computer in an array.

C. You must install a configuration storage server prior to installing the first ISA Server 2004 Enterprise Edition computer in an array.

D. A configuration storage server cannot be installed on the same computer as ISA Server 2004, Enterprise Edition.

E. You can install a configuration storage server without installing ISA Server services as long as it is installed on a domain controller.

Objective 1.2 Answers

1.   Correct Answers: A and B

    A. Correct: ISA Server 2004, Enterprise Edition, installed on Windows Server 2003, Enterprise Edition, supports the use of L2TP and IPSec with preshared keys for VPN.

    B. Correct: ISA Server 2004, Standard Edition, installed on Windows Server 2003, Enterprise Edition, supports the use of L2TP and IPSec with pre-shared keys for VPN.

    C. Incorrect: When ISA Server 2004 is installed on Windows 2000 Server, L2TP and IPSec using pre-shared keys are not supported.

    D. Incorrect: When either edition of ISA Server 2004 is installed on Windows 2000 Advanced Server, L2TP and IPSec using pre-shared keys are not supported.

    E. Incorrect: When either version of ISA Server 2004 is installed on Windows 2000 Advanced Server, L2TP and IPSec using pre-shared keys are not supported.

2.   Correct Answers: C and D

    A. Incorrect: IIS 5.0 is not required for the installation of ISA Server 2004.

    B. Incorrect: SUS Server is used to distribute updates and service packs to computers on the local network. It is not required for the installation of ISA Server 2004.

    C. Correct: Service Pack 4 or later must be installed on a Windows 2000 Server computer prior to the installation of ISA Server 2004.

    D. Correct: Internet Explorer 6 or later must be installed on a Windows 2000 Server computer prior to the installation of ISA Server 2004.

    E. Incorrect: The .NET framework does not need to be installed on a computer running Windows 2000 Server to support the installation of ISA Server 2004.

3.   Correct Answers: B and D

    A. Incorrect: The external interface on an ISA Server 2004 computer functioning as an edge firewall can use dynamically assigned IP address information.

    B. Correct: The external interface on an ISA Server 2004 computer functioning as an edge firewall can use dynamically assigned IP address information.

    C. Incorrect: The internal and perimeter network interfaces of an ISA Server 2004 server functioning as an edge firewall must have statically assigned IP address information.

    D. Correct: The internal and perimeter network interfaces of an ISA Server 2004 server functioning as an edge firewall must have statically assigned IP address information.

4.   Correct Answers: E

   A. Incorrect: Changing the subnet mask to this value would still mean that the IP address and default gateway were on different TCP/IP subnets. This would not resolve the connectivity problem.

   B. Incorrect: Changing the subnet mask to this value would still mean that the IP address and the default gateway were on different TCP/IP subnets. This would not resolve the connectivity problem.

   C. Incorrect: This would not resolve the connectivity problem as the IP address and default gateways would still be on different TCP/IP subnets.

   D. Incorrect: This would not resolve the connectivity problem as the IP address and default gateways would still be on different TCP/IP subnets. Also, the question does not hint at problems with DNS resolution.

   E. Correct: Changing the default gateway address to 190.168.0.65 would mean that the IP address and the default gateway are now on the same TCP/IP subnet. Of the solutions presented, this is the only one that meets this particular goal and hence is the only one likely to resolve the described problem.

5.   Correct Answers: E

   A. Incorrect: The Certificate Services component allows Windows Server 2003 to function as a Certificate Authority. This functionality is not required to install the Message Screener component of ISA Server 2004.

   B. Incorrect: The E-Mail Services component allows Windows Server 2003 to function as a simple POP3 server. Although POP3 is mail-related, it is the SMTP service component, not the POP3 service component, that is required for the Message Screener component of ISA Server 2004 to be installed.

   C. Incorrect: The ASP.NET allows Windows Server 2003 to run ASP.NET application. This functionality is not required to install the Message Screener component of ISA Server 2004.

   D. Incorrect: The Message Queuing component of Windows Server 2003 provides guaranteed message delivery, efficient routing, security, and transactional support. Although mail-related, only the SMTP service, which is separate from the messaging queuing component, is required for the Message Screener component of ISA Server 2004 to be installed.

   E. Correct: The SMTP Service component of IIS must be installed prior to installing the Message Screener component of ISA Server 2004.

6. **Correct Answers: A and D**

   A. **Correct:** To function as an edge firewall, ISA Server 2004 will require at least two network cards.

   B. **Incorrect:** The minimum required amount of RAM for ISA Server 2004 is 256 MB of RAM, which is currently installed in the test Windows 2000 Server computer.

   C. **Incorrect:** ISA Server 2004 only requires 150 MB of hard disk space. Currently there is 10 times that amount available, so a new 10 GB hard disk drive is not required.

   D. **Correct:** The minimum processor requirement for ISA Server 2004 is a 550 MHz Pentium III. The current 300 MHz Pentium II is not powerful enough and must be upgraded.

   E. **Incorrect:** ISA Server 2004 retains almost all the functionality on the Windows 2000 platform as it has on Windows Server 2003.

7. **Correct Answers: C and E**

   A. **Incorrect:** The enterprise configuration storage server software cannot be installed on a domain controller.

   B. **Incorrect:** The enterprise configuration storage server software must be installed on a server that is a member of a domain.

   C. **Correct:** The enterprise configuration storage server software must be installed on a server that is a member of a domain.

   D. **Incorrect:** The enterprise configuration storage server software cannot be installed on a domain controller.

   E. **Correct:** The enterprise configuration storage server software must be installed on a server that is a member of a domain. This can be either a Windows Server 2003 member server or a Windows 2000 member server.

8. **Correct Answers: A and B**

   A. **Correct:** Configuration storage servers store ISA Server 2004 Enterprise Edition configuration within Active Directory. Although the ISA Server computers themselves don't need to be members of a domain, the configuration storage server does.

   B. **Correct:** When you install the first ISA Server 2004 computer in an array, you have the option of selecting a pre-existing configuration storage server or installing one. The second ISA Server 2004 computer in an array must have access to the configuration storage server used by the first ISA Server 2004 computer in the array.

C. **Incorrect:** You can install a configuration storage server at the same time as you install the first ISA Server 2004 Enterprise Edition computer in an array.

D. **Incorrect:** You can install a configuration storage server at the same time as you install the first ISA Server 2004 Enterprise Edition computer in an array.

E. **Incorrect:** A server can function as a configuration storage server without having to install ISA Server services such as the firewall, VPN server, and proxy and Web caching services. However, the enterprise configuration storage server cannot be installed on a domain controller.

Objective 1.3

Deploy ISA Server 2004

To complete the Deploy ISA Server 2004 objective of the 70-350 exam successfully, you need to have an in-depth understanding of the ways in which ISA Server 2004 can be deployed. You need to understand how to migrate configuration data from a pre-existing ISA Server 2000 installation to ISA Server 2004. You also need to understand what upgrades you must make to Windows 2000 to allow for the successful installation of ISA Server 2004. You need to understand the process by which you install ISA Server 2004, including how to perform an unattended installation. You need to have an understanding of the differences involved between installing the standard and enterprise versions of ISA Server 2004. Finally, you must be able to verify that the installation of ISA Server 2004 has occurred without any problems, generate performance data for a post-installation baseline, and prepare configuration backups in the event of server failure.

Objective 1.3 Questions

1. Contoso, Ltd. has a Windows 2000 Advanced Server computer located on its screened subnet running ISA Server 2000 with Service Pack 1. The Windows 2000 Advanced Server computer is patched to Service Pack 3. Its hardware includes 256 MB of RAM, 5 GB of free disk space, and a 600 MHz Pentium III CPU.

Management at Contoso has decided to upgrade this server to ISA Server 2004 while using as much of the existing hardware as possible. Avoiding unnecessary administrative effort, which of the following steps must be taken before the upgrade can occur? (Choose the correct answer.)

   A. Upgrade Windows 2000 Advanced Server to Windows Server 2003, Enterprise Edition.

   B. Install Service Pack 4 or higher on the Windows 2000 Advanced Server computer.

   C. Upgrade the processor to a 1.2 GHz Pentium IV.

   D. Upgrade the server so that it has 512 MB of RAM.

   E. Install ISA Server 2000 Service Pack 2.

2. Tailspin Toys has an ISA 2000 Server computer that is to be decommissioned. A new computer installed with Windows Server 2003 and ISA Server 2004 will replace the original ISA 2000 Server computer. The configuration will be migrated using the ISA Server Migration Wizard, which creates an .xml file with the ISA 2000 configuration information that will be imported to the ISA Server 2004 computer. Which of the following settings will be migrated when this technique is used? (Choose the correct answer.)

   A. The IP address of the external network adapter of the original ISA Server 2000 computer

   B. Bandwidth rules applied to the original ISA Server 2000 computer

   C. Logging configuration used on the original ISA Server 2000 computer

   D. System access control lists (SACLs) used on the original ISA Server 2000 computer

   E. Report configuration used on the original ISA Server 2000 computer

3. You are preparing to install four ISA Server 2004 computers using an unattended installation. The ISA Server 2004 media will be located on each computer's CD-ROM E drive. The unattended installation file will be located on a removable universal serial bus (USB) disk drive F. You want the installation to proceed quietly without you needing to input any information into dialog boxes. Which of the following commands should you issue from the command prompt of each of the Windows Server 2003 computers on which you will install ISA Server? (Choose the correct answer.)

    A. F:\SETUP.EXE /X /QN E:\MSISAUND.INI

    B. E:\WINNT32.EXE /X /QN F:\MSISAUND.INI

    C. E:\SETUP.EXE /X /QN F:\MSISAUND.INI

    D. E:\SETUP.EXE /X /QN F:\UNATTEND.TXT

4.   Your organization is about to deploy 10 ISA Server 2004 computers running on Windows Server 2003. After assessing the technical material available on the ISA Server 2004 Web site, you have recommended to your manager that your organization implement ISA Server 2004, Enterprise Edition, rather than Standard Edition. After receiving your recommendation, your manager has asked you to prepare a report detailing why your organization should pay the extra licensing costs involved in purchasing the Enterprise Edition of ISA Server. Which of the following benefits does ISA Server 2004, Enterprise Edition, provide over ISA Server 2004, Standard Edition? (Select all that apply.)

    A. Support for NLB

    B. Support for Cache Array Routing Protocol (CARP)

    C. Support for more than three networks

    D. Support for RSA SecurID authentication

    E. Centralized storage of configuration data

5.   You are planning the installation of six ISA Server 2004 Enterprise Edition computers in your organization. You have the following goals: You want to be able to make configuration changes centrally on these servers, and you also want to support RSA SecurID authentication. Of the following conditions, which must be met to meet these goals? (Select all that apply.)

    A. Each ISA Server 2004 Enterprise Edition computer must be a member of the same Active Directory forest.

    B. Each ISA Server 2004 Enterprise Edition computer must be a member of a Windows Server 2003 domain running at the Windows Server 2003 functional level.

    C. Each ISA Server 2004 Enterprise Edition computer must be located within the same Active Directory site.

    D. Each ISA Server 2004 Enterprise Edition computer must be located on the same IP subnet.

    E. Each ISA Server 2004 Enterprise Edition computer must be able to communicate with an RSA ACE server located on your internal network.

6.   Which of the following IP addresses are unlikely to be used as the IP address of your ISA Server 2004 edge firewall's external interface? (Choose all that apply.)

    A.   10.38.128.134

    B.   172.36.97.8

    C.   192.168.101.224

    D.   169.252.36.28

    E.   226.194.34.28

7.   You have recently completed an unattended installation of four branch-office ISA Server 2004 computers. You want to verify that the installation has completed correctly on each computer. Which of the following files contains a brief summary that you can open using Notepad to verify the installation's success? (Choose the correct answer.)

    A.   %Windir%\Temp\Isainstall_###.log

    B.   %Windir%\Temp\Isawrap_###.log

    C.   %Windir%\Temp\Isamsde_###.log

    D.   %Windir%\Temp\Isafwse_###.log.

8.   You have performed a default installation of ISA Server 2004 on a computer running Windows 2000 Server. After the installation has completed, particular services are installed and visible in the services Microsoft Management Console (MMC). By default, which of the following services are *not* configured to start automatically after ISA Server 2004 is installed? (Select all that apply.)

    A.   Microsoft Firewall

    B.   Microsoft ISA Server Control

    C.   Microsoft ISA Server Job Scheduler

    D.   Microsoft ISA Server Storage

    E.   MSSQLServerADHelper

9.   Which of the following tools would be useful in generating a post-installation baseline for ISA Server 2004? (Choose the correct answer.)

    A.   Event Viewer

    B.   Task Manager

    C.   Network Monitor

    D.   Performance Monitor

10.   You are planning on making several significant changes to the configuration of an ISA Server 2004 computer currently used as an edge firewall. ISA Server 2004 is installed on a computer running Windows Server 2004. Which of the following procedures will allow you to roll back the changes you make to the current configuration with a minimum amount of administrative effort? (Choose the correct answer.)

   A. Create an Automated System Recovery (ASR) backup set.

   B. Create a backup of the system state data.

   C. Export the configuration using the ISA Management Console.

   D. Back up the configuration using the ISA Management Console.

Objective 1.3 Answers

1. **Correct Answers: B**

  A. Incorrect: ISA Server 2004 can be installed on Windows 2000 Server as long as Service Pack 4 or higher has been installed. Although upgrading Windows 2000 Advanced Server to Windows Server 2003, Enterprise Edition, is a possibility, it would entail additional administrative effort. Although there is some functionality that is not available when using Windows 2000 as an operating system platform, these features are not required in this particular scenario.

  B. Correct: Currently the Windows 2000 Advanced Server computer is patched to Service Pack 3. ISA Server 2004 requires Windows 2000 to be patched to at least Service Pack 4 before upgrade can commence.

  C. Incorrect: The minimum requirement for ISA Server 2004 is a 550 MHz Pentium II–compatible CPU. Although the server would certainly run quicker with a 1.2 GHz Pentium IV, upgrading the processor would entail unnecessary administrative effort.

  D. Incorrect: ISA Server 2004 has a minimum requirement of 256 MB of RAM, the same requirement as ISA Server 2000. Although the server would certainly function better with more RAM, upgrading to 512 MB would entail unnecessary administrative effort.

  E. Incorrect: ISA Server 2000 can be upgraded to ISA Server 2004 so long as ISA Server 2000 has Service Pack 1 installed. Installation of ISA Server 2000 Service Pack 2 is unnecessary in this situation.

2. **Correct Answers: A**

  A. Correct: The IP address of the external network adapter of the original ISA Server 2000 computer will be migrated if the ISA Server Migration Wizard is used. If the IP address of the external network adapter has changed after the migration to the new computer, you must correct this after the .xml file is imported on the new computer.

  B. Incorrect: Bandwidth rules are not supported by ISA Server 2004.

  C. Incorrect: Logging configuration is not migrated when you use the ISA Server Migration Wizard.

  D. Incorrect: SACLs and other permission settings are not upgraded when you use the ISA Server Migration Wizard.

  E. Incorrect: Reporting configuration is not migrated when you use the ISA Server Migration Wizard.

3.   Correct Answers: C

   A. Incorrect: This answer is incorrect because it states that the installation files are on F:\ rather than E:\ as specified in the question.

   B. Incorrect: ISA Server 2004 setup is not invoked using the Winnt32.exe command.

   C. Correct: The syntax is PathToMedia\Setup.exe /X /QN F:\PathToIniFile\MSISAUND.INI. The /X switch performs an unattended installation, as opposed to a reinstallation. /QN performs a quiet setup without requiring input into dialog boxes.

   D. Incorrect: The name of the ISA Server unattended installation file is MSISAUND. INI. Unattend.txt is commonly used for the unattended installation of the server operating system.

4.   Correct Answers: B and E

   A. Incorrect: NLB can be configured manually for the Standard Edition of ISA Server 2004. The difference between Enterprise Edition and Standard Edition is that Enterprise Edition more closely integrates NLB into the management of ISA Server. The Enterprise Edition console contains an area for the management and monitoring of NLB, a function not supported by ISA Server 2004, Standard Edition.

   B. Correct: CARP is used to determine which server in an array will request and cache a page. It is also used to remember which server holds that page so that if the page is requested again, the client retrieves it from the appropriate server. This functionality is not supported by ISA Server 2004, Standard Edition.

   C. Incorrect: Although ISA Server 2000 supported only three networks, both the Standard and Enterprise Editions of ISA Server 2004 support more than three networks.

   D. Incorrect: Both the Standard and Enterprise Editions of ISA Server 2004 support RSA SecurID authentication.

   E. Correct: ISA Server 2004, Enterprise Edition, can store configuration on a special server called a Configuration Storage server, which integrates with Active Directory. This allows the configuration of all ISA Server 2004 Enterprise Edition computers in an organization to be managed centrally. Configuration for ISA Server 2004, Standard Edition, is stored locally on each computer and cannot be managed centrally.

5.   Correct Answers: E

   A. Incorrect: To centralize configuration, each ISA Server 2004 Enterprise Edition computer must be able to contact a configuration storage server. Although the configuration storage server must be a member of an Active Directory domain, the ISA Server 2004 Enterprise Edition computers need not be.

B. Incorrect: To centralize configuration, each ISA Server 2004 Enterprise Edition computer must be able to contact a configuration storage server. Although the configuration storage server must be a member of an Active Directory domain, the ISA Server 2004 Enterprise Edition computers need not be.

C. Incorrect: To centralize configuration, each ISA Server 2004 Enterprise Edition computer must be able to contact a configuration storage server. This does not necessitate the computers being located within the same Active Directory site.

D. Incorrect: To centralize configuration, each ISA Server 2004 Enterprise Edition computer must be able to contact a configuration storage server. This does not necessitate the computers being located on the same IP subnet.

E. Correct: An RSA ACE server is required to support RSA SecurID authentication. If communication cannot be established between an ISA Server 2004 computer and an RSA ACE server located on your internal network, RSA SecurID authentication cannot be implemented.

6.   Correct Answers: A, C, and E

A. Correct: 10.38.128.134 is located within the private address space. The private IP address space is not routable from the public IP address space and is used only on internal networks.

B. Incorrect: 172.36.97.8 is a part of the public IP address space and hence is a possible candidate for an edge firewall's external interface.

C. Correct: 192.168.101.224 is located within the private address space. The private IP address space is not routable from the public IP address space and is used only on internal networks.

D. Incorrect: 169.252.36.28 is a part of the public IP address space and hence is a possible candidate for an edge firewall's public interface.

E. Correct: 226.194.34.28 is a part of the multicast IP address space and hence is unable to be used either as your public interface address or your private interface address.

7.   Correct Answers: B

A. Incorrect: This log does not exist. The log that you can use to confirm successful installation is %Windir%\Temp\Isawrap_###.log

B. Correct: The %Windir%\Temp\Isawrap_###.log will have an entry detailing whether or not the installation was successful.

C. Incorrect: The Isamsde_###.log file contains information about the installation of the MSDE component.

    D. Incorrect: Although the Isafwse_####.log file can be used to verify installation, this is a complete log file of the entire installation, which is over 1 MB in size and is not as succinct as the Isawrap_###.log file for verification purposes.

8.   **Correct Answers: E**

    A. Incorrect: The Microsoft Firewall service is installed and configured to start automatically during the default installation of ISA Server 2004.

    B. Incorrect: The Microsoft ISA Server Control service is installed and configured to start automatically during the default installation of ISA Server 2004.

    C. Incorrect: The Microsoft ISA Server Job Scheduler service is installed and configured to start automatically during the default installation of ISA Server 2004.

    D. Incorrect: The Microsoft ISA Server Storage service is installed and configured to start automatically during the default installation of ISA Server 2004.

    E. Correct: Although this service is installed during the default installation of ISA Server 2004, it is configured to start manually rather than automatically.

9.   **Correct Answers: D**

    A. Incorrect: Event Viewer records events. Although events can provide information about the system, the best tool for establishing a performance baseline is Performance Monitor.

    B. Incorrect: Although Task Manager can provide point-in-time data about current processor and network usage, it cannot provide information about disk, network, and processor usage over a sustained period of time as Performance Monitor can.

    C. Incorrect: Network Monitor is a useful tool for getting an idea of the protocols in use on a network. You would not use Network Monitor to generate baseline information about the operation of a server.

    D. Correct: Performance Monitor allows you to set up counters and record values over a period of time. This is very useful in generating baseline operating information as you can record values over several periods of normal operation for the server. You should store this information somewhere safe. If you suspect in the future that the server is not operating properly, you can compare the current values to the baseline values.

10.   **Correct Answers: C**

    A. Incorrect: ASR is perhaps the most invasive way to go about undoing a configuration change. It involves making a large backup and creating a special configuration disk. To roll back to a previous configuration involves rebooting the server using the installation media and inserting the ASR backup diskette at the appropriate time. Then the ASR backup is restored over the existing configuration.

B. Incorrect: Although this would work, restoring the system state data is far more invasive than importing the exported configuration.

C. Correct: Exporting the configuration prior to making any changes allows you to roll back the changes by simply re-importing the exported configuration.

D. Incorrect: Backing up the configuration using the ISA Management Console backs up the entire configuration. Although this is similar to exporting the configuration, restoring from a backup requires more administrative effort than importing a configuration.

14 Installing and Configuring Client Computers (2.0)

Successfully implementing Microsoft Internet and Security Acceleration (ISA) Server 2004 requires more than just configuring ISA Server 2004 itself. The clients that will use ISA Server 2004 must also be configured properly. Computers that are not correctly configured to utilize the ISA Server 2004 computer cannot access a whole range of local network and Internet resources. There are many aspects to the successful deployment of ISA Server clients. You must decide how to deploy the **ISA Server 2004 Firewall Client** software, assuming that you are not configuring the client to use Web proxy or secure network address translation (SecureNAT). In small organizations, it might be simplest to install the software manually. In large organizations, an automated deployment method is appropriate. Once client software is deployed, there are several ways to configure it, the simplest of which is to configure the software using the ISA Server 2004 computer. However, in some cases, especially if custom applications are in use, you may have to perform a manual setup by editing the configuration files located on the client computer. The process of ISA Server 2004 Firewall Client deployment can be greatly simplified if configuration is automated. This means that the ISA Server settings on large numbers of clients can be updated automatically rather than manually. When clients are mobile, this takes on even greater importance. With automatic configuration fully deployed, clients need only connect to the network to receive their configuration, rather than have it set manually or by using a script. Finally, it is important to understand the types of problems that can result in a client being incorrectly configured, and the areas that you should check first to resolve these problems.

Testing Skills and Suggested Practices

The skills that you need to master the Installing and Configuring Client Computers objective on Exam 70-350, *Implementing Microsoft Internet Security and Acceleration (ISA) Server 2004,* include:

- Install Firewall Client software.
    - ❏ Practice 1: Place a computer in your domain into a new organizational unit (OU) named Test. Create a Group Policy Object (GPO) and link it to the Test OU. Configure the OU to assign the ISA Server 2004 firewall software using the Computer Configuration\Software Settings node of the GPO. Log on to the target computer and check that the installation was successful.

❏ Practice 2: Write a logon script to perform an unattended installation of the ISA Server 2004 Firewall Client software. Remember that the user account to which the logon script maps must be a member of the Administrator group for the logon script to work.

■ Configure ISA Server 2004 for automatic client configuration by using Web Proxy Automatic Discovery (WPAD).

❏ Practice 1: Configure Domain Name System (DNS) and Dynamic Host Configuration Protocol (DHCP) on your network to support WPAD. Check the ISA Server 2004 help files for the exact steps required to achieve this.

❏ Practice 2: Configure the ISA Server 2004 computer to publish automatic client configuration information. For information about how to do this, consult the ISA Server 2004 help files. On the computer on which you performed the unattended installation of Firewall Client, open Firewall Client and check whether it can automatically detect the ISA Server 2004 computer.

■ Configure a local domain table (LDT).

❏ Practice 1: Open the ISA Server 2004 Management Console and edit the properties of the internal network. Examine the Domains tab and add the name of the domain used on the internal network.

❏ Practice 2: Open the ISA Server 2004 Management Console and edit the properties of the internal network. Examine the Web Browser tab. Locate the area where you would add the servers or domains for internal network clients to access directly, without using the ISA Server 2004 proxy.

Further Reading

This section lists supplemental readings by objective. We recommend that you study these sources thoroughly before taking this exam.

Objective 2.1   Review Chapter 4, "Installing and Managing ISA Server Clients."

ISA Server 2004 FAQ: Clients: *http://www.microsoft.com/technet/prodtechnol/isa/2004/plan/faq-clients.mspx*

Objective 2.2   Review Chapter 4, "Installing and Managing ISA Server Clients."

ISA Server 2004 Help, "Advanced Firewall Client configuration file settings."

Objective 2.3   Review Chapter 4, "Installing and Managing ISA Server Clients."

ISA Server 2004 Help, "Configure domains included in a network."

Objective 2.4   Review Chapter 4, "Installing and Managing ISA Server Clients."

ISA Server 2004 Help, "Automatic Discovery."

Objective 2.5   Review Chapter 4, "Installing and Managing ISA Server Clients."

Objective 2.1

Install Firewall Client Software

The ISA Server 2004 Firewall Client software enables clients on an internal network to access a range of approved network protocols. As with any software, how you choose to install the ISA Server 2004 Firewall Client software depends on the number of computers that you manage and the amount of time that you have. The simplest, but most labor-intensive, way is to copy the installation files to a CD-ROM or to a network location and then visit each computer in your organization to install the software manually. This is fine if you only have a few computers to visit, but if you manage several hundred, there are better ways for you to utilize your time. Another option is to perform an unattended installation. This tends to be quicker, but has the drawback of requiring the person running the installation to have **local administrator privileges** on the computer on which the Firewall Client is being installed. In most organizations, the average user does not have such privileges, which means that you will be unable to add the unattended installation commands to a logon script. The simplest way to deploy the ISA Server 2004 Firewall Client software to computers within a large organization is to use the software installation and maintenance facility of Active Directory directory service. This overcomes the limitations of the unattended installation and is likely to produce the desired results. Gaining an understanding of the benefits and drawbacks of each type of installation method is something that will help candidates when they attempt the 70-350 exam.

Objective 2.1 Questions

1. Contoso, Ltd. has five locations. The headquarters is located in Wangaratta, and there are branch offices in Wodonga, Wagga Wagga, Traralgon, and Moonee Ponds. Contoso has a single Microsoft Windows Server 2003 functional-level domain called *contoso.internal*. There are five Active Directory sites, one for each of Contoso's locations. Branch offices are connected to headquarters over a virtual private network (VPN). You have recently installed ISA Server 2004 at the Wangaratta and Traralgon sites. The Wodonga, Wagga Wagga, and Moonee Ponds sites are currently using Microsoft Proxy Server 2.0. All client computers at Contoso use Microsoft Windows 2000 Professional as their operating system. All client computers at Contoso are members of the Clients OU. All employees at Contoso are members of the Engineers, Marketing, Management, or Production OU. You wish to deploy the ISA Server 2004 clients using Active Directory. Which of the following strategies should you employ? (Choose the correct answer.)

   A. Create a GPO and link it to the Contoso.internal domain. Set the GPO to assign the ISA Server 2004 Firewall Client software.

   B. Create a GPO and link it to the Clients OU. Set the GPO to assign the ISA Server 2004 Firewall Client software.

   C. Create a GPO and link it to the Wangaratta and Traralgon sites. Set the GPO to assign the ISA Server 2004 Firewall Client software.

   D. Create a GPO and link it to the Engineers, Marketing, Managers, and Production OUs. Set the GPO to assign the ISA Server 2004 Firewall Client software.

2. You are the security administrator for Tailspin Toys, a company that has 15 offices located throughout Australia. You have recently installed ISA Server 2004 at several of your offices. You want to use a logon script to install the ISA Server 2004 Firewall Client to all users at the Traralgon and Wangaratta sites, because these were the first sites at which you deployed ISA Server 2004. There are 40 users at the Wangaratta site and 15 users at the Traralgon site. All users are members of their local computer's Power Users group. You have copied the installation files to the following locations: \\Trgfiles\\Install and \\Wngfiles\\Install. You have the following goals:

Primary Goal: Install the ISA Server 2004 Firewall Client using a logon script.

Secondary Goal: Users at the Wangaratta site should use the ISA Server 2004 server that is located at Internet Protocol (IP) address 192.168.10.1.

Secondary Goal: Users at the Traralgon site should use the ISA Server 2004 server that is located at IP address 192.168.15.1.

You take the following actions: You create two scripts. The first script contains the command

```
\\WNGFILES\\INSTALL\setup.exe /v "SERVER_NAME_OR_IP=192.168.10.1" REFRESH_WEB_PROXY=1 /qn
```

The second script contains the command

```
\\TRGFILES\\INSTALL\setup.exe /v "SERVER_NAME_OR_IP=192.168.15.1" REFRESH_WEB_PROXY=1 /qn
```

You then configure the 40 Wangaratta user accounts to use the first script, and then configure the 15 Traralgon user accounts to use the second script.

Which of your goals have you achieved? (Choose the correct answer.)

A. The primary and both secondary goals have been achieved.

B. The primary goal and one secondary goal have been achieved.

C. Only the primary goal has been achieved.

D. Both secondary goals have been achieved.

E. None of the listed goals has been achieved.

3. Which of the following features is available to Microsoft Windows XP clients using the ISA Server 2004 Firewall Client software, as opposed to Windows XP clients using the ISA Server 2000 Firewall Client software? (Choose the correct answer.)

A. ISA Server 2004 Firewall Clients are able to connect to ISA Server 2000 and Proxy Server 2.0 using the default configuration.

B. ISA Server 2000 Firewall Clients cannot use encrypted connections to ISA Server 2004.

C. ISA Server 2000 Firewall Clients do not support the use of WPAD.

D. ISA Server 2000 Firewall Clients cannot be deployed using Group Policy.

Objective 2.1 Answers

1.   Correct Answers: C

   A. Incorrect: You should not assign the ISA Server 2004 client to all computers in the organization, but only to computers that will use ISA Server 2004 as their proxy server. Assigning the ISA Server 2004 client to all the organization's computers will cause problems at the sites that still use Proxy Server 2.0. Using the ISA Server 2004 client with Proxy Server 2.0 requires editing the registry on each computer.

   B. Incorrect: You should not assign the ISA Server 2004 client to all computers in the organization, but only to those that will use ISA Server 2004 as their proxy server. Assigning the ISA Server 2004 client to all the organization's computers will cause problems at the sites that still use Proxy Server 2.0. Using the ISA Server 2004 client with Proxy Server 2.0 requires editing the registry on each computer.

   C. Correct: Because only the Wangaratta and Traralgon sites have ISA Server 2004, you should install the ISA Server 2004 Firewall Client software only on computers at these locations.

   D. Incorrect: You should not assign the ISA Server 2004 client to all computers in the organization, but only to those that are going to use ISA Server 2004 as their proxy server. Assigning the ISA Server 2004 client to all of the organization's computers will cause problems at the sites that still use Proxy Server 2.0. Using the ISA Server 2004 client with Proxy Server 2.0 requires editing the registry on each computer.

2.   Correct Answers: E

   A. Incorrect: The problem with using a logon script to install the ISA Server 2004 Firewall Client in this instance is that the installation requires local administrator privileges. Because the users are only members of the Power Users group, installation will not occur, and the primary goal will not be achieved. Because installation has not occurred, neither secondary goal can be achieved.

   B. Incorrect: The problem with using a logon script to install the ISA Server 2004 Firewall Client in this instance is that the installation requires local administrator privileges. Because the users are only members of the Power Users group, installation will not occur, and the primary goal will not be achieved. Because installation has not occurred, neither secondary goal can be achieved.

   C. Incorrect: The problem with using a logon script to install the ISA Server 2004 Firewall Client in this instance is that the installation requires local administrator privileges. Because the users are only members of the Power Users group, installation will not occur, and the primary goal will not be achieved. Because installation has not occurred, neither secondary goal can be achieved.

D. **Incorrect:** The problem with using a logon script to install the ISA Server 2004 Firewall Client in this instance is that the installation requires local administrator privileges. Because the users are only members of the Power Users group, installation will not occur, and the primary goal will not be achieved. Because installation has not occurred, neither secondary goal can be achieved.

E. **Correct:** The problem with using a logon script to install the ISA Server 2004 Firewall Client in this instance is that the installation requires local administrator privileges. Because the users are only members of the Power Users group, installation will not occur, and the primary goal will not be achieved. Because installation has not occurred, neither secondary goal can be achieved.

3.   Correct Answers: B

A. **Incorrect:** ISA Server 2004 Firewall Clients cannot be used to connect to ISA Server 2000 or Proxy Server 2.0 computers without enabling the User Datagram Protocol (UDP) control port which, by default, is disabled. This port must be enabled by modifying the registry.

B. **Correct:** The Firewall Clients that shipped with Proxy 2.0 and ISA Server 2000 can still connect to ISA Server 2004, but these connections will not be encrypted.

C. **Incorrect:** ISA Server 2000 Firewall Clients support WPAD.

D. **Incorrect:** ISA Server 2000 Firewall Clients can be deployed using Group Policy.

Objective 2.2

Configure Client Computers for ISA Server 2004

A certain level of client configuration can be achieved using the ISA Server 2004 Management Console. In most cases, this will be more than adequate and no further configuration will be necessary. In specialized circumstances, however, it is likely that you might need to perform an advanced configuration of the ISA Server 2004 Firewall Client software. This advanced configuration is performed by editing specific text files located in the Documents and Settings\All Users\Application Data\Microsoft\Firewall Client 2004\ directory. Using these text files, you can configure the client to support applications at the individual client level, rather than making a change that influences every computer within the organization. In preparation for the exam, you should study each of these text files and understand what they can and cannot be used for.

Objective 2.2 Questions

1. You have 15 Windows XP Professional Tablet PCs on which you need to use a custom client local address table (LAT) file, in addition to the ISA Server 2004 Firewall Client settings. Which of the following files should you configure in the \Documents and Settings\All Users\Application Data\Firewall Client 2004 folder on the Windows XP Professional Table PCs? (Choose the correct answer.)

    A. Application.ini

    B. Common.ini

    C. Management.ini

    D. Locallat.txt

    E. ISAconfig.txt

2. You are the security administrator for Tailspin Toys. Tailspin Toys has 1,000 employees that use the internal network. All Tailspin Toys user and computer accounts are located in the default Active Directory containers, and 10 of your Windows XP Professional clients use a custom application created by contract programmers. You want to configure the computers of these 10 contractors to allow for the use of this application with the ISA Server 2004 Firewall Client. You do not want to change the settings on any of the other 990 computers used at Tailspin Toys. Which of the following files in the \Documents and Settings\All Users\Application Data\Firewall Client 2004 folder should you change? (Choose the correct answer.)

    A. Application.ini

    B. Configuration.ini

    C. Management.ini

    D. Locallat.txt

3. Orin and Rooslan are two users of a Windows XP Professional workstation that has the ISA Server 2004 Firewall Client installed. On each computer are several versions of the Common.ini file. Each file has different content, and this is represented as follows:

    \Documents and Settings\All Users\Application Data\Firewall Client 2004\Common.ini

    ```
    [Common]

    ServerName=Contoso-ISA-01

    NameResolution=L
    ```

\Documents and Settings\Orin\Application Data\Firewall Client 2004\Common.ini

```
[Common]
```

```
ServerName=Contoso-ISA-02
```

```
NameResolution=R
```

\Documents and Settings\Rooslan\Application Data\Firewall Client 2004\Common.ini

```
[Common]
```

```
ServerName=Contoso-ISA-03
```

```
NameResolution=L
```

Given this information, which of the following statements is true? (Select all that apply.)

A. When Rooslan is logged on to the computer, the Firewall Client will be configured to use the ISA Server computer that is named Contoso-ISA-04.

B. When Orin is logged on to the computer, the Firewall Client will be configured to use the ISA Server computer that is named Contoso-ISA-01.

C. When a new user who has not logged on before logs on to this particular computer, the Firewall Client will be configured to use the ISA Server computer named Contoso-ISA-01.

D. When Orin is logged on to the computer, the Firewall Client uses Contoso-ISA-02 for DNS name resolution.

E. When Rooslan is logged on to the computer, the Firewall Client uses Contoso-ISA-03 for DNS name resolution.

Objective 2.2 Answers

1. **Correct Answers: D**

    A. **Incorrect:** Application.ini is used to specify application-specific configuration settings. It is not used to set custom LAT settings.

    B. **Incorrect:** Common.ini is used to specify common configurations for all applications. It is not used to set custom LAT settings.

    C. **Incorrect:** Management.ini is used to specify Firewall Client Management configuration settings. It is not used to set custom LAT settings.

    D. **Correct:** Locallat.txt is a text file that is used to create a custom client LAT. When editing this file, enter IP address pairs into the file.

    E. **Incorrect:** There is no ISAconfig.txt file located in the \Documents and Settings\All Users\Application Data\Firewall Client 2004 folder.

2. **Correct Answers: A**

    A. **Correct:** Application.ini is used to specify application-specific configuration settings. You should modify this file rather than Configuration.ini, which is used to specify configurations for all applications.

    B. **Incorrect:** Configuration.ini is used to set general configuration options for all applications. In this instance it would be more appropriate to edit the Application.ini file, because this application is used by only a few people.

    C. **Incorrect:** Management.ini is used to specify Firewall Client Management configuration settings. You would not use this file in this situation.

    D. **Incorrect:** Locallat.txt is a text file that is used to create a custom client LAT. This file is not used to set application-specific settings.

3. **Correct Answers: C & D**

    A. **Incorrect:** Configuration files in a user's directory override those in the All Users directory. The configuration file in Rooslan's directory sets the computer running ISA Server to Contoso-ISA-03 rather than to Contoso-ISA-04.

    B. **Incorrect:** Configuration files in a user's directory override those in the All Users directory. The configuration file in Orin's directory sets the ISA Server computer to Contoso-ISA-02 rather than to Contoso-ISA-01.

    C. **Correct:** Any new user will not have a configuration setting located in his or her user directory; therefore, the user will use the configuration settings located in the All Users directory. The configuration file in this directory specifies that the ISA Server computer named Contoso-ISA-01 should be used.

D. Correct: Orin's configuration file specifies that DNS resolution should be handled by the ISA Server computer. The configuration file specifies that Contoso-ISA-02 should be used as the ISA Server computer.

E. Incorrect: Rooslan's configuration file specifies that DNS resolution should be handled by the client computer, not by the ISA Server computer.

Objective 2.3

Configure a Local Domain Table (LDT)

The **local domain table (LDT)** is a list of servers and domains that the ISA Server 2004 computer has been configured to recognize as residing on internal, rather than on remote, networks. You should add any **internal domains** to the LDT. If you do not, it may be difficult for some ISA Server 2004 clients to contact servers on the internal network. Similar to the LDT, the Web browser settings on the internal network properties lets you specify specific sites and domains on the Internet for which you can grant internal network clients direct access. This can be important because not every Web site located on the Internet functions correctly for clients when traffic to them passes through the proxy on ISA Server 2004. Understanding how to configure both LDT and Web proxy settings is an important skill for candidates undertaking the ISA Server 2004 exam.

1. You are the security administrator for Contoso, Ltd. Recently your company merged with Fabrikam Inc. Both Fabrikam and Contoso are now located in the same building and share a local area network (LAN). Fabrikam's computers are located in a Windows Server 2003 functional-level forest. Contoso's computers are currently in a separate forest with all domain controllers, servers, and clients running Windows 2000 Professional. A single ISA Server 2004 server has been configured as an Internet-edge firewall. All computers in the Fabrikam and Contoso building have the ISA Server 2004 client installed. Management at Fabrikam has recently started publishing company policy documents on an intranet server. The intranet server is located in the domain *hr.fabrikam.internal* and has the host name Intranet. Unfortunately, none of the users in the Contoso and Fabrikam building is able to access the Intranet server. You've checked the Web server yourself and verified that the service is functioning. You suspect that a problem exists because connections are being routed through the ISA Server 2004 computer. What configuration changes must you make to allow access to the Intranet server? (Choose the correct answer.)

A. Edit the LAT file and add the IP address for *intranet.hr.fabrikam.internal*.

B. Edit the Configuration.ini file and add the IP address for *intranet.hr.fab rikam.internal*.

C. On the ISA Server 2004 server, edit the properties of the internal network. On the Domains tab of the Internal Network Properties dialog box, type **intranet.hr.fab-rikam.internal**.

D. On the ISA Server 2004 server, navigate to the Configuration\General node and open the Define Firewall Client Settings option. On the Domains tab of the Internal Network Properties dialog box, type **intranet.hr.fabrikam.internal**.

2. The properties of the internal network of a ISA Server 2004 computer that is configured as an Internet-edge firewall, Web proxy, and Web cache are configured as shown here.

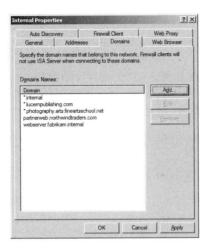

You have three clients on the internal network. Client Alpha has the Firewall Client installed and is configured to connect to the ISA Server 2004 computer. Client Beta does not have the Firewall Client installed, but has the ISA Server 2004 computer configured as a Web proxy. Client Gamma does not have the Firewall Client installed, nor is it configured to use the ISA Server 2004 computer as a Web proxy. It is, however, configured with the Internal IP address of the ISA Server 2004 computer as its default gateway. Given this information, which of the following statements is true? (Choose the correct answer.)

A. When Client Alpha accesses the Web server located at *intranet.contoso.internal*, it will do so using the ISA Server 2004 computer.

B. When Client Beta accesses the Web server located at *webserver.fabrikam.com*, it will do so directly without using the ISA Server 2004 computer.

C. When Client Gamma attempts to access the Web server located at *intranet.lucern publishing.com* located on a remote subnet, traffic will not pass through the ISA Server 2004 computer.

D. When Client Alpha attempts to access the Web server located at *intranet.partner web.northwindtraders.com*, access will not be mediated through the ISA Server 2004 computer.

3. Your company has recently implemented ISA Server 2004 and the accompanying Firewall Client. All Web traffic bound for the Internet now passes through the ISA Server 2004 proxy, firewall, and caching server. Since the implementation, some staff members have found that they are unable to access several important corporate sites on the Internet. These sites are *www.tailspintoys.com*, *www.treyresearch.net*, and *www.proseware.com*. Your manager has asked you to devise a way to allow staff members to access these sites by bypassing the ISA Server 2004 server. No other Web sites should be bypassed. Which of the following methods can you use to achieve this goal? (Choose the correct answer.)

   A. Configure the LDT with the FQDNs *www.tailspintoys.com*, *www.treyresearch.net*, and *www.proseware.com*.

   B. Configure the LAT with the FQDNs *www.tailspintoys.com*, *www.treyresearch.net*, and *www.proseware.com*.

   C. On the Web browser tab of the Internal Network Properties dialog box on the ISA Server 2004 computer, leave the default settings and add the following servers to the Directly Access These Servers Or Domains box: *www.tailspintoys.com*, *www.treyresearch.net*, and *www.proseware.com*.

   D. Configure Application.ini on each client with the IP address of *www.tailspin toys.com*, *www.treyresearch.net*, and *www.proseware.com*.

Objective 2.3 Answers

1. **Correct Answers: C**

A. Incorrect: The LAT file is a list of IP addresses and ranges that map to local IP addresses. You cannot use the LAT to map fully qualified domain names (FQDNs) to IP addresses, or to exclude particular FQDNs from being processed by ISA Server 2004.

B. Incorrect: The LDT, rather than the Configuration.ini file, is where you should make modifications to allow direct access to *intranet.br.fabrikam.internal*.

C. Correct: The Domains tab of the Internal Network Properties dialog box allows you to enter whole domains, or single FQDNs, that Firewall Clients can then access without using ISA Server 2004.

D. Incorrect: The Domains tab is not located in the Define Firewall Client Settings option. The Domains tab, which contains the LDT, can only be accessed through the Internal Network Properties dialog box.

2. **Correct Answers: B**

A. Incorrect: The first line of the LDT has the entry *.internal. This means that traffic to any FQDN ending with the suffix .internal will not be mediated by the ISA Server 2004 computer.

B. Correct: The final entry in the LDT is *webserver.fabrikam.internal*. Any Firewall or Web Proxy client on the internal network will directly access this Web server without using the ISA Server 2004 computer.

C. Incorrect: Client Gamma uses the ISA Server 2004 computer as a default gateway. Because the Web server *intranet.lucernpublishing.com* is located on a remote subnet, Transmission Control Protocol/Internet Protocol (TCP/IP) traffic will pass through the ISA Server 2004 computer, even if it is routed to another host on the internal network.

D. Incorrect: The entry in the LDT specifies only the FQDN *partnerweb.north windtraders.com*. If the entry in the LDT had specified *.partnerweb.north windtraders.com*, access would occur without going through the ISA Server 2004 computer.

3. Correct Answers: C

A. Incorrect: This would work only if the computers to which these addresses map are located on the internal network. Rather than use the Domains tab of the Internal Network Properties dialog box, you must use the Web browser tab to add the addresses of Internet locations that should be accessible without going through the ISA Server Web proxy.

B. Incorrect: The LAT is used for configuring IP address mappings on a local client; it cannot be used to bypass the ISA Server Web proxy for Internet addresses.

C. Correct: To configure ISA Server to allow clients from the internal network to access sites on the Internet directly without using the Web proxy, you must add the addresses of these sites to the Directly Access These Servers Or Domains Box on the Web browser tab of the Internal Network Properties dialog box.

D. Incorrect: Application.ini is used to configure application-specific mappings on each client. It is not used to allow clients to bypass the ISA Server proxy for specific sites on the Internet.

Configure ISA Server 2004 for Automatic Client Configuration by Using Web Proxy Automatic Discovery (WPAD)

Web Proxy Automatic Discovery (WPAD) significantly simplifies the process of configuring clients. Rather than having to specify proxy configuration manually, clients can receive their configuration automatically at startup. This is especially useful when you have a mobile workforce that might be moving from site to site, with each site having its own unique configuration. There are three aspects to preparing a successful WPAD deployment. The first is to configure DNS correctly by entering the appropriate new records. The second is to configure the DHCP server to provide information about WPAD to clients receiving automatic IP addressing information. The third aspect is to ensure that the ISA Server 2004 server is publishing this information so that clients can apply it to their configuration.

Objective 2.4 Questions

1. Microsoft Internet Explorer refreshes WPAD every 6 hours. Assuming that a computer running Windows XP Professional has been in use for 12 hours, in which of the following orders does it attempt to obtain information? (Choose the correct answer.)

    A. First: Server listed in Common.ini file. Second: Server listed as DHCP option 252. Third: Try to access the file http://Wpad.*<dns search suffix>*/Wpad.dat.

    B. First: Server listed in Common.ini file. Second: Try to access the file http://wpad.*<dns search suffix>*/Wpad.dat. Third: Server listed as DHCP option 252.

    C. First: Server listed as DHCP option 252. Second: Server listed in Common.ini file. Third: Try to access the file http://Wpad.*<dns search suffix>*/Wpad.dat.

    D. First: Try to access the file http://Wpad.*<dns search suffix>*/Wpad.dat. Second: Server listed in Common.ini file. Third: Server listed as DHCP option 252.

2. You want to configure your ISA Server 2004 computer to publish automatic discovery information for clients on the internal network. Which of the following methods can you use to do this? (Choose the correct answer.)

    A. Edit the properties of the internal network. On the Auto Discovery tab, check the Publish Automatic Discovery Information check box.

    B. Open the Firewall Client. Select Automatically Detect ISA Server.

    C. Edit the Common.ini file. Set Autodetection=1.

    D. Edit the Common.ini file. Set Autodetection=0.

3. You are the security administrator for Contoso, Ltd. Contoso has a single-domain Windows Server 2003 functional-level forest. The domain name is *contoso.internal* and is served by an Active Directory Integrated Zone replicated to all domain controllers within the forest. Contoso has a single ISA Server 2004 computer. The IP address of the public interface of this computer resolves to the FQDN *gateway.contoso.com*. The IP address of the internal network interface of this computer resolves to the FQDN *gateway.contoso.internal*. You are currently in the process of configuring WPAD for all Windows clients located in the Contoso corporation domain. To do this you need to create the appropriate record in DNS. Which of the following steps should you take? (Choose the correct answer.)

    A. On a DNS server that hosts the *contoso.com* zone, create an MX record for *gateway.contoso.internal*.

    B. On a DNS server that hosts the *contoso.internal* zone, create an MX record for *gateway.contoso.com*.

    C. On a DNS server that hosts the *contoso.com* zone, create an alias named WPAD that points to *gateway.contoso.com*.

    D. On a DNS server that hosts the *internal.contoso.com* zone, create an alias named WPAD that points to *gateway.internal.contoso.com*.

    E. On a DNS server that hosts the *contoso.internal* zone, create an alias named WPAD that points to *gateway.contoso.internal*.

4. You are configuring the options on the Contoso DHCP server necessary to support WPAD. You have already configured DNS to support WPAD for the *contoso.internal* zone. Which of the following settings will you use in configuring setting up the predefined options for WPAD? (Select all that apply.)

    A. Set the code to 250.

    B. Set the code to 252.

    C. Set the Data type to String and set the String to *http://wpad.contoso.internal/ wpad.dat*.

    D. Set the data type to Hex and set the Hex value to 7A69.

    E. Set the data type to Oct and set the Oct value to 75151.

5. Your ISA Server 2004 server has recently been configured to publish client configuration settings. DHCP and DNS have also been configured to support WPAD. Which of the following configuration settings can you make to a Windows XP Service Pack 2 computer with the Firewall Client installed so that it attempts to locate the ISA Server 2004 proxy and firewall automatically? (Select all that apply.)

    A. Open the Firewall Client from the system tray. Select the Automatically Detect ISA Server radio button. Click Detect Now. Click OK.

    B. Edit the Common.ini file located in \Documents and Settings\All Users\Application Data\Firewall Client 2004. Add the following line: Autodetection=1.

    C. Edit the Common.ini file located in \Documents and Settings\All Users\Application Data\Firewall Client 2004. Add the following line: Autodetection=0.

    D. Edit the Locallat.txt file located in \Documents and Settings\All Users\Application Data\Firewall Client 2004. Add the following line: Autodetection=0.

    E. Edit the Locallat.txt file located in \Documents and Settings\All Users\Application Data\Firewall Client 2004. Add the following line: Autodetection=1.

1.   Correct Answers: A

    A. Correct: The first place the computer will check is the server listed in the Common.ini file. If this server is unavailable, the server listed as DHCP option 252 will be checked. If this option is not set or if the server is unavailable, the computer will attempt to access the file at http://Wpad.*<dns search suffix>*/Wpad.dat.

    B. Incorrect: The server listed as DHCP option 252 is checked before attempting to access the file http://Wpad.*<dns search suffix>*/Wpad.dat.

    C. Incorrect: A computer that is just starting will try DHCP option 252 first, but one that has been in operation for 12 hours will try the server listed in the Common.ini file first.

    D. Incorrect: A computer that has been operating for 12 hours will try to access the file at http://Wpad.*<dns search suffix>*/Wpad.dat as a last resort.

2.   Correct Answers: A

    A. Correct: To publish automatic discovery information on the ISA Server 2004 computer for clients on the internal network, edit the properties of the internal network. On the Auto Discovery tab, check the Publish Automatic Discovery Information check box.

    B. Incorrect: This will configure an ISA Server client, not configure the ISA Server 2004 server itself, to publish the automatic discovery information.

    C. Incorrect: Common.ini is a file located on ISA Server clients. Making changes to this file will not configure an ISA Server 2004 computer to publish discovery information automatically for clients.

    D. Incorrect: Common.ini is a file located on ISA Server clients. Making changes to this file will not configure an ISA Server 2004 computer to publish discovery information automatically for clients.

3.   Correct Answers: E

    A. Incorrect: MX records are used for SMTP servers. The *contoso.com* zone is used by clients outside the Contoso network to access public Contoso resources. If you were creating an MX record in this zone, you would create it for the FQDN linked to the external interface.

    B. Incorrect: MX records are used for SMTP servers. Although this zone is used by clients on the internal Contoso network only, you don't use a MX record to configure WPAD.

C. Incorrect: The required alias should be created in the *contoso.internal* domain and should point to the FQDN of the internal interface, which in this case is *gateway.contoso.internal*.

D. Incorrect: The required alias should be created in the *contoso.internal* domain and should point to the FQDN of the internal interface, which in this case is *gateway.contoso.internal*.

E. Correct: The required alias should be created in the *contoso.internal* domain and should point to the FQDN of the internal interface, which in this case is *gateway.contoso.internal*.

4.   Correct Answers: B and C

A. Incorrect: The code needs to be set to 252, because that is the DHCP option code of WPAD.

B. Correct: The DHCP option for WPAD is 252.

C. Correct: The data type should be set to String. If DNS has been configured correctly, there will be an alias for WPAD pointing to the ISA Server 2004 computer.

D. Incorrect: The data type should be set to String rather than hex.

E. Incorrect: The data type should be set to String rather than to Oct.

5.   Correct Answers: A and B

A. Correct: This is one way of configuring the ISA Server 2004 Firewall Client to detect the ISA Server 2004 server automatically.

B. Correct: Adding the line Autodetection=1 sets the ISA Server 2004 Firewall Client up to detect the ISA Server 2004 server automatically.

C. Incorrect: Adding the line Autodetection=0 to Common.ini disables automatic detection of the ISA Server 2004 firewall.

D. Incorrect: The Locallat.txt file is used for configuring the LAT. It has nothing to do with setting whether the ISA Server 2004 Firewall Client attempts to contact the ISA Server 2004 server automatically.

E. Incorrect: The Locallat.txt file is used for configuring the LAT. It has nothing to do with setting whether the ISA Server 2004 Firewall Client attempts to contact the ISA Server 2004 server automatically.

Diagnose and Resolve Client Computer Connectivity Issues

When clients aren't functioning correctly—perhaps they can't connect to the Internet, or perhaps they can't connect to any servers on remote internal networks—you need to have some idea of where to start looking to resolve the problem. This particular exam objective looks at the common areas where ISA Server 2004 clients have configuration issues. There are several things you should check, such as name resolution. If a name cannot be correctly resolved to an IP address, the rest of the communication process cannot proceed. To diagnose problems, you must also understand some of the protocols that are used by the client software to communicate with the ISA Server computer. In some cases, the newer client software is not entirely compatible with previous versions of ISA Server, such as ISA Server 2000 or Proxy Server 2.0. You must also understand how clients on your network use ISA Server, as this differs between Firewall Client, Web Proxy, and SecureNAT. When using **SecureNAT** clients, it is very important to get the routers configured correctly. Implementing SecureNAT is relatively simple on a single TCP/IP subnet that contains an ISA Server. However, things become far more complex when you attempt to implement SecureNAT where the ISA Server 2004 computer is located on a remote TCP/IP subnet.

Objective 2.5 Questions

1. There are two domain controllers located on the Tailspin Toys network. The first domain controller has the DNS service installed. It hosts the *tailspintoys.internal* network and is configured as a root server. ISA Server 2004 is installed on a stand-alone Windows Server 2003 computer. The DNS service is installed on the ISA Server 2004 computer and it is configured as a caching-only server. The Root Hints tab of the DNS server on the ISA Server 2004 computer contains 13 entries. The Forwarders tab is configured to forward all queries for the *tailspintoys.internal* network to the second domain controller. The LDT on the ISA Server computer includes the entry **.tailspin toys.internal*. Tailspin Toys uses a single TCP/IP subnet. The IP address of the internal network interface of the ISA Server 2004 computer is 192.168.10.1. The IP address of the first domain controller is 192.168.10.5. The IP address of the second domain controller is 192.168.10.6. Currently clients are able to connect to hosts on the Tailspin Toys network, but are unable to connect to hosts on the Internet. Which of the following changes could you make to resolve this? (Choose the correct answer.)

   A. Configure the clients to use 192.168.10.6 as their preferred DNS server.

   B. Configure the clients to use 192.168.10.1 as their preferred DNS server.

   C. Configure the Forwarders tab on DNS service on the first DC to forward all requests for the *tailspintoys.internal* zone to 192.168.10.1. Configure all clients to use 192.168.10.1 as their preferred DNS server.

   D. Configure the Forwarders tab on the DNS service on the ISA Server 2004 server and ensure that it forwards all requests for the *tailspintoys.internal* zone to 192.168.10.5. Configure all clients to use IP address 192.168.10.1 for their preferred DNS server.

2. You receive a call from a laptop user who spends two days a week at your company's Wagga Wagga site and three days a week at your company's headquarters in Wangaratta. All computers at the Wangaratta site, including the laptop in question, use either Windows XP Professional or Windows Server 2003. All computers at the Wagga Wagga site, except for that of the employee who travels there from Wangaratta, use Windows 2000 Professional or Windows 2000 Server. The Wagga Wagga and Wangaratta sites are connected through a VPN. You have recently installed ISA Server 2004 at the Wangaratta site. All computers at the Wangaratta site have the ISA Server 2004 Firewall Client software installed. Currently the Wagga Wagga site uses ISA Server 2000 and the clients there use the version of the client software that came with that product. The user who calls you tells you that he is able to access all network resources and the Internet from the Wangaratta location, but when he travels to Wagga Wagga, he cannot access the Internet. Access to other network resources at Wagga Wagga occurs without problem. So far as the user can recall, the problem arose around the same week that you rolled out ISA Server 2004 at the Wangaratta location. Other users at Wagga Wagga do not have this problem and there are no plans to upgrade the Wagga Wagga ISA Server to the 2004 version of the software in the foreseeable future. Which of the following steps would allow you to provide this user with Internet access with the least amount of administrative effort? (Choose the correct answer.)

A. Install ISA Server 2004 at the Wagga Wagga site.

B. Install the ISA Server 2004 client on all computers at the Wagga Wagga site.

C. Edit the registry of the user's Windows XP laptop. Set the HKEY_ LOCAL_MACHINE\Software\Microsoft\Firewall Client 2004\EnableUdpControl Channel value to 1.

D. Remove the ISA Server 2004 client from the laptop and reinstall the ISA Server 2000 client.

3. Your building has three separate TCP/IP subnets, as illustrated here:

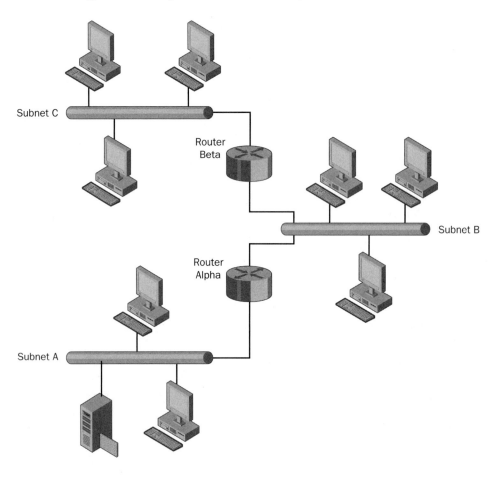

Subnet A is 192.168.10.0, subnet mask 255.255.255.0. Subnet B is 192.168.20.0, subnet mask 255.255.255.0. Subnet C is 192.168.30.0, subnet mask 255.255.255.0. You have an ISA Server 2004 server configured as a proxy and a firewall. The IP address of this server is 192.168.10.15. Subnet A is connected to Subnet B through Router Alpha. One interface of Router Alpha is IP address 192.168.10.1, the other interface of Router Alpha is IP address 192.168.20.1. Subnet B is connected to Subnet C through Router Beta. One interface of Router Beta is IP address 192.168.20.2, the other interface of Router Alpha is IP address 192.168.30.1. You wish to configure a Windows XP Professional workstation as a SecureNAT client. The IP address of the client is 192.168.30.25, the subnet mask is 255.255.255.0, and the default gateway is set to 192.168.10.10. All routers have been configured to support SecureNAT traffic. Currently the Windows XP Professional workstation cannot access clients on remote networks in your building or hosts on the Internet. Which of the following changes should you make? (Choose the correct answer.)

  A. Change the subnet mask of the client to 255.255.0.0.

  B. Change the default gateway to 192.168.10.15.

  C. Change the default gateway to 192.168.10.1.

  D. Change the default gateway to 192.168.20.1.

  E. Change the default gateway to 192.168.30.1.

4.   Your LAN has two TCP/IP subnets, one for each building. Building One is connected to the Internet. Building Two is connected to Building One through a router. An ISA Server 2004 computer is located in Building One. The IP address of the internal network interface of the ISA Server 2004 computer is 172.16.30.21. The IP address of the public network interface of the ISA Server 2004 computer is 207.46.130.108. The IP address of one router interface is 172.16.30.1. The IP address of the second router interface is 127.16.30.33. You want to configure all the clients in Building One and Building Two as SecureNAT clients but still have them be able to contact servers located in both buildings. Currently all clients in Building One have the default gateway 172.16.30.1, and all clients in Building Two have the default gateway 172.16.30.33. Clients are able to access each other, but are unable to access the Internet. What should you do to resolve this problem? (Choose the correct answer.)

  A. Configure the router to forward all traffic not destined for the Building One or Building Two networks to IP address 172.16.30.21.

  B. Configure the router to forward all traffic not destined for the Building One or Building Two networks to IP address 207.46.130.109.

  C. Configure all clients in Building One and Building Two to use IP address 127.160.30.21 as their default gateway.

  D. Configure all clients in Building One and Building Two to use IP address 207.46.130.109 as their default gateway.

5.   Your network currently uses Windows 2000 Professional clients and Windows 2000 Server computers. You have recently upgraded from ISA Server 2000 to ISA Server 2004. You are continuing to use the ISA Server 2000 Firewall Client. You have recently become concerned about the possibility that authentication traffic between the Windows 2000 Professional clients and the ISA Server 2004 computer might be intercepted. You want to ensure that the authentication process between the ISA Server 2004 computer and the Firewall Clients is encrypted. Which of the following steps should you take? (Select two.)

   A. Edit the Application.ini file on the Windows 2000 Professional clients. Add the line ForceCredentials=1.

   B. Edit the Application.ini file on the Windows 2000 Professional clients. Add the line ForceCredentials=0.

   C. Edit the properties of the Internal Network on the ISA Server 2004 computer. Ensure that the Enable Firewall Client Support For This Network box is checked.

   D. Upgrade the Firewall Clients to the ISA Server 2004 Firewall Client on all computers.

   E. In the Configuration\General node of the ISA Server 2004 Management Console, open the Define Firewall Client Settings option and ensure that the Allow Non-encrypted Firewall Client Connections box is unchecked.

Objective 2.5 Answers

1.   Correct Answers: D

A.   Incorrect: Currently there is no DNS service installed on the second domain controller, which is located at IP address 192.168.10.6.

B.   Incorrect: Currently the ISA Server is configured to forward DNS requests for the *tailspintoys.internal* zone to a server that does not host a DNS server. This will mean that there will be name-resolution issues on the internal network.

C.   Incorrect: This will not work as queries to the *tailspintoys.internal* zone should be resolved by the first domain controller.

D.   Correct: This course of action solves both problems. It clears up the forwarding issue for the *tailspintoys.internal* zone, which currently is set to a DNS server that doesn't exist, and also allows clients to use the DNS service on the ISA Server 2004 computer to resolve FQDNs on the Internet.

2.   Correct Answers: C

A.   Incorrect: Although this would work, it would require significant administrative effort. It is much easier to alter a single key in the laptop's registry than it is to upgrade a server from ISA Server 2000 to ISA Server 2004.

B.   Incorrect: This would worsen the problem. The ISA Server 2004 client, by default, does not work with Proxy Server 2.0 and ISA Server 2000 that use the UDP-only control channel. Because this is the issue in question, it would mean that no computers at Wagga Wagga could access the Internet.

C.   Correct: ISA Server 2000 and Proxy Server 2.0 have the Firewall Client control channel listening on TCP and UDP Port 1745. As a security measure for ISA Server 2004, the UDP channel was disabled by default. This means that the ISA Server 2004 client cannot connect to a Proxy 2.0 or ISA Server 2000 computer that requires a UDP-only control channel. The control channel can be updated by changing the above registry value.

D.   Incorrect: Although this would work, it requires significantly more administrative effort than changing the value of a registry key.

3.   Correct Answers: E

A.   Incorrect: The networks are bounded by routers. If you change the subnet mask to 255.255.0.0, the client will incorrectly believe that all the networks in your building can be contacted without forwarding traffic to a default gateway.

B. Incorrect: You can set the default gateway of a SecureNAT client to the IP address of the ISA Server computer only if both computers are located on the same TCP/IP subnet. When a SecureNAT client is located on a remote TCP/IP subnet, you need to configure it to use the local default gateway and configure the router's routing table to forward all Internet traffic to the ISA Server computer.

C. Incorrect: You can set the default gateway of a SecureNAT client to the IP address of the computer running ISA Server only if both computers are located on the same TCP/IP subnet. When a SecureNAT client is located on a remote TCP/IP subnet, you must configure it to use the local default gateway and configure the router's routing table to forward all Internet traffic to the ISA Server computer.

D. Incorrect: You can set the default gateway of a SecureNAT client to the IP address of the computer running ISA Server only if both computers are located on the same TCP/IP subnet. When a SecureNAT client is located on a remote TCP/IP subnet, you need to configure it to use the local default gateway and configure the router's routing table to forward all Internet traffic to the ISA Server computer.

E. Correct: Address 192.168.30.1 is the client's local default gateway. You can only set the default gateway of a SecureNAT client to the IP address of the ISA Server computer if both computers are located on the same TCP/IP subnet. When a SecureNAT client is located on a remote TCP/IP subnet, you need to configure it to use the local default gateway and configure the router's routing table to forward all Internet traffic to the ISA Server computer. The question states that the routers are already configured to support SecureNAT; hence the only change that needs to be made is to set the correct default gateway.

4.   Correct Answers: A

A. Correct: If configured in this way, traffic will still pass properly between the two buildings. If the router is asked to forward traffic to an IP address other than those on the Building One or Building Two network, it will forward it to the internal network interface of the ISA Server computer, allowing the computer to process it.

B. Incorrect: The router needs to be configured to forward all traffic not destined for the local networks to the internal network interface of the ISA Server computer rather than to the public network interface.

C. Incorrect: Although this would grant Internet access to the Building One clients, it would mean that problems would occur contacting Building Two clients. Because the default gateway for Building Two clients would be on a remote network, they could not communicate with hosts outside their subnet.

D. Incorrect: This would result in clients in Building One being able to contact only other clients in Building One and clients in Building Two being able to contact only other clients in Building Two. Any computer that is configured with a default gateway located on a subnet different than its own will be unable to communicate with computers located on remote networks. Default gateways must always be located on the same TCP/IP subnet as the host itself.

5.   **Correct Answers: D & E**

   A. Incorrect: This will not force the authentication process to be encrypted. The ForceCredentials=1 option means that alternative user credentials are used. This is useful if the ISA Server computer is hosted on a stand-alone server and you are authenticating using a local account on that server rather than your domain account.

   B. Incorrect: This will not force the authentication process to be encrypted. The ForceCredentials=0 option means that alternative user credentials are not used. Alternative credentials are useful if the ISA Server computer is hosted on a stand-alone server and you are authenticating using a local account on that server rather than your domain account.

   C. Incorrect: Having this box checked will not ensure that authentication between Firewall Clients and the ISA Server 2004 computer is encrypted.

   D. Correct: The ISA Server 2000 Firewall Client does not support encrypted connections, and hence encrypted authentication. You will need to upgrade to the ISA Server 2004 Firewall Client to meet this goal.

   E. Correct: To force encrypted connections, and hence encrypted authentication, you must ensure that non-encrypted Firewall Client connections are not allowed. To do this, edit the Firewall Client Settings located in the Configuration\General node of the ISA Server 2004 Management Console.

15 Configuring and Managing ISA Server 2004 (3.0)

There are several important areas to be aware of when configuring and managing Microsoft Internet Security and Acceleration (ISA) Server 2004. The first area is the **system policy**, which is used to configure all the communication between the ISA Server 2004 computer and external networks. You can use the system policy to set which domain controllers can be used for authentication. You can also use the system policy to create a list of remote client IP addresses, and use that list to restrict who can and cannot connect to the server using Terminal Services or the Microsoft Management Console (MMC).

The second area is backing up and restoring ISA Server 2004 configuration. This is made relatively simple by the fact that ISA Server 2004 can export its configuration to **Extensible Markup Language (XML)** format. As any administrator knows, you should always perform some type of backup prior to making a configuration change. That way, if the change goes haywire, you can quickly roll back to the previous settings.

The third area is the use of **administrative roles**. Administrative roles are sets of rights that are defined or established in advance. Rights are not set on a per-right basis, but are conferred in sets through the delegation of administrative roles. In small organizations, you are unlikely to have much use for these roles because it is likely that a sole person is responsible for the ISA Server 2004 computer. Among larger organizations, in which support teams are in place, there may be several people who are responsible for aspects of the ISA Server 2004 computer, and the use of these administrative roles becomes more likely.

The fourth area, configuring **firewall settings**, provides another way of customizing ISA Server 2004. **Intrusion detection** allows you to maintain a record of the types of detected attacks that are being launched against your network infrastructure. Internet Protocol (IP) options filtering allows you to drop packets that contain particular configuration flags. **IP fragmentation** settings allow you to configure the ISA Server 2004 computer to drop fragmented packets, which attackers may use in attempts to compromise your computer.

The fifth and sixth areas are **network load balancing (NLB)** and particular network topology. Network load balancing allows you to create a cluster to share ISA Server duties. The benefit of NLB is that if one server fails, other servers in the cluster will pick up the load, providing a seamless experience for the client. To deal with the most common sorts of network topologies, ISA Server 2004 introduces the concept of **network templates.** These templates can be used to quickly configure ISA Server 2004 for the most common deployment types.

Testing Skills and Suggested Practices

The skills that you need to master the "Installing and Configuring Client Computers" objective on Exam 70-350, *Implementing Microsoft Internet Security and Acceleration (ISA) Server 2004,* include:

- Configure the system policy.

    ❑ Practice 1: Open the ISA Server 2004 Management Console. Navigate to the Firewall Policy node and select the Edit System Policy task. Navigate to the Authentication Services node and examine the default settings for Active Directory, Remote Authentication Dial-In User Service (RADIUS), RSA SecurID and CRL Download. Disable RADIUS authentication, and then click OK. Apply the changes to the firewall.

    ❑ Practice 2: Open the ISA Server 2004 Management Console. Navigate to the Firewall Policy node and select the Edit System Policy task. Navigate to Remote Management, and open the Terminal Server node. Click on the From tab. Select the Remote Management Computers group and then click Edit. Use the dialog to add a computer named Admin with IP address 192.168.10.21 to this group. Click OK to close the System Policy Editor. Apply the changes to the firewall.

- Back up and restore ISA Server 2004.

    ❑ Practice 1: Open the ISA Server 2004 Management Console. Right-click on the ISA Server 2004 computer and select Export. Set the filename to Myisaconfig.xml. Check the Export User Permission Settings and Export Confidential Information boxes and then click Export. Type an eight-character password to continue. When the export completes, click OK.

    ❑ Practice 2: Open the ISA Server 2004 Management Console. Navigate to the Firewall Policy node and select the Export System Policy task. For the file name, type **mysystempolicy.xml**. Ensure that the Export Confidential Information box is checked and then click Export. Type an eight-character password to continue. When the export completes, click OK.

- Define administrative roles.

    ❑ Practice 1: Create a local group on your Windows Server 2003 computer named ISA-MONITORS. Open the ISA Server 2004 Management Console. Navigate to the General node located under the Configuration node. Open Administration Delegation. This launches the Administration Delegation Wizard. Click Add and select the newly created ISA-MONITORS group. Assign this group the ISA Server Extended Monitoring role.

- Configure firewall settings.

  ❏ Practice 1: Open the ISA Server 2004 Management Console. Navigate to the General node located under the Configuration node. Open Define IP Preferences. Navigate to the IP Fragments tab and click the Question Mark to get a description of what this means. Navigate to the IP Routing tab and perform the same action.

  ❏ Practice 2: Open the ISA Server 2004 Management Console. Navigate to the General node located under the Configuration node. Open Enable Intrusion Detection and DNS Attack Detection. Ensure that Enable Intrusion Detection is selected. Click the question mark to get a description of all the options.

- Configure ISA Server 2004 for NLB.

  ❏ Practice 1: From the Windows Server 2003 Administrative Tools menu, open the Network Load Balancing Manager. From the Cluster menu select New. Enter the IP address as **192.168.99.101**. Enter the subnet mask as **255.255.255.0**. Click Next three times until you reach the Connect screen. In the dialog box, enter the IP address as **127.0.0.1** and then click Connect. Select the primary network interface to be used by the cluster and then click Next. Click Finish. This will create an NLB cluster, though one with only a single member. Once the hourglass disappears, delete the cluster.

- Configure ISA Server 2004 to support a network topology.

  ❏ Practice 1: Open the ISA Server 2004 Management Console. Navigate to the Networks node located under the Configuration node. Open the Templates tab and change from the currently selected template to a 3-Leg Perimeter or Back Firewall template.

Further Reading

This section lists supplemental readings by objective. We recommend that you study these sources thoroughly before taking this exam.

Objective 3.1   Review the article "System Policy" in Microsoft ISA Server 2004 Help and the three related articles located under it.

Review the following articles:

ISA Server 2004 System Policy, *http://www.microsoft.com/technet/prodtechnol/isa/2004/plan/systempolicy.mspx*

ISA Server 2004 FAQ: Administering, *http://www.microsoft.com/technet/prodtechnol/isa/2004/plan/faq-administering.mspx*

Objective 3.2   Review the following articles in ISA Server 2004 Help: "Export and Import," "Back Up and Restore," "Export a Configuration," "Export a Partial Configuration," and "Import a Configuration."

Review the following article:

Export, Import, and Backup Functionality in ISA Server 2004, *http://www.microsoft.com/technet/prodtechnol/isa/2004/plan/exportimportsettings.mspx*

Objective 3.3   Review the following articles in ISA Server 2004 Help: "Administrative Roles" and "Assign Administrative Roles."

Review the following articles:

What Is New in ISA Server 2004? *http://www.microsoft.com/isaserver/evaluation/whatsnew.asp*

Objective 3.4   Review the following articles in ISA Server 2004 Help: "Firewall Chaining," "Dial-Up Connections," "Network for Automatic Dialing," "Dial-Up Connection Configuration Steps," "Enable IP Fragment Filtering," "Enable IP Options Filtering," and "Enable IP Routing."

Objective 3.5   Review the following articles:

Windows Network Load Balancing: Configuration—Best Practices, *http://www.microsoft.com/technet/prodtechnol/windowsserver2003/technologies/clustering/nlbbp.mspx*

Network Load Balancing: Frequently Asked Questions, *http://www.microsoft.com/technet/prodtechnol/windowsserver2003/technologies/clustering/nlbfaq.mspx*

Objective 3.6   Review the following articles in ISA Server 2004 Help: "Network Templates," "Edge Firewall Network Template," "3-Leg Perimeter Network Template," "Front Firewall Network Template," "Back Firewall Network Template," "Single Network Adapter Network Template," "Network Rules."

Configure the System Policy

System policy is used to ensure that adequate access exists between the ISA Server 2004 computer and the connected networks so that the server may function correctly and be administered remotely. System policies deal with access between the Local Network, which is the ISA Server computer, and the networks connected to it. Unlike firewall access rules, system policy rules are defined in advance. You simply need to choose whether to enable a rule and to which networks or hosts the rule applies. By default, certain system policies are enabled. The enabled policies are the ones most commonly used to ensure network functionality.

Objective 3.1 Questions

1.   You have just become aware of an intrusion attempt against your organization's network from an array of hosts located on the Internet. With the permission of management, you have manually shut down the firewall service on your ISA Server 2004 computer so that you can reconfigure ISA Server 2004 to deal with the specific attack that is occurring. Your organization has seven site-to-site virtual private networks (VPNs), which are used to connect branch offices to headquarters that traverse the ISA Server computer. Client computers on your organization's internal network use the ISA Server computer as a proxy to speed access to resources on the Internet. You manage the server through the remote desktop client in Windows XP or the MMC. Which of the following statements correctly describe the functionality of ISA Server 2004 when the firewall service is shut down manually? (Select all that apply.)

   A. The ISA Server 2004 computer can be remotely managed through Remote Desktop Protocol (RDP).

   B. You can only mange the ISA Server 2004 computer by logging on using the console.

   C. You can manage ISA Server using the ISA MMC installed on your Windows XP Professional computer.

   D. The seven site-to-site VPNs that connect branch offices to headquarters will remain functional.

   E. Clients on your internal network can still access Web content using the cache on the ISA Server 2004 computer.

2.   You want to manage a stand-alone ISA Server 2004 computer using the RDP client built in to Windows XP Professional. You go to the server room, where the ISA Server 2004 computer resides. From the console of the server, you edit the system policy. On the Terminal Server node, you check the Enable box. You lock the screen of the ISA Server 2004 computer. You then attempt to open an RDP session on the ISA Server from a Windows XP Professional computer that is also located in the server room. You are unable to establish a connection. Which of the following steps should you take to resolve this problem? (Select two, both of which are necessary steps.)

   A. Click Apply to enforce the changed configuration.

   B. In the Firewall Policy node, select the Create New Access Rule task. Set the following Rule properties:

   - Applies to: All Outbound Traffic
   - When rule conditions are met: Allow

- This rule applies to traffic from these sources: Computer Sets\Remote Management Computers

- This rule applies to traffic sent to these destinations: Computer Sets\Remote Management Computers

■ User Sets: All Users

C. In the Firewall Policy node, select Create New Access Rule task. Set the following rule properties:

- When rule conditions are met: Deny

- Applies to: All Outbound Traffic

- This rule applies to traffic from these sources: Computer Sets\Remote Management Computers

- This rule applies to traffic sent to these destinations: Computer Sets\Remote Management Computers

■ User Sets: Administrators

D. Edit the Firewall Client settings to Allow Non-Encrypted Firewall Client Connections.

E. Edit the system policy. On the Terminal Server node, ensure that the IP address of the Windows XP computer is entered in the Remote Management Computers group on the From tab.

3. You want to ensure that all the ISA Server 2004 Enterprise Edition computers in the Contoso array use a domain controller at IP address 10.0.0.10 only for authentication, rather than the default settings. The internal network is currently defined as 10.0.0.0 through 10.255.255.255. The Contoso internal network has domain controllers at IP addresses 10.0.0.10, 10.0.0.11, 10.0.0.12, and 10.0.0.13. Assuming that installation default settings apply, which of the following changes must you make to the system policy? (Select two; each selection forms a part of the answer.)

A. In the To box of the Authentication node located under the Active Directory node of the System Policy, remove the Internal Network.

B. Remove IP addresses 10.0.0.10, 10.0.0.11, 10.0.0.12, and 10.0.0.13 from the Remote Management Computers group.

C. In the To box of the Authentication node located under the Active Directory node of the System Policy, click Add. In the Network Entities dialog box, select New ... Computer and then enter a computer name and IP address 10.0.0.10. Add this newly named computer to the list in the To box.

D. In the Exceptions dialog box on the To box of the Authentication node located under the Active Directory node of the System Policy, click Add and enter the IP addresses: 10.0.0.10, 10.0.0.11, 10.0.0.12, and 10.0.0.13.

4. You are in the process of locking down the system policy on an ISA Server 2004, Enterprise Edition, configuration storage server, specifically the section dealing with authentication services for the array. Your ISA Server 2004 array currently has the default system policy configuration. In locking down the system policy, you have the following goals:

- Primary Goal: To enable the array to authenticate using RSA SecurID to the configured RSA ACE/Server at IP address 10.0.0.50.

- Secondary Goal: Disable RADIUS authentication.

- Secondary Goal: Allow RPC protocols such as Distributed Component Object Model (DCOM) to be used in the Active Directory authentication process.

You perform the following steps:

Log on to the ISA Server 2004 Enterprise Edition configuration storage server. From the Firewall Policy node, select the Edit System Policy task. Navigate to the Authentication Services node. On the Active Directory node, ensure that the Enforce Strict RPC Compliance check box is checked. On the RADIUS node, clear the Enable check box. On the RSA SecurID node, select the To tab. Click Add and, in the Network Entities dialog box, create an entry for the RSA ACE/Server at IP address 10.0.0.50. Select this entry. Click OK to close the System Policy Editor dialog box, and then click Apply to enforce the changes.

By performing these actions, which goals have you achieved?

A. The primary and both secondary goals have been achieved.

B. The primary goal and one secondary goal have been achieved.

C. The primary goal has not been achieved. Both secondary goals have been achieved.

D. The primary goal has not been achieved. Only one secondary goal has been achieved.

E. None of the goals has been achieved.

5. Rooslan, your junior administrator, shares with you the administration duties of the organization's ISA Server 2004 computer. Both you and Rooslan manage the ISA Server 2004 computer using a copy of the ISA Server 2004 Management Console installed on each of your Windows XP Professional computers. No one else in your organization should be able to perform this function. Rooslan has just returned from a four-week vacation. He informs you that although he can still access all network resources, he currently cannot use his local copy of the ISA Server 2004 Management Console to manage ISA Server 2004 remotely, something he was able to do prior to his vacation. You check and find that you are still able to manage ISA Server 2004 remotely using this method from your computer, but when you try to perform the same function from Rooslan's computer, it does not work. Rooslan is able to manage ISA Server 2004 using your computer. Rooslan's computer was shut down during his vacation and no configuration changes were made to it. Likewise, no configuration changes were made to ISA Server 2004 during Rooslan's absence. Which of the following steps can you take to resolve this issue so that it does not occur again?

A. Edit the Configuration.ini file on Rooslan's computer and enter the IP address of the ISA Server 2004 computer.

B. Add Rooslan to the Local Administrators group on the ISA Server 2004 computer.

C. Delegate the ISA Server Full Administrator role to Rooslan's user account.

D. Configure both your computer and Rooslan's computer with static IP addresses. Ensure that these static IP addresses are included in the list of Remote Management Computers in the ISA Server 2004's system policy.

E. Reinstall the ISA Server 2004 Firewall Client software on Rooslan's computer.

6. The Remote Management Computer properties are configured as shown here:

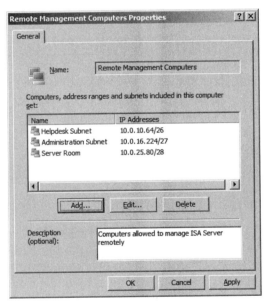

Given that the Terminal Server option in the Remote Management node is set to Enabled, which of the following host IP addresses will be able to establish connections to the ISA Server 2004 computer using an RDP client? (Select all that apply.)

A. 10.0.10.120

B. 10.0.25.97

C. 10.0.16.220

D. 10.0.10.130

E. 10.0.25.90

Objective 3.1 Answers

1.   **Correct Answers: A and C**

   A. Correct: When the firewall service is shut down manually, ISA Server 2004 enters lockdown mode. In lockdown mode, clients, such as the Remote Desktop client on Windows XP and Windows Server 2003, can still connect to an ISA Server 2004 computer.

   B. Incorrect: When the firewall service is shut down manually, ISA Server 2004 enters lockdown mode. Although this places a significant restriction on the network traffic that can traverse the server, the computer can still be managed using RDP and MMC.

   C. Correct: Port 3847, used for MMC management of ISA Server 2004, remains open to the internal network in the event that ISA Server 2004 enters lockdown mode.

   D. Incorrect: When the firewall service is shut down manually, ISA Server 2004 enters lockdown mode. When in lockdown mode, VPN remote-access clients and site-to-site VPN connections cannot traverse the ISA Server computer.

   E. Incorrect: When the firewall service is shut down manually, ISA Server 2004 enters lockdown mode. All incoming traffic, except remote procedure call (RPC), RDP, and Internet Control Message Protocol (ICMP) from trusted servers, and Dynamic Host Configuration Protocol (DHCP) traffic can reach the ISA Server computer. This means that HTTP requests routed through the server will not be granted until the firewall service restarts.

2.   **Correct Answers: A and E**

   A. Correct: At no point was it mentioned that you actually applied the changes made to the system policy.

   B. Incorrect: This is a general traffic rule that allows traffic from the Remote Management Computers to the Remote Management Computers. It will not enable RDP traffic to reach the ISA Server. Access rules are used to allow traffic to pass through the ISA Server 2004 computer to remote networks. The hint that this answer is wrong is that the source and destination are the same.

   C. Incorrect: This is a general traffic rule that denies traffic from the Remote Management Computers to the Remote Management Computers. It will not enable RDP traffic to reach the ISA Server. Access rules are used to allow traffic to pass through the ISA Server 2004 computer to remote networks. The hint that this answer is wrong is that the source and destination are the same.

D. Incorrect: This is used to support the ISA Server 2000 firewall client and the Microsoft Proxy 2.0 firewall client. It will not allow computers to connect to the ISA Server 2004 computer using an RDP client.

E. Correct: By default, the Remote Management Computers group is empty. You must populate it with the IP addresses of hosts that you wish to manage the server remotely. Until this group is populated, remote management of the terminal server will not be possible.

3.   Correct Answers: A and C

A. Correct: By default, all domain controllers on the internal network can be used for Active Directory directory service authentication. To ensure that the other domain controllers on the Contoso internal network are not used for authentication, you must remove this default option.

B. Incorrect: By default, domain controllers will not be members of the remote management group. Because the remote management group is not used by default to locate domain controllers against which to authenticate, this change will not achieve the desired results.

C. Correct: You will need to use the New ... Computer option to add the domain controller located at IP address 10.0.0.10 to the list of locations that can be used for Active Directory authentication. You cannot simply enter the IP address of the domain controller at the Add dialog box; instead, you must select an existing object or create a new object in the network entities list.

D. Incorrect: This answer is incorrect because it excludes the domain controller against which you wish to authenticate. Also, you cannot simply enter IP addresses, but must select an existing object or create a new object in the network entities list.

4.   Correct Answers: D

A. Incorrect: By default, RSA SecurID is not enabled. At no point in the question was it enabled, hence the primary goal is not achieved. By default, RADIUS authentication is enabled. By clearing the check box on the RADIUS authentication, it becomes disabled, meeting the first of the two secondary goals. Enforcing strict RPC compliance means that Active Directory authentication using DCOM is disabled, and therefore the second secondary goal is not achieved.

B. Incorrect: By default, RSA SecurID is not enabled. At no point in the question was it enabled, hence the primary goal is not achieved. By default, RADIUS authentication is enabled. By clearing the check box on the RADIUS authentication, it becomes disabled, meeting the first of the two secondary goals. Enforcing strict RPC compliance means that Active Directory authentication using DCOM is disabled, and therefore the second secondary goal is not achieved.

C. **Incorrect:** By default, RSA SecurID is not enabled. At no point in the question was it enabled, hence the primary goal is not achieved. By default, RADIUS authentication is enabled. By clearing the check box on the RADIUS authentication, it becomes disabled, meeting the first of the two secondary goals. Enforcing strict RPC compliance means that Active Directory authentication using DCOM is disabled, and therefore the second secondary goal is not achieved.

D. **Correct:** By default, RSA SecurID is not enabled. At no point in the question was it enabled, hence the primary goal is not achieved. By default RADIUS authentication is enabled. By clearing the check box on the RADIUS authentication, it becomes disabled, meeting the first of the two secondary goals. Enforcing strict RPC compliance means that Active Directory authentication using DCOM is disabled, and therefore the second secondary goal is not achieved.

E. **Incorrect:** By clearing the check box on the RADIUS authentication, it becomes disabled, meeting the first of the two secondary goals.

5.   Correct Answers: D

A. **Incorrect:** The problem is that during Rooslan's absence, his DHCP lease expired. Upon return, a new IP address was allocated to his computer. This IP address does not match any listed on the Remote Management Computers property. Configuration.ini is used by the Firewall client and is irrelevant to managing ISA Server 2004 through MMC in this situation.

B. **Incorrect:** Because Rooslan can administer ISA Server 2004 from your computer, this is not likely to be the problem.

C. **Incorrect:** Because Rooslan is able to administer ISA Server 2004 from your computer, this is not likely to be the problem.

D. **Correct:** The Remote Management Computers group in ISA Server 2004's system policy contains a list of IP addresses or subnets. Hosts with these addresses are allowed to connect to the ISA Server computer for the purposes of remote management. During Rooslan's absence, it is likely that his DHCP lease expired. If Rooslan's DHCP-allocated IP address was entered into the Remote Management Computers group, it would remain relevant only until the DHCP lease again expired. To circumvent this, assign a static IP address to both Rooslan and your computer so that you will always be able to manage the ISA Server 2004 computer remotely.

E. **Incorrect:** The ISA Server 2004 Firewall Client software is not used to establish remote MMC connections to the ISA Server computer.

6.   Correct Answers: A and E

A. Correct: The Helpdesk Subnet includes the IP address range 10.0.10.64 through 10.0.10.127.

B. Incorrect: The Server Room subnet includes the IP address range 10.0.25.80 through 10.0.25.95.

C. Incorrect: The Administration subnet includes the IP address range 10.0.16.224 through 10.0.16.255.

D. Incorrect: The Helpdesk Subnet includes the IP address range 10.0.10.64 through 10.0.10.127.

E. Correct: The Server Room subnet includes the IP address range 10.0.25.80 through 10.0.25.95.

Back Up and Restore ISA Server 2004

There is a reason that when servers crash, the term "disaster recovery" is used instead of something more neutral such as "configuration rescue" or "server restoration." When something goes wrong with servers in the real world, the problems tend to be of the worst sort, hence the appropriate use of the word "disaster." When administering ISA Server 2004, you should prepare for the worst. Make regular backups of the computer, and ensure that you export the configuration prior to making any changes, so you can roll back the changes in the event that they have unintended consequences. It takes only a moment to export an ISA Server configuration. If you don't do this before making changes and something goes wrong, it may be several hours before you can correct the problem. Rectifying the problem with an exported configuration may take only a few minutes. Another benefit to exporting configurations is that you can import them on other ISA Server 2004 computers. This makes cloning ISA Server 2004 computers relatively simple, a task that was more difficult with ISA Server 2000.

Objective 3.2 Questions

1. You are about to make significant changes to the system policy of an ISA Server 2004 array. You want to make sure that you can roll back to the current configuration in the event that something goes wrong. Which of the following steps can you take to ensure that you have the ability to roll back to the current configuration? (Choose the correct answer.)

   A. On a configuration storage server in the array, right-click the Enterprise node in the ISA Server Management Console and select Export.

   B. On a configuration storage server in the array, right-click the Array node in the ISA Server Management Console and select Export.

   C. On a configuration storage server in the array, in the Firewall Policy node, select the Export System Policy task.

   D. On a configuration storage server in the array, right-click the Virtual Private Networks (VPN) node in the ISA Server Management Console and select Export VPN Clients Configuration.

2. In the last few hours, several shared Internet Protocol Security (IPSec) keys used by your organization's ISA Server 2004 computer have become corrupt. ISA Server 2004 is installed on a computer running Windows Server 2003. Prior to the corruption, the backup utility was used to create an Automated System Recovery (ASR) set. It was also used to create a separate backup of the system state data. In addition, you exported and backed up the entire configuration using the ISA server console to two separate locations. Since the backups were made, you have installed some new hardware on the server. The software installed with this hardware has made significant modifications to the registry. Which of the following methods could you use to recover the shared IPSec keys used by ISA Server 2004? (Select all that apply.)

   A. Restart the computer in directory services restore mode and perform an authoritative restore.

   B. Restore the system state data.

   C. Perform ASR.

   D. Import the exported configuration using the ISA Server Management Console.

   E. Restore the backed-up configuration through the ISA Server Management Console.

3. You are the administrator of an ISA Server 2004 Enterprise Edition array that comprises three servers and a separate ISA Server 2004 Configuration Storage server. The configuration storage server does not have the firewall component of ISA Server installed. All servers run Windows Server 2003. The array has a complex configuration that has been developed over the last year of use. There is a fire in the server room one Saturday morning, and ISA Server computers 1 and 3 are completely destroyed. Unfortunately, the junior administrator that works for you forgot to take the backup tapes off-site. This means that the last two months of backup tapes have also been destroyed. You have two replacement servers available. You install Windows Server 2003 on the replacement servers and configure these computers with the Transmission Control Protocol/ Internet Protocol (TCP/IP) configuration of the destroyed systems. Which of the following methods will allow you to replace the configurations of ISA Server computers 1 and 3? (Choose the correct answer.)

A. Export the configuration of ISA Server computer 2. Install ISA Server 2004, Enterprise Edition, on replacement servers 1 and 3. Import the configuration of ISA Server computer 2 to replacement ISA Server computers 1 and 3. Join replacement servers 1 and 3 to the array.

B. Export the configuration and system policy of ISA Server computer 2. Install ISA Server 2004, Enterprise Edition, on replacement servers 1 and 3. Import the configuration and system policy of ISA Server computer 2 on to replacement ISA Server computers 1 and 3. Join replacement servers 1 and 3 to the array.

C. Export the configuration of the ISA Server 2004 configuration storage server. Install ISA Server 2004, Enterprise Edition, on replacement servers 1 and 3. Import the exported configuration on to replacement ISA Server computers 1 and 3. Join replacement servers 1 and 3 to the array.

D. Export the configuration and system policy of the ISA Server 2004 configuration storage server. Install ISA Server 2004, Enterprise Edition, on replacement servers 1 and 3. Import the exported configuration and system policy on to replacement ISA Server computers 1 and 3. Join replacement servers 1 and 3 to the array.

E. Install ISA Server 2004, Enterprise Edition, on replacement servers 1 and 3. During installation, specify the location of the configuration storage server and join the array.

4.   Contoso Ltd. currently has a branch site located in Wangaratta. ISA Server 2004 is installed and configured as a branch office firewall at this site on a computer that barely meets the minimum specifications for both ISA Server 2004 and Windows Server 2003. This server has been functioning erratically for the last few months and management has decided that it should be upgraded. You have a new Pentium IV computer running Windows Server 2003 and ISA Server 2004 with the same number of network interfaces that you can use to replace the old branch office firewall.

You have the following goals:

■ Primary Goal: The new computer will use the same highly customized system policy that exists on the old branch office firewall.

- Secondary Goal: The 50 SecureNAT clients located at the Wangaratta site will not require updates to their configuration.

- Secondary Goal: The current administrative role delegation settings that exist on the old branch office firewall are replicated on the replacement computer.

- You perform the following tasks:

- In the ISA Server 2004 Management Console of the old branch office firewall, right-click the server node and select Export. Select the appropriate removable media as the export location and ensure that you export the user permission settings and confidential information.

- Record the TCP/IP configuration of the old branch office firewall, then shut down the firewall and replace it with the newer computer. Set the TCP/IP configuration of the new server to that of the old branch office firewall.

- In the ISA Server 2004 Management Console of the new branch office firewall, right-click the server node and select Import, choosing the removable media onto which you saved the old server's configuration.

Given this information, which of your goals have you accomplished? (Choose the correct answer.)

A. You have accomplished the primary goal and both secondary goals.

B. You have accomplished the primary goal and one secondary goal.

C. You have accomplished only the primary goal.

D. You have not accomplished the primary goal. You have accomplished both secondary goals.

E. None of your goals have been accomplished.

5. Your organization has a single array of three ISA Server 2004, Enterprise Edition, computers. Which of the following configuration settings are shared between them? (Select all that apply.)

A. Local User and Group configuration

B. DNS Server settings

C. Domains that belong to the internal network

D. Allowing Firewall client connections from the Microsoft Proxy 2.0 and ISA Server 2000 firewall clients

E. Delegation of administrative roles

Objective 3.2 Answers

1.   Correct Answers: C

   A. Incorrect: This action will export the Enterprise policy. It will not export the fire-wall policies of an array within the enterprise.

   B. Incorrect: This action will back up all settings except the system policy settings. To back up the system policy settings, use the Export System Policy task.

   C. Correct: This action will export the system policy configuration, enabling you to roll it back if something goes wrong.

   D. Incorrect: This action will export the VPN clients' configuration. It will not export the system policy configuration.

2.   Correct Answers: D and E

   A. Incorrect: Directory services restore mode is only used on domain controllers when an Active Directory object is accidentally deleted and must be restored.

   B. Incorrect: The question stated that significant changes had been made to the registry since the system state data had been backed up. If the system state data was restored, the registry would be overwritten and these changes would be lost.

   C. Incorrect: The ASR set does include important configuration settings for the Windows Server 2003 computer. However, if an ASR restore was performed, the significant changes made to the registry after the installation of new hardware and associated software would be lost.

   D. Correct: As the entire configuration was exported, the original shared IPSec keys will be stored in this exported configuration. Importing this configuration again will overwrite the corrupted shared IPSec keys.

   E. Correct: When you back up the configuration using the ISA Server Management Console, all configuration settings, including shared IPSec keys, are backed up. When you restore the backed-up configuration using the ISA Server Management Console it overwrites the existing configuration in its entirety.

3.   Correct Answers: E

   A. Incorrect: The configuration storage server stores the ISA Server configuration. There is no need to export from the other servers. On installation, simply join the replacement servers to the array and the configuration will be set.

   B. Incorrect: The configuration storage server stores the ISA Server configuration. There is no need to export from the other servers. On installation, simply join the replacement servers to the array and the configuration will be set.

C. Incorrect: The configuration storage server stores the ISA Server configuration. There is no need to export from the other servers. On installation, simply join the replacement servers to the array and the configuration will be set.

D. Incorrect: The configuration storage server stores the ISA Server configuration. There is no need to export from the other servers. On installation, simply join the replacement servers to the array and the configuration will be set.

E. Correct: The configuration storage server stores the ISA Server configuration. On installation, simply join the replacement servers to the array and the configuration will be set.

4.   Correct Answers: D

A. Incorrect: The system policy must be exported independently of all other configuration settings using the export system policy tasks. In the actions listed in the question, the system policy is never exported, so the primary goal has not been met. Because the TCP/IP configuration of the old server is applied to the new server, SecureNAT clients will not require any additional changes. Exporting a configuration when using the options specified, while not saving the system policy, does include administrative role delegation settings.

B. Incorrect: The system policy must be exported independently of all other configuration settings using the export system policy tasks. In the actions listed in the question, the system policy is never exported, so the primary goal has not been met. Because the TCP/IP configuration of the old server is applied to the new server, SecureNAT clients will not require any additional changes. Exporting a configuration when using the options specified, while not saving the system policy, does include administrative role delegation settings.

C. Incorrect: The system policy must be exported independently of all other configuration settings using the export system policy tasks. In the actions listed in the question, the system policy is never exported, so the primary goal has not been met. Because the TCP/IP configuration of the old server is applied to the new server, SecureNAT clients will not require any additional changes. Exporting a configuration when using the options specified, while not saving the system policy, does include administrative role delegation settings.

D. Correct: The system policy must be exported independently of all other configuration settings using the export system policy tasks. In the actions listed in the question, the system policy is never exported, so the primary goal has not been met. Because the TCP/IP configuration of the old server is applied to the new server, SecureNAT clients will not require any additional changes. Exporting a configuration when using the options specified, while not saving the system policy, does include administrative role delegation settings.

E. **Incorrect:** The system policy must be exported independently of all other configuration settings using the export system policy tasks. In the actions listed in the question, the system policy is never exported, so the primary goal has not been met. Because the TCP/IP configuration of the old server is applied to the new server, SecureNAT clients will not require any additional changes. Exporting a configuration when using the options specified, while not saving the system policy, does include administrative role delegation settings.

5. **Correct Answers: C, D, and E**

A. **Incorrect:** Local users and groups are unique to each individual member of the array.

B. **Incorrect:** DNS Server settings are configured on a per-server, rather than on a per-array, basis.

C. **Correct:** Domains that belong to the internal network are specified for the entire array.

D. **Correct:** Whether non-encrypted Firewall client connections are allowed is set at the array level, rather than the individual server level, when using ISA Server 2004, Enterprise Edition.

E. **Correct:** Roles can be delegated at the array and Enterprise level, but not at the individual server level, when an ISA Server 2004 Enterprise Edition computer is a member of an array.

Objective 3.3
Define Administrative Roles

Permissions in ISA Server 2004 are not assigned on an individual basis; rather, they are bundled into administrative roles. To grant a user or group a particular set of permissions, you delegate a specific administrative role to that group. ISA Server 2004, Enterprise Edition, differs from Standard Edition in that you are able to delegate administrative roles only to accounts and groups that are members of the domain or forest to which the Enterprise Edition server belongs. The three administrative roles are ISA Server Basic Monitoring, ISA Server Extended Monitoring, and ISA Server Full Administrator.

Objective 3.3 Questions

1. You are the senior systems administrator at Contoso Ltd. The Contoso network contains four ISA Server 2004 computers, all of which are members of the *contoso.com* domain. You are training one of your junior administrators to share some of the maintenance duties on the ISA Server 2004 computers. Management of the servers is performed using RDP. You want the junior administrator to be able to export confidential information such as shared IPSec keys and passwords to an XML file in a secure folder on a daily basis. You do not want the junior administrator to be able to configure the cache or firewall policy. Which of the following steps should you take? (Choose the correct answer.)

A. Assign the ISA Server Basic Monitoring role to the junior administrator's domain account.

B. Assign the ISA Server Extended Monitoring role to the junior administrator's domain account.

C. Assign the ISA Server Full Administrator role to the junior administrator's domain account.

D. Add the junior administrator's domain account to the local ISA Server Extended Monitoring group.

2. Rooslan is the junior security administrator at your company. You are currently teaching him how to administrate a stand-alone Windows Server 2003 computer running ISA Server 2004. To this end, you have configured a local user account for him on the computer running ISA Server 2004 and delegated the ISA Server Extended Monitoring role to this account. This will enable Rooslan to explore many of the settings without accidentally making vital configuration changes. When logged on to the server through Remote Desktop, Rooslan has found that he can view policy, stop and start sessions and services, and create reports. When he runs the ISA Server Performance Monitor, however, he is unable to add any counters or get the monitor to work. Which of the following steps could you take to rectify this situation? (Select all that apply.)

A. Delegate the ISA Server Basic Monitoring role to Rooslan's local user account.

B. Delegate the ISA Server Full Administrator role to Rooslan's local user account.

C. Add Rooslan's user account to the local Power Users group.

D. Add Rooslan's user account to the local Performance Log Users group.

E. Add Rooslan's user account to the local Performance Monitor Users group.

3.   You have delegated roles on your ISA Server 2004 computer as shown here:

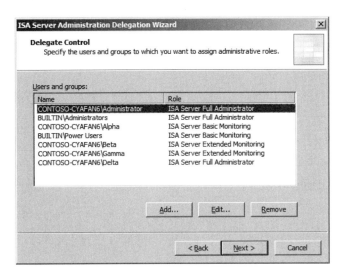

You wish to ensure that only the local Administrators and Delta groups can create alert definitions. For which of the following groups will you need to alter delegated permissions? (Select all that apply.)

A. Power Users

B. Gamma

C. Beta

D. Alpha

E. Delta

4. You are assigning administrative roles on a Configuration Storage server used to support an ISA Server 2004 Enterprise Edition array for Coho Vineyards. The administrative roles that are currently defined for the configuration server are shown here:

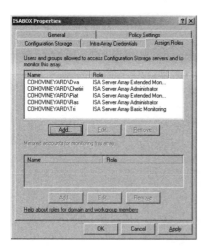

Which of the domain groups listed in the screen shot are able to create reports when connected to the Coho Vineyards member server that hosts the Configuration Storage server? (Select all that apply.)

A. Dva

B. Chetiri

C. Piat

D. Ras

E. Tri

5. You want to restrict members of your help desk team to acknowledging alerts on a stand-alone ISA Server 2004 computer. All members of the help desk team are members of the Helpdesk and Power Users local groups on the ISA Server 2004 Standard Edition computer. The computer has ISA Server 2004 installed and hosted by Windows Server 2003. You do not want the help desk team to be able to view ISA Server 2004 log information. Which of the following administrative roles should you assign to the Helpdesk local group? (Choose the correct answer.)

A. Assign no role.

B. Assign the ISA Server Basic Monitoring role to the Helpdesk local group.

C. Assign the ISA Server Extended Monitoring role to the Helpdesk local group.

D. Assign the ISA Server Full Administrator role to the Helpdesk local group.

6.   You wish to allow 10 domain users to view ISA Server logs and firewall policy, and have the ability to generate reports using the ISA Server 2004 Enterprise Edition Management Console. These users should not be able to set firewall policy. Your organization has a single ISA Server 2004 Enterprise Edition computer that functions as an edge firewall. ISA Server 2004 is installed on a server running Windows Server 2003, Enterprise Edition. Which of the following steps should you take to give the 10 users the required access with a minimum amount of administrative effort? (Choose the correct answer.)

   A. Add the 10 users to the Power Users local group on the Windows Server 2003 Enterprise Edition computer.

   B. Create a local group on the ISA Server 2004 computer named Policyreport. Add the 10 domain user accounts to the Policyreport group. Use the ISA Server 2004 Enterprise Edition Management Console to delegate the ISA Server Basic Monitoring role to this group.

   C. Create a local group on the ISA Server 2004 computer named Policyreport. Add the 10 domain user accounts to the Policyreport group. Use the ISA Server 2004 Enterprise Edition Management Console to delegate the ISA Server Extended Monitoring role to this group.

   D. Create a local group on the ISA Server 2004 computer named Policyreport. Add the 10 domain user accounts to the Policyreport group. Use the ISA Server 2004 Enterprise Edition Management Console to delegate the ISA Server Full Administrator role to this group.

   E. Use the ISA Server 2004 Enterprise Edition Management Console to delegate the ISA Server Extended Monitoring role to each of the 10 individual domain accounts.

Objective 3.3 Answers

1.   Correct Answers: B

   A. Incorrect: User accounts that are assigned the ISA Server Basic Monitoring role can monitor ISA Server and network activity but are unable to perform more advanced functions such as the exporting of confidential configuration information.

   B. Correct: The ISA Server Extended Monitoring role provides a middle ground between the Basic Monitoring role and the Full Administrator role. It allows user accounts assigned the role to perform functions such as exporting and importing confidential configuration information without being able to configure advanced settings such as cache and firewall policy.

   C. Incorrect: User accounts assigned the ISA Server Full Administrator role are able to perform all administrative functions on the ISA Server computer, including configuration of cache and firewall policy. The question stated that the junior administrator should not be able to configure the cache or firewall policy, so this answer is incorrect.

   D. Incorrect: Roles are assigned using the ISA Server 2004 Management Console. Roles are not assigned by adding users to local groups, unless the local group has been specifically assigned a particular role. Because nothing was mentioned in the question about such an existing situation, and this group does not exist by default, this answer is incorrect.

2.   Correct Answers: D and E

   A. Incorrect: The problem does not exist within the administrative roles. To use Performance Monitor, a user must be a member of the local Performance Log Users or Performance Monitor Users group.

   B. Incorrect: The problem does not exist within the administrative roles. To use Performance Monitor, a user must be a member of the local Performance Log Users or Performance Monitor Users group. Delegating this role would provide Rooslan with more privileges than you are willing to give him.

   C. Incorrect: Members of the local Power Users group do not automatically have permission to use Performance Monitor and Performance Logs on Windows Server 2003 computers.

   D. Correct: The problem does not exist within the administrative roles. To use Performance Monitor, a user must be a member of the local Performance Log Users or Performance Monitor Users group.

E. Correct: The problem does not exist within the administrative roles. To use Performance Monitor, a user must be a member of the local Performance Log Users or Performance Monitor Users group.

3.   **Correct Answers: B and C**

   A. Incorrect: Accounts and groups delegated the ISA Server Extended Monitoring and ISA Server Full Administrator roles have the ability to create alert definitions. Because the Power Users group has neither of these roles, no alteration to the role delegated to them is necessary.

   B. Correct: Accounts and groups delegated the ISA Server Extended Monitoring and ISA Server Full Administrator roles have the ability to create alert definitions. This means that the role delegated to group Gamma must be altered.

   C. Correct: Accounts and groups delegated the ISA Server Extended Monitoring and ISA Server Full Administrator roles have the ability to create alert definitions. This means that the role delegated to group Beta must be altered.

   D. Incorrect: Accounts and groups delegated the ISA Server Extended Monitoring and ISA Server Full Administrator roles have the ability to create alert definitions. As the Alpha group has neither of these roles, no alteration to the role delegated to them is necessary.

   E. Incorrect: The question specified that the Delta group should retain the ability to create alert definitions. As the role delegated to this group already confers that right, no change should be made.

4.   **Correct Answers: A, B, C, and D**

   A. Correct: When delegated, the ISA Server Array Extended Monitoring role allows those that access a Configuration Storage server to view logs or generate reports.

   B. Correct: When delegated, the ISA Server Array Administrator role allows those that access a Configuration Storage server to view logs or generate reports.

   C. Correct: When delegated, the ISA Server Array Extended Monitoring role allows those that access a Configuration Storage server to view logs or generate reports.

   D. Correct: When delegated, the ISA Server Array Administrator role allows those that access a Configuration Storage server to view logs or generate reports.

   E. Incorrect: When delegated, the ISA Server Array Basic Monitoring role does not allow those that access a Configuration Storage server to view logs or generate reports.

5.   Correct Answers: B

A. Incorrect: If no role is assigned, the members of the help desk team will be unable to acknowledge alerts.

B. Correct: The ISA Server Basic Monitoring role will allow members of the Help-desk local user group to acknowledge alerts but will not allow them to view ISA Server 2004 log information.

C. Incorrect: Although the ISA Server Extended Monitoring role will enable members of the Helpdesk local user group to acknowledge alerts, it will also allow them to view ISA Server 2004 log information.

D. Incorrect: Assigning the ISA Server Full Administrator role to the Helpdesk local user group will mean that the members of that group will be able to view logs as well as perform more important administrative functions such as changing firewall policy.

6.   Correct Answers: E

A. Incorrect: Adding the 10 domain user accounts to the Power Users local group on the Windows Server 2003 Enterprise Edition computer will not immediately confer the ability to view ISA Server. This must be done through the delegation of administrative roles.

B. Incorrect: Administrative roles in an ISA Server 2004 Enterprise Edition computer can only be delegated to user and group accounts that are members of the domain. The Extended Monitoring, rather than Basic Monitoring, role should be delegated.

C. Incorrect: Administrative roles in an ISA Server 2004 Enterprise Edition computer can be delegated only to user and group accounts that are members of the domain.

D. Incorrect: Administrative roles in an ISA Server 2004 Enterprise Edition computer can only be delegated to user and group accounts that are members of the domain. The Extended Monitoring rather than Full Administrator role should be delegated.

E. Correct: The key to this question is the fact that you can only delegate administrative roles on ISA Server 2004, Enterprise Edition, to domain accounts or groups. The Extended Monitoring role confers the appropriate rights without providing the 10 users with the ability to configure firewall policy.

Objective 3.4
Configure Firewall Settings

You can configure ISA Server 2004 to generate alerts if certain types of attacks against it are attempted. When intrusion detection is configured, the ISA Server computer will generate an alert whether the attack is sent from a host on the Internet or from the internal network. IP options filtering allows an administrator to configure the ISA Server 2004 computer to drop packets that contain particular flags. The use of these flags does not always signify an attack. That being said, their use is so unusual and attackers can use them so effectively that many administrators believe it is safest to drop any packets that contain them. Similarly, ISA Server 2004 can be configured to drop IP fragments. Configuring ISA Server 2004 to drop IP fragments can have a deleterious effect on some types of network activity, specifically those types of traffic that do not retransmit dropped packets. ISA Server also has the option of being able to be configured to use the dial-up adapter to connect to specific remote networks. In addition, you can configure ISA Server to create a dial-up connection in the event that the primary Internet connection fails. Another important firewall configuration option is firewall chaining. Firewall chaining allows you to have traffic forwarded from a downstream firewall to an upstream firewall for clients configured as ISA Server 2004 firewall clients or SecureNAT clients.

Objective 3.4 Questions

1. You have enabled intrusion detection on your ISA Server 2004 computer. The ISA Server 2004 computer is configured using the Edge Firewall template. There is a new worm on the Internet that sends IP fragments to hosts that contain more data than the maximum packet size. Your goal is to be notified each time the ISA Server 2004 computer is the target of such an attack. To this end, you enable intrusion detection on the ISA Server 2004 computer. When configuring intrusion detection, which of the following attack types should you enable detection of to meet your goal? (Choose the correct answer.)

    A. Windows out-of-band (WinNuke)

    B. Land

    C. Ping of death

    D. IP half scan

    E. UDP bomb

2. Intrusion detection is configured on the Contoso Ltd. ISA Server 2004 computer as shown here.

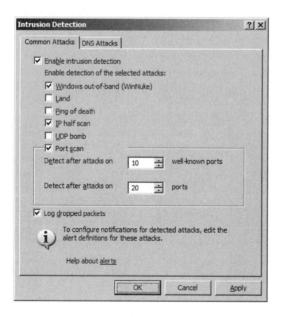

Given this configuration, which of the following traffic events will cause ISA Server 2004 to generate an alert? (Choose the correct answer.)

    A. An attacker sends an illegal UDP packet.

    B. An attacker scans ports 20, 21, 25, 53, 80, 110, 137, 143, and 443 looking for available services.

    C. An attacker sends TCP packets with invalid flags in such a way that the TCP three-way handshake is never completed.

    D. An attacker sends an IP fragment that contains more data than the maximum IP packet size.

3. By default, IP options filtering is enabled on a computer running ISA Server 2004. What type of traffic does IP options filtering deal with? (Choose the correct answer.)

    A. IP options filtering ensures that IP fragments are dropped.

    B. IP options filtering ensures that IP packets that contain specified IP options flags are dropped.

    C. IP options filtering ensures that IP fragments containing more data than the maximum IP packet size are dropped.

    D. IP options filtering ensures that DNS host names exceeding 255 bytes will be dropped.

4. Your goal is to configure ISA Server to use the dial-up adapter rather than the normal network adapter to connect to any internal hosts that are located on the 192.168.99.0 / 24 and 192.168.100.0 /24 networks. These address ranges represent a remote site to which you need to connect using dial-up, because it does not have its own Internet connection. The name of the dial-up connection used to connect to this remote site is Remotedial. Which of the following steps should you take to meet this goal? (Choose two answers; each forms a part of the solution.)

    A. In the ISA Server Management Console, create a new internal network named RemotesiteA. Set the starting address to 192.168.99.0 and the ending address to 192.168.100.255.

    B. In the ISA Server Management Console, create an internal network named RemotesiteB. Set the starting address to 192.168.99.0 and the ending address to 192.168.101.255.

    C. Edit the System Policy. Ensure that RemotesiteA is a member of the Remote Management Computers group.

    D. Edit the System Policy. Ensure that RemotesiteB is a member of the Remote Management Computers group.

    E. In the ISA Server management console, open Specify Dial-Up Preferences. Check the Allow Automatic Dialing To This Network radio button and set the network to RemotesiteA. In the Use The Following Dial-up Connection drop-down list, select the Remotedial connection.

    F. In the ISA Server Management Console, open Specify Dial-Up Preferences. Select the Allow Automatic Dialing To This Network option and set the network to RemotesiteB. In the Use The Following Dial-up Connection drop-down list, select the Remotedial connection.

5. Contoso Ltd. has several branch offices and a main headquarters. You want branch office client connections to the Internet to be routed through the local branch office ISA Server 2004 firewall and then routed through the headquarters ISA Server 2004 firewall. To achieve this, which of the following steps must you take? (Select all that apply.)

    A. Ensure that all clients at the branch offices are configured to use the ISA Server 2004 firewall client or are SecureNAT clients.

    B. Ensure that all clients at the branch offices are configured as Web Proxy clients.

    C. Configure firewall chaining on each of the branch office ISA Server computers. Chain each branch office's ISA Server computer to the fully qualified domain name (FQDN) of the headquarters' ISA Server 2004 firewall.

    D. Configure firewall chaining on the headquarters ISA Server 2004 firewall. Chain the headquarters' ISA Server 2004 firewall to the FQDN of one of the branch office's ISA Server 2004 firewalls.

6. The Contoso Ltd. ISA Server 2004 computer is configured with the Edge Firewall template. This computer also performs caching and proxy functions. You are considering configuring this computer to drop all IP fragments as a way of tightening security. Which of the following consequences might occur if you do this? (Select all that apply.)

    A. VPN connections using Point-to-Point Tunneling Protocol (PPTP) may not be successfully established.

    B. Hosts on the internal network accessing streaming audio or video servers on the Internet may encounter problems.

    C. Hosts on the internal network accessing dynamic Web pages hosted by servers on the Internet may encounter problems.

    D. Hosts on the internal network attempting to download video files using the FTP protocol may encounter problems.

    E. VPN connections using L2TP over IPSec connections may not be successfully established.

Objective 3.4 Answers

1.   Correct Answers: C

A. Incorrect: An out-of-band attack occurs when a host receives a packet with the "URGENT" flag set but receives no follow-up data.

B. Incorrect: A land attack occurs when a TCP SYN packet is sent with a spoofed source IP address and port number that matches those of the destination IP address and port number.

C. Correct: Ping of death attacks involve the host's receiving an IP fragment that contains more data than the maximum IP packet size. When successful, this attack leads to a kernel buffer overflow, halting the computer.

D. Incorrect: IP half-scan attacks involve an attacker's sending TCP packets with invalid flags leading to the TCP three-way handshake not being completed.

E. Incorrect: The UDP bomb attack involves the attacker sending an illegal User Datagram Protocol (UDP) packet. Older operating systems can fail when this type of packet is received.

2.   Correct Answers: C

A. Incorrect: This attack is known as a UDP bomb, and it is not one of the attacks configured on the Contoso Ltd. ISA Server computer.

B. Incorrect: Although the screen shot indicates that the ISA Server 2004 computer will generate an alert when ports are scanned, the alert will only occur after 10 well-known ports or 20 ports in total are scanned. In this answer, only nine ports are scanned, all of which are well-known ports and are the FTP control and data ports, SMTP, DNS, HTTP, POP3, NETBIOS, IMAP4, and HTTPS.

C. Correct: IP half-scan attacks involve an attacker sending TCP packets with invalid flags, leading to incompletion of the TCP three-way handshake. This attack is also known as a *stealth scan*.

D. Incorrect: Ping of death attacks involve the host receiving an IP fragment that contains more data than the maximum IP packet size. When successful, this attack leads to a kernel buffer overflow, halting the computer. This is not one of the attacks configured on the Contoso Ltd. ISA Server computer.

3. **Correct Answers: B**

    A. **Incorrect:** IP options filtering is used to deny packets that contain particular IP options flags.

    B. **Correct:** IP options filtering is used to deny packets that contain particular IP options flags. IP options flags can be used to allow an attacker to override routing decisions made by routers between the source and destination hosts. This may enable access to the internal network.

    C. **Incorrect:** IP fragments containing more data than the maximum IP packet size are used in ping of death attacks. IP options filtering is used to deny packets that contain particular IP options flags.

    D. **Incorrect:** Defeating a DNS host name overflow attack is done by configuring the DNS intrusion detection filter. IP options filtering is used to deny packets that contain particular IP options flags.

4. **Correct Answers: A and E**

    A. **Correct:** To get ISA Server 2004 to use the dial-up adapter to connect to a particular network, you first need to define that network. The combined IP address range of these two networks will go from a starting address of 192.168.99.0 through an ending address of 192.168.100.255.

    B. **Incorrect:** The combined IP address range of these two networks will go from a starting address of 192.168.99.0 through an ending address of 192.168.100.255, rather than the values specified in this answer.

    C. **Incorrect:** This would allow the network range encompassed by RemotesiteA to connect and manage the ISA Server 2004 computer. This would not configure the ISA Server 2004 computer to use the dial-up adapter to connect to a specific remote network.

    D. **Incorrect:** This would allow the network range encompassed by RemotesiteB to connect and manage the ISA Server 2004 computer. This would not configure the ISA Server 2004 computer to use the dial-up adapter to connect to a specific remote network.

    E. **Correct:** RemotesiteA correctly represents the network range used at the remote site. To configure the ISA Server 2004 computer to connect through the dial-up adapter when it needs to access an IP address within this range, use the Specify Dial-Up preferences option in the General node of the ISA Server 2004 Management Console.

    F. **Incorrect:** RemotesiteB contains IP addresses that are not used at the remote location. The network must instead be set to RemotesiteA.

5.   **Correct Answers: A and C**

    A. Correct: Firewall chaining can only be used with ISA Server 2004 firewall clients or SecureNAT clients.

    B. Incorrect: Only ISA Server 2004 firewall and SecureNAT clients support firewall chaining. Web Proxy clients do not support firewall chaining.

    C. Correct: This will ensure that branch office connections to the Internet are routed through the local branch offices' ISA Server 2004 firewalls and then routed to the headquarter's ISA Server 2004 firewall.

    D. Incorrect: Although this would configure firewall chaining, it would do so in such a way that traffic from the headquarter's site would go to the headquarter's firewall and then be forwarded to the branch office's firewall.

6.   **Correct Answers: B and E**

    A. Incorrect: PPTP is not sensitive to IP fragment filtering in the way that Layer Two Tunneling Protocol (L2TP) over IPSec can be. If you institute a policy dropping all IP fragments, it may be necessary to configure VPN clients to use PPTP rather than L2TP over IPSec because packet fragmentation may occur during certificate exchange.

    B. Correct: Audio and video streaming can be adversely influenced by instituting a policy whereby all IP fragments are dropped. This is because streaming servers do not retransmit dropped packets in the way that most other forms of network communications do.

    C. Incorrect: Dynamic Web pages change on the basis of user input. This communication is standard, and any dropped IP fragments are likely to be retransmitted without causing any degradation of the user experience.

    D. Incorrect: Being one of the Internet's oldest protocols, FTP is extremely robust. In the case that an FTP transfer is interrupted by an IP fragment's being dropped, the offending packet, like most communication, will be retransmitted once the host determines that it has not arrived.

    E. Correct: If packet fragmentation occurs during certificate exchange, an L2TP over IPSec VPN connection cannot be established.

Configure ISA Server 2004 for Network Load Balancing

Network Load Balancing (NLB) is a clustering technique that allows two or more servers to share a processing load. The cluster has a virtual IP address that is shared among all nodes. Each node has its own individual IP addresses assigned to each adapter. Clients of the cluster see only a single computer, when in fact there are between two and eight nodes. NLB clusters can reconfigure themselves, redirecting traffic if a node fails, and redistributing traffic if a new cluster node comes online. Windows Server 2003 supports NLB out of the box. One of the benefits of choosing ISA Server 2004, Enterprise Edition, over Standard Edition is that it supports clustering out of the box. If you use Standard Edition, you must set up the cluster configuration manually.

Objective 3.5 Questions

1. You are considering implementing ISA Server 2004 on your network. After performing some simulations, you have determined that you will need four computers configured as an NLB cluster to support the estimated traffic load. Which of the following options would allow you to deploy a four-node ISA Server 2004 NLB cluster with a minimum amount of administrative effort? (Choose the correct answer.)

    A. Install ISA Server 2004, Standard Edition, on an Active/Passive four-node cluster running Windows 2000 Server.

    B. Install ISA Server 2004, Standard Edition, on an Active/Passive four-node cluster running Windows Server 2003, Enterprise Edition.

    C. Install ISA Server 2004, Standard Edition, on four separate Windows Server 2003 Enterprise Edition computers. Configure NLB manually.

    D. Implement ISA Server 2004, Enterprise Edition, on four separate Windows Server 2003 Enterprise Edition computers. Ensure that the servers are all members of the same array.

2. You want to configure ISA Server 2004, Standard Edition, to use NLB for two ISA Server 2004 computers. Given your requirements, you must determine which server platform you will use to host ISA Server 2004. Which of the following Windows Server platforms will support the installation of ISA Server 2004 and NLB? (Select all that apply.)

    A. Windows 2000 Server

    B. Windows 2000 Advanced Server

    C. Windows Server 2003

    D. Windows Server 2003, Web Edition.

    E. Windows Server 2003, Enterprise Edition

3. You are configuring four Windows Server 2003 computers running ISA Server 2004, Standard Edition, as an NLB cluster. Each server has two network adapters. Each server should have a common system policy and configuration. Which of the following steps do you need to take after installing ISA Server 2004 on each computer? (Select all that apply.)

    A. Ensure that each of the four computers has the same cluster IP address configured in Network Load Balancing Manager.

    B. In the Network Load Balancing Manager, ensure that each computer has a unique cluster IP address.

  C. Use DNS round-robin to map the cluster FQDN to the IP addresses of each network adapter.

  D. Configure a DNS host record to map the FQDN of the cluster to the cluster IP address.

  E. In the Network Load Balancing Manager, create a new cluster. Specify a cluster IP address and a cluster FQDN. Export the system policy and configuration. Import the system policy and configuration on the other three nodes of the cluster.

Objective 3.5 Answers

1.   Correct Answers: D

   A. Incorrect: Active/Passive node clustering requires a shared storage medium and is quite different from NLB.

   B. Incorrect: Active/Passive node clustering requires a shared storage medium and is quite different from NLB.

   C. Incorrect: Although this would work, it is far more administratively intensive than using ISA Server 2004, Enterprise Edition, which has NLB configuration built in.

   D. Correct: ISA Server 2004, Enterprise Edition, has NLB built in for servers that are members of the same array. This makes setting up NLB far less intensive than it would be if you were configuring it on computers running ISA Server 2004, Standard Edition.

2.   Correct Answers: B, C, and E

   A. Incorrect: Windows 2000 Server does not support NLB and cannot be used as a platform in this case.

   B. Correct: Windows 2000 Advanced Server does support NLB and can be used as a platform in this scenario.

   C. Correct: Windows Server 2003 supports NLB and can be used as a platform in this scenario.

   D. Incorrect: Although Windows Server 2003, Web Edition, supports NLB, you cannot install ISA Server 2004 on this scaled-down Windows Server 2003 platform.

   E. Correct: Windows Server 2003 Enterprise Edition supports NLB and can be used as a platform in this scenario.

3.   Correct Answers: A, D, and E

   A. Correct: If computers have separate IP addresses configured in Network Load Balancing Manager, they will be members of separate NLB clusters.

   B. Incorrect: If computers have separate IP addresses configured in Network Load Balancing Manager, they will be members of separate NLB clusters. Although you can configure multiple cluster IP addresses, these must be shared across the cluster and not be unique to cluster nodes. Cluster IP addresses are separate from the IP addresses assigned to network adapters.

C. **Incorrect:** DNS round-robin is a way of distributing traffic, but it is not NLB. The cluster FQDN should be mapped to the cluster IP address, not the IP address of the network adapters attached to nodes in the cluster.

D. **Correct:** As you will generally want your hosts to address the cluster using FQDN, you need to ensure that the cluster FQDN maps to the cluster IP address in the relevant DNS zone.

E. **Correct:** This is the first step involved in setting up an NLB cluster. It also ensures that you have a common configuration and system policy throughout the cluster. The administration of a cluster is greatly simplified if ISA Server 2004, Enterprise Edition, is in use, so those organizations that require clustering functionality should strongly consider implementing Enterprise Edition to reduce administrative overhead.

Configure ISA Server 2004 to Support a Network Topology

ISA Server 2004 ships with a set of configured network templates that allow administrators to deploy the server quickly and easily. The network templates reflect the most common types of ISA Server configuration. These templates include Edge Firewall, 3-Leg Perimeter, Front Firewall, Back Firewall, and Single Network Adapter. The template that you choose to implement is dependent on the configuration of the network to which you are deploying the ISA Server 2004 computer. Setting up networks in ISA Server 2004 is relatively simple; an administrator merely needs to specify the start and end of the IP address range. If given a network range in CIDR notation, an administrator may need to calculate the range. There are two types of relationships that can be configured between networks on an ISA Server 2004 computer. The first type of relationship, known as a *route relationship*, is used when hosts on both networks require the ability to communicate directly with each other. The second type of relationship, known as the *NAT relationship*, is used when the hosts on one network need to contact the hosts on a second network, but the second network hosts need to be restricted from contacting the hosts on the first.

Objective 3.6 Questions

1. Your organization has an existing hardware firewall that your manager does not want to decommission. You want to implement ISA Server 2004 as a firewall and, after careful planning, have decided that the best place to do this is behind the existing firewall. Which of the following network templates should you apply to ISA Server 2004 in this situation? (Choose the correct answer.)

    A. Edge firewall template

    B. 3-Leg perimeter template

    C. Front firewall template

    D. Single network adapter template

    E. Back firewall template

2. You are a consultant about to set up the Internet infrastructure for a brand-new company named Tailspin Toys. Tailspin Toys management has provided you with the following information:

They want to use only one computer as a firewall, proxy, and cache. They want to use the ISA Server 2004 software. They want to locate two Web servers and an SMTP server on a network that is available to hosts on the Internet and hosts on the internal network. They do not want any hosts on the internal network accessible to hosts on the Internet.

Given this information, which of the following network templates would you apply in this situation? (Choose the correct answer.)

    A. Edge firewall template

    B. Front firewall template

    C. Back firewall template

    D. 3-Leg perimeter template

3. You are installing an ISA Server 2004 computer for a new branch office of Tailspin Toys. You have requested the range of IP addresses that will be in use on this network. The network administrator has replied in an e-mail that the internal network should use the IP network 192.168.10.80 /28. When configuring the IP address range for the internal network on the ISA Server computer, which of the following values should you use? (Select all that apply.)

    A. Start address: 192.168.10.64

    B. Start address: 192.168.10.80

   C. End address: 192.168.10.87

   D. End address: 192.168.10.95

   E. End address: 192.168.10.111

4. You are configuring the IP address range to be used on the internal network at Contoso Ltd.'s head office. The head-office campus consists of three buildings, each of which is configured with its own individual IP subnet. The network administrator informs you that the following IP networks are in use:

Building One: 192.168.28.32 /27

Building Two: 192.168.28.64 /28

Building Three: 192.168.28.0 /27

When configuring the IP address range for the internal network on the ISA Server computer, which of the following values should you use? (Choose the correct answer.)

   A. Start address: 192.168.28.0; end address: 192.168.28.111

   B. Start address: 192.168.28.32; end address: 192.168.28.95

   C. Start address: 192.168.28.0; end address: 192.168.28.79

   D. Start address: 192.168.28.32; end address: 192.168.28.111

5. You have configured an ISA Server 2004 computer using the 3-leg perimeter network template. Hosts on the perimeter network have public IP addresses and need to be accessible to hosts on the Internet. Hosts on the internal network use the private IP address space and should not be accessed directly by hosts on the Internet or the perimeter network; however, hosts on the internal network should be able to access hosts on the Internet and the perimeter network. VPN clients should be able to access and be accessed by hosts on the internal network. Given this information, which of these relationships should be configured to use a route relationship as opposed to a NAT relationship? (Select all that apply.)

   A. Internal network to perimeter network

   B. VPN clients to internal network

   C. Internal network to Internet

   D. Internet to perimeter network

Objective 3.6 Answers

1.   Correct Answers: E

   A. Incorrect: The edge firewall template is used for ISA Server computers that are connected directly to the Internet. This template is inappropriate if a firewall exists between the deployed ISA Server computer and the Internet.

   B. Incorrect: The 3-Leg perimeter template is appropriate when you wish to connect your internal network to the Internet, protect it from intruders, and publish services to the Internet from a perimeter network (also known as a demilitarized zone, or DMZ). This template is inappropriate if a firewall exists between the deployed ISA Server computer and the Internet.

   C. Incorrect: When using this template, ISA Server is configured as the front-line defense in a back-to-back perimeter network configuration. This template is inappropriate if a firewall exists between the deployed ISA Server and the Internet.

   D. Incorrect: When using this template, ISA Server is able to function only in a Web proxying, caching, Web publishing, and Microsoft Outlook Web Access (OWA) publishing role. When so configured, ISA Server cannot function as a firewall, which is what the question specifies.

   E. Correct: When using this template, ISA Server functions as the back-line defense in a back-to-back perimeter network configuration. This option should be used when there is an existing firewall and you want to configure a perimeter network between the existing firewall and the newly deployed ISA Server firewall.

2.   Correct Answers: D

   A. Incorrect: The desire to locate Web servers and an SMTP server on a network that is available to hosts on the Internet and hosts on the internal network, while not allowing hosts on the internal network to be available to hosts on the Internet, hints at the necessity for a perimeter network. You can not use a perimeter network when ISA Server 2004 is configured using the edge firewall template.

   B. Incorrect: Although configuring ISA Server using the front firewall template allows for the existence of a perimeter network, it also necessitates the existence of a second firewall to take on the back firewall role. As Tailspin Toys management has specified, only one computer is to be used, so the choice of this particular template is incorrect.

   C. Incorrect: Configuring ISA Server using the back firewall template allows for the existence of a perimeter network, but also necessitates the existence of a front firewall between the perimeter network and the Internet. As Tailspin Toys management has specified, only one computer is to be used, so the choice of this particular template is incorrect.

   D. Correct: A single ISA Server 2004 computer configured with the 3-Leg perimeter template allows for the existence of a perimeter network while using only a single computer. This computer must be configured with three network interfaces. One interface connects to the Internet, one to the internal network, and one to the perimeter network.

3.   **Correct Answers: B and D**

   A. Incorrect: The IP network 192.168.10.80 /28 has a starting address of 192.168.10.80 and an end address of 192.168.10.95.

   B. Correct: The IP network 192.168.10.80 /28 has a starting address of 192.168.10.80 and an end address of 192.168.10.95.

   C. Incorrect: The IP network 192.168.10.80 /28 has a starting address of 192.168.10.80 and an end address of 192.168.10.95.

   D. Correct: The IP network 192.168.10.80 /28 has a starting address of 192.168.10.80 and an end address of 192.168.10.95.

   E. Incorrect: The IP network 192.168.10.80 /28 has a starting address of 192.168.10.80 and an end address of 192.168.10.95.

4.   **Correct Answers: C**

   A. Incorrect: The three networks together form a contiguous range from 192.168.28.0 through to 192.168.28.79.

   B. Incorrect: The three networks together form a contiguous range from 192.168.28.0 through to 192.168.28.79.

   C. Correct: The three networks together form a contiguous range from 192.168.28.0 through to 192.168.28.79.

   D. Incorrect: The three networks together form a contiguous range from 192.168.28.0 through to 192.168.28.79.

5.   **Correct Answers: B and D**

   A. Incorrect: There is no requirement for bidirectional communication between networks.

   B. Correct: By default, a route relationship exists between the internal network and the VPN clients network. VPN clients need to be able to have bidirectional communication with hosts on the internal network and do not use a NAT relationship.

C. **Incorrect:** Internal networks have their IP address information hidden from hosts on the Internet through NAT. NAT relationships are unidirectional, whereas route relationships are bidirectional.

D. **Correct:** Hosts on the Internet and perimeter require the ability to contact each other. Bidirectional communication implies that a route relationship should be configured, as opposed to a NAT relationship.

16 Configuring Web Caching (4.0)

Caching enables organizations to limit the amount of Web traffic crossing their Internet link by storing copies of commonly accessed Web content. Analysis of Web browsing patterns has shown that, in almost every organization, a small number of sites accounts for the vast majority of traffic. Rather than retrieve the same information from Internet Web servers time and again, caching stores retrieved pages centrally. When a second user accesses the same content, the cache forwards the second user to the locally stored content rather than downloading it again from the Internet. This can save an organization a significant amount of money, as incoming Internet traffic is often metered on a per-megabyte or per-gigabyte basis. For large organizations, such as universities, effective Web caching can strip tens of thousands of dollars from their Internet bills.

Tested Skills and Suggested Practices

The skills that you need to master the Configuring Web Caching objective domain on the *Implementing Microsoft Internet Security and Acceleration (ISA) Server 2004* exam include:

- Configure forward caching and reverse caching.
    - ❑ Practice 1: Enable Caching on a volume on your server by allocating disk space to the cache. In the Configuration\Cache node of the ISA Server 2004 Management Console, click the Define Cache Drives tasks. On the Define Cache Drives page, enter a figure of 100 MB and then click Set. Then click OK. When applying the changes, select the Save The Changes And Restart The Services option.
    - ❑ Practice 2: Create a Cache Rule by clicking the Create A Cache Rule task in the Configuration\Cache node of the ISA Server 2004 Management Console. This will run the New Cache Rule Wizard. Apply the following settings: Name: Temp-rule. Cache Rule Destination: External Network. Retrieve From Cache: Default Value. Cache Content: Default Value. Cache Advanced Configuration: Default Value. HTTP Caching: Default Value. FTP Caching: Default Value.

- Optimize performance of the ISA Server 2004 cache.
    - ❑ Practice 1: Enable Active Caching by opening the ISA Server 2004 Management Console and right-clicking the Configuration\Cache node. Navigate to the Active Caching tab and select the Enable Active Caching check box. Examine the different options for updating active objects in the cache, leaving the default choice active. Click OK and then apply the changes.

❑ Practice 2: Configure the Advanced Cache Settings by opening the ISA Server 2004 Management Console and right-clicking the Configuration\Cache node. Navigate to the Advanced Tab. Click the question mark to be provided with an explanation of each of the options that you can configure in this tab.

■ Diagnose and resolve caching issues.

❑ Practice : From the Start menu, navigate to the Administrative Tools menu and select Performance. Ensure that the System Monitor node is selected. Clear any existing counters by selecting them and pressing the DELETE key. Click the "+" button on the toolbar to open the Add Counters dialog box. Ensure that the Use Local Computer Counters option is selected. Use the Performance object drop-down list to select ISA Server Cache. Select each of the counters in the list and click Explain to view an explanation of the counter's function. When you have finished, add the Byres Retrieved Rate from Disk Cache, Bytes Retrieved Rate from Memory Cache, Max URLs Cached, and URLs in Cache performance counters by selecting them and clicking Add. When finished, click Close to close the Add Counters dialog box. Use a computer with the ISA Server 2004 Firewall Client software installed to retrieve Web pages from the Internet. Note the influence this has on the performance counters.

Further Reading

This section lists supplemental readings by objective. We recommend that you study these sources thoroughly before taking this exam.

Objective 4.1 ISA Server 2004 FAQ: Caching *http://www.microsoft.com/technet/prodtechnol/isa/2004/plan/faq-caching.mspx*

Outlook Web Access Server Publishing in ISA Server 2004 *http://www.microsoft.com/technet/prodtechnol/isa/2004/plan/owapublishing.mspx*

About the ISA Server Cache *http://msdn.microsoft.com/library/default.asp?url=/library/en-us/isasdk/isa/about_the_isa_server_cache.asp*

ISA Server Help: Cache Configuration

ISA Server Help: Cache Overview

Objective 4.2 How ISA Server 2004 caches responses to Web publishing client requests in reverse proxy mode *http://support.microsoft.com/?kbid=837737*

White Paper: Accelerating the Internet with ISA Server 2004 Web Caching *http://www.microsoft.com/isaserver/evaluation/whitepapers/default.asp*

ISA Server 2004 Technical Overview: Technet Briefing *http://www.microsoft.com/technet/community/events/isa/TNT1-111.mspx*

Objective 4.3   Deleting Cache Contents *http://www.microsoft.com/technet/prodtech nol/isa/2004/plan/deletecachecontents.mspx*

Introduction to the ISA Server Cache Objects *http://msdn.microsoft.com/library/ default.asp?url=/library/en-us/isasdk/isa/ introduction_to_the_isa_server_cache_objects.asp*

HOW TO: Prevent Caching in Internet Explorer, in the Microsoft Knowledge Base at *http://support.microsoft.com/support/kb/articles/Q234/0/67.asp*

Objective 4.1

Configure Forward Caching and Reverse Caching

Forward caching is what most people think about when they consider Web caching. Forward caching occurs when Web content hosted on Internet servers is stored on the **caching server** after it was requested by hosts on the **Internal network**. Future requests for the same content by hosts on the Internal network will be served from the cache rather than being downloaded from the Internet again. **Reverse caching** occurs when the caching server works as an intermediary for hosts on the Internet requesting content from Web servers located on the Internal or **perimeter network** (also known as a demilitarized zone, or DMZ, or a screened subnet). When configuring caching on a computer running ISA Server 2004, the administrator must consider the size of the cache and the volume on which it is stored and what content to cache preemptively. If using an array of computers with ISA Server 2004, Enterprise Edition, you will need to consider the configuration of **Cache Array Routing Protocol (CARP)**.

Objective 4.1 Questions

1. Your Microsoft Windows Server 2003 computer has its operating system installed on a single 50-gigabyte (GB) small computer system interface (SCSI) disk drive. The operating system volume spans the entire disk. ISA Server 2004 is installed on the operating system volume. In addition to the operating system volume, there are three 80-GB SCSI disk drives installed on the computer. At present, no volumes have been created on these 80-GB disk drives and they are configured as dynamic disks. You wish to configure a cache on the ISA Server 2004 computer that totals 150 GB. What is the best way to do this on this particular hardware configuration? (Choose the best answer.)

    A. Configure a redundant array of independent disks (RAID) 0 volume of 240 GB. Format this volume as FAT32. Configure a 150-GB cache on the new volume.

    B. Configure a RAID 0 volume of 240 GB. Format this volume as NTFS. Configure a 150-GB cache on the new volume.

    C. Configure a RAID 5 volume of 160 GB. Format this volume as FAT32. Configure a 150-GB cache on the new volume.

    D. Configure a RAID 5 volume of 160 GB. Format this volume as NTFS. Configure a 150-GB cache on the new volume.

    E. Create three separate 80-GB volumes, one to each SCSI disk. Format volumes as NTFS. Configure caching so that there are 50 GB allocated to each disk.

2. You are the security administrator for Contoso Ltd. You have installed ISA Server 2004 on a Windows Server 2003 computer, which has functioned well as a firewall. Now you want to have the ISA Server 2004 computer function in a caching role. Your computer is configured with four 20-GB SCSI disk drives. The first drive contains a single 20-GB NTFS volume and hosts the Windows Server 2003 and ISA Server 2004 installation. Other than being converted to dynamic disks, no configuration has been performed on the three remaining 20-GB SCSI disk drives. How should you configure the remaining three SCSI disk drives to maximize cache size and performance? (Choose the best answer.)

    A. Configure a single 60-GB spanned volume. Format using NTFS. In the ISA Server 2004 Management Console, create a 60-GB cache on this new volume.

    B. Configure a single 60-GB RAID 0 volume. Format using NTFS. In the ISA Server 2004 Management Console, create a 60-GB cache on this new volume.

    C. Configure a single 40-GB RAID 5 volume. Format using NTFS. In the ISA Server 2004 Management Console, create a 40-GB cache on this new volume.

    D. Configure three single 20-GB volumes. Format each using NTFS. In the ISA Server 2004 Management Console, create a 20-GB cache file on each volume.

3.   Contoso Ltd. has a single 128-kilobit per second (Kbps) link to the Internet. Several users at Contoso are downloading a data file from the Internet using File Transfer Protocol (FTP). The file that they are downloading is 100 megabytes (MB) in size and this file is accessed by at least 20 different users on the Internal network over the course of a week. Updates to this data file occur only once every 10 days. After analyzing Contoso's traffic, you have noticed that the same file is downloaded once each day, significantly affecting other users' Internet experience. You want to configure a cache rule to ensure that the file is downloaded at most once a week. Which of the following settings should you configure in the New Cache Rule Wizard on the Contoso ISA Server 2004 computer? (Choose the best answer.)

   A. Select Enable FTP Caching. Leave the default values in place.

   B. Select Enable FTP Caching. Set Time-to-Live (TTL) for FTP objects to five days.

   C. Select Do Not Cache Objects Larger Than: and set the value to 10 MB.

   D. Select Enable FTP Caching. Set TTL for FTP objects to eight days.

4.   Your organization has a strict Internet access policy. You want to ensure that users access only content that has been downloaded during the night. Users should not be able to access any site outside those that exist within the cache. Which of the following steps can you take when creating a cache rule using the New Cache Rule Wizard to ensure this? (Choose one.)

   A. Set Retrieve The Requested Object From The Cache: to Only If A Valid Version Of The Object Exists In The Cache. If no valid version exists, route the request to the server.

   B. Set Retrieve The Requested Object From The Cache: to If Any Version Of The Object Exists In The Cache. If none exists, route the request to the server.

   C. Set Retrieve The Requested Object From The Cache: to If Any Version Of The Object Exists In The Cache. If none exists, drop the request.

   D. Set Select When Content Should Be Stored In The Cache: to Never, No Content Will Ever Be Cached.

5.   Which of the following conditions must be met before a Content Download Job can be scheduled? (Choose all that apply.)

   A. The External network is configured to listen for Web Proxy client requests.

   B. The Local Host network is configured to listen for Web Proxy client requests.

   C. System policy rules allowing content download must be enabled.

   D. The Edge Firewall, 3-Leg Perimeter, or Front Firewall network templates must be in use.

   E. The Microsoft ISA Server Job Scheduler service must be running.

6.   Your ISA Server 2004 server is configured to reverse cache a Web server located on your perimeter network for hosts located on the Internet. To facilitate this, you created a Content Download Job named Localcache to replicate the content of the Web server to the ISA Server 2004 cache using default settings. The ISA Server 2004 computer is configured using the 3-Leg Perimeter template. The pages on the perimeter network ISA Server 2004 computer are updated hourly. You receive a complaint from a user on the Internet that the user continually gets the same page, which doesn't seem to update. Which of the following steps can you take to rectify this problem? (Choose the correct answer.)

   A. Edit the properties of the Localcache rule. On the Cache tab, select the All Content Will Be Cached option.

   B. Edit the properties of the Localcache rule. On the Cache tab, select If Source And Request Headers Indicate To Cache, Then The Content Will Be Cached.

   C. Edit the properties of the Localcache rule. On the Schedule tab, change the Download Frequency to Daily. Set the Daily Frequency to repeat once every hour.

   D. Edit the properties of the Localcache rule. On the Cache tab, use the Override object's TTL and set Mark Downloaded Objects with a new TTL of 120 minutes.

7.   You are the security administrator for Tailspin Toys, which has four ISA Server 2004 Enterprise Edition computers that are members of the same array. The first computer has a 600-megahertz (MHz) Pentium III processor and 256 MB of RAM. The second of these computers has a 1-GHz Pentium IV processor and 512 MB of RAM. The final two computers in the array are configured with 3-GHz Pentium IV processors and 1 GB of RAM. After benchmarking each of the servers, you have determined that the two 3-gigahertz (GHz) Pentium IV computers provides a 300 percent improvement over the performance of the 600-MHz Pentium III computer and a 200 percent improvement on the performance of the 1-GHz Pentium IV computer. You want to configure the CARP load factor on the basis of the benchmark figures so that load is distributed on the basis of relative performance. Which of the following actions should you take? (Select two answers, each of which forms a part of the answer.)

   A. Set the CARP load factor of the 600-MHz Pentium III to 30 and the CARP load factor of the 1-GHz Pentium IV to 45.

   B. Set the CARP load factor on the 1-GHz Pentium IV to 60 and the CARP load factor of the 600-MHz Pentium IV to 40.

   C. Set the CARP load factor of the 600-MHz Pentium III to 50 and the CARP load factor of the 1-GHz Pentium IV to 75.

   D. Set the CARP load factor of both the 3-GHz computers to the default value.

   E. Set the CARP load factor of both the 3-GHz computers to 120.

8.   You want to use CARP to distribute Web requests from client systems to a five-server ISA Server 2004 Enterprise Edition array. Each of the computers hosing ISA Server 2004, Enterprise Edition, is identical and none currently has caching enabled. Which of the following must you do to enable CARP? (Choose all that apply.)

   A. Enable caching on each of the five servers in the array.

   B. Enable CARP at the array level.

   C. Enable CARP on each member of the array.

   D. Enable CARP at the enterprise level.

   E. Enable caching on one server in the array.

Objective 4.1 Answers

1. **Correct Answers: E**

  A. **Incorrect:** ISA Server caches can be configured only on NTFS file system volumes. The maximum size of an ISA Server cache file is 64 GB. If you require a cache size larger than 64 GB, it must be spread across several different volumes. Although RAID 0 will improve access speed, it is inappropriate to use it in this circumstance because of the 64-GB limit.

  B. **Incorrect:** The maximum size of an ISA Server cache file is 64 GB. If you require a cache size larger than 64 GB, it must be spread across several different volumes. Although RAID 0 will improve access speed, it is inappropriate to use it in this circumstance because of the 64-GB limit.

  C. **Incorrect:** ISA Server caches can only be configured on NTFS file system volumes. The maximum size of an ISA Server cache file is 64 GB. If you require a cache size larger than 64 GB, it must be spread across several different volumes. Although RAID 0 will improve access speed, it is inappropriate to use it in this circumstance because of the 64-GB limit. Moreover, because caching data is not as critical as other data, there is no need for RAID 5's redundancy. Caching data can be easily regenerated by downloading content from the Internet.

  D. **Incorrect:** The maximum size of an ISA Server cache file is 64 GB. If you require a cache size larger than 64 GB, it must be spread across several different volumes. Although RAID 5 will improve access speed and provide redundancy, it is inappropriate to use it in this circumstance because of the 64-GB limit. Moreover, because caching data is not as critical as other data, there is no need for RAID 5's redundancy. Caching data can be easily regenerated by downloading content from the Internet.

  E. **Correct:** The key to this question is knowing that the maximum size of a cache file is 64 GB. If a cache larger than 64 GB is required, it is necessary to distribute the cache over separate volumes. Allocating 50 GB over each disk creates a cache of 150 GB.

2. **Correct Answers: B**

  A. **Incorrect:** Although this answer maximizes the cache size, it does not maximize the performance. Spanned volumes do not perform as quickly as RAID 5 or RAID 0 volumes.

  B. **Correct:** This answer has the benefit of maximizing cache size and maximizing performance. RAID 0 volumes have better read/write speed than RAID 5 volumes because they do not have to generate parity information.

C. **Incorrect:** This answer does not maximize the cache size, though it will provide good performance. Generally cache data should be considered as temporary data and hence should not be stored using disk redundancy. If a disk is lost, new cache data can be generated through normal Internet use.

D. **Incorrect:** Although this solution will maximize cache size, the performance of three separate cache files will not be as good as a single cache file mounted on a volume using RAID 0. When using RAID 0, cache objects are stored and read off three disks at once, maximizing read speed. When using three separate drives, cache objects are stored and read off individual single disks, which does not exploit the advantage of having disks work in parallel.

3. **Correct Answers: D**

A. **Incorrect:** By default, FTP objects have a Time-to-Live (TTL) of one day. After one day, they expire and must be downloaded again from the Internet.

B. **Incorrect:** Although setting the TTL for FTP objects to five days will reduce the number of times the object is downloaded from once a day to once every five days, this does not meet the goal of the file's being downloaded at most once per week.

C. **Incorrect:** Altering this setting will not reduce the amount of times that the data file is downloaded during the week. If the data file grows above this limit, it will mean that it will be downloaded each time it is requested from the Internet server because it will not be stored in the cache.

D. **Correct:** Setting the TTL to eight days means that the file will remain in cache for eight days before expiring. This means that the file will be downloaded once every eight days rather than once daily, which is the default.

4. **Correct Answers: C**

A. **Incorrect:** With this content retrieval rule in place, if a valid version of a page does not exist in the cache the page will be downloaded automatically from the Internet, bypassing your organization's strict Internet access policy.

B. **Incorrect:** With this content retrieval rule in place, anything that does not exist in the cache will be automatically downloaded from the Internet, bypassing your organization's strict Internet access policy.

C. **Correct:** This content retrieval rule means that if an object is not in the cache, the request will be dropped. The only way that new content can enter the cache is if it does so through a new download job.

D. **Incorrect:** Altering this setting will have no influence on whether content not located in the cache can be accessed by users on the Internal network.

5.   Correct Answers: B, C, and E

A. Incorrect: For content download jobs to be enabled, the Local Host network must be configured to listen for Web Proxy client requests, system policy rules must allow content download, and the ISA Job Scheduler must be enabled. The External network cannot be configured to listen for Web Proxy client requests.

B. Correct: For content download jobs to be enabled, the Local Host network must be configured to listen for Web Proxy client requests, system policy rules must allow content download, and the ISA Job Scheduler must be enabled.

C. Correct: For content download jobs to be enabled, the Local Host network must be configured to listen for Web Proxy client requests, system policy rules must allow content download, and the ISA Job Scheduler must be enabled.

D. Incorrect: Content download jobs can be enabled if any of the network templates is in use, including Back Firewall and Single Network Adapter.

E. Correct: For content download jobs to be enabled, the Local Host network must be configured to listen for Web Proxy client requests, system policy rules must allow content download, and the ISA Job Scheduler must be enabled.

6.   Correct Answers: C

A. Incorrect: The problem is not that the content is not being cached correctly, but that the content in the cache is not being updated frequently enough. This can be solved by modifying the frequency at which content is retrieved from the server on the perimeter network.

B. Incorrect: The problem is not that the content is not being cached correctly, but that the content in the cache is not being updated frequently enough. This can be solved by modifying the frequency at which content is retrieved from the server on the perimeter network.

C. Correct: Configuring this setting will mean that the content in the cache will be updated through a download from the source on an hourly basis. Clients that are served pages from the cache for this site will never view items more than 1 hour old.

D. Incorrect: Configuring this setting would mean that objects that arrived in the cache through this download rule would expire in 120 minutes. Depending on the cache settings, which are not detailed in this question, this might mean that the cache routes a new request to the host server or it may simply drop the request.

7.   Correct Answers: B and E

A. Incorrect: Load factor indicates the relative cache availability of this server compared to the rest of the array members. In answering this question, you must choose two different load factors for the 600-MHz and 1-GHz computers that are in the correct ratio for the load factor that you have selected for the two 3-GHz computers.

B. Correct: Load factor indicates the relative cache availability of this server compared to the rest of the array members. In answering this question you must choose two different load factors for the 600-MHz and 1-GHz computers that are in the correct ratio for the load factor that you have selected for the two 3-GHz computers. Because a CARP load of 120 for the 3-GHz computers is an option, and the other CARP load option for these computers fits correctly with the specified benchmarks, this answer is correct.

C. Incorrect: Load factor indicates the relative cache availability of this server compared to the rest of the array members. In answering this question, you must choose two different load factors for the 600-MHz and 1-GHz computers that are in the correct ratio for the load factor that you have selected for the two 3-GHz computers. Although the ratio to each other is correct, because there is no option to set the CARP load of the two 3-GHz computers to 150, this answer is incorrect.

D. Incorrect: In general, there is no problem leaving the default values. In the case of this question, you would only leave the default value if the CARP load for the 600-MHz computer were set to 33 and the CARP load for the 1-GHz computer were set to 50. These options are not present, hence this answer is wrong.

E. Correct: Load factor indicates the relative cache availability of this server compared to the rest of the array members. In answering this question, you must choose two different load factors for the 600-MHz and 1-GHz computers that are in the correct ratio for the load factor that you have selected for the two 3-GHz computers. A CARP load factor of 120 for the 3-GHz computers, when paired with the option of 40 for the 600-MHz computer and 60 for the 1-GHz computer meets the load-balancing requirements set out in the question.

8.   Correct Answers: B and E

A. Incorrect: CARP becomes available when you enable caching on any ISA Server 2004 Enterprise Edition computer in an array.

B. Correct: CARP is enabled at the array level rather than the individual server level.

C. Incorrect: CARP is enabled at the array level rather than at the individual server level. You cannot enable CARP at the individual server level.

D. Incorrect: CARP is enabled at the array level and cannot be enabled at the enterprise level.

E. Correct: CARP can be enabled at the array level once caching is enabled on any single server within the array.

Objective 4.2

Optimize Performance on the ISA Server 2004 Cache

Implementing caching requires an understanding of the type of content that users in an organization must access. When a user is served a Web page from a cache instead of from the server on which it was originally hosted, there is a chance that the page that they will view will be out of date. Most Web sites update their pages infrequently, but others update their Web pages almost all the time. You must fine-tune the performance of your ISA Server 2004 computer so that users get the most up-to-date information when they access sites. You must balance such access criteria with the need to retain efficient caching policies so that the content that is not updated frequently is not constantly downloaded from the Internet. **Active caching** is a feature that allows ISA Server to preempt users automatically by downloading objects within the cache that are accessed often before the objects expire. The advanced caching options allow you to configure the amount of free memory to use for caching, as well as how to deal with requests for Web sites that cannot be reached, but for which an expired version exists within the cache.

Objective 4.2 Questions

1. You are the security administrator at Tailspin Toys located in Melbourne, Australia. You have a single ISA Server 2004 computer that is configured using the 3-Leg Perimeter template and is also configured as a caching server. Tailspin Toys is a medium-sized organization that has a single site connected to the Internet using a 10-megabit-per-second (Mbps) link. During business hours, the link averages 35 percent use, half of which is Web traffic. You estimate that 60 percent of requests for Web content are met from the cache rather than being routed to the Internet. Of those requests routed to the Internet, roughly 80 percent are for objects that have been in the cache within the last three days. Requests routed to the Internet take slightly longer to be returned to the users because generally they are for non-Australian sites and they must travel across the ocean to be received by international servers. The Cache Settings are currently configured using the defaults. You are tuning the cache in an attempt to provide the best browsing experience for users on your network. Which of the following steps should you take? (Choose the best answer.)

   A. Do not enable active caching. Leave the Cache Settings unchanged.

   B. Enable active caching. Set the Update Active Objects In Cache: option to Frequently.

   C. Enable active caching. Set the Update Active Objects In Cache: option to Normally.

   D. Enable active caching. Set the Update Active Objects In Cache: option to Less Frequently.

2. You are the network administrator for an Antarctic research station that has 20 researchers who spend the dark winter months tending scientific instruments. One of the researchers' main forms of relaxation is to spend an hour or so each day surfing the Internet. The research station is connected to the Internet by a 1.544-Mbps T1 line. ISA Server 2004 is installed on a Windows Server 2003 computer, which is configured as an Internet-edge firewall. Caching is also enabled with default settings. During working hours the Internet link is at approximately 50 percent usage, which drops to 10 percent usage during the research station's rest period. Due to the distance of Antarctica from most of the Web sites accessed by the station's personnel, there is a significant delay between requesting a page and its download from the remote server. Requested content that exists within the cache is served immediately, but content that does not exist within the cache can take quite some time to appear on the screen. You want to configure the cache to update itself automatically without configuring hundreds of separate download jobs to take into account each researcher's favorite sites. And you believe that network usage can safely increase, but not by a dramatic amount. Which of the following configuration changes should you make? (Choose the correct answer.)

   A. Do not enable active caching. Leave the default caching settings unchanged.

    B. Enable active caching. Set the Update Active Objects In Cache: option to Frequently.

    C. Enable active caching. Set the Update Active Objects In Cache: option to Normally.

    D. Enable active caching. Set the Update Active Objects In Cache: option to Less Frequently.

3. The advanced cache settings of an ISA Server 2004 computer are shown here:

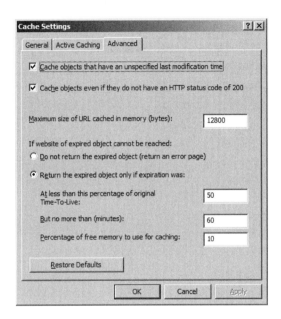

Having performed baseline analysis of this server, you have determined that, of the 2 GB of RAM installed, when ISA Server 2004 is in normal operation, 1024 MB of memory are free and that 500 MB of the page file are used. Clients on your internal network are trying to access content on the Contoso public Web server at *www.contoso.com*. This server crashed 90 minutes ago, and clients were able to access content for the first time today just before this server crashed. The TTL of pages on the Contoso Web server was set to 70 minutes. All Web pages on the Contoso public Web server have unspecified last modification times. Given this information, which of the following statements is correct? (Choose all that apply.)

    A. 204.8 MB of RAM will be allocated by ISA Server 2004 for caching.

    B. Clients attempting to access *www.contoso.com* will see an error page.

    C. Clients attempting to access *www.contoso.com* will be returned objects from the cache.

    D. Web pages hosted on *www.contoso.com* will not be cached.

    E. 102.4 MB of RAM will be allocated by ISA Server 2004 for caching.

4. Web pages on the Tailspin Toys Internet Web server *www.tailspintoys.com* are configured with a TTL of 90 minutes. The Tailspin Toys Web server crashed at 13:13 CST. The server will not be operational for the next few hours. A user on your internal network accessed Web pages on the Tailspin Toys site at 13:10 CST. You have an ISA Server 2004 computer configured as a Web caching server. Your advanced cache settings are displayed here:

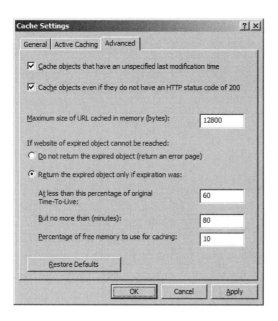

At which of the following times will the cached version of the Tailspin Toys Web pages be returned to clients on the internal network? (Choose all that apply.)

   A. 14:38 CST

   B. 16:04 CST

   C. 15:38 CST

   D. 15:28 CST

   E. 14:48 CST

Objective 4.2 Answers

1. **Correct Answers: B**

    A. Incorrect: An improvement could be made to the browsing experience by implementing active caching. Although the figures are confusing, currently 40 percent of requests are routed to the Internet and are slower than the 60 percent that are not. If active caching were implemented using the Frequently setting, it is possible that the 40 percent figure could be reduced to 20 percent, with 80 percent of requests being serviced by the cache. The link usage of 35 percent indicates that there is adequate bandwidth to allow frequent active caching.

    B. Correct: Although the figures are confusing, currently 40 percent of requests are routed to the Internet and are slower than the 60 percent that are not. If active caching were implemented using the Frequently setting, it is possible that the 40 percent figure could be reduced to 20 percent, with 80 percent of requests being serviced by the cache. The link utilization of 35 percent indicates that there is adequate bandwidth to allow frequent active caching.

    C. Incorrect: The currently low link usage of 35 percent (17.5 percent of which is Web traffic) means that client cache-to-hit ratio can take precedence over network traffic insofar as even a doubling of current Web traffic would not strain the link. You would consider this option if the link usage were between 50 percent and 60 percent. Generally it is good practice not to push link usage above 80 percent because, although below the theoretical limit of the link, in practice 80 percent usage is the equivalent of the link's taking a full load.

    D. Incorrect: The currently low link usage of 35 percent (17.5 percent of which is Web traffic) means that client cache-to-hit ratio can take precedence over network traffic insofar as even a doubling of current Web traffic would not strain the link. You would consider this option if the link usage were between 50 percent and 60 percent. Generally it is good practice not to push link utilization much above 80 percent because, although below the theoretical limit of the link, in practice 80 percent usage is the equivalent of the link's taking a full load.

2. **Correct Answers: C**

    A. Incorrect: Because you can take a slight hit in terms of increasing network usage, you should enable active caching.

    B. Incorrect: Using this setting will improve the user experience, but also has a significant impact on network performance. Because you can only allow a small increase in network usage, using the Normally setting, rather than Frequently, is more appropriate.

C. **Correct:** This setting is appropriate because it will lead to only a slight increase in network usage while providing a significant improvement in the user experience.

D. **Incorrect:** Using this setting will mean that very commonly accessed objects will be cached in advance, but the majority of objects in the cache will be allowed to expire. The Less Frequently setting has no impact on network performance. Because a better result can be generated with a slight impact on network performance and is still within the constraints of the scenario, this answer is incorrect.

3. **Correct Answers: A and C**

A. **Correct:** Although the wording is somewhat confusing, "percentage of free memory to use for caching" refers to the percentage of total RAM that ISA Server 2004 uses for caching. Because the server has 2 GB (or 2048 MB) of RAM, and by default ISA Server uses 10 percent of installed physical memory for caching when caching is enabled, this means that 204.8 MB of RAM will be allocated to the ISA Server 2004 computer for caching.

B. **Incorrect:** Because the original objects had a TTL of 70 minutes and were accessed just before the server crashed 90 minutes ago, the cached objects from *www.contoso.com* would have expired 20 minutes ago. In the screenshot, the settings indicate that an expired object will be returned if the period is less than 50 percent of the original TTL, which in this case is 35 minutes (50 percent of 70 minutes). Because 35 minutes is longer than 20 minutes, the expired object will be returned to the client.

C. **Correct:** Because the original objects had a TTL of 70 minutes and were accessed just before the server crashed 90 minutes ago, the cached objects from *www.contoso.com* would have expired 20 minutes ago. In the screenshot, the settings indicate that an expired object will be returned if the period is less than 50 percent of the original TTL, which in this case is 35 minutes (50 percent of 70 minutes). Because 35 minutes is longer than 20 minutes, the expired object will be returned to the client.

D. **Incorrect:** According to the screenshot, objects with an unspecified last modification time will be cached. This means that there is no reason why Web pages hosted on *www.contoso.com* will not be cached.

E. **Incorrect:** Although the wording is somewhat confusing, "percentage of free memory to use for caching" refers to the percentage of total RAM that ISA Server 2004 uses for caching. Because the server has 2 GB (or 2048 MB) of RAM, and by default ISA Server uses 10 percent of installed physical memory for caching when caching is enabled, this means that 204.8 MB of RAM will be allocated to the ISA Server 2004 computer for caching.

4.   Correct Answers: A, D, and E

    A. Correct: Given that the Web pages have a TTL of 90 minutes and that they were last accessed at 13:10 CST, the Web pages in the ISA Server 2004 cache will expire at 14:40 CST. However the settings indicate that the object will be returned after it has expired for a period of up to 60 percent of the original TTL unless that period exceeds 80 minutes. In this case, 60 percent of the original TTL of 90 minutes is 54 minutes, meaning that the object will be returned up to 144 minutes after it was originally cached if the Web site that hosted the object cannot be contacted. Because the objects entered the cache at 13:10 CST, they will be returned from the cache, assuming that the Web server is unavailable, until 15:34 CST.

    B. Incorrect: Given that the Web pages have a TTL of 90 minutes and that they were last accessed at 13:10 CST, the Web pages in the ISA Server 2004 cache will expire at 14:40 CST. However the settings indicate that the object will be returned after it has expired for a period of up to 60 percent of the original TTL unless that period exceeds 80 minutes. In this case, 60 percent of the original TTL of 90 minutes is 54 minutes, meaning that the object will be returned up to 144 minutes after it was originally cached if the Web site that hosted the object cannot be contacted. Because the objects entered the cache at 13:10 CST, they will be returned from the cache, assuming that the Web server is unavailable, until 15:34 CST.

    C. Incorrect: Given that the Web pages have a TTL of 90 minutes and that they were last accessed at 13:10 CST, the Web pages in the ISA Server 2004 cache will expire at 14:40 CST. However the settings indicate that the object will be returned after it has expired for a period of up to 60 percent of the original TTL unless that period exceeds 80 minutes. In this case, 60 percent of the original TTL of 90 minutes is 54 minutes, meaning that the object will be returned up to 144 minutes after it was originally cached if the Web site that hosted the object cannot be contacted. Because the objects entered the cache at 13:10 CST, they will be returned from the cache, assuming that the Web server is unavailable, until 15:34 CST.

    D. Correct: Given that the Web pages have a TTL of 90 minutes and that they were last accessed at 13:10 CST, the Web pages in the ISA Server 2004 cache will expire at 14:40 CST. However the settings indicate that the object will be returned after it has expired for a period of up to 60 percent of the original TTL unless that period exceeds 80 minutes. In this case, 60 percent of the original TTL of 90 minutes is 54 minutes, meaning that the object will be returned up to 144 minutes after it was originally cached if the Web site that hosted the object cannot be contacted. Because the objects entered the cache at 13:10 CST, they will be returned from the cache, assuming that the Web server is unavailable, until 15:34 CST.

E. Correct: Given that the Web pages have a TTL of 90 minutes and that they were last accessed at 13:10 CST, the Web pages in the ISA Server 2004 cache will expire at 14:40 CST. However the settings indicate that the object will be returned after it has expired for a period of up to 60 percent of the original TTL unless that period exceeds 80 minutes. In this case, 60 percent of the original TTL of 90 minutes is 54 minutes, meaning that the object will be returned up to 144 minutes after it was originally cached if the Web site that hosted the object cannot be contacted. Because the objects entered the cache at 13:10 CST, they will be returned from the cache, assuming that the Web server is unavailable, until 15:34 CST.

Diagnose and Resolve Caching Issues

Once a cache is functional, it is important to monitor it to see whether there is any way that you can improve performance by tuning the ISA Server 2004 computer. The performance monitor contains a range of ISA Server Cache performance objects that can be useful in monitoring the function of the cache. Reports generated in the Monitoring node of the ISA Server 2004 Management Console also can provide more general information about how effectively the cache is being used. Given this information, you may consider altering the way in which active caching or the advanced cache settings are configured.

Objective 4.3 Questions

1. You want to get an idea of the number of Uniform Resource Locators (URLs) kept in the ISA Server 2004 cache at any one time as a way of base-lining cache performance. Which of the following methods should you use? (Choose the best answer.)

   A. Generate a report using the default report settings.

   B. Add the Total URLs Cached counter to Performance Monitor.

   C. Add the Total URLs Retrieved From Disk counter to Performance Monitor

   D. Add the URL Commit Rate counter to Performance Monitor.

2. You are the security administrator at Contoso Ltd., which has an ISA Server 2004 computer with the 3-Leg Perimeter network template applied. On the perimeter network is Contoso's World Wide Web server, *www.contoso.com*. This server is updated regularly with important information that should be disseminated to Contoso investors and is published through the ISA Server 2004 computer. Since enabling Web caching last week, you have had complaints from investors connecting from the Internet that they are not being given the most recently updated information. On the other hand, since instituting caching, usage of the Contoso Internet link has dropped considerably and your manager projects that this will save the company several thousand dollars this quarter. What can you do to retain the savings realized by instituting caching while also ensuring that investors are not receiving outdated information when they connect to *www.contoso.com* from hosts on the Internet? (Choose the best answer.)

   A. Set the size of the Web cache on the ISA Server 2004 computer to zero.

   B. Disable reverse caching.

   C. Create a cache rule that disables caching for *http://www.contoso.com/** URLs.

   D. Increase the TTL on pages located on the *www.contoso.com* Web server.

3.   Users on your network have noticed a great difference between accessing normal Web sites and accessing Secure Sockets Layer (SSL) Web sites on the Internet. After some analysis, you determine that performance for normal Web sites is good because the content is being cached. The performance for SSL Web sites, on the other hand, is bad because the content must be retrieved from the Internet each time. You examine the traffic carefully and notice that 95 percent of the SSL traffic is bridged, rather than tunneled. Besides the default, there is a single cache rule configured named Cacherule. Which of the following steps will increase the speed of 95 percent of the SSL traffic for users on your internal network? (Choose the correct answer.)

A. Install a stand-alone certificate authority (CA) on the ISA Server 2004 computer.

B. This cannot be done.

C. Edit the Cacherule cache rule. Ensure that Cache SSL Responses is selected.

D. Set the size of the cache to zero on the ISA Server 2004 computer.

Objective 4.3 Answers

1.   Correct Answers: B

> **A. Incorrect:** The default report settings do not list the total number of URLs cached. Instead, it provides information about the number of objects returned from the Internet and cache over the period of the report.
>
> **B. Correct:** The Total URLs Cached counter will provide you with the total number of URLs in the cache from moment to moment. This is the best way to meet your goal.
>
> **C. Incorrect:** Using the Total URLs Retrieved From Disk counter will provide only information about the number of URLs being retrieved from the Disk cache at a particular time.
>
> **D. Incorrect:** Adding the URL Commit Rate counter to Performance Monitor will provide you with information about the per-second rate at which URLs are being stored in the cache. It will not provide information about the total number of URLs cached.

2.   Correct Answers: C

> **A. Incorrect:** Although this will allow investors to see up-to-date information, it effectively disables caching, which you do not want to do because it saves several thousand dollars per quarter.
>
> **B. Incorrect:** Reverse caching cannot be disabled independently of forward caching. Either both are enabled or both are disabled. The solution to this problem lies in disabling reverse caching for specific sites by creating a cache rule that disables caching for *http://www.contoso.com/** URLs.
>
> **C. Correct:** Reverse caching cannot be disabled independently of forward caching. Either both are enabled or both are disabled. The solution to this problem lies in disabling reverse caching for specific sites by creating a cache rule that disables caching for *http://www.contoso.com/** URLs. Requests for these URLs will simply be routed straight through without use of the cache, and the investors will be provided with up-to-date information.
>
> **D. Incorrect:** This will lead to outdated pages staying in the cache longer than you want, because it will take them more time to expire.

3.   Correct Answers: C

   A. Incorrect: Installing a stand-alone CA will not allow the caching of bridged SSL traffic; it will merely allow you to issue digital certificates.

   B. Incorrect: It is possible to cache bridged SSL traffic by selecting the Cache SSL responses on the Advanced tab of a cache rule.

   C. Correct: It is possible to cache bridged SSL traffic by selecting the Cache SSL responses on the Advanced tab of a cache rule.

   D. Incorrect: This will remove the cache; it will not allow SSL bridged traffic to be cached.

17 Configuring Firewall Policy (5.0)

Firewall policy enables you to mediate access on the basis of protocol and user identification from your protected networks to External networks through **access rules**. **Server publishing rules** allow you to mediate access from hosts on external networks such as the Internet to hosts on protected networks such as the perimeter or internal network. The benefit of using access rules is that they allow you to restrict your organization's users' access to the external network. By default, all access is denied to and from any network. Through adding access rules, you can slowly grant access to Internet protocols as is required by your organization. Restricting all but specially configured access ensures that only approved protocols are in use. This is important for organizations because copyright holders are increasingly litigious and it is better to limit content at the firewall than it is to learn, after the organization has been served with a lawsuit, that certain users have been downloading restricted content. In publishing servers, the ISA Server 2004 computer acts as an intermediary. Hosts on the Internet are unable to directly access the server hosting content; they can access only the specific protocols that you have published through your ISA Server 2004 computer. This reduces the likelihood of attackers on the Internet exploiting a service that administrators were unaware was running because only published services are available to those on External networks.

Tested Skills and Suggested Practices

The skills that you need to master the Configuring Firewall Policy objective domain on the Implementing *Microsoft Internet Security and Acceleration (ISA) Server 2004* exam include:

■ Plan a firewall policy.

❑ Practice: On a computer running ISA Server 2004, Enterprise Edition, open the ISA Server Management Console. Navigate to the Enterprise Policies node under the Enterprise node. From the Tasks pane, select the Create New Enterprise Policy task. This will open the Enterprise Policy Wizard. Enter the policy name ALPHA and click Next. Click Finish to close the wizard. Select the new ALPHA node under the Enterprise Policies node. Create an access rule allowing HTTP traffic from All Protected Networks to External networks for All Users. Click Apply to save the changes to the ISA Server 2004 Enterprise Edition server. Open the Arrays node. Select the Firewall Policy node. From the Tasks pane, select the Show Enterprise Policy Rules task. Create an Array access rule denying POP3 access from the Internal network to the External network for all users. Note the order in which policy rules are applied. Navigate back to the ALPHA node. Use the Move Selected Rules Down task to move the rule allowing HTTP traffic that you created earlier to the category of Enterprise Policy Rules Applied After Array Firewall Policy.

■ Create policy elements, access rules, and connection limits.

❑ Practice: Click the Create New Access Rule task in the Firewall Policy node of the ISA Server 2004 Management Console. Set the Access rule name to NNTP and then click Next. Set the rule condition to Allow and then click Next. In the This Rule Applies To drop-down box, choose the Selected Protocols option, then click Add. In the Add Protocols dialog box, expand the All Protocols node. Scroll to NNTP, and then click Add. Click Close, and then click Next. Add the Internal network as a source by clicking Add, expanding the Networks node, and then selecting Internal and clicking Add again. Click Close, and then click Next. Add the External network as a destination by clicking Add, expanding the Networks node, and then selecting External and clicking Add again. Click Close, and then click Next. Click Next to leave the default as All Users. Click Finish.

■ Create policy rules for Web publishing.

❑ Practice 1: Right-click a Web publishing rule in the Firewall Policy node of the ISA Server 2004 Management Console and select Configure HTTP. Navigate through each of the available tabs, clicking on the question mark box to describe the function of each configurable option.

❑ Practice 2: Select the Publish A Secure Web Server task in the Firewall Policy node of the ISA Server 2004 Management Console. Give the rule the name TEST-SSL and then click Next. On the Publishing Mode page of the wizard, click Link To Help About SSL Bridging And Tunneling. This will open a link to a help file providing information about SSL bridging and tunneling. Review the text and then close the help file. On the Publishing Mode page Select SSL Bridging and click Next. Set the Action To Take When Rule Conditions Are Met to Allow and then click Next. On the Bridging Mode page, examine all three options and try to understand the differences between them. The graphic shown as part of the dialog box should assist you. Instead of completing the wizard, close the dialog box.

■ Create policy rules for mail server publishing.

❑ Practice: In the Firewall Policy node of the ISA Server 2004 Management Console, select the Publish A Mail Server task. Set the name of the rule as TEMPUS and then click Next. Set the Client Access to RPC, IMAP, POP3, SMTP and click Next. Allow secure POP3 and Outlook (RPC) and click Next. Enter the network IP address of the mail server (for example 10.99.98.97) and then click Next. Listen only to requests from the External network and click Next. To close the wizard, click Finish.

■ Create policy rules for server publishing.

❑ Practice 1: Navigate to the Firewall Policy node of the ISA Server 2004 Management Console. Click Create New Server Publishing Rule. This will start the New Server Publishing Rule Wizard. Enter the name as TEST-NNTP and then click Next. Enter the IP address of the server as 10.9.8.7 and then click Next. Use the drop-down Selected Protocol menu and select NNTP Server. Click Next. On the Listen For Requests From These Networks, check the External Network check box. Click Next. Click Finish.

Further Reading

This section lists supplemental readings by objective. We recommend that you study these sources thoroughly before taking this exam.

Objective 5.1   ISA Server Publishing *http://www.microsoft.com/isaserver/techinfo/guidance/2004/publishing.asp*

Digital Certificates for ISA Server 2004   *http://www.microsoft.com/technet/prodtechnol/isa/2004/plan/digitalcertificates.mspx*

ISA Server Help: Cache Configuration

ISA Server Help: Cache Overview

Objective 5.2   HTTP Filtering in ISA Server 2004 *http://www.microsoft.com/technet/prodtechnol/isa/2004/plan/httpfiltering.mspx*

Objective 5.3   How ISA Server 2004 caches responses to Web publishing client requests in reverse proxy mode   *http://support.microsoft.com/?kbid=837737*

White paper: Unique Protection for Microsoft Exchange Server, Internet Information Server, and Windows-Based Virtual Private Networking *http://www.microsoft.com/isaserver/evaluation/whitepapers/default.asp*

White paper: Protecting Microsoft Internet Information Services Web Servers with ISA Server 2004 *http://www.microsoft.com/isaserver/evaluation/whitepapers/default.asp*

Objective 5.4   Outlook Web Access Server Publishing in ISA Server 2004 *http://www.microsoft.com/technet/prodtechnol/isa/2004/plan/owapublishing.mspx*

Using the ISA Server 2004 SMTP Filter and Message Screener   *http://www.microsoft.com/technet/prodtechnol/isa/2004/plan/smtpfilter.mspx*

Objective 5.5   ISA Server Publishing   *http://www.microsoft.com/isaserver/techinfo/guidance/2004/publishing.asp*

Common Application Signatures   *http://www.microsoft.com/tech net/prodtechnol/isa/2004/plan/commonapplicationsignatures.mspx*

Publishing FTP Servers Using ISA Server 2004   *http://www.microsoft.com/technet/prodtechnol/isa/2004/plan/publishingFTPservers.mspx*

Publishing a VPN Server in ISA Server 2004   *http://www.microsoft.com/technet/prodtechnol/isa/2004/plan/publishingVPNservers.mspx*

Plan a Firewall Policy

Planning firewall policy carefully, especially in situations where you are implementing ISA Server 2004, Enterprise Edition, can save you many headaches when it comes to rollout. The most important rule about policy application is that, once a set of conditions is met, rules further down the list that also apply to the same conditions are not enforced. Enterprise-level policies can be applied both before and after array-level policies. The default enterprise policy, Deny All Traffic, is applied after all other policies. Any traffic that meets none of the earlier policy conditions will be discarded by this final rule.

Objective 5.1 Questions

1. You are the administrator of an ISA Server 2004 enterprise that includes three distinct ISA Server 2004 Enterprise Edition arrays. Each array consists of two ISA Server 2004 Enterprise Edition computers. You have created five new enterprise policies. Given the existing enterprise policies, what is the maximum number of enterprise policies that can be applied to an individual array? (Choose the best answer.)

    A. One

    B. Two

    C. Three

    D. Four

    E. Five

    F. Six

2. Your ISA Server 2004 enterprise has 12 servers spread over four separate arrays. Your organization has the following requirements:

- All users, except those using the fourth array, should be allowed SMTP and POP3 access to servers on the Internet.

- All users, except the Pragmatics user set using the third array, should be denied access to external DNS servers.

Given this information, which of the following policies should you apply? (Choose all that apply.)

    A. Configure an enterprise-level policy to allow all users external SMTP and POP3 access. Ensure that this policy is applied before array level policies. Configure an array-level policy on the fourth array to deny external access to SMTP and POP3 for all users.

    B. Configure an enterprise-level policy to allow all users external SMTP and POP3 access. Ensure that this policy is applied after array level policies. Configure an array-level policy on the fourth array to deny external access to SMTP and POP3 for all users.

    C. Configure an enterprise-level policy denying external DNS access for all users. Ensure that this policy is applied before array-level policies. Configure an array-level policy allowing the Pragmatics user set external DNS access. Apply this policy to the third array.

   D. Configure an enterprise-level policy granting access to external DNS for the Prag-matics user set. Apply this policy prior to array level policies. Configure an enter-prise-level policy denying access to external DNS for all users. Apply this policy after array-level policies.

   E. Configure an enterprise-level policy denying external DNS access for all users. Ensure that this policy is applied after array-level policies. Configure an array-level policy allowing the Pragmatics user set external DNS access. Apply this policy to the third array.

3. Your organization has a single array in its enterprise. Enterprise- and array-level policy is configured as shown here.

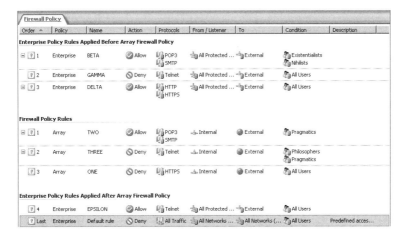

Which of the following policy rules are unnecessary because they will never be enforced? (Choose all that apply.)

   A. DELTA

   B. TWO

   C. ONE

   D. THREE

   E. EPSILON

4. Your ISA Server 2004 enterprise has four arrays. Each separate array is used by a dif-ferent branch office in your organization. Which of the following policy rules would be more appropriate at the array level rather than the enterprise level? (Choose all that apply.)

   A. You need a policy rule that denies HTTP access to all users at a specific branch office.

B. You need a policy rule that denies access to external DNS servers for a particular set of user groups throughout the organization.

C. You need a policy that allows managers that commute between several locations to access a single specific telnet server on the Internet.

D. You need to grant MSN Messenger access for all users at a particular branch office.

E. You need to deny access to SSL Web sites for all users at two branch offices.

5. Your ISA Server 2004 enterprise has five separate arrays. A separate array is used for each geographic region in which your organization has a presence. You have delegated the ISA Server Array Administrator role to local personnel in each geographic region. It is the responsibility of these administrators to set firewall policy, determining which protocols can be used to access services on the Internet for users of their particular array. You do not, however, want these administrators to be able to publish any servers on the internal network to the Internet. How can you impose this limitation without removing the administrator's ability to set other types of firewall policy? (Choose all that apply.)

A. Assign the ISA Server Array Auditor role.

B. Assign the ISA Server Array Monitoring Auditor role.

C. In the Array Firewall Policy Rule Types box of the Policy Settings tab of the Array Properties dialog box, remove the check box next to Deny Access Rules.

D. In the Array Firewall Policy Rule Types box of the Policy Settings tab of the Array Properties dialog box, remove the check box next to Allow Access Rules.

E. In the Array Firewall Policy Rule Types box of the Policy Settings tab of the Array Properties dialog box, remove the check box next to Publishing Rules.

6. Enterprise- and array-level policy is configured as shown here.

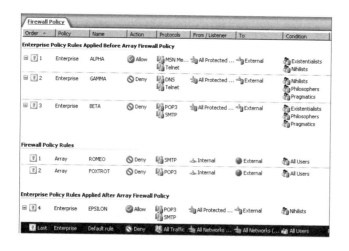

Members of the Nihilists user set should be able to access mail servers on the Internet using POP3 and SMTP but are currently unable to do so. Which of the following changes should you make to correct this problem? (Choose the best answer.)

A. Move array-level firewall policy rules ROMEO and FOXTROT below enterprise policy Rule Epsilon.

B. Move policy rule EPSILON to the position above policy rule ROMEO in the Array-level Firewall Policy Rules.

C. Move enterprise policy rule EPSILON to the position below enterprise policy rule BETA.

D. Edit the enterprise policy rule BETA and change the action from Deny to Allow.

7. Oksana and Rooslan are members of Microsoft Windows Server 2003 groups that are members of the Philosophers user set. They should be allowed to access Web servers on the Internet, but are currently unable to do so. Enterprise- and array-level firewall policy is configured as shown here.

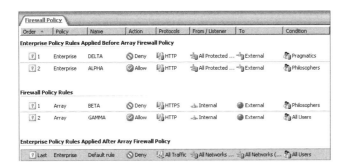

Which of the following steps could you take to ensure that Oksana and Rooslan get access? (Choose the best answer.)

A. Change Rule BETA from Deny to Allow.

B. Move Rule GAMMA to the position above Rule BETA.

C. Move Rule ALPHA to the position above Rule DELTA.

D. Change Rule GAMMA from Allow to Deny.

Objective 5.1 Answers

1.   Correct Answers: A

   A. Correct: Only a single enterprise policy can be applied to an individual array, irrespective of the number of servers in the array.

   B. Incorrect: Only a single enterprise policy can be applied to an individual array, irrespective of the number of servers in the array.

   C. Incorrect: Only a single enterprise policy can be applied to an individual array, irrespective of the number of servers in the array.

   D. Incorrect: Only a single enterprise policy can be applied to an individual array, irrespective of the number of servers in the array.

   E. Incorrect: Only a single enterprise policy can be applied to an individual array, irrespective of the number of servers in the array.

   F. Incorrect: Although there are six enterprise policies in total, the five you created and the default policy, only one enterprise policy can be applied to an individual array.

2.   Correct Answers: B and E

   A. Incorrect: If the enterprise policy is applied before array level policies, users of the fourth array will be granted SMTP and POP3 access.

   B. Correct: By applying the deny policy to the fourth array only, users of this array will be unable to access SMTP and POP3. Even though an allow policy will apply to all arrays through enterprise policy, it will be enforced after the array-level policy. Later policies do not apply when conditions are met. This means that users of all other arrays will be able to access these services on the Internet.

   C. Incorrect: By denying external DNS access for all users in an Enterprise-level policy prior to the implementation of an array-level policy, you will deny access to the Pragmatics user set, which should be granted external DNS access.

   D. Incorrect: Although this does grant external DNS access to the Pragmatics user set, it would do so on all arrays, when this access should only occur when the third array is providing access to the Pragmatics user set.

   E. Correct: The policy for the Pragmatics user set gaining external DNS access via the third array should be enforced prior to any enterprise level policy denying external DNS access. Generally a policy denying access to all users for a particular protocol is not necessary because of the default policy explicitly denying access.

3.   Correct Answers: C, D, and E

A. **Incorrect:** Rule DELTA means that Rule ONE will not be enforced. No rule overrides Rule DELTA.

B. **Incorrect:** Although Rule BETA does deal with POP3 and SMTP traffic as well, it applies to the Existentialists and Nihilists user sets. Rule TWO applies to the Pragmatics user set and hence will be enforced, because no other prior rule deals with POP3 and SMTP traffic for this particular user set.

C. **Correct:** Rule DELTA means that Rule ONE will not be enforced.

D. **Correct:** Enterprise Rule GAMMA denies telnet at the enterprise level, meaning that Rule THREE is not necessary insofar as there is no need to deny access to the Pragmatics and Philosophers user set because they could not access the protocol anyway.

E. **Correct:** Enterprise Rule GAMMA denies telnet at the enterprise level, meaning that Rule EPSILON, applied after array-level rules, will never be enforced.

4.   Correct Answers: A, D, and E

A. **Correct:** Because this policy would apply only to the users of one of the four arrays, it would be more appropriate at the array level.

B. **Incorrect:** Because the set of user groups exists throughout the organization, it would be better to apply this policy at the Enterprise level.

C. **Incorrect:** Rather than apply array-level policies granting this access on each array, it would be simpler to apply an Enterprise-level policy.

D. **Correct:** Because this policy rule would apply only to users at a particular branch office, you should only implement it on the array at that branch office.

E. **Correct:** Because the restriction is based on branch office location, you would use an array-level, rather than an Enterprise-level, policy rule.

5.   Correct Answers: E

A. **Incorrect:** Users assigned the ISA Server Array Auditor role cannot set firewall policy.

B. **Incorrect:** Users assigned the ISA Server Array Monitoring Auditor role cannot set firewall policy

C. **Incorrect:** This will mean that array administrators will be unable to create deny-access rules. You must remove their ability to create publishing rules.

D. **Incorrect:** This will mean that array administrators will be unable to create allow access rules. You must remove their ability to create publishing rules.

    E. **Correct:** Removing the check box next to Publishing Rules in the Array Firewall Policy Rules Types of the Policy Settings tab of the Array Properties dialog box will allow array administrators to create deny and allow rules, but not publish any servers located on the Internal network.

6.   **Correct Answers: C**

    A. **Incorrect:** Array-level policy rules are separate from enterprise-level policy rules. You cannot move an array-level policy rule into the list of enterprise-level policy rules.

    B. **Incorrect:** Enterprise-level policy rules can be moved into place before or after the array-level firewall policy rules, but cannot be moved into the array-level firewall policy rules. Array-level policy rules are separate from enterprise policy.

    C. **Correct:** You can move enterprise policy rules between the groups applied before or after the array firewall policies. Because the array-level firewall policy rules ROMEO and FOXTROT deny use of SMTP and POP3 to all users, to allow the Nihilists user set to access these protocols, a rule allowing this access must be applied prior to the enforcement of the array-level firewall policy rules.

    D. **Incorrect:** Enterprise policy rule BETA applies to the Existentialists, Philosophers, and Pragmatics user set. Changing this rule will not grant the requisite access to the Nihilists user set.

7.   **Correct Answers: C**

    A. **Incorrect:** Rule BETA is not the problem because it would not be enforced due to the presence of Rule ALPHA. With the configuration as shown, the only way that Oksana and Rooslan could not get access, given that they are members of the Philosophers user set, is if they are also members of the Pragmatics user set.

    B. **Incorrect:** The Philosophers user set, of which Oksana and Rooslan are members, already has access through Enterprise Rule ALPHA. Moving Rule GAMMA will not solve the problem. With the configuration as shown, the only way that Oksana and Rooslan could not get access, given that they are members of the Philosophers user set, is if they are also members of the Pragmatics user set.

    C. **Correct:** With the configuration as shown, the only way that Oksana and Rooslan could not get access, given that they are members of the Philosophers user set, is if they are also members of the Pragmatics user set. By moving ALPHA, which grants access to the Philosophers user set, above Rule DELTA, they will be granted the requisite access.

    D. **Incorrect:** With the configuration as shown, the only way that Oksana and Rooslan could not get access, given that they are members of the Philosophers user set, is if they are also members of the Pragmatics user set. The problem is the ordering of Rule DELTA and Rule ALPHA. Changing Rule GAMMA will not grant access to anyone; in fact it is likely to deny access to a large group of users who should have it.

Create Policy Elements, Access Rules, and Connection Limits

Access rules are used to grant users on protected networks access to resources located on External networks. Protected networks include the Internal, Perimeter, and Quarantined virtual private network (VPN) Client networks. Access rules are built using the Create New Access Rule task located in the Firewall Policy node of the ISA Server 2004 Management Console.

Objective 5.2 Questions

1. You want to restrict Web access on your site for all users except those in the IT Support user set to a list of approved Web sites. When configuring the Access Rule Destinations dialog box of a new HTTP access rule, which of the following network entities should you create to include the list of approved sites? (Choose the best answer.)

   A. Domain Name sets

   B. Network sets

   C. Address ranges

   D. URL sets

2. Your organization's users perform their work on multiple operating system platforms. The Linux users have one user directory and the Windows users use Active Directory directory service. Approximately 10 percent of users in your organization have been issued RSA SecurID accounts. Dial-up access for both Linux and Windows users is authenticated by a Remote Authentication Dial-In User Service (RADIUS) protocol server. Your ISA Server 2004 Internet-edge firewall is configured as a stand-alone server. All incoming and outgoing network traffic for your organization will pass through the ISA Server 2004 computer. Which of the following user sets can you configure for application to server publishing and access rules? (Choose all that apply.)

   A. A user set composed of all users in the RSA SecurID namespace

   B. A user set composed of groups local to the ISA Server 2004 computer

   C. A user set composed of domain users and groups

   D. A user set composed of all users in the RADIUS namespace

3. You want to allow members of the Engineers Active Directory user group to access MSN Messenger servers on the Internet from the internal network, but deny access to all other users. Which of the following steps should you take to do this? (Choose two.)

   A. Use the Create New Server Publishing Rule task to publish an MMS Server. Configure the rule to listen to requests from the Internal network.

   B. Create a user set named Engineers that includes only the Engineers Active Directory User group.

   C. Create an access rule for the MSN Messenger protocol from the Internal network to the External network. Grant access to the All Users user set and deny access to the Engineers user set.

   D. Create an access rule for the MSN Messenger protocol from the External network to the Internal network. Grant access to the Engineers user set and deny access to the All Users user set.

   E. Create an access rule for the MSN Messenger protocol from the Internal network to the External network. Grant access to the Engineers user set.

4. Firewall Policy on your organization's ISA Server 2004 computer is configured as shown here.

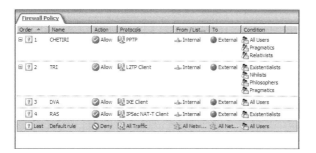

Users in your organization regularly access remote VPN servers. Given the information above, which of the following statements is correct? (Choose the correct answer.)

   A. All users in the organization will be able to establish Point-to-Point Tunneling Protocol (PPTP) connections to VPN servers located on the Internet.

   B. Users who are members of the Philosophers user set will be able to use a Layer Two Tunneling Protocol/Internet Protocol Security (L2TP/IPSec) connection to VPN servers published through remote ISA Server 2004 computers.

   C. Members of the Relativists user set will be able to establish an L2TP connection to VPN servers located on the Internet.

   D. Members of the Existentialists user set will be able to use an L2TP/IPSec connection to VPN servers published through remote ISA Server 2004 computers.

5. The firewall policy on your ISA Server 2004 computer is configured as shown here.

Given the information in the graphic, which of the following statements is true? (Choose all that apply.)

A. Members of the Pragmatics user set will be able to access Network News Transfer Protocol (NNTP) servers on the Internet.

B. Members of the Nihilists user set will be able to access NNTP servers on the Internet.

C. Members of the Existentialists user set are able to access Internet Relay Chat (IRC) servers on the Internet according to the Work Hours schedule.

D. Members of the Existentialists user set can access MSN Messenger servers on the Internet according to the Weekends schedule.

E. Members of the Engineers user set cannot access the MSN Messenger service on the Internet according to the Weekends schedule, but will be able to access these servers at other times.

Objective 5.2 Answers

1.   Correct Answers: D

   A. Incorrect: Uniform Resource Locator (URL) sets, rather than Domain Name Sets, are the best way to restrict Web traffic to a list of approved sites.

   B. Incorrect: URL sets are the best way to restrict Web traffic to a list of approved sites. Network sets are far too general to be used in this way.

   C. Incorrect: URL sets are the best way to restrict Web traffic to a list of approved sites. Address ranges are far too general to be used in this way.

   D. Correct: URL sets are the best way to restrict Web traffic to a list of approved sites. You simply enter the list of sites that you want to allow users to visit.

2.   Correct Answers: A, B, and D

   A. Correct: RSA SecurID can be used on a stand-alone ISA Server 2004 computer to populate user sets. You can select individual users or all users within the SecureID namespace.

   B. Correct: Local users and groups can be used to populate user sets.

   C. Incorrect: Because the server is a stand-alone server, domain users and groups cannot be used to populate user sets.

   D. Correct: A user set can consist of all users in the RADIUS namespace.

3.   Correct Answers: B and E

   A. Incorrect: Access rules are used to grant access from protected networks (such as Internal networks) to unprotected networks (such as the Internet). Publishing rules are used to grant access from unprotected networks to protected networks. In this situation, an access rule is appropriate.

   B. Correct: User sets are the means of assigning permissions to access and publishing rules. You must create this user set if you want to restrict access to this particular user group.

   C. Incorrect: Creating this access rule would allow everyone but the members of the Engineers user set to use MSN Messenger.

   D. Incorrect: This access rule does not meet the specified goals because it would allow MSN traffic from the Internet to traverse the ISA Server to an MSN Messenger server on the Internal network. The question states that the MSN Messenger servers are on the Internet.

   E. Correct: Once the Engineers user set is created, you can grant access to the MSN Messenger protocol. There is no need to specify that other users are denied, because ISA Server Firewall Policy has an explicit deny-as-the-default rule, which pertains to all traffic that is not addressed by existing rules.

4.   Correct Answers: D

A. Incorrect: Users who are members of the Pragmatics user set and the Relativists user set are specifically excluded from the PPTP according to Rule Chetiri.

B. Incorrect: The key to why this answer is incorrect is the Network Address Translation–Traversal (NAT-T) protocol. Any VPN server published through a remote ISA Server 2004 computer will require use of the NAT-T protocol, which can only be used by the Existentialists group.

C. Incorrect: Rule Trio does not grant access to the Relativists user set, only to the Existentialists, Nihilists, Philosophers, and Pragmatics user sets.

D. Correct: Use of L2TP/IPSec to servers published through remote ISA Server 2004 computers requires Internet Key Exchange (IKE) Client and IPSec NAT-T Client connections. Rule Dva and Ras grant the appropriate access.

5.   Correct Answers: A and C

A. Correct: Rule GAMMA specifies that all users except the Pragmatics user set are denied access to NNTP. Rule BETA allows the Nihilists user set access. Because the Pragmatics user set members weren't denied access earlier, they will still be able to access servers on the Internet.

B. Incorrect: Unlike the Pragmatics user set, the Nihilists user set is not excluded from Rule GAMMA. This means that although they are granted access in Rule BETA, the position of Rule BETA following Rule GAMMA means that Rule GAMMA takes precedence.

C. Correct: Rule DELTA allows the Existentialists user set to access the IRC protocol according to the Work Hours schedule.

D. Incorrect: According to Rule ALPHA, only members of the Philosophers user set can access MSN Messenger according to the Weekends schedule.

E. Incorrect: Although the Engineers user set is the exception in Rule ALPHA, this does not grant the Engineers user set access to the MSN Messenger service.

Create Policy Rules for Web Publishing

Web sites are an organization's public face to the world. Web sites must be both accessible to and protected from people using the Internet. ISA Server 2004 makes it relatively simple to **publish** Web sites located on hosts on the internal or perimeter network (also known as a demilitarized zone, or DMZ) by providing administrators with special publishing tasks to ease configuration. The ISA Server 2004 computer will mediate access, ensuring that although the Web site is accessible to the public, other services hosted on the same computer are not. You can either configure a Web site to be published normally or securely. If a Web site is published securely, access occurs through **Hypertext Transfer Protocol Secure (HTTPS)** rather than **Hypertext Transfer Protocol (HTTP)**. HTTPS uses **Secure Sockets Layer** (SSL) to digitally encrypt communication. HTTPS requires the use of an SSL digital certificate. Although you can use your organization's own **certification authority** (CA) to generate an SSL certificate, it would mean that you would need to configure clients accessing the secure site to trust certificates issued by your CA. It is often simpler to obtain an SSL certificate signed by a commercial CA because such certificates will already be trusted by Web clients across the Internet.

Objective 5.3 Questions

1. You want to configure your ISA Server 2004 computer to support HTTPS to HTTPS bridging for several Web sites published on your organization's perimeter network. The people who will access these Web sites will do so from the Internet and are not necessarily affiliated with your organization. Their access should involve a minimum of configuration changes on their part. From which of the following CAs should you obtain a certificate? (Choose the best answer.)

   A. Enterprise Root CA on your perimeter network

   B. Enterprise Subordinate CA on your perimeter network

   C. Stand Alone Root CA on your perimeter network

   D. Commercial CA located on the Internet

2. You have recently obtained and installed a commercially signed SSL certificate on your organization's ISA Server 2004 computer. The certificate is for computer *secureweb.contoso.com*. This computer is used to publish a single secure Web site on your organization's perimeter network using HTTPS to HTTPS bridging. The computer hosting the secure Web server has the fully qualified domain names (FQDNs) *secureweb.contoso.com* and *perimeterwww.contoso.com* mapped to it using external and internal Domain Name System (DNS) respectively. Both of these names can be correctly resolved to the secure Web server's IP address from the ISA Server 2004 computer. These are the only names that map to the secure Web server's IP address. When you attempt to access the secure Web site *secureweb.contoso.com* from the Internet you receive the message 500 Internal Server Error: Principle name is incorrect. Which of the following methods can you use to resolve this issue? (Choose the best answer.)

   A. Renew the digital certificate.

   B. Obtain a new certificate that matches the name of the ISA Server 2004 computer.

   C. On the To tab of the Web publishing rule, alter the server name to *secureweb.contoso.com*.

   D. Delete the DNS record for *secureweb.contoso.com*.

   E. On the To tab of the Web publishing rule, alter the server name to *perimeter www.contoso.com*.

3. You are the security administrator for a local hospital. You have four different Web sites published through your organization's ISA Server 2004 Internet-edge firewall. The first of these Web sites contains highly confidential organizational information that should be protected with the strongest possible authentication method. The second contains information that should be restricted to medical records administrators. The third Web site contains information that should be restricted to doctors and nursing staff. The fourth Web site should be accessible to the general public over the Internet. The hospital uses a Windows Server 2003 domain. The domain contains the following user groups: Records Administrators, Nurses, Doctors, Management, and Secretariat. Only those personnel who are allowed to access the highly confidential information have been issued with RSA SecurID hardware authenticators, typically referred to as *fobs*. You wish to restrict access to the Web sites at the ISA Server 2004 computer. Not including any default user sets, how many user sets will you use to secure the four Web sites published through the ISA Server 2004 computer? (Choose the best answer.)

   A. One

   B. Two

   C. Four

   D. Three

   E. Five

4. Users in your domain are often members of multiple user groups. You wish to allow access to a Web server published through ISA Server 2004 to members of your domain's Engineers, Researchers, and Scientists groups, but do not want to allow access to members of the Accountants group. Which of the following actions should you perform to achieve this goal? (Choose the best answer.)

   A. Create two user sets. Add the Engineers, Researchers, and Scientists groups to the first set. Add the Accountants group to the second user set. Add the second set to the Rule Applies To Requests From The Following User Sets list. Add the first set to the Exceptions list.

   B. Create two user sets. Add the Engineers, Researchers, and Scientists groups to the first set. Add the Accountants group to the second user set. Add the first set to the This Rule Applies To Requests From The Following User Sets list. Add the second set to the Exceptions list.

   C. Add the Engineers, Researchers, and Scientists groups to the This Rule Applies To Requests From The Following User Sets list. Add the Accountants group to the Exceptions list.

   D. Add the Engineers, Researchers, and Scientists groups to the Exceptions list. Add the Accountants group to the This Rule Applies To Requests From The Following User Sets list.

5. You are setting up a customer feedback discussion board for Tailspin Toys. The discussion board will be hosted on a Windows Server 2003 computer located on the Tailspin Toys perimeter network. You have published the discussion board Web server through ISA Server 2004, which is configured using the 3-Leg Perimeter template. You want to ensure that inappropriate language is not posted on the board. To ensure this, when editing the Web publishing rule used to publish the discussion board server, which of the following should you block? (Choose the best answer.)

    A. HTTP methods

    B. HTTP extensions

    C. HTTP headers

    D. HTTP signatures

6. Which of the following statements about HTTP filtering is correct? (Choose all that apply.)

    A. HTTP filtering cannot be applied to deny rules.

    B. Setting the Maximum Headers Length in the HTTP Properties dialog box for a specific rule will apply globally to all Web publishing rules.

    C. Web sites that use Russian language URLs will remain available if the Block High-Bit Characters filter is selected.

    D. Any actions configured for specific file extensions on a rule's HTTP properties will apply globally to all Web publishing rules.

    E. Any signatures configured by editing a Web publishing rule's HTTP properties will apply globally to all Web publishing rules.

7. Which of the following statements about digital certificates and bridging from an ISA Server 2004 computer to a Microsoft Internet Information Services (IIS) 6.0 server located on the perimeter network is correct? (Choose the best answer.)

    A. HTTPS-to-HTTPS bridging requires certificates on both the ISA Server computer and the IIS 6.0 computer. HTTPS-to-HTTP bridging, however, requires a certificate only on the IIS 6.0 computer.

    B. HTTPS-to-HTTPS bridging requires certificates on both the ISA Server computer and the IIS 6.0 computer. HTTPS-to-HTTP bridging, however, requires a certificate only on the ISA Server computer.

    C. HTTPS-to-HTTPS bridging requires only a certificate on the ISA Server computer. HTTPS-to-HTTP bridging requires a certificate only on the IIS 6.0 computer.

    D. HTTPS-to-HTTPS bridging requires only a certificate on the IIS 6.0 computer. HTTPS-to-HTTP bridging requires a certificate only on the ISA Server computer.

    E. HTTPS-to-HTTPS bridging requires only a certificate on the ISA Server computer. HTTPS-to-HTTP bridging, however, requires a certificate on both the ISA Server computer and the IIS 6.0 computer.

8. You are publishing an IIS 6.0 Web server located on the perimeter network using an ISA Server 2004 computer. This server will be accessed primarily by hosts on the Internet. You want to use HTTPS-to-HTTPS bridging, but neither the ISA Server 2004 nor the Web server has digital certificates installed. The ISA Server 2004 computer has no IIS components installed. How should you configure digital certificates in this situation? (Choose all that apply.)

    A. Run the IIS Web Server Certificate Wizard on the Web server computer to prepare a request to a commercial CA. Install the commercial certificate on the Web server computer and then export it to the ISA Server 2004 computer.

    B. Run the IIS Web Server Certificate Wizard on the ISA Server 2004 computer to prepare a request to a commercial CA. Install the commercial certificate on the ISA Server 2004 computer and then export it to the Web server computer.

    C. When using the SSL Web Publishing Rule Wizard, ensure that the bridging mode is set to Secure Connection To Clients.

    D. When using the SSL Web Publishing Rule Wizard, ensure that the bridging mode is set to Secure Connection To Web Server.

    E. When using the SSL Web Publishing Rule Wizard, ensure that the bridging mode is set to Secure Connection To Clients And Web Server.

9. For the last 12 months, your organization has used the intranet Web server *www.tailspin toys.internal*. You now want to grant access, through your ISA Server 2004 Internet-edge firewall, to selected clients on the Internet. A problem you face is that many pages on the intranet Web server include *www.tailspintoys.internal* as part of the URLs rather than relative pathnames. You want the selected clients on the Internet to access the server as intranet.tailspintoys.com. Which of the following methods will allow Internet clients to access the Web server seamlessly, without problems occurring when a page that uses the *www.tailspintoys.internal* URL is requested? (Choose the best answer.)

    A. Edit each Web page that contains the URL *www.tailspintoys.internal* and convert it to a relative pathname.

    B. Get the selected clients on the Internet to access the server as *www.tailspintoys. internal* rather than as *intranet.tailspintoys.com*.

    C. Edit each Web page that contains the URL *www.tailspintoys.internal* and convert it to *intranet.tailspintoys.com*.

    D. Configure link translation on the ISA Server 2004 computer to map *www.tailspin toys.internal* to *intranet.tailspintoys.com*.

    E. Configure link translation on the ISA Server 2004 computer to map *intranet.tailspin toys.com* to *www.tailspintoys.internal*.

10. Last week you created a Web publishing rule named Test. Today your assistant has edited the Web publishing rule to configure Link translation. The Link Translation tab of the publishing rule properties with the new entries configured by your assistant is shown here.

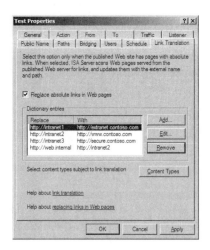

Since configuring link translation, your assistant has been unable to save this rule and has asked for your assistance. Which of the following configuration changes must you make to the rule to allow it to be saved with link translation enabled? (Choose the best answer.)

A. Delete the entry http://intranet3.

B. Delete the entry http://intranet1.

C. Ensure that the Web publishing rule specifies an explicit public domain name.

D. Ensure that the Web publishing rule specifies an explicit private domain name.

E. Delete the entry http://web.internal.

Objective 5.3 Answers

1. **Correct Answers: D**

   A. **Incorrect:** An Enterprise Root CA is used within an Active Directory environment and is therefore not an appropriate place to obtain a certificate to communicate securely with users who are not affiliated with your organization.

   B. **Incorrect:** An Enterprise Subordinate CA is used within an Active Directory environment and is therefore not an appropriate place to obtain a certificate to communicate securely with users who are not affiliated with your organization.

   C. **Incorrect:** A Stand Alone Root CA managed by your organization is unlikely to issue certificates that will automatically be trusted by users who are not affiliated with your organization.

   D. **Correct:** A certificate signed by a commercial CA located on the Internet is the most likely to be automatically trusted by users who are not affiliated with your organization.

2. **Correct Answers: C**

   A. **Incorrect:** Although you will receive a 500 Internal Server Error page if the certificate has expired, the fact that the certificate being used was recently obtained suggests that it has not expired. Further, the error message accompanying the 500 Internal Server Error page will not include the message Principle Name Is Incorrect in the case of certificate expiration.

   B. **Incorrect:** Obtaining a new certificate that matches the name of the secure Web server would resolve this problem, but obtaining a new certificate that matches the name of the ISA Server 2004 computer would not. The problem is that the server name provided in the Web publishing rule does not match the name on the SSL certificate.

   C. **Correct:** The problem that you have encountered is that the Web publishing rule is configured with a name that does not match the name on the digital certificate. You know that the name of the certificate is *secureweb.contoso.com*. The easiest solution is to change the Web publishing rule, although it is also possible to request a new digital certificate using the alternative name listed on the To tab of the secure Web publishing rule.

   D. **Incorrect:** This would not resolve the problem because the ISA Server 2004 computer must be able to resolve *secureweb.contoso.com* to perform the bridging function.

   E. **Incorrect:** The question asks to resolve the issue when accessing using the server name *secureweb.contoso.com* rather than *perimeterwww.contoso.com*. You know from the question that the certificate matches *secureweb.contoso.com*, hence you will need to change the server name on the Web publishing rule to match that name rather than another one.

3.   **Correct Answers: D**

A. **Incorrect:** Not including the default user sets, you will use three user sets to meet the security requirements listed in this question. A user set containing all Users in the hospital's SecurID namespace must be created to meet the security requirements of the first Web site. A user set containing all members of the Records Administrators Active Directory group must be created to meet the security requirements of the second Web site. A user set containing all Users in the Nurses and Doctors Active Directory group must be created. The default All Users user set can be applied to meet the security requirements of the fourth Web site and hence is not included in the figure.

B. **Incorrect:** Not including the default user sets, you will use three user sets to meet the security requirements listed in this question. A user set containing all Users in the hospital's SecurID namespace must be created to meet the security requirements of the first Web site. A user set containing all members of the Records Administrators Active Directory group must be created to meet the security requirements of the second Web site. A user set containing all Users in the Nurses and Doctors Active Directory group must be created. The default All Users user set can be applied to meet the security requirements of the fourth Web site and hence is not included in the figure.

C. **Incorrect:** Not including the default user sets, you will use three user sets to meet the security requirements listed in this question. A user set containing all Users in the hospital's SecurID namespace must be created to meet the security requirements of the first Web site. A user set containing all members of the Records Administrators Active Directory group must be created to meet the security requirements of the second Web site. A user set containing all Users in the Nurses and Doctors Active Directory group must be created. The default All Users user set can be applied to meet the security requirements of the fourth Web site and hence is not included in the figure.

D. **Correct:** Not including the default user sets, you will use three user sets to meet the security requirements listed in this question. A user set containing all Users in the hospital's SecurID namespace must be created to meet the security requirements of the first Web site. A user set containing all members of the Records Administrators Active Directory group must be created to meet the security requirements of the second Web site. A user set containing all Users in the Nurses and Doctors Active Directory group must be created. The default All Users user set can be applied to meet the security requirements of the fourth Web site and hence is not included in the figure.

E. Incorrect: Not including the default user sets, you will use three user sets to meet the security requirements listed in this question. A user set containing all Users in the hospital's SecurID namespace must be created to meet the security requirements of the first Web site. A user set containing all members of the Records Administrators Active Directory group must be created to meet the security requirements of the second Web site. A user set containing all Users in the Nurses and Doctors Active Directory group must be created. The default All Users user set can be applied to meet the security requirements of the fourth Web site and hence is not included in the figure.

4. **Correct Answers: B**

    A. Incorrect: ISA Server 2004 uses user sets rather than user groups when determining which users are granted or denied access to a particular published resource. You will need to create two user sets, one to grant access to and one to deny access to. In general, everyone who isn't specifically granted access is denied access. For this reason, you would not have to create a user set for users who have been denied access. You only need to use deny access when there is a smaller group of people who shouldn't have access contained in a larger group that has been granted access. In this specific case, you want to deny access to the Accountants group because there are members of the Accountants group who have been given access because they are also members of the Engineers, Researchers, and Scientists groups.

    B. Correct: ISA Server 2004 uses user sets rather than user groups when determining which users are granted or denied access to a particular published resource. You will need to create two user sets, one to grant access to and one to deny access to. In general, everyone who isn't specifically granted access is denied access. For this reason, you would not have to create a user set for users who have been denied access. You only need to use deny access when there is a smaller group of people who shouldn't have access contained in a larger group that has been granted access. In this specific case, you want to deny access to the Accountants group because there are people that are members of the Accountants group who have been given access because they are also members of the Engineers, Researchers, and Scientists groups.

    C. Incorrect: ISA Server 2004 uses user sets rather than user groups when determining which users are granted or denied access to a particular published resource. User sets can include Active Directory groups, RADIUS users, or RSA SecurID users.

    D. Incorrect: ISA Server 2004 uses user sets rather than user groups when determining which users are granted or denied access to a particular published resource. User sets can include Active Directory groups, RADIUS users, or RSA SecurID users.

5.   Correct Answers: D

A. Incorrect: HTTP methods control interactions between the Web client and Web server. Although you can use HTTP methods filtering to stop postings to the Web discussion board by disallowing POST and PUT methods, you cannot use HTTP methods to allow posting while disallowing certain inappropriate words.

B. Incorrect: HTTP extensions can be used to determine which file extensions are allowed. This is not the method you would use to block inappropriate words. To block inappropriate words posted to a discussion board, you must examine the body of HTTP traffic, and the best way of doing this is by filtering HTTP signatures.

C. Incorrect: HTTP headers would not contain the inappropriate words. To block inappropriate words posted to a discussion board, you must examine the body of HTTP traffic, and the best way of doing this is by filtering HTTP signatures.

D. Correct: You can create a signature entry that contains the list of inappropriate words. HTTP traffic that contains these words will be discarded.

6.   Correct Answers: A and C

A. Correct: HTTP filtering can only be applied to allow rules; it cannot be applied to deny rules.

B. Incorrect: If you set the Maximum Headers Length (done by selecting Configure HTTP for a rule from the Context menu) of a rule, it applies to all Web publishing rules.

C. Correct: High-bit characters are used in URLs that contain double-byte character sets, such as those used in Japanese, Russian, and other non-English languages. Blocking high-bit characters blocks the use of non-English-character URLs.

D. Incorrect: Unlike the Maximum Headers Length setting, actions configured for specific file extensions apply only to the specific rules rather than to all rules globally.

E. Incorrect: Unlike the Maximum Headers Length setting, signatures configured and applied to Web publishing rules influence only that rule and do not apply globally.

7.   Correct Answers: B

A. Incorrect: HTTPS-to-HTTPS bridging requires certificates on both the ISA Server computer and the IIS 6.0 computer. HTTPS-to-HTTP bridging, however, requires a certificate only on the ISA Server computer. A certificate is not required for the IIS

6.0 computer. The key to this question is remembering that, when HTTPS bridging is in use, the ISA Server computer always requires a certificate.

B. Correct: HTTPS-to-HTTPS bridging requires certificates on both the ISA Server computer and the IIS 6.0 computer. HTTPS-to-HTTP bridging, however, requires a certificate only on the ISA Server computer. A certificate is not required for the IIS 6.0 computer. The key to this question is remembering that, when HTTPS is in use, the ISA Server computer always requires a certificate.

C. Incorrect: HTTPS-to-HTTPS bridging requires certificates on both the ISA Server computer and the IIS 6.0 computer. HTTPS-to-HTTP bridging, however, requires a certificate only on the ISA Server computer. A certificate is not required for the IIS 6.0 computer. The key to this question is remembering that, when HTTPS is in use, the ISA Server computer always requires a certificate.

D. Incorrect: HTTPS-to-HTTPS bridging requires certificates on both the ISA Server computer and the IIS 6.0 computer. HTTPS-to-HTTP bridging, however, requires a certificate only on the ISA Server computer. A certificate is not required for the IIS 6.0 computer. The key to this question is remembering that, when HTTPS is in use, the ISA Server computer always requires a certificate.

E. Incorrect: HTTPS-to-HTTPS bridging requires certificates on both the ISA Server computer and the IIS 6.0 computer. HTTPS-to-HTTP bridging, however, requires a certificate only on the ISA Server computer. A certificate is not required for the IIS 6.0 computer. The key to this question is remembering that, when HTTPS is in use, the ISA Server computer always requires a certificate.

8.   Correct Answers: A and E

A. Correct: You will be unable to request the certificate from the ISA Server 2004 computer because it has no IIS components installed. Requesting the certificate from the Web server computer and then exporting the certificate to the ISA Server 2004 computer will ensure that both computers have an SSL certificate, which is necessary for HTTPS-to-HTTPS bridging.

B. Incorrect: Because none of the IIS components is installed on the ISA Server 2004 computer, you will not be able to run the IIS Web Server Certificate Wizard on this computer.

C. Incorrect: When the bridging mode is set to Secure Connection To Clients, HTTPS-to-HTTP bridging is in effect rather than HTTPS-to-HTTPS bridging. The difference is that, in HTTPS-to-HTTP bridging, the connection between the client and the ISA Server is encrypted using SSL, but the connection between the ISA Server and the Web server is not encrypted using SSL.

D. Incorrect: When the bridging mode is set to Secure Connection To Web Server, HTTP-to-HTTPS bridging rather than HTTPS-to-HTTPS bridging is in effect. The difference between the two is that, with HTTP-to-HTTPS bridging, the client's request to the ISA Server remains unencrypted and the ISA Server's communication with the Web server remains encrypted.

    E. Correct: HTTPS-to-HTTPS bridging means that the traffic between client, ISA Server, and Web server is all encrypted using SSL.

9.   Correct Answers: D

    A. Incorrect: Although this would work, it would also require a significant amount of effort compared to instituting link translation and hence is not the best answer.

    B. Incorrect: This is unlikely to work because the selected clients on the Internet will be unable to resolve www.tailspintoys.internal insofar as it is not a part of the Internet DNS namespace.

    C. Incorrect: Although this would work, it would also require a significant amount of effort compared to instituting link translation.

    D. Correct: Link translation can be used when the published Web site has pages that contain absolute links. You must map www.tailspintoys.internal to intranet.tailspin toys.com. Each time a page is encountered on the Intranet server with the name www.tailspintoys.internal, it will be translated to the client accessing the server through ISA Server 2004 as internal.tailspintoys.com.

    E. Incorrect: Although link translation is the appropriate technology to use, you need to map www.tailspintoys.internal to intranet.tailspintoys.com rather than the other way around.

10.   Correct Answers: C

    A. Incorrect: None of the mappings shown in the graphic will prevent the rule's being saved, hence deleting this entry will not resolve the problem. You can create and save a Web publishing rule without an explicit public domain name, however if you wish to enable link translation, you must also ensure that an explicit public domain name exists. If no explicit public domain name is set and link translation is enabled, you will be unable to save the rule. To resolve this issue, disable link translation or specify an explicit public domain name on the Public Name tab of the rule Properties dialog box.

    B. Incorrect: None of the mappings shown in the graphic will prevent the rule's being saved, hence deleting this entry will not resolve the problem. You can create and save a Web publishing rule without an explicit public domain name, however if you wish to enable link translation, you must also ensure that an explicit public domain name exists. If no explicit public domain name is set and link translation is enabled, you will be unable to save the rule. To resolve this issue, disable link translation or specify an explicit public domain name on the Public Name tab of the rule Properties dialog box.

C. **Correct:** Link translation cannot be enabled unless an explicit public domain name is contained within the Web publishing rule. Adding an explicit public domain name to this Web publishing rule will mean that the rule can be saved.

D. **Incorrect:** Link translation cannot be enabled unless an explicit public, rather than private, domain name is contained within the Web publishing rule.

E. **Incorrect:** None of the mappings shown in the graphic will prevent the rule's being saved, hence deleting this entry will not solve the problem. You can create and save a Web publishing rule without an explicit public-domain name, however if you wish to enable link translation, you must also ensure that an explicit public-domain name exists. If no explicit public-domain name is set and link translation is enabled, you will be unable to save the rule. To resolve this problem, disable link translation or specify an explicit public-domain name on the Public Name tab of the Rule Properties dialog box.

Objective 5.4

Create Policy Rules for Mail Server Publishing

E-mail is the lifeblood of most modern organizations. It also can represent a security threat because e-mail must not only pass from the internal network to the Internet; it must pass from unknown third parties on the Internet to at least one exposed host on your organization's network. ISA Server 2004 can be configured to screen **Simple Mail Transfer Protocol (SMTP)**, the transport protocol used to shift e-mail across the Internet, to ensure that protocol-level strikes, such as buffer overflow attacks, do not reach your organization's e-mail server. ISA Server can also be configured to allow hosts on the Internet to access e-mail servers on the perimeter or internal networks. There are several methods by which this can be done. **Outlook Web Access (OWA)** allows users to access e-mail, contacts, Exchange folders, and calendars through any computer on which Internet Explorer is installed.

1. Tailspin Toys, a manufacturer of remote-controlled toy aircraft, has released a new remote-controlled hovering jet. Sales representatives are about to start traveling the world to visit influential trade shows to demonstrate this addition to the company's catalogue. All sales representatives are issued laptop computers running Microsoft Windows XP Professional and have dial-up connections configured for all the cities that they will visit. Management has asked you to develop a list of what the company must do to allow the sales representatives to use Microsoft Outlook to access the company's Exchange Server 2003 server. Management wants this access to occur through the existing ISA Server 2004 Internet-edge firewall by using remote procedure call (RPC) over HTTP. Management does not want to allow direct Internet Message Access Protocol 4 (IMAP4) access to the Exchange Server 2003 server. The Exchange Server 2003 server is located on the company's internal network. The host operating system for Exchange Server 2003 is Windows Server 2003. Which of the following steps must you take to satisfy management's demands? (Choose all that apply.)

   A. Configure Exchange Server 2003 as an RPC proxy server.

   B. Configure ISA Server 2004 to publish an IMAP4 server using the Exchange Server 2003 computer's IP address. Enable SMTP message screening.

   C. Configure ISA Server 2004 to publish an RPC proxy server using the Exchange Server 2003 computer's IP address and enable RPC over HTTP communications.

   D. Ensure that all sales representatives have Outlook 2000 or later installed on their laptops.

   E. Ensure that Outlook 2003 or later is installed on each sales representative's laptop computer.

2. You are the systems administrator for Contoso, Ltd. Contoso has a single ISA Server 2004 computer configured using the 3-Leg Perimeter network template. Located on the perimeter network is a mail server that supports Post Office Protocol 3 (POP3) and SMTP. The mail server has a public IP address and can send and receive e-mail to other SMTP servers located on the Internet. The IP address of the ISA Server 2004 computer's public interface is 131.107.10.1. The IP address of the ISA Server 2004 computer's perimeter network interface is 131.107.10.9. The IP address of the ISA Server 2004 computer's Internal network interface is 10.0.0.1. The IP address of the mail server located on the perimeter network is 131.107.10.10. The mail server is configured to use the ISA Server 2004 computer as its default gateway. The host record *mail.contoso.com* points to IP address 131.107.10.10. The host record *gateway.contoso.com* points to IP address 131.107.10.1. A mail exchange (MX) record in the *contoso.com* zone points to this host name. ISA Server 2004 is configured so that this mail server is published with the SMTP protocol to the external network. The name of this policy rule is Alpha. The mail server is published to the internal network using SMTP and POP3. The name of these policy rules are Rule BETA and Rule GAMMA. The mail server located on the perimeter network is the sole SMTP and POP3 server at Contoso. After a recent buffer overflow attack on your SMTP server, you wish to enable SMTP message screening on the ISA Server 2004 computer. A diagram of the network is shown here.

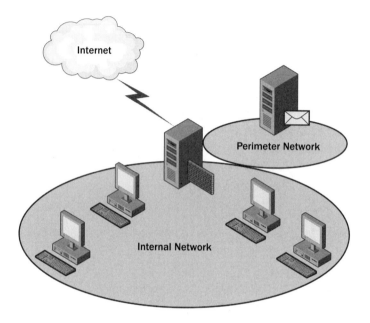

You have the following goals:

■ First Goal: To ensure that all SMTP traffic entering and exiting the Contoso network is screened by the ISA Server 2004 computer.

■ Second Goal: All SMTP traffic entering the Contoso network addressed to Contoso.com users is forwarded from the ISA Server 2004 computer to the mail server.

■ Third Goal: All SMTP traffic exiting the Contoso network is screened by the ISA Server 2004 computer.

■ You take the following steps:

■ Ensure that the SMTP service component of Windows Server 2003 and message screening component of ISA Server 2004 is installed on the ISA Server computer.

■ Update the MX record in the Contoso.com zone to point to gateway.contoso.com

■ Modify Rule ALPHA to use IP address 131.107.10.1

■ Modify Rule BETA to use IP address 10.0.0.1

Configure all mail clients on the Internal network to use IP address 10.0.0.1 as their SMTP server.

In the SMTP Service in the IIS 6.0 console of the ISA Server computer, configure a remote domain for *contoso.com* and forward all mail addressed to this domain to the smart host at 131.107.10.10

Which of your goals have you achieved? (Choose the correct answer.)

   A. The first, second, and third goals have been achieved.

   B. The first and third goals have been achieved.

   C. The first goal has been achieved.

   D. The second and third goals have been achieved.

   E. The third goal has been achieved.

3. You want to use forms-based authentication in publishing OWA running on an Exchange Server 2003 computer through an ISA Server 2004 Internet-edge firewall. While reading the product documentation, you have learned that you can configure forms-based authentication on either the ISA Server 2004 computer or the Exchange Server 2003 computer, but not both at the same time. Which of the following is an advantage of configuring forms-based authentication on the ISA Server 2004 computer as opposed to on the Exchange Server 2003 computer? (Choose the best answer.)

   A. Request headers can be inspected by ISA Server 2004.

   B. The Exchange data compression feature can be used.

   C. Response headers can be inspected by ISA Server 2004.

   D. Request bodies can be inspected by ISA Server 2004.

   E. Response bodies can be inspected by ISA Server 2004.

4. You have a Windows Server 2003 computer that has ISA Server 2004 installed on it and on which you wish to use the SMTP filter and Message Screening. Which of the following conditions must be met on the Windows Server 2003 computer before the Message-Screening component of ISA Server 2004 can be installed? (Choose the best answer.)

   A. The E-mail Services component must be installed.

   B. Certificate Services must be installed.

   C. The SMTP service must be installed.

   D. Exchange Server 2003 must be installed.

Objective 5.4 Answers

1. **Correct Answers: A, C, and E**

    A. Correct: To use RPC over HTTP, the Exchange Server 2003 server must be configured as an RPC proxy server.

    B. Incorrect: Management explicitly stated that direct IMAP4 access must not be allowed. SMTP message screening was not mentioned in the text of the question.

    C. Correct: You should publish the Exchange Server 2003 computer as an RPC proxy server, once it is configured as an RPC proxy server, rather than as an IMAP4 server, which was explicitly discouraged by management.

    D. Incorrect: Only Outlook 2003 or later supports the use of RPC over HTTP. Earlier versions of Outlook do not support this access method.

    E. Correct: Only Outlook 2003 or later supports the use of RPC over HTTP. Earlier versions of Outlook do not support this access method.

2. **Correct Answers: A**

    A. Correct: The first goal is achieved by ensuring that the message-screening component and SMTP service are installed, that the contoso.com MX record now points at the ISA Server rather than at the mail server and by modifying existing publishing rules. The second goal is achieved by configuring the remote domain within IIS 6.0. The third goal is met by configuring all mail clients on the internal network to use the ISA Server 2004 computer as their SMTP server.

    B. Incorrect: The first goal is achieved by ensuring that the message-screening component and SMTP service are installed, that the contoso.com MX record now points at the ISA Server rather than at the mail server and by modifying existing publishing rules. The second goal is achieved by configuring the remote domain within IIS 6.0. The third goal is met by configuring all mail clients on the internal network to use the ISA Server 2004 computer as their SMTP server.

    C. Incorrect: The first goal is achieved by ensuring that the message-screening component and SMTP service are installed, that the contoso.com MX record now points at the ISA Server rather than at the mail server and by modifying existing publishing rules. The second goal is achieved by configuring the remote domain within IIS 6.0. The third goal is met by configuring all mail clients on the internal network to use the ISA Server 2004 computer as their SMTP server.

    D. Incorrect: The first goal is achieved by ensuring that the message-screening component and SMTP service are installed, that the contoso.com MX record now points at the ISA Server rather than at the mail server and by modifying existing publishing rules. The second goal is achieved by configuring the remote domain within IIS 6.0. The third goal is met by configuring all mail clients on the internal network to use the ISA Server 2004 computer as their SMTP server.

E. Incorrect: The first goal is achieved by ensuring that the message-screening component and SMTP service are installed, that the contoso.com MX record now points at the ISA Server rather than at the mail server and by modifying existing publishing rules. The second goal is achieved by configuring the remote domain within IIS 6.0. The third goal is met by configuring all mail clients on the internal network to use the ISA Server 2004 computer as their SMTP server.

3.   Correct Answers: E

A. Incorrect: Request headers will be inspected regardless of whether forms-based authentication is configured on the Exchange Server 2003 computer or on the ISA Server 2004 computer.

B. Incorrect: Exchange data compression can be used only when forms-based authentication is configured on Exchange Server 2003 rather than on ISA Server 2004.

C. Incorrect: Response headers will be inspected regardless of whether forms-based authentication is configured on the Exchange Server 2003 computer or on the ISA Server 2004 computer.

D. Incorrect: Request bodies will be inspected regardless of whether forms-based authentication is configured on the Exchange Server 2003 computer or on the ISA Server 2004 computer.

E. Correct: Response bodies can be inspected only if forms-based authentication is enabled on the ISA Server 2004 computer as opposed to on the Exchange Server 2003 computer.

4.   Correct Answers: C

A. Incorrect: The E-mail Services component installs a POP3 server on the Windows Server 2003 computer. Message Screening works on the SMTP rather than the POP3 protocol.

B. Incorrect: The Message-Screening component of ISA Server 2004 functions independently of Certificate Services.

C. Correct: For Message Screening and SMTP filtering to be enabled, the SMTP service must be installed on the computer running ISA Server 2004.

D. Incorrect: It is recommended that you do not install Message Screening on Exchange Server 2003 because it will interfere with Exchange Server's connection and recipient filtering feature.

Create Policy Rules for Server Publishing

Server publishing allows servers other than e-mail and Web servers to be published to the Internet. Server publishing can also be used to allow more complex configurations for e-mail and Web servers than are allowed under the simplified Web and e-mail server publishing rules. Setting up server publishing is generally more complicated than Web and e-mail server publishing; on the other hand, it can also be more finely configured, enabling an administrator to configure options not available in the simpler rules.

Objective 5.5 Questions

1. Which of the following correctly delineates the differences between publishing a Web server using the Web publishing rules (including secure Web publishing) as opposed to using the Server publishing rules? (Choose all that apply.)

   A. Server publishing rules allow IP address logging for the client computer on the Web server.

   B. Server publishing rules allow access to multiple protocols in one rule.

   C. Secure Web publishing rules support encryption.

   D. Server publishing rules do not use the Web Proxy filter.

   E. Server publishing rules support link translation.

2. You have created an RPC access rule using the Create New Access Rule Wizard. You want to ensure that RPC type protocols such as Distributed Component Object Model (DCOM) are not permitted by clients using this access rule. Which of the following steps should you take? (Choose the best answer.)

   A. Edit the RPC Application Filter properties. Ensure that the RPC Compliance check box is checked.

   B. Edit the RPC Application Filter properties. Ensure that the RPC Compliance check box is unchecked.

   C. On the RPC access rule, configure the RPC protocol. Ensure that the Enforce Strict RPC Compliance check box is checked.

   D. On the RPC access rule, configure the RPC protocol. Ensure that the Enforce Strict RPC Compliance check box is unchecked.

   E. Edit the System Policy. In the Authentication Services\Active Directory node, ensure that the Enforce Strict RPC Compliance check box is checked.

3. You are the security administrator for a small publishing company. The company has recently instituted ISA Server 2004 as an Internet-edge firewall. Located on the internal company network is an IIS 6.0 FTP server. The FTP server is configured to allow anonymous users as well as those that have logged in to upload and download files. The server has been in use for some time and users report no difficulties storing or retrieving files on it. You have decided that you would like users on the Internet to access this FTP server. You create a new Server Publishing Rule and use the defaults for the FTP server, entering its IP address on the Internal network and configuring the rule to listen on the External network. After the publishing rule has been active for several hours, you receive reports from users who say that they can download files from the FTP server over the Internet fine, but when they try to upload files to the FTP server they are unable to do so. Users on the internal network report no problems. Which of the following steps can you take to rectify this situation? (Choose the best answer.)

   A. Restart the FTP service on the internal network FTP server.

   B. On the ISA Server 2004 computer, right-click the FTP server publishing rule and select Properties. On the Networks tab, ensure that the Internal rather than External network is selected.

   C. On the ISA Server 2004 computer, right-click the FTP server publishing rule and select Configure FTP. Remove the check from the Read Only check box.

   D. On the ISA Server 2004 computer, right-click the FTP server publishing rule and select Properties. On the To tab, ensure that the Requests Appear To Come From The ISA Server Computer check box is selected.

   E. On the ISA Server 2004 computer, right-click the FTP server publishing rule and select Properties. Navigate to the Schedule tab. Change the Schedule from Always to Weekends.

4. Concerned about security, you have configured a Server Publishing rule to allow Terminal Server or Remote Desktop connections from the Internet to a particular server located on your organization's perimeter network. The server's FQDN is moward.contoso.com. The rule is set to allow traffic from the External network. The rules schedule is shown here.

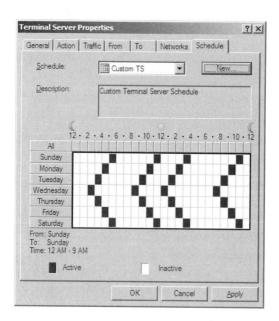

The unusual schedule is for security purposes, so that connections can only be established at specific times rather the server being accessible 24 hours a day. Given the information in the schedule, which of the following statements is correct? (Choose all that apply.)

A. This rule is active at 4:12 A.M. on Sunday, according to the ISA Server computer's clock.

B. If the host *moward.contoso.com* were located in a time zone one hour ahead of the ISA Server computer's time zone, a client would be able to access the terminal server at 11:30 A.M. on a Monday, according to the ISA Server computer's clock.

C. A Remote Desktop Protocol (RDP) client is located in a time zone two hours behind that of the ISA Server 2004 computer. The client will be able to access the terminal server at 6:14 A.M. on Wednesday, according to the ISA Server computer's clock.

D. A client that successfully connects to the terminal server at 9:55 A.M. on Thursday according to the ISA Server computer's clock will lose that connection five minutes later.

5. Rather than use your ISA Server 2004 Internet-edge firewall to be the end point for VPN connections, you have decided to set up a server on the Internal network to serve as the VPN terminus. All the VPN connections from the Internet to this server will be initiated from computers running Windows XP Professional. Which of the following conditions must be met for VPNs using L2TP/IPSec with NAT-T to be successfully established? (Choose all that apply.)

A. The VPN server must be running Windows Server 2003.

B. Two publishing rules must be configured on the ISA Server computer, one for IKE and the second to publish NAT-T.

C. Two publishing rules must be configured on the ISA Server computer, one for IKE and the second to publish PPTP.

D. Ensure that all VPN clients have the NAT-T update installed.

E. One publishing rule must be configured to publish the L2TP server

Objective 5.5 Answers

1.   Correct Answers: B and D

A. Incorrect: Although not enabled by default, Web publishing can be configured to allow the Web server to log the client computer's IP address rather than the IP address of the ISA Server's internal interface. Server publishing has this behavior enabled by default.

B. Correct: You can customize a server publishing rule to take into account multiple protocols within the same rule. On a Web server that provides content using other protocols, this means that you do not have to configure multiple rules, because all protocol transactions can be handled by one rule.

C. Incorrect: Both server publishing and secure Web publishing rules support encryption.

D. Correct: Web publishing rules use the Web Proxy filter. Server publishing rules forward authorized client requests directly to the published server.

E. Incorrect: Server publishing rules do not support link translation. Link translation is only supported by Web server publishing rules.

2.   Correct Answers: C

A. Incorrect: The only option that you have with any application filter is to either enable it or disable it. You cannot configure most Application Filter properties. RPC compliance is ensured by Configuring the RPC Protocol in the Firewall Policy on specific access rules.

B. Incorrect: The only option that you have with any application filter is to either enable it or disable it. You cannot configure most Application Filter properties. RPC compliance is ensured by Configuring the RPC Protocol in the Firewall Policy on specific access rules.

C. Correct: When this check box is checked, clients using the access rule will need to use strict RPC compliance rather than protocols such as DCOM.

D. Incorrect: Unchecking the check box will allow the type of traffic that you are trying to block.

E. Incorrect: This check box is used for configuring authentication between the ISA Server itself and Active Directory. Enabling this check box will not force clients using the separate RPC access rule from using methods such as DCOM.

3. **Correct Answers: C**

A. Incorrect: Users on the Internal network are experiencing no problems with the FTP server, so it is reasonable to assume that the problem does not lie there, but lies instead on the ISA Server 2004 computer.

B. Incorrect: By changing the listener to listen on the Internal rather than the External network, all access, both downloading and uploading from the Internet would be blocked.

C. Correct: By default, the FTP server publishing rule does not allow uploads. To allow uploads, clear the Read Only check box on the FTP protocol policy.

D. Incorrect: The IIS 6.0 FTP service cannot mediate read/write permissions based on a client IP address. If clients on the Internal network can perform read/write operations, clients on the External network should be able to perform write operations if they can perform read operations. Changing this setting will only change information in the log; it will not resolve this issue.

E. Incorrect: This will mean that the FTP server will be available to Internet clients only on weekends rather than on weekdays. It will do nothing to resolve the issue about Internet clients being unable to upload content.

4. **Correct Answers: D**

A. Incorrect: The schedule is dependent on the ISA Server computer's clock. The schedule indicates that the server is available at 5 A.M. to 6 A.M., 11 A.M. to 12 noon, 3 P.M. to 4 P.M., and 10 P.M. to 11 P.M. on Sundays.

B. Incorrect: The schedule is dependent on the time at the ISA Server computer rather than the time at the published server. On Mondays, the rule is active on the ISA Server computer from 4 A.M. to 5 A.M., 10 A.M. to 11 A.M., 2 P.M. to 3 P.M., and 9 P.M. to 10 P.M. A client attempting to access the terminal server at 11:30 A.M. at the ISA Server computer would be unable to gain access.

C. Incorrect: The schedule is dependent on the time at the ISA Server computer rather than the time at the published server. The time at the client's location is irrelevant. According to the schedule in the graphic, the terminal server is available on Wednesdays from 2 A.M. to 3 A.M., 8 A.M. to 9 A.M., 12 noon to 1 P.M., and 7 P.M. to 8 P.M.

D. Correct: The schedule determines when a rule is active. When a rule becomes inactive, current connections are dropped and new connections are refused. Connections can exist only within the windows of the schedule. The schedule in the graphic stipulates that connections can exist on Thursday only from 3 A.M. to 4 A.M., 9 A.M. to 10 A.M., 1 P.M. to 2 P.M., and 8 P.M. to 9 P.M.

5.   Correct Answers: B and D

A. Correct: A VPN server running Windows 2000 Server can support L2TP/IPSec but cannot support NAT-T. Only Windows Server 2003 can support NAT-T.

B. Correct: For a VPN server supporting L2TP/IPSec on the Internal network to be published on the ISA Server 2004 computer, a publishing rule for IKE and a publishing rule for NAT-T must be configured.

C. Incorrect: PPTP is a tunneling protocol separate from L2TP and is therefore not relevant in this situation.

D. Correct: Operating systems prior to Windows Server 2003, including Windows XP Professional, do not natively support NAT-T. To enable this support, install the NAT-T update or the most recent service pack.

E. Incorrect: When L2TP is used without IPSec, only one publishing rule needs to be configured. When L2TP is used with IPSec, two publishing rules, one for IKE and the other for NAT-T, must be configured.

18 Configuring and Managing Remote Network Connectivity (6.0)

Virtual private networks (VPNs) allow the Internet to become a medium over which your organization securely transmits data to remote branch locations. Data transmission is secured by sending it through encrypted tunnels. Each end of the tunnel can encrypt the data that it is to transmit and decrypts the data that it receives. Users are unaware of this process other than when they manually initiate a VPN connection.

Tested Skills and Suggested Practices

The skills that you need to master the Configuring and Managing Remote Network Connectivity objective domain on the *Implementing Microsoft Internet Security and Acceleration (ISA) Server 2004* exam include:

- Configure ISA Server 2004 for site-to-site VPN.
  - ❑ Practice: On the ISA Server 2004 Management Console, navigate to the Networks node under the Configuration node. On the Tasks tab, click Create A New Network task. This will start the New Network Wizard. Enter the Network Name as **REMOTENET** and click Next. In the Network Type dialog box, select VPN Site-To-Site Network. Click Next. In the VPN Protocol dialog box, select IPSecurity (IPSec) Tunnel Mode. Click Next. Set the remote VPN gateway IP address as **131.107.0.1**. Set the local VPN gateway Internet Protocol (IP) address as the IP address of the network interface on the Internal network. Click Next. On the IPSec Authentication page, select Use Pre-shared Key For Authentication and type **"The Quick Brown Fox Jumped Over The Lazy Dog"** (including the quotes) and then click Next. On the Network Addresses page, click Add and then enter a starting address of **10.90.0.1** and an ending address of **10.90.0.255**. Click OK and then click Next. If you receive an error stating that the range that you have entered is within your internal network, use another part of the private address space such as 192.168.10.1 to 192.168.10.255. Click Finish to exit the New Network Wizard.

- Configure ISA Server 2004 as a remote access VPN server.
  - ❑ Practice: On the ISA Server 2004 Management Console, navigate to the Virtual Private Networks node. On the Tasks tab, open the Enable VPN Client Access task. Click Apply to save changes and update ISA Server configuration. On

the Tasks tab, open the Configure VPN Client Access task. This opens the VPN Client Properties dialog box. On the General tab, set the Maximum Number of VPN Clients Allowed to 20. On the Protocols tab, disable PPTP and enable L2TP/IPSec. Click OK to close the VPN Clients Properties dialog box. You will be prompted to restart the ISA Server computer. Apply the changes and then restart the computer. Once the server has restarted, open the ISA Server 2004 Management Console, right-click the Virtual Private Networks node and select Properties. Navigate to the Address Assignment tab and configure the IP address assignment method as Static Address Pool. Enter a start IP address of **192.168.100.1** and a finish address of **192.168.100.254**. If these addresses are part of your internal network, select other addresses from the private address space. Navigate to the Authentication tab and check the Allow Custom IPSec Policy for L2TP Connection check box. Type **"The Quick Brown Fox Jumped Over The Lazy Dog"** (including the quotation marks) as the pre-shared key. Click **OK**.

■ Diagnose and resolve VPN connectivity issues.

❑ Practice: On the ISA Server Management Console, navigate to the Monitoring node and select the Sessions tab. On the Tasks tab, open the Edit Filter task. This opens the Edit Filter dialog box. Use the drop-down Filter to select Session Type. Set the Condition to Equals and the Value to VPN Client. Click Add To List. Repeat this procedure using the settings Filter By Session type, Condition to Equals and the Value to VPN Remote Site. Click Add To List and then click Start Query.

Further Reading

This section lists supplemental readings by objective. We recommend that you study these sources thoroughly before taking this exam.

Objective 6.1   Site-To-Site VPN in ISA Server 2004   *http://www.microsoft.com/tech net/prodtechnol/isa/2004/plan/sitetositevpn.mspx*

Configuring IPSec Site-to-Site Connections Between ISA Server 2004 and Third-Party Gateways   *http://www.microsoft.com/technet/prodtechnol/isa/2004/plan/ sitetositeipsec.mspx*

Objective 6.2   VPN Roaming Clients and Quarantine Control in ISA Server 2004   *http:// www.microsoft.com/technet/prodtechnol/isa/2004/plan/vpnroamingquarantine.mspx*

Authenticating VPN Clients with RSA SecurID Authentication   *http://www. microsoft.com/technet/prodtechnol/isa/2004/plan/vpnrsa.mspx*

Objective 6.3   ISA Server 2004 FAQ: VPN   *http://www.microsoft.com/technet/ prodtechnol/isa/2004/plan/faq-vpn.mspx*

ISA Server 2004 VPN Deployment Kit   *http://www.microsoft.com/isaserver/ techinfo/productdoc/2004.asp*

Excluding Specific Addresses from VPN Source Networks in ISA Server 2004   *http:// www.microsoft.com/technet/prodtechnol/isa/2004/plan/excludingaddressesfromvpn. mspx*

Objective 6.1

Configure ISA Server 2004 for Site-to-Site VPNs

Until relatively recently, if an organization wanted to connect a branch-office network to a headquarters network over a significant distance, it would have to make its own direct connection over the public telephone network. This could be done through a permanent connection such as an Integrated Services Digital Network (ISDN) leased line or an intermittent dial-up modem connection. On very distant connections—from Seattle to Miami, for example—this could incur significant long-distance telephone charges. Site-to-site VPNs are a relatively new development and use the Internet as a medium over which to transmit this information. Rather than make a long-distance call from Seattle to Miami, a connection is made to the Internet at each location and the data is transmitted across the Internet. The drawback of this method is that the Internet is a public network and hence all data transmitted across the Internet can theoretically be intercepted and read. The solution to this problem is the VPN, which creates an encryption-protected tunnel across the Internet through which an organization's site-to-site data can travel. In the event that the data transmitted between the sites is intercepted, the encryption protects it from being read.

Objective 6.1 Questions

1. You are creating a site-to-site VPN prior to configuring a site-to-site VPN using the New Network Wizard. You must choose a VPN protocol to protect the traffic sent between the sites. Which of the following VPN protocols provides the highest security while retaining interoperability with third-party VPN equipment? (Choose the best answer.)

    A. IPSec tunnel mode

    B. RPC over HTTP

    C. L2TP over IPSec

    D. PPTP

2. You are creating a VPN site-to-site network prior to configuring a site-to-site VPN using the New Network Wizard. You have decided that IPSec tunnel mode will be used to protect site-to-site traffic passing across the Internet. When configuring IPSec tunnel mode, you must select an authentication method for establishing the tunnel between local and remote VPN servers. Which of the following authentication methods is compatible with IPSec tunnel mode? (Choose all that apply.)

    A. RSA SecurID authentication

    B. Digital Certificate

    C. RADIUS

    D. Kerberos V5

    E. Pre-shared Key

3. You are configuring the user account that will be used to establish an L2TP over IPSec tunnel from a branch office to your organization's headquarters. For the connection to succeed, which of the following properties must this user account always have? (Choose all that apply.)

    A. The password meets complexity requirements.

    B. The User Cannot Change Password option is set.

    C. The Store Password Using Reversible Encryption option is set.

    D. User name and site-to-site network name must be identical.

    E. User account properties must be set to allow remote access.

4. Contoso, Ltd. has 22 locations throughout Australasia. You are configuring VPNs between the Contoso headquarters, located in Sydney, and the 21 branch offices. The branch offices have differing hardware and therefore support different tunneling technology. Each branch office has its own separate network. Of the branch offices, 11 will use IPSec tunneling-mode tunnels, 7 branch offices will use L2TP over IPSec tunnels, and 3 will use PPTP tunnels. How many separate user accounts must you configure so that remote access connections can be successfully initiated to establish these site-to-site VPN links? (Choose the best answer.)

A. 1

B. 11

C. 10

D. 7

E. 21.

5. You are the administrator of an ISA Server 2004 Enterprise Edition computer array that has three member computers. The computers are clustered so that hosts on the Internet use only a single IP address to access resources published on your organization's perimeter network. You wish to configure the array to also manage incoming VPN traffic. As part of this process, you are configuring VPN client address assignment. You want addresses assigned regardless of which ISA Server 2004 Enterprise Edition computer handles the request. In which of the following ways should you do this? (Choose the best answer.)

A. You should configure all three servers in the array to use a Dynamic Host Configuration Protocol (DHCP) server to assign addresses.

B. Configure one server in the array to use a DHCP server to assign addresses.

C. Configure all three servers in the array to assign addresses from a static pool.

D. Configure one server in the array to assign addresses from a static pool.

6. You are a consultant who has been asked to configure five L2TP-over-IPSec connections from the Contoso, Ltd. head office to its branch locations. There are six ISA Server 2004 computers functioning as Internet-edge firewalls. One is located at the head office site and one at each of five branch-office locations. You will use pre-shared keys for authentication. How many unique pre-shared keys must you configure? (Choose the best answer.)

A. 1

B. 5

C. 6

D. 10

E. 12

7.   You have configured an IPSec tunnel-mode connection between Contoso's headquarters and the Wangaratta branch-office site. You have configured a route relationship between these two networks named HQ-Wangaratta. You have created five different access rules as shown here.

The rules are currently disabled. Which rules should you enable to allow all traffic from the Wangaratta site to the Internal network and all traffic from the Internal network to the Wangaratta network over the VPN site-to-site link? (Choose all that apply.)

   A.   Rule-One

   B.   Rule-Two

   C.   Rule-Three

   D.   Rule-Four

   E.   Rule-Five

Objective 6.1 Answers

1. **Correct Answers: A**

   A. **Correct:** IPSec tunnel mode provides high security and interoperability with third-party VPN vendors.

   B. **Incorrect:** Remote procedure call (RPC) over Hypertext Transfer Protocol (HTTP) is not a VPN protocol. RPC over HTTP provides a way of tunneling RPC traffic using HTTP.

   C. **Incorrect:** Although Layer Two Tunneling Protocol (L2TP) over Internet Protocol Security (IPSec) does provide high security, it is only supported by Microsoft ISA Server 2004 or Routing and Remote Access Service (RRAS) on Microsoft Windows Server 2003 and Windows 2000 Server.

   D. **Incorrect:** Point-to-Point Tunneling Protocol (PPTP) requires Microsoft ISA Server 2004 or RRAS on Windows Server 2003 and Windows 2000 Server. PPTP is not as secure as L2TP over IPSec or IPSec tunnel mode.

2. **Correct Answers: B and E**

   A. **Incorrect:** RSA SecurID cannot be used to authenticate the establishment of a site-to-site VPN tunnel that uses IPSec tunnel mode. Authentication methods for this type of tunnel are restricted to digital certificate or pre-shared key.

   B. **Correct:** Digital certificates issued by a certification authority (CA) that is trusted by both local and remote VPN servers can be used to authenticate IPSec tunnel-mode VPN tunnels.

   C. **Incorrect:** Remote Authentication Dial-In User Service (RADIUS) cannot be used to authenticate the establishment of a site-to-site VPN tunnel that uses IPSec tunnel mode. Authentication methods for this type of tunnel are restricted to digital certificate or pre-shared key.

   D. **Incorrect:** Kerberos version 5 authentication protocol cannot be used to authenticate the establishment of a site-to-site VPN tunnel that uses IPSec tunnel mode. Authentication methods for this type of tunnel are restricted to digital certificate or pre-shared key.

   E. **Correct:** Digital certificates from a mutually trusted CA and pre-shared keys can be used to authenticate IPSec tunnel mode VPN tunnels. A pre-shared key is a set of characters typed into a dialog box with which both the local and remote VPN server are configured. In many situations, it is simpler to use a pre-shared key than it is to configure digital certificates.

3.   Correct Answers: D and E

A. Incorrect: Password complexity is only required if the server on which the account is held has the Enforce Password Complexity policy set.

B. Incorrect: Although it may be wise to set this particular option for the user account that is used to establish an L2TP over IPSec tunnel, it is not mandatory.

C. Incorrect: This option is not required for a user account that's used to establish an L2TP over IPSec tunnel. This option also makes a password less secure.

D. Correct: To establish an L2TP over IPSec tunnel, the account used to initiate the remote-access connection must have a name that is identical to the name of the site-to-site network.

E. Correct: The Remote Access Permission (dial-in or VPN) option on the Dial-In tab of the User Account properties must be set to Allow Access.

4.   Correct Answers: C

A. Incorrect: No user accounts will need to be configured for the IPSec tunneling-mode tunnels because these connections use certificates or pre-shared keys for authentication. A total of 7 user accounts must be configured to support the L2TP over IPSec tunnels, because each account name must match the remote network name. For the same reason, 3 accounts will be required to support the PPTP tunnels.

B. Incorrect: No user accounts will need to be configured for the IPSec tunneling-mode tunnels because these connections use certificates or pre-shared keys for authentication. A total of 7 user accounts must be configured to support the L2TP over IPSec tunnels, because each account name must match the remote network name. For the same reason, 3 accounts will be required to support the PPTP tunnels.

C. Correct: No user accounts will need to be configured for the IPSec tunneling-mode tunnels because these connections use certificates or pre-shared keys for authentication. A total of 7 user accounts must be configured to support the L2TP over IPSec tunnels, because each account name must match the remote network name. For the same reason, 3 accounts will be required to support the PPTP tunnels.

D. Incorrect: No user accounts will need to be configured for the IPSec tunneling-mode tunnels because these connections use certificates or pre-shared keys to authenticate. A total of 7 user accounts must be configured to support the L2TP over IPSec tunnels, because each account name must match the remote network name. For the same reason, 3 accounts will be required to support the PPTP tunnels.

E. **Incorrect:** No user accounts will need to be configured for the IPSec tunneling-mode tunnels because these connections use certificates or pre-shared keys for authentication. A total of 7 user accounts must be configured to support the L2TP over IPSec tunnels, because each account name must match the remote network name. For the same reason, 3 accounts will be required to support the PPTP tunnels.

5. **Correct Answers: C**

A. **Incorrect:** A DHCP server can only be used to assign addresses if the array contains a single ISA Server 2004 Enterprise Edition computer. Where there are three such servers, static address pools must be used.

B. **Incorrect:** A DHCP server can only be used to assign addresses if the array contains a single ISA Server 2004 Enterprise Edition computer. Where there are three such servers, static address pools must be used.

C. **Correct:** A DHCP server can only be used to assign addresses if the array contains a single ISA Server 2004 Enterprise Edition computer. Where there are three such servers, static address pools must be used. Because any server in the array can be called upon to service the address request, all must have a static address pool configured.

D. **Incorrect:** A DHCP server can only be used to assign addresses if the array contains a single ISA Server 2004 Enterprise Edition computer. Where there are three such servers, static address pools must be used. Because any server in the array can be called upon to service the address request, all must have a static address pool configured.

6. **Correct Answers: A**

A. **Correct:** A VPN server can use only one pre-shared key for all L2TP-over-IPSec connections. This means that all connections must use the same key. It also means that all branch offices that will be the other end of the site-to-site connection must use that key as well.

B. **Incorrect:** A VPN server can use only one pre-shared key for all L2TP-over-IPSec connections. This means that all connections must use the same key. It also means that all branch offices that will be the other end of the site-to-site connection must use that key as well.

C. **Incorrect:** A VPN server can use only one pre-shared key for all L2TP-over-IPSec connections. This means that all connections must use the same key. It also means that all branch offices that will be the other end of the site-to-site connection must use that key as well.

D. Incorrect: A VPN server can use only one pre-shared key for all L2TP-over-IPSec connections. This means that all connections must use the same key. It also means that all branch offices that will be the other end of the site-to-site connection must use that key as well.

E. Incorrect: A VPN server can use only one pre-shared key for all L2TP-over-IPSec connections. This means that all connections must use the same key. It also means that all branch offices that will be the other end of the site-to-site connection must use that key as well.

7. **Correct Answers: B and E**

A. Incorrect: Enabling Rule-One would deny all traffic from the Wangaratta network to the Internal network.

B. Correct: Enabling Rule-Two would allow all traffic from the Internal network to pass to the Wangaratta network.

C. Incorrect: Enabling Rule-Three would allow all traffic from the Wangaratta network to pass to the VPN clients' network rather than to the Internal network.

D. Incorrect: Enabling Rule-Four would allow all traffic from the VPN clients' network to pass to the Internal network. Although a VPN is in use, it is the Wangaratta network, rather than the VPN clients' network, that is germane to this question.

E. Correct: Enabling Rule-Five would allow all traffic from the Wangaratta network to pass through to the Internal network.

Objective 6.2

Configure ISA Server 2004 as a Remote-Access VPN Server

Remote-access VPNs have become an increasingly popular way of allowing people to access an organization's network remotely. In the past, this access would have been granted by means of a dial-up modem. Remote-access VPNs mean that clients first connect to their own Internet service providers (ISPs). Once that connection is established, clients then connect to the VPN server. As anyone who has worked on the help desk at an organization that has provided a modem bank to which its members connect will attest, shifting the burden of establishing that initial connection from the organization to an ISP can save the support team many hours of frustration. In implementing VPNs, administrators must consider how to assign IP addresses to incoming VPN clients, how those clients should authenticate, determine whether to quarantine clients, and decide which protocols and networks VPN clients can access.

Objective 6.2 Questions

1. Your network administrator has suggested that you use the 192.168.10.64 /28 subnet when you configure a static address pool for an ISA Server 2004 computer that will function as a VPN server. Which start address and end address should you configure for this particular subnet in the Address Assignment tab of the Virtual Private Networks (VPN) Properties dialog box? (Choose two.)

   A. Start address: 192.168.10.65

   B. Start address: 192.168.10.64

   C. Start address: 192.168.10.1

   D. End address: 192.168.10.80

   E. End address: 192.168.10.78

   F. End address: 192.168.10.79

2. In which of the following situations can you use a DHCP server to assign IP addresses to VPN clients? (Choose all that apply.)

   A. A single ISA Server 2004 Standard Edition computer configured as an Internet-edge firewall

   B. Two ISA Server 2004 Standard Edition computers configured with network load balancing (NLB)

   C. A single ISA Server 2004 Enterprise Edition computer

   D. Two ISA Server 2004 Enterprise Edition computers that are members of the same array

   E. Three ISA Server 2004 Enterprise Edition computers that are members of the same array

3. You are configuring access policy for VPN client computers. You have created five rules as shown here.

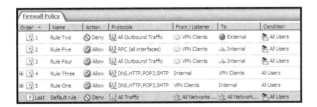

These five rules are all currently disabled. What is the minimum number of rules that you must enable to allow VPN clients to access the organization's internal Web server, Post Office Protocol 3 (POP3) and Simple Mail Transport Protocol (SMTP) server, Domain Name System (DNS) servers and file servers while denying VPN clients access to the Internet? (Choose the correct answer.)

    A. One

    B. Three

    C. Four

    D. Five

    E. Two

4. You have installed ISA Server 2004 on a stand-alone Windows Server 2003 computer. You want to ensure that passwords, even in encrypted form, are not transmitted across the Internet. Which of the following Authentication methods can you enable, given these limitations? (Choose all that apply.)

    A. MS-CHAPv2

    B. Extensible Authentication Protocol (EAP)

    C. MS-CHAP

    D. CHAP

    E. Shiva Password Authentication Protocol (SPAP)

5. Which of the following must you do to use RSA SecurID to authenticate VPN client connections to an ISA Server 2004 computer? (Choose all that apply.)

    A. Configure the ISA Server 2004 computer as an RSA ACE/Agent.

    B. Configure client computers as RSA ACE/Agents.

    C. Configure the ISA Server 2004 system policy rule to allow the ISA Server computer access to the RSA SecurID server.

    D. Configure EAP (RSA SecurID) authentication.

    E. Disable MS-CHAPv2 as an authentication method on the ISA Server 2004 computer.

6. Which of the following must you configure to use ISA Server 2004 Quarantine Control on a Windows Server 2003 computer with ISA Server 2004, Standard Edition, installed? (Choose all that apply.)

    A. Enterprise Root CA.

    B. A group of users configured to authenticate against an RSA SecurID Server.

    C. A listener component such as Rqs.exe installed on the ISA Server 2004 computer.

    D. A quarantine-compatible, remote-access client with installed quarantine Connection Manager profile.

    E. Client-side quarantine script that executes Rqc.exe when the appropriate conditions are met.

7. The Quarantined VPN Clients Properties is configured as shown here.

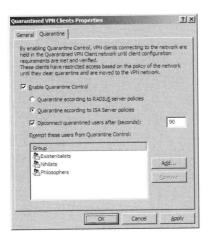

Given this information, which of the following statements is true? (Choose the best answer.)

    A. Members of the Existentialists user group will be automatically transferred to the VPN clients' network once they authenticate their connections.

    B. A client that does not have an appropriately configured Connection Manager profile will be disconnected from the VPN server after 60 seconds.

    C. ISA Server 2004 must be configured to use RADIUS authentication.

    D. ISA Server 2004 must be configured to use RSA SecurID authentication.

Objective 6.2 Answers

1.   Correct Answers: A and E

   A. Correct: The subnet 192.168.10.64 uses the IP addresses 192.168.10.65 through to 192.168.10.78. IP address 192.168.10.64 is reserved as the network address, and 192.168.10.79 will be used as that subnet's broadcast address.

   B. Incorrect: When using this particular subnet mask, IP address 192.168.10.64 becomes a network address rather than an address that can be used by a host. If a host were assigned this address by the VPN server, it would experience connectivity problems.

   C. Incorrect: The subnet 192.168.10.64 uses the IP addresses 192.168.10.65 through to 192.168.10.78. IP address 192.168.10.64 is reserved as the network address and 192.168.10.79 will be used as that subnet's broadcast address.

   D. Incorrect: The subnet 192.168.10.64 uses the IP addresses 192.168.10.65 through to 192.168.10.78. IP address 192.168.10.64 is reserved as the network address and 192.168.10.79 will be used as that subnet's broadcast address. 192.168.10.80 is the network address of the next subnet after 192.168.10.64 /28.

   E. Correct: The subnet 192.168.10.64 uses the IP addresses 192.168.10.65 through to 192.168.10.78. IP address 192.168.10.64 is reserved as the network address and 192.168.10.79 will be used as that subnet's broadcast address.

   F. Incorrect: The subnet 192.168.10.64 uses the IP addresses 192.168.10.65 through to 192.168.10.78. IP address 192.168.10.64 is reserved as the network address and 192.168.10.79 will be used as that subnet's broadcast address.

2.   Correct Answers: A, B, and C

   A. Correct: Single or multiple ISA Server 2004 Standard Edition computers can be configured to use a DHCP server to assign IP addresses to VPN clients. The only time that you cannot use a DHCP server to assign IP addresses to VPN clients is when using an array of two or more ISA Server 2004 Enterprise Edition computers.

   B. Correct: Single or multiple ISA Server 2004 Standard Edition computers can be configured to use a DHCP server to assign IP addresses to VPN clients. The only time that you cannot use a DHCP server to assign IP addresses to VPN clients is when using an array of two or more ISA Server 2004 Enterprise Edition computers.

   C. Correct: Single or multiple ISA Server 2004 Standard Edition computers can be configured to use a DHCP server to assign IP addresses to VPN clients. The only time that you cannot use a DHCP server to assign IP addresses to VPN clients is when using an array of two or more ISA Server 2004 Enterprise Edition computers.

D. **Incorrect:** Single or multiple ISA Server 2004 Standard Edition computers can be configured to use a DHCP server to assign IP addresses to VPN clients. The only time that you cannot use a DHCP server to assign IP addresses to VPN clients is when using an array of two or more ISA Server 2004 Enterprise Edition computers.

E. **Incorrect:** Single or multiple ISA Server 2004 Standard Edition computers can be configured to use a DHCP server to assign IP addresses to VPN clients. The only time that you cannot use a DHCP server to assign IP addresses to VPN clients is when using an array of two or more ISA Server 2004 Enterprise Edition computers.

3. **Correct Answers: A**

A. **Correct:** Enabling Rule-Four will meet the requirement. You need not enable a rule to deny access to the Internet because the already enabled Default Rule at the bottom of the graphic implicitly handles that access denial.

B. **Incorrect:** Enabling Rule-Four will meet the requirement. You need not enable a rule to deny access to the Internet because the already enabled Default Rule at the bottom of the graphic implicitly handles that access denial.

C. **Incorrect:** Enabling Rule-Four will meet the requirement. You need not enable a rule to deny access to the Internet because the already enabled Default Rule at the bottom of the graphic implicitly handles that access denial.

D. **Incorrect:** Enabling Rule-Four will meet the requirement. You need not enable a rule to deny access to the Internet because the already enabled Default Rule at the bottom of the graphic implicitly handles that access denial.

E. **Incorrect:** Enabling Rule-Four will meet the requirement. You need not enable a rule to deny access to the Internet because the already enabled Default Rule at the bottom of the graphic implicitly handles that access denial.

4. **Correct Answers: A, C, and D**

A. **Correct:** Microsoft Challenge Handshake Authentication Protocol version 2 (MS-CHAPv2) does not transmit the password across the Internet in any form, and it can be used on a stand-alone server.

B. **Incorrect:** EAP can be used only if the ISA Server computer is a member of a domain.

C. **Correct:** MS-CHAP does not transmit the password across the Internet in any form.

D. **Correct:** CHAP does not transmit the password across the Internet in any form.

E. **Incorrect:** SPAP sends the password in an encrypted form and hence does not meet the requirements of the scenario.

5. **Correct Answers: A, C, and D**

   A. Correct: To use RSA SecurID authentication, an ISA Server 2004 computer must be configured as an RSA ACE/Agent.

   B. Incorrect: To use RSA SecurID authentication, client computers need not be configured as RSA ACE/Agents.

   C. Correct: Not only does the ISA Server 2004 computer need to be configured as an RSA ACE/Agent; it must also have access to the RSA SecurID server, typically installed on the Internal network.

   D. Correct: Once the ISA Server 2004 computer is configured as an RSA ACE/Agent and is allowed access to the RSA SecurID server, you must enable this form of authentication by entering the RSA SecurID server in the EAP Providers dialog box.

   E. Incorrect: There is no need to disable MS-CHAPv2 as an authentication method to enable RSA SecurID as an authentication method.

6. **Correct Answers: C, D, and E**

   A. Incorrect: CAs are not required to implement ISA Server 2004 Quarantine Control.

   B. Incorrect: An RSA SecurID server is not required to implement ISA Server 2004 Quarantine Control.

   C. Correct: The listener component listens for messages from quarantine-compatible remote access clients that indicate that their scripts have been run successfully.

   D. Correct: VPN clients must have a quarantine-compatible, remote-access client that is configured with the appropriate Connection Manager quarantine profile. Connection Manager is an add-on component to Windows Server 2003 that can be downloaded from Microsoft's Web site.

   E. Correct: The client-side quarantine script performs a series of checks on the remote-access client's configuration to ascertain whether it is safe to move the client off the quarantine network to the VPN clients network. Such checks could include whether the client's antivirus definitions are up-to-date. Once the script has executed correctly, RQC.EXE sends the successful notification to the listener installed on the ISA Server computer.

7.   Correct Answers: A

A. Correct: According to the graphic, users in the Existentialists, Nihilists, and Philosophers groups will be exempt from the quarantine-control process.

B. Incorrect: According to the graphic, clients who do not have appropriately configured Connection Manager profiles or clients whose script does not validate an appropriate configuration will be disconnected from the VPN server after 90 seconds, rather than 60 seconds.

C. Incorrect: According to the graphic, quarantine occurs according to ISA Server policies rather than RADIUS server policies. Although RADIUS may be used for authentication of users, it is not a necessity, given this configuration.

D. Incorrect: According to the graphic, quarantine occurs according to ISA Server policies. Nothing is stated about requiring RSA SecurID authentication in this instance.

Objective 6.3

Diagnose and Resolve VPN Connectivity Issues

VPN connections can fail for a variety of reasons. If the routing between the Internal and remote networks is incorrectly configured, traffic will not cross the VPN link. If the correct CA is not trusted, connections that require certificates for authentication will not be established. In some cases, enabling network security options such as dropping IP fragments, commonly used in attacks such as the teardrop attack, will mean that certain VPN connections cannot be established because the two endpoints cannot authenticate against each other. Even when VPN connections are successfully established, it is important to know which tunneling protocols natively support name resolution and which protocols require extra DNS configuration for resolution of host names on the remote network.

Objective 6.3 Questions

1. For the last 12 months, your headquarters has been connected to a remote branch office using a site-to-site VPN link. All hosts at the branch office use the DNS suffix *branch.contoso.com*. All hosts at the headquarters office use the DNS suffix *hq.con toso.com*. Each location has its own separate DNS server. For the last 12 months, clients have been able to access servers on the remote branch-office network using both fully qualified domain names (FQDN) and IP addresses. In the last week you have upgraded the site-to-site VPN link from PPTP to IPSec tunneling mode because PPTP did not provide several features that you required, such as data integrity and origin authentication. Since the switch to IPSec tunneling mode, clients at the headquarters site have been unable to access branch-office servers using FQDN, though they are accessible using IP address. What can you do to resolve this situation? (Choose the best answer.)

    A. Configure the headquarters DNS to use conditional forwarding to forward all queries made to the *branch.contoso.com* zone to the DNS server at the branch office.

    B. Configure the branch-office DNS server to act as a secondary server to the primary zone, which is stored on the headquarters DNS server.

    C. Issue an IPSec certificate to the branch-office DNS server.

    D. Issue an IPSec certificate to the headquarters DNS server.

    E. Configure the headquarters DNS server with a remote-access VPN connection to the branch-office network.

2. You are the network administrator for A. Datum Corp. You have configured two IPSec tunnel-mode, site-to-site VPN connections to two partner organizations. The first partner organization uses the zone name *tailspintoys.internal* for hosts on its Internal network. The second partner organization uses the zone name *contoso.internal* for hosts on its Internal network. All organizations use Windows Server 2003 as their DNS servers and have ISA Server 2004 configured as their Internet-edge firewall. You want to ensure that hosts on the A. Datum Internal network can resolve host names on the Tailspintoys and Contoso Internal networks. Which of the following methods would work? (Choose all that apply.)

    A. Configure conditional forwarding for the partner zones on the A. Datum DNS server.

    B. Configure stub zones for the partner zones on the A. Datum DNS server.

    C. Configure the A. Datum DNS server as a root server.

    D. Configure secondary zones of the partner zones on the A. Datum DNS server.

    E. Configure the partner zones as Active Directory Integrated zones and ensure that they replicate to all domain controllers within the forest.

3. You are setting up a site-to-site VPN between Contoso Ltd. and Coho Vineyard. The Internal network at Contoso uses the address range 10.0.0.0 /22. The Internal network at Coho Vineyard uses the address range 10.0.4.0 /24. Each network uses a ISA Server 2004 Internet-edge firewall. The Coho Vineyard site-to-site VPN network using IPSec tunneling is configured on the Contoso ISA Server 2004 computer using the appropriate IP address range. The Contoso site-to-site VPN network using IPSec tunneling is configured on the Coho Vineyard ISA Server 2004 computer using the appropriate IP address range. You now wish to configure network rules on both of these ISA Server computers. Which of the following network relationships can be used? (Choose all that apply.)

   A. Configure a network address translation (NAT) relationship on the Coho Vineyard ISA Server 2004 computer. Configure a NAT relationship on the Contoso ISA Server 2004 computer.

   B. Configure a NAT relationship on the Coho Vineyard ISA Server 2004 computer. Configure a route relationship on the Contoso ISA Server 2004 computer.

   C. Configure a route relationship on the Coho Vineyard ISA Server 2004 computer. Configure a NAT relationship on the Contoso ISA Server 2004 computer.

   D. Configure a route relationship on the Coho Vineyard ISA Server 2004 computer. Configure a route relationship on the Contoso ISA Server 2004 computer.

4. Your organization has five sites, four branch-office sites, and a headquarters site. You have configured four separate networks, BRANCHONE, BRANCHTWO, BRANCHTHREE, and BRANCHFOUR, to use IPSec tunneling mode to connect. The Network Rules on the headquarters site ISA Server 2004 Internet-edge firewall are configured as shown here.

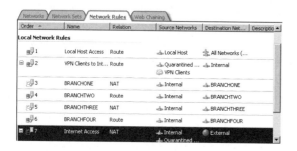

Bidirectional communication is possible between the headquarters site, BRANCHONE, BRANCHTWO, and BRANCHFOUR. Currently it is not possible to establish a site-to-site VPN link to BRANCHTHREE. Which of the following actions might resolve this issue? (Choose the best answer.)

A. Reset the password on the BRANCHTHREE user account.

B. Rename the user account used to authenticate the BRANCHTREE site-to-site connection to BRANCHTHREE.

C. Change the route relationship for the BRANCHTHREE rule from NAT to Route.

D. Change the source network for the BRANCHTHREE rule to include VPN Clients.

5. You are attempting to set up an L2TP-over-IPSec site-to-site VPN connection, but you are having no success. Each endpoint of the L2TP-over-IPSec site-to-site VPN is a computer running ISA Server 2004. You have determined that a problem occurs during the certificate-exchange process. The certificates used for this connection are issued by the same commercial CA. A route relationship exists on each ISA Server 2004 computer between its Internal network and the remote network being used for the VPN site-to-site connection. Which of the following steps resolves this problem? (Choose the best answer.)

A. Reset the passwords on the user accounts used to support the L2TP-over-IPSec VPN connections.

B. Change the route relationship to a NAT relationship on both ISA Server 2004 computers.

C. Ensure that fragment filtering is disabled on both ISA Server 2004 computers.

D. Ensure that the Verify That Incoming Client Certificates Are Not Revoked option is set.

6. You want to set the Maximum Transmission Unit (MTU) after determining that VPN connections are not successful when the MTU size exceeds 1400 bytes. How can you limit the MTU size on your ISA Server computer to 1400 bytes? (Choose the correct answer.)

A. In the Specify Dial-Up Preferences dialog box, set the MTU to 1400.

B. In the Define IP Preferences dialog box, set the MTU to 1400.

C. Edit the VPN Clients Properties and set the MTU to 1400.

D. Edit the registry. Create an entry named MTU of type REG_DWORD. Enter the decimal value 1400.

7. Your organization is about to open a second branch office. You have been successfully using a site-to-site VPN connection using L2TP over IPSec for the last 12 months to connect your headquarters site with the first branch office. You have configured a remote network for the new branch office. All the settings for each remote network are the same, except for the following:

Network name	BranchOne	BranchTwo
Remote VPN Server Name or IP Address	gatewayone.contoso.com	gatewaytwo.contoso.com
Network Addresses	10.50.0.1 to 10.50.0.255	10.60.0.1 to 10.60.0.255

Which of the following must you do to resolve this issue? (Choose the best answer.)

A. On the BranchTwo network, change the remote VPN server name to *gatewayone.contoso.com*.

B. On the BranchOne network, change the remote VPN server name to *gatewaytwo.contoso.com*.

C. Configure a user account named Gatewaytwo, and ensure that the user account properties are set to allow remote access. Configure the BranchTwo network to use the Gatewaytwo user account for authentication.

D. Configure a user account named BranchTwo, and ensure that the user account properties are set to allow remote access. Configure the BranchTwo network to use the BranchTwo user account for authentication.

8.   Your junior administrator has been trying, with no success, to configure site-to-site VPN links from your headquarters in Wagga Wagga to branch offices in Kooweerup, Melbourne, Traralgon, Victoria, Wangaratta, and Warragul. All accounts used for site-to-site VPN link authentication are located in the Site-To-Site organizational unit (OU) as shown here.

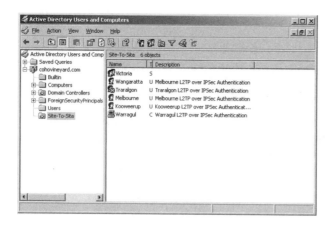

In resolving these problems, which of the following steps should you take? (Choose all that apply.)

   A. Ensure that all accounts have the Dial-In Remote Access Permission set to Allow Access.

   B. Ensure that all accounts have the Dial-In Remote Access Permission set to Control Access through Remote Access Policy.

   C. Enable the Traralgon user account.

   D. Make all accounts members of the Victoria group.

   E. Delete the Warragul computer account and recreate it as a user account.

9. You wish to set up bidirectional site-to-site VPN connections from Contoso Ltd. to Tailspin Toys. Both Tailspin Toys and Contoso Ltd. have their own unique Enterprise CA. The host name of the Contoso CA is ent-ca.contoso.internal. The host name of the Tailspin Toys CA is ent-ca.tailspintoys.internal. Both Tailspin Toys and Contoso Ltd. use ISA Server 2004 Enterprise Edition installed on Windows Server 2003 computers. You wish to configure IPSec tunnel mode to be authenticated by digital certificate. How can you configure the Tailspin Toys ISA Server computer to trust the Contoso CA and the Contoso ISA Server computer to trust the Tailspin Toys CA? (Choose two.)

   A. Obtain an SSL certificate from *ent-ca.contoso.internal*. Install this certificate on the Tailspin Toys ISA Server computer.

   B. Obtain an SSL certificate from *ent-ca.tailspintoys.internal*. Install this certificate on the Contoso ISA Server computer.

   C. Obtain a root certificate from *ent-ca.tailspintoys.internal*. Install this certificate on the Contoso ISA Server computer.

   D. Obtain a root certificate from *ent-ca.contoso.internal*. Install this certificate on the Tailspin Toys ISA Server computer.

   E. Obtain an IPSec certificate from *ent-ca.contoso.internal*. Install this certificate on the Tailspin Toys ISA Server computer.

   F. Obtain an IPSec certificate from *ent-ca.tailspintoys.internal*. Install this certificate on the Contoso ISA Server computer.

10. You are the security administrator for Coho Vineyard. You wish to set up a site-to-site VPN connection using IPSec tunneling mode between your organization and Tailspin Toys. Tailspin Toys has a complex CA infrastructure. The stand-alone root CA *root-ca.tailspintoys.com* issued a signing certificate to CA *level-one.tailspintoys.com*. CA *level-one.tailspintoys.com* issued signing certificates to CA *level-two.tailspintoys.com* and CA *level-three.tailspintoys.com*. CA *level-four.tailspintoys.com* is responsible for issuing IPSec certificates, one of which was issued to the Tailspin Toys ISA Server computer.

Level-four.tailspintoys.com was issued a signing certificate by CA *level-two.tailspintoys.com*. There is a new CA *level-five.tailspintoys.com*, which was issued a signing certificate by CA *level-four.tailspintoys.com*. Both Coho Vineyard and Tailspin Toys use ISA Server 2004 computers as VPN servers. Coho Vineyard has a single stand-alone root CA that is responsible for issuing all Coho Vineyard certificates. Which certificates could you install on the Coho Vineyard ISA Server 2004 computer so that it will trust the certificate used by the Tailspin Toys ISA Server computer? (Choose the best answer.)

A. IPSec certificate issued by *level-four.tailspintoys.com*.

B. IPSec certificate issued by *level-two.tailspintoys.com*.

C. Root certificate issued by *level-three.tailspintoys.com*.

D. Root certificate issued by *level-five.tailspintoys.com*.

E. Root certificate issued by *level-one.tailspintoys.com*.

F. Root certificate issued by *level-two.tailspintoys.com*.

Objective 6.3 Answers

1.   Correct Answers: A

    A.   Correct: When PPTP and L2TP over IPSec are used, the remote site provides the local site with the remote-site DNS server address. This does not occur with IPSec tunneling mode. One solution is to configure the headquarters DNS server to forward all queries for the remote-site zone to the DNS server located at the remote site.

    B.   Incorrect: Replicating the headquarters DNS zone to the branch office will not resolve the problem that the headquarters clients cannot resolve branch-office FQDNs.

    C.   Incorrect: Issuing the branch-office DNS server with an IPSec certificate will not resolve this problem. The problem exists because PPTP and L2TP over IPSec provide remote network DNS information, where IPSec tunneling mode does not.

    D.   Incorrect: Issuing the headquarters DNS server with an IPSec certificate will not resolve this problem. The problem exists because PPTP and L2TP over IPSec provide remote network DNS information, where IPSec tunneling mode does not.

    E.   Incorrect: Because a VPN site-to-site tunnel exists, there is no reason to establish a second VPN connection to the branch-office network. Unless the DNS server is configured further, using either stub zones, secondary zones, or conditional forwarding, this issue will not be resolved.

2.   Correct Answers: A, B, and D

    A.   Correct: Conditional forwarding allows forwarding of queries based on domain names. Queries to *tailspintoys.internal* and *contoso.internal* could be forwarded to the respective partner DNS servers, allowing hosts on the A. Datum Internal network to resolve host names.

    B.   Correct: A stub zone hosts the authoritative name servers for the target zone. This would mean that clients who queried the A. Datum DNS server would be redirected to the DNS servers that hosted the target zones, which, in this case, are the partner DNS servers at Tailspin Toys and Contoso.

    C.   Incorrect: This would not enable hosts on the A. Datum internal network to resolve host names on the partner network. Root servers sit at the top of the DNS namespace and would not be appropriate in this situation.

    D.   Correct: If secondary zones of the partner zones were hosted on the A. Datum DNS server, clients using that server could resolve partner host names to IP addresses.

E. Incorrect: The question stated nothing about the partner organizations' being a part of the same Active Directory forest, hence this option would not work.

3.   Correct Answers: B, C, and D

A. Incorrect: A NAT relationship from each VPN network to the other will mean that communication cannot be established. If a route relationship is defined by one network, the other network can use a NAT relationship. Communication also works if both networks have a route relationship configured.

B. Correct: A NAT relationship from each VPN network to the other will mean that communication cannot be established. If a route relationship is defined by one network, the other network can use a NAT relationship. Communication also works if both networks have a route relationship configured.

C. Correct: A NAT relationship from each VPN network to the other will mean that communication cannot be established. If a route relationship is defined by one network, the other network can use a NAT relationship. Communication also works if both networks have a route relationship configured.

D. Correct: A NAT relationship from each VPN network to the other will mean that communication cannot be established. If a route relationship is defined by one network, the other network can use a NAT relationship. Communication also works if both networks have a route relationship configured.

4.   Correct Answers: C

A. Incorrect: IPSec tunneling mode does not require user accounts for authentication.

B. Incorrect: IPSec tunneling mode does not require user accounts for authentication.

C. Correct: A NAT relationship from each VPN network to the other will mean that communication cannot be established. If a route relationship is defined by one network, the other network can use a NAT relationship. Communication also works if both networks have a route relationship configured.

D. Incorrect: The issue is not access by VPN clients to a particular network, but access from one network to another using a site-to-site VPN link. You would only add the VPN clients if you wanted them to use the site-to-site VPN link.

5.   Correct Answers: C

A. Incorrect: The question specifies that the problem occurs during the certificate-exchange process. The user-account passwords used to support L2TP-over-IPSec are not relevant at this point.

B. Incorrect: If both computers are configured to use NAT relationships rather than route relationships, a connection cannot be established. Connections can only be established when the relationship is route-route, route-NAT, or NAT-route.

C. Correct: Fragment filtering adversely affects the certificate-exchange process and must be disabled on the ISA Server 2004 computers for L2TP-over-IPSec VPN connections to be established.

D. Incorrect: Setting this option, which is not enabled by default, is likely to cause problems rather than resolve them. If there is a problem with the certificate-exchange process, it is unlikely that it is because certificates are not being checked for validity. This option can be configured by selecting the Specify Certificate Revocation option in the General node.

6.   Correct Answers: D

A. Incorrect: MTU can only be set in the registry, and only by adding an entry named MTU of type REG_DWORD with the appropriate value. MTU cannot be set by editing Dial-Up Preferences.

B. Incorrect: MTU can only be set in the registry, and only by adding an entry named MTU of type REG_DWORD with the appropriate value. MTU cannot be changed by altering the IP Preferences.

C. Incorrect: MTU can only be set in the registry, and only by adding an entry named MTU of type REG_DWORD with the appropriate value. MTU cannot be set by editing the VPN Clients Properties.

D. Correct: MTU can only be set in the registry, and only by adding an entry named MTU of type REG_DWORD with the appropriate value.

7.   Correct Answers: D

A. Incorrect: This will attempt to connect to the first branch office's ISA Server rather than resolve the issue, which is due to the BranchOne user account's being used to attempt authentication for the BranchTwo network, when both user account name and network name must match for L2TP-over-IPSec authentication to occur.

B. Incorrect: According to the question, there is no problem with the site-to-site connection to the first branch office, hence you should not alter the settings of the first branch office's remote network. The problem is due to the BranchOne user account's being used to attempt authentication for the BranchTwo network, when both user account name and network name must match for L2TP-over-IPSec authentication to occur.

    C. Incorrect: The network name must match the user account name used for authentication. *Gatewaytwo.contoso.com* is the name of the remote VPN gateway, not the name of the remote network configured in ISA Server 2004.

    D. Correct: The network name must match the user account name used for authentication. Because you had copied the original remote-access network settings, the problem was that the BranchOne user account was being used to attempt to authenticate the BranchTwo network connection.

8.   Correct Answers: A, C, and E

    A. Correct: All accounts should have the Dial-In Remote Access Permission set to Allow rather than to Control Access Through Remote Access Policy. By setting this permission manually, you will override any possible policy conflicts, which is important because VPN site-to-site links should always be available.

    B. Incorrect: All accounts should have the Dial-In Remote Access Permission set to Allow rather than to Control Access Through Remote Access Policy because there may be times when the policy does not allow access, something that you do not want for site-to-site VPN links.

    C. Correct: According to the graphic, the Traralgon user account is currently disabled. This account must be enabled if it is to be used to authenticate L2TP-over-IPSec connections.

    D. Incorrect: There is no reason why these user accounts would need to be members of the Victoria group.

    E. Correct: Computer accounts cannot be used to authenticate L2TP-over-IPSec site-to-site VPN connections.

9.   Correct Answers: C and D

    A. Incorrect: You need to obtain a root certificate from *ent–ca.contoso.internal* and install it on the Tailspin Toys ISA Server computer for that computer to trust certificates issued by the Contoso CA.

    B. Incorrect: You need to obtain a root certificate from *ent–ca.tailspintoys.internal* and install it on the Contoso ISA Server computer for that computer to trust certificates issued by the Tailspin Toys CA.

    C. Correct: For a computer to trust a noncommercial CA, you must install a root certificate from that CA on the computer. Once that is done, certificates directly issued from that CA, or from CAs that have been issued a signing certificate by that CA, will be trusted by the computer.

    D. Correct: For a computer to trust a noncommercial CA, you must install a root certificate from that CA on the computer. Once that is done, certificates directly issued from that CA, or from CAs that have been issued a signing certificate by that CA, will be trusted by the computer.

E. **Incorrect:** A root certificate, rather than an IPSec certificate, is required for the Tailspin Toys ISA Server computer to trust the Contoso CA.

F. **Incorrect:** A root certificate, rather than an IPSec certificate, is required for the Contoso ISA Server computer to trust the Tailspin Toys CA.

10.   Correct Answers: E and F

A. **Incorrect:** To trust certificates issued from a CA, you must install a root certificate from that CA or the root certificate of a CA further up the CA chain. In this scenario, if you installed a root certificate from *level-four.tailspintoys.com*, *level-two.tailspintoys.com*, *level-one.tailspintoys.com*, or *root-ca.tailspintoys.com* on the Coho Vineyard ISA Server 2004 computer, the computer would trust certificates issued by *level-four.tailspintoys.com*.

B. **Incorrect:** To trust certificates issued from a CA, you must install a root certificate from that CA or the root certificate of a CA further up the CA chain. In this scenario, if you installed a root certificate from *level-four.tailspintoys.com*, *level-two.tailspintoys.com*, *level-one.tailspintoys.com*, or *root-ca.tailspintoys.com* on the Coho Vineyard ISA Server 2004 computer, the computer would trust certificates issued by *level-four.tailspintoys.com*.

C. **Incorrect:** To trust certificates issued from a CA, you must install a root certificate from that CA or the root certificate of a CA further up the CA chain. In this scenario, if you installed a root certificate from *level-four.tailspintoys.com*, *level-two.tailspintoys.com*, *level-one.tailspintoys.com*, or *root-ca.tailspintoys.com* on the Coho Vineyard ISA Server 2004 computer, the computer would trust certificates issued by *level-four.tailspintoys.com*. A root certificate from *level-three.tailspintoys.com* would not work because this CA is not in the signing chain that *level-four.tailspintoys.com* is.

D. **Incorrect:** To trust certificates issued from a CA, you must install a root certificate from that CA or the root certificate of a CA further up the CA chain. In this scenario, if you installed a root certificate from *level-four.tailspintoys.com*, *level-two.tailspin toys.com*, *level-one.tailspintoys.com*, or *root-ca.tailspintoys.com* on the Coho Vineyard ISA Server 2004 computer, the computer would trust certificates issued by *level-four.tailspintoys.com*. A root certificate from *level-five.tailspintoys.com* would not work because it is below this CA and cannot be used to verify certificates from above it in the chain.

E. **Correct:** To trust certificates issued from a CA, you must install a root certificate from that CA or the root certificate of a CA further up the CA chain. In this scenario, if you installed a root certificate from *level-four.tailspintoys.com*, *level-two.tailspintoys.com*, or *level-one.tailspintoys.com* on the Coho Vineyard ISA Server 2004 computer, the computer would trust certificates issued by *level-four.tailspintoys.com*.

F. Correct: To trust certificates issued from a CA, you must install a root certificate from that CA or the root certificate of a CA further up the CA chain. In this scenario, if you installed a root certificate from *level-four.tailspintoys.com, level-two.tailspintoys.com, level-one.tailspintoys.com,* or *root-ca.tailspintoys.com* on the Coho Vineyard ISA Server 2004 computer, the computer would trust certificates issued by *level-four.tailspintoys.com.*

19 Monitoring and Reporting ISA Server 2004 Activity (7.0)

In the realm of information security, the best defense is to have as much information as possible about what is occurring on your network. Microsoft Internet Security and Acceleration (ISA) Server 2004 often sits as a bastion between the anarchy of the Internet and the managed tranquility of the Internal network. To keep that bastion strong, you, as an administrator, should constantly monitor what is happening, from the traffic that is allowed to pass through the ISA Server 2004 computer to the types of traffic that the ISA Server 2004 computer is configured to block. It is one thing to configure an ISA Server 2004 computer to perform functions X, Y, and Z. It is only through monitoring and reporting that you can verify that functions X, Y, and Z are being carried out. ISA Server 2004 can be configured to provide the administrator with a copious amount of information. It can be configured to send an e-mail alert when a service fails or a nefarious intrusion is detected. It can also be configured to generate management-friendly reports that quickly break down how ISA Server 2004 is performing with nice graphics for whoever wishes to avoid being bogged down with details. It is important that you, as an administrator, monitor and tune your ISA Server 2004 computer based on what is actually occurring at the network level, rather than assuming that the initial configuration that you set up is the best way to proceed and requires no modification.

Tested Skills and Suggested Practices

The skills that you need to master the Monitoring and Reporting ISA Server 2004 Activity objective domain on the Implementing Microsoft Internet Security and Acceleration (ISA) Server 2004 exam include:

- Monitor ISA Server 2004 Activity.
    - ❑ Practice: On the ISA Server Management Console, navigate to the Monitoring node. Click the Dashboard tab. Examine each of the following areas: Connectivity, Services, Reports, Alerts, Sessions and System Performance. Note what information is present. When finished, open the Performance Console from the Administrative Tools menu. Click the Plus ("+") symbol button and change the Performance Object to ISA Server Firewall Service. Examine each of the possible counters by selecting it and then clicking Explain. When you are finished, click Close to exit the Add Counters dialog box.

- Configure and run reports.

  ❑ Practice: On the ISA Server Management Console, navigate to the Monitoring node. Click the Reports tab. From the Tasks sidebar, click Create And Configure Report Jobs. The Report Jobs Properties dialog box will open. Click Add. This will launch the New Report Job Wizard. In the Report Job Name: field, enter **Report1** and then click Next. On the Report Content page, view all available options and then remove the check next to the Summary check box. Click Next. On the Report Job Schedule page, select the Weekly, On Specified Days option and select Monday, Wednesday, and Friday. Click Next. On the Report Publishing page, examine the default settings and click Next. On the Send E-mail Notification page, examine the default settings and then click Next. On the Completing The New Report Job Wizard page, click Finish. On the Report Jobs Properties page, click OK.

- Configure logging and alerts.

  ❑ Practice: On the ISA Server Management Console, navigate to the Monitoring node. Click the Alerts tab. On the Tasks sidebar, select the Configure Alerts Definitions task. On the Alerts Properties dialog box, click Add. This will start the New Alert Wizard. In the Alert Name field, enter **RedAlert** and then click Next. On the Events And Conditions page, in the Event drop-down menu, select Intrusion Detected. On the Additional Condition drop-down menu, select UDP Bomb Attack. Click Next. On the Category And Severity page, examine the default values and then click Next. On the Actions page, check the Send An E-Mail Message check box and then click Next. On the Sending E-Mail Messages page, set the SMTP Server field to localhost. Set the From: field to *isaserver@cohovineyard.com*. Set the To field to *isa.administrator@cohovineyard.com*. Click Next to continue. Click Finish to exit the wizard. Click OK to close the Alerts Properties dialog box.

Further Reading

This section lists supplemental readings by objective. We recommend that you study these sources thoroughly before taking this exam.

Objective 7.1 ISA Server 2004 Performance Best Practices *http://www.microsoft.com/technet/prodtechnol/isa/2004/plan/bestpractices.mspx*

ISA Server 2004 FAQ: Monitoring and Logging *http://www.microsoft.com/technet/prodtechnol/isa/2004/plan/faq-monitoring.mspx*

ISA Server 2004 Monitoring Features *http://www.microsoft.com/technet/prodtechnol/isa/2004/plan/monitoringfeatures.mspx*

ISA Server 2004 Help: Expand and read all topics under the Monitoring section.

Objective 7.2 ISA Server 2004 Monitoring Features *http://www.microsoft.com/tech net/prodtechnol/isa/2004/plan/monitoringfeatures.mspx*

Objective 7.3 ISA Server 2004 FAQ: Monitoring and Logging *http://www.microsoft. com/technet/prodtechnol/isa/2004/plan/faq-monitoring.mspx*

Troubleshooting Alert Action Failures *http://www.microsoft.com/technet/prodtech nol/isa/2004/plan/troubleshootingAlertActionFailures.mspx*

Objective 7.1

Monitor ISA Server 2004 Activity

Monitoring is essentially keeping an eye on things in real time. ISA Server 2004, through the Dashboard, Alerts, Sessions, Connectivity, and Services sections of the Monitoring node allows an administrator to keep track of the minute-to-minute operation of the ISA Server 2004 computer. The Dashboard provides a bird's-eye view of what is occurring. Information contained in the other areas is summarized here. Alerts allow you to configure the ISA Server computer to notify you automatically if a particular set of conditions is met. Sessions allow you to view which clients are connected to the ISA Server 2004 computer at any moment. Connectivity is used to regularly check that the ISA Server 2004 computer is able to maintain contact with important infrastructure servers. The Services section allows you to keep an eye on the particular services used by ISA Server 2004, including data such as uptime.

Objective 7.1 Questions

1. You have noticed that a particular user in your organization is accessing confidential content on a competitor's Web site using a connection made through the ISA Server 2004 computer that you are responsible for managing. The user is located in a remote building and has not answered the telephone for five minutes. Because each minute that the user continues this access increases your organization's exposure to litigation, you want to shut down the user's session now. You contact your manager who is attending a corporate function and the manager instructs you to do whatever is necessary to limit the organization's exposure to legal liability. All computers in your organization have the Firewall Client software installed. From the Sessions tab of the Monitoring node of the ISA Server 2004 Management Console, select the user's session. From the Tasks sidebar, click the Disconnect Session task. Which of the following statements about the user's connection to the ISA Server 2004 computer is true? (Choose the best answer.)

    A. The user will be unable to establish a new session until the user logs off and then logs on to the computer.

    B. The user will be unable to establish a new session until the user restarts the firewall client.

    C. The user will not be able to establish a new session until the user restarts the computer.

    D. The user will not be able to establish a new session until you reactivate the user's account in Firewall Policy.

    E. The user can instantly reestablish the session by attempting to connect again.

2. Which of the following statements is true about monitoring sessions to an ISA Server 2004 computer? (Choose the best answer.)

    A. The Sessions tab of the Monitoring node of the ISA Server 2004 Management Console will always show more sessions than the Firewall Service Sessions counter in Performance Monitor.

    B. The Sessions tab of the Monitoring node of the ISA Server 2004 Management Console will always show fewer sessions than the number shown by issuing the Netstat command from the command prompt of the ISA Server computer.

    C. The number of sessions shown by issuing the Netstat command from the command prompt of the ISA Server computer will equal the number of sessions shown by the Firewall Service Sessions counter in Performance Monitor.

    D. The Sessions tab of the Monitoring node of the ISA Server 2004 Management Console will always show the same number of sessions as displayed by the Firewall Service Sessions counter in Performance Monitor.

3.   Which of the following statistics can be monitored from the ISA Server 2004 Monitoring Dashboard? (Choose all that apply.)

    A. Number of Firewall Client sessions

    B. Processor Time

    C. Number of Site-to-Site VPN links

    D. Dropped Packets/Second

    E. VPN Quarantined Client sessions.

4.   You have assigned the ISA Server Array Monitoring Auditor role to Oksana's user account. The ISA Server 2004 Enterprise Edition array comprises two servers, with the Configuration Storage server installed on the first computer. Both servers are members of the same Active Directory directory services domain. Oksana is able to connect through a remote desktop to the first computer and can run the ISA Server 2004 Management Console and view the Monitoring Dashboard. When she tries to add Firewall Service counters to the Performance Monitor, she cannot do so. Which of the following steps should you take to allow Oksana to use the Firewall Service counters in Performance Monitor for both servers in the array without unnecessarily elevating Oksana's rights to computers in the array? (Choose the best answer.)

    A. Delegate the ISA Server Enterprise Auditor role to Oksana's user account.

    B. Delegate the ISA Server Enterprise Administrator role to Oksana's account.

    C. Delegate the ISA Server Array Auditor role to Oksana's user account.

    D. Delegate the ISA Server Administrator role to Oksana's user account.

    E. Add Oksana's user account to the Performance Monitor user group on each ISA Server computer.

5.   Which of the following tools can you use to monitor network performance? (Choose the best answer.)

    A. ISA Server 2004 Dashboard

    B. ISA Server 2004 Sessions

    C. ISA Server 2004 Logging

    D. Performance Monitor

6.   A connectivity verifier configured on your ISA Server computer reports that the Post Office Protocol 3 (POP3) service on host *pop3.cohovineyard.internal* is currently inaccessible. You wish to verify this manually. Which of the following commands, issued from the command prompt, can you use to verify that the POP3 service on host *pop3.cohovineyard.internal* is indeed unavailable? (Choose the best answer.)

   A. ping –i 25 pop3.cohovineyard.internal.

   B. ping –i 110 pop3.cohovineyard.internal.

   C. telnet pop3.cohovineyard.internal 110.

   D. telnet pop3.cohovineyard.internal 25.

7.   You are configuring an Alert so that you are sent an e-mail after three Internet Protocol (IP) fragments are received containing more data than the maximum packet size. On the Events tab of the Alert properties, you have chosen the Intrusion Detected event. You only want this alert triggered if IP fragments with more data than the maximum packet size are received, not when a TCP SYN packet is sent with a spoofed IP address and port number that matches the destination IP address and port number. Which of the following Additional Conditions should you set for this particular alert? (Choose the best answer.)

   A. Any Intrusion

   B. IP Half Scan Attack

   C. Land Attack

   D. Ping of Death Attack

8.   The IntruderIntruder alert Events properties are configured as shown here.

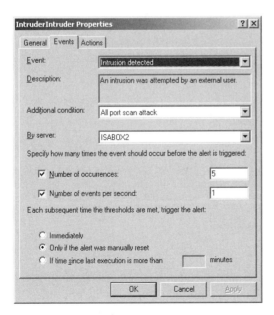

All other ISA Server 2004 defaults are set. The Actions tab is configured to send an e-mail to *intruder@contoso.com*. Under which of the following conditions will an e-mail be sent to *intruder@contoso.com*? (Choose all that apply.)

A. Five scans of 15 random Transmission Control Protocol (TCP) ports each are conducted over a 10-minute period.

B. Three scans of 25 random TCP ports each are conducted over a 5-minute period.

C. Five scans of 25 random TCP ports each are conducted over a 25-minute period.

D. Six scans of 21 random TCP ports each are conducted over a 40-minute period.

E. Five scans of 40 random TCP ports each are conducted in a five-minute window after the alert was triggered sending an e-mail.

9. Your ISA Server 2004 Internet-edge firewall publishes the Web server *http://www.cohovineyard.com* to hosts on the Internet. The site *www.cohovineyard.com* is located on your organization's internal network. Hosts on the Internal network access this Web site using the URL *http://externalweb.cohovineyard.internal*, though some also use the traditional *http://www.cohovineyard.com* URL. You want to be notified in the event that the ISA Server computer cannot establish a connection to the Web site. To this end, you have configured the Connect1 Connectivity Verifier as shown here.

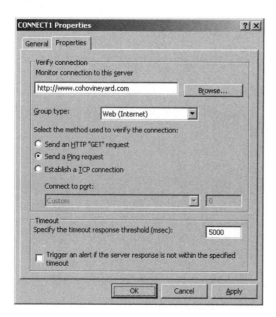

You shut down Microsoft Internet Information Services (IIS) on the server hosting *www.cohovineyard.com*, yet you do not receive an alert. After checking, you determine that the alert is configured correctly and that the problem must lie with the Connectivity Verifier. Which of the following changes should you make to the properties of the Connect1 Connectivity Verifier to make it function correctly? (Choose all that apply.)

   A. Change the Select The Method Used To Verify The Connection option to Establish a TCP connection. On the Connect To Port drop-down list, select HTTPS.

   B. Change the Group Type to Published Servers.

   C. Check the Trigger An Alert If The Server Response Is Not Within The Specified Timeout check box.

   D. Change the Monitor Connection To This Server dialog to *http://externalweb. cohovineyard.internal.*

   E. Change the Select The Method Used To Verify The Connection option to Send An HTTP "GET" Request.

10. You wish to know when the SMTP service on server *smtp.cohovineyard.com* is not accessible to your organization's ISA Server 2004 computer. You are configuring a connectivity verifier to this end. When configuring the verification method, which of the following should you choose? (Choose the best answer.)

   A. Send an HTTP "GET" request.

   B. Send a Ping request.

   C. Establish a TCP connection to Port: Custom 23.

   D. Establish a TCP connection to Port: Custom 110.

   E. Establish a TCP connection to Port: Custom 25.

Objective 7.1 Answers

1. **Correct Answers: E**

   A. **Incorrect:** Disconnecting a session does not stop a user from reestablishing a session. To block a user temporarily or permanently requires a change in firewall policy.

   B. **Incorrect:** Disconnecting a session does not stop a user from reestablishing a session. To block a user temporarily or permanently requires a change in firewall policy.

   C. **Incorrect:** Disconnecting a session does not stop a user from reestablishing a session. To block a user temporarily or permanently requires a change in firewall policy.

   D. **Incorrect:** Disconnecting a session does not stop a user from reestablishing a session, nor does it influence firewall policy. To block a user temporarily or permanently requires a change in firewall policy.

   E. **Correct:** Disconnecting a session disconnects only that particular session. It does not stop a user from initiating a new session if the prior one is disconnected.

2. **Correct Answers: B**

   A. **Incorrect:** The Sessions tab lists a session by unique username and client IP address. The Firewall Service Sessions counter in Performance Monitor shows total sessions. Because a single user can initiate more than one session, this means that multiple sessions will be recorded by the Performance Monitor, which will not be recorded on the Sessions tab.

   B. **Correct:** Netstat displays all TCP/IP network connections to the ISA Server computer, not just sessions connected to the firewall service. For this reason, the number of sessions displayed by Netstat will always exceed the number displayed by the Monitoring node of the ISA Server 2004 Management Console and the Firewall Service Sessions counter in Performance Monitor.

   C. **Incorrect:** Netstat displays all TCP/IP network connections to the ISA Server computer, not just sessions connected to the firewall service. For this reason, the number of sessions displayed by Netstat will always exceed the number displayed by the Monitoring node of the ISA Server 2004 Management Console and the Firewall Service Sessions counter in Performance Monitor.

   D. **Incorrect:** The Sessions tab lists a session by unique username and client IP address. The Firewall Service Sessions counter in Performance Monitor shows total sessions. Because a single user can initiate more than one session, this means that multiple sessions will be recorded by the Performance Monitor, which will not be recorded on the Sessions tab.

3.   Correct Answers: A, C, D, and E

    A.   Correct: The total number of sessions, including the number of Web Proxy, Firewall Client, SecureNAT, VPN Remote Client, VPN Quarantine, and VPN Site-to-Site sessions can be monitored from the ISA Server 2004 Monitoring Dashboard.

    B.   Incorrect: Processor Time can only be measured using the Performance Monitor or Task Manager; this information is not available in the ISA Server 2004 Monitoring Dashboard.

    C.   Correct: The total number of sessions, including the number of Web Proxy, Firewall Client, SecureNAT, VPN Remote Client, VPN Quarantine, and VPN Site-to-Site sessions can be monitored from the ISA Server 2004 Monitoring Dashboard.

    D.   Correct: The Monitoring Dashboard provides a display of the number of Dropped Packets/Second.

    E.   Correct: The total number of sessions, including the number of Web Proxy, Firewall Client, SecureNAT, VPN Remote Client, VPN Quarantine, and VPN Site-to-Site sessions can be monitored from the ISA Server 2004 Monitoring Dashboard.

4.   Correct Answers: E

    A.   Incorrect: Whether a user can use Performance Monitor is independent of any administrative role delegated to the user's account. To add counters to Performance Monitor, a user's account must be a member of either the local Administrators, Performance Log, or Performance Monitor user group.

    B.   Incorrect: Whether a user can use Performance Monitor is independent of any administrative role delegated to the user's account. To add counters to Performance Monitor, a user's account must be a member of the local Administrators, Performance Log, or Performance Monitor user group.

    C.   Incorrect: Whether a user can use Performance Monitor is independent of any administrative role delegated to the user's account. To add counters to Performance Monitor, a user's account must be a member of the local Administrators, Performance Log, or Performance Monitor user group.

    D.   Incorrect: Whether a user can use Performance Monitor is independent of any administrative role delegated to the user's account. To add counters to Performance Monitor, a user's account must be a member of the local Administrators, Performance Log, or Performance Monitor user group.

    E.   Correct: Whether a user can use Performance Monitor is independent of any administrative role delegated to the user's account. To add counters to Performance Monitor, a user's account must be a member of the local Administrators, Performance Log, or Performance Monitor user group.

5.   Correct Answers: D

A. Incorrect: ISA Server 2004 Dashboard provides information about the number of allowed and dropped packets per second, but does not do it on a per-interface basis. This means that the Dashboard cannot be used to determine the network performance.

B. Incorrect: ISA Server 2004 Sessions cannot be used to measure network performance.

C. Incorrect: Although ISA Server 2004 Logging can provide some insight as to what traffic is passing through the ISA Server 2004 computer, it cannot be used to estimate network performance.

D. Correct: Bytes Total (which includes bytes sent and received) per second through an interface can be used to determine bandwidth use.

6.   Correct Answers: C

A. Incorrect: Issuing this command will send a ping request with a Time-to-Live (TTL) of 25 to host *pop3.cohovineyard.internal*.

B. Incorrect: Issuing this command will send a ping request with a TTL of 110 to host *pop3.cohovineyard.internal*.

C. Correct: If you issue the command telnet *pop3.cohovineyard.internal* 110, you will be greeted by a connection string announcing something similar to "+OK Microsoft Windows POP3 Service Version 1.0 (15177892@pop3.cohovine yard.internal) ready" if the service is available. If the service is unavailable, you will receive the message "Could not open connection to the host, on Port 110: Connect failed".

D. Incorrect: If you issue the command telnet *pop3.cohovineyard.internal* 25 it will connect to the Simple Mail Transport Protocol (SMTP) service, rather than the POP3 service.

7.   Correct Answers: D

A. Incorrect: Although this will trigger an alert when the ISA Server computer receives an IP fragment with more data than the maximum packet size, it will also trigger an alert when a TCP SYN packet is sent with a spoofed IP address.

B. Incorrect: IP Half Scan attacks occur when connections are made to a destination computer and no corresponding ACK packets are communicated. The type of attack mentioned in the question is a Ping of Death attack.

C. Incorrect: A land attack occurs when a TCP SYN packet is sent with a spoofed IP address and port number that matches that of the destination IP address and port number.

D. Correct: Ping of Death attacks occur when the ISA Server 2004 computer receives an IP fragment with more data than the maximum IP packet size.

8. **Correct Answers: C and D**

    A. **Incorrect:** By default, an All Port Scan Attack condition is met when 20 TCP ports are scanned in succession. Because 15 random ports are scanned at a time, none of these would register as a port scan attack.

    B. **Incorrect:** Although a scan of 25 random TCP ports meets the default threshold for an All Port Scan Attack, there must be five occurrences for the alert to be triggered.

    C. **Correct:** There is no limitation on the amount of time that must pass between the occurrences, hence five scans of 25 random TCP ports meets the requirements to trigger this alert.

    D. **Correct:** There is no limit on the amount of time that must pass between the occurrences, hence six scans of 21 random TCP ports meets the requirements to trigger this alert.

    E. **Incorrect:** According to the dialog box, the alert can only be triggered again once the alert is manually reset. This means that, once the alert is issued, no further e-mails will be sent until the alert is manually reset.

9. **Correct Answers: B, C, and E**

    A. **Incorrect:** This will cause the Connectivity Verifier to attempt a connection to an HTTPS site rather than to a standard Web site using Port 80 through HTTP.

    B. **Correct:** The question states that the Web site *http://www.cohovineyard.com* is a server published to clients on the Internet, hence the Published Servers group type is more appropriate than the Web (Internet) group type.

    C. **Correct:** This check box needs to be checked so that the alert can be used to notify you.

    D. **Incorrect:** Changing this will not influence the functionality of the Connectivity Verifier because the ISA Server 2004 computer can resolve both host names.

    E. **Correct:** Sending a ping request only verifies that the server responds to Internet Control Message Protocol (ICMP). This could mean that the server is functioning, but that the Web site is shut down. Sending an HTTP "GET" Request ensures that the Web server is actually functioning.

10. **Correct Answers: E**

    A. **Incorrect:** An HTTP "GET" request is used to determine whether a functioning Web server is present. It cannot be used to verify that the SMTP service on a particular server is accessible.

    B. **Incorrect:** Although a Ping request will verify connectivity to a particular server, it will not be able to verify whether the SMTP service is accessible.

C. Incorrect: TCP Port 23 is used for Telnet rather than SMTP. SMTP uses TCP Port 25.

D. Incorrect: TCP Port 110 is used for the POP3 protocol. POP3 is used to retrieve e-mail, but it is not used to send e-mail. SMTP on Port 25 is used to send and relay e-mail.

E. Correct: SMTP uses Port 25. Configuring a Connectivity Verifier to check that Port 25 is accessible will allow the ISA Server to determine whether the SMTP service is accessible.

Objective 7.2

Configure and Run Reports

Reports are user-friendly summaries of the information contained within the log files. Reports are generated from the data contained within log files, hence there is nothing contained within a report that you could not find by examining log file data. Reports are great for "at-a-glance" information about how ISA Server 2004 is performing. Reports often contain information such as lists of the top Web sites accessed and the top Web users, information that is not necessarily apparent at first glance when viewing log data. Reports are published in Hypertext Markup Language (HTML) format, either directly on the ISA Server 2004 computer on which they are generated, or to a convenient shared folder where they can be accessed by interested parties. Reports can be published manually, or you can configure them to be published on a regular basis.

Objective 7.2 Questions

1. Which of the following properties is displayed when you generate a new report and select only the security content to be included? (Choose all that apply.)

   A. The number of network intrusion attempts that occurred during the reporting period

   B. The number of dropped packets by the user

   C. The number of authorization failures by the user

   D. The number of DNS intrusion attempts

   E. The number of successful authorizations by the user

2. Which of the following traffic types can be included in reports generated by ISA Server 2004? (Choose all that apply.)

   A. FTP traffic, including destination site and username, from SecureNAT clients

   B. Web traffic, including destination URL and user name, from SecureNAT clients

   C. Web traffic, including destination URL and user name, from Web Proxy clients

   D. FTP traffic, including destination site and user name, from Firewall clients

   E. Web traffic, including destination URL and user name, from Firewall clients

3. You are the security administrator for an array of four ISA Server 2004 Enterprise Edition computers that are configured using the Internet-edge firewall template. Your manager is under pressure to cut the cost of the Internet traffic bill. To this end, she has requested that you generate a weekly report detailing which employees are accessing the Web most frequently. Your manager has no administrative rights to the ISA Server 2004 Enterprise Edition Enterprise or Array. How can you make this information available to your manager with a minimum amount of administrative effort? (Choose the best answer.)

   A. Every Monday, manually generate a report on the Configuration Storage server.

   B. Configure a recurring report job to create a report on the Configuration Storage server each Monday.

   C. Assign the ISA Server Enterprise Auditor role to your manager's user account.

   D. Assign the ISA Server Array Monitoring Auditor role to your manager's user account.

   E. Configure a recurring report job to publish a report every Monday to a shared folder accessible to your manager.

4.   Which of the following statements is true about the default settings of a Web Usage Content report created on the Configuration Storage server of an ISA Server 2004 Enterprise Edition array? (Choose the best answer.)

   A. The Top Site is the site that has received the most requests from clients on the Internal network.

   B. The Top User is the one that has made the most HTTP requests through the ISA Server 2004 computer.

   C. The Top Browser is that which is used by the largest number of users.

   D. The Top Protocol is the one used to transfer the largest amount of data.

Objective 7.2 Answers

1.   **Correct Answers: B and C**

   A. Incorrect: When you include security content in an ISA Server 2004 report, you will be able to view Authorization Failures By User and Dropped Packets By User. You will not be provided with the number of network intrusion attempts that occurred during the reporting period.

   B. Correct: When you include security content in an ISA Server 2004 report, you will be able to view Authorization Failures By User and Dropped Packets By User.

   C. Correct: When you include security content in an ISA Server 2004 report, you will be able to view Authorization Failures By User and Dropped Packets By User.

   D. Incorrect: When you include security content in an ISA Server 2004 report, you will be able to view Authorization Failures By User and Dropped Packets By User.

   E. Incorrect: When you include security content in an ISA Server 2004 report, you will be able to view Authorization Failures By User and Dropped Packets By User. You cannot view data in the report on the number of successful authorizations.

2.   **Correct Answers: D**

   A. Incorrect: All traffic from SecureNAT and Web Proxy clients is not included in reports generated by ISA Server 2004.

   B. Incorrect: All traffic from SecureNAT and Web Proxy clients is not included in reports generated by ISA Server 2004.

   C. Incorrect: All traffic from SecureNAT and Web Proxy clients is not included in reports generated by ISA Server 2004.

   D. Correct: All traffic from Firewall clients, including FTP traffic, can be included in reports generated by ISA Server 2004.

   E. Incorrect: All traffic from Firewall clients, including FTP traffic, can be included in reports generated by ISA Server 2004.

3.   **Correct Answers: E**

   A. Incorrect: Although this will generate the report, your manager will not be able to view the report because she has no administrative rights to the Enterprise or Array.

   B. Incorrect: Although this will generate the report, your manager will not be able to view the report because she has no administrative rights to the Enterprise or Array.

C. **Incorrect:** The ISA Server Enterprise Auditor role assigns read-only privileges to the entirety of the enterprise, which includes all array configurations. Although assigning this role would allow your manager to view information on the Configuration Management server, it would not provide her with the necessary weekly information with the stated minimum of administrative effort.

D. **Incorrect:** The ISA Server Array Monitoring Auditor role assigns the ability to monitor network activity, but is unable to configure any monitoring functionality. Assigning this role does not provide your manager with the necessary weekly information with the stated minimum of administrative effort.

E. **Correct:** This will enable your manager to view the required reports once a week with a minimum amount of administrative effort.

4. **Correct Answers: D**

A. **Incorrect:** Top Sites are ordered in terms of the total bytes sent and received, which may mean that a site from which a few users download a lot of data will rank higher than one that many users use, but doesn't have a high bandwidth requirement.

B. **Incorrect:** The Top User is the one that has sent and received the most traffic during the reporting period. A user who downloads a single very large file and doesn't use the Web for the rest of the period will be ranked higher than one who uses it often, but doesn't download files.

C. **Incorrect:** By default, the Top Browser is the one that makes the most HTTP requests regardless of how many people actually use it.

D. **Correct:** By default, the Top Protocol is measured by the total number of bytes sent and received through the ISA Server 2004 array.

Objective 7.3

Configure Logging and Alerts

There are four ways to configure log files. The first two ways are to have a log written to a traditional text file, the first in ISA Server 2004 format, the second in a format that complies with the World Wide Web Consortium (W3C) standard. The second way is to write the log in a format that complies with the Microsoft SQL Server Desktop Engine (MSDE) standard, which has the benefit of allowing analysis through the ISA Server 2004 log viewing tool. The final way is to write log files directly to a SQL Server computer. This provides the greatest flexibility for log file analysis, because queries can easily be structured in SQL. The downside is that the process is not as user-friendly as the other formats and requires that the administrator have the ability to generate appropriate SQL queries to retrieve the desired data.

Alerts are set to trigger an action when a specified set of conditions has occurred. The actions are to send an e-mail, run a program, write an event to a log, or start or shut down a particular service. The action that you configure will be relevant to the conditions that trigger the alert. In some cases, it is appropriate merely that an event is written to a log; in other cases, it is necessary for services to be shut down and for an administrator to be immediately informed by e-mail that something on the ISA Server 2004 computer is amiss.

1.   The Contoso Ltd mail administrator has configured the e-mail address *isa_alert@ contoso.com* to forward immediately the text of any e-mail that it receives through Short Message Service (SMS) to your cellular phone. You are the administrator of an ISA Server 2004 Enterprise Edition array that contains three computers. In the event that the Microsoft Firewall Service becomes inoperative, you want to be immediately notified by SMS. Which of the following ISA Server 2004 monitoring functionalities should you take advantage of? (Choose the best answer.)

   A.   Logging

   B.   Connectivity Verification

   C.   Alerts

   D.   Reports

2.   The Events tab of the DNS Intrusion alert definition is configured as shown here.

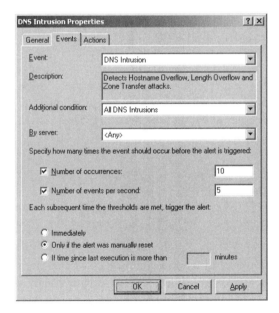

The Actions tab is configured to send you an e-mail when this alert has triggered. As yet, you have received no e-mails from ISA Server 2004 in relation to this alert, even though your logs show that there has been an average of 35 DNS intrusion attempts per minute in the last hour. You want to receive an e-mail once 30 successive DNS intrusion attempts are detected. The Actions tab is configured correctly. Which of the following changes should you make to the Events tab of the DNS Intrusion alert definition? (Choose all that apply.)

    A. Change the Number Of Occurrences property to 30.

    B. Change the Each Subsequent Time The Thresholds Are Met, Trigger The Alert property to Immediately.

    C. Change the Number Of Events Per Second property to 2.

    D. Clear the Number Of Events Per Second check box.

    E. Clear the Number Of Occurrences check box.

3. Which of the following statements about using a SQL database to store logs from your ISA Server 2004 computer are true? (Choose all that apply.)

    A. Logs can be viewed using the ISA Server log viewer.

    B. Firewall logs can be written to a SQL database.

    C. Web Proxy logs can be written to a SQL database.

    D. SMTP Message Screener logs can be written to a SQL database.

    E. Logs written to a SQL database can be stored on remote servers.

4. Your organization has branch offices located in Honolulu, Portland, Phoenix, Atlanta, Sioux Falls, S.D., and Newport News, Va. Because each branch office is located in a separate time zone, you want to ensure that Web Proxy logs are written in GMT or Universal Time Coordinate (UTC), rather than in local time. Which of the following log formats can you use? (Choose all that apply.)

    A. File: ISA Server File Format

    B. File: W3C Extended Log File Format

    C. MSDE Database

    D. SQL Database

5. Your ISA Server 2004 computer is configured using the 3-Leg Perimeter network template. You are currently using the MSDE Database log storage format for your Firewall and Web Proxy logs. You have configured the Logging Filter as shown on the following page.

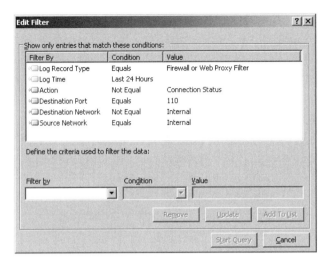

The Internal network range is 192.168.10.0 /26. The query has been running continuously for the last week. It is currently 3 P.M. on Wednesday. Which of the following events will be visible in the Log viewer? (Choose the best answer.)

A. On Tuesday evening, a host on the VPN Clients network with IP address 192.168.10.212 attempts to send e-mail to an SMTP server located on the perimeter network.

B. On Wednesday morning, a host on the VPN Clients network with IP address 192.168.10.230 attempts to download mail from a POP3 server located on the perimeter network.

C. On Monday evening, a host on the Internet attempts to access an Internet Message Access Protocol 4 (IMAP4) server located on the perimeter network.

D. On Tuesday evening, a host on the internal network attempts to access a POP3 server located on the perimeter network.

E. On Wednesday morning, a host on the internal network attempts to access an IMAP4 server located on the perimeter network.

Objective 7.3 Answers

1.   Correct Answers: C

A. Incorrect: Logging cannot be configured to send an alert by e-mail in the event that a particular service fails.

B. Incorrect: Connectivity Verification is used to determine whether a particular computer can be contacted by the ISA Server 2004 computer. Although there are three computers in the ISA Server array, you would not use Connectivity Verification because Connectivity Verification is used to detect non-responsive computers rather than non-responsive remote services. You can configure alerts for services located on any server in an array from the Enterprise Edition configuration server.

C. Correct: C. The Actions tab of an ISA Server 2004 Alert's properties can be configured so that an e-mail message is sent to a particular address. Because your mail administrator has already configured all e-mail sent to *isa_alert@contoso.com* to be forwarded using SMS to your mobile phone, this meets your goals. Alerts can be configured on the ISA Server 2004 Enterprise Edition configuration server for all servers within an array.

D. Incorrect: Reports cannot be configured to send an alert by e-mail in the event that a particular service fails.

2.   Correct Answers: A and D

A. Correct: To have an alert generated once 30 successive DNS intrusion attempts are detected, you must configure the Number Of Occurrences property to 30.

B. Incorrect: The question discusses the first time that the alert is triggered, rather than subsequent alert triggers.

C. Incorrect: The question says nothing about the frequency of alerts. When both Number Of Occurrences and Number Of Events Per Second options are set, both conditions must be met before an alert is triggered.

D. Correct: The question says nothing about frequency of alerts. In removing the check in the Number Of Events Per Second check box, only the total number of occurrences will be relevant with respect to the issuing of alerts.

E. Incorrect: If you clear the Number Of Occurrences check box, there is no way that an alert can be issued once a threshold of 30 attempts is reached.

3. **Correct Answers: B, C, and E**

> **A. Incorrect:** The ISA Server log viewer can be used only to view logs that are stored in MSDE format.
>
> **B. Correct:** Both Firewall logs and Web Proxy logs can be configured to write to a SQL database; only SMTP Message Screener logs cannot be written to a SQL database.
>
> **C. Correct:** Both Firewall logs and Web Proxy logs can be configured to write to a SQL database; only SMTP Message Screener logs cannot be written to a SQL database.
>
> **D. Incorrect:** SMTP Message Screener logs can be written only to text file format; they cannot be written to a SQL database or in MSDE format.
>
> **E. Correct:** There are two significant benefits to writing logs to a SQL database. The first is that you can perform a more comprehensive analysis of logs by using custom SQL queries. The second is that you can store logs on a remote server, which is not possible using the text file or MSDE format.

4. **Correct Answers: B and D**

> **A. Incorrect:** File: ISA Server File Format uses local time, not UTC, when writing events to the log.
>
> **B. Correct:** File: W3C Extended Log File Format uses UTC, not local time, when writing events to the log.
>
> **C. Incorrect:** The MSDE Database log storage format uses local time, not UTC, when writing events to the log.
>
> **D. Correct:** The SQL Database log storage format uses UTC, not local time, when writing events to the log.

5. **Correct Answers: D**

> **A. Incorrect:** The filter will display attempts from hosts on the Internal network attempting to access hosts on networks other than the Internal network through the ISA Server 2004 computer using POP3 made within the last 24 hours. All conditions in the filter must be met for an entry to be displayed.
>
> **B. Incorrect:** The filter will display attempts from hosts on the Internal network attempting to access hosts on networks other than the Internal network through the ISA Server 2004 computer using POP3 made within the last 24 hours. All conditions in the filter must be met for an entry to be displayed.
>
> **C. Incorrect:** The filter will display attempts from hosts on the Internal network attempting to access hosts on networks other than the Internal network through the ISA Server 2004 computer using POP3 made within the last 24 hours. All conditions in the filter must be met for an entry to be displayed.

D. Correct: The filter will display attempts from hosts on the Internal network attempting to access hosts on networks other than the Internal network through the ISA Server 2004 computer using POP3 made within the last 24 hours. All conditions in the filter must be met for an entry to be displayed.

E. Incorrect: The filter will display attempts from hosts on the Internal network attempting to access hosts on networks other than the Internal network through the ISA Server 2004 computer using POP3 made within the last 24 hours. All conditions in the filter must be met for an entry to be displayed.

Glossary

access rule   Defines the conditions stipulating when traffic will be allowed or denied between networks defined on the Microsoft ISA Server computer.

access rule element   A Microsoft ISA Server configuration object that you can use when creating an access rule. Access rule elements include protocols, user sets, network objects, and schedules.

active caching   A process by which the Microsoft ISA Server 2000 computer preemptively caches objects within the cache that are frequently accessed by users. Active caching is disabled in ISA Server 2004.

Active Directory   The Microsoft Windows–based directory service. Active Directory directory service stores information about objects on a network and makes this information available to users and network administrators. Active Directory gives network users access to permitted resources anywhere on the network using a single-logon process. It provides network administrators with an intuitive, hierarchical view of the network and a single point of administration for all network objects.

Active Directory Application Mode (ADAM)   ADAM is a special mode of the Active Directory directory service that is designed for directory-enabled applications. The ADAM directory service, which is compatible with the Lightweight Directory Access Protocol (LDAP), runs on servers on which Microsoft Windows Server 2003 is installed.

ADAM   *See* Active Directory Application Mode (ADAM).

administrative roles   Used to assign permissions on Microsoft ISA Server. Each administrative role has a predefined set of permissions that allow the user to perform specific tasks on the ISA Server computer.

affinity   The method used by network load balancing (NLB) to associate client requests to cluster hosts. When no affinity is specified, all network requests are load-balanced across the cluster without respect to their source. Affinity is implemented by directing all client requests from the same Internet Protocol (IP) address to the same cluster host.

alert   A notification of an event or action that has occurred on a Microsoft ISA Server computer. When the event occurs, an alert is triggered according to the conditions and trigger thresholds specified for the event.

API *See* application programming interface (API).

application-layer filtering A type of filtering in which a firewall examines the actual content of a network packet to determine whether the packet will be forwarded through the firewall. The firewall opens the entire packet and examines the actual data in the packet before making a forwarding decision.

application programming interface (API) A set of routines that an application uses to request and carry out lower-level services performed by a computer's operating system. These routines usually execute maintenance tasks such as managing files and displaying information.

array An array is a group of Microsoft ISA Server 2004 Enterprise Edition computers that share the same configuration. An array includes one or more Configuration Storage servers that store the configuration information for the array and one or more array members which are computers with ISA Server services installed.

authentication The process of validating the credentials of a person, computer process, or device. Authentication requires that the person, process, or device making the request provides a credential that proves it is what or who it says it is. Common forms of credentials are digital signatures, smart cards, biometric data, and a combination of user names and passwords.

automatic discovery Automatic discovery is a feature of Microsoft ISA Server that enables Firewall and Web Proxy clients to discover an ISA Server computer automatically.

Background Intelligent Transfer Service (BITS) A service that transfers files between a client and server in the background. Used by Software Update Services and Microsoft Windows Update Services to download hot fixes, updates, and service packs.

Basic authentication An authentication mechanism that is supported by most browsers, including Microsoft Internet Explorer. Basic authentication encodes, but does not encrypt, user name and password data before transmitting it over the network. Also known as plaintext authentication.

BITS *See* Background Intelligent Transfer Service (BITS).

buffer A region of random access memory (RAM) reserved for use with data that is temporarily held while waiting to be transferred between two locations, such as between an application's data area and an input/output device.

buffer overrun A condition that results from adding more information to a buffer than it was designed to contain. An attacker may exploit this vulnerability to take over a system.

CA   *See* certification authority (CA).

Cache Array Routing Protocol (CARP)   Distributes the cache used by Web Proxy clients across an array of Microsoft ISA Server computers. CARP uses hash-based routing to determine which ISA Server computer will respond to a client request and cache specific Web content.

cache rule   Define the types of Web content that is stored in the cache and how Web content is stored and returned to users from the cache. Rules can be configured to allow or deny caching from particular sites.

caching   The process of storing a copy of a requested Web object on a local server so that other clients on the local network can be served the copy of the object rather than have it be retrieved again from a remote server.

CARP   *See* Cache Array Routing Protocol (CARP).

CDDI   *See* Copper Data Distribution Interface (CDDI).

certificate   A digital file containing user or server identification information that is used to verify identity and to help establish a security-enhanced link.

certification authority (CA)   A server responsible for establishing and vouching for the authenticity of public keys belonging to users or computers or other certification authorities. Activities of a certification authority can include assigning certificates, binding public keys to distinguished names through signed certificates, managing certificate serial numbers, and certificate revocation.

Challenge Handshake Authentication Protocol (CHAP)   A challenge-response authentication protocol for Point-to-Point Protocol (PPP) connections described in RFC 1994. CHAP uses the industry-standard Message Digest 5 (MD5) hashing algorithm to hash the combination of a challenge string issued by the authenticating server and the user's password in the response.

CHAP   *See* Challenge Handshake Authentication Protocol (CHAP).

Configuration Storage server   A server that stores the configuration for an enterprise of Microsoft ISA Server 2004 Enterprise Edition computers. The enterprise configuration is modified on this server rather than on the individual Microsoft ISA Server 2004 computers that comprise the arrays in the enterprise.

connectivity verifier   A Microsoft ISA Server object used to regularly test connections from the ISA Server computer to any computer or Uniform Resource Locator (URL) on any network. When you configure a connectivity verifier, you can configure the method that the verifier will use to determine connectivity.

content download job Used to retrieve Web content from selected Web sites in advance to provide faster response for internal clients. Jobs can be configured to download any content on a flexible schedule.

Copper Data Distribution Interface (CDDI) A technology used to carry data over copper cable at high speed.

credentials Information that includes identification and proof of identification that is used to gain access to local and network resources. Examples of credentials are user names and passwords, smart cards, and certificates.

denial-of-service (DoS) attack An attempt by a malicious (or unwitting) user, process, or system to prevent legitimate users from accessing a resource (usually a network service) by exploiting a weakness or design limitation in an information system. Examples of DoS attacks include flooding network connections, filling disk storage, disabling ports, or removing power.

DHCP *See* Dynamic Host Configuration Protocol (DHCP)

Digest authentication An authentication mechanism that hashes user name, password, and other data before transmitting it over the network.

DNS *See* Domain Name System (DNS).

DNS forwarder A Domain Name System (DNS) server designated by other internal DNS servers to be used to forward queries for resolving external or offsite DNS domain names.

domain controller In an Active Directory forest, a server that contains a writable copy of the Active Directory database, participates in Active Directory replication, and controls access to network resources. Administrators can manage user accounts, network access, shared resources, site topology, and other directory objects from any domain controller in the forest.

Domain Name System (DNS) A hierarchical, distributed database that contains mappings of DNS domain names to various types of data, such as Internet Protocol (IP) addresses. DNS enables the location of computers and services by user-friendly names, and it also enables the discovery of other information stored in the database.

Dynamic Host Configuration Protocol (DHCP) A Transmission Control Protocol/Internet Protocol (TCP/IP) service protocol that offers dynamic leased configuration of host IP addresses and distributes other configuration parameters to eligible network clients.

EAP *See* Extensible Authentication Protocol (EAP).

edge firewall   A two-interface firewall. The first interface is connected to the trusted network, and the second interface is connected to the untrusted network. In almost all cases, the untrusted network is the Internet.

encryption   The process of converting data into a coded form (ciphertext) to prevent it from being read and understood by an unauthorized party.

enterprise   A collection of all Microsoft ISA Server 2004 Enterprise Edition computers that use the same Configuration Storage directory to store configuration information. An enterprise includes one or more arrays.

enterprise policy   A policy defined at the enterprise level that can be applied to any array.

Extensible Authentication Protocol (EAP)   An extension to the Point-to-Point Protocol (PPP) that allows for arbitrary authentication mechanisms to be employed for the validation of a PPP connection.

Extensible Markup Language (XML)   A meta-markup language that provides a format for describing structured data. XML allows customized tags, enabling precise declarations of content between applications and between organizations.

File Transfer Protocol (FTP)   A member of the Transmission Control Protocol/Internet Protocol (TCP/IP) suite of protocols, used to copy files between two computers on the Internet. Both computers must support their respective FTP roles: one must be an FTP client and the other an FTP server.

firewall   A device that is located between one network and another, and allows only authorized network traffic to pass between the networks. The firewall is configured with traffic filtering rules that define what types of network traffic will be allowed to pass through the firewall.

firewall access rule   A configuration object on Microsoft ISA Server that defines what types of network traffic will be allowed on the ISA Server computer. By default, all network traffic is blocked unless a firewall access rule allows the specific traffic.

Firewall client   A computer that has Firewall Client software installed and enabled. Firewall clients provide the highest level of functionality and security of the types of clients.

firewall policy   A collection of access and publishing rules that govern the passage of traffic across the Microsoft ISA Server 2004 computer's network interfaces.

forward caching   Forward caching occurs when a user on the corporate network makes a request for Web content located on an Internet Web server and the request is intercepted by a caching server. The caching server retrieves the content from the Internet Web server, stores it in its cache, and returns the content to the user.

FQDN   *See* fully qualified domain name (FQDN).

FTP   *See* File Transfer Protocol (FTP).

fully qualified domain name (FQDN)   A Domain Name System (DNS) host name that includes a host and domain name, including the top-level domain.

hardware-based firewall   A network appliance that performs no other function than that of a firewall. It has a basic operating system used for configuration and management of firewall functions. Often more expensive than a software-based firewall like Microsoft ISA Server 2004.

host   Any device on a Transmission Control Protocol/Internet Protocol (TCP/IP) network that has an IP address. Examples of hosts include servers, workstations, network-interface print devices, and routers.

Hosts file   A local text file, stored in the \%Systemroot%\System32\Drivers\Etc folder, that maps host names to Internet Protocol (IP) addresses.

HTTP   *See* Hypertext Transfer Protocol (HTTP).

HTTPS   *See* Hypertext Transfer Protocol Secure (HTTPS).

Hypertext Transfer Protocol (HTTP)   The protocol used to transfer Web content from Web servers such as Microsoft Internet Information Services (IIS) 6.0 to Web clients such as Microsoft Internet Explorer 6.0

Hypertext Transfer Protocol Secure (HTTPS)   A secure version of the HTTP protocol that uses Secure Sockets Layer (SSL) to encrypt bidirectional communication between server and client.

IAS   *See* Internet Authentication Service (IAS).

internal domain   A domain name that exists on the internal network rather than on external networks such as the Internet.

Internal network   A protected network that is not accessible to hosts on External networks, such as the Internet, except through a firewall.

Internet Authentication Service (IAS)   The Microsoft implementation of a Remote Authentication Dial-In User Service (RADIUS) server and proxy, which provides authentication and accounting for network access.

Internet Protocol security (IPSec)   A set of industry-standard, cryptography-based protection services and protocols. IPSec protects all protocols in the Transmission Control Protocol/Internet Protocol (TCP/IP) protocol suite and Internet communications.

IPSec   *See* Internet Protocol security (IPSec).

IPSec tunnel mode A protocol used to secure site-to-site virtual private network (VPN) connections, for which IPSec provides the encapsulation for IP traffic sent across a public network.

Internet usage policy A policy defined by an organization that sets restrictions on the types of activities users at the organization can perform on the Internet.

intrusion detection A means of detecting when an attack is attempted or in progress against a network.

ISA Server 2004 Firewall Client software Special software that can be installed on Microsoft Windows 2000, Windows XP, and Windows Server 2003 computers to enable them to route all requests for external network resources through a Microsoft ISA Server 2004 computer.

ISA Server client A client computer that accesses network resources by passing the request through a Microsoft ISA Server computer. ISA Server 2004 supports three types of clients: secure network-address translation (SecureNAT) clients, Web Proxy clients, and Firewall clients.

Internet Protocol (IP) A routable protocol in the Transmission Control Protocol/Internet Protocol (TCP/IP) protocol suite that is responsible for IP addressing, routing, and the fragmentation and reassembly of IP packets.

L2TP over IPSec (Layer-Two Tunneling Protocol over Internet Protocol security) A virtual private network (VPN) connection method that provides session authentication, address encapsulation, and strong encryption of private data between remote access servers and clients. L2TP provides address encapsulation and user authentication, and Internet Protocol security (IPSec) provides computer authentication and encryption of the L2TP session.

LAT *See* local address table (LAT).

Layer-Two Tunneling Protocol (L2TP) An industry-standard Internet tunneling protocol that provides encapsulation for sending Point-to-Point Protocol (PPP) frames across packet-oriented media. In Microsoft operating systems, L2TP is used in conjunction with Internet Protocol security (IPSec) as a virtual private network (VPN) technology to provide remote access or router-to-router VPN connections. L2TP is described in RFC 2661.

LDAP *See* Lightweight Directory Access Protocol (LDAP).

LDT *See* local domain table (LDP).

Lightweight Directory Access Protocol (LDAP) LDAP is an industry-standard protocol, established by the Internet Engineering Task Force (IETF), that allows users to query and update information in a directory service. Active Directory and Active Directory Application Mode (ADAM) support both LDAP version 2 and LDAP version 3.

link translation   A Microsoft ISA Server configuration object that enables ISA Server to replace internal server names on Web pages with server names that are accessible from the Internet.

local address table (LAT)   A table used by Microsoft ISA Server Firewall clients that defines the Internal network addresses.

Local administrator privileges   Assigned to members of the local Administrators group. Gives members full control over a single computer, but confers no rights to other computers on the network.

local domain table (LDT)   A table used by Microsoft ISA Server Firewall clients that contains a list of domains and server names that are on the internal network rather than on a remote network.

log   Provides detailed information about the Web proxy, Microsoft Firewall service, or Simple Mail Transfer Protocol (SMTP) Message Screener. Microsoft ISA Server logs all client connections and all blocked client connections by default.

Mail Exchanger (MX) record   An entry in a domain name database that identifies the mail server that is responsible for handling e-mails for a domain name.

mail relaying   A practice in which an attacker sends e-mail messages from another system's e-mail server so as to use its resources or to make it appear that the messages originated from the other system.

malicious code   Software that, when run, fulfills the deliberately harmful intent of an attacker. Examples of malicious code are viruses, worms, and Trojan horses.

MAPI   *See* Messaging Application Programming Interface (MAPI).

Messaging Application Programming Interface (MAPI)   The application programming interface (API) used by Microsoft Outlook clients when connecting to a Microsoft Exchange server. MAPI clients use remote procedure calls (RPCs) to connect to the Exchange server.

Microsoft Challenge Handshake Authentication Protocol (MS-CHAP)   A non-reversible, encrypted password authentication protocol that can be used with Microsoft Point-to-Point Encryption (MPPE) to encrypt data.

Microsoft Point-to-Point Encryption (MPPE)   A 128-bit key or 40-bit key encryption algorithm using RSA RC4. MPPE provides for packet confidentiality between the remote access client and the remote access or tunnel server.

MPPE   *See* Microsoft Point-to-Point Encryption (MPPE).

MS-CHAP   *See* Microsoft Challenge Handshake Authentication Protocol (MS-CHAP).

MS-CHAP version 2 (MS-CHAPv2)   An authentication protocol that uses mutual authentication, so both the client and the server are authenticated. Also uses separate session keys for encrypting transmitted and received data.

MS Firewall Control Protocol   An outbound Transmission Control Protocol (TCP) defined on Port 3847. It is used for communications between the Microsoft ISA Server Management Console and computers running ISA Server services.

MS Firewall Storage Protocol   An inbound LDAP-based protocol that uses Port 2172 (for Secure Sockets Layer, or SSL, connections) and Port 2171 (for non-SSL connections). Array members communicate with the Configuration Storage server using the MS Firewall Storage protocol. Computers running Microsoft ISA Server Management also use the MS Firewall Storage protocol to read from and write to the Configuration Storage server.

MS Firewall Storage Replication Protocol   An outbound Transmission Control Protocol (TCP) that is defined on Port 2173. MS Firewall Storage Replication is used for configuration replication between Configuration Storage servers.

multimaster, or multiple-master, replication   A replication model in which any computer hosting a directory service accepts and replicates directory changes. This model differs from single-master replication models, in which one domain controller stores the single modifiable copy of the directory and other domain controllers store backup copies.

MX   *See* Mail Exchanger record (MX).

network address translation (NAT)   An Internet Protocol (IP) translation process that allows a network with private addresses to access information on the Internet.

network load balancing (NLB)   A Microsoft Windows network component that is used to create a cluster of computers that can be addressed by a single cluster Internet Protocol (IP) address. NLB provides load balancing and high availability for IP-based services.

network rule   Defines how network packets will be passed between networks. Network rules determine whether there is a relationship between two network entities and what type of relationship is defined.

network template   A set of Microsoft ISA Server configuration options that define networks and network sets, network rules, access rule elements, and access rules.

NLB   *See* network load balancing (NLB).

Outlook Web Access (OWA) An Exchange Server feature that provides access to the mailboxes on a Microsoft Exchange Server computer through a Web browser.

OWA *See* Outlook Web Access (OWA).

OWA forms-based authentication A cookie-based authentication method that ensures that user credentials are not cached on the client computer after the user logs off or after a timeout period expires. In addition, Outlook Web Access (OWA) forms-based authentication can be used to restrict whether users can view or download e-mail attachments.

packet filtering Filters network packets by inspecting and allowing or denying the Internet Protocol (IP) packets based on information in the IP packet network layer header.

PAP *See* Password Authentication Protocol (PAP).

Password Authentication Protocol (PAP) A simple, plaintext authentication scheme for authenticating Point-to-Point Protocol (PPP) connections. The user name and password are requested by the remote-access server and returned by the remote-access client in plaintext.

pass-through authentication The ability of Microsoft ISA Server to pass a client's authentication information to the destination server.

path mapping A Microsoft ISA Server feature that enables ISA Server to redirect user requests to multiple internal Web servers or to multiple locations on the same Web server.

perimeter network A network that is separated from an internal network and the Internet. Perimeter networks allow external users to gain access to specific servers that are located on the perimeter network while preventing direct access from the Internet to the internal network.

PKI *See* public key infrastructure (PKI).

Point-to-Point Protocol (PPP) An industry standard suite of protocols for the use of point-to-point links to transport multiprotocol datagrams. PPP is documented in RFC 1661.

Point-to-Point Tunneling Protocol (PPTP) A virtual private network (VPN) connection method that uses Point-to-Point Protocol (PPP) user authentication methods and Microsoft Point-to-Point Encryption (MPPE) to encrypt IP traffic.

port The method that Transmission Control Protocol (TCP) and User Datagram Protocol (UDP) use to specify which program running on the system is sending or receiving the data.

port scanning   A method that is used to identify services or programs that respond to service requests that are made over a network port.

PPP   *See* Point-to-Point Protocol (PPP).

PPTP   *See* Point-to-Point Tunneling Protocol (PPTP).

pre-shared key   An Internet Protocol security (IPSec) technology in which a shared secret key is used for authentication.

private key   One of two keys used in public-key encryption. The user keeps the private key secret and typically uses it to digitally sign data or to decrypt data that has been encrypted with the corresponding public key.

proxy server   A firewall component that manages Internet traffic to and from a local area network (LAN) and can provide other functions, such as caching and access control. The proxy server is situated between a client application, such as a Web browser, and a server to which the client connects.

public key   One of two keys used in public-key encryption. The user releases this key to the public, who can use it to encrypt messages to be sent to the user and to verify the user's digital signature.

public-key encryption   A method of encryption that uses a pair of mathematically related keys: a public key and a corresponding private key. Either key can be used to encrypt data, but the corresponding key must be used to decrypt it. Also called asymmetric encryption.

public key infrastructure (PKI)   A framework encompassing the laws, policies, standards, hardware, and software to provide and manage the use of public key cryptography on public networks such as the Internet.

publishing rule   A Microsoft ISA Server configuration object that is used to make a resource on the internal or perimeter network available to clients on unprotected networks such as the Internet.

quarantine control   A remote-access feature that can be used to restrict virtual private network (VPN) client access. Quarantine control allows you to screen VPN client machines using a client-side script before allowing them access to the organization's network.

Quarantined VPN Clients network   Contains the IP addresses of all the Virtual Private Network (VPN) clients that have connected using VPN client access but have not yet cleared quarantine.

RADIUS   *See* Remote Authentication Dial-In User Service (RADIUS).

Remote Authentication Dial-In User Service (RADIUS)   An industry-standard protocol used to provide authentication in heterogeneous environments.

Remote Management Computers   A computer set that is used to provide remote management access to Microsoft ISA Server. This computer set should include all the IP addresses of the computers that are used to perform remote administration on the ISA Server computer.

remote procedure call (RPC)   A communication mechanism that allows computers to communicate with one another over a network. An RPC consists of a procedure identifier, parameters passed to the procedure, and a value returned to the caller (client computer) after the procedure has executed on the remote system (server computer).

remote-site network   Contains the Internet Protocol (IP) addresses of all the computers in remote sites when a site-to-site Virtual Private Network (VPN) connection is configured. Additional remote-site networks are created for each remote-site connection.

replication   The process of copying updated data from a data store or file system on a source computer to a matching data store or file system on one or more destination computers to synchronize the data.

report   Provides summarized information about the usage patterns on Microsoft ISA Server. The report information is extracted from the ISA Server logs.

resource record (RR)   A standard Domain Name System (DNS) database structure containing information used to process DNS queries. For example, an address (A) resource record contains an IP address corresponding to a host name.

reverse caching   Reverse caching occurs when users on the Internet request Web content located on the corporate network. When an Internet user requests content from the internal server, the caching server forwards the request to the Web server. The caching server will cache a copy of the requested information so that the next request for the same information can be provided from the cache rather than accessing the internal Web server again.

RPC   *See* remote procedure call (RPC).

RR   *See* resource record (RR).

RSA SecurID authentication   An authentication mechanism requiring that a remote user have two factors, such as a personal identification number (PIN), and a physical token to gain access to protected resources.

Secure Sockets Layer (SSL)   A protocol that provides secure data communication through data encryption. This protocol enables authentication, integrity, and data privacy over networks through a combination of digital certificates, public-key cryptography, and bulk data encryption. This protocol does not provide authorization or nonrepudiation.

SecureNAT client A Microsoft ISA Server client that does not have the Firewall Client software installed and is not configured as a Web Proxy client. In this configuration, the client uses the ISA Server 2004 computer as the default gateway in its Transmission Control Protocol/Internet Protocol (TCP/IP) configuration.

server publishing rule A firewall rule that specifies how Microsoft ISA Server will route requests from hosts on external networks to hosts on protected networks using any available protocol.

service account A user account in a Windows-based operating system that is used to run services on the computer.

session A logical connection created between two hosts to exchange data. Typically, sessions use sequencing and acknowledgments to send data reliably.

session monitoring Used to provide real-time information about the users or computers that are connected to the Microsoft ISA Server computer. These clients may be internal SecureNAT, Firewall, or Web Proxy clients, or they may be Internet clients connected to an internal Web resource, or through a virtual private network (VPN) connection.

Simple Mail Transfer Protocol (SMTP) A Transmission Control Protocol/Internet Protocol (TCP/IP) protocol that is used to transfer e-mail between servers on the Internet.

single affinity Specifies that network load balancing (NLB) should direct multiple requests from the same client Internet Protocol (IP) address to the same cluster host. This is the default setting for affinity.

site-to-site VPN A point-to-point secure tunnel created through the Internet between a virtual private network (VPN) gateway server in one location and a VPN gateway server in another location.

smart card A credit card–sized device with an embedded microprocessor and a small amount of storage that is used, with an access code, to enable certificate-based authentication. Smart cards securely store certificates, public and private keys, passwords, and other types of personal information.

SMTP *See* Simple Mail Transfer Protocol (SMTP).

SMTP application filter Provides application-layer filtering that can be used to block buffer overflow attacks and to disable SMTP commands that are not required.

SMTP Message Screener Provides application layer filtering that can be used to filter Simple Mail Transfer Protocol (SMTP) mail. The Message Screener can scan the messages and examine the attachments and then block or hold messages for later inspection.

split DNS   Uses two different Domain Name System (DNS) servers with the same DNS domain name to provide name resolution for internally and externally accessible resources. Both DNS servers are authoritative for the same domain name.

SSL   *See* Secure Sockets Layer (SSL).

SSL bridging   Occurs when the Microsoft ISA Server computer operates as the endpoint for an SSL connection. The Secure Sockets Layer (SSL) connection could be between ISA Server and the client or between ISA Server and the internal Web server.

SSL tunneling   Occurs when a client establishes a Secure Sockets Layer (SSL) tunnel through the Microsoft ISA Server computer directly to the server protected by the ISA Server computer.

stateful filtering   Filters network packets by using information about the Transmission Control Protocol (TCP) session to determine if a packet should be blocked or allowed through the firewall.

system policy   A set of firewall access rules that controls how the Microsoft ISA Server computer communicates with computers on the attached networks.

TCP/IP   *See* Transmission Control Protocol/Internet Protocol (TCP/IP).

TLS   *See* Transport Layer Security (TLS).

Transmission Control Protocol/Internet Protocol (TCP/IP)   A set of networking protocols widely used on the Internet that provide communications across interconnected networks of computers with diverse hardware architectures and various operating systems. TCP/IP includes standards for how computers communicate and conventions for connecting networks and routing traffic.

Transport Layer Security (TLS)   A protocol that provides communications privacy and security between two applications communicating over a network. TLS provides a secure channel by encrypting communications and enables clients to authenticate servers or, optionally, servers to authenticate clients.

tunneling protocol   Uses encryption protocols to provide data security as the data is sent across the public network. The two virtual private network (VPN) protocols supported by Microsoft ISA Server are Microsoft Point-to-Point Tunneling Protocol (PPTP) or the Layer-Two Tunneling Protocol (L2TP).

UDP   *See* User Datagram Protocol (UDP).

unattended installation   An automated installation method in which a setup information file provides the information required by the installation program to complete the product installation.

universally unique identifier (UUID)   A unique number assigned to a particular device, component, or service. Used to identify remote procedure call–based applications running on servers.

User Datagram Protocol (UDP)   A protocol that offers a connectionless datagram service that guarantees neither delivery nor correct sequencing of delivered packets.

UUID   *See* universally unique identifier (UUID).

virtual IP address   An Internet Protocol (IP) address that is shared among the hosts of a Network Load Balancing cluster.

virtual private network (VPN)   A virtual network that enables communication between a remote-access client and computers on the internal network or between two remote sites separated by a public network such as the Internet.

VPN   *See* virtual private network (VPN).

VPN Clients network   Contains the Internet Protocol (IP) addresses of all the virtual private network (VPN) clients that have connected using VPN client access.

Web-based Distributed Authoring and Versioning (WebDAV)   A technology that allows users to edit and manage files on remote Web servers. Has the benefit that when publishing content to remote servers, authentication can occur in an encrypted manner, unlike File Transfer Protocol (FTP) publishing, where authentication occurs in clear text.

Web Filter   A feature that extends the functionality of the firewall service in Microsoft ISA Server by providing advanced filtering capability for Hypertext Transfer Protocol (HTTP) packets as they pass through ISA Server.

Web listener   A Microsoft ISA Server configuration object that defines how the ISA Server computer listens for Hypertext Transfer Protocol (HTTP) requests and Secure Sockets Layer (SSL) requests. The Web listener defines the network, Internet Protocol (IP) address and the port number on which ISA Server listens for client connections.

Web Proxy Automatic Discovery   A process by which the Web proxy settings of client browsers are automatically configured.

Web Proxy client   Any computer that runs Hypertext Transfer Protocol (HTTP) 1.1–compatible Web applications such as Web browsers. The Web applications must be configured to use the Microsoft ISA Server computer as a proxy server.

Web publishing rule   A firewall rule that specifies how Microsoft ISA Server will route incoming requests to internal Web servers.

WebDAV *See* Web-based Distributed Authoring and Versioning (WebDAV).

Winsock applications Applications that use sockets to communicate with services running on other computers. The Firewall Client intercepts Winsock application requests and redirects them to the Microsoft ISA Server computer.

workgroup A simple grouping of computers that do not offer the centralized user accounts and authentication offered by Active Directory–based domains.

XML *See* Extensible Markup Language (XML).

zone transfer The synchronization of authoritative Domain Name System (DNS) data between DNS servers. A DNS server configured with a secondary zone periodically queries the master DNS servers to synchronize its zone data.

Index

Symbols

* (asterisk)
  content type configuration, 5-34
  specifying set of computers with, 5-37
/ (slash), content type configuration, 5-34

A

access control
  access rule configuration, 4-24
  Firewall clients and, 4-5
  restricting Internet access, 5-8 to 5-9
  Web Proxy clients and, 4-7
access control lists (ACLs), 2-33, 3-5
access policies, networks, 1-19
access rule elements, 5-29 to 5-40
  defined, 5-65
  exercises configuring, 5-38 to 5-39
  network object configuration, 5-35 to 5-37
  overview of, 5-29
  protocol element configuration, 5-30 to 5-31
  questions and answers, 5-67
  review, 5-39 to 5-40
  schedule configuration, 5-34
  types of, 5-29
  user set configuration, 5-31 to 5-32
access rules
  actions, 5-50
  applying, 7-18 to 7-19
  content types, 5-53
  configuring new, 5-49
  destination, 5-52
  defined, 5-65
  DNS lookup, 5-56
  employees, 5-58
  enterprise networks, 12-53
  exercises, 5-56 to 5-59
  multiple networks, 7-14
  inbound access, 7-33
  managers, 5-57
  modifying, 7-32
  network templates and, 7-32
  overview, 5-48
  priorities, 5-53 to 5-54

  protocols, 5-51
  questions and answers, 5-69
  remote site netpworks, 10-41, 10-46
  review, 5-59 to 5-60
  source, 5-51
  structure or format, 5-48
  testing, 5-59
  troubleshooting access, 5-55 to 5-56
  users, 5-53
accounts. See user accounts
ACE Server, RSA, 10-25
acknowledge registered alerts, 11-24
acknowledgement (ACK), 7-5
ACLs (access control lists), 2-33, 3-5
actions, alert
  configuring, 11-20
  defined, 11-20
activation information, session monitoring, 11-29
Active Directory
  ADAM as special mode of, 12-6
  Authentication and, 1-12
  configuration information stored in, 1-20
  dial-in permissions, 10-26
  DNS servers and, 2-8
  domain controllers, 12-10
  Enterprise CA integrated with, 8-36
  Enterprise Edition and, 12-4
  Group Policy. See Group Policy
Active Directory Application Mode (ADAM)
  configuration storage, 1-18
  Configuration Storage servers, 12-3, 12-23
  defined, 12-75
  overview of, 12-6
  replication, 12-38
  site configuration, 12-38
Active Directory Users and Computers
  groups, 5-2
  user accounts, 10-27
ActiveSync
  as mobile service component, 9-27
  configuring, 9-33
ADAM. See Active Directory Application Mode (ADAM)
Adamsites.exe, 12-38

Address Resolution Protocol (ARP), 10-20 to 10-21

administration
distributed, 12-4
centralized, 12-29
remote, 12-26

Administration Delegation Wizard
administrative roles, 3-23
user and group permissions, 1-20

administrative roles, 3-21 to 3-23
arrays, 12-57
assigning, 3-23
configuring for enterprise networks, 12-26 to
12-27
default, 3-21
defined, 3-42
Enterprise Edition and, 12-50
exercise configuring, 3-25
tasks associated with, 3-22

administrator permissions, Enterprise Edition, 12-50

Administrators group, 3-15

advanced settings
caching, 6-15, 6-22
proxy servers, 5-16
Web listeners, 8-18

alerts, 11-15 to 11-28
actions, 11-20
application filters generating, 7-47
configuring, 11-17 to 11-22
dashboard view, 11-5
defined, 11-17, 11-61
events and conditions, 11-18
exercises for configuring and managing, 11-24 to 11-26
intrusion detection and, 11-23
ISA Server Management Console, 11-4
managing, 11-23, 11-24
monitoring, 1-36, 11-8
overview of, 11-15
questions and answers, 11-63
review, 11-27 to 11-28
testing, 11-26
thresholds, 11-8
types of, 11-15
viewing, 11-16

algorithms, 10-9

All Authenticated Users
access rules and, 7-32
user sets, 5-32

All Users
authentication and, 8-63
user sets, 5-32

allowed sites, system policies, 3-19

anonymous access, to public Web sites, 1-7

antivirus software, 10-53

API (application programming interface), Winsock, 4-4

application layer, intrusion detection at, 7-9

application logs, 2-29

application programming interface (API), Winsock, 4-4

Application.ini file, 4-39 to 4-41

application filters, 7-7 to 7-8, 7-46 to 7-48
advantages and disadvantages, 7-7
alert and log events, 7-47
compatibility problems, 2-35
configuring SMTP application filters, 9-10
defined, 1-41
complex protocols and, 7-47
HTTP application filter, 8-4
ISA Server 2004 features, 1-20
overview, 1-9, 7-7, 7-46
protocol-level content filtering, 7-47
protocol-level intrusion detection, 7-47
questions and answers, 7-73
real world example, 1-9
reasons for using, 7-7 to 7-8
RPC application filter, 9-40
SecureNAT clients and, 4-6
securing applications, 3-5
security inspection with, 2-15
server publishing rules and, 8-6
SMTP application filter, 9-55
SMTP traffic, 9-7
Web Proxy clients and, 4-8

applications
application names in session monitoring, 11-30
application transparency in VPNs, 10-6
secure Internet access and, 5-4
security in defense-in-depth, 3-5
usage reports, 11-47
Web applications, 5-13

ARP proxy, 10-20 to 10-21

array policies
effectiveness of, 12-12 to 12-13
overview of, 12-11
planning, 12-25

arrays
  administrative roles, 12-57
  back-end, 12-34 to 12-35
  centralizing management with, 12-20
  Configuration Storage settings, 12-56
  configuring, 12-8, 12-10, 12-55 to 12-57
  creating, 12-53
  defined, 12-75
  delegation of administrative rights and, 12-4
  DNS and, 12-69
  enterprise networks enabling communication between, 12-9
  enterprise policies applied to 12-54
  exercise creating and configuring, 12-59 to 12-60
  front-end, 12-32 to 12-34
  intra-array authentication, 12-30
  intra-array addressing, 12-65 to 12-67
  intra-array credentials, 12-56
  membership, 12-61
  overview of, 12-8
  planning network configuration for
  back-to-back firewalls, 12-31
  policies, 12-8, 12-11 to 12-13, 12-25, 12-55
  policy rules, 12-57
  workgroups, 12-21, 12-30
asterisk (*)
  configuring content types and, 5-34
  specifying set of computers with, 5-37
attacks
  buffer-overflow, 9-3
  denial-of-service (DoS), 9-3
  DNS, 7-40
  intrusion detection and, 7-8, 7-37
  investigating, 11-3
  malicious e-mail, 9-5
  SMTP command, 9-4
  unwanted e-mail, 9-4
audit policies, 3-10
AUTH command, SMTP, 9-10
authentication
  access rules and, 5-55
  accessing private Web sites, 1-7
  back-to-back firewalls, 12-34
  basic authentication, 9-45
  client authentication, 8-33

Configuration Storage servers, 12-61
  configuring, 5-44 to 5-46, 8-64 to 8-66
  domain authentication, 12-24
  deciding which type to use, 5-43 to 5-44
  enhancements, 1-20
  exercise configuring ISA Server authentication, 8-71 to 8-73
  exercise testing RADIUS authentication, 8-73
  forms-based for OWA connections, 9-30 to 9-33
  intra-array, 12-30
  ISA Server clients and, 5-42 to 5-43
  ISA Server options for, 2-11
  methods, 1-12
  options, 5-41 to 5-42
  overview of, 5-41
  questions and answers, 5-68, 8-84
  RADIUS, 7-48, 8-67 to 8-69
  review, 5-46 to 5-47, 8-73 to 8-75
  SecureNAT clients and, 4-6
  SecurID, 8-70
  server authentication, 8-33
  site-to-site VPNs, 10-37
  troubleshooting VPN connections, 10-28
  user authentication, 5-11
  user set configuration and, 5-32
  VPN infrastructure planning, 10-13
  VPNs, 1-14, 10-8 to 10-9, 10-23 to 10-27
  Web listener configuration, 8-15
  Web Proxy clients and, 4-7
  Web publishing rules and, 8-4, 8-63 to 8-64
authentication services, system policies, 3-18
automatic discovery
  defined, 4-47
  enabling, 4-21 to 4-24
  how it works, 4-21
  overview of, 4-20 to 4-24
  Web Proxy clients configured for, 4-10
availability
  deployment planning, 2-5, 2-17
  high availability with NLB, 12-13

B

back-end
  arrays, 12-33 to 12-35
  firewalls, 1-24 to 1-25

network template, 7-28
back-to-back, perimeter network configuration, 7-27
back-to-back firewalls, 12-27 to 12-35
    authentication, 12-34
    back-end arrays, 12-33 to 12-35
    case scenario, 12-72
    case scenario questions, 12-81 to 12-82
    domain or workgroup options, 12-28 to 12-31
    front-end arrays, 12-32 to 12-33
    overview of, 12-27
    planning array configuration, 12-31
    SSL publishing and, 12-33
backup files, 12-37
backups
    backing up configuration, 3-31
    security updates and, 3-13
    Web chaining and, 5-22
bandwidth
    bandwidth rules supported, 2-33
    caching and, 6-4
    Internet connections and, 2-15
basic authentication
    overview of, 5-41
    publishing rules supporting, 8-5
    RPC over HTTP and, 9-45
    support for, 5-43
bastion hosts, 7-26
batch files, 10-55
bidirectional affinity, in ISA Server, 12-14
branch offices, 12-35 to 12-38
    deployment planning and, 2-4
    firewalls, 1-25 to 1-26
    overview of, 12-35
    remote office connectivity, 12-36 to 12-37
    site-to-site VPNs, 12-22
    Web chaining, 5-19, 6-9 to 6-10
    buffer-overflow attacks, 9-3
business
    business needs justifying ISA Server deployment, 2-1
    transaction confidentiality, 1-11

C

CA. *See* certificate authority (CA)
Cache Array Routing Protocol (CARP)
    benefits of, 12-16
    configuring, 12-70
    defined, 12-76
    distributing caching over multiple computers, 6-8
    Enterprise Edition and, 1-18, 12-2, 12-15 to 12-16, 12-69 to 12-70
    how it works, 12-16
    intra-array addressing and, 12-65
    scalability as benefit of, 12-21
    Web caching with, 12-4
cache files, 6-7
cache rules, 6-17 to 6-25
    advanced settings, 6-22
    basic settings, 6-17
    content caching settings, 6-21
    content retrieval settings, 6-20
    creating, 6-18 to 6-19
    defined, 6-41
    disabling and deleting, 6-25
    exercise configuring, 6-26
    exporting and importing, 6-25
    HTTP settings, 6-22
    modifying, 6-24
    rule order, 6-24
caching
    advanced settings, 6-15
    benefits, 6-3
    case scenario questions, 6-45
    case scenarios, 6-39 to 6-40
    configuring, 1-27, 6-29 to 6-30
    content caching for Web servers, 8-5
    content download jobs, 6-5 to 6-7, 6-31 to 6-38
    content restrictions, 6-8
    content settings, 6-15
    default configuration, 3-17
    defined, 6-3
    DNS cache, 2-10, 4-24
    drive configuration, 6-13 to 6-14
    exam objectives, 6-1
    exercise configuring, 6-26
    exercise creating content download job, 6-36
    exercise monitoring, 6-27 to 6-29
    forward caching, 6-5, 6-41
    future of, 6-38 to 6-39
    hardware requirements, 6-2
    how it works, 6-4 to 6-5
    optimizing, 6-7 to 6-8
    overview of, 6-3
    questions and answers, 6-42 to 6-44

reverse caching, 6-5, 6-41
review, 6-11
troubleshooting, 6-25 to 6-26
Web chaining and, 5-19, 6-9 to 6-10
caching servers
  ISA Server as, 1-10
  ISA Server as integrated firewall, proxy, and caching
    server, 1-26 to 1-27
  ISA Server deployed as proxy and caching server, 1-27
    to 1-28
capacity planning, 2-14 to 2-17
  connection bandwidths, 2-15
  firewall policies, 2-15 to 2-16
  overview, 2-14
CARP. *See* Cache Array Routing Protocol (CARP)
.cdat files, 6-14
cell phones, secure connections, 7-25
certificate authority (CA)
  accessing CA Web site, 8-43
  commercial vs. creating own, 8-35
  domain authentication and, 12-30
  Enterprise CA, 8-42
  installing digital certificates on ISA Server, 8-36
  private and public keys, 8-34
  server authentication, 8-33
certificate-based authentication, PPTP, 10-13
Challenge Handshake Authentication Protocol (CHAP),
    10-9
chat rooms, 5-5
cHTML (compact HTML), 9-27
clear text, 9-27
Client for Microsoft Networks
  accessing resources on internal network, 3-7
  SMB/CIFS and, 3-6
clients. *See also* Outlook client connections, Web client
    connections
  authentication, 8-33
  authentication methods for Web listeners, 8-15
  connection settings for Web listeners, 8-15
  deployment planning, 2-5
  digital certificates and, 8-35
  installating and configuring, 1-32
  hostnames, 11-30
  IP addresses, 8-6, 11-29
  network access for remote, 10-5
  Outlook Express, 9-46
  remote VPN clients. *See* remote clients, VPNs
  request filtering, 5-11

SecurID, 8-70
securing connection to Internet, 1-10
session monitoring, 11-29
user names, 11-29
VPN quarantine and, 10-11
Web site access enabled for internal and Internet clients,
    8-7
clients, ISA Server
  authentication, 5-42 to 5-43
  case scenario, 4-46
  case scenario question, 4-51
  choosing, 4-10
  comparing, 4-8
  configuring, 4-12 to 4-15, 4-25 to 4-26
  configuring Firewall clients, 4-33 to 4-39, 4-43
  configuring SecureNAT clients, 4-12 to 4-15, 4-25
  configuring Web Proxy clients, 4-15 to 4-20, 4-25
  Firewall clients, 4-3, 4-4 to 4-5
  guidelines for choosing, 4-9
  installing Firewall Client, 4-28 to 4-33, 4-43
  logging client connections, 4-25
  managing ISA Server client sessions, 11-31
  questions and answers, 4-49
  review, 4-10 to 4-11
  SecureNAT clients, 4-3, 4-5 to 4-7
  troubleshooting Firewall clients, 4-42 to 4-43
  troubleshooting SecureNAT and Web Proxy clients, 4-
    23 to 4-25
  types, 2-39, 4-3
  Web Proxy clients, 4-3, 4-7 to 4-8
client-side script, 10-53 to 10-54, 10-62
cloning ISA Server configuration, 3-28
clusters, NLB, 1-18, 12-4
CMAK. *See* Connection Manager Administration Kit
    (CMAK)
COM (Component Object Model), 7-46
command files, 10-55
  command filters, SMTP, 9-8 to 9-11
  Common.ini file, 4-39 to 4-40
Communication, testing in enterprise networks,
    12-24
compact HTML (cHTML), 9-27
compatibility, Firewall clients with proxy servers,
    4-42
Component Object Model (COM), 7-46
computer sets
  access based on, 7-32
  configuring network objects, 5-37

exercise configuring, 5-39
conditions
    alerts, 11-18
    remote access policies, 10-59
confidentiality
    business transactions, 1-11
    personal data, 1-10
configuration
    Enterprise Edition vs. Standard Edition, 12-3
    exporting and importing settings, 1-20
    scripts,Web Proxy clients, 4-17 to 4-18
    settings stored in Active Directory, 1-20
    storage in Enterprise Edition, 1-17
configuration, clients, 4-12 to 4-24
    exercise configuring client connection logs, 4-25
    exercise configuring Firewall clients, 4-43
    exercise configuring SecureNAT clients, 4-25
    exercise configuring Web Proxy clients, 4-26
    Firewall clients, 4-33 to 4-39
    questions and answers, 4-49
    review, 4-26 to 4-27
    SecureNAT clients, 4-12 to 4-15
    Web Proxy clients, 4-15 to 4-20
Configuration Storage servers
    ADAM and, 12-3, 12-6
    array settings, 12-56
    authentication, 12-61
    back-to-back firewalls and, 12-28
    branch office/main office communication and,
        12-37
    deploying, 12-6 to 12-7, 12-22 to 12-24
    domain and workgroup membership and, 12-4
    domain controllers and, 12-48
    Enterprise Edition deployment and, 12-22 to 12-24
    exercise installing on DC1, 12-49
    exercise installing required user and group accounts, 12-
        49
    mixed workgroup/domain configuration, 12-30
    installation process, 12-45 to 12-48
    ISA Server installation and, 12-60
    replication management, 12-37
    workgroups and, 12-21
Configurerqsforisa.vbs script, 10-57
Connection Manager
    configuring CM profile, 10-64 to 10-66
    configuring VPN clients for quarantine control,
        10-55 to 10-56
    distributing CM profile, 10-56

installing CM profile, 10-66
Connection Manager Administration Kit (CMAK)
    creating Connection Manager profile, 10-52
    installing, 10-64
    VPN quarantine control, 10-11
connection rules, ISA Server, 7-6
connectivity
    dashboard view, 11-5
    dial-up connections, 1-27
    front office and back office, 12-36 to 12-37
    ISA Server Management Console and, 11-4
    monitoring, 1-36
    securing against hackers, 1-6
    securing client connections, 1-10
    securing Internet connections, 1-7, 1-10, 5-3
    troubleshooting network connectivity, 4-24, 11-3
    Web listener configuration, 8-15
connectivity, monitoring, 11-34 to 11-37
    configuring, 11-34
    exercise configuring, 11-36 to 11-37
    review, 11-38 to 11-39
connectivity, verifying
    configuring, 11-35 to 11-37
    defined, 11-61
    types of, 11-34
connectivity, VPN connections
    from client computers, 10-27
    remote-access clients, 10-5, 10-11
    remote-site networks, 10-12
    site-to-site connections, 10-12
    VPN clients network, 10-12
ConnName parameter, Rqc.exe, 10-54
content
    access rule configuration and, 5-33 to 5-34, 5-53
    choosing report content type, 11-50
    configuring content type set, 5-34
    creating new types, 5-33
    exercise configuring content types, 5-38
    filtering at protocol level, 7-47
    inspection with proxy servers, 5-11
    preconfigured types, 5-33
    securing e-mail content, 9-27
    securing e-mail content on wireless devices, 9-28
content caching
    caching rules, 6-21
    configuring, 6-15
    restrictions, 6-8
    retrieval rules, 6-20

Web publishing rules and, 8-5
content download jobs, 6-5 to 6-38
  benefits of, 6-6
  caching, 6-34
  configuring, 6-31 to 6-32
  disabling and deleting, 6-36
  exercise creating, 6-36
  frequency of, 6-32
  how it works, 6-6 to 6-7
  managing, 6-35 to 6-36
  modifying, 6-35
  overview of, 6-5
  questions and answers, 6-44 to 6-45
  review, 6-37 to 6-38
  scheduling, 6-31 to 6-33
  starting and stopping, 6-36
  testing, 6-37
context-sensitive tasks, in ISA Server Managment
      Console, 1-35
Contoso Pharmaceuticals case study, 1-38 to 1-39
credit cards, secure data transfer, 1-10
Custom Installation, ISA Server, 2-22

D

Dashboard nodes, monitoring with, 11-5
data
  defense-in-depth, 3-5
  secure Internet access and, 5-4
  secure transfer over Internet, 1-10
date and time formats, 11-41
dedicated servers, Configuration Storage servers,
      12-23
default configuration, ISA Server, 3-15 to 3-17
default policy, enterprise policies, 12-11
defense-in-depth, 3-3 to 3-5
  components, 7-25
  overview, 3-3
  strategy, 3-4 to 3-5
definitions, alert
  configuring, 11-18
  configuring new, 11-22
  creating new, 11-25
  modifying existing, 11-26
  overview of, 11-17
delegation of rights. *See* distributed administration
demilitarized zones (DMZs), 12-9. *See also* perimeter
      networks
denial-of-service (DoS) attacks

buffer overflow attacks and, 9-3
  responding to, 11-9
deployment planning, 2-3 to 2-18
  availability and fault tolerance, 2-5
  branch office plan, 2-4
  clients, 2-5
  DHCP requirements, 2-12 to 2-13
  DNS requirements, 2-8 to 2-11
  domain controller requirements, 2-11 to 2-12
  Enterprise Edition requirements, 2-14
  exam objectives, 2-1
  firewall policies, 2-15 to 2-16
  hardware requirements, 2-13 to 2-14
  implementation plan, 2-6 to 2-7
  Internet access, 2-5
  Internet connection bandwidth, 2-15
  logging requirements, 2-16
  network infrastructure plan, 2-3 to 2-4
  operating system requirements, 2-13
  overview, 2-3
  questions and answers, 2-40 to 2-41
  redundancy and availability, 2-17
  review, 2-17 to 2-18
  security policies, 2-3
  server publishing, 2-5
  VPN deployment, 2-6
deployment scenarios
  caching and, 6-3
  Web chaining combined with caching, 6-10
destination addresses, 7-3
destination rules, 5-20
DHCP. *See* Dynamic Host Control Protocol (DHCP)
diagnostic services, 3-19
Dial-in permissions, Active Directory, 10-26
dial-up connections
  ISA Server as proxy server, 5-24 to 5-25
  ISA Server support for, 1-27
digest authentication
  certificates, 5-42
  overview of, 5-41
  publishing rules and, 8-5
  support for, 5-43
digital certificates
  certificate-based authentication for VPNs, 10-13
  client computers, 8-35
  enabling SSL and, 8-34
  exercise installing on ISA Server, 8-43

installing on Exchange Server, 9-34
installing on ISA Server, 8-36 to 8-37
PPTP and, 10-7
publishing rules supporting, 8-5
sources for, 8-35
SSL and, 8-34
SSL bridging, 8-35
SSL tunneling, 8-34
troubleshooting, 8-58
disaster recovery, 3-31 to 3-32
disk drives
cache drive configuration, 6-13 to 6-14
disk caching, 6-7
distributed administration, 12-4
DLLs (dynamic link libraries), 2-15, 7-46
DMZs (demilitarized zones), 12-9. *See also* perimeter
networks
DNS. *See* Domain Name System (DNS)
DNSCacheSize registry settings, 2-11
Domain Admins group, 12-48
domain controllers
Active Directory, 12-10
Configuration Storage servers and, 12-48
exercise installing Configuration Storage servers on
DC1, 12-49
ISA Server configuration and, 5-2
network infrastructure requirements, 2-11 to 2-12
domain members
accessing resources on back-end array, 12-35
deploying ISA Server components on, 12-29
ISA Server configuration and, 5-2
Domain Name System (DNS)
ADAM and, 12-6
arrays and, 12-69
automatic discovery, 4-21, 4-23
attack detection, 7-40
automatic name registration, 3-6 to 3-7
DNS cache, 2-10
DNS forwarding, 2-9, 2-39
DNS host name overflow attacks, 7-38
DNS intrusion, 7-38, 11-15
DNS length overflow attacks, 7-38
DNS records, 8-58
DNS zone transfer attacks, 7-39
DNS Servers, external, 2-9 to 2-11
DNS Servers, internal, 2-8 to 2-9
enterprise policies and, 12-13

exercise creating DNS records, 8-9 to 8-10
exercise testing internal access to Web sites, 8-10
implementing split DNS, 8-8
internal interface configuration and, 2-20
ISA Server and, 5-2
lookup rules, 5-56
overview, 2-8
SecureNAT clients and, 4-14 to 4-15
system policies, 3-18
troubleshooting Internet access, 5-55
troubleshooting SecureNAT and Web Proxy clients, 4-
24 to 4-25
troubleshooting VPN connections, 10-29
Web and Server publishing and, 8-6 to 8-10
domain names, 5-37, 5-39
domain parameter, Rqc.exe, 10-54
domains
authentication, 12-30
array configuration and, 12-10
back-to-back firewalls and, 12-28
Configuration Storage servers and, 12-4, 12-23
dial-in access and, 10-26
domain membership vs. stand alone, 2-11
Enterprise Edition configuration, 12-21
Internal network configuration, 4-37
ISA Server deployment options, 12-47
site-to-site VPNs and, 12-22
workgroup/domain mixed configuration, 12-30
DoS. *See* denial-of-service (DoS) attacks
download jobs, 3-19
dynamic addresses, VPN clients, 10-21
Dynamic Host Control Protocol (DHCP)
automatic discovery, 4-21 to 4-23
network infrastructure requirements, 2-12 to 2-13
SecureNAT clients and, 4-13
system policies, 3-18
VPN clients and, 10-20
dynamic link libraries (DLLs), 2-15, 7-46

E
EAP (Extensible Authentication Protocol), 10-9
EAP/TLS (Extensible Authentication Protocol/
Transport Level Security), 10-7
edge firewalls
access and network rules created by, 7-34
applying, 7-30
exercise applying network templates to 7-33

as network template, 7-28
policies, 7-29
EFS (Encrypting File System), 3-5
e-mail. *See also* Exchange Server
    alerts, 11-20
    content security, 9-27
    filters, 9-4
    notification for reports, 11-51
    POP3 and IMAP4 clients, 9-46
    preventing unwanted, 9-18
    receiving, 9-3
    SMTP Message Screener and, 9-8, 9-12
    unwanted or malicious, 9-4 to 9-5
    viruses and worms and, 9-1, 9-5
e-mail servers
    publishing with ISA Server, 1-13 to 1-14
    receiving e-mail via SMTP servers, 9-3
    remote access to 1-7
employees
    Internet access, 5-58
    remote access to internal network resources, 1-7
Encrypting File System (EFS), 3-5
encryption
    EFS and, 3-5
    HTTP packets, 7-48
    server publishing rules, 8-6
    SSL and, 1-12, 8-34, 12-30
    VPNs and, 1-14
    Web publishing rules and, 8-5
End-User License Agreement (EULA), 2-30
Enterprise CAs, 8-36, 8-42
Enterprise Edition
    administrator permissions, 12-50
    array configuration, 12-10, 12-55 to 12-57
    array creation, 12-53
    CARP and, 1-18, 12-15 to 12-16, 12-69 to 12-70
    configuration components, 12-8
    configuration storage, 1-17, 12-5 to 12-7
    deployment, 12-2 to 12-5
    enterprise network configuration, 12-9 to 12-10, 12-51
    enterprise policies, 12-52
    exercise creating and configuring arrays, 12-59 to 12-60
    exercises installing ISA Server, 12-62 to 12-65
    exerice configuring enterprise policies, 12-57 to 12-59
    features, 1-17
    installation requirements, 2-14, 12-43 to 12-44

installing Configuration Storage server, 12-45 to 12-50
    intra-array addressing, 12-65 to 12-67
    ISA Server installation, 12-60 to 12-65
    NLB and, 1-18, 12-13 to 12-14, 12-67 to 12-68
    overview of, 12-1, 12-43
    policies, 12-11 to 12-13
    questions and answers, 12-77 to 12-78, 12-80
    review, 12-17 to 12-18, 12-70 to 12-72
    unattended setup, 12-62
    vs. Standard edition, 1-17 to 1-19
    VPNs and, 12-15
    Web chaining and, 5-17
Enterprise Edition, planning deployment, 12-20 to 12-42
    back-to-back firewalls, 12-27 to 12-35
    branch offices, 12-22, 12-35 to 12-38
    centralized monitoring and management, 12-26 to 12-27
    Configuration Storage servers, 12-22 to 12-24
    deployment scenarios, 12-20
    enterprise and array policies, 12-24 to 12-26
    multiple ISA Server computers in identical roles, 12-20 to 12-21
    questions and answers, 12-78 to 12-79
    review, 12-39 to 12-42
    upgrading from ISA Server 2000 to ISA Server 2004, 12-38
    workgroups, 12-21 to 12-22
enterprise networks
    configuring, 12-9 to 12-10, 12-51
    defined, 12-76
    IP address ranges, 12-8
    predefined, 12-9
    scenarios for using, 12-9
    testing communication in, 12-24
    using temporary enterprise, 12-37

enterprise policies
    applying to arrays, 12-54
    creating, 12-52
    default policy, 12-11
    defined, 12-76
    effectiveness of, 12-12 to 12-13
    exerice configuring, 12-57 to 12-59
    overview of, 12-8
    planning, 12-24
error messages
    installation troubleshooting and, 2-28

publishing rules and, 8-58

reporting to Microsoft, 3-19

EULA (End-User License Agreement), 2-30

event logs, 3-10

Event Viewer, 1-35

events

   alert events, 11-18 to 11-19

   monitoring in real-time, 11-8

   responding to critical events, 11-9

Exchange Server. *See also* Outlook client connections, Web
     client connections

   as e-mail server, 1-13

   case scenarios, 9-49

   configuring Exchange RPC Server, 9-42

   configuring for RPC over HTTP, 9-44

   installing certificate on, 9-34

   local, 1-26

   overview of, 9-1

   prerequisites, 9-2

   RPC application filter, 9-40

   RPC over HTTP, 9-43

   securing SMTP traffic. *See* Simple Mail Transport
     Protocol (SMTP)

   support for wireless devices, 9-27 to 9-28

exporting and importing

   ISA Server configuration, 3-29 to 3-30

   cache rules, 6-25

Extensible Authentication Protocol (EAP), 10-9

Extensible Authentication Protocol/Transport Level
     Security (EAP/TLS), 10-7

Extensions, HTTP filters, 7-54 to 7-56

external interface

   configuring external network interface, 2-21

   securing external Internet interface, 3-6

external networks, 12-32. *See also* perimeter networks

F

failover, Enterprise Edition and, 12-5

fault tolerance, in deployment planning, 2-5

features, new in ISA Server 2004, 1-19 to 1-21

File and Printer Sharing, Microsoft networks, 3-6
     to 3-7

File Transfer Protocol (FTP)

   application filters, 7-47

   content type elements and, 5-33

   disabled during installation, 2-24

   forward caching and, 6-5

   FTP server publishing rules, 8-55 to 8-56

packet direction and, 7-3

SecureNAT clients and, 4-6

troubleshooting SecureNAT and Web Proxy clients, 4-
   24

Web Proxy clients and, 4-5, 4-8

files

   extensions, 1-9

   log formats, 11-45

   logs, 2-16

   saving ISA Server logs to 11-41

   single cache file, 6-7

filters. *See also* Web filters

   application filters, 3-5, 7-7 to 7-8, 7-46 to 7-48

   client request filters, 5-11

   content filters, 7-47

   e-mail filters, 9-4

   HTTP application filters, 8-4

   HTTP Web filters, 2-16

   intrusion detection and, 7-9

   log filters, 11-46

   packet filters, 7-3 to 7-5

   RPC application filters, 9-40

   rules instead of, 2-16

   security inspection with application filters, 2-15

   server publishing rules for application filters, 8-6

   session monitoring filters, 11-32 to 11-33

   SMTP application filters, 9-7, 9-10, 9-55

   Spam filters, 9-18

   stateful filters, 7-5 to 7-7

Firewall Client application

   advanced configuration options, 4-38 to 4-42

   automating installation of, 4-30

   automating Web browser settings, 4-19

   configuring, 4-33 to 4-34

   deploying, 4-10

   exercise installing, 4-43

   installing manually, 4-28 to 4-30

   installing on client computers, 4-4, 4-5

   installing with Group Policy, 4-32

   installing with SMS, 4-32 to 4-33

   modifying settings with ISA Server Management
     Console, 4-19

   publishing servers to Internet, 4-6

   system policies, 3-17, 3-18

   unattended installation, 4-30 to 4-31

   Web Proxy browser configured with, 4-5

Web Proxy client configuration and, 4-20
Winsock and, 4-4
Firewall Client Tools for ISA Server 2004, 4-43
firewall clients
advantages and disadvantages, 4-5
authentication, 5-42
choosing, 4-9 to 4-10
defined, 4-48
DNS and, 2-9
Enterprise Edition and, 12-69
Firewall Client Installation Share, 2-22
installing, 4-28 to 4-33
ISA Server support for, 2-39
overview of, 4-3, 4-4
session monitoring, 11-29
software versions, 2-23 to 2-24
Firewall Server 2004, 7-1
Firewall Service, Configuration Storage servers, 12-7
firewalls. *See also* back-to-back firewalls
access rules, 3-42, 10-20
application filters, 1-9, 7-7 to 7-9
applying firewall policy, 7-18
back-end firewall, 1-24 to 1-25
branch office firewall, 1-25 to 1-26
breaches of, 7-27
chaining, 5-23
client options in ISA Server installation, 2-23
default configuration, 3-16
defined, 1-41
Enterprise Edition vs. Standard Edition, 12-3
Firewall Policy, 12-12
implementing ISA Server as, 5-8
Internet-edge firewall, 1-22 to 1-23
intrusion detection, 7-8
ISA Server as, 1-3
ISA Server as integrated firewall, proxy, and caching
server, 1-26 to 1-28
ISA Server Management Console interface for, 1-35
logging, 11-40
Microsoft Firewall, 2-25
overview, 7-3
packet filtering, 1-8, 7-3 to 7-5
perimeter security, 3-4, 7-24
policies, 2-15 to 2-16, 7-29, 7-32, 8-64, 9-41, 9-47
questions and answers, 7-69 to 7-70
review, 7-9 to 7-11
services, 2-22

stateful filtering, 1-8, 7-5 to 7-6
three-legged configuration, 7-13, 7-26
fixes, security updates, 3-13
flexibility, VPN benefits, 10-6
Flushdns command, ipconfig, 4-24
formats
date and time, 11-41
file format for logs, 11-45
W3C log files, 11-41
MSDE log files, 11-46
forms-based authentication
configuring, 9-30 to 9-33
defined, 9-55
OWA and, 7-48
forward caching
defined, 6-41
overview of, 6-5
scenario, 6-4 to 6-5
forward proxy servers, 5-12 to 5-14
FQDNs (fully qualified domain names), 5-55, 8-6
front-end
arrays, 12-32 to 12-34
network template, 7-28
FTP. *See* File Transfer Protocol (FTP)
Full Installation, ISA Server, 2-21
fully qualified domain names (FQDNs), 5-55, 8-6

G
gateway servers, VPNs, 10-42 to 10-43
GET command, HTTP, 1-9, 11-34
Getting Started page, ISA Server Management Console, 1-
34
GPO (Group Policy Object), 3-12
Group Policy
automating installation of Firewall Client, 4-30, 4-32
configuring Web Proxy clients, 4-10
exercise managing system services, 3-14 to 3-15
Group Policy Object (GPO), 3-12
groups
access rules and, 5-55
Configuration Storage servers, 12-49
creating with Active Directory Users and Computers, 5-
2
Domain Admins and, 12-48
permissions, 1-20

H
hackers, 1-6
hardware requirements

caching, 6-2

deployment planning, 2-13 to 2-14

headers

    HTTP, 7-56 to 7-58

    link translation, 8-22

    packet filtering and, 1-8

    stateful inspection of IP and TCP headers, 1-8

HIDS (host-based intrusion-detection system), 3-5

host-based intrusion-detection system (HIDS), 3-5

HTML (Hypertext Markup Language), 9-27

HTTP filters

    exercises configuring, 7-61 to 7-63

    extensions, 7-54 to 7-56

    headers, 7-56 to 7-58

    methods, 7-52 to 7-54

    options, 7-49 to 7-50

    policy signatures, 7-58 to 7-61

    properties, 7-50 to 7-52

    review, 7-63 to 7-64

    scenarios, 7-49

HTTPS. *See* Hypertext Transfer Protocol Secure (HTTPS)

Hypertext Markup Language (HTML), 9-27

Hypertext Transfer Protocol (HTTP). *See also* RPC over HTTP

    access rules, 5-29

    application filters, 7-7

    cache rules, 6-22

    content type elements, 5-33

    enabling and disabling HTTP connections, 5-16

    enterprise policies and, 12-11, 12-13

    extensions, 7-54 to 7-56

    forward caching and, 6-5

    GET command, 1-9, 11-34

    headers, 7-56 to 7-58

    HTTP 1.1 compliance, 4-7

    methods, 7-52, 7-53 to 7-54

    packets filters, 7-48

    policy signatures, 7-58 to 7-61

    POST command, 1-9

    publishing rules, 8-2, 8-4

    security risks vs. benefits, 5-5

    troubleshooting SecureNAT and Web Proxy clients, 4-24

    verbs, 7-52

    viruses and malicous code, 1-9

    Web filters, 2-16

    Web Proxy clients and, 4-3, 4-5, 4-8

Web publishing rules, 1-11

Hypertext Transfer Protocol Secure (HTTPS)

    enterprise policies and, 12-11, 12-13

    forward caching and, 6-5

    publishing rules and, 8-2, 8-4

    securing e-mail content, 9-27

    security risks vs. benefits, 5-5

    system policy rules for traffic, 11-34

    SecureNAT clients, 4-24

    Web Proxy clients and, 4-5, 4-8, 4-24

I

IAS. *See* Internet Authentication Server (IAS)

ICMP (Internet Control Message Protocol), 3-19, 7-3

ICQ, 5-5

IDS (intrusion detection system), 7-9

IIS. *See* Internet Information Services (IIS)

IKE (Internet Key Exchange), 10-28

IMAP4 clients, 9-46

IMAPS (secure Internet Message Access Protocol), 8-6

implementation, ISA Server

    administration design, 1-31 to 1-32

    minimizing impact of change on users, 2-6

    side-by-side (parallel), 2-6

    testing before deploying, 2-7

    upgrade, 2-7

    user training and, 2-7

importing. *See* exporting and importing

information

    configuration in AD, 1-20

    monitoring long-term, 11-8

    security related, 11-9

    session monitoring and, 11-29

infrastructure. *See* networks, infrastructure

in-place upgrade, 2-33 to 2-34

installing Firewall clients

    exercise, 4-43

    overview of, 4-28 to 4-33

    questions and answers, 4-50

    review, 4-44 to 4-45

installing ISA Server. *See also* upgrade installation

    case scenario questions, 2-42

    case scenarios, 2-37 to 2-38

    exam objectives, 2-1

    exercise installing, 2-29 to 2-30

    exercise verifying, 2-30 to 2-31

    firewall client options, 2-23

installation types, 2-21 to 2-22

internal network IP address configuration, 2-22 to 2-23

network interface configuration, 2-20 to 2-21

overview, 2-19

preparation checklist, 2-19

questions and answers, 2-41

review, 2-31 to 2-32

scenarios, 2-40 to 2-41

services disabled during, 2-24

troubleshooting, 2-28 to 2-29

tasks in, 1-32

unattended installation, 2-26 to 2-28

upgrades, 12-44

verification of successful install, 2-25 to 2-26

with Remote Desktop, 2-24

installing ISA Server clients, 1-32

Integrated Windows authentication, 5-42 to 5-43

internal interfaces. *See also* network interfaces

configuring internal network interface, 2-20

securing internal Internet interface, 3-6 to 3-7

internal networks

Configuration Storage servers deployed on, 12-24

configuring multiple, 7-14

default configuration, 3-16

domain configuration, 4-37

firewall protection, 1-8

hiding with proxy servers, 5-12

hiding with Web publishing rules, 1-12

IP address configuration, 2-22 to 2-23, 4-37

ISA Server deployment and, 1-5

network connectivity and, 7-25

publishing rules and, 8-4

resource access, 1-7

resource access on back-end arrays, 12-33, 12-35

security of, 3-4

SSL for publishing network servers, 12-33

Web browser settings, 4-18 to 4-20

Web site access enabled for internal clients, 8-7

internal servers, remote access to, 1-4

Internet

access in deployment planning, 2-5

access in network configuration, 3-16

authenticating Internet requests, 5-44

benefits and hazards of, 1-6

connection bandwidths, 2-15

organizations providing employee access to, 1-4

as public network, 1-4

routing Internet requests with SecureNAT clients, 4-12 to 4-13

securing access to, 1-9 to 1-11

securing client connections, 1-10

securing data transferred over, 1-10

security policies, 1-7

server protection and, 7-24

testing access to, 7-35

user access, 1-7, 1-10, 1-32

Web site access for Internet clients, 8-7

Internet Authentication Server (IAS)

installing and configuring, 8-71

quarantine control and, 10-59, 10-60

Remote Access Policies, 8-72

Windows servers, 10-10

Internet Connection Firewall, 2-24

Internet Connection Sharing, 2-24

Internet Control Message Protocol (ICMP), 3-19, 7-3

Internet Explorer

Web Proxy configuration and, 4-10, 4-16 to 4-20

Windows Integrated authentication and, 5-43

Internet Information Services (IIS)

Admin service disabled during installation, 2-24

OWA virtual directories and, 9-34

SMTP Message Screener and, 9-12

Web filters and, 7-48

Internet Key Exchange (IKE), 10-28

Internet Protocol (IP)

intrusion detection for IP attacks, 7-37 to 7-38

configuring IP options, 7-42

packet filters and, 7-3

preferences, 7-40 to 7-45

routing, 7-41, 7-43

spoofing, 7-4, 11-15

stateful inspection of IP headers, 1-8

Internet Protocol Security (IPSec)

advanced configuration, 10-39

encrypted traffic, 7-27

guidelines for choosing, 10-35

L2TP and, 10-7

troubleshooting VPN connections, 10-28

tunnel mode, 1-26, 10-35

VPN connections, 10-13

Internet Security and Acceleration Server. *See* ISA Server

Internet usage policy, 5-5 to 5-7

case scenarios, 5-61

components of, 5-6

defined, 5-65
guidelines, 5-6 to 5-7
implementing with ISA Server, 5-8
Internet-edge firewalls, 1-22 to 1-23
intrusion detection
    alerts, 11-15, 11-23
    application layer, 7-38 to 7-39
    configuration, 7-37 to 7-40
    defined, 7-68
    exercise configuring, 7-43
    exercise testing, 7-43
    IP level, 7-37 to 7-38
    ISA Server and, 7-9
    overview of, 7-8
    process of, 7-39
    questions and answers, 7-72 to 7-73
    review, 7-44 to 7-45
intrusion detection system (IDS), 7-9
IP. *See* Internet Protocol (IP)
IP addresses
    adding to internal network, 2-23
    address spoofing attacks, 7-4, 11-15
    assigning to internal network, 2-23
    assignments for VPN clients, 10-20 to 10-23
    computer clusters and, 12-4
    configuring for Internal network, 4-37
    configuring for internal network, 2-22 to 2-23
    configuring ISA Server to assign, 10-21
    configuring using network template, 7-31
    dynamic, 10-21
    enterprise networks and, 12-8, 12-9, 12-51
    enterprise-level administration of, 12-9
    intra-array addressing, 12-67
    logging client computers, 8-6
    multiple Web sites and, 8-5
    packet filtering and, 7-4
    ranges of private IP addresses, 2-20
    SecureNAT clients and, 4-3
    static, 10-21
    troubleshooting Internet access, 5-55
    VPN remote sites, 10-38
    Web publishing rules and, 8-29
IP fragments
    configuring, 7-42
    IP preferences, 7-40
    packet filtering for IP fragement attacks, 7-4
IP preferences, 7-40 to 7-45

configuring, 7-41
IP fragments, 7-40
IP option, 7-40
IP routing, 7-41
questions and answers, 7-72 to 7-73
review, 7-44 to 7-45
Ipconfig command, 4-24
IPSec. *See* Internet Protocol Security (IPSec)
ISA Server
    arrays. *See* arrays
    authentication, 8-66
    default services, 11-12
    digital certificates, 8-36 to 8-37
    editions, 1-17 to 1-21
    Enterprise Edition. *See* Enterprise Edition
    enterprises, 12-8
    exercises installing, 12-62 to 12-65
    as firewall, 1-7 to 1-9
    how it works, 1-4 to 1-7
    installation overview, 12-44
    Internet access security, 1-9 to 1-11
    IP addresses, 10-21
    ISA Server 2000 compared with ISA Server 2004, 1-19
        to 1-21
    ISA Server 2000, Service Pack 1 (SP1), 2-33
    log types, 11-42
    Microsoft Firewall Server 2004 and, 7-1
    monitoring, 11-8
    overview of, 1-4, 1-17
    OWA enabled, 9-28 to 9-30
    as proxy server. *See* proxy servers
    performance monitoring, 11-10 to 11-11
    publishing. *See* publishing
    publishing e-mail servers with, 1-13 to 1-14
    questions and answers, 1-42 to 1-43
    RADIUS and, 10-24
    resource publishing, 1-11 to 1-13
    review, 1-15 to 1-16, 1-21
    RPC over HTTP, 9-45
    security. *See* securing ISA Server
    service monitoring, 11-12
    SMTP service, 9-5, 9-21
    Standard Edition. *See* Standard Edition
    Standard Edition compared with Enterprise Edition, 1-
        17 to 1-19
    as VPN Server, 1-14 to 1-15, 10-11 to 10-12
ISA Server, administering, 1-31 to 1-37

administrative roles, 12-27
client configuration, 1-32
implementation design, 1-31 to 1-32
installing and securing ISA Server, 1-32
Internet access, 1-32
ISA Server Management Console, 1-34 to 1-35
monitoring, 1-33, 1-35 to 1-36
overview, 1-31
questions and answers, 1-44 to 1-45
review, 1-36 to 1-37
VPN access, 1-33
ISA Server, deploying, 1-22 to 1-30
   as back-end firewall, 1-24 to 1-25
   as branch office firewall, 1-25 to 1-26
   as integrated firewall, proxy, and caching server, 1-26 to
      1-27
   as Internet-edge firewall, 1-22 to 1-23
   as proxy and caching server, 1-27 to 1-28
   case scenario, 1-37 to 1-39
   case scenario question, 1-45
   overview of, 1-22
   questions and answers, 1-43 to 1-44
   review, 1-29 to 1-30
ISA Server, maintaining, 3-28 to 3-37
   backing up and restoring configuration, 3-31
      to 3-32
   exercise using ISA Management Console for remote
      administration, 3-34 to 3-35
   exercise using Remote Desktop for remote
      administration, 3-35 to 3-36
   exporting and importing configuration, 3-28
      to 3-30
   overview, 3-28
   questions and answers, 3-45 to 3-46
   remote administration, 3-32 to 3-34
   review, 3-36 to 3-37
ISA Server Administrator, 12-27
ISA Server Array Auditor, 12-27
ISA Server Array Monitoring Auditor, 12-27
ISA Server Basic Monitoring, 3-21
ISA Server Control, 2-25
ISA Server Enterprise Administrator, 12-26
ISA Server Enterprise Auditor, 12-26
ISA Server Extended Monitoring, 3-21
ISA Server Full Administrator, 3-21
ISA Server Job Scheduler, 2-25
ISA Server Management Console

access rules, 5-49
administration, 1-34 to 1-35
alerts, 11-16
cache drive configuration, 6-13
client connection logging, 4-25
client session monitoring, 11-30
Configuration Storage servers and, 12-7
content download jobs, 6-31, 6-36 to 6-37
Dashboard nodes, 11-5
enterprise policies, 12-52
exporting and importing configuration, 3-30
Firewall Client application, 4-19, 4-33, 4-36 to 4-37
intrusion detection, 7-39
IP address assignments, 10-21
monitoring, 11-4, 11-8, 1-35
network configuration, 5-15
NLB configuration, 12-14
protocol creation, 5-31
remote administration, 3-33 to 3-35, 12-26
Remote Management Computers, 3-34
VPN authentication, 10-23
Web Proxy clients, 4-7
ISA Server Manager, 12-8
ISA Server Migration Wizard, 2-34
ISA Server Performance Monitor, 11-10
ISA Server Storage, 2-25
Isaautorun.exe, 12-45
ISALOG_yyyymmdd_FWS_nnn.iis, 11-45
ISALOG_yyyymmdd_FWS_nnn.w3c, 11-45

J
junk mail filters, 9-4

K
keyword option, SMTP Message Screener, 9-14

L
LANs (local area networks), 1-4
languages, array configuration, 12-10
LATs (local address tables), 4-38 to , 4-39
Layer Two Tunneling Protocol (L2TP)
   guidelines for choosing L2TP/IPSec, 10-35
   overview of L2TP/IPSec, 10-7
   PPTP compared with L2TP/IPSec, 10-8
   RRAS and, 2-35
   troubleshooting VPN connections, 10-28
   tunneling protocols supported by ISA Server, 1-26
   VPNs and, 10-4, 10-13

LDAP. *See* Lightweight Directory Access Protocol (LDAP)

licenses, EULA, 2-30

Lightweight Directory Access Protocol (LDAP)
ADAM and, 12-6

member servers and, 2-11

network connectivity and, 11-34

link directories, Web publishing rules, 8-23

link translation
configuring, 8-22

defined, 8-79

levels, 8-22

overview of, 8-21

Web publishing rules and, 8-5

LMHOSTS lookup, 3-6

load balancing, 12-21. *See also* network load balancing (NLB)

local address table (LAT), 4-38 to 4-39

local area network (LAN), 1-4

Local Host, 3-16

Local Host Access, 3-16

locales, array configuration, 12-10

logs. *See also* server logs
access rules and, 5-56

alert actions, 11-20

application filters, 7-47

application logs, 2-29

array configuration and, 12-10

client connection logs, 4-25

configuring ISA Server logging, 10-25

configuring log filters, 11-46

configuring log summaries, 11-49

defined, 11-61

deployment planning, 2-16

file formats, 11-45

file logging, 2-16

Firewall clients and, 4-5

installation logs, 2-29

IP address logs, 8-6

ISA Server Management Console, 11-4

monitoring, 1-36

MSDE logs, 2-16

report summary database, 11-48

system policies, 3-19

user access logs, 5-12

long-term information, monitoring, 11-8

M

Mail Exchanger (MX) records, 9-19

MAIL FROM command, SMTP, 9-10, 9-12

Mail Server Wizard, 9-6 to 9-7

mail servers. *See* Simple Mail Transport Protocol (SMTP)

malicous code, HTTP, 1-9

malicious content, 5-4

malicious e-mail, SMTP, 9-5

malicious software (malware), 9-1, 10-54

malicious traffic, 1-11

malicious users, 7-39

management. *See also* ISA Server Management Console
enterprise networks, 12-26 to 12-27

manageability as reason for deploying Enterprise Edition, 12-5

management.ini file, 4-39 to 4-40

managers, Internet access rule for, 5-57

MAPI. *See* Messaging Application Programming Interface (MAPI)

Maximum Transmission Units (MTUs), 10-28, 10-44

member servers, LDAP, 2-11

Message Digest 5 (MD5), 10-9

Message Screener. *See* SMTP Message Screener

Messaging Application Programming Interface (MAPI)
as Outlook client, 9-38

RPC application filters, 9-40

vulnerabilities, 9-39

Microsoft
error reporting, 3-19

Exchange Server. *See* Exchange Server

File And Printer Sharing, 3-6 to 3-7

Firewall, 2-25

Firewall Client, 4-43

Firewall Control, 12-7, 12-65, 12-76

Firewall Server 2004, 7-1

Firewall Storage, 12-7, 12-24, 12-76

Internet Security and Acceleration Security Center, 3-13

ISA Server Control, 2-25

ISA Server Job Scheduler, 2-25

ISA Server Storage, 2-25

OMA. *See* Outlook Mobile Access (OMA)

OWA. *See* Outlook Web Access (OWA)

Security Bulletin Search, 3-13

Security Notification Service, 3-12

Security Web site, 3-13

SharePoint Portal Server, 1-26

System Mangement Server (SMS), 4-30

Windows. *See* Windows

Microsoft CHAP (MS-CHAP), 10-9
Microsoft CHAP Version 2 (MS-CHAP v2), 10-7
Microsoft Data Engine (MSDE)
    database logging, 11-40
    logging, 2-16, 11-46
    security updates, 3-12
migration. *See* upgrade installation
MIME (Multipurpose Internet Mail Extensions), 5-33 to
    5-34
mobile clients, 7-25
monitoring. *See also* session monitoring
    administration, 1-35 to 1-36
    caching, 6-27 to 6-29
    components for, 1-36, 11-4 to 11-5
    dashboard, 1-34, 11-5
    enterprise networks, 12-26 to 12-27
    Enterprise Edition computers, 12-21
    Event Viewer and, 1-35
    ISA Server, 1-33
    ISA Server Management Console, 1-34 to 1-35
    long-term information, 11-8
    options, 1-36
    overview, 1-35, 11-3
    planning strategy for, 11-6
    prerequisites, 11-2
    questions and answers, 11-62 to 11-63
    real-time information, 11-8
    reasons for implementing, 11-3
    remotely, 3-19
    response strategy, 11-9
    review, 11-12 to 11-14
    scenario question, 11-66
    security updates, 3-12
    services, 11-12
    server performance, 1-35, 11-10 to 11-11
    vulnerabilities, 7-9
    Msisaund.ini file, 2-26 to 2-28
MS-Quarantine to IPFilter setting, 10-60
MS-Quarantine to Session-Timeout, 10-60
MSSQL$MSFW, 2-25
MSSQLServerADHelper, 2-25
MTUs (Maximum Transmission Units), 10-28, 10-44
multiple networks, 7-12 to 7-23
    configuration options, 7-12 to 7-14
    default networks enabled in ISA Server, 7-15
    exercises, 7-20
    ISA Server support for, 7-12
    network objects, 7-16 to 7-17

network rules, 7-17 to 7-18
    overview of, 7-12
    questions and answers, 7-70 to 7-71
    review, 7-22 to 7-23
Multipurpose Internet Mail Extensions (MIME), 5-33 to
    5-34
MX (Mail Exchanger) records, 9-19

N

name resolution. *See also* Domain Name System (DNS)
    DNS service, 2-8
    SecureNAT clients, 4-12, 4-14 to 4-15
    troubleshooting SecureNAT and Web Proxy clients, 4-
        24 to 4-25
    troubleshooting VPN connections, 10-28
    VPN clients, 10-23
NAT. *See* Network Address Translation (NAT)
negative cache, DNS, 2-10
NetBIOS, 3-19
NetBIOS over TCP/IP, 3-6, 3-7
Netstat utility, 8-58
network adapters, 2-23, 12-10
Network Address Translation (NAT)
    disabled during installation, 2-24
    internal interface configuration and, 2-20
    network rules and, 7-17
    SecureNAT. *See* SecureNat
network interface card (NIC), 1-23
network interfaces
    configuring in ISA Server installation, 2-20 to 2-21
network interfaces *continued*
    exercise securing, 3-14
    securing external Internet interfaces, 3-6
    securing internal Internet interfaces, 3-6 to 3-7
network layer, intrusion detection at, 7-9
network load balancing (NLB)
    balancing network traffic, 12-16, 12-21
    benefits of, 12-13
    defined, 12-76
    Enterprise Edition and, 1-8, 12-2, 12-13 to 12-14, 12-67
        to 12-69
    failover and, 12-5
    integrating with ISA Server, 12-4, 12-14
    intra-array addressing and, 12-65
    redundancy and, 12-21
    VPNs and, 12-15
Network News Transfer Protocol (NNTP), 2-24
network objects, 5-35 to 5-37
    back-to-back firewalls, 12-34

creating and modifying, 7-16 to 7-17
  enterprise policy and, 12-8
network packets, 1-5
network perimeter. *See also* perimeter networks
  access points, 1-7
  defense-in-depth strategy, 3-4
  firewalls deployed at, 1-8
  securing, 1-4, 1-7
Network Quarantine Service, 10-56, 10-62
network routing, on front-end array, 12-32
network rules
  applying, 7-18 to 7-19
  creating new, 7-19 to 7-20
  defined, 7-68
  exercise configuring, 7-21
  VPN remote clients, 10-20
  VPN remote sites, 10-41
network sets, 5-37
Network Template Wizard
  exporting firewall settings, 7-30
  implementing network templates, 7-29
  overview of, 7-28
network templates, 7-28 to 7-35
  defined, 7-68
  exercise applying Edge Firewall, 7-33 to 7-34
  implementing, 7-29 to 7-32
  in ISA Server Management Console, 1-35
  modifying access rules applied by, 7-32 to 7-33
  provided by ISA Server, 1-27
  questions and answers, 7-71 to 7-72
  review, 7-35 to 7-36
  stored in XML files, 7-28
  testing Internet access, 7-35
  types of, 7-28
Network Time Protocol (NTP), 3-18
network traffic. *See also* SMTP traffic
  balancing with NLB, 12-16, 12-21
  blocking malicious traffic, 1-11
  enrypted with IPSec, 7-27
  filtering, 1-7
  firewalls and, 7-3
  monitoring, 11-3
  redirecting to internal servers, 1-11
  system policies, 11-34
networks
  access policies and rules, 1-19, 7-17 to 7-18, 10-5, 10-46
  configuration options, 7-12 to 7-14

Contoso Pharmaceuticals case study, 1-38 to 1-39
  creating and modifying network objects, 7-16
       to 7-17
  default configuration, 3-16
  default networks enabled in ISA Server, 7-15
  enterprise. *See* enterprise networks
  exercise configuring, 7-21
  external, 12-32
  internal. *See* internal networks
  monitoring traffic, 11-3
  multiple. *See* multiple networks
  multiple network support, 1-19, 7-12
  network rules, 7-17 to 7-20
  network objects, 5-35 to 5-37
  open vs. controlled communication between, 10-41
  perimeter. *See* perimeter networks
  relationship settings, 3-16
  remote sites, 10-45
  SecureNAT client settings, 4-13
  site-to-site. *See* site-to-site VPNs
  speed as consideration in deploying Configuration
       Storage servers, 12-24
  system policies, 3-18
  troubleshooting connectivity, 11-3
  types of, 7-16

networks, connectivity
  internal networks and, 7-25
  troubleshooting, 4-24, 11-3
  verifying, 11-34
networks, infrastructure
  deployment planning and, 2-3
  DHCP service, 2-12 to 2-13
  DNS service, 2-8 to 2-11
  domain controller requirements, 2-11 to 2-12
  modifying, 11-4
  planning, 2-4
  services required, 2-7
  VPNs, 10-13 to 10-14
nework option, Web listeners, 8-15
NIC (network interface card), 1-23
NLB. *See* network load balancing (NLB)
NNTP (Network News Transfer Protocol), 2-24
NSLookup, 4-24
NTP (Network Time Protocol), 3-18

O

objects
  caching, 6-8
  network objects, 5-35 to 5-37
  performance objects, 11-10
Office Web Components 2002 (OWC), 3-12
operating systems
  deployment planning, 2-13
  security in defense-in-depth, 3-5
  security updates and, 3-12
organizations
  Internet access provided by, 1-4
  Internet access requirements of small organizations, 1-27
  large organizations deploying Enterprise Edition, 12-1
  secure Internet access and, 5-5
outbound traffic, SMTP, 9-20
Outlook, as Exchange Server client, 1-14
Outlook 2003, 9-45
Outlook client connections, 9-38 to 9-49
  exercises configuring, 9-47 to 9-48
  how RPC application filter works, 9-40
  known security issues, 9-39
  overview of, 9-38
  POP3 and IMAP4 clients, 9-46
  publishing rules, 9-41, 9-47
  questions and answers, 9-58
  review, 9-48
  RPC Server protocol, 9-42
  RPC over HTTP, 9-43 to 9-46
Outlook Express, 9-46
Outlook Mobile Access (OMA)
  client access to Exchange Server, 1-14
  configuring, 9-33
  as mobile service component, 9-27
Outlook Web Access (OWA)
  accessing secure Web sites, 9-51 to 9-53
  client access to Exchange Server, 1-14
  defined, 9-55
  enabling, 9-28 to 9-30
  exercises configuring, 9-34 to 9-36
  features and security, 9-26
  forms-based authentication, 7-48, 9-55
  Outlook clients compared with, 9-39
  publishing rules, 9-29
  SSL required on virtual directories, 9-34
  testing access to OWA sites, 9-53

OMA. *See* Outlook Mobile Access (OMA)
OWA. *See* Outlook Web Access (OWA)
OWC (Office Web Components) 2002, 3-12

P

packet filters, 7-3 to 7-5
  advantages and disadvantages, 7-4
  criteria for evaluating IP packets, 7-3
  defined, 7-68
  IP, 2-34
  ISA Server 2004 and, 7-4
  overview of, 1-8
packet sniffers, 1-5
packets. *See* network packets
PAP (Password Authentication Protocol), 10-9
partitions, array configuration, 12-10
pass-through authentication, 8-79
Password Authentication Protocol (PAP), 10-9
password authentiction, VPN clients, 10-13
patches, security, 3-13
path mapping
  configuring, 8-20
  defined, 8-79
  how it works, 8-19
  overview of, 8-19
  Web publishing rules, 8-4
PDAs (personal digital assistants), 9-27
peer-to-peer file sharing, 5-5
performance
  caching and, 6-3
  collecting performance-related information, 11-9
  dashboard view, 11-5
  improving Internet access, 5-12
  ISA Server Management Console, 11-4
  monitoring, 1-36, 11-10 to 11-11
  objects, 11-10
Performance Monitor, 11-8 to 11-9
perimeter network interface, 2-21
perimeter networks. *See also* network perimeter
  back-to-back firewalls and, 12-34
  benefits of, 7-25
  characteristics of, 7-24 to 7-25
  configuration options, 7-26 to 7-27
  configuring multiple, 7-14
  firewall protection, 1-8
  front-end arrays and, 12-32
  IP addresses in, 12-9
  overview of, 7-24

publishing rules and, 8-4
questions and answers, 7-71 to 7-72
resource access on, 12-32
review, 7-35 to 7-36
SSL publishing for network servers, 12-33
permissions
administrator, 12-50
dial-in, 10-26
remote access, 10-59
secure Internet access and, 5-4
user and group, 1-20
VPN remote clients, 10-18
personal digital assistants (PDAs), 9-27
physical security, in defense-in-depth strategy, 3-4
ping
connectivity verification, 11-34
DNS name resolution and, 5-55
PKI (Public Key Infrastructure), 8-34
Point-to-Point Tunneling Protocol (PPTP), 1-26
certificate-based authentication, 10-13
compared with L2TP/IPSec, 10-8
guidelines for choosing, 10-35
overview of, 10-7
RRAS and, 2-35
VPNS and, 10-4
policies. *See also* security policies
array, 12-8, 12-25, 12-57
enterprise, 12-8, 12-24
Enterprise Edition, 12-11 to 12-13
firewall, 7-18
Internet access, 5-5 to 5-9
network access, 1-19
planning, 12-24 to 12-25
quarantine control, 10-50
remote-access for VPNs, 10-20
POP. *See* Post Office Protocol (POP)
Port Scan, 7-39
ports
checking with Netstat utility, 8-58
numbers, 7-4, 8-5, 8-15, 8-17
port override options for server publishing rules, 8-48, 8-50
TCP/UDP, 7-4
POST command, HTTP, 1-9
Post Office Protocol (POP)
intrusion detection and, 7-38
POP buffer overflow attacks, 7-39

POP3 clients, 9-46
secure publishing rules, 8-6
PPTP. *See* Point-to-Point Tunneling Protocol (PPTP)
private computers, OWA forms-based authentication, 9-32
private Web sites, 1-7
production environment, deploying security updates in, 3-13
profiles, remote access, 10-59
protected network. *See* internal network
protocol-level exploits, SMTP security issues, 9-3
protocols
access rule configuration, 5-51
access rule elements, 5-30 to 5-31
Exchange RPC Server protocol, 9-42
intrusion detection at protocol level, 7-47
ISA Server and, 1-13, 1-20
network templates and, 7-32
secure Internet access and, 5-4
server publishing rules and, 8-5, 8-50
VPN remote clients, 10-20
proxy requests, 8-27
proxy servers, 5-11 to 5-28
caching and, 6-1
compatibility with Firewall clients, 4-42
configuration, 5-15 to 5-17
defined, 1-41
dial-up connections, 5-24 to 5-25
DNS, 2-9
exercise configuring ISA Server as proxy server, 5-26
exercise configuring Web Chaining, 5-26
firewall chaining rules, 5-23
forward proxy servers, 5-12 to 5-14
functions of, 5-11 to 5-12
how they work, 5-12 to 5-15
implementing, 5-8
ISA Server as, 1-10
ISA Server as integrated firewall, proxy, and caching server, 1-26 to 1-27
ISA Server computer as, 4-15
ISA Server deployed as proxy and caching server, 1-27 to 1-28
overview, 5-11
questions and answers, 5-66
reverse proxy servers, 5-14
review, 5-27 to 5-28
Web chaining, 5-17 to 5-22

public computers, OWA forms-based authentication, 9-31

Public Key Infrastructure (PKI), 8-34

public names, Web publishing rules, 8-26

public networks, 1-4

public Web sites

  anonymous access, 1-7

  organization providing access to 1-11

publishing

  checking publishing rule configuration, 8-58

  digital certificates on ISA Server, 8-36 to 8-37

  DNS configured for Web and Server publishing, 8-6 to 8-10

  default configuration, 3-16

  exercise configuring Secure Web publishing rules, 8-42 to 8-45

  link translation, 8-21 to 8-23

  overview, 8-4

  path mapping, 8-19 to 8-21

  planning for, 2-5

  questions and answers, 8-81

  review, 8-11 to 8-12

  resources. *See* resource publishing

  Secure Web publishing rules, 8-33 to 8-34

  server publishing rules, 8-5 to 8-6

  servers to Internet, 4-6

  SSL enabled on ISA Server, 8-34 to 8-36

  SSL bridging, 8-37 to 8-38

  SSL tunneling, 8-39

  Web listeners, 8-14 to 8-19

  Web publishing rules, 8-4 to 8-5, 8-13 to 8-14, 8-39 to 8-41

publishing rules

  checking configuration of publishing rules, 8-58

  exercise configuring Secure Web publishing rules, 8-42 to 8-45

  network access and, 7-33

  OWA, 9-29, 9-35, 9-36

  RPC, 9-41, 9-47

  Secure Web publishing rules, 8-33 to 8-34

  server publishing rules, 8-5 to 8-6

  SMTP, 9-23

  Web publishing rules, 8-4 to 8-5, 8-13 to 8-14, 8-39 to 8-41

Q

quarantine control, VPNs, 10-50 to 10-69

  client-side script for, 10-53 to 10-54

  configuring VPN clients with Connection Manager, 10-55 to 10-56

  defined, 10-72

  enabling, 10-63

  enforcing remote access policies, 10-10

  Enterprise Edition support of, 12-15

  exercises configuring, 10-61 to 10-67

  how to enable, 10-57 to 10-59

  IAS for, 10-59 to 10-60

  implementing with ISA Server, 10-51 to 10-52

  integration and, 1-20

  listener component, 10-56 to 10-57

  questions and answers, 10-76

  review, 10-67 to 10-69

  testing, 10-66

  VPN client access rules, 10-60 to 10-61

  what it is, 10-50 to 10-51

quarantined VPN clients network, 10-12, 10-72

questions and answers

  access rule elements, 5-67

  access rules for Internet, 5-69

  alerts, 11-63

  application filters, 7-73

  authentication, 5-68, 8-84

  caching, 6-42, 6-43 to 6-44

  client configuration, 4-49

questions and answers *continued*

  clients, ISA Server, 4-49

  content download jobs, 6-44 to 6-45

  deployment planning, 2-40 to 2-41, 12-78 to 12-79

  Enterprise Edition, 12-77 to 12-80

  firewalls, 7-69 to 7-70

  Firewall clients, 4-50

questions and answers *continued*

  intrusion detection, 7-72 to 7-73

  IP preferences, 7-72 to 7-73

  ISA Server, 1-42 to 1-45, 2-41

  maintaining ISA Server, 3-45 to 3-46

  monitoring, 11-62 to 11-63

  multiple networking, 7-70 to 7-71

  network templates, 7-71 to 7-72

  Outlook clients, 9-58

  perimeter networks, 7-71 to 7-72

  proxy servers, 5-66

  publishing, 8-81

  quarantine control, VPNs, 10-76

remote clients, VPNs, 10-73 to 10-74

remote sites, VPNs, 10-75

reports, 11-65 to 11-66

secure access to Internet, 5-66

secure Web publishing rules, 8-82

securing ISA Server, 3-43 to 3-45

server logging, 11-65 to 11-66

server publishing rules, 8-83

session monitoring, 11-64 to 11-65

SMTP traffic, 9-56

upgrade installation, 2-41

VPNs, 10-73

Web clients, 9-57

Web filters, 7-73

Web Publishing rules, 8-82

R

RADIUS. *See* Remote Authentication Dial-In User Service (RADIUS)

RAM, 6-7

RDP (Remote Desktop Protocol), 8-56

real-time block list (RBL), 9-18

real-time information, monitoring, 11-8

recovery, of cached objects, 6-8

redundancy

    Configuration Storage servers providing, 12-23

    deployment planning, 2-17

    Enterprise Edition and, 12-5

    NLB and, 12-21

remote access

    e-mail servers, 1-7

    employees to internal network resources, 1-7

    permissions, 10-59

    users to internal servers, 1-4

    VPNs, 1-14

remote access policies

    conditions, 10-59

    dial-in access, 10-26

    IAS, 8-72

    VPNs, 10-10

    VPN clients, 10-20

remote administration

    branch office connectivity, 12-36 to 12-37

    exercise preparing workstation for, 3-39 to 3-40

    exercise using ISA Server Management Console for, 3-34 to 3-35

    maintaining ISA Server, 3-32 to 3-34

    Remote Desktop, 3-35 to 3-36, 12-26

    troubleshooting, 3-40

Remote Authentication Dial-In User Service (RADIUS)

    authentication, 1-12, 2-11, 7-48, 8-67 to 8-69

    authentication server for VPNs, 10-10

    clients, 8-67

    configuring ISA Server to use, 8-68, 10-24

    defined, 8-80

    exercise configuring ISA Server for, 8-71

    publishing rules supporting, 8-5

    servers, 8-67

    system policies, 3-18

    testing, 8-73

    VPN connections, 10-14

remote clients, VPNs, 10-16 to 10-32

    access configuration, 10-11, 10-16

    connections, 10-27

    default access configuration, 10-19

    exercises configuring, 10-29 to 10-30

    network access for, 10-5

    permissions, 10-18

    questions and answers, 10-73 to 10-74

    review, 10-30

    user mapping, 10-19

Remote Desktop

    installing ISA Server, 2-24

    remote administration, 3-32, 3-35 to 3-36, 12-26

Remote Desktop Protocol (RDP), 8-56

Remote Management Computers

    defined, 3-42

    ISA Server Management Console and, 3-34

remote monitoring, system policies, 3-19

Remote Procedure Call (RPC). *See also* RPC over HTTP

    application filters, 9-40

    Configuration Storage servers and, 12-7

Remote Procedure Call (RPC) *continued*

    Exchange Server client connections and, 1-14

    intra-array communication and, 12-65

    ISA Server computers communicating over, 12-24

    RPC publishing rules, 9-47

    server publishing rules, 8-52 to 8-55

remote sites, VPNs, 10-33 to 10-49

    access rules, 10-41

    creating, 10-36

    configuring, 10-19

    defined, 10-72

    exercises configuring, 10-44 to 10-47

    gateway servers, 10-42 to 10-43

    IP address ranges, 10-38

network rules, 10-41

questions and answers, 10-75

remote site networks, 10-12, 10-36 to 10-39

review, 10-47 to 10-49

site-to-site VPNs, 10-33 to 10-34, 10-39

replication

ADAM, 12-38

managing with Configuration Storage servers, 12-37

reports. *See also* monitoring

content, 11-47, 11-50

configuring, 11-48 to 11-54

dashboard view, 11-5

defined, 11-61

e-mail notification, 11-51

exercises configuring, 11-54

generating, 11-49, 11-54

how they work, 11-48

ISA Server Management Console and, 11-4

log summary database for, 11-48

monitoring, 1-36

planning strategy for, 11-6

publishing, 11-53

questions and answers, 11-65 to 11-66

recurring, 11-52, 11-54

review, 11-55 to 11-57

usage reports, 11-9

viewing, 11-51

Request for Comment (RFC), 9-10

request scanning, Web filters, 7-48

reset registered alerts, 11-24

Resource Kit, ISA Server, 12-38

resource publishing

e-mail server publishing, 1-13 to 1-14

overview of, 1-11

server publishing rules, 1-13

Web publishing rules, 1-11 to 1-13

resources

accessing between branch and main offices, 1-7

accessing non-Web-based, 1-11

checking availability, 8-58

selective access to internal, 1-3

response scanning, Web filters, 7-48

response strategy, security, 11-9

restore, ISA Server configuration, 3-31

restrictions, Internet access, 5-8 to 5-9

reverse cache

defined, 6-41

DNS, 2-10

overview of, 6-5

reverse proxy servers, 5-14

RFC (Request for Comment), 9-10

roles

administrator role for enterprise networks, 12-50

assigning ISA Server, 12-30

roll back, ISA Server configuration, 3-29

route, network relationships, 7-17

Routing and Remote Access Service (RRAS)

migrating RRAS VPNs to ISA Server, 2-35

remote site connections, 10-44

VPN clients and, 10-11

VPN functionality of, 10-12

VPN tunnels, 12-36

routing Internet requests, with SecureNAT clients, 4-12 to 4-13

RPC. *See* Remote Procedure Call (RPC)

RPC over HTTP

case scenario question, 9-59

configuring Exchange Server 2003 for, 9-44

configuring ISA Server for, 9-45

configuring Outlook 2003 for, 9-45

overview, 9-43

requirements, 9-43

Rqc.exe, 10-54.

Rqs.exe, 10-56, 10-62

RRAS. *See* Routing and Remote Access Service (RRAS)

RSA. *See* SecurID

rules. *See also* policies

access. *See* access rules

enterprise-level, 12-9

filters compared with, 2-16

publishing. *See* publishing rules

S

SACLs (system access control lists), 2-33

SANS Institute Security Policy Project, 2-4

scalability

CARP and, 12-21

Enterprise Edition vs. Standard Edition, 12-3

NLB and, 12-14

schedules

access rule elements, 5-34

content download jobs, 6-31 to 6-34

download jobs, 3-19

exercise configuring, 5-38

modifying, 5-35

recurring reports, 11-53

scripts
 CARP algorithm, 12-16
 configuration scripts for Web Proxy clients, 4-17 to 4-18
 Configurerqsforisa.vbs, 10-57
ScriptVersion parameter, Rqc.exe, 10-54
Secedit, 3-10
secure access, to Internet, 5-3 to 5-10
 case scenario, 5-61
 case scenario questions, 5-70, 5-71, 7-73
 overview of, 5-3 to 5-5
 policy guidelines, 5-5 to 5-7
 policy implementation, 5-8 to 5-9
 questions and answers, 5-66
 review, 5-9 to 5-10
 security risks vs. benefits, 5-4 to 5-5
Secure HTTP. See Hypertext Transfer Protocol Secure (HTTPS)
secure Internet Message Access Protocol (IMAPS), 8-6
secure network address translation. See SecureNAT
Secure Sockets Layer (SSL)
 array configuration and, 12-10
 bridging. See SSL bridging
 connections, 5-16
 digital certificates, 8-34
 encrypted channels, 12-30
 encrypting user sessions, 9-27
 features, 8-33 to 8-34
 OWA required on virtual directories, 9-34
 packet filtering, 8-4
 publishing network servers, 12-33
 RPC over HTTP and, 9-45
 secure Web publishing rules, 1-12, 8-5
 server publishing rules, 8-49
 troubleshooting configuration and certificates, 8-58
 tunneling. See SSL tunneling
 Web publishing security, 12-33
secure Web publishing rules
 authentication, 8-63
 configuring new rule, 8-39 to 8-41
 digital certificates, installing on ISA Server, 8-36 to 8-37
 enabling SSL on ISA Server, 8-34 to 8-36
 exercise configuring new rule, 8-42 to 8-45
 exercise testing new rule, 8-45
 overview of, 1-12 to 1-13, 8-33
 path mapping and, 8-19
 questions and answers, 8-82
 review, 8-45 to 8-46

SSL configuration, 8-34, 8-37-39
 SSL features, 8-33 to 8-34
secure Web sites, 9-51 to 9-53
SecureNAT
 caching and, 6-4
 DNS and, 2-10
SecureNAT clients
 advantages and disadvantages, 4-6
 authentication, 5-42
 choosing in real world, 4-10
 comparing with other clients, 4-9
 defined, 4-48
 exercise configuring and testing, 4-25
 guidelines for choosing, 4-9
 ISA Server support, 2-39
 name resolution, 4-14 to 4-15
 network settings, 4-13
 overview of, 4-3, 4-5 to 4-6
 routing Internet requests, 4-12 to 4-13
 session monitoring, 11-29
 troubleshooting, 4-23 to 4-25

SecurID
 advantages and disadvantages, 10-14
 authentication methods, 1-12, 2-12
 choosing authentication server, 10-10
 configuring, 10-25
 implementing, 8-70
securing ISA Server, 3-3 to 3-27
 administrative roles, 3-21 to 3-23
 case scenario questions, 3-46
 case scenarios, 3-38
 default configuration, 3-15 to 3-17
 defense-in-depth, 3-3 to 3-5
 exam objectives, 3-1
 exercise configuring administrative roles, 3-25
 exercise examining default configuration, 3-24
 exercise examining and modifying system policies, 3-24
 exercise securing network interface, 3-14
 hardening the server, 3-5
 network interfaces, 3-6 to 3-7
 questions and answers, 3-43 to 3-45
 review, 3-26 to 3-27
 security options, 3-10
 security updates, 3-12 to 3-13
 system policies, 3-17 to 3-21
 system services, 3-7 to 3-12

security
  beyond perimeter security, 1-5
  collecting security-related information, 11-9
  Internet connections, 1-10
  out of box security for ISA Server 2004, 1-27
  perimeter security, 1-7
  responding to breaches, 11-9
  tradeoffs in Internet security, 5-5
  VPN benefits for, 10-6
Security Configuration and Analysis snap-in, 3-10
security policies
  deployment planning and, 2-3
  defense-in-depth strategy, 3-4
  Internet access, 1-7
  SANS Institute Security Policy Project, 2-4
  user access, 1-4
security reports, 11-48
security templates, 3-10 to 3-12
  applying to ISA Server, 3-11
  configuring for ISA Server, 3-12
  exercise using Group Policy to manage system services,
      3-14 to 3-15
  implementing, 3-10 to 3-11
  settings configured with, 3-10
Security Templates snap-in, 3-11
security updates, 3-12 to 3-13
  deploying on ISA Server, 3-13
  monitoring, 3-12
  overview, 3-12
Security Web site, Microsoft, 3-13
server logs, 11-40 to 11-46
  configuring, 11-41 to 11-44
  questions and answers, 11-65 to 11-66
  review, 11-55 to 11-57
  troubleshooting client connections, 11-45
  viewing, 11-44
Server Message Block/Common Internet File System
      (SMB/CIFS), 3-6
server publishing rules, 8-47 to 8-62
  configuring, 8-48 to 8-51
  defined, 8-80
  DNS, 8-6 to 8-10
  exercises configuring, 8-59 to 8-60
  FTP servers, 8-55 to 8-56
  overview of, 1-13, 8-5 to 8-6
  OWA, 9-35
  path mapping and, 8-19
    port override options, 8-48
    questions and answers, 8-83
    review, 8-61 to 8-62
    RPC servers, 8-52 to 8-55
    scenarios, 8-52 to 8-57
    SMTP, 9-6, 9-19
    SSL and, 8-49
    Terminal Services server, 8-56 to 8-57
    testing, 8-60
    troubleshooting, 8-58 to 8-59
    VPN servers, 8-57
    Web servers, 8-52
server publishing wizards, 1-27
servers
  authentication, 8-33
  deployment when multiple servers require same
      configuration, 12-4
  isolating from internal and Internet networks, 7-25
  monitoring client sessions by server name, 11-30
  monitoring performance, 1-35
servers continued
  planning for server publishing, 2-5
  protecting servers accessible from Internet, 7-24
  protecting servers in perimeter networks, 7-24
  rebuilding failed, 2-26
  Web servers. See Web servers
Service Pack 1 (SP1), ISA Server 2000, 2-33
services
  dashboard view, 11-5
  disabled during ISA Server installation, 2-24
  monitoring ISA Server, 11-12
  start up alerts, 11-15
  verifying installation of, 2-25
session monitoring. See also monitoring
  defined, 11-61
  disconnecting sessions, 11-31
  exercise monitoring sessions, 11-36
  filtering sessions, 11-32 to 11-33
  how to apply, 11-30
  managing client sessions, 11-31
  options, 1-36
  overview of, 11-29
  pausing, 11-31
  questions and answers, 11-64 to 11-65
  review, 11-38 to 11-39
  stopping, 11-31
  type of information in, 11-29

sessions
   client, 11-31
   dashboard view, 11-5
   disconnecting, 11-31
   filtering, 11-32 to 11-33
   ISA Server Management Console, 11-4
setup, unattended, 2-28
SharePoint Portal Server, 1-26
Shiva Password Authentication Protocol (SPAP), 10-9
side-by-side deployment, 2-6
Simple Mail Transport Protocol (SMTP), 9-3 to 9-25
   application filters, 7-7, 7-47, 9-7, 9-10, 9-55
   case scenario question, 9-59
   clients sending mail with, 9-46
   command attacks at protocol-level, 9-4
   command filters, 9-8 to 9-10
   e-mail server publishing and, 1-13
   exercises securing SMTP traffic, 9-19 to 9-23
   known security issues, 9-3 to 9-5
   Mail Server Wizard, 9-6 to 9-7
   Message Screener. *See* SMTP Message Screener
   messages, commands for sending, 9-4
   preventing unwanted mail, 9-18
   protocol-level exploits, 9-3
   questions and answers, 9-56
   review, 9-23 to 9-25
   service, installing on ISA Server, 9-21
   system policies, 3-19
   traffic. *See* SMTP traffic
   unwanted or malicious e-mail attacks, 9-4 to 9-5
Simple Network Management Protocol (SNMP), 2-24
single cache file, 6-7
single network adapter, 7-29
site and content rules, in-place upgrades, 2-34
site-to-site tunneling protocols, 10-35
site-to-site VPNs, 10-33 to 10-34
   branch office site-to-site VPN scenario, 12-22
   components, 10-33
   connections, 10-12
   defined, 10-72
   Enterprise Edition support of, 12-15
   network and access rules, 10-40 to 10-42
   overview of, 1-15, 10-5
   remote authentication, 10-37
   system policies, 10-40
   third-party solution, 12-36
   troubleshooting, 10-43
   what they are, 10-34

slash (/), content type configuration, 5-34
smart cards
   PKI and, 10-7
   VPN authentication and, 10-13
smart phones, 9-27
SMB/CIFS (Server Message Block/Common Internet File System), 3-6
SMS (Systems Mangement Server) , 4-30, 4-32 to 4-33
SMTP. *See* Simple Mail Transport Protocol (SMTP)
SMTP Message Screener, 1-14
   configuring, 9-13
   deciding where to install, 9-16
   defined, 9-55
   guidelines for implementing, 9-16 to 9-17
   how it works, 9-12
   implementing, 9-12
   inbound and outbound messages, 9-17
   inbound messages only, 9-17
   installation options, 2-22
   installing, 9-22
   keyword option, 9-14
   logging, 11-40
   overview of, 9-7
   publishing rules, 9-23
   testing, 9-23
   third-party tools for, 9-18
   user/groups option, 9-15
SMTP traffic. *See also* network traffic
   configuring outbound, 9-20
   exercises securing, 9-19 to 9-23
   questions and answers, 9-56
   testing flow, 9-21
   security of, 9-6 to 9-7, 9-25
SNMP (Simple Network Management Protocol), 2-24
source address, packet filters, 7-3
source network, session monitoring, 11-29
spam filters, 9-18
SPAP (Shiva Password Authentication Protocol), 10-9
split DNS, 8-8, 8-80
SQL database, 11-41
SSL. *See* Secure Sockets Layer (SSL)
SSL bridging
   configuration options, 8-38
   defined, 8-80
   digital certificates, 8-35
   how it works, 8-37
   mode, 8-41
   overview of, 8-34

Web chaining rules, 5-22
SSL publishing mode, 8-40
SSL tunneling
  configuring, 8-39
  defined, 8-80
  digital certificates, 8-34
  how it works, 8-39
  installing digital certificates on ISA Server, 8-37
  overview of, 8-34
stand-alone computers vs. domain members, 2-11
Standard Edition
  compared with Enterprise Edition, 1-17 to 1-19, 12-1
  decision making regarding purchase of, 12-5
  reasons for deploying Enterprise Edition instead of, 12-3
  Web chaining and, 5-17
start up alerts, 11-15
stateful filtering, 7-5 to 7-7
  advantages and disadvantages, 7-6
  defined, 7-68
  overview of, 1-8
  TCP and, 2-16, 7-5
stateful inspection
  ISA Server connection rules, 7-6
  VPN clients, 1-20
static address assignment, VPN clients, 10-21
summary reports
  database logs, 11-48
  overview of, 11-47
SYN, TCP sessions, 7-5
system access control lists (SACLs), 2-33
System and Network Service, user sets, 5-32
Systems Mangement Server (SMS), 4-30, 4-32 to 4-33
system policies, 3-17 to 3-21
  configuring, 3-18 to 3-19
  defined, 3-42
  exercise examining and modifying, 3-24
  exporting, 3-29
  firewall access rules, 3-16
  Firewall Client Share, 3-17
  ISA Server Management Console and, 1-35
  modifying default settings, 3-19 to 3-20
  overview, 3-17
  site-to-site VPNs, 10-40
  VPN client access, 10-19
system services, 3-7 to 3-12
  exercise managing with Group Policy, 3-14 to 3-15
  optional, 3-9
  managing, 3-7, 3-9
  required, 3-8 to 3-9
  security templates for, 3-10 to 3-12
  settings, 3-10

T

TCP. *See* Transmission Control Protocol (TCP)
TCP/IP. *See* Transmission Control Protocol/Internet Protocol (TCP/IP)
TCPPort parameter, Rqc.exe, 10-54
templates
  network. *See* network templates
  security. *See* security templates
Terminal Services
  installing ISA Server remotely, 2-24
  remote administration with, 3-32
  system policies, 3-18
Terminal Services server, 8-56 to 8-57

tests
  communication in enterprise networks, 12-24
  implementation before deploying, 2-7
  Internet access rules, 5-59
  security updates, 3-13
  Web chaining, 5-19
three-legged configuration
  firewalls, 7-13
  perimeter networks, 7-26
  templates for perimeter network, 7-28
thresholds, alerts, 11-8
time zones, array configuration, 12-10
Time-to-Live (TTL), 2-10, 6-5

traffic
  network. *See* network traffic
  SMTP. *See* SMTP traffic
training, user education plan, 2-7
Transmission Control Protocol (TCP)
  application filtering, 2-16
  packet filters and, 7-3
  port numbers, 7-4
  stateful filtering, 2-16
  stateful inspection of TCP headers, 1-8
  three-way handshake for establishing sessions, 7-5
  verifying connections, 11-34
Transmission Control Protocol/Internet Protocol (TCP/IP)
  application filters, 7-7

SecureNAT clients, 4-6
tunneling protocols based on, 10-4
troubleshooting
  caching, 6-25 to 6-26
  client connections, 11-45
  Firewall clients, 4-42 to 4-43
  Internet access, 5-55 to 5-56
  ISA Server configuration, 3-29
  ISA Server installation, 2-28 to 2-29
  remote administration, 3-40
  SecureNAT clients, 4-23 to 4-25
  server publishing rules, 8-58 to 8-59
  site-to-site VPNs, 10-43
  VPN connections, 10-28
  Web Proxy clients, 4-23 to 4-25
  Web publishing rules, 8-58 to 8-59
TTL (Time-to-Live), 2-10, 6-5
TunnelConnName parameter, Rqc.exe, 10-54
tunneling protocols
  choosing VPN tunneling protocol, 10-37
  comparing, 10-35
  defined, 10-72
  guidelines for choosing, 10-34 to 10-36
  ISA Server support for, 1-26
  VPN clients and, 10-4
Typical Installation, ISA Server, 2-21

U

unattended installation
  defined, 2-39
  Msisaund.ini file and, 2-26 to 2-28
  running unattended setup, 2-28
  scenarios, 2-26
unattended setup, 2-28, 12-62
Uniform Resource Locators (URLs)
  application filters and, 1-9
  configuring proxy serves and, 4-17
  limiting URLs that ISA Server responds to, 1-11
  URL sets, 5-37, 5-39
Universal Time Coordinate (UTC), 11-41
universally unique identifiers (UUIDs), 9-39
unwanted e-mail, 9-4, 9-18
updates, 12-10. *See also* security updates
upgrade installation, 2-33 to 2-36
  configuration migration, 2-34
  implementing, 2-7
  in-place upgrade, 2-33 to 2-34
  ISA Server 2000 to ISA Server 2004, 12-38

migrating RRAS VPN to ISA Server 2004, 2-35
  overview, 2-33
  questions and answers, 2-41
  review, 2-35 to 2-36
URLs. *See* Uniform Resource Locators (URLs)
usability vs. security, 5-5
usage reports, 11-9
user accounts
  Configuration Storage servers, 12-49
  dial-in access, 10-26
  mirroring for centralized administration, 12-29
  remote site connections, 10-44
user authentication
  proxy servers providing, 5-11
  VPN connections, 10-28
  Web publishing rules, 8-4
User Datagram Protocol (UDP)
  packet direction and, 7-3
  packet filters and, 7-3
  port numbers, 7-4
user logon, 9-27, 9-28
user mapping, remote VPN clients, 10-19
user name parameter, Rqc.exe, 10-54
user sets
  access based on, 7-32
  authentication of All Users, 8-63
  configuring access rule elements, 5-31 to 5-32
  exercise configuring, 5-38
user/groups option, SMTP Message Screener, 9-15
users
  access rules and, 5-55
  accessing internal network from Internet, 1-7
  accessing Internet resources, 1-10
  configuring access to Internet, 1-32
  education in deployment planning, 2-7
  Internet usage policy, 5-6
  logging user access to Internet, 5-12
  malicious content and, 5-4
  permissions, 1-20
  rights assignments, 3-10
  secure Internet access and, 5-3 to 5-5
  security policies, 1-4
UTC (Universal Time Coordinate), 11-41
utilization reports, 11-47
UUIDs (universally unique identifiers), 9-39

V

VBScript, 10-53
verbs (command filters, SMTP), 9-8 to 9-11

verification, ISA Server installation, 2-25, 2-30
virtual private networks (VPNs)
   access configuration, 1-33
   authentication, 10-8 to 10-9, 10-23 to 10-27
   authentication servers, 10-10
   benefits of, 10-6
   branch offfice site-to-site VPN scenario, 12-22
   case scenario questions, 10-77
   case scenarios, 10-69
   client configuration, 3-16, 10-19
   client IP addresses, 10-20 to 10-23
   connections, 10-27 to 10-28, 10-30
   defined, 10-72
   deployment planning, 2-6
   Enterprise Edition and, 12-15
   exercises configuring for remote clients, 10-29 to 10-30
   how they work, 10-4
   implementing with ISA Server, 10-11 to 10-12
   infrastructure implementation guidelines, 10-12 to 10-14
   ISA Server Mangement Console and, 1-35
   ISA Server as VPN server, 1-14 to 1-15
   multiple networks and, 7-14
   network configuration, 3-16
   overview of, 10-4
   perimeter security and, 1-7, 3-4
   prerequisites, 10-2
   proptocol options, 10-7 to 10-8
   quarantine control. See quarantine control, VPNs
   questions and answers, 10-73
   remote access policies, 10-10
   remote clients. See remote clients, VPNs
   remote sites. See remote sites, VPNs
   review, 10-14 to 10-15, 10-30 to 10-32
   RRAS VPN migration to ISA Server, 2-35
   scenarios for using, 10-5
   server publishing rules, 8-57
   stateful inspection of VPN clients, 1-20
   third-party site-to-site solution, 12-36
   troubleshooting VPN connections, 10-28
   tunneling protocol selection guidelines, 10-34 to 10-36
viruses
   antivirus scanning, 9-18
   application filtering and, 1-9, 7-7
   damage caused by, 9-5
   HTTP and, 1-9, 7-48

   spreading via e-mail, 9-1, 9-5
VPNs. See virtual private networks (VPNs)
VPN clients. See also remote clients, VPNs
   accessing ISA Server, 10-29
   authentication, 10-23 to 10-27
   configuring, 3-16, 10-19
   defined, 10-72
   dial-in permissions, 10-26
   IP addresses, 10-20 to 10-23
   name resolution, 10-23
   network for VPN connections, 10-12
   quarantine control, 10-55 to 10-56, 10-60 to 10-61
   RADIUS, 10-24
   SecurID, 10-25
   stateful inspection, 1-20
   tunneling protocols, 10-4
vulnerabilities
   identifying, 5-6
   monitoring, 7-9
   Outlook clients, 9-39
   SMTP, 9-3 to 9-5

W

W3C (World Wide Web Consortium), 11-41
WANs (wide area networks), 6-10, 10-2
WDigest authentication, 5-41
Web applications, proxy servers, 5-13
Web browsers
   authentication and, 5-43
   HTTP 1.1 compliance, 4-7
   Internal network settings, 4-18 to 4-20
   Web Proxies and, 4-7, 4-15
Web caching, CARP, 12-4
Web chaining, 5-17 to 5-22, 6-9 to 6-10
   actions, 5-21
   backup actions, 5-22
   benefits of, 6-9
   branch offices and, 5-19, 6-10
   combining with caching, 6-9
   destination rules, 5-20
   exercise configuring, 5-26
   primary route configuration, 5-22
   reasons for using, 5-18
   rule configuration, 5-19 to 5-23
Web client connections, 9-26 to 9-37
   access to non-OWA clients, 9-33
   configuring OWA, 9-28 to 9-30, 9-34 to 9-36

forms-based authentication, 9-30 to 9-33
known security issues, 9-26 to 9-28
OWA features and security, 9-26
questions and answers, 9-57
review, 9-36 to 9-37
wireless device support, 9-27 to 9-28
Web filters, 7-48 to 7-63
compatibility problems, 2-35
defined, 7-68
exercise configuring HTTP filter, 7-61 to 7-63
HTTP extensions, 7-54 to 7-56
HTTP filter options, 7-49 to 7-50
HTTP headers, 7-56 to 7-58
HTTP methods, 7-52 to 7-54
HTTP policy properties, 7-50 to 7-52
HTTP policy signatures, 7-58 to 7-61
HTTP Web filter scenarios, 7-49
overview, 7-48
questions and answers, 7-73
review, 7-63 to 7-64
tasks performed by, 7-48
Web listeners
advanced settings, 8-18
authentication, 8-63
configuration options, 8-15
creating, 8-15
defined, 8-80
network configuration for, 8-16
overview of, 8-14
preferences, 8-18
protocols and port numbers, 8-17
publishing rules for, 8-14 to 8-15, 8-29
RADIUS authentication, 8-69
Web pages, link translation, 8-22
Web Proxy
DNS and, 2-9
logs, 11-40
Web Proxy Automatic Discovery (WPAD), 4-20
Web Proxy clients
advantages and disadvantages, 4-7 to 4-8
authentication, 5-42
automatic configuration, 4-17 to 4-20
automatic discovery, 4-20 to 4-21
choosing in real world, 4-10
comparing with other clients, 4-9
configuring, 4-15
defined, 4-48

Enterprise Edition and, 12-69
exercise configuring and testing, 4-25
guidelines for choosing, 4-9
ISA Server configured for, 4-15 to 4-16
ISA Server support, 2-39
manual configuration, 4-16 to 4-17
overview of, 4-3, 4-7
session monitoring, 11-29
troubleshooting, 4-23 to 4-25
Web publishing
in-place upgrades and, 2-34
SSL security, 12-33
Web publishing rules
authentication, 8-63 to 8-64
complex scenarios, 8-28 to 8-29
configuring, 8-13 to 8-14, 8-23 to 8-27
creating, 8-24
defined, 8-80
DNS configuration, 8-6 to 8-10
DNS resolution errors, 8-6
exercise configuring new rule, 8-30
exercise configuring Web listener, 8-29
exercise testing Web site access, 8-30
link directories, 8-23
link translation, 8-23
modifying, 8-26
overview of, 1-11 to 1-12, 8-4 to 8-5
path mapping and, 8-19, 8-20
questions and answers, 8-82
redirecting client requests, 8-19
review, 8-31 to 8-32
RPC over HTTP and, 9-45
secure publishing rules, 8-5
SSL bridging and, 8-37
troubleshooting, 8-58 to 8-59
Web listener configuration, 8-14 to 8-19
Web servers
access control with firewalls, 1-8
authentication on internal, 8-65, 8-66
content caching, 8-5
digital certificates on, 8-36 to 8-37
proxy request configuration, 8-27
publishing rules for HTTP protocol, 8-4
server publishing rules, 8-52
Web sites
access enabled for internal and Internet clients, 8-7

accessing public and private, 1-7
allowed sites, 3-19
Microsoft Security Web site, 3-13
path mapping, 8-4
publishing rules, 8-4, 8-5, 8-24, 8-28
securing, 1-12
testing access to secure, 9-51, 9-53
Web usage reports, 11-47
weekends, access rule elements, 5-34
wide area networks (WANs), 6-10, 10-2
wildcards, proxy servers, 4-17
Windows Backup, 12-37
Windows Installer, 4-33
Windows Internet Naming Service (WINS), 3-6,
    10-21
Windows Management Instrumentation (WMI),
    10-53
Windows networking, 3-19
Windows, clients
  Firewall clients and, 4-5
  VPN quarantine and, 10-11
Windows, servers
  DNS required by, 2-8
  installing ISA Server on remotely, 2-24
  IAS and, 10-10
  L2TP/IPSec support, 10-7
  Windows Server 2003 Security Guide, 3-11
Winsock applications
  connecting with services on other computers, 4-4
  defined, 4-48
  Firewall Client application and, 4-4, 4-39
  Firewall clients supporting, 4-5
WINS (Windows Internet Naming Service), 3-6,
    10-21
Winsock Proxy AutoDetect (WSPAD), 4-20
wireless devices, 7-25, 9-27 to 9-28
WMI (Windows Management Instrumentation), 10-53
work hours, access rule elements, 5-34
workgroups
  arrays, 12-30
  back-to-back firewalls and, 12-28
  Configuration Storage servers and, 12-4, 12-23
  domain/workgroup mixed configurations, 12-30
  Enterprise Edition deployment, 12-21 to 12-22
  ISA Server deployment options, 12-29, 12-47
workstations
  preparing for remote administration, 3-39 to 3-40
  monitoring Enterprise Edition computers from,
    12-21

World Wide Web Consortium (W3C), 11-41
World Wide Web Publishing service, 2-24
worms
  application filters and, 7-7
  damage caused by, 9-5
  spreading via e-mail, 9-5
WPAD (Web Proxy Automatic Discovery), 4-20
WSPAP (Winsock Proxy AutoDetect), 4-20

X

XML files, templates stored in, 7-28

Z

zone transfer attacks, 7-39

For *Windows Server 2003* administrators

Microsoft® Windows® Server 2003 Administrator's Companion
ISBN 0-7356-1367-2

The comprehensive, daily operations guide to planning, deployment, and maintenance. Here's the ideal one-volume guide for anyone who administers Windows Server 2003. It offers up-to-date information on core system-administration topics for Windows, including Active Directory® services, security, disaster planning and recovery, interoperability with NetWare and UNIX, plus all-new sections about Microsoft Internet Security and Acceleration (ISA) Server and scripting. Featuring easy-to-use procedures and handy workarounds, it provides ready answers for on-the-job results.

Microsoft Windows Server 2003 Administrator's Pocket Consultant
ISBN 0-7356-1354-0

The practical, portable guide to Windows Server 2003. Here's the practical, pocket-sized reference for IT professionals who support Windows Server 2003. Designed for quick referencing, it covers all the essentials for performing everyday system-administration tasks. Topics covered include managing workstations and servers, using Active Directory services, creating and administering user and group accounts, managing files and directories, data security and auditing, data back-up and recovery, administration with TCP/IP, WINS, and DNS, and more.

Microsoft IIS 6.0 Administrator's Pocket Consultant
ISBN 0-7356-1560-8

The practical, portable guide to IIS 6.0. Here's the eminently practical, pocket-sized reference for IT and Web professionals who work with Internet Information Services (IIS) 6.0. Designed for quick referencing and compulsively readable, this portable guide covers all the basics needed for everyday tasks. Topics include Web administration fundamentals, Web server administration, essential services administration, and performance, optimization, and maintenance. It's the fast-answers guide that helps users consistently save time and energy as they administer IIS 6.0.

To learn more about the full line of Microsoft Press® products for IT professionals, please visit:

microsoft.com/mspress/IT

In-depth technical information for
Microsoft Windows Server 2003

Microsoft® Windows® TCP/IP Protocols and Services Technical Reference
ISBN 0-7356-1291-9

The in-depth technical guide to TCP/IP protocols and services and their implementation in Windows .NET Server 2003. Get the in-depth details you need to support TCP/IP on the Windows .NET Server 2003 platform with this comprehensive technical guide. Combining concepts with packet examples, it steps layer by layer through the TCP/IP protocols and services that Windows .NET Server 2003 supports to help you understand how they work and how they're implemented in the operating system. With the latest information about Point-to-Point Protocol (PPP), Remote Authentication Dial-In User Service (RADIUS), IP Security (IPSec), and Virtual Private Networks (VPNs), it's a must-have for any technical professional who works with Windows .ENT Server 2003 and TCP/IP.

Active Directory® Services for Microsoft Windows Server 2003 Technical Reference
ISBN 0-7356-1577-2

The in-depth reference for network architects and administrators implementing enterprise directory services. Get the focused, in-depth technical expertise you need to implement and optimize your Microsoft directory services infrastructure. As two Active Directory experts guide you through advanced design and deployment issues for the Windows Server 2003 environment, you'll develop a thorough understanding of the underlying concepts, architectural components, and real-world functionality of Active Directory directory service. Whether you're upgrading from Microsoft Windows NT® 4.0 or later, or performing a clean installation, you'll learn the best ways to exploit Active Directory capabilities for your organization—and deliver new levels of network performance and productivity.

Deploying Virtual Private Networks with Microsoft Windows Server 2003 Technical Reference
ISBN 0-7356-1576-4

The essential guide to designing and deploying Windows based VPN solutions. Get the focused, in-depth technical expertise you need to deploy virtual private networks (VPNs) using the Windows Server 2003 operating system. The authors—networking specialists from the Microsoft Windows Server team—thoroughly detail VPN components, capabilities, and security considerations for remote access and site-to-site connections. From planning and design to deploying and troubleshooting your solution, you get expert technical guidance through all key decision points and procedures. This guide also features an end-to-end deployment example and best practices information, with additional resources on CD.

To learn more about the full line of Microsoft Press® products for IT professionals, please visit:

microsoft.com/mspress/IT

System Requirements

Hardware Requirements

Each computer must have the following minimum configuration. All hardware should be on the Microsoft Windows Server 2003 or Windows XP Hardware Compatibility List.

- A personal computer with a 550 megahertz (MHz) or higher Pentium III–compatible CPU.

- 256 megabytes (MB) of memory.

- For the computers that will be configured as Microsoft Internet Security and Acceleration (ISA) Server computers, you need one network adapter for communication with the internal network and an additional network adapter for each network directly connected to the ISA Server 2004 computer. You need two network adapters for most exercises, with a third network adapter required for one exercise.

- One local hard disk partition that is formatted with the NTFS file system and that has at least 150 megabytes (MB) of available hard disk space. If you enable caching and logging, you will need additional hard disk space.

- CD-ROM drive.

- Microsoft Mouse or compatible pointing device.

Software Requirements

The following software is required to complete the procedures in this training kit. (A 180-day evaluation edition of Windows Server 2003, Enterprise Edition, is included on the CD-ROM that accompanies this book.)

- Windows Server 2003, Enterprise Edition

- ISA Server 2004, Standard Edition

- ISA Server 2004, Enterprise Edition

- Microsoft Exchange Server 2003, either Standard or Enterprise Edition

- Microsoft Windows XP, Professional Edition

- Microsoft Outlook 2003

What do you think of this book?
We want to hear from you!

Do you have a few minutes to participate in a brief online survey? Microsoft is interested in hearing your feedback about this publication so that we can continually improve our books and learning resources for you.

To participate in our survey, please visit:

www.microsoft.com/learning/booksurvey

And enter this book's ISBN, 0-7356-2169-1. As a thank-you to survey participants in the United States and Canada, each month we'll randomly select five respondents to win one of five $100 gift certificates from a leading online merchant.* At the conclusion of the survey, you can enter the drawing by providing your e-mail address, which will be used for prize notification *only*.

Thanks in advance for your input. Your opinion counts!

Sincerely,

Microsoft Learning

Learn More. Go Further.

To see special offers on Microsoft Learning products for developers, IT professionals, and home and office users, visit: *www.microsoft.com/learning/booksurvey*

Save 15%
on your MCSA/MCSE Exam testing!

Get certified

You invested in your future with the purchase of this book. Now take the opportunity to get a full return on your investment and get the recognition your skills deserve. A Microsoft® certification validates your technical expertise and enhances your credibility in the marketplace. It's a great way to invest in your IT future!

Test at any Certified Microsoft Exam Provider—worldwide!

Use this voucher to save 15% on MCSA/MCSE Exam 70-350 at any Certified Microsoft Exam Provider.

Redeem your discount voucher

Present the discount voucher on the back of this page in-person at a Certified Microsoft Exam Provider testing center, or use the voucher discount code to register online or via phone at the Certified Microsoft Exam Provider of your choice. For complete information on how to register for MCSA/MCSE Exam 350: Microsoft® Internet Security and Acceleration Server 2004, see the Certified Microsoft Exam Provider Web site:

http://www.microsoft.com/mcp/exams

Microsoft
CERTIFIED
Professional
15% off
exam voucher
Redeemable at Certified Microsoft Exam Providers worldwide.
See **http://www.microsoft.com/mcp/exams** for a complete list.

Turn the page to find your exam voucher discount codes and for promotion details.

Microsoft

Present this discount voucher to any of 5,000 testing centers worldwide in 130 countries for 15% off your exam fee. Or, use the discount code on the voucher to register online or via phone at the Certified Microsoft Exam Provider of your choice.

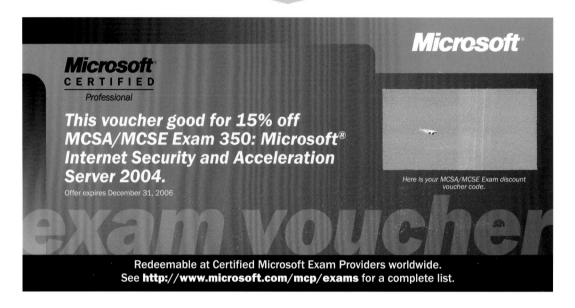

Microsoft

Microsoft
C E R T I F I E D
Professional

This voucher good for 15% off MCSA/MCSE Exam 350: Microsoft® Internet Security and Acceleration Server 2004.

Offer expires December 31, 2006

Here is your MCSA/MCSE Exam discount voucher code.

Redeemable at Certified Microsoft Exam Providers worldwide.
See **http://www.microsoft.com/mcp/exams** for a complete list.

For more information or the location of a Certified Microsoft Exam Provider near you, visit:
http://www.microsoft.com/mcp/exams

Promotion Terms and Conditions:

- Voucher can be redeemed online or at Certified Microsoft Exam Providers worldwide.
- Discounted exam must be taken on or before December 31, 2006.
- Promotion is limited to one discounted exam per candidate for each book purchased.
- Inform your Certified Microsoft Exam Provider at the time you register for the exam that you want to use this voucher as payment for your exam.
- This 15% discount is valid only on MCSA/MCSE Exam 350: Microsoft® Internet Security and Acceleration Server 2004.

Voucher Terms and Conditions

- Expired voucher has no value.
- Voucher code must be used at time of registration.
- This voucher may not be combined with other vouchers or discounts.
- This voucher is nontransferable and is void if altered or revised in any way. It may not be redeemed for cash, credit, or refund, and may not be used for any other exam.
- Any transfer or resale of this voucher is expressly prohibited.

X11-10422

EXAM 70-350